Lecture Notes in Computer Science 11822

Advanced Research in Computing and Software Science

Subline of Lecture Notes in Computer Science

More information about this series at http://www.springer.com/series/7408

Bor-Yuh Evan Chang (Ed.)

Static Analysis

26th International Symposium, SAS 2019
Porto, Portugal, October 8–11, 2019
Proceedings

Springer

Editor
Bor-Yuh Evan Chang
University of Colorado
Boulder, CO, USA

ISSN 0302-9743 ISSN 1611-3349 (electronic)
Lecture Notes in Computer Science
ISBN 978-3-030-32303-5 ISBN 978-3-030-32304-2 (eBook)
https://doi.org/10.1007/978-3-030-32304-2

LNCS Sublibrary: SL2 – Programming and Software Engineering

This Springer imprint is published by the registered company Springer Nature Switzerland AG
The registered company address is: Gewerbestrasse 11, 6330 Cham, Switzerland

Preface

This volume contains the proceedings of the 26th International Static Analysis Symposium (SAS 2019) held on October 8–11, 2019 in Porto, Portugal as part of the Third World Congress on Formal Methods.

Static analysis is widely recognized as a fundamental tool for program verification, bug detection, compiler optimization, program understanding, and software maintenance. The series of Static Analysis Symposia has served as the primary venue for the presentation of theoretical, practical, and application advances in the area. Previous symposia were held in Freiburg, New York, Edinburgh, Saint-Malo, Munich, Seattle, Deauville, Venice, Perpignan, Los Angeles, Valencia, Kongens Lyngby, Seoul, London, Verona, San Diego, Madrid, Paris, Santa Barbara, Pisa, Aachen, Glasgow, and Namur.

SAS 2019 employed a double-blind reviewing process with an author-response period. Within the review period, the Program Committee used an internal two-round review process where each submission received three first-round reviews to drive the possible selection of additional expert reviews as needed before the author response period. All submissions received at least three reviews with over a third of the submissions receiving four. The author response period was followed by a one-and-a-half-week Program Committee discussion period with over 600 comments generated and culminating in a synchronous, virtual Program Committee meeting on June 12, 2019, to finalize the selection of papers.

New in 2019, SAS solicited papers on a trending topic in static analysis: the emerging convergence of static analysis and machine learning. The conference received 50 submissions, including nine Trends in Static Analysis papers. After thoroughly evaluating the relevance and quality of each paper, the Program Committee decided to accept 20 contributions, including two Trends in Static Analysis papers.

Authors were also encouraged to submit artifacts accompanying their papers to strengthen evaluations and reproducibility of results in static analysis. The conference received 13 submissions with artifacts of which five were accepted. Each of the artifacts was evaluated by two or three members of the Artifact Evaluation Committee, whose comments were available to the Program Committee.

We were also honored to include four invited talks by the following distinguished researchers:

- Mayur Naik (University of Pennsylvania, USA) on "Rethinking Static Analysis by Combining Discrete and Continuous Reasoning"
- Caterina Urban (Inria/ENS, France) on "Static Analysis of Data Science Software"
- Somesh Jha (University of Wisconsin-Madison, USA) on "Towards Semantic Adversarial Examples"
- Suresh Jagannathan (Purdue University, USA) on "Learning Verifiers and Verifying Learners"

SAS 2019 featured three associated workshops held on the day before the conference, October 8, 2019:

- 10th Workshop on Static Analysis and Systems Biology (SASB 2019)
  - Chairs: Pedro T. Monteiro (INESC-ID/IST - Universidade de Lisboa) and Jean Krivine (CNRS)
- 10th Workshop on Tools for Automatic Program Analysis (TAPAS 2019)
  - Chair: David Delmas (Airbus and Sorbonne Université)
- 8th Workshop on Numerical and Symbolic Abstract Domains (NSAD 2019)
  - Chair: Laure Gonnord (Université de Lyon)

This program would not have been possible without the substantial efforts of many people, whom we sincerely thank. The Program Committee, Artifact Evaluation Committee, subreviewers, and external expert reviewers worked tirelessly to select the strongest possible program while simultaneously offering constructive and supportive comments in their reviews. The Organizing Committee of FM Week chaired by José Nuno Oliveira (INESC TEC and University of Minho) were tremendous. We also graciously thank the SAS Steering Committee for their leadership and timely advice. Finally, we thank our platinum sponsor Google for supporting our invited speakers, as well as Springer for bronze sponsorship and publishing these proceedings.

August 2019

Bor-Yuh Evan Chang
Hakjoo Oh

Organization

Program Chair

Bor-Yuh Evan Chang	University of Colorado Boulder, USA

Program Committee

Josh Berdine	Facebook, UK
Marc Brockschmidt	Microsoft Research, UK
Yu-Fang Chen	Academia Sinica, Taiwan
Roberto Giacobazzi	Università di Verona, Italy
Ben Hardekopf	University of California, Santa Barbara, USA
Thomas Jensen	Inria, France
Ranjit Jhala	University of California, San Diego, USA
Andy King	University of Kent, UK
Shuvendu Lahiri	Microsoft Research, USA
Akash Lal	Microsoft Research, India
Francesco Logozzo	Facebook, USA
Jan Midtgaard	University of Southern Denmark, Denmark
Antoine Miné	Sorbonne Université, France
Anders Møller	Aarhus University, Denmark
David Monniaux	VERIMAG/CNRS/Université Grenoble Alpes, France
Kedar Namjoshi	Bell Labs, Nokia, USA
Sylvie Putot	LIX, École polytechnique, France
Veselin Raychev	DeepCode AG, Switzerland
Xavier Rival	Inria/CNRS/ENS/PSL*, France
Sriram Sankaranarayanan	University of Colorado Boulder, USA
Tachio Terauchi	Waseda University, Japan
Aditya Thakur	University of California, Davis, USA
Tomas Vojnar	FIT, Brno University of Technology, Czech Republic
Kwangkeun Yi	Seoul National University, South Korea
Xin Zhang	Massachusetts Institute of Technology, USA
Florian Zuleger	TU Wien, Austria

Artifact Evaluation Chair

Hakjoo Oh	Korea University, South Korea

Artifact Evaluation Committee

François Bidet	LIX, École polytechnique, France
Liqian Chen	National University of Defense Technology, China

Mehmet Emre	University of California, Santa Barbara, USA
John K. Feser	Massachusetts Institute of Technology, USA
Kihong Heo	University of Pennsylvania, USA
Maxime Jacquemin	LIX, École polytechnique, France
Sehun Jeong	Korea University, South Korea
Matthieu Journault	Sorbonne Université, France
Yue Li	Aarhus University, Denmark
Viktor Malik	FIT, Brno University of Technology, Czech Republic
Suvam Mukherjee	Microsoft Research, India
Abdelraouf Ouadjaout	Sorbonne Université, France
Saswat Padhi	University of California, Los Angeles, USA
Jiasi Shen	Massachusetts Institute of Technology, USA
Gagandeep Singh	ETH Zurich, Switzerland
Benno Stein	University of Colorado Boulder, USA
Yulei Sui	University of Technology Sydney, Australia
Tian Tan	Aarhus University, Denmark
Xinyu Wang	University of Texas at Austin, USA

Steering Committee

Bor-Yuh Evan Chang	University of Colorado Boulder, USA
Andreas Podelski	University of Freiburg, Germany
Francesco Ranzato	University of Padoa, Italy
Xavier Rival	Inria/CNRS/ENS/PSL*, France
Thomas Jensen	Inria Rennes, France
Sandrine Blazy	University of Rennes 1, France
Patrick Cousot	New York University, USA

Additional Reviewers

Bjorner, Nikolaj
Ceska, Milan
Chevalier, Marc
Churchill, Berkeley
Darulova, Eva
Ghorbal, Khalil
Havlena, Vojtěch
Holik, Lukas
Katelaan, Jens
Kim, Jinyung
Lee, Woosuk
Lin, Hsin-Hung
Lång, Magnus
Maréchal, Alexandre
Pani, Thomas
Rogalewicz, Adam
Seed, Tom

Abstracts of Invited Contributions

Towards Semantic Adversarial Examples

Somesh Jha

University of Wisconsin-Madison, USA
jha@cs.wisc.edu

Abstract. Fueled by massive amounts of data, models produced by machine-learning (ML) algorithms, especially deep neural networks, are being used in diverse domains where trustworthiness is a concern, including automotive systems, finance, health care, natural language processing, and malware detection. Of particular concern is the use of ML algorithms in cyber-physical systems (CPS), such as self-driving cars and aviation, where an adversary can cause serious consequences.

However, existing approaches to generating adversarial examples and devising robust ML algorithms mostly ignore the semantics and context of the overall system containing the ML component. For example, in an autonomous vehicle using deep learning for perception, not every adversarial example for the neural network might lead to a harmful consequence. Moreover, one may want to prioritize the search for adversarial examples towards those that significantly modify the desired semantics of the overall system. Along the same lines, existing algorithms for constructing robust ML algorithms ignore the specification of the overall system. In this talk, we argue that the semantics and specification of the overall system has a crucial role to play in this line of research. We present preliminary research results that support this claim.

Learning Verifiers and Verifying Learners

Suresh Jagannathan

Purdue University, West Lafayette, IN 47907, USA
suresh@cs.purdue.edu

Abstract. On the surface, modern-day machine learning and program verification tools appear to have very different and contradictory goals - machine learning emphasizes generality of the hypotheses it discovers over soundness of the results it produces, while program verification ensures correctness of the claims it makes, even at the expense of the generality of the problems it can handle.

Nonetheless, it would also appear that machine learning pipelines have much to offer program verifiers precisely because they are structured to extract useful, albeit hidden, information from their subject domain. When applied to software, data-driven methods may help discover facts and properties critical to program verification that would otherwise require tedious human involvement to state and prove. Conversely, program verification methods would seem to have much to offer machine learning pipelines. Neural networks, the building blocks of modern ML methods, are opaque and uninterpretible, characteristics that make them vulnerable to safety violations and adversarial attacks. Suitably-adapted verification methods may help to identify problematic behavior in these networks, an indispensable need in safety-critical environments.

This talk explores two point instances to support these claims. Our first example considers how machine learning tools can facilitate solutions to Constrained Horn Clauses (CHCs), a popular formalism for encoding verification conditions that capture sophisticated safety properties. We demonstrate how data-driven techniques can be used for efficient invariant discovery over complex recursive CHCs in which the structure of the discovered invariants are drawn from expressive feature spaces (e.g., polyhedra domains). Our second example considers how program verification and synthesis tools can be used to guarantee safety of reinforcement learning-based neural controllers. We suggest a black-box technique that uses the neural network as an oracle to guide the search for a similarly-behaving deterministic program, more amenable to verification, that is guaranteed to satisfy a desired safety specification. This program can then be effectively used within a runtime monitoring framework as a safety shield, overriding proposed actions of the network whenever such actions can cause the system to violate safety conditions.

The results of these investigations give us confidence that there are significant synergies to be had by judiciously combining learning and verification techniques. We envision learners as a mechanism to complement the expressivity of program verifiers by enabling improved efficiency and generality, while verifiers can be used to guarantee the safety of machine learning artifacts without compromising accuracy and utility.

Contents

Invited Contributions

Rethinking Static Analysis by Combining Discrete and Continuous Reasoning

Mayur Naik(✉)

Department of Computer and Information Science,
University of Pennsylvania, Philadelphia, USA
mhnaik@cis.upenn.edu

Abstract. Static analyses predominantly use discrete modes of logical reasoning to derive facts about programs. Despite significant strides, this form of reasoning faces new challenges in modern software applications and practices. These challenges concern not only traditional analysis objectives such as scalability, accuracy, and soundness, but also emerging ones such as tailoring analysis conclusions based on relevance or severity of particular code changes, and needs of individual programmers.

We advocate seamlessly extending static analyses to leverage continuous modes of logical reasoning in order to address these challenges. Central to our approach is expressing the specification of the static analysis in a constraint language that is amenable to computing provenance information. We use the logic programming language Datalog as proof-of-concept for this purpose. We illustrate the benefits of exploiting provenance even in the discrete setting. Moreover, by associating weights with constraints, we show how to amplify these benefits in the continuous setting.

We also present open problems in aspects of analysis usability, language expressiveness, and solver techniques. The overall process constitutes a fundamental rethinking of how to design, implement, deploy, and adapt static analyses.

Keywords: Static analysis · Constraint solving · Provenance · Probabilistic logics · Alarm ranking · Inductive logic programming

1 Introduction

Static analysis has made remarkable strides in theory and practice over the decades since the seminal work of Cousot and Cousot on abstract interpretation [10]. The practical impact of static analysis tools includes triumphs such as Astrée [11] for verifying memory safety properties of C programs used in Airbus controller software, SLAM [6] for verifying temporal safety properties that device drivers on the Windows operating system must obey, Coverity [7] for checking a wide variety of programming errors based on semantic inconsistencies in large enterprise C/C++ applications, and Infer [9] for modularly checking various

B.-Y. E. Chang (Ed.): SAS 2019, LNCS 11822, pp. 3–16, 2019.
https://doi.org/10.1007/978-3-030-32304-2_1

safety properties of C, C++, Objective C, and Java code in Android and iOS mobile applications.

At the same time, new programming languages with rich dynamic features, such as Javascript and Python, and new software engineering practices such as continuous integration and continuous deployment (CI/CD) are becoming increasingly popular. These settings favor programmer productivity but pose new challenges to static analysis, such as tailoring analysis conclusions based on relevance or severity of code changes by individual developers in large teams [19,30]. The resulting trend in the growth and diversity of software applications is challenging even traditional objectives of static analysis, such as scalability, accuracy, and soundness [21].

Static analyses predominantly use discrete modes of logical reasoning to derive facts about programs: the facts and the process of deriving them are discrete in nature. For instance, such analyses typically work by applying deductive rules of the form $A \Rightarrow B$ on program text. The undecidability of the static analysis problem lends such rules to be necessarily incomplete, deriving consequent B which may be false even if antecedent A is true.

In this paper, we argue that leveraging continuous modes of logical reasoning opens promising avenues to address the above challenges. For instance, we can extend the syntax of the above deductive rule with a real-valued weight $w \in [0,1]$, and extend its semantics to the continuous domain, which allows to selectively violate instances of the rule as well as associate a *confidence score* with each derived fact. This enables to leverage inference procedures for conventional probabilistic graphical models such as Bayesian networks [31] (e.g. [32]) or Markov Logic Networks (MLN) [35] (e.g. [24]). We can even learn the weights and structure of the rules from (possibly partial or noisy) input-output data (e.g. labeled alarms on program text) rather than being hand-engineered by human experts. By replacing the traditional operations ($\wedge$, $\vee$) and values $\{true, false\}$ of the Boolean semiring with the corresponding operations ($\times$, max) and values [0, 1] of the Viterbi semiring [14], we can leverage ideas from numerical relaxation in optimization problems, such as Newton's root-finding method, MCMC-based random sampling, and stochastic gradient descent [36]. This opens the door to the invention of new program approximations and to the customization of static analyses by end-users.

Crucially, we advocate to seamlessly *extend* rather than *replace* existing methods, by synergistically combining discrete and continuous forms of logical reasoning in static analysis. In particular, we presume that the analysis is expressed in a constraint language that is amenable to computing provenance information in the form of proof trees that explain how the analysis derives output facts (e.g., alarms) from input facts (e.g., program text). Such information allows to answer questions such as whether a particular alarm is relevant to a particular code change in a continuously evolving codebase. Such information is useful even in the discrete setting but its benefits are amplified in the continuous setting—for instance, allowing to answer questions such as the *extent* to which an alarm is relevant to a code change. Throughout, we use the logic programming language Datalog [1] as proof-of-concept for the constraint language, since it suffices to express a wide range of analyses in the literature, and efficient procedures exist for evaluating Datalog programs, computing provenance information, and extending the Datalog language and solvers with capabilities such as statistical relational models and mathematical optimization procedures [3].

The rest of the paper is organized as follows. Section 2 illustrates the key ingredients of our approach on the problem of improving the effective accuracy of a static analysis by incorporating user feedback. Section 3 outlines the landscape of challenges in static analysis where similar ideas are applicable and discusses open problems. Finally, Sect. 4 concludes.

2 Illustrative Overview

We illustrate our approach using an example from [32] which applies a static analysis to a multi-threaded Java program called Apache FTP server. Figure 1 shows a code fragment from the program. The `RequestHandler` class is used to handle client connections. An object of this class is created for every incoming connection to the server. The `close()` method is used to clean up and close an open client connection, and the `getRequest()` method is used to access the `request` field. Both these methods can be invoked from other parts of the program by multiple threads in parallel on the same `RequestHandler` object.

Dataraces are a common and insidious kind of error that plague multi-threaded programs. Since `getRequest()` and `close()` may be called on the same `RequestHandler` object by different threads in parallel, there exists a datarace between lines 10 and 20: the first thread may read the `request` field while the second thread concurrently sets the `request` field to `null`.

On the other hand, even though the `close()` method may also be simultaneously invoked by multiple threads on the same `RequestHandler` object, the atomic test-and-set operation on lines 13–16 ensures that for each object instance, lines 17–24 are executed at most once. There is therefore no datarace between the pair of accesses to `controlSocket` on lines 17 and 18, and similarly no datarace between the accesses to `request` on lines 19 and 20, and so forth.

We may use a static analysis to find dataraces in this program. However, due to the undecidable nature of the problem, the analysis may also report alarms on lines 17–24. In the rest of this section, we illustrate how our approach generalizes from user feedback to guide the analysis away from the false positives and towards the actual datarace.

A Static Datarace Analysis. Fig. 1 shows a simplified version of the analysis in Chord, a static datarace detector for Java programs [29]. The analysis is expressed in Datalog as a set of logical rules over relations.

The analysis takes relations $\mathcal{N}(p_1, p_2)$, $\mathcal{U}(p_1, p_2)$, and $\mathcal{A}(p_1, p_2)$ as input, and produces relations $\mathcal{P}(p_1, p_2)$ and $\mathcal{R}(p_1, p_2)$ as output. In all relations, variables p_1 and p_2 range over the domain of program points. Each relation may be visualized as the set of tuples indicating some known facts about the program.

```
1   package org.apache.ftpserver;
2
3   public class RequestHandler {
4     FtpRequestImpl request;
5     FtpWriter writer;
6     BufferedReader reader;
7     Socket controlSocket;
8     boolean isClosed;
9     public FtpRequest getRequest() {
10      return request;          // l0
11    }
12    public void close() {
13      synchronized(this) {     // l1
14        if (isClosed) return;  // l2
15        isClosed = true;       // l3
16      }
17      controlSocket.close();   // l4
18      controlSocket = null;    // l5
19      request.clear();         // l6
20      request = null;          // l7
21      writer.close();
22      writer = null;
23      reader.close();
24      reader = null;
25    }
26  }
```

Input relations:

$\mathcal{N}(p_1, p_2)$ (program point p_1 is an immediate successor of program point p_2)

$\mathcal{U}(p_1, p_2)$ (no common lock guards program points p_1 and p_2)

$\mathcal{A}(p_1, p_2)$ (instructions at program points p_1 and p_2 may access the same memory location, and constitute a possible datarace)

Output relations:

$\mathcal{P}(p_1, p_2)$ (different threads may reach program points p_1 and p_2 in parallel)

$\mathcal{R}(p_1, p_2)$ (datarace may occur between different threads while executing the instructions at program points p_1 and p_2)

Analysis rules:

$r_1: \mathcal{P}(p_1, p_3) :\!- \mathcal{P}(p_1, p_2), \mathcal{N}(p_2, p_3), \mathcal{U}(p_1, p_3)$

$r_2: \mathcal{P}(p_2, p_1) :\!- \mathcal{P}(p_1, p_2)$

$r_3: \mathcal{R}(p_1, p_2) :\!- \mathcal{P}(p_1, p_2), \mathcal{A}(p_1, p_2)$

Fig. 1. Java program and simplified static datarace analysis in Datalog.

For our example program, $\mathcal{N}(p_1, p_2)$ may contain the tuples $\mathcal{N}(l_1, l_2)$, $\mathcal{N}(l_2, l_3)$, etc. While some input relations, such as $\mathcal{N}(p_1, p_2)$, may be directly obtained from the text of the program being analyzed, other input relations, such as $\mathcal{U}(p_1, p_2)$ or $\mathcal{A}(p_1, p_2)$, may themselves be the result of earlier analyses (in this case, a lockset analysis and a pointer analysis, respectively).

The rules are intended to be read from right-to-left, with all variables universally quantified, and the :- operator interpreted as implication. For example, the rule r_1 may be read as saying, "For all program points p_1, p_2, p_3, if p_1 and p_2 may execute in parallel ($\mathcal{P}(p_1, p_2)$), and p_3 may be executed immediately after p_2 ($\mathcal{N}(p_2, p_3)$), and p_1 and p_3 are not guarded by a common lock ($\mathcal{U}(p_1, p_3)$), then p_1 and p_3 may themselves execute in parallel."

Observe that the analysis is *flow-sensitive*, i.e. it takes into account the order of program statements, represented by the relation $\mathcal{N}(p_1, p_2)$, but *path-insensitive*, i.e. it disregards the satisfiability of path conditions and predicates along branches. This is an example of an approximation to enable the analysis to scale to large programs.

Applying the Analysis to a Program. To apply the above analysis to our example program, one starts with the set of input tuples, and repeatedly applies the inference rules r_1, r_2, and r_3, until no new facts can be derived. Starting with the tuple $\mathcal{P}(l_4, l_2)$, we show a portion of the derivation graph thus obtained in Fig. 2. Each box represents a tuple and is shaded gray if it is an input tuple. Nodes identified with rule names represent grounded clauses: for example, the node $r_1(l_4, l_2, l_3)$ indicates the "*grounded instance*" of the rule r_1 with $p_1 = l_4$, $p_2 = l_2$, and $p_3 = l_3$. This clause takes as hypotheses the tuples $\mathcal{P}(l_4, l_2)$, $\mathcal{N}(l_2, l_3)$, and $\mathcal{U}(l_4, l_3)$, and derives the conclusion $\mathcal{P}(l_4, l_3)$, and the arrows represent these dependencies.

Observe that clause nodes are conjunctive: a rule fires iff all of its antecedents are derivable. On the other hand, tuple nodes are disjunctive: a tuple is derivable iff there exists at least one derivable clause of which it is the conclusion. For instance, the tuple $\mathcal{P}(l_6, l_7)$ can be derived in one of two ways: either by instantiating r_1 with $p_1 = l_6$, $p_2 = l_6$, and $p_3 = l_7$ (as shown in Fig. 2), or by instantiating r_2 with $p_1 = l_7$ and $p_2 = l_6$ (not shown).

Observe that lines l_4 and l_2 can indeed execute in parallel, and the original conclusion $\mathcal{P}(l_4, l_2)$, in Fig. 2, is true. However, the subsequent conclusion $\mathcal{P}(l_4, l_3)$ is spurious, and is caused by the analysis being incomplete: the second thread to enter the `synchronized` block will necessarily leave the method at line l_2. Among others, four subsequent false alarms—$\mathcal{R}(l_4, l_5)$, $\mathcal{R}(l_5, l_5)$, $\mathcal{R}(l_6, l_7)$, and $\mathcal{R}(l_7, l_7)$—result from the analysis incorrectly concluding $\mathcal{P}(l_4, l_3)$.

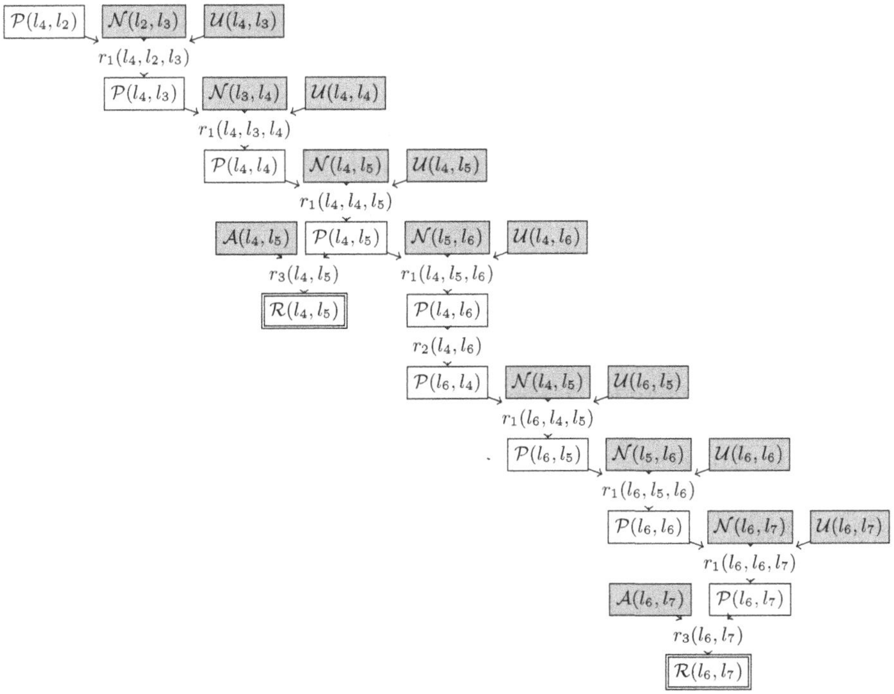

Fig. 2. A portion of the derivation graph obtained by applying the static datarace analysis to the program in Fig. 1. The central focus of this section is following: if the user identifies $\mathcal{R}(l_4, l_5)$ as a false alarm, then how should this affect our confidence in the remaining alarms?

Quantifying Incompleteness using Probabilities. Incomplete analysis rules are the principal cause of false alarms: although $\mathcal{P}(l_4, l_2)$, $\mathcal{N}(l_2, l_3)$, and $\mathcal{U}(l_4, l_3)$ are all true, it is not the case that $\mathcal{P}(l_4, l_3)$. To address this problem, we relax the interpretation of clause nodes, and treat them probabilistically:

$$\Pr(r_1(l_4, l_2, l_3) \mid h_1) = 0.95, \text{ and} \tag{1}$$
$$\Pr(\neg r_1(l_4, l_2, l_3) \mid h_1) = 1 - 0.95 = 0.05, \tag{2}$$

where $h_1 = \mathcal{P}(l_4, l_2) \wedge \mathcal{N}(l_2, l_3) \wedge \mathcal{U}(l_4, l_3)$ is the event indicating that all the hypotheses of $r_1(l_4, l_2, l_3)$ are true, and $p_1 = 0.95$ is the probability of the clause "correctly firing". By setting p_1 to a value strictly less than 1, we make it possible for the conclusion of $r_1(l_4, l_2, l_3)$, $\mathcal{P}(l_4, l_3)$ to still be false, even though all the hypotheses in h_1 hold.

In this new setup, as before, if any of the antecedents of $r_1(l_4, l_2, l_3)$ is false, then it is itself definitely false:

$$\Pr(r_1(l_4, l_2, l_3) \mid \neg h_1) = 0, \text{ and} \tag{3}$$
$$\Pr(\neg r_1(l_4, l_2, l_3) \mid \neg h_1) = 1. \tag{4}$$

We also continue to treat tuple nodes as regular disjunctions:

$$\Pr(\mathcal{P}(l_6, l_7) \mid r_1(l_6, l_6, l_7) \vee r_2(l_7, l_6)) = 1, \tag{5}$$
$$\Pr(\mathcal{P}(l_6, l_7) \mid \neg(r_1(l_6, l_6, l_7) \vee r_2(l_7, l_6))) = 0, \tag{6}$$

and treat all input tuples t as being known with certainty: $\Pr(t) = 1$.

These rule probabilities can be learnt using an expectation maximization (EM) algorithm from training data. For now, we associate the rule r_3 with firing probability $p_3 = 0.95$, and r_2 with probability $p_2 = 1$. Finally, to simplify the discussion, we treat $\mathcal{P}(l_0, l_1)$ and $\mathcal{P}(l_1, l_1)$ as input facts, with $\Pr(\mathcal{P}(l_0, l_1)) = 0.40$ and $\Pr(\mathcal{P}(l_1, l_1)) = 0.60$.

From Derivation Graphs to Bayesian Networks. By attaching conditional probability distributions (CPDs) such as Eqs. 1–6 to each node of Fig. 2, we view the derivation graph as a Bayesian network. Specifically, we perform marginal inference on the network to associate each alarm with the probability, or *belief*, that it is a true datarace. This procedure generates a list of alarms ranked by probability, shown in Table 1a. For example, it computes the probability of $\mathcal{R}(l_4, l_5)$ as follows:

$$\begin{aligned}
\Pr(\mathcal{R}(l_4, l_5)) &= \Pr(\mathcal{R}(l_4, l_5) \wedge r_3(l_4, l_5)) + \Pr(\mathcal{R}(l_4, l_5) \wedge \neg r_3(l_4, l_5)) \\
&= \Pr(\mathcal{R}(l_4, l_5) \wedge r_3(l_4, l_5)) \\
&= \Pr(\mathcal{R}(l_4, l_5) \mid r_3(l_4, l_5)) \cdot \Pr(r_3(l_4, l_5)) \\
&= \Pr(r_3(l_4, l_5) \mid \mathcal{P}(l_4, l_5) \wedge \mathcal{A}(l_4, l_5)) \cdot \Pr(\mathcal{P}(l_4, l_5)) \cdot \Pr(\mathcal{A}(l_4, l_5)) \\
&= 0.95 \cdot \Pr(\mathcal{P}(l_4, l_5)) = 0.95^4 \cdot \Pr(\mathcal{P}(l_4, l_2)) \\
&= 0.95^8 \cdot \Pr(\mathcal{P}(l_1, l_1)) = 0.398.
\end{aligned}$$

The user now inspects the top-ranked report, $\mathcal{R}(l_4, l_5)$, and classifies it as a false alarm. The key idea underlying our approach is that *generalizing from feedback is conditioning on evidence*. By replacing the prior belief $\Pr(a)$, for each alarm a, with the posterior belief, $\Pr(a \mid \neg\mathcal{R}(l_4, l_5))$, our approach effectively propagates the user feedback to the remaining conclusions of the analysis.

This results in the updated list of alarms shown in Table 1b. Observe that the belief in the closely related alarm $\mathcal{R}(l_6, l_7)$ drops from 0.324 to 0.030, while the belief in the unrelated alarm $\mathcal{R}(l_0, l_7)$ remains unchanged at 0.279. As a result, the entire family of false alarms drops in the ranking, so that the only true datarace is now at the top.

The computation of the updated confidence values occurs by a similar procedure as before. For example:

$$\begin{aligned}
&\Pr(\mathcal{R}(l_6, l_7) \mid \neg\mathcal{R}(l_4, l_5)) \\
&\quad = \Pr(\mathcal{R}(l_6, l_7) \wedge \mathcal{P}(l_4, l_5) \mid \neg\mathcal{R}(l_4, l_5)) + \Pr(\mathcal{R}(l_6, l_7) \wedge \neg\mathcal{P}(l_4, l_5) \mid \neg\mathcal{R}(l_4, l_5)) \\
&\quad = \Pr(\mathcal{R}(l_6, l_7) \wedge \mathcal{P}(l_4, l_5) \mid \neg\mathcal{R}(l_4, l_5)).
\end{aligned}$$

Next, $\mathcal{R}(l_4, l_5)$ and $\mathcal{R}(l_6, l_7)$ are conditionally independent given $\mathcal{P}(l_4, l_5)$ as it occurs on the unique path between them. So,

$$\begin{aligned}
&\Pr(\mathcal{R}(l_6, l_7) \wedge \mathcal{P}(l_4, l_5) \mid \neg\mathcal{R}(l_4, l_5)) \\
&\quad = \Pr(\mathcal{R}(l_6, l_7) \mid \mathcal{P}(l_4, l_5)) \cdot \Pr(\mathcal{P}(l_4, l_5) \mid \neg\mathcal{R}(l_4, l_5)) \\
&\quad = 0.95^5 \cdot \Pr(\mathcal{P}(l_4, l_5) \mid \neg\mathcal{R}(l_4, l_5)).
\end{aligned}$$

Finally, by Bayes' rule, we have:

$$\begin{aligned}
\Pr(\mathcal{P}(l_4, l_5) \mid \neg\mathcal{R}(l_4, l_5)) &= \frac{\Pr(\neg\mathcal{R}(l_4, l_5) \mid \mathcal{P}(l_4, l_5)) \cdot \Pr(\mathcal{P}(l_4, l_5))}{\Pr(\neg\mathcal{R}(l_4, l_5))} \\
&= \frac{0.05 \cdot 0.95^7 \cdot 0.60}{0.60} = 0.03.
\end{aligned}$$

Our prior belief in $\mathcal{P}(l_4, l_5)$ was $\Pr(\mathcal{P}(l_4, l_5)) = 0.42$, so that $\Pr(\mathcal{P}(l_4, l_5) \mid \neg\mathcal{R}(l_4, l_5)) \ll \Pr(\mathcal{P}(l_4, l_5))$, but is still strictly greater than 0. This is because one eventuality by which $\neg\mathcal{R}(l_4, l_5)$ may occur is for $\mathcal{P}(l_4, l_5)$ to be true, but for the clause $r_3(l_4, l_5)$ to misfire. We may now conclude that $\Pr(\mathcal{R}(l_6, l_7) \mid \neg\mathcal{R}(l_4, l_5)) = 0.95^5 \cdot 0.03 = 0.030$.

The Interaction Model. In summary, given an analysis and a program to be analyzed, our approach takes as input the set of tuples and grounded clauses produced by the Datalog solver at fixpoint, and constructs the belief network. Next, it performs Bayesian inference to compute the probability of each alarm, and presents the alarm with highest probability for inspection by the user. The user then indicates its ground truth, and our approach incorporates this feedback as evidence for subsequent iterations.

There are several possible stopping criteria by which the user could cease interaction, e.g., only inspect alarms with confidence higher than some threshold p_0, and stop once the confidence of the highest ranked alarm drops below p_0; or only inspect n alarms, and stop after n iterations. In all these situations, we lose any soundness guarantees provided by the underlying analysis, but given the large number of alarms typically emitted by analysis tools, this approach strikes a useful tradeoff between accuracy and soundness.

Table 1. List of alarms produced (a) before and (b) after the feedback $\neg\mathcal{R}(l_4, l_5)$. Observe how the real datarace $\mathcal{R}(l_0, l_7)$ rises in ranking as a result of feedback.

(a) $\Pr(a)$.

Rank	Belief	Program points
1	0.398	l_4, l_5
2	0.378	l_5, l_5
3	0.324	l_6, l_7
4	0.308	l_7, l_7
5	0.279	l_0, l_7

(b) $\Pr(a \mid \neg\mathcal{R}(l_4, l_5))$.

Rank	Belief	Program points
1	0.279	l_0, l_7
2	0.035	l_5, l_5
3	0.030	l_6, l_7
4	0.028	l_7, l_7
5	0	l_4, l_5

3 A Taxonomy of Research Directions

In this section, we outline the landscape of challenges in static analysis, argue how techniques similar to those in the preceding section can be used to address them, and discuss open problems. We classify the landscape into three broad categories: (i) balancing analysis tradeoffs (Sect. 3.1), (ii) tailoring analysis results (Sect. 3.2), and (iii) specifying and implementing analyses (Sect. 3.3). Note that these challenges are agnostic of specific analyses and apply broadly to a variety of different analyses.

3.1 Balancing Analysis Tradeoffs

The undecidability of the static analysis problem necessitates tradeoffs between accuracy, cost, and soundness. We focus on two of the most common tradeoffs: accuracy vs. cost, and accuracy vs. soundness.

Analysis Accuracy vs. Cost. This tradeoff concerns balancing the cost of the program abstraction against the accuracy of the analysis result. A popular paradigm to suitably strike this tradeoff is counterexample-guided abstraction refinement (CEGAR).

In [39], we show how to enable CEGAR for arbitrary analyses specified in Datalog. It uses a formulation of maximum satisfiability (MaxSAT), an optimization extension of the Boolean satisfiability problem, wherein the hard constraints encode provenance information relating analysis results (e.g. alarms) to abstractions, while the soft constraints encode the relative costs of different abstractions. The objective is to either find the cheapest abstraction that suffices to prove a program property of interest or show that no such abstraction exists.

Open problems in this space include supporting richer analyses, such as those that employ widening, and considering not only the costs of different abstractions but also their likelihood of success (e.g. [15]).

Analysis Accuracy vs. Soundness. This tradeoff concerns balancing the accuracy of the analysis result against the soundness of the analysis. Arguably the most common tradeoff struck by static analyses in practice, it incurs false positives as well as false negatives, unlike the accuracy vs. cost tradeoff which only incurs false positives.

In [24] and [32], we show how to enable this tradeoff for arbitrary analyses specified in Datalog. The approach in [32] was illustrated in Sect. 2 wherein we perform marginal inference on a Bayesian network induced by provenance constraints to rank alarms produced by the analysis. In [24], we employ a different approach by performing MAP inference on a Markov Logic Network (MLN). The main difference between the two approaches, besides the different probabilistic models, is that we obtain a confidence score for each derived fact in [32], whereas we obtain the "most likely world" in [24]. The former is more amenable to user interaction both because it allows to rank analysis alarms and because incorporating user feedback translates into conditioning on evidence (in contrast, [24] requires additional constraints to propagate the user feedback).

Open problems in this space include how to transfer user feedback across programs, providing a rigorous semantics of rule weights, and richer probabilistic models which allow rule weights to depend on finer-grained program contexts.

3.2 Tailoring Analysis Results

A relatively recent area of exploration in static analysis concerns how to improve usability by tailoring analysis results. We consider unguided vs. interactive approaches, batch vs. continuous approaches, classification vs. ranking approaches, and different metrics for ranking.

Unguided vs. Interactive. Conventional static analyses are unguided in that they cannot tailor results to individual users. As we illustrated in Sect. 2, continuous modes of logical reasoning allow analyses to incorporate and generalize user feedback, but no longer guarantee soundness. Our earlier work [38] enables interaction while preserving soundness, but does not generalize user feedback; instead, the objective is to minimize the user burden by prioritizing questions that maximize the alarms to be resolved. Even in this discrete setting, provenance information is used to relate alarms to questions.

Open problems in this space include coping with noise inherent in interactive approaches, how to generalize user feedback effectively within a program, and how to transfer the knowledge learnt from interaction across programs.

Batch vs. Continuous Reasoning. Conventional static analyses operate in batch mode in that different parts of the program are presumed to be equally relevant to the user. However, in prevalent settings of continuous integration and continuous deployment, the user is interested only in alarms relevant to their code change [19,30].

In [16], we show how to compute differential provenance information between two program versions in order to prioritize alarms relevant to the code change, even in discrete modes of reasoning. Moreover, by incorporating continuous modes of reasoning, we show how to amplify the benefits by ranking the alarms, and by incorporating and generalizing user feedback.

Open problems in this arena include how to guarantee the soundness of differential analysis even in the discrete setting, and the related problem of what code granularity to use for identifying the changes between two program versions (e.g. AST-based vs. line-based).

Alarm Clustering vs. Ranking. Another dimension to tailor analysis results is to cluster related alarms in order to reduce inspection effort. Provenance information can be used to identify dependencies between alarms and cluster correlated alarms together (e.g. [20]). However, clustering treats all alarms uniformly, which is seldom useful in practice.

Ranking alarms on the other hand opens the door to different metrics to prioritize alarms. We showed in Sect. 2 how continuous modes of reasoning can be combined with provenance information to rank alarms based on *ground truth*. However, alternative metrics of ranking are possible, such as *relevance* to code changes, and alarm *severity*. An important open problem in this setting is how to quantify severity.

3.3 Analysis Specification and Implementation

Another set of challenges concerns how to specify and implement constraint-based analyses to effectively support the use-cases discussed above. We discuss how to synthesize analyses automatically from data, expressiveness issues of the language for specifying analyses, and capabilities required of analysis solvers.

Synthesizing Analyses from Data. The problem of synthesizing analyses from input-output data (e.g., programs with labeled alarms) is motivated by two reasons: first, allowing end-users to customize analyses to diverse settings, and secondly, overcoming limitations of hand-engineered analyses that hinder use-cases discussed above. For example, the effectiveness of generalizing user feedback across alarms relies heavily on the quality of analysis rules, as rule weights can only go so far to compensate for it.

In recent work [2,33,36], we have developed increasingly scalable approaches to synthesize Datalog programs from input-output data. Provenance information is crucial to scaling the approach in [33] which follows the counterexample-guided inductive synthesis (CEGIS) paradigm for program synthesis. The key idea is to use a Datalog solver to not only produce counterexamples for the candidate Datalog program with respect to given input-output data, but also explain them using "why" and "why-not" provenance. This in turn allows the iterative CEGIS process to converge faster and scale better.

The Datalog synthesis problem can also be seen as an instance of the classic Inductive Logic Programming (ILP) problem [26,28]. A key difference is that ILP techniques focus on learning relations, often probabilistic ones, from vast amounts of mined data, e.g., biological data [27]. On the other hand, in our setting, and in a large class of synthesis techniques, the goal is to interactively infer a program from a small, representative set of input-output examples.

Open problems in this arena include active learning to reduce the burden on providing labeled data upfront, coping with noisy data, avoiding the need for syntactic rule templates, and synthesizing analyses with expressive features such as invented predicates, recursion, negation, and aggregation. Note that coping with noisy data is fundamentally necessary because, even if the data perfectly captures the concrete semantics of program behavior, the synthesized analysis must follow an abstract semantics that approximates the data.

Expressiveness of Analysis Language. The use of Datalog for static analysis dates back to Reps's work on demand-driven analysis [34]. The desire to express a wide variety of analyses in Datalog has led to extending the language with features such as value construction, negation, aggregation, and higher-order predicates. These extensions include LogicBlox's LogiQL [3] which forms the basis of the Doop static analysis framework [8], Semmle's QL [5] which allows Datalog programs to be written over the target program's syntax, the higher-order functional Datalog language Datafun [4], and Flix for specifying static analyses [22]. Finally, many works extend the semantics of logic programming to the continuous domain, such as Markov Logic Networks [35], ProbLog [12], and its extensions such as DeepProbLog [25] and aProbLog [18].

Capabilities of Analysis Solvers. A benefit of constraint-based analysis lies in the ability to leverage off-the-shelf solvers. The need for more expressive features in the constraint language is counterbalanced by the need to efficiently execute analyses specified in the language. Moreover, the use-cases discussed above require features besides just efficient execution, notably efficient computation of provenance information. Efficient algorithms for "why" and "why not" provenance for Datalog remain areas of active research [37,40], and notions of provenance for more expressive logics are further beyond [13]. Finally, another interesting direction of exploration is the integration of Datalog solvers with solvers for other theories, such as SMT solvers [17] and solvers for mathematical optimization (e.g. MaxSAT and Integer Linear Programming) [3,23].

4 Conclusions

We proposed a new approach to static analysis that builds upon the long-standing constraint-based approach while providing fundamentally new capabilities. The approach aims to seamlessly combine discrete and continuous modes of logical reasoning. To this end, it relies on static analyses being specified in a constraint language that is amenable to computing provenance information. We showed how provenance plays a crucial role in a rich variety of applications of our approach. Finally, we outlined a taxonomy of research directions and described open problems in the field.

Acknowledgments. I thank the following for making vital contributions to the body of research summarized in this paper: PhD students Sulekha Kulkarni, Xujie Si, and Xin Zhang; postdocs Kihong Heo, Woosuk Lee, and Mukund Raghothaman; and collaborators Radu Grigore, Aditya Nori, and Hongseok Yang. I am grateful to Peter O'Hearn for providing useful feedback at various stages of this work. This research was supported by DARPA award #FA8750-15-2-0009, NSF awards #1253867 and #1526270, ONR award #N00014-18-1-2021, and gifts from Facebook, Google, and Microsoft.

References

1. Abiteboul, S., Hull, R., Vianu, V.: Foundations of Databases. Addison-Wesley, Boston (1995)
2. Albarghouthi, A., Koutris, P., Naik, M., Smith, C.: Constraint-based synthesis of Datalog programs. In: Proceedings of the 23rd International Conference on Principles and Practice of Constraint Programming (CP) (2017)
3. Aref, M., et al.: Design and implementation of the LogicBlox system. In: Proceedings of the ACM SIGMOD International Conference on Management of Data (SIGMOD) (2015)
4. Arntzenius, M., Krishnaswami, N.: Datafun: A functional Datalog. In: Proceedings of the ACM SIGPLAN International Conference on Functional Programming (ICFP) (2016)
5. Avgustinov, P., de Moor, O., Jones, M.P., Schäfer, M.: QL: Object-oriented queries on relational data. In: Proceedings of the 30th European Conference on Object-Oriented Programming (ECOOP) (2016)
6. Ball, T., Rajamani, S.: The SLAM project: debugging system software via static analysis. In: Proceedings of the 29th ACM SIGPLAN-SIGACT Symposium on Principles of Programming Languages (POPL) (2002)
7. Bessey, A., et al.: A few billion lines of code later: using static analysis to find bugs in the real world. Commun. ACM **53**(2), 66–75 (2010)
8. Bravenboer, M., Smaragdakis, Y.: Strictly declarative specification of sophisticated points-to analyses. In: Proceedings of the ACM SIGPLAN Conference on Object Oriented Programming Systems Languages and Applications (OOPSLA) (2009)
9. Calcagno, C., et al.: Moving fast with software verification. In: Havelund, K., Holzmann, G., Joshi, R. (eds.) NFM 2015. LNCS, vol. 9058, pp. 3–11. Springer, Cham (2015). https://doi.org/10.1007/978-3-319-17524-9_1
10. Cousot, P., Cousot, R.: Abstract interpretation: a unified lattice model for static analysis of programs by construction or approximation of fixpoints. In: Proceedings of the 4th ACM SIGPLAN-SIGACT Symposium on Principles of Programming Languages (POPL) (1977)
11. Cousot, P., et al.: The ASTRÉE analyzer. In: Proceedings of the 14th European Symposium on Programming (ESOP) (2005)
12. De Raedt, L., Kimmig, A., Toivonen, H.: Problog: A probabilistic Prolog and its application in link discovery. In: Proceedings of the 20th International Joint Conference on Artificial Intelligence (2007)
13. Grädel, E., Tannen, V.: Semiring provenance for first-order model checking (2017). http://arxiv.org/abs/1712.01980
14. Green, T., Karvounarakis, G., Tannen, V.: Provenance semirings. In: Proceedings of the 26th Symposium on Principles of Database Systems (PODS) (2007)
15. Grigore, R., Yang, H.: Abstraction refinement guided by a learnt probabilistic model. In: Proceedings of the 43rd ACM SIGPLAN-SIGACT Symposium on Principles of Programming Languages (POPL) (2016)
16. Heo, K., Raghothaman, M., Si, X., Naik, M.: Continuously reasoning about programs using differential bayesian inference. In: Proceedings of the 40th ACM SIGPLAN Conference on Programming Language Design and Implementation (PLDI) (2019)
17. Hoder, K., Bjørner, N., De Moura, L.: μz: An efficient engine for fixed points with constraints. In: Proceedings of the 23rd International Conference on Computer-Aided Verification (CAV) (2011)

18. Kimmig, A., den Broeck, G.V., De Raedt, L.: An algebraic Prolog for reasoning about possible worlds. In: Proceedings of the 25th AAAI Conference on Artificial Intelligence (2011)
19. Lahiri, S., Vaswani, K., Hoare, C.A.R.: Differential static analysis: opportunities, applications, and challenges. In: Proceedings of the FSE/SDP Workshop on Future of Software Engineering Research (FoSER) (2010)
20. Lee, W., Lee, W., Yi, K.: Sound non-statistical clustering of static analysis alarms. In: Proceedings of the 13th International Conference on Verification, Model Checking, and Abstract Interpretation (VMCAI) (2012)
21. Livshits, B., et al.: In defense of soundiness: a manifesto. Commun. ACM **58**(2), 44–46 (2015)
22. Madsen, M., Yee, M.H., Lhoták, O.: From datalog to Flix: a declarative language for fixed points on lattices. In: Proceedings of the 37th ACM SIGPLAN Conference on Programming Language Design and Implementation (PLDI) (2016)
23. Mangal, R., Zhang, X., Naik, M., Nori, A.V.: Volt: A lazy grounding framework for solving very large MaxSAT instances. In: Proceedings of the International Conference on Theory and Applications of Satisfiability Testing (SAT) (2015)
24. Mangal, R., Zhang, X., Nori, A., Naik, M.: A user-guided approach to program analysis. In: Proceedings of the Joint Meeting on European Software Engineering Conference and Symposium on the Foundations of Software Engineering (ESEC/FSE) (2015)
25. Manhaeve, R., Dumancic, S., Kimmig, A., Demeester, T., De Raedt, L.: Deepproblog: neural probabilistic logic programming. In: Advances in Neural Information Processing Systems (2018)
26. Muggleton, S.: Inductive logic programming. New Gener. Comput. **8**(4), 295–318 (1991)
27. Muggleton, S.: Scientific knowledge discovery using inductive logic programming. Commun. ACM **42**(11), 42–46 (1999)
28. Muggleton, S., et al.: ILP turns 20 - biography and future challenges. Mach. Learn. **86**(1), 3–23 (2012)
29. Naik, M., Aiken, A., Whaley, J.: Effective static race detection for Java. In: Proceedings of the 27th ACM SIGPLAN Conference on Programming Language Design and Implementation (PLDI) (2006)
30. O'Hearn, P.W.: Continuous reasoning: scaling the impact of formal methods. In: Proceedings of the 33rd Annual ACM/IEEE Symposium on Logic in Computer Science (LICS) (2018)
31. Pearl, J.: Probabilistic Reasoning in Intelligent Systems: Networks of Plausible Inference. Morgan Kaufmann, Burlington (1988)
32. Raghothaman, M., Kulkarni, S., Heo, K., Naik, M.: User-guided program reasoning using Bayesian inference. In: Proceedings of the 39th ACM SIGPLAN Conference on Programming Language Design and Implementation (PLDI) (2018)
33. Raghothaman, M., Mendelson, J., Zhao, D., Scholz, B., Naik, M.: Provenance-guided synthesis of Datalog programs. Technical report (2019)
34. Reps, T.: Demand interprocedural program analysis using logic databases. In: Ramakrishnan, R. (ed.) Applications of Logic Databases, vol. 296. Springer, Boston (1995). https://doi.org/10.1007/978-1-4615-2207-2_8
35. Richardson, M., Domingos, P.: Markov logic networks. Mach. Learn. **62**(1–2), 107–136 (2006)
36. Si, X., Raghothaman, M., Heo, K., Naik, M.: Synthesizing Datalog programs using numerical relaxation. In: Proceedings of the 28th International Joint Conference on Artificial Intelligence (IJCAI) (2019)

37. Xu, J., Zhang, W., Alawini, A., Tannen, V.: Provenance analysis for missing answers and integrity repairs. IEEE Data Eng. Bull. **41**(1), 39–50 (2018)
38. Zhang, X., Grigore, R., Si, X., Naik, M.: Effective interactive resolution of static analysis alarms. In: Proceedings of the ACM SIGPLAN International Conference on Systems, Programming, Languages, and Applications (OOPSLA) (2017)
39. Zhang, X., Mangal, R., Grigore, R., Naik, M., Yang, H.: On abstraction refinement for program analyses in Datalog. In: Proceedings of the 35th ACM SIGPLAN Conference on Programming Language Design and Implementation (PLDI) (2014)
40. Zhao, D., Subotic, P., Scholz, B.: Provenance for large-scale Datalog (2019). http://arxiv.org/abs/1907.05045

Static Analysis of Data Science Software

Caterina Urban[1,2(✉)]

[1] INRIA, Paris, France
caterina.urban@inria.fr
[2] DIENS, École Normale Supérieure, CNRS, PSL University, Paris, France

Abstract. Data science software is playing an increasingly important role in every aspect of our daily lives and is even slowly creeping into mission critical scenarios, despite being often opaque and unpredictable. In this paper, we will discuss some key challenges and a number of research questions that we are currently addressing in developing static analysis methods and tools for data science software.

1 Introduction

Nowadays, thanks to advances in machine learning and the availability of vast amounts of data, computer software plays an increasingly important role in assisting or even autonomously performing tasks in our daily lives.

As data science software becomes more and more widespread, we become increasingly vulnerable to *programming errors*. In particular, programming errors that do not cause failures can have serious consequences since code that produces an erroneous but plausible result gives no indication that something went wrong. This issue becomes particularly worrying knowing that machine learning software, thanks to its ability to efficiently approximate or simulate more complex systems [22], is slowly creeping into mission critical scenarios[1].

However, programming errors are not the only concern. Another important issue is the vulnerability of machine learning models to *adversarial examples* [39], that is, small input perturbations that cause the model to misbehave in unpredictable ways. More generally, a critical issue is the notorious difficulty to interpret and explain machine learning software[2].

Finally, as we are witnessing widespread adoption of software with far-reaching societal impact — i.e., to automate decision-making in fields such as social welfare, criminal justice, and even health care — a number of recent cases have evidenced the importance of ensuring software *fairness* and non-discrimination[3] as well as data *privacy*[4]. Going forward, data science software

[1] https://www.airbus.com/innovation/future-technology/artificial-intelligence.html.
[2] http://www.technologyreview.com/s/604087/the-dark-secret-at-the-heart-of-ai.
[3] https://www.nytimes.com/2017/10/26/opinion/algorithm-compas-sentencing-bias.html.
[4] https://www.nytimes.com/2012/02/19/magazine/shopping-habits.html.

B.-Y. E. Chang (Ed.): SAS 2019, LNCS 11822, pp. 17–23, 2019.
https://doi.org/10.1007/978-3-030-32304-2_2

will be subject to more and more legal regulations (e.g., the European General Data Protection Regulation adopted in 2016) as well as administrative audits.

It is thus paramount to develop method and tools that can keep up with these developments and enhance our understanding of data science software and ensure it behaves correctly and reliably. In this paper, we will discuss challenges and a number of research questions that we are currently addressing in this area.

2 Key Challenges

A number of key challenges differentiate static analysis methods for data science software from static analysis of regular software. We discuss them below.

Dirty Data. Data is often incorrect, inaccurate, incomplete, or inconsistent and needs to be cleaned before it can be used. According to recent surveys, data preparation occupies between 50% and 80% of the time of a data scientist[5]. Moreover, data preparation code is the most fragile in a data science pipeline as it generally heavily relies on implicit assumptions on the data. For this latter reason, static analysis methods for data preparation code involve an *additional level of indirection* compared to more classical static analysis that infer properties about program variables.

Inscrutability. The behavior of machine learning models is poorly understood [15]. Some mathematical properties of these models have been discovered [26] but the mathematical theory generally still lacks behind. Therefore, static analysis methods for machine learning have *no semantics to build upon* as in traditional application scenarios, e.g. [11].

Meaningless Accuracy. The performance of machine learning models is measured by their accuracy on the testing data. However, this measure does not provide any general guarantee on the model behavior on other, previously unseen, data. Thus, static analysis methods for machine learning must be data-independent, lest they remain limited to local properties, e.g., [14].

Lack of Specifications. It is often hard to formally specify the correct behavior of a machine learning model, e.g., it is not obvious how to specify an obstacle that a machine learning model should recognize[6]. Generally, some specification is reconstructed at the system level, by combining together information coming from multiple system components, e.g., from a machine learning model and multiple sensors. Similarly, without a formal specification to refer to, static analysis methods also *need to be decomposed*, each component dedicated to a well-identified property that can be formalized.

Scalability and Precision. Static analysis methods for machine learning models only need to handle relatively simple operations such as matrix multiplications and activation functions. However, scaling to certain model architectures

[5] https://www.nytimes.com/2014/08/18/technology/for-big-data-scientists-hurdle-to-insights-is-janitor-work.html.

[6] https://www.tesla.com/blog/tragic-loss.

used in practice while retaining enough precision to prove useful properties, remains a challenge. To this end, new static analysis methods should be designed that employ dedicated and clever partitioning strategies [34] or specialized new (combinations of) abstract domains [37].

3 Research Questions

To address the above challenges we are currently working in the four main directions that we present below.

Implicit Assumptions on Data. Data preparation code is generally disregarded as glue code and, for this reason, is usually poorly tested. This, together with the fact that this code is often written in a rush and is highly dependent on the data (e.g., the use of magic constants is not uncommon for this kind of code), greatly increases the likelihood for programming errors to remain unnoticed.

To address these issues, we have developed a static analysis that automatically the infers implicit assumptions on the data that are embedded in the code. Specifically, we infer assumptions on the *structure* of the data as well as on the data *values* and the *relations* between the data. The analysis uses a combination of existing abstract domains [7,8,29, etc.] extended to indirectly reason about the data rather than simply reasoning about program variables.

The inferred assumptions can simply provide feedback on one's expectations on both the program and the data. Alternatively, they can be leveraged for testing the data, e.g., via grammar-based testing [18]. Finally and more interestingly, they can be used to automatically check and guide the cleaning of the data.

Data Usage. A common source of errors in data science software is data being mistakenly ignored. A notable example is economists Reinhart and Rogoff's paper "Growth in a Time of Debt", which was widely cited in political debates and was later demonstrated to be flawed. Indeed, one of the flaws was a programming error, which entirely excluded some data from the analysis [19]. Its critics hold that this paper led to unjustified adoption of austerity policies in the European Union [27]. The likelihood of data remaining accidentally unused becomes particularly high for long data science pipelines.

In recent work [41], we have proposed a static analysis framework for automatically detecting unused data. They key ingredient of the framework is the notion of *dependency* between the data and the outcome of the program. This yields a *unifying framework* that encompasses dependency-based analysis that arise in many other contexts, such as secure information flow [38], program slicing [42], as well as provenance and lineage analysis [5], to name a few.

Algorithmic Bias. It is not difficult to envision that in the future most of the decisions in society will be delegated to software. It is thus becoming increasingly important to be able to detect whether the software is operating fairly or it is reinforcing biases and perpetuating prejudices.

To this end, we have designed a general static analysis framework for proving *causal fairness* [24]. Within this framework we have developed a scalable static analysis for feed-forward multi-layer neural networks. The analysis is a combination of a forward and backward analysis; the forward analysis effectively splits the analysis into independent parallelizable tasks and overall reduces the analysis effort. One can tune the precision and cost of the analysis by adjusting the size of the tasks and the total time allotted to the analysis. In this way, one can adapt the analysis to the context in which it is being deployed and even make it incremental, i.e., by resuming the tasks on which the analysis is imprecise once more resources become available.

Global Robustness. Finally, we are working on generalizing the framework discussed above to proving *global robustness* of machine learning models. Note that this property is concerned with certifying the whole input space and is thus much harder than local robustness [14,32]. Specifically, we are designing a framework parametric in the chosen notion of (abstract) distance between input data points. In order to scale to larger neural networks with more complex architectures, we are studying new combinations of existing abstract domains [28] as well as new specialized abstract domains.

4 Related Work

We now quickly survey some of the related work in the area, broadly defined. The discussion is by no means exhaustive but only intended to suggest some useful reference pointers for further exploration.

Spreadsheet Analyses. There has been considerable work on testing, analyzing, and debugging spreadsheets [2,6,35, etc.]. These mostly target errors (e.g., type errors) in the data rather than in the software (i.e., the spreadsheet formulas).

Adversarial Examples. Since neural networks were shown to be vulnerable to them [39], a lot of work has been focused on constructing adversarial examples [31,40, etc.] and harnessing them for adversarial training [16,20,30, etc.].

Robustness Analyses. Comparatively little work instead has been dedicated to testing [32] and verifying [21,23,33, etc.] neural network robustness. The challenge remains to scale to large and complex network architectures used in practice, with a few recent notable exceptions, e.g., [14,37]. On the other hand, robustness analyses for neural networks deal with much simpler control structures compared to regular programs [4,17,25, etc.].

Fairness and Privacy. Work on testing and verifying other properties such as fairness and privacy [1, 10, 13, etc.] is generally limited to standard machine learning software or rather small neural networks, with recent exceptions, e.g., [3].

Probabilistic Programs. Finally, data science programs can also be seen as probabilistic programs, for which a vast literature exists [9, 12, 36, etc.]. We refer to [36] for an in-depth discussion of the related work in this area.

5 Conclusion

We discussed the challenges and some of our progress in developing static analyses for data science software. Much more work remains to be done and, as our automated future presses for results, we hope that this exposition encourages the formal methods community as a whole to contribute to this effort.

References

1. Albarghouthi, A., D'Antoni, L., Drews, S., Nori, A.V.: FairSquare: probabilistic verification of program fairness. In: PACMPL, vol. 1(OOPSLA), pp. 80:1–80:30 (2017)
2. Barowy, D.W., Gochev, D., Berger, E.D.: CheckCell: data debugging for spreadsheets. In: OOPSLA, pp. 507–523 (2014)
3. Bastani, O., Zhang, X., Solar-Lezama, A.: Verifying Fairness Properties via Concentration. CoRR, abs/1812.02573 (2018)
4. Chaudhuri, S., Gulwani, S., Lublinerman, R.: Continuity and robustness of programs. Commun. ACM **55**(8), 107–115 (2012)
5. Cheney, J., Ahmed, A., Acar, U.A.: Provenance as dependency analysis. Math. Struct. Comput. Sci. **21**(6), 1301–1337 (2011)
6. Cheng, T., Rival, X.: An abstract domain to infer types over zones in spreadsheets. In: Miné, A., Schmidt, D. (eds.) SAS 2012. LNCS, vol. 7460, pp. 94–110. Springer, Heidelberg (2012). https://doi.org/10.1007/978-3-642-33125-1_9
7. Costantini, G., Ferrara, P., Cortesi, A.: A suite of abstract domains for static analysis of string values. Softw. - Pract. Experience **45**(2), 245–287 (2015)
8. Cousot, P., Cousot, R.: Static determination of dynamic properties of programs. In: Second International Symposium on Programming, pp. 106–130 (1976)
9. Cousot, P., Monerau, M.: Probabilistic abstract interpretation. In: ESOP, pp. 169–193 (2012)
10. Datta, A., Fredrikson, M., Ko, G., Mardziel, P., Sen, S.: Use privacy in data-driven systems: theory and experiments with machine learnt programs. In: CCS, pp. 1193–1210 (2017)
11. Feret, J.: Static analysis of digital filters. In: ESOP, pp. 33–48 (2004)
12. Filieri, A., Pasareanu, C.S., Visser, W.: Reliability analysis in symbolic pathfinder. In: ICSE, pp. 622–631 (2013)
13. Galhotra, S., Brun, Y., Meliou, A.: Fairness testing: testing software for discrimination. In: FSE, pp. 498–510 (2017)
14. Gehr, T., et al.: AI2: safety and robustness certification of neural networks with abstract interpretation. In: S & P, pp. 3–18 (2018)

15. Gilpin, L.H., Bau, D., Yuan, B.Z., Bajwa, A., Specter, M., Kagal, L.: Explaining Explanations: An Approach to Evaluating Interpretability of Machine Learning. CoRR, abs/1806.00069 (2018)
16. Goodfellow, I.J., Shlens, J., Szegedy, C.: Explaining and harnessing adversarial examples. In: ICLR (2015)
17. Goubault, E., Putot, S.: Robustness analysis of finite precision implementations. In: APLAS, pp. 50–57 (2013)
18. Hennessy, M., Power, J.F.: An analysis of rule coverage as a criterion in generating minimal test suites for grammar-based software. In: ASE, pp. 104–113 (2005)
19. Herndon, T., Ash, M., Pollin, R.: Does high public debt consistently stifle economic growth? a critique of reinhart and rogoff. Cambridge J. Econ. **38**(2), 257–279 (2014)
20. Huang, R., Xu, B., Schuurmans, D., Szepesvári, C.: Learning with a Strong Adversary. CoRR, abs/1511.03034 (2015)
21. Huang, X., Kwiatkowska, M., Wang, S., Wu, M.: Safety verification of deep neural networks. In: CAV, pp. 3–29 (2017)
22. Julian, K.D., Lopez, J., Brush, J.S., Owen, M.P., Kochenderfer, M.J.: Policy compression for aircraft collision avoidance systems. In: DASC, pp. 1–10 (2016)
23. Katz, G., Barrett, C.W., Dill, D.L., Julian, K., Kochenderfer, M.J.: Reluplex: an efficient SMT solver for verifying deep neural networks. In: CAV, pp. 97–117 (2017)
24. Kusner, M., Loftus, J., Russell, C., Silva, R.: Counterfactual fairness. In: NIPS, pp. 4069–4079 (2017)
25. Majumdar, R., Saha, I.: Symbolic robustness analysis. In: RTSS, pp. 355–363 (2009)
26. Mallat, S.: Understanding deep convolutional networks. Phil. Trans. Royal Soc. A: Math., Phys. Eng. Sci. **374**, 20150203 (2016)
27. Mencinger, J., Aristovnik, A., Verbič, M.: The impact of growing public debt on economic growth in the european union. Amfiteatru Econ. **16**(35), 403–414 (2014)
28. Miné, A.: Symbolic methods to enhance the precision of numerical abstract domains. In: VMCAI, pp. 348–363 (2006)
29. Miné, A.: The octagon abstract domain. Higher-Order Symb. Comput. **19**(1), 31–100 (2006)
30. Mirman, M., Gehr, T., Vechev, M.T.: Differentiable abstract interpretation for provably robust neural networks. In: ICML, pp. 3575–3583 (2018)
31. Nguyen, A.M., Yosinski, J., Clune, J.: Deep neural networks are easily fooled: high confidence predictions for unrecognizable images. In: CVPR, pp. 427–436 (2015)
32. Pei, K., Cao, Y., Yang, J., Jana, S.: DeepXplore: automated whitebox testing of deep learning systems. In: SOSP, pp. 1–18 (2017)
33. Pulina, L., Tacchella, A.: An abstraction-refinement approach to verification of artificial neural networks. In: CAV, pp. 243–257 (2010)
34. Rival, X., Mauborgne, L.: The trace partitioning abstract domain. Trans. Program. Lang. Syst. **29**(5), 26 (2007)
35. Rothermel, G., Burnett, M.M., Li, L., DuPuis, C., Sheretov, A.: A methodology for testing spreadsheets. Trans. Softw. Eng. Methodol. **10**(1), 110–147 (2001)
36. Sankaranarayanan, S., Chakarov, A., Gulwani, S.: Static analysis for probabilistic programs: inferring whole program properties from finitely many paths. In: PLDI, pp. 447–458 (2013)
37. Singh, G., Gehr, T., Püschel, M., Vechev, M.T.: An abstract domain for certifying neural networks. In: PACMPL, vol. 3(POPL), pp. 41:1–41:30 (2019)
38. Smith, G.: Principles of secure information flow analysis. Malware Detection, vol. 27. Springer, Boston (2007). https://doi.org/10.1007/978-0-387-44599-1_13

39. Szegedy, C., et al.: Intriguing properties of neural networks. In: ICLR (2014)
40. Tabacof, P., Valle, E.: Exploring the space of adversarial images. In: IJCNN, pp. 426–433 (2016)
41. Urban, C., Müller, P.: An abstract interpretation framework for input data usage. In: ESOP, pp. 683–710 (2018)
42. Weiser, M.: Program slicing. Trans. Softw. Eng. **10**(4), 352–357 (1984)

Pointers and Dataflow

Fast and Precise Handling of Positive Weight Cycles for Field-Sensitive Pointer Analysis

Yuxiang Lei and Yulei Sui(✉)

School of Computer Science, University of Technology, Sydney, Australia
yuxiang.lei@student.uts.edu.au, Yulei.Sui@uts.edu.au

Abstract. By distinguishing the fields of an object, Andersen's field-sensitive pointer analysis yields better precision than its field-insensitive counterpart. A typical field-sensitive solution to inclusion-based pointer analysis for C/C++ is to add positive weights to the edges in Andersen's constraint graph to model field access. However, the precise modeling is at the cost of introducing a new type of constraint cycles, called *positive weight cycles* (*PWC*s). A *PWC*, which contains at least one positive weight constraint, can cause infinite and redundant field derivations of an object unless the number of its fields is bounded by a pre-defined value. *PWC*s significantly affect analysis performance when analyzing large C/C++ programs with heavy use of structs and classes.

This paper presents Dea, a fast and precise approach to handling of *PWC*s that significantly accelerates existing field-sensitive pointer analyses by using a new field collapsing technique that captures the *derivation equivalence* of fields derived from the same object when resolving a *PWC*.

Two fields are derivation equivalent in a *PWC* if they are always pointed to by the same variables (nodes) in this *PWC*. A stride-based field representation is proposed to identify and collapse derivation equivalent fields into one, avoiding redundant field derivations with significantly fewer field objects during points-to propagation. We have conducted experiments using 11 open-source C/C++ programs. The evaluation shows that Dea is on average 7.1X faster than Pearce et al.'s field-sensitive analysis (Pkh), obtaining the best speedup of 11.0X while maintaining the same precision.

Keywords: Pointer analysis · Field-sensitive · Cycle elimination · Positive weight cycle

1 Introduction

Pointer analysis, which statically approximates the runtime values of a pointer, is an important enabling technology that paves the way for many other program analyses, such as program understanding, bug detection and compiler

B.-Y. E. Chang (Ed.): SAS 2019, LNCS 11822, pp. 27–47, 2019.
https://doi.org/10.1007/978-3-030-32304-2_3

optimisations. Andersen's analysis (or inclusion-based analysis) represents one of the most commonly used pointer analyses for Java and C/C++ programs. Field-sensitivity is an important precision enhancement that is naturally used in Andersen's analysis for analyzing Java [1–4], but is rarely used in many Andersen's analyses for C/C++ [5–9].

```
typedef struct A {int idx; /* f0 */ A* next; /* f1 */ } A;
```

```
A* p, q;
for(...){
p=malloc(...);//o
q=&p->next;
p=q;
}
```

$$\{o\} \subseteq p$$
$$p+1 \subseteq q$$
$$q \subseteq p$$

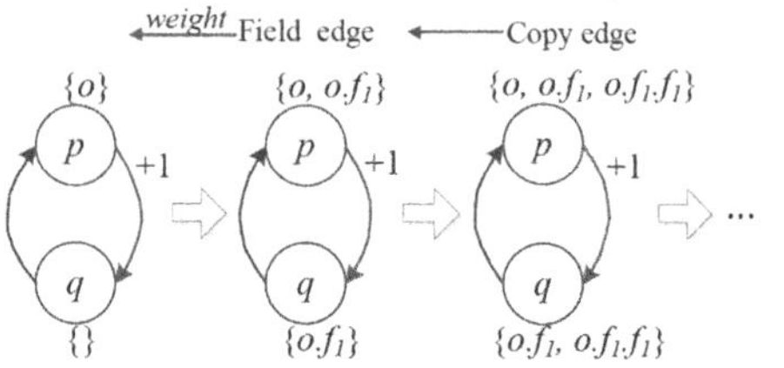

(a) C code (b) Constraints (c) Solving a *PWC* on the constraint graph

Fig. 1. A positive weight cycle example in Pearce's field-sensitive analysis.

Developing field-sensitive analysis for C/C++ is much harder than that for Java. The key difficulty, as also mentioned in [10,11], is that the address of a field can be taken in C/C++ (via an *address-of-field* instruction `q=&p→f`), whereas Java does not permit taking the address of a field. Accessing the value of a field in Java is through the load/store instruction associated with an extra field specifier in Java's bytecode given its strongly-typed language feature. However, in the C/C++ intermediate representation (e.g., LLVM IR), a load/store only accepts a single pointer operand without a field specifier even for the reading/writing values of a field. The address taken by the pointer operand needs to be computed by the analysis itself to identify which field of an object the load/store may access.

To simplify the complicated field-sensitivity in C/C++, the majority of the works on Andersen's analysis are field-insensitive (i.e., accessing a field of an object is treated as accessing the entire object). One representative field-sensitive analysis proposed by Pearce et al. [10] offers a field-index-based object modeling, which distinguishes the fields of an object by their unique indices (with nested structs expanded), yielding better precision than field-insensitive analysis [10,11]. The approach extends Andersen's inclusion constraints [12] to differentiate an *address-of-field* instruction `q=&p→f`$_i$ from a simple *copy* instruction `q=p` by adding a positive weight i to the field-insensitive constraint $p \subseteq q$ to obtain the field-sensitive one $p + i \subseteq q$, indicating that q points to i-th field of an object o that p points to. In contrast, field-insensitive analysis imprecisely assumes that p and q both point to object o based on the non-weighted constraint $p \subseteq q$.

The field-sensitive points-to relations are resolved by computing the dynamic transitive closure on top of the extended Andersen's constraint graph, where each node represents a variable and each edge denotes an inclusion constraint between two variables. One key challenge for field-sensitive analysis is to detect and resolve a new type of cycles, called *positive weight cycles* (*PWCS*) on the constraint graph. A *PWC* is a cycle containing at least one positive weighted constraint edge. A *PWC* differs from a normal constraint cycle (or non-*PWC* containing only copy constraints) in two fundamental ways: (1) the points-to sets of variables in a non-*PWC* are identical after constraint resolution, but the points-to sets of variables in a *PWC* can be different, and (2) computing the transitive closure of a non-*PWC* terminates once a fixed-point is reached, but a *PWC* can cause infinite derivations unless a maximum number of fields of each object is specified.

Figure 1 gives an example from [10, §4.1] to illustrate a PWC that incurs infinite derivations during constraint resolution. Figure 1(b) gives the constraints transformed from the code via Pearce et al.'s modeling [10]. Figure 1(c) shows its corresponding constraint graph with a *PWC* containing a positive weighted edge from p to q ($p+1 \subseteq q$) and a simple copy edge from q back to p ($q \subseteq p$). An abstract object o allocated at line 3 is initially added to p's points-to set. Note that the object is modeled per allocation site (e.g., `malloc`) in Andersen's analysis. The constraint $p+1 \subseteq q$ derives a new field object given each object that p points to. The new object is then propagated back to p via $q \subseteq p$ for a new round of field derivation due to this *PWC*, resulting in infinitely deriving fields $o.f_1, o.f_1.f_1, ...$ from the base object o.

To avoid infinite derivations, Pearce et al. [10] set a maximum number of fields for each object to ensure that field access via an index is always within the scope of an object. For a stack and global object, its number of fields can be statically determined based on its declared types. However, a dynamically allocated heap object may have an unknown number of fields and is thus assumed to have as many as the largest struct in the program, causing redundant derivations.

To accelerate the constraint resolution, cycle elimination is a commonly used technique that merges nodes within a cycle into one node if the point-to sets of the nodes in this cycle are identical. However, the existing cycle elimination approaches [5,6,13,14] in field-insensitive analysis can not be directly applied to solve *PWC*s in field-sensitive analysis. Unlike nodes in a non-*PWC*, nodes in a *PWC* may not have identical points-to sets, thus collapsing all nodes in a *PWC* leads to precision loss. Collapsing only non-*PWC*s following previous algorithms cannot solve the infinite derivation problem in field-sensitive analysis.

This paper presents DEA, a fast and precise approach to handling of *PWC*s in field-sensitive Andersen's analysis. Rather than cycle elimination, we present a field collapsing technique to solve *PWC*s by capturing *derivation equivalence*. Two fields derived from the same object are derivation equivalent when solving a *PWC* if these fields are always pointed to by the same variables (nodes) in this *PWC*. A new *stride-based field representation* (SFR) is proposed to identify and collapse derivation equivalent fields when field-sensitive constraints.

Our handling of *PWC*s significantly boosts the performance of existing field-sensitive analysis (e.g., [10] proposed by Pearce et al.), while achieving the same precision. By capturing derivation equivalence, DEA avoids redundant field derivations with greatly reduced overhead during points-to propagation, making constraint solving converge more quickly. Our precision-preserving handling of *PWC*s can be easily integrated into existing Andersen's field-sensitive analyses, and is also complementary to the state-of-the-art cycle elimination methods for non-*PWC*s. Our evaluation shows that DEA on average achieves a speed up of 7.1X over PKH equipped with a recent cycle elimination technique, wave propagation [6] for analyzing 11 open-source large-scale C/C++ programs.

Table 1. Analysis domains, LLVM instructions, and constraint edges

Analysis Domains		Instruction	Constraint	Type
$i, j, w \in \mathbb{Z}$	Integer constants	`p = &o`	$p \xleftarrow{\text{AddrOf}} o$	AddrOf
$o \in \mathcal{O}$	Abstract objects	`p = q`	$p \xleftarrow{\text{Copy}} q$	Copy
$o.f_i \in \mathcal{F}$	Abstract field objects	`p = &q→fi`	$p \xleftarrow{\text{Field}_i} q$	Field
$a, b, c \in \mathcal{A} = \mathcal{O} \cup \mathcal{F}$	Address-taken variables	`p = *q`	$p \xleftarrow{\text{Load}} q$	Load
$p, q, r \in \mathcal{P}$	Top-level variables	`*p = q`	$p \xleftarrow{\text{Store}} q$	Store
$u, v \in \mathcal{V} = \mathcal{A} \cup \mathcal{P}$	Variables			

The key contributions of this paper are:

- We present a fast and precise handling of positive weight cycles to significantly boost the existing field-sensitive Andersen's analysis by capturing derivation equivalence when solving *PWC*s.
- We propose a new stride-based field abstraction to identify and collapse a sequence of derivation equivalent fields.
- We have implemented DEA in LLVM-7.0.0 and evaluated using 11 real-world large C/C++ programs. The results show that DEA on average is 7.1X faster than Pearce et al.'s field-sensitive analysis with the best speedup of 11.0X.

2 Background and Motivating Example

This section introduces the background of field-sensitive Andersen's analysis, including program representation, abstract object modeling and inference rules. We then give a motivating example to explain the key idea of derivation equivalence when resolving *PWC*s.

2.1 Program Representation and Field-Sensitive Analysis

We perform our pointer analysis on top of the LLVM-IR of a program, as in [11, 15–18]. The domains and the LLVM instructions relevant to field-sensitive pointer analysis are given in Table 1. The set of all variables $\mathcal{V}$ is separated into two subsets, $\mathcal{A} = \mathcal{O} \cup \mathcal{F}$ which contains all possible abstract objects and their fields, i.e., *address-taken variables* of a pointer, and $\mathcal{P}$ which contains all *top-level variables*, including stack virtual registers (symbols starting with "%") and global variables (symbols starting with "@") which are explicit, i.e., directly accessed. Address-taken variables in $\mathcal{A}$ are implicit, i.e., accessed indirectly at LLVM's load or store instructions via top-level variables.

After the SSA conversion, a program is represented by five types of instructions: $p = \&o$ (AddrOf), $p = q$ (Copy), $p = \&q \rightarrow f_i$ (Field or Address-of-field) $p = *q$ (Load) and $*p = q$ (Store), where $p, q \in \mathcal{P}$ and $o \in \mathcal{O}$. Top-level variables are put directly in SSA form, while address-taken variables are only accessed indirectly via Load or Store. For an AddrOf $p = \&o$, known as an *allocation site*, o is a stack or global variable with its address taken or a dynamically created abstract heap object (e.g., via `malloc()`). Parameter passings and returns are treated as Copys.

C code	LLVM IR

`p = &a;`
`a = &b;`
	`p = &a;`
	`t1 = &b;`
	`*p = t1;`

`q = &c;`
`*p = *q;`
	`q = &c;`
	`t2 = *q;`
	`*p = t2;`

Fig. 2. C code fragment and its LLVM IR.

```
struct A{                 struct B{
  int x;                    int v0;
  struct B y;               int v1;
  ...                       int v2;
}                         }
```

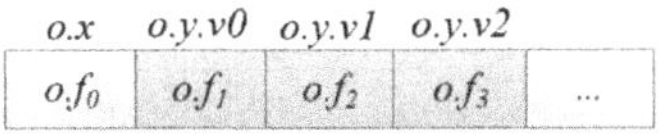

Fig. 3. The flattened fields with their unique indices (i.e., $o.f_0$, $o.f_1$, $o.f_2$, $o.f_3$, ...) for object o of type **struct A**.

Figure 2 shows a code fragment and its corresponding partial SSA form, where $\mathtt{p}, \mathtt{q}, \mathtt{t1}, \mathtt{t2} \in \mathcal{P}$ and $\mathtt{a}, \mathtt{b}, \mathtt{c} \in \mathcal{A}$. Note that `a` is indirectly accessed at a store `*p = t1` by introducing a top-level pointer `t1` in the partial SSA form. Complex statements such as `*p = *q` are decomposed into basic instructions by introducing a top-level pointer `t2`.

Our handling of field-sensitivity is ANSI-compliant [19]. For each struct allocation e.g., $p = \&o$, a field-insensitive object o is created to represent the entire struct object. The fields of a struct are distinguished by their unique indices [10,11] with the fields of nested structs flattened as illustrated in Fig. 3. A field object denoted by $o.f_i$ is derived from o when analyzing Field $\mathtt{q}{=}\&\mathtt{p}{\rightarrow}\mathtt{f_i}$ (LLVM's getelementptr instruction), where f_i denotes the i-th field of o and i is a constant value. Following [10], the address of o is modeled by the address of its first field with index 0. All other fields are modeled using distinct subobjects. Two pointer dereferences are aliased if one refers to o and another refers to one of its fields e.g., $o.f_i$, since it is the sub component of o. However, dereferences refer to distinct fields of o (e.g., $o.f_2$ and $o.f_3$) which are distinguished and not aliased.

For a C pointer arithmetic (e.g., $q = p{+}j$), if p points to a struct object o, we conservatively assume that q can point to any field of this struct object, i.e., the entire object o. This is based on the assumption that the pointer arithmetic is not across the boundary of the object. Similar to previous practices for analyzing C/C++, the analysis can be unsound if a pointer arithmetic used to access an aggregate object is out of the boundary or arbitrary castings between a pointer and an integer. Arrays are treated monolithically, i.e., accessing any element of an array is treated as accessing the entire array object.

In Andersen's analysis [12], resolving the points-to sets $pts(v)$ of a variable v is formalized as a set-constraint problem on top of the constraint graph $G = \langle V, E\rangle$, where each node $v \in V$ represents a variable, and an edge $e \in E$ between two nodes represents one of the five types of constraints (Table 1). Figure 4 gives the inference rules of field-sensitive analysis, which solves a dynamic transitive closure on G by propagating points-to information following the established Copy/Field edges and by adding new Copy edges until a fixed-point is reached [12].

$$[\text{ADDROF}]\ \frac{p \xleftarrow{\text{AddrOf}} o}{o \in pts(p)} \qquad [\text{COPY}]\ \frac{v \xleftarrow{\text{Copy}} u}{pts(u) \subseteq pts(v)}$$

$$[\text{FIELD-1}]\ \frac{p \xleftarrow{\text{Field}_i} q \quad o \in pts(q)}{o.f_i \in pts(p)} \qquad [\text{FIELD-2}]\ \frac{p \xleftarrow{\text{Field}_i} q \quad o.f_j \in pts(q)}{o.f_{i+j} \in pts(p)}$$

$$[\text{STORE}]\ \frac{p \xleftarrow{\text{Store}} q \quad a \in pts(p)}{a \xleftarrow{\text{Copy}} q} \qquad [\text{LOAD}]\ \frac{p \xleftarrow{\text{Load}} q \quad a \in pts(q)}{p \xleftarrow{\text{Copy}} a}$$

Fig. 4. Inference rules of Pearce et al.'s field-sensitive Andersen's analysis

2.2 A Motivating Example

Figure 5 gives an example to show the redundant derivations when solving a *PWC* on the constraint graph by PKH [10] (Pearce et al.'s field-sensitive analysis) based on its inference rules (Fig. 4). We illustrate how our idea captures the derivation equivalence by using a stride-based representation to collapse fields which are always pointed to by all the pointers in this *PWC*. The example consists of five types of constant edges corresponding to the five types of instructions in Table 1 with one *PWC* involving nodes p_1 and p_2. Pointer r initially points to o (`[ADDROF]`). The points-to set of p_2 has the field $o.f_1$ derived from the object o when resolving $p_2 \xleftarrow{\text{Field}_1} r$ (`[FIELD-1]`). Since $p_1 \xleftarrow{\text{Field}_2} p_2$ and $p_2 \xleftarrow{\text{Copy}} p_1$ form a *PWC* with a positive weight +2, a sequence of field objects starting from $o.f_3$ with a stride 2 are iteratively derived and added into p_1's points-to set (`[FIELD-2]`) and then propagated back to p_2 (`[COPY]`). These field objects are derivation equivalent because all the fields are always pointed to by both p_1 and p_2 in this *PWC*, incurring redundant derivations. Even worse, the edge $p_1 \xleftarrow{\text{Store}} q_1$ flowing into and the edge $q_2 \xleftarrow{\text{Load}} p_1$ going out of this *PWC* add redundant Copy edges (e.g., $o.f_3 \xleftarrow{\text{Copy}} q_1$ and $q_2 \xleftarrow{\text{Copy}} o.f_3$)) based on `[STORE]` and `[LOAD]`, causing redundant points-to propagation, as also illustrated in Fig. 5(a).

To avoid redundant field derivations and unnecessary **Copy** edges when resolving **Load** and **Store**. Our idea is to merge derivation equivalent fields into a stride-based polynomial representation $o.f_{i+ks}$, where i is the starting field, s is the stride corresponding to the weight of the PWC, and $k \in \mathbb{N}$. Figure 5(b) illustrates the new representation $o.f_{3+2k}$ for collapsing equivalent fields $\{o.f_3, o.f_5, ...\}$ in Fig. 5(a). The new representation successfully reduces the number of points-to targets during points-to propagation and the number of **Copy** edges added into the constraint graph when solving **Store**/**Load** edges, while maintaining the same precision, i.e., the points-to sets of r, p_1, p_2 (after expanding the fields based on the polynomial representation) are identical to those produced by PKH.

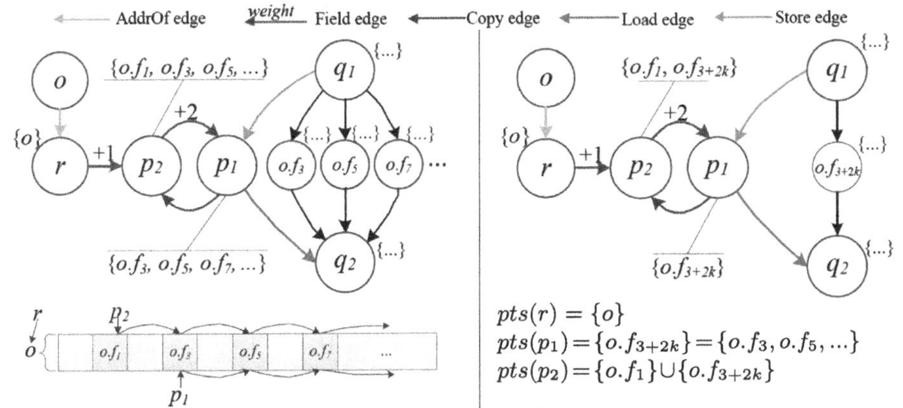

$pts(r) = \{o\}$
$pts(p_1) = \{o.f_{3+2k}\} = \{o.f_3, o.f_5, ...\}$
$pts(p_2) = \{o.f_1\} \cup \{o.f_{3+2k}\}$

(a) *PWC* resolved by Pearce et al.'s method (b) *PWC* resolved by our approach

Fig. 5. A motivating example.

3 Our Approach

This section details our approach to handling of *PWC*s in field-sensitive pointer analysis, including the stride-based field abstraction to represent derivation equivalent fields and the inference rules based on the new field representation.

3.1 Stride-Based Field Representation

Definition 1 (Stride-based Field Representation (SFR)). *We use $\sigma = \langle o, i, S\rangle$ to denote a single object or a sequence of fields in Pearce et al.'s modeling starting from i-th field following the strides in S. The field expansion of $\langle o, i, S\rangle$ is as follows:*

$$FX(\langle o,i,S\rangle) = \begin{cases} \{o\} & \text{if } S=\emptyset \wedge i=0 \\ \{o.f_j \,|\, j=i+\sum_{n=1}^{|S|} k_n s_n,\ j \le max, k_n \in \mathbb{N}, s_n \in S\} & \text{otherwise} \end{cases}$$

where max denotes the maximum number of fields of object o and s_n is the n-th element of the stride set S which models precisely field derivations when a **Field** edge resides in one or multiple PWCs. We use $\langle o, 0, \emptyset \rangle$ to represent the entire object o and its single field $o.f_i$ is denoted by $\langle o, i, \{0\} \rangle$. SFR unifies the notations of an object and its fields. The expansion of an SFR fully represents the objects and fields in Pearce et al.'s modeling, while it reduces the number of points-to targets during constraint solving. Two SFRs can be disjointed or overlapping (Definition 2).

$$\text{[E-ADDROF]} \ \frac{p \xleftarrow{\text{AddrOf}} o \quad \sigma = \langle o, 0, \emptyset \rangle}{\sigma \in pts(p)} \qquad \text{[E-COPY]} \ \frac{v \xleftarrow{\text{Copy}} u}{pts(u) \subseteq pts(v)}$$

$$\text{[E-FIELD]} \ \frac{p \xleftarrow{\text{Field}_i} q \quad \langle o, j, S \rangle \in pts(q) \quad S' = Strides(p \xleftarrow{\text{Field}_i} q) \quad \sigma = \langle o, i+j, S \cup S' \rangle}{\nexists\, \sigma' \in pts(p) : \sigma \sqsubseteq \sigma' \Rightarrow \sigma \in pts(p)}$$

$$\text{[E-STORE]} \ \frac{p \xleftarrow{\text{Store}} q \quad \sigma \in pts(p)}{\sigma \xleftarrow{\text{Copy}} q} \qquad \text{[E-LOAD]} \ \frac{p \xleftarrow{\text{Load}} q \quad \sigma \in pts(q)}{\forall \sigma' : \sigma \sqcap \sigma' \neq \emptyset \Rightarrow p \xleftarrow{\text{Copy}} \sigma'}$$

$$Strides(e) = \begin{cases} \{0\} & \text{if edge } e \text{ is not in any } PWC \\ \{\mathcal{W}_{\mathcal{C}} \mid \forall \mathcal{C} \subseteq E : e \in \mathcal{C}\} & \text{otherwise} \quad \text{(Definition 4)} \end{cases}$$

Fig. 6. Inference rules of our approach

Definition 2 (Overlapping and disjointed SFRs). *Two* SFRs *are overlapping, denoted as* $\sigma \sqcap \sigma' \neq \emptyset$ *if* $\sigma = \sigma'$ *or two different* SFRs *derived from the same object* o *have at least one common field, i.e.,* $FX(\langle o, i, S \rangle) \cap FX(\langle o, i', S' \rangle) \neq \emptyset$. *A special case is the subset relation between two overlapping* SFRs, *denoted as* $\sigma \sqsubseteq \sigma'$, *i.e.,* $FX(\langle o, i, S \rangle) \subseteq FX(\langle o, i', S' \rangle)$. *We say that two* SFRs *are disjointed if* $\sigma \sqcap \sigma' = \emptyset$.

Example 1 (Field expansion). The expanded fields of $\langle o, 1, \{2\} \rangle$ are $FX(\sigma) = \{o.f_1, o.f_3, o.f_5 ...\}$. Likewise, the fields represented by $\langle o, 1, \{5, 6\} \rangle$ are $FX(\sigma) = \{o.f_j \mid j = 1 + 5k_1 + 6k_2, k_1, k_2 \in \mathbb{N}\} = \{o.f_1, o.f_6, o.f_7, o.f_{11}, o.f_{12}, ...\}$.

3.2 Inference Rules

Figure 6 gives the inference rules of our field-sensitive points-to analysis based on the stride-based field representation for resolving the five types of constraints. Object and field nodes on the constraint graph are now represented by the unified SFRs. Rule [E-ADDROF] initializes the points-to set of p with object o represented by $\langle o, 0, \emptyset \rangle$ (Definition 1) for each $p \xleftarrow{\text{AddrOf}} o$. Similar to [COPY] in Fig. 4, [E-COPY] simply propagates the points-to set of u to that of v when analyzing $v \xleftarrow{\text{Copy}} u$.

Definition 3 (Path and cycle). *A path* $u \overset{*}{\Leftarrow} v$ *on the constraint graph* $G = \langle V, E \rangle$ *is a sequence of edges leading from* v *to* u. *A path* $v \overset{*}{\Leftarrow} v$ *is called a closed path. A closed path* $v \overset{*}{\Leftarrow} v$ *is a* ***cycle*** *if all its edges are distinct and the only node to occur twice in this path is* v.

Definition 4 (Weight of a PWC). *A PWC, denoted as $\mathcal{C}$, is a cycle containing only* **Copy** *and* **Field** *edges and at least one edge is a* **Field** *with a positive weight. The weight of $\mathcal{C}$ is $\mathcal{W}_\mathcal{C} = \sum_{e \in \mathcal{C}} wt_e$, where e is a* **Field** *or* **Copy** *and wt_e is its weight (wt_e is 0 if e is a* **Copy***). The set of weights of all the PWCs containing e is $\{\mathcal{W}_\mathcal{C} \mid \forall \mathcal{C} \subseteq E : e \in \mathcal{C}\}$*

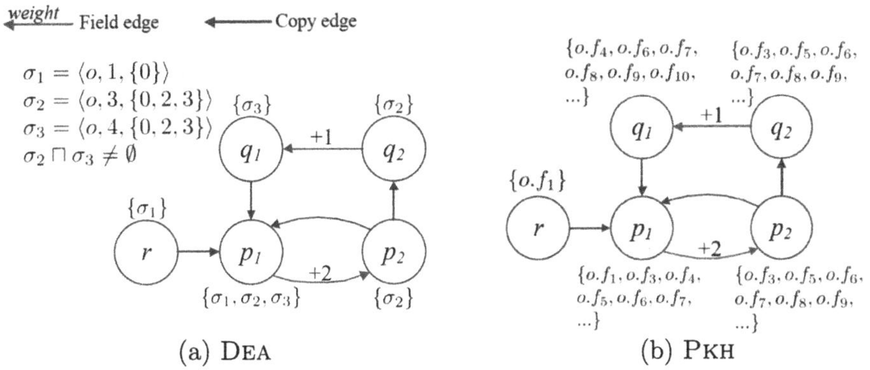

Fig. 7. Solving the FIELD edge $p_2 \xleftarrow{\text{Field}_2} p_1$ which involves in multiple PWCs

Unlike rule [FIELD-1] and [FIELD-2] in Fig. 4 which generate a single field object when analyzing $p \xleftarrow{\text{Field}_i} q$, [E-FIELD] generates an SFR $\sigma = \langle o, j+w, S \cup S'\rangle$ representing a sequence of fields starting from $(i+j)$-th field following strides $S \cup S'$, where $S' = \{0\}$ if $p \xleftarrow{\text{Field}_i} q$ is not involved in any PWC, otherwise $S' = \{\mathcal{W}_\mathcal{C} \mid \forall \mathcal{C} \subseteq E : (p \xleftarrow{\text{Field}_i} q) \in \mathcal{C}\}$, a set of the weights of all the positive weight cycles with each $\mathcal{C}$ containing $p \xleftarrow{\text{Field}_i} q$ on the constraint graph (Definitions 3 and 4). If $p \xleftarrow{\text{Field}_i} q$ is involved in multiple PWCs, σ is derived to collapse as many equivalent fields as possible by considering the set of weights S' of all the PWCs containing $p \xleftarrow{\text{Field}_i} q$. The premise of [E-FIELD] ensures that σ represents the derivation equivalent fields such that the targets added to the points-to sets of all these fields are always identical when solving each cycle $\mathcal{C}$. The conclusion of [E-FIELD] ensures early termination and avoids redundant derivations, since an SFR σ can only be generated and added to $pts(p)$ if there no SFR σ' already exists in $pts(p)$ such that σ' can represent σ, i.e., $\sigma \sqsubseteq \sigma'$ (Definition 2). Examples 2 and 3 give two scenarios in which a **Field** edge resides in single and multiple PWCs.

Example 2 ([E-FIELD] for a single PWC). Let us revisit our motivating example in Fig. 5 to explain [E-FIELD]. The **Field** edge $p_2 \xleftarrow{\text{Field}_1} r$ is not involved in any PWC, therefore, [E-FIELD] generates an SFR $\sigma = \langle o, 1, \{0\}\rangle$ with $S' = \{0\}$, representing only field $o.f_1$ and it then adds σ into $pts(p_2)$. Together with $p_2 \xleftarrow{\text{Copy}} p_1$, the second **Field** edge $p_1 \xleftarrow{\text{Field}_2} p_2 \in \mathcal{C}$ forms a positive weight cycle $\mathcal{C}$

with its weight $\mathcal{W}_\mathcal{C} = 2$. A new SFR $\sigma = \langle o, 1+2, \{0\} \cup \{2\}\rangle = \langle o, 3, \{0,2\}\rangle$ is derived and added into $pts(p_1)$ given $\langle o, 1, \{0\}\rangle \in pts(p_2)$. The SFR $\langle o, 3, \{0,2\}\rangle$ is then propagated back to p_2. In the second iteration for resolving $p_1 \xleftarrow{\mathsf{Field}_2} p_2$, the newly derived SFR $\langle o, 5, \{0,2\}\rangle$ is discarded and not added into $pts(p_1)$ since $\langle o, 5, \{0,2\}\rangle$ can be represented by $\langle o, 3, \{0,2\}\rangle$, i.e., a subset relation $\langle o, 5, \{0,2\}\rangle \sqsubseteq \langle o, 3, \{0,2\}\rangle$ (Definition 2) holds.

Example 3 (`[E-FIELD]` *for multiple PWCs).* Figure 7 compares DEA with PKH to show that `[E-FIELD]` requires significantly fewer field derivations to resolve $p_2 \xleftarrow{\mathsf{Field}_2} p_1$ when it is involved in two PWCs, i.e., cycle $\mathcal{C}_1$ formed by p_1 and p_2, and $\mathcal{C}_2$ formed by p_1, p_2, q_2 and q_1. The weights of $\mathcal{C}_1$ and $\mathcal{C}_2$ are 2 and 3 respectively, therefore $S' = \{2, 3\}$. Initially, p_1 points to $\sigma_1 = \langle o, 1, \{0\}\rangle$, which is propagated to p_1 along $p_1 \xleftarrow{\mathsf{Copy}} r$. We first take a look at resolving $\mathcal{C}_1$. A new SFR $\sigma_2 = \langle o, 1+2, \{0\} \cup \{2,3\}\rangle = \langle o, 3, \{0,2,3\}\rangle$ is derived and added to $pts(p_2)$ when analyzing $p_2 \xleftarrow{\mathsf{Field}_2} p_1$, as shown in Fig. 7(a). σ_2 is then propagated back and added to $pts(p_1)$ along $p_1 \xleftarrow{\mathsf{Copy}} p_2$. The second iteration for analyzing $p_2 \xleftarrow{\mathsf{Field}_2} p_1$ avoids adding $\langle o, 5, \{0,2,3\}\rangle$ because it is a subset of σ_2, into $pts(p_2)$, resulting in early termination. Similarly, when resolving $\mathcal{C}_2$ which contains two **Field** edges, DEA generates $\sigma_3 = \langle o, 3+1, \{0,2,3\}\rangle$ when analyzing $q_1 \xleftarrow{\mathsf{Field}_1} q_2$ and then propagates σ_3 to p_1. Given this new σ_3 in $pts(p_1)$, $\langle o, 4+1, \{0,2,3\}\rangle$ is derived when again analyzing $p_2 \xleftarrow{\mathsf{Field}_2} p_1$ in $\mathcal{C}_2$. However, $\langle o, 4+1, \{0,2,3\}\rangle$, which is a subset of σ_2, is not added to $pts(p_2)$. Note that though σ_2 and σ_3 are overlapping due to the intersecting PWCs, σ_2 successfully captures the equivalent fields that are always pointed by p_1, p_2, q_2 and σ_3 captures the equivalent fields that are always pointed by p_1, q_1, avoiding redundant derivations. For each PWC, DEA generates only one SFR, requiring at most two iterations to converge the analysis. In contrast, PKH performs redundant derivations until it reaches the maximum number of fields of this object, as also illustrated in Fig. 7(b).

Let us move to rules `[E-LOAD]` and `[E-STORE]`. Unlike `[STORE]` and `[LOAD]` in Fig. 4, our handling of **Store** and **Load** is asymmetric for both efficiency and precision-preserving purposes. For $p \xleftarrow{\mathsf{Store}} q$, `[E-STORE]` is similar to `[STORE]` by propagating $pts(q)$ to $pts(\sigma)$, where σ is pointed to by p. For an SFR σ pointed to by q at $p \xleftarrow{\mathsf{Load}} q$, `[LOAD]` propagates the points-to set of any σ' which overlaps with σ (Definition 2) to $pts(p)$. This is because a field $o.f_i$ in PKH may belong to one or multiple SFRs. For example, in Fig. 7, $o.f_6$ belongs to σ_2 and σ_3 when resolving a **Field** edge which is involved in multiple cycles or in one PWC containing multiple **Field** edges. We use $\mathcal{M}_{o.f_i}$ to denote a set of all SFRs containing $o.f_i$, i.e., any two SFRs in $\mathcal{M}_{o.f_i}$ share common fields including at least $o.f_i$. According to Definition 1, any change to the point-to sets of $\sigma \in \mathcal{M}_{o.f_i}$ also applies to those of $o.f_i$ during our constraint resolution. If $*q$ at a **Load** refers to an SFR σ, it also refers $\sigma' \in \mathcal{M}_{o.f_i}$ that overlaps with σ for each field $o.f_i \in FX(\sigma)$ (Definition 2). Therefore, `[LOAD]` maintains the correctness that $pts(o.f_i)$ obtains the union of the points-to sets of all SFRs in $\mathcal{M}_{o.f_i}$. Since a points-to target in $pts(\sigma)$ must be in the points-to set of every field in $FX(\sigma)$ (i.e, for any $\sigma \in \mathcal{M}_{o.f_i}$, $pts(\sigma)$ is always a subset of $pts(o.f_i)$), ensuring that no spurious points-to targets other than $pts(o.f_i)$ will be propagated to p at the Load. Thus, our handling of PWCs is precision preserving, i.e., the points-to set of a variable after field expansion resolved by DEA is the same as that of PKH.

Example 4 ([E-LOAD] and [E-STORE]). Figure 8 illustrates the resolving of $p \xleftarrow{\text{Store}} q$ and $r \xleftarrow{\text{Load}} p$ with the initial points-to sets $pts(p) = \{\sigma_1\}$, $pts(q) = \{\sigma_3\}$ and $pts(\sigma_2) = \{\sigma_4\}$. σ_1 and σ_2 are both derived from object o with overlapping fields, e.g., $o.f_4$, as highlighted in orange in Fig. 8. When resolving $p \xleftarrow{\text{Store}} q$, [E-STORE] adds a new Copy edge $\sigma_1 \xleftarrow{\text{Copy}} q$, propagating $\sigma_3 \in pts(q)$ to $pts(\sigma_1)$, but not $pts(\sigma_2)$ though $\sigma_1 \sqcap \sigma_2 \neq \emptyset$. This avoids, for example, introducing the spurious target σ_3 to the points-to set of $o.f_2$ (in green), which only resides in σ_2 but not in σ_1. In contrast, [E-LOAD] resolves $r \xleftarrow{\text{Load}} p$ by adding two Copy edges $r \xleftarrow{\text{Copy}} \sigma_1$ and $r \xleftarrow{\text{Copy}} \sigma_2$, as also depicted in Fig. 8. Since $\sigma_1 \sqcap \sigma_2 = \{o.f_4, ...\}$ and $\sigma_1 \in pts(p)$, if $*p$ at Load $r = *p$ refers to an overlapping field e.g., $o.f_4$ shared by σ_1 and σ_2, the points-to set of r is the union of $pts(\sigma_1)$ and $pts(\sigma_2)$, i.e., $pts(r) = \{\sigma_3, \sigma_4\}$, achieving the precise field-sensitive results.

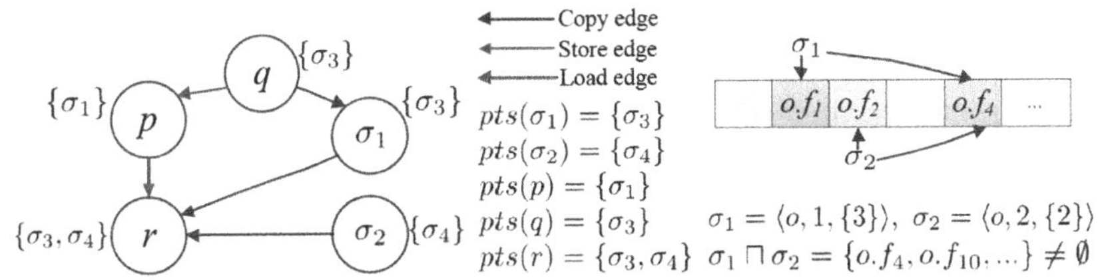

Fig. 8. Resolving Store $p \xleftarrow{\text{Store}} q$ and Load $r \xleftarrow{\text{Load}} p$ for overlapping SFRs (Color figure online)

3.3 An Algorithm

Our precision-preserving handling of PWCs (i.e., the inference rules in Fig. 6) can be integrated into existing constraint solving algorithms for field-insensitive Andersen's analysis, e.g., the state-of-the-art cycle elimination approaches [5,6, 13,14]. This section gives an overall algorithm of our approach by instantiating our inference rules on top of *wave propagation* [6], a constraint solving strategy with better or comparable performance as HCD/LCD [5] for analyzing large size programs.

In Algorithm 1, all the AddrOf edges are processed only once to initialize the worklist W (lines 2–5), followed by a *while* loop for the main phase of constraint solving, which has three phases.

(1) SCC (strongly connected component) detection and weight calculation for PWCs (lines 7–9). We use Nuutilia et al.'s algorithm [20] to detect SCCs,

Algorithm 1. An Algorithm

```
Function DEA (G = ⟨V, E⟩)
    W := ∅; W_ind := ∅
    for each e : v ←AddrOf− o ∈ E do                                  } ▷[E-ADDROF]
        ⟨o, 0, ∅⟩ ∈ pts(v)
        W.push(v)
    while W ≠ ∅ do
        Compute SCC on G using Nuutilia's algorithm [20]
        Collapse nodes in one SCC that contains only COPY edges
        Calculate W_C for each cycle in SCCs
        while W ≠ ∅ do
            v := W.pop_front()
            for each u ←Copy− v ∈ E do                                 } ▷[E-COPY]
                pts(v) ⊆ pts(u)
                if pts(u) changed then
                    W.push(u)
            for each u ←Field_i− v ∈ E do                              } ▷[E-FIELD]
                S' := Strides(u ←Field_i− v)
                for each ⟨o, j, S⟩ ∈ pts(v) do
                    σ := ⟨o, i+j, S∪S'⟩
                    if ∄ σ' ∈ pts(u) : σ ⊑ σ' then
                        σ ∈ pts(u)
                        W.push(u)
            if ∃ v ←Store− u ∈ E or ∃ u ←Load− v ∈ E then
                push v into W_ind
        while W_ind ≠ ∅ do
            q := W_ind.pop_front()
            for each v ←Store− u ∈ E do                                } ▷[E-STORE]
                for each σ ∈ pts(v) do
                    if σ ←Copy− u then
                        E := E ∪ σ ←Copy− u
                        W.push(u)
            for each u ←Load− v ∈ E do                                 } ▷[E-LOAD]
                for each σ' ∈ {σ' ⊓ σ ≠ ∅ | σ ∈ pts(v)} do
                    if u ←Copy− σ' then
                        E := E ∪ u ←Copy− σ'
                        W.push(σ')
        for each u ←Copy− v added by UPDATECALLGRAPH do
            W.push(v)
```

which is an improvement over the original algorithm developed by Tarjan et al. [21]. The weight W_C of each positive weight cycle C is then calculated given the detected SCCs.

(2) Points-to propagation along Copy and Field edges (lines 10–24). We propagate points-to information along each Copy edge based on [E-COPY] (lines 12–15). New SFRs are derived and added to the points-to sets of the destination node of each Field edge based on [E-FIELD] (lines 16–22). A variable v is pushed into a new worklist W_{ind} if there exists an incoming Store edge to v or an outgoing Load edge from v for later handling of Loads/Stores (lines 23–24)

(3) Processing Store and Load edges (lines 25–36). New Copy edges are added to G, and the source node of each newly added Copy edge is added to worklist W for points-to propagation in the next iteration. Lines 37–38 update the callgraph by creating new Copy edges (e.g., $u \xleftarrow{\text{Copy}} v$) for parameter/return passings when a new callee function is discovered at a callsite using the points-to results of function pointers obtained from this points-to resolution round. The source node v of the Copy edge is added to W to be processed in the next iteration until a fixed point is reached, i.e., no changes are made to the points-to set of any node.

Table 2. Basic characteristics of the benchmarks (IR's lines of code, number of pointers, number of five types of instructions on the initial constraint graph, and maximum number of fields of the largest struct in each program).

	LOC	#Pointers	MaxFields	#Field	#Copy	#Store	#Load	#AddrOf
git-checkout	1253K	624K	302	93201	88406	41620	60723	33380
json-conversions	355K	264K	64	27685	36557	37960	36872	43448
json-ubjson	330K	233K	64	24064	35813	34577	26288	34165
llvm-as-new	729K	597K	121	307167	77944	287634	41960	17435
llvm-dwp	1796K	897K	632	100877	101849	116205	142943	121541
llvm-objdump	728K	353K	121	61117	57743	56493	40314	16767
opencv_perf_core	1014K	715K	64	122744	192419	59599	79466	24450
opencv_test_dnn	889K	635K	64	105550	174080	52304	70332	22786
python	539K	420K	171	84779	74524	49215	56434	18340
redis-server	706K	374K	332	52178	60111	24542	39205	13175
Xalan	2192K	807K	133	110184	181804	35940	68812	53926

Other field-sensitive analyses (e.g., PKH [10]) can also be implemented under the same constraint solving algorithm by simply replacing the lines for handling the five types of constraints with the inference rules in Fig. 4.

4 Experimental Evaluation

The objective of our evaluation is to show that our field-sensitive analysis is significantly faster than Pearce et al.'s analysis (PKH) yet maintains the same precision in analyzing large size C/C++ programs.

4.1 Implementation and Experimental Setup

Our approach is implemented on top of LLVM-7.0.0 and its sub-project SVF [18, 22,23]. A state-of-the-art constraint resolution algorithm, *wave propagation* [6] is used for cycle detection and computing dynamic transitive closures on top of the same constraint graph for both PKH and DEA. Indirect calls via function pointers are resolved on-the-fly during points-to resolution. A C++ virtual call $p \rightarrow foo()$ is translated into four low-level LLVM instructions for our pointer analysis. (1) a Load $vtptr = *p$, obtaining virtual table pointer *vtptr* by dereferencing pointer *p* to the object, (2) a Field $vfn = \&vtptr \rightarrow idx$, obtaining the entry in the vtable at a designated offset *idx* for the target function, (3) a Load $fp = *vfn$, obtaining the address of the function, and (4) a function call *fp*(*p*). Following [22,24,25], a white list is maintained to summarize all the side-effects of external calls (e.g., `memcpy`, `xmalloc` and `_Znwm` for C++ `new`) [26].

To evaluate the effectiveness of our implementation, we chose 11 large-scale open-source C/C++ projects downloaded from Github, including `git-checkout` (a sub project of Git for version control), `json-conversions` and `json-ubjson` (two main Json libraries for modern C++ environment, version 3.6.0), `llvm-as-new` and `llvm-dwp` (tools in LLVM-7.0.0 compiler), `opencv_perf_core` and `opencv_ test_dnn` (two main libraries in OpenCV-3.4), `python` (version 3.4.2) and `redis-server` (a distributed database server, version 5.0). The source code of each program is compiled into bit code files Clang-7.0.0 [27] and then linked together using `WLLVM` [28] to produce whole program bc files.

Table 2 collects the basic characteristics about the 11 programs before the main pointer analysis phase. The statistics include the LLVM IR's lines of code (LOC) of a program, the number of pointers (#Pointers), the number of fields of the largest struct in the program, also known as the maximum number of fields using the upper bound for deriving fields of a heap object, and the number of each of the five types of constraint edges in the initial constraint graph. The reason that *#Field* is not much smaller than *#Copy* is twofold (1) Field refers to LLVM's getelementptr instruction, which is used to get the addresses of subelements of aggregates, including not only structs but also arrays and nested aggregates (Fig. 3). (2) In low-level LLVM IR, a Copy only refers to an assignment between two virtual registers, such as casting or parameter passing (Sect. 2.1). An assignment "p = q" in high-level C/C++ is not translated into a Copy, but a Store/Load manipulated indirectly through registers on LLVM's partial SSA form.

All our experiments were conducted on a platform consisting of a 3.50 GHz Intel Xeon Quad Core CPU with 128 GB memory, running Ubuntu Linux (kernel version 3.11.0).

4.2 Results and Analysis

Table 3 compares DEA with PKH for each of the 11 programs evaluated in terms of the following three analysis results after constraint resolution, the total number of address-taken variables (*#AddrTakenVar*), the total number of fields derived when resolving all Field edges (*#Field*), and the number of fields derived only when resolving Field edges involving *PWC*s (*#FieldByPWC*). Both DEA and PKH use `LLVM Sparse Bitvectors` as the points-to set implementation. The peak memory usage by DEA is 7.33G observed in git-checkout. DEA produces identical points-to results as those by PKH, confirming that DEA's precision is preserved.

From the results produced by PKH, we can see that the number of fields (Column 4 in Table 3) occupies a large proportion of the total address-taken variables (Column 2) in modern large-scale C/C++ programs. On average, 72.5% of the address-taken variables are field objects. In programs `git-checkout` (written in C) and `json-ubjson` (written in C++) with heavy use of structs and classes, the percentages for both are higher than 80%. In 8 of the 11 programs, over 50% of the fields are derived from *PWC*s.

Columns 4–5 of Table 3 compare the total number of field objects produced by PKH and DEA respectively. Columns 6–7 give more information about the number of fields derived only when resolving *PWC*s by PKH and DEA, we can see that these fields are significantly reduced by DEA with an average reduction rate of 86.6%, demonstrating that DEA successfully captured the derivation equivalence to collapse a majority of fields into SFRs when resolving *PWC*s.

Table 3. Comparing the results produced by DEA with those by PKH, including the total number of address-taken variables, number of fields and the number of fields derived when resolving *PWC*s, and the number of Copy edges connected to/from the field object nodes derived when resolving *PWC*s

	#AddrTakenVar		#Field		#FieldByPWC	
	PKH	DEA	PKH	DEA	PKH	DEA
git-checkout	135576	73967	121574	59965	68045	6436
json-conversions	62397	40993	40943	19539	22330	926
json-ubjson	60721	34987	49211	23477	27000	1266
llvm-as-new	24427	16124	19304	11001	9770	1467
llvm-dwp	145247	91945	109650	56348	62383	9081
llvm-objdump	16130	12007	11235	7112	5119	996
opencv_perf_core	60625	44061	40196	23632	18894	2330
opencv_test_dnn	53064	37957	35177	20070	17366	2259
python	30848	23713	21530	14395	9531	2396
redis-server	13109	9581	8165	4637	4234	706
Xalan	90314	62859	61466	34011	32226	4771
Max reduction	45.4%		52.3%		95.9%	
Average reduction	32.4%		44.4%		86.6%	

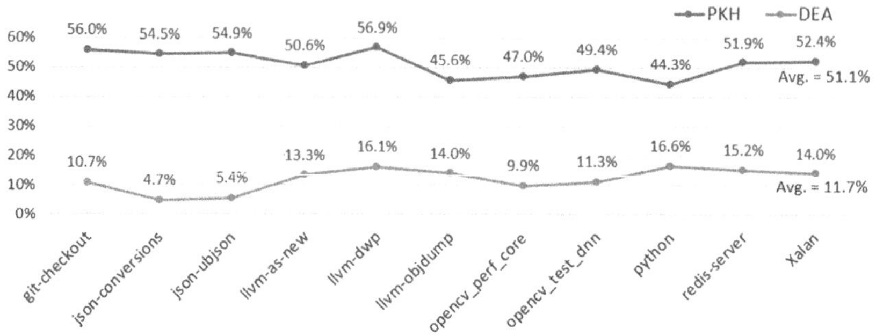

Fig. 9. Percentages of fields derived when solving *PWC*s out of the total number of fields, i.e., $\frac{\#FieldByPWC}{\#Field} * 100$ (Color figure online)

Figure 9 further compares DEA with PKH in terms of percentages of fields derived from resolving *PWC*s out of the total number of fields for the 11 programs. The average percentage of 51.1% in PKH (blue line) is reduced to only 11.7% (orange line) in DEA with a reduction of 39.4%.

Table 4. Constraint graph information (*#NodeInPWC* denotes the number of nodes involving *PWC*s by PKH; *#SFR* denotes the number of stride-based field representatives, generated by DEA; *#CopyByPWC*, denotes the number of Copy edges flowing into and going out of fields derived when solving *PWC*s; *#CopyProcessed* denotes the number of processing times of Copy edges.)

	#NodeInPWC	*#SFR*	*#CopyByPWC*		*#CopyProcessed*	
	PKH	DEA	PKH	DEA	PKH	DEA
git-checkout	2840	2172	12372	2046	3868834	1128617
json-conversions	3631	1641	13490	2622	2253266	319960
json-ubjson	4271	1753	4311	1037	5621768	575884
llvm-as-new	1752	2085	9739	2789	2513940	688238
llvm-dwp	7263	1463	15062	2128	2802988	779424
llvm-objdump	1581	1761	7105	2013	2177990	647582
opencv_perf_core	1373	2030	4948	1973	4800563	655095
opencv_test_dnn	1007	777	4008	1577	5095795	460127
python	3817	1942	8530	3854	3495769	971376
redis-server	2783	1405	3380	1408	1288753	390783
Xalan	4874	2909	21935	7671	5143418	1554627
Max reduction			85.9%		91.0%	
Avg. reduction			70.3%		77.3%	

In `git-checkout`, `json-conversions` and `json-ubjson`, DEA achieves over 90% reduction in solving *PWC*s because these programs have relatively large numbers of address-taken variables (Table 3) and relatively more nodes involving *PWC*s (Table 4). On average, over 85% of redundant field derivations involving *PWC*s are avoided with the maximum reduction rate of 95.9% in `json-conversions`, confirming the effectiveness of our field collapsing in handling *PWC*s.

Table 4 gives the constraint graph information after points-to resolution. Column 2 lists the number of nodes involving *PWC*s by PKH. For each SFR σ generated by DEA, Column 3 gives the numbers of SFRs generated by DEA. The average numbers of overlapping SFRs for the 11 programs evaluated are all below 1, which means that the majority of the SFRs either represent a single object/field or represent a sequence of fields that do not overlap with one another.

Columns 4–5 give the numbers of **Copy** edges flowing into and going out of field nodes derived when resolving *PWC*s by PKH and DEA respectively. DEA on average reduces the **Copy** edges in Column 4 by 70.3% with a maximum reduction rate of 85.9% Columns 6–7 give the number of processing times of **Copy** edges during points-to propagation by the two approaches. Since the number of **Copy** edges is significantly reduced by DEA, the processing times of **Copy** edges are reduced accordingly with an average/maximum reduction rate of 77.3%/91.0%.

Table 5 compares DEA with PKH in terms of the overall analysis times and the times collected for each of the three analysis phases. The total pointer analysis time consists of three major parts, as also discussed in Algorithm 1, and

Table 5. Total analysis times and the times of the three analysis stages, including *CycleDec* cycle detection (Lines 7–9 of Algorithm 1), *PtsProp*, propagating point-to information via **Copy** and **Field** edges (Lines 11–24), *ProcessLdSt*, adding new **Copy** edges when processing **Loads**/**Stores** (Lines 25–36)

	CycleDec		*PtsProp*		*ProcessLdSt*		TotalTime		Speed
	PKH	DEA	PKH	DEA	PKH	DEA	PKH	DEA	*up*
git-checkout	3117.8	4600.0	138233.5	26668.1	3870.2	1472.5	145221.6	32740.6	4.4
json-conversions	4436.2	561.6	12248.2	939.2	17.6	11.5	16702.0	1512.3	11.0
json-ubjson	25.1	6.0	18635.2	1817.3	52.4	23.2	18712.7	1846.6	10.1
llvm-as-new	22.6	11.9	10920.4	1728.9	541.9	221.2	11484.9	1962.0	5.9
llvm-dwp	3134.1	1457.7	120654.4	22177.2	1671.2	747.5	125459.8	24382.4	5.1
llvm-objdump	22.2	22.2	10617.3	2158.4	254.8	109.7	10894.4	2290.2	4.8
opencv_perf_core	338.5	299.3	30049.9	3018.5	2125.5	991.7	32513.9	4309.5	7.5
opencv_test_dnn	67.0	64.2	3145.5	248.8	366.1	122.2	3578.6	435.2	8.2
python	51.6	18.8	167556.9	22674.4	939.9	474.8	168548.3	23168.0	7.3
redis-server	525.1	428.6	11088.3	1315.2	99.8	49.8	11713.2	1793.5	6.5
Xalan	412.3	118.1	146617.8	21729.4	352.5	218.1	147382.7	22065.6	6.7
Average speedup									7.1

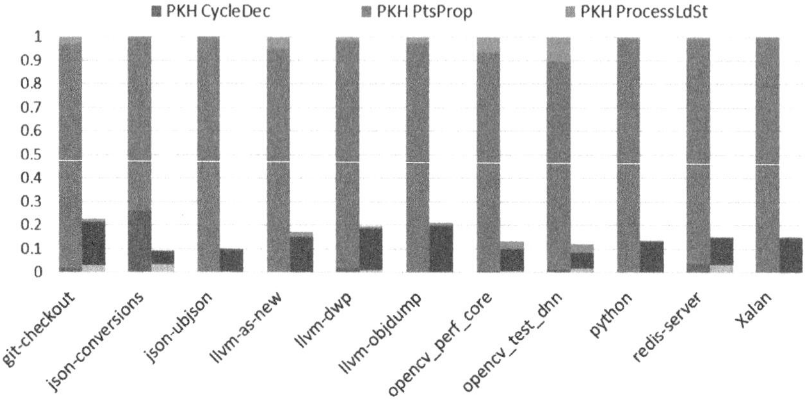

Fig. 10. Comparing the time distribution of the three analysis phases of DEA with that of PKH (normalized with PKH as the base). (Color figure online)

comprises (1) cycle detection, (2) propagating point-to sets via Copy and Field edges, and (3) processing Stores and Loads by adding new Copy edges into the constraint graph. Overall, DEA has a best speed up of 11.0X (observed in `json-conversions`) with an average speed up of 7.1X among the 11 programs.

Figure 10 gives the analysis time distributions of the three analysis phases in Table 5 for both PKH and DEA, where the phases are highlighted in different colors. The time cost of *PtsProp* (Columns 4–5) occupies a large percentage in resolution time by PKH. This is because *PtsProp* in field-sensitive pointer analysis needs to perform heavy set union operations for handling both Copy and Field edges. Worse, *PWC*s which need to be fully resolved by PKH incur a large number of redundant field derivations and unnecessary Copy edges until a pre-defined maximum number is reached, resulting in high analysis overhead in the *PtsProp* phase. In contrast, as depicted in Fig. 10, the analysis overhead introduced by *PtsProp* is greatly reduced by DEA, though it occupies a noticeable portion of the total analysis time, showing that DEA effectively cuts down the overhead introduced by *PWC*s (i.e., redundant points-to propagation, and unnecessary Copy edges connecting to/from derivation equivalent fields) to help constraint resolution converge more quickly.

5 Related Work

Andersen's inclusion-based analysis [12] is one of the most commonly used pointer analyses. Resolving points-to relations in Andersen's analysis is formalized as a set-constraint problem by computing a dynamic transitive closure on top of the constraint graph of a program. The majority of works on Andersen's analysis for C/C++ programs are field-insensitive [1,5,6,13,14,29]. Faehndrich et al. [29] introduced a partial online cycle elimination while processing complex constraints (e.g., Load/Store) and demonstrated that cycle detection is critical for scaling inclusion-based pointer analysis. Heintze and Tardieu [13] proposed a new field-based Andersen's analysis that can analyze large-scale programs with one million lines of code. Compared to field-sensitive analysis, field-based analysis imprecisely treats all instances of a field as one. For example, $o_1.f$ and $o_2.f$ are treated as one variable f, even if o_1 and o_2 are two different base objects allocated from different allocation sites.

To reduce the overhead of repeatedly finding cycles on the constraint graph during points-to resolution, *Lazy Cycle Detection* [5] triggers an SCC detection only when a visited **Copy** edge whose source and destination node have the same point-to information during points-to propagation. In addition to the online cycle elimination techniques, a number of preprocessing techniques, such as *Offline Variable Substitution* [30] and HVN [7], have also been proposed. The techniques explore pointer and location equivalence to reduce the size of the constraint graph for subsequent pointer analysis without losing any precision. *Hybrid Cycle Detection* [5] presented a hybrid cycle elimination algorithm by combing linear-time offline preprocessing with online cycle detection to further accelerate constraint resolution. Pereira et al. [6] proposed *Wave Propagation* by separating the constraint resolution of Andersen's analysis into three stages, i.e., collapsing of cycles, points-to propagation and insertion of new edges. The three phases are repeated until no more changes are detected in the constraint graph. The approach differentiates the existing (old) and new points-to information of a pointer to reduce set union overhead on an acyclic constraint graph in topological order during points-to propagation.

Field-sensitive analysis distinguishes fields of a struct object improving its field-insensitive counterpart [10,11,31–34]. The challenges of field-sensitivity in for C/C++ is that the address of a field can be taken, stored to some pointer and later read at an arbitrary load. To tackle this challenge, Pearce et al. [10] proposes PKH, a representative field-sensitive analysis by employing a field-index-based abstraction modeling in which the fields of an object are distinguished using unique indices. The Andersen's constraint graph is extended by adding a new **Field** constraint to model address-of-field instructions for deriving fields during constraint resolution. Miné [34] presented a field- and array-sensitive analysis that translates field and array accesses to pointer arithmetic in the abstract interpretation framework. LPA [35] presented a loop-oriented pointer analysis for automatic SIMD vectorization. DSA [31] supports field-sensitivity using byte offsets object modeling, however, the approach is based on Steensgarrd's unification-based analysis, using a coarser abstract object/points-to than Andersen's analysis.

CCLYZER [11] presents a precision enhancement approach to Pearce's field-sensitive analysis (PKH) by lazily inferring the types of heap objects by leveraging the type casting information to filter out spurious field derivations. CCLYZER improves the precision of PKH in the presence of factory methods and heap allocation wrappers in a program, achieving the heap cloning results without explicit context-sensitivity, but at the expense of more analysis time since an order of magnitude more type-augmented objects are introduced into the analysis. Rather than sacrificing performance to enhance analysis precision, DEA maintains the same precision as PKH, but significantly reduces its analysis overhead by fast and precise handling of positive weight cycles, a key challenge in field-insensitive pointer analysis. Our approach is also complementary to other cycle elimination resolution algorithms and fits well into existing constraint resolution frameworks for Andersen's analysis.

6 Conclusion

This paper presents a fast and precise handling of positive weight cycles to significantly boost the existing field-sensitive Andersen's analysis by capturing derivation equivalence. A new stride-based field abstraction is proposed to represent a sequence of derivation equivalent fields when resolving *PWC*s. DEA has been implemented in LLVM-7.0.0 and evaluated using 11 real-world large C/C++ programs. The evaluation results show that DEA on average is 7.1X faster than Pearce et al.'s field-sensitive analysis with the best speedup of 11.0X.

Acknowledgements. We would like to thank the anonymous reviewers for their helpful comments. This research is supported by Australian Research Grant DE170101081.

References

1. Berndl, M., Lhoták, O., Qian, F., Hendren, L., Umanee, N.: Points-to analysis using BDDs. In: PLDI 2003, vol. 38, pp. 103–114. ACM (2003)
2. Rountev, A., Milanova, A., Ryder, B.G.: Points-to analysis for java using annotated constraints. In: OOPSLA 2001, vol. 36, pp. 43–55. ACM (2001)
3. Milanova, A., Rountev, A., Ryder, B.G.: Parameterized object sensitivity for points-to and side-effect analyses for Java. ACM SIGSOFT Software Eng. Not. **27**(4), 1–11 (2002)
4. Bravenboer, M., Smaragdakis, Y.: Strictly declarative specification of sophisticated points-to analyses. In: OOPSLA 2009, vol. 44, pp. 243–262. ACM (2009)
5. Hardekopf, B., Lin, C.: The ant and the grasshopper: fast and accurate pointer analysis for millions of lines of code. In: PLDI 2007, vol. 42, pp. 290–299. ACM (2007)
6. Pereira, F.M.Q., Berlin, D.: Wave propagation and deep propagation for pointer analysis. In: CGO 2009, pp. 126–135. IEEE (2009)
7. Hardekopf, B., Lin, C.: Exploiting pointer and location equivalence to optimize pointer analysis. In: Nielson, H.R., Filé, G. (eds.) SAS 2007. LNCS, vol. 4634, pp. 265–280. Springer, Heidelberg (2007). https://doi.org/10.1007/978-3-540-74061-2_17
8. Blackshear, S., Chang, B.-Y.E., Sankaranarayanan, S., Sridharan, M.: The flow-insensitive precision of Andersen's analysis in practice. In: Yahav, E. (ed.) SAS 2011. LNCS, vol. 6887, pp. 60–76. Springer, Heidelberg (2011). https://doi.org/10.1007/978-3-642-23702-7_9
9. Zhang, Q., Xiao, X., Zhang, C., Yuan, H., Su, Z.: Efficient subcubic alias analysis for C. In OOPSLA 2014, vol. 49, pp. 829–845. ACM (2014)
10. Pearce, D.J., Kelly, P.H.J., Hankin, C.: Efficient field-sensitive pointer analysis of C. TOPLAS **30**(1), 4 (2007)
11. Balatsouras, G., Smaragdakis, Y.: Structure-sensitive points-to analysis for C and C++. In: Rival, X. (ed.) SAS 2016. LNCS, vol. 9837, pp. 84–104. Springer, Heidelberg (2016). https://doi.org/10.1007/978-3-662-53413-7_5

12. Andersen, L.O.: Program analysis and specialization for the C programming language. Ph.D. thesis, University of Cophenhagen (1994)
13. Heintze, N., Tardieu, O.: Ultra-fast aliasing analysis using cla: a million lines of c code in a second. In: PLDI 2001, vol. 36, pp. 254–263. ACM (2001)
14. Pearce, D.J., Kelly, P.H.J., Hankin, C.: Online cycle detection and difference propagation for pointer analysis. In: Proceedings Third IEEE International Workshop on Source Code Analysis and Manipulation, pp. 3–12. IEEE (2003)
15. Lhoták, O., Chung, K.-C.A.: Points-to analysis with efficient strong updates. In: POPL 2011, pp. 3–16 (2011)
16. Li, L., Cifuentes, C., Keynes, N.: Boosting the performance of flow-sensitive points-to analysis using value flow. In: FSE 2011, pp. 343–353 (2011)
17. Ye, S., Sui, Y., Xue, J.: Region-based selective flow-sensitive pointer analysis. In: SAS 2014, pp. 319–336 (2014)
18. Sui, Y., Xue, J.: On-demand strong update analysis via value-flow refinement. In: FSE 2016, pp. 460–473. ACM (2016)
19. ISO90. ISO/IEC. international standard ISO/IEC 9899, programming languages - C (1990)
20. Nuutila, E., Soisalon-Soininen, E.: On finding the strongly connected components in a directed graph. Inf. Process. Lett. **49**(1), 9–14 (1994)
21. Tarjan, R.: Depth-first search and linear graph algorithms. SIAM J. Comput. **1**(2), 146–160 (1972)
22. Sui, Y., Xue, J.: SVF: interprocedural static value-flow analysis in LLVM. In: CC 2016, pp. 265–266 (2016)
23. Sui, Y., Ye, D., Xue, J.: Detecting memory leaks statically with full-sparse value-flow analysis. IEEE Trans. Software Eng. **40**(2), 107–122 (2014)
24. Implementing next generation points-to in open64. www.affinic.com/documents/open64workshop/2010/slides/8_Ravindran.ppt
25. Hardekopf, B., Lin, C.: Semi-sparse flow-sensitive pointer analysis. In: POPL 2009, vol. 44, pp. 226–238. ACM (2009)
26. Side-effects of external apis. https://github.com/SVF-tools/SVF/blob/master/lib/Util/ExtAPI.cpp
27. Clang-7.0.0. http://releases.llvm.org/7.0.0/cfe-7.0.0.src.tar.xz
28. Whole-program llvm. http://github.com/travitch/whole-program-llvm
29. Fähndrich, M., Foster, J.S., Su, Z., Aiken, A.: Partial online cycle elimination in inclusion constraint graphs. In: PLDI 2098, vol. 33, pp. 85–96. ACM (1998)
30. Rountev, A., Chandra, S.: Off-line variable substitution for scaling points-to analysis. In: PLDI 2000, vol. 35, pp. 47–56. ACM (2000)
31. Lattner, C., Lenharth, A., Adve, V.: Making context-sensitive points-to analysis with heap cloning practical for the real world. In: PLDI 2007, vol. 42, pp. 278–289. ACM (2007)
32. Avots, D., Dalton, M., Livshits, V.B., Lam, M.S.: Improving software security with a C pointer analysis. In: ICSE 2005, pp. 332–341. ACM (2005)
33. Nystrom, E.M., Kim, H.-S., Hwu, W.W.: Importance of heap specialization in pointer analysis. In: PASTE 2004, pp. 43–48. ACM (2004)
34. Miné, A.: Field-sensitive value analysis of embedded c programs with union types and pointer arithmetics. In: LCTES 2006, vol. 41, pp. 54–63. ACM (2006)
35. Sui, Y., Fan, X., Zhou, H., Xue, J.: Loop-oriented array-and field-sensitive pointer analysis for automatic SIMD vectorization. In: LCTES 2016, pp. 41–51. ACM (2016)

Per-Dereference Verification of Temporal Heap Safety via Adaptive Context-Sensitive Analysis

Hua Yan[1,4,5](✉), Shiping Chen[2], Yulei Sui[3], Yueqian Zhang[1,2], Changwei Zou[1](✉), and Jingling Xue[1](✉)

[1] University of New South Wales, Sydney, Australia
[2] Data61, CSIRO, Sydney, Australia
[3] University of Technology Sydney, Sydney, Australia
[4] Sangfor Technologies Inc., Shenzhen, China
[5] Shenzhen Institutes of Advanced Technology, CAS, Shenzhen, China
yanhuacs@outlook.com, changwei.zou@student.unsw.edu.au, j.xue@unsw.edu.au

Abstract. We address the problem of verifying the temporal safety of heap memory at each pointer dereference. Our whole-program analysis approach is undertaken from the perspective of pointer analysis, allowing us to leverage the advantages of and advances in pointer analysis to improve precision and scalability. A dereference ω, say, via pointer q is unsafe iff there exists a deallocation ψ, say, via pointer p such that on a control-flow path ρ, p aliases with q (with both pointing to an object o representing an allocation), denoted $\mathcal{A}_\omega^\psi(\rho)$, and ψ reaches ω on ρ via control flow, denoted $\mathcal{R}_\omega^\psi(\rho)$. Applying directly any existing pointer analysis, which is typically solved separately with an associated control-flow reachability analysis, will render such verification highly imprecise, since $\exists\rho.\mathcal{A}_\omega^\psi(\rho) \wedge \exists\rho.\mathcal{R}_\omega^\psi(\rho) \nRightarrow \exists\rho.\mathcal{A}_\omega^\psi(\rho) \wedge \mathcal{R}_\omega^\psi(\rho)$ (i.e., $\exists$ does not distribute over $\wedge$). For precision, we solve $\exists\rho.\mathcal{A}_\omega^\psi(\rho) \wedge \mathcal{R}_\omega^\psi(\rho)$, with a control-flow path ρ containing an allocation o, a deallocation ψ and a dereference ω abstracted by a tuple of three contexts (c_o, c_ψ, c_ω). For scalability, a demand-driven full context-sensitive (modulo recursion) pointer analysis, which operates on pre-computed def-use chains with adaptive context-sensitivity, is used to infer (c_o, c_ψ, c_ω), without losing soundness or precision. Our evaluation shows that our approach can successfully verify the safety of 81.3% (or $\frac{93,141}{114,508}$) of all the dereferences in a set of ten C programs totalling 1,166 KLOC.

1 Introduction

Unmanaged programming languages such as C/C++ still remain irreplaceable in developing performance-critical systems such as operating systems, databases and web browsers. Such languages, however, suffer from memory safety issues. While spatial errors (e.g., buffer overflows) result in disastrous consequences (e.g., crashes, data corruption, information leakage, privilege escalation and control-flow hijacking), their temporal counterparts have also been shown to be

B.-Y. E. Chang (Ed.): SAS 2019, LNCS 11822, pp. 48–72, 2019.
https://doi.org/10.1007/978-3-030-32304-2_4

equally deadly [28,54]. In particular, verifying absence of dangling pointer dereferences, an important temporal heap safety (referred to TH-safety hereafter), is thus desirable.

A quite flourishing research thread focuses on separation logic [15,42,59], which enables precise shape analysis for pointer-based data structures. Much research effort has been devoted to improving scalability and automation of separation-logic-based verification [13,58]. In particular, bi-abduction [8] empowers separation-logic-based verification to generate program specifications automatically for large programs with millions of lines of code, in a compositional manner rather than as a whole-program analysis. However, one of its inevitable downsides (from the perspective of whole-program analysis) is the loss of precision due to a maximum size limit imposed on disjunctions of pre-conditions manipulated in order to improve performance [7,8].

Memory errors can also be found by other techniques, such as data-flow analysis [14,41] and model checking [24,26,38]. Notably, pointer analysis [25,31,45,47,49,62] has recently made significant strides, providing a solid foundation for developing many pointer-analysis-based static analyses for detecting memory errors [9,30,44,56,57,60]. In this paper, we present a fully-automated pointer-analysis-based approach, called D^3 (a **D**isprover of **D**angling pointer **D**ereferences), to verifying absence of (i.e., disproving presence of) dangling pointers on a per dereference basis. Compared to separation-logic-based approaches, our approach tackles this verification task from a different angle. Instead of focusing on reasoning about a variety of pointer-based data structures precisely in separation logic, we focus on reasoning about pointer aliasing and control-flow reachability context-sensitively in a whole-program setting *on-demand.*

Challenges. We highlight three challenges, from the perspective of pointer analysis:

Challenge 1: Modeling the Triple Troublemakers. A TH-safety violation involves three distinct program locations, an allocation o (representing an allocation site), a deallocation ψ and a dereference ω , which must be all modelled precisely.

Challenge 2: Resolving Aliases. A dereference ω (via pointer q) is unsafe iff there exists a deallocation ψ (via pointer p) such that on a control-flow path ρ, p aliases with q (with both pointing to an object o), denoted $\mathcal{A}_{\omega}^{\psi}(\rho)$, and ψ reaches ω on ρ via control flow, denoted $\mathcal{R}_{\omega}^{\psi}(\rho)$. Pointer aliasing, a well-known difficult static analysis problem, must be solved to guarantee both soundness and precision scalably for large programs. For the TH-safety verification, this is particularly challenging. Any existing k-limited context-sensitive pointer analysis that scales for large programs [25,45] (where $k \leq 3$ currently) is not precise enough (as o, ψ and ω can often span across more than three functions). In addition, off-the-shelf pointer analyses provide the alias information between ψ and ω but are oblivious to the control-flow reachability information from ψ to ω (even if solved flow-sensitively), causing potentially a significant precision loss, since $\exists\rho.\mathcal{A}_{\omega}^{\psi}(\rho) \wedge \exists\rho.\mathcal{R}_{\omega}^{\psi}(\rho) \nRightarrow \exists\rho.\mathcal{A}_{\omega}^{\psi}(\rho) \wedge \mathcal{R}_{\omega}^{\psi}(\rho)$ (i.e., $\exists$ does not distribute over $\wedge$). Thus, increasing precision in our verification task requires pointer analysis to be not only more precise (with longer calling-contexts) but also synergistic with control-flow reachability analysis.

Challenge 3: Pruning the Search Space. To achieve high precision, a fine abstraction of control-flow paths (e.g., with adequate context-sensitivity) is required, but at a risk for causing path explosion. Furthermore, the presence of a large number of deallocation-dereference (ψ, ω) pairs that need to be checked further exacerbates the problem. Pruning the search space without any loss of precision is essential.

Our Solution. In this paper, we present a whole-program analysis approach that verifies TH-safety for each dereference ω. Specifically, ω is considered safe iff there exists no deallocation ψ such that the pair (ψ, ω) causes a dangling pointer dereference at ω.

To meet Challenge 1, we model this verification problem context-sensitively with three contexts. We identify an allocation o, a deallocation ψ (via pointer p) and a dereference ω (via pointer q) by a context tuple (c_o, c_ψ, c_ω) so that $\langle\!\langle c_o, o \rangle\!\rangle$ represents a context-sensitive heap object, i.e, an object o created under c_o, (c_ψ, p) deallocates what is pointed to by p under c_ψ, and (ω, q) dereferences pointer q under context c_ω. We verify TH-safety with respect to (o, ψ, ω) by disproving the presence of a control-flow path that contains a context tuple, (c_o, c_ψ, c_ω), such that $\langle\!\langle c_o, o \rangle\!\rangle$, once deallocated at (c_ψ, p), is still accessed subsequently at (c_ω, q) along the path.

To meet Challenge 2, we introduce a demand-driven pointer analysis that automatically infers the context information in pointer aliases so that the resulting alias analysis can correlate with an associated control-flow reachability analysis as required. Given a pointer p at a deallocation (resp. a pointer q at a dereference) without any context given, our pointer analysis will infer a context c_ψ (resp. c_ω), together with a context-sensitive object $\langle\!\langle c_o, o \rangle\!\rangle$, such that the context-sensitive pointer (c_ψ, p) (resp. (c_ω, q)) points to $\langle\!\langle c_o, o \rangle\!\rangle$, implying that $\exists \rho. \mathcal{A}_\omega^\psi(\rho)$. In addition, c_ψ and c_ω are also required to satisfy the control-flow reachability constraint $\exists \rho. \mathcal{R}_\omega^\psi(\rho)$ simultaneously so that $\exists \rho. \mathcal{A}_\omega^\psi(\rho) \wedge \mathcal{R}_\omega^\psi(\rho)$ holds. This avoids false positives that satisfy $\mathcal{R}_\omega^\psi$ and $\mathcal{A}_\omega^\psi$ only for two distinct paths, respectively, which happens when $\exists \rho. \mathcal{A}_\omega^\psi(\rho) \wedge \exists \rho. \mathcal{R}_\omega^\psi(\rho) \nRightarrow \exists \rho. \mathcal{A}_\omega^\psi(\rho) \wedge \mathcal{R}_\omega^\psi(\rho)$. Finally, points-to queries are raised on-demand by traversing pre-computed def-use chains (in order to improve efficiency) and by supporting full context-sensitivity (modulo recursion) to transcend k-limiting (in order to improve precision).

To meet Challenge 3, we make our context-sensitive analysis adaptive. A context tuple (c_o, c_ψ, c_ω) is reduced to $(c'_o, c'_\psi, c'_\omega)$ if c_o, c_ψ and c_ω share a common prefix c_{pre}, so that $c_o = cons(c_{pre}, c'_o)$, $c_\psi = cons(c_{pre}, c'_\psi)$, and $c_\omega = cons(c_{pre}, c'_\omega)$, where *cons* denotes string concatenation. This adaptive analysis aims to reduce exponentially many prefixes starting from `main()`, which would otherwise significantly impede scalability.

Program P	::=	F^+
Function F	::=	^{l}`def` $f(\vec{x})$ { S; }
Statement S	::=	$^l x = y$
	|	$^l x = {*}y$
	|	$^l {*}x = y$
	|	$^l x = \&y$
	|	$^l x =$ `malloc()`
	|	^{l}`free(`y`)`
	|	$^l x = fp(\vec{y})$
	|	^{l}`ret` x
	|	^{l}`if (*)` S_1 `else` S_2
	|	^{l}`while (*)` S
	|	$S_1; S_2$

Fig. 1. A small unmanaged imperative language.

Contributions. This paper makes the following main contributions:

- We propose a fully automated approach to TH-safety verification on a per dereference basis, with a precise context-sensitive model, which enables a control-flow path to be abstracted by three contexts for its allocation, deallocation and dereference. This provides a balanced trade-off between precision and scalability.
- We present a static whole-program analysis that solves this three-point verification problem in the presence of both data-dependence and control-flow constraints. To this end, we develop a demand-driven pointer analysis with full context-sensitivity (modulo recursion) that automatically infers the context information required.
- We present an adaptive context-sensitive policy for TH-safety verification that automatically truncates redundant context prefixes without losing soundness or precision. This enables our approach to scale to some large real-world programs.
- We have implemented D^3 in LLVM and evaluated it using a suite of ten real-world programs. Our results show that D^3 scales to hundreds of KLOC, with a capability of verifying 81.3% of all the 114,508 dereferences to be safe.

2 Preliminaries

We describe our techniques using a small language in Fig. 1. Function definitions and statements are identified by their labels or line numbers. The language is standard. Pointers are propagated via copy ($x = y$), load ($x = {*}y$), store (${*}x = y$) and address-taking ($x = \&y$) statements; heap objects are allocated and deallocated by `malloc()` and `free()`, respectively; the callee of a function call ($x = fp(\vec{y})$) is specified by a function pointer (fp) with its parameters ($\vec{y}$) passed by value (as in LLVM-IR); and `ret`, `if` and `while` represent standard return, branching and looping statements.

As with previous work [8,34,36,58], we currently do not handle concurrent programs.

Inter-Procedural Control-Flow Graph (ICFG). This is a directed graph (N, E), where each node $n \in N$ represents a statement and each edge $e = (src, dst) \in E$ represents the control flow from statement src to statement dst. In particular, if e represents a function call/return, then e is labeled with the corresponding call-site ID κ.

Contexts. Given any statement in function f, a *calling context* (or *context*, for short) $c = [\kappa_1, \kappa_2, ..., \kappa_n]$ is a sequence of n call-site IDs in their invocation order that uniquely specifies an abstract call-path to f on the ICFG of the program.

Allocation, Deallocation and Dereference. A context-sensitive (abstract) *object*, denoted $\langle\!\langle c_o, o \rangle\!\rangle$, represents the set of concrete objects created at allocation site o under context c_o. We write $\psi(c_\psi, l_\psi, p)$ to signify a context-sensitive *deallocation* of the object pointed to by p at line l_ψ under context c_ψ. Similarly, a context-sensitive *dereference* $\omega(c_\omega, l_\omega, q)$ accesses the object pointed to by q at line l_ω under context c_ω. Context-insensitively, these notations are simplified to o, $\psi(l_\psi, p)$ and $\omega(l_\omega, q)$, respectively.

Pointer Analysis. A context-sensitive pointer analysis conservatively computes a function $pt_{cs} : \mathrm{C} \times \mathrm{V} \rightarrow 2^{\mathrm{C} \times \mathrm{O}}$ that relates each context-sensitive pointer $(c, v) \in \mathrm{C} \times \mathrm{V}$ to the set of context-sensitive objects $\langle\!\langle c_o, o \rangle\!\rangle \in \mathrm{C} \times \mathrm{O}$ pointed to by (c, v). A pointer analysis is formulated by a set of inference rules that can be solved using a standard fixed-point algorithm. Andersen-style [4] subset-based context-insensitive pointer analysis $pt : \mathrm{V} \rightarrow 2^{\mathrm{O}}$ is given in Fig. 2. $\mathcal{P}[\![s]\!]$ signifies that statement s appears in program $\mathcal{P}$.

We consider only field-sensitive pointer analysis techniques. As with previous techniques [6,22,39,58], we assume that our programs are ANSI-compliant that are devoid of buffer overflows and data misalignments. Arrays are handled monolithically. Any access to a member of an array or struct object with a statically unknown offset is viewed to be a non-deterministic operation on the given object (soundly but imprecisely).

TH-Safety Violation. A context-sensitive *TH-safety violation*, denoted $\langle \langle\!\langle c_o, o \rangle\!\rangle, \psi(c_\psi, l_\psi, p), \omega(c_\omega, l_\omega, q) \rangle$, occurs when $\langle\!\langle c_o, o \rangle\!\rangle$, which is deallocated at l_ψ under c_ψ, is accessed later at l_ω under c_ω. Our context-insensitive notation is $\langle o, \psi(l_\psi, p), \omega(l_\omega, q) \rangle$.

3 Illustrating Examples

In Sect. 3.1, we explain why aliasing and control-flow reachability must be solved synergistically rather than separately in order to achieve high precision in our verification task, no matter how precise pointer analysis is. In Sect. 3.2, we

$$\text{[Addr]}\frac{\mathcal{P}[\![x = \&y]\!]}{y \in pt(x)} \qquad \text{[Alloc]}\frac{\mathcal{P}[\![{}^{o}x = \texttt{malloc()}]\!]}{o \in pt(x)}$$

$$\text{[Copy]}\frac{\mathcal{P}[\![x = y]\!]}{pt(y) \subseteq pt(x)}$$

$$\text{[Load]}\frac{\mathcal{P}[\![x = *y]\!] \quad o \in pt(y)}{pt(o) \subseteq pt(x)} \qquad \text{[Store]}\frac{\mathcal{P}[\![*x = y]\!] \quad o \in pt(x)}{pt(y) \subseteq pt(o)}$$

Fig. 2. Andersen-style subset-based, flow- and context-insensitive pointer analysis [4]. Passing arguments into and returning results from functions are handled as copy statements.

describe how our synergistic approach works on top of a demand-driven pointer analysis, by taming path explosion with full context-sensitivity (modulo recursion) adaptively.

```
1: def alloc() {                8: def Reach_But_NoAlias() {
2:     x=malloc(); //o2         9:     a=alloc();      //κ9 , 《[κ9 ],o2》
3:     ret x; }                10:     b=alloc();      //κ10, 《[κ10],o2》
                               11:     dealloc(a);     //κ11
4: def dealloc(y) {            12:     deref(b); }     //κ12
5:     free(y); } //ψ(l5,y)    13: def Alias_But_NoReach() {
                               14:     c=alloc();      //κ14, 《[κ14],o2》
6: def deref(z) {              15:     deref(c);       //κ15
7:     temp=*z; } //ω(l7,z)    16:     dealloc(c); }   //κ16
```

(a) Safe code, with a dereference in line 7

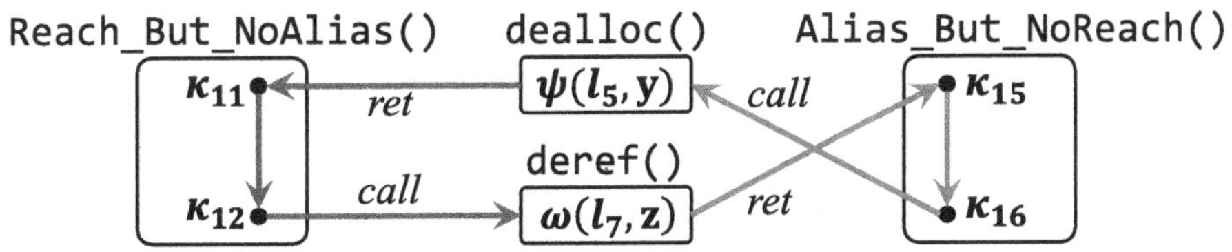

(b) ICFG (with relevant edges given), showing that $\psi(l_5, \mathrm{y})$ reaches $\omega(l_7, \mathrm{z})$ on the blue path but $\psi(l_5, \mathrm{y})$ aliases with $\omega(l_7, \mathrm{z})$ on the orange path, implying that the dereference at l_7 is safe

Fig. 3. An example without any TH-safety violation.

3.1 Aliasing and Control-Flow Reachability: Separately vs. Synergistically

Figure 3(a) gives a program, in which $\psi(l_5, y)$ does not cause a TH-safety violation at $\omega(l_7, z)$ (Fig. 3(b)). The wrappers, `alloc()`, `dealloc()` and `deref()`, allocate o_2, deallocate the object pointed by y at $\psi(l_5, \texttt{y})$ and dereference z at $\omega(l_7, \texttt{z})$, respectively. In `Reach_But_NoAlias()`, $\langle\!\langle[\kappa_9], o_2\rangle\!\rangle$ is first deallocated in l_{11} and then another object $\langle\!\langle[\kappa_{10}], o_2\rangle\!\rangle$ is accessed indirectly in l_{12}. In `Alias_But_NoReach()`, $\langle\!\langle[\kappa_{14}], o_2\rangle\!\rangle$ is first accessed indirectly in l_{15} and then deallocated in l_{16}.

If aliasing and control-flow reachability for $\psi(l_5, y)$ and $\omega(l_7, z)$ are solved separately, a TH-safety violation will be reported (but as a false positive), no matter how precise the underlying pointer analysis is used. As illustrated in Fig. 3(b), aliasing (the orange path) and reachability (the blue path) happen along two different paths in the ICFG, and consequently, cannot be satisfied simultaneously in the same path.

To avoid false positives like this, aliasing and control-flow reachability must be solved together. In our synergistic approach, we identify o_2, $\psi(l_5, \texttt{y})$ and $\omega(l_7, \texttt{z})$ by their respective contexts c_o, c_ψ and c_ω, and disprove the presence of a context tuple (c_o, c_ψ, c_ω), such that $\langle\!\langle c_o, o_2\rangle\!\rangle$ is first deallocated in l_5 under c_ψ and subsequently accessed in l_7 under c_ω along the same path. Therefore, our approach will report no TH-safety violation for this program. Note that any context-insensitive analysis that merges $\langle\!\langle[\kappa_9], o_2\rangle\!\rangle$ and $\langle\!\langle[\kappa_{10}], o_2\rangle\!\rangle$ into o_2 (by disregarding their contexts) will report a false violation as $\langle o_2, \psi(l_5, \texttt{y}), \omega(l_7, \texttt{z})\rangle$.

```
def foo() {
    d=bar();        //κ18
    deref(d); }//κ19

def bar() {
    e=alloc(); //κ21, 《[κ21],o2》
    dealloc(e);//κ22
    ret e; }
```

(a) Allocation and deallocation (via wrappers) in the same function `bar()`

```
def baz() {
    f=alloc(); //κ25, 《[κ25],o2》
    qux(f); }   //κ26

def qux(g) {
    dealloc(g);//κ28
    deref(g); }//κ29
```

(b) Deallocation and dereference (via wrappers) in the same function `qux()`

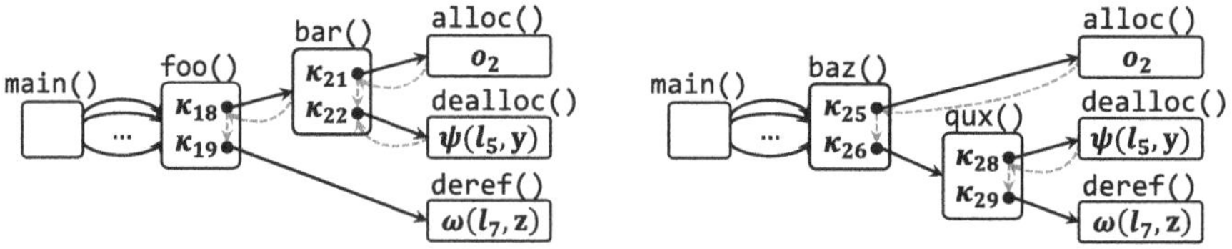

(c) ICFG for (a) (d) ICFG for (b)

Fig. 4. Two representative TH-safety violations caused by $\psi(l_5, y)$ and $\omega(l_7, z)$ appearing in Fig. 3, where the three wrappers, `alloc()`, `dealloc()` and `deref()` are defined.

3.2 Synergizing Pointer Analysis and Control-Flow Reachability Analysis: On-Demand with Adaptive Context-Sensitivity

Let us illustrate our approach further by expanding Fig. 3 into Fig. 4 by examining how it detects two representative TH-safety violations caused now by $\psi(l_5, y)$

and $\omega(l_7, z)$ considered earlier. In Fig. 4(a) (with its relevant ICFG given in Fig. 4(c)), o_2 and $\psi(l_5, y)$ are reached transitively via the two call sites in the same function, `bar()`, which is called by `foo()`, in which $\omega(l_7, z)$ is reached via a call to `deref()` transitively. In Fig. 4(b) (with its relevant ICFG given in Fig. 4(d)), $\psi(l_5, y)$ and $\omega(l_7, z)$ are reached transitively via the two call sites in the same function, `qux()`, which is called by `baz()`, in which o_2 is reached via a call to `alloc()` transitively.

We will only discuss Fig. 4(a) below as Fig. 4(b) can be understood similarly.

Verifying TH-Safety by Synergizing Pointer and Reachability Analyses On-Demand. Our approach relies on pt_{cs}^{dd}, a *demand-driven* version of pointer analysis pt_{cs} introduced in Sect. 2. For Fig. 4(a), we report a TH-safety violation $\langle\langle\!\langle[\kappa_{18}, \kappa_{21}], o_2\rangle\!\rangle, \psi([\kappa_{18}, \kappa_{22}], l_5, \mathtt{y}), \omega([\kappa_{19}], l_7, \mathtt{z})\rangle$. To obtain this, we check to see if `y` aliases `z` by querying pt_{cs}^{dd} for the points-to sets of `y` and `z`, i.e., $pt_{cs}^{dd}([\,], \mathtt{y})$ and $pt_{cs}^{dd}([\,], \mathtt{z})$, respectively, where their initial unknown contexts $[\,]$ will be eventually filled up by pt_{cs}^{dd}. On-demand, pt_{cs}^{dd} traces backwards the flow of objects along the pre-computed def-use chains (obtained by a pre-analysis) in the program. To compute $pt_{cs}^{dd}([\,], \mathtt{y})$, for example, starting from l_5, pt_{cs}^{dd} traces back to l_4 where `y` is defined; moves to the call-site κ_{22} where `y` receives the value of `e` via parameter passing; reaches l_{21} where `e` is defined; encounters l_3 where `x` is returned (by entering `alloc()` from its exit at κ_{21}); and finally, arrives at l_2 where `x` is defined, giving rise to $\langle\!\langle[\kappa_{21}], o_2\rangle\!\rangle \in pt_{cs}^{dd}([\kappa_{22}], \mathtt{y})$. Note that the initial unknown context $[\,]$ has been inferred to be $[\kappa_{22}]$ as desired. This implies that $\langle\!\langle[\kappa_{18}, \kappa_{21}], o_2\rangle\!\rangle \in pt_{cs}^{dd}([\kappa_{18}, \kappa_{22}], \mathtt{y})$. Similarly we obtain $\langle\!\langle[\kappa_{18}, \kappa_{21}], o_2\rangle\!\rangle \in pt_{cs}^{dd}([\kappa_{19}], \mathtt{z})$. Thus, $\psi([\kappa_{18}, \kappa_{22}], l_5, \mathtt{y})$ aliases with $\omega([\kappa_{19}], l_7, \mathtt{z})$ (with `y` and `z` both pointing to $\langle\!\langle[\kappa_{18}, \kappa_{21}], o_2\rangle\!\rangle$), and in addition, the former also reaches the latter along the same path identified by $[\kappa_{18}, \kappa_{21}]$, $[\kappa_{18}, \kappa_{22}]$ and $[\kappa_{19}]$. As a result, our approach reports this violation as $\langle\langle\!\langle[\kappa_{18}, \kappa_{21}], o_2\rangle\!\rangle, \psi([\kappa_{18}, \kappa_{22}], l_5, \mathtt{y}), \omega([\kappa_{19}], l_7, \mathtt{z})\rangle$.

Taming Path Explosion with Adaptive Context-Sensitivity. In our approach, pt_{cs}^{dd} applies context-sensitivity adaptively without analyzing the callers of `foo()`, avoiding the possible path explosion that may occur between `main()` and `foo()` in Fig. 4(c). Soundness is still guaranteed, since the context elements between `main()` and `foo()` do not affect the value-flows of $\langle\!\langle[\kappa_{18}, \kappa_{21}], o_2\rangle\!\rangle$ and are thus redundant. To see this, if we extend the two contexts in $\psi([\kappa_{18}, \kappa_{22}], l_5, \mathtt{y})$ and $\omega([\kappa_{19}], l_7, \mathtt{z})$ with two distinct prefixes, $[\kappa_{a1}]$ and $[\kappa_{a2}]$, we will fail to obtain any additional violation witness, since both are no longer aliased: $pt_{cs}^{dd}([\kappa_{a1}, \kappa_{18}, \kappa_{22}], \mathtt{y}) = \{\langle\!\langle[\kappa_{a1}, \kappa_{18}, \kappa_{21}], o_2\rangle\!\rangle\} \neq \{\langle\!\langle[\kappa_{a2}, \kappa_{18}, \kappa_{21}], o_2\rangle\!\rangle\} = pt_{cs}^{dd}([\kappa_{a2}, \kappa_{19}], \mathtt{z})$. If we use the same prefix instead, we will end up with a finer abstraction, yielding the results already subsumed.

4 Our Approach

The workflow of our four-stage approach is given in Fig. 5. To start with (①), we perform a fast but imprecise pre-analysis for a program using Andersen's pointer analysis pt (Fig. 2). Then (②), we build a value-flow graph to capture the flow of values across the program based on the points-to information obtained in the pre-analysis (Sect. 4.1). Next (③), we obtain the points-to set at each dereference by querying pt^{dd}_{cs}, a demand-driven version of pt_{cs} (discussed in Sect. 2) that now operates on the value-flow graph (Sect. 4.2). This way, pt^{dd}_{cs} will traverse pre-computed def-use chains rather than control-flow, achieving better efficiency. Finally (④), we verify absence of a TH-safety violation at a dereference by considering aliasing and control-flow reachability synergistically with adaptive context-sensitivity (Sects. 4.3 and 4.4).

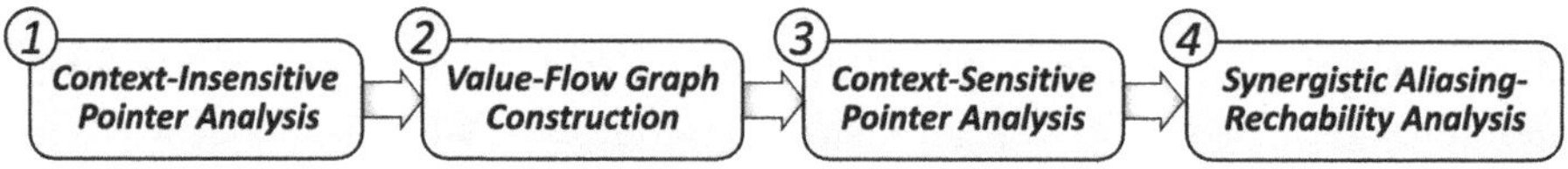

Fig. 5. The workflow of our approach on synergizing pointer analysis with reachability analysis.

4.1 Value-Flow Graph Construction

We construct a *value-flow graph* for a program, following [12,44,49], based on the points-to information discovered during the pre-analysis to capture the flow of values across the program. This entails building the def-use chains for its top-level variables (which are conceptually regarded as register variables) and address-taken variables (which are all referred to as memory objects or objects for short in this paper).

The def-use chains for top-level variables are readily available. However, those for address-taken variables (accessed indirectly at loads, stores and call sites) are implicit. To make such indirect memory accesses explicit, we resort to the rules in Fig. 6. For an address-taken variable o, there are two types of annotations: $[\![\mu(o)]\!]$, which represents a potential use of o, and $[\![o = \chi(o)]\!]$, which represents both a potential definition and a potential use of o. We define $\Delta : \mathrm{L} \times \mathrm{ORD} \rightarrow 2^{\mathrm{ANNOT}}$, where ANNOT is the set of annotations (shown in brackets), L is the set of statement labels, and ORD $= \{\prec, \succ\}$ indicates if an annotation appears immediately before ($\prec$) or after ($\succ$) a statement.

Let us go through the rules in Fig. 6, where allow us to soundly model both strong updates (by killing old values) and weak updates (by preserving old values) for address-taken variables. For a load statement $x = *y$ at l, if y points to o, then $[\![\mu(o)]\!]$ is added before l to indicate that o may be used at this load (Rule [Mu]). For a store statement $*x = y$ at l, if x points to o, then $[\![o = \chi(o)]\!]$ is added after l to indicate that o (LHS) may be redefined in terms of both o (RHS) in the case of a weak update and y at this store (Rule [Chi]). Rules [Ref] and [Mod] prescribe the standard inter-procedural MOD/REF analysis. Let a function f be defined at l_f and called at a call site l via a function pointer fp. Consider [Ref] first. If $[\![\mu(o)]\!]$ is annotated inside f, then $[\![\mu(o)]\!]$ is added before l (as o may be used in f directly or indirectly), and $[\![o = \chi(o)]\!]$ is added before f's definition at l_f (as o may be passed indirectly as a parameter to f). Consider

$$[\text{Mu}]\ \frac{\mathcal{P}[\![^{l}\ x = *y]\!] \qquad o \in pt(y)}{[\![\mu(o)]\!] \in \Delta(l, \prec)} \qquad\qquad [\text{Chi}]\ \frac{\mathcal{P}[\![^{l}\ *x = y]\!] \qquad o \in pt(x)}{[\![o{=}\chi(o)]\!] \in \Delta(l, \succ)}$$

$$[\text{Ref}]\ \frac{\begin{array}{c}\mathcal{P}[\![^{l}\ \_ = fp(\_)]\!] \qquad f \in pt(fp) \\ \mathcal{P}[\![^{l_f}\texttt{def}\ f(\_)\{...\}]\!] \qquad l_s \in L(f) \\ [\![\mu(o)]\!] \in \Delta(l_s, \prec)\end{array}}{[\![\mu(o)]\!] \in \Delta(l, \prec) \quad [\![o{=}\chi(o)]\!] \in \Delta(l_f, \prec)} \qquad [\text{Mod}]\ \frac{\begin{array}{c}\mathcal{P}[\![^{l}\ \_ = fp(\_)]\!] \qquad f \in pt(fp) \\ \mathcal{P}[\![^{l_f}\texttt{def}\ f(\_)\{...\}]\!] \qquad l_s \in L(f) \\ [\![o{=}\chi(o)]\!] \in \Delta(l_s, \succ)\end{array}}{\begin{array}{c}[\![\mu(o)]\!] \in \Delta(l, \prec) \quad [\![o{=}\chi(o)]\!] \in \Delta(l_f, \prec) \\ [\![\mu(o)]\!] \in \Delta(l_f, \succ) \quad [\![o{=}\chi(o)]\!] \in \Delta(l, \succ)\end{array}}$$

Fig. 6. Rules for adding two types of annotations, $[\![\mu(o)]\!]$ and $[\![o = \chi(o)]\!]$, to make explicit the accesses of a memory object o. $L(f)$ denotes the set of statement labels in function f. $\Delta(l, \prec)$ and $\Delta(l, \succ)$ represent the sets of annotations added just before and after l, respectively.

[Mod] now. If $[\![o = \chi(o)]\!]$ is annotated inside f, then we add not only the same annotations at l and l_f as in [Ref], but also $[\![\mu(o)]\!]$ after l_f (as o may be returned to its call sites) and $[\![o = \chi(o)]\!]$ after l (as o may be modified at l).

Once a program has been annotated, its top-level variables and objects appearing in the annotations are put into SSA form [11], with their versions denoted in *superscripts*.

Example 1. Let us see how to add o_5-related annotations in Fig. 7. For now, the value-flow edges shown are irrelevant. In line 8, $[\![o_5^2 = \chi(o_5^1)]\!]$ is added after l_8, i.e., as $8^{\succ}$, in `put()` as `pctn` is found to point to o_5 by the pre-analysis in Fig. 2 (Rule [Chi]). As a result, this inter-procedural MOD/REF effect needs to be reflected at its definition and call sites, by adding $7^{\prec}$, $7^{\succ}$, $14^{\prec}$, $14^{\succ}$, $15^{\prec}$, and $15^{\succ}$ (Rule [Mod]). In line 16, $[\![\mu(o_5^2)]\!]$ is added before l_{16} since `tray` is found to point to o_5 (Rule [Mu]).

Given an annotated program in SSA form, we build its value-flow graph, $G_{\text{vfg}} = (\text{L} \times \text{V}, \text{E})$, to capture the flow of values through its def-use chains and inter-procedural call/return edges, by using the rules in Fig. 8 to construct its value-flow edges. We make use of two mappings, $\mathcal{D} : \text{V} \to 2^{\text{L}}$ and $\mathcal{U} : \text{V} \to 2^{\text{L}}$, that map a variable $v \in \text{V}$ to the set of its definition sites $l_{def} \in L$ and use sites $l_{use} \in L$, respectively. We write $\langle l_{src}, v\rangle \longrightarrow \langle l_{dst}, v'\rangle$ to denote the flow of a value initially in v at l_{src} to v' at l_{dst}. For a top-level variable $x \in \text{V}^{\text{T}}$, Rule [$\text{D}^{\text{T}}$] adds the definition site l to $\mathcal{D}(x)$ and Rules [$\text{U}^{\text{T}}_{\text{Copy}}$], [$\text{U}^{\text{T}}_{\text{Load}}$], [$\text{U}^{\text{T}}_{\text{Store}}$], [$\text{U}^{\text{T}}_{\text{Addr}}$], [$\text{U}^{\text{T}}_{\text{Free}}$] and [$\text{U}^{\text{T}}_{\text{Call}}$] add the use site l to $\mathcal{U}(x)$. For an address-taken variable $o \in \text{V}^{\text{A}}$, Rules [$\text{D}^{\text{A}}$] and [$\text{U}^{\text{A}}_{\chi}$]/[$\text{U}^{\text{A}}_{\mu}$] simply collect its definition and use sites into $\mathcal{D}(o)$ and $\mathcal{U}(o)$, respectively. The last five rules construct the edges in G_{vfg} by connecting a definition site with all its use sites. [VF^{Intra}] adds intra-procedural value-flow edges while the other four add inter-procedural value-flow edges (with [$\text{VF}^{\text{T}}_{\text{Call}}$] and [$\text{VF}^{\text{T}}_{\text{Ret}}$] for top-level variables and [$\text{VF}^{\text{A}}_{\text{Call}}$] and [$\text{VF}^{\text{A}}_{\text{Ret}}$] for address-taken variables).

```
1: def mkFd() {                        9:  def feedPets() {
2:     fd=malloc();      // o₂        10:      bone=mkFd();    // ⟪[κ₁₀],o₂⟫
3:     ret fd;                        11:      fish=mkFd();    // ⟪[κ₁₁],o₂⟫
   }                                  12:      tray=mkCtn();   // ⟪[κ₁₂],o₅⟫
                                      13:      bowl=mkCtn();   // ⟪[κ₁₃],o₅⟫
4: def mkCtn() {                      14:      ⟦μ(o₅⁰)⟧
5:     ctn=malloc();     // o₅        14:      put(bone, tray);// κ₁₄
6:     ret ctn;                       14:      ⟦o₅¹ = χ(o₅⁰)⟧
   }
                                      15:      ⟦μ(o₅¹)⟧
7: ⟦o₅¹ = χ(o₅⁰)⟧                     15:      put(fish, bowl);// κ₁₅
7: def put(pfd, pctn) {               15:      ⟦o₅² = χ(o₅¹)⟧
8:     *pctn=pfd;
8: ⟦o₅² = χ(o₅¹)⟧                     16:      ⟦μ(o₅²)⟧
   }                                  16:      feedDog=*tray;
7: ⟦μ(o₅²)⟧                              }
```

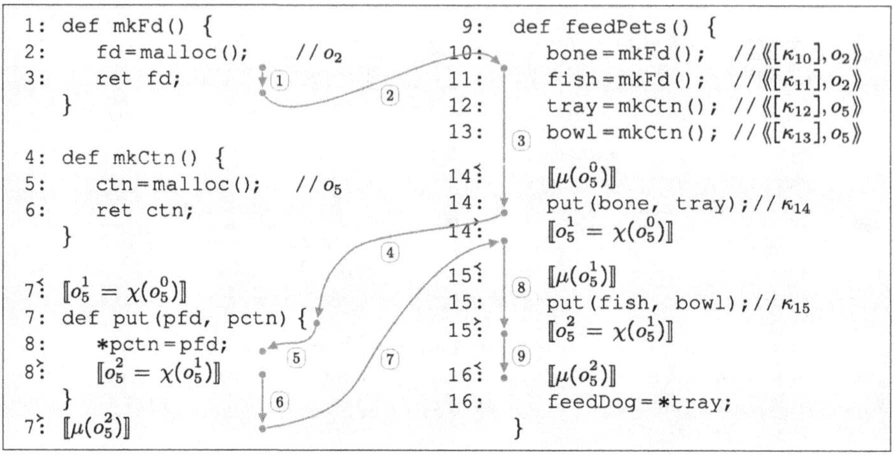

Fig. 7. A program (referred to in Example 1 (annotations), Example 2 (value-flow edges) and Example 3 (pointer analysis)), decorated with μ and χ annotations and all the value-flow edges ①–⑨ that capture the flow of o_2 from bone in line 10 through to feedDog in line 16.

Once G_{vfg} has been constructed, the SSA versions of a variable will be ignored.

Example 2. Figure 7 shows all the value-flow edges ①–⑨ capturing the flow of o_2 via fd, bone, pfd, o_5 and feedDog. We obtain these edges by applying the following rules (Fig. 8): ① for $\langle l_2, \text{fd} \rangle \longrightarrow \langle l_3, \text{fd} \rangle$ ([VF^{Intra}]); ② for $\langle l_3, \text{fd} \rangle \longrightarrow \langle l_{10}, \text{bone} \rangle$ ([VF$^{\text{T}}_{\text{Ret}}$]); ③ for $\langle l_{10}, \text{bone} \rangle \longrightarrow \langle l_{14}, \text{bone} \rangle$ ([VF^{Intra}]); ④ for $\langle l_{14}, \text{bone} \rangle \longrightarrow \langle l_7, \text{pfd} \rangle$ ([VF$^{\text{T}}_{\text{Call}}$]); ⑤ for $\langle l_7, \text{pfd} \rangle \longrightarrow \langle l_8, \text{pfd} \rangle$ and ⑥ for $\langle l_8^{\succ}, o_5^2 \rangle \longrightarrow \langle l_7^{\succ}, o_5^2 \rangle$ ([VF^{Intra}]); ⑦ for $\langle l_7^{\succ}, o_5^2 \rangle \longrightarrow \langle l_{14}^{\succ}, o_5^0 \rangle$ ([VF$^{\text{A}}_{\text{Ret}}$]); and ⑧ for $\langle l_{14}^{\succ}, o_5^1 \rangle \longrightarrow \langle l_{15}^{\succ}, o_5^1 \rangle$ and ⑨ for $\langle l_{15}^{\succ}, o_5^2 \rangle \longrightarrow \langle l_{16}^{\prec}, o_5^2 \rangle$ ([VF^{Intra}]).

In Fig. 10 (discussed in Sect. 4.2), we will give a version of Fig. 7 with all the value-flow edges included for the program.

4.2   Demand-Driven Context-Sensitive Pointer Analysis

Our context-sensitive pointer analysis pt_{cs}^{dd} operates on the value-flow graph G_{vfg} of a program. We write $pt_{cs}^{dd}(c, l, v) = \diamondsuit$ to signify a demand query for the points-to set of variable v at statement l under context c. In the case of $pt_{cs}^{dd}([\ ], l, v) = \diamondsuit$ with an empty context $[\ ]$, pt_{cs}^{dd} will find all pointed-to objects $\langle\!\langle c_o, o \rangle\!\rangle \in pt_{cs}^{dd}(c, l, v)$, where c is also inferred automatically. This automatic context inference is essential for achieving high precision as it provides a mechanism for us to synergize alias and control-flow reachability analyses as needed. As $pt_{cs}^{dd}(c, l, v) = \diamondsuit$ is solved on-demand (with possibly many other points-to queries raised along the way), by traversing backwards only the value-flow edges

$$[\mathrm{D}^{\mathrm{T}}]\ \frac{\mathcal{P}[\![{}^{l}\, x = \_]\!]}{l \in \mathcal{D}(x)} \qquad [\mathrm{U}^{\mathrm{T}}_{\mathrm{Copy}}]\ \frac{\mathcal{P}[\![{}^{l}\, \_ = x]\!]}{l \in \mathcal{U}(x)} \qquad [\mathrm{U}^{\mathrm{T}}_{\mathrm{Load}}]\ \frac{\mathcal{P}[\![{}^{l}\, \_ = *x]\!]}{l \in \mathcal{U}(x)} \qquad [\mathrm{U}^{\mathrm{T}}_{\mathrm{Store}}]\ \frac{\mathcal{P}[\![{}^{l}\, *x = \_]\!]}{l \in \mathcal{U}(x)}$$

$$[\mathrm{U}^{\mathrm{T}}_{\mathrm{Addr}}]\ \frac{\mathcal{P}[\![{}^{l}\, \_ = \&x]\!]}{l \in \mathcal{U}(x)} \qquad [\mathrm{U}^{\mathrm{T}}_{\mathrm{Free}}]\ \frac{\mathcal{P}[\![{}^{l}\, \mathtt{free}(x)]\!]}{l \in \mathcal{U}(x)} \qquad [\mathrm{U}^{\mathrm{T}}_{\mathrm{Call}}]\ \frac{\mathcal{P}[\![{}^{l}\, \_ = fp(\vec{x})]\!] \quad x \in \vec{x}}{l \in \mathcal{U}(x)}$$

$$[\mathrm{D}^{\mathrm{A}}]\ \frac{[\![o = \_]\!] \in \Delta(l, \succ)}{l^{\succ} \in \mathcal{D}(o)} \qquad [\mathrm{U}^{\mathrm{A}}_{\chi}]\ \frac{[\![\_ = \chi(o)]\!] \in \Delta(l, \succ)}{l^{\succ} \in \mathcal{U}(o)} \qquad [\mathrm{U}^{\mathrm{A}}_{\mu}]\ \frac{[\![\mu(o)]\!] \in \Delta(l, \prec)}{l^{\prec} \in \mathcal{U}(o)}$$

$$[\mathrm{VF}^{\mathrm{Intra}}]\ \frac{l_d \in \mathcal{D}(o) \quad l_u \in \mathcal{U}(o) \quad F(l_d) = F(l_u)}{\langle l_d, o\rangle \longrightarrow \langle l_u, o\rangle}$$

$$[\mathrm{VF}^{\mathrm{T}}_{\mathrm{Call}}]\ \frac{\begin{array}{c}\mathcal{P}[\![{}^{l}\, \_ = fp(\vec{x})]\!] \quad x_i \in \vec{x} \quad y_i \in \vec{y} \\ \mathcal{P}[\![{}^{l_f}\, \mathtt{def}\ f(\vec{y})\{...\}]\!] \quad f \in pt(fp)\end{array}}{\langle l, x_i\rangle \longrightarrow \langle l_f, y_i\rangle} \qquad [\mathrm{VF}^{\mathrm{T}}_{\mathrm{Ret}}]\ \frac{\begin{array}{c}\mathcal{P}[\![{}^{l}\, y = fp(\_)]\!] \quad f \in pt(fp) \\ \mathcal{P}[\![{}^{l_f}\, \mathtt{def}\ f(\_)\{...\ {}^{l_r}\, \mathtt{ret}\ x;\}]\!]\end{array}}{\langle l_r, x\rangle \longrightarrow \langle l, y\rangle}$$

$$[\mathrm{VF}^{\mathrm{A}}_{\mathrm{Call}}]\ \frac{\begin{array}{c}\mathcal{P}[\![{}^{l}\, \_ = fp(\_)]\!] \quad [\![\mu(o^i)]\!] \in \Delta(l, \prec) \\ \mathcal{P}[\![{}^{l_f}\, \mathtt{def}\ f(\_)\{...\}]\!] \quad f \in pt(fp) \\ [\![\_ = \chi(o^j)]\!] \in \Delta(l_f, \prec)\end{array}}{\langle l^{\prec}, o^i\rangle \longrightarrow \langle l_f^{\prec}, o^j\rangle} \qquad [\mathrm{VF}^{\mathrm{A}}_{\mathrm{Ret}}]\ \frac{\begin{array}{c}\mathcal{P}[\![{}^{l}\, \_ = fp(\_)]\!] \quad [\![\_ = \chi(o^j)]\!] \in \Delta(l, \succ) \\ \mathcal{P}[\![{}^{l_f}\, \mathtt{def}\ f(\_)\{...\}]\!] \quad f \in pt(fp) \\ [\![\mu(o^i)]\!] \in \Delta(l_f, \succ)\end{array}}{\langle l_f^{\succ}, o^i\rangle \longrightarrow \langle l^{\succ}, o^j\rangle}$$

Fig. 8. Rules for building the value-flow graph G_{vfg} for an annotated program in SSA form (with the version of an SSA variable omitted when it is irrelevant to avoid cluttering). $\mathcal{D}(v)$ ($\mathcal{U}(v)$) denotes the set of definition (use) sites of a variable v. $F(l)$ identifies the function containing l.

in G_{vfg} established on the fly, imprecision in G_{vfg} (due to spurious value-flow edges) will affect only the efficiency but not precision of pt^{dd}_{cs}.

Figure 9 gives the rules for answering $pt^{dd}_{cs}(c, l, v) = \diamondsuit$, where $\rightsquigarrow$, which is transitive by [VF$_{\mathrm{Trans}}$], represents the flow of a value across one or more value-flow edges in G_{vfg} actually traversed. Note that $\langle\!\langle c_o, o\rangle\!\rangle$ is essentially $\langle c_o, o, o\rangle$ since o is the line number for the corresponding allocation site. We say that x *flows to* y if $\langle \_, \_, x\rangle \rightsquigarrow \langle \_, \_, y\rangle$. To solve $pt^{dd}_{cs}(c, l, v) = \diamondsuit$, we solve $\diamondsuit \rightsquigarrow \langle c, l, v\rangle$, i.e., find what flows to $\langle c, l, v\rangle$ (Rule [QRY]). If $\langle\!\langle c_o, o\rangle\!\rangle$ flows to $\langle c, l, v\rangle$, then $\langle c, l, v\rangle$ points to $\langle\!\langle c_o, o\rangle\!\rangle$ (Rule [PT]). If $\langle c, l, v\rangle$ has been reached, we need to continue exploring backwards what may flow to $\langle c, l, v\rangle$ on-demand (Rule [DD$_{\mathrm{Back}}$]). Rules [VF$_{\mathrm{Addr}}$] and [VF$_{\mathrm{Alloc}}$] handle allocation statements that allocate memory for an address-taken variable on the stack and in the heap, respectively.

For a load ${}^{l}x = *y$ with a query $\diamondsuit \rightsquigarrow \langle c, l, x\rangle$, pt^{dd}_{cs}, pt^{dd}_{cs} first checks to see if $\langle\!\langle c_o, o\rangle\!\rangle \rightsquigarrow \langle c, l, y\rangle$ holds by issuing a demand query $\diamondsuit \rightsquigarrow \langle c, l, y\rangle$ (Rule [DD$_{\mathrm{Load}}$]), and if this is the case, then $\langle c, l^{\prec}, \langle\!\langle c_o, o\rangle\!\rangle\rangle \rightsquigarrow \langle c, l, x\rangle$ is

$$[\text{QRY}]\ \frac{pt^{dd}_{cs}(c,l,v) = \diamond}{\diamond \rightsquigarrow \langle c,l,v\rangle} \qquad [\text{PT}]\ \frac{\langle\!\langle c_o,o\rangle\!\rangle \rightsquigarrow \langle c,l,v\rangle}{\langle\!\langle c_o,o\rangle\!\rangle \in pt^{dd}_{cs}(c,l,v)} \qquad [\text{DD}_{\text{Back}}]\ \frac{\langle c,l,v\rangle \rightsquigarrow \_}{\diamond \rightsquigarrow \langle c,l,v\rangle}$$

$$[\text{VF}_{\text{Addr}}]\ \frac{\mathcal{P}\llbracket^{l}\ x = \&y\rrbracket \quad \diamond \rightsquigarrow \langle c,l,x\rangle}{\langle\!\langle c,y\rangle\!\rangle \rightsquigarrow \langle c,l,x\rangle} \qquad [\text{VF}_{\text{Alloc}}]\ \frac{\mathcal{P}\llbracket^{o}\ x = \texttt{malloc()}\rrbracket \quad \diamond \rightsquigarrow \langle c,l,x\rangle}{\langle\!\langle c,o\rangle\!\rangle \rightsquigarrow \langle c,l,x\rangle}$$

$$[\text{DD}_{\text{Load}}]\ \frac{\mathcal{P}\llbracket^{l}\ x = *y\rrbracket \quad \diamond \rightsquigarrow \langle c,l,x\rangle}{\diamond \rightsquigarrow \langle c,l,y\rangle} \qquad [\text{VF}_{\text{Load}}]\ \frac{\begin{array}{c}\mathcal{P}\llbracket^{l}\ x = *y\rrbracket \quad \diamond \rightsquigarrow \langle c,l,x\rangle\\ \langle\!\langle c_o,o\rangle\!\rangle \rightsquigarrow \langle c,l,y\rangle\end{array}}{\langle c,l^{<},\langle\!\langle c_o,o\rangle\!\rangle\rangle \rightsquigarrow \langle c,l,x\rangle}$$

$$[\text{DD}_{\text{Store}}]\ \frac{\mathcal{P}\llbracket^{l}\ *x = y\rrbracket \quad \diamond \rightsquigarrow \langle c,l^{>},\langle\!\langle c_o,o\rangle\!\rangle\rangle}{\diamond \rightsquigarrow \langle c,l,x\rangle} \qquad [\text{VF}_{\text{Store}}]\ \frac{\begin{array}{c}\mathcal{P}\llbracket^{l}\ *x = y\rrbracket \quad \diamond \rightsquigarrow \langle c,l^{>},\langle\!\langle c_o,o\rangle\!\rangle\rangle\\ \langle\!\langle c_o,o\rangle\!\rangle \rightsquigarrow \langle c,l,x\rangle\end{array}}{\langle c,l,y\rangle \rightsquigarrow \langle c,l^{>},\langle\!\langle c_o,o\rangle\!\rangle\rangle}$$

$$[\text{VF}_{\text{Copy}}]\ \frac{\mathcal{P}\llbracket^{l}\ x = y\rrbracket \quad \diamond \rightsquigarrow \langle c,l,x\rangle}{\langle c,l,y\rangle \rightsquigarrow \langle c,l,x\rangle} \qquad [\text{VF}_{\text{Trans}}]\ \frac{\begin{array}{c}\langle c',l',v'\rangle \rightsquigarrow \langle c'',l'',v''\rangle\\ \langle c'',l'',v''\rangle \rightsquigarrow \langle c''',l''',v'''\rangle\end{array}}{\langle c',l',v'\rangle \rightsquigarrow \langle c''',l''',v'''\rangle}$$

$$[\text{VF}^{\text{T}}]\ \frac{\begin{array}{c}\langle l',x\rangle \longrightarrow \langle l,x\rangle \qquad x \in \text{V}^{\text{T}}\\ \diamond \rightsquigarrow \langle c,l,x\rangle\end{array}}{\langle c,l',x\rangle \rightsquigarrow \langle c,l,x\rangle} \qquad [\text{VF}^{\text{A}}]\ \frac{\begin{array}{c}\langle l',o\rangle \longrightarrow \langle l,o\rangle \qquad o \in \text{V}^{\text{A}}\\ \diamond \rightsquigarrow \langle c,l,\langle\!\langle c_o,o\rangle\!\rangle\rangle\end{array}}{\langle c,l',\langle\!\langle c_o,o\rangle\!\rangle\rangle \rightsquigarrow \langle c,l,\langle\!\langle c_o,o\rangle\!\rangle\rangle}$$

$$[\text{VF}^{\text{T}}_{\text{Call}}]\ \frac{\begin{array}{c}\mathcal{P}\llbracket^{l}\ \_ = fp(\vec{x})\rrbracket \quad \mathcal{P}\llbracket^{l_f}\ \texttt{def}\ f(\vec{y})\{...\}\rrbracket\\ \diamond \rightsquigarrow \langle c,l_f,y\rangle \qquad c^{-} = c \ominus l\\ \langle l,x\rangle \longrightarrow \langle l_f,y\rangle\end{array}}{\langle c^{-},l,x\rangle \rightsquigarrow \langle c,l_f,y\rangle} \qquad [\text{VF}^{\text{T}}_{\text{Ret}}]\ \frac{\begin{array}{c}\mathcal{P}\llbracket^{l}\ x = fp(\_)\rrbracket \quad \mathcal{P}\llbracket^{l_r}\ \texttt{ret}\ y\rrbracket\\ \diamond \rightsquigarrow \langle c,l,x\rangle \qquad c^{+} = c \oplus l\\ \langle l_r,y\rangle \longrightarrow \langle l,x\rangle\end{array}}{\langle c^{+},l_r,y\rangle \rightsquigarrow \langle c,l,x\rangle}$$

$$[\text{VF}^{\text{A}}_{\text{Call}}]\ \frac{\begin{array}{c}\mathcal{P}\llbracket^{l}\ \_ = fp(\_)\rrbracket \quad \mathcal{P}\llbracket^{l_f}\ \texttt{def}\ f(\_)\ \{...\}\rrbracket\\ \diamond \rightsquigarrow \langle c,l_f^{<},\langle\!\langle c_o,o\rangle\!\rangle\rangle \qquad c^{-} = c \ominus l\\ \langle l,o\rangle \longrightarrow \langle l_f^{<},o\rangle\end{array}}{\langle c^{-},l,\langle\!\langle c_o,o\rangle\!\rangle\rangle \rightsquigarrow \langle c,l_f^{<},\langle\!\langle c_o,o\rangle\!\rangle\rangle} \qquad [\text{VF}^{\text{A}}_{\text{Ret}}]\ \frac{\begin{array}{c}\mathcal{P}\llbracket^{l}\ \_ = fp(\_)\rrbracket \quad \mathcal{P}\llbracket^{l_f}\ \texttt{def}\ f(\_)\ \{...\}\rrbracket\\ \diamond \rightsquigarrow \langle c,l,\langle\!\langle c_o,o\rangle\!\rangle\rangle \qquad c^{+} = c \oplus l\\ \langle l_f^{>},o\rangle \longrightarrow \langle l,o\rangle\end{array}}{\langle c^{+},l_f^{>},\langle\!\langle c_o,o\rangle\!\rangle\rangle \rightsquigarrow \langle c,l,\langle\!\langle c_o,o\rangle\!\rangle\rangle}$$

Fig. 9. Rules for demand-driven context-sensitive pointer analysis pt^{dd}_{cs} (with $\diamond$ denoting a demand query issued and $n_{src} \rightsquigarrow n_{dst}$ denoting the flow of a value from n_{src} to n_{dst} on G_{vfg}).

established (Rule [VF_{Load}]). Similarly, for a store $^{l}*x = y$ with a query $\diamond \rightsquigarrow \langle c,l^{>},\langle\!\langle c_o,o\rangle\!\rangle\rangle$, pt^{dd}_{cs}, pt^{dd}_{cs} checks to see if $\langle\!\langle c_o,o\rangle\!\rangle \rightsquigarrow \langle c,l,x\rangle$ holds by issuing a demand query $\diamond \rightsquigarrow \langle c,l,x\rangle$ (Rule [DD_{Store}]), and if this is the case, then $\langle c,l,y\rangle \rightsquigarrow \langle c,l^{>},\langle\!\langle c_o,o\rangle\!\rangle\rangle$ is established (Rule [VF_{Store}]).

Rules $[\mathrm{VF_{Copy}}]$, $[\mathrm{VF^{T}}]$ and $[\mathrm{VF^{A}}]$ simply propagate values across assignments (with the former for copy statements and the latter two for def-use chains). In particular, $[\mathrm{VF^{A}}]$ performs a weak update at a store. Note that pt_{cs}^{dd} is also flow-sensitive with strong updates performed for singleton objects as is standard [19,29,49].

To support the inter-procedural analysis at the function calls and returns, $[\mathrm{VF^{T}_{Call}}]$ and $[\mathrm{VF^{T}_{Ret}}]$ handle top-level variables while $[\mathrm{VF^{A}_{Call}}]$ and $[\mathrm{VF^{A}_{Ret}}]$ handle address-taken variables. Context-sensitivity is achieved by maintaining a context with push ($\oplus$) and pop ($\ominus$) operations in a stack-like manner. When handling a function call at a call site l, a new context c^{-} is generated by popping off l from the current context c, denoted $c^{-} = c \ominus l$, to track the value-flow backwards outside the callee (c^{-}) from inside the callee (c). Conversely, when handling a callee function's return statement that returns to a call site l, a new context c^{+} is created by pushing l to the top of the current context c, denoted $c^{+} = c \oplus l$, to represent the fact that the backward analysis will now enter the callee (c^{+}) at its return statement from the call-site l outside the callee (c).

Example 3. Given $pt_{cs}^{dd}([\,], 16, \texttt{feedDog}) = \Diamond$ for the program in Fig. 7, pt_{cs}^{dd} yields the following facts related to the nine value-flow edges marked as ① – ⑨:

$$
\begin{array}{llll}
\langle\!\langle [\kappa_{10}], o_2 \rangle\!\rangle & \rightsquigarrow \langle [\kappa_{10}], 2, \texttt{fd} \rangle & \overset{1}{\rightsquigarrow} \langle [\kappa_{10}], 3, \texttt{fd} \rangle & \\
\overset{2}{\rightsquigarrow} \langle [\,], 10, \texttt{bone} \rangle & \overset{3}{\rightsquigarrow} \langle [\,], 14, \texttt{bone} \rangle & \overset{4}{\rightsquigarrow} \langle [\kappa_{14}], 7, \texttt{pfd} \rangle & \\
\overset{5}{\rightsquigarrow} \langle [\kappa_{14}], 8, \texttt{pfd} \rangle & \rightsquigarrow \langle [\kappa_{14}], 8^{\succ}, \langle\!\langle [\kappa_{12}], o_5 \rangle\!\rangle \rangle & \overset{6}{\rightsquigarrow} \langle [\kappa_{14}], 7^{\succ}, \langle\!\langle [\kappa_{12}], o_5 \rangle\!\rangle \rangle & \\
\overset{7}{\rightsquigarrow} \langle [\,], 14^{\succ}, \langle\!\langle [\kappa_{12}], o_5 \rangle\!\rangle \rangle & \overset{8}{\rightsquigarrow} \langle [\,], 15^{\succ}, \langle\!\langle [\kappa_{12}], o_5 \rangle\!\rangle \rangle & \overset{9}{\rightsquigarrow} \langle [\,], 16^{\prec}, \langle\!\langle [\kappa_{12}], o_5 \rangle\!\rangle \rangle & \rightsquigarrow \langle [\,], 16, \texttt{feedDog} \rangle
\end{array}
$$

This means that $\langle\!\langle [\kappa_{10}], o_2 \rangle\!\rangle \rightsquigarrow \langle [\,], 16, \texttt{feedDog} \rangle$ by Rule $[\mathrm{VF_{Trans}}]$. Finally, we can conclude that $\langle\!\langle [\kappa_{10}], o_2 \rangle\!\rangle \in pt_{cs}^{dd}([\,], 16, \texttt{feedDog})$ by Rule [PT].

In addition to ① – ⑨, there are other facts generated on-demand, in an (unsuccessful) attempt to identify some other objects pointed to by **feedDog**. Table 1 gives a step-by-step trace of $pt_{cs}^{dd}([\,], 16, \texttt{feedDog}) = \Diamond$ when operating on Fig. 10, a version of Fig. 7 with a complete value-flow graph for the same program. For Table 1, we would like to highlight the following three aspects:

1. **Value-Flow Transitivity.** The flow of $\langle\!\langle [\kappa_{10}], o_2 \rangle\!\rangle$ into $\langle [\,], 16, \texttt{feedDog} \rangle$, i.e., $\langle\!\langle [\kappa_{10}], o_2 \rangle\!\rangle \rightsquigarrow \langle [\,], 16, \texttt{feedDog} \rangle$, discussed in Example 3, is obtained by Steps #11 – #13 – #32 – #34 – #36 – #51 – #53 – #55 – #57 – #59 – #61 – #63.
2. **Generating Demand Points-to Queries.** In addition to $pt_{cs}^{dd}([\,], 16, \texttt{feedDog}) = \Diamond$, the other demand queries $\Diamond$ are issued in by firing ① Rule $[\mathrm{DD_{Back}}]$ (e.g., Steps #4, #6 and #8) to start a new backward traversal, and ② Rules $[\mathrm{DD_{Load}}]$ and $[\mathrm{DD_{Store}}]$ (e.g., Steps #2 and #19) at a load or store statement to resolve a dereferenced pointer.

3. **Context-sensitivity.** Starting with $pt_{cs}^{dd}([\,], 16, \texttt{feedDog}) = \diamond$, i.e., $\diamond \rightsquigarrow \langle[\,], 16, \texttt{feedDog}\rangle$ at Step #1, we obtain $\langle\!\langle[\kappa_{12}], o_5\rangle\!\rangle \rightsquigarrow \langle[\,], 16, \texttt{tray}\rangle$ in Steps #2–#10. There are two call sites, κ_{14} and κ_{15}, for `put()`. Once we know what `tray` points to, we can enter `put()` backwards from its exit at line $7^{\succ}$ in two ways, depending on whether it is called from κ_{15} or κ_{14}.

By performing Steps #11–#18 (with the assumption that `put()` is called from κ_{15}), we reach line 8, where we issue a demand query at Step #19, $\diamond \rightsquigarrow \langle[\kappa_{15}], 8, \texttt{pctn}\rangle$, but only to find that $\langle\!\langle[\kappa_{13}], o_5\rangle\!\rangle \rightsquigarrow \langle[\kappa_{15}], 8, \texttt{pctn}\rangle$, i.e., $\langle\!\langle[\kappa_{12}], o_5\rangle\!\rangle \not\rightsquigarrow \langle[\kappa_{15}], 8, \texttt{pctn}\rangle$ at the end of Steps #19–#31.

Alternatively, after having performed Steps #32–#37 (with the assumption that `put()` is called from κ_{14}), we reach line 8 again, where we issue another query at Step #38, $\diamond \rightsquigarrow \langle[\kappa_{14}], 8, \texttt{pctn}\rangle$. This time, however, we obtain $\langle\!\langle[\kappa_{12}], o_5\rangle\!\rangle \rightsquigarrow \langle[\kappa_{14}], 8, \texttt{pctn}\rangle$, i.e., at the end of Steps #38–#50. By completing Steps #51–#64, as already demonstrated in Example 3, we obtain $\langle\!\langle[\kappa_{10}], o_2\rangle\!\rangle \in pt_{cs}^{dd}([\,], 16, \texttt{feedDog})$.

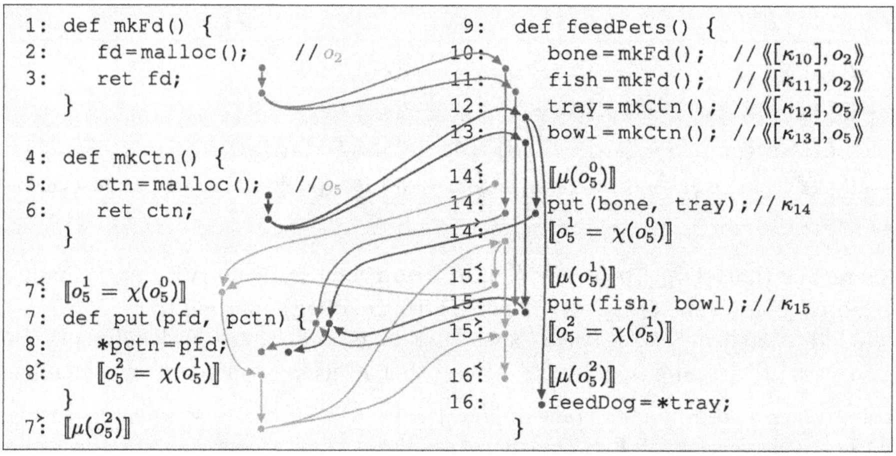

Fig. 10. The program given in Fig. 7 decorated with all the value-flow edges.

4.3 Synergizing Aliasing and Control-Flow Reachability

Given a pair of deallocation $\psi(l_\psi, p)$ and dereference $\omega(l_\omega, q)$, we proceed to prove absence of $\langle\langle\!\langle c_o, o\rangle\!\rangle, \psi(c_\psi, l_\psi, p), \omega(c_\omega, l_\omega, q)\rangle$ on all the control-flow paths ρ across the ICFG of the program, where $c_\psi \in C_\psi$ and $c_\omega \in C_\omega$ are calling contexts for l_ψ and l_ω, respectively. We abstract ρ with a context tuple (c_o, c_ψ, c_ω), which is shortened to (c_ψ, c_ω), since c_o can be automatically inferred by pt_{cs}^{dd} from c_ψ and c_ω.

The following two properties are checked context-sensitively:

Table 1. A step-by-step trace of $pt^{dd}_{cs}([\,], 16, \mathtt{feedDog}) = \Diamond$, for computing $\langle\!\langle[\kappa_{10}], o_2\rangle\!\rangle \in pt^{dd}_{cs}([\,], 16, \mathtt{feedDog})$, with pt^{dd}_{cs} operating on the value-flow graph of the program in Fig. 10 by applying the rules given in Fig. 9.

Step #	$\rightsquigarrow$	Rule	Step #	$\rightsquigarrow$	Rule
1	$\Diamond \rightsquigarrow \langle[\,], 16, \mathtt{feedDog}\rangle$	[QRY]	33	$\Diamond \rightsquigarrow \langle[\,], 14^{>}, \langle\!\langle[\kappa_{12}], o_5\rangle\!\rangle\rangle$	$[\mathrm{DD}_{\mathrm{Back}}]$
2	$\Diamond \rightsquigarrow \langle[\,], 16, \mathtt{tray}\rangle$	$[\mathrm{DD}_{\mathrm{Load}}]$	34	$\langle[\kappa_{14}], 7^{>}, \langle\!\langle[\kappa_{12}], o_5\rangle\!\rangle\rangle \rightsquigarrow \langle[\,], 14^{>}, \langle\!\langle[\kappa_{12}], o_5\rangle\!\rangle\rangle$	$[\mathrm{VF}^{\mathrm{A}}_{\mathrm{Ret}}]$
3	$\langle[\,], 12, \mathtt{tray}\rangle \rightsquigarrow \langle[\,], 16, \mathtt{tray}\rangle$	$[\mathrm{VF}^{\mathrm{T}}]$	35	$\Diamond \rightsquigarrow \langle[\kappa_{14}], 7^{>}, \langle\!\langle[\kappa_{12}], o_5\rangle\!\rangle\rangle$	$[\mathrm{DD}_{\mathrm{Back}}]$
4	$\Diamond \rightsquigarrow \langle[\,], 12, \mathtt{tray}\rangle$	$[\mathrm{DD}_{\mathrm{Back}}]$	36	$\langle[\kappa_{14}], 8^{>}, \langle\!\langle[\kappa_{12}], o_5\rangle\!\rangle\rangle \rightsquigarrow \langle[\kappa_{14}], 7^{>}, \langle\!\langle[\kappa_{12}], o_5\rangle\!\rangle\rangle$	$[\mathrm{VF}^{\mathrm{A}}]$
5	$\langle[\kappa_{12}], 6, \mathtt{ctn}\rangle \rightsquigarrow \langle[\,], 12, \mathtt{tray}\rangle$	$[\mathrm{VF}^{\mathrm{T}}_{\mathrm{Ret}}]$	37	$\Diamond \rightsquigarrow \langle[\kappa_{14}], 8^{>}, \langle\!\langle[\kappa_{12}], o_5\rangle\!\rangle\rangle$	$[\mathrm{DD}_{\mathrm{Back}}]$
6	$\Diamond \rightsquigarrow \langle[\kappa_{12}], 6, \mathtt{ctn}\rangle$	$[\mathrm{DD}_{\mathrm{Back}}]$	38	$\Diamond \rightsquigarrow \langle[\kappa_{14}], 8, \mathtt{pctn}\rangle$	$[\mathrm{DD}_{\mathrm{Store}}]$
7	$\langle[\kappa_{12}], 5, \mathtt{ctn}\rangle \rightsquigarrow \langle[\kappa_{12}], 6, \mathtt{ctn}\rangle$	$[\mathrm{VF}^{\mathrm{T}}]$	39	$\langle[\kappa_{14}], 7, \mathtt{pctn}\rangle \rightsquigarrow \langle[\kappa_{14}], 8, \mathtt{pctn}\rangle$	$[\mathrm{VF}^{\mathrm{T}}]$
8	$\Diamond \rightsquigarrow \langle[\kappa_{12}], 5, \mathtt{ctn}\rangle$	$[\mathrm{DD}_{\mathrm{Back}}]$	40	$\Diamond \rightsquigarrow \langle[\kappa_{14}], 7, \mathtt{pctn}\rangle$	$[\mathrm{DD}_{\mathrm{Back}}]$
9	$\langle\!\langle[\kappa_{12}], o_5\rangle\!\rangle \rightsquigarrow \langle[\kappa_{12}], 5, \mathtt{ctn}\rangle$	$[\mathrm{VF}_{\mathrm{Alloc}}]$	41	$\langle[\,], 14, \mathtt{tray}\rangle \rightsquigarrow \langle[\kappa_{14}], 7, \mathtt{pctn}\rangle$	$[\mathrm{VF}^{\mathrm{T}}_{\mathrm{Call}}]$
10	$\langle\!\langle[\kappa_{12}], o_5\rangle\!\rangle \rightsquigarrow \langle[\,], 16, \mathtt{tray}\rangle$	$[\mathrm{VF}_{\mathrm{Trans}}]$	42	$\Diamond \rightsquigarrow \langle[\,], 14, \mathtt{tray}\rangle$	$[\mathrm{DD}_{\mathrm{Back}}]$
11	$\langle[\,], 16^{<}, \langle\!\langle[\kappa_{12}], o_5\rangle\!\rangle\rangle \rightsquigarrow \langle[\,], 16, \mathtt{feedDog}\rangle$	$[\mathrm{VF}_{\mathrm{Load}}]$	43	$\langle[\,], 12, \mathtt{tray}\rangle \rightsquigarrow \langle[\,], 14, \mathtt{tray}\rangle$	$[\mathrm{VF}^{\mathrm{T}}]$
12	$\Diamond \rightsquigarrow \langle[\,], 16^{<}, \langle\!\langle[\kappa_{12}], o_5\rangle\!\rangle\rangle$	$[\mathrm{DD}_{\mathrm{Back}}]$	44	$\Diamond \rightsquigarrow \langle[\,], 12, \mathtt{tray}\rangle$	$[\mathrm{DD}_{\mathrm{Back}}]$
13	$\langle[\,], 15^{>}, \langle\!\langle[\kappa_{12}], o_5\rangle\!\rangle\rangle \rightsquigarrow \langle[\,], 16^{<}, \langle\!\langle[\kappa_{12}], o_5\rangle\!\rangle\rangle$	$[\mathrm{VF}^{\mathrm{A}}]$	45	$\langle[\kappa_{12}], 6, \mathtt{ctn}\rangle \rightsquigarrow \langle[\,], 12, \mathtt{tray}\rangle$	$[\mathrm{VF}^{\mathrm{T}}_{\mathrm{Ret}}]$
14	$\Diamond \rightsquigarrow \langle[\,], 15^{>}, \langle\!\langle[\kappa_{12}], o_5\rangle\!\rangle\rangle$	$[\mathrm{DD}_{\mathrm{Back}}]$	46	$\Diamond \rightsquigarrow \langle[\kappa_{12}], 6, \mathtt{ctn}\rangle$	$[\mathrm{DD}_{\mathrm{Back}}]$
15	$\langle[\kappa_{15}], 7^{>}, \langle\!\langle[\kappa_{12}], o_5\rangle\!\rangle\rangle \rightsquigarrow \langle[\,], 15^{>}, \langle\!\langle[\kappa_{12}], o_5\rangle\!\rangle\rangle$	$[\mathrm{VF}^{\mathrm{A}}_{\mathrm{Ret}}]$	47	$\langle[\kappa_{12}], 5, \mathtt{ctn}\rangle \rightsquigarrow \langle[\kappa_{12}], 6, \mathtt{ctn}\rangle$	$[\mathrm{VF}^{\mathrm{T}}]$
16	$\Diamond \rightsquigarrow \langle[\kappa_{15}], 7^{>}, \langle\!\langle[\kappa_{12}], o_5\rangle\!\rangle\rangle$	$[\mathrm{DD}_{\mathrm{Back}}]$	48	$\Diamond \rightsquigarrow \langle[\kappa_{12}], 5, \mathtt{ctn}\rangle$	$[\mathrm{DD}_{\mathrm{Back}}]$
17	$\langle[\kappa_{15}], 8^{>}, \langle\!\langle[\kappa_{12}], o_5\rangle\!\rangle\rangle \rightsquigarrow \langle[\kappa_{15}], 7^{>}, \langle\!\langle[\kappa_{12}], o_5\rangle\!\rangle\rangle$	$[\mathrm{VF}^{\mathrm{A}}]$	49	$\langle\!\langle[\kappa_{12}], o_5\rangle\!\rangle \rightsquigarrow \langle[\kappa_{12}], 5, \mathtt{ctn}\rangle$	$[\mathrm{VF}_{\mathrm{Alloc}}]$
18	$\Diamond \rightsquigarrow \langle[\kappa_{15}], 8^{>}, \langle\!\langle[\kappa_{12}], o_5\rangle\!\rangle\rangle$	$[\mathrm{DD}_{\mathrm{Back}}]$	50	$\langle\!\langle[\kappa_{12}], o_5\rangle\!\rangle \rightsquigarrow \langle[\kappa_{14}], 8, \mathtt{pctn}\rangle$	$[\mathrm{VF}_{\mathrm{Trans}}]$
19	$\Diamond \rightsquigarrow \langle[\kappa_{15}], 8, \mathtt{pctn}\rangle$	$[\mathrm{DD}_{\mathrm{Store}}]$	51	$\langle[\kappa_{14}], 8, \mathtt{pfd}\rangle \rightsquigarrow \langle[\kappa_{14}], 8^{>}, \langle\!\langle[\kappa_{12}], o_5\rangle\!\rangle\rangle$	$[\mathrm{VF}_{\mathrm{Store}}]$
20	$\langle[\kappa_{15}], 7, \mathtt{pctn}\rangle \rightsquigarrow \langle[\kappa_{15}], 8, \mathtt{pctn}\rangle$	$[\mathrm{VF}^{\mathrm{T}}]$	52	$\Diamond \rightsquigarrow \langle[\kappa_{14}], 8, \mathtt{pfd}\rangle$	$[\mathrm{DD}_{\mathrm{Back}}]$
21	$\Diamond \rightsquigarrow \langle[\kappa_{15}], 7, \mathtt{pctn}\rangle$	$[\mathrm{DD}_{\mathrm{Back}}]$	53	$\langle[\kappa_{14}], 7, \mathtt{pfd}\rangle \rightsquigarrow \langle[\kappa_{14}], 8, \mathtt{pfd}\rangle$	$[\mathrm{VF}^{\mathrm{T}}]$
22	$\langle[\,], 15, \mathtt{bowl}\rangle \rightsquigarrow \langle[\kappa_{15}], 7, \mathtt{pctn}\rangle$	$[\mathrm{VF}^{\mathrm{T}}_{\mathrm{Call}}]$	54	$\Diamond \rightsquigarrow \langle[\kappa_{14}], 7, \mathtt{pfd}\rangle$	$[\mathrm{DD}_{\mathrm{Back}}]$
23	$\Diamond \rightsquigarrow \langle[\,], 15, \mathtt{bowl}\rangle$	$[\mathrm{DD}_{\mathrm{Back}}]$	55	$\langle[\,], 14, \mathtt{bone}\rangle \rightsquigarrow \langle[\kappa_{14}], 7, \mathtt{pfd}\rangle$	$[\mathrm{VF}^{\mathrm{T}}_{\mathrm{Call}}]$
24	$\langle[\,], 13, \mathtt{bowl}\rangle \rightsquigarrow \langle[\,], 15, \mathtt{bowl}\rangle$	$[\mathrm{VF}^{\mathrm{T}}]$	56	$\Diamond \rightsquigarrow \langle[\,], 14, \mathtt{bone}\rangle$	$[\mathrm{DD}_{\mathrm{Back}}]$
25	$\Diamond \rightsquigarrow \langle[\,], 13, \mathtt{bowl}\rangle$	$[\mathrm{DD}_{\mathrm{Back}}]$	57	$\langle[\,], 10, \mathtt{bone}\rangle \rightsquigarrow \langle[\,], 14, \mathtt{bone}\rangle$	$[\mathrm{VF}^{\mathrm{T}}]$
26	$\langle[\kappa_{13}], 6, \mathtt{ctn}\rangle \rightsquigarrow \langle[\,], 13, \mathtt{bowl}\rangle$	$[\mathrm{VF}^{\mathrm{T}}_{\mathrm{Ret}}]$	58	$\Diamond \rightsquigarrow \langle[\,], 10, \mathtt{bone}\rangle$	$[\mathrm{DD}_{\mathrm{Back}}]$
27	$\Diamond \rightsquigarrow \langle[\kappa_{13}], 6, \mathtt{ctn}\rangle$	$[\mathrm{DD}_{\mathrm{Back}}]$	59	$\langle[\kappa_{10}], 3, \mathtt{fd}\rangle \rightsquigarrow \langle[\,], 10, \mathtt{bone}\rangle$	$[\mathrm{VF}^{\mathrm{T}}_{\mathrm{Ret}}]$
28	$\langle[\kappa_{13}], 5, \mathtt{ctn}\rangle \rightsquigarrow \langle[\kappa_{13}], 6, \mathtt{ctn}\rangle$	$[\mathrm{VF}^{\mathrm{T}}]$	60	$\Diamond \rightsquigarrow \langle[\kappa_{10}], 3, \mathtt{fd}\rangle$	$[\mathrm{DD}_{\mathrm{Back}}]$
29	$\Diamond \rightsquigarrow \langle[\kappa_{13}], 5, \mathtt{ctn}\rangle$	$[\mathrm{DD}_{\mathrm{Back}}]$	61	$\langle[\kappa_{10}], 2, \mathtt{fd}\rangle \rightsquigarrow \langle[\kappa_{10}], 3, \mathtt{fd}\rangle$	$[\mathrm{VF}^{\mathrm{T}}]$
30	$\langle\!\langle[\kappa_{13}], o_5\rangle\!\rangle \rightsquigarrow \langle[\kappa_{13}], 5, \mathtt{ctn}\rangle$	$[\mathrm{VF}_{\mathrm{Alloc}}]$	62	$\Diamond \rightsquigarrow \langle[\kappa_{10}], 2, \mathtt{fd}\rangle$	$[\mathrm{DD}_{\mathrm{Back}}]$
31	$\langle\!\langle[\kappa_{13}], o_5\rangle\!\rangle \rightsquigarrow \langle[\kappa_{15}], 8, \mathtt{pctn}\rangle$	$[\mathrm{VF}_{\mathrm{Trans}}]$	63	$\langle\!\langle[\kappa_{10}], o_2\rangle\!\rangle \rightsquigarrow \langle[\kappa_{10}], 2, \mathtt{fd}\rangle$	$[\mathrm{VF}_{\mathrm{Alloc}}]$
32	$\langle[\,], 14^{>}, \langle\!\langle[\kappa_{12}], o_5\rangle\!\rangle\rangle \rightsquigarrow \langle[\,], 15^{>}, \langle\!\langle[\kappa_{12}], o_5\rangle\!\rangle\rangle$	$[\mathrm{VF}^{\mathrm{A}}]$	64	$\langle\!\langle[\kappa_{10}], o_2\rangle\!\rangle \rightsquigarrow \langle[\,], 16, \mathtt{feedDog}\rangle$	$[\mathrm{VF}_{\mathrm{Trans}}]$

- **Aliasing**, $\mathcal{A}^{\psi}_{\omega} : C_{\psi} \times C_{\omega} \to \{\mathit{true}, \mathit{false}\}$, indicating if (c_{ψ}, p) aliases (c_{ω}, q), and
- **Reachability**, $\mathcal{R}^{\psi}_{\omega} : C_{\psi} \times C_{\omega} \to \{\mathit{true}, \mathit{false}\}$, indicating if l_{ψ} reaches l_{ω} on the ICFG by going through first the return edges specified by c_{ψ} and then the call edges specified by c_{ω}.

$$[\text{AliasingAndReaching}]\ \frac{\mathcal{R}^{\psi}_{\omega}(c_{\psi}, c_{\omega}) \quad \mathcal{A}^{\psi}_{\omega}(c_{\psi}, c_{\omega})}{\mathcal{S}^{\psi}_{\omega}(c_{\psi}, c_{\omega})}$$

$$[\text{Aliasing}]\ \frac{\begin{array}{c} pt^{dd}_{cs}(c_{\psi}, l_{\psi}, p) = \diamond \vdash \langle\!\langle hc_{\psi}, o \rangle\!\rangle \in pt(c_{\psi}, l_{\psi}, p) \\ pt^{dd}_{cs}(c_{\omega}, l_{\omega}, q) = \diamond \vdash \langle\!\langle hc_{\omega}, o \rangle\!\rangle \in pt(c_{\omega}, l_{\omega}, q) \\ cons(\_, hc_{\psi}) = hc_{\omega} \ \vee \ cons(\_, hc_{\omega}) = hc_{\psi} \end{array}}{\mathcal{A}^{\psi}_{\omega}(c_{\psi}, c_{\omega})}$$

$$[\text{Reaching}]\ \frac{\overline{l_{\psi}} = car(cons(c_{\psi}, l_{\psi})) \quad \overline{l_{\omega}} = car(cons(c_{\omega}, l_{\omega})) \quad \mathcal{R}_{Intra}(\overline{l_{\psi}}, \overline{l_{\omega}})}{\mathcal{R}^{\psi}_{\omega}(c_{\psi}, c_{\omega})}$$

Fig. 11. Rules for synergizing aliasing and control-flow reachability.

We consider aliasing and reachability together, $\mathcal{S}^{\psi}_{\omega} : C_{\psi} \times C_{\omega} \rightarrow \{true, false\}$, by requiring $\mathcal{A}^{\psi}_{\omega}$ and $\mathcal{R}^{\psi}_{\omega}$ to be satisfied for the same context pair (c_{ψ}, c_{ω}). We report a TH-safety violation at the dereference iff $\mathcal{S}^{\psi}_{\omega}$ is satisfied, thereby avoiding false-positives that satisfy both constraints on two different paths only.

Figure 11 gives our rules. Rule [Aliasing] computes an abstract path, (c_{ψ}, c_{ω}), on which p aliases q. Note that $\langle\!\langle hc_{\psi}, o \rangle\!\rangle$ and $\langle\!\langle hc_{\omega}, o \rangle\!\rangle$ may represent the same (concrete) object if one of these two contexts is a suffix of (i.e., coarser than) the other. Rule [Reaching] computes an abstract path, (c_{ψ}, c_{ω}), on which l_{ψ} reaches l_{ω}, which happens if l_{ψ} first reaches $\overline{l_{\psi}}$ inter-procedurally via the return edges specified by c_{ψ}, then $\overline{l_{\psi}}$ reaches $\overline{l_{\omega}}$ intra-procedurally in the same function (denoted $\mathcal{R}_{Intra}(\overline{l_{\psi}}, \overline{l_{\omega}})$), and finally, $\overline{l_{\omega}}$ reaches l_{ω} inter-procedurally via the call edges specified by c_{ω}.

4.4 Adaptive Context-Sensitivity

To guarantee soundness, all context pairs $(c_{\psi}, c_{\omega}) \in C_{\psi} \times C_{\omega}$ in the program must be considered, making [Aliasing] in Fig. 11 prohibitively costly to verify. To tame path explosion, we use the two rules in Fig. 12 instead with adaptive context-sensitivity, thereby reducing significantly the number of context pairs considered without losing soundness or precision. We explain these two rules, illustrated in Fig. 13, below.

The key insight behind is that $pt^{dd}_{cs}([\,], l, v)$, when asked to compute the points-to set of (l, v) with an empty context $[\,]$, which represents an abstraction of all possible contexts (from `main()`), will return $\langle\!\langle hc, o \rangle\!\rangle \in pt^{dd}_{cs}(c, l, v)$, where the contexts c and hc are automatically inferred. In particular, c and hc are appropriately k-limited (with any unnecessary context prefix c_{pre} from `main()` truncated), since we have: $pt^{dd}_{cs}([\,], l, v) = \diamond \vdash \langle\!\langle hc, o \rangle\!\rangle \in pt^{dd}_{cs}(c, l, v) \iff \langle\!\langle cons(c_{pre}, hc), o \rangle\!\rangle \in pt^{dd}_{cs}(cons(c_{pre}, c), l, v)$

$$\text{[Aliasing-EqHeapCtx]}\ \frac{\begin{array}{ll} pt^{dd}_{cs}([\,], l_\psi, p) = \diamond \ \vdash\ \langle\!\langle hc, o\rangle\!\rangle \in pt^{dd}_{cs}(c_\psi, l_\psi, p) & c_\psi = cons(c_{pre}, \overline{c_\psi}) \\ pt^{dd}_{cs}([\,], l_\omega, q) = \diamond \ \vdash\ \langle\!\langle hc, o\rangle\!\rangle \in pt^{dd}_{cs}(c_\omega, l_\omega, q) & c_\omega = cons(c_{pre}, \overline{c_\omega}) \end{array}}{\mathcal{A}^{\psi}_{\omega}(\overline{c_\psi}, \overline{c_\omega})}$$

$$\text{[Aliasing-NeqHeapCtx]}\ \frac{\begin{array}{ll} pt^{dd}_{cs}([\,], l_\psi, p) = \diamond \ \vdash\ \langle\!\langle hc_\psi, o\rangle\!\rangle \in pt^{dd}_{cs}(c_\psi, l_\psi, p) & \overline{c_\psi} = cons(c_{pre}, c_\psi) \\ pt^{dd}_{cs}([\,], l_\omega, q) = \diamond \ \vdash\ \langle\!\langle hc_\omega, o\rangle\!\rangle \in pt^{dd}_{cs}(c_\omega, l_\omega, q) & hc_\omega = cons(c_{pre}, hc_\psi) \end{array}}{\mathcal{A}^{\psi}_{\omega}(\overline{c_\psi}, c_\omega)}$$

Fig. 12. Two rules for replacing [Aliasing] in Fig. 11 with adaptive context-sensitivity.

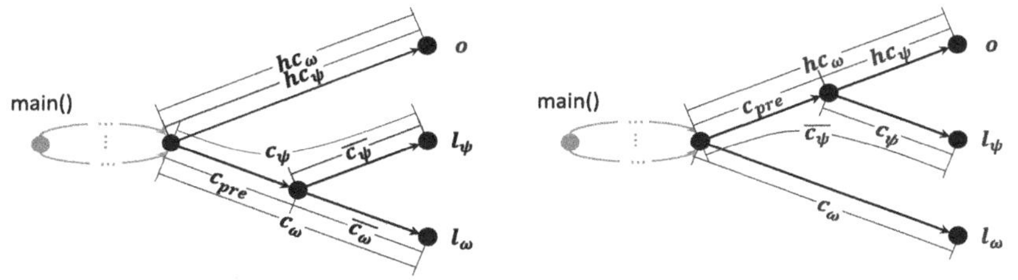

(a) [Aliasing-EqHeapCtx] ($hc_\psi = hc_\omega$)   (b) [Aliasing-NeqHeapCtx] ($hc_\psi \neq hc_\omega$)

Fig. 13. An illustration of the two rules in Fig. 12, where a fat dot represents a function and an arrow represents a sequence of (transitive) function calls across the functions in the program.

In [Aliasing], there are three possibilities for $\langle\!\langle hc_\psi, o\rangle\!\rangle$ and $\langle\!\langle hc_\omega, o\rangle\!\rangle$ to be aliases:

1. $hc = hc_\psi = hc_\omega$. This case, illustrated in Fig. 13(a), is handled by [Aliasing-EqHeapCtx], which says that it suffices to consider only $(\overline{c_\psi}, \overline{c_\omega})$ by removing any common prefix c_{pre} from c_ψ and c_ω, since $(\overline{c_\psi}, \overline{c_\omega})$ is coarser than (c_ψ, c_ω). In addition, all context pairs $(cons(c^1_{pre}, c_\psi), cons(c^2_{pre}, c_\omega))$, where $c^1_{pre} \neq c^2_{pre}$, can also be soundly removed, since $\langle\!\langle cons(c^1_{pre}, hc), o\rangle\!\rangle$ cannot be aliased with $\langle\!\langle cons(c^2_{pre}, hc), o\rangle\!\rangle$. By construction, $car(cons(\overline{c_\psi}, l_\psi))$ and $car(cons(\overline{c_\omega}, l_\omega))$ are guaranteed to be in the same function, allowing $\mathcal{R}^\psi_\omega$ in [Reaching] to be checked trivially.
2. $hc_\omega = cons(c, hc_\psi)$. To check $\mathcal{R}^\psi_\omega$ in [Reaching] efficiently, [Aliasing-NeqHeapCtx], as shown in Fig. 13(b), constructs $\overline{c_\psi}$ by extending c_ψ such that $car(cons(\overline{c_\psi}, l_\psi))$ and $car(cons(c_\omega, l_\omega))$ reside in the same function. As in [Aliasing-EqHeapCtx], all context-pairs $(cons(c^1_{pre}, \overline{c_\psi}), cons(c^2_{pre}, c_\omega))$, where $c^1_{pre} \neq c^2_{pre}$, are ignored soundly. In addition, $car(cons(\overline{c_\psi}, l_\psi))$ and $car(cons(c_\omega, l_\omega))$ always reside in the same function, allowing $\mathcal{R}^\psi_\omega$ in [Reaching] to be checked trivially as above.
3. $hc_\psi = cons(c, hc_\omega)$. This case, which indicates a use-before-free, is always safe.

Our approach D^3 is adaptive since its search space exploration selects calling contexts with appropriate lengths adaptively without losing soundness or precision.

Example 4. Let us apply our rules to the program in Fig. 4(a) to detect the TH-safety violation $\langle\!\langle\!\langle [\kappa_{18}, \kappa_{21}], o_2 \rangle\!\rangle, \psi([\kappa_{18}, \kappa_{22}], l_5, \mathtt{y}), \omega([\kappa_{19}], l_7, \mathtt{z})\rangle\!\rangle$. Let us consider [Aliasing-NeqHeapCtx] first. For the two points-to queries $pt^{dd}_{cs}([\,], l_5, \mathtt{y}) = \diamond$ and $pt^{dd}_{cs}([\,], l_7, \mathtt{z}) = \diamond$ issued, we obtain $\langle\!\langle [\kappa_{21}], o_2 \rangle\!\rangle \in pt^{dd}_{cs}([\kappa_{22}], l_5, \mathtt{y})$ and $\langle\!\langle [\kappa_{18}, \kappa_{21}], o_2 \rangle\!\rangle \in pt^{dd}_{cs}([\kappa_{19}], l_7, \mathtt{z})$. As $hc_\omega = [\kappa_{18}, \kappa_{21}] = cons([\kappa_{18}], [\kappa_{21}]) = cons(c_{pre}, hc_\psi)$, we have $\overline{c_\psi} = cons(c_{pre}, c_\psi) = [\kappa_{18}, \kappa_{21}]$. By applying [Aliasing-NeqHeapCtx], $\mathcal{A}^{\psi}_{\omega}([\kappa_{18}, \kappa_{21}], [\kappa_{19}])$ holds. Let $\overline{l_\psi} = \kappa_{18}$ and $\overline{l_\omega} = \kappa_{19}$. By applying [Reaching], $\mathcal{R}^{\psi}_{\omega}([\kappa_{18}, \kappa_{21}], [\kappa_{19}])$ holds. Finally, by [AliasingAndReaching], $\mathcal{S}([\kappa_{18}, \kappa_{21}], [\kappa_{19}])$ holds, triggering this as a TH-safety violation.

4.5 Soundness

For a program P considered in Sect. 2, D^3 (Fig. 5) is sound. First, G_{vfg} constructed for P, based on the rules in Fig. 8, over-approximates the flow of any value in P as Andersen's analysis (Fig. 2) is sound. Second, pt^{dd}_{cs} (Fig. 9) is sound as it over-approximates the points-to information in P. Third, we suppress a TH-safety violation warning soundly according to [AliasingAndReaching] (Fig. 11). Finally, our adaptive analysis (Fig. 12) is sound as the context pairs (c_ψ, c_ω) pruned for [AliasingAndReaching] during the search space exploration are redundant (Sect. 4.4).

5 Evaluation

We show that D^3 can accomplish our TH-safety verification task for reasonably large C programs efficiently with good precision in the context of the prior work.

5.1 Methodology

We have implemented D^3 in the open-source program analysis framework, SVF [50], which is implemented in LLVM [27]. Given a program, its source files are first compiled individually into LLVM IR by the Clang compiler front-end, before linked together into a single whole-program IR file by the LLVM Gold Plugin. Our TH-safety verification task is then performed statically on the whole-program LLVM IR file.

Two sets of benchmark are used. One set consists of 138 test cases with the ground truth for use-after-free vulnerabilities (CWE-416) from the NIST Juliet Test Suite for C [1], which are all TH-safety violations extracted from real-world scenarios, with one per test case. The other set consists of ten popular open-source C programs (with 40–260 KLOC) given in Table 2, containing a total of 114,508 pointer dereferences.

Table 2. Results for verifying 10 open-source C programs. D^{SEP} is a version of D^3 with aliasing $\mathcal{A}_\omega^\psi$ and reachability $\mathcal{R}_\omega^\psi$ checked separately. %Impr is computed as $\frac{D^3.\#Safe - D^{SEP}.\#Safe}{\#Deref - D^{SEP}.\#Safe} \times 100\%$.

Program	Characteristics		Value-Flow Graph		D^{SEP}			D^3			
	KLOC	#Derefs	#Nodes	#Edges	Time (s)	#Safe	%Safe	Time (s)	#Safe	%Safe	%Impr
a2ps-4.14	65	12,601	35,201	58,255	428	7,000	55.6%	5,653	9,944	78.9%	52.6%
cpio-2.12	94	5,211	13,486	23,379	10	3,805	73.0%	180	4,964	95.3%	82.4%
ctags-5.8	42	14,628	56,320	152,846	54	10,538	72.0%	520	14,014	95.8%	85.0%
MCSim-6.0.1	60	8,718	17,914	28,365	64	5,233	60.0%	1,010	8,105	93.0%	82.4%
parted-3.2	138	1,493	7,703	16,415	9	1,133	75.9%	14	1,371	91.8%	66.1%
patch-2.7.6	88	5,334	16,926	35,269	50	4,065	76.2%	480	4,961	93.0%	70.6%
sendmail-8.15	260	21,536	128,312	328,892	1,332	12,368	57.4%	3,277	15,570	72.3%	34.9%
tar-1.31	191	11,671	54,594	109,269	225	7,741	66.3%	7,672	9,200	78.8%	37.1%
tmux-2.8	54	24,877	91,373	185,594	166	12,366	49.7%	12,295	18,266	73.4%	47.2%
wget-1.20	174	8,439	31,460	63,738	100	5,957	70.6%	1,920	6,746	79.9%	31.8%
Avg	117	11,451	45,329	100,202	244	7,021	65.7%	3,302	9,314	85.2%	59.0%
Total	1,166	114,508	453,289	1,002,022	2,438	70,206	61.3%	33,022	93,141	81.3%	51.8%

We compare D^3 with a C bounded model checker, CBMC (version 5.11) [26]. CBMC, as confirmed by the authors, does not provide an option to verify TH-safety only by disabling other types of memory errors. Thus, we have configured it with the "pointercheck" option to detect all pointer-related errors and then manually extracted all the TH-safety violations reported. For the small test cases in the NIST Juliet Test Suite, loops are not bounded. For the ten real-world programs, loops are unwound by using "unwind 2" to accelerate termination (at the expense of losing soundness).

Infer [7] (i.e., Abductor earlier [8]) has evolved into a bug detector by sacrificing soundness, with its older verification-oriented versions no longer available (as confirmed by its authors), The latest version of SLAyer [6] does not compile (as also confirmed by its authors) since it relies on a specific yet unknown old subversion of the Z3 SMT-solver. So we will not compare with such separation-logic-based verifiers, as Infer, for example, is now designed to lower its false positive rate by tolerating for false negatives.

In addition, we also evaluate D^3 against a version of D^3, denoted D^{SEP}, for which aliasing and control-flow reachability are considered separately.

As pt_{cs}^{dd} is demand-driven, the time budget for a points-to query issued from [Aliasing] (Fig. 12) is set to be a maximum of 10,000 value-flow edges traversed. On time out, pt_{cs}^{dd} will fall back to the result computed by Andersen's pointer analysis, *pt*, soundly (Fig. 2). We have done our experiments on a machine with a 3.5 GHz Intel Xeon 16-core CPU and 256 GB memory, running Ubuntu OS (version 16.04 LTS). The analysis time of a program is the average of five runs. For D^3/D^{SEP}, the analysis times from all its stages (Fig. 5) are included, except the pre-analysis, since Andersen's analysis is expected to be reused by many other static analyses for the program.

5.2 Results and Analysis

5.2.1 Juliet Test Suite: Soundness

Both CBMC and D^3 report soundly all the 138 use-after-free bugs without any false positives. Each test case is small, with a few hundreds of LOC, costing less than one second to verify by either tool.

5.2.2 The Ten Open-Source Programs: Precision and Scalability

For any of these programs, CBMC, which is bounded by even "unwind 2", cannot terminate within a 1-day time budget. We have decided to evaluate D^3 against a version, D^{SEP}, in which both aliasing and control-flow reachability are considered separately, as shown in Table 2.

- **Precision.** For a total of 114,508 dereferences in the ten programs, D^3 proves successfully 81.3% (or $\frac{93,141}{114,508}$) to be safe. This translates into an average of 85.2% per program, ranging from 72.3% in `sendmail` to 95.8% for `ctags`. For the remaining 14.8%, anout an average of 33% fail due to the out-of-budget problem. In contrast, D^{SEP} finds only 61.3% of all the dereferences to be safe, with an average of 65.7% per program, ranging from 49.7% for `tmux` to 76.2% for `patch`.
  D^3 is significantly more precise than D^{SEP} (as measured by %Impr). For a total of 44,302 dereferences that cannot be verified to be safe by D^{SEP}, D^3 recognizes 51.8% of these (i.e., $\frac{22,935}{44,302}$) as being safe. The largest improvements are observed for `ctags` (85.0%), `cpio` (82.4%) and `MCSim` (82.4%), which contain many cases as illustrated in Fig. 3, causing D^{SEP} to fail but D^3 to succeed, since aliasing and reachability must be considered together. On the other hand, the precision improvements for `wget` (31.8%) and `sendmail` (34.9%), where linked lists are heavily used, are the least impressive.
- **Scalability.** For a given program, the size of its value-flow graph affects the time complexity of our approach. D^3 scales reasonably well to these programs, spending a total of 33,022 s on analyzing a total of 1,166 KLOC, while D^{SEP} is faster (finishing in 2,438 s) but less precise. For `sendmail` (the largest with 260 KLOC), D^3 takes 3,277 s to complete. For `ctags` (the smallest with 42 KLOC), D^3 finishes in 520 s. D^3 is the fastest for `parted`, which has the smallest value-flow graph with the smallest number of dereferences. D^3 is the slowest for `tmux`, which has the second largest value-flow graph with the largest number of dereferences.

6 Related Work

Pointer Analysis. Substantial progress has been made for whole-program [23,33,48] and demand-driven [20,47,51] pointer analyses, with flow-sensitivity [19,31], call-site-sensitivity [40,61], object-sensitivity [37,55] and type-sensitivity [25,45]). These recent advances in both precision and scalability have resulted in their widespread adoption in detecting memory bugs [2,17], such as memory leaks [9,52], null dereferences [34,36], uninitialized variables [35,60], buffer overflows [10,30], and typestate verification [12,16]. Pointer-analysis-based tools [44,57] can detect TH-safety violations with low false-positive rates, but at the expense of missing true bugs. Some recent advances on pointer analysis for object-oriented languages [32,46] improve the efficiency of the traditional k-object-sensitivity by analyzing some methods context-insensitively, but due to the lack of flow-insensitivity, such techniques are unsuitable for analyzing TH-safety. In contrast, D^3 is designed to be a verifier for finding TH-safety violations with good precision soundly by considering aliasing and control-flow reachability synergistically.

Separation Logic. As an extension of Hoare logic for heap-manipulating programs, separation logic [42] provides the basis for a long line of research on memory safety verification. At its core is the separating conjunction $*$ that splits the heap into disjoint heaplets, allowing program reasoning to be confined in heaplets [15,59]. For separation-logic-based verification, scalability has considerably improved with techniques like bi-abduction at the expense of sacrificing some precision [8,58], leading to industrial-strength tools such as Microsoft's SLAyer [6] and Facebook's Infer [7]. By giving up also some soundness, many industrial-strength static analyzers, such as Clang Static Analyzer [3,43] and Infer (the current release 0.15.0) are bug detectors, which reduce false positives at the expense of exhibiting false negatives as well. Unlike separation-logic-based approaches that support compositional and modular reasoning, D^3 takes a pointer-analysis-based approach by analyzing also only the relevant code on-demand.

Model Checking. Model checking represents a powerful framework for reasoning about a wide range of properties [24]. To analyze pointer-intensive C programs, model checkers such as SLAM [5] and BLAST [21] rely on pre-computed points-to information. Goal-driven techniques like SMACK+Corral [18] aim at improving scalability by simplifying verification conditions. However, as pointed out in [26], model checking still suffers from limitations in fully automated TH-safety verification for large-sized programs, partly due to complex pointer aliasing. Model checkers with symbolic execution (e.g., Symbiotic [53]) can find bugs precisely but with limited scalability for large-sized programs due to path explosion.

7 Conclusion

This paper presents D^3, a novel approach for addressing the TH-safety verification problem based on a demand-driven context-sensitive pointer analysis. D^3 achieves its precision (by considering both aliasing and control-flow reachability simultaneously) and scalability (with adaptive context-sensitivity). In future work, we plan to empower D^3 by also considering (partial) path-sensitivity and shape analysis.

Acknowledgement. We would like to thank the anonymous reviewers for their valuable comments. This research is supported by an Australian Research Grant DP180104169.

References

1. Juliet Test Suite 1.2. https://samate.nist.gov/srd/testsuite.php
2. Aiken, A., Bugrara, S., Dillig, I., Dillig, T., Hackett, B., Hawkins, P.: An overview of the Saturn project. In: PASTE 2007, pp. 43–48 (2007)
3. Clang Static Analyzer. http://clang-analyzer.llvm.org/
4. Andersen, L.O.: Program analysis and specialization for the C programming language. Ph.D. thesis, DIKU, University of Copenhagen (1994)
5. Ball, T., Majumdar, R., Millstein, T., Rajamani, S.K.: Automatic predicate abstraction of C programs. In: PLDI 2001, pp. 203–213 (2001)
6. Berdine, J., Cook, B., Ishtiaq, S.: SLAYER: memory safety for systems-level code. In: Gopalakrishnan, G., Qadeer, S. (eds.) CAV 2011. LNCS, vol. 6806, pp. 178–183. Springer, Heidelberg (2011). https://doi.org/10.1007/978-3-642-22110-1_15
7. Calcagno, C., Distefano, D.: Infer: an automatic program verifier for memory safety of C programs. In: Bobaru, M., Havelund, K., Holzmann, G.J., Joshi, R. (eds.) NFM 2011. LNCS, vol. 6617, pp. 459–465. Springer, Heidelberg (2011). https://doi.org/10.1007/978-3-642-20398-5_33
8. Calcagno, C., Distefano, D., O'Hearn, P., Yang, H.: Compositional shape analysis by means of bi-abduction. In: POPL 2009, pp. 289–300 (2009)
9. Cherem, S., Princehouse, L., Rugina, R.: Practical memory leak detection using guarded value-flow analysis. In: PLDI 2007, pp. 480–491 (2007)
10. Cifuentes, C., et al.: Static deep error checking in large system applications using parfait. In: ESEC/FSE 2011, pp. 432–435 (2011)
11. Cytron, R., Ferrante, J., Rosen, B.K., Wegman, M.N., Kenneth Zadeck, F.: Efficiently computing static single assignment form and the control dependence graph. ACM Trans. Program. Lang. Syst. (TOPLAS) **13**(4), 451–490 (1991)
12. Das, M., Lerner, S., Seigle, M.: ESP: path-sensitive program verification in polynomial time. In: PLDI 2002, pp. 57–68 (2002)
13. Dillig, I., Dillig, T.: EXPLAIN: a tool for performing abductive inference. In: Sharygina, N., Veith, H. (eds.) CAV 2013. LNCS, vol. 8044, pp. 684–689. Springer, Heidelberg (2013). https://doi.org/10.1007/978-3-642-39799-8_46
14. Dillig, I., Dillig, T., Aiken A.: Sound, complete and scalable path-sensitive analysis. In: PLDI 2008, pp. 270–280 (2008)
15. Distefano, D., O'Hearn, P.W., Yang, H.: A local shape analysis based on separation logic. In: Hermanns, H., Palsberg, J. (eds.) TACAS 2006. LNCS, vol. 3920, pp. 287–302. Springer, Heidelberg (2006). https://doi.org/10.1007/11691372_19
16. Fink, S.J., Yahav, E., Dor, N., Ramalingam, G., Geay, E.: Effective typestate verification in the presence of aliasing. ACM Trans. Softw. Eng. Methodol. (TOSEM) **17**, 9 (2008)
17. Hackett, B., Aiken, A.: How is aliasing used in systems software? In: FSE 2006, pp. 69–80 (2006)
18. Haran, A., Carter, M., Emmi, M., Lal, A., Qadeer, S., Rakamarić, Z.: SMACK+Corral: a modular verifier. In: Baier, C., Tinelli, C. (eds.) TACAS 2015. LNCS, vol. 9035, pp. 451–454. Springer, Heidelberg (2015). https://doi.org/10.1007/978-3-662-46681-0_42

19. Hardekopf, B., Lin, C.: Semi-sparse flow-sensitive pointer analysis. In: POPL 2009, pp. 226–238 (2009)
20. Heintze, N., Tardieu, O.: Demand-driven pointer analysis. In: PLDI 2001, pp. 24–34 (2001)
21. Henzinger, T.A., Jhala, R., Majumdar, R., McMillan, K.L.: Abstractions from proofs. In: POPL 2004, pp. 232–244 (2004)
22. Henzinger, T.A., Necula, G.C., Jhala, R., Sutre, G., Majumdar, R., Weimer, W.: Temporal-safety proofs for systems code. In: Brinksma, E., Larsen, K.G. (eds.) CAV 2002. LNCS, vol. 2404, pp. 526–538. Springer, Heidelberg (2002). https://doi.org/10.1007/3-540-45657-0_45
23. Jeong, S., Jeon, M., Cha, S., Oh, H.: Data-driven context-sensitivity for points-to analysis. In: OOPSLA 2014, pp. 100:1–100:28 (2017)
24. Jhala, R., Majumdar, R.: Software model checking. ACM Comput. Surv. (CSUR) **41**(4), 21 (2009)
25. Kastrinis, G., Smaragdakis, Y.: Hybrid context-sensitivity for points-to analysis. In: PLDI 2013, pp. 423–434 (2013)
26. Kroening, D., Tautschnig, M.: CBMC – C bounded model checker. In: Ábrahám, E., Havelund, K. (eds.) TACAS 2014. LNCS, vol. 8413, pp. 389–391. Springer, Heidelberg (2014). https://doi.org/10.1007/978-3-642-54862-8_26
27. Lattner, C., Adve, V.: LLVM: a compilation framework for lifelong program analysis & transformation. In: CGO 2004, pp. 75–86 (2004)
28. Lee, B., et al.: Preventing use-after-free with dangling pointers nullification. In: NDSS 2015 (2015)
29. Lhoták, O., Chung, K.-C.A.: Points-to analysis with efficient strong updates. In: POPL 2011, pp. 3–16 (2011)
30. Li, L., Cifuentes, C., Keynes, N.: Practical and effective symbolic analysis for buffer overflow detection. In: FSE 2010, pp. 317–326 (2010)
31. Li, L., Cifuentes, C., Keynes, N.: Boosting the performance of flow-sensitive points-to analysis using value flow. In: ESEC/FSE 2011, pp. 343–353 (2011)
32. Li, Y., Tan, T., Møller, A., Smaragdakis, Y.: Precision-guided context sensitivity for pointer analysis. In: OOPSLA 2018, p. 141 (2018)
33. Liang, P., Tripp, O., Naik, M.: Learning minimal abstractions. In: POPL 2011, pp. 31–42 (2011)
34. Loginov, A., Yahav, E., Chandra, S., Fink, S., Rinetzky, N., Nanda, M.: Verifying dereference safety via expanding-scope analysis. In: ISSTA 2008, pp. 213–224 (2008)
35. Lu, K., Song, C., Kim, T., Lee, W.: UniSan: proactive kernel memory initialization to eliminate data leakages. In: CCS 2016, pp. 920–932 (2016)
36. Madhavan, R., Komondoor, R.: Null dereference verification via over-approximated weakest pre-conditions analysis. In: OOSPLA 2011, pp. 1033–1052 (2011)
37. Milanova, A., Rountev, A., Ryder, B.G.: Parameterized object sensitivity for points-to analysis for java. ACM Trans. Softw. Eng. Methodol. (TOSEM) **14**(1), 1–41 (2005)
38. Musuvathi, M., Park, D.Y.W., Chou, A., Engler, D.R., Dill, D.L.: CMC: a pragmatic approach to model checking real code. In: OSDI 2002, pp. 75–88 (2002)
39. Nagarakatte, S., Zhao, J., Martin, M.M.K., Zdancewic, S.: CETS: compiler enforced temporal safety for C. In: ISMM 2010, pp. 31–40 (2010)
40. Oh, H., Lee, W., Heo, K., Yang, H., Yi, K.: Selective context-sensitivity guided by impact pre-analysis. In: PLDI 2014, pp. 475–484 (2014)
41. Reps, T., Horwitz, S., Sagiv, M.: Precise interprocedural dataflow analysis via graph reachability. In: POPL 1995, pp. 49–61 (1995)

42. Reynolds, J.C.: Separation logic: a logic for shared mutable data structures. In: LICS 2002, pp. 55–74 (2002)
43. Coverity Scan. https://scan.coverity.com/
44. Shi, Q., Xiao, X., Wu, R., Zhou, J., Fan, G., Zhang, C.: Pinpoint: fast and precise sparse value flow analysis for million lines of code. In: PLDI 2018, pp. 693–706 (2018)
45. Smaragdakis, Y., Bravenboer, M., Lhoták, O.: Pick your contexts well: understanding object-sensitivity. In: POPL 2011, pp. 17–30 (2011)
46. Smaragdakis, Y., Kastrinis, G., Balatsouras, G.: Introspective analysis: context-sensitivity, across the board. In: PLDI 2014, pp. 485–495 (2014)
47. Späth, J., Do, L.N.Q., Ali, K., Bodden, E.: Boomerang: demand-driven flow-and context-sensitive pointer analysis for Java. In: ECOOP 2016, pp. 22:1–22:26 (2016)
48. Sridharan, M., Bodík, R.: Refinement-based context-sensitive points-to analysis for Java. In: PLDI 2016, pp. 387–400 (2006)
49. Sui, Y., Xue, J.: On-demand strong update analysis via value-flow refinement. In: FSE 2016, pp. 460–473 (2016)
50. Sui, Y., Xue, J.: SVF: interprocedural static value-flow analysis in LLVM. In: CC 2016, pp. 265–266 (2016)
51. Sui, Y., Xue, J.: Value-flow-based demand-driven pointer analysis for C and C++. IEEE Trans. Softw. Eng. (TSE) (2018)
52. Sui, Y., Ye, D., Xue, J.: Static memory leak detection using full-sparse value-flow analysis. In: ISSTA 2012, pp. 254–264 (2012)
53. Symbiotic. https://github.com/staticafi/symbiotic
54. Szekeres, L., Payer, M., Wei, T., Song, D.: SoK: eternal war in memory. In: SP 2013, pp. 48–62 (2013)
55. Tan, T., Li, Y., Xue, J.: Efficient and precise points-to analysis: modeling the heap by merging equivalent automata. In: PLDI 2017, pp. 278–291 (2017)
56. Yan, H., Sui, Y., Chen, S., Xue, J.: Machine-learning-guided typestate analysis for static use-after-free detection. In: ACSAC 2017, pp. 42–54 (2017)
57. Yan, H., Sui, Y., Chen, S., Xue, J.: Spatio-temporal context reduction: a pointer-analysis-based static approach for detecting use-after-free vulnerabilities. In: ICSE 2018, pp. 327–337 (2018)
58. Yang, H., et al.: Scalable shape analysis for systems code. In: Gupta, A., Malik, S. (eds.) CAV 2008. LNCS, vol. 5123, pp. 385–398. Springer, Heidelberg (2008). https://doi.org/10.1007/978-3-540-70545-1_36
59. Yang, H., O'Hearn, P.: A semantic basis for local reasoning. In: Nielsen, M., Engberg, U. (eds.) FoSSaCS 2002. LNCS, vol. 2303, pp. 402–416. Springer, Heidelberg (2002). https://doi.org/10.1007/3-540-45931-6_28
60. Ye, D., Sui, Y., Xue, J.: Accelerating dynamic detection of uses of undefined values with static value-flow analysis. In: CGO 2014, pp. 154–164 (2014)
61. Yu, H., Xue, J., Huo, W., Feng, X., Zhang, Z.: Level by level: making flow-and context-sensitive pointer analysis scalable for millions of lines of code. In: CGO 2010, pp. 218–229 (2010)
62. Zhang, X., Mangal, R., Grigore, R., Naik, M., Yang, H.: On abstraction refinement for program analyses in datalog. In: PLDI 2014, pp. 239–248 (2014)

A Change-Based Heuristic for Static Analysis with Policy Iteration

Marcus Völker(✉) and Stefan Kowalewski

Informatik 11 - RWTH Aachen University, Aachen, Germany
{voelker,kowalewski}@embedded.rwth-aachen.de
http://www.embedded.rwth-aachen.de

Abstract. We improve the *policy iteration*-based algorithm for value set analysis by giving a new heuristic for policy selection based on a local static analysis. In particular, we detect loops in the program and perform an analysis to discover the *relative changes* of variables in the loop, that is, whether a variable is constant or whether its value rises, falls or both. We use these relative changes to improve the old heuristic, achieving better (that is, smaller) fixed points than the original approach.

Keywords: Data flow analysis · Value set analysis · Policy iteration

1 Introduction

Static analysis in the form of dataflow analysis is classically done with the algorithm of Kleene iteration [3]. To that end, the program is transformed into a set of *dataflow equations*. These equations are then solved via Kleene iteration, with the solution representing some information about the program. If the analysis is a value set analysis, these equations typically give an assignment of abstract values to program variables for every location in the program.

Since Kleene iteration is not guaranteed to terminate, techniques such as widening and narrowing [3] have been developed which guarantee termination at the cost of precision and partially recover lost precision, respectively.

To improve precision and run times of the classical algorithm, the algorithm of policy iteration [6] was reformulated to be used for dataflow analysis [2] with the interval domain and later expanded to relational domains [4]. This algorithm replaces the set of dataflow equations with a set of sets of simpler to solve equations called *policies* that have the property of overapproximating the solution. Then one of the policies is chosen heuristically with the goal of finding a solution that is also a solution of the original set of equations. The policy is solved with Kleene iterations. If the solution is also a solution of the original set, the algorithm terminates, otherwise, it is used as a starting point for the next heuristically chosen policy. As we approach the least fixpoint from below, the variant of policy iteration used in this paper is *min-policy iteration* [5].

The reason why this algorithm is powerful is that if the policy is chosen well, a drastically simpler dataflow problem has to be solved, reducing

B.-Y. E. Chang (Ed.): SAS 2019, LNCS 11822, pp. 73–95, 2019.
https://doi.org/10.1007/978-3-030-32304-2_5

running times. Also, it is possible that a fixed point is reached without using widening, improving precision in comparison with classical Kleene iteration. Note that policy iteration is guaranteed to find a fixed point, provided the algorithm used to solve the policies terminates. On the other hand, if the policy is chosen poorly, the algorithm has to solve multiple dataflow equation systems instead of just one, potentially increasing run time. Alternatively, an equation system may be chosen that gives a correct but unnecessarily big fixed point. Consequently, a policy iteration-based algorithm's performance strongly depends on a good heuristic.

In the basic version detailed in [2], the algorithm is executed with interval abstraction, i.e. the value sets are abstracted as intervals. To get a policy, each intersection operation $\sqcap$ in the program is replaced by another function. These intersections are typically generated to model branches. For instance, a branch depending on $x \leq 16$ would be represented as $x' = x \sqcap [-\infty, 16]$ and its dual branch as $x' = x \sqcap [17, \infty]$. There are four functions that may replace $\sqcap$:

- $l(a, b) = a$
- $r(a, b) = b$
- $m(a, b) = [a.l, b.u]$
- $i(a, b) = [b.l, a.u]$

where $x.l$ is the lower bound and $x.u$ is the upper bound of interval x. If interval a or b are empty, the result of any of the four functions is empty. Furthermore, if a policy would result in an illegal interval such as $[1, 0]$, the result is also treated as empty.

The standard heuristic for choosing a policy given in [2] is very simple: At each bound, compare both possible bounds. Constant bounds trump variable bounds, and variable bounds trump infinite bounds. If both bounds are constant, take the tighter bound. If both bounds are variable, take the left bounds. To illustrate, consider again the intersections $x \sqcap [-\infty, 16]$ and $x \sqcap [17, \infty]$. With this heuristic, the bounds of x trump ∞ and $-\infty$, while 16 and 17 trump the bounds of x. Therefore the policies are:

$$[\mathbf{x.l}, x.u] \sqcap [-\infty, \mathbf{16}] \Rightarrow [x.l, 16] \mathrel{\hat{=}} m$$
$$[x.l, \mathbf{x.u}] \sqcap [\mathbf{17}, \infty] \Rightarrow [17, x.u] \mathrel{\hat{=}} i$$

This heuristic is based on the fact that when there is a branch, it usually is there for a good reason. For example, consider the example program in Fig. 1. The branch in the loop is there to check whether the loop terminates. Since x is incremented in each step, it will reach the loop bound 16 at some point, so $[0, 15]$ is the correct interval for the loop body. Therefore it makes sense to set it to 15 right at the beginning of the loop, which is what the deduced m policy achieves.

However, this assumption is only correct if the program behaves as expected. This is an assumption that does not need to hold - indeed we use static analysis in the first place to find out whether the program behaves as expected. The places in which it does not behave as expected are precisely the points that are of most interest to us. By assuming the program behaves as expected, we may choose policies that either do not give correct solutions, costing time for policy refinement, or policies that give larger solutions than necessary, losing precision at the important places.

Take again the program in Fig. 1. If we were to change it only slightly, initialising y with -1 instead of 1, the loop would count downward, yet the interval $[0, 15]$ would still be used for the loop body, eventually reaching $[-\infty, 15]$ after infinitely many steps or widening, even though the values $[1, 15]$ are spurious. If we knew, however, how x is going to change throughout the loop, we could use this to improve the heuristic, chosing i instead of m, immediately leading to $[-\infty, 0]$, the correct fixed point.

Another problem is the intersection of two variable-based expressions, such as $x \leq y$. This assumption would, for the purposes of policy iteration, be converted into the following two equations:

$$x' = x \sqcap [-\infty, y.u]$$
$$y' = y \sqcap [x.l, \infty]$$

If y is constant inside the loop but variable in general (such as the length of a dynamic data structure over which is iterated), the best choice of policy would treat y no different from an explicit constant and therefore pick m and l as policies for the two equations, respectively. However, standard heuristic has no way to know whether x or y is constant over the loop and picks the default left bound, which results in the policy l being chosen for both equations, giving the equations

$$x' = x$$
$$y' = y$$

which effectively removes the assumption from the program and causes x to increment to ∞, taking infinitely many normal iteration steps to reach convergence.

Therefore, in this paper we introduce a dataflow analysis we call *relative change analysis* which is capable of detecting the direction in which a variable changes, and how we can use that information to build a better heuristic for important cases. In Sect. 2, we detail how the RCA works. In Sect. 3, we build a heuristic from the RCA results which can be used with policy iteration and finds smaller solutions in many cases. In Sect. 4, we evaluate the algorithm on multiple programs, both qualitative (i.e. with respect to solution size) and quantitative (i.e. with respect to run time). Finally, in Sect. 5 we sum up the results presented in this paper and give an outlook on future improvements to the presented heuristic, both qualitatively and quantitatively.

We only consider the interval domain in this paper. However, due to the relational nature of the relative change analysis, it seems reasonable that policy iteration on certain relational domains such as template polyhedra domains [10], the octagon abstract domain [8] or the zone abstract domain [7] would also benefit from our heuristic.

```
x := 0;
y := 1;
WHILE x < 16 DO
  x := x + y
OD
```

(a) Source code

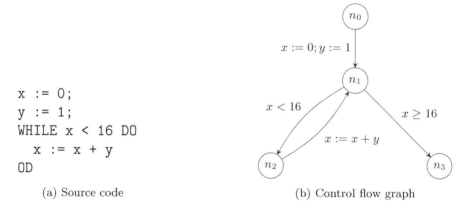

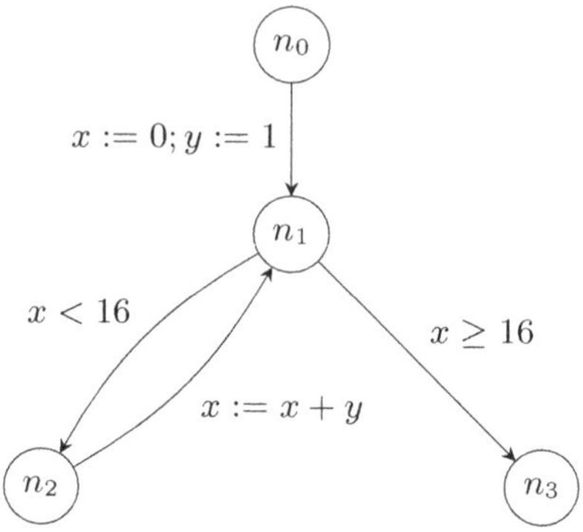

(b) Control flow graph

Fig. 1. The worked example. Note that from n_1, the edge (n_1, n_2) leads into the loop, while the edge (n_1, n_3) leads out of the loop.

Furthermore, our current implementation only considers programs that operate on a single, numerical domain, such as integers. Other authors have investigated how to use policy iteration on logico-numerical programs, i.e. programs that contain Boolean variables in addition to numerical variables [11].

2 Relative Change Analysis

Before we formally define and explain the analysis we use to find the heuristic, we will give an intuition about how this analysis is supposed to work to make it more understandable. To that end, we take the worked example from Figure and go through it step-by-step, performing the same operations as in the formal part further down, but in an intutive rather than a formal way.

The very first step is to identify loops and the part of the program that leads to a loop, which we call the loop prefix. In the worked example, the loop is the nodes $\{n_1, n_2\}$ with the two edges between them and the prefix is the edge (n_0, n_1). We also note that the two edges we have to apply the heuristic to are the edge (n_1, n_2) which goes into the loop body, and (n_1, n_3), which is taken once the loop terminates. As the assumptions on these edges are both based on x, we are especially interested in how the value of x changes over the course of the loop.

We start at n_1 with the information that $x = x_0$ and then go through the loop. Assumptions do not change values, therefore this information is also annotated at n_2. Now, we have the assignment $x := x + y$, i.e, x is modified in a way determined by y, so we need information about the value of y, more exactly, about the sign of y to figure out if x stays the same, grows or shrinks.

With a pre-analysis to identify constants and signs, we can determine that y is 1 at the start of the loop and keeps a positive sign throughout the loop and therefore, $x \geq x_0$ is propagated back to n_1, which also turns out to be the final value, so we have now determined that x grows over the course of the loop and can use this information in the actual heuristic.

2.1 Formal Definition

Formally, we build a specialised dataflow analysis we call *relative change analysis* (RCA) which tracks the values of an expression relative to the valuations of all program variables. Formally, we represent this as a mapping $\tau : Var_0 \to \mathcal{R}$ with set $\mathcal{R} := \{r_=, r_\leq, r_\geq, r_?\}$. The semantics of this mapping are as follows: If a value v is described with a mapping τ, it means that v compares to x_0, i.e., the value of $x \in Var$ at the start of the program fragment, with the comparison operator $\tau(x_0)$.

Example 1. Let $v := x + 1$. Then $\tau(x_0) = r_\geq$, i.e. $x + 1 \geq x_0$.
Let $v := -x$. Then $\tau(x_0) = r_?$, i.e. the relation between $-x$ and x_0 is unknown, since negation may increase or decrease a value, depending on its sign.

$\mathcal{R}$ forms a lattice $(\mathcal{R}, \sqsubseteq)$ with $\bot = r_=$, $\top = r_?$ and $r_\leq$ and $r_\geq$ incomparable, as shown in Fig. 2. Consequently, $\{\tau : Var_0 \to \mathcal{R}\}$ and $\{\rho : Var \to (Var_0 \to \mathcal{R})\}$ also form lattices with the usual pointwise mapping for functions. Results in the latter lattice, with the semantics $\rho(x)(y_0) = r_\circ \Rightarrow x \circ y_0$ are sufficient for retrieving information about the variable change direction and can be considered as a very simple relational lattice storing difference constraints of the form $x - y_0 \leq 0$ and $x_0 - y \leq 0$, i.e. strongly restricted zones [7]. If, at the end of the loop, a variable x is valuated with $\rho(x)$, then $\rho(x)(x_0)$ is the change of x over the course of the loop execution. However, an analysis on this lattice alone does not yield sufficiently precise results. To illustrate this, consider the assignment $x := x + y$. To know whether x is increased or decreased, the relation between y and (x_0, y_0) is not relevant. Instead, we need to know the *sign* of y. Therefore, we augment our analysis by storing the set of possible signs $\in \mathbb{S} := 2^{\{+,0,-\}}$ as well, which gives us the analysis domain of

$$Var \to ((Var_0 \to \mathcal{R}) \times \mathbb{S})$$

which can be rewritten as

$$(Var \to (Var_0 \to \mathcal{R})) \times (Var \to \mathbb{S})$$

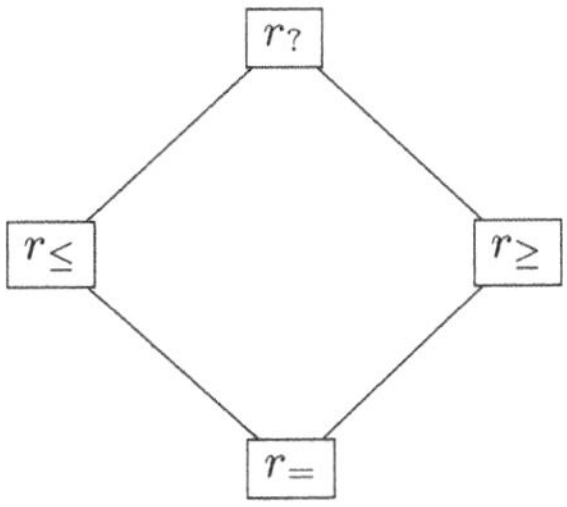

Fig. 2. Lattice $(\mathcal{R}, \sqsubseteq)$ as Hasse diagram

Therefore, an analysis on this domain can be considered a reduced product of a simple relational analysis and a sign analysis. With this domain, we can construct transfer functions that calculate the relative change of variables with sufficient accuracy for common operations on loop variables and small changes to them. To this end, we define the valuation function $val_\rho : Expr \rightarrow ((Var_0 \rightarrow \mathcal{R}) \times \mathbb{S})$ that calculates the value of an expression in relation to the initial valuations, as well as the sign, to actually get a reduced product analysis as opposed to a regular product between the relational and the sign information.

- If $e \in \mathbb{Z}$,

$$val_\rho(e) = ([x_0 \mapsto \mathrm{comp}_\mathbb{S}([\rho(x)]_2, \mathrm{sgn}(e)) \mid x \in Var], \mathrm{sgn}(e))$$

  where comp : $\mathbb{S} \times \mathbb{S} \rightarrow \mathcal{R}$ computes the relation between two sets of signs (see Appendix C for the definition). and $[.]_1$ and $[.]_2$ are the first and second element of a pair, respectively.
- If $e \in Var$,

$$val_\rho(e) = \rho(e)$$

- If $e := e_1 + e_2$,

$$val_\rho(e) = val_\rho(e_1) \oplus val_\rho(e_2)$$

$$(\tau_1, S_1) \oplus (\tau_2, S_2) = \big([x_0 \mapsto \tau_1(x_0) \oplus S_2 \sqcap \tau_2(x_0) \oplus S_1 \mid x \in Var], S_1 +^\# S_2\big)$$

$$r \oplus S = \begin{cases} r_= & r = r_= \wedge \{+, -\} \cap S = \emptyset \\ r_\geq & - \notin S \wedge (r = r_\geq \vee (r = r_= \wedge + \in S)) \\ r_\leq & + \notin S \wedge (r = r_\leq \vee (r = r_= \wedge - \in S)) \\ r_? & otherwise \end{cases}$$

- If $e := e_1 - e_2$,

$$val_\rho(e) = val_\rho(e_1) \ominus val_\rho(e_2)$$

$$(\tau_1, S_1) \ominus (\tau_2, S_2) = \big(\big[x_0 \mapsto \tau_1(x_0) \oplus (-^\# S_2) \mid x \in Var\big], S_1 -^\# S_2\big)$$

- Valuation functions for other operators $(\cdot, /, ...)$ can be built in a similar fashion.

The idea for the addition function is that we either consider the result of the addition as the relation of the left summand modified by the sign of the right summand, or vice-versa. Since both ways of looking at the addition are valid overapproximations of the correct behaviour, we then take the intersection of the results, which is guaranteed to still give us a valid overapproximation. If we subtract, on the other hand, we only take the first interpretation, since the second interpretation (subtracting a relation from a sign) involves negating a relation, which always gives $r_?$. We can therefore reuse the $\oplus$ operator by simply negating the signs in S_2. Now we only need to calculate the initial information ι to build our dataflow framework. For this, we perform a simple combination of constant propagation and sign analysis on the *prefix* of the loop. That is, we take the fragment of the program that leads up to the loop and perform the pre-analysis only on that. If the analysis is to be part of a larger analysis framework that also performs a reaching definitions analysis [9], the results of that can be used to shorten that prefix to the part relevant for the loop. We obtain, for each program variable at the loop entry point, either a constant valuation or a set of signs in case of non-constant values. From these, we then build the ι as follows, assuming the result is given as $c : Var \to \mathbb{Z} \cup \mathbb{S}$:

$$\iota = [x \mapsto ([y \mapsto \text{comp}(c(x), c(y)) \mid y \in Var \setminus \{x\}] \cup [x \mapsto r_=], s(c(x))) \mid x \in Var]$$

where comp : $(\mathbb{Z} \cup \mathbb{S}) \times (\mathbb{Z} \cup \mathbb{S}) \to \mathcal{R}$ computes the relation between two values in $\mathbb{Z} \cup \mathbb{S}$ (see Appendix C for the definition) and $s(k) = \begin{cases} k & k \in \mathbb{S} \\ \{\text{sgn}(k)\} & k \in \mathbb{Z} \end{cases}$

This ι takes the given values to construct relations between program variables in the entries $[\rho(x)]_1(y_0)$, while leaving the diagonal $[\rho(x)]_1(x_0)$ as $r_=$, since it is known that every variable starts out equal to itself. The sign information $[\rho(x)]_2$ is taken straight from the pre-analysis. This information at the entry of the loop might be not sound if we only take a short prefix of the loop or if we deal with a reactive program where the program itself runs in an infinite loop. However, since we are building a heuristic with this information, this does not matter for the soundness of the resulting policy iteration algorithm, since that algorithm is sound regardless of the heuristic chosen, as long as the policies generated fulfill the requirements of that algorithm.

Starting the dataflow analysis with this, we obtain a final valuation ρ at the loop entry, containing the relations of all variables after executing the loop compared to before executing the loop. Now we simply have to take the diagonal of the relations, i.e. $\tau_{loop} = [x \mapsto [\rho(x)]_1(x_0) \mid x \in Var]$ and we know how each variable changes over the course of the loop execution.

We will now demonstrate how the RCA works by reconsidering the worked example from Fig. 1. The prefix of the loop is just the edge (n_0, n_1), so that single edge is the fragment to run the combined constant propagation and sign analysis on. The result will be (at location n_1): $[x \mapsto 0, y \mapsto 1]$. From this we construct the extremal information

$$\iota = [x \mapsto ([x_0 \mapsto r_=, y_0 \mapsto r_\leq], \{0\}), y \mapsto ([x_0 \mapsto r_\geq, y_0 \mapsto r_=], \{+\})]$$

We use ι to run the RCA on the program loop between n_1 and n_2. The assumption $x < 16$ does not change the abstract value, so the only transfer function we have to apply is $x := x + y$. For this, we calculate $\rho(x) \oplus \rho(y)$, i.e.

$$\begin{aligned}
&([x_0 \mapsto r_=, y_0 \mapsto r_\leq], \{0\}) \oplus ([x_0 \mapsto r_\geq, y_0 \mapsto r_=], \{+\}) \\
&\quad = ([x_0 \mapsto (r_= \oplus \{+\} \sqcap r_\geq \oplus \{0\}), y_0 \mapsto (r_\leq \oplus \{+\} \sqcap r_= \oplus \{0\})], \{0\} +^\# \{+\}) \\
&\quad = ([x_0 \mapsto (r_\geq \sqcap r_\geq), y_0 \mapsto (r_? \sqcap r_=)], \{+\}) \\
&\quad = ([x_0 \mapsto r_\geq, y_0 \mapsto r_=], \{+\})
\end{aligned}$$

This abstract value is assigned to x and merged back into the initial information ι resulting in new information

$$[x \mapsto ([x_0 \mapsto r_{\geq}, y_0 \mapsto r_{\leq}], \{0,+\}), y \mapsto ([x_0 \mapsto r_{\geq}, y_0 \mapsto r_{=}], \{+\})]$$

Another loop execution gives

$$\begin{aligned}
&([x_0 \mapsto r_{\geq}, y_0 \mapsto r_{\leq}], \{0,+\}) \oplus ([x_0 \mapsto r_{\geq}, y_0 \mapsto r_{=}], \{+\}) \\
&= \left([x_0 \mapsto (r_{\geq} \oplus \{+\} \sqcap r_{\geq} \oplus \{0,+\}), y_0 \mapsto (r_{\leq} \oplus \{+\} \sqcap r_{=} \oplus \{0,+\})], \{0,+\} +^{\#} \{+\}\right) \\
&= ([x_0 \mapsto (r_{\geq} \sqcap r_{\geq}), y_0 \mapsto (r_{?} \sqcap r_{\geq})], \{+\}) \\
&= ([x_0 \mapsto r_{\geq}, y_0 \mapsto r_{\geq}], \{+\})
\end{aligned}$$

After merging:

$$[x \mapsto ([x_0 \mapsto r_{\geq}, y_0 \mapsto r_{?}], \{0,+\}), y \mapsto ([x_0 \mapsto r_{\geq}, y_0 \mapsto r_{=}], \{+\})]$$

Which is the loop entry information of the fixed point. Extracting the diagonal leaves us with the relative change of the variables

$$\tau_{loop} = [x \mapsto r_{\geq}, y \mapsto r_{=}]$$

which tells us that x is growing over the course of the loop, while y is constant.

3 Change-Based Heuristic

To obtain the policy we will use, we first have to decompose the program into loops and prefixes as mentioned above. This can be accomplished with a simple DFS-based approach on the CFG. If the input program is in a structured form (i.e. no gotos) we can use information about loops present in it to accelerate loop detection. We then sort the list of loops with respect to inclusion, that is, we make sure to analyse inner loops before we analyse outer loops so that we can reuse the information from the inner loop for the outer loop. The prefix of the inner loop, as far as the outer loop is considered, is just the path from the entry of the outer loop to the entry of the inner loop, as well as the prefix of the outer loop. In particular, this means that the parts of the outer loop that can only be reached after reaching the inner loop are not part of the inner loop's prefix. For an example illustrating this, see Fig. 3. When analysing the outer loop, we condense the inner loop into a single edge which applies (i.e. merges) the relative change of the inner loop to the input. At the end of this step, we will obtain a relative change τ_{loop} for each program loop. In the next step, we take the heuristic defined by [2] and improve it with τ_{loop}. For this purpose, we define three classes of interval bounds: $\mathcal{B} = \{K, G, I\}$ with the semantics:

K is a *keep*-bound, i.e. a bound that does not change over the course of the loop.
G is a *grow*-bound, i.e. a bound that grows over the course of the loop.
I is an *inf*-bound, i.e. a bound that is infinite from the start.

These classes can be derived from the arguments of the $\sqcap$ and τ_{loop}. If a bound is constant or infinite, its class is K or I respectively. If a bound is dependent on a variable, it is either K or G, depending on that variable's relative change:

$$\begin{aligned} r_= &\Rightarrow [K, K] \\ r_\geq &\Rightarrow [K, G] \\ r_\leq &\Rightarrow [G, K] \\ r_? &\Rightarrow [G, G] \end{aligned}$$

Another relevant part of the heuristic is whether the assumption we inspect is on the edge that leads into the loop or on the edge that leads out of the loop, since they have different expected behaviours. Table 1 shows the selected bound based on the bound classes in both cases. Tighter means that we take the bound resulting in a smaller interval, as long as it's possible (i.e. if we have constant valuations or easily comparable signs for both left over from the pre-analysis). Don't care means we choose either bound, since we don't have enough information to know the better one (in the case of $G \sqcap G$) or they are equal (in the case of $I \sqcap I$). In our implementation, we use left for the $G \sqcap G$ case on the in-loop edge and right on the out-of-loop edge. The general rule here is that we prefer to take K, if possible. If we have to choose between G and I instead, we take I in the in-loop case (since a variable grows against an infinite bound) and G in the out-of-loop case (since we left the loop and therefore don't grow any further).

To sum up, the algorithm for obtaining a policy is as follows:

1. Split the program into (inclusion-ordered) loops and their prefixes
2. For each pair (prefix, loop):
   (a) Perform a joint constant propagation and sign analysis on the prefixes
   (b) Perform the RCA on the loop, condensing subloops to the results of their RCAs
   (c) Calculate τ_{loop} from $\rho_{entry(loop)}$
   (d) Use τ_{loop} to calculate bound classes and calculate the local policies for this loop
3. Assemble all local policies into the global policy

Example 2. Take $x < 16$ as the loop condition, which translates to the transfer function $x_{in} = x \sqcap [-\infty, 15]$ for the in-loop edge and $x_{out} = x \sqcap [16, \infty]$ for the out-of-loop edge. Furthermore, take $\tau_{loop}(x) = r_\geq$. This leads to the classifications (with chosen bounds in bold face)

$$\begin{aligned} x_{in} &= [\mathbf{K}, G] \sqcap [I, \mathbf{K}] \mathrel{\hat{=}} [x.l, 15] \mathrel{\hat{=}} m \\ x_{out} &= [K, \mathbf{G}] \sqcap [\mathbf{K}, I] \mathrel{\hat{=}} [16, x.u] \mathrel{\hat{=}} i \end{aligned}$$

which aligns with the standard heuristic for intervals, since the loop behaves as expected. If we change the relative change as $\tau_{loop}(x) = r_\leq$ instead (which on

Table 1. Bound selection based on bound classes

left \ right	K	G	I
K	tighter	left	left
G	right	don't care	right
I	right	left	don't care

(a) in-loop

left \ right	K	G	I
K	tighter	left	left
G	right	don't care	left
I	right	right	don't care

(b) out-of-loop

the worked example would result from accidentially writing $x := x - y$ instead of $x := x + y$), however, we get

$$x_{in} = [G, \mathbf{K}] \sqcap [\mathbf{I}, K] \mathrel{\hat{=}} [-\infty, x.u] \mathrel{\hat{=}} i$$
$$x_{out} = [G, \mathbf{K}] \sqcap [\mathbf{K}, I] \mathrel{\hat{=}} [16, x.u] \mathrel{\hat{=}} i$$

which gives the correct fixed point $[-\infty, 0]$ for the in-loop edge and $[16, 0] = \bot$ for the out-of-loop edge within one loop iteration, compared to $[-\infty, 15]$ and $\bot$ from the standard heuristic after infinitely many iterations or alternatively applying widening. With a relative change of as $\tau_{loop}(x) = r_=$ instead (which on the worked example would result from accidentially writing $x := x$ instead of $x := x + y$), we get

$$x_{in} = [\mathbf{K}, \mathbf{K}] \sqcap [I, K] \mathrel{\hat{=}} x \mathrel{\hat{=}} l$$
$$x_{out} = [K, \mathbf{K}] \sqcap [\mathbf{K}, I] \mathrel{\hat{=}} [16, x.u] \mathrel{\hat{=}} i$$

which gives the correct fixed point $[0, 0]$ for the in-loop edge and $[16, 0] = \bot$ for the out-of-loop edge within one loop iteration, compared to $[0, 15]$ and $\bot$ within one loop iteration.

With this, we have a heuristic for the initial policy selection. For the improved policy selection, we follow the idea in [2] and simply generate a policy p' that conforms with the constraint that $p'(p^-) = \Phi(p^-)$ for the currently obtained fixed point p^-. We accomplish this by going over all the equations in p and keeping the local policies the same if $p(p^-)_l = \Phi(p^-)_l$ at location l, and switching them to match otherwise. If we have multiple choices (such as switching from l to m or r), we choose the policy that is closest to the already chosen policy, i.e. we try to keep one of the bounds the same if possible (in this case m, which keeps the lower bound as opposed to r, which switches both bounds).

Nested Loops. To see how the algorithm performs on a program with nested loops, we look at two nested loops that increment their respective variables, with the inner loop termination dependent on the outer loop variable. Program and CFG are depicted in Fig. 3. Decomposing this program gives

$$(\{n_0, n_1, n_2, n_3\}, \{n_3, n_4\})$$

as inner prefix and loop and

$$(\{n_0, n_1\}, \{n_1, n_2, n_3, n_4, n_5\})$$

as outer prefix and loop. We therefore first analyse the inner loop with result $\tau_{inner} = [x \mapsto r_{=}, y \mapsto r_{\geq}]$ and afterwards the outer loop resulting in $\tau_{outer} = [x \mapsto r_{\geq}, y \mapsto r_{?}]$. The policies obtained by the standard heuristic and our heuristic are shown in Table 2. The results here show that for the outer loop, the standard heuristic already gives the optimal policy, since the behaviour of the outer loop is the expected behaviour for a loop condition $x < 16$. However, for the inner loop, the standard heuristic gives a non-optimal policy since the constraint contains two variables and the heuristic cannot infer which one is the one that changes over the course of the loop. Here, our heuristic knows that y is growing and x is constant and therefore selects the optimal policy in a single step. The obtained fixed points are displayed in Table 3. Note that the fixed point obtained via the standard heuristic is not a fixed point of the original program and would trigger a policy improvement step, eventually giving the correct result.

```
x := 0;
WHILE x < 16 DO
  y := 0;
  WHILE y < x DO
    y := y + 1
  OD;
  x := x + 1
OD
```

(a) Source code

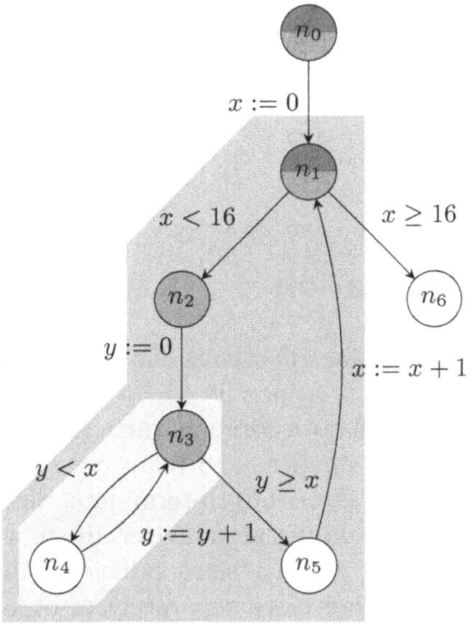

(b) Control flow graph with loops and prefixes

Fig. 3. Two-dimensional loop

Table 2. Policies with standard heuristic and our heuristic for the program in Fig. 3

v_e	Transfer Function	Standard	Ours
$x_{(3,4)}$	$x_4 := [y_3.l + 1, \infty] \sqcap x_3$	m	r
$y_{(3,4)}$	$y_4 := y_3 \sqcap [-\infty, x_3.u - 1]$	l	m
$x_{(3,5)}$	$x_5 := [-\infty, y_3.u] \sqcap x_3$	i	r
$y_{(3,5)}$	$y_5 := y_3 \sqcap [x_3.l, \infty]$	l	i
$x_{(1,2)}$	$x_2 := x_2 \sqcap [-\infty, 15]$	m	m
$x_{(1,6)}$	$x_6 := x_6 \sqcap [16, \infty]$	i	i

Table 3. Fixed points found by the two heuristics on the program in Fig. 3. Improved bounds have been marked in boldface

v	Standard	Ours
x_0	$\top$	$\top$
y_0	$\top$	$\top$
x_1	$[0, 16]$	$[0, 16]$
y_1	$\top$	$\top$
x_2	$[0, 15]$	$[0, 15]$
y_2	$\top$	$\top$
x_3	$[0, 15]$	$[0, 15]$
y_3	$[0, \infty]$	$[0, \mathbf{15}]$
x_4	$[0, 15]$	$[0, 15]$
y_4	$[0, \infty]$	$[0, \mathbf{14}]$
x_5	$[0, 15]$	$[0, 15]$
y_5	$[0, \infty]$	$[\mathbf{1}, \mathbf{15}]$
x_6	$[16, 16]$	$[16, 16]$
y_6	$\top$	$\top$

4 Evaluation

To evaluate the effectivity of our approach, we have first written a set of simple programs (c.f. Appendix A) by hand to compare the standard heuristic to our heuristic. We both compare the quality of the results by checking which heuristic leads to the smaller fixed point once both algorithms terminate and the time it took for the algorithm to terminate. Since policy iteration allows for selection of policies that do not actually terminate without employing other techniques such as widening, we have set a sufficiently high timeout to detect when this occurs and view these cases separately in order to evaluate the improvements to the policy iteration algorithm itself. Note that the termination guarantee from [2] is only valid if the policies terminate, so using a technique such as widening is necessary. Our implementation uses simple Kleene iterations to solve the policies themselves, without using widening, since we have encountered problems when employing widening; particularly, if widening finds a post-fixed point as opposed to a fixed point, the termination guarantee of policy iteration does no longer hold, since it requires fixed points of the policies for a correct policy improvement step. The results of this benchmark are depicted in Fig. 4.

Starting from this set of 16 programs, we have then put each of these programs through our program fuzzer twenty times which, while leaving the structure of the program intact, randomly modifies operators, variables and constants in the program. This simulates mistakes such as off-by-one errors or using the wrong variable in a loop condition. The aggregated results for this benchmark are presented in Fig. 5, normalised for the maximal time of the corresponding program for better readability. The full evaluation for each program can be found in the appendix in Figs. 8 and 9. As we can see from Fig. 5, using the relative change analysis to build the heuristic slows down the analysis by a factor between 2 and 4 in most cases. In exchange, we get two advantages: In most cases, we find either the same or a smaller fixed point as the standard heuristic. Also, in

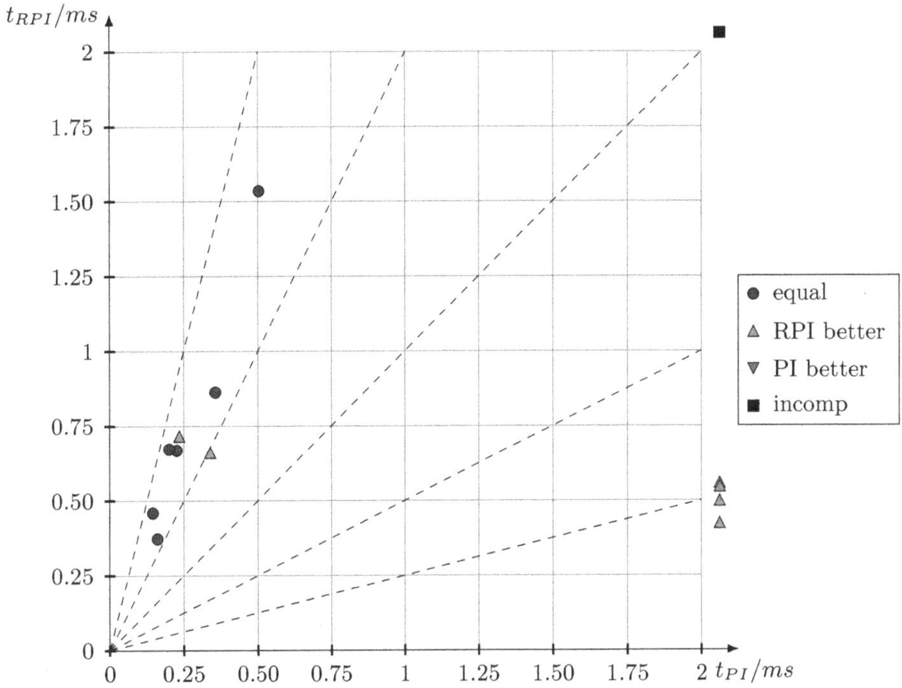

Fig. 4. Evaluation results of handwritten programs. The color and shape of the symbols refers to the size of the obtained fixed points. PI denotes the policy iteration with the standard heuristic, while RPI denotes the policy iteration with our heuristic. Accordingly, t_{PI} is the time the analysis took with the standard heuristic, while t_{RPI} is the time it took with our heuristic. (Color figure online)

Table 4. Program counts for Fig. 5, with the same classes of programs as in the legend there. *improvement* means that a fixed point found with the standard heuristic has been improved upon by our heuristic, while *termination* means that our heuristic found a fixed point on a program where the standard heuristic selected a policy that does not terminate.

Kind	Count	Percentage
Equal	163	50.9%
RPI better	98	30.7%
improvement	53	16.6%
termination	45	14.1%
PI better	1	0.3%
Incomparable	58	18.1%
Σ	320	100%

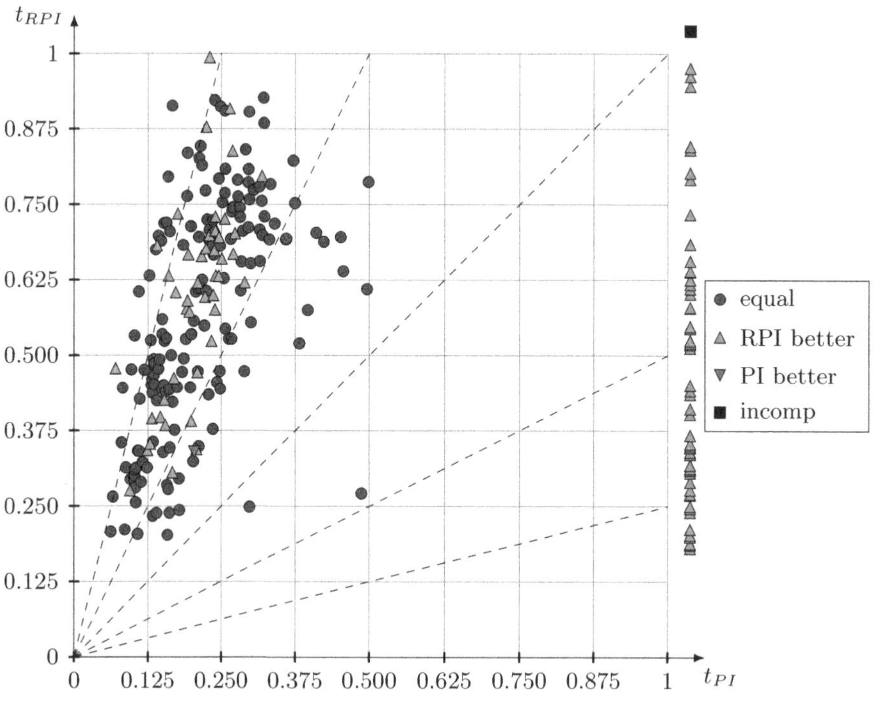

Fig. 5. Evaluation results of fuzzed benchmark, normalised per benchmark for readability. t_{PI} is the time for the standard heuristic, while t_{RPI} is the time for our heuristic on the same program. Results outside the coordinate grid denote that the corresponding analysis did not terminate. There are no cases in which the standard heuristic gave a terminating analysis where our heuristic did not. (Color figure online)

some of the cases where the standard heuristic fails to find a fixed point because the chosen policy does not terminate, our heuristic manages to find a fixed point by choosing a better policy (Table 4).

To investigate the slowdown, we have also tracked the time taken for the heuristic and the Kleene solver, respectively, as well as the number of policy improvement steps that were necessary to find a fixed point. Since we do not believe partial results to be worthwile for this analysis, we only focus on those cases where both analyses terminated. The results are depicted in Fig. 6. There is a bit of a bias there for our heuristic causing less policy iteration steps than

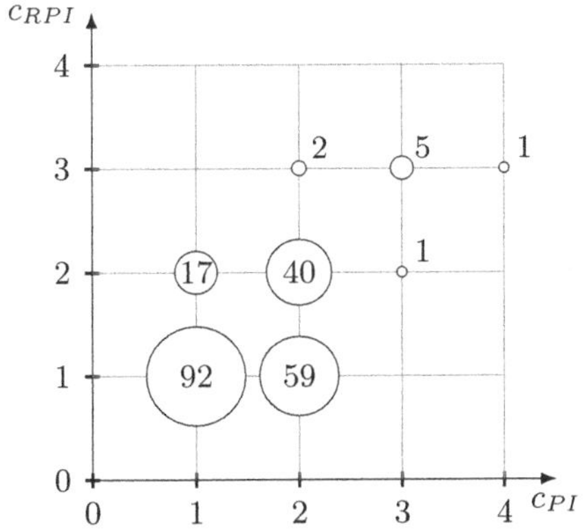

Fig. 6. Comparison between policy iteration steps for the standard heuristic (c_{PI}) and our heuristic (c_{RPI}). Numbers and size of circles indicate how many programs fall into that group.

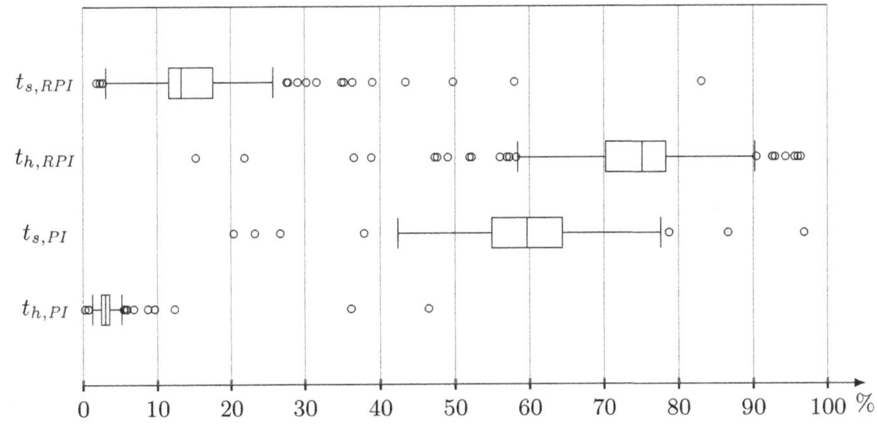

Fig. 7. Percentage of time taken for heuristic calculation (h) and Kleene solutions (s), with the standard heuristic (PI) and our heuristic (RPI). Time to check fixpoint candidates not taken into account. Whisker length is ≤ 1.5 IQR.

the standard heuristic, but overall, cases where both heuristics needed the same amount of iteration steps to terminate were the most common. The timings of heuristic calculation and Kleene solution are graphed in Fig. 7. The values there are in percent of the whole analysis. Median values are $\approx 3\%$ for calculating the standard heuristic and $\approx 59\%$ for solving the policies obtained from the standard heuristic with Kleene iteration. For our heuristic, we get $\approx 75\%$ of the run time for calculation of the heuristic and $\approx 13\%$ for Kleene iteration. The time missing for 100% is spent for setup and for checking if the fixpoint of the policy obtained through Kleene iteration is a fixpoint of the program. Since this part is equally expensive for both approaches, we have not measured it. The result is that in our approach, the heuristic takes most of the time, which was expected from the slowdown we experienced.

5 Conclusion

In policy iteration-based value set analysis, the selection of the proper policy is crucial to both getting a small fixed point and finding it as quickly as possible. To that end, the algorithm utilises a heuristic with the goal of selecting such a policy. The standard heuristic given by [2] seeks to accomplish this by looking at the conditional the policy is used in and selecting a policy with the assumption that the conditional is a good predictor of the surrounding program's behaviour, e.g., that the condition of a while loop starts off being fulfilled and becomes unfulfilled during the loop's execution. As we have seen, if the program contains faulty code, this assumption might easily be violated by simple mistakes, such as a wrong variable in nested loops, an off-by-one error or by using the wrong operator. To that end, we have developed a heuristic that does analyse the loop's body to find out the ways in which a loop's body modifies the variables relevant to its condition, based on the abstract interpretation framework that we already utilise for value set analysis in general. The effect of using this heuristic is a tradeoff between speed and accuracy. The analysis with our heuristic typically takes between 2 and 4 times as long to perform, but often gives more accurate results in the case that the program contains the type of programming errors mentioned above, or contains conditionals between two variables, where the standard heuristic cannot obtain any clues about the behaviour of the loop. Furthermore, only in very rare, specifically constructed cases do we obtain worse results with our heuristic.

5.1 Future Work

Now that the basic heuristic based on relative changes is implemented and yields promising results, there are a few avenues in which we will continue our research. First off, we have two improvements for the algorithm to calculate the relative changes in mind: On one hand, we expect speed-up by using a template-based approach as a pre-analysis. The idea here is to first scan for the variables in the loop condition whether they are only operated on trivially, e.g. with an operation such as $x := x + 1$. If we detect only such operations on the condition-relevant variables in the loop body, we can forego the expensive analysis and obtain the relative changes for use in the heuristic easily. As we have seen in Sect. 4, 75% of the run time of the algorithm with our heuristic is due to heuristic calculation, so a significant speedup in this part could improve runtimes enough to compete with the standard heuristic, at least on programs with simple loop variable manipulation. The other improvement aims to increase accuracy by employing an SMT-solver. Here, we would encode the loop body as an SMT formula using large block encoding [1] and query, for each variable, whether the variable can have a value greater than or less than its initial value. Another interesting topic is the generation of improved policies; the original approach only describes a heuristic for the initial policy, which we have improved upon in this paper for relevant cases. However, for the policy improvement, i.e. the case where the first attempt does not find a fixed point and a new policy has to be chosen to continue the algorithm, we only know the requirements that the improved policy has to fulfill, but no heuristic to determine a promising improvement. A better heuristic in that regard, with the knowledge that the RCA information is flawed (since policy improvement is necessary) should be able to speed up a few corner cases where our heuristic fails to provide a fixed point on the first attempt.

A Evaluated programs

Listing 1.1.

```
x := 0;
WHILE x <= 16 DO
    x := x
OD
```

Listing 1.2.

```
x := 1;
WHILE x < 16 DO
    x := x + 1
OD
```

Listing 1.3.

```
x := 0;
y := 1;
WHILE x < 16 DO
    x := x + y
OD
```

Listing 1.4.

```
x := 0;
y := 1;
WHILE x < 16 DO
    x := x - y
OD
```

Listing 1.5.

```
x := 0;
WHILE x > 16 DO
    x := x + 1
OD
```

Listing 1.6.

```
x = 0;
WHILE x < 16 DO
    x := x - 1
OD
```

Listing 1.7.

```
x := 0;
y := undef();
WHILE x <= 16 DO
    x := y
OD
```

Listing 1.8.

```
x := 0;
y := undef();
WHILE x < y DO
    x := x + 1
OD
```

Listing 1.9.

```
x := 0;
y := 16;
WHILE x < y DO
    x := x + 1;
    y := y - 1
OD
```

Listing 1.10.

```
x := 0;
WHILE x < 16 DO
    IF x < 8 THEN
        x := x + 1
    FI
OD
```

Listing 1.11.

```
x := 0;
WHILE x < 16 DO
    IF x < 8 THEN
        x := x + 1
    ELSE
        x := x - 1
    FI
OD
```

Listing 1.12.

```
x := 0;
WHILE x < 16 DO
  y := 0;
  WHILE y < x DO
    y := y + 1
  OD;
  x := x + 1
OD
```

Listing 1.13.

```
x := 0;
y := 1;
z := 16;
WHILE x < z DO
    x := x - y
OD
```

Listing 1.14.

```
x0 := 0;
x1 := 0;
WHILE x0 <= x1 DO
    x1 := x1 + 1;
    x0 := x1
OD
```

Listing 1.15.

```
x0 := 0;
x1 := 0;
x2 := 0;
x3 := 0;
x4 := 0;
WHILE x0 <= 16 DO
    x4 := x4 + 1;
    x3 := x4;
    x2 := x3;
    x1 := x2;
    x0 := x1
OD
```

Listing 1.16.

```
x := 0;
y := undef();
WHILE x < 16 DO
    y := y + 1
OD
```

B Detailed Evaluation Results

In each of the following graphs, a program and twenty randomly mutated variations of it were analysed with policy iteration, once with the standard heuristic and once with our heuristic. Each symbol represents one analysed program, with the time it took to analyse it with the standard heuristic plotted on the x-axis and with our heuristic on the y-axis. Since our heuristic incurs a runtime cost of at least factor 2 in most cases, the x-axis has been scaled for better readability.

The shape and color of the symbols denotes the quality of the results. A blue circle denotes equal results, a green triangle pointing upwards denotes better results with our heuristic, a red triangle pointing downwards denotes worse results with our heuristic and a black square denotes incomparable results. The last symbol only occurs in our graph when both analyses hit a timeout.

Since the standard Kleene iteration without widening can run into infinite chains, it is possible for the policy iteration algorithm to not terminate when naive Kleene iteration is applied. We have chosen to denote this with the symbols that appear outside the grid. If a symbol appears at the right side of the grid, that means that the standard heuristic chose a non-terminating policy, but our heuristic did not. Since a non-terminating policy yields no results, our heuristic's result is considered better in these cases. Theoretically, it is also possible for the other case to appear (our heuristic not terminating, but the standard heuristic giving results), but that case did not occur in our benchmarking. Finally, the black square in the top-right corner of some of the diagrams denotes that a program there hit non-termination with both our and the standard heuristic.

C Formulas

$$comp : (\mathbb{Z} \cup \mathbb{S}) \times (\mathbb{Z} \cup \mathbb{S}) \to \mathcal{R}$$

$$comp_{\mathbb{S}} : \mathbb{S} \times \mathbb{S} \to \mathcal{R}$$

$$comp(c_x, c_y) = \bigsqcup \{comp_{\mathbb{Z}}(z_x, z_y) \mid z_x \in \gamma(c_x), z_y \in \gamma(c_y)\}$$

$$comp_{\mathbb{Z}}(z_x, z_y) = \begin{cases} r_= & z_x = z_y \\ r_\leq & z_x < z_y \\ r_\geq & z_x > z_y \end{cases}$$

$$comp_{\mathbb{S}}(s_x, s_y) = \bigsqcup \{comp_{\mathbb{Z}}(z_x, z_y) \mid z_x \in \gamma(c_x), z_y \in \gamma(c_y)\}$$

$$\gamma(c) = \begin{cases} \{c\} & c \in \mathbb{Z} \\ \bigcup \{\gamma_{\mathbb{S}}(s) \mid s \in c\} & otherwise \end{cases}$$

$$\gamma_{\mathbb{S}}(c) = \begin{cases} \{z \mid z \in \mathbb{Z}, z < 0\} & s = - \\ \{0\} & s = 0 \\ \{z \mid z \in \mathbb{Z}, z > 0\} & s = + \end{cases}$$

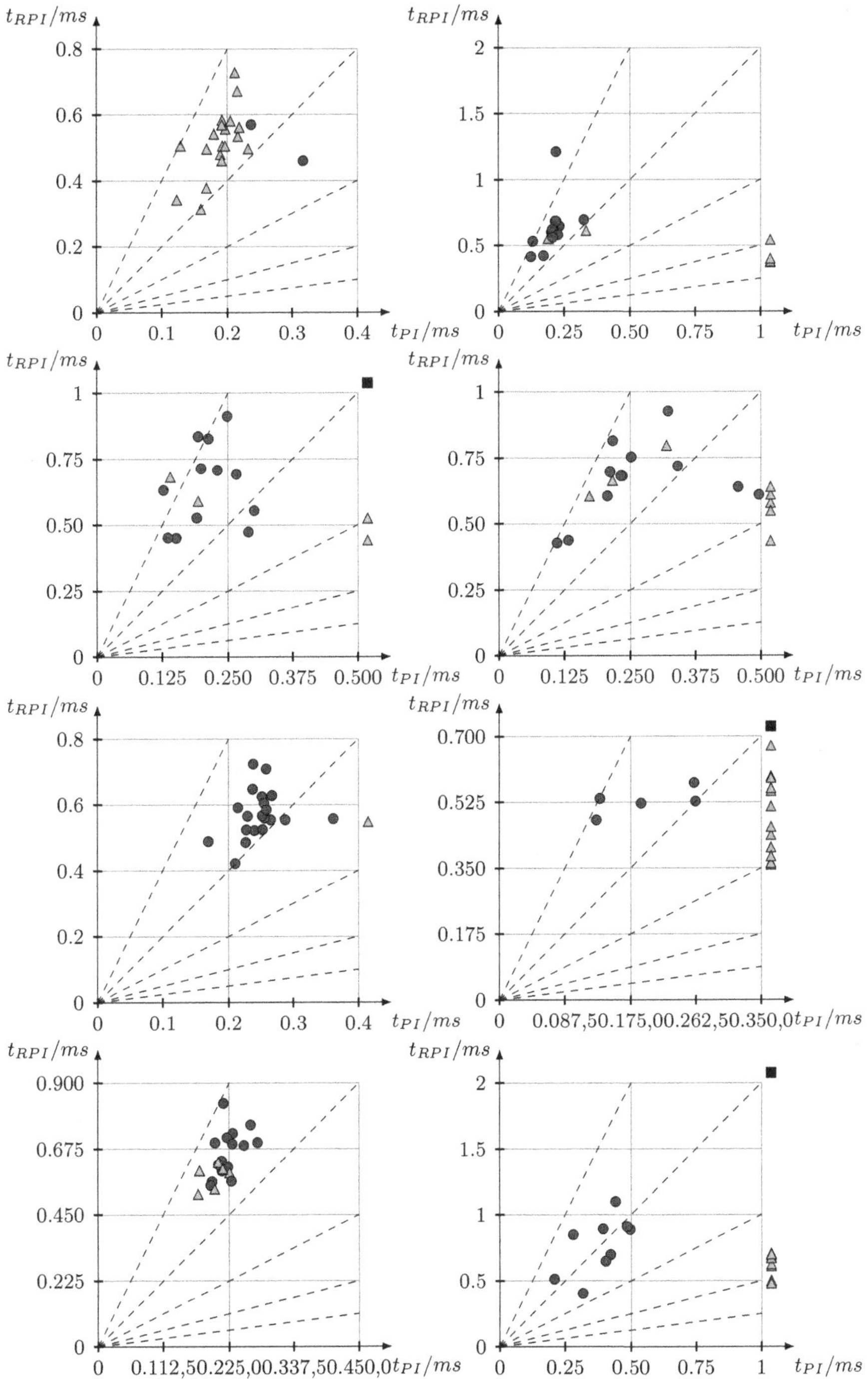

Fig. 8. Evaluation results of Mutator benchmark, programs 1–8. For an explanation, see Sect. B (Color figure online)

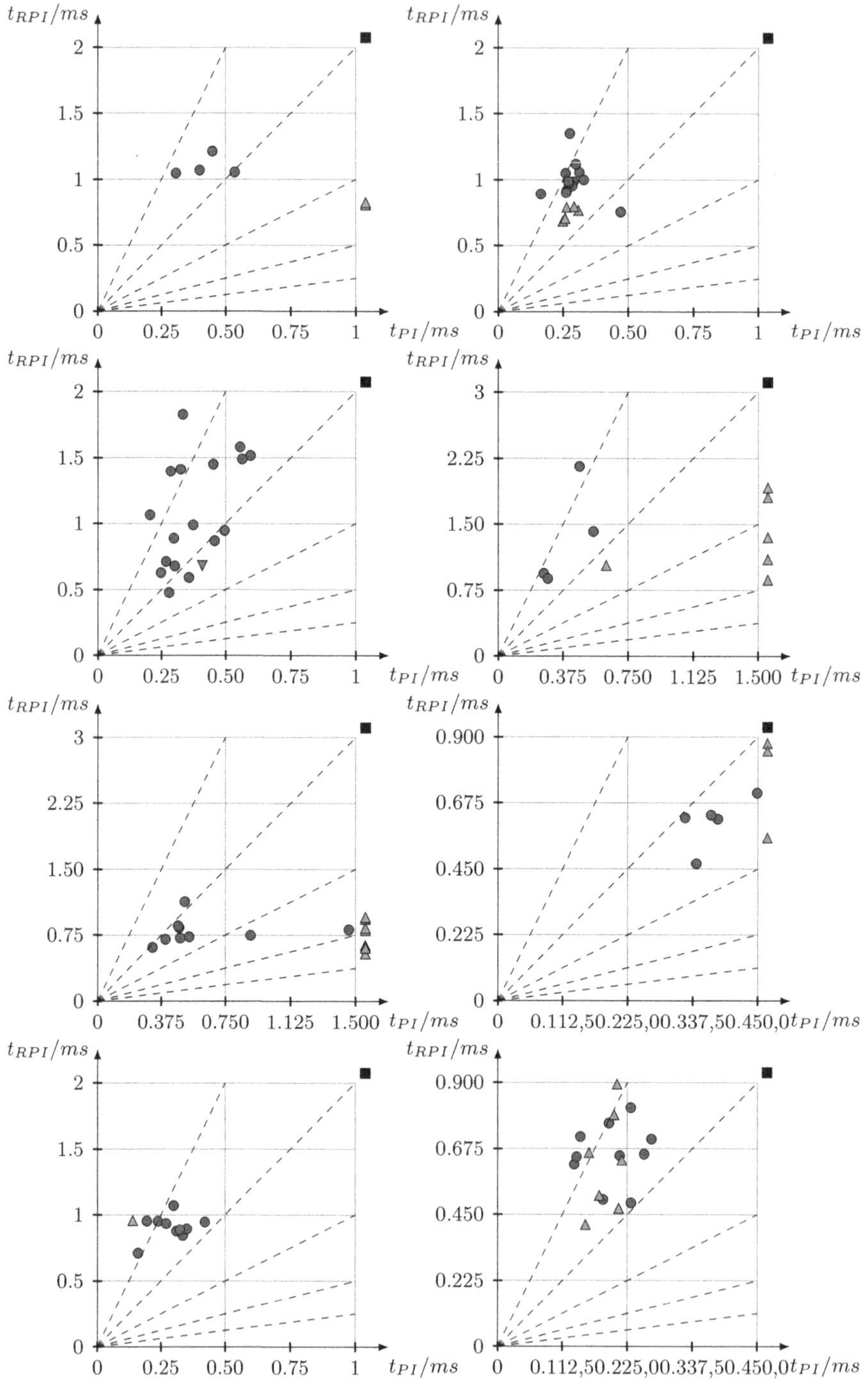

Fig. 9. Evaluation results of Mutator benchmark, programs 9–16. For an explanation, see Sect. B (Color figure online)

References

1. Beyer, D., Cimatti, A., Griggio, A., Keremoglu, M.E., Sebastiani, R.: Software model checking via large-block encoding. In: 2009 Formal Methods in Computer-Aided Design, pp. 25–32, November 2009. https://doi.org/10.1109/FMCAD.2009.5351147
2. Costan, A., Gaubert, S., Goubault, E., Martel, M., Putot, S.: A policy iteration algorithm for computing fixed points in static analysis of programs. In: Etessami, K., Rajamani, S.K. (eds.) CAV 2005. LNCS, vol. 3576, pp. 462–475. Springer, Heidelberg (2005). https://doi.org/10.1007/11513988_46
3. Cousot, P., Cousot, R.: Abstract interpretation: a unified lattice model for static analysis of programs by construction or approximation of fixpoints. In: Conference Record of the Fourth Annual ACM SIGPLAN-SIGACT Symposium on Principles of Programming Languages, Los Angeles, California, pp. 238–252. ACM Press, New York (1977)
4. Gaubert, S., Goubault, E., Taly, A., Zennou, S.: Static analysis by policy iteration on relational domains. In: De Nicola, R. (ed.) ESOP 2007. LNCS, vol. 4421, pp. 237–252. Springer, Heidelberg (2007). https://doi.org/10.1007/978-3-540-71316-6_17
5. Gawlitza, T., Seidl, H.: Precise fixpoint computation through strategy iteration. In: De Nicola, R. (ed.) ESOP 2007. LNCS, vol. 4421, pp. 300–315. Springer, Heidelberg (2007). https://doi.org/10.1007/978-3-540-71316-6_21
6. Howard, R.A.: Dynamic Programming and Markov Processes. MIT Press, Cambridge (1960)
7. Miné, A.: A new numerical abstract domain based on difference-bound matrices. In: Danvy, O., Filinski, A. (eds.) PADO 2001. LNCS, vol. 2053, pp. 155–172. Springer, Heidelberg (2001). https://doi.org/10.1007/3-540-44978-7_10
8. Miné, A.: The octagon abstract domain. Higher Order Symbol. Comput. **19**(1), 31–100 (2006)
9. Nielson, F., Nielson, H.R., Hankin, C.: Principles of Program Analysis. Springer, Heidelberg (1999). https://doi.org/10.1007/978-3-662-03811-6
10. Sankaranarayanan, S., Colón, M.A., Sipma, H., Manna, Z.: Efficient strongly relational polyhedral analysis. In: Emerson, E.A., Namjoshi, K.S. (eds.) VMCAI 2006. LNCS, vol. 3855, pp. 111–125. Springer, Heidelberg (2005). https://doi.org/10.1007/11609773_8
11. Schrammel, P., Subotic, P.: Logico-numerical max-strategy iteration. In: Giacobazzi, R., Berdine, J., Mastroeni, I. (eds.) VMCAI 2013. LNCS, vol. 7737, pp. 414–433. Springer, Heidelberg (2013). https://doi.org/10.1007/978-3-642-35873-9_25

Syntactic and Semantic Soundness of Structural Dataflow Analysis

Patrick Cousot
Courant Institute of Mathematical Sciences, New York University, New York, USA
pcousot@cs.nyu.edu

Abstract. We show that the classical approach to the soundness of dataflow analysis is with respect to a syntactic path abstraction that may be problematic with respect to a semantics trace-based specification. The fix is a rigorous abstract interpretation based approach to formally construct dataflow analysis algorithms by calculational design.

Keywords: Abstract interpretation · Dataflow analysis · Model-checking · Soundness

1 Introduction

The very first data flow analysis algorithms [1,2,3,4] were postulated: map the program to a control flow graph (CFG), derive binary vector fixpoint equations using transfer functions/transformers to abstract the actions in the CFG, solve iteratively or by elimination, the result is postutaled to be the abstract information available on the program semantics. We call this approach "syntactic" since the values of the variables are not taken into account at all by the transfer functions/transformers in the equations.

Gary Kildall proposed to reason on paths in the CFG [22]: define the abstract information available on any path in the CFG by composition of syntactic transfer functions/transformers along that path and then merge/join/meet the information on all paths. In general, this yields more precise results than the fixpoint equations (except for distributive frameworks where transformers preserve joins/meets and the results are the same). This is an abstract form of soundness since one can prove that the solution of the equations over-approximates the merge over all paths solution. [12, Section 9] showed that the merge over all paths solution is also the solution of fixpoint equations taken over the disjunctive completion [12,16] of the original abstract domain. So the imprecision is not due to the equations but to the abstract domain [17].

Bernhard Steffen observed that by considering the CFG as a transition system, the information along a path can be specified by a modal/temporal logic formula [28,29]. Model-checking over all paths yields the abstract information available about the program semantics. The specification is concise and an existing model-checker can be reused for the implementation. Fixpoint iterates convergence requires the abstract domain to be finite (which excludes *e.g.* Kildall's constant propagation [22] for which the model checker would not be guaranteed to terminate). The information on the program semantics is still defined with respect to a syntactic abstraction of the semantics, not the semantics itself.

To solve this problem, David Schmidt proposed to get the abstraction of the paths by abstract interpretation of a trace semantics [25]. Now the information

B.-Y. E. Chang (Ed.): SAS 2019, LNCS 11822, pp. 96–117, 2019.
https://doi.org/10.1007/978-3-030-32304-2_6

extracted from the program is related to the semantics, but indirectly, since it is postulated syntactically on abstract paths, not on the traces of the semantics itself.

David Schmidt used his model to explore "Why some flow analyzes are unsound?" and claimed that the live variable analysis is unsound [25, Section 7]. As shown in [13] this is because the analysis is about potential liveness while David Schmidt's counter-example is on definite liveness. David Schmidt claims that this is not a problem in practice since the information is used dually [25]. If a variable is not potentially live, it is definitely dead and its value need not be stored *e.g.* in a register. But if a data flow analysis were wrong, its dual would be wrong too. As shown by this erroneous reasoning, the syntactic modal/temporal specification on abstract paths but not directly on the semantics may be problematic.

In this paper, we explore the definition of dataflow analyses by direct abstraction of the trace semantics. So the abstract information extracted by the static analysis is directly related to the program trace semantics, not to an abstraction of this semantics. In this way, values of variables can be taken into account, which is not the case with temporal specifications on abstract paths. The analyzes should therefore be more precise and provably sound.

Surprisingly, this approach shows that the abstract syntactic definition of liveness is unsound with respect to its semantic definition. The problem is both for definite and potential liveness. The problem comes from the fact that the semantic definition takes values into account while the abstract definition hence the resulting dataflow analysis algorithm captures that incorrectly.

Example 1 For definite liveness, consider for example `if` ℓ_1 `(x==0)` ℓ_2 `x = x-x ;` where `x` is dead on exit. The syntactic equational and path-based definitions of definite liveness both yield `x` is live at ℓ_1 and ℓ_2. However, this program is equivalent to `if` ℓ_1 `(x==0)` ℓ_2 `x = 0 ;` so `x` is not live at ℓ_2. Moreover, this last program is itself equivalent to ℓ_1`;` (skip) so that no variable, in particular `x` is live at ℓ_1. Therefore the semantic definition of definite liveness at ℓ_1 and ℓ_2 in the original program `if` ℓ_1 `(x==0)` ℓ_2 `x = x-x ;` should be that `x` is not live, in contradiction with the syntactic equational and path-based definite liveness. □

Potential liveness or, dually, definite deadness is not better.

Example 2 For definite deadness, consider ℓ_1 `x = y-y ;`ℓ_2 where `x` is live at ℓ_2 on exit. Syntactically, `x` is not used in `y-y` and `x` is modified by the assignment so `x` is syntactically dead at ℓ_1. Semantically, `x` is not used in `y-y` since changing the value of `x` at ℓ_1 will not change the value of `y-y` which is always 0. However, assume `x` = 0 at ℓ_1 then the assignment ℓ_1 `x = y-y ;` does not modify this value. So in that case `x` is not modified by the assignment and therefore `x` is live at ℓ_1 *i.e.* if the precondition `x` = 0 is always true, the compiler is allowed to remove the assignment. For all other initial values `x` ≠ 0 at ℓ_1, the assignment does modify this value by assigning 0 in which case `x` is dead at ℓ_1. So syntactically, `x` is definitely dead at ℓ_1 while, semantically, this is not always the case (*i.e.* when `x` is 0 at ℓ_1). □

To solve these soundness problems, we first define a structural fixpoint trace semantics in Section **2**. Then, in Section **3**, we first provide an intuitive semantic definition of liveness by abstraction of a trace semantics: "a variable is live at some point if its value may be read before the next time it is modified". The above examples 1 and 2 show that the classical syntactic liveness algorithm is unsound with respect to this definition. At that point we could change the algorithm or the liveness definition. We choose the second alternative (so as not to have to change compilers, but this choice is arbitrary!). This second definition "a variable is live at some point if its value may be read before the next time it is assigned to" mixes a syntactic (assignment) and a semantic (value) points of view (thus preventing meaningful program syntactic transformation such as useless assignment elimination). It specifies exactly in what sense the classical syntactic deadness/liveness algorithm [20,19,21] is sound. Then by a further purely syntactic abstraction "a variable is live at some point if its value may be used before the next time it is assigned to" (where use and assigned to are defined syntactically, thus preventing expression and assignment optimizations), we get, by calculational design [8], the classical syntactic potential liveness algorithm [20,19,21] in Section **4**, and the dual definite deadness algorithm in Section **5**. The definition of the trace semantics is structural, so we get the classical syntactic deadness/liveness algorithm in structural form. Surprisingly, there is no fixpoint iteration and the (implicit) equations are solved by elimination, which is more efficient. This is comparable to equation resolution by elimination for reducible flowcharts [27,24,26] but much simpler and efficient. In Section **6**, we discuss whether liveness analysis is correctly used for code optimization. We conclude in Section **7**.

2 Syntax and Trace Semantics

Programs are a subset of `C` with the following context-free syntax.

$\mathtt{x}, \mathtt{y}, \ldots \in \mathbb{V}$	variable ($\mathbb{V}$ not empty)
$\mathtt{A} \in \mathbb{A} ::= \mathtt{1} \mid \mathtt{x} \mid \mathtt{A}_1 - \mathtt{A}_2$	arithmetic expression
$\mathtt{B} \in \mathbb{B} ::= \mathtt{A}_1 < \mathtt{A}_2 \mid \mathtt{B}_1 \ \mathtt{nand} \ \mathtt{B}_2$	boolean expression
$\mathtt{S} \in \mathbb{S} ::=$	statement
$\quad \mathtt{x = A ;}$	assignment
$\quad \mid \ \mathtt{;}$	skip
$\quad \mid \ \mathtt{if\ (B)\ S} \mid \mathtt{if\ (B)\ S\ else\ S}$	conditionals
$\quad \mid \ \mathtt{while\ (B)\ S} \mid \mathtt{break\ ;}$	iteration and break
$\quad \mid \ \mathtt{\{\ Sl\ \}}$	compound statement
$\mathtt{Sl} \in \mathbb{Sl} ::= \mathtt{Sl}\ \mathtt{S} \mid \epsilon$	statement list
$\mathtt{P} \in \mathbb{P} ::= \mathtt{Sl}$	program

A break exits the closest enclosing loop, if none this is a syntactic error. If `P` is a program then `int main () { P }` is a valid `C` program. We call "[program] component" $\mathtt{S} \in \mathbb{Pc} \triangleq \mathbb{S} \cup \mathbb{Sl} \cup \mathbb{P}$ either a statement, a statement list, or a program.

2.1 Program labels

Labels are not part of the language, but useful to discuss program points reached during execution. For each program component S, we define informally

at⟦S⟧	the program point at which execution of S starts;
aft⟦S⟧	the program exit point after S, at which execution of S is supposed to normally terminate, if ever;
esc⟦S⟧	a boolean indicating whether or not the program component S contains a **break ;** statement escaping out of that component S;
brk-to⟦S⟧	the program point at which execution of the program component S goes to when a **break ;** statement escapes out of that component S;
brks-of⟦S⟧	the set of labels of all **break ;** statements that can escape out of S;
in⟦S⟧	the set of program points inside S (including at⟦S⟧ but excluding aft⟦S⟧ and brk-to⟦S⟧);
labs⟦S⟧	the potentially reachable program points while executing S either at, in, or after the statement, or resulting from a break.

2.2 Traces

Because liveness analysis at a program point relates the past, present, and future of a computation, we use a trace semantics relating the past computation reaching that program point to the future computation continuing this past computation. For simplicity, the program point where liveness is calculated is the entry point at⟦S⟧ at a program component S.

A trace $\pi \in \mathbb{T}^{+\infty}$ is a sequence of states separated by events. States are program labels designating the next action to be executed in the program. The events record the effect of this execution *i.e.* the value assigned to a variable, a test B which is true (marked (B)) or false (marked (¬B)), a **break ;** exiting from a loop, or a skip when execution goes on with no variable modification. For example, the program

$$\ell_1\ \texttt{x = x + 1 ; if}\ \ell_2\ \texttt{(x < 0)}\ \ell_3\ \texttt{x = 0 ;}\ \ell_4 \tag{1}$$

executed with initial value 0 of x has execution trace $\ell_1 \xrightarrow{\texttt{x = x + 1 = 1}} \ell_2 \xrightarrow{\neg(\texttt{x} < 0)} \ell_4$. A trace π can be finite $\pi \in \mathbb{T}^+$ or infinite $\pi \in \mathbb{T}^\infty$ (recording a non-terminating computation) so $\mathbb{T}^{+\infty} \triangleq \mathbb{T}^+ \cup \mathbb{T}^\infty$ [1]. Trace concatenation $\frown$ is defined as follows

$$\pi_1\ell_1 \frown \ell_2\pi_2 \quad \text{undefined if } \ell_1 \neq \ell_2 \qquad \pi_1 \frown \ell_2\pi_2 \triangleq \pi_1 \quad \text{if } \pi_1 \in \mathbb{T}^\infty \text{ is infinite}$$
$$\pi_1\ell_1 \frown \ell_1\pi_2 \triangleq \pi_1\ell_1\pi_2 \quad \text{if } \pi_1 \in \mathbb{T}^+ \text{ is finite}$$

In pattern matching, we sometimes need the empty trace $\ni$. For example if $\ell\pi\ell' = \ell$ then $\pi = \ni$ and so $\ell = \ell'$.

States do not record the value of variables x. $\varrho(\pi)\texttt{x}$ is the last value assigned to x on trace π (or 0 at initialization).

$$\varrho(\ell)\texttt{x} \triangleq 0 \qquad \varrho(\pi\ell \xrightarrow{\texttt{x = A =}\ \nu} \ell')\texttt{x} \triangleq \nu \qquad \varrho(\pi\ell \xrightarrow{\ \cdots\ } \ell')\texttt{x} \triangleq \varrho(\pi\ell)\texttt{x} \ \text{ otherwise} \tag{2}$$

[1] Abstracting program label states would yield Stephen Brookes trace semantics [6].

2.3 Trace semantics

The trace semantics of a program component S is a relation between past traces reaching the entry point at⟦S⟧ and future traces recording the computation of S from at⟦S⟧. For example, program S in (1) has the following two pairs of traces in its trace semantics.

$$\langle \ell_0 \xrightarrow{\texttt{x = 0} = 0} \ell_1,\ \ell_1 \xrightarrow{\texttt{x = x + 1} = 1} \ell_2 \xrightarrow{\neg(\texttt{x} < 0)} \ell_4\rangle \in \mathcal{S}^{+\infty}[\![\texttt{S}]\!]$$

$$\langle \ell_0 \xrightarrow{\texttt{x = 1} = 1} \ell_1,\ \ell_1 \xrightarrow{\texttt{x = x + 1} = 2} \ell_2 \xrightarrow{\neg(\texttt{x} < 0)} \ell_4\rangle \in \mathcal{S}^{+\infty}[\![\texttt{S}]\!]$$

In the *maximal trace semantics* $\mathcal{S}^{+\infty}[\![\texttt{S}]\!]$, the observation of the future computation is maximal. It is finite when the program execution stops and infinite when the execution does not terminate. In the *prefix trace semantics* $\mathcal{S}^{*}[\![\texttt{S}]\!]$, the observation of the future computation is finite and can stop at any time during the execution (in particular just at the program entry). For example, program S in (1) has the following two pairs of traces in its prefix trace semantics.

$$\langle \ell_0 \xrightarrow{\texttt{x = 0} = 0} \ell_1,\ \ell_1\rangle \in \mathcal{S}^{*}[\![\texttt{S}]\!] \qquad \langle \ell_0 \xrightarrow{\texttt{x = 1} = 1} \ell_1,\ \ell_1 \xrightarrow{\texttt{x = x + 1} = 2} \ell_2\rangle \in \mathcal{S}^{*}[\![\texttt{S}]\!]$$

It follows from this discussion that the prefix trace semantics is a relation between finite traces $\mathcal{S}^{*}[\![\texttt{S}]\!] \in \wp(\mathbb{T}^{+} \times \mathbb{T}^{+})$ while the maximal trace semantics is a relation between finite traces and finite or infinite traces $\mathcal{S}^{+\infty}[\![\texttt{S}]\!] \in \wp(\mathbb{T}^{+} \times \mathbb{T}^{+\infty})$.

2.4 Formal definition of the prefix trace semantics

The prefix trace semantics is defined in fixpoint form by structural induction on the syntax of program components.

- A prefix future trace of an assignment S ::= ℓ x = A ; (where at⟦S⟧ = ℓ) continuing some past trace $\pi\ell$ either stops at ℓ or is ℓ followed by the event x = A = v where $v \in \mathbb{V}$ is the value assigned to x (that is the value of the arithmetic expression A evaluated on $\pi\ell$) and finishing at the label aft⟦S⟧ after the assignment.

$$\mathcal{S}^{*}[\![\texttt{S}]\!] \triangleq \{\langle \pi\ell,\ \ell\rangle, \langle \pi\ell,\ \ell \xrightarrow{\texttt{x = A} = v} \mathsf{aft}[\![\texttt{S}]\!]\rangle \mid \pi\ell \in \mathbb{T}^{+} \wedge v = \mathcal{A}[\![\texttt{A}]\!]\varrho(\pi\ell)\} \tag{3}$$

We often write $\ell \xrightarrow{\texttt{x} = v} \ell'$ for $\ell \xrightarrow{\texttt{x = A} = v} \ell'$ (since ℓ x = A ; can be recovered from the program text and the unique program label ℓ). The value of an arithmetic expression A in environment $\rho \in \mathbb{E}\mathbb{v} \triangleq V \to \mathbb{V}$ is $\mathcal{A}[\![\texttt{A}]\!]\rho \in \mathbb{V}$:

$$\mathcal{A}[\![\texttt{1}]\!]\rho \triangleq 1 \qquad \mathcal{A}[\![\texttt{x}]\!]\rho \triangleq \rho(\texttt{x}) \qquad \mathcal{A}[\![\texttt{A}_1 - \texttt{A}_2]\!]\rho \triangleq \mathcal{A}[\![\texttt{A}_1]\!]\rho - \mathcal{A}[\![\texttt{A}_2]\!]\rho \tag{4}$$

- A prefix trace of a break statement S ::= ℓ **break ;** continuing some initial trace $\pi\ell$ either stops at ℓ or is the trace ℓ followed by the **break ;** event and ending at the break label brk-to⟦S⟧ (which is defined as the exit label of the closest enclosing iteration).

$$\mathcal{S}^{*}[\![\texttt{S}]\!] \triangleq \{\langle \pi\ell,\ \ell\rangle, \langle \pi\ell,\ \ell \xrightarrow{\textbf{break}} \mathsf{brk\text{-}to}[\![\texttt{S}]\!]\rangle \mid \pi\ell \in \mathbb{T}^{+}\} \tag{5}$$

- A prefix trace of a conditional statement S ::= **if** ℓ **(B)** $\texttt{S}_t$ continuing some initial trace $\pi_1\ell$ is

- either ℓ when the observation of the execution stops on entry of the program component;
- or, when the value of the boolean expression B on $\pi_1\ell$ is ff, ℓ followed by the event ¬(B) and finishing at the label aft⟦S⟧ after the conditional statement;
- or finally, when the value of the boolean expression B on $\pi_1\ell$ is tt, ℓ followed by the test event B followed by a prefix trace of S_t continuing $\pi_1\ell \xrightarrow{\texttt{B}} \mathsf{at}[\![S_t]\!]$.

$$
\begin{aligned}
\mathcal{S}^*[\![S]\!] &\triangleq \{\langle \pi_1\ell, \ell\rangle \mid \pi_1\ell \in \mathbb{T}^+\} && (6)\\
&\cup \{\langle \pi_1\ell, \ell \xrightarrow{\neg(\texttt{B})} \mathsf{aft}[\![S]\!]\rangle \mid \mathcal{B}[\![B]\!]\varrho(\pi_1\ell) = \mathrm{ff} \wedge \pi_1\ell \in \mathbb{T}^+\}\\
&\cup \{\langle \pi_1\ell, \ell \xrightarrow{\texttt{B}} \mathsf{at}[\![S_t]\!] \mathbin{\hat{}} \pi_2\rangle \mid \mathcal{B}[\![B]\!]\varrho(\pi_1\ell) = \mathrm{tt} \wedge \langle \pi_1\ell \xrightarrow{\texttt{B}} \mathsf{at}[\![S_t]\!], \pi_2\rangle \in \mathcal{S}^*[\![S_t]\!]\}
\end{aligned}
$$

Notice that if π_2 starting at⟦S_t⟧ is a maximal trace of S_t terminating aft⟦S_t⟧ then $\ell \xrightarrow{\texttt{B}} \mathsf{at}[\![S_t]\!] \mathbin{\hat{}} \pi_2$ is also a maximal trace of S terminating aft⟦S⟧ since aft⟦S_t⟧ = aft⟦S⟧.

Observe also that definition (6) includes the case of a conditional within an iteration and containing a break statement in the true branch S_t. Since brk-to⟦S⟧ = brk-to⟦S_t⟧, from $\langle \pi_1\ell \xrightarrow{\texttt{B}} \mathsf{at}[\![S_t]\!], \pi_2 \xrightarrow{\texttt{break}} \textsf{brk-to}[\![S_t]\!]\rangle \in \mathcal{S}^*[\![S_t]\!]$, we infer that $\langle \pi_1\ell, \ell \xrightarrow{\texttt{B}} \mathsf{at}[\![S_t]\!] \mathbin{\hat{}} \pi_2 \xrightarrow{\texttt{break}} \textsf{brk-to}[\![S]\!]\rangle \in \mathcal{S}^*[\![S]\!]$.

- A prefix trace π of the empty statement list Sl ::= ϵ is reduced to the program label at that empty statement.

$$
\mathcal{S}^*[\![Sl]\!] \triangleq \{\langle \pi\mathsf{at}[\![Sl]\!], \mathsf{at}[\![Sl]\!]\rangle \mid \pi\mathsf{at}[\![Sl]\!] \in \mathbb{T}^+\} \qquad (7)
$$

- A prefix trace of a statement list Sl ::= Sl′ S continuing an initial trace π_1 can be a prefix trace of Sl′ or a finite maximal trace of Sl′ followed by a prefix trace of S.

$$
\begin{aligned}
\mathcal{S}^*[\![Sl]\!] &\triangleq \mathcal{S}^*[\![Sl']\!] && (8)\\
&\cup \{\langle \pi_1, \pi_2 \mathbin{\hat{}} \pi_3\rangle \in \mathcal{S}^*[\![Sl]\!] \mid \langle \pi_1, \pi_2\rangle \in \mathcal{S}^*[\![Sl']\!] \wedge \langle \pi_1 \mathbin{\hat{}} \pi_2, \pi_3\rangle \in \mathcal{S}^*[\![S]\!]\}
\end{aligned}
$$

Notice that if $\langle \pi_1 \mathbin{\hat{}} \pi_2, \pi_3\rangle \in \mathcal{S}^*[\![S]\!]$ then trace π_3 starts at⟦S⟧ = aft⟦Sl′⟧ so the trace π_2 in $\langle \pi_1, \pi_2\rangle \in \mathcal{S}^*[\![Sl']\!]$ must end aft⟦Sl′⟧. Therefore π_2 must be a maximal terminating execution of Sl′ *i.e.* S is executed only if Sl′ terminates.

- The prefix finite trace semantic definition $\mathcal{S}^*[\![S]\!]$ (9) of an iteration statement of the form S ::= **while** ℓ (B) S_b is the ⊆-least solution $\mathsf{lfp}^{\subseteq}\,\mathcal{F}^*[\![S]\!]$ to the equation $X = \mathcal{F}^*[\![S]\!](X)$. Since $\mathcal{F}^*[\![S]\!] \in \wp(\mathbb{T}^+ \times \mathbb{T}^+) \to \wp(\mathbb{T}^+ \times \mathbb{T}^+)$ is ⊆- monotone (if $X \subseteq X'$ then $\mathcal{F}^*[\![S]\!](X) \subseteq \mathcal{F}^*[\![S]\!](X')$ and $\langle \wp(\mathbb{T}^+ \times \mathbb{T}^+), \subseteq, \emptyset, \mathbb{T}^+ \times \mathbb{T}^+, \cup, \cap\rangle$ is a complete lattice, $\mathsf{lfp}^{\subseteq}\,\mathcal{F}^*[\![S]\!]$ exists by Tarski's fixpoint theorem [30] and can be defined as the limit of iterates [11], which is useful to abstract into iterative static analysis algorithms. In definition (9) of the transformer $\mathcal{F}^*[\![S]\!]$, case (9.a) corresponds to a loop execution observation stopping on entry, (9.b) corresponds to an observation of a loop exiting after 0 or more iterations, and (9.c) corresponds to a loop execution observation that stops anywhere in the body S_b after 0 or more iterations. This last case covers the case of an iteration terminated by a break statement (to aft⟦S⟧ after the iteration statement).

$$\mathcal{S}^*[\![\mathsf{S}]\!] = \mathsf{lfp}^{\subseteq}\, \mathcal{F}^*[\![\mathsf{S}]\!] \tag{9}$$

$$\mathcal{F}^*[\![\mathtt{while}\ \ell\ \mathtt{(B)}\ \mathtt{S}_b]\!](X) \triangleq \{\langle \pi_1\ell',\ \ell'\rangle \mid \pi_1\ell' \in \mathbb{T}^+ \wedge \ell' = \ell\}\ ^2 \tag{a}$$

$$\cup\, \{\langle \pi_1\ell',\ \ell'\pi_2\ell' \xrightarrow{\neg(\mathtt{B})} \mathsf{aft}[\![\mathsf{S}]\!]\rangle \mid \langle \pi_1\ell',\ \ell'\pi_2\ell'\rangle \in X \wedge \mathcal{B}[\![\mathtt{B}]\!]\varrho(\pi_1\ell'\pi_2\ell') = \mathsf{ff} \wedge \ell' = \ell\} \tag{b}$$

$$\cup\, \{\langle \pi_1\ell',\ \ell'\pi_2\ell' \xrightarrow{\mathtt{B}} \mathsf{at}[\![\mathtt{S}_b]\!] \frown \pi_3\rangle \mid \langle \pi_1\ell',\ \ell'\pi_2\ell'\rangle \in X \wedge \mathcal{B}[\![\mathtt{B}]\!]\varrho(\pi_1\ell'\pi_2\ell') = \mathsf{tt} \wedge \langle \pi_1\ell'\pi_2\ell' \xrightarrow{\mathtt{B}} \mathsf{at}[\![\mathtt{S}_b]\!],\ \pi_3\rangle \in \mathcal{S}^*[\![\mathtt{S}_b]\!] \wedge \ell' = \ell\} \tag{c}$$

- The prefix trace semantics of the other program components is similar. It follows that for each program component S, we have

$$\{\langle \pi_1\mathsf{at}[\![\mathsf{S}]\!],\ \mathsf{at}[\![\mathsf{S}]\!]\rangle \mid \pi_1\mathsf{at}[\![\mathsf{S}]\!] \in \mathbb{T}^+\} \subseteq \mathcal{S}^*[\![\mathsf{S}]\!] \tag{10}$$

2.5 Definition of the maximal trace semantics

The maximal trace semantics $\mathcal{S}^{+\infty}[\![\mathsf{S}]\!] = \mathcal{S}^{+}[\![\mathsf{S}]\!] \cup \mathcal{S}^{\infty}[\![\mathsf{S}]\!]$ is derived from the prefix trace semantics $\mathcal{S}^*[\![\mathsf{S}]\!]$ by keeping the longest finite traces $\mathcal{S}^{+}[\![\mathsf{S}]\!]$ and passing to the limit $\mathcal{S}^{\infty}[\![\mathsf{S}]\!]$ of prefix-closed traces for infinite traces.

$$\mathcal{S}^{+}[\![\mathsf{S}]\!] \triangleq \{\langle \pi_1,\ \pi_2\ell\rangle \in \mathcal{S}^*[\![\mathsf{S}]\!] \mid (\ell = \mathsf{aft}[\![\mathsf{S}]\!]) \vee (\mathsf{esc}[\![\mathsf{S}]\!] \wedge \ell = \mathsf{brk\text{-}to}[\![\mathsf{S}]\!])\} \tag{11}$$

$$\mathcal{S}^{\infty}[\![\mathsf{S}]\!] \triangleq \lim(\mathcal{S}^*[\![\mathsf{S}]\!]) \tag{12}$$

where the limit is $\lim \mathcal{T} \triangleq \{\langle \pi,\ \pi'\rangle \mid \pi' \in \mathbb{T}^{\infty} \wedge \forall n \in \mathbb{N}\ .\ \langle \pi,\ \pi'[0..n]\rangle \in \mathcal{T}\}$. (13)

The intuition for (13) is the following. Let S be an iteration. $\langle \pi,\ \pi'\rangle \in \mathcal{S}^{\infty}[\![\mathsf{S}]\!] = \lim \mathcal{S}^*[\![\mathsf{S}]\!]$ where π' is infinite if and only if, whenever we take a prefix $\pi'[0..n]$ of π', it is a possible finite observation of the execution of S and so belongs to the prefix trace semantics $\langle \pi,\ \pi'[0..n]\rangle \in \mathcal{S}^*[\![\mathsf{S}]\!]$.

3 The semantic and syntactic liveness/deadness abstractions

3.1 The generic liveness/deadness abstractions

Informally "a variable is (potentially/definitely) live at some point if it holds a value that may/must be used in the future before the next time the variable is modified". The liveness abstraction $\alpha^{l}_{use,mod}[\![\mathsf{S}]\!]\ L_b, L_e\ \langle \pi_0,\ \pi\rangle$ of a program trace π continuing an initial trace π_0 of a program component S is parameterized by

[2] A definition of the form $d(\vec{x}) \triangleq \{f(\vec{x}') \mid P(\vec{x}', \vec{x})\}$ has the variables $\vec{x}'$ in $P(\vec{x}', \vec{x})$ bound to those of $f(\vec{x}')$ whereas $\vec{x}$ is free in $P(\vec{x}', \vec{x})$ since it appears neither in $f(\vec{x}')$ nor (by assumption) under quantifiers in $P(\vec{x}', \vec{x})$. The $\vec{x}$ of $P(\vec{x}', \vec{x})$ is therefore bound to the $\vec{x}$ of $d(\vec{x})$.

- *use* defining the set $use[\![a]\!]\rho$ of variables which value is used when executing action a in environment ρ;
- *mod* defining the set $mod[\![a]\!]\rho$ of variables which value is modified when executing action a in environment ρ.

Liveness depends on the set L_b of variables assumed to be live on exit of the program component S by a break statement and L_e by a normal exit after S. It is defined inductively on a finite trace (or co-inductively for an infinite trace) as follows

$$\alpha^l_{use,mod}[\![\mathtt{S}]\!]\ L_b, L_e\ \langle\pi_0,\ \ell\rangle \triangleq \{\mathtt{x} \in \mathbb{V} \mid (\ell = \mathsf{aft}[\![\mathtt{S}]\!] \wedge \mathtt{x} \in L_e) \vee (\mathsf{esc}[\![\mathtt{S}]\!] \wedge \ell = \mathsf{brk\text{-}to}[\![\mathtt{S}]\!] \wedge \mathtt{x} \in L_b)\} \quad \text{(a)} \quad (14)$$

$$\alpha^l_{use,mod}[\![\mathtt{S}]\!]\ L_b, L_e\ \langle\pi_0,\ \ell \xrightarrow{a} \ell'\pi_1\rangle \triangleq \{\mathtt{x} \in \mathbb{V} \mid \mathtt{x} \in use[\![a]\!]\varrho(\pi_0) \vee (\mathtt{x} \notin mod[\![a]\!]\varrho(\pi_0) \wedge \mathtt{x} \in \alpha^l_{use,mod}[\![\mathtt{S}]\!]\ L_b, L_e\ \langle\pi_0 \mathbin{\hat{\ }} \ell \xrightarrow{a} \ell',\ \ell'\pi_1\rangle)\} \quad \text{(b)}$$

The potential and definite liveness are abstractions of the maximal trace semantics $\mathcal{S} = \mathcal{S}^{+\infty}[\![\mathtt{S}]\!]$ is by merge over all traces

$$\alpha^{\exists l}_{use,mod}[\![\mathtt{S}]\!]\ \mathcal{S}\ L_b, L_e = \bigcup_{\langle\pi_0,\ \pi\rangle \in \mathcal{S}} \alpha^l_{use,mod}[\![\mathtt{S}]\!]\ L_b, L_e\ \langle\pi_0,\ \pi\rangle \qquad \text{potential liveness} \quad (15)$$

$$\alpha^{\forall l}_{use,mod}[\![\mathtt{S}]\!]\ \mathcal{S}\ L_b, L_e = \bigcap_{\langle\pi_0,\ \pi\rangle \in \mathcal{S}} \alpha^l_{use,mod}[\![\mathtt{S}]\!]\ L_b, L_e\ \langle\pi_0,\ \pi\rangle \qquad \text{definite liveness} \quad (16)$$

Potential and definite deadness are defined dually.

$$\alpha^{\exists d}_{use,mod}[\![\mathtt{S}]\!]\ \mathcal{S}\ D_b, D_e = \neg\alpha^{\forall l}_{use,mod}[\![\mathtt{S}]\!]\ \mathcal{S}\ \neg D_b, \neg D_e \qquad \text{potential deadness} \quad (17)$$

$$\alpha^{\forall d}_{use,mod}[\![\mathtt{S}]\!]\ \mathcal{S}\ D_b, D_e = \neg\alpha^{\exists l}_{use,mod}[\![\mathtt{S}]\!]\ \mathcal{S}\ \neg D_b, \neg D_e \qquad \text{definite deadness} \quad (18)$$

If S and S′ have the same aft, esc, and brk-to labelling, they have the same $\alpha^l_{use,mod}$, $\alpha^{\exists l}_{use,mod}$, $\alpha^{\forall l}_{use,mod}$, $\alpha^{\exists d}_{use,mod}$, and $\alpha^{\exists l}_{use,mod}$.

Unfolding the recursive definition (14) , we get

Lemma 1 *If* $\pi_1 = \ell_1 \xrightarrow{a_1} \ell_2 \xrightarrow{a_2} \ldots \xrightarrow{a_{n-1}} \ell_n$ *and* $\langle\pi_0,\ \pi_1\rangle \in \mathcal{S}^*[\![\mathtt{S}]\!]$ *then*

$$\alpha^l_{use,mod}[\![\mathtt{S}]\!]\ L_b, L_e\ \langle\pi_0,\ \pi_1\rangle = \{\mathtt{x} \in \mathbb{V} \mid \exists i \in [1, n-1]\ .\ \forall j \in [1, i-1]\ .\ \mathtt{x} \notin mod[\![a_j]\!]\varrho(\pi_0 \mathbin{\hat{\ }} \ell_1 \xrightarrow{a_1} \ell_2 \ldots \xrightarrow{a_{j-1}} \ell_j) \wedge \mathtt{x} \in use[\![a_i]\!]\varrho(\pi_0 \mathbin{\hat{\ }} \ell_1 \xrightarrow{a_1} \ell_2 \ldots \xrightarrow{a_{i-1}} \ell_i)\} \cup (\!|\ \ell_n = \mathsf{aft}[\![\mathtt{S}]\!]\ ?\ L_e \mathbin{⸗} \varnothing\ |\!) \cup (\!|\ \mathsf{esc}[\![\mathtt{S}]\!] \wedge \ell_n = \mathsf{brk\text{-}to}[\![\mathtt{S}]\!]\ ?\ L_b \mathbin{⸗} \varnothing\ |\!). \quad \square$$

Proof (of Lem. 1) For the basis $n = 1$, only the first clause (a) of (14) is applicable with $\pi_1 = \ell_1$, $[1, n-1]$ is empty, and $\alpha^l_{use,mod}[\![\mathtt{S}]\!]\ L_b, L_e\ \langle\pi_0,\ \pi_1\rangle = (\!|\ \ell_1 = \mathsf{aft}[\![\mathtt{S}]\!]\ ?\ L_e \mathbin{⸗} \varnothing\ |\!) \cup (\!|\ \mathsf{esc}[\![\mathtt{S}]\!] \wedge \ell_1 = \mathsf{brk\text{-}to}[\![\mathtt{S}]\!]\ ?\ L_b \mathbin{⸗} \varnothing\ |\!)$ which is precisely what is given by Lem. 1 since $[1, n-1] = \varnothing$ so the first term is empty.

For the induction step $n+1 > 1$, we have $\pi_1 = \ell_1 \xrightarrow{a_1} \ell_2 \xrightarrow{a_2} \ell_3 \xrightarrow{a_3} \ldots \xrightarrow{a_n} \ell_{n+1}$ and only the second clause (b) of (14) is applicable so we get

$\alpha^{l}_{use,mod}[\![\mathsf{S}]\!]\ L_b, L_e\ \langle \pi_0,\ \pi_1 \rangle$ $\quad$ (assuming $n + 1 \geqslant 2$)

$= \{\mathsf{x} \in \mathbb{V} \mid \mathsf{x} \in use[\![a_1]\!]\varrho(\pi_0) \vee (\mathsf{x} \notin mod[\![a_1]\!]\varrho(\pi_0)) \wedge \mathsf{x} \in \alpha^{l}_{use,mod}[\![\mathsf{S}]\!]\ L_b, L_e\ \langle \pi_0 \mathbin{\hat{}}\ \ell_1 \xrightarrow{a_1} \ell_2,\ \ell_2 \xrightarrow{a_2} \ell_3 \xrightarrow{a_3} \ldots \xrightarrow{a_n} \ell_{n+1} \rangle)\}$ $\quad$ ((14.b) when $n > 1$)

$= \{(\mathsf{x} \in \mathbb{V} \mid \mathsf{x} \in use[\![a_1]\!]\varrho(\pi_0)) \vee (\mathsf{x} \notin mod[\![a_1]\!]\varrho(\pi_0) \wedge \exists i \in [2, n]\ .\ \forall j \in [2, i-1]\ .\ \mathsf{x} \notin mod[\![a_j]\!]\varrho(\pi_0 \mathbin{\hat{}} \ell_1 \xrightarrow{a_1} \ell_2 \ldots \xrightarrow{a_{j-1}} \ell_j) \wedge \mathsf{x} \in use[\![a_i]\!]\varrho(\pi_0 \mathbin{\hat{}} \ell_1 \xrightarrow{a_1} \ell_2 \ldots \xrightarrow{a_{i-1}} \ell_i)) \vee (\!| \ell_{n+1} = \mathsf{aft}[\![\mathsf{S}]\!]\ ?\ \mathsf{x} \in L_e : \mathsf{ff} |\!) \vee (\!| \mathsf{esc}[\![\mathsf{S}]\!] \wedge \ell_{n+1} = \mathsf{brk\text{-}to}[\![\mathsf{S}]\!]\ ?\ \mathsf{x} \in L_b : \mathsf{ff} |\!)\}$

(since $\alpha^{l}_{use,mod}[\![\mathsf{S}]\!]\ L_b, L_e\ \langle \pi_0 \mathbin{\hat{}} \ell_1 \xrightarrow{a_1},\ \ell_2 \xrightarrow{a_2} \ldots \xrightarrow{a_n} \ell_{n+1} \rangle = \{\mathsf{x} \in \mathbb{V} \mid \exists i \in [2, n]\ .\ \forall j \in [2, i-1]\ .\ \mathsf{x} \notin mod[\![a_j]\!]\varrho(\pi_0 \mathbin{\hat{}} \ell_1 \xrightarrow{a_1} \ell_2 \ldots \xrightarrow{a_{j-1}} \ell_j) \wedge \mathsf{x} \in use[\![a_i]\!]\varrho(\pi_0 \mathbin{\hat{}} \ell_1 \xrightarrow{a_1} \ell_2 \ldots \xrightarrow{a_{i-1}} \ell_i)\} \cup (\!| \ell_{n+1} = \mathsf{aft}[\![\mathsf{S}]\!]\ ?\ L_e : \varnothing |\!) \cup (\!| \mathsf{esc}[\![\mathsf{S}]\!] \wedge \ell_{n+1} = \mathsf{brk\text{-}to}[\![\mathsf{S}]\!]\ ?\ L_b : \varnothing |\!)$ by ind. hyp. for Lem. 1)

$= \{\mathsf{x} \in \mathbb{V} \mid \exists i \in [1, n]\ .\ \forall j \in [1, i-1]\ .\ \mathsf{x} \notin mod[\![a_j]\!]\varrho(\pi_0 \mathbin{\hat{}} \ell_1 \xrightarrow{a_1} \ell_2 \ldots \xrightarrow{a_{j-1}} \ell_j) \wedge \mathsf{x} \in use[\![a_i]\!]\varrho(\pi_0 \mathbin{\hat{}} \ell_1 \xrightarrow{a_1} \ell_2 \ldots \xrightarrow{a_{i-1}} \ell_i)\} \cup (\!| \ell_{n+1} = \mathsf{aft}[\![\mathsf{S}]\!]\ ?\ L_e : \varnothing |\!) \cup (\!| \mathsf{esc}[\![\mathsf{S}]\!] \wedge \ell_{n+1} = \mathsf{brk\text{-}to}[\![\mathsf{S}]\!]\ ?\ L_b : \varnothing |\!)$

(incorporating $(\mathsf{x} \in \mathbb{V} \mid \mathsf{x} \in use[\![a_1]\!]\varrho(\pi_0))$ in the case $i = 1$ for which $[1, i-1] = \varnothing$ and $\varrho(\pi_0 \mathbin{\hat{}} \ell_1 \xrightarrow{a_1} \ell_2 \ldots \xrightarrow{a_{i-1}} \ell_i) = \varrho(\pi_0 \mathbin{\hat{}} \ell_1) = \varrho(\pi_0)$.)

This proves Lem. 1 for the induction step and we conclude by recurrence on n. ☐

We also observe that potential liveness (hence dually definite deadness) can be equivalently defined using maximal or prefix traces.

Lemma 2 $\alpha^{\exists l}_{use,mod}[\![\mathsf{S}]\!]\ (\mathcal{S}^{+\infty}[\![\mathsf{S}]\!]) = \alpha^{\exists l}_{use,mod}[\![\mathsf{S}]\!]\ (\mathcal{S}^{*}[\![\mathsf{S}]\!])$. ☐

Proof of Lem. 2. To show that $\alpha^{\exists l}_{use,mod}[\![\mathsf{S}]\!]\ (\mathcal{S}^{+\infty}[\![\mathsf{S}]\!]) = \alpha^{\exists l}_{use,mod}[\![\mathsf{S}]\!]\ (\mathcal{S}^{*}[\![\mathsf{S}]\!])$ we must, by (15), prove that

$$A = \bigcup_{\langle \pi_0,\ \pi \rangle \in \mathcal{S}^{+\infty}[\![\mathsf{S}]\!]} \alpha^{l}_{use,mod}[\![\mathsf{S}]\!]\ L_b, L_e \langle \pi_0,\ \pi \rangle = \bigcup_{\langle \pi_0,\ \pi' \rangle \in \mathcal{S}^{*}[\![\mathsf{S}]\!]} \alpha^{l}_{use,mod}[\![\mathsf{S}]\!]\ L_b, L_e \langle \pi_0,\ \pi' \rangle = B.$$

- Assume $\mathsf{x} \in A$ because of some $\langle \pi_0,\ \pi \rangle \in \mathcal{S}^{+\infty}[\![\mathsf{S}]\!]$. There are two cases.
  - Either $\mathsf{x} \in A$ follows from (14.a) and so the second alternative in (14.b) has always been chosen before reaching the end of the trace π with a label $\ell = \mathsf{aft}[\![\mathsf{S}]\!]$ or $\mathsf{esc}[\![\mathsf{S}]\!] = \mathsf{tt}$ and $\ell = \mathsf{brk\text{-}to}[\![\mathsf{S}]\!]$. In both cases, π is maximal by (11), $\langle \pi_0,\ \pi \rangle \in \mathcal{S}^{*}[\![\mathsf{S}]\!]$, and so $\mathsf{x} \in B$ by (14).
  - Otherwise, $\mathsf{x} \in A$ follows from (14.b) where the second alternative has been chosen finitely many times (so x is unmodified) until the first alternative is chosen because x is used. Consider the prefix of π up to that point of use. By (13), it is, or an extension of it, π' is in the prefix semantics $\langle \pi_0,\ \pi' \rangle \in \mathcal{S}^{*}[\![\mathsf{S}]\!]$ and so from this trace we derive from (14.b) that $\mathsf{x} \in B$.

It follows that $A \subseteq B$.

- Conversely, assume $\mathsf{x} \in B$. Then there exists $\langle \pi_0, \pi' \rangle \in \mathcal{S}^*[\![\mathsf{S}]\!]$ such that $\mathsf{x} \in \alpha^l_{use,mod}[\![\mathsf{S}]\!]\ L_b, L_e\ \langle \pi_0, \pi' \rangle$. Consider a maximal extension of π' so that there exists π'' with $\langle \pi_0, \pi' \cdot \pi'' \rangle \in \mathcal{S}^{+\infty}[\![\mathsf{S}]\!]$. There are two cases, depending of whether $\mathsf{x} \in B$ in (14.a) or (14.b).
  - If $\mathsf{x} \in B$ because of (14.a) then the π' ends at $\mathsf{aft}[\![\mathsf{S}]\!]$ or at $\mathsf{brk\text{-}to}[\![\mathsf{S}]\!]$ and so π' is maximal that is $\langle \pi_0, \pi' \rangle \in \mathcal{S}^{+\infty}[\![\mathsf{S}]\!]$ and so $\mathsf{x} \in A$.
  - If $\mathsf{x} \in B$ because of (14.b) then $\mathsf{x} \in B$ is used in π' without being modified before and so this is also the case in $\langle \pi_0, \pi' \cdot \pi'' \rangle \in \mathcal{S}^{+\infty}[\![\mathsf{S}]\!]$, $\pi'' = \ni$, and then $\mathsf{x} \in A$ by (14).

  In both cases, $B \subseteq A$.
- By antisymmetry, $A = B$. □

3.2 The semantic liveness/deadness abstractions

Semantically, an action a uses variable y in a given environment ρ if and only if it is possible to change the value of y so as to change the effect of action a on program execution. For an assignment, the assigned value will be changed. For a test, which has no side effect, the branch taken will be different. For example, $\mathsf{y} \notin \mathsf{use}[\![\mathsf{x = y - y}]\!]\,\rho$ and $\mathsf{x} \notin \mathsf{use}[\![\mathsf{x = x}]\!]\,\rho$. Formally,

$$\begin{aligned} \mathsf{use}[\![\mathsf{skip}]\!]\,\rho &\triangleq \emptyset \\ \mathsf{use}[\![\mathsf{x = A}]\!]\,\rho &\triangleq \{\mathsf{y} \mid \exists v \in \mathbb{V}\,.\, \mathcal{A}[\![\mathsf{A}]\!]\,\rho \neq \mathcal{A}[\![\mathsf{A}]\!]\,\rho[\mathsf{y} \leftarrow v] \wedge \rho(\mathsf{x}) \neq \mathcal{A}[\![\mathsf{A}]\!]\,\rho\} \\ \mathsf{use}[\![a]\!]\,\rho &\triangleq \{\mathsf{y} \mid \exists v \in \mathbb{V}\,.\, \mathcal{B}[\![a]\!]\,\rho \neq \mathcal{B}[\![a]\!]\,\rho[\mathsf{y} \leftarrow v]\} \qquad a \in \{\mathsf{B}, \neg(\mathsf{B})\} \end{aligned} \tag{19}$$

Notice that $\mathsf{x} \in \mathsf{use}[\![a]\!]$ in (19) compares two executions of action a in different environments so that (14) is a dependency analysis involving a trace and the abstraction of another one by a different environment [10]. An action a modifies variable x in an environment ρ if and only the execution of action a in environment ρ changes the value of x. This corresponds to

$$\mathsf{mod}[\![a]\!]\,\rho \triangleq \{\mathsf{x} \mid a = (\mathsf{x = A}) \wedge (\rho(\mathsf{x}) \neq \mathcal{A}[\![\mathsf{A}]\!]\,\rho)\}$$

So the semantic potential liveness abstract semantics is

$$\mathcal{S}^{\exists l}[\![\mathsf{S}]\!] \triangleq \alpha^{\exists l}_{\mathsf{use,mod}}[\![\mathsf{S}]\!]\ (\mathcal{S}^{+\infty}[\![\mathsf{S}]\!]) \tag{20}$$

instantiating (15) with *use* as use and *mod* as mod (and similarly for the other cases).

3.3 The classical syntactic liveness/deadness abstractions

Classical dataflow analysis as considered in [25] is purely syntactic *i.e.* approximates semantic properties by coarser syntactic ones based on the program syntax only. The set $\mathbb{use}[\![a]\!]$ of variables used and the set $\mathbb{mod}[\![a]\!]$ of variables assigned to/modified in an action $a \in \mathbb{A}$ are postulated to be as follows (the parameter ρ is useless but added for consistency with (14)).

$$\mathbb{use}[\![\mathsf{x} = \mathsf{A}]\!]\,\rho \triangleq \mathbb{vars}[\![\mathsf{A}]\!] \quad \mathbb{use}[\![\mathsf{skip}]\!]\,\rho \triangleq \varnothing \quad \mathbb{use}[\![\mathsf{B}]\!]\,\rho \triangleq \mathbb{use}[\![\neg(\mathsf{B})]\!]\,\rho \triangleq \mathbb{vars}[\![\mathsf{B}]\!]$$
$$\mathbb{mod}[\![\mathsf{x} = \mathsf{A}]\!]\,\rho \triangleq \{\mathsf{x}\} \quad \mathbb{mod}[\![\mathsf{skip}]\!]\,\rho \triangleq \varnothing \quad \mathbb{mod}[\![\mathsf{B}]\!]\,\rho \triangleq \mathbb{mod}[\![\neg(\mathsf{B})]\!]\,\rho \triangleq \varnothing \qquad (21)$$

where $\mathbb{vars}[\![\mathsf{E}]\!]$ is the set of program variables occurring in arithmetic or boolean expression E.

So the classical syntactic potential liveness abstract semantics is

$$\mathcal{S}^{\exists \mathbb{l}}[\![\mathsf{S}]\!] \triangleq \alpha^{\exists l}_{\mathbb{use},\mathbb{mod}}[\![\mathsf{S}]\!]\ (\mathcal{S}^{+\infty}[\![\mathsf{S}]\!]) \qquad (22)$$

instantiating (15) with *use* as $\mathbb{use}$ and *mod* as $\mathbb{mod}$ (and similarly for the other cases).

3.4 Unsoundness of the syntactic liveness/deadness abstractions

One would expect soundness that is the potentially live variables determined syntactically by [25] is a pointwise over-approximation of the potentially live variables determined semantically but this is wrong $\mathcal{S}^{\exists l}[\![\mathsf{S}]\!] \not\dot{\subseteq} \mathcal{S}^{\exists \mathbb{l}}[\![\mathsf{S}]\!]$, as shown by Ex. 2. The problem is that

$$\exists \rho \in \mathbb{E}\mathbb{v}\ .\ \mathsf{y} \in \mathsf{use}[\![a]\!]\,\rho \Rightarrow \forall \rho \in \mathbb{E}\mathbb{v}\ .\ \mathsf{y} \in \mathbb{use}[\![a]\!]\,\rho \qquad (23)$$

but in general, as shown by Ex. 2, $\exists \rho \in \mathbb{E}\mathbb{v}\ .\ \mathsf{x} \in \mathbb{mod}[\![a]\!]\,\rho \wedge \mathsf{x} \notin \mathsf{mod}[\![a]\!]\,\rho$.

Proof of (23). Let us first remark that if $\mathsf{x} \notin \mathbb{vars}[\![\mathsf{B}]\!]$ and $\forall \mathsf{y} \in \mathbb{V} \setminus \{\mathsf{x}\}\ .\ \rho'(\mathsf{y}) = \rho(\mathsf{y})$ then $\mathcal{B}[\![\mathsf{B}]\!]\rho = \mathcal{B}[\![\mathsf{B}]\!]\rho'$ and similarly for arithmetic expressions.

(23) is trivial for skip since $\mathsf{use}[\![\mathsf{skip}]\!]\,\rho\ \mathsf{y} = \mathsf{ff}$ in (19). Otherwise, by contraposition, assume that $\mathsf{y} \notin \mathbb{use}[\![a]\!]\rho$.

— If $a = \mathsf{x} = \mathsf{A}$ then $\mathsf{y} \notin \mathbb{vars}[\![\mathsf{A}]\!]$ by (21) so $\forall \nu \in \mathbb{V}\ .\ \mathcal{A}[\![\mathsf{A}]\!]\,\rho = \mathcal{A}[\![\mathsf{A}]\!]\,\rho[\mathsf{y} \leftarrow \nu]$, proving $\neg(\mathsf{use}[\![\mathsf{x} = \mathsf{A}]\!]\,\rho\ \mathsf{y})$ by (19).

— Similarly if $a = \mathsf{B}$ or $a = \neg(\mathsf{B})$ then changing y does not change the value of the boolean expression so y is not semantically used by (19). □

3.5 Soundness of the syntactic liveness/deadness abstractions with respect to revised syntactic/semantic liveness/deadness abstractions

To fix the problem $\mathcal{S}^{\exists l}[\![\mathsf{S}]\!] \not\dot{\subseteq} \mathcal{S}^{\exists \mathbb{l}}[\![\mathsf{S}]\!]$, we can either change $\alpha^{\exists l}_{\mathsf{use},\mathsf{mod}}$ or $\alpha^{\exists l}_{\mathbb{use},\mathbb{mod}}$. Changing $\alpha^{\exists l}_{\mathbb{use},\mathbb{mod}}$ would mean changing the classical potential live variable algorithm [20,19,21] and all compilers using it. So we change $\alpha^{\exists l}_{\mathsf{use},\mathsf{mod}}$ so as to explain exactly in what sense the unchanged classical potential live variable algorithm is sound (even if this is not the most semantically intuitive one). We remark that we have $\alpha^{\exists l}_{\mathsf{use},\mathbb{mod}} \dot{\subseteq} \alpha^{\exists l}_{\mathbb{use},\mathbb{mod}}$ so the classical potential live variable algorithm $\mathcal{S}^{\exists \mathbb{l}}[\![\mathsf{S}]\!]$ which over-approximates $\alpha^{\exists l}_{\mathbb{use},\mathbb{mod}}[\![\mathsf{S}]\!]\ (\mathcal{S}^{+\infty}[\![\mathsf{S}]\!])$ is sound. However, the program transformations that preserve mod but not $\mathbb{mod}$ may change the liveness analysis. Therefore we define

$$\mathcal{S}^{\exists \mathsf{l}}[\![\mathsf{S}]\!] \triangleq \alpha^{\exists l}_{\mathsf{use},\mathbb{mod}}\ (\mathcal{S}^{+\infty}[\![\mathsf{S}]\!]) \qquad (24)$$

Theorem 1 *If* $\alpha^{\exists l}_{\mathsf{use,mod}}[\![\mathsf{S}]\!]\ (\mathcal{S}^{+\infty}[\![\mathsf{S}]\!]) \mathrel{\dot{\subseteq}} \mathcal{S}^{\exists l}[\![\mathsf{S}]\!]$ *then* $\mathcal{S}^{\exists l}[\![\mathsf{S}]\!] \mathrel{\dot{\subseteq}} \mathcal{S}^{\exists l}[\![\mathsf{S}]\!]$.

Proof of Th. 1. We have to prove that $\alpha^{\exists l}_{\mathsf{use,mod}}[\![\mathsf{S}]\!] \mathrel{\dot{\subseteq}} \alpha^{\exists l}_{\mathsf{use,mod}}[\![\mathsf{S}]\!]$, pointwise. We first prove that $\alpha^{l}_{\mathsf{use,mod}}[\![\mathsf{S}]\!] \mathrel{\dot{\subseteq}} \alpha^{l}_{\mathsf{use,mod}}[\![\mathsf{S}]\!]$. We proceed by induction (more precisely bi-induction [15] to account for infinite traces).

— For the basis

$$
\begin{aligned}
& \alpha^{l}_{\mathsf{use,mod}}[\![\mathsf{S}]\!]\ L_b, L_e\ \langle \pi_0,\ \ell \rangle \\
= {} & \{\mathsf{x} \in \mathbb{V} \mid (\ell = \mathsf{aft}[\![\mathsf{S}]\!] \wedge \mathsf{x} \in L_e) \vee (\mathsf{esc}[\![\mathsf{S}]\!] \wedge \ell = \mathsf{brk\text{-}to}[\![\mathsf{S}]\!] \wedge \mathsf{x} \in L_b)\} && \text{(14.a)} \\
\subseteq {} & \alpha^{l}_{\mathsf{use,mod}}[\![\mathsf{S}]\!]\ L_b, L_e\ \langle \pi_0,\ \ell \rangle && \text{(14.a) and } \subseteq \text{ reflexive}
\end{aligned}
$$

— For the induction step

$$
\begin{aligned}
& \alpha^{l}_{\mathsf{use,mod}}[\![\mathsf{S}]\!]\ L_b, L_e\ \langle \pi_0,\ \ell \xrightarrow{a} \ell'\pi_1 \rangle \\
= {} & \{\mathsf{x} \in \mathbb{V} \mid \mathsf{x} \in \mathsf{use}[\![a]\!]\varrho(\pi_0) \vee (\mathsf{x} \notin \mathsf{mod}[\![a]\!]\varrho(\pi_0) \wedge \mathsf{x} \in \alpha^{l}_{\mathsf{use,mod}}[\![\mathsf{S}]\!]\ L_b, L_e\ \langle \pi_0 \mathbin{\hat{}} \ell \xrightarrow{a} \ell', \\
& \ell'\pi_1 \rangle)\} && \text{(14.b)} \\
\subseteq {} & \{\mathsf{x} \in \mathbb{V} \mid \mathsf{x} \in \mathsf{use}[\![a]\!]\varrho(\pi_0) \vee (\mathsf{x} \notin \mathsf{mod}[\![a]\!]\varrho(\pi_0) \wedge \mathsf{x} \in \alpha^{l}_{\mathsf{use,mod}}[\![\mathsf{S}]\!]\ L_b, L_e\ \langle \pi_0 \mathbin{\hat{}} \ell \xrightarrow{a} \ell', \\
& \ell'\pi_1 \rangle)\} && \text{(23)} \\
\subseteq {} & \{\mathsf{x} \in \mathbb{V} \mid \mathsf{x} \in \mathsf{use}[\![a]\!]\varrho(\pi_0) \vee (\mathsf{x} \notin \mathsf{mod}[\![a]\!]\varrho(\pi_0) \wedge \mathsf{x} \in \alpha^{l}_{\mathsf{use,mod}}[\![\mathsf{S}]\!]\ L_b, L_e\ \langle \pi_0 \mathbin{\hat{}} \ell \xrightarrow{a} \ell', \\
& \ell'\pi_1 \rangle)\} && \text{ind. hyp.} \\
= {} & \alpha^{l}_{\mathsf{use,mod}}[\![\mathsf{S}]\!]\ L_b, L_e\ \langle \pi_0,\ \ell \xrightarrow{a} \ell'\pi_1 \rangle && \text{(14.b)}
\end{aligned}
$$

It follows that

$$
\begin{aligned}
& \alpha^{\exists l}_{\mathsf{use,mod}}[\![\mathsf{S}]\!]\ \mathcal{S}\ L_b, L_e \\
= {} & \bigcup_{\langle \pi_0,\ \pi \rangle \in \mathcal{S}} \alpha^{l}_{\mathsf{use,mod}}[\![\mathsf{S}]\!]\ L_b, L_e\ \langle \pi_0,\ \pi \rangle && \text{(15)} \\
\subseteq {} & \bigcup_{\langle \pi_0,\ \pi \rangle \in \mathcal{S}} \alpha^{l}_{\mathsf{use,mod}}[\![\mathsf{S}]\!]\ L_b, L_e\ \langle \pi_0,\ \pi \rangle && \alpha^{l}_{\mathsf{use,mod}}[\![\mathsf{S}]\!] \mathrel{\dot{\subseteq}} \alpha^{l}_{\mathsf{use,mod}}[\![\mathsf{S}]\!] \\
= {} & \alpha^{\exists l}_{\mathsf{use,mod}}[\![\mathsf{S}]\!]\ \mathcal{S}\ L_b, L_e && \text{(15)}
\end{aligned}
$$

If $\alpha^{\exists l}_{\mathsf{use,mod}}[\![\mathsf{S}]\!]\ (\mathcal{S}^{+\infty}[\![\mathsf{S}]\!]) \mathrel{\dot{\subseteq}} \mathcal{S}^{\exists l}[\![\mathsf{S}]\!]$ then $\alpha^{\exists l}_{\mathsf{use,mod}}[\![\mathsf{S}]\!]\ (\mathcal{S}^{+\infty}[\![\mathsf{S}]\!]) \mathrel{\dot{\subseteq}} \mathcal{S}^{\exists l}[\![\mathsf{S}]\!]$ and therefore, by (24), $\mathcal{S}^{\exists l}[\![\mathsf{S}]\!] \triangleq \alpha^{\exists l}_{\mathsf{use,mod}}\ (\mathcal{S}^{+\infty}[\![\mathsf{S}]\!]) \mathrel{\dot{\subseteq}} \mathcal{S}^{\exists l}[\![\mathsf{S}]\!]$.

The other cases $\mathcal{S}^{\forall l}[\![\mathsf{S}]\!]$, $\mathcal{S}^{\exists d}[\![\mathsf{S}]\!]$, and $\mathcal{S}^{\forall d}[\![\mathsf{S}]\!]$ are similar.

4 Calculational design of the structural syntactic potential liveness static analysis

By Th. 1, a liveness inference algorithm $\mathcal{S}^{\exists l}[\![\mathtt{S}]\!]$ is sound whenever

$$\alpha^{\exists l}_{\mathbf{use},\mathbf{mod}}[\![\mathtt{S}]\!]\ (\mathcal{S}^{+\infty}[\![\mathtt{S}]\!]) \mathrel{\dot\subseteq} \mathcal{S}^{\exists l}[\![\mathtt{S}]\!],$$

equivalently

$$\alpha^{\exists l}_{\mathbf{use},\mathbf{mod}}[\![\mathtt{S}]\!]\ (\mathcal{S}^{*}[\![\mathtt{S}]\!]) \mathrel{\dot\subseteq} \mathcal{S}^{\exists l}[\![\mathtt{S}]\!]$$

by Lem. 2. So we can construct this algorithm $\mathcal{S}^{\exists l}[\![\mathtt{S}]\!]$ by a calculus that simplifies the term $\alpha^{\exists l}_{\mathbf{use},\mathbf{mod}}[\![\mathtt{S}]\!]\ (\mathcal{S}^{*}[\![\mathtt{S}]\!])$. Since the semantics $\mathcal{S}^{*}[\![\mathtt{S}]\!]$ is structural, we get a structural algorithm which proceeds by elimination, without any fixpoint iteration. We first give the result in Figure 1 and then show the systematic calculational design [8]. Notice that although the semantics is forward, the analysis is backward (see *e.g.* the statement list and iteration). We omit the unused environment parameter of $\mathbf{use}$ and $\mathbf{mod}$.

Structural syntactic potential liveness analysis

$$\widehat{\mathcal{S}}^{\exists l}[\![\mathtt{Sl}\ \ell]\!]\ L_e \triangleq \widehat{\mathcal{S}}^{\exists l}[\![\mathtt{Sl}\ \ell]\!]\ \varnothing, L_e \tag{25}$$

$$\widehat{\mathcal{S}}^{\exists l}[\![\mathtt{x = A ;}]\!]\ L_b, L_e \triangleq \mathbf{use}[\![\mathtt{x = A}]\!] \cup (L_e \setminus \mathbf{mod}[\![\mathtt{x = A}]\!])$$

$$\widehat{\mathcal{S}}^{\exists l}[\![\mathtt{;}]\!]\ L_b, L_e \triangleq L_e$$

$$\widehat{\mathcal{S}}^{\exists l}[\![\mathtt{Sl'}\ \mathtt{S}]\!]\ L_b, L_e \triangleq \widehat{\mathcal{S}}^{\exists l}[\![\mathtt{Sl'}]\!]\ L_b, (\widehat{\mathcal{S}}^{\exists l}[\![\mathtt{S}]\!]\ L_b, L_e)$$

$$\widehat{\mathcal{S}}^{\exists l}[\![\epsilon]\!]\ L_b, L_e \triangleq L_e$$

$$\widehat{\mathcal{S}}^{\exists l}[\![\mathtt{if\ (B)\ S}_t]\!]\ L_b, L_e \triangleq \mathbf{use}[\![\mathtt{B}]\!] \cup L_e \cup \widehat{\mathcal{S}}^{\exists l}[\![\mathtt{S}_t]\!]\ L_b, L_e$$

$$\widehat{\mathcal{S}}^{\exists l}[\![\mathtt{if\ (B)\ S}_t\ \mathtt{else}\ \mathtt{S}_f]\!]\ L_b, L_e \triangleq \mathbf{use}[\![\mathtt{B}]\!] \cup \widehat{\mathcal{S}}^{\exists l}[\![\mathtt{S}_t]\!]\ L_b, L_e \cup \widehat{\mathcal{S}}^{\exists l}[\![\mathtt{S}_f]\!]\ L_b, L_e$$

$$\widehat{\mathcal{S}}^{\exists l}[\![\mathtt{while\ (B)\ S}_b]\!]\ L_b, L_e \triangleq \mathbf{use}[\![\mathtt{B}]\!] \cup L_e \cup \widehat{\mathcal{S}}^{\exists l}[\![\mathtt{S}_b]\!]\ L_b, L_e$$

$$\widehat{\mathcal{S}}^{\exists l}[\![\mathtt{break ;}]\!]\ L_b, L_e \triangleq L_b$$

$$\widehat{\mathcal{S}}^{\exists l}[\![\mathtt{\{\ Sl\ \}}]\!]\ L_b, L_e \triangleq \widehat{\mathcal{S}}^{\exists l}[\![\mathtt{Sl}]\!]\ L_b, L_e \qquad \square$$

Fig. 1. Potential liveness

Theorem 2 *$\widehat{\mathcal{S}}^{\exists l}[\![\mathtt{S}]\!]$ defined by* (25) *is syntactically sound that is* $\mathcal{S}^{\exists l}[\![\mathtt{S}]\!] = \alpha^{\exists l}_{\mathbf{use},\mathbf{mod}}[\![\mathtt{S}]\!]\ (\mathcal{S}^{*}[\![\mathtt{S}]\!]) \mathrel{\dot\subseteq} \widehat{\mathcal{S}}^{\exists l}[\![\mathtt{S}]\!]$.

Proof of Th. 2. By structural induction on $\mathtt{S}$. We provide an example of a base case (assignment) and an inductive case (iteration), all other cases are similar.

– For the ***assignment*** $\mathtt{S} ::= \ell\ \mathtt{x = A ;}$, let us calculate $\mathcal{S}^{\exists l}[\![\mathtt{S}]\!]\ L_b, L_e$

$= \alpha^{\exists l}_{\mathbf{use},\mathbf{mod}}[\![\mathtt{S}]\!](\mathcal{S}^{*}[\![\mathtt{S}]\!])\ L_b, L_e$ 〈(22) and Lem. 2〉

$= \bigcup\{\alpha^{l}_{\mathbf{use},\mathbf{mod}}[\![\mathtt{S}]\!]\ L_b, L_e\ \langle\pi_0, \pi_1\rangle \mid \langle\pi_0, \pi_1\rangle \in \widehat{\mathcal{S}}^{*}[\![\mathtt{S}]\!]\}$ 〈def. (15) of $\alpha^{\exists l}_{\mathbf{use},\mathbf{mod}}[\![\mathtt{S}]\!]$〉

$= \bigcup\{\alpha^l_{\mathrm{use,mod}}[\![S]\!]\ L_b, L_e\ \langle\pi_0\mathsf{at}[\![S]\!],\ \mathsf{at}[\![S]\!]\rangle\} \cup \bigcup\{\alpha^l_{\mathrm{use,mod}}[\![S]\!]\ L_b, L_e\ \langle\pi_0\mathsf{at}[\![S]\!],\ \mathsf{at}[\![S]\!] \xrightarrow{\mathtt{x = A} = \mathscr{A}[\![A]\!]\varrho(\pi_0\mathsf{at}[\![S]\!])} \mathsf{aft}[\![S]\!]\rangle\}$ ⟨def. (3) of $\mathcal{S}^*[\![S]\!]$⟩

$= \bigcup\{\alpha^l_{\mathrm{use,mod}}[\![S]\!]\ L_b, L_e\ \langle\pi_0\mathsf{at}[\![S]\!],\ \mathsf{at}[\![S]\!] \xrightarrow{\mathtt{x = A} = \mathscr{A}[\![A]\!]\varrho(\pi_0\mathsf{at}[\![S]\!])} \mathsf{aft}[\![S]\!]\rangle\}$
⟨def. (14.a) of $\alpha^l_{\mathrm{use,mod}}[\![S]\!]\ L_b, L_e\ \langle\pi_0\mathsf{at}[\![S]\!],\ \mathsf{at}[\![S]\!]\rangle = \varnothing$⟩

$= \bigcup\{\mathtt{y} \in \mathbb{V} \mid \mathtt{y} \in \mathbb{use}[\![\mathtt{x = A}]\!]\varrho(\pi_0\mathsf{at}[\![S]\!]) \vee (\mathtt{y} \notin \mathbb{mod}[\![\mathtt{x = A}]\!]\varrho(\pi_0\mathsf{at}[\![S]\!]) \wedge \mathtt{y} \in \alpha^l_{\mathrm{use,mod}}[\![S]\!]\ L_b, L_e\ \langle\pi_0\mathsf{at}[\![S]\!] \mathbin{\smallfrown} \mathsf{at}[\![S]\!] \xrightarrow{\mathtt{x = A} = \mathscr{A}[\![A]\!]\varrho(\pi_0\mathsf{at}[\![S]\!])} \mathsf{aft}[\![S]\!],\ \mathsf{aft}[\![S]\!]\rangle)\}$
⟨def. (14.b) of $\alpha^l_{\mathrm{use,mod}}\ L_b, L_e\ \langle\pi_0\mathsf{at}[\![S]\!],\ \mathsf{at}[\![S]\!] \xrightarrow{\mathtt{x = A} = \mathscr{A}[\![A]\!]\varrho(\pi_0\mathsf{at}[\![S]\!])} \mathsf{aft}[\![S]\!]\rangle$⟩

$= \{\mathtt{y} \in \mathbb{V} \mid \mathtt{y} \in \mathbb{use}[\![\mathtt{x = A}]\!] \vee (\mathtt{y} \notin \mathbb{mod}[\![\mathtt{x = A}]\!] \wedge \mathtt{y} \in L_e)\}$
⟨def. (14.a) of $\alpha^l_{\mathrm{use,mod}}[\![S]\!]\ L_b, L_e\ \langle\pi_0,\ \mathsf{aft}[\![S]\!]\rangle \triangleq \{\mathtt{x} \in \mathbb{V} \mid \mathtt{x} \in L_e\} = L_e$ since $\mathsf{esc}[\![S]\!] = \mathsf{ff}$ and omitting the useless parameters of $\mathbb{use}$ and $\mathbb{mod}$⟩

$= \mathbb{use}[\![\mathtt{x = A}]\!] \cup (L_e \setminus \mathbb{mod}[\![\mathtt{x = A}]\!])$ ⟨def. $\in$⟩

$= \widehat{\mathcal{S}}^{\exists l}[\![\mathtt{x = A ;}]\!]\ L_b, L_e$ ⟨(25), Q.E.D.⟩

$\subseteq$ is never used in this derivation so $\widehat{\mathcal{S}}^{\exists l}[\![\mathtt{x = A ;}]\!]\ L_b, L_e = \mathcal{S}^{\exists l}[\![\mathtt{x = A ;}]\!]\ L_b, L_e$ is the best (most precise) abstraction for the assignment.

– For the ***iteration*** $\mathtt{S} ::= \mathtt{while}\ \ell\ \mathtt{(B)}\ \mathtt{S}_b$, we apply the semi-commutation fixpoint approximation Theorem 1 of [9] to the fixpoint definition (9) of the prefix trace semantics of the iteration. For the semi-commutation where we can assume that X is an iterate of $\mathcal{F}^*[\![\mathtt{while}\ \ell\ \mathtt{(B)}\ \mathtt{S}_b]\!]$ from $\varnothing$ and therefore $X \subseteq \mathcal{S}^*[\![S]\!]$, we have

$\alpha^{\exists l}_{\mathrm{use,mod}}[\![S]\!]\ (\mathcal{F}^*[\![\mathtt{while}\ \ell\ \mathtt{(B)}\ \mathtt{S}_b]\!](X))\ L_b, L_e$

$= \bigcup\{\alpha^l_{\mathrm{use,mod}}[\![S]\!]\ L_b, L_e\ \langle\pi_0,\ \pi_1\rangle \mid \langle\pi_0,\ \pi_1\rangle \in \mathcal{F}^*[\![\mathtt{while}\ \ell\ \mathtt{(B)}\ \mathtt{S}_b]\!](X)\}$ ⟨(15)⟩

$= \bigcup\{\alpha^l_{\mathrm{use,mod}}[\![S]\!]\ L_b, L_e\ \langle\pi_0,\ \pi_1\rangle \mid \langle\pi_0,\ \pi_1\rangle \in \{\langle\pi_1\ell',\ \ell'\rangle \mid \pi_1\ell' \in \mathbb{T}^+ \wedge \ell' = \ell\}\} \cup$ (a)
$\bigcup\{\alpha^l_{\mathrm{use,mod}}[\![S]\!]\ L_b, L_e\ \langle\pi_0,\ \pi_1\rangle \mid \langle\pi_0,\ \pi_1\rangle \in \{\langle\pi_1\ell',\ \ell'\pi_2\ell' \xrightarrow{\neg(\mathtt{B})} \mathsf{aft}[\![S]\!]\rangle \mid \langle\pi_1\ell',\ \ell'\pi_2\ell'\rangle \in X \wedge \mathcal{B}[\![\mathtt{B}]\!]\varrho(\pi_1\ell'\pi_2\ell') = \mathsf{ff} \wedge \ell' = \ell\}\} \cup$ (b)
$\bigcup\{\alpha^l_{\mathrm{use,mod}}[\![S]\!]\ L_b, L_e\ \langle\pi_0,\ \pi_1\rangle \mid \langle\pi_0,\ \pi_1\rangle \in \{\langle\pi_1\ell',\ \ell'\pi_2\ell' \xrightarrow{\mathtt{B}} \mathsf{at}[\![\mathtt{S}_b]\!] \mathbin{\smallfrown} \pi_3\rangle \mid \langle\pi_1\ell',\ \ell'\pi_2\ell'\rangle \in X \wedge \mathcal{B}[\![\mathtt{B}]\!]\varrho(\pi_1\ell'\pi_2\ell') = \mathsf{tt} \wedge \langle\pi_1\ell'\pi_2\ell' \xrightarrow{\mathtt{B}} \mathsf{at}[\![\mathtt{S}_b]\!],\ \pi_3\rangle \in \mathcal{S}^*[\![\mathtt{S}_b]\!] \wedge \ell' = \ell\}\}$ (c)
⟨(9)⟩

We go on by cases.

- For the case (a), we have

$\bigcup\{\alpha^l_{\mathrm{use,mod}}[\![S]\!]\ L_b, L_e\ \langle\pi_0,\ \pi_1\rangle \mid \langle\pi_0,\ \pi_1\rangle \in \{\langle\pi_1\ell',\ \ell'\rangle \mid \pi_1\ell' \in \mathbb{T}^+ \wedge \ell' = \ell\}\}$ ⟨(a)⟩

$= \bigcup\{\alpha^l_{\mathrm{use,mod}}[\![S]\!]\ L_b, L_e\ \langle\pi_1\ell,\ \ell\rangle \mid \pi_1\ell \in \mathbb{T}^+\}$ ⟨where $\ell = \mathsf{at}[\![\mathtt{while}\ \ell\ \mathtt{(B)}\ \mathtt{S}_b]\!]$⟩

$= \{\mathtt{x} \in \mathbb{V} \mid (\ell = \mathsf{aft}[\![S]\!] \wedge \mathtt{x} \in L_e) \vee (\mathsf{esc}[\![S]\!] \wedge \ell = \mathsf{brk\text{-}to}[\![S]\!] \wedge \mathtt{x} \in L_b)\}$ ⟨(14.a)⟩

$= \varnothing$ ⟨$\ell = \mathsf{at}[\![S]\!] \neq \mathsf{aft}[\![S]\!]$ and $\ell = \mathsf{at}[\![S]\!] \neq \mathsf{brk\text{-}to}[\![S]\!]$ for iteration⟩

- For the case (b) where $X \subseteq \mathcal{S}^*[\![S]\!]$ is a subset of the iterates, we have

$\bigcup\{\alpha^{l}_{\mathrm{use,mod}}[\![\mathsf{S}]\!]\ L_b, L_e\ \langle\pi_0,\ \pi_1\rangle \mid \langle\pi_0,\ \pi_1\rangle\ \in\ \{\langle\pi_1\ell',\ \ell'\pi_2\ell' \xrightarrow{\neg(\mathsf{B})} \mathsf{aft}[\![\mathsf{S}]\!]\rangle \mid \langle\pi_1\ell',\ \ell'\pi_2\ell'\rangle \in X \wedge \mathcal{B}[\![\mathsf{B}]\!]\varrho(\pi_1\ell'\pi_2\ell') = \mathrm{ff} \wedge \ell' = \ell\}\}$

$= \bigcup\{\alpha^{l}_{\mathrm{use,mod}}[\![\mathsf{S}]\!]\ L_b, L_e\ \langle\pi_1\ell,\ \ell\pi_2\ell \xrightarrow{\neg(\mathsf{B})} \mathsf{aft}[\![\mathsf{S}]\!]\rangle \mid \langle\pi_1\ell,\ \ell\pi_2\ell\rangle \in X \wedge \mathcal{B}[\![\mathsf{B}]\!]\varrho(\pi_1\ell\pi_2\ell) = \mathrm{ff}\}$ ⦃def. $\in$ and $\ell' = \ell = \mathsf{at}[\![\mathsf{S}]\!]$⦄

$= \bigcup\{\{\mathsf{x} \in \mathbb{V} \mid \exists i \in [1,n-1]\ .\ \forall j \in [1,i-1]\ .\ \mathsf{x} \notin \mathrm{mod}[\![a_j]\!] \wedge \mathsf{x} \in \mathrm{use}[\![a_i]\!]\} \cup L_e \cup \mid \langle\pi_1\ell,\ \ell\pi_2\ell\rangle \in X \wedge \mathcal{B}[\![\mathsf{B}]\!]\varrho(\pi_1\ell\pi_2\ell) = \mathrm{ff}\}$

⦃by Lem. 1 where $\ell\pi_2\ell \xrightarrow{\neg(\mathsf{B})} \mathsf{aft}[\![\mathsf{S}]\!] = \ell_1 \xrightarrow{a_1} \ell_2 \xrightarrow{a_2} \ldots \xrightarrow{a_{n-2}} \ell_{n-1} = \ell \xrightarrow{a_{n-1} = \neg(\mathsf{B})} \ell_n$ where $\ell = \ell_1$ and $\ell_n = \mathsf{aft}[\![\mathsf{S}]\!]$, $\langle\pi_1\ell,\ \ell\pi_2\ell\rangle \in X \subseteq \mathcal{S}^*[\![\mathsf{S}]\!]$ so $\langle\pi_1\ell,\ \ell\pi_2\ell \xrightarrow{\neg(\mathsf{B})} \mathsf{aft}[\![\mathsf{S}]\!]\rangle \in \mathcal{S}^*[\![\mathsf{S}]\!]$, and $\mathsf{esc}[\![\mathsf{S}]\!] = \mathrm{ff}$⦄

$= \bigcup\{\{\mathsf{x} \in \mathbb{V} \mid \exists i \in [1,n-2]\ .\ \forall j \in [1,i-1]\ .\ \mathsf{x} \notin \mathrm{mod}[\![a_j]\!] \wedge \mathsf{x} \in \mathrm{use}[\![a_i]\!]\} \cup \{\mathsf{x} \in \mathbb{V} \mid \forall j \in [1,n-2]\ .\ \mathsf{x} \notin \mathrm{mod}[\![a_j]\!] \wedge \mathsf{x} \in \mathrm{use}[\![\mathsf{B}]\!]\} \cup L_e \mid \langle\pi_1\ell, \ell\pi_2\ell\rangle \in X \wedge \mathcal{B}[\![\mathsf{B}]\!]\varrho(\pi_1\ell\pi_2\ell) = \mathrm{ff}\}$ ⦃$[1,n-1] = [1,n-2] \cup \{n-1\}$, $a_{n-1} = \neg(\mathsf{B})$, and $\mathrm{use}[\![\neg(\mathsf{B})]\!] = \mathrm{use}[\![\mathsf{B}]\!]$⦄

$\subseteq \bigcup\{\{\mathsf{x} \in \mathbb{V} \mid \exists i \in [1,n-2]\ .\ \forall j \in [1,i-1]\ .\ \mathsf{x} \notin \mathrm{mod}[\![a_j]\!] \wedge \mathsf{x} \in \mathrm{use}[\![a_i]\!] \mid \langle\pi_1\ell,\ \ell\pi_2\ell\rangle \in X\}\} \cup \mathrm{use}[\![\mathsf{B}]\!] \cup L_e$

⦃ignoring the check $\forall j \in [1,n-2]\ .\ \mathsf{x} \notin \mathrm{mod}[\![a_j]\!]$ that x has not been modified before its use in $\neg(\mathsf{B})$, that the test B is false, and $\ell\pi_2\ell \triangleq \ell_1 \xrightarrow{a_1} \ell_2 \xrightarrow{a_2} \ldots \xrightarrow{a_{n-2}} \ell_{n-1}$ with $\ell = \ell_1$ and $\ell_{n-1} = \ell$⦄

$\subseteq \bigcup\{\alpha^{l}_{\mathrm{use,mod}}[\![\mathsf{S}]\!]\ L_b, L_e\ \langle\pi_0,\ \pi_1\rangle \mid \langle\pi_0,\ \pi_1\rangle\ \in\ X\} \cup \mathrm{use}[\![\mathsf{B}]\!] \cup L_e$ ⦃Lem. 1⦄

$= \alpha^{\exists l}_{\mathrm{use,mod}}[\![\mathsf{S}]\!]\ (X)\ L_b, L_e \cup \mathrm{use}[\![\mathsf{B}]\!] \cup L_e$ ⦃(15)⦄

- For the case (c) where $X \subseteq \mathcal{S}^*[\![\mathsf{S}]\!]$ is a subset of the iterates, we have

$\bigcup\{\alpha^{l}_{\mathrm{use,mod}}[\![\mathsf{S}]\!]\ L_b, L_e\ \langle\pi_0,\ \pi_1\rangle \mid \langle\pi_0,\ \pi_1\rangle\ \in\ \{\langle\pi_1\ell',\ \ell'\pi_2\ell' \xrightarrow{\mathsf{B}} \mathsf{at}[\![\mathsf{S}_b]\!] \frown \pi_3\rangle \mid \langle\pi_1\ell',\ \ell'\pi_2\ell'\rangle \in X \wedge \mathcal{B}[\![\mathsf{B}]\!]\varrho(\pi_1\ell'\pi_2\ell') = \mathrm{tt} \wedge \langle\pi_1\ell'\pi_2\ell' \xrightarrow{\mathsf{B}} \mathsf{at}[\![\mathsf{S}_b]\!],\ \pi_3\rangle \in \mathcal{S}^*[\![\mathsf{S}_b]\!] \wedge \ell' = \ell\}\}$

$= \bigcup\{\alpha^{l}_{\mathrm{use,mod}}[\![\mathsf{S}]\!]\ L_b, L_e\ \langle\pi_1\ell,\ \ell\pi_2\ell \xrightarrow{\mathsf{B}} \mathsf{at}[\![\mathsf{S}_b]\!] \frown \pi_3\rangle \mid \langle\pi_1\ell,\ \ell\pi_2\ell\rangle \in X \wedge \mathcal{B}[\![\mathsf{B}]\!]\varrho(\pi_1\ell\pi_2\ell) = \mathrm{tt} \wedge \langle\pi_3,\ \pi_1\ell\pi_2\ell \xrightarrow{\mathsf{B}} \mathsf{at}[\![\mathsf{S}_b]\!]\rangle \in \mathcal{S}^*[\![\mathsf{S}_b]\!]\}$

⦃def. $\in$ and $\ell' = \ell = \mathsf{at}[\![\mathsf{S}]\!]$⦄

$= \bigcup\{\{\mathsf{x} \in \mathbb{V} \mid \exists i \in [1,n-1]\ .\ \forall j \in [1,i-1]\ .\ \mathsf{x} \notin \mathrm{mod}[\![a_j]\!] \wedge \mathsf{x} \in \mathrm{use}[\![a_i]\!]\} \cup (\!|\ \ell_n = \mathsf{aft}[\![\mathsf{S}]\!]\ ?\ L_e\ :\ \varnothing\ |\!) \cup (\!|\ \mathsf{esc}[\![\mathsf{S}]\!] \wedge \ell_n = \mathsf{brk\text{-}to}[\![\mathsf{S}]\!]\ ?\ L_b\ :\ \varnothing\ |\!) \mid \langle\pi_1\ell,\ \ell\pi_2\ell\rangle \in X \wedge \mathcal{B}[\![\mathsf{B}]\!]\varrho(\pi_1\ell\pi_2\ell) = \mathrm{tt} \wedge \langle\pi_3,\ \pi_1\ell\pi_2\ell \xrightarrow{\mathsf{B}} \mathsf{at}[\![\mathsf{S}_b]\!]\rangle \in \mathcal{S}^*[\![\mathsf{S}_b]\!] \wedge \ell\pi_2\ell \xrightarrow{\mathsf{B}} \mathsf{at}[\![\mathsf{S}_b]\!] \frown \pi_3 = \ell_1 \xrightarrow{a_1} \ell_2 \xrightarrow{a_2} \ldots \xrightarrow{a_{n-1}} \ell_n\}$ ⦃by Lem. 1⦄

$= \bigcup\{\{\mathsf{x} \in \mathbb{V} \mid \exists i \in [1,n-1] \,.\, \forall j \in [1,i-1] \,.\, \mathsf{x} \notin \mathbb{mod}[\![a_j]\!] \wedge \mathsf{x} \in \mathbb{use}[\![a_i]\!]\} \mid \langle \pi_1\ell, \ell\pi_2\ell\rangle \in X \wedge \mathscr{B}[\![\mathsf{B}]\!]\varrho(\pi_1\ell\pi_2\ell) = \mathrm{tt} \wedge \langle \pi_3, \pi_1\ell\pi_2\ell \xrightarrow{\mathsf{B}} \mathsf{at}[\![\mathsf{S}_b]\!]\rangle \in \mathcal{S}^*[\![\mathsf{S}_b]\!] \wedge \ell\pi_2\ell = \ell_1 \xrightarrow{a_1} \ell_2 \xrightarrow{a_2} \ldots \xrightarrow{a_{m-1}} \ell_m \wedge \ell \xrightarrow{\mathsf{B}} \mathsf{at}[\![\mathsf{S}_b]\!] = \ell_m \xrightarrow{a_m\,=\,\mathsf{B}} \ell_{m+1} \wedge \pi_3 = \ell_{m+1} \xrightarrow{a_{m+1}} \ldots \xrightarrow{a_{n-1}} \ell_n\}$

(by decomposing the trace according to its pattern, $\langle \pi_3, \pi_1\ell\pi_2\ell \xrightarrow{\mathsf{B}} \mathsf{at}[\![\mathsf{S}_b]\!]\rangle \in \mathcal{S}^*[\![\mathsf{S}_b]\!]$ so $\ell_n \neq \mathsf{aft}[\![\mathsf{S}]\!]$, and $\mathsf{esc}[\![\mathsf{S}]\!] = \mathrm{ff}$)

$= \bigcup\{\{\mathsf{x} \in \mathbb{V} \mid \exists i \in [1,m-1] \,.\, \forall j \in [1,i-1] \,.\, \mathsf{x} \notin \mathbb{mod}[\![a_j]\!] \wedge \mathsf{x} \in \mathbb{use}[\![a_i]\!]\} \cup \{\mathsf{x} \in \mathbb{V} \mid \forall j \in [1,m-1] \,.\, \mathsf{x} \notin \mathbb{mod}[\![a_j]\!] \wedge \mathsf{x} \in \mathbb{use}[\![a_m]\!]\} \cup \{\mathsf{x} \in \mathbb{V} \mid \exists i \in [m+1,n-1] \,.\, \forall j \in [1,i-1] \,.\, \mathsf{x} \notin \mathbb{mod}[\![a_j]\!] \wedge \mathsf{x} \in \mathbb{use}[\![a_i]\!]\} \mid \langle \pi_1\ell, \ell\pi_2\ell\rangle \in X \wedge \mathscr{B}[\![\mathsf{B}]\!]\varrho(\pi_1\ell\pi_2\ell) = \mathrm{tt} \wedge \langle \pi_3, \pi_1\ell\pi_2\ell \xrightarrow{\mathsf{B}} \mathsf{at}[\![\mathsf{S}_b]\!]\rangle \in \mathcal{S}^*[\![\mathsf{S}_b]\!] \wedge \ell\pi_2\ell = \ell_1 \xrightarrow{a_1} \ell_2 \xrightarrow{a_2} \ldots \xrightarrow{a_{m-1}} \ell_m \wedge \ell \xrightarrow{\mathsf{B}} \mathsf{at}[\![\mathsf{S}_b]\!] = \ell_m \xrightarrow{a_m\,=\,\mathsf{B}} \ell_{m+1} \wedge \pi_3 = \ell_{m+1} \xrightarrow{a_{m+1}} \ldots \xrightarrow{a_{n-1}} \ell_n\}$

(by decomposing $[1,n-1] = [1,m-1] \cup \{m\} \cup [m+1,n-1]$)

$\subseteq \bigcup\{\{\mathsf{x} \in \mathbb{V} \mid \exists i \in [1,m-1] \,.\, \forall j \in [1,i-1] \,.\, \mathsf{x} \notin \mathbb{mod}[\![a_j]\!] \wedge \mathsf{x} \in \mathbb{use}[\![a_i]\!]\} \mid \langle \pi_1\ell, \ell\pi_2\ell\rangle \in X \wedge \ell\pi_2\ell = \ell_1 \xrightarrow{a_1} \ell_2 \xrightarrow{a_2} \ldots \xrightarrow{a_{m-1}} \ell_m\} \cup \mathbb{use}[\![\mathsf{B}]\!] \cup \bigcup\{\{\mathsf{x} \in \mathbb{V} \mid \exists i \in [m+1,n-1] \,.\, \forall j \in [1,i-1] \,.\, \mathsf{x} \notin \mathbb{mod}[\![a_j]\!] \wedge \mathsf{x} \in \mathbb{use}[\![a_i]\!]\} \mid \langle \pi_3, \pi_1\ell\pi_2\ell \xrightarrow{\mathsf{B}} \mathsf{at}[\![\mathsf{S}_b]\!]\rangle \in \mathcal{S}^*[\![\mathsf{S}_b]\!] \wedge \pi_3 = \ell_{m+1} \xrightarrow{a_{m+1}} \ldots \xrightarrow{a_{n-1}} \ell_n\}$

(def. $\cup$, ignoring the check $\forall j \in [1,m-1] \,.\, \mathsf{x} \notin \mathbb{mod}[\![a_j]\!]$ that x has not been modified before its use in $a_m = \mathsf{B}$, ignoring the value of $\mathscr{B}[\![\mathsf{B}]\!]\varrho(\pi_1\ell\pi_2\ell) = \mathrm{tt}$)

$\subseteq \bigcup\{\alpha^l_{\mathbb{use},\mathbb{mod}}[\![\mathsf{S}]\!]\ L_b, L_e\ \langle \pi_1\ell, \ell\pi_2\ell\rangle \mid \langle \pi_1\ell, \ell\pi_2\ell\rangle \in X\} \cup \mathbb{use}[\![\mathsf{B}]\!] \cup \bigcup\{\{\mathsf{x} \in \mathbb{V} \mid \exists i \in [m+1,n-1] \,.\, \forall j \in [1,i-1] \,.\, \mathsf{x} \notin \mathbb{mod}[\![a_j]\!] \wedge \mathsf{x} \in \mathbb{use}[\![a_i]\!]\} \cup (\!|\, \ell_n = \mathsf{aft}[\![\mathsf{S}_b]\!] \mathrel{?} L_e \mathrel{:} \varnothing \,|\!) \cup (\!|\, \mathsf{esc}[\![\mathsf{S}_b]\!] \wedge \ell_n = \mathsf{brk\text{-}to}[\![\mathsf{S}_b]\!] \mathrel{?} L_b \mathrel{:} \varnothing \,|\!) \mid \langle \pi_3, \pi_1\ell\pi_2\ell \xrightarrow{\mathsf{B}} \mathsf{at}[\![\mathsf{S}_b]\!]\rangle \in \mathcal{S}^*[\![\mathsf{S}_b]\!] \wedge \pi_3 = \ell_{m+1} \xrightarrow{a_{m+1}} \ldots \xrightarrow{a_{n-1}} \ell_n\}$

(by Lem. 1 for the first term since $\mathsf{aft}[\![\mathsf{S}]\!] \neq \ell$ and $\mathsf{brk\text{-}to}[\![\mathsf{S}]\!] \neq \ell$ and over-approximating the third term)

$\subseteq \bigcup\{\alpha^l_{\mathbb{use},\mathbb{mod}}[\![\mathsf{S}]\!]\ L_b, L_e\ \langle \pi_1\ell, \ell\pi_2\ell\rangle \mid \langle \pi_1\ell, \ell\pi_2\ell\rangle \in X\} \cup \mathbb{use}[\![\mathsf{B}]\!] \cup \bigcup\{\alpha^l_{\mathbb{use},\mathbb{mod}}[\![\mathsf{S}_b]\!]\ L_b, L_e\ \langle \pi_1\ell\pi_2\ell \xrightarrow{\mathsf{B}} \mathsf{at}[\![\mathsf{S}_b]\!], \pi_3\rangle \mid \langle \pi_1\ell\pi_2\ell \xrightarrow{\mathsf{B}} \mathsf{at}[\![\mathsf{S}_b]\!], \pi_3\rangle \in \mathcal{S}^*[\![\mathsf{S}_b]\!]\}$ (by Lem. 1)

$\subseteq \bigcup\{\alpha^l_{\mathbb{use},\mathbb{mod}}[\![\mathsf{S}]\!]\ L_b, L_e\langle \pi_0, \pi_1\rangle \mid \langle \pi_0, \pi_1\rangle \in X\} \cup \mathbb{use}[\![\mathsf{B}]\!] \cup \bigcup\{\alpha^l_{\mathbb{use},\mathbb{mod}}[\![\mathsf{S}_b]\!]\ L_b, L_e\langle \pi_0, \pi_1\rangle \mid \langle \pi_0, \pi_1\rangle \in \mathcal{S}^*[\![\mathsf{S}_b]\!]\}$ (over-approximating the semantics X and $\mathcal{S}^*[\![\mathsf{S}_b]\!]$)

$\subseteq (\alpha^{\exists l}_{\mathbb{use},\mathbb{mod}}[\![\mathsf{S}]\!]\ (X)\ L_b, L_e) \cup \mathbb{use}[\![\mathsf{B}]\!] \cup (\alpha^{\exists l}_{\mathbb{use},\mathbb{mod}}\mathsf{S}_b]\ (\mathcal{S}^*[\![\mathsf{S}_b]\!])\ L_b, L_e)$ ((15))

$\subseteq (\alpha^{\exists l}_{\mathbb{use},\mathbb{mod}}[\![\mathsf{S}]\!]\ (X)\ L_b, L_e) \cup \mathbb{use}[\![\mathsf{B}]\!] \cup \widehat{\mathcal{S}}^{\exists l}[\![\mathsf{S}_b]\!]\ L_b, L_e$

≀structural induction hypothesis of Th. 2≀

- Gathering the three cases (*a*), (*b*), and (*c*), we have proved the semi-commutation condition

  $\alpha^{\exists l}_{\mathsf{use,mod}}[\![\mathtt{S}]\!]\ (\mathscr{F}^*[\![\mathtt{while}\ \ell\ \mathtt{(B)}\ \mathtt{S}_b]\!](X))\ L_b, L_e \subseteq$
  $L_e \cup (\alpha^{\exists l}_{\mathsf{use,mod}}[\![\mathtt{S}]\!]\ (X)\ L_b, L_e \cup \mathsf{use}[\![\mathtt{B}]\!] \cup L_e) \cup (\alpha^{\exists l}_{\mathsf{use,mod}}[\![\mathtt{S}]\!]\ (X)\ L_b, L_e) \cup \mathsf{use}[\![\mathtt{B}]\!] \cup$
  $\widehat{\mathcal{S}}^{\exists l}[\![\mathtt{S}_b]\!]\ L_b, L_e$

  So we define

  $$\mathscr{B}^{\exists l}[\![\mathtt{while}\ \mathtt{(B)}\ \mathtt{S}_b]\!]\ L_b, L_e\ X \triangleq L_e \cup X \cup \mathsf{use}[\![\mathtt{B}]\!] \cup \widehat{\mathcal{S}}^{\exists l}[\![\mathtt{S}_b]\!]\ L_b, L_e$$

  to get $\widehat{\mathcal{S}}^{\exists l}[\![\mathtt{while}\ \mathtt{(B)}\ \mathtt{S}_b]\!]\ L_b, L_e \triangleq \mathsf{lfp}^{\subseteq}\ \mathscr{B}^{\exists l}[\![\mathtt{while}\ \mathtt{(B)}\ \mathtt{S}_b]\!]\ L_b, L_e$. The iterates are
  - $X^0 = \varnothing$
  - $X^1 = \mathscr{B}^{\exists l}[\![\mathtt{while}\ \mathtt{(B)}\ \mathtt{S}_b]\!]\ L_b, L_e\ X^0 = L_e \cup \mathsf{use}[\![\mathtt{B}]\!] \cup \widehat{\mathcal{S}}^{\exists l}[\![\mathtt{S}_b]\!]\ L_b, L_e$
  - $X^2 = \mathscr{B}^{\exists l}[\![\mathtt{while}\ \mathtt{(B)}\ \mathtt{S}_b]\!]\ L_b, L_e\ X^2 = L_e \cup \mathsf{use}[\![\mathtt{B}]\!] \cup \widehat{\mathcal{S}}^{\exists l}[\![\mathtt{S}_b]\!]\ L_b, L_e = X^1$

  Therefore the least fixpoint is the constant

  $$\widehat{\mathcal{S}}^{\exists l}[\![\mathtt{while}\ \mathtt{(B)}\ \mathtt{S}_b]\!]\ L_b, L_e = L_e \cup \mathsf{use}[\![\mathtt{B}]\!] \cup \widehat{\mathcal{S}}^{\exists l}[\![\mathtt{S}_b]\!]\ L_b, L_e$$

  as stated in (25), Q.E.D. □

We conclude that algorithm (25) is sound with respect to the revised syntactic/semantic definition $\mathcal{S}^{\exists l}[\![\mathtt{S}]\!]$ of liveness in (24).

Theorem 3 $\mathcal{S}^{\exists l}[\![\mathtt{S}]\!] = \alpha^{\exists l}_{\mathsf{use,mod}}\ (\mathcal{S}^{+\infty}[\![\mathtt{S}]\!]) \mathrel{\dot{\subseteq}} \widehat{\mathcal{S}}^{\exists l}[\![\mathtt{S}]\!]$.

Proof (of Th. 3)

$\alpha^{\exists l}_{\mathsf{use,mod}}\ (\mathcal{S}^{+\infty}[\![\mathtt{S}]\!])$

$= \alpha^{\exists l}_{\mathsf{use,mod}}\ (\mathcal{S}^{*}[\![\mathtt{S}]\!])$ ≀Lem. 2≀

$\dot{\subseteq}\ \widehat{\mathcal{S}}^{\exists l}[\![\mathtt{S}]\!]$ ≀Th. 2 and Th. 1≀ □

5 Calculational design of the syntactic structural deadness static analysis

By duality we obtain the syntactic definite deadness analysis which is the information actually needed in compilers.

Structural syntactic definite deadness analysis

$$\widehat{\mathcal{S}}^{\forall d}[\![\texttt{sl}\ \ell]\!]\ D_e = \widehat{\mathcal{S}}^{\forall d}[\![\texttt{sl}\ \ell]\!]\ \mathbb{V}, D_e \tag{26}$$

$$\widehat{\mathcal{S}}^{\forall d}[\![\texttt{x = A ;}]\!]\ D_b, D_e = \neg\,\mathbb{use}[\![\texttt{x = A}]\!] \cap (D_e \cup \mathbb{mod}[\![\texttt{x = A}]\!])$$

$$\widehat{\mathcal{S}}^{\forall d}[\![\texttt{;}]\!]\ D_b, D_e = D_e$$

$$\widehat{\mathcal{S}}^{\forall d}[\![\texttt{sl}'\ \texttt{s}]\!]\ D_b, D_e = \widehat{\mathcal{S}}^{\forall d}[\![\texttt{sl}']\!]\ D_b, (\widehat{\mathcal{S}}^{\forall d}[\![\texttt{s}]\!]\ D_b, D_e)$$

$$\widehat{\mathcal{S}}^{\forall d}[\![\ \epsilon\ ]\!]\ D_b, D_e = D_e$$

$$\widehat{\mathcal{S}}^{\forall d}[\![\texttt{if (B) s}_t]\!]\ D_b, D_e = \neg\,\mathbb{use}[\![\texttt{B}]\!] \cap D_e \cap \widehat{\mathcal{S}}^{\forall d}[\![\texttt{s}_t]\!]\ D_b, D_e$$

$$\widehat{\mathcal{S}}^{\forall d}[\![\texttt{if (B) s}_t\ \texttt{else s}_f]\!]\ D_b, D_e = \neg\,\mathbb{use}[\![\texttt{B}]\!] \cap \widehat{\mathcal{S}}^{\forall d}[\![\texttt{s}_t]\!]\ D_b, D_e \cap \widehat{\mathcal{S}}^{\forall d}[\![\texttt{s}_f]\!]\ D_b, D_e$$

$$\widehat{\mathcal{S}}^{\forall d}[\![\texttt{while (B) s}_b]\!]\ D_b, D_e = \neg\,\mathbb{use}[\![\texttt{B}]\!] \cap D_e \cap \widehat{\mathcal{S}}^{\forall d}[\![\texttt{s}_b]\!]\ D_b, D_e$$

$$\widehat{\mathcal{S}}^{\forall d}[\![\texttt{break ;}]\!]\ D_b, D_e = D_b$$

$$\widehat{\mathcal{S}}^{\forall d}[\![\texttt{\{ sl \}}]\!]\ D_b, D_e = \widehat{\mathcal{S}}^{\forall d}[\![\texttt{sl}]\!]\ D_b, D_e \qquad \square$$

Theorem 4 (Structural syntactic definite deadness analysis) *For all program components* s, *define* $\mathcal{S}^{\forall d}[\![\texttt{s}]\!]\ D_b, D_e \triangleq \neg\mathcal{S}^{\exists l}[\![\texttt{s}]\!]\ \neg D_b, \neg D_e$. $\mathcal{S}^{\forall d}$ *is equivalently defined by* $\widehat{\mathcal{S}}^{\forall d}$ *in* (26).

Proof of Th. 4. The proof is by structural induction and essentially consists in applying De Morgan laws for complement. For example,

$$\begin{aligned}
&\mathcal{S}^{\forall d}[\![\texttt{if (B) s}_t]\!]\ D_b, D_e\\
= {}&\neg\mathcal{S}^{\exists l}[\![\texttt{if (B) s}_t]\!]\ \neg D_b, \neg D_e && \text{(definition of } \mathcal{S}^{\forall d}[\![\texttt{s}]\!] \text{ as dual of } \mathcal{S}^{\exists l}[\![\texttt{s}]\!]\text{)}\\
= {}&\neg(\mathbb{use}[\![\texttt{B}]\!] \cup \neg D_e \cup \mathcal{S}^{\exists l}[\![\texttt{s}_t]\!]\ \neg D_b, \neg D_e) && \text{((25))}\\
= {}&\neg\,\mathbb{use}[\![\texttt{B}]\!] \cap \neg\neg D_e \cap \neg\mathcal{S}^{\exists l}[\![\texttt{s}_t]\!]\ \neg D_b, \neg D_e) && \text{(De Morgan laws)}\\
= {}&\neg\,\mathbb{use}[\![\texttt{B}]\!] \cap D_e \cap \mathcal{S}^{\forall d}[\![\texttt{s}_t]\!]\ D_b, D_e && \text{(structural induction hypothesis)}
\end{aligned}$$

All other cases are similar. $\square$

6 Is liveness analysis correctly used for code optimization?

6.1 Liveness specification

We have considered three possible specifications of liveness. A purely semantic one $\mathcal{S}^{\exists l}$ in (20) with respect to which the liveness analysis algorithm (25) is unsound and a syntactic one $\mathcal{S}^{\exists l}$ in (22) as well as a revised syntactic/semantic liveness specification $\mathcal{S}^{\exists l}$ in (24) for which, by Th. 1 and 2, the liveness analysis algorithm (25) is sound. The problem is that, as shown in Section **3.4**, the syntactic specification of liveness $\mathcal{S}^{\exists l}$ in (22) is unsound with respect to the purely semantic specification $\mathcal{S}^{\exists l}$ in (20). This is problematic since applications of the liveness analysis algorithm (25) are not designed with respect to what the algorithm does, but with respect to the specification of what it is supposed to do. Therefore, a potential problem is in the use of the liveness analysis algorithm (25) with a semantic definition $\mathcal{S}^{\exists l}$ in (20) of soundness for which it is incorrect.

6.2 What could go wrong when optimizing programs?

Consider a compiler that successively performs

1. a (syntactic) liveness analysis $\mathcal{S}^{\exists\mathbb{l}}$;
2. next, a code optimization by removal
   (a) of assignments to variables that are dead after this assignment,
   (b) of assignments to variables that do not change the value of this variable (using Kildall's constancy analysis [22] or a more precise symbolic constancy analysis [18,31]);
3. next, a register allocation such that
   (a) simultaneously live variables are stored in different registers,
   (b) when no register is left and one is needed, one of those containing the value of a dead variable is preferred (to avoid saving the value of the variable to its memory location as would be needed for live variables).

For the following program (where all variables are dead on exit)

		semantically live	semantically dead	syntactically live	syntactically dead
`x=0; scanf(y);`					
`if (x==0){`					
ℓ_1 `...` x and y neither used nor modified `...`	ℓ_1	{x}	{y}	{y}	{x}
ℓ_2 `x = y - y; }`	ℓ_2	{x}	{y}	{y}	{x}
`else {`					
`x=42;`					
`}`					
ℓ_3 `print(x);`	ℓ_3	{x}	{y}	{x}	{y}

x is semantically live at ℓ_1, ℓ_2, and ℓ_3 since it is never modified (in particular not modified at ℓ_2) before being used at ℓ_3. However it is syntactically dead at ℓ_1 and ℓ_2 since it is not used before being assigned at ℓ_2. Code elimination (2b) will suppress the assignment at ℓ_2 since the value of x is unchanged. Assume x is in a register at ℓ_1 and a fresh register is needed but none is left available. By (3b) the register containing x may be selected since its value need not be saved to memory because x is syntactically dead at ℓ_1. Then the value of x is lost at ℓ_3, a compilation bug. The problem is the notion of modification assimilated to an assignment in (21) and syntactic liveness $\mathcal{S}^{\exists\mathbb{l}}$ in (22) when this assignment is redundant and may be eliminated from the object program.

This error does not occur with semantic liveness $\mathcal{S}^{\exists l}$ in (20) which declares x live at ℓ_1 so the register containing its value will be saved to memory (and reloaded at ℓ_3).

6.3 Why does it not go wrong?

One solution is to prevent program transformations (such as (2b) and (3b) above) that do not preserve the soundness of the semantic liveness $\mathcal{S}^{\exists l}$ in (20). Since (2b) does not depend on the liveness analysis, it can be moved before. Another solution is to redo the liveness analysis after any program transformation that does not preserve the information. A better solution is adopted in CompCert [23]: the liveness analysis and code elimination are performed simultaneously and the liveness analysis is designed to be valid *after* code elimination. The soundness of the liveness analysis is stated and proved as "after code elimination, the program execution does not depend on the values of the variables declared dead by the analysis". More generally, a program transformation based on a sound static program analysis must be formally proved to be correct. This can be done in the framework of abstract interpretation [14].

7 Conclusion

We have shown that Gary Kildall approach to data flow analysis by abstraction over a path and merge over all paths [22] as well as Bernhard Steffen's approach "Data Flow Analysis is Model Checking" [28,29] (requiring finite abstract domains) formalized by David Schmidt as "Data Flow Analysis is Model Checking of Abstract Interpretations" [28,29], (including its recent reformulation [5]), hide subtleties in the definition of soundness, which may lead to incorrect semantics-based compiler optimizations.

Moreover, the use of transition systems in model checking forgets about the program structure and so cannot be used directly to formally derive structural elimination algorithms which may be more efficient than fixpoint algorithms. Of course elimination would not be necessarily feasible in presence of arbitrary branching in or out of loops. But nevertheless, by the chaotic iteration theorem [7], the result remains valid for all loops with forward branching only.

We have argued that "Data Flow Analysis is an Abstract Interpretation of a Trace Semantics", as first propounded by [12, Section 7.2.0.6.3] solves the soundness and design problems thanks to a not so natural replacement of "semantically modified" by "syntactically assigned to". Therefore liveness analysis must be performed after program assignment transformations.

Since the program cannot be modified after the classical syntactic liveness analysis since the analysis can become wrong after the transformation, an alternative, à la CompCert [23], is to use dependency: the soundness of the liveness analysis is stated and proved as "the program execution does not depend on the values of the variables declared dead by the analysis".

More generally, this is another illustration that program property specification is better performed directly on a semantics rather than, as is the case in dataflow analysis, on any of its abstractions.

Let us leave the conclusion to an anonymous reviewer. "It is an old story that the dataflow analysis framework ("syntactic" dataflow analysis in paper's characterization) is way too weak. For modern programming languages, control flow is not syntactic but a part of semantics. Dataflow analysis assumes the control flow to be available before the analysis hence a stalemate for modern languages with higher order functions, dynamic bindings, or dynamic gotos; dataflow analysis has neither a systematic guide to prove the correctness of an analysis nor systematic approach to manage the precision of the analysis. On the other hand, the semantics-based design theory (abstract interpretation) is general enough to handle any kind of source languages and powerful enough to prove the correctness and to manage its precision."

Acknowledgement. I thank Sandrine Blazy, Xavier Leroy, and Francesco Ranzato for lively discussions. I thank the reviewers for their livable comments. This work was supported in part by NSF Grant CNS-1446511. Any opinions, findings, and conclusions or recommendations expressed in this material are those of the author and do not necessarily reflect the views of the National Science Foundation.

References

1. Allen, F.E.: Control flow analysis. SIGPLAN Not. **5**(7), 1–19 (1970)
2. Allen, F.E.: A basis for program optimization. In: IFIP Congress, vol. 1, pp. 385–390 (1971)
3. Allen, F.E.: Interprocedural data flow analysis. In: Rosenfeld, J.L. (ed.) Information Processing 1974, pp. 398–402. North-Holland Pub. Co., Amsterdam (1974)
4. Allen, F.E., Cocke, J.: A program data flow analysis procedure. Commun. ACM **19**(3), 137–147 (1976)
5. Beyer, D., Gulwani, S., Schmidt, D.A.: Combining model checking and data-flow analysis. In: Clarke, E.M., Henzinger, T.A., Veith, H., Bloem, R. (eds.) Handbook of Model Checking, pp. 493–540. Springer, Cham (2018). https://doi.org/10.1007/978-3-319-10575-8_16
6. Brookes, S.: Traces, pomsets, fairness and full abstraction for communicating processes. In: Brim, L., Křetínský, M., Kučera, A., Jančar, P. (eds.) CONCUR 2002. LNCS, vol. 2421, pp. 466–482. Springer, Heidelberg (2002). https://doi.org/10.1007/3-540-45694-5_31
7. Cousot, P.: Asynchronous iterative methods for solving a fixed point system of monotone equations in a complete lattice. Res. rep. R.R. 88, Laboratoire IMAG, Université scientifique et médicale de Grenoble, Grenoble, France, September 1977. 15 pages
8. Cousot, P.: The calculational design of a generic abstract interpreter. In: Broy, M., Steinbrüggen, R. (eds.) Calculational System Design. NATO ASI Series F. IOS Press, Amsterdam (1999)
9. Cousot, P.: Constructive design of a hierarchy of semantics of a transition system by abstract interpretation. Theor. Comput. Sci. **277**(1–2), 47–103 (2002)
10. Cousot, P.: Abstract semantic dependency. In: Chang, B.-Y.E. (ed.) SAS 2019. LNCS, vol. 11822, pp. 389–410. Springer, Cham (2019)
11. Cousot, P., Cousot, R.: Constructive versions of Tarski's fixed point theorems. Pac. J. Math. **81**(1), 43–57 (1979)

12. Cousot, P., Cousot, R.: Systematic design of program analysis frameworks. In: POPL, pp. 269–282. ACM Press (1979)
13. Cousot, P., Cousot, R.: Temporal abstract interpretation. In: POPL, pp. 12–25. ACM (2000)
14. Cousot, P., Cousot, R.: Systematic design of program transformation frameworks by abstract interpretation. In: POPL, pp. 178–190. ACM (2002)
15. Cousot, P., Cousot, R.: Bi-inductive structural semantics. Inf. Comput. **207**(2), 258–283 (2009)
16. Filé, G., Ranzato, F.: The powerset operator on abstract interpretations. Theor. Comput. Sci. **222**(1–2), 77–111 (1999)
17. Giacobazzi, R., Ranzato, F., Scozzari, F.: Making abstract interpretations complete. J. ACM **47**(2), 361–416 (2000)
18. Haghighat, M.R., Polychronopoulos, C.D.: Symbolic analysis for parallelizing compilers. ACM Trans. Program. Lang. Syst. **18**(4), 477–518 (1996)
19. Kennedy, K.: Node listings applied to data flow analysis. In: POPL, pp. 10–21. ACM Press (1975)
20. Kennedy, K.: A comparison of two algorithms for global data flow analysis. Int. J. Comput. Math. Section A **3**, 5–15 (1976)
21. Kennedy, K.: A comparison of two algorithms for global data flow analysis. SIAM J. Comput. **5**(1), 158–180 (1976)
22. Kildall, G.A.: A unified approach to global program optimization. In: POPL, pp. 194–206. ACM Press (1973)
23. Leroy, X.: Formal verification of a realistic compiler. Commun. ACM **52**(7), 107–115 (2009)
24. Ryder, B.G., Paull, M.C.: Elimination algorithms for data flow analysis. ACM Comput. Surv. **18**(3), 277–316 (1986)
25. Schmidt, D.A.: Data flow analysis is model checking of abstract interpretations. In: POPL, pp. 38–48. ACM (1998)
26. Scholz, B., Blieberger, J.: A new elimination-based data flow analysis framework using annotated decomposition trees. In: Krishnamurthi, S., Odersky, M. (eds.) CC 2007. LNCS, vol. 4420, pp. 202–217. Springer, Heidelberg (2007). `https://doi.org/10.1007/978-3-540-71229-9_14`
27. Sharir, M.: Structural analysis: a new approch to flow analysis in optimizing compilers. Comput. Lang. **5**(3), 141–153 (1980)
28. Steffen, B.: Data flow analysis as model checking. In: Ito, T., Meyer, A.R. (eds.) TACS 1991. LNCS, vol. 526, pp. 346–364. Springer, Heidelberg (1991). `https://doi.org/10.1007/3-540-54415-1_54`
29. Steffen, B.: Generating data flow analysis algorithms from modal specifications. Sci. Comput. Program. **21**(2), 115–139 (1993)
30. Tarski, A.: A lattice theoretical fixpoint theorem and its applications. Pac. J. Math. **5**, 285–310 (1955)
31. Wegman, M.N., Zadeck, F.K.: Constant propagation with conditional branches. ACM Trans. Program. Lang. Syst. **13**(2), 181–210 (1991)

Languages and Decidability

Abstract Interpretation of Indexed Grammars

Marco Campion(✉), Mila Dalla Preda, and Roberto Giacobazzi

Dipartimento di Informatica, University of Verona, Verona, Italy
{marco.campion,mila.dallapreda,roberto.giacobazzi}@univr.it

Abstract. Indexed grammars are a generalization of context-free grammars and recognize a proper subset of context-sensitive languages. The class of languages recognized by indexed grammars are called indexed languages and they correspond to the languages recognized by nested stack automata. For example indexed grammars can recognize the language $\{a^n b^n c^n \mid n \geqslant 1\}$ which is not context-free, but they cannot recognize $\{(ab^n)^n \mid n \geqslant 1\}$ which is context-sensitive. Indexed grammars identify a set of languages that are more expressive than context-free languages, while having decidability results that lie in between the ones of context-free and context-sensitive languages. In this work we study indexed grammars in order to formalize the relation between indexed languages and the other classes of languages in the Chomsky hierarchy. To this end, we provide a fixpoint characterization of the languages recognized by an indexed grammar and we study possible ways to abstract, in the abstract interpretation sense, these languages and their grammars into context-free and regular languages.

1 Introduction

Chomsky's hierarchy [6] drove most of the research in theoretical computer science for decades. Its structure, and its inner separation results between formal languages, represent the corner stone to understand the expressive power of symbolic structures. In this paper we show how abstract interpretation can be used for studying formal languages, in particular we consider indexed languages as our concrete semantics. This because of two reasons: (1) they lack, to the best of our knowledge, of a fixpoint semantics and (2) they represent an intermediate family of languages between context-free (CF) and context-sensitive (CS), therefore including CF and regular (REG) languages as subclasses.

Indexed languages have been introduced in [2] as an extension of CF languages in order to include languages such as $\{a^n b^n c^n \mid n \geqslant 1\}$. It is known that indexed languages are strictly less expressive than CS languages, e.g., the language $\{(ab^n)^n \mid n \geqslant 1\}$ is CS but not indexed. This intermediate class between CF and CS has interesting properties, e.g., decidable emptiness test and NP-complete membership check, where the first is undecidable and the latter is PSPACE-complete in CS.

B.-Y. E. Chang (Ed.): SAS 2019, LNCS 11822, pp. 121–139, 2019.
https://doi.org/10.1007/978-3-030-32304-2_7

Indexed languages are described by indexed grammars which differ from CF grammars in that each non-terminal is equipped with a stack on which push and pop instructions can be performed. Moreover, the stack can be copied to all non-terminals on the right side of each production.

Although sporadically used in the literature (we can mention its use in natural language analysis [20] and in logic programming [5]) indexed languages represent an ideal concrete semantics for rebuilding part of Chomsky's hierarchy by abstract interpretation, in particular for the case of regular and CF languages.

Abstract interpretation [10,11] is a general theory for the approximation of dynamic systems. It generalizes most existing methodologies for static program analysis into a unique sound-by-construction framework which is based on a simple but striking idea: *extracting properties of a system is approximating its semantics* [10]. In this paper we show that abstract interpretation can be used for studying the relation between formal languages in Chomsky's hierarchy.

The first step in our construction is to give a fixpoint semantics to indexed languages (Sect. 4). The construction follows the one known for CS languages, and derives a system of equations associated with each indexed grammar. We prove that the fixpoint solution of this system of equations corresponds precisely to the language generated by the grammar. This will provide the base fixpoint semantics for making abstract interpretation.

We show in Sect. 5 that no best abstraction, which in abstract interpretation are represented by Galois Insertions, is possible between indexed languages and respectively CF and regular languages, w.r.t. set inclusion. This means that we need to act at the level of grammar structures (i.e., on the way languages are generated and represented in grammatical form) in order to generate languages as abstract interpretations of an index grammar. It is therefore necessary to weaken the structure of Galois insertion-based abstract interpretation and consider abstractions that do not admit adjoint [12]. This is a quite widespread phenomenon in program analysis, e.g., the polyhedra abstract domain does not form a Galois insertion with the concrete semantics [14]. We introduce several abstractions of grammatical structures in such a way that the abstract language transformer associated with the system of equations of the indexed language generates the desired language. We show that certain simplifications of the productions of indexed grammars can be specified as abstractions, now in the standard Galois insertion based framework, and that the corresponding abstract semantics coincides precisely to classes of languages in Chomsky's hierarchy, in our case the class of CF languages. The main advantage is that known fixpoint characterisation and algorithms for CF languages can be extracted in a *calculational* way by abstract interpretation of the fixpoint semantics of the more concrete indexed grammars. This shows that standard methods for the design of static program analyses and hierarchy of semantics (e.g., see [9,15,16]) can be applied to systematically derive fixpoint presentations for families of formal languages and to let abstract interpretation methods to be applicable to Chomsky's hierarchy.

Section 6 concludes the paper with a discussion of related future works.

2 Background

Mathematical Notation. We denote with $\mathbf{X} = (X_1, \ldots, X_n)$ a tuple $\mathbf{X}$ of n elements. We define with $\texttt{proj}_i$ the projection function of the i-th element of a tuple such that $\texttt{proj}_i(\mathbf{X}) = X_i$ and $\texttt{proj}_{-1}(\mathbf{X}) = X_n$.

Given two sets S and T, we denote with $\wp(S)$ the powerset of S, with $S \subset T$ strict inclusion and with $S \subseteq T$ inclusion. $\langle P, \leqslant_P \rangle$ denotes a poset P with ordering relation $\leqslant_P$. A function $f : P \to Q$ on poset is additive when for any $Y \subseteq P$: $f(\bigvee_P Y) = \bigvee_Q f(Y)$, and co-additive when for any $Y \subseteq P : f(\bigwedge_P Y) = \bigwedge_Q f(Y)$. A poset $\langle P, \leqslant_P \rangle$ with $P \neq \emptyset$, is a lattice if $\forall x, y \in P$ we have that $x \vee y, x \wedge y \in P$. A lattice is complete if for every $S \subseteq P$ we have that $\bigvee S \in P$ and $\bigwedge S \in P$. A lattice is denoted $\langle C, \leqslant_C, \vee_C, \wedge_C, \top_C, \bot_C \rangle$.

Abstract Domains. The Abstract Interpretation (AI) framework is based on the correspondence between a domain of concrete or exact properties and a domain of abstract or approximate properties [11]. The concrete is specified by a set C called the concrete semantic domain and a partial function $F_C : C \to C$ which is the concrete semantic transfer function with fixpoint solution starting from a basic element $\bot_C \in C$ such that $F_C^0(\bot_C) = \bot_C$ and $F_C^{i+1}(\bot_C) = F_C(F_C^i(\bot_C))$. In particular, the concrete iterates may be in increasing order for a partial order $\leqslant_C \in \wp(C \times C)$. This partial order relation may induce a partial order $\langle C, \leqslant_C \rangle$ or even a complete lattice structure on C [11].

The abstract is specified by an abstract semantic domain A which is an approximate version of the concrete semantic domain C. The objective of an abstract interpretation is to find an abstract property $a \in A$, if any, which is a correct approximation of the concrete semantics $c \in C$. Abstract semantics can be specified by transfinite recursion using an abstract basis $\bot_A \in A$ and an abstract semantic function $F_A : A \to A$ such that $F_A^0(\bot_A) = \bot_A$ and $F_A^{i+1}(\bot_A) = F_A(F_A^i(\bot_A))$. The abstract iterates may be in increasing order for a partial order $\leqslant_A \in \wp(A \times A)$ which may induce an order structure $\langle A, \leqslant_A, \bot_A, \cup_A \rangle$ ensuring that the abstract iteration is convergent [11].

The correspondence between the concrete and abstract properties is specified by a soundness relation $\sigma \in \wp(C \times A)$ where $\langle c, a \rangle \in \sigma$ means that the concrete semantics c has the abstract property a. A common assumption is that every concrete property has an abstract approximation: $\forall c \in C : \exists a \in A : \langle c, a \rangle \in \sigma$ [11].

The Galois Insertion approach to AI is based on a Galois Insertion (or equivalently closure operators, Moore families, complete join congruence relations or families of principal ideals [11]) correspondence between concrete and abstract properties. Galois Insertions (GI) are defined between a concrete domain $\langle C, \leqslant_C \rangle$ and an abstract domain $\langle A, \leqslant_A \rangle$ which are assumed to be at least posets [10]. A GI is a tuple (C, α, γ, A) where the abstraction map $\alpha : C \to A$ and the concretization map $\gamma : A \to C$ give rise to an adjunction: $\forall a \in A, c \in C : \alpha(c) \leqslant_A a \Leftrightarrow c \leqslant_C \gamma(a)$. Thus, $\alpha(c) \leqslant_A a$ and, equivalently $c \leqslant_C \gamma(a)$, means that a is a sound approximation of c in A. A tuple (C, α, γ, A) is a GI iff α is additive iff γ is co-additive [10]. A GI is a Galois Connection (GC) where $\alpha \circ \gamma = id$. Indeed, GIs ensure that $\alpha(c)$ actually provides the best possible approximation of the concrete value $c \in C$ on A. Whenever we have an additive (resp. co-additive) function f between two domains we can always build a GI by considering the right (resp. left) adjoint map induced by f. In fact, every abstraction map induces a concretization map and viceversa, formally $\gamma(a) = \bigvee_C \{c \mid \alpha(c) \leqslant_A a\}$ and $\alpha(a) = \bigwedge_A \{a \mid \gamma(a) \leqslant_C c\}$ [10].

An Upper Closure Operator (uco) $\varphi \in C \to C$ on a poset $\langle C, \leqslant \rangle$ is an operator that is monotone, idempotent and extensive (i.e. $\forall c \in C\ c \leqslant \varphi(c)$) [11]. Closures are uniquely determined by the set of their fixpoints $\varphi(C)$. The set of all closures on C is denoted by $uco(C)$. The lattice of abstract domains of C is therefore isomorphic to $uco(C)$ [11]. If C is a complete lattice, then $\langle uco(C), \sqsubseteq, \sqcup, \sqcap, \lambda x.\top, id \rangle$ is a complete lattice, where $id = \lambda x.x$ and for every $\rho, \eta \in uco(C)$, $\rho \sqsubseteq \eta \leftrightarrow \forall y \in C\ \rho(y) \leqslant \eta(y) \leftrightarrow \eta(C) \subseteq \rho(C)$. The glb $\sqcap$ is isomorphic to the so called reduced product, i.e. $\bigsqcap_{i \in I} \rho_i$ is the most abstract common concretization of all ρ_i.

Given $X \subseteq C$, the least abstract domain containing X is the least closure including X as fixpoints, which is the Moore-closure $M(X) = \{\bigwedge S \mid S \subseteq X\}$. Note that $\bigsqcap_{i \in I} \rho_i = M(\bigcup_{i \in I} \rho_i)$. If (C, α, γ, A) is a GI then $\varphi = \gamma \circ \alpha$ is the closure associated with A, such that $\varphi(C)$ is a complete lattice isomorphic to A.

Abstract Interpretation. The least fixpoint (lfp) of an operator F on a poset $\langle P, \leqslant \rangle$, when it exists, is denoted by $lfp^{\leqslant} F$, or by $lfp F$ when $\leqslant$ is clear. Any continuous operator $F \in C \to C$ on a given complete lattice $\langle C, \leqslant, \sqcup, \sqcap, \top, \bot \rangle$ admits a lfp: $lfp^{\leqslant}_{\bot} F = \bigvee_{n \in \mathbb{N}} F^i(\bot)$, where for any $i \in \mathbb{N}$ and $x \in C$: $F^0(x) = x$ and $F^{i+1}(x) = F(F^i(x))$. Given an abstract domain $\langle A, \leqslant_A \rangle$ of $\langle C, \leqslant_C \rangle$, $F^\# \in A \to A$ is a correct (sound) approximation of $F \in C \to C$ when $\alpha(lfp^{\leqslant_C} F) \leqslant_A lfp^{\leqslant_A} F^\#$. To this end it is enough to have a monotone map $\alpha : C \to A$ such that $\alpha(\bot_C) = \bot_A$ and $\alpha \circ F \leqslant_A F^\# \circ \alpha$ [12]. An abstraction is complete when $\alpha \circ F = F^\# \circ \alpha$. In this case of complete abstractions we have $\alpha(lfp^{\leqslant_C} F) = lfp^{\leqslant_A} F^\#$ [11,21].

3 Indexed Languages

Indexed grammars were introduced by Aho in the late 1960s to model a natural subclass of context-sensitive languages, more expressive than context-free grammars with interesting closure properties [2]. In this paper we use the definition of indexed grammar provided in [1].

Definition 1. *An Indexed Grammar is a 5-tuple* $G = (N, T, I, P, S)$ *such that:*

(1) N, T *and* I *are three mutually disjoint finite sets of symbols: the set* N *of non-terminals, the set* T *of terminals and the set* I *of indices, where* ϵ *is a designated symbol for the empty sequence;*
(2) $S \in N$ *is a distinguished symbol in* N*, namely the start symbol;*
(3) P *is a finite set of productions, each having the form of one of the following:*
  (a) $A \to \alpha$ *(Stack copy)*
  (b) $A \to B_f$ *(Push)*
  (c) $A_f \to \beta$ *(Pop)*

where $A, B \in N$ *are non-terminal symbols,* $f \in I$ *is an index symbol and* $\alpha, \beta \in (N \cup T)^*$.

Observe the similarity to context-free grammars which are only defined by production rules of type (*3a*). The above definition is a finite representation of rules that rewrite pairs of non-terminal and sequences of index symbols that we call stacks. A key feature of indexed grammars is that their productions in P expand non-terminal/stack pairs of the form (A, σ), where $A \in N$ and $\sigma \in I^*$. So each non-terminal symbol $A \in N$ together with its stack $\sigma \in I^*$, can be viewed as a pair (A, σ) and the start symbol S is shorthand for the pair (S, ϵ). Therefore, with a slight abuse of notation, in the rest of the paper we use α to denote a string of terminal symbols and non-terminals symbols with its stack, namely $\alpha \in ((N \times I^*) \cup T)^*$. The string α is often referred to as a *sentential form*. Given any non-empty stack $\sigma \in I^+$, the top symbol is the left-most index. The stack is implicit and is copied, to all non-terminals only, when the production is applied. So, for example, the type (*3a*) production rule $A \to aBC$ is shorthand for $(A, \sigma) \to a(B, \sigma)(C, \sigma)$ with $A, B, C \in N$, $a \in T$ and $\sigma \in I^*$. A production rule of the form (*3b*) implements a push onto the stack while a production rule of the form (*3c*) encodes a pop off of the stack. For example, the production rule $A \to B_f$ applied to (A, σ) expands to $(B, f\sigma)$ where $f\sigma$ is the stack with the index $f \in I$ pushed on. Likewise, $A_f \to \beta$ can only be applied to (A, σ) if the top of the stack string σ is f. The result is β such that any non-terminal $B \in \beta$ is of the form (B, σ'), where σ' is the stack with the top character popped off. Push and Pop productions differ from the original definition given by Aho [2] in which, by Definition 1, at most one index symbol is loaded or unloaded in any production.

Let $G = (N, T, I, P, S)$ be an indexed grammar. A derivation in G is a sequence of strings $\alpha_1, \alpha_2, \dots, \alpha_n$ with $\alpha_i \in ((N \times I^*) \cup T)^*$, where α_{i+1} is derived from α_i by the application of one production in P, written $\alpha_i \to_G \alpha_{i+1}$. The subscript G is dropped whenever G is clearly understood. Let $\to_G^*$ be the reflexive and transitive closure of $\to_G$ defined as usual: $\alpha \to_G^0 \alpha$ for $n \geqslant 0$, $\alpha \to_G^{n+1} \gamma$ if $\exists \beta : \alpha \to_G^n \beta$ and $\beta \to_G \gamma$; $\alpha \to_G^* \beta$ iff $\alpha \to_G^i \beta$ for some $i \geqslant 0$.

The language $\mathcal{L}(G)$ recognized by an indexed grammar G is

$$\mathcal{L}(G) = \{w \in T^* \mid (S, \epsilon) \to_G^* w\}.$$

We denote with *IL* the set of indexed languages.

From now on the set of non-terminals N will range on superscript symbols such as $A, B, \dots$, the set of terminals T on symbols a, b, c, d, e while indices I on f, g.

Example 1. The language $L = \{a^n b^n c^n \mid n \geqslant 1\}$ is generated by the indexed grammar $G = (\{S, T, A, B, C\}, \{a, b, c\}, \{f\}, P, S)$, with productions:

$$\begin{array}{lll} S \to T & A_f \to aA & B_\epsilon \to b \\ T \to T_f & A_\epsilon \to a & C_f \to cC \\ T \to ABC & B_f \to bB & C_\epsilon \to c \end{array}$$

For example, the word "$aabbcc$" can be generated by the following derivation: $(S, \epsilon) \to (T, \epsilon) \to (T, f) \to (A, f)(B, f)(C, f) \to a(A, \epsilon)(B, f)(C, f) \to aa(B, f)(C, f) \to^* aabbcc$.

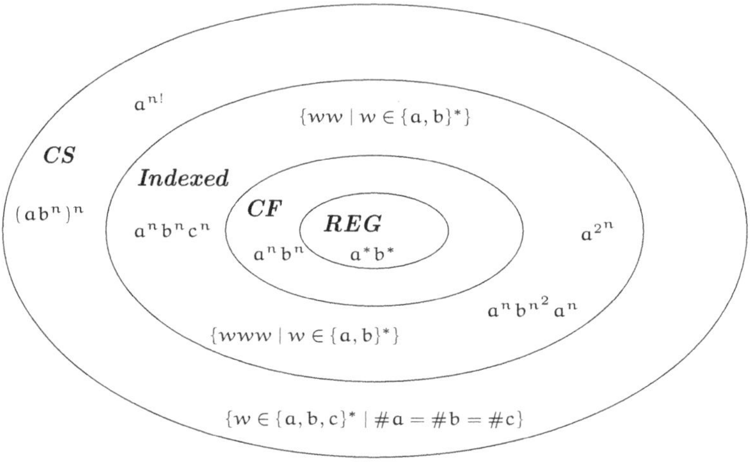

Fig. 1. Chomsky hierarchy

Indexed languages are recognized by nested stack automata [3]. A nested stack automaton is a finite automaton that can make use of a stack containing data which can be additional stacks. Like a stack automaton, a nested stack automaton may step up or down in the stack, and read the current symbol; in addition, it may at any place create a new stack, operate on that one, eventually destroy it, and continue operating on the old stack. In this way, stacks can be nested recursively to an arbitrary depth; however, the automaton always operates on the innermost stack only. For more details on nested stack automata see [3].

As argued above, the class of indexed languages properly includes the one of CF languages, while being properly included in the one of CS languages. Figure 1 represents these different classes and highlights some of the languages that characterize the different classes [24].

Table 1 reports some decidability and computational complexity properties of indexed languages and of the others formal languages in the Chomsky hierarchy. As expected, the decidability results of indexed languages lay in between the ones of CS and CF languages.

4 Fixpoint Characterization of Indexed Languages

In order to study the existence of abstraction functions between context-sensitive, indexed and context-free languages we need to provide a fixpoint

Table 1. Decidability and complexity results

Class	Emptiness	Membership	Equivalence
Regular	$\mathbb{P}$ ($O(n)$)	$\mathbb{P}$ ($O(n)$)	NL-complete
Context-free	$\mathbb{P}$ ($O(n^3)$)	$\mathbb{P}$ ($O(n^3)$)	Undecidable
Indexed	EXP-complete	NP-complete	Undecidable
Context-sensitive	Undecidable	PSPACE-complete	Undecidable

characterization of indexed languages. The fixpoint characterizations of CF languages, well known as the ALGOL-like theorem, and CS languages are already constructed and proved [22,23].

The fixpoint characterization that we present is mainly derived from the one of CS languages [23]. Essentially it consists of two elements: a substitution function that simulates a context-free rule for the pair non-terminal/stack (productions of type (*3a*) and (*3b*)) and a regular expression to verify the context of the stack in case of a pop production (*3c*).

Before showing the theorem, let us give some notations and definitions. Let V be the set of variables of an indexed grammar: an element of V is either a pair of non-terminal/stack or a terminal symbol, namely $V = (N \times I^*) \cup T$. Therefore, if α is a sentential form of an indexed grammar, then $\alpha \in V^*$.

Definition 2. *An indexed state* $\mathbf{X}$ *is a m-tuple* $\mathbf{X} = (X_1, \ldots, X_m)$ *of sets of sentential forms* $X_i \in \wp(V^*)$ *with* $i \in [1, m]$.

Thus, the set of possible m-tuples of indexed states is $\underbrace{\wp(V^*) \times \cdots \times \wp(V^*)}_{m}$.

Definition 3. *A substitution function* h *is a map* $h\colon \wp(V^*) \to \wp(V^*)$.

Functions h will be defined in the proof of Theorem 1 and will be used to simulate an application of a CF-like production.

Regular sets over V are denoted by regular expressions $R \in \wp(V^*)$ and will be used to verify the top character of the stack for pop productions.

Definition 4. *Given a substitution function* h *and a regular set* R, *we define a pair* $\pi = (h, R)$ *called a* π*-function. A* π*-function is a map*

$$\pi : \underbrace{\wp(V^*) \times \cdots \times \wp(V^*)}_{m} \to \wp(V^*)$$

defined as follows:

$$\pi(\mathbf{X}) = h(\bigcup \mathbf{X} \cap R)$$

where $\bigcup \mathbf{X} = X_1 \cup \cdots \cup X_m$ *is the set corresponding to the union of all components of the indexed state* $\mathbf{X}$. *We denote with the bold symbol*

$$\boldsymbol{\pi} : \underbrace{\wp(V^*) \times \cdots \times \wp(V^*)}_{m} \to \underbrace{\wp(V^*) \times \cdots \times \wp(V^*)}_{m}$$

a vector function of π-functions $\boldsymbol{\pi} = (\pi_1, \ldots, \pi_m)$ *such that*

$$\boldsymbol{\pi}(\mathbf{X}) = (\pi_1(\mathbf{X}), \ldots, \pi_m(\mathbf{X})).$$

As we will see in the proof of Theorem 1, a π-function allows us to simulate an application of an indexed production.

Theorem 1. *Let* G *be an indexed grammar, then* $\mathcal{L}(G)$ *is a component of the least fixpoint of a system of equations on indexed states:*

$$\mathbf{X}_G^{j+1} = \boldsymbol{\pi}_G(\mathbf{X}_G^j) \tag{1}$$

where $\mathbf{X}_G^0 = \underbrace{(\{(S, \epsilon)\}, \emptyset, \ldots, \emptyset)}_{n}$ *is the initial indexed state and the vector function of π-functions induced by* G *is* $\boldsymbol{\pi}_G = (\pi_{G,1}, \ldots, \pi_{G,n})$.

Proof. The proof considers an indexed grammar $G = (N, T, I, P, S)$ with m productions in P. Let $[\tau]_i \in P$ be an enumeration of all productions in P with $i \in [1, m]$, where $\tau \in P$ could be in one of the three forms of Definition 1. We build a system of equations having the form (1) where each indexed state $\mathbf{X}_G$ has $n = m + 2$ components: one for each production in P, namely $X_{G,1}, \ldots, X_{G,m}$ and two additional components $X_{G,0}$ and $X_{G,t}$, where t is a variable symbol denoting the "terminals" set and it is always at position $m + 1$ of $\mathbf{X}_G$. So the components of each indexed state are $\mathbf{X}_G = (X_{G,0}, X_{G,1}, \ldots, X_{G,m}, X_{G,t})$. The least fixpoint computation of the so obtained system of equations is calculated by the iterative application of the vector function $\boldsymbol{\pi}_G = (\pi_{G,0}, \pi_{G,1}, \ldots, \pi_{G,m}, \pi_{G,t})$ associated to the grammar G. The sets from $X_{G,1}$ to $X_{G,m}$ are associated to the m productions in P while $X_{G,t}$ contains only terminal symbols and $X_{G,0}$ initialize a sentential form. In particular, given the initial indexed state $\mathbf{X}_G^0$, the language is iteratively built in the last element $X_{G,t}$ of $\mathbf{X}_G$ such that at fixpoint $X_{G,t}^{FIX} = \mathcal{L}(G)$. From now on, the subscript G is dropped whenever it is clearly understood.

We introduce a barred version of the set of non-terminals N: $\bar{N} = \{\bar{A} \mid A \in N\}$ where $\bar{A}$ is the corresponding "marked" non-terminal to A. We also extend the set of variables V in order to contain marked non-terminals: $V = (N \cup \bar{N}, I^*) \cup T$. Marked non-terminals are the only symbols which can be rewritten by an indexed production.

In detail, given an indexed grammar G, the vector of π-functions induced by G is $\boldsymbol{\pi}_G = (\pi_0, \pi_1, \ldots, \pi_m, \pi_t)$. For $i \in [1, m]$, we associate the π_i-function $\pi_i = (h_i, R_i)$ with the i-th production in the enumeration of P. Each substitution function h_i, with $i \in [1, m]$, is defined inductively as follows where $\alpha, \beta \in V^*$ and $\sigma \in I^*$:

$h_i(\emptyset) = \emptyset$
$h_i(\{\epsilon\}) = \{\epsilon\}$
$h_i(\{a\}) = \{a\}$, if $a \in T$

$$h_i(\{(\bar{A},\sigma)\}) = \begin{cases} \{\alpha\} & \text{if } (\bar{A},\sigma) \in V \text{ and } [A \to \alpha]_i \in P \textit{ (Stack copy rule)} \\ \{(B, f\sigma)\} & \text{if } (\bar{A},\sigma) \in V \text{ and } [A \to B_f]_i \in P \textit{ (Push rule)} \\ \{\beta\} & \text{if } (\bar{A},\sigma) \in V \text{ and } [A_f \to \beta]_i \in P \textit{ (Pop rule)} \\ \{(\bar{A},\sigma)\} & \text{otherwise} \end{cases}$$

$h_i(\{\alpha Y\}) = h_i(\{\alpha\})h_i(\{Y\})$, if $\alpha \in V^+$ and $Y \in V$
$h_i(Q) = \bigcup_{\alpha \in Q} h_i(\{\alpha\})$, if $Q \in \wp(V^*)$, $Q \neq \emptyset$ and $\alpha \notin Q$.

Intuitively, the substitution function h_i will apply the i-th production to the marked non-terminal corresponding to the non-terminal of the associated production, without checking the stack symbols, i.e. in a context-free way. The other non-terminals remain untouched.

Given G, each regular expression R_i associated to the i-th production of P, with $i \in [1, m]$, is defined as follows, with $f \in I$ and $\sigma \in I^*$:

$$R_i = \begin{cases} V^*(\bar{A}, f\sigma)V^* & \text{if } [A_f \to \beta]_i \in P \textit{ (Pop rule)} \\ V^* & \text{otherwise.} \end{cases}$$

Intuitively, if the i-th indexed production $A_f \to \beta$ associated to R_i is of type (*3c*), then only the sentential forms containing the signed non-terminal $\bar{A}$ and having f as the top symbol of its stack, will be selected from intersection.

Now an application of $\pi_i = (h_i, R_i)$, with $i \in [1, m]$, to an indexed state corresponds to an application of the i-th indexed production.

We define the π-function π_0: its role is to mark the leftmost non-terminal of each sentential form (this marked non-terminal is the one used in the next iteration). Formally, $\pi_0 = (h_0, R_0)$ is inductively defined as follows for $\alpha \in V^+$:

$h_0(\emptyset) = \emptyset$
$h_0(\{\epsilon\}) = \{\epsilon\}$

$$h_0(\{Y\alpha\}) = \begin{cases} Y\,h_0(\{\alpha\}) & \text{if } Y \in T \\ (\bar{A},\sigma)\,\mathtt{unmark}(\{\alpha\}) & \text{if } Y = (A,\sigma) \text{ and } A \in N \\ (A,\sigma)\,h_0(\{\alpha\}) & \text{if } Y = (\bar{A},\sigma) \text{ and } \bar{A} \in \bar{N} \end{cases}$$

$h_0(Q) = \bigcup_{\alpha \in Q} h_0(\{\alpha\})$, if $Q \in \wp(V^*)$, $Q \neq \emptyset$ and $\alpha \notin Q$.

and function $\mathtt{unmark} : \wp(V^*) \to \wp(V^*)$ differs from h_0 in:

$$\mathtt{unmark}(\{Y\alpha\}) = \begin{cases} (A,\sigma)\,\mathtt{unmark}(\{\alpha\}) & \text{if } Y = (\bar{A},\sigma) \text{ and } \bar{A} \in \bar{N} \\ Y\,\mathtt{unmark}(\{\alpha\}) & \text{otherwise.} \end{cases}$$

The regular expression associated to h_0 is $R_0 = V^*$. Function h_0 marks the leftmost unmarked non-terminal while it unmarks any previously marked ones.

We define the π-function π_t to be applied to the last element of the state $\mathbf{X}$ that collects in X_t all the terminal words. Formally, $\pi_t = (h_t, R_t)$ where h_t is the identity function, namely $h_t = id$, and $R_t = T^*$. This leads us to the following system of equations where $0 \leqslant i \leqslant m$ and $j \geqslant 1$:

$$\begin{cases} \mathbf{X}^0 = (\{(S,\epsilon)\}, \emptyset, \ldots, \emptyset) \\ X_t^{j+1} = \pi_t(\mathbf{X}^j) \\ X_i^{j+1} = \pi_i(\mathbf{X}^j) \end{cases}$$

Let $(S, \epsilon) \to^n w$, with $w \in T^*$ and $n \geqslant 1$, be a derivation of G after n steps. We can construct a sequence of π-functions that exactly simulate the derivations in G such that the word $w \in X_{G,t}^{2n+1}$. Indeed, an application of the i-th production in P is exactly simulated by an application of two π-functions: $\pi_{G,0}$ to mark the non-terminal used in the production and $\pi_{G,i}$ to apply the i-th index production. After $2n$ steps, an application of the π-function $\pi_{G,t}$ at step $2n+1$ yields $w \in X_{G,t}^{2n+1}$.

Conversely it is straightforward to show by induction on n that, for every $w \in T^*$, if $w \in X_{G,t}^n$, with $n \geqslant 1$, then there exists a derivation in G yielding w after $(n-1)/2$ steps, namely $(S, \epsilon) \to^{(n-1)/2} w$. This means that $X_{G,t}^{FIX} = \mathcal{L}(G)$. □

Example 2. Consider the indexed language $L = \{a^n b^n c^n \mid n \geqslant 1\}$ and the indexed grammar $G = (\{S, T, A, B, C\}, \{a, b, c\}, \{f\}, P, S)$ generating it presented in Example 1. Let the productions in P be enumerated as follow:

$$\begin{array}{lll} [S \to T]_1 & [A_f \to aA]_4 & [B_\epsilon \to b]_7 \\ [T \to T_f]_2 & [A_\epsilon \to a]_5 & [C_f \to cC]_8 \\ [T \to ABC]_3 & [B_f \to bB]_6 & [C_\epsilon \to c]_9 \end{array}$$

We denote a substitution as a list of replacements, e.g. $\{(\bar{S}, \sigma) \to (T, \sigma)\}$ denotes the substitution h_1 defined by $h_1(\{(\bar{S}, \sigma)\}) = \{(T, \sigma)\}$ and identity otherwise. Following Theorem 1, the fixpoint characterization of the indexed grammar of Example 1 is:

$$\begin{aligned}
X_0^{j+1} &= \pi_0(h_0, R_0) = h_0(V^* \cap \bigcup \mathbf{X}^j) \\
X_1^{j+1} &= \pi_1(h_1, R_1) = \{(\bar{S}, \sigma) \to (T, \sigma)\}(V^* \cap \bigcup \mathbf{X}^j) \\
X_2^{j+1} &= \pi_2(h_2, R_2) = \{(\bar{T}, \sigma) \to (T, f\sigma)\}(V^* \cap \bigcup \mathbf{X}^j) \\
X_3^{j+1} &= \pi_3(h_3, R_3) = \{(\bar{T}, \sigma) \to (A, \sigma)(B, \sigma)(C, \sigma)\}(V^* \cap \bigcup \mathbf{X}^j) \\
X_4^{j+1} &= \pi_4(h_4, R_4) = \{(\bar{A}, f\sigma) \to a(A, \sigma)\}(V^*(\bar{A}, f\sigma)V^* \cap \bigcup \mathbf{X}^j) \\
X_5^{j+1} &= \pi_5(h_5, R_5) = \{(\bar{A}, \epsilon) \to a\}(V^*(\bar{A}, \epsilon)V^* \cap \bigcup \mathbf{X}^j) \\
X_6^{j+1} &= \pi_6(h_6, R_6) = \{(\bar{B}, f\sigma) \to b(B, \sigma)\}(V^*(\bar{B}, f\sigma)V^* \cap \bigcup \mathbf{X}^j) \\
X_7^{j+1} &= \pi_7(h_7, R_7) = \{(\bar{B}, \epsilon) \to b\}(V^*(\bar{B}, \epsilon)V^* \cap \bigcup \mathbf{X}^j) \\
X_8^{j+1} &= \pi_8(h_8, R_8) = \{(\bar{C}, f\sigma) \to c(C, \sigma)\}(V^*(\bar{C}, f\sigma)V^* \cap \bigcup \mathbf{X}^j) \\
X_9^{j+1} &= \pi_9(h_9, R_9) = \{(\bar{C}, \epsilon) \to c\}(V^*(\bar{C}, \epsilon)V^* \cap \bigcup \mathbf{X}^j) \\
X_t^{j+1} &= \pi_t(h_t, R_t) = (T^* \cap \bigcup \mathbf{X}^j)
\end{aligned}$$

where $\sigma \in I^*$, $\mathbf{X}^0 = (\{(S, \epsilon)\}, \emptyset, \emptyset, \emptyset, \emptyset, \emptyset, \emptyset, \emptyset, \emptyset, \emptyset, \emptyset)$ and the union of all components is given by $\bigcup \mathbf{X}^j = \bigcup \{X_y^j \mid y \in \{0, 1, 2, 3, 4, 5, 6, 7, 8, 9, t\}\}$. We have $X_t^{FIX} = \mathcal{L}(G) = \{a^n b^n c^n \mid n \geqslant 1\}$.

For example, the word "$aabbcc$" can be generated in X_t, after 19 steps, by the following derivation:

$$aabbcc \in \pi_t \pi_9 \pi_0 \pi_8 \pi_0 \pi_7 \pi_0 \pi_6 \pi_0 \pi_5 \pi_0 \pi_4 \pi_0 \pi_3 \pi_0 \pi_2 \pi_0 \pi_1 \pi_0(\mathbf{X}^0)$$

5 Abstract Indexed Grammars

We want to investigate if the relation that exists between regular, CF, indexed and CS languages can be expressed as GIs, namely if less expressive languages can be seen as abstractions of more expressive ones.

Given a finite set of alphabet symbols Σ, we consider the complete lattice of all possible languages on Σ, namely $\langle \wp(\Sigma^*), \subseteq, \cup, \cap, \Sigma^*, \emptyset \rangle$. Suppose that we want to model the relation between Indexed and CF languages as a GI. This means that we want to abstract an indexed language into the best (w.r.t. set inclusion) CF language that includes it. However, this is not possible since CF languages are not closed under intersection, and therefore the abstract domain of CF languages $\langle CF, \subseteq \rangle$ is not a Moore family. The same holds when analyzing the relation between CS and indexed languages, and the one between CF and regular languages: the families of indexed languages and of regular languages do not form a Moore family of $\langle \wp(\Sigma^*), \subseteq \rangle$, as shown in the following three examples.

Example 3. Consider the following family of languages: $\forall i \geqslant 0 : \mathsf{L}_i = \overline{\{\mathsf{a}^i\mathsf{b}^i\}}$. Each set L_i is a regular language since its complement language $\overline{\mathsf{L}_i}$ is a finite set and regular languages are closed under complement operation, this means that $\forall i \geqslant 0 : \mathsf{L}_i \in REG$. Taking the intersection of all L_i, namely $\mathsf{L} = \bigcap_{i=0}^{\infty} \mathsf{L}_i$, we get $\mathsf{L} = \overline{\{\mathsf{a}^n\mathsf{b}^n \mid n \geqslant 0\}}$ where the $\overline{w}$ is the complement operation. $\mathsf{L} \in CF$ since it can be created from the union of several simpler languages:

$$\mathsf{L} = \{\mathsf{a}^i\mathsf{b}^j \mid i > j\} \cup \{\mathsf{a}^i\mathsf{b}^j \mid i < j\} \cup (\mathsf{a} \cup \mathsf{b})^*\mathsf{b}(\mathsf{a} \cup \mathsf{b})^*\mathsf{a}(\mathsf{a} \cup \mathsf{b})^*$$

that is, all strings of as followed by bs in which the number of as and bs differ, joined with all strings not of the form $\mathsf{a}^i\mathsf{b}^j$. The language $\{\mathsf{a}^i\mathsf{b}^j \mid i > j\} \in CF$ and a CF grammar generating it is $\mathsf{S} \to \mathsf{aSb} \mid \mathsf{aS} \mid \mathsf{a}$ similarly $\{\mathsf{a}^i\mathsf{b}^j \mid i < j\} \in CF$, while $(\mathsf{a} \cup \mathsf{b})^*\mathsf{b}(\mathsf{a} \cup \mathsf{b})^*\mathsf{a}(\mathsf{a} \cup \mathsf{b})^* \in REG$ since it is a regular expression. Observe that we have obtained a CF language from an (infinite) intersection of regular languages.

Example 4. Consider the following two CF languages and their corresponding CF grammars:

$\mathsf{L}_1 = \{\mathsf{a}^n\mathsf{b}^n\mathsf{c}^m \mid n, m \geqslant 0\}$	$\mathsf{L}_2 = \{\mathsf{a}^n\mathsf{b}^m\mathsf{c}^m \mid n, m \geqslant 0\}$
$\mathsf{S} \to \mathsf{AC}$	$\mathsf{S} \to \mathsf{AB}$
$\mathsf{A} \to \mathsf{aAb} \mid \epsilon$	$\mathsf{A} \to \mathsf{aA} \mid \epsilon$
$\mathsf{C} \to \mathsf{cC} \mid \epsilon$	$\mathsf{B} \to \mathsf{bBc} \mid \epsilon$

Note that $\mathsf{L}_1 \cap \mathsf{L}_2 = \mathsf{L} = \{\mathsf{a}^n\mathsf{b}^n\mathsf{c}^n \mid n \geqslant 0\}$ and L is an indexed language but not CF, namely $\mathsf{L} \in IL \setminus CF$.

Example 5. Consider the following indexed languages $\mathsf{L}_1 = \{w \in \{\mathsf{a}, \mathsf{b}, \mathsf{c}\}^* \mid \#\mathsf{a} = \#\mathsf{b}\}$ and $\mathsf{L}_2 = \{w \in \{\mathsf{a}, \mathsf{b}, \mathsf{c}\}^* \mid \#\mathsf{b} = \#\mathsf{c}\}$ where $\#\mathsf{a}$ means the number of symbols a in a word. L_1 can be generated by the following CF grammar:

$$\mathsf{S} \to \mathsf{SS} \qquad \mathsf{S} \to \mathsf{aSb} \qquad \mathsf{S} \to \mathsf{bSa} \qquad \mathsf{S} \to \mathsf{c} \qquad \mathsf{S} \to \epsilon$$

and similarly for L_2. Consider the language

$$L = L_1 \cap L_2 = \{w \in \{a, b, c\}^* \mid \#a = \#b = \#c\}.$$

$L \in CS$ but $L \notin IL$. A CS grammar generating L is:

$$\begin{array}{llllll} S \to ABC & AB \to BA & BC \to CB & CA \to AC & A \to a & C \to c \\ S \to ABCS & AC \to CA & BA \to AB & CB \to BC & B \to b & \end{array}$$

Observe that we have obtained a CS language from an intersection of two indexed languages.

The examples above show that it is not possible to specify GIs between the domains of languages in the Chiomsky hierarchy. However, this does not exclude the possibility of approximating the fixpoint semantics of indexed grammars by acting on the productions of the grammars. This corresponds to constraining the structures of productions or the way the memory (stack) of the productions of indexed grammars are used, by acting on the indexed states of the equational characterization associated. We provide abstractions of indexed grammars, namely of the mechanism used to generate the indexed languages, with the aim of transforming an indexed language into a more abstract (namely a less expressive) language in Chomsky's hierarchy, such as CF or REG languages. We start in Sect. 5.1 with a simple abstraction, stack elimination, which eliminates completely the stack of all non-terminals. Then, with the purpose of refining the abstraction, we present two other abstractions: stack limitation (Sect. 5.2), which limits the stack capacity, and stack copy limitation (Sect. 5.3), which limits stack copy productions.

5.1 Stack Elimination

Definition 5. *Stack elimination removes the stack of each non-terminal in a sentential form of an indexed grammar. Namely, given a sentential form* α, *each pair* $(A, \sigma) \in \alpha$, *with* $A \in N$ *and* $\sigma \in I^*$, *is replaced by* (A, I^*).

The idea of stack elimination is to abstract away from the stack, namely, to abstract the stack to top in the sentential form. In the concrete domain, the abstract value top of the stack precisely corresponds to the set of all possible stacks. In other words, this corresponds to have a set of sentential forms one for each possible stack value. A major consequence of applying stack elimination is that the three kinds of indexed productions (stack copy, push and pop) in an indexed grammar are turned into a single context-free production.

We want to demonstrate that stack elimination is a sound abstraction of indexed grammars. In the following we denote with Φ_G the domain $\wp(V^*)^m$ of possible indexed states of an indexed grammar $G = (N, T, I, P, S)$ with m productions in P, used in the fixpoint characterization of Theorem 1. It is possible to define a function on the concrete domain $\langle \Phi_G, \sqsubseteq \rangle$ that iteratively computes the language of an indexed grammar G. The partial order $\sqsubseteq$ over Φ_G is defined as follows:

$$\forall \mathbf{X}, \mathbf{Y} \in \Phi_G : \mathbf{X} \sqsubseteq \mathbf{Y} \iff \mathtt{proj}_{\text{-}1}(\mathbf{X}) \subseteq \mathtt{proj}_{\text{-}1}(\mathbf{Y})$$

The transition relation between two indexed states $\mathbf{X}^i, \mathbf{X}^{i+1} \in \Phi_G$ corresponds to the application of the vector function $\pi_G : \Phi_G \to \Phi_G$, namely $\mathbf{X}^{i+1} = \pi_G(\mathbf{X}^i)$.

We formalize the abstract domain as a closure $\rho^E : \Phi_G \to \Phi_G$ on $\langle \Phi_G, \sqsubseteq \rangle$, as follows:

$$\rho^E(\mathbf{X}) = (\rho^E(X_1), \ldots, \rho^E(X_m))$$

and, with a slight abuse of notation, $\rho^E(X_i) = \{\rho^E(s_i) \mid s_i \in X_i\}$ where for $s_i = \lambda_{i1} \ldots \lambda_{iw}$ with $\lambda_{ij} \in V$ we have:

$$\rho^E(\lambda_{i1})\rho^E(\lambda_{i2} \ldots \lambda_{iw}) = \begin{cases} (A, I^*) \text{ if } \lambda_{i1} = (A, \sigma) \\ \lambda_{i1} \quad\quad \text{otherwise.} \end{cases}$$

Intuitively, the stack of all non-terminal symbols is set to I^*. This means that there is no restrictions on the symbol on the top of the stack when performing a pop operation, turning push and pop productions to stack copy productions.

Lemma 1. *The function ρ^E on domain $\langle \Phi_G, \sqsubseteq \rangle$ is an upper closure operator. Moreover, we have that* $\mathtt{lfp}^{\sqsubseteq}\pi_G(\mathbf{X}^0) = \rho^E \circ \mathtt{lfp}^{\sqsubseteq}\pi_G(\mathbf{X}^0)$ *while* $\mathtt{lfp}^{\sqsubseteq}\pi_G(\mathbf{X}^0) \sqsubseteq \mathtt{lfp}^{\sqsubseteq}\pi_G(\rho^E(\mathbf{X}^0))$.

Lemma 2. *Let $\widetilde{G}$ be the indexed grammar obtained by stack elimination from an indexed grammar* G, *then* $\mathtt{lfp}^{\sqsubseteq}\pi_{\widetilde{G}}(\mathbf{X}^0) = \mathtt{lfp}^{\sqsubseteq}\pi_G(\rho^E(\mathbf{X}^0))$.

This allows us to prove the soundness of the abstraction showing that any language obtained by stack elimination from an indexed grammar is an over approximation of its original indexed language:

Theorem 2. *Let $\widetilde{G}$ be the indexed grammar obtained by stack elimination from the indexed grammar* G, *then* $\mathcal{L}(G) \subseteq \mathcal{L}(\widetilde{G})$.

The loss of precision is due to the fact that, when eliminating the stack, an indexed grammar can no longer count or store occurrences of an index symbol, thus it is reduced to a CF grammar. Moreover, it turns out that if the original indexed grammar G is such that $\mathcal{L}(G) \in \mathit{IL}$ but $\mathcal{L}(G) \notin \mathit{CF}$ then $\mathcal{L}(\widetilde{G})$ is a CF language but not indexed.

Corollary 1. *Let $\widetilde{G}$ be the indexed grammar obtained from* G *by stack elimination such that $\mathcal{L}(G) \in \mathit{IL} \setminus \mathit{CF}$, then $\mathcal{L}(\widetilde{G}) \notin \mathit{IL} \setminus \mathit{CF}$.*

Example 6. The language $L = \{a^n b^n c^n \mid n \geqslant 1\}$ in Example 1 is an indexed language but not CF, namely $L \in \mathit{IL} \setminus \mathit{CF}$. If we apply stack elimination as described above, we obtain a new language $\mathcal{L}(\widetilde{G})$ generated by the new grammar $\widetilde{G}$ with the following productions:

$$\begin{array}{lll} \mathsf{S} \to \mathsf{T} & \mathsf{A} \to \mathsf{aA} & \mathsf{B} \to \mathsf{b} \\ \mathsf{T} \to \mathsf{T} & \mathsf{A} \to \mathsf{a} & \mathsf{C} \to \mathsf{cC} \\ \mathsf{T} \to \mathsf{ABC} & \mathsf{B} \to \mathsf{bB} & \mathsf{C} \to \mathsf{c} \end{array}$$

The language generated from $\widetilde{G}$ is $\mathcal{L}(\widetilde{G}) = \{a^*b^*c^*\}$ and it is a regular language, $\mathcal{L}(\widetilde{G}) \in \mathsf{REG}$.

Although some examples may be deceiving, in general it is not true that any indexed languages become regular by stack elimination. Indeed, indexed grammars could contain context-free characteristic rules that do not affect stacks and so, after stack elimination, still remain, turning the language to a CF language and not regular. The following is an example of such an indexed grammar.

Example 7. The language $L = \{a^n b^n c^n \mid n \geqslant 1\}$ could be generated also by the following indexed grammar:

$$\begin{array}{ll} S \to aS_f c & T_f \to Tb \\ S \to T & T_\epsilon \to \epsilon \end{array}$$

If we apply stack elimination, we obtain the language $\widetilde{L} = \{a^n b^* c^n \mid n \geqslant 1\}$. Note that $L \subseteq \widetilde{L}$ and $\widetilde{L} \in \mathit{CF}$ but $\widetilde{L} \notin \mathit{REG}$.

It is indeed obvious to observe that stack elimination produces precisely the class of CF languages.

Corollary 2. *For any CF grammar* $\widetilde{G}$ *there exists an indexed grammar* G *such that:* $\mathrm{lfp}^{\sqsubseteq} \boldsymbol{\pi}_{\widetilde{G}}(\mathbf{X}^0) = \mathrm{lfp}^{\sqsubseteq} \boldsymbol{\pi}_G(\rho^E(\mathbf{X}^0))$.

5.2 Stack Limitation

Definition 6. *Stack limitation limits the numbers of symbols on the stack of each non-terminal by a constant* $k \geqslant 0$. *This means that each stack can contain at most* k *symbols and all others* $k+1$ *symbols pushed on to the stack will be discarded.*

We want to demonstrate that stack limitation is a sound abstraction of indexed grammars. As in the previous section, we operate on the concrete domain $\langle \Phi_G, \sqsubseteq \rangle$. We formalize the abstract domain as an upper closure operator ρ_k^L, with $k \geqslant 0$, on the concrete domain $\langle \Phi_G, \sqsubseteq \rangle$. We define $\rho_k^L : \Phi_G \to \Phi_G$:

$$\rho_k^L(\mathbf{X}) = (\rho_k^L(X_1), \ldots, \rho_k^L(X_m))$$

and, with a slight abuse of notation, $\rho_k^L(X_i) = \{\rho_k^L(s_i) \mid s_i \in X_i\}$ where for $s_i = \lambda_{i1} \ldots \lambda_{iw}$ with $\lambda_{ij} \in V$ we have:

$$\rho_k^L(\lambda_{i1})\rho_k^L(\lambda_{i2} \ldots \lambda_{iw}) = \begin{cases} (A, \hat{\sigma}) \text{ if } \lambda_{i1} = (A, \sigma) \text{ and } |\sigma| > k \\ \lambda_{i1} \quad \text{ otherwise.} \end{cases}$$

where $|\sigma| = z$ if $\sigma = q_z \ldots q_{k+1} q_k \ldots q_1$ and $|\epsilon| = 0$ with $\sigma \in I^*$, and for $1 \leqslant i \leqslant z$, $q_i \in I$, q_z top symbol and $\hat{\sigma} = q_k \ldots q_1$. Intuitively, by function ρ_k^L, the stack of each non-terminal is limited to k symbols and each additional push of others symbols will be discarded. Observe that this technique corresponds to limiting push productions only.

Lemma 3. *The function* ρ_k^L *on the domain* $\langle \Phi_G, \sqsubseteq \rangle$ *is an upper closure operator. Moreover,* $\mathrm{lfp}^{\sqsubseteq} \pi_G(\mathbf{X}^0) = \rho_k^L \circ \mathrm{lfp}^{\sqsubseteq} \pi_G(\mathbf{X}^0)$.

Lemma 4. *Let* $\widetilde{G}_k$ *be the indexed grammar obtained by stack limitation with the constant* k *from an indexed grammar* G*, then* $\mathrm{lfp}^{\sqsubseteq} \pi_{\widetilde{G}_k}(\mathbf{X}^0) = \mathrm{lfp}^{\sqsubseteq} \pi_G(\rho_k^L(\mathbf{X}^0))$.

In the following theorem we prove that stack limitation, as defined by function ρ_k^L, is not sound, namely, at fixpoint, the language generated is not always an over approximation of the original concrete language.

Theorem 3. $\mathrm{lfp}^{\sqsubseteq} \pi_G(\mathbf{X}^0) \not\sqsubseteq \mathrm{lfp}^{\sqsubseteq} \pi_G(\rho_k^L(\mathbf{X}^0))$.

Proof. The proof is made by providing a counterexample. The language $L = \{a^n b^n c^n \mid n \geqslant 1\}$ in Example 1 has only one push production: $T \to T_f$. Therefore, after stack limitation, each stack can contain at most k index symbols of f and the following family of languages is generated:

$$\forall k \geqslant 0\ ,\ L_k = \{a^n b^n c^n \mid 1 \leqslant n \leqslant k+1\}$$

For all $k \geqslant 0$, the language L_k is a regular language since each family contains a finite number of words: for $k = 0$ then $\{abc\}$, $k = 1$ then $\{abc, aabbcc\}$, ... Moreover, each L_k is not an over approximation of the original language since $L \not\subseteq L_k$, this leads to $\mathrm{lfp}^{\sqsubseteq} \pi_G(\mathbf{X}^0) \not\sqsubseteq \mathrm{lfp}^{\sqsubseteq} \pi_G(\rho_k^L(\mathbf{X}^0))$. □

Observe that the infinite intersection of all family of languages L_k obtained by stack limitation from a language L, corresponds to L_0, namely $\bigcap_{k=0}^{\infty} L_k = L_0$, while the infinite union of all L_k is a superset of the original language L, namely $L \subseteq \bigcup_{k=0}^{\infty} L_k$.

At first glance, the family of languages generated from a language non-stack-limited is regular, as the previous example showed but, in general, this is not always true: the next example shows a counterexample, similar to Example 7:

Example 8. The language $L = \{a^n b^n c^n \mid n \geqslant 1\}$ could be generated also by the following indexed grammar:

$$S \to aS_f c \qquad T_f \to Tb$$
$$S \to T \qquad T_\epsilon \to \epsilon$$

If we apply stack limitation we get the following family of languages:

$$\forall k \geqslant 1\ ,\ L_k = \{a^n b^m c^n \mid n \geqslant 1 \wedge m \leqslant k\}$$

Note that $\forall k \geqslant 1\ L_k \in \mathit{CF}$ while for $k = 0\ \ L_0 = \{\epsilon\}$ the empty word ϵ is not accepted by L.

We can force the soundness of stack limitation abstraction by modifying the upper closure operator ρ_k^L as follows, obtaining the new uco ρ_k^{LE}:

$$\rho_k^{LE}(\mathbf{X}) = \cdots = \rho_k^{LE}(\lambda_{ij}) = \begin{cases} (A, I^*) & \text{if } \lambda_{i1} = (A, \sigma) \text{ and } |\sigma| > k \text{ or } k = 0 \\ \lambda_{i1} & \text{otherwise.} \end{cases}$$

Intuitively, ρ_k^{LE} eliminates completely the stack of a non-terminal if and only if $k = 0$ or the size of the stack exceeds the parameter k.

Lemma 5. $\mathsf{lfp}^{\sqsubseteq}\pi_{\mathsf{G}}(\mathbf{X}^0) \sqsubseteq \mathsf{lfp}^{\sqsubseteq}\pi_{\mathsf{G}}(\rho_k^{LE}(\mathbf{X}^0))$.

By Lemma 5 and by substituting ρ_k^L with the new uco ρ_k^{LE} in Lemmas 3 and 4, we can prove the soundness of this new abstraction.

Theorem 4. *Let* $\widetilde{\mathsf{G}}_k$ *be the indexed grammar obtained by stack limitation with the constant* k *from an indexed grammar* G*, then* $\mathcal{L}(\mathsf{G}) \subseteq \mathcal{L}(\widetilde{\mathsf{G}}_k)$.

5.3 Stack Copy Limitation

Definition 7. *Stack copy limitation limits the copy of the stack, from the right-side of a production, to a finite number of non-terminals symbols in a given set* H*. The contents of the other stacks are set to* I^* *meaning that you can do push and pop operations with no limits as in Sect. 5.1.*

As before, we want to demonstrate that stack copy limitation is a sound abstraction of indexed grammars. As in the previous sections, we formalize the abstract domain as an upper closure operator ρ_H^C on the concrete domain $\langle \Phi_G, \sqsubseteq \rangle$ with $\mathsf{H} \subseteq \mathsf{N}$ where N is the set of non-terminals of the indexed grammar. We define $\rho_H^C : \Phi_G \to \Phi_G$ as:

$$\rho_H^C(\mathbf{X}) = (\rho_H^C(X_1), \ldots, \rho_H^C(X_m))$$

and, with a slight abuse of notation, $\rho_H^C(X_i) = \{\rho_H^C(s_i) \mid s_i \in X_i\}$ where for $s_i = \lambda_{i1} \ldots \lambda_{iw}$ with $\lambda_{ij} \in V$ we have:

$$\rho_H^C(\lambda_{i1})\rho_H^C(\lambda_{i2} \ldots \lambda_{iw}) = \begin{cases} (A, I^*) \text{ if } \lambda_{i1} = (A, \sigma) \text{ and } A \notin H \\ \lambda_{i1} \qquad \text{otherwise.} \end{cases}$$

Intuitively, the function ρ_H^C eliminates the stack of only a restricted set of non-terminals, namely those not in the set H, while for all non-terminals in H the stack will be copied and so all the indices symbols on it still remain. Observe that if $\mathsf{H} = \mathsf{N}$ then $\rho_H^C = id$ where id is the identity function, while if $\mathsf{H} = \emptyset$ then $\rho_H^C = \rho^E$ where ρ^E is the stack elimination technique presented in Sect. 5.1.

Lemma 6. *The function* ρ_H^C *on the domain* $\langle \Phi_G, \sqsubseteq \rangle$ *is an uco. Moreover, we have* $\mathsf{lfp}^{\sqsubseteq}\pi_{\mathsf{G}}(\mathbf{X}^0) = \rho_H^C \circ \mathsf{lfp}^{\sqsubseteq}\pi_{\mathsf{G}}(\mathbf{X}^0)$ *while* $\mathsf{lfp}^{\sqsubseteq}\pi_{\mathsf{G}}(\mathbf{X}^0) \sqsubseteq \mathsf{lfp}^{\sqsubseteq}\pi_{\mathsf{G}}(\rho_H^C(\mathbf{X}^0))$.

Lemma 7. *Let* $\widetilde{\mathsf{G}}_H$ *be the indexed grammar obtained by stack copy limitation from an indexed grammar* G*, with* $\mathsf{H} \subseteq \mathsf{N}$ *where* N *is the set of non-terminals of* G*, then* $\mathsf{lfp}^{\sqsubseteq}\pi_{\widetilde{\mathsf{G}}_H}(\mathbf{X}^0) = \mathsf{lfp}^{\sqsubseteq}\pi_{\mathsf{G}}(\rho_H^C(\mathbf{X}^0))$.

The following theorem asserts the soundness of the abstraction by showing that any language obtained by stack copy limitation from an indexed grammar is an over approximation of its original indexed language:

Theorem 5. *Let* $\widetilde{\mathsf{G}}_H$ *be the indexed grammar obtained by stack copy limitation of a subset of non-terminals* H *from an indexed grammar* G*, then* $\mathcal{L}(\mathsf{G}) \subseteq \mathcal{L}(\widetilde{\mathsf{G}}_H)$.

As expected, the quality of this abstraction, in terms of classification in the Chomsky hierarchy, may be better then stack elimination, depending on which non-terminals form the set $H \subseteq N$.

Example 9. Consider the language $L = \{a^n b^n c^n \mid n \geqslant 1\}$ in Example 1 and let $H = \{A\}$, then by stack copy limitation we obtain: $\widetilde{L} = \{a^n b^* c^* \mid n \geqslant 1\}$. Observe that $\widetilde{L} \in REG$ and $L \subseteq \widetilde{L}$, indeed, if H contains one of the three non-terminals then stack copy limitation is equivalent to stack elimination. However, if $H = \{A, B\}$, then by stack copy limitation we obtain $\widetilde{L}' = \{a^n b^n c^* \mid n \geqslant 1\}$. Note that $L \subseteq \widetilde{L}' \subseteq \widetilde{L}$, $\widetilde{L}' \in CF$ and $\widetilde{L}' \notin REG$.

We conclude by showing in Fig. 2 the three sound abstractions presented in this section applied to Example 6.

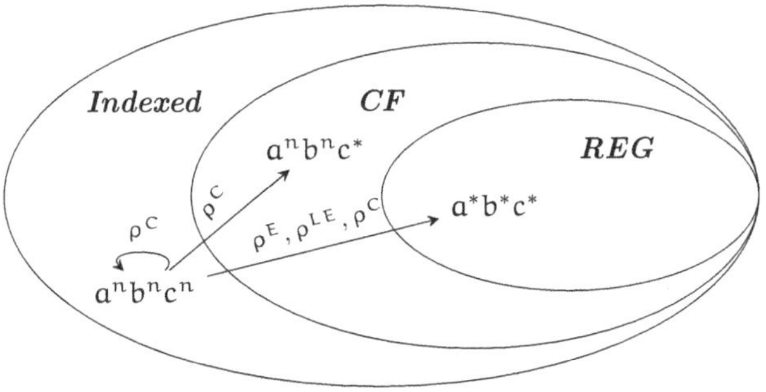

Fig. 2. Sound abstractions of indexed grammars presented in Sect. 5 and applied to Example 6

6 Related and Future Works

The approximation of grammar structures by abstract interpretation is not new. In [13] and [15] the authors introduced the idea of abstracting formal languages by abstract interpretation for the design of static analysers that manipulate symbolic structures. This provided both the source for new symbolic abstract domains for program analysis and the possibility of formalising known algorithms, such as parsers, as abstract interpreters. Abstractions into regular languages have been used in formal verification (e.g., see [7]). In program analysis non-regular approximations of formal languages have been used in aliasing analysis [19]. The idea of grammar abstraction as a relation between CF grammars has been also used for relating concrete and abstract syntax in [4]. We exploit this latter line of research by establishing a relation, formalised here by abstract interpretation, between indexed grammars with the aim of relating languages in Chomsky's hierarchy [6].

None of the above mentioned approaches considered the more general problem of correlating languages in Chomsky's hierarchy by the theory of fixpoint abstraction by abstract interpretation. We believe that a systematic reconstruction of Chomsky's hierarchy by fixpoint abstract interpretation may provide both new insights into a fundamental field of computer science and new algorithms and methods for approximating structures described by grammars. Indeed, the current work originated from the desire of finding suitable abstract domains for expressing the invariant properties among obfuscated malware variants [17,18]. We reformulated the Chomsky's hierarchy by using the standard abstract interpretation methods: we provided a fixpoint semantics for indexed languages and we characterised classes of less expressive languages in terms of fixpoint abstractions of this semantics. In our case, the approximation of indexed languages shows how it is possible to systematically and constructively derive all fixpoint descriptions for CF languages as abstract interpretations. In particular, we proved that a *calculational design*, in the style of [8], of these fixpoint representation for CF languages is possible, and how new families of languages can be derived in this form. As future work we plan to generalize known separation results between classes of languages, e.g., the Pumping Lemmata, as instances of incompleteness of language abstractions. The idea is that, if a family of languages corresponds to a suitable abstraction of the fixpoint semantics of a more concrete family of languages–in our case indexed languages, then languages not expressible in one family should correspond to witnesses of the incompleteness of this abstraction [21]. The interest in this perspective over Chomsky's hierarchy is in the fact that we can reformulate most of this hierarchy, including separation results, in terms of abstract interpretation, providing powerful tools for comparing symbolic abstract domains with respect to their expressive power.

References

1. Adams, J., Freden, E., Mishna, M.: From indexed grammars to generating functions. RAIRO Theor. Inform. Appl. **47**(4), 325–350 (2013)
2. Aho, A.V.: Indexed grammars - an extension of context-free grammars. J. ACM **15**(4), 647–671 (1968)
3. Aho, A.V.: Nested stack automata. J. ACM **16**(3), 383–406 (1969)
4. Ballance, R.A., Butcher, J., Graham, S.L.: Grammatical abstraction and incremental syntax analysis in a language-based editor. In: Proceedings of the ACM SIGPLAN 1988 Conference on Programming Language Design and Implementation, PLDI 1988, pp. 185–198. ACM, New York (1988)
5. Bertsch, E.: On the relationship between indexed grammars and logic programs. J. Log. Program. **18**(1), 81–98 (1994)
6. Chomsky, N.: On certain formal properties of grammars. Inf. Control. **2**(2), 137–167 (1959)
7. Clarke, E.M., Grumberg, O., Jha, S.: Verifying parameterized networks. ACM Trans. Program. Lang. Syst. **19**(5), 726–750 (1997)
8. Cousot, P.: The calculational design of a generic abstract interpreter. In: Broy, M., Steinbrüggen, R. (eds.) Calculational System Design, vol. 173, pp. 421–505. NATO Science Series, Series F: Computer and Systems Sciences. IOS Press, Amsterdam (1999)

9. Cousot, P.: Constructive design of a hierarchy of semantics of a transition system by abstract interpretation. Theor. Comput. Sci. **277**(1–2), 47–103 (2002)
10. Cousot, P., Cousot, R.: Abstract interpretation: a unified lattice model for static analysis of programs by construction or approximation of fixpoints. In: Conference Record of the 4th ACM Symposium on Principles of Programming Languages (POPL 1977), pp. 238–252. ACM Press (1977)
11. Cousot, P., Cousot, R.: Systematic design of program analysis frameworks. In: Conference Record of the 6th ACM Symposium on Principles of Programming Languages (POPL 1979), pp. 269–282. ACM Press (1979)
12. Cousot, P., Cousot, R.: Abstract interpretation frameworks. J. Log. Comput. **2**(4), 511–547 (1992)
13. Cousot, P., Cousot, R.: Compositional and inductive semantic definitions in fixpoint, equational, constraint, closure-condition, rule-based and game-theoretic form (Invited Paper). In: Wolper, P. (ed.) CAV 1995. LNCS, vol. 939, pp. 293–308. Springer, Heidelberg (1995). https://doi.org/10.1007/3-540-60045-0_58
14. Cousot, P., Halbwachs, N.: Automatic discovery of linear restraints among variables of a program. In: POPL 1978: Proceedings of the 5th ACM SIGACT-SIGPLAN Symposium on Principles of Programming Languages, pp. 84–96. ACM Press (1978)
15. Cousot, P., Cousot, R.: Grammar semantics, analysis and parsing by abstract interpretation. Theor. Comput. Sci. **412**(44), 6135–6192 (2011)
16. Cousot, P., Cousot, R.: Abstract interpretation: past, present and future. In: Henzinger, T.A., Miller, D. (eds.) Joint Meeting of the Twenty-Third EACSL Annual Conference on Computer Science Logic (CSL) and the Twenty-Ninth Annual ACM/IEEE Symposium on Logic in Computer Science (LICS), CSL-LICS 2014, Vienna, Austria, 14–18 July 2014, pp. 2:1–2:10. ACM (2014)
17. Dalla Preda, M., Giacobazzi, R., Debray, S., Coogan, K., Townsend, G.M.: Modelling metamorphism by abstract interpretation. In: Cousot, R., Martel, M. (eds.) SAS 2010. LNCS, vol. 6337, pp. 218–235. Springer, Heidelberg (2010). https://doi.org/10.1007/978-3-642-15769-1_14
18. Dalla Preda, M., Giacobazzi, R., Debray, S.K.: Unveiling metamorphism by abstract interpretation of code properties. Theor. Comput. Sci. **577**, 74–97 (2015)
19. Deutsch, A.: Interprocedural may-alias analysis for pointers: beyond k-limiting. SIGPLAN Not. **29**(6), 230–241 (1994)
20. Gazdar, G.: Applicability of indexed grammars to natural languages. In: Reyle, U., Rohrer, C. (eds.) Natural Language Parsing and Linguistic Theories, pp. 69–94. Springer, Dordrecht (1988). https://doi.org/10.1007/978-94-009-1337-0_3
21. Giacobazzi, R., Ranzato, F., Scozzari, F.: Making abstract interpretation complete. J. ACM. **47**(2), 361–416 (2000)
22. Ginsburg, S.: The Mathematical Theory of Context Free Languages. McGraw-Hill Book Company, New York (1966)
23. Istrail, S.: Generalization of the Ginsburg-Rice Schützenberger fixed-point theorem for context-sensitive and recursive-enumerable languages. Theor. Comput. Sci. **18**(3), 333–341 (1982)
24. Partee, B.B., ter Meulen, A.G., Wall, R.: Mathematical Methods in Linguistics, vol. 30. Springer, Dordrecht (2012). https://doi.org/10.1007/978-94-009-2213-6

Language Inclusion Algorithms as Complete Abstract Interpretations

Pierre Ganty[1], Francesco Ranzato[2], and Pedro Valero[1,3](✉)

[1] IMDEA Software Institute, Madrid, Spain
{pierre.ganty,pedro.valero}@imdea.org
[2] Dipartimento di Matematica, University of Padova, Padova, Italy
francesco.ranzato@unipd.it
[3] Universidad Politécnica de Madrid, Madrid, Spain

Abstract. We study the language inclusion problem $L_1 \subseteq L_2$ where L_1 is regular. Our approach relies on abstract interpretation and checks whether an overapproximating abstraction of L_1, obtained by successively overapproximating the Kleene iterates of its least fixpoint characterization, is included in L_2. We show that a language inclusion problem is decidable whenever this overapproximating abstraction satisfies a completeness condition (i.e. its loss of precision causes no false alarm) and prevents infinite ascending chains (i.e. it guarantees termination of least fixpoint computations). Such overapproximating abstraction function on languages can be defined using quasiorder relations on words where the abstraction gives the language of all words "greater than or equal to" a given input word for that quasiorder. We put forward a range of quasiorders that allow us to systematically design decision procedures for different language inclusion problems such as regular languages into regular languages or into trace sets of one-counter nets. In the case of inclusion between regular languages, some of the induced inclusion checking procedures correspond to well-known state-of-the-art algorithms like the so-called antichain algorithms. Finally, we provide an equivalent greatest fixpoint language inclusion check which relies on quotients of languages and, to the best of our knowledge, was not previously known.

1 Introduction

Language inclusion is a fundamental and classical problem which consists in deciding, given two languages L_1 and L_2, whether $L_1 \subseteq L_2$ holds. We consider languages of finite words over a finite alphabet Σ.

The basic idea of our approach for solving a language inclusion problem $L_1 \subseteq L_2$ is to leverage Cousot and Cousot's abstract interpretation [6,7] for checking the inclusion of an overapproximation (i.e. a superset) of L_1 into L_2. This idea draws inspiration from the work of Hofmann and Chen [18], who used abstract interpretation to decide language inclusion between languages of infinite words.

Assuming that L_1 is specified as least fixpoint of an equation system on $\wp(\Sigma^*)$, an approximation of L_1 is obtained by applying an overapproximating

B.-Y. E. Chang (Ed.): SAS 2019, LNCS 11822, pp. 140–161, 2019.
https://doi.org/10.1007/978-3-030-32304-2_8

abstraction function for sets of words $\rho : \wp(\Sigma^*) \to \wp(\Sigma^*)$ at each step of the Kleene iterates converging to the least fixpoint. This ρ is an upper closure operator which is used in standard abstract interpretation for approximating an input language by adding words (possibly none) to it. This abstract interpretation-based approach provides an abstract inclusion check $\rho(L_1) \subseteq L_2$ which is always sound by construction. We then give conditions on ρ which ensure a *complete* abstract inclusion check, namely, the answer to $\rho(L_1) \subseteq L_2$ is always exact (no "false alarms" in abstract interpretation terminology): (i) $\rho(L_2) = L_2$; (ii) ρ is a complete abstraction for symbol concatenation $\lambda X \in \wp(\Sigma^*).aX$, for all $a \in \Sigma$, according to the standard notion of completeness in abstract interpretation [6,16,23]. This approach leads us to design in Sect. 4 an algorithmic framework for language inclusion problems which is parameterized by an underlying language abstraction (cf. Theorem 4.5).

We then focus on overapproximating abstractions ρ which are induced by a quasiorder relation $\leqslant$ on words in Σ^*. Here, a language L is overapproximated by adding all the words which are "greater than or equal to" some word of L for $\leqslant$. This allows us to instantiate the above conditions (i) and (ii) for having a complete abstract inclusion check in terms of the quasiorder $\leqslant$. Termination, which corresponds to having finitely many Kleene iterates in the fixpoint computations, is guaranteed by requiring that the relation $\leqslant$ is a well-quasiorder.

We define quasiorders satisfying the above conditions which are directly derived from the standard Nerode equivalence relations on words. These quasiorders have been first investigated by Ehrenfeucht et al. [11] and have been later generalized and extended by de Luca and Varricchio [8,9]. In particular, drawing from a result by de Luca and Varricchio [8], we show that the language abstractions induced by the Nerode quasiorders are the most general ones which fit in our algorithmic framework for checking language inclusion. While these quasiorder abstractions do not depend on some language representation (e.g., some class of automata), we provide quasiorders which instead exploit an underlying language representation given by a finite automaton. In particular, by selecting suitable well-quasiorders for the class of language inclusion problems at hand we are able to systematically derive decision procedures for the inclusion problem $L_1 \subseteq L_2$ when: (i) both L_1 and L_2 are regular and (ii) L_1 is regular and L_2 is the trace language of a one-counter net.

These decision procedures that we systematically derive here by instantiating our framework are then related to existing language inclusion checking algorithms. We study in detail the case where both languages L_1 and L_2 are regular and represented by finite state automata. When our decision procedure for $L_1 \subseteq L_2$ is derived from a well-quasiorder on Σ^* by exploiting the automaton-based representation of L_2, it turns out that we obtain the well-known "antichain algorithm" by De Wulf et al. [10]. Also, by including a simulation relation in the definition of the well-quasiorder we derive a decision procedure that partially matches the inclusion algorithm by Abdulla et al. [2], hence also that by Bonchi and Pous [4]. For the case in which L_1 is regular and L_2 is the set of traces of a one-counter net we derive an alternative proof for the decidability of the language inclusion problem [19].

Finally, we leverage a standard duality result in abstract fixpoint checking [5] and put forward a greatest fixpoint approach (instead of the above least fixpoint-based procedure) for the case where both L_1 and L_2 are regular languages. In this case, we exploit the properties of the overapproximating abstraction induced by the quasiorder in order to show that the Kleene iterates of this greatest fixpoint computation are finitely many. Interestingly, the Kleene iterates of the greatest fixpoint are finitely many whether you apply the overapproximating abstraction or not, which we show relying on forward complete abstract interpretations [15]. An extended version of this paper is available on-line [14].

2 Background

Order Theory Basics. If X is a subset of some universe set U then X^c denotes the complement of X with respect to U, and U is implicitly given by the context.

$\langle D, \leqslant\rangle$ is a *quasiordered set* (qoset) when $\leqslant$ is a quasiorder relation on D, i.e. a reflexive and transitive binary relation. A qoset satisfies the *ascending* (resp. *descending*) *chain condition* (ACC, resp. DCC) if there is no countably infinite sequence of distinct elements $\{x_i\}_{i\in\mathbb{N}}$ such that, for all $i \in \mathbb{N}$, $x_i \leqslant x_{i+1}$ (resp. $x_{i+1} \leqslant x_i$). A qoset is called ACC (DCC) when it satisfies the ACC (DCC).

A qoset $\langle D, \leqslant\rangle$ is a *partially ordered set* (poset) when $\leqslant$ is antisymmetric. A subset of a poset is *directed* if it is nonempty and every pair of elements has an upper bound in it. A poset $\langle D, \leqslant\rangle$ is a *directed-complete partial order* (CPO) if it has the least upper bound (lub) of all its directed subsets. A poset is a *join-semilattice* if it has the lub of all its nonempty finite subsets (so that binary lubs are enough). A poset is a *complete lattice* if it has the lub of all its arbitrary (possibly empty) subsets (so that it also has the greatest lower bound (glb) of all its arbitrary subsets).

A qoset $\langle D, \leqslant\rangle$ is a *well-quasiordered set* (wqoset) when for every countably infinite sequence of elements $\{x_i\}_{i\in\mathbb{N}}$ there exist $i, j \in \mathbb{N}$ such that $i < j$ and $x_i \leqslant x_j$. For every qoset $\langle D, \leqslant\rangle$ with $X, Y \subseteq D$, we define the following relation:

$$X \sqsubseteq Y \stackrel{\triangle}{\Longleftrightarrow} \forall x \in X, \exists y \in Y,\ y \leqslant x .$$

A *minor* of a subset $X \subseteq D$, denoted by $\lfloor X \rfloor$, is a subset of minimal elements of X w.r.t. $\leqslant$, i.e. $\lfloor X \rfloor \triangleq \{x \in X \mid \forall y \in X, y \leqslant x \text{ implies } y = x\}$. The *minor* of X satisfies the following properties: (i) $X \sqsubseteq \lfloor X \rfloor$ and (ii) $\lfloor X \rfloor$ is an *antichain*, that is, $x_1 \leqslant x_2$ for no distinct $x_1, x_2 \in \lfloor X \rfloor$. Let us recall that every subset of a wqoset $\langle D, \leqslant\rangle$ has at least one minor set, all minor sets are finite and if $\langle D, \leqslant\rangle$ is additionally a poset then there exists exactly one minor set. We denote the set of antichains of a qoset $\langle D, \leqslant\rangle$ by $\mathrm{AC}_{\langle D,\leqslant\rangle} \triangleq \{X \subseteq D \mid X \text{ is an antichain}\}$. It turns out that $\langle \mathrm{AC}_{\langle D,\leqslant\rangle}, \sqsubseteq\rangle$ is a qoset, it is ACC if $\langle D, \leqslant\rangle$ is a wqoset and it is a poset if $\langle D, \leqslant\rangle$ is a poset.

Kleene Iterates. Let $\langle X, \leqslant\rangle$ be a qoset, $f : X \to X$ be a function and $b \in X$. Then, the trace of values of the variable $x \in X$ computed by the following iterative procedure:

$$\texttt{Kleene}(f, b) \triangleq \begin{cases} x := b; \\ \textbf{while } f(x) \neq x \textbf{ do } x := f(x); \\ \textbf{return } x; \end{cases}$$

provides the possibly infinite sequence of so-called Kleene iterates of the function f starting from the basis b. When $\langle X, \leqslant \rangle$ is a ACC (resp. DCC) CPO, $b \leqslant f(b)$ (resp. $f(b) \leqslant b$) and f is monotonic then $\texttt{Kleene}(f, b)$ terminates and returns the least (resp. greatest) fixpoint of the function f which is greater (resp. less) than or equal to b.

Let us also recall that given a monotonic function $f : C \to C$ on a complete lattice C, its least and greatest fixpoints always exist, and we denote them, resp., by $\text{lfp}(f)$ and $\text{gfp}(f)$.

For the sake of clarity, we overload the notation and use the same symbol for an operator/relation and its componentwise (i.e. pointwise) extension on product domains. A vector $\vec{\boldsymbol{Y}}$ in some product domain $D^{|S|}$ might be also denoted by $\langle Y_i \rangle_{i \in S}$ and $\vec{\boldsymbol{Y}}_q$ denotes its component Y_q.

Language Theory Basics. Let Σ be an *alphabet* (that is, a finite nonempty set of symbols). Words are finite sequences of symbols where ϵ denote the empty sequence. Languages are sets of words where Σ^* is the set of all words. Concatenation in Σ^* is simply denoted by juxtaposition, both for concatenating words uv, languages $L_1 L_2$ and words with languages such as uLv. We sometimes use the symbol $\cdot$ to refer explicitly to the concatenation operation.

A *finite automaton* (FA) is a tuple $\mathcal{A} = \langle Q, \delta, I, F, \Sigma \rangle$ where Σ is the *alphabet*, Q is the finite set of *states*, $I \subseteq Q$ are the *initial states*, $F \subseteq Q$ are the *final states*, and $\delta : Q \times \Sigma \to \wp(Q)$ is the *transition relation*. If $u \in \Sigma^*$ and $q, q' \in Q$ then $q \overset{u}{\rightsquigarrow} q'$ means that the state q' is reachable from q by following the string u. Therefore, $q \overset{\epsilon}{\rightsquigarrow} q'$ holds iff $q = q'$. The *language generated by a FA* $\mathcal{A}$ is $\mathcal{L}(\mathcal{A}) \triangleq \{u \in \Sigma^* \mid \exists q_i \in I, \exists q_f \in F, q_i \overset{u}{\rightsquigarrow} q_f\}$. Figure 1 depicts an example of FA.

3 Inclusion Check by Complete Abstractions

The *language inclusion problem* consists in checking whether $L_1 \subseteq L_2$ holds where L_1 and L_2 are two languages over an alphabet Σ. In this section, we show how (backward) complete abstractions ρ can be used to compute an overapproximation $\rho(L_1)$ of L_1 such that $\rho(L_1) \subseteq L_2 \Leftrightarrow L_1 \subseteq L_2$.

Let $\text{uco}(C)$ denote the set of upper closure operators (or simply closure operators) on a poset $\langle C, \leq_C \rangle$, that is, the set of monotonic, idempotent (i.e., $\rho(x) = \rho(\rho(x))$) and increasing (i.e., $x \leq_C \rho(x)$) functions in $C \to C$. We often write $c \in \rho(C)$ (or simply $c \in \rho$ when C is clear from the context) to denote that there exists $c' \in C$ with $c = \rho(c')$, and let us recall that this happens iff $\rho(c) = c$.

Closure-based abstract interpretation [7] can be applied to solve a generic inclusion checking problem stated through least fixpoints as follows. Let $\rho \in \text{uco}(C)$ and $c_2 \in C$ such that $c_2 \in \rho$. Then, for all $c_1 \in C$, it turns out that

$$c_1 \leq_C c_2 \Leftrightarrow \rho(c_1) \leq_C \rho(c_2) \Leftrightarrow \rho(c_1) \leq_C c_2. \tag{1}$$

We apply here the notion of backward completeness in abstract interpretation [6,7,16,23]. In abstract interpretation, a closure operator $\rho \in \text{uco}(C)$ on a concrete domain C plays the role of abstraction function for objects of C. A closure $\rho \in \text{uco}(C)$ is called backward complete for a concrete monotonic function $f : C \to C$ when $\rho f = \rho f \rho$ holds. The intuition is that backward completeness models an ideal situation where no loss of precision is accumulated in the computations of ρf when its concrete input objects are approximated by ρ. It is well-known [7] that in this case backward completeness implies completeness of least fixpoints, namely, $\rho(\text{lfp}(f)) = \text{lfp}(\rho f) = \text{lfp}(\rho f \rho)$ holds by assuming that these least fixpoints exist (this is the case, e.g., when C is a CPO). Theorem 3.1 states that in order to check an inclusion $c_1 \leq_C c_2$ for some $c_1 = \text{lfp}(f)$ and $c_2 \in \rho$, it is enough to perform an inclusion check $\text{lfp}(\rho f) \leq_C c_2$ which is defined on the abstraction $\rho(C)$.

Theorem 3.1. *If C is a CPO, $f : C \to C$ is monotonic, $\rho \in \text{uco}(C)$ is backward complete for f and $c_2 \in \rho$, then $\text{lfp}(f) \leq_C c_2 \Leftrightarrow \text{lfp}(\rho f) \leq_C c_2$. In particular, if $\langle \rho, \leq_C \rangle$ is ACC then the Kleene iterates of $\text{lfp}(\rho f)$ are finitely many.*

In the following sections we apply this general abstraction technique for a number of different language inclusion problems, by designing decision algorithms which rely on specific backward complete abstractions of $\wp(\Sigma^*)$.

4 An Algorithmic Framework for Language Inclusion

4.1 Languages as Fixed Points

Let $\mathcal{A} = \langle Q, \delta, I, F, \Sigma \rangle$ be a FA. Given $S, T \subseteq Q$, define

$$W^{\mathcal{A}}_{S,T} \triangleq \{u \in \Sigma^* \mid \exists q \in S, \exists q' \in T, q \overset{u}{\leadsto} q'\}.$$

When $S = \{q\}$ or $T = \{q'\}$ we abuse the notation and write $W^{\mathcal{A}}_{q,T}$, $W^{\mathcal{A}}_{S,q'}$, or $W^{\mathcal{A}}_{q,q'}$. Also, we omit the automaton $\mathcal{A}$ in superscripts when this is clear from the context. The language accepted by $\mathcal{A}$ is therefore $\mathcal{L}(\mathcal{A}) = W^{\mathcal{A}}_{I,F}$. Observe that

$$\mathcal{L}(\mathcal{A}) = \bigcup_{q \in I} W^{\mathcal{A}}_{q,F} = \bigcup_{q \in F} W^{\mathcal{A}}_{I,q} \tag{2}$$

where, as usual, $\bigcup \varnothing = \varnothing$. Let us recall how to define the language accepted by an automaton as a solution of a set of equations [24]. Given a Boolean predicate $p(x)$ (typically a membership predicate) and two sets T and F, we define the following parametric choice function:

$$\psi^T_F(p(x)) \triangleq \begin{cases} T & \text{if } p(x) \text{ holds} \\ F & \text{otherwise} \end{cases}.$$

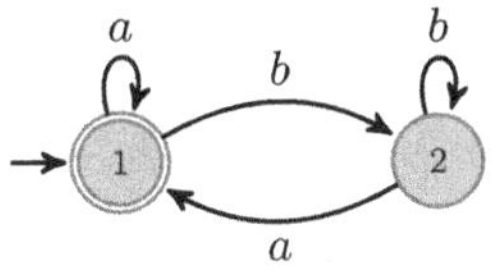

Fig. 1. A finite automaton $\mathcal{A}$ with $\mathcal{L}(\mathcal{A}) = (a + (b^+a))^*$.

The FA $\mathcal{A}$ induces the following set of equations, where the X_q's are variables of type $X_q \in \wp(\Sigma^*)$ indexed by states $q \in Q$:

$$\mathrm{Eqn}(\mathcal{A}) \triangleq \{X_q = \psi_{\varnothing}^{\{\epsilon\}}(q \in F) \cup \bigcup_{a\in\Sigma, q'\in\delta(q,a)} aX_{q'} \mid q \in Q\}.$$

Thus, the functions in the right-hand side of the equations in $\mathrm{Eqn}(\mathcal{A})$ have type $\wp(\Sigma^*)^{|Q|} \to \wp(\Sigma^*)$. Since $\langle \wp(\Sigma^*)^{|Q|}, \subseteq\rangle$ is a (product) complete lattice (as $\langle \wp(\Sigma^*), \subseteq\rangle$ is a complete lattice) and all the right-hand side functions in $\mathrm{Eqn}(\mathcal{A})$ are monotonic, the least solution $\langle Y_q\rangle_{q\in Q}$ of $\mathrm{Eqn}(\mathcal{A})$ does exist and it is easily seen that for every $q \in Q$, $Y_q = W^{\mathcal{A}}_{q,F}$ holds.

Note that, by using right (rather than left) concatenations, one could also define an equivalent set of equations whose least solution coincides with $\langle W^{\mathcal{A}}_{I,q}\rangle_{q\in Q}$ instead of $\langle W^{\mathcal{A}}_{q,F}\rangle_{q\in Q}$.

Example 4.1. Let us consider the automaton $\mathcal{A}$ in Fig. 1. The set of equations induced by $\mathcal{A}$ are as follows:

$$\mathrm{Eqn}(\mathcal{A}) = \begin{cases} X_1 = \{\epsilon\} \cup X_1a \cup X_2a \\ X_2 = \varnothing \cup X_1b \cup X_2b \end{cases} . \qquad \Diamond$$

Equivalently, the equations in $\mathrm{Eqn}(\mathcal{A})$ can be stated using an "initial" vector $\vec{\epsilon}^F \in \wp(\Sigma^*)^{|Q|}$ and the function $\mathrm{Pre}_{\mathcal{A}} \colon \wp(\Sigma^*)^{|Q|} \to \wp(\Sigma^*)^{|Q|}$ defined as follows:

$$\vec{\epsilon}^F \triangleq \langle \psi_{\varnothing}^{\{\epsilon\}}(q \in F)\rangle_{q\in Q}, \qquad \mathrm{Pre}_{\mathcal{A}}(\langle X_q\rangle_{q\in Q}) \triangleq \langle \bigcup_{a\in\Sigma, q'\in\delta(q,a)} aX_{q'}\rangle_{q\in Q}.$$

Since $\epsilon \in W^{\mathcal{A}}_{q,F}$ for all $q \in F$, the least fixpoint computation can start from the vector $\vec{\epsilon}^F$ and iteratively apply $\mathrm{Pre}_{\mathcal{A}}$, that is, it turns out that

$$\langle W^{\mathcal{A}}_{q,F}\rangle_{q\in Q} = \mathrm{lfp}(\lambda \vec{\boldsymbol{X}}.\, \vec{\epsilon}^F \cup \mathrm{Pre}_{\mathcal{A}}(\vec{\boldsymbol{X}})). \tag{3}$$

Together with Equation (2), it follows that $\mathcal{L}(\mathcal{A})$ equals the union of the component languages of the vector $\mathrm{lfp}(\lambda \vec{\boldsymbol{X}}.\, \vec{\epsilon}^F \cup \mathrm{Pre}_{\mathcal{A}}(\vec{\boldsymbol{X}}))$ indexed by initial states in I.

Example 4.2 (Continuation of Example 4.1). The fixpoint characterization of $\langle W^{\mathcal{A}}_{q,F}\rangle_{q\in Q}$ is:

$$\begin{pmatrix} W^{\mathcal{A}}_{q_1,q_1} \\ W^{\mathcal{A}}_{q_2,q_1} \end{pmatrix} = \mathrm{lfp}\left(\lambda \begin{pmatrix} X_1 \\ X_2 \end{pmatrix} . \begin{pmatrix} \{\epsilon\} \cup aX_1 \cup bX_2 \\ \varnothing \cup aX_1 \cup bX_2 \end{pmatrix}\right) = \begin{pmatrix} (a + (b^+a))^* \\ (a+b)^*a \end{pmatrix} . \qquad \Diamond$$

Fixpoint-Based Inclusion Check. Consider the language inclusion problem $L_1 \subseteq L_2$, where $L_1 = \mathcal{L}(\mathcal{A})$ for some FA $\mathcal{A} = \langle Q, \delta, I, F, \Sigma \rangle$. The language L_2 can be formalized as a vector in $\wp(\Sigma^*)^{|Q|}$ as follows:

$$\overrightarrow{\boldsymbol{L_2}}^I \triangleq \langle \psi_{\Sigma^*}^{L_2}(q \in I) \rangle_{q \in Q}. \tag{4}$$

Using (2), (3) and (4), it is routine to prove that

$$\mathcal{L}(\mathcal{A}) \subseteq L_2 \Leftrightarrow \mathrm{lfp}(\lambda \overrightarrow{\boldsymbol{X}}. \overrightarrow{\boldsymbol{\epsilon}}^F \cup \mathrm{Pre}_{\mathcal{A}}(\overrightarrow{\boldsymbol{X}})) \subseteq \overrightarrow{\boldsymbol{L_2}}^I. \tag{5}$$

4.2 Abstract Inclusion Check Using Closures

In what follows we will use Theorem 3.1 for solving the language inclusion problem, where we will have that $C = \langle \wp(\Sigma^*)^{|Q|}, \subseteq \rangle$, $f = \lambda \overrightarrow{\boldsymbol{X}}. \overrightarrow{\boldsymbol{\epsilon}}^F \cup \mathrm{Pre}_{\mathcal{A}}(\overrightarrow{\boldsymbol{X}})$ and $\rho : \wp(\Sigma^*)^{|Q|} \to \wp(\Sigma^*)^{|Q|}$ is an upper closure operator.

Theorem 4.3. *Let Σ be an alphabet. If $\rho \in \mathrm{uco}(\wp(\Sigma^*))$ is backward complete for $\lambda X \in \wp(\Sigma^*). aX$ for all $a \in \Sigma$, then, for all FAs $\mathcal{A} = \langle Q, \delta, I, F, \Sigma \rangle$, the closure ρ is backward complete for $\mathrm{Pre}_{\mathcal{A}}$ and $\lambda \overrightarrow{\boldsymbol{X}}. \overrightarrow{\boldsymbol{\epsilon}}^F \cup \mathrm{Pre}_{\mathcal{A}}(\overrightarrow{\boldsymbol{X}})$.*

Corollary 4.4. *If $\rho \in \mathrm{uco}(\wp(\Sigma^*))$ is backward complete for $\lambda X \in \wp(\Sigma^*). aX$ for all $a \in \Sigma$ then $\rho(\mathrm{lfp}(\lambda \overrightarrow{\boldsymbol{X}}. \overrightarrow{\boldsymbol{\epsilon}}^F \cup \mathrm{Pre}_{\mathcal{A}}(\overrightarrow{\boldsymbol{X}}))) = \mathrm{lfp}(\lambda \overrightarrow{\boldsymbol{X}}. \rho(\overrightarrow{\boldsymbol{\epsilon}}^F \cup \mathrm{Pre}_{\mathcal{A}}(\overrightarrow{\boldsymbol{X}})))$.*

Note that if ρ is backward complete for $\lambda X.aX$ for all $a \in \Sigma$ and $L_2 \in \rho$ then, as a consequence of Theorem 3.1 and Corollary 4.4, the equivalence (5) becomes

$$\mathcal{L}(\mathcal{A}) \subseteq L_2 \Leftrightarrow \mathrm{lfp}(\lambda \overrightarrow{\boldsymbol{X}}. \rho(\overrightarrow{\boldsymbol{\epsilon}}^F \cup \mathrm{Pre}_{\mathcal{A}}(\overrightarrow{\boldsymbol{X}}))) \subseteq \overrightarrow{\boldsymbol{L_2}}^I. \tag{6}$$

4.3 Abstract Inclusion Check Using Galois Connections

To solve a language inclusion problem $\mathcal{L}(\mathcal{A}) \subseteq L_2$ using equivalence (6) we must first compute the corresponding least fixpoint and then decide its inclusion in $\overrightarrow{\boldsymbol{L_2}}^I$. Since closure operators are fully isomorphic to Galois connections [7, Section 6], they allow us to conveniently define and reason on abstract domains independently of their representation. Recall that a *Galois Connection* (GC) or *adjunction* between two posets $\langle C, \leq_C \rangle$ (called concrete domain) and $\langle A, \leq_A \rangle$ (called abstract domain) consists of two functions $\alpha : C \to A$ and $\gamma : A \to C$ such that $\alpha(c) \leq_A a \Leftrightarrow c \leq_C \gamma(a)$ always holds. A Galois Connection is denoted by $\langle C, \leq_C \rangle \underset{\alpha}{\overset{\gamma}{\leftrightarrows}} \langle A, \leq_A \rangle$. In an adjunction, α is called the left-adjoint of γ, and, dually, γ is called the right-adjoint of α. This terminology is justified by the fact that if some function $\alpha : C \to A$ admits a right-adjoint $\gamma : A \to C$ then this is unique (and this dually holds for left-adjoints).

The next result shows that there exists an algorithm that solves the language inclusion problem $\mathcal{L}(\mathcal{A}) \subseteq L_2$ on an abstraction D of the concrete domain of languages $\langle \wp(\Sigma^*), \subseteq \rangle$ whenever D satisfies a list of requirements related to backward completeness and computability.

Theorem 4.5. *Let $\mathcal{A} = \langle Q, \delta, I, F, \Sigma \rangle$ be a FA and let L_2 be a language over Σ. Let $\langle \wp(\Sigma^*), \subseteq \rangle \overset{\gamma}{\underset{\alpha}{\leftrightarrows}} \langle D, \leq_D \rangle$ be a GC where $\langle D, \leq_D \rangle$ is a poset. Assume that the following properties hold:*

(i) $L_2 \in \gamma(D)$ and for every $a \in \Sigma$ and $X \in \wp(\Sigma^*)$, $\alpha(aX) = \alpha(a\gamma\alpha(X))$.
(ii) $(D, \leq_D, \sqcup)$ is an effective domain, meaning that: $(D, \leq_D, \sqcup)$ is an ACC join-semilattice, every element of D has a finite representation, $\leq_D$ is decidable and $\sqcup$ is a computable binary lub.
(iii) There is an algorithm, say $\mathrm{Pre}^\sharp(\vec{\boldsymbol{X}})$, which computes $\alpha(\mathrm{Pre}_{\mathcal{A}}(\gamma(\vec{\boldsymbol{X}})))$, for all $\vec{\boldsymbol{X}} \in \wp(\Sigma^*)^{|Q|}$.
(iv) There is an algorithm, say $\epsilon^\sharp$, computing $\alpha(\vec{\boldsymbol{\epsilon}}^F)$.
(v) There is an algorithm, say $\mathrm{Incl}^\sharp(\vec{\boldsymbol{X}})$, deciding the abstract inclusion $\vec{\boldsymbol{X}} \leq_D \alpha(\vec{\boldsymbol{L_2}}^I)$, for every vector $\vec{\boldsymbol{X}} \in \alpha(\wp(\Sigma^*)^{|Q|})$.

Then, the following algorithm decides whether $\mathcal{L}(\mathcal{A}) \subseteq L_2$:
$\langle Y_q \rangle_{q \in Q} :=$ `Kleene`$(\lambda \vec{\boldsymbol{X}}.\, \epsilon^\sharp \sqcup \mathrm{Pre}^\sharp(\vec{\boldsymbol{X}}), \vec{\boldsymbol{\varnothing}})$;
return $\mathrm{Incl}^\sharp(\langle Y_q \rangle_{q \in Q})$;

Quasiorder Galois Connections. It turns out that Theorem 4.5 still holds for abstract domains which are mere qosets rather than posets.

Definition 4.6 (Quasiorder GC). A *quasiorder GC* (QGC) $\langle C, \leq_C \rangle \overset{\gamma}{\underset{\alpha}{\leftrightarrows}} \langle D, \leq_D \rangle$ consists of: (a) two qosets $\langle C, \leq_C \rangle$ and $\langle D, \leq_D \rangle$ such that one of them is a poset; (b) two functions $\alpha \colon C \to D$ and $\gamma \colon D \to C$ such that $\alpha(c) \leq_D d \Leftrightarrow c \leq_C \gamma(d)$ holds for all $c \in C$ and $d \in D$. ■

Analogously to GCs, it is easily seen that in QGCs both α and γ are monotonic as well as $c \leq_C \gamma(\alpha(c))$ and $\alpha(\gamma(d)) \leq_D d$ always hold. Observe that if C is a poset and $d \leq_D d' \leq_D d$ with $d \neq d'$ then $\gamma(d) = \gamma(d')$, because γ is monotonic, and conversely, if D is a poset and $c \leq_C c' \leq_C c$ with $c \neq c'$ then $\alpha(c) = \alpha(c')$ holds. Similarly to GCs, if C is a poset then $\gamma \circ \alpha \in \mathrm{uco}(\langle C, \leq_C \rangle)$ holds for QGCs.

In the following, we apply all the standard order-theoretic notions used for posets also to a qoset $\langle D, \leq_D \rangle$ by implicitly referring to the quotient poset $\langle D_{/\cong_D}, \leq_{D/\cong_D} \rangle$ where $\cong_D \triangleq \leq_D \cap \leq_D^{-1}$.

For example:

- $\langle D, \leq_D \rangle$ is ACC (CPO) means that the poset $\langle D_{/\cong_D}, \leq_{D/\cong_D} \rangle$ is ACC (CPO).
- $\langle D, \leq_D \rangle$ is a join-semilattice means that $\langle D_{/\cong_D}, \leq_{D/\cong_D} \rangle$ is a join-semilattice; a binary lub for D (one could have several binary lubs) is a map $\lambda \langle d, d' \rangle . d \sqcup d'$ such that $\lambda \langle [d]_{\cong_D}, [d']_{\cong_D} \rangle . [d \sqcup d']_{\cong_D}$ is the lub in the poset $\langle D_{/\cong_D}, \leq_{D/\cong_D} \rangle$.

Corollary 4.7. *Theorem 4.5 still holds for a QGC $\langle \wp(\Sigma^*), \subseteq \rangle \overset{\gamma}{\underset{\alpha}{\leftrightarrows}} \langle D, \leq_D \rangle$ where $\langle D, \leq_D \rangle$ is a qoset.*

5 Instantiating the Framework

In this section we focus on a particular class of closures on sets of words: those induced by quasiorder relations on words. Then, we provide a list of conditions on quasiorders such that the induced closures fit our framework. In addition, we study some instances of such quasiorders and compare them.

5.1 Word-Based Abstractions

Let $\leqslant \subseteq \Sigma^* \times \Sigma^*$ be a quasiorder relation on words. The corresponding closure operator $\rho_{\leqslant} \in \text{uco}(\wp(\Sigma^*))$ is defined as follows:

$$\rho_{\leqslant}(X) \triangleq \{v \in \Sigma^* \mid \exists u \in X,\, u \leqslant v\}. \tag{7}$$

Thus, $\rho_{\leqslant}(X)$ is the $\leqslant$-upward closure of X and it is easy to check that $\rho_{\leqslant}$ is indeed a closure on $\langle \wp(\Sigma^*), \subseteq \rangle$.

A quasiorder $\leqslant$ on Σ^* is called *left-monotonic* (resp. *right-monotonic*) if $\forall y, x_1, x_2 \in \Sigma^*,\ x_1 \leqslant x_2 \Rightarrow yx_1 \leqslant yx_2$ (resp. $x_1 y \leqslant x_2 y$). Also, $\leqslant$ is called monotonic if it is both left- and right-monotonic.

Definition 5.1 (L-Consistent Quasiorder). Let $L \in \wp(\Sigma^*)$. A quasiorder $\leqslant_L$ on Σ^* is called *left* (resp. *right*) *L-consistent* when: (a) $\leqslant_L \cap (L \times \neg L) = \varnothing$ and (b) $\leqslant_L$ is left- (resp. right-) monotonic. Also, $\leqslant_L$ is called *L-consistent* when it is both left and right L-consistent. ■

It turns out that a L-consistent quasiorder induces a closure which includes L and is backward complete for concatenation.

Lemma 5.2. *Let L be a language over Σ and $\leqslant_L$ be a left (resp. right) L-consistent quasiorder on Σ^*. Then,*

(a) $\rho_{\leqslant_L}(L) = L$.
(b) $\rho_{\leqslant_L}$ is backward complete for $\lambda X.\, aX$ (resp. $\lambda X.\, Xa$) for all $a \in \Sigma$.

Moreover, we show that the $\leqslant$-upward closure $\rho_{\leqslant}$ in (7) can be equivalently defined through the qoset of antichains. In fact, the qoset of antichains $\langle \text{AC}_{\langle \Sigma^*, \leqslant \rangle}, \sqsubseteq \rangle$ can be viewed as a language abstraction through the minor abstraction map. Let $\alpha_{\leqslant} : \wp(\Sigma^*) \to \text{AC}_{\langle \Sigma^*, \leqslant \rangle}$ and $\gamma_{\leqslant} : \text{AC}_{\langle \Sigma^*, \leqslant \rangle} \to \wp(\Sigma^*)$ be defined as follows:

$$\alpha_{\leqslant}(X) \triangleq \lfloor X \rfloor, \qquad \gamma_{\leqslant}(Y) \triangleq \rho_{\leqslant}(Y). \tag{8}$$

Theorem 5.3. *Let $\langle \Sigma^*, \leqslant \rangle$ be a qoset.*

(a) $\langle \wp(\Sigma^*), \subseteq \rangle \underset{\alpha_{\leqslant}}{\overset{\gamma_{\leqslant}}{\leftrightarrows}} \langle \text{AC}_{\langle \Sigma^*, \leqslant \rangle}, \sqsubseteq \rangle$ *is a QGC.*
(b) $\gamma_{\leqslant} \circ \alpha_{\leqslant} = \rho_{\leqslant}$.

The QGC $\langle \wp(\Sigma^*), \subseteq \rangle \underset{\alpha_\leqslant}{\overset{\gamma_\leqslant}{\longleftrightarrow}} \langle \mathrm{AC}_{\langle \Sigma^*, \leqslant \rangle}, \sqsubseteq \rangle$ allows us to represent and manipulate $\leqslant$-upward closed sets in $\wp(\Sigma^*)$ using finite subsets, as already shown by Abdulla et al. [1].

We are now in position to show that, given a language L_2 whose membership decision problem is decidable, for every decidable L_2-consistent wqo relation $\leqslant_{L_2}$, the QGC $\langle \wp(\Sigma^*), \subseteq \rangle \underset{\alpha_{\leqslant_{L_2}}}{\overset{\gamma_{\leqslant_{L_2}}}{\longleftrightarrow}} \langle \mathrm{AC}_{\langle \Sigma^*, \leqslant_{L_2} \rangle}, \sqsubseteq \rangle$ of Theorem 5.3 (a) yields an algorithm for deciding the inclusion $\mathcal{L}(\mathcal{A}) \subseteq L_2$ where $\mathcal{A}$ is a FA. In particular, for a left L_2-consistent wqo $\leqslant^l_{L_2}$, the algorithm `FAIncW` solves this inclusion problem. `FAIncW` is called "word-based" algorithm because the vector $\langle Y_q \rangle_{q \in Q}$ used by `FAIncW` consists of finite sets of words.

`FAIncW`: Word-based algorithm for $\mathcal{L}(\mathcal{A}) \subseteq L_2$

Data: FA $\mathcal{A} = \langle Q, \delta, I, F, \Sigma \rangle$; a decision procedure for membership in L_2; a decidable left L_2-consistent wqo $\leqslant^l_{L_2}$.

$\langle Y_q \rangle_{q \in Q} :=$ `Kleene`$(\lambda \vec{X}.\, \lfloor \vec{\epsilon}^F \rfloor \sqcup \lfloor \mathrm{Pre}_{\mathcal{A}}(\vec{X}) \rfloor, \vec{\varnothing})$;
forall the $q \in I$ **do**
  forall the $u \in Y_q$ **do**
    if $u \notin L_2$ **then return** *false*
return *true*;

Theorem 5.4. *Let $\mathcal{A}$ be a FA and let L_2 be a language such that: (i) membership in L_2 is decidable; (ii) there exists a decidable left L_2-consistent wqo on Σ^*. Then, the algorithm* `FAIncW` *decides the inclusion $\mathcal{L}(\mathcal{A}) \subseteq L_2$.*

A symmetric version of algorithm `FAIncW` (and of Theorem 5.4) for *right* L_2-consistent wqos, which relies on equations concatenating to the right (instead of to the left as in $\mathrm{Eqn}(\mathcal{A})$), can be found in the extended version of this paper [14].

In what follows, we will consider different quasiorders and we will show that they fulfill the requirements of Theorem 5.4 (or its symmetric version for right quasiorders), so that they yield algorithms for solving the language inclusion problem.

5.2 Nerode Quasiorders

Given $w \in \Sigma^*$ and $X \in \wp(\Sigma^*)$, left and right quotients are defined as usual: $w^{-1}X \triangleq \{u \in \Sigma^* \mid wu \in X\}$ and $Xw^{-1} \triangleq \{u \in \Sigma^* \mid uw \in X\}$. Given a language $L \subseteq \Sigma^*$, let us define the following quasiorder relations on Σ^*:

$$u \leqq^l_L v \overset{\triangle}{\Longleftrightarrow} Lu^{-1} \subseteq Lv^{-1}, \qquad u \leqq^r_L v \overset{\triangle}{\Longleftrightarrow} u^{-1}L \subseteq v^{-1}L.$$

De Luca and Varricchio [8] call them, resp., the *left* ($\leqq^l_L$) and *right* ($\leqq^r_L$) *Nerode quasiorders relative to* L. The following result shows that Nerode quasiorders are the most general (i.e., greatest for set inclusion) L_2-consistent quasiorders for which the algorithm `FAIncW` can be instantiated to decide a language inclusion $\mathcal{L}(\mathcal{A}) \subseteq L_2$.

Lemma 5.5. *Let $L \subseteq \Sigma^*$ be a language.*

(a) $\leqq^l_L$ and $\leqq^r_L$ are, resp., left and right L-consistent quasiorders. If L is regular then $\leqq^l_L$ and $\leqq^r_L$ are, additionally, decidable wqos.
(b) Let $\leqslant$ be a quasiorder on Σ^*. If $\leqslant$ is left (resp. right) L-consistent then $\rho_{\leqq^l_L} \subseteq \rho_{\leqslant}$ (resp. $\rho_{\leqq^r_L} \subseteq \rho_{\leqslant}$).

Let us now consider a first instantiation of Theorem 5.4. Because membership is decidable for regular languages, Lemma 5.5 (a) for $\leqq^l_{L_2}$ implies that the hypotheses (i) and (ii) of Theorem 5.4 are satisfied, so that the algorithm `FAIncW` decides the inclusion $\mathcal{L}(\mathcal{A}) \subseteq L_2$. Furthermore, under these hypotheses, Lemma 5.5 (b) shows that $\leqq^l_{L_2}$ is the most general (i.e., greatest for set inclusion) left L_2-consistent quasiorder relation on Σ^* for which the algorithm `FAIncW` can be instantiated for deciding an inclusion $\mathcal{L}(\mathcal{A}) \subseteq L_2$.

Remark 5.6 (On the Complexity of Nerode quasiorders). For the inclusion problem between languages generated by finite automata, deciding the (left or right) Nerode quasiorder can be easily shown[1] to be as hard as the language inclusion problem, which is PSPACE-complete. For the inclusion problem of a language generated by an automaton within the trace set of a one-counter net (cf. Sect. 5.3) the right Nerode quasiorder is a right language-consistent well-quasiorder but it turns out to be undecidable (cf. Lemma 5.12). More details can be found in the extended version of this paper [14]. ■

5.3 State-Based Quasiorders

Consider the inclusion problem $\mathcal{L}(\mathcal{A}_1) \subseteq \mathcal{L}(\mathcal{A}_2)$ where $\mathcal{A}_1$ and $\mathcal{A}_2$ are FAs. In the following, we study a class of well-quasiorders based on $\mathcal{A}_2$, called state-based quasiorders. This is a strict subclass of Nerode quasiorders defined in Sect. 5.2 and sidesteps the untractability or undecidability of Nerode quasiorders (cf. Remark 5.6) yet allowing to define an algorithm solving the language inclusion problem.

Inclusion in Regular Languages. We define the quasiorders $\leq^l_{\mathcal{A}}$ and $\leq^r_{\mathcal{A}}$ on Σ^* induced by a FA $\mathcal{A} = \langle Q, \delta, I, F, \Sigma\rangle$ as follows:

$$u \leq^l_{\mathcal{A}} v \overset{\triangle}{\Longleftrightarrow} \mathrm{pre}^{\mathcal{A}}_u(F) \subseteq \mathrm{pre}^{\mathcal{A}}_v(F), \qquad u \leq^r_{\mathcal{A}} v \overset{\triangle}{\Longleftrightarrow} \mathrm{post}^{\mathcal{A}}_u(I) \subseteq \mathrm{post}^{\mathcal{A}}_v(I), \qquad (9)$$

where, for all $X \subseteq Q$ and $u \in \Sigma^*$, $\mathrm{pre}^{\mathcal{A}}_u(X) \triangleq \{q \in Q \mid u \in W^{\mathcal{A}}_{q,X}\}$ and $\mathrm{post}^{\mathcal{A}}_u(X) \triangleq \{q' \in Q \mid u \in W^{\mathcal{A}}_{X,q'}\}$.

Lemma 5.7. *Let $\mathcal{A}$ be a FA. Then, $\leq^l_{\mathcal{A}}$ and $\leq^r_{\mathcal{A}}$ are, resp., decidable left and right $\mathcal{L}(\mathcal{A})$-consistent wqos.*

[1] Sketch: Given $\mathcal{A}_1 = (Q_1, \delta_1, I_1, F_1, \Sigma)$ and $\mathcal{A}_2 = (Q_2, \delta_2, I_2, F_2, \Sigma)$ define $\mathcal{A}_3 = (Q_1 \cup Q_2 \cup \{q^\dagger\}, \delta_3, \{q^\dagger\}, F_1 \cup F_2)$ where δ_3 maps $(q^\dagger, a)$ to I_1, $(q^\dagger, b)$ to I_2 and like δ_1 or δ_2 elsewhere. Then, it turns out that $a \leqq^r_{\mathcal{L}(\mathcal{A}_3)} b \Leftrightarrow a^{-1}\mathcal{L}(\mathcal{A}_3) \subseteq b^{-1}\mathcal{L}(\mathcal{A}_3) \Leftrightarrow \mathcal{L}(\mathcal{A}_1) \subseteq \mathcal{L}(\mathcal{A}_2)$.

It follows from Lemma 5.7 that Theorem 5.4 applies to $\leq^l_{\mathcal{A}_2}$ (and $\leq^r_{\mathcal{A}_2}$), so that one can instantiate the algorithm FAIncW with the wqo $\leq^l_{\mathcal{A}_2}$ for deciding $\mathcal{L}(\mathcal{A}_1) \subseteq \mathcal{L}(\mathcal{A}_2)$. Turning back to the left Nerode wqo $\leqq^l_{\mathcal{L}(\mathcal{A}_2)}$ we find that:

$$u \leqq^l_{\mathcal{L}(\mathcal{A}_2)} v \Leftrightarrow \mathcal{L}(\mathcal{A}_2)u^{-1} \subseteq \mathcal{L}(\mathcal{A}_2)v^{-1} \Leftrightarrow W_{I,\mathrm{pre}_u^{\mathcal{A}_2}(F)} \subseteq W_{I,\mathrm{pre}_v^{\mathcal{A}_2}(F)}.$$

Since $\mathrm{pre}_u^{\mathcal{A}_2}(F) \subseteq \mathrm{pre}_v^{\mathcal{A}_2}(F) \Rightarrow W_{I,\mathrm{pre}_u^{\mathcal{A}_2}(F)} \subseteq W_{I,\mathrm{pre}_v^{\mathcal{A}_2}(F)}$, it follows that $u \leq^l_{\mathcal{A}_2} v \Rightarrow u \leqq^l_{\mathcal{L}(\mathcal{A}_2)} v$. Moreover, by Lemmas 5.5 (b) and 5.7, we have that $\rho_{\leqq^l_{\mathcal{L}(\mathcal{A}_2)}} \subseteq \rho_{\leq^l_{\mathcal{A}_2}}$.

Simulation-Based Quasiorders. Recall that, given a FA $\mathcal{A} = \langle Q, \delta, I, F, \Sigma\rangle$, a *simulation* on $\mathcal{A}$ is a binary relation $\preceq \subseteq Q \times Q$ such that if $p \preceq q$ then: (i) $p \in F$ implies $q \in F$ and (ii) for every transition $p \xrightarrow{a} p'$, there exists a transition $q \xrightarrow{a} q'$ such that $p' \preceq q'$. It is well-known that simulation implies language inclusion, i.e., if $\preceq$ is a simulation on $\mathcal{A}$ then

$$q \preceq q' \Rightarrow W^{\mathcal{A}}_{q,F} \subseteq W^{\mathcal{A}}_{q',F}.$$

We lift a quasiorder $\preceq$ on Q to a quasiorder $\preceq^{\forall\exists}$ on $\wp(Q)$ as follows:

$$X \preceq^{\forall\exists} Y \stackrel{\triangle}{\Longleftrightarrow} \forall x \in X, \exists y \in Y,\ x \preceq y$$

so that $X \preceq^{\forall\exists} Y \Rightarrow W^{\mathcal{A}}_{X,F} \subseteq W^{\mathcal{A}}_{Y,F}$ holds. Therefore, we define the *right simulation-based quasiorder* $\preceq^r_{\mathcal{A}}$ on Σ^* as follows:

$$u \preceq^r_{\mathcal{A}} v \stackrel{\triangle}{\Longleftrightarrow} \mathrm{post}_u^{\mathcal{A}}(I) \preceq^{\forall\exists} \mathrm{post}_v^{\mathcal{A}}(I). \tag{10}$$

Lemma 5.8. *Given a simulation relation $\preceq$ on $\mathcal{A}$, the right simulation-based quasiorder $\preceq^r_{\mathcal{A}}$ is a decidable right $\mathcal{L}(\mathcal{A})$-consistent wqo.*

Thus, once again, Theorem 5.4 applies to $\preceq^r_{\mathcal{A}_2}$ and this allows us to instantiate the algorithm FAIncW to $\preceq^r_{\mathcal{A}_2}$ for deciding $\mathcal{L}(\mathcal{A}_1) \subseteq \mathcal{L}(\mathcal{A}_2)$.

Observe that $u \preceq^r_{\mathcal{A}_2} v$ implies $W_{\mathrm{post}_u^{\mathcal{A}_2}(I),F} \subseteq W_{\mathrm{post}_v^{\mathcal{A}_2}(I),F}$, which is equivalent to the right Nerode quasiorder $u \leqq^r_{\mathcal{L}(\mathcal{A}_2)} v$, so that $u \preceq^r_{\mathcal{A}_2} v \Rightarrow u \leqq^r_{\mathcal{L}(\mathcal{A}_2)} v$. Moreover, $u \leq^r_{\mathcal{A}_2} v \Rightarrow u \preceq^r_{\mathcal{A}_2} v$ trivially holds. Summing up, the following containments relate (the right versions of) state-based, simulation-based and Nerode quasiorders:

$$\leq^r_{\mathcal{A}_2} \subseteq \preceq^r_{\mathcal{A}_2} \subseteq \leqq^r_{\mathcal{L}(\mathcal{A}_2)}.$$

All these quasiorders are decidable $\mathcal{L}(\mathcal{A}_2)$-consistent wqos so that the algorithm FAIncW can be instantiated for each of them for deciding $\mathcal{L}(\mathcal{A}_1) \subseteq \mathcal{L}(\mathcal{A}_2)$.

Inclusion in Traces of One-Counter Nets. We show that our framework can be instantiated to systematically derive an algorithm for deciding the inclusion

$\mathcal{L}(\mathcal{A}) \subseteq L_2$ where L_2 is the trace set of a one-counter net. This is accomplished by defining a decidable L_2-consistent quasiorder so that Theorem 5.4 can be applied.

Intuitively, a one-counter net is a FA equipped with a nonnegative integer counter. Formally, a One-Counter Net (OCN) [17] is a tuple $\mathcal{O} = \langle Q, \Sigma, \delta \rangle$ where Q is a finite set of states, Σ is an alphabet and $\delta \subseteq Q \times \Sigma \times \{-1, 0, 1\} \times Q$ is a set of transitions A *configuration* of $\mathcal{O}$ is a pair qn consisting of a state $q \in Q$ and a value $n \in \mathbb{N}$ for the counter. Given two configurations qn and $q'n'$ we write $qn \xrightarrow{a} q'n'$ and call it a a-step (or simply step) if there exists a transition $(q, a, d, q') \in \delta$ such that $n' = n + d$. Given $qn \in Q \times \mathbb{N}$, the *trace set* $T(qn) \subseteq \Sigma^*$ of an OCN is defined as follows:

$$T(qn) \triangleq \{u \in \Sigma^* \mid Z_u^{qn} \neq \varnothing\} \quad \text{where}$$
$$Z_u^{qn} \triangleq \{q_k n_k \mid qn \xrightarrow{a_1} q_1 n_1 \xrightarrow{a_2} \cdots \xrightarrow{a_k} q_k n_k,\ a_1 \cdots a_k = u\}.$$

Observe that $Z_\epsilon^{qn} = \{qn\}$ and Z_u^{qn} is a finite set for every word $u \in \Sigma^*$.

Let $\mathbb{N}_\bot \triangleq \mathbb{N} \cup \{\bot\}$ where $\bot \leq_{\mathbb{N}_\bot} n$ holds for all $n \in \mathbb{N}_\bot$, while for all $n, n' \in \mathbb{N}$, $n \leq_{\mathbb{N}_\bot} n'$ is the standard ordering relation. For a finite set of states $S \subseteq Q \times \mathbb{N}$ define the so-called macro state $M_S \colon Q \to \mathbb{N}_\bot$ as follows:

$$M_S(q) \triangleq \max\{n \in \mathbb{N} \mid qn \in S\},$$

where $\max \varnothing \triangleq \bot$. Define the following quasiorder on Σ^*:

$$u \leqq_{qn}^r v \overset{\triangle}{\iff} \forall q' \in Q,\ M_{Z_u^{qn}}(q') \leq_{\mathbb{N}_\bot} M_{Z_v^{qn}}(q').$$

Lemma 5.9. *Given a OCN $\mathcal{O}$ together with a configuration qn, $\leqq_{qn}^r$ is a right $T(qn)$-consistent decidable wqo.*

Thus, as a consequence of Theorem 5.4, Lemma 5.9 and the decidability of membership in $T(qn)$, we derive the following known decidability result [19, Theorem 3.2] by resorting to our framework.

Theorem 5.10. *Given a FA $\mathcal{A}$ and a OCN $\mathcal{O}$ together with a configuration qn, the problem $\mathcal{L}(\mathcal{A}) \subseteq T(qn)$ is decidable.*

Moreover, the following result closes a conjecture made by de Luca and Varricchio [8, Section 6].

Lemma 5.11. *The right Nerode quasiorder $\leqq_{T(qn)}^r$ is a well-quasiorder.*

It is worth remarking that, by Lemma 5.5 (a), the left and right Nerode quasiorders relative to $T(qn)$ are $T(qn)$-consistent. However, the left Nerode quasiorder does not need to be a wqo for otherwise $T(qn)$ would be regular.

Lemma 5.12. *The right Nerode quasiorder for the trace set of OCN is undecidable.*

We conjecture that, using our framework, Theorem 5.10 can be extended to traces of Petri Nets, which is already known to be true [19].

6 A Novel Perspective on the Antichain Algorithm

Let $\mathcal{A}_1 = \langle Q_1, \delta_1, I_1, F_1, \Sigma\rangle$ and $\mathcal{A}_2 = \langle Q_2, \delta_2, I_2, F_2, \Sigma\rangle$ be two FAs and consider the left $\mathcal{L}(\mathcal{A}_2)$-consistent wqo $\leq^l_{\mathcal{A}_2}$ defined in (9). Theorem 5.4 shows that the algorithm `FAIncW` solves the inclusion problem $\mathcal{L}(\mathcal{A}_1) \subseteq \mathcal{L}(\mathcal{A}_2)$ by computing on the qoset abstraction $\langle \mathrm{AC}_{\langle \Sigma^*, \leq^l_{\mathcal{A}_2}\rangle}, \sqsubseteq\rangle$ of antichains of $\langle \Sigma^*, \leq^l_{\mathcal{A}_2}\rangle$.

Since $u \leq^l_{\mathcal{A}_2} v \Leftrightarrow \mathrm{pre}^{\mathcal{A}_2}_u(F_2) \subseteq \mathrm{pre}^{\mathcal{A}_2}_v(F_2)$ holds, we can equivalently consider the set of states $\mathrm{pre}^{\mathcal{A}_2}_u(F_2)$ rather than a word $u \in \Sigma^*$. This leads us to design an algorithm analogous to `FAIncW` but computing on the poset $\langle \mathrm{AC}_{\langle \wp(Q_2), \subseteq\rangle}, \sqsubseteq\rangle$ of antichains of sets of states of $\langle \wp(Q_2), \subseteq\rangle$. In order to do this, the poset $\langle \mathrm{AC}_{\langle \wp(Q_2), \subseteq\rangle}, \sqsubseteq\rangle$ is viewed as an abstraction of the qoset $\langle \mathrm{AC}_{\langle \Sigma^*, \leq^l_{\mathcal{A}_2}\rangle}, \sqsubseteq'\rangle$ (where $\sqsubseteq'$ is used for distinguishing the two ordering relations on antichains) through the abstraction and concretization maps $\alpha_{\mathcal{A}_2} : \mathrm{AC}_{\langle \Sigma^*, \leq^l_{\mathcal{A}_2}\rangle} \to \mathrm{AC}_{\langle \wp(Q_2), \subseteq\rangle}$ and $\gamma_{\mathcal{A}_2} : \mathrm{AC}_{\langle \wp(Q_2), \subseteq\rangle} \to \mathrm{AC}_{\langle \Sigma^*, \leq^l_{\mathcal{A}_2}\rangle}$ defined as follows:

$$\alpha_{\mathcal{A}_2}(X) \triangleq \{\mathrm{pre}^{\mathcal{A}_2}_u(F_2) \in \wp(Q_2) \mid u \in X\},$$
$$\gamma_{\mathcal{A}_2}(Y) \triangleq \lfloor\{u \in \Sigma^* \mid \mathrm{pre}^{\mathcal{A}_2}_u(F_2) \in Y\}\rfloor.$$

Lemma 6.1. *$\langle \mathrm{AC}_{\langle \Sigma^*, \leq^l_{\mathcal{A}_2}\rangle}, \sqsubseteq'\rangle \xleftrightarrows[\alpha_{\mathcal{A}_2}]{\gamma_{\mathcal{A}_2}} \langle \mathrm{AC}_{\langle \wp(Q_2), \subseteq\rangle}, \sqsubseteq\rangle$ is a QGC.*

Combining the word-based algorithm `FAIncW` with $\alpha_{\mathcal{A}_2}$ and $\gamma_{\mathcal{A}_2}$ we are able to systematically derive a new algorithm which solves the inclusion $\mathcal{L}(\mathcal{A}_1) \subseteq \mathcal{L}(\mathcal{A}_2)$ using the abstract domain $\langle \mathrm{AC}_{\langle \wp(Q_2), \subseteq\rangle}, \sqsubseteq\rangle$ which is viewed as an abstraction of $\langle \wp(\Sigma^*), \subseteq\rangle$ by composing the following two QGCs:

$$\langle \wp(\Sigma^*), \subseteq\rangle \xleftrightarrows[\alpha_{\leq^l_{\mathcal{A}_2}}]{\gamma_{\leq^l_{\mathcal{A}_2}}} \langle \mathrm{AC}_{\langle \Sigma^*, \leq^l_{\mathcal{A}_2}\rangle}, \sqsubseteq'\rangle, \qquad \text{[by Theorem 5.3(a)]}$$
$$\langle \mathrm{AC}_{\langle \Sigma^*, \leq^l_{\mathcal{A}_2}\rangle}, \sqsubseteq'\rangle \xleftrightarrows[\alpha_{\mathcal{A}_2}]{\gamma_{\mathcal{A}_2}} \langle \mathrm{AC}_{\langle \wp(Q_2), \subseteq\rangle}, \sqsubseteq\rangle. \qquad \text{[by Lemma 6.1]}$$

Let $\alpha\colon \wp(\Sigma^*) \to \mathrm{AC}_{\langle \wp(Q_2), \subseteq\rangle}$, $\gamma\colon \mathrm{AC}_{\langle \wp(Q_2), \subseteq\rangle} \to \wp(\Sigma^*)$ and $\mathrm{Pre}^{\mathcal{A}_2}_{\mathcal{A}_1} : \wp(Q_2)^{|Q_1|} \to \wp(Q_2)^{|Q_1|}$ be defined as follows:

$$\alpha(X) \triangleq \lfloor\{\mathrm{pre}^{\mathcal{A}_2}_u(F_2) \in \wp(Q_2) \mid u \in X\}\rfloor,$$
$$\gamma(Y) \triangleq \{u \in \Sigma^* \mid \exists S \in Y, S \subseteq \mathrm{pre}^{\mathcal{A}_2}_u(F_2)\},$$
$$\mathrm{Pre}^{\mathcal{A}_2}_{\mathcal{A}_1}(\langle X_q\rangle_{q \in Q_1}) \triangleq \langle \lfloor\{\, \mathrm{pre}^{\mathcal{A}_2}_a(S) \mid \exists a \in \Sigma, q' \in Q_1,\, q' \in \delta_1(q,a) \wedge S \in X_{q'}\}\rfloor\rangle_{q \in Q_1}.$$

Lemma 6.2. *The following properties hold:*

(a) $\alpha = \alpha_{\mathcal{A}_2} \circ \alpha_{\leq^l_{\mathcal{A}_2}}$
(b) $\gamma = \gamma_{\leq^l_{\mathcal{A}_2}} \circ \gamma_{\mathcal{A}_2}$
(c) $\langle \wp(\Sigma^*), \subseteq\rangle \xleftrightarrows[\alpha]{\gamma} \langle \mathrm{AC}_{\langle \wp(Q_2), \subseteq\rangle}, \sqsubseteq\rangle$ *is a GC*
(d) $\gamma \circ \alpha = \rho_{\leq^l_{\mathcal{A}_2}}$

(e) For all $\vec{\boldsymbol{X}} \in \alpha(\wp(\Sigma^*)^{|Q_1|})$, $\mathrm{Pre}^{\mathcal{A}_2}_{\mathcal{A}_1}(\vec{\boldsymbol{X}}) = \alpha_{\mathcal{A}_2} \circ \alpha_{\leq^l_{\mathcal{A}_2}} \circ \mathrm{Pre}_{\mathcal{A}_1} \circ \gamma_{\leq^l_{\mathcal{A}_2}} \circ \gamma_{\mathcal{A}_2}(\vec{\boldsymbol{X}})$

It follows from Lemma 6.2 that the GC $\langle \wp(\Sigma^*), \subseteq \rangle \overset{\gamma}{\underset{\alpha}{\leftrightarrows}} \langle \mathrm{AC}_{\langle \wp(Q_2), \subseteq \rangle}, \sqsubseteq \rangle$ together with the abstract function $\mathrm{Pre}^{\mathcal{A}_2}_{\mathcal{A}_1}$ satisfy the hypotheses (i)–(iv) of Theorem 4.5. Thus, in order to obtain an algorithm for deciding $\mathcal{L}(\mathcal{A}_1) \subseteq \mathcal{L}(\mathcal{A}_2)$ it remains to show that requirement (v) of Theorem 4.5 holds, i.e., there is an algorithm to decide whether $\vec{\boldsymbol{Y}} \sqsubseteq \alpha(\overrightarrow{\boldsymbol{L_2}^{I_2}})$ for every $\vec{\boldsymbol{Y}} \in \alpha(\wp(\Sigma^*))^{|Q_1|}$.

Let us notice that the Kleene iterates of the function $\lambda \vec{\boldsymbol{X}}.\, \alpha(\vec{\boldsymbol{\epsilon}}^{F_1}) \sqcup \mathrm{Pre}^{\mathcal{A}_2}_{\mathcal{A}_1}(\vec{\boldsymbol{X}})$ of Theorem 4.5 are vectors of antichains in $\langle \mathrm{AC}_{\langle \wp(Q_2), \subseteq \rangle}, \sqsubseteq \rangle$, where each component indexed by some $q \in Q_1$ represents (through its minor set) a set of sets of states that are predecessors of F_2 in $\mathcal{A}_2$ by a word generated by $\mathcal{A}_1$ from that state q (i.e., $\mathrm{pre}^{\mathcal{A}_2}_u(F_2)$ with $u \in W^{\mathcal{A}_1}_{q,F_1}$). Since $\epsilon \in W^{\mathcal{A}_1}_{q,F_1}$ for all $q \in F_1$ and $\mathrm{pre}^{\mathcal{A}_2}_{\epsilon}(F_2) = F_2$ the iterations of the procedure `Kleene` begin with $\alpha(\vec{\boldsymbol{\epsilon}}^{F_1}) = \langle \psi^{F_2}_{\varnothing}(q \in F_1) \rangle_{q \in Q_1}$. By taking the minor of each vector component, we are considering smaller sets which still preserve the relation $\sqsubseteq$ (because $A \sqsubseteq B \Leftrightarrow \lfloor A \rfloor \sqsubseteq B \Leftrightarrow A \sqsubseteq \lfloor B \rfloor \Leftrightarrow \lfloor A \rfloor \sqsubseteq \lfloor B \rfloor$). Let $\vec{\boldsymbol{Y}}$ be the fixpoint computed by the `Kleene` procedure. We have that, for each component $q \in Q_1$, $\vec{\boldsymbol{Y}}_q = \lfloor \{ \mathrm{pre}^{\mathcal{A}_2}_u(F_2) \mid u \in W^{\mathcal{A}_1}_{q,F_1} \} \rfloor$. Whenever $\mathcal{L}(\mathcal{A}_1) \subseteq \mathcal{L}(\mathcal{A}_2)$ holds, all the sets of states in $\vec{\boldsymbol{Y}}_q$ for $q \in I_1$ are predecessors of F_2 in $\mathcal{A}_2$ by words in $\mathcal{L}(\mathcal{A}_2)$, so that they all contain at least one initial state in I_2. As a result, we obtain the following algorithm `FAIncS`, a "state-based" inclusion algorithm for deciding $\mathcal{L}(\mathcal{A}_1) \subseteq \mathcal{L}(\mathcal{A}_2)$.

`FAIncS`: State-based algorithm for $\mathcal{L}(\mathcal{A}_1) \subseteq \mathcal{L}(\mathcal{A}_2)$

Data: FAs $\mathcal{A}_1 = \langle Q_1, \delta_1, I_1, F_1, \Sigma \rangle$ and $\mathcal{A}_2 = \langle Q_2, \delta_2, I_2, F_2, \Sigma \rangle$.

$\langle Y_q \rangle_{q \in Q_1} :=$ `Kleene`$(\lambda \vec{\boldsymbol{X}}.\, \alpha(\vec{\boldsymbol{\epsilon}}^{F_1}) \sqcup \mathrm{Pre}^{\mathcal{A}_2}_{\mathcal{A}_1}(\vec{\boldsymbol{X}}), \vec{\boldsymbol{\varnothing}})$;
forall the $q \in I_1$ **do**
  forall the $s \in Y_q$ **do**
    if $s \cap I_2 = \varnothing$ **then return** *false*;
return *true*;

Theorem 6.3. *Let* $\mathcal{A}_1, \mathcal{A}_2$ *be FAs. The algorithm* `FAIncS` *decides the inclusion* $\mathcal{L}(\mathcal{A}_1) \subseteq \mathcal{L}(\mathcal{A}_2)$.

De Wulf et al. [10] introduced two antichain algorithms, called forward and backward, for deciding the universality of the language generated by a FA, i.e., whether the language is Σ^* or not. Then, they extended the backward algorithm in order to decide language inclusion. In what follows we show that `FAIncS` is equivalent to the corresponding extension of the forward algorithm and, therefore, dual to the antichain algorithm of De Wulf et al. [10].

To do that, we first define the poset of antichains in which the forward antichain algorithm computes its fixpoint. Then, we give a formal definition of the forward antichain algorithm for deciding language inclusion and show that this algorithm coincides with `FAIncS` when applied to the reverse automata.

Since the language inclusion between two languages holds iff it holds between the reverse languages generated by the reverse automata, we conclude that the algorithm FAIncS is equivalent to the forward antichain algorithm.

Let us consider the following poset of antichains $\langle \mathrm{AC}_{\langle \wp(Q_2),\subseteq\rangle}, \widetilde{\sqsubseteq}\rangle$ where

$$X \widetilde{\sqsubseteq} Y \stackrel{\triangle}{\Longleftrightarrow} \forall y \in Y, \exists x \in X,\ x \subseteq y.$$

It is easy to see that $\widetilde{\sqsubseteq}$ and $\sqsubseteq^{-1}$ coincides. As observed by De Wulf et al. [10], it turns out that $\langle \mathrm{AC}_{\langle \wp(Q_2),\subseteq\rangle}, \widetilde{\sqsubseteq}\rangle$ is a finite lattice, where $\widetilde{\sqcap}$ and $\widetilde{\sqcup}$ denote, resp., glb and lub of antichains. The lattice $\langle \mathrm{AC}_{\langle \wp(Q_2),\subseteq\rangle}, \widetilde{\sqsubseteq}\rangle$ is the domain in which the forward antichain algorithm computes on for deciding universality. The following result extends this forward algorithm in order to decide language inclusion.

Theorem 6.4 *bf ([10,* **Theorems 3 and 6]** *). Let* $\overrightarrow{\mathcal{FP}} \triangleq \widetilde{\bigsqcap}\{\overrightarrow{X} \in (\mathrm{AC}_{\langle \wp(Q_2),\subseteq\rangle})^{|Q_1|} \mid \overrightarrow{X} = \mathrm{Post}_{\mathcal{A}_1}^{\mathcal{A}_2}(\overrightarrow{X})\ \widetilde{\sqcap}\ \langle \psi_{\varnothing}^{\{I_2\}}(q \in I_1)\rangle_{q\in Q_1}\}$ *with* $\mathrm{Post}_{\mathcal{A}_1}^{\mathcal{A}_2}(\langle X_q\rangle_{q\in Q_1}) \triangleq \langle \lfloor\{\mathrm{post}_a^{\mathcal{A}_2}(X) \mid \exists a \in \Sigma, q' \in Q_1, X \in X_{q'},\ q \in \delta_1(q', a)\}\rfloor\rangle_{q\in Q_1}$. *Then,* $\mathcal{L}(\mathcal{A}_1) \nsubseteq \mathcal{L}(\mathcal{A}_2)$ *iff* $\exists q \in F_1, \overrightarrow{\mathcal{FP}}_q \widetilde{\sqsubseteq} \{F_2^c\}$.

Let $\mathcal{A}^R$ denote the reverse of $\mathcal{A}$, where arrows are flipped and the initial/final states become final/initial. Note that language inclusion can be decided by considering the reverse automata since $\mathcal{L}(\mathcal{A}_1) \subseteq \mathcal{L}(\mathcal{A}_2) \Leftrightarrow \mathcal{L}(\mathcal{A}_1^R) \subseteq \mathcal{L}(\mathcal{A}_2^R)$ holds. Furthermore, it is straightforward to check that $\mathrm{Post}_{\mathcal{A}_1}^{\mathcal{A}_2} = \mathrm{Pre}_{\mathcal{A}_1^R}^{\mathcal{A}_2^R}$. We therefore obtain the following result.

Theorem 6.5. *Let* $\overrightarrow{\mathcal{FP}} \triangleq \widetilde{\bigsqcap}\{\overrightarrow{X} \in (\mathrm{AC}_{\langle \wp(Q_2),\subseteq\rangle})^{|Q_1|} \mid \overrightarrow{X} = \mathrm{Pre}_{\mathcal{A}_1}^{\mathcal{A}_2}(\overrightarrow{X})\ \widetilde{\sqcap}\ \langle \psi_{\varnothing}^{\{F_2\}}(q \in F_1)\rangle_{q\in Q_1}\}$. *Then,* $\mathcal{L}(\mathcal{A}_1) \nsubseteq \mathcal{L}(\mathcal{A}_2)$ *iff* $\exists q \in I_1, \overrightarrow{\mathcal{FP}}_q \widetilde{\sqsubseteq} \{I_2^c\}$.

Since $\widetilde{\sqsubseteq} = \sqsubseteq^{-1}$, we have that $\widetilde{\sqcap} = \sqcup$. Moreover, by definition of α we have that $\langle \psi_{\varnothing}^{\{F_2\}}(q \in F_1)\rangle_{q\in Q_1} = \alpha(\overrightarrow{\epsilon}^{F_1})$. Therefore, we can rewrite the vector $\overrightarrow{\mathcal{FP}}$ of Theorem 6.5 as $\overrightarrow{\mathcal{FP}} = \bigsqcup\{\overrightarrow{X} \mid \overrightarrow{X} = \mathrm{Pre}_{\mathcal{A}_1}^{\mathcal{A}_2}(\overrightarrow{X}) \sqcup \alpha(\overrightarrow{\epsilon}^{F_1})\}$, which is the least fixpoint for $\sqsubseteq$ of $\mathrm{Pre}_{\mathcal{A}_1}^{\mathcal{A}_2}$ above $\alpha(\overrightarrow{\epsilon}^{F_1})$. It turns out that the Kleene iterates of this least fixpoint computation that converge to $\overrightarrow{\mathcal{FP}}$ exactly coincide with the iterates computed by the Kleene procedure of the state-based algorithm FAIncS. In particular, if $\overrightarrow{Y}$ is the output vector of the call to Kleene in FAIncS then $\overrightarrow{Y} = \overrightarrow{\mathcal{FP}}$. Furthermore, $\overrightarrow{\mathcal{FP}}_q \widetilde{\sqsubseteq} \{I_2^c\} \Leftrightarrow \exists S \in \overrightarrow{\mathcal{FP}}_q,\ S \cap I_2 = \varnothing$. Summing up, the $\sqsubseteq$-lfp algorithm FAIncS coincides with the $\widetilde{\sqsubseteq}$-gfp antichain algorithm of Theorem 6.5.

We can also derive an algorithm equivalent to FAIncS by considering the antichain poset $\langle \mathrm{AC}_{\langle \wp(Q_2),\supseteq\rangle}, \sqsubseteq\rangle$ for the dual lattice $\langle \wp(Q_2), \supseteq\rangle$ and by replacing the functions $\alpha_{\mathcal{A}_2}$, $\gamma_{\mathcal{A}_2}$, α, γ and $\mathrm{Pre}_{\mathcal{A}_1}^{\mathcal{A}_2}$ of Lemma 6.2, resp., with:

$$\alpha_{\mathcal{A}_2}^c(X) \triangleq \{\mathrm{cpre}_u^{\mathcal{A}_2}(F_2^c) \mid u \in X\},\ \gamma_{\mathcal{A}_2}^c(Y) \triangleq \lfloor\{u \in \Sigma^* \mid \mathrm{cpre}_u^{\mathcal{A}_2}(F_2^c) \in Y\}\rfloor,$$
$$\alpha^c(X) \triangleq \lfloor\{\mathrm{cpre}_u^{\mathcal{A}_2}(F_2^c) \mid u \in X\}\rfloor,\ \gamma^c(Y) \triangleq \{u \in \Sigma^* \mid \exists y \in Y, y \supseteq \mathrm{cpre}_u^{\mathcal{A}_2}(F_2^c)\},$$

$$\mathrm{CPre}_{\mathcal{A}_1}^{\mathcal{A}_2}(\langle X_q\rangle_{q\in Q_1}) \triangleq \langle \lfloor \{\mathrm{cpre}_a^{\mathcal{A}_2}(S) \mid \exists a \in \Sigma, q' \in Q_1,\, q' \in \delta_1(q,a) \wedge S \in X_{q'}\}\rfloor \rangle_{q\in Q_1}.$$

where $\mathrm{cpre}_u^{\mathcal{A}_2}(F_2^c) = (\mathrm{pre}_u^{\mathcal{A}_2}(F_2))^c$. When using these functions, we obtain a lfp algorithm computing on the domain $\langle \mathrm{AC}_{\langle \wp(Q_2), \supseteq\rangle}, \sqsubseteq\rangle$. Indeed, it turns out that $\mathcal{L}(\mathcal{A}_1) \subseteq \mathcal{L}(\mathcal{A}_2)$ iff $\mathtt{Kleene}(\lambda \vec{\boldsymbol{X}}.\, \alpha^c(\vec{\boldsymbol{\epsilon}}^{F_1}) \sqcup \mathrm{CPre}_{\mathcal{A}_1}^{\mathcal{A}_2}(\vec{\boldsymbol{X}}), \vec{\boldsymbol{\varnothing}}) \sqsubseteq \alpha^c(\overrightarrow{\boldsymbol{L_2}}^{I_1})$. It is straightforward to check that this algorithm coincides with the backward antichain algorithm defined by De Wulf et al. [10, Algorithm 1, Theorem 6] since both compute on the same domain, $\lfloor X \rfloor$ corresponds to the maximal (w.r.t. set inclusion) elements of X, $\alpha^c(\{\epsilon\}) = \{F_2^c\}$ and for all $X \in \alpha^c(\wp(\Sigma^*))$, we have that $X \sqsubseteq \alpha^c(L_2) \Leftrightarrow \forall S \in X,\, I_2 \not\subseteq S$.

We have thus shown that the two forward/backward antichain algorithms introduced by De Wulf et al. [10] can be systematically derived by instantiating our framework. The original antichain algorithms were later improved by Abdulla et al. [2] and, subsequently, by Bonchi and Pous [4]. Among their improvements, they showed how to exploit a precomputed binary relation between pairs of states of the input automata such that language inclusion holds for all pairs in the relation. When that binary relation is a simulation relation, our framework allows to partially match their results by using the quasiorder $\preceq_{\mathcal{A}}^r$ defined in Sect. 5.3. However, this quasiorder relation $\preceq_{\mathcal{A}}^r$ does not consider pairs of states $Q_2 \times Q_2$ whereas the aforementioned works do.

7 An Equivalent Greatest Fixpoint Algorithm

Let us recall a result from Cousot [5, Theorem 4] that if $g\colon C \to C$ is a monotonic function on a complete lattice $\langle C, \leq, \vee, \wedge\rangle$ which admits its unique right-adjoint $\widetilde{g}\colon C \to C$ (i.e., $g(c) \leq c' \Leftrightarrow c \leq \widetilde{g}(c')$ holds) then the following equivalence holds: for all $c, c' \in C$,

$$\mathrm{lfp}(\lambda x.\, c \vee g(x)) \leq c' \Leftrightarrow c \leq \mathrm{gfp}(\lambda y.\, c' \wedge \widetilde{g}(y)). \quad (11)$$

This property has been exploited to derive equivalent least/greatest fixpoint-based invariance proof methods for programs [5]. In the following, we use (11) to derive an algorithm for deciding the inclusion $\mathcal{L}(\mathcal{A}_1) \subseteq \mathcal{L}(\mathcal{A}_2)$, which relies on the computation of a greatest fixpoint rather than a least fixpoint. This can be achieved by exploiting the following simple observation, which provides an adjunction between concatenation and quotients of sets of words.

Lemma 7.1. *For all $X, Y \subseteq \Sigma^*$ and $w \in \Sigma^*$, $wY \subseteq Z \Leftrightarrow Y \subseteq w^{-1}Z$ and $Yw \subseteq Z \Leftrightarrow Y \subseteq Zw^{-1}$.*

Given the set of equations induced by a FA $\mathcal{A} = \langle Q, \delta, I, F, \Sigma\rangle$, we define the function $\widetilde{\mathrm{Pre}}_{\mathcal{A}} : \wp(\Sigma^*)^{|Q|} \to \wp(\Sigma^*)^{|Q|}$ as follows:

$$\widetilde{\mathrm{Pre}}_{\mathcal{A}}(\langle X_q \rangle_{q\in Q}) \triangleq \langle \bigcap_{a\in\Sigma, q'\in\delta(q,a)} a^{-1}X_q \rangle_{q'\in Q},$$

where, as usual, $\bigcap \varnothing = \Sigma^*$. It turns out that $\widetilde{\mathrm{Pre}}_{\mathcal{A}}$ is the right-adjoint of $\mathrm{Pre}_{\mathcal{A}}$.

Lemma 7.2. *For all* $\vec{\boldsymbol{X}}, \vec{\boldsymbol{Y}} \in \wp(\Sigma^*)^{|Q|}$, $\mathrm{Pre}_{\mathcal{A}}(\vec{\boldsymbol{X}}) \subseteq \vec{\boldsymbol{Y}} \Leftrightarrow \vec{\boldsymbol{X}} \subseteq \widetilde{\mathrm{Pre}}_{\mathcal{A}}(\vec{\boldsymbol{Y}})$.

Hence, from equivalences (5) and (11) we obtain:

$$\mathcal{L}(\mathcal{A}_1) \subseteq L_2 \Leftrightarrow \vec{\boldsymbol{\epsilon}}^{F_1} \subseteq \mathrm{gfp}(\lambda\vec{\boldsymbol{X}}.\,\vec{\boldsymbol{L_2}}^{I_1} \cap \widetilde{\mathrm{Pre}}_{\mathcal{A}_1}(\vec{\boldsymbol{X}})). \tag{12}$$

The following algorithm `FAIncGfp` decides the inclusion $\mathcal{L}(\mathcal{A}_1) \subseteq L_2$ by implementing the greatest fixpoint computation in equivalence (12). The intuition behind algorithm `FAIncGfp` is that

$$L_1 \subseteq L_2 \Leftrightarrow \forall w \in L_1, (\epsilon \in w^{-1}L_2 \Leftrightarrow \epsilon \in \bigcap_{w\in L_1} w^{-1}L_2),$$

where $L_1 = \mathcal{L}(\mathcal{A}_1)$. Therefore, `FAIncGfp` computes the set $\bigcap_{w\in L_1} w^{-1}L_2$ by using the automaton $\mathcal{A}_1$ and by considering prefixes of L_1 of increasing lengths. This means that after n iterations of `Kleene`, the algorithm `FAIncGfp` has computed $\bigcap_{wu\in L_1, |w|\leq n, q_0\in I_1, q_0 \stackrel{w}{\rightsquigarrow} q} w^{-1}L_2$, for every state $q \in Q_1$.

`FAIncGfp`: Greatest fixpoint algorithm for $\mathcal{L}(\mathcal{A}_1) \subseteq L_2$

Data: FA $\mathcal{A}_1 = \langle Q_1, \delta_1, I_1, F_1, \Sigma\rangle$; regular language L_2.

1 $\langle Y_q \rangle_{q\in Q} :=$ `Kleene`$(\lambda\vec{\boldsymbol{X}}.\,\vec{\boldsymbol{L_2}}^{I_1} \cap \widetilde{\mathrm{Pre}}_{\mathcal{A}_1}(\vec{\boldsymbol{X}}), \vec{\boldsymbol{\Sigma^*}})$;
2 **forall the** $q \in F_1$ **do**
3   **if** $\epsilon \notin Y_q$ **then return** *false*;
4 **return** *true*;

The regularity of L_2 clanguages of being closed under intersections and quotients show that each iterate computed by `Kleene`$(\lambda\vec{\boldsymbol{X}}.\,\vec{\boldsymbol{L_2}}^{I_1} \cap \widetilde{\mathrm{Pre}}_{\mathcal{A}_1}(\vec{\boldsymbol{X}}), \vec{\boldsymbol{\Sigma^*}})$ is a (computable) regular language. To the best of our knowledge, this language inclusion algorithm `FAIncGfp` has never been described in the literature before.

Next, we discharge the fundamental assumption on which the correctness of this algorithm `FAIncGfp` depends on: the Kleene iterates computed by `FAIncGfp` are finitely many. In order to do that, we consider an abstract version of the greatest fixpoint computation exploiting a closure operator which guarantees that the abstract Kleene iterates are finitely many. This closure operator $\rho_{\leq_{\mathcal{A}_2}}$ will be defined by using an ordering relation $\leq_{\mathcal{A}_2}$ induced by a FA $\mathcal{A}_2$ such that $L_2 = \mathcal{L}(\mathcal{A}_2)$ and will be shown to be *forward complete* for the function $\lambda\vec{\boldsymbol{X}}.\,\vec{\boldsymbol{L_2}}^{I_1} \cap \widetilde{\mathrm{Pre}}_{\mathcal{A}_1}(\vec{\boldsymbol{X}})$ used by `FAIncGfp`.

Forward completeness of abstract interpretations [15] is different from and orthogonal to backward completeness introduced in Sect. 3 and used in Sects. 4 and 5. In particular, a remarkable consequence of exploiting a forward complete abstraction is that the Kleene iterates of the concrete and abstract greatest fixpoint computations coincide. The intuition here is that this forward complete closure $\rho_{\leq_{\mathcal{A}_2}}$ allows us to establish that all Kleene iterates of $\mathrm{gfp}(\overrightarrow{\boldsymbol{X}}.\, \overrightarrow{\boldsymbol{L_2}}^{I_1} \cap \widetilde{\mathrm{Pre}}_{\mathcal{A}_1}(\overrightarrow{\boldsymbol{X}}))$ belong to the image of the closure $\rho_{\leq_{\mathcal{A}_2}}$, more precisely that every Kleene iterate is a language which is upward closed for $\leq_{\mathcal{A}_2}$. Interestingly, a similar phenomenon occurs in well-structured transition systems [1,13].

Let us now describe in detail this abstraction. A closure $\rho \in \mathrm{uco}(C)$ on a concrete domain C is forward complete for a monotonic function $f : C \to C$ if $\rho f \rho = f\rho$ holds. The intuition here is that forward completeness means that no loss of precision is accumulated when the output of a computation of $f\rho$ is approximated by ρ, or, equivalently, f maps elements of ρ into elements of ρ. Dually to the case of backward completeness, forward completeness implies that $\mathrm{gfp}(f) = \mathrm{gfp}(f\rho) = \mathrm{gfp}(\rho f \rho)$ holds, when these greatest fixpoints exist (this is the case, e.g., when C is a complete lattice). It turns out that forward and backward completeness are related by the following duality on the function f.

Lemma 7.3 (**[15, Corollary 1]**). *Let $\langle C, \leq_C\rangle$ be a complete lattice and assume that $f\colon C \to C$ admits the right-adjoint $\widetilde{f}\colon C \to C$, i.e., $f(c) \leq_C c' \Leftrightarrow c \leq_C \widetilde{f}(c')$ holds. Then, ρ is backward complete for f iff ρ is forward complete for $\widetilde{f}$.*

Thus, by Lemma 7.3, in the following result instead of assuming the hypotheses implying that a closure ρ is forward complete for the right-adjoint $\widetilde{\mathrm{Pre}}_{\mathcal{A}_1}$ we state some hypotheses which guarantee that ρ is backward complete for its left-adjoint $\mathrm{Pre}_{\mathcal{A}_1}$.

Theorem 7.4. *Let $\mathcal{A}_1 = \langle Q_1, \delta_1, I_1, F_1, \Sigma\rangle$ be a FA, L_2 be a regular language and $\rho \in \mathrm{uco}(\wp(\Sigma^*))$. Let us assume that:*

(1) $\rho(L_2) = L_2$;
(2) ρ is backward complete for $\lambda X.\, aX$ for all $a \in \Sigma$.

Then, $\mathcal{L}(\mathcal{A}_1) \subseteq L_2$ iff $\vec{\epsilon}^{F_1} \subseteq \mathrm{gfp}(\overrightarrow{\boldsymbol{X}}.\, \rho(\overrightarrow{\boldsymbol{L_2}}^{I_1} \cap \widetilde{\mathrm{Pre}}_{\mathcal{A}_1}(\overrightarrow{\boldsymbol{X}})))$. Moreover, the Kleene iterates computed by $\mathrm{gfp}(\overrightarrow{\boldsymbol{X}}.\, \rho(\overrightarrow{\boldsymbol{L_2}}^{I_1} \cap \widetilde{\mathrm{Pre}}_{\mathcal{A}_1}(\overrightarrow{\boldsymbol{X}})))$ coincide in lockstep with those of $\mathrm{gfp}(\overrightarrow{\boldsymbol{X}}.\, \overrightarrow{\boldsymbol{L_2}}^{I_1} \cap \widetilde{\mathrm{Pre}}_{\mathcal{A}_1}(\overrightarrow{\boldsymbol{X}}))$.

We can now establish that the sequence of Kleene iterates computed by $\mathrm{gfp}(\overrightarrow{\boldsymbol{X}}.\, \overrightarrow{\boldsymbol{L_2}}^{I_1} \cap \widetilde{\mathrm{Pre}}_{\mathcal{A}_1}(\overrightarrow{\boldsymbol{X}}))$ is finite. Let $L_2 = \mathcal{L}(\mathcal{A}_2)$, for some FA $\mathcal{A}_2$, and consider the corresponding left state-based quasiorder $\leq^l_{\mathcal{A}_2}$ on Σ^* as defined by (9). Lemma 5.7 tells us that $\leq^l_{\mathcal{A}_2}$ is a left L_2-consistent wqo. Furthermore, since Q_2 is finite we have that both $\leq^l_{\mathcal{A}_2}$ and $(\leq^l_{\mathcal{A}_2})^{-1}$ are wqos, so that, in turn, $\langle \rho_{\leq^l_{\mathcal{A}_2}}, \subseteq\rangle$ is a poset which is both ACC and DCC. In particular, the definition of $\leq^l_{\mathcal{A}_2}$ implies that every chain in $\langle \rho_{\leq^l_{\mathcal{A}_2}}, \subseteq\rangle$ has at most $2^{|Q_2|}$ elements, so that if we compute $2^{|Q_2|}$ Kleene iterates then we have necessarily computed the greatest fixpoint. Moreover, as a consequence of the DCC property we have that the Kleene iterates of $\mathrm{gfp}(\lambda\overrightarrow{\boldsymbol{X}}.\, \rho_{\leq_{\mathcal{A}_2}}(\overrightarrow{\boldsymbol{L_2}}^{I_1} \cap \widetilde{\mathrm{Pre}}_{\mathcal{A}_1}(\overrightarrow{\boldsymbol{X}})))$ are finitely many, hence so are the iterates of $\mathrm{gfp}(\lambda\overrightarrow{\boldsymbol{X}}.\, \overrightarrow{\boldsymbol{L_2}}^{I_1} \cap \widetilde{\mathrm{Pre}}_{\mathcal{A}_1}(\overrightarrow{\boldsymbol{X}}))$ because they go in lockstep as stated by Theorem 7.4.

Corollary 7.5. *Let $\mathcal{A}_1$ be a FA and let L_2 be a regular language. Then, the algorithm* `FAIncGfp` *decides the inclusion $\mathcal{L}(\mathcal{A}_1) \subseteq L_2$*

Finally, it is worth citing that Fiedor et al. [12] put forward an algorithm for deciding WS1S formulae which relies on the same lfp computation used in `FAIncS`. Then, they derive a dual gfp computation by relying on Park's duality [22]: $\text{lfp}(\lambda X. f(X)) = (\text{gfp}(\lambda X. (f(X^c)^c))^c$. Their approach differs from ours since we use the equivalence (11) to compute a gfp, different from the lfp, which still allows us to decide the inclusion problem. Furthermore, their algorithm decides whether a given automaton accepts ϵ and it is not clear how their algorithm could be extended for deciding language inclusion.

8 Conclusion and Future Work

We believe that this work only scratched the surface of the use of well-quasiorders on words for solving language inclusion problems. In particular, our approach based on complete abstract interpretations allowed us to systematically derive within our framework well-known algorithms, such as the antichain algorithms by De Wulf et al. [10], as well as novel algorithms, such as `FAIncGfp`, for deciding the inclusion of regular languages. Due to lack of space, we deliberately omitted from this paper the study of the inclusion problem $\mathcal{L}(\mathcal{G}) \subseteq L$ where $\mathcal{G}$ is a context-free grammar, in exchange for a deeper understanding of the $\mathcal{L}(\mathcal{A}) \subseteq L$ case. The case $\mathcal{L}(\mathcal{G}) \subseteq \mathcal{L}(\mathcal{A})$ is covered in the extended version [14].

Future directions include leveraging well-quasiorders for infinite words [21] to shed new light on the inclusion problem between ω languages. Our results could also be extended to inclusion of tree languages by relying on the extensions of Myhill-Nerode theorems for tree languages [20]. Another interesting topic for future work is the enhancement of quasiorders using simulation relations. Even though we already showed in this paper that simulations can be used to refine our language inclusion algorithms, we are not on par with the thoughtful use of simulation relations made by Abdulla et al. [2] and Bonchi and Pous [4]. Finally, let us mention that the correspondence between least and greatest fixpoint-based inclusion checks assuming complete abstractions was studied by Bonchi et al. [3] with the aim of formally connecting sound up-to techniques and complete abstract interpretations. Further possible developments include the study of our abstract interpretation-based algorithms for language inclusion from the point of view of sound up-to techniques.

Acknowledgements. We would like to thank the reviewers for their insightful feedback that allowed us to find a simpler connection between our work and the antichain algorithms. Pierre Ganty completed this work with the support of the Spanish Ministry of Economy and Competitiveness project No. PGC2018-102210-B-I00, the Madrid Regional Government project No. S2018/TCS-4339 and the Ramón y Cajal fellowship RYC-2016-20281. The work of Francesco Ranzato has been partially funded by the University of Padova, SID2018 project "Analysis of STatic Analyses (ASTA)", and by the Italian Ministry of Research MIUR, project No. 201784YSZ5 "AnalysiS of PRogram Analyses (ASPRA)".

References

1. Abdulla, P.A., Cerans, K., Jonsson, B., Tsay, Y.-K.: General decidability theorems for infinite-state systems. In: Proceedings of the 11th Annual IEEE Symposium on Logic in Computer Science (LICS 1996), pp. 313–321. IEEE Computer Society (1996)
2. Abdulla, P.A., Chen, Y.-F., Holík, L., Mayr, R., Vojnar, T.: When simulation meets antichains. In: Esparza, J., Majumdar, R. (eds.) TACAS 2010. LNCS, vol. 6015, pp. 158–174. Springer, Heidelberg (2010). https://doi.org/10.1007/978-3-642-12002-2_14
3. Bonchi, F., Ganty, P., Giacobazzi, R., Pavlovic, D.: Sound up-to techniques and complete abstract domains. In: Proceedings of the 33rd Annual ACM/IEEE Symposium on Logic in Computer Science (LICS 2018). ACM Press (2018)
4. Bonchi, F., Pous, D.: Checking NFA equivalence with bisimulations up to congruence. In: Proceedings of the 40th Annual ACM SIGPLAN-SIGACT Symposium on Principles of Programming Languages (POPL 2013), pp. 457–468. ACM Press (2013)
5. Cousot, P.: Partial completeness of abstract fixpoint checking. In: Choueiry, B.Y., Walsh, T. (eds.) SARA 2000. LNCS (LNAI), vol. 1864, pp. 1–25. Springer, Heidelberg (2000). https://doi.org/10.1007/3-540-44914-0_1
6. Cousot, P., Cousot, R.: Abstract interpretation: a unified lattice model for static analysis of programs by construction or approximation of fixpoints. In: Proceedings of the 4th ACM SIGACT-SIGPLAN Symposium on Principles of Programming Languages (POPL 1977), pp. 238–252. ACM Press (1977)
7. Cousot, P., Cousot, R.: Systematic design of program analysis frameworks. In: Proceedings of the 6th ACM SIGACT-SIGPLAN Symposium on Principles of Programming Languages (POPL 1979), pp. 269–282. ACM, New York (1979)
8. de Luca, A., Varricchio, S.: Well quasi-orders and regular languages. Acta Informatica **31**(6), 539–557 (1994)
9. de Luca, A., Varricchio, S.: Finiteness and Regularity in Semigroups and Formal Languages. Springer, Heidelberg (2011). https://doi.org/10.1007/978-3-642-59849-4
10. De Wulf, M., Doyen, L., Henzinger, T.A., Raskin, J.-F.: Antichains: a new algorithm for checking universality of finite automata. In: Ball, T., Jones, R.B. (eds.) CAV 2006. LNCS, vol. 4144, pp. 17–30. Springer, Heidelberg (2006). https://doi.org/10.1007/11817963_5
11. Ehrenfeucht, A., Haussler, D., Rozenberg, G.: On regularity of context-free languages. Theor. Comput. Sci. **27**(3), 311–332 (1983)
12. Fiedor, T., Holík, L., Lengál, O., Vojnar, T.: Nested antichains for WS1S. Acta Informatica **56**(3), 205–228 (2019)
13. Finkel, A., Schnoebelen, P.: Well-structured transition systems everywhere!. Theor. Comput. Sci. **256**(1–2), 63–92 (2001)
14. Ganty, P., Ranzato, F., Valero, P.: Complete abstractions for checking language inclusion. arXiv e-prints, arXiv:1904.01388, April 2019
15. Giacobazzi, R., Quintarelli, E.: Incompleteness, counterexamples, and refinements in abstract model-checking. In: Cousot, P. (ed.) SAS 2001. LNCS, vol. 2126, pp. 356–373. Springer, Heidelberg (2001). https://doi.org/10.1007/3-540-47764-0_20
16. Giacobazzi, R., Ranzato, F., Scozzari, F.: Making abstract interpretations complete. J. ACM **47**(2), 361–416 (2000)

17. Hofman, P., Totzke, P.: Trace inclusion for one-counter nets revisited. Theor. Comput. Sci. **735**, 50–63 (2018)
18. Hofmann, M., Chen, W.: Abstract interpretation from Büchi automata. In: Proceedings of the Joint Meeting of the Twenty-Third EACSL Annual Conference on Computer Science Logic (CSL 2014) and the Twenty-Ninth Annual ACM/IEEE Symposium on Logic in Computer Science (LICS 2014). ACM Press (2014)
19. Jančar, P., Esparza, J., Moller, F.: Petri nets and regular processes. J. Comput. Syst. Sci. **59**(3), 476–503 (1999)
20. Kozen, D.: On the Myhill-Nerode theorem for trees. Bull. EATCS **47**, 170–173 (1992)
21. Ogawa, M.: Well-quasi-orders and regular ω-languages. Theor. Comput. Sci. **324**(1), 55–60 (2004)
22. Park, D.: Fixpoint induction and proofs of program properties. Mach. Intell. **5**, 59–78 (1969)
23. Ranzato, F.: Complete abstractions everywhere. In: Giacobazzi, R., Berdine, J., Mastroeni, I. (eds.) VMCAI 2013. LNCS, vol. 7737, pp. 15–26. Springer, Heidelberg (2013). https://doi.org/10.1007/978-3-642-35873-9_3
24. Schützenberger, M.P.: On context-free languages and push-down automata. Inf. Control **6**(3), 246–264 (1963)

On the Monniaux Problem in Abstract Interpretation

Nathanaël Fijalkow[1], Engel Lefaucheux[2(✉)], Pierre Ohlmann[3], Joël Ouaknine[2,4], Amaury Pouly[5], and James Worrell[4]

[1] CNRS, LaBRI, France and The Alan Turing Institute, London, UK
[2] Max Planck Institute for Software Systems, Saarland Informatics Campus, Saarbrücken, Germany
elefauch@mpi-sws.org
[3] IRIF, Université Paris 7, Paris, France
[4] Department of Computer Science, Oxford University, Oxford, UK
[5] CNRS, IRIF, Université Paris Diderot, Paris, France

Abstract. The Monniaux Problem in abstract interpretation asks, roughly speaking, whether the following question is decidable: given a program P, a safety (*e.g.*, non-reachability) specification φ, and an abstract domain of invariants $\mathcal{D}$, does there exist an inductive invariant $\mathcal{I}$ in $\mathcal{D}$ guaranteeing that program P meets its specification φ. The Monniaux Problem is of course parameterised by the classes of programs and invariant domains that one considers.

In this paper, we show that the Monniaux Problem is undecidable for unguarded affine programs and semilinear invariants (unions of polyhedra). Moreover, we show that decidability is recovered in the important special case of simple linear loops.

1 Introduction

Invariants are one of the most fundamental and useful notions in the quantitative sciences, appearing in a wide range of contexts, from gauge theory, dynamical systems, and control theory in physics, mathematics, and engineering to program verification, static analysis, abstract interpretation, and programming language semantics (among others) in computer science. In spite of decades of scientific work and progress, automated invariant synthesis remains a topic of active research, especially in the fields of program analysis and abstract interpretation, and plays a central role in methods and tools seeking to establish correctness properties of computer programs; see, *e.g.*, [20], and particularly Sect. 8 therein.

Nathanaël Fijalkow, Pierre Ohlmann, and Amaury Pouly were supported by the Agence Nationale de la Recherche through the project Codys (ANR-18-CE40-0007). Joël Ouaknine was supported by ERC grant AVS-ISS (648701) and by DFG grant 389792660 as part of TRR 248 (see https://perspicuous-computing.science). James Worrell was supported by EPSRC Fellowship EP/N008197/1.

B.-Y. E. Chang (Ed.): SAS 2019, LNCS 11822, pp. 162–180, 2019.
https://doi.org/10.1007/978-3-030-32304-2_9

The focus of the present paper is the ***Monniaux Problem*** on the decidability of the existence of separating invariants, which was formulated by David Monniaux in [22,23] and also raised by him in a series of personal communications with various members of the theoretical computer science community over the past five years or so. There are in fact a multitude of versions of the Monniaux Problem—indeed, it would be more appropriate to speak of a *class* of problems rather than a single question—but at a high level the formulation below is one of the most general:

> Consider a program P operating over some numerical domain (such as the integers or rationals), and assume that P has an underlying finite control-flow graph over the set of nodes $Q = \{q_1, \ldots, q_r\}$. Let us assume that P makes use of d numerical variables, and each transition $q \xrightarrow{t} q'$ comprises a function $f_t : \mathbb{R}^d \to \mathbb{R}^d$ as well as a guard $g_t \subseteq \mathbb{R}^d$. Let $x, y \in \mathbb{Q}^d$ be two points in the ambient space. By way of intuition and motivation, we are interested in the reachability problem as to whether, starting in location q_1 with variables having valuation x, it is possible to reach location q_r with variables having valuation y, by following the available transitions and under the obvious interpretation of the various functions and guards. Unfortunately, in most settings this problem is well-known to be undecidable.
>
> Let $\mathcal{D} \subseteq 2^{\mathbb{R}^d}$ be an 'abstract domain' for P, *i.e.*, a collection of subsets of $\mathbb{R}^d$. For example, $\mathcal{D}$ could be the collection of all convex polyhedra in $\mathbb{R}^d$, or the collection of all closed semialgebraic sets in $\mathbb{R}^d$, etc.
>
> The Monniaux Problem can now be formulated as a decision question: is it possible to adorn each control location q with an element $\mathcal{I}_q \in \mathcal{D}$ such that:
>
> 1. $x \in \mathcal{I}_{q_1}$;
> 2. The collection of $\mathcal{I}_q$'s forms an *inductive invariant*: for each transition $q \xrightarrow{t} q'$, we have that $f_t(\mathcal{I}_q \cap g_t) \subseteq \mathcal{I}_{q'}$; and
> 3. $y \notin \mathcal{I}_{q_r}$.
>
> We call such a collection $\{\mathcal{I}_q : q \in Q\}$ a *separating inductive invariant* for program P. (Clearly, the existence of a separating inductive invariant constitutes a proof of non-reachability for P with the given x and y.)
>
> Associated with this decision problem, in positive instances one is also potentially interested in the synthesis problem, *i.e.*, the matter of algorithmically producing a suitable separating invariant $\{\mathcal{I}_q : q \in Q\}$.[1]

The Monniaux Problem is therefore parameterised by a number of items, key of which are (i) the abstract domain $\mathcal{D}$ under consideration, and (ii) the kind of functions and guards allowed in transitions.

Our main interest in this paper lies in the *decidability* of the existence of separating invariants for various instances of the Monniaux Problem. We give below a cursory cross-sectional survey of existing work and results in this direction.

---

[1] In the remainder of this paper, the term 'invariant' shall always refer to the inductive kind.

Arguably the earliest positive result in this area is due to Karr, who showed that strongest affine invariants (conjunctions of affine equalities) for affine programs (no guards, and all transition functions are given by affine expressions) could be computed algorithmically [19]. Note that the ability to synthesise strongest (*i.e.*, smallest with respect to set inclusion) invariants immediately entails the decidability of the Monniaux Problem instance, since the existence of *some* separating invariant is clearly equivalent to whether the *strongest* invariant is separating. Müller-Olm and Seidl later extended this work on affine programs to include the computation of strongest polynomial invariants of fixed degree [24], and a randomised algorithm for discovering affine relations was proposed by Gulwani and Necula [16]. More recently, Hrushovski *et al.* showed how to compute a basis for *all* polynomial relations at every location of a given affine program [16].

The approaches described above all compute invariants consisting exclusively of conjunctions of *equality* relations. By contrast, an early and highly influential paper by Cousot and Halbwachs considers the domain of convex closed polyhedra [8], for programs having polynomial transition functions and guards. Whilst no decidability results appear in that paper, much further work was devoted to the development of restricted polyhedral domains for which theoretical guarantees could be obtained, leading (among others) to the *octagon domain* of Miné [21], the *octahedron domain* of Clarisó and Cortadella [5], and the *template polyhedra* of Sankaranarayanan *et al.* [25]. In fact, as observed by Monniaux [23], if one considers a domain of convex polyhedra having a *uniformly bounded* number of faces (therefore subsuming in particular the domains just described), then for any class of programs with polynomial transition relations and guards, the existence of separating invariants becomes decidable, as the problem can equivalently be phrased in the first-order theory of the reals.

One of the central motivating questions for the Monniaux Problem is whether one can always compute separating invariants for the full domain of polyhedra. Unfortunately, on this matter very little is known at present. In recent work, Monniaux showed undecidability for the domain of convex polyhedra and the class of programs having affine transition functions and polynomial guards [23]. One of the main results of the present paper is to show undecidability for the domain of *semilinear sets*[2] and the class of affine programs (without any guards)—in fact, affine programs with only a single control location and two transitions:

Theorem 1. *Let $A, B \in \mathbb{Q}^{d\times d}$ be two rational square matrices of dimension d, and let $x, y \in \mathbb{Q}^d$ be two points in $\mathbb{Q}^d$. Then the existence of a semilinear set $\mathcal{I} \subseteq \mathbb{R}^d$ having the following properties:*

1. $x \in \mathcal{I}$;
2. $A\mathcal{I} \subseteq \mathcal{I}$ *and* $B\mathcal{I} \subseteq \mathcal{I}$; *and*
3. $y \notin \mathcal{I}$

is an undecidable problem.

[2] A semilinear set consists of a finite union of polyhedra, or equivalently is defined as the solution set of a Boolean combination of linear inequalities.

Remark 2. It is worth pointing out that the theorem remains valid even for sufficiently large fixed d (our proof shows undecidability for $d = 336$, but this value could undoubtedly be improved). If moreover one requires $\mathcal{I}$ to be topologically closed, one can lower d to having fixed value 27 (which again is unlikely to be optimal). Finally, an examination of the proof reveals that the theorem also holds for the domain of semialgebraic sets, and in fact for any domain of o-minimal sets in the sense of [1]. The proof also carries through whether one considers the domain of semilinear sets having rational, algebraic, or real coordinates.

Although the above is a negative (undecidability) result, it should be viewed in a positive light; as Monniaux writes in [23], *"We started this work hoping to vindicate forty years of research on heuristics by showing that the existence of polyhedral inductive separating invariants in a system with transitions in linear arithmetic (integer or rational) is undecidable."* Theorem 1 shows that, at least as regards non-convex invariants, the development and use of heuristics is indeed vindicated and will continue to remain essential. Related questions of *completeness* of given abstraction scheme have also been examined by Giaccobazzi *et al.* in [13,14].

It is important to note that our undecidability result requires at least *two* transitions. In fact, much research work has been expended on the class of simple *affine* loops, *i.e.*, one-location programs equipped with a single self-transition. In terms of invariants, Fijalkow *et al.* establish in [10,11] the decidability of the existence of *semialgebraic* separating invariants, and specifically state the question of the existence of separating *semilinear* invariants as an open problem. Almagor *et al.* extend this line of work in [1] to more complex targets (in lieu of the point y) and richer classes of invariants. The second main result of the present paper is to settle the open question of [10,11] in the affirmative:

Theorem 3. *Let $A \in \mathbb{Q}^{d\times d}$ be a rational square matrix of dimension d, and let $x, y \in \mathbb{Q}^d$ be two points in $\mathbb{Q}^d$. It is decidable whether there exists a closed semilinear set $\mathcal{I} \subseteq \mathbb{R}^d$ having algebraic coordinates such that:*

1. $x \in \mathcal{I}$;
2. $A\mathcal{I} \subseteq \mathcal{I}$; *and*
3. $y \notin \mathcal{I}$.

Remark 4. The proof shows that, in fixed dimension d, the decision procedure runs in polynomial time. It is worth noting that one also has decidability if A, x, and y are taken to have real-algebraic (rather than rational) entries.

Let us conclude this section by briefly commenting on the important issue of *convexity.* At its inception, abstract interpretation had a marked preference for domains of *convex* invariants, of which the interval domain, the octagon domain, and of course the domain of convex polyhedra are prime examples. Convexity confers several distinct advantages, including simplicity of representation, algorithmic tractability and scalability, ease of implementation, and better termination heuristics (such as the use of widening). The central drawback of convexity, on the other hand, is its poor expressive power. This has been noted time and again: *"convex polyhedra [...] are insufficient for expressing certain invariants, and what is often needed is a disjunction of convex polyhedra."* [2]; *"the ability to express non-convex properties is sometimes required in order to achieve a precise analysis of some numerical properties"* [12]. Abstract interpretation can accommodate non-convexity either by introducing disjunctions (see, *e.g.*, [2] and references therein), or via the development of special-purpose domains of non-convex invariants such as *donut domains* [12]. The technology, data structures, algorithms, and heuristics supporting the use of disjunctions in the leading abstract-interpretation tool ASTRÉE are presented in great detail in [7]. In the world of software verification, where predicate abstraction is the dominant paradigm, disjunctions—and hence non-convexity—are nowadays native features of the landscape.

It is important to note that the two main results presented in this paper, Theorems 1 and 3, have only been proven for families of invariants that are not necessarily convex. The Monniaux Problem restricted to families of *convex* invariants remains open and challenging.

Full proofs can be found in the companion arXiv report [9].

2 Preliminaries

2.1 Complex and Algebraic Numbers

The set of complex numbers is $\mathbb{C}$, and for a complex number z its modulus is $|z|$, its real part is $\mathrm{Re}\,(z)$ and its imaginary part is $\mathrm{Im}\,(z)$.

Let $\mathbb{C}^*$ denote the set of non-zero complex numbers. We write S^1 for the complex unit circle, *i.e.* the set of complex numbers of modulus 1. We let $\mathbb{U}$ denote the set of roots of unity, *i.e.* complex numbers $z \in S^1$ such that $z^n = 1$ for some $n \in \mathbb{N}$.

When working in $\mathbb{C}^d$, the norm of a vector z is $||z||$, defined as the maximum of the moduli of each complex number z_i for i in $\{1, \ldots, d\}$. For $\varepsilon > 0$ and z in $\mathbb{C}^d$, we write $B(z, \varepsilon)$ for the open ball centered in z of radius ε. The topological closure of a set $\mathcal{I} \subseteq \mathbb{C}^d$ is $\overline{\mathcal{I}}$, its interior $\mathcal{I}^\circ$, and its frontier $\partial\mathcal{I}$, defined as $\overline{\mathcal{I}} \cap \overline{\mathbb{C}^d \setminus \mathcal{I}}$.

We will mostly work in the field $\mathbb{A} \subseteq \mathbb{C}$ of algebraic numbers, that is, roots of polynomials with coefficients in $\mathbb{Z}$. It is possible to represent and manipulate algebraic numbers effectively, by storing their minimal polynomial and a sufficiently precise numerical approximation. An excellent reference in computational algebraic number theory is [6]. All standard algebraic operations such as sums, products, root-finding of polynomials, or computing Jordan normal forms of matrices with algebraic entries can be performed effectively.

2.2 Semilinear Sets

We now define semilinear sets in $\mathbb{C}^d$, by identifying $\mathbb{C}^d$ with $\mathbb{R}^{2d}$. A set $\mathcal{I} \subseteq \mathbb{R}^{2d}$ is semilinear if it is the set of real solutions of some finite Boolean combination of linear inequalities with algebraic coefficients. We give an equivalent definition now using half-spaces and polyhedra. A half-space $\mathcal{H}$ is a subset of $\mathbb{C}^d$ of the form

$$\mathcal{H} = \left\{ z \in \mathbb{C}^d \mid \sum_{i=1}^{d} \mathrm{Re}\,(z\overline{u}) \succ a \right\},$$

for some u in $\mathbb{A}^d$, a in $\mathbb{A} \cap \mathbb{R}$ and $\succ \in \{\geq, >\}$. A polyhedron is a finite intersection of half-spaces, and a semilinear set a finite union of polyhedra.

We recall some well known facts about semilinear sets which will be useful for our purposes.

Lemma 5 (Projections of Semilinear Sets). *Let $\mathcal{I}$ be a semilinear set in $\mathbb{C}^{d+d'}$. Then the projection of $\mathcal{I}$ on the first d coordinates, defined by*

$$\Pi(\mathcal{I}, d) = \left\{ z \in \mathbb{C}^d \mid \exists t \in \mathbb{C}^{d'}, (z,t) \in \mathcal{I} \right\}$$

is a semilinear set.

Lemma 6 (Sections of Semilinear Sets). *Let $\mathcal{I}$ be a semilinear set in $\mathbb{C}^{d+d'}$ and t in $\mathbb{C}^{d'}$. Then the section of $\mathcal{I}$ along t, defined by*

$$\mathit{Section}\,(\mathcal{I}, t) = \left\{ z \in \mathbb{C}^d \mid (z,t) \in \mathcal{I} \right\},$$

is a semilinear set.

Furthermore, there exists a bound B in $\mathbb{R}$ such that for all t in $\mathbb{C}^{d'}$ of norm at most 1, if Section$(\mathcal{I}, t)$ is non-empty, then it contains some z in $\mathbb{C}^d$ of norm at most B.

For the reader's intuitions, note that the last part of this lemma does not hold for more complicated sets. For instance, consider the hyperbola defined by $\mathcal{I} = \{(x,y) \in \mathbb{R}^2 \mid xy = 1\}$. Choosing a small x forces to choose a large y, hence there exist no bound B as stated in the lemma for $\mathcal{I}$.

The dimension of a set X of $\mathbb{R}^d$ is the minimal k in $\mathbb{N}$ such that X is included in a finite union of affine subspaces of dimension at most k.

Lemma 7 (Dimension of Semilinear Sets). *Let $\mathcal{I}$ be a semilinear set in $\mathbb{R}^d$. If $\mathcal{I}^\circ = \emptyset$, then $\mathcal{I}$ has dimension at most $d-1$.*

3 Main Results Overview

We are interested in instances of the Monniaux Problem in which there are no guards, all transitions are affine (or equivalently linear, since affine transitions can be made linear by increasing the dimension of the ambient space by 1), and invariants are semilinear. This gives rise to the *semilinear invariant problem*, where an instance is given by a set of square matrices $A_1, \ldots, A_k \in \mathbb{A}^{d\times d}$ and two points $x, y \in \mathbb{A}^d$. A semilinear set $\mathcal{I} \subseteq \mathbb{C}^d$ is a *separating invariant* if

1. $x \in \mathcal{I}$,
2. $A_i\mathcal{I} \subseteq \mathcal{I}$ for all $i \leq k$,
3. $y \notin \mathcal{I}$.

The semilinear invariant problem asks whether such an invariant exists.

We need to introduce some terminology. The triple $((A_i)_{i\leq k}, x, y)$ is a *reach* instance if there exists a matrix M belonging to the semigroup generated by $(A_i)_{i\leq k}$ such that $Mx = y$, and otherwise it is a *non-reach* instance. Clearly a separating invariant can only exist for non-reach instances. An instance for $k = 1$ is called an *Orbit instance.*

3.1 Undecidability for Several Matrices

Our first result is the undecidability of the semilinear invariant problem. We start by showing it is undecidable in fixed dimension, with a fixed number of matrices and requiring that the invariant be closed. We defer the proofs until Sect. 4.

Theorem 8. *The semilinear invariant problem is undecidable for 9 matrices of dimension 3 and closed invariants.*

In establishing the above, we used many matrices of small dimension. One could instead use only two matrices, but increasing the dimension to 27.

Theorem 9. *The semilinear invariant problem is undecidable for 2 matrices of dimension 27 and closed invariants.*

In the above results, it can happen that the target belongs to the closure of the set of reachable points. We now show that we can ignore those "non-robust" systems and maintain undecidability.

Theorem 10. *The semilinear invariant problem is undecidable for "robust" instances,* i.e. *instances in which the target point does not belong to the closure of the set of reachable points.*

The proof of the above result does not require that the invariants be closed. We can therefore establish Theorem 1 by making use of the same construction as in the proof of Theorem 9 to encode all the matrices of Theorem 10 into only two distinct matrices.

3.2 Decidability for Simple Linear Loops

In this section, we are only concerned with Orbit instances. Since it is possible to decide (in polynomial time) whether an Orbit instance is reach or non-reach [17,18], we can always assume that we are given a non-reach instance. All decidability results are only concerned with *closed invariants*, this is crucial in several proofs.

Theorem 11. *There is an algorithm that decides whether an Orbit instance admits a closed semilinear invariant. Furthermore, it runs in polynomial time assuming the dimension d is fixed.*

We now comment a few instructive examples to illustrate the different cases that arise. The proof of Theorem 11 is postponed to Sect. 5.

Example 12. Consider the Orbit instance $\ell = (A, x, y)$ in dimension 2 where

$$A = \frac{1}{2}\begin{bmatrix} 1 & -2 \\ 2 & 1 \end{bmatrix},$$

$x = (1, 0)$ and $y = (3, 3)$. The orbit is depicted on Fig. 1. Here, A is a counter-clockwise rotation around the origin with an expanding scaling factor. A suitable semilinear invariant can be constructed by taking the complement of the convex hull of a large enough number of points of the orbit, and adding the missing points. In this example, we can take

$$\mathcal{I} = \{x, Ax\} \cup \text{Conv}\left(\{A^n x, n \leq 8\}\right)^{\mathsf{c}}.$$

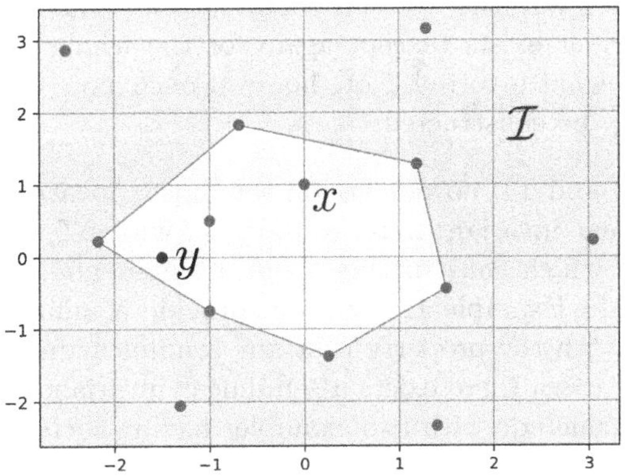

Fig. 1. An invariant for Example 12.

Constructing an invariant of this form will often be possible, for instance when A has an eigenvalue of modulus > 1. A similar (yet more involved) construction gives the same result when A has an eigenvalue of modulus < 1. The case in which all eigenvalues have modulus 1 is more involved. Broadly speaking, invariant properties in such cases are often better described by sets involving equations or inequalities of higher degree [10], which is why interesting semilinear invariants do not exist in many instances. However, delineating exactly which instances admit separating semilinear invariants is challenging, and is our main technical contribution on this front. The following few examples illustrate some of the phenomena that occur.

Example 13. Remove the expanding factor from the previous instance, that is, put instead

$$A = \frac{1}{\sqrt{5}} \begin{bmatrix} 1 & -2 \\ 2 & 1 \end{bmatrix}.$$

Now A being a rotation of an irrational angle, the orbit of x is dense in the circle of radius 1. It is quite easy to prove that no semilinear invariant exists (except for the whole space $\mathbb{R}^2$) for this instance, whatever the value of y. This gives a first instance of non-existence of a semilinear invariants. Many such examples exist, and we shall now supply a more subtle one. Note that simple invariants do exist, such as the unit circle, which is a semialgebraic set but not a semilinear one.

Example 14. Consider $\ell = (A, x, y)$ in dimension 4 with

$$A = \begin{bmatrix} A' & I_2 \\ 0 & A' \end{bmatrix},$$

where A' is the matrix from Example 13, $x = (0, 0, 1, 0)$ and y is arbitrary. When repeatedly applying A to x, the last two coordinates describe a circle of radius 1 as in the previous example. However, the first two coordinates diverge: at each step, they are rotated and the last two coordinates are added. In this instance, no semilinear invariant exists (except again for the whole space $\mathbb{R}^4$), however proving this is somewhat involved. Note however once more that a semialgebraic invariant may easily be constructed.

In Examples 13 and 14, no non-trivial semilinear invariant exist, or equivalently any semilinear invariant must contain $\mathcal{I}_0$, where $\mathcal{I}_0$ is the whole space. In all instances for which constructing an invariant is not necessarily immediate (as is the case in Example 12), we will provide a minimal invariant, that is, a semilinear $\mathcal{I}_0$ with the property that any semilinear invariant will have to contain $\mathcal{I}_0$. In such cases there exists a semilinear invariant (namely $\mathcal{I}_0$) if and only if $y \notin \mathcal{I}_0$. We conclude with two examples having such minimal semilinear invariants (Fig. 2).

Example 15. Consider $\ell = (A, x, y)$ in dimension 3 with

$$A = \begin{bmatrix} A' & 0 \\ 0 & -1 \end{bmatrix},$$

where A' is the matrix of Example 13, a 2-dimensional rotation by an angle which is not a rational multiple of 2π and $x = (1, 0, 1)$. As we iterate matrix A, the two first coordinates describe a circle, and the third coordinate alternates between 1 and -1: the orbit is dense in the union of two parallel circles. Yet the minimal semilinear invariant comprises the union of the two planes containing these circles.

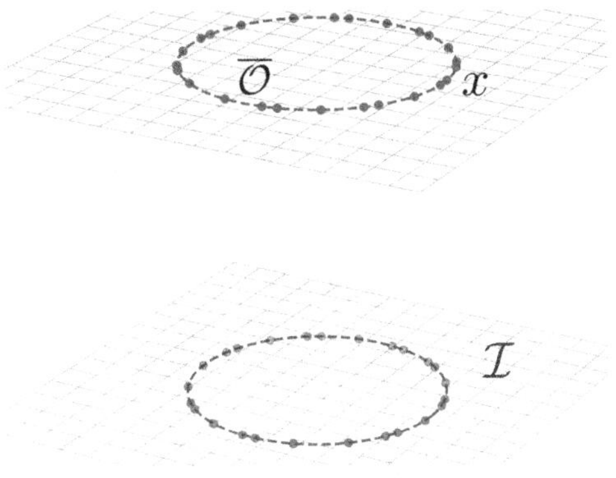

Fig. 2. The minimal invariant for Example 15. Here, $\bar{\mathcal{O}}$ denotes the topological closure of the orbit of x.

Example 16. Consider $\ell = (A, x, y)$ in dimension 8 with

$$A = \begin{bmatrix} A' & 0 \\ 0 & -A' \end{bmatrix},$$

where A' is the matrix from Example 14. This can be seen as two instances of Example 14 running in parallel. Let $x = (0, 0, 1, 0, 0, 0, -7, 0)$, and note that both blocks of x are initially related by a multiplicative factor, namely $-7(x_1, x_2, x_3, x_4) = (x_5, x_6, x_7, x_8)$. Moreover, as the first block is multiplied by the matrix A' while the second one is multiplied by $-A'$, the multiplicative factor relating the two blocks alernates between 7 and -7. Thus, the minimal semilinear invariant in this setting is

$$\mathcal{I}_0 = \{u \in \mathbb{R}^8 \mid (u_1, u_2, u_3, u_4) = \pm 7(u_5, u_6, u_7, u_8)\},$$

which has dimension 4. If however, we had $x = (0, 0, 1, 0, 1, 0, -7, 0)$, then the minimal semilinear invariant would be

$$\{u \in \mathbb{R}^8 \mid (u_3, u_4) = \pm 7(u_7, u_8)\},$$

which has dimension 6. Roughly speaking, no semilinear relation holds between (u_1, u_2) and (u_5, u_6).

4 Undecidability Proofs

4.1 Proof of Theorem 8

We reduce an instance of the ω-PCP problem defined as follows: given nine pairs of non-empty words $\{(u^{(1)}, v^{(1)}), \ldots, (u^{(9)}, v^{(9)})\}$ on alphabet $\{0, 2\}$, does there exist an infinite word $w = w_1 w_2 \ldots$ on alphabet $\{1, \ldots, 9\}$ such that $u^{(w_1)} u^{(w_2)} \cdots = v^{(w_1)} v^{(w_2)} \ldots$. This problem is known to be undecidable [15].

In order to simplify future notations, given a finite or infinite word w, we denote $|w|$ the length of the word w and given an integer $i \leq |w|$, we write w_i for the i'th letter of w. Given a finite or infinite word w on alphabet $\{1,\ldots,9\}$ we denote $u^{(w)}$ and $v^{(w)}$ the words on the alphabet $\{0,2\}$ such that $u^{(w)} = u^{(w_1)}u^{(w_2)}\ldots$ and $v^{(w)} = v^{(w_1)}v^{(w_2)}\ldots$. Given a (finite or infinite) word w on the alphabet $\{0,2\}^*$, denote by $[w] = \sum_{i=1}^{|w|} w_i 4^{1-i}$ the quaternary encoding of w. It is clear that it satisfies $[ww'] = [w] + 4^{-|w|}[w']$ and that $[w] \in [0, \frac{8}{3}]$.

Let $\{(u^{(1)},v^{(1)}),\ldots,(u^{(9)},v^{(9)})\}$ be an instance of the ω-PCP problem. For all $i \leq 9$, for readibility, we denote $|u^{(i)}| = n_i$ and $|v^{(i)}| = m_i$. We build the matrices $M_1,\ldots,M_9$ where

$$M_i = \begin{bmatrix} 1 & [u^{(i)}] & -[v^{(i)}] \\ 0 & 4^{-n_i} & 0 \\ 0 & 0 & 4^{-m_i} \end{bmatrix}$$

In the following, we write M_w for $w = w_1\ldots w_k \in \{1,\ldots,9\}^*$ the matrix $M = M_{w_k}\ldots M_{w_1}$, which can be checked to satisfy

$$M_w = \begin{bmatrix} 1 & [u^{(w)}] & -[v^{(w)}] \\ 0 & 4^{-|u^{(w)}|} & 0 \\ 0 & 0 & 4^{-|v^{(w)}|} \end{bmatrix}, \qquad M_w \begin{bmatrix} 0 \\ 1 \\ 1 \end{bmatrix} = \begin{bmatrix} [u^w]-[v^w] \\ 4^{-|u^w|} \\ 4^{-|v^w|} \end{bmatrix}.$$

Let us show that there exists a separating invariant of $((M_i)_{i\leq 9}, x, y)$ where $x = (0,1,1)$ and $y = (0,0,0)$ iff the ω-PCP instance has no solution.

Let us first assume the ω-PCP instance has a solution w. Fix $r \in \mathbb{N}$ and let $w\restriction_r = w_1\cdots w_r$ and $x_r = M_{w\restriction_r} x$. We have that $x_r = ([u^{(w\restriction_r)}] - [v^{(w\restriction_r)}], 4^{-|u^{(w\restriction_r)}|}, 4^{-|v^{(w\restriction_r)}|})$ and since $u^{(w)} = v^{(w)}$, it is clear that $x_r \to 0 = y$ as $r \to \infty$. Any separating invariant $\mathcal{I}$ must contain this sequence x_r since $\mathcal{I}$ contains the initial point and is stable under $(M_i)_{i\leq 9}$. Moreover, $\mathcal{I}$ is closed so it must contain the limit of the sequence, $(0,0,0)$, which is the target point. Thus $\mathcal{I}$ cannot be a separating invariant. Therefore there is no separating invariant of $((M_i)_{i\leq 9}, (0,1,1), (0,0,0))$.

Now, let us assume the ω-PCP instance has no solution. There exists $n_0 \in \mathbb{N}$ such that for every infinite word w on alphabet $\{0,\ldots,9\}$ there exists $n \leq n_0$ such that $u_n^{(w)} \neq v_n^{(w)}$. Indeed, consider the tree which root is labelled by $(\varepsilon,\varepsilon)$ and, given a node (u,v) of the tree, if for all $n \leq \min(|u|,|v|)$ we have $u_n = v_n$, then this node has 9 children: the nodes $(uu^{(i)}, vv^{(i)})$ for $i = 1\ldots 9$. This tree is finitely branching and does not contain any infinite path (which would induce a solution to the ω-PCP instance). Thus, according to König's lemma, it is finite. We can therefore choose the height of this tree as our n_0.

We define the invariant $\mathcal{I} = \mathcal{I}' \cup \mathcal{I}''$ where[3]

$$\mathcal{I}' = \left\{(s,c,d) : |s| \geq 4(c+d) + 4^{-n_0-1} \wedge c \geq 0 \wedge d \geq 0\right\}$$

[3] This is a semilinear invariant since $|x| \geqslant y$ if and only if $x \geqslant y \vee -x \geqslant y$.

and

$$\mathcal{I}'' = \left\{M_w x : w \in \{1,\dots,9\}^* \wedge |w| \leq n_0 + 1\right\}$$

Let us show that $\mathcal{I}$ is a separating invariant of $((M_i)_{i\leq 9}, (0,1,1), (0,0,0))$. By definition, $\mathcal{I}$ is closed, semilinear, contains x and does not contain y. The difficult point is to show stability under M_i for $i \leq 9$.

- Let $M_w x \in \mathcal{I}''$, for some w: there are two cases. Either $|w| \leqslant n_0$, then $|wi| \leqslant n_0+1$, therefore $M_i M_w x = M_{wi} z \in \mathcal{I}''$. Otherwise, $M_i M_w x = M_{wi} x = (s,c,d)$ where $s = \left[u^{(wi)}\right] - \left[v^{(wi)}\right]$, $c = 4^{-|u^{(wi)}|}$ and $d = 4^{-|v^{(wi)}|}$. But then, there exists $n \leqslant n_0$ such that $u_n^{(wi)} \neq v_n^{(wi)}$. Let n be the smallest such number, then

$$\begin{aligned} s &= \left[u^{(wi)}\right] - \left[v^{(wi)}\right] \\ &= (u_n^{(wi)} - v_n^{(wi)})4^{1-n} + \sum_{j=n+1}^{|wi|} (u_j^{(wi)} - v_j^{(wi)})4^{1-j} \end{aligned}$$

since $u_j^{(wi)} = v_j^{(wi)}$ for $j < n$. Thus,

$$\begin{aligned} |s| &\geqslant 2\cdot 4^{1-n} - \tfrac{8}{3}4^{-n} && \text{since } |u_n^{(wi)} - u_n^{(wi)}| = 2 \text{ and } [\cdot] \in [0, \tfrac{8}{3}] \\ &\geqslant 4^{1-n} + 4^{-n} \\ &\geqslant 4(c+d) + 4^{-n_0-1} && \text{since } n \leqslant n_0 \text{ and } |u^{(wi)}|, |v^{(wi)}| \geqslant n_0 + 2. \end{aligned}$$

This shows that $M_i(M_w x) \in \mathcal{I}' \subseteq \mathcal{I}$.
- Let $z = (s,c,d) \in \mathcal{I}'$, then $|s| \geqslant 4(c+d) + 4^{-n_0-1}$. Without loss of generality, assume that $d \geqslant c$ (this is completely symmetric in c and d). Let $(s',c',d') = M_i z$, and we check that then

$$\begin{aligned} |s'|. &= |s + c\left[u^{(i)}\right] - d\left[v^{(i)}\right]| && \text{by applying the matrix } M_i \\ &\geqslant |s| - d\max(\left[u^{(i)}\right], \left[v^{(i)}\right]) \\ &\geqslant 4(c+d) + 4^{-n_0-1} - d\max(\left[u^{(i)}\right], \left[v^{(i)}\right]) && \text{by assumption on } s \\ &\geqslant 4(c+d) + 4^{-n_0-1} - d\tfrac{8}{3} && \text{since } [\cdot] \in [0, \tfrac{8}{3}] \\ &= 4(c+d/3) + 4^{-n_0-1} \\ &\geqslant 4(c'+d') + 4^{-n_0-1} && \text{since } c \geqslant c' \text{ and } d/4 \geqslant d' \end{aligned}$$

since $c' = c4^{-|u^{(i)}|}$ and $d' = d4^{-|v^{(i)}|}$. This shows that $M_i z \in \mathcal{I}' \subseteq \mathcal{I}$.

This shows that $\mathcal{I}$ is thus stable and concludes the reduction.

4.2 Proof of Theorem 9

We reduce the instances of Theorem 8 to 2 matrices of size 27. The first matrix M_s shifts upwards the position of the values in the point by 3, while the second matrix M_p applies one of the matrices of the previous reduction, depending on the position of the values within the matrices, then put the obtained value at the top. In other words, $M_p M_s^{i-1}$ for $1 \leq i \leq 9$ intuitively has the same effect as M_i had in the proof of Theorem 8. In the following, we reuse the notations and results of the proof of Theorem 8.

Define matrices M_s and M_p, where I_3 is the identity matrix of size 3×3, and for any $z \in \mathbb{R}^3$ and $i \in \{0, \dots, 8\}$, the ith shift $z^{\downarrow i} \in \mathbb{R}^{27}$ of z, where $\mathbf{0}_n \in \mathbb{R}^n$ denotes the zero vector of size n, as follows:

$$M_s = \begin{bmatrix} 0 & \cdots & 0 & I_3 \\ I_3 & & & \\ & \ddots & & \\ & & I_3 & 0 \end{bmatrix}, \qquad M_p = \begin{bmatrix} M_1 & \cdots & M_9 \\ 0 & \cdots & 0 \\ \vdots & & \vdots \\ 0 & \cdots & 0 \end{bmatrix}, \qquad z^{\downarrow i} = \begin{bmatrix} \mathbf{0}_{3i} \\ z \\ \mathbf{0}_{24-3i} \end{bmatrix}.$$

It follows that $M_s z^{\downarrow i} = z^{\downarrow i+1 \bmod 9}$ and $M_p z^{\downarrow i} = (M_{i+1} z)^{\downarrow 0}$. Assume that there exists a separating invariant $\mathcal{I}$ for $(M_1, \dots, M_9, x, y)$ and let

$$\mathcal{J} = \bigcup_{i=0}^{8} \{z^{\downarrow i} : z \in \mathcal{I}\}$$

which is a closed semilinear set. Then for any $z^{\downarrow i} \in \mathcal{J}$, we have $M_s z^{\downarrow i} = z^{\downarrow i+1 \bmod 9} \in \mathcal{I}$ by definition and $M_p z^{\downarrow i} = (M_i z)^{\downarrow 0} \in \mathcal{J}$ since $M_i z \in \mathcal{I}$ by virtue of $z \in \mathcal{I}$ and $\mathcal{I}$ being invariant. Furthermore, $x' = x^{\downarrow 0} \in \mathcal{I}$ since $x \in \mathcal{I}$, and $y' = y^{\downarrow 0} \notin \mathcal{J}$ for otherwise we would have $y \in \mathcal{I}$. Therefore $\mathcal{J}$ is a separating invariant for (M_s, M_p, x', y').

Assume that there exists a separating invariant $\mathcal{J}$ for (M_s, M_p, x', y') and let $\mathcal{I} = \{z : z^{\downarrow 0} \in \mathcal{J}\}$ which is a closed semilinear set. Clearly $x \in \mathcal{I}$ since $x' = x^{\downarrow 0} \in \mathcal{J}$ and $y \notin \mathcal{I}$ since $y' = y^{\downarrow 0} \notin \mathcal{J}$. Let $z \in \mathcal{I}$ and $i \in \{1, \dots, 9\}$, then $(M_i z)^{\downarrow 0} = M_p M_s^{i-1} z^{\downarrow 0} \in \mathcal{J}$ and since $z^{\downarrow 0} \in \mathcal{J}$ and $\mathcal{J}$ is invariant under M_s and M_p, thus $M_i z \in \mathcal{I}$. Therefore $\mathcal{I}$ is a non-reachability invariant for $(M_1, \dots, M_9, x, y)$.

4.3 Proof Sketch of Theorem 10

We do the proof of Theorem 10 twice: first we use linear guards in order to limit the selection of the matrices. The added power of the guards allows for a relatively simple proof. This first proof can be seen as an extended sketch of the second one, that can be found in the companion arXiv report, where we remove the guards to obtain the result claimed. We do so by emulating the guards using extra variables.

We reduce from the ω-PCP problem and reuse some of the notations of the proof of Theorem 8. Let $\{(u^{(1)}, v^{(1)}), \dots, (u^{(9)}, v^{(9)})\}$ be an instance of the ω-PCP problem. We build the matrices $\hat{M}_1, \dots, \hat{M}_9, M_e, M_-$ where

$$\hat{M}_i = \begin{bmatrix} M_i & & \\ & 1 & 2 \\ & 0 & 1 \end{bmatrix}, \qquad M_e = \begin{bmatrix} \mathbf{0}_{3\times 3} & & \\ & 1 & 0 \\ & 0 & 1 \end{bmatrix}, \qquad M_- = \begin{bmatrix} I_3 & & \\ & 1 & -2 \\ & 0 & 1 \end{bmatrix}$$

and $M_1, \ldots, M_9$ are from the proof of Theorem 8. Moreover, when in (s, c, d, n, a), the matrices $\hat{M}_i$ and M_e can only be selected if the linear guard $|s| < 4(c + d)$ holds, and the matrix M_- can only be selected if $s = c = d = 0$.

Informally, in state (s, c, d, n, a), the subvector (s, c, d) has the same role as before: s contains the difference of the values of the numbers obtained using the v_i and u_i, while c and d are used in order to help compute this value. In the proof of Theorem 8, we showed that when the ω-PCP instance had no solution, there existed a value n_0 such that any pair of words created with the alphabet $(u^{(i)}, v^{(i)})$ differed on one of the first n_0 terms. The variable n is used with the guards in order to detect this value n_0: if such an n_0 exists, then at most $n_0 + 1$ matrices M_i can be selected before the guard stops holding. Moreover, firing a matrix M_i adds 2 to n ensuring that when the guard stops holding, n is smaller or equal to $2(n_0 + 1)$. Conversely, if no such n_0 exist, then there is a way to select matrices M_i such that the guard always holds, allowing the variable n to become an even number as high as one wants. The existence of an upper bound on the value of n is used to build an invariant or to prove that there cannot exist an invariant. Finally, the value a is only here in order to allow for affine modification of the values. It is never modified.

Let $\hat{x} = (x, 0, 1)$ and $\hat{y} = (y, 1, 1)$. Note that $\hat{y}$ is not in the adherence of the reachable set as the fourth variable of any reachable point is an even number while y's is an odd one.

Assume the ω-PCP instance does not possess a solution. Then there exists $n_0 \in \mathbb{N}$ such that any pair of words $(u^{(w)}, v^{(w)})$ differs on one of the first n_0 letters. Define the invariant $\mathcal{I} = \mathcal{I}' \cup \mathcal{I}''$ where

$$\mathcal{I}' = \{\hat{M}_w \hat{x} : w \in \{1, \ldots, 9\}^* \wedge |w| \leqslant n_0 + 1\}$$
$$\mathcal{I}'' = \{(0, 0, 0, n, 1) : n \leqslant 0 \vee (\exists k \in \mathbb{N}, n = 2k \wedge n \leqslant 2(n_0 + 1))\}.$$

This invariant is clearly semilinear, it contains $\hat{x}$ and does not contain $\hat{y}$. If $z = (0, 0, 0, n, 1) \in \mathcal{I}''$ then only M_- can be triggered due to the guards and $M_- z = (0, 0, 0, n - 2, 1) \in \mathcal{I}''$. Now if $z = (s, c, d, n, a) = \hat{M}_w \hat{x} \in \mathcal{I}'$ for some $w \in \{1, \ldots, 9\}^*$, then M_- cannot be fired as the guard does not hold. If one fires M_e, by construction of $\mathcal{I}'$, n is an even number smaller than $2(n_0 + 1)$, thus $M_e z \in \mathcal{I}''$. Now in order to fire a matrix $\hat{M}_i$, one needs $|s| < 4(c + d)$ to hold. We showed in the proof of Theorem 8 that, from the initial configuration x, after $n_0 + 1$ transitions using one of the matrices M_i then $1/4^{n_0+1} \leqslant |s| - 4(c + d)$. As a consequence, if the guard holds, then $|w| \leqslant n_0$ and $\hat{M}_i z = \hat{M}_{wi} \hat{x} \in \mathcal{I}'$. Therefore, $\mathcal{I}$ is a separating invariant of $(\hat{M}_1, \ldots \hat{M}_9, M_e, M_-, \hat{x}, \hat{y})$.

Now assume the ω-PCP possesses a solution $w \in \{1, \ldots, 9\}^\omega$. For $k \in \mathbb{N}$, we denote $w \restriction_k$ the prefix of length k of w. Let $k \in \mathbb{N}$ and $(s, c, d, n, a) = \hat{M}_{w \restriction_k} x$, then $|s| < 4(c + d)$. Indeed, assume that $u^{(w \restriction_k)}$ is longer than $v^{(w \restriction_k)}$. Then $u^{(w \restriction_k)} = v^{(w \restriction_k)} t$ for some word $t \in \{0, 2\}^*$ because $u^w(w) v^{(w)}$. Let $\ell = |u^{(w \restriction_k)}|$ and recall that $c = 4^{-\ell}$, then

$$s = |[u^{(w \restriction_k)}] - [v^{(w \restriction_k)}]| = 4^{-\ell}[t] \leqslant 4^{-\ell}\tfrac{8}{3} \leqslant 4c < 4(c + d).$$

The symmetric case is similar but uses d instead. Therefore the guard is satisfied and $M_e \hat{M}_{w\restriction_k} \hat{x} = (0,0,0,2k,1) \in \mathcal{I}$ is reachable for all $k \in \mathbb{N}$. Let $\mathcal{I}$ be a semilinear invariant containing the reachability set, then $\mathcal{I} \cap \{(0,0,0,x,1) : x \in \mathbb{R}\}$ is semilinear and contains $(0,0,0,2k,1)$ for all $k \in \mathbb{N}$. This implies that it necessarily contains an unbounded interval and there must exists $k_0 \in \mathbb{N}$ such that $(0,0,0,2k_0+1,1) \in \mathcal{I}$. Since $\mathcal{I}$ is stable by the matrix M_-, $\mathcal{I}$ contains the target y. Therefore, $\mathcal{I}$ is not a separating invariant of $((\hat{M}_1, \ldots \hat{M}_9, M_e, M_-), x, y)$.

5 Decidability Proofs

This section is aimed at sketching the main ideas of the proof of Theorem 11 while avoiding technicalities and details. We point to the appendix for full proofs. Recall that we only consider closed semilinear invariants.

- We first normalize the Orbit instance, which amounts to putting matrix A in Jordan normal form, and eliminating some easy instances. This is described in Sect. 5.1.
- We then eliminate some positive cases in Sect. 5.2. More precisely, we construct invariants whenever one of the three following conditions is realized:
  - A has an eigenvalue of modulus > 1.
  - A has an eigenvalue of modulus < 1.
  - A has a Jordan block of size ≥ 2 with an eigenvalue that is a root of unity.
- We are now left with an instance where all eigenvalues are of modulus 1 and not roots of unity, which is the most involved part of the paper. In this setting, we exhibit the minimal semilinear invariant $\mathcal{I}$ containing x. In particular, there exists a semilinear invariant (namely, $\mathcal{I}$) if and only if $y \notin \mathcal{I}$. This part is explained in Sect. 5.3.

5.1 Normalization

As a first step, recall that every matrix A can be written in the form $A = Q^{-1}JQ$, where Q is invertible and J is in Jordan normal form. The following lemma transfers semilinear invariants through the change-of-basis matrix Q.

Lemma 17. *Let $\ell = (A, x, y)$ be an Orbit instance, and Q an invertible matrix in $\mathbb{A}^{d\times d}$. Construct the Orbit instance $\ell_Q = (QAQ^{-1}, Qx, Qy)$. Then $\mathcal{I}$ is a semilinear invariant for ℓ_Q if, and only if, $Q^{-1}\mathcal{I}$ is a semilinear invariant for ℓ.*

Proof. First of all, $Q^{-1}\mathcal{I}$ is semilinear if, and only if, $\mathcal{I}$ is semilinear. We have:

- $QAQ^{-1}\mathcal{I} \subseteq \mathcal{I}$ if, and only if, $AQ^{-1}\mathcal{I} \subseteq Q^{-1}\mathcal{I}$,
- $Qx \in \mathcal{I}$ if, and only if, $x \in Q^{-1}\mathcal{I}$,
- $Qy \notin \mathcal{I}$, if, and only if, $y \notin Q^{-1}\mathcal{I}$.

This concludes the proof.

Thanks to Lemma 17, we can reduce the problem of the existence of semilinear invariants for Orbit instances to cases in which the matrix is in Jordan normal form, *i.e.*, is a diagonal block matrix, where the blocks (called Jordan blocks) are of the form:

$$\begin{bmatrix} \lambda & 1 & & \\ & \lambda & \ddots & \\ & & \ddots & 1 \\ & & & \lambda \end{bmatrix}$$

Note that this transformation can be achieved in polynomial time [3,4]. Formally, a Jordan block is a matrix $\lambda I + N$ with $\lambda \in \mathbb{C}$, I the identity matrix and N the matrix with 1's on the upper diagonal, and 0's everywhere else. The number λ is an eigenvalue of A. We will use notation $\mathcal{J}_d(\lambda)$ for the Jordan block of size d with eigenvalue λ. A Jordan block of dimension one is called diagonal, and A is diagonalisable if, and only if, all Jordan blocks are diagonal.

The d dimensions of the matrix A are indexed by pairs (J, k), where J ranges over the Jordan blocks and $k \in \{1, \ldots, d(J)\}$ where $d(J)$ is the dimension of the Jordan block J. For instance, if the matrix A has two Jordan blocks, J_1 of dimension 1 and J_2 of dimension 2, then the three dimensions of A are $(J_1, 1)$ (corresponding to the Jordan block J_1) and $(J_2, 1), (J_2, 2)$ (corresponding to the Jordan block J_2).

For a point v and a subset S of $\{1, \ldots, d\}$, let v_S be the projection of v on the dimensions in S, and extend this notation to matrices. For instance, v_J is the point corresponding to the dimensions of the Jordan block J, and $v_{J,>k}$ is projected on the coordinates of the Jordan block J whose index is greater than k. We write S^c for the coordinates which are not in S.

There are a few degenerate cases which we handle now. We say that an Orbit instance $\ell = (A, x, y)$ in Jordan normal form is normalized if:

- There is no Jordan block associated with the eigenvalue 0, or equivalently A is invertible.
- For each Jordan block J, the last coordinate of the point x_J is not zero, *i.e.* $x_{J,d(J)} \neq 0$.
- There is no diagonal Jordan block with an eigenvalue which is a root of unity,
- Any Jordan block J with an eigenvalue of modulus < 1 has $y_J \neq 0$.

Lemma 18. *The existence of semilinear invariants for Orbit instances reduces to the same problem for normalized Orbit instances in Jordan normal form.*

5.2 Positive Cases

Many Orbit instances present a divergence which we can exploit to construct a semilinear invariant. Such behaviours are easily identified once the matrix is in Jordan Normal Form, as properties of its Jordan blocks. We isolate three such cases.

- If there is an eigenvalue of modulus > 1. Call J its Jordan block. Projecting to the last coordinate of J the orbit of x diverges to ∞ in modulus (see Example 12). A long enough "initial segment" $\{x, Ax, \ldots, A^k x\}$ together with the complement of its convex hull (on the last coordinate of J) constitutes a semilinear invariant.
- If there is an eigenvalue of modulus < 1 in block J, the situation is quite similar with a convergence towards 0. However, the construction we give is more involved, the reason being that we may not just concentrate on the last nonzero coordinate $x_{J,l}$ of x_J, since $y_{J,l}$ may very well be 0, which belongs to the adherence of the orbit on this coordinate. Yet on the full block, $y_J \neq 0$. We show how to construct, for any $0 < \varepsilon$, a semilinear invariant $\mathcal{I}$ such that $B(0, \varepsilon') \subseteq \mathcal{I} \subseteq B(0, \varepsilon)$ for some $\varepsilon' > 0$. Picking ε small enough we make sure that $y \notin \mathcal{I}$, and then $\{x, Ax, \ldots, A^k x\} \cup \mathcal{I}$ is a semilinear invariant if k is large enough so that $||A^k x|| \leq \varepsilon'$.
- Finally, if there is an eigenvalue which is a root of unity, say $\lambda^n = 1$, on a Jordan block J of size at least 2 (that is, a non diagonal block), then penultimate coordinate on J of the orbit goes to ∞ in modulus. In this case, the orbit on this coordinate is contained in a union of n half-lines which we cut far enough away from 0 and add an initial segment to build a semilinear invariant.

Note that in each of these cases, we concentrate on the corresponding (stable) eigenspace, construct a separating semilinear invariant for this restriction of the problem, and extend it to the full space by allowing any value on other coordinates.

5.3 Minimal Invariants

We have now reduced to an instance where all eigenvalues have modulus 1 and are not roots of unity. Intuitively, in this setting, semilinear invariants fail, as they are not precise enough to exploit subtle multiplicative relations that may hold among eigenvalues. However, it may be the case that some coarse information in the input can still be stabilised by an semilinear invariant, for instance if two synchronised blocks are exactly identical (see Examples 15 and 16 for more elaborate cases).

We start by identifying exactly where semilinear invariants fail. Call two eigenvalues equivalent if their quotient is a root of unity (that is, they have a multiplicative relationship of degree 1). We show that whenever no two different eigenvalues are even non-equivalent, the only stable semilinear sets are trivial. As a consequence, computing the minimal semilinear invariant in this setting is easy, as it is basically the whole space (except where x is 0). However, this lower bound (non-existence of semilinear invariant) constitutes the most technically involved part. Our proof is inductive with as base case the diagonal case, where it makes crucial use of the Skolem-Mahler-Lech theorem.

When the matrix has several equivalent eigenvalues, we show how to iteratively reduce the dimension in order to eventually fall into the previous scenario.

Rougly speaking, if A is comprised of two identical blocks B, we show that it suffices to compute a minimal invariant $\mathcal{I}_B$ for B, since $\{z \mid \tilde{z}_1 \in \mathcal{I}_B \text{ and } \tilde{z}_2 = \tilde{z}_1\}$ (with obvious notations) is a minimal invariant for A. This is achieved, by first assuming that all equivalent eigenvalues are in fact equal and then easily reducing to this case by considering a large enough iterations of A.

References

1. Almagor, S., Chistikov, D., Ouaknine, J., Worrell, J.: O-minimal invariants for linear loops. In: Proceedings of ICALP. LIPIcs, vol. 107, pp. 114:1–114:14. Schloss Dagstuhl - Leibniz-Zentrum fuer Informatik (2018)
2. Bakhirkin, A., Monniaux, D.: Extending constraint-only representation of polyhedra with boolean constraints. In: Podelski, A. (ed.) SAS 2018. LNCS, vol. 11002, pp. 127–145. Springer, Cham (2018). https://doi.org/10.1007/978-3-319-99725-4_10
3. Cai, J.-Y.: Computing Jordan normal forms exactly for commuting matrices in polynomial time. Technical report, SUNY at Buffalo (2000)
4. Cai, J.-Y., Lipton, R.J., Zalcstein, Y.: The complexity of the A B C problem. SIAM J. Comput. **29**(6), 1878–1888 (2000)
5. Clarisó, R., Cortadella, J.: The octahedron abstract domain. In: Giacobazzi, R. (ed.) SAS 2004. LNCS, vol. 3148, pp. 312–327. Springer, Heidelberg (2004). https://doi.org/10.1007/978-3-540-27864-1_23
6. Cohen, H.: A Course in Computational Algebraic Number Theory. Springer-Verlag, Heidelberg (1993). https://doi.org/10.1007/978-3-662-02945-9
7. Cousot, P., Cousot, R., Feret, J., Mauborgne, L., Miné, A., Rival, X.: Why does Astrée scale up? Formal Meth. Syst. Des. **35**(3), 229–264 (2009)
8. Cousot, P., Halbwachs, N.: Automatic discovery of linear restraints among variables of a program. In: Proceedings of POPL, pp. 84–96. ACM Press (1978)
9. Fijalkow, N., Lefaucheux, E., Ohlmann, P., Ouaknine, J., Pouly, A., Worrell, J.: On the monniaux problem in abstract interpretation. CoRR, abs/1907.08257 (2019)
10. Fijalkow, N., Ohlmann, P., Ouaknine, J., Pouly, A., Worrell, J.: Semialgebraic invariant synthesis for the Kannan-Lipton Orbit Problem. In: Proceedings of STACS. LIPIcs, vol. 66, pp. 29:1–29:13. Schloss Dagstuhl - Leibniz-Zentrum fuer Informatik (2017)
11. Fijalkow, N., Ohlmann, P., Ouaknine, J., Pouly, A., Worrell, J.: Complete semialgebraic invariant synthesis for the Kannan-LiptonOrbit Problem. Theory of Computing Systems (2019)
12. Ghorbal, K., Ivančić, F., Balakrishnan, G., Maeda, N., Gupta, A.: Donut domains: efficient non-convex domains for abstract interpretation. In: Kuncak, V., Rybalchenko, A. (eds.) VMCAI 2012. LNCS, vol. 7148, pp. 235–250. Springer, Heidelberg (2012). https://doi.org/10.1007/978-3-642-27940-9_16
13. Giacobazzi, R., Logozzo, F., Ranzato, F.: Analyzing program analyses. In: Proceedings POPL, pp. 261–273. ACM (2015)
14. Giacobazzi, R., Ranzato, F., Scozzari, F.: Making abstract interpretations complete. J. ACM **47**(2), 361–416 (2000)
15. Halava, V., Harju, T.: Undecidability of infinite Post correspondence problem for instances of size 9. RAIRO - Theoret. Inf. Appl. Informatique Théorique Appl. **40**(4), 551–557 (2006)

16. Hrushovski, E., Ouaknine, J., Pouly, A., Worrell, J.: Polynomial invariants for affine programs. In: Proceedings of LICS, pp. 530–539. ACM (2018)
17. Kannan, R., Lipton, R.J.: The Orbit Problem is decidable. In: Proceedings of STOC, pp. 252–261 (1980)
18. Kannan, R., Lipton, R.J.: Polynomial-time algorithm for the Orbit Problem. J. ACM **33**(4), 808–821 (1986)
19. Karr, M.: Affine relationships among variables of a program. Acta Inf. **6**, 133–151 (1976)
20. Kincaid, Z., Cyphert, J., Breck, J., Reps, T.W.: Non-linear reasoning for invariant synthesis. PACMPL **2**(POPL), 54:1–54:33 (2018)
21. Miné, A.: The octagon abstract domain. In: Proceedings of WCRE, p. 310. IEEE Computer Society (2001)
22. Monniaux, D.: On the decidability of the existence of polyhedral invariants in transition systems. CoRR, abs/1709.04382 (2017)
23. Monniaux, D.: On the decidability of the existence of polyhedral invariants in transition systems. Acta Inf. **56**(4), 385–389 (2019)
24. Müller-Olm, M., Seidl, H.: A note on Karr's Algorithm. In: Díaz, J., Karhumäki, J., Lepistö, A., Sannella, D. (eds.) ICALP 2004. LNCS, vol. 3142, pp. 1016–1028. Springer, Heidelberg (2004). https://doi.org/10.1007/978-3-540-27836-8_85
25. Sankaranarayanan, S., Sipma, H.B., Manna, Z.: Scalable analysis of linear systems using mathematical programming. In: Cousot, R. (ed.) VMCAI 2005. LNCS, vol. 3385, pp. 25–41. Springer, Heidelberg (2005). https://doi.org/10.1007/978-3-540-30579-8_2

Numerical

Revisiting Polyhedral Analysis for Hybrid Systems

Anna Becchi[1(✉)] and Enea Zaffanella[2(✉)]

[1] University of Udine, Udine, Italy
becchi.anna@spes.uniud.it
[2] University of Parma, Parma, Italy
enea.zaffanella@unipr.it

Abstract. Thanks to significant progress in the adopted implementation techniques, the recent years have witnessed a renewed interest in the development of analysis tools based on the domain of convex polyhedra. In this paper we revisit the application of this abstract domain to the case of reachability analysis for hybrid systems, focusing on the lesson learned during the development of the tool PHAVerLite. In particular, we motivate the implementation of specialized versions of several well known abstract operators, as well as the adoption of a heuristic technique (*boxed polyhedra*) for the handling of finite collections of polyhedra, showing their impact on the efficiency of the analysis tool.

1 Introduction

Hybrid automata model dynamic systems exhibiting both discrete and continuous behaviors. Due to the intrinsic complexity of these systems, soon after their introduction several approaches have been put forward to apply formal methods, so as to support the developer when reasoning about their correctness. Most notably, in [21,22] it was shown how abstract interpretation [9] based on the domain of convex polyhedra [12] can be used to compute correct approximations of the reachable states for the class of linear hybrid automata.

During the following years, many tools for the automatic analysis of hybrid systems have been implemented. In particular, PHAVer (Polyhedral Hybrid Automaton Verifier, [13,14]) represented a significant progress with respect to its predecessor HyTech [23]. The applicability of the approach was extended from the piecewise constant to the affine class of automata, by on-the-fly over-approximation of the continuous dynamics tailored by a systematic partitioning of the state space. Building on the PPL (Parma Polyhedra Library [4,5]), PHAVer features a robust and relatively efficient backend for computing on the domain of NNC (not necessarily closed) polyhedra. Moreover, it is characterized by the systematic adoption of heuristic techniques meant to overcome the inherent limitations affecting the implemented analysis: the excessive complexity of operators based on convex polyhedra; the loss of accuracy caused by the convex approximation; and the slow convergence of the fixpoint computation,

B.-Y. E. Chang (Ed.): SAS 2019, LNCS 11822, pp. 183–202, 2019.
https://doi.org/10.1007/978-3-030-32304-2_10

in particular when relying on partitioning techniques while using exact arithmetic. Since 2011, PHAVer is included as a plug-in (PHAVer/SX) in SpaceEx [17]. Several other verification tools for hybrid systems that are based on different abstract domains and/or approximation algorithms have been developed [31]. Here we only mention another SpaceEx plug-in, the LGG scenario [17, 18], based on a domain of template polyhedra, which however sacrifices formal soundness due to the adoption of floating point computations.

In recent years, we are witnessing new momentum in the development of efficient algorithms for the domain of convex polyhedra:

- by revisiting the Cartesian factoring technique proposed in [19, 20], it was shown that a static analysis tool based on convex polyhedra [32] is able to obtain impressive speedups when analyzing benchmarks taken from the software verification competition SV-COMP;
- a constraint-only version of the domain of convex polyhedra has been implemented in the VPL (Verimag Polyhedra Library), exploiting Parametric Linear Programming to quickly identify and remove redundancies [26];
- a new conversion algorithm has been proposed in [6] for the domain of NNC polyhedra, improving upon the previous approaches [2, 21]; this lead to the development of the PPLite library [7], which is shown to obtain remarkable efficiency improvements on the static analysis of C programs.

This progress motivated new interest in revisiting the application of polyhedral computations in the context of the analysis and verification of hybrid systems. In particular, choosing PHAVer/SX as a starting point, a new plug-in PHAVer-lite/SX [16] has been implemented for the SpaceEx platform, mainly characterized by the replacement of the PPL backend with the newly developed library PPLite [7]. Building on the encouraging efficiency results obtained by PHAVer-lite/SX, in this paper we describe the new tool PHAVerLite [15].

While providing the same formal soundness guarantees, PHAVerLite differs from PHAVer-lite/SX in that it is designed as a *stand-alone* tool, like the original PHAVer. The independence from the SpaceEx platform simplifies the application of more significant changes to the underlying algorithm for reachability analysis, so as to easily experiment with novel computational heuristics, design tradeoffs and specialized operators on the underlying domain of NNC polyhedra. In Fig. 1 we summarize the efficiency improvements obtained, with respect to both PHAVer/SX and PHAVer-lite/SX, when analyzing the benchmarks coming from the HPWC (hybrid systems with piecewise constant dynamics) category of the ARCH-COMP friendly competition [15, 16]. In the 2019 edition, the HPWC category had a total of 25 tests: 15 'safe' tests (aiming at *proving* a safety property, so that a reachability analysis is permitted to compute overapproximations) and 10 'unsafe' tests (aiming at *disproving* a safety property, meaning that no overapproximation is permitted). For the 13 tests on which PHAVer/SX is able to terminate[1] the overall speedup factor obtained by PHAVerLite is ~337; moreover,

[1] The tests on PHAVer-lite/SX and PHAVerLite have been executed on an Intel Core i7-3632QM CPU; the tests on PHAVer/SX were executed on a faster CPU (~25%).

PHAVerLite is able to complete the analysis (successfully proving or disproving the corresponding property as required) of all but one of the 25 benchmarks in ~224 s.

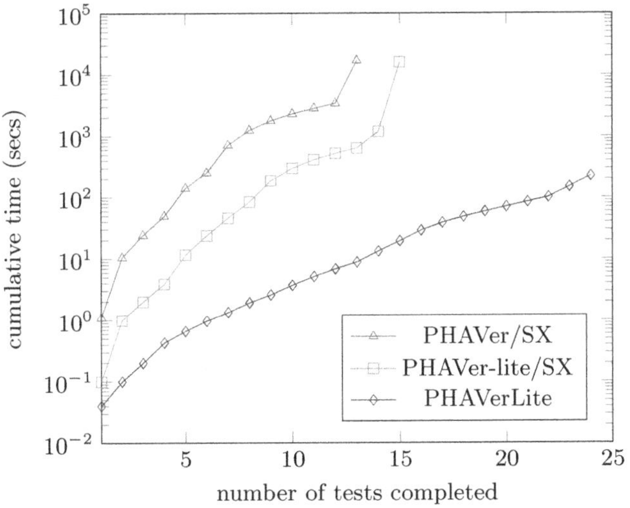

Fig. 1. Comparing the tools PHAVer/SX, PHAVer-lite/SX and PHAVerLite on the ARCH-COMP HPWC benchmarks.

The main contribution of this paper, however, is not the presentation of the tool itself: rather, we describe in detail a few of the specific improvements implemented in PHAVerLite, highlighting their impact on the overall efficiency. In particular,

- we propose specialized implementations for several "common" abstract operators on the domain of convex polyhedra: the computation of affine images (Sect. 3.1); the approximation of the convex polyhedral hull (Sect. 3.2); and the splitting of a polyhedron according to a constraint (Sect. 5);
- we propose a novel heuristic approach (*boxed polyhedra*) for a more efficient handling of finite collections of polyhedra (Sect. 4.2), which can also be viewed as an instance of an online meta-analysis [11].

In summary, our investigation shows that, when adopting an abstract domain sacrificing some performance to favor precision, a good portion of the inefficiencies can often be eliminated by the identification of suitable heuristic techniques.

The paper is structured as follows. Section 2 briefly recalls some preliminary concepts. Section 3 reconsiders the implementation of affine images for convex polyhedra and discusses ways to overapproximate the expensive convex polyhedral hull. Section 4 tackles the problem of the efficient handling of finite collections of polyhedra, showing the effectiveness of a new heuristics.

Section 5 proposes a new operator for polyhedra libraries based on the Double Description framework, motivated by the usage of location partitioning techniques. We conclude in Sect. 6.

2 Preliminaries

A non-trivial, non-strict linear inequality constraint β defines a closed half-space $\mathrm{con}(\{\beta\})$ of the vector space $\mathbb{R}^n$; we write $\neg\beta$ to denote the complement of β, i.e., the open half-space $\mathrm{con}(\{\neg\beta\}) = \mathbb{R}^n \setminus \mathrm{con}(\{\beta\})$. A not necessarily closed (NNC) convex polyhedron $\phi = \mathrm{con}(\mathcal{C}) \subseteq \mathbb{R}^n$ is defined as the set of solutions of a finite system $\mathcal{C}$ of (strict or non-strict) linear inequality constraints; equivalently, $\phi = \mathrm{gen}(\mathcal{G})$ can be defined as the set obtained by suitably combining the elements (lines, rays, points and closure points) of a generator system $\mathcal{G}$. The Double Description framework [28] exploits both representations; we write $\phi \equiv (\mathcal{C}, \mathcal{G})$ to denote that $\phi = \mathrm{con}(\mathcal{C}) = \mathrm{gen}(\mathcal{G})$. The set $\mathbb{P}_n$ of all NNC polyhedra on $\mathbb{R}^n$, partially ordered by set inclusion, is a lattice $\langle \mathbb{P}_n, \subseteq, \emptyset, \mathbb{R}^n, \cap, \uplus \rangle$, where the emptyset and $\mathbb{R}^n$ are the bottom and top elements, the binary meet operator is set intersection and the binary join operator '$\uplus$' is the convex polyhedral hull.

The use of the domain of convex polyhedra for static analyses based on abstract interpretation has been introduced in [12]. The semantics of the analyzed system is modeled by suitably combining the lattice operators mentioned above with other operators that approximate the concrete behavior of the system. For instance, the effect of a conditional guard described by linear constraints can be modeled by the meet of the lattice, whereas the convex polyhedral hull can be used to approximate the merging of control flow paths. The effect of affine assignments on state variables can be modeled by computing the image of a domain element under an affine transformation; the addition of k new state variables is modeled by operator $\mathrm{add\_dims}_k \colon \mathbb{P}_n \to \mathbb{P}_{n+k}$, embedding the input polyhedron in a higher dimension space, where the newly added dimensions are unconstrained; similarly, the removal of a set V of state variables, where $|V| = k$, can be modeled by a projection operator $\mathrm{rem\_dims}_V \colon \mathbb{P}_{n+k} \to \mathbb{P}_n$.

The set $\mathbb{CP}_n$ of closed polyhedra on the vector space $\mathbb{R}^n$ is a sublattice of $\mathbb{P}_n$; $\mathbb{CB}_n$ denotes the set of closed boxes on $\mathbb{R}^n$, i.e., those polyhedra that can be defined by inequality constraints having the form $\pm x_i \leq k$. Note that $\langle \mathbb{CB}_n, \subseteq, \emptyset, \mathbb{R}^n, \cap \rangle$ is a meet-sublattice of $\mathbb{CP}_n$.

For a set S, $\wp(S)$ denotes the powerset of S; we will write $\wp_\mathrm{f}(S)$ to denote the *finite* powerset of S, i.e., the set of all the finite subsets of S. The cardinality of S is denoted by $|S|$. The finite powerset construction [3] is a domain refinement similar to disjunctive completion [10]. It can be used to lift a base-level abstract domain to model disjunctions by explicit (hence, finite) collections of base-level elements. In the following, we instantiate the finite powerset construction by fixing $\mathbb{P}_n$ as the base-level abstract domain, thereby trading some generality for concreteness and readability. The reader interested in obtaining more details and some links to the relevant literature is referred to [3]. For efficiency, it is important that these finite collections of elements do not contain redundancies.

A set $S \in \wp_{\mathrm{f}}(\mathbb{P}_n)$ is *non-redundant* (with respect to the base-level partial order $\subseteq$) if and only if $\emptyset \notin S$ and $\forall \phi_1, \phi_2 \in S : \phi_1 \subseteq \phi_2 \implies \phi_1 = \phi_2$. The set of finite non-redundant subsets of $\mathbb{P}_n$ is denoted $\wp_{\mathrm{fn}}(\mathbb{P}_n)$. The reduction function $\Omega\colon \wp_{\mathrm{f}}(\mathbb{P}_n) \to \wp_{\mathrm{fn}}(\mathbb{P}_n)$ is defined, for each $S \in \wp_{\mathrm{f}}(\mathbb{P}_n)$ by

$$\Omega(S) \stackrel{\mathrm{def}}{=} S \setminus \{\phi_1 \in S \mid \phi_1 = \emptyset \vee \exists \phi_2 \in S \,.\, \phi_1 \subset \phi_2\}.$$

Definition 1 (Finite powerset over $\mathbb{P}_n$). *The finite powerset domain over $\mathbb{P}_n$ is the join-semilattice $\langle \wp_{\mathrm{fn}}(\mathbb{P}_n), \vdash, \bot, \oplus_\Omega \rangle$, where the bottom element is $\bot = \emptyset$ and the binary join operator is defined by $S_1 \oplus_\Omega S_2 \stackrel{\mathrm{def}}{=} \Omega(S_1 \cup S_2)$.*

Note that $S_1 \vdash S_2$ if and only if $\forall \phi_1 \in S_1 : \exists \phi_2 \in S_2 \,.\, \phi_1 \subseteq \phi_2$ (i.e., '$\vdash$' is the Hoare powerdomain partial order).

We adopt a tailored definition for hybrid automata. In particular, we assume that: initial states and state invariants are modeled by NNC polyhedra having a fixed space dimension n; the discrete post operator is modeled by a linear relation on pre-state and post-state variables (hence, having space dimension $2n$); and the continuous flow operator is modeled by linear constraints on the first-order derivatives of the variables (i.e., piecewise constant dynamics).

Definition 2. *Let Loc, Lab and Var be finite sets of locations, synchronization labels and state variables, respectively, where $n = |\mathit{Var}|$. A hybrid automaton $H = \langle \mathit{Loc}, \mathit{Lab}, \mathit{Var}, \mathrm{init}, \mathrm{inv}, \longrightarrow, \mathrm{flow} \rangle$ is defined by:*

- *initial states* $\mathrm{init}\colon \mathit{Loc} \to \mathbb{P}_n$ *and invariant states* $\mathrm{inv}\colon \mathit{Loc} \to \mathbb{P}_n$*, satisfying* $\mathrm{init}(\ell) \subseteq \mathrm{inv}(\ell)$*;*
- *a finite set $\longrightarrow \subseteq (\mathit{Loc} \times \mathit{Lab} \times \mathbb{P}_{2n} \times \mathit{Loc})$ of discrete transitions between locations; we write $\ell_1 \xrightarrow{a,\mu} \ell_2$ to denote that $(\ell_1, a, \mu, \ell_2) \in \longrightarrow$;*
- *a continuous flow relation* $\mathrm{flow}\colon \mathit{Loc} \to \mathbb{P}_n$ *specifying the constraints on the first order derivatives of the state variables.*

Note that we consider the case where all initial states and invariants are convex. Finite disjunctions can still be modeled by splitting locations; as an alternative, one may explicitly choose $\wp_{\mathrm{f}}(\mathbb{P}_n)$ as the codomain of 'init' and/or 'inv'.

The goal of reachability analysis is to compute or overapproximate the reachable set of configurations for the automaton. The reachable set is defined as the fixpoint of a system of semantic equations, one for each location of the automaton, having the following form [21]:

$$\mathrm{reach}(\ell) \stackrel{\mathrm{def}}{=} \left(\left(\mathrm{init}(\ell) \cup \bigcup_{\ell' \xrightarrow{a,\mu} \ell} \mathrm{dpost}\big(\mathrm{reach}(\ell'), \mu, \mathrm{inv}(\ell)\big) \right) \nearrow \mathrm{flow}(\ell) \right) \cap \mathrm{inv}(\ell)$$

Informally, this equation means that the reachable state at location ℓ satisfies its invariant predicate $\mathrm{inv}(\ell)$ and is obtained by letting the state evolve according to the continuous relation $\mathrm{flow}(\ell)$ (using the *time-elapse* operator $\nearrow$), starting from either an initial state in $\mathrm{init}(\ell)$ or from a state that can reach ℓ through any incoming transition, via the discrete post operator dpost.

Depending on the desired precision/efficiency tradeoff, on the domain of NNC polyhedra the set reach(ℓ) can be modeled by using either a single polyhedron or a finite set of polyhedra: analysis tools such as PHAVer let the user choose the approach. Convergence may be enforced by using widening operators [1,3,12,21], but it is often the case that no widening is applied (e.g., when overapproximations are not permitted), thereby obtaining a potentially non-terminating analysis.

3 Improving Polyhedra Operators

An approximation of the reachable set of a hybrid automaton can be computed by iterating a suitable composition of well known operators on the domain of NNC polyhedra [21,22]. In this section we focus our attention on the efficient (exact or approximated) implementation of some of these operators.

3.1 Computing the Discrete Post Operator

The discrete post operator models the effect of a transition $\ell_1 \xrightarrow{a,\mu} \ell_2$ mapping the automaton state from the source location ℓ_1 to the target location ℓ_2. Namely, if $S_1 = \{\phi_1, \dots, \phi_{m_1}\}$ is the current reachable state at ℓ_1, each disjunctive component $\phi_i \in \mathbb{P}_n$ is mapped by $\mu \in \mathbb{P}_{2n}$ to a disjunctive component $\psi_j \in \mathbb{P}_n$, contributing to the formation of the reachable state $S_2 = \{\psi_1, \dots, \psi_{m_2}\}$ of the target location ℓ_2.[2]

Focusing now on a single disjunctive component $\phi \in \mathbb{P}_n$, the *relational approach* to compute the corresponding target component $\psi \in \mathbb{P}_n$ is by a straightforward application of the relational constraints in μ, which amounts to the following abstract domain operations:

- state $\phi \in \mathbb{P}_n$ is embedded in space $\mathbb{P}_{2n}$, by adding n unconstrained primed variables V', yielding $\mu_1 = \text{add\_dims}_n(\phi)$;
- the constraints in μ are added to $\mu_1 \in \mathbb{P}_{2n}$, obtaining $\mu_2 = \mu_1 \cap \mu$;
- μ_2 is brought back to $\mathbb{P}_n$, by projecting away the n unprimed variables V, obtaining $\psi_2 = \text{rem\_dims}_V(\mu_2)$;
- finally, ψ_2 is intersected with the target invariant, yielding $\psi = \psi_2 \cap \text{inv}(\ell_2)$.

While generally applicable, this relational approach may incur a high computational overhead, due to the temporary doubling of the number of variables. As a consequence, most analysis tools provide optimized implementations for those special cases when the relational constraints in μ happen to encode a rather simple relation between the pre- and post- values of state variables. A common approach is to classify the constraints in μ as follows:

- *guard constraints*: these are constraints that mention unprimed (i.e., source-state) variables only; they are meant to filter the source state, possibly disabling the transition altogether;

[2] The synchronization label $a \in \mathit{Lab}$ only plays a role when a hybrid automaton is defined as the parallel composition of several smaller automata.

- *identity relations*: these are constraints having the form $x'_i = x_i$, modeling the fact that state variable x_i is not affected by the transition;
- *simple resets* and *increments*: these have the form $x'_i = k$ and $x'_i = x_i \pm k$, respectively.

If all the constraints defining μ have one of the forms above, then the discrete transition can be implemented rather efficiently, without the addition of new variables. However, there are cases escaping from the given classification.

Example 1. The Dutch Railway Network benchmark (DRNW) is one of the test in the HPWC category of the ARCH-COMP competition [15]. The automaton specified in this benchmark is rather peculiar: being derived from a MPL (max-plus-linear) system specified using difference-bound constraints, it happens to be a purely discrete automaton (i.e., it has a trivial continuous flow dynamics). The automaton tracks the value of 14 variables $Var = \{x_1, \ldots, x_{14}\}$, each one representing the departure time of trains from given railway stations. It has a single location, featuring 12 self-loop discrete transitions, each one corresponding to a different "region". An example of linear relation $\mu \in \mathbb{P}_{28}$ (modeling the discrete transition for Region 1) is described by the following constraint system where x_i and x'_i denote the pre- and post- values of state variable x_i, respectively:

$$
\begin{array}{ll}
40 + x_1 \geq 72 + x_6, & 55 + x_7 \geq 54 + x_8, \\
55 + x_7 \geq 37 + x_5, & 90 + x_{11} \geq 93 + x_{12}, \\
x'_1 = 38 + x_6, & x'_2 = 40 + x_1, \\
x'_3 = 50 + x_2, & x'_4 = 41 + x_3, \\
x'_5 = 41 + x_4, & x'_6 = 53 + x_5, \\
x'_7 = 38 + x_{14}, & x'_8 = 36 + x_{14}, \\
x'_9 = 55 + x_7, & x'_{10} = 35 + x_9, \\
x'_{11} = 54 + x_{10}, & x'_{12} = 58 + x_{10}, \\
x'_{13} = 90 + x_{11}, & x'_{14} = 16 + x_{13}.
\end{array}
$$

The first 4 constraints describing μ, mentioning unprimed variables only, form the transition guard. The remaining 14 constraints of μ bind a distinct primed variable to a linear expression on unprimed variables only; these can be seen as implementing a (non-simple) reset of all the state variables. Note that these resets are meant to be computed simultaneously: in particular, due to the presence of circular dependencies (e.g., $x_1 \to x_6 \to x_5 \to x_4 \to x_3 \to x_2 \to x_1$), the semantics of the overall parallel reset operation is not equivalent to a sequential composition of the individual resets.

Due to the problem with variable dependencies, tools such as PHAVer/SX implement the discrete transition $\ell_1 \xrightarrow{a,\mu} \ell_2$ following the relational approach.

An alternative, *parallel approach*, which can be adopted whenever μ is a combination of linear guard and reset constraints as in Example 1, relies on polyhedra libraries implementing the *parallel affine image* operator. In this case, after intersecting the source state ϕ with the guard constraints, this specific operator is applied, avoiding the intermediate changes of space dimension.

While being more efficient than the relational approach, even in this case the computational overhead may be significant; this is due to the fact that, in libraries based on the Double Description method, the parallel affine image operator is often implemented by rewriting the generator system: in order to obtain the constraint description, a *non-incremental* application of the conversion algorithm by Chernikova is required.[3]

To avoid the problem above, we propose the *compiled parallel approach*, based on an alternative implementation of the parallel affine image operator (available in PPLite 0.4), only requiring *incremental* applications of the Chernikova algorithm. To this end, we "compile" the set of parallel bindings into a carefully chosen sequence of calls to the non-parallel affine image operator (whose incremental computation is simple). We initially build a dependency graph where each arc $x_i \rightarrow x_j$ means that the new value of x_i depends on x_j (hence, a binding resetting x_j can be processed only after having processed the binding for x_i). Using the graph, we process those bindings having no dependencies, keeping the graph up-to-date. When identifying a circular dependency (i.e., a cycle in the graph), we break it by introducing a minimal number of primed variables, so as to allow continuing with the sequential processing of the bindings. The unprimed versions of these additional variables are later projected away. By following this technique, all of the bindings can be processed by adding only a few variables, thereby better exploiting the incremental nature of Chernikova algorithm.

Example 2. Considering Example 1, the new approach to compute the discrete post operator starts, as before, by adding to ϕ the guard constraints. Then we compute the dependency graph for the reset constraints, identifying cycles

$$x_1 \rightarrow x_6 \rightarrow x_5 \rightarrow x_4 \rightarrow x_3 \rightarrow x_2 \rightarrow x_1,$$

$$x_{14} \rightarrow x_{13} \rightarrow x_{11} \rightarrow x_{10} \rightarrow x_9 \rightarrow x_7 \rightarrow x_{14},$$

as well as the non-circular dependencies $x_8 \rightarrow x_{14}$ and $x_{12} \rightarrow x_{14}$.

Since x_8 and x_{12} have no entering arcs, the corresponding bindings $x_8' = 36 + x_{14}$ and $x_{12}' = 58 + x_{10}$ can be processed (in any order). After that no other binding can be processed, since we are left with the two cycles. Considering the first cycle, we add a new space dimension for variable x_1'; as a consequence, we can process the sequence of bindings $x_1' = 38 + x_6$, $x_6' = 53 + x_5$, $x_5' = 41 + x_4$, $x_4' = 41 + x_3$, $x_3' = 50 + x_2$, $x_2' = 40 + x_1$ (in this order) and then project away the unprimed variable x_1. The bindings forming the other cycle are handled similarly, for instance adding (and then projecting away) a single space dimension for x_{14}'.

In Table 1 we show the time spent in PHAVerLite when computing the reachable states for the specific benchmark DRNW-BDR01, when adopting the classical relational and the compiled parallel approaches. As said before, since this benchmark has a trivial continuous dynamics, almost all of the analysis time is actually spent in the 96 calls to the discrete post operator. By exploiting incrementality, the new approach is able to obtain a significant speedup factor (column 'Ratio'). It is worth stressing that, even though the relational constraints

[3] This is the case for the Apron library [24] and for PPLite up to version 0.3.

$\mu \in \mathbb{P}_{28}$ of Example 1 are all difference-bound constraints, the approach we are proposing is more general, as it can handle all kinds of affine constraints.

Table 1. Efficiency of the discrete post operator for the DRNW-BDR01 benchmark.

	Discrete post		Overall analysis	
Implementation	Calls	Time	Time	Ratio
Relational	96	129.28	129.60	11.86
Compiled parallel	96	10.64	10.93	1.00

3.2 Approximating the Convex Polyhedral Hull

As briefly recalled in Sect. 2, in principle the computation of reach(ℓ) requires to compute the *set union* of the initial states and the contributes of incoming transitions. Since this may incur high computational costs, the classical approach [21,22] maintains a single polyhedron per location and systematically overapproximates set unions using the convex polyhedral hull '$\uplus$'.

As a matter of fact, there are cases when even the computation of the convex polyhedral hull can be regarded as an overkill, so that more aggressive approximations are applied. One approach is to replace the abstract domain of NNC polyhedra with some further abstraction (such as octagons [27] or even boxes). Another possibility is to keep computing on the domain of NNC polyhedra, but use an approximate version of the convex polyhedral hull operator. Letting $\phi_1 = \text{con}(\mathcal{C}_1)$ and $\phi_2 = \text{con}(\mathcal{C}_2)$, there are several options:

- the *envelope* $\phi_1 \sqcup_{\text{env}} \phi_2$, proposed in [8], is defined by keeping only those constraints $\beta \in \mathcal{C}_1 \cup \mathcal{C}_2$ that are valid for both ϕ_1 and ϕ_2;
- the *weak join* $\phi_1 \sqcup_{\text{w}} \phi_2$, formalized in [30], is the smallest polyhedron containing $\phi_1 \cup \phi_2$ which is defined by constraints sharing the same slope with the ones occurring in $\mathcal{C}_1 \cup \mathcal{C}_2$;
- the *inversion join* $\phi_1 \sqcup_{\text{inv}} \phi_2$ [30] further improves on the weak join by also inferring some constraint slopes not occurring in $\mathcal{C}_1 \cup \mathcal{C}_2$.

Note that $(\phi_1 \cup \phi_2) \subseteq (\phi_1 \uplus \phi_2) \subseteq (\phi_1 \sqcup_{\text{inv}} \phi_2) \subseteq (\phi_1 \sqcup_{\text{w}} \phi_2) \subseteq (\phi_1 \sqcup_{\text{env}} \phi_2)$.

In the following we consider the operator adopted in the original PHAVer, named *constraint hull*, which happens to be equivalent to the weak join of [30]. Given a constraint $\beta_1 \in \mathcal{C}_1$, the problem of finding the tightest constraint β_2 having the same slope of β_1 and satisfying $\phi_2 \subseteq \text{con}(\beta_2)$ can be addressed either as a Linear Programming problem or, if the chosen representation allows it, by enumerating the generators defining ϕ_2. In both cases, we can obtain a significant efficiency improvement with respect to the computation of the convex polyhedral hull, which may either require a high number of iterations of the Chernikova conversion algorithm or a high number of redundancy checks when adopting a constraint-only approach.

Example 3. The Fischer protocol benchmark (FISC) is one of the tests from the HPWC category of the ARCH-COMP competition [15]; it models a time based protocol for mutual exclusion between processes described in [25]. For the instance FISCS06, whose composed automaton has 6 variables and 28672 locations, the verification goal is to prove that, during the interaction of 6 processes, no two processes can be in the critical section at the same time. In order to prove this property it is sufficient to keep a single polyhedron for each location. In Table 2 we compare the overall analysis time obtained when using different implementations to compute (exact or approximated) unions of NNC polyhedra. Column 'Iters' reports the number of iterations of the fixpoint computation; column 'Poly' reports the number of polyhedra in the reachable set (which equals the number of reachable locations when using '$\uplus$' or '$\sqcup_w$'). The analysis exceeds a 20 min timeout threshold when adopting exact unions (i.e., when computing on the finite powerset domain of NNC polyhedra); the "constraint hull" approach performs significantly better than the convex polyhedral hull, also because it causes the analysis to converge after fewer iterations. Note that the one reported is the *total time* spent by PHAVerLite, including the parsing phase and the generation of the automaton by parallel composition of its components; together, these consume almost 40% of the 11.42 s spent on FISCS06.

Table 2. Comparing exact and approximated unions for the FISCS06 benchmark.

Implementation	Iters	Poly	Time	Time ratio
$\cup$	>184040	>137072	>1200.00	>100.0
$\uplus$	27289	2378	261.00	22.9
$\sqcup_w$	8738	2378	11.42	1.0

The results above have been obtained after replacing the original constraint hull implementation in PHAVer with a *specialized operator* (based on the enumeration of generators) made available in version 0.4 of the PPLite library. While this change has a negligible effect on the FISCS06 benchmark itself, we have observed impressive speedups on those benchmarks characterized by a higher number of state variables. For example, the time to compute the 917 applications of the constraint hull operator for the DISC04 benchmark (having 17 state variables) dropped from 675.50 to 2.14 s.

When using PHAVerLite on the experiments of Fig. 1, 3 of the 15 'safe' tests require the full precision of the set union operator; for 11 tests the overapproximation provided by the constraint hull operator is precise enough to prove the property of interest; for the remaining test, a timeout is obtained no matter the considered approach.

4 Handling Sets of Polyhedra

As discussed in the previous section, when the analyzed system can be verified by approximating disjunctions using a single polyhedron (either by applying the convex polyhedral hull or by more aggressive forms of approximation), then this is usually the most efficient approach. There are however cases (e.g., when disproving the safety property in an 'unsafe' test) when in order to complete successfully the verification task at hand the analysis needs to (explicitly or implicitly) maintain a collection of elements of the chosen abstract domain. Therefore, in this section we consider an analysis that models disjunctions using explicit, finite collections of polyhedra in $\mathbb{P}_n$.

In this context, it can be seen that most of the operators defining the semantics of the system happens to be *additive*, so that they can be modeled by an element-wise application of the corresponding approximation operator defined on the base-level domain $\mathbb{P}_n$. For instance, the meet (i.e., set intersection) operator on $\mathbb{P}_n$ can be lifted on finite sets S_1, S_2 of polyhedra as follows:

$$S_1 \sqcap S_2 \stackrel{\text{def}}{=} \{\, \phi_1 \cap \phi_2 \mid \phi_1 \in S_1, \phi_2 \in S_2 \,\}. \tag{1}$$

If $n_1 = |S_1|$ and $n_2 = |S_2|$, this approach requires $n_1 \cdot n_2$ applications of the base-level meet operator. In order to keep efficiency under control, it is therefore important that these finite collections of elements do not encode redundant information.

4.1 On Redundancy Removal

The intuitive notion of "redundancy" needs some clarification. In the context of reachability analysis, the concrete semantics of a finite set $S \in \wp_{\mathrm{f}}(\mathbb{P}_n)$ is defined by the set union operator $[\![S]\!] = \bigcup S$. Hence, strictly speaking, S may be encoding redundant information in several, distinct ways:

1. an element $\phi \in S$ can be said to be redundant in S when it can be simply dropped without affecting the semantics, so that $[\![S]\!] = [\![S \setminus \{\phi\}]\!]$;
2. if there exists $\phi_1, \phi_2 \in S$ such that $\phi_1 \cap \phi_2 \neq \emptyset$, then ϕ_1 and/or ϕ_2 could be *partitioned* in sets S_1' and S_2' of smaller, pairwise disjoint polyhedra such that $[\![S]\!] = [\![S \setminus \{\phi_1, \phi_2\} \cup S_1' \cup S_2']\!]$; after partitioning, some of the elements in $S_1' \cup S_2'$ may become redundant according to 1 and hence removed;
3. a subset $S' \subseteq S$, where $|S'| > 1$, could be *merged* into a single polyhedron $\phi = \biguplus S'$ such that $[\![S]\!] = [\![S \setminus S' \cup \{\phi\}]\!]$, decreasing the cardinality of the finite collection.

Note that the first form of redundancy listed above corresponds to the one used when introducing the finite powerset construction (see Sect. 2). Since maintaining non-redundancy has its own computational cost, most analysis tools usually choose this lighter definition.

As a matter of fact, the original code in PHAVer was sometimes adopting an even weaker form of redundancy removal when joining two finite sets of polyhedra; namely, $S_1 \oplus_{\mathrm{w}} S_2 \stackrel{\mathrm{def}}{=} S_1 \cup \{\, \phi_2 \in S_2 \mid \nexists \phi_1 \in S_1 \,.\, \phi_2 \subseteq \phi_1 \,\}$. Note that '$\oplus_{\mathrm{w}}$' is not symmetric: thus, it may fail to remove some elements in S_1 that are made redundant by elements coming from S_2. On the other hand, the application of the symmetric operator '$\oplus_{\Omega}$' requires a higher number of inclusion tests: in the worst case, which is always attained when ϕ is not redundant in S, $S \oplus_{\mathrm{w}} \{\phi\}$ requires $|S|$ inclusion tests, whereas $S \oplus_{\Omega} \{\phi\}$ requires $2 \cdot |S|$ tests.

Example 4. The Distributed Controller (DISC) is one of the tests coming from the HPWC category of the ARCH-COMP competition [15]; it models the distributed controller for a robot that reads and processes data from a number of sensors having different priorities. In Table 3 we show some statistics collected during the analysis of instance DISC03 of the benchmark (i.e., using 3 sensors, so that the automaton is defined on 11 variables and 258 locations), where we have prevented PHAVerLite from computing the poly hull approximation and rather maintain a finite set of polyhedra for each location.[4] Distinguishing between those calls that actually add ϕ to S and those calls that detect ϕ to be redundant, we report the total number of calls to the semantic operator $S \oplus \{\phi\}$, the resulting total number of inclusion tests performed, as well as their average number and the average size of S. By detecting and removing redundant elements in S, operator '$\oplus_{\Omega}$' is able to significantly reduce the average size of S; moreover, since some of the removed elements were in the "waiting list", they no longer need to be processed by the reachability algorithm, resulting in a significant decrease of the number of calls to $S \oplus_{\Omega} \{\phi\}$. As a result, the total number of inclusion tests is reduced by a factor of more than 20.

Table 3. The effectiveness of operators '$\oplus_{\mathrm{w}}$' and '$\oplus_{\Omega}$' on the DISC03 benchmark.

	ϕ not redundant (added)			ϕ redundant (not added)		
	$\oplus_{\mathrm{w}}$	$\oplus_{\Omega}$	Ratio	$\oplus_{\mathrm{w}}$	$\oplus_{\Omega}$	Ratio
Calls to $S \oplus \{\phi\}$	63738	15131	4.2	109827	14945	7.3
Total $\subseteq$ tests	79312223	4112746	19.3	11613424	331650	35.0
Avg $\lvert S \rvert$	1244.3	135.9	9.2	792.0	113.1	7.0
Avg $\subseteq$ tests	1244.3	271.8	4.6	105.7	22.2	4.8
Total rem from S	0	9692	—	0	0	—

4.2 Improving Efficiency of the Inclusion Tests

As seen in the previous section, Ω-reduction can significantly decrease the number of inclusion tests that need to be performed. In our quest for efficiency, the next step is to try and improve the efficiency of the inclusion test itself.

Assuming that we are computing on a polyhedra library based on the Double Description approach, the inclusion test $\phi_1 \subseteq \phi_2$ on polyhedra $\phi_1, \phi_2 \in \mathbb{P}_n$ is

[4] This was done for exposition purposes, since this specific benchmark can be successfully verified, more efficiently, by using a single polyhedron for each location.

usually implemented by checking that all the generators of $\phi_1 = \text{gen}(\mathcal{G}_1)$ satisfy all the constraints of $\phi_2 = \text{con}(\mathcal{C}_2)$. In the worst case, this amounts to the computation of $|\mathcal{G}_1| \cdot |\mathcal{C}_2|$ scalar products, each one requiring $n + 1$ multiplications and n additions of (arbitrary precision) integral coefficients, where n is the dimension of the vector space.

By observing again the data in Table 3, we can see that most of the inclusion tests are *failing*: for instance, in order to detect that ϕ is redundant in S (last but one column in the table), we perform 331650 inclusion tests, among which the successful ones are 14945, i.e., only 4.5%; things are even worse when ϕ is not redundant (3rd column of the table), since in this case we perform 4112746 inclusion tests, among which the successful ones are 9692, i.e., only 0.24%. Therefore, in order to improve efficiency, we look for heuristic procedures that allow to quickly identify cases when the polyhedra inclusion test will necessarily fail. To this end, we associate further abstractions to our polyhedra.

Definition 3. *The* bounding box *function* $\text{bbox}\colon \mathbb{P}_n \to \mathbb{CB}_n$ *is defined, for each polyhedron* $\phi \in \mathbb{P}_n$*, as follows:*

$$\text{bbox}(\phi) = \bigcap \{ B \in \mathbb{CB}_n \mid \phi \subseteq B \}.$$

Note that the bounding box is required to be *tight*, i.e., it is the most precise box in $\mathbb{CB}_n$ containing ϕ.

Lemma 1. *Let* $\phi_1, \phi_2 \in \mathbb{P}_n$*. If* $\text{bbox}(\phi_1) \not\subseteq \text{bbox}(\phi_2)$*, then* $\phi_1 \not\subseteq \phi_2$*.*

Thus, a correct (but incomplete) test for non-inclusion on $\mathbb{P}_n$ can be obtained by checking non-inclusion of the bounding boxes. Since non-inclusion on boxes can be checked by performing at most $2 \cdot n$ (arbitrary precision) extended rational comparisons, the efficiency gain with respect to the test on $\mathbb{P}_n$ may be significant.

The same approach can be iterated by further abstracting the bounding box information into an even lighter approximation.

Definition 4. *For each 1-dimensional box* $B \in \mathbb{CB}_1$*, the* pseudo volume *and the* number of rays *of* B *are defined as*

$$\text{pvol}(B) \stackrel{\text{def}}{=} \begin{cases} 0, & \textit{if } B \textit{ is empty;} \\ 1 + (ub - lb), & \textit{if} B = [lb, ub] \neq \emptyset \textit{ is bounded;} \\ +\infty, & \textit{otherwise;} \end{cases}$$

$$\text{nrays}(B) \stackrel{\text{def}}{=} \begin{cases} 0, & \textit{if } B = [lb, ub] \textit{ is bounded;} \\ 2, & \textit{if } B = \mathbb{R}\textit{;} \\ 1, & \textit{otherwise.} \end{cases}$$

These are extended to n-dimensional boxes $B \in \mathbb{CB}_n$ *as follows:*

$$\text{pvol}(B) \stackrel{\text{def}}{=} \prod_{i=1}^{n} \text{pvol}(\pi_i(B)), \qquad \text{nrays}(B) \stackrel{\text{def}}{=} \sum_{i=1}^{n} \text{nrays}(\pi_i(B)),$$

where $\pi_i(B)$ *is the projection of box* B *on the i-th coordinate of the vector space.*

Note that, in the definition of 'pvol', the systematic addition of 1 to the length of each 1-dimensional box is meant to force the computation of a positive pseudo volume even for those boxes having some projections of length zero.

Lemma 2. *Let* $B_1, B_2 \in \mathbb{CB}_n$. *If* $\mathrm{pvol}(B_1) > \mathrm{pvol}(B_2)$ *or* $\mathrm{nrays}(B_1) > \mathrm{nrays}(B_2)$, *then* $B_1 \not\subseteq B_2$.

Hence, a correct (but incomplete) test for non-inclusion on $\mathbb{CB}_n$ can be obtained by performing a constant number of comparisons.

This is the main idea behind the *boxed polyhedra* domain, where each polyhedron $\phi \in \mathbb{P}_n$ in the finite collection is matched by information on the corresponding bounding box. Note that the approach we are proposing can also be viewed as the application of a dynamic meta-analysis [11].

Definition 5. *A* boxed polyhedron *is a tuple* $\langle v, r, B, \phi \rangle$ *such that* $\phi \in \mathbb{P}_n$, $B = \mathrm{bbox}(\phi)$, $r = \mathrm{nrays}(B)$ *and* $v = \mathrm{pvol}(B)$. *The set of boxed polyhedra is partially ordered by the lexicographic composition of the orders defined on its components.*

In Table 4 we evaluate the effectiveness of Lemmas 1 and 2 in reducing the number of polyhedra inclusion tests for the DISC03 benchmark. Note that we are using the '$\oplus_\Omega$' operator, so that the total number of inclusion tests has already been reduced from 90.9M to 4.4M, as reported in Table 3. It can be seen that, for the considered benchmark, the semi-decision procedures are effective on more than 95% of the inclusion tests performed. Also note that the non-inclusion tests based on the number of rays never succeeds: this is due to the fact that, in test DISC03, all polyhedra happen to be polytopes.

Table 4. The effectiveness of the semi-decision procedures for inclusion tests on boxed polyhedra $\langle v_i, r_i, B_i, \phi_i \rangle$ for the DISC03 benchmark.

	Lemma 2		Lemma 1	
	$v_1 > v_2$	$r_1 > r_2$	$B_1 \not\subseteq B_2$	$\phi_1 \not\subseteq \phi_2$
Num tests	4444396	2274428	2274428	212357
$\subseteq$ decided	2169968	0	2062071	212357
%	48.82	0.00	46.40	4.78

When implementing the inclusion test on boxed polyhedra, an optimization can be obtained even when Lemma 1 fails to apply.[5] In fact, by exploiting the knowledge that $\mathrm{bbox}(\phi_1) \subseteq \mathrm{bbox}(\phi_2)$, we can replace the full inclusion test $\phi_1 \subseteq \phi_2$ with a lighter one, where we avoid to check the interval constraints of ϕ_2 against the generators of ϕ_1. The effect of this heuristics can be significant: for

[5] Note that this implies that neither Lemma 2 applies.

instance, when computing the inclusion tests $\phi_1 \subseteq \phi_2$ for the DISC03 benchmark, about 70% of the constraints are interval constraints.

A further improvement can be obtained if the finite collections are sorted according to a suitable variant of the partial order relation defined on boxed polyhedra: this enables the application of binary search (rather than linear search) to quickly detect the subrange of boxed polyhedra that actually need to be checked for inclusion. In our experiments, we sorted these lists in increasing order of the v_i component (the bounding box pseudo-volume). For the DISC03 benchmark, this reduces the total number of tests for applicability of Lemma 2 by more than 90% (from 4444396 to 314722).

Table 5. Comparing efficiency for the DISCS03 benchmark.

Reduction	Num iter	Boxing	Time	Ratio
$\oplus_{\mathrm{w}}$	63805	Unboxed	1492.79	141.77
		Boxed	108.76	10.33
$\oplus_{\Omega}$	9625	Unboxed	93.28	8.86
		Boxed	10.53	1.00

In Table 5 we report the timings obtained for the DISC03 benchmark when varying the reduction strategy and the choice of the powerset element (boxed or unboxed polyhedra). The improvements provided by the two techniques carry over to computation times; moreover, the two techniques provide almost orthogonal efficiency improvements.

In our implementation of boxed polyhedra, the bounding box information is computed on-demand and cached. Some care has to be taken to invalidate these caches after applying semantic operators that change the polyhedra.

4.3 Improving Other Operators

When adopting the finite powerset of boxed polyhedra, we can improve the efficiency of other semantic operators. For instance, consider the implementation of the lattice meet: as discussed before (see Eq. 1), after the element-wise application of the polyhedra intersections, the resulting powerset needs to be checked for redundancies; in particular, some of the computed intersections $\phi_1 \cap \phi_2$ may be empty. In principle, the generation of these empty elements could be avoided by checking if the two arguments ϕ_1 and ϕ_2 are disjoint, but on the domain of polyhedra $\mathbb{P}_n$ this check happens to be as expensive as the computation of the intersection itself. With boxed polyhedra, the following result applies.

Lemma 3. *Let* $\phi_1, \phi_2 \in \mathbb{P}_n$. *If* $\mathrm{bbox}(\phi_1) \cap \mathrm{bbox}(\phi_2) = \emptyset$, *then* $\phi_1 \cap \phi_2 = \emptyset$.

Lemma 3 can be used, for instance, to quickly detect that $\phi_1 \in \mathrm{reach}(\ell_1)$ is disjoint from the guard component of an outgoing transition $\ell_1 \xrightarrow{a,\mu} \ell_2$ (i.e., the transition is disabled). For the DISC03 benchmark this happens in about 34% of cases (15374 times on a total of 45514 checks). However, the efficiency gain obtained is negligible.

5 Splitting Polyhedra

In Sects. 3.2 and 4 we revisited different ways to model, in the abstract semantic construction, the merging of different execution paths. The efficient handling of this merge operator is quite often one of the main concerns when designing a static analysis tool. In this section, we turn our attention to the "dual" semantic operator, which intuitively *splits* an execution path in two branches.

In a classical (forward semantics) program static analysis, splitting typically occurs when approximating the effect of conditional branching: for instance, the analysis of an `if-then-else` statement splits the current approximation into a `then`-component (satisfying the conditional guard) and an `else`-component (satisfying its complement). In the context of the verification of hybrid systems, a similar semantic operator may be needed when a location state is partitioned according to some constraints, so as to better approximate a continuous flow relation which is not piecewise constant. Similarly, the split operator can be used in the *abstract solving* of a geometric CSP [29], where the current search space is partitioned into subdomains, refining the following propagation steps. Splits are also relevant for powerset domains: for instance, given two sets of polyhedra $S_1, S_2 \in \wp_f(\mathbb{P}_n)$, the algorithm checking whether S_1 is *geometrically covered* by S_2, i.e., $(\cup S_1) \subseteq (\cup S_2)$, typically requires the splitting of those polyhedra in S_1 that are not included in a polyhedron in S_2.

Depending on the application and the underlying abstract domain, different variants of this operator may be defined.

Definition 6. *Let β be a non-strict linear inequality constraint on $\mathbb{R}^n$ and β' be the non-strict version of its (strict) complement $\neg\beta$. The* strict *and the* non-strict *split operators are defined, for each $\phi \in \mathbb{P}_n$, as* $\mathrm{split}^{\mathrm{s}}_{\beta}(\phi) = (\phi_1, \phi_2)$ *and* $\mathrm{split}^{\mathrm{ns}}_{\beta}(\phi) = (\phi_1, \phi'_2)$*, where* $\phi_1 = \phi \cap \mathrm{con}(\{\beta\})$*,* $\phi_2 = \phi \cap \mathrm{con}(\{\neg\beta\})$ *and* $\phi'_2 = \phi \cap \mathrm{con}(\{\beta'\})$*.*

Note that $\phi = \phi_1 \cup \phi_2 = \phi_1 \cup \phi'_2$; also, $\phi_1 \cap \phi_2 = \emptyset$, while ϕ_1 and ϕ'_2 may overlap. The non-strict operator '$\mathrm{split}^{\mathrm{ns}}_{\beta}$' can also be defined on the domain of topologically closed polyhedra $\mathbb{CP}_n$.

Available polyhedra libraries do not provide a direct implementation for the split operator: it is typically implemented by the user, by first cloning the input polyhedron and then separately adding the constraint β and its (strict or non-strict) complement to the constraint systems of the two polyhedra. Such an approach, however, easily results in a *duplication* of the computational work.

To see this, consider an implementation based on the Double Description method[6] and, for ease of exposition, consider the *non-strict* split operator applied

[6] To some extent, the reasoning should also apply to constraint-only representations, if the implementation attempts to identify and remove redundant constraints.

to a *closed* polyhedron $\phi \equiv \langle \mathcal{C}, \mathcal{G} \rangle \in \mathbb{CP}_n$. The addition of β to constraint system $\mathcal{C}$ requires a call to the incremental Chernikova conversion algorithm. The core of this procedure partitions the generator system $\mathcal{G}$ into $\mathcal{G}^+$, $\mathcal{G}^0$ and $\mathcal{G}^-$, according to the sign of the scalar product of each generator with β, and then linearly combines $\mathcal{G}^+$ and $\mathcal{G}^-$ to produce $\mathcal{G}^\star$; the resulting polyhedron $\phi_1 \equiv \langle \mathcal{C} \cup \{\beta\}, \mathcal{G}_1 \rangle$ is defined by the new generator system $\mathcal{G}_1 = \mathcal{G}^+ \cup \mathcal{G}^0 \cup \mathcal{G}^\star$. Since β and β' only differ in the sign of their coefficients, when adding β' to $\mathcal{C}$ (so as to obtain ϕ_2') we end up recomputing the same partition of $\mathcal{G}$, modulo exchanging the roles of $\mathcal{G}^+$ and $\mathcal{G}^-$; also, the previously computed set $\mathcal{G}^\star$ can be reused as is, since the linear combination procedure is symmetric. Hence, $\phi_2' \equiv \langle \mathcal{C} \cup \{\beta'\}, \mathcal{G}_2' \rangle$ is easily obtained by reusing the computation done before, letting $\mathcal{G}_2' = \mathcal{G}^- \cup \mathcal{G}^0 \cup \mathcal{G}^\star$, with no additional scalar products or linear combinations.

When encoding NNC polyhedra using the *direct* representation proposed in [6], the implementation of the strict operator '$\text{split}^{\text{s}}_\beta$' is more complicated, but it essentially preserves all of the computational savings mentioned above. This is not the case when the NNC polyhedra are encoded by using an additional slack variable [2,21], which is the classical approach implemented in Apron and PPL. In such a case, the NNC polyhedron $\phi \in \mathbb{P}_n$ would be encoded by a closed representation $\psi \in \mathbb{CP}_{n+1}$, violating a basic assumption underlying our optimization. The following example describes the problem in more detail.

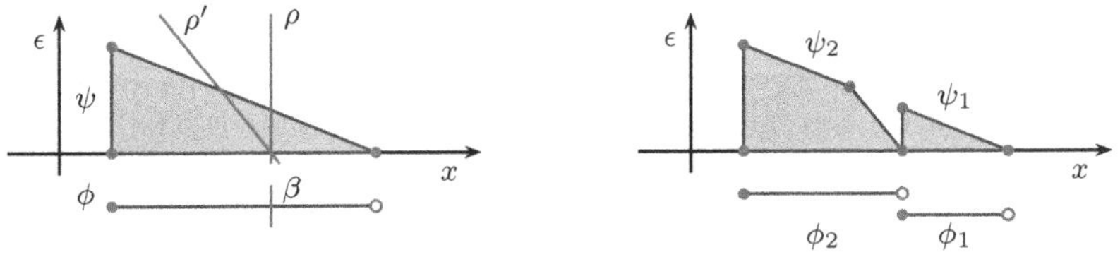

Fig. 2. When using the ϵ-representation approach, the complementary constraints β and $\neg\beta$ are encoded by ρ and ρ', which are not complementary in $\mathbb{R}^2$.

Example 5. On the upper left portion of Fig. 2 we show the topologically closed ϵ-representation $\psi \in \mathbb{CP}^2$ for the 1-dimensional, half-open interval $\phi = \text{con}(\{1 \leq x < 6\}) \in \mathbb{P}_1$, which is depicted below ψ. The (closure) points of the polyhedra are denoted by (unfilled) circles. Consider the constraint $\beta \equiv (x \geq 4)$, so that $\neg\beta \equiv (x < 4)$ and $\text{split}^{\text{s}}_\beta(\mathcal{P}) = (\phi_1, \phi_2)$, where $\phi_1 = \text{con}(\{4 \leq x < 6\})$ and $\phi_2 = \text{con}(\{1 \leq x < 4\})$, represented on the lower right portion of the figure. Working on the ϵ-representations though, the two (non-strict and strict) inequalities β and $\neg\beta$ are respectively encoded by $\rho \equiv (4 \leq x + 0 \cdot \epsilon)$ and $\rho' \equiv (x + \epsilon \leq 4)$, which are both non-strict and not complementary on $\mathbb{R}^2$. Hence, a proper computation of the split operator on the ϵ-representation ψ (shown on the upper right portion of Fig. 2) requires two distinct calls to the incremental conversion procedure to obtain ψ_1 and ψ_2.

In Table 6 we show the efficiency of different implementations of the split operation: we compare the 'standard', user-defined implementation (on both the PPL and the PPLite libraries) with the newly defined abstract operator (only available in PPLite). The polyhedron chosen for the test is a half-open hypercube $\mathcal{H} \in \mathbb{P}_{12}$, defined by constraints of the form $-1 < x_i \leq 1$; for the tests on $\mathbb{CP}_{12}$ we use its topological closure $\mathrm{cl}(\mathcal{H})$; we also perform a test on $\mathcal{H}' \in \mathbb{P}_{12}$, which is obtained from $\mathcal{H}$ by adding three *non-skeleton* points [6] (that is, $\mathcal{H}'$ also contains the relative interior of three of the facets that are disjoint from $\mathcal{H}$). In all cases, the polyhedron is split by constraint $\beta \equiv (x_0 + 2x_1 - 2x_{10} - x_{11} \geq 0)$; when splitting $\mathcal{H}$, we test both the strict and non-strict variant of the split operation.

Table 6. Splitting $\mathcal{H}$, $\mathrm{cl}(\mathcal{H})$ and $\mathcal{H}'$ using β. Units: Time (s), Vec (K), Sat (M).

		$\mathrm{split}^{\mathrm{ns}}_{\beta}(\mathcal{H})$			$\mathrm{split}^{\mathrm{s}}_{\beta}(\mathcal{H})$			$\mathrm{split}^{\mathrm{ns}}_{\beta}(\mathrm{cl}(\mathcal{H}))$			$\mathrm{split}^{\mathrm{s}}_{\beta}(\mathcal{H}')$		
Library	Impl	Time	Vec	Sat	Time	Vec	Sat	Time	Vec	Sat	Time	Vec	Sat
PPL	standard	0.450	244	43.65	0.457	245	43.66	0.167	10	9.45	7.823	283	1742.13
PPLite	standard	0.068	10	4.73	0.069	10	4.73	0.066	10	4.73	0.070	10	4.81
	split	0.035	5	2.36	0.036	5	2.37	0.035	5	2.36	0.038	5	2.44

In columns 'Vec' and 'Sat' we report the number of operations performed on vectors (scalar products and linear combinations) and saturation rows (population counts, unions and tests for inclusion on bit-vectors): it can be seen that the newly implemented operator systematically halves the values of these counters. Note that, since this test is characterized by low magnitude coefficients, the efficiency gain on vector operations is probably underestimated. The comparison with the PPL implementation confirms that libraries based on the ϵ-dimension approach are significantly less efficient, in particular when the input polyhedron contains non-skeleton constraints/generators.

6 Conclusion

Starting from PHAVer, we have developed a new tool PHAVerLite for the analysis of hybrid systems characterized by piecewise constant continuous dynamics. While revisiting the application of the domain of NNC polyhedra to the problem of computing or overapproximating the reachable states, we focused our attention on several well known abstract operators, showing that remarkable efficiency improvements can be obtained by providing implementations that are specialized for the considered context. For a more efficient handling of sets of polyhedra, we have proposed a new heuristic approach, where we couple each polyhedron in the set with information corresponding to further approximations (bounding box and pseudo volume). As future work, we plan to extend our investigation to other semantic operators, including those that are needed when extending the analysis to more general classes of hybrid systems.

Acknowledgment. The work of Enea Zaffanella has been partially supported by *Gruppo Nazionale per il Calcolo Scientifico* of *Istituto Nazionale di Alta Matematica*.

References

1. Bagnara, R., Hill, P.M., Ricci, E., Zaffanella, E.: Precise widening operators for convex polyhedra. Sci. Comput. Program. **58**(1–2), 28–56 (2005)
2. Bagnara, R., Hill, P.M., Zaffanella, E.: Not necessarily closed convex polyhedra and the double description method. Formal Aspects Comput. **17**(2), 222–257 (2005)
3. Bagnara, R., Hill, P.M., Zaffanella, E.: Widening operators for powerset domains. Softw. Tools Technol. Transfer **8**(4/5), 449–466 (2006)
4. Bagnara, R., Hill, P.M., Zaffanella, E.: The Parma Polyhedra Library: toward a complete set of numerical abstractions for the analysis and verification of hardware and software systems. Sci. Comput. Program. **72**(1–2), 3–21 (2008)
5. Bagnara, R., Hill, P.M., Zaffanella, E.: Applications of polyhedral computations to the analysis and verification of hardware and software systems. Theoret. Comput. Sci. **410**(46), 4672–4691 (2009)
6. Becchi, A., Zaffanella, E.: A direct encoding for NNC polyhedra. In: Computer Aided Verification - 30th International Conference, CAV 2018, Held as Part of the Federated Logic Conference, FloC 2018, Oxford, UK, July 14–17, 2018, Proceedings, Part I, pp. 230–248 (2018)
7. Becchi, A., Zaffanella, E.: An efficient abstract domain for not necessarily closed polyhedra. In: Podelski, A. (ed.) SAS 2018. LNCS, vol. 11002, pp. 146–165. Springer, Cham (2018). https://doi.org/10.1007/978-3-319-99725-4_11
8. Bemporad, A., Fukuda, K., Torrisi, F.D.: Convexity recognition of the union of polyhedra. Comput. Geom. Theory Appl. **18**(3), 141–154 (2001)
9. Cousot, P., Cousot, R.: Abstract interpretation: a unified lattice model for static analysis of programs by construction or approximation of fixpoints. In: Proceedings of the Fourth Annual ACM Symposium on Principles of Programming Languages, pp. 238–252. ACM Press, Los Angeles (1977)
10. Cousot, P., Cousot, R.: Systematic design of program analysis frameworks. In: Proceedings of the Sixth Annual ACM Symposium on Principles of Programming Languages, pp. 269–282. ACM Press, San Antonio (1979)
11. Cousot, P., Giacobazzi, R., Ranzato, F.: A^2I: abstract^2 interpretation. PACMPL **3**(POPL), 42:1–42:31 (2019)
12. Cousot, P., Halbwachs, N.: Automatic discovery of linear restraints among variables of a program. In: Conference Record of the Fifth Annual ACM Symposium on Principles of Programming Languages, pp. 84–96. ACM Press, Tucson (1978)
13. Frehse, G.: PHAVer: algorithmic verification of hybrid systems past HyTech. In: Morari, M., Thiele, L. (eds.) HSCC 2005. LNCS, vol. 3414, pp. 258–273. Springer, Heidelberg (2005). https://doi.org/10.1007/978-3-540-31954-2_17
14. Frehse, G.: PHAVer: algorithmic verification of hybrid systems past HyTech. Softw. Tools Technol. Transfer **10**(3), 263–279 (2008)
15. Frehse, G., et al.: ARCH-COMP19 category report: Hybrid systems with piecewise constant dynamics. In: 6th International Workshop on Applied Verification of Continuous and Hybrid Systems ARCH19. EPiC Series in Computing, vol. 61, pp. 1–13. EasyChair (2019)
16. Frehse, G., et al.: ARCH-COMP18 category report: Hybrid systems with piecewise constant dynamics. In: 5th International Workshop on Applied Verification of Continuous and Hybrid Systems ARCH18. EPiC Series in Computing, vol. 54, pp. 1–13. EasyChair (2018)
17. Frehse, G., et al.: Spaceex: scalable verification of hybrid systems. In: Computer Aided Verification - 23rd International Conference, CAV 2011, Snowbird, UT, USA. Proceedings, pp. 379–395 (2011)

18. Guernic, C.L., Girard, A.: Reachability analysis of hybrid systems using support functions. In: 21st International Conference on Computer Aided Verification, CAV 2009, Grenoble, France. Proceedings, pp. 540–554 (2009)
19. Halbwachs, N., Merchat, D., Gonnord, L.: Some ways to reduce the space dimension in polyhedra computations. Formal Meth. Syst. Des. **29**(1), 79–95 (2006)
20. Halbwachs, N., Merchat, D., Parent-Vigouroux, C.: Cartesian factoring of polyhedra in linear relation analysis. In: Cousot, R. (ed.) SAS 2003. LNCS, vol. 2694, pp. 355–365. Springer, Heidelberg (2003). https://doi.org/10.1007/3-540-44898-5_20
21. Halbwachs, N., Proy, Y.-E., Raymond, P.: Verification of linear hybrid systems by means of convex approximations. In: Le Charlier, B. (ed.) SAS 1994. LNCS, vol. 864, pp. 223–237. Springer, Heidelberg (1994). https://doi.org/10.1007/3-540-58485-4_43
22. Halbwachs, N., Proy, Y.E., Roumanoff, P.: Verification of real-time systems using linear relation analysis. Formal Meth. Syst. Des. **11**(2), 157–185 (1997)
23. Henzinger, T.A., Ho, P.H., Wong-Toi, H.: HyTech: a model checker for hybrid systems. Softw. Tools Technol. Transfer **1**(1+2), 110–122 (1997)
24. Jeannet, B., Miné, A.: Apron: a library of numerical abstract domains for static analysis. In: 21st International Conference on Computer Aided Verification, CAV 2009, Grenoble, France. Proceedings, pp. 661–667 (2009)
25. Lamport, L.: A fast mutual exclusion algorithm. ACM Trans. Comput. Syst. **5**(1), 1–11 (1987)
26. Maréchal, A., Monniaux, D., Périn, M.: Scalable minimizing-operators on polyhedra via parametric linear programming. In: Static Analysis - 24th International Symposium, SAS 2017, New York, NY, USA, Proceedings, pp. 212–231 (2017)
27. Miné, A.: The octagon abstract domain. Higher-Order Symbolic Comput. **19**(1), 31–100 (2006)
28. Motzkin, T.S., Raiffa, H., Thompson, G.L., Thrall, R.M.: The double description method. In: Contributions to the Theory of Games. Annals of Mathematics Studies, vol. II, No. 28, pp. 51–73. Princeton University Press, Princeton (1953)
29. Pelleau, M., Miné, A., Truchet, C., Benhamou, F.: A constraint solver based on abstract domains. In: 14th International Conference Verification, Model Checking, and Abstract Interpretation, VMCAI 2013, Rome, Italy. Proceedings, pp. 434–454 (2013)
30. Sankaranarayanan, S., Colón, M.A., Sipma, H., Manna, Z.: Efficient strongly relational polyhedral analysis. In: Emerson, E.A., Namjoshi, K.S. (eds.) VMCAI 2006. LNCS, vol. 3855, pp. 111–125. Springer, Heidelberg (2005). https://doi.org/10.1007/11609773_8
31. Schupp, S., Ábrahám, E., Chen, X., Ben Makhlouf, I., Frehse, G., Sankaranarayanan, S., Kowalewski, S.: Current challenges in the verification of hybrid systems. In: Berger, C., Mousavi, M.R. (eds.) CyPhy 2015. LNCS, vol. 9361, pp. 8–24. Springer, Cham (2015). https://doi.org/10.1007/978-3-319-25141-7_2
32. Singh, G., Püschel, M., Vechev, M.T.: Fast polyhedra abstract domain. In: Proceedings of the 44th ACM SIGPLAN Symposium on Principles of Programming Languages, POPL 2017, Paris, France, January 18–20, 2017, pp. 46–59 (2017)

An Efficient Parametric Linear Programming Solver and Application to Polyhedral Projection

Hang Yu(✉) and David Monniaux

Univ. Grenoble Alpes, CNRS, Grenoble INP, 38000 Grenoble, France
{Hang.Yu,David.Monniaux}@univ-grenoble-alpes.fr

Abstract. Polyhedral projection is a main operation of the polyhedron abstract domain. It can be computed via parametric linear programming (PLP), which is more efficient than the classic Fourier-Motzkin elimination method.

In prior work, PLP was done in arbitrary precision rational arithmetic. In this paper, we present an approach where most of the computation is performed in floating-point arithmetic, then exact rational results are reconstructed.

We also propose a workaround for a difficulty that plagued previous attempts at using PLP for computations on polyhedra: in general the linear programming problems are degenerate, resulting in redundant computations and geometric descriptions.

Keywords: Polyhedral projection · Parametric linear programming · Floating-point arithmetic

1 Introduction and Related Work

Abstract interpretation [6] is an approach for obtaining invariant properties of programs, which may be used to verify their correctness. Abstract interpretation searches for invariants within an *abstract domain*. For numerical properties, a common and cheap choice is one interval per variable per location in the program, but this cannot represent relationships between variables. Such imprecision often makes it impossible to prove properties of the program using that domain. If we retain linear equalities and inequalities between variables, we obtain the domain of *convex polyhedra* [7], which is more expensive, but more precise.

Several implementations of the domain of convex polyhedra over the field of rational numbers are available. The most popular ones for abstract interpretation are NewPolka[1] and the Parma Polyhedra Library (PPL) [1]. These libraries, and others, use the *double description* of polyhedra: as *generators* (vertices, and for unbounded polyhedra, rays and lines) and constraints (linear equalities

Grenoble INP—Institute of Engineering Univ. Grenoble Alpes

[1] Now distributed as part of APRON http://apron.cri.ensmp.fr/library/.

B.-Y. E. Chang (Ed.): SAS 2019, LNCS 11822, pp. 203–224, 2019.
https://doi.org/10.1007/978-3-030-32304-2_11

and inequalities). Some operations are easier on one representation than on the other, and some, such as removing redundant constraints or generators, are easier if both are available. One representation is computed from the other using Chernikova's algorithm [4,16]. This algorithm is expensive in some cases, and, furthermore, in some cases, one representation is exponentially larger than the other. This is in particular the case of the generator representation of hypercubes or, more generally, products of intervals; thus interval analysis which simulate using convex polyhedra in the double description has cost exponential in the dimension.

In 2012 Verimag started implementing a library using constraints only, called VPL (Verified Polyhedra Library) [11,17]. There are several reasons for using only constraints; we have already cited the high generator complexity of some polyhedra commonly found in abstract interpretation, and the high cost of Chernikova's algorithm. Another reason was to be able to certify the results of the computation, in particular that the obtained polyhedra includes the one that should have been computed, which is the property that ensures the soundness of abstract interpretation. One can certify that each constraint is correct by exhibiting coefficients, as in Farkas' lemma.

In the first version of VPL, all main operations boiled down to projection, performed using Fourier-Motzkin elimination [9], but this method generates many redundant constraints which must be eliminated at high cost. Also, for projecting out many variables $x_1, \ldots, x_n$, it computes all intermediate steps (projection of x_1, then of $x_2 \ldots$), even though they may be unneeded and have high description complexity. In the second version, projection and convex hull both boil down to *parametric linear programming* [14]. The current version of VPL is based on a parametric linear programming solver implemented in arbitrary precision arithmetic in OCaml [18].

In this paper, we improved on this approach in two respects.

- We replace most of the exact computations in arbitrary precision rational numbers by floating-point computations performed using an off-the-shelf linear programming solver. We can however recover exact solutions and check them exactly, an approach that has previously been used for SMT-solving [15,20].
- We resolve some difficulties due to geometric degeneracy in the problems to be solved, which previously resulted in many redundant computations.

Furthermore, the solving is divided into independent tasks, which may be scheduled in parallel. The parallel implementation is covered in [5].

2 Notations and Preliminaries

2.1 Notations

Capital letters (e.g. A) denote matrices, small bold letters (e.g. $\boldsymbol{x}$) denote vectors, small letters (e.g. b) denote scalars. The ith row of A is $\boldsymbol{a}_{i\bullet}$, its jth column is

$\boldsymbol{a}_{\bullet j}$. $\mathcal{P} : A\boldsymbol{x} + \boldsymbol{b} \geq 0$ denotes a polyhedron and $\mathcal{C}$ a constraint. The ith constraint of $\mathcal{P}$ is $\mathcal{C}_i$: $\boldsymbol{a}_{i\bullet}\boldsymbol{x} \geq b_i$, where b_i is the ith element of $\boldsymbol{b}$. a_{ij} denotes the element at the ith row and the jth column of A. $\mathbb{Q}$ denotes the field of rational numbers, and $\mathbb{F}$ is the set of finite floating-point numbers, considered as a subset of $\mathbb{Q}$.

2.2 Linear Programming

Linear programming (LP) consists in getting the optimal value of a linear function $Z(\boldsymbol{\lambda})$ subject to a set of linear constraints $A\boldsymbol{\lambda} = \boldsymbol{b}$, $\boldsymbol{\lambda} \geq 0$[2], where $\boldsymbol{\lambda}$ is the vector of variables. The optimal value Z^* is reached at $\boldsymbol{\lambda}^*$: $Z^* = Z(\boldsymbol{\lambda}^*)$.

2.3 Basic and Non-basic Variables

We use the implementation of the simplex algorithm in GLPK[3] as LP solver. In the simplex algorithm each constraint is expressed in the form $(\lambda_B)_i = \sum_{j=1}^{n} a_{ij}(\lambda_N)_j + c_i$, where $(\lambda_B)_i$ is known as a *basic variable*, the $(\lambda_N)_j$ is *non-basic variable*, and c_i is a constant. The basic variables constitute a *basis*. The basic and non-basic variables form a partition of the variables, and the objective function is obtained by substituting the basic variables with non-basic variables.

2.4 Parametric Linear Programming

A parametric linear program (PLP) is a linear program, subjecting to $A\boldsymbol{\lambda} = \boldsymbol{b}$, $\boldsymbol{\lambda} \geq 0$, whose objective function $Z(\boldsymbol{\lambda}, \boldsymbol{x})$ contains parameters $\boldsymbol{x}$ appearing linearly.[4] The PLP reaches optimum at the vertex $\boldsymbol{\lambda}^*$, and the optimal solution is a set of $(\mathcal{R}_i, Z_i^*(\boldsymbol{x}))$. $\mathcal{R}_i$ is the region of parameters $\boldsymbol{x}$, in which the basis does not change. $Z_i^*(\boldsymbol{x})$ is the optimal function corresponding to $\mathcal{R}_i$, meaning that all the parameters in $\mathcal{R}_i$ will lead to the same optimal function $Z_i^*(\boldsymbol{x})$. In the case of *primal degeneracy* (Sect. 4), the optimal vertex $\boldsymbol{\lambda}^*$ has multiple partitions of basic and non-basic variables, thus an optimal function can be obtained by different bases, i.e., several regions share the same optimal function.

2.5 Redundant Constraints

Definition 1 (Redundant). *A constraint is said to be redundant if it can be removed without changing the shape of the polyhedron.*

In our algorithms, there are several steps at which redundant constraints must be removed, which we call *minimization* of the polyhedron. For instance

---

2 This is the canonical form of the LP problem. All the LP problems can be transformed into this form.

3 The GNU Linear Programming Toolkit (GLPK) is a linear programming solver implemented in floating-point arithmetic. https://www.gnu.org/software/glpk/.

4 There also exist parametric linear programs where the parameters are in the constant terms of the inequalities, we do not consider them here.

we have $P = \{C_1 : x_1 - 2x_2 \leq -2, C_2 : -2x_1 + x_2 \leq -1, C_3 : x_1 + x_2 \leq 8, C_4 : -2x_1 - 4x_2 \leq -7\}$, and C_4 is a redundant constraint.

The redundancy can be tested by Farkas' Lemma: a redundant constraint can be expressed as the combination of some other constraints.

Theorem 1 (Farkas' Lemma). *Let* $A \in \mathbb{R}^{m\times n} A \in \mathbb{R}^{m\times n}$ *and* $\boldsymbol{b} \in \mathbb{R}^m \boldsymbol{b} \in \mathbb{R}^m$. *Then exactly one of the following two statements is true:*

- *There exists an* $\boldsymbol{x} \in \mathbb{R}^n$ *such that* $A\boldsymbol{x} = \boldsymbol{b}$ *and* $\boldsymbol{x} \geq 0$.
- *There exists a* $\boldsymbol{y} \in \mathbb{R}^m$ *such that* $A^\mathsf{T}\boldsymbol{y} \geq 0$ *and* $\boldsymbol{b}^\mathsf{T}\boldsymbol{y} < 0$.

It is easy to determine the redundant constraints using Farkas' lemma, but in our case we have much more irredundant constraints than redundant ones, in which case using Farkas' lemma is not efficient. A new minimization algorithm which can find out the irredundant constraints more efficiently is explained in [19].

3 Algorithm

As our PLP algorithm is implemented with mix of rational numbers and floating-point numbers, we will make explicit the type of data used in the algorithm. In the pseudo-code, we annotate data with ($name^{type}$), where *name* is the name of data and *type* is either $\mathbb{Q}$ or/and $\mathbb{F}$. $\mathbb{Q} \times \mathbb{F}$ means that the data is stored in both rational and floating-point numbers.

Floating-point computations are imprecise, and thus the floating-point LP solver may provide an incorrect answer: it may report that the problem is infeasible whereas it is feasible, that it is feasible even though it is infeasible, and it may provide an "optimal" solution that is not truly optimal. What our approach guarantees is that, whatever the errors committed by the floating-point LP solvers, the polyhedron that we computed is a valid over-approximation: it always includes the polyhedron that should have been computed. Details will be explained later in this section and in Sect. 5.

In this section we do not consider the *degeneracy*, which will be talked in Sect. 4.

3.1 Flow Chart

The Fig. 1 shows the flow chart of our algorithm. The rectangles are processes and diamonds are decisions. The processes/decisions colored by orange are computed by floating-point arithmetic, and that by green uses rational numbers. The dotted red frames show the cases that rarely happen, which means that most computation in our approach uses floating-point numbers.

In Sect. 3 we will present the overview of the algorithm. Then we will explain into details the processes/decisions framed by dashed blue rectangles in Sect. 5.

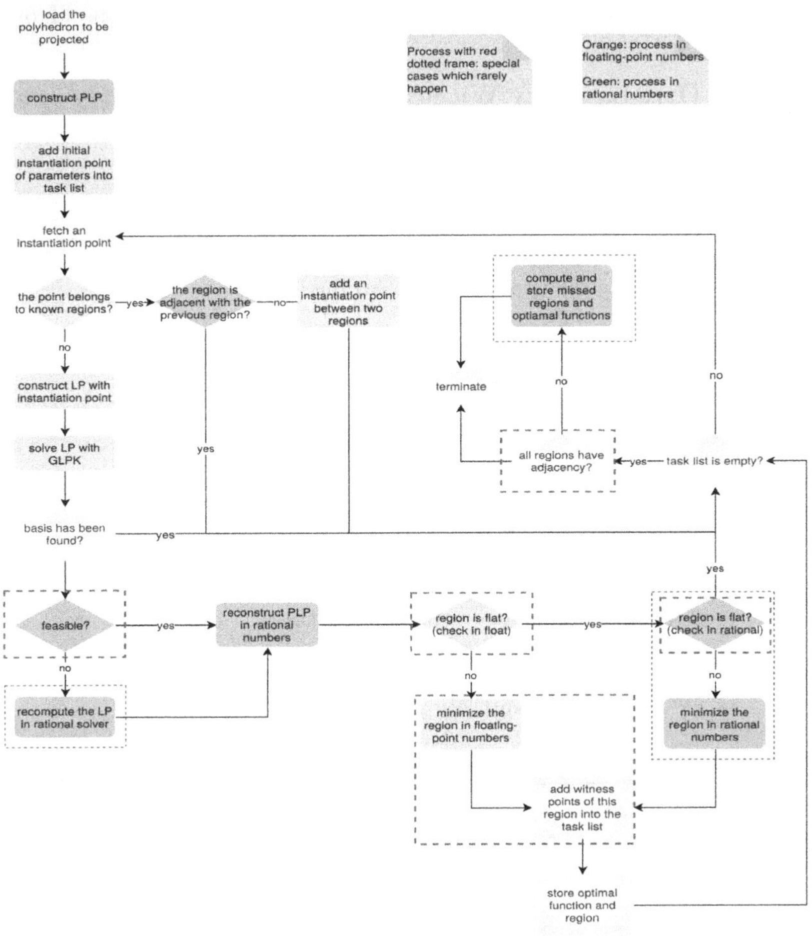

Fig. 1. Flow chart

3.2 Ray-Tracing Minimization

At several steps we need to remove redundant constraints from the description of a polyhedron. We here present an efficient ray-tracing minimization method based on [19]. Their approach used rational computations, while ours uses floating-point arithmetic. The use of floating-point numbers here will not cause a soundness problem: in the worst case, we will eliminate constraints that should not be removed. In other words, when the floating-point algorithm cannot determine the redundancy, the corresponding constraints will be reported as redundant.

There are two phases in ray-tracing minimization. In the first phase we launch rays to the constraints, and the first hit constraints are irredundant. The remaining constraints will be determined in the second phase: if we can find the *irredundancy witness* point, then the constraint is irredundant. The algorithm is shown in Algorithm 1.

Definition 2 (Irredundancy Witness). *The irredundancy witness of a constraint C_i is a point that violates C_i but satisfies the other constraints.*

Algorithm 1. Ray-tracing minimization algorithm.

```
Input: poly^F: the polyhedron to be minimized
Output: the index of the irredundant constraints
Function Minimize(poly^F)
    p^F = GetInternalPoint(poly^F)
    rays^F = LaunchRays(poly^F, p^F)
    foreach ray^F in rays^F do
        constraintIdx = FirstHitConstraint(poly^F, ray^F, p^F)
        SetAsIrredundant(poly^F, constraintIdx)
    foreach constraint idx in undetermined constraints do
        if cannot determine then
            SetAsRedundant(poly^F, idx)
        else
            if found irredundancy witness point then
                SetAsIrredundant(poly^F, idx)
            else
                SetAsRedundant(poly^F, idx)
    return the irredundant constraints
```

3.3 Parametric Linear Programming Solver

The algorithm is shown in Algorithm 2. Firstly we construct the PLP problem, and then we solve it by solving a set of LP problems via floating-point LP solver. Then the rational solution will be reconstructed based on the information obtained from the LP solver. We will explain each step in the following sections. Our focus will be on the cooperation of rational and floating-point numbers, and the tricks for dealing with floating-point arithmetic.

Constructing PLP for Projection. The polyhedron to be projected is $\mathcal{P}$: $A\boldsymbol{x} + \boldsymbol{b} \geq 0$. To perform projection, we can construct a PLP problem shown in Problem 1. In this problem, $\boldsymbol{x}$ are parameters, and $\boldsymbol{\lambda}$ are decision variables, where $\boldsymbol{x} = [x_1, \cdots, x_m]^\mathsf{T}$, $\boldsymbol{\lambda} = [\lambda_0, \cdots, \lambda_n]^\mathsf{T}$. Assume that we wish to eliminate $x_p, \cdots, x_q$, where $1 \leq p \leq q \leq m$.

Algorithm 2. Parametric linear programming algorithm.

Input: $poly^{\mathbb{Q}}$: the polyhedron to be projected
$[x_p, ..., x_q]$: the variables to be eliminated
n: number of initial points

Output: $optimums^{\mathbb{Q}}$ the set of optimal function
$regions^{\mathbb{Q}\times\mathbb{F}}$ the corresponding regions

Function Plp($poly^{\mathbb{Q}}$, $[x_p, ..., x_q]$, n)
- $plp^{\mathbb{Q}\times\mathbb{F}}$ = ConstructPlp($poly^{\mathbb{Q}}$, $[x_p, ..., x_q]$)
- $worklist^{\mathbb{F}}$ = GetInitialPoints($poly^{\mathbb{Q}}$, n)
- $optimums^{\mathbb{Q}}$ = none
- $regions^{\mathbb{Q}\times\mathbb{F}}$ = none
- **while** $worklist^{\mathbb{F}} \neq$ none **do**
  - $(w^{\mathbb{F}}, R_{from}{}^{\mathbb{Q}}, F_{from})$ = getTask($worklist^{\mathbb{F}}$)
  - $R_{curr}{}^{\mathbb{Q}}$ = CheckCovered($regions^{\mathbb{F}}$, $w^{\mathbb{F}}$)
  - **if** $R_{curr}{}^{\mathbb{Q}}$ == none **then**
    - ($basicIndices$, $nonbasicIndices$) = GlpkSolveLp($w^{\mathbb{F}}$, $plp^{\mathbb{F}}$)
    - $reconstructMatrix^{\mathbb{Q}}$ = Reconstruct($plp^{\mathbb{Q}}$, $basicIndices$)
    - ($newOptimum^{\mathbb{Q}}$, $newRegion^{\mathbb{Q}\times\mathbb{F}}$) = ExtractResult($reconstructMatrix^{\mathbb{Q}}$, $nonbasicIndices$)
    - ($activeIndices$, $witnessList^{\mathbb{F}}$) = Minimize($newRegion^{\mathbb{F}}$)
    - $minimizedR^{\mathbb{Q}}$ = GetRational($newRegion^{\mathbb{Q}}$, activeIndices)
    - Insert($optimums^{\mathbb{Q}}$, $newOptimum^{\mathbb{Q}}$)
    - Insert($regions^{\mathbb{Q}}$, $newRegion^{\mathbb{Q}}$)
    - AddWitnessPoints($witnessList^{\mathbb{F}}$, $worklist$)
    - $R_{curr}{}^{\mathbb{Q}}$=$minimizedR^{\mathbb{Q}}$
  - **if** Adjacent($R_{curr}{}^{\mathbb{Q}}$, $R_{from}{}^{\mathbb{Q}}$, F_{from}) **then**
    - F_{curr} = GetCrossFrontier($R_{curr}{}^{\mathbb{Q}}$, $R_{from}{}^{\mathbb{Q}}$, F_{from})
    - StoreAdjacencyInfo($R_{from}{}^{\mathbb{Q}}$, F_{from}, $R_{curr}{}^{\mathbb{Q}}$, F_{curr})
  - **else**
    - AddExtraPoint($worklist$, $R_{curr}{}^{\mathbb{Q}}$, $R_{from}{}^{\mathbb{Q}}$)

$$
\begin{array}{rll}
\text{minimize} & \sum_{i=1}^{n}(\boldsymbol{a}_{i\bullet}\boldsymbol{x}+b_i)\lambda_i+\lambda_0 & \\
\text{subject to} & \sum_{i=1}^{n}(\boldsymbol{a}_{i\bullet}\boldsymbol{p}+b_i)\lambda_i+\lambda_0=1 \quad (*) & \\
 & \sum_{i=1}^{n}a_{ij}\lambda_i=0 \quad (\forall j\in\{p,\cdots,q\}) \quad (**) & \\
\text{and} & \lambda_i\geq 0 \quad (\forall i\in\{0,\cdots,n\}) &
\end{array}
\tag{1}
$$

where $\boldsymbol{p}=[p_1,\cdots,p_m]$ is a point inside $\mathcal{P}$. The constraint $(*)$ is called normalization constraint. To compute the convex hull of $\mathcal{P}$ and $\mathcal{P}'$: $A'\boldsymbol{x}+\boldsymbol{b}'\geq 0$, we just replace the constraints $(**)$ with $A^T\boldsymbol{\lambda}-A'^T\boldsymbol{\lambda}'=0$, $\boldsymbol{b}^T\boldsymbol{\lambda}+\lambda_0-\boldsymbol{b}'^T\boldsymbol{\lambda}'-\lambda_0'=0$. For more details about constructing the PLP problem of projection, please refer to [14,18].

Solving PLP. The PLP problem represents a set of LP problems, whose constraints are the same and objective function varies with the instantiation of the parameters. Here is a brief sketch of our solver. We maintain a working set of tasks yet to be performed. At the beginning, a random vector of parameters (or a fixed one) is chosen as the initial task to trigger the algorithm. Then, as long as the working set is not empty, a vector of parameters $\boldsymbol{w}$ is taken from the working set. We solve the (non-parametric) linear programming problem for this vector of parameters, using an off-the-shelf floating-point solver. From the information of the final basis reached, we obtain a polyhedral region $\mathcal{R}$ of parameters, to which $\boldsymbol{w}$ belongs, that all share the same optimum and the same basis, as it will be explained below. In general, this region is obtained with redundant constraints, so we minimize its representation. The witness points $\boldsymbol{w}_1, \ldots, \boldsymbol{w}_m$ of the irredundant constraints lie outside of $\mathcal{R}$, and are inserted into the working set. We also maintain a set of already created regions: a vector $\boldsymbol{w}$ of parameters is ignored if it lies inside one of them. The algorithm stops when the working set is empty, meaning that the full set of parameters is covered by regions.

Here is how we process a vector $\boldsymbol{w}$ from the working set. We solve the LP problem:

$$\begin{aligned} \text{minimize} \quad & \sum_{i=1}^{n} (\boldsymbol{a}_{i\bullet}\boldsymbol{w} + b_i)\lambda_i + \lambda_0 \\ \text{subject to} \quad & \sum_{i=1}^{n} (\boldsymbol{a}_{i\bullet}\boldsymbol{p} + b_i)\lambda_i + \lambda_0 = 1 \quad (*) \\ & \sum_{i=1}^{n} a_{ij}\lambda_i = 0 \quad (\forall j \in \{p, \cdots, q\}) \\ \text{and} \quad & \lambda_i \geq 0 \quad (\forall i \in \{0, \cdots, n\}) \end{aligned} \tag{2}$$

Obtaining Rational Solution. We solve this LP problem in floating-point using GLPK. Had the solving been done in exact arithmetic, one could retain the optimal point $\boldsymbol{\lambda}^*$, but here we cannot use it directly. Instead, we obtain the final partition of the variables into basic and non-basic variables, and from this partition we can recompute exactly, in rational numbers, the optimum $\boldsymbol{\lambda}^*$, as well as a certificate that it is feasible.

Let M denote the matrix of constraints and O that of the PLP objective function. The last column of the each matrix represents the constant.

$$M = \begin{bmatrix} (A\boldsymbol{p} + \boldsymbol{b})^\top & 1 & 1 \\ (\boldsymbol{a}_{\bullet p})^\top & 0 & 0 \\ \vdots & \vdots & \vdots \\ (\boldsymbol{a}_{\bullet q})^\top & 0 & 0 \end{bmatrix} \qquad O = \begin{bmatrix} A^\top & 0 & 0 \\ \boldsymbol{b}^\top & 1 & 0 \end{bmatrix} \tag{3}$$

To generate the result of PLP, we need to reconstruct the matrices M and O to make sure the objective function of PLP contains the same basis as the final tableau of the simplex algorithm: the coefficients of the basic variables in the objective function should be 0. We extract the indices of the basic variables from that tableau; M_B and O_B denote the sub-matrices from M and B containing only the columns corresponding to the basic variables. By linear algebra in rational arithmetic[5] we compute a matrix Θ, representing the substitution performed by the simplex algorithm. Then we apply this substitution to the objective matrix O to get the new objective function O': $\Theta = O_B M_B^{-1}$, $O' = O - \Theta M$, where M_B^{-1} denotes the inverse of M_B (actually, we do not inverse that matrix but instead call a solver for systems of linear equations).

In our LP problem 2, the variables $\boldsymbol{\lambda}$ have lower bound 0, which means that when the objective function reaches the optimal, all the non-basic variables should reach their lower bound and their coefficients should be non-negative, otherwise the optimal value can decrease furthermore. The same applies to the parametric linear problems, except that the coefficients of the objective function may contain parameters; thus the sign conditions on these coefficients is translated to linear inequalities on these parameters. Each non-zero column in O' represents a function in $\boldsymbol{x}$, which is the coefficient of a non-basic variable. The conjunction of constraints $(O'_{\bullet j})^{\mathsf{T}}\boldsymbol{x} \geq 0$ constitute the region of $\boldsymbol{x}$ where j belongs to the indices of non-basic variables. This conjunction of constraints may be redundant: we thus call the minimization procedure over it.

4 Overlapping Regions and Degeneracy

Ideally, the parametric linear programming outputs a quasi-partition of the space of parameters, meaning that the produced regions do not have overlap except at their boundary (we shall from now on say "do not overlap" for short) and cover the full space of parameters. This may not be the case due to two reasons: geometric degeneracy, leading to overlapping regions, and imprecision due to floating-point arithmetic, leading to insufficient coverage. The latter will be dealt with by rational checker, which will be explained in Sect. 5.

If regions do not overlap, it is possible to verify that the space of parameters is fully covered by checking that each boundary of a region is also a boundary of an adjacent region (proof in Sect. 5.4); otherwise, this means we have a boundary with nothing on the other side, thus the space is not fully covered. This simple test does not work if regions overlap. Furthermore, overlapping regions may be needlessly more numerous than those in a quasi-partition. We thus have two reasons to modify our algorithm to get rid of overlapping regions.

Let us see how overlapping regions occur. In a non-degenerate parametric linear program, for a given optimization function, there is only one optimal vertex (no *dual degeneracy*), and this optimal vertex is described by only one optimal basis (no *primal degeneracy*), i.e., there is a single optimal partition of variables into basic and non-basic. Thus, in a non-degenerate parametric linear program, for a given vector of parameters there is one single optimal basis (except

---

[5] We use Flint, which provides exact rational scalar, vector and matrix computations, including solving of linear systems. http://www.flintlib.org/.

at boundaries), meaning that each optimal function corresponds to one region. However when there is degeneracy, there will be multiple bases corresponding to one optimal function, and each of them computes a region. These regions may be overlapping. We call the regions corresponds to the same optimal function *degeneracy regions.*

Theorem 2. *There will be no overlapping regions if there is no degeneracy.*

Proof. In parametric linear programming, the regions are yielded by the partition of variables into basic and non-basic, i.e., each region corresponds to one basis. The parameters within one region lead the PLP problem to the same partition of variables. If there are overlapping regions, say $\mathcal{R}_i$ and $\mathcal{R}_j$, the PLP problem will be optimized by multiple bases when the parameters belong to $\mathcal{R}_i \cap \mathcal{R}_j$. In this case there must be degeneracy: these multiple bases may lead to multiple optimal vertex when we have dual degeneracy, or the same optimal vertex when we have primal degeneracy. By transposition, we know that if there is no degeneracy the PLP problem will always obtain a unique basis with given parameters, and there will be no overlapping regions. □

We thus need to get rid of degeneracy. We shall first prove that there is no dual degeneracy in our PLP algorithm, and then deal with the primal degeneracy.

4.1 Dual Degeneracy

Theorem 3. *For projection and convex hull, the parametric linear program exhibits no dual degeneracy.*

Proof. We shall see that the *normalization constraint* (the constraint (∗) in Problem 1) present in the parametric linear programs defining projection and convex hull prevents dual degeneracy.

Assume that at the optimum $Z^*(\boldsymbol{x})$ we have the simplex tableau in Table 1. λ_k denote the decision variables: $\lambda_k \geq 0$. In the current dictionary, the parametric coefficients of the objective function is $f_k = \boldsymbol{a}'_{i\bullet}\boldsymbol{x} + b'_i$. Assuming the variable leaving the basis is λ_r, and the entering variable is λ_q. Then λ_r is defined by the jth row as $\sum_j m_{jp}\lambda_p + \lambda_r = c_j$, where λ_p are nonbasic variables. That means $\lambda_r = c_j$ when the nonbasic variables reach their lower bound, which is 0 here.

Now we look for another optimum by doing one pivoting. As the current dictionary is feasible, we must have $c_j \geq 0$. To maintain the feasibility, we must choose λ_q such that $m_{jq} > 0$. As we only choose the non-basic variable whose coefficient is negative to enter the basis, then we know $f_q < 0$. By pivoting we obtain the new objective function $Z'(\boldsymbol{\lambda}, \boldsymbol{x}) = Z(\boldsymbol{\lambda}, \boldsymbol{x}) - f_q \frac{c_j}{m_{jq}}$. The new optimal function is:

$$Z^{*'}(\boldsymbol{x}) = Z^*(\boldsymbol{x}) - f_q \frac{c_j}{m_{jq}} \tag{4}$$

Let us assume that a dual degeneracy occurs, which means that we obtain the same objective function after the pivoting, i.e., $Z^{*'}(\boldsymbol{x}) = tZ^*(\boldsymbol{x})$, where t is a positive constant. Due to the normalization constraint at the point $\boldsymbol{x}_0$ enforcing $Z^{*'}(\boldsymbol{x}_0) = Z^*(\boldsymbol{x}_0) = 1$, we have $t = 1$. Hence we will obtain

$$Z^{*'}(\boldsymbol{x}) = Z^*(\boldsymbol{x}) \tag{5}$$

Considering the Eqs. 4 and 5 we obtain

$$f_q \frac{c_j}{m_{jq}} = 0 \tag{6}$$

Since $f_q \neq 0$, c_j must equal to 0, which means that we in fact faced a primal degeneracy.

Let $D_1 = f_q \frac{c_j}{m_{jq}}$, where the subscript of D_1 denotes the first pivoting. As $c_j \geq 0, f_q < 0$ and $m_{jq} > 0$, we know $D_1 \leq 0$. Similarly in each pivoting we have $D_i \leq 0$.

If we generalize the situation above to N rounds of pivoting, we will obtain:

$$Z^{*'}(\boldsymbol{x}) = Z^*(\boldsymbol{x}) - \sum_{i=1}^{N} D_i \tag{7}$$

If there is dual degeneracy $Z^{*'}(\boldsymbol{x}) = Z^*(\boldsymbol{x})$, and then

$$\sum_{i=1}^{N} D_i = 0 \tag{8}$$

As $\forall i, D_i \leq 0$, Eq. 8 implies $\forall i, D_i = 0$, which is possible if and only if all the c_j equal to 0. For the same reason as above, in this case we can only have primal degeneracy. □

4.2 Primal Degeneracy

Many methods to deal with primal degeneracy in non-parametric linear programming are known [3,8,10]; fewer in parametric linear programming [13]. We implemented an approach to avoid overlapping regions based on the work of

Table 1. Simplex tableau.

	non-basic variables				basic variables		constants
	λ_1	$\cdots$	λ_q	$\cdots$	$\cdots\ \lambda_r \cdots \lambda_s \cdots$	λ_n	
objective	f_1	$\cdots$	f_q	$\cdots$	$\cdots\ 0 \cdots 0 \cdots$	0	$Z^*(\boldsymbol{x})$
$\vdots$	....	....	....	....	....	....	....
row j	....	....	m_{jq}	$\cdots$	$\cdots\ 1 \cdots 0 \cdots$	0	c_j
$\vdots$	....	....	....	....	....	....	....
row k	....	....	m_{kq}	$\cdots$	$\cdots\ 0 \cdots 1 \cdots$	0	c_k
$\vdots$	....	....	....	....	....	....	....

Jones et al. [13], which used the perturbation method [10]. The algorithm is shown in Algorithm 3. Once entering a new region, we check if there is primal degeneracy: it occurs when one or several basic variables equal zero. In this case we will explore all *degeneracy regions* for the same optimum, using, as explained below, a method avoiding overlaps.

Let us consider a projected polyhedra in 3 dimensions with primal degeneracy, because of which there are multiple regions corresponding to the same face. Figure 2 shows the 2D view of the face. The yellow and red triangles represent the intersection of the regions with their face. Figure 2a shows the disappoint case where the regions are overlapping. The reason is that when the parameters locate in the orange part, two different bases will lead the constructed LP problem to optimum. We aim to avoid the overlap and obtain the result either in Fig. 2b or in Fig. 2c.

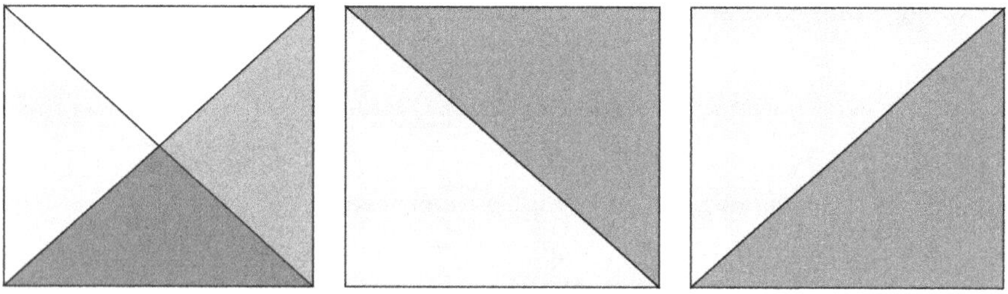

(a) (b) (c)

Fig. 2. Example of overlapping regions.

Our solution against overlaps is to make the optimal basis unique for given parameters of the objective function by adding perturbation terms to the right side of the constraints [13]. These perturbation terms are "infinitesimal", meaning that the right-hand side, instead of being a vector of rational scalars, becomes a matrix where the first column corresponds to the original vector, the second column corresponds to the first infinitesimal, the third column to the second infinitesimal, etc. The same applies to $\boldsymbol{\lambda}$. Instead of comparing scalar coordinates using the usual ordering on rational numbers, we compare line vectors of rationals with the lexicographic ordering. After the perturbation, there will be no primal degeneracy as all the right-hand side of the constraints cannot be equal.

The initial perturbation matrix is a $k * k$ identity matrix: $M_p = I$, where k is the number of constraints. Then the perturbation matrix will be updated as the reconstruction of the constraint matrix. After adding this perturbation matrix, the right-hand side becomes $B = [\boldsymbol{b}|M_p]$. The new constants are vectors in the form of $\boldsymbol{v}_i = [b_i \; 0 \; \cdots \; 1 \; \cdots \; 0]$. We compare the vectors by lexico-order: $\boldsymbol{v}_i > \boldsymbol{v}_j$ if the first non-zero element of $\boldsymbol{v}_i$ is larger than that of $\boldsymbol{v}_j$.

To obtain a new basis, in contrast to working with non-degeneracy regions, we do not solve the problem using floating point solver. Instead, we pivot directly on the perturbed rational matrix. Each non-basic variable will be chosen as entering variable. Then from all the constraints in which $b_i = 0$, we select the basic variable λ_l in C_i whose ratio $\frac{v_i}{a_{ij}}$ is smallest as the leaving variable, where j is the index of the entering variable. If such a leaving variable exist, we will obtain a degeneracy region: as $b_i = 0$, the new optimal function will remain the same. Otherwise it means that a new optimal function will be obtained by crossing the corresponding frontier. The latter will not be treated by this algorithm, but will be computed with a task point by Algorithm 2. We maintain a list of bases which have been explored. The algorithm terminates when all the degeneracy regions of the same optimal function are found.

5 Checkers and Rational Solvers

We compared our results with those from NewPolka. We tested about 1.75 million polyhedra in our benchmarks. In only 3 cases, round-off errors caused 1 face being missed. In this section, we explain how we modified our algorithm to work around this difficulty. The resulting implementation then computes exactly solutions to parametric linear programs, and thus exactly the same polyhedra as NewPolka.

5.1 Verifying Feasibility of the Result from GLPK

GLPK uses a threshold (10^{-7} by default) to check feasibility, that is, if the solution it proposes truly is a solution. It may report a feasible result when the problem is in fact infeasible. Assume that we have an LP problem whose constraints are $C_1 : \lambda_1 \geq 0, C_2 : \lambda_2 \geq 0, C_3 : \lambda_1 + \lambda_2 \leq 10^{-8}$, GLPK will return $(0, 0)$ as a solution, whereas it is not.

We use FLINT to compute the row echelon form of the rational matrix of constraints, so that the pivots are the coefficients of basic variables. We obtain $[I\ A'] = [\boldsymbol{b}]$[6], where A' are the coefficients of the non-basic variables. When the LP problem reaches an optimum, the non-basic variables are at their lower bound 0, so the value of the basic variables are just the value of $\boldsymbol{b}$. As we have the constraints that the variables are non-negative, we thus just need to verify that all coordinates in $\boldsymbol{b}$ are non-negative. If it is not in this case, it means that GLPK does not have enough precision, which is likely due to an ill-conditioned subproblem. In this case, we start a textbook implementation of the simplex algorithm in rational arithmetic.

GLPK may also report an optimal solution which is in fact not optimized. We did not provide a checker for this situation, as even if the solution is not optimized in the required region, it is optimized in anther region which is probably adjacent to the expected one. We keep the obtained solution, and add extra task points between the regions if they are not adjacent. Besides the adjacency checker guarantees there will be no missed face.

[6] There may be rows of all zeros in the bottom of the matrix.

Algorithm 3. Algorithm to avoid overlapping regions.

```
Input: w^F: the task point
       plp^Q: the PLP problem to be solved
Output: degeneracy regions correspond to the same optimal solution
Function DiscoverNewRegion(w^F, plp^F)
    basicIdx = GlpkSolveLp(w^F, plp^F)
    if degenerate then
        size = GetSize(basicIdx)
        perturbM^Q = GetIdentityMatrix(size, size)
        basisList = none
        Insert(basisList, basicIdx)
        degBasic = none
        foreach basic variable v do
            if v == 0 then
                Insert(degBasic, GetIdx(v))
        while basisList ≠ none do
            currBasis = GetBasis(basisList)
            if currBasis has been found then
                continue
            nonBasicIdx = GetNonBasic(currBasis)
            (reconstructM^Q, perturbM^Q) = Reconstruct(plp^Q, basicIdx,
            perturbM^Q)
            (newOptimum^Q, newRegion^{Q×F}) = ExtractResult(reconstructM^Q,
            nonbasicIdx)
            activeIdx=Minimize(newRegion^F)
            minimizedR^Q = GetRational(newRegion^Q, avtiveIdx)
            Insert(optimums^Q, newOptimum^Q)
            Insert(regions^Q, newRegion^Q)
            foreach constraint i in minimizedR^Q do
                enteringV = GetIdx(i)
                leavingV = SearchLeaving(degBasic, perturbM^Q)
                if leavingV ≠ none then
                    newBasis = GetNewBasis(basicIdx, enteringV, leavingV)
                    Insert(basisList, newBasis)
```

5.2 Flat Regions

Our regions are obtained from the rational matrix, and then they are converted into floating-point representation. As the regions are normalized and intersect at the same point, they are in the shape of cones. During the conversion, the constrains will lose accuracy, and thus a cone could be misjudged as flat, meaning it has empty interior. For instance, we have a cone $\{\mathcal{C}_1 : -\frac{100000001}{10000000}x_1 + x_2 \leq 0, \mathcal{C}_2 : \frac{100000000}{10000000}x_1 - x_2 \leq 0\}$, which is not flat. After conversion, $\mathcal{C}_1$ and $\mathcal{C}_2$ will be represented in floating-point numbers as $\{\mathcal{C}_1 : -10.0x_1 + x_2 \leq 0, \mathcal{C}_2 : 10.0x_1 - x_2 \leq 0\}$, and the floating-point cone is flat.

In this case we invoke a rational simplex solver to check the region by shifting all the constraints to the interior direction. If the region becomes infeasible after shifting, then the region is really flat; otherwise we launch a rational minimization algorithm, which is implemented using Farkas' Lemma, to obtain the minimized region.

5.3 Computing an Irredundancy Witness Point

In the minimization algorithm, the checker makes sure that the constraints which cannot be determined by floating-point algorithm will be regarded as redundant constraints. In the meantime these constraints are marked as uncertainty. If the polyhedron to be minimized is also represented by rational numbers, a rational solver will be launched to determine the uncertain constraints. As in our PLP algorithm all the regions are represented by both floating-point and rational numbers, the rational solver can always be executed when there are uncertain constrains.

Consider the case of computing the irredundant witness point of the constraint $\mathcal{C}_i$, we need to solve a feasibility problem: $\mathcal{C}_i : \boldsymbol{a}_i\boldsymbol{x} < b_i$ and $\mathcal{C}_j : \boldsymbol{a}_j\boldsymbol{x} \leq b_j, \forall j \neq i$. For efficiency, we solve this problem in floating point. However, GLPK does not support strict inequalities, thus we need tricks to deal with them.

One method is to shift the inequality constraint a little and obtain a non-strict inequality $\mathcal{C}'_1 : \boldsymbol{a}_1\boldsymbol{x} \leq b_1 - \epsilon$, where ϵ is a positive constant. This method is however difficult to apply properly because of the need to find a suitable ϵ. If ϵ is small, we are likely to obtain a point too close to the constraint $\mathcal{C}_1$; if ϵ is too large, perhaps we cannot find any point. One exception is that when the polyhedron is a cone, we can always find a satisfiable point by shifting the constraints, no matter how large ϵ is.

We thus adopted another method for non-conic polyhedra. Instead of solving a satisfiability problem, we solve an optimization problem:

$$\begin{array}{ll} \text{maximize} & -\boldsymbol{a}_i\boldsymbol{x} \\ \text{subject to} & \boldsymbol{a}_j\boldsymbol{x} \leq b_j \quad \forall j \neq i \\ & \boldsymbol{a}_i\boldsymbol{x} \leq b_i \end{array} \tag{9}$$

The found optimal vertex is the solution we are looking for.

Assuming we have the polyhedron: $-x_1+x_2 \leq 0, x_1+x_2 \leq 7, -2x_2 < -3$. The two methods are shown in Fig. 3. If we compute the optimum in the direction x_2 with constraints $-x_1 + x_2 \leq 0, x_1 + x_2 \leq 7$, we obtain a feasible point $(3.5, 3.5)$.

However the floating-point solver could misjudge, thus the found optimal vertex $\boldsymbol{p}$ could be infeasible. Hence we need to test $\boldsymbol{a}_i\boldsymbol{p} \leq b_i - t$, where t is the GLPK threshold. If the test fails, we will use the rational simplex algorithm to compute the Farkas combination: the constraint is really irredundant if the combination does not exist.

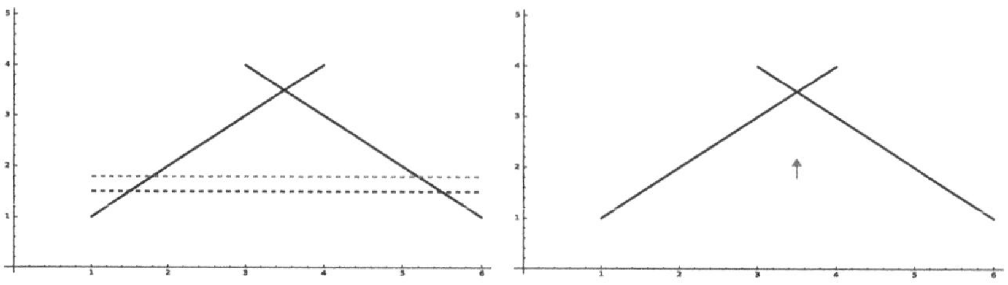

Fig. 3. Solving an optimization problem instead of a feasibility problem.

5.4 Adjacency Checker

We shall now prove that no face is missed if and only if for each region and each boundary of this region, another region is found which shares that boundary.

Assuming we have a situation shown in Fig. 4: the four regions correspond to different optimal functions. $\mathcal{R}_1, \mathcal{R}_2$ and $\mathcal{R}_3$ all found their adjacencies, but $\mathcal{R}_4$ is missed. In this case there exist two adjacent regions for some boundaries. We here show that this situation will not happen.

Theorem 4. *No face will be missed if each region finds all the adjacent regions.*

Proof. Assume that we cross the boundary $\mathcal{F}$ of the region $\mathcal{R}_i$, and the adjacent regions are $\mathcal{R}_j$ and $\mathcal{R}_k$. The corresponding optimal functions are Z_j and Z_k, and $Z_j \neq Z_k$ (otherwise no face will be missed). From $\mathcal{R}_i$ to its adjacency, we need to do one pivoting. Consider the simplex tableau in Table 1. Assuming the entering variable is λ_q. If there are two adjacent regions, there will be two possible leaving variables, say λ_r and λ_s. In the simplex algorithm we always choose the variable with the smallest ratio of the constant and the coefficient as the leaving variable. When there are two possible leaving variables, the value of these two ratios must be equal, that is $\frac{b_j}{a_{jq}} = \frac{b_k}{a_{kq}}$. In this case we face the primal degeneracy, and $f^*(\boldsymbol{x}) - \frac{b_j}{a_{jq}} f_q = f^*(\boldsymbol{x}) - \frac{b_k}{a_{kq}} f_q$. This is a contradictory to the assumption $Z_j \neq Z_k$. Hence the situation will not happen. □

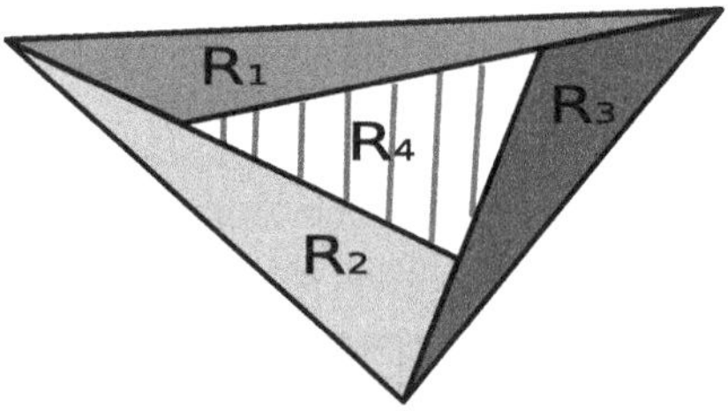

Fig. 4. Example of missing faces.

To find out all the faces, we just need to ensure that all the regions have their adjacencies. Although we tried to add task points between the regions which are not adjacent, there may be still missed region because of floating-point arithmetic. Hence we invoke an adjacency checker at the end of the algorithm. The information of adjacency has been saved in Algorithm 2: if the regions $\mathcal{R}_i$ and $\mathcal{R}_j$ are adjacent by crossing the boundaries $\mathcal{F}_m$ and $\mathcal{F}_n$, we set true to $(\mathcal{R}_i, \mathcal{F}_m)$ and $(\mathcal{R}_j, \mathcal{F}_n)$ in the adjacency table. The checker will find out the pair $(\mathcal{R}_k, \mathcal{F}_p)$ whose flag of adjacency is false. Then we cross the boundary $\mathcal{F}_p$ and use Algorithm 3 to compute the missed region and the corresponding optimal function. The adjacencies of the new obtained region will be checked then, and the algorithm terminates when all the obtained regions have complete adjacencies.

6 Experiments

In this section, we analyze the performance of our parametric linear programming solver on projection operations. We compare its performance with that of the NewPolka library of Apron[7] and ELINA library [21]. Since NewPolka and ELINA do not exploit parallelism, we compare it to our library running with only one thread.

We used three libraries in our implementation:

- Eigen 3.3.2 for floating-point vector and matrix operations;
- FLINT 2.5.2 for rational arithmetic, vector and matrix operations;
- GLPK 4.6.4 for solving linear programs in floating-point.

The experiments are carried out on 2.30 GHz Intel Core i5-6200U CPU.

6.1 Experiments on Random Polyhedra

Benchmarks. The benchmark contains randomly-generated polyhedra, in which the coefficients of constraints are in the range of −50 to 50. Each polyhedron has 4 parameters: number of constraints (CN), number of variables (VN), projection ratio(PR) and density (D). The projection ratio is the proportion of eliminated variables: for example if we eliminate 6 variables out of 10, the projection ratio is 60%. Density represents the ratio of zero coefficients: if there are 2 zeros in 10 coefficients, density is 20%. In each experiment, we project 10 polyhedra generated with the same parameters. To smooth out experimental noise, we do each experiment 5 times, i.e., 50 executions for each set of parameters. Then we calculate the average execution time of the 50 executions.

Experimental Results. We illustrate the execution time (in seconds) by line charts. The blue line is the performance of NewPolka library of Apron, and the red line is that of our serial PLP algorithm. To illustrate the performance benefits from the floating-point arithmetic, we turned off GLPK and always use

[7] https://github.com/antoinemine/apron.

the rational LP solver, and the execution time is shown by the orange lines[8]. It is shown that solving the LP problems in floating-point numbers and reconstructing the rational simplex tableau leads to significant improvement of performance.

By a mount of experiments, we found that when the parameters $CN = 19, VN = 8, PR = 62.5\%$ and $D = 37.5\%$, the execution time of PLP and Apron are similar, so we maintain three of them and vary the other to analyze the variation of performance.

Recall that in order to give a constraint description of the projection of a convex polyhedron P in constraint description, Apron (and all libraries based on the same approach, including PPL) computes a generator description of P, projects it and then computes a minimized constraint description.

Projection Ratio. In Fig. 5a we can see that execution time of PLP is almost the same for all the cases, whereas that of Apron changes significantly. Apron incurs a large cost when it computes the generator representation of each polyhedron. We plot the execution time of PLP (Fig. 5c) and the number of regions (Fig. 5d), which vary with the same trend. That means the cost of our approach depends mostly on the number of regions to be explored. To illustrate it more clearly, the zoomed figure is shown in Fig. 5b.

The more variables are eliminated, the lower dimension the projected polyhedron has. Then the cost of chernikova's algorithm to convert from the generators into the constraints will be less. This explains why Apron is slow when the projection ratio is low, and becomes faster when the number of eliminated variable is larger.

Number of Constraints. Keep the other parameters, we increase the number of constraints from 12 to 30. The result is shown in Fig. 6. We can see that Apron is faster than PLP when constraints are fewer than 19; beyond that, its execution time increases significantly. In contrast, the execution time of PLP grows much more slowly.

Number of Variables. Here the range of variables is 3 to 15. Figure 7a shows that the performance are similar for Apron and PLP when variables are fewer than 11, but after that the execution time of Apron explodes as the variable number increases. The zoomed figure is shown in Fig. 7b.

Our understanding is that the execution time of Apron is dominated by the conversion to the generator description, which is exponential in the number of constraints for polyhedra resembling hypercubes—likely for a nonempty polyhedron built from m random constraints in a space of dimension less than m.

Density. The Fig. 8 shows the effect of density. The execution time varies for both Apron and PLP with the increase of density, with the same trend.

[8] The minimization is still computed in floating-point numbers.

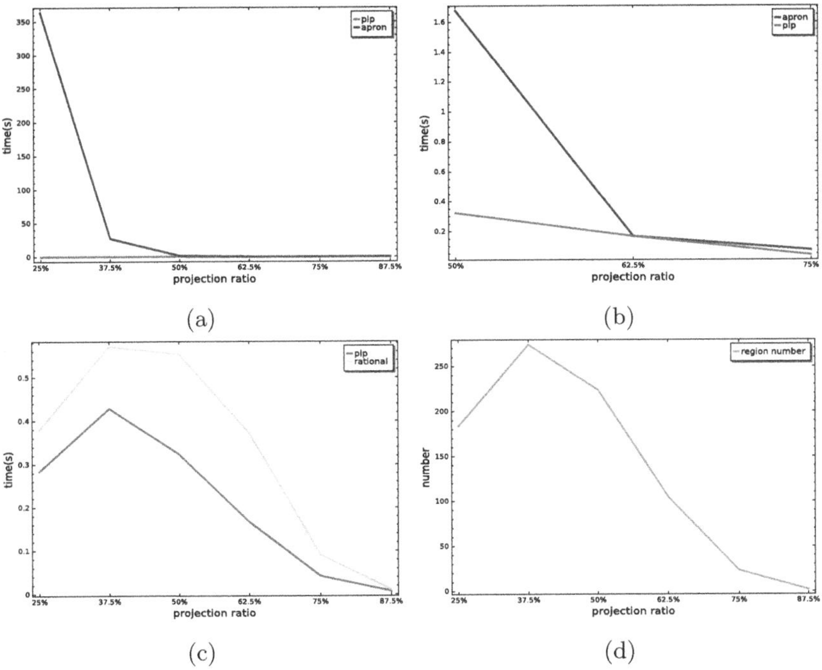

Fig. 5. CN = 19, VN = 8, D = 37.5%, PR = [25%, 87.5%]

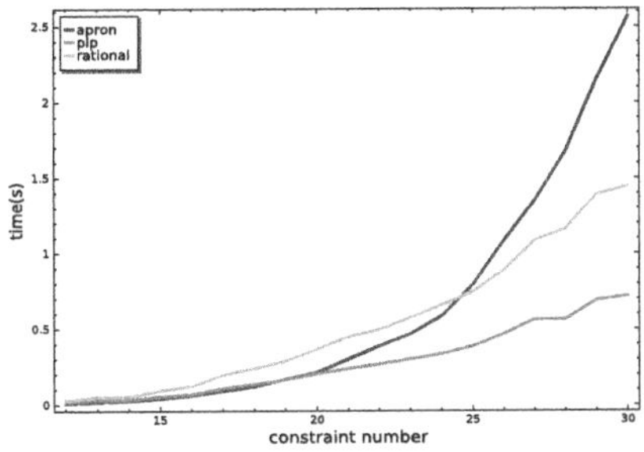

Fig. 6. CN = [12, 30], VN = 8, D = 37.5%, PR = 62.5%

6.2 Experiments on SV-COMP Benchmarks

In this experiment we used the analyzer Pagai [12] and SV-COMP benchmarks [2]. We randomly selected C programs from the category of Concurrency Safety, Software System and Reach Safety. The result is compared with NewPolka and ELINA. In Table 2, we show the name of programs, the number of polyhedra to be projected (Num), the total and average time (AveT) spent on projection, the average constraint number (ACN) and the average variable number (AVN).

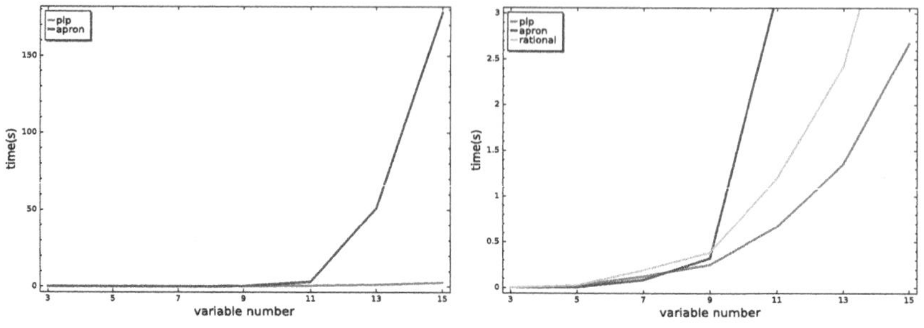

(a) (b)

Fig. 7. CN = 19, VN = [3, 15], D = 37.5%, PR = 62.5%

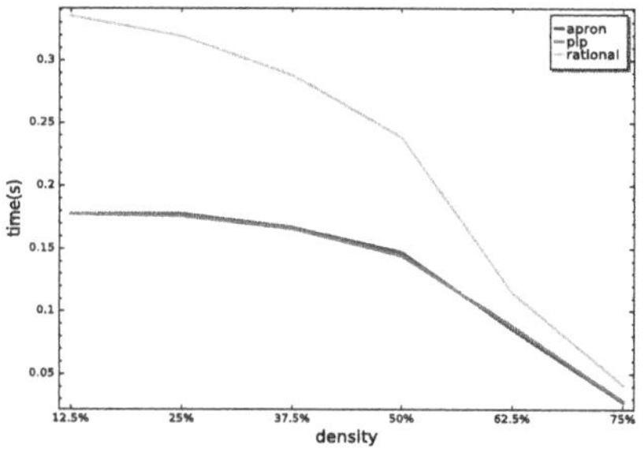

Fig. 8. CN = 19,VN = 8, D = [12.5%,75%], PR = 62.5%

The time is in milliseconds. As it is shown, our algorithm has advantage over Apron when the polyhedra contain more constraints and/or in higher dimension, e.g, polyhedra in ldv-linux-3.0-module-loop and ldv-linux-3.0-bluetooth, as we get rid of maintaining double description. ELINA is the most efficient.

6.3 Analysis

We conclude that our approach has remarkable advantage over Apron for projecting polyhedra in large dimension (large number of constraints or/and variables); it is not good choice for solving problems with few constraints in small dimension.

Our serial algorithm is less efficient than ELINA, but our approach is parallelable and is able to speed up with multiple threads.

Table 2. Performance on SV-COMP benchmarks.

Program	Num	Apron	AveT	ELINA	AveT	PLP	AveT	ACN	AVN
pthread-complex-buffer	405	116.03	0.29	71.46	0.18	128.56	0.32	3.25	3.06
ldv-linux-3.0-module-loop	10745	**6148.74**	0.57	2346.16	0.22	**3969.44**	0.37	3.16	**16.19**
ssh-clnt-01.csv	17655	5081.45	0.29	3123.7	0.18	5664.97	0.32	3.53	2.61
ldv-consumption-firewire	30650	13763.71	0.45	8574.01	0.28	21493.57	0.7	7.19	6.14
busybox-1.22.0-head3	18340	13686.23	0.75	6930.74	0.38	23971.92	1.31	10.94	6.14
ldv-linux-3.0-magicmouse	20	6.6	0.33	4.24	0.21	10.3	0.52	5	5
ldv-linux-3.0-usb-input	1230	327.22	0.27	198.0	0.16	356.71	0.29	3	2
bitvector-gcd	240	78.14	0.33	46.06	0.19	174.55	0.73	5	3
array-example-sorting	5395	1769.75	0.33	1081.45	0.2	3413.21	0.63	4.78	3.67
ldv-linux-3.0-bluetooth	15250	**3898819.28**	255.66	37477.14	2.46	**190001.11**	12.46	**20.62**	**17.66**
ssh-srvr-01	82500	35806.67	0.43	20170.35	0.24	98763.8	1.2	5.91	4.68

7 Conclusion and Future Work

We have presented an algorithm to project convex polyhedra via parametric linear programming. It internally uses floating-point numbers, and then the exact result is constructed over the rationals. Due to floating-point round-off errors, some faces may be missed by the main pass of our algorithm. However, we can detect this situation and recover the missing faces using an exact solver.

We currently store the regions that have been explored into an unstructured array; checking whether an optimization direction is covered by an existing region is done by linear search. This could be improved in two ways: (i) regions corresponding to the same optimum (primal degeneracy) could be merged into a single region; (ii) regions could be stored in a structure allowing fast search. For instance, we could use a binary tree where each node is labeled with a hyperplane, and each path from the root corresponds to a conjunction of half-spaces; then each region is stored only in the paths such that the associated half-spaces intersects the region.

References

1. Bagnara, R., Hill, P.M., Zaffanella, E.: The parma polyhedra library: toward a complete set of numerical abstractions for the analysis and verification of hardware and software systems. Sci. Comput. Program. **72**(1), 3–21 (2008)
2. Beyer, D.: Automatic verification of C and Java programs: SV-COMP 2019. In: Beyer, D., Huisman, M., Kordon, F., Steffen, B. (eds.) TACAS 2019. LNCS, vol. 11429, pp. 133–155. Springer, Cham (2019). https://doi.org/10.1007/978-3-030-17502-3_9
3. Bland, R.G.: New finite pivoting rules for the simplex method. Math. Oper. Res. **2**(2), 103–107 (1977)
4. Chernikova, N.: Algorithm for discovering the set of all the solutions of a linear programming problem. USSR Comput. Math. Math. Phys. **8**(6), 282–293 (1968)
5. Coti, C., Monniaux, D., Yu, H.: Parallel parametric linear programming solving, and application to polyhedral computations. In: Rodrigues, J.M.F., et al. (eds.) ICCS 2019. LNCS, vol. 11540, pp. 566–572. Springer, Cham (2019). https://doi.org/10.1007/978-3-030-22750-0_52

6. Cousot, P., Cousot, R.: Abstract interpretation: a unified lattice model for static analysis of programs by construction or approximation of fixpoints. In: Proceedings of the 4th ACM SIGACT-SIGPLAN Symposium on Principles of Programming Languages, pp. 238–252. ACM (1977)
7. Cousot, P., Halbwachs, N.: Automatic discovery of linear restraints among variables of a program. In: Proceedings of the 5th ACM SIGACT-SIGPLAN Symposium on Principles of Programming Languages, pp. 84–96. ACM (1978)
8. Dantzig, G.B.: Application of the simplex method to a transportation problem. In: Activity Analysis and Production and Allocation (1951)
9. Dantzig, G.B.: Fourier-motzkin elimination and its dual. Technical report, Stanford Univ CA Dept of Operations Research (1972)
10. Dantzig, G.B., Thapa, M.N.: Linear Programming 2: Theory and Extensions. Springer, New York (2006)
11. Fouilhé, A.: Revisiting the abstract domain of polyhedra: constraints-only representation and formal proof. Ph.D. thesis, Université Grenoble Alpes (2015)
12. Henry, J., Monniaux, D., Moy, M.: PAGAI: a path sensitive static analyser. Electron. Notes Theor. Comput. Sci. **289**, 15–25 (2012)
13. Jones, C.N., Kerrigan, E.C., Maciejowski, J.M.: Lexicographic perturbation for multiparametric linear programming with applications to control. Automatica **43**(10), 1808–1816 (2007)
14. Jones, C.N., Kerrigan, E.C., Maciejowski, J.M.: On polyhedral projection and parametric programming. J. Optim. Theory Appl. **138**(2), 207–220 (2008)
15. King, T., Barrett, C., Tinelli, C.: Leveraging linear and mixed integer programming for SMT. In: Proceedings of the 14th Conference on Formal Methods in Computer-Aided Design, pp. 139–146. FMCAD Inc. (2014)
16. Le Verge, H.: A note on Chernikova's algorithm. Technical report 635, IRISA (1992). https://www.irisa.fr/polylib/document/cher.ps.gz
17. Maréchal, A.: New Algorithmics for Polyhedral Calculus via Parametric Linear Programming. Theses, UGA - Université Grenoble Alpes, December 2017. https://hal.archives-ouvertes.fr/tel-01695086
18. Maréchal, A., Monniaux, D., Périn, M.: Scalable minimizing-operators on polyhedra via parametric linear programming. In: Ranzato, F. (ed.) SAS 2017. LNCS, vol. 10422, pp. 212–231. Springer, Cham (2017). https://doi.org/10.1007/978-3-319-66706-5_11
19. Maréchal, A., Périn, M.: Efficient elimination of redundancies in polyhedra by raytracing. In: Bouajjani, A., Monniaux, D. (eds.) VMCAI 2017. LNCS, vol. 10145, pp. 367–385. Springer, Cham (2017). https://doi.org/10.1007/978-3-319-52234-0_20
20. Monniaux, D.: On using floating-point computations to help an exact linear arithmetic decision procedure. In: Bouajjani, A., Maler, O. (eds.) CAV 2009. LNCS, vol. 5643, pp. 570–583. Springer, Heidelberg (2009). https://doi.org/10.1007/978-3-642-02658-4_42
21. Singh, G., Püschel, M., Vechev, M.: Fast polyhedra abstract domain. ACM SIGPLAN Not. **52**, 46–59 (2017)

Analysis of Software Patches Using Numerical Abstract Interpretation

David Delmas[1,2(✉)] and Antoine Miné[2,3]

[1] Airbus Operations S.A.S, 316 route de Bayonne, 31060 Toulouse Cedex 9, France
david.delmas@airbus.com
[2] Sorbonne Université, CNRS, LIP6, 75005 Paris, France
antoine.mine@lip6.fr
[3] Institut universitaire de France, 1 rue Descartes, 75231 Paris Cedex 5, France

Abstract. We present a static analysis for software patches. Given two syntactically close versions of a program, our analysis can infer a semantic difference, and prove that both programs compute the same outputs when run on the same inputs. Our method is based on abstract interpretation, and parametric in the choice of an abstract domain. We focus on numeric properties only. Our method is able to deal with unbounded executions of infinite-state programs, reading from infinite input streams. Yet, it is limited to comparing terminating executions, ignoring non terminating ones.

We first present a novel concrete collecting semantics, expressing the behaviors of both programs at the same time. Then, we propose an abstraction of infinite input streams able to prove that programs that read from the same stream compute equal output values. We then show how to leverage classic numeric abstract domains, such as polyhedra or octagons, to build an effective static analysis. We also introduce a novel numeric domain to bound differences between the values of the variables in the two programs, which has linear cost, and the right amount of relationality to express useful properties of software patches.

We implemented a prototype and experimented on a few small examples from the literature. Our prototype operates on a toy language, and assumes a joint syntactic representation of two versions of a program given, which distinguishes between common and distinctive parts.

1 Introduction

The problem of proving the functional equivalence of programs, or program parts, is fundamental [7]. It aims at comparing the behaviors of two programs running in the same environment, *i.e.* their input-output relationships. In this paper, we describe a static analysis which aims at inferring that two syntactically close versions of a program compute equal outputs, when run on equal inputs.

This work is performed as part of a collaborative partnership between Sorbonnne Université/CNRS (LIP6) and Airbus. This work is partially supported by the European Research Council under the Consolidator Grant Agreement 681393 – MOPSA.

B.-Y. E. Chang (Ed.): SAS 2019, LNCS 11822, pp. 225–246, 2019.
https://doi.org/10.1007/978-3-030-32304-2_12

```
     /* Like fstatat, but cache the result.  If ST->st_size is -1, the
        status has not been gotten yet.  If less than -1, fstatat failed
-       with errno == -1 - ST->st_size.  Otherwise, the status has already
+       with errno == ST->st_ino.  Otherwise, the status has already
        been gotten, so return 0.  */
     static int
     cache_fstatat (int fd, char const *file, struct stat *st, int flag)
     {
       if (st->st_size == -1 && fstatat (fd, file, st, flag) != 0)
-        st->st_size = -1 - errno;
+        {
+          st->st_size = -2;
+          st->st_ino = errno;
+        }
       if (0 <= st->st_size)
         return 0;
-      errno = -1 - st->st_size;
+      errno = (int) st->st_ino;
       return -1;
     }
```

Fig. 1. Patch on remove.c of Coreutils (between v6.10 and v6.11)

The main application of this analysis is regression verification [8]: prove that a program change does not add any undesirable behavior. Take, for instance, the commit shown on Fig. 1, extracted from a revision control repository of the GNU core utilities. It describes a change in a library implementing core functions for removing files and directories, and used by the POSIX rm command. The main function of this library uses the POSIX fstatat function to read information on the file to delete. As the same status information is needed in several contexts, the library implements a caching mechanism. At initialization, the main function calls a cache_stat_init function, which initializes the st_size field of the stat structure *st to -1. Then, it calls the cache_fstatat function shown on Fig. 1 repeatedly, whenever status information is needed. Indeed, cache_fstatat caches the results of the fstatat function. In revision v6.10 of Coreutils, this function used the st_size field of the stat structure *st to store information on the error value returned by fstatat upon the first call. It did it in a way that ensures that st_size<0 whenever errno > 0, so as to use the sign of st_size upon subsequent calls, to distinguish between successful and erroneous executions. This scheme works for operating systems where errno is always set to positive values. However, some systems, such as BeOS [1] and Haiku [2], allow for negative errno values. The fix displayed on Fig. 1 aims at accommodating such systems. It consists in storing errno directly in the st_ino field of the stat structure.

On this example, non regression verification amounts to proving that the behavior of the main function of the library is unchanged on systems with only positive error values. This is, indeed, validated by our analysis. The analyzed

```
for (c=0; c<n; c++) cache_stat_init (&file[c].st);

while ((c=getchar()) >= 0 && c < n)
  r = cache_fstatat (AT_FDCWD, file[c].name, &file[c].st,
        AT_SYMLINK_NOFOLLOW);
```

Fig. 2. Execution environments for cache_fstatat

source code includes a stub variable for errno, and stub code for the fstatat function. The stub for fstatat updates errno with a non-deterministic value, ranging over positive integers. Note that a separate analysis of the cache_fstatat function, as opposed to an analysis of the whole library, makes it necessary to model its possible execution environments with an unbounded loop, calling cache_fstatat an arbitrary number of times, with parameters taken from an arbitrary sequence of file names and stat structures. This unbounded sequence is modeled, in practice, using an unbounded number of reads from an input stream. Figure 2 shows an example for n files, where n may be unbounded.

More generally, we are interested in analyzing patches of programs reading an unbounded number of input values, e.g. programs reading from file or I/O streams, and embedded reactive software with internal state, which no related work addresses. Or goal is to prove that the original and patched versions of such programs compute equal outputs, when run with the same sequence of inputs. We therefore model streams directly in the semantics on which our analysis is based (see Sect. 2).

Running Example. In the following, we sketch our approach to the analysis of semantic differences between two syntactically similar programs P_1 and P_2. We are interested in proving that P_1 and P_2 compute equal outputs when run on equal inputs. P_1 and P_2 are represented together in the syntax of a so-called double program P. Simple programs P_1 and P_2 are referred to as the left and right projections of P. Figure 3 shows the Unchloop example, taken from [24], and translated into our syntax of double programs. The $\|$ symbol is used to represent syntactic difference. It is available at expression, condition, and statement levels in our syntax for double programs. For instance at line 3, $c \leftarrow 1 \| 0$ means $c \leftarrow 1$ for P_1, and $c \leftarrow 0$ for P_2. In contrast, line 4 means $i \leftarrow 0$ for both P_1 and P_2.

Let us describe the example program. Both versions P_1 and P_2 read inputs in the range $[-1000, 1000]$ into a and b at lines 1 and 2. At line 3, the counter c is being initialised with value 1 for program P_1, and value 0 for program P_2. Then, both programs add a times the value of b to c in a loop. Finally, they both store the result into r at line 9: c for P_1, c+1 for P_2. The assertion at line 10 expresses the property we would like to check: if both programs reach it, then they should have computed equal values for r.

We assume here that both programs read the same input value in a, and the same input value in b. More generally, the semantics of P is parameterized by a (possibly infinite) sequence of input values, and we wish to prove that, given the same sequence of input values, P_1 and P_2 have the same result in r.

```
1 :  a ← input(−1000, 1000);
2 :  b ← input(−1000, 1000);
3 :  c ← 1 || 0;
4 :  i ← 0;
5 :  while (i < a) {
6 :      c ← c + b;
7 :      i ← i + 1;
8 :  }
9 :  r ← c || c + 1;
10 : assert_sync(r);
```

Fig. 3. Unchloop example

```
1 : x ← input(−100, 100);
2 : if (x < 0) x ← −1;
3 : else {
4 :      if (x ≥ 2 || x ≥ 4) {} // x > 4 in original paper
5 :      else {
6 :         while (i = 2) x ← 2;
7 :         x ← 3;
8 :      }
9 :  }
10 : assert_sync(x); // x = 2 ignored
```

Fig. 4. Modified [24, Fig. 2] example.

The assertion at line 10 of our example is thus valid. It is, indeed, validated by our analysis.

Limitations. Our analysis is based on abstractions of a concrete collecting semantics which will be presented in Sect. 2. This semantics relates pairs of terminating executions of projections of a double program. It is suitable to prove a number of properties, including that two terminating programs starting from equal initial states will produce equal outputs, a notion called partial equivalence in [8]. In contrast, an analysis based on this collecting semantics will fail to report differences between pairs of executions where at least one of the programs does not terminate. For instance, in the example on Fig. 4, our analysis does not report any difference between P_1 and P_2, although P_1 terminates on input $x = 2$, and P_2 does not.

As opposed to [21,22], which develop algorithms to automate the construction of a correlating program $P_1 \bowtie P_2$, on which to run the static analysis, we assume for now the joint representation of P_1 and P_2 given, as part of a double program in our toy language.

Related Work. [11] pioneered the field of semantic differencing between two versions of a procedure by comparing dependencies between input and output variables. Symbolic execution methods [19,23,24] have proposed analysis techniques for programs with small state space and bounded loops, which may support modular regression verification. On the contrary, we can handle programs with unbounded loops and an infinite number of execution paths, like the example of Figs. 1 and 2. Some approaches [16] combine symbolic execution and program analysis techniques to improve the coverage of patches with tests suites, but such testing coverage criteria bring no formal guarantee of correctness, unlike our method.

RVT [8] and SymDiff [14,15] combine two versions of the same program, with equality constraints on their inputs, and compile equivalence properties into verification conditions to be checked by SMT solvers. On the contrary, we rely on abstract domains to infer equivalence properties.

The DIZY [21,22] tool leverages numerical abstract interpretation to establish equivalence under abstraction. In particular, the authors give a semi-formal description of an operational concrete trace semantics. This semantics is not defined by induction on the syntax, and does not support streams. Our main contribution, with respect to this work, is a novel, fully formalized, denotational concrete collecting semantics by induction on the syntax, which can deal with programs reading from infinite input streams, and a novel numeric domain to bound differences between the values of the variables in the two programs. Another difference is that [21,22] rely on program transformations to build a correlating program, which they analyze according to simple program semantics, while our semantics is defined for double programs directly.

The Fluctuat [9,17] static analyser compares the real and floating-point semantics of numeric programs to bound errors in floating-point computations. The authors use the zonotope abstract domain to bound the difference between real and floating-point values. Like in our concrete semantics, they also address unstable test analysis [10].

Contributions. The main contributions of this work are:

- We present a novel concrete collecting semantics, expressing the behaviors of two versions of a program at the same time. This semantics deals with programs reading from unbounded input streams.
- We propose an abstraction of infinite input streams able to prove that programs that read from the same stream compute equal output values.
- We introduce a novel numeric domain to bound differences between the values of the variables in the two programs, which has linear cost, and the right amount of relationality to express useful properties of software patches.
- We implemented a prototype static analyzer which exhibits significant speedups with respect to previous works.

We build on previous work [6]. The main contributions of the current paper, with respect to this work, is a formal treatment of infinite input streams, in the concrete and abstract semantics.

The paper is organised as follows. Section 2 formalizes the concrete collecting semantics, and illustrates it on the example from Fig. 3. Section 3 describes the abstract semantics, discusses the choice of numeric abstract domains, and introduces a novel numeric domain. Section 4 presents experimental results with a prototype implementation. Section 5 concludes.

$$\begin{array}{rcll} stat & ::= & V \leftarrow expr & V \in \mathcal{V} \\ & | & V \leftarrow \mathbf{input}(a, b) & a, b \in \mathbb{R} \\ & | & \mathbf{if}\ cond\ \mathbf{then}\ stat\ \mathbf{else}\ stat & \\ & | & \mathbf{while}\ cond\ \mathbf{do}\ stat & \\ & | & stat; stat & \\ & | & \mathbf{skip} & \end{array}$$

(a) Simple statements

$$\begin{array}{rcll} expr & ::= & V & V \in \mathcal{V} \\ & | & c & c \in \mathbb{R} \\ & | & -expr & \\ & | & expr \diamond expr & \diamond \in \{+, -, \times, /\} \\ & | & \mathbf{rand}(a, b) & a, b \in \mathbb{R} \\ cond & ::= & expr \bowtie expr & \bowtie \in \{\leq, \geq, =, \neq, <, >\} \\ & | & \neg cond & \\ & | & cond \diamond cond & \diamond \in \{\wedge, \vee\} \end{array}$$

(b) Simple expressions and conditions

$$\begin{array}{rcll} dstat & ::= & stat & \\ & | & stat \parallel stat & \\ & | & V \leftarrow dexpr & V \in \mathcal{V} \\ & | & \mathbf{assert\_sync}(V) & \\ & | & dstat; dstat & \\ & | & \mathbf{if}\ dcond\ \mathbf{then}\ dstat\ \mathbf{else}\ dstat & \\ & | & \mathbf{while}\ dcond\ \mathbf{do}\ dstat & \end{array}$$

(c) Double statements

$$\begin{array}{rcl} dexpr & ::= & expr \\ & | & expr \parallel expr \\ dcond & ::= & cond \\ & | & cond \parallel cond \end{array}$$

(d) Double expressions and conditions

Fig. 5. Syntax of simple and double programs

2 Syntax and Concrete Semantics

Following the standard approach to abstract interpretation [4], we developed a concrete collecting semantics for a toy While language for double programs. The $\parallel$ operator may occur anywhere in the parse tree, to denote syntactic differences between the left and right projections of a double program. However, $\parallel$ operators cannot be nested: a double program only describes a pair of programs.

Given double program P with variables in $\mathcal{V}$, consider its left (resp. right) projection $P_1 = \pi_1(P)$ (resp. $P_2 = \pi_2(P)$), where π_1 (resp. π_2) is a projection operator defined by induction on the syntax, keeping only the left (resp. right) side of $\parallel$ symbols. For instance, $\pi_1(c \leftarrow 1 \parallel 0) = c \leftarrow 1$, and $\pi_2(c \leftarrow 1 \parallel 0) = c \leftarrow 0$, while $\pi_1(i \leftarrow 0) = i \leftarrow 0 = \pi_2(i \leftarrow 0)$.

2.1 Simple Programs

P_1 and P_2 are simple programs, with concrete memory states in $\mathcal{E} \triangleq \mathcal{V} \to \mathbb{R}$. Let $k \in \{1; 2\}$. The syntax of simple program P_k is standard. Statements *stat* are presented in Fig. 5(a). They are built on top of numeric expressions *expr* and Boolean conditions *cond*, defined in Fig. 5(b). To define the semantics of simple program P_k, we leverage standard, relational, input-output semantics, defined by induction on the syntax, in denotational style. Given $\mathbb{E}[\![e]\!] \in \mathcal{E} \to \mathcal{P}(\mathbb{R})$ for non-deterministic expression $e \in expr$, and $\mathbb{C}[\![c]\!] \in \mathcal{E} \to \mathcal{P}(\{\text{true}, \text{false}\})$ for condition $c \in cond$, we let $\mathbb{S}[\![s]\!]$ describe the relation between input and output states of statement $s \in stat$. Because of the **input** command, which reads some input stream, $\mathbb{S}[\![s]\!]$ is parameterised by a sequence of values, and program states record the current index in this sequence. Note that this sequence has to be infinite: indeed, due to non-determinism, the concrete semantics maps every input stream to a (possibly infinite) set of executions, which can execute an unbounded number of input statements. Therefore $\mathbb{S}[\![s]\!] \in \mathbb{R}^\omega \to \mathcal{P}(\mathcal{E}' \times \mathcal{E}')$, where $\mathcal{E}' \triangleq \mathcal{E} \times \mathbb{N}$, and:

$$\mathbb{S}[\![V \leftarrow \textbf{input}(a,b)]\!]\sigma \triangleq \{ ((\rho,n),(\rho[V \mapsto \sigma_n], n+1)) \mid (\rho,n) \in \mathcal{E}' \wedge a \leq \sigma_n \leq b \}$$

Note that we model one input stream only, but the generalization to several input streams is obvious. We do not display the semantics for other commands, as the semantics for assignments and tests are standard for memory environments, and leave indexes unchanged. For instance, $\mathbb{S}[\![V \leftarrow e]\!]\sigma \triangleq \{ ((\rho,n),(\rho[V \mapsto v],n)) \mid (\rho,n) \in \mathcal{E}' \wedge v \in \mathbb{E}[\![e]\!]\rho \}$.

2.2 Double Programs

We then lift the semantics $\mathbb{S}$ to double programs. As P_1 and P_2 have concrete states in $\mathcal{E}'$, P has concrete states in $\mathcal{D}' \triangleq \mathcal{E}' \times \mathcal{E}'$. The syntax of double statements *dstat* is shown in Fig. 5(c). They are built on top of double expressions *dexpr* and double conditions *dcond*, defined in Fig. 5(d). The semantics of a double statement $s \in dstat$, denoted $\mathbb{D}[\![s]\!] \in \mathbb{R}^\omega \rightarrow \mathcal{P}(\mathcal{D}' \times \mathcal{D}')$, describes the relation between input and output states of s, which are pairs of states of simple programs, for a given shared sequence of input values. The definition for $\mathbb{D}[\![s]\!]$ is shown on Fig. 6, in relational style. It is defined by induction on the syntax, so as to allow for modular, joint analyses of double programs that maintain input-output relations on the variables. Note that $\mathbb{D}$ is parametric in $\mathbb{S}$.

The semantics for the empty program is the diagonal, identity relation $\Delta_{\mathcal{D}'}$. The semantics $\mathbb{D}[\![s_1 \parallel s_2]\!]$ for the composition of two syntactically different statements reverts to the pairing of the simple program semantics of individual simple statements s_1 and s_2. Note that $\mathbb{D}[\![s_1 \parallel s_2]\!]\sigma = \mathbb{D}[\![s_1 \parallel \textbf{skip}]\!]\sigma \,⨾\, \mathbb{D}[\![\textbf{skip} \parallel s_2]\!]\sigma$ for any $\sigma \in \mathbb{R}^\omega$, where we use the symbol ⨾ to denote the left composition of relations: $R_1 ⨾ R_2 \triangleq \{ (x,z) \mid \exists y : (x,y) \in R_1 \wedge (y,z) \in R_2 \}$. The semantics for assignments of double expressions $\mathbb{D}[\![V \leftarrow e_1 \parallel e_2]\!]$ (different expressions to the same variable) is defined using this construct. The interest of double expressions in the syntax is to allow for simple symbolic simplifications in later abstraction steps, when computing differences between expressions assigned to a variable. The semantics of **assert_sync**(V) statements asserts that the left and right projections of a double program agree on the value of variable V. The semantics for the sequential composition of statements boils down to the composition of the semantics of individual statements. The semantics for selection statements relies on the filter $\mathbb{F}[\![c_1 \parallel c_2]\!]$ to distinguish between cases where both projections agree on the value of the controlling expression, and cases where they do not (*a.k.a.* unstable tests). There are two stable and two unstable test cases, according to the evaluations of the two conditions. The semantics for stable test cases is standard. The semantics for unstable test cases is defined by composing the left restriction of the left projection $\pi_1(s) \parallel \textbf{skip}$ and the right restriction of the right projection $\textbf{skip} \parallel \pi_2(t)$ of the **then** s and **else** t branches. Intuitively, $\pi_1(s) \parallel \textbf{skip}$ means that the left projection of the double program executes s, while the right projection of the double program does nothing. The semantics for (possibly unbounded) iteration statements is defined using the least fixpoint of a function defined similarly.

$$\mathbb{D}[\![\, dstat \,]\!] \in \mathbb{R}^{\omega} \to \mathcal{P}(\mathcal{D}' \times \mathcal{D}')$$

$$\begin{array}{ll}
\mathbb{D}[\![\, \mathbf{skip} \,]\!]\sigma & \triangleq \Delta_{\mathcal{D}'} \\
\mathbb{D}[\![\, s_1 \parallel s_2 \,]\!]\sigma & \triangleq \{\, ((i_1, i_2), (o_1, o_2)) \mid (i_1, o_1) \in \mathbb{S}[\![\, s_1 \,]\!]\sigma \wedge (i_2, o_2) \in \mathbb{S}[\![\, s_2 \,]\!]\sigma \,\} \\
\mathbb{D}[\![\, V \leftarrow e_1 \parallel e_2 \,]\!]\sigma & \triangleq \mathbb{D}[\![\, V \leftarrow e_1 \parallel V \leftarrow e_2 \,]\!]\sigma \\
\mathbb{D}[\![\, V \leftarrow e \,]\!]\sigma & \triangleq \mathbb{D}[\![\, V \leftarrow e \parallel V \leftarrow e \,]\!]\sigma \\
\mathbb{D}[\![\, V \leftarrow \mathbf{input}(a, b) \,]\!]\sigma & \triangleq \mathbb{D}[\![\, V \leftarrow \mathbf{input}(a, b) \parallel V \leftarrow \mathbf{input}(a, b) \,]\!]\sigma \\
\mathbb{D}[\![\, \mathbf{assert_sync}(V) \,]\!]\sigma & \triangleq \{\, (((\rho_1, n_1), (\rho_2, n_2)), ((\rho_1, n_1), (\rho_2, n_2))) \mid \rho_1(V) = \rho_2(V) \,\} \\
\mathbb{D}[\![\, s\, ;\, t \,]\!]\sigma & \triangleq \mathbb{D}[\![\, s \,]\!]\sigma \,;\, \mathbb{D}[\![\, t \,]\!]\sigma \\
\mathbb{D}[\![\, \mathbf{if}\ c_1 \parallel c_2\ \mathbf{then}\ s\ \mathbf{else}\ t \,]\!]\sigma & \triangleq \mathbb{F}[\![\, c_1 \parallel c_2 \,]\!] \,;\, \mathbb{D}[\![\, s \,]\!]\sigma \\
& \cup\, \mathbb{F}[\![\, c_1 \parallel \neg c_2 \,]\!] \,;\, \mathbb{D}[\![\, \pi_1(s) \parallel \mathbf{skip} \,]\!]\sigma \,;\, \mathbb{D}[\![\, \mathbf{skip} \parallel \pi_2(t) \,]\!]\sigma \\
& \cup\, \mathbb{F}[\![\, \neg c_1 \parallel c_2 \,]\!] \,;\, \mathbb{D}[\![\, \pi_1(t) \parallel \mathbf{skip} \,]\!]\sigma \,;\, \mathbb{D}[\![\, \mathbf{skip} \parallel \pi_2(s) \,]\!]\sigma \\
& \cup\, \mathbb{F}[\![\, \neg c_1 \parallel \neg c_2 \,]\!] \,;\, \mathbb{D}[\![\, t \,]\!]\sigma \\
\mathbb{D}[\![\, \mathbf{if}\ c\ \mathbf{then}\ s\ \mathbf{else}\ t \,]\!]\sigma & \triangleq \mathbb{D}[\![\, \mathbf{if}\ c \parallel c\ \mathbf{then}\ s\ \mathbf{else}\ t \,]\!]\sigma \\
\mathbb{D}[\![\, \mathbf{while}\ c_1 \parallel c_2\ \mathbf{do}\ s \,]\!]\sigma & \triangleq (\mathrm{lfp}\ H) \,;\, \mathbb{F}[\![\, \neg c_1 \parallel \neg c_2 \,]\!] \\
\mathbb{D}[\![\, \mathbf{while}\ c\ \mathbf{do}\ s \,]\!]\sigma & \triangleq \mathbb{D}[\![\, \mathbf{while}\ c \parallel c\ \mathbf{do}\ s \,]\!]\sigma
\end{array}$$

$$\text{where}\quad \mathbb{F}[\![\, c_1 \parallel c_2 \,]\!] \triangleq \{\, (((\rho_1, n_1), (\rho_2, n_2)), ((\rho_1, n_1), (\rho_2, n_2))) \mid \mathrm{true} \in \mathbb{C}[\![\, c_1 \,]\!]\rho_1 \cap \mathbb{C}[\![\, c_2 \,]\!]\rho_2 \,\}$$

$$\text{and}\qquad H(R) \triangleq \Delta_{\mathcal{D}'} \cup R \,;\, \left(\begin{array}{l} \mathbb{F}[\![\, c_1 \parallel c_2 \,]\!] \,;\, \mathbb{D}[\![\, s \,]\!]\sigma \quad \cup \\ \mathbb{F}[\![\, c_1 \parallel \neg c_2 \,]\!] \,;\, \mathbb{D}[\![\, \pi_1(s) \parallel \mathbf{skip} \,]\!]\sigma \cup \\ \mathbb{F}[\![\, \neg c_1 \parallel c_2 \,]\!] \,;\, \mathbb{D}[\![\, \mathbf{skip} \parallel \pi_2(s) \,]\!]\sigma \end{array} \right)$$

Fig. 6. Denotational concrete semantics of double programs

Note that the semantics $\mathbb{D}[\![\, V \leftarrow \mathbf{input}(a, b) \,]\!]$ of input statements is different from the semantics $\mathbb{D}[\![\, V \leftarrow \mathbf{rand}(a, b) \,]\!]$ of non-deterministic assignments. The latter entails no relationship between the values read by the two projections of a double program, besides the fact that they range in the same interval. On the contrary, the former reads from a shared input stream σ, hence the left and right projections P_1 and P_2 read equal values if their input indexes n_1 and n_2 are equal. This is the case when P_1 and P_2 have called **input** equal numbers of times. On the contrary, if one projection, say P_1, has called **input** more often than the other, then P_1 is ahead of P_2 in the stream, and the two projections are desynchronized. Nonetheless, they may resynchronize later if P_2 catches up with P_1, hence read equal values again. Also, owing to the semantics $\mathbb{S}[\![\, V \leftarrow \mathbf{input}(a, b) \,]\!]$ of simple input statements, $\mathbf{input}(a, b)$ returns only if the input value at the current index is in the range $[a, b]$. Therefore, it should be considered a semantic error if P_1 and P_2 use different ranges $[a_1, b_1] \neq [a_2, b_2]$ to read the input at the same index. For the sake of simplicity, we do not check this in our semantics (altough our implementation performs this check).

The presence of both **input** and **rand** primitives makes the semantics very expressive, and useful for modeling many practical problems. Non-determinism allows to abstract unknown parts of a program: for instance, $\mathbf{rand}(0, 10)$ is a sound stub for $f()$, when function f is only known to return values between 0 and 10. Also, combining **input** and **rand** allows to model information flow problems. For instance, the $\mathbb{D}$ semantics distinguishes the two programs (a) and (b) shown on Fig. 21, and presented in Sect. 5.

2.3 Properties of Interest

We wish to prove the functional equivalence of the left and right projections of a given double program $P \in dstat$, restricted to a set of distinguished variables $\mathcal{V}_0 \in \mathcal{P}(\mathcal{V})$, specified with the **assert_sync** primitive. Let $I_0 \triangleq \{((\lambda V.\, 0, 0), (\lambda V.\, 0, 0))\}$ be the singleton state with all variables and input indexes initialized to zero. The set of states reachable by P from I_0 with input stream σ is $(\mathbb{D}[\![P]\!]\sigma)I_0$. Therefore the property of interest may be formalized as:

$$\forall \sigma \in \mathbb{R}^\omega : \forall V \in \mathcal{V}_0 : \forall((\rho_1, n_1), (\rho_2, n_2)) \in (\mathbb{D}[\![P]\!]\sigma)I_0 : \rho_1(V) = \rho_2(V)$$

Coming back to our running example Unchloop on Fig. 3, the concrete semantics of the program from line 3 to 9 is displayed on Fig. 7, for any sequence of inputs $\sigma \in \mathbb{R}^\omega$. With the additional assumption that both program projections compute with equal inputs ($a_1 = a_2 = \sigma_0 \wedge b_1 = b_2 = \sigma_1$), ensured by the semantics of line 1 and 2, and the initial environment I_0, the two projections can be proved to compute equal values for r.

$$\begin{array}{ll}
\mathbb{D}[\![\mathit{Unchloop}_{3..9}]\!]\sigma = & \\
\quad \{\, s_0, ((a_1, b_1, 1, 0, 1, n_1), (a_2, b_2, 0, 0, 1, n_2)) & | \, a_1 \leq 0 \wedge a_2 \leq 0 \wedge H_0 \,\} \\
\cup \{\, s_0, ((a_1, b_1, 1 + a_1 \times b_1, a_1, 1 + a_1 \times b_1, n_1), (a_2, b_2, 0, 0, 1, n_2)) & | \, a_1 > 0 \wedge a_2 \leq 0 \wedge H_0 \,\} \\
\cup \{\, s_0, ((a_1, b_1, 1, 0, 1, n_1), (a_2, b_2, a_2 \times b_2, a_2, 1 + a_2 \times b_2, n_2)) & | \, a_1 \leq 0 \wedge a_2 > 0 \wedge H_0 \,\} \\
\cup \{\, s_0, ((a_1, b_1, 1 + a_1 \times b_1, a_1, 1 + a_1 \times b_1, n_1), (a_2, b_2, a_2 \times b_2, a_2, 1 + a_2 \times b_2, n_2)) & | \, a_1 > 0 \wedge a_2 > 0 \wedge H_0 \,\}
\end{array}$$

where $s_0 \triangleq ((a_k, b_k, c_k, i_k, r_k), n_k)_{k \in \{1,2\}}$
and $H_0 \triangleq s_0 \in \mathbb{R}^4 \times \mathbb{N}$

Fig. 7. Concrete semantics of the Unchloop example from Fig. 3

Unfortunately, our concrete collecting semantics $\mathbb{D}$ is not computable in general. A particular difficulty of the Unchloop example is that the input-ouptut relation is non linear: $(a \leq 0 \Rightarrow r = 1) \wedge (a \geq 0 \Rightarrow r = 1 + a \times b)$. Hence, inferring such information is beyond classic numeric domains, such as polyhedra. We will provide a new analysis method which avoids resorting to more complex, non-linear numeric domains. An additional difficulty, not shown in the Unchloop example, is that the programs can read an unbounded number of values from their input stream.

3 Abstract Semantics

We therefore tailor an abstract semantics suitable for the analysis of program differences.

$$(\mathbb{R}^\omega \to \mathcal{P}(\mathcal{D}' \times \mathcal{D}'), \dot{\subseteq}) \xleftarrow[\alpha_{\mathfrak{F}}]{\gamma_{\mathfrak{F}}} (\mathcal{P}(\hat{\mathcal{D}} \times \hat{\mathcal{D}}), \subseteq)$$

$$\alpha_{\mathfrak{F}}(f) \triangleq \{ (\beta_\sigma(s), \beta_\sigma(s')) \mid (s, s') \in f(\sigma) \wedge \sigma \in \mathbb{R}^\omega \}$$

$$(\gamma_{\mathfrak{F}}(R))(\sigma) \triangleq \{ (s, s') \mid (\beta_\sigma(s), \beta_\sigma(s')) \in R \}$$

where $\forall\, \sigma \in \mathbb{R}^\omega : \beta_\sigma \in \mathcal{D}' \to \hat{\mathcal{D}}$

$$\beta_\sigma(((\rho_1, n_1), (\rho_2, n_2))) \triangleq (\rho_1, \rho_2, \delta, q)$$

$$\text{with} \quad \delta = n_2 - n_1 \wedge |q| = |\delta| \wedge \forall\, 0 \le n < |\delta| : q_n = \sigma_{\max\{n_1, n_2\} - n - 1}$$

Fig. 8. Abstraction of shared input sequences with unbounded FIFO queues

3.1 Wrapping up Infinite Input Sequences

A first observation is that we do not need to recall the whole input sequence $\sigma \in \mathbb{R}^\omega$ shared by the left and right projections P_1 and P_2 of a double program P. Indeed, we only aim at inferring equalities between the input values read by P_1 and P_2. We therefore only need to record, at any point in the analysis, the input subsequence that has been read by one program, but not the other one yet. This ensures that, when a program that has read less values than the other catches up with it, it reads the same values. Values read by both programs can be discarded, and values not read by any program do not need to be known in advance, as they can be chosen non-deterministically. This subsequence of input values read by one program only forms an (unbounded) FIFO queue, as inputs are read in order. We therefore abstract the input sequence σ, and indexes n_1 and n_2 of P_1 and P_2 in this sequence, defined in $\mathcal{D}'$, as the difference $\delta \triangleq n_2 - n_1$, and a FIFO queue of length $|\delta|$ in $\hat{\mathcal{D}} \triangleq \mathcal{E} \times \mathcal{E} \times \mathbb{N} \times \mathbb{R}^\star$. This abstraction does not lose information. A formalization of this abstraction is shown on Fig. 8. Note that we use the symbol $\dot{\subseteq}$ to denote the pointwise lifting of $\subseteq$: $f \dot{\subseteq} f' \equiv \forall \sigma \in \mathbb{R}^\omega : f(\sigma) \subseteq f'(\sigma)$.

Proposition 1. *The pair $(\alpha_{\mathfrak{F}}, \gamma_{\mathfrak{F}})$ defined in Fig. 8 is a Galois isomorphism.*

Note that this abstraction includes some redundancy: indeed, it would be enough to record only the sign of δ, instead of its value, as its absolute value is given by the length of the queue. However, keeping the value simplifies subsequent abstraction steps.

Simple Programs. Starting from the concrete semantics $\mathbb{D}$, let us now formalize the semantics resulting from this first abstraction step. To start with, we first define the simple program semantics. The behaviors of the left and right projections P_1 and P_2 of a double program P depend on which is ahead in the input sequence, and which is behind. P_1 is ahead if $\delta < 0$, and P_2 is ahead if $\delta > 0$. Therefore, we need to particularize the simple program semantics $\hat{\mathbb{S}}_k[\![s]\!] \in \mathcal{P}(\hat{\mathcal{E}} \times \hat{\mathcal{E}})$, where $\hat{\mathcal{E}} \triangleq \mathcal{E} \times \mathbb{N} \times \mathbb{R}^\star$, and $k \in \{1, 2\}$. Figure 9 shows the semantics for $\hat{\mathbb{S}}_k[\![V \leftarrow \textbf{input}(a, b)]\!]$. Note that we write $q \cdot q'$ to denote concatenation of queues q and q'. Intuitively, this semantics distinguishes between two cases:

$$\hat{\mathbb{S}}_k[\![s]\!] \in \mathcal{P}(\hat{\mathcal{E}} \times \hat{\mathcal{E}}) \qquad ; \qquad k \in \{1, 2\}$$

$$\begin{aligned}
\hat{\mathbb{S}}_1[\![V \leftarrow \mathbf{input}(a, b)]\!] \triangleq & \\
& \{ ((\rho, \delta, q), (\rho[V \mapsto \nu], \delta - 1, \nu \cdot q)) \mid (\rho, \delta, q) \in \hat{\mathcal{E}} \wedge \delta \leq 0 \wedge a \leq \nu \leq b \} \\
\cup & \{ ((\rho, \delta, q \cdot v), (\rho[V \mapsto v], \delta - 1, q)) \mid (\rho, \delta, q) \in \hat{\mathcal{E}} \wedge \delta > 0 \wedge a \leq v \leq b \}
\end{aligned}$$

$$\begin{aligned}
\hat{\mathbb{S}}_2[\![V \leftarrow \mathbf{input}(a, b)]\!] \triangleq & \\
& \{ ((\rho, \delta, q), (\rho[V \mapsto \nu], \delta + 1, \nu \cdot q)) \mid (\rho, \delta, q) \in \hat{\mathcal{E}} \wedge \delta \geq 0 \wedge a \leq \nu \leq b \} \\
\cup & \{ ((\rho, \delta, q \cdot v), (\rho[V \mapsto v], \delta + 1, q)) \mid (\rho, \delta, q) \in \hat{\mathcal{E}} \wedge \delta < 0 \wedge a \leq v \leq b \}
\end{aligned}$$

Fig. 9. Abstract semantics of simple programs P_1 and P_2 with unbounded queues

1. If program P_k is ahead of the other program in the input sequence, or at the same point, then a new successful input read operation produces a fresh input value, and adds it at the head of the queue.
2. If program P_k is behind the other program in the input sequence, then a new successful input read operation retrieves the value at the tail of the queue.

In both cases, an input read operation is only successful if the value read matches the bounds specified for the **input** statement. We do not display the semantics for other commands, as the semantics for assignments and tests are standard for memory environments, and leave input index differences and queues unchanged. For instance, $\hat{\mathbb{S}}_k[\![V \leftarrow e]\!] \triangleq \{ ((\rho, \delta, q), (\rho[V \mapsto v], \delta, q)) \mid (\rho, \delta, q) \in \hat{\mathcal{E}} \wedge v \in \mathbb{E}[\![e]\!]\rho \}$.

Double Programs. We then lift the semantics $\hat{\mathbb{S}}_1[\![s]\!]$ and $\hat{\mathbb{S}}_2[\![s]\!]$ to double programs. The definition of $\hat{\mathbb{D}}[\![s]\!] \in \mathcal{P}(\hat{\mathcal{D}} \times \hat{\mathcal{D}})$ is very similar to that of $\mathbb{D}[\![s]\!]$. It can be obtained by removing σ parameters from Fig. 6, except for the composition of syntactically different statements $\hat{\mathbb{D}}[\![s_1 \parallel s_2]\!]$ and conditions $\hat{\mathbb{F}}[\![c_1 \parallel c_2]\!]$ We thus only show the definitions of these relations on Fig. 10. Following the particularization of simple statement semantics, the semantics for double statements and conditions compose the semantics of their left and right projections $\hat{\mathbb{D}}_k[\![s_k]\!]$ and $\hat{\mathbb{F}}_k[\![c_k]\!]$, where $\hat{\mathbb{D}}_k$ and $\hat{\mathbb{F}}_k$ operate on simple statements and conditions only. Note that the order of the composition is arbitrary, and not significant, as $\hat{\mathbb{D}}_1[\![s]\!] \mathbin{⨾} \hat{\mathbb{D}}_2[\![t]\!] = \hat{\mathbb{D}}_2[\![t]\!] \mathbin{⨾} \hat{\mathbb{D}}_1[\![s]\!]$, and likewise for $\hat{\mathbb{F}}_1[\![c]\!]$ and $\hat{\mathbb{F}}_2[\![d]\!]$. Finally, we formalize the relation between the abstract semantics $\hat{\mathbb{D}}$ and the concrete collecting semantics $\mathbb{D}$.

Proposition 2. *$\hat{\mathbb{D}}$ is a sound and complete abstraction of $\mathbb{D}$: $\hat{\mathbb{D}} = \alpha_{\mathfrak{F}}(\mathbb{D})$.*

3.2 Bounding Input Queues

The abstract semantics $\hat{\mathbb{D}}$ features unbounded queues. We aim at abstracting the concrete collecting semantics $\mathbb{D}$ in numeric domains, so we need to deal with a bounded number of variables. As it is also simpler to deal with a fixed number

$\hat{\mathbb{D}}[\![s]\!] \in \mathcal{P}(\hat{\mathcal{D}} \times \hat{\mathcal{D}})$

$$\hat{\mathbb{D}}[\![s_1 \parallel s_2]\!] \triangleq \hat{\mathbb{D}}_1[\![s_1]\!] \fatsemi \hat{\mathbb{D}}_2[\![s_2]\!]$$

$$\hat{\mathbb{D}}_1[\![s]\!] \triangleq \{ ((\rho_1, \rho_2, \delta, q), (\rho_1', \rho_2, \delta', q')) \mid ((\rho_1, \delta, q), (\rho_1', \delta', q')) \in \hat{\mathbb{S}}_1[\![s]\!] \wedge \rho_2 \in \mathcal{E} \}$$

$$\hat{\mathbb{D}}_2[\![s]\!] \triangleq \{ ((\rho_1, \rho_2, \delta, q), (\rho_1, \rho_2', \delta', q')) \mid ((\rho_2, \delta, q), (\rho_2', \delta', q')) \in \hat{\mathbb{S}}_2[\![s]\!] \wedge \rho_1 \in \mathcal{E} \}$$

$$\hat{\mathbb{F}}[\![c_1 \parallel c_2]\!] \triangleq \hat{\mathbb{F}}_1[\![c_1]\!] \fatsemi \hat{\mathbb{F}}_2[\![c_2]\!]$$

$$\hat{\mathbb{F}}_k[\![c]\!] \triangleq \{ ((\rho_1, \rho_2, \delta, q), (\rho_1, \rho_2, \delta, q)) \mid (\rho_1, \rho_2, \delta, q) \in \hat{\mathcal{D}} \wedge \text{true} \in \mathbb{C}[\![c]\!]\rho_k \} \; ; \; k \in \{1; 2\}$$

Fig. 10. Abstract semantics of double programs with unbounded queues

$$(\mathcal{P}(\hat{\mathcal{D}} \times \hat{\mathcal{D}}), \subseteq) \underset{\alpha_p}{\overset{\gamma_p}{\leftrightarrows}} (\mathcal{P}(\hat{\mathcal{D}}_p \times \hat{\mathcal{D}}_p), \subseteq)$$

$$\alpha_p(R) \triangleq \{ (\beta_p(s), \beta_p(s')) \mid (s, s') \in R \}$$

$$\gamma_p(R) \triangleq \{ (s, s') \mid (\beta_p(s), \beta_p(s')) \in R \}$$

$$\text{where } \beta_p \in \hat{\mathcal{D}} \to \hat{\mathcal{D}}_p$$

$$\beta_p((\rho_1, \rho_2, \delta, q)) \triangleq (\rho_1, \rho_2, \delta, \tilde{q}) \text{ with } \tilde{q}_n = \begin{cases} q_n & \textbf{if } 0 \le n < |\delta| \\ 0 & \textbf{if } |\delta| \le n < p \end{cases}$$

Fig. 11. Abstraction of FIFO queues to fixed length $p \geq 1$

of variables, we parameterize our abstract semantics with some predetermined integer $p \geq 1$, used to define the lengths of abstract FIFO queues in domain $\hat{\mathcal{D}}_p \triangleq \mathcal{E} \times \mathcal{E} \times \mathbb{N} \times \mathbb{R}^p$. Queues from $\hat{\mathcal{D}}$ are truncated whenever $|\delta| > p$, and padded with zeros whenever $|\delta| < p$. A formalization of this abstraction is shown on Fig. 11.

Proposition 3. *For all $p \geq 1$, the pair (α_p, γ_p) defined in Fig. 11 is a Galois embedding.*

Let $p \geq 1$. Starting from semantics $\hat{\mathbb{D}}$, we now give a formal definition for the abstract double program semantics $\hat{\mathbb{D}}^p$ resulting from this second abstraction step.

Simple Programs. To this aim, we first define the semantics $\hat{\mathbb{S}}_k^p[\![s]\!] \in \mathcal{P}(\hat{\mathcal{E}}_p \times \hat{\mathcal{E}}_p)$ of simple programs, where $\hat{\mathcal{E}}_p \triangleq \mathcal{E} \times \mathbb{N} \times \mathbb{R}^p$, and $k \in \{1, 2\}$. Figure 12 shows the semantics of $\hat{\mathbb{S}}_1^p[\![V \leftarrow \textbf{input}(a, b)]\!]$. *Mutatis mutandis*, the case of $\hat{\mathbb{S}}_2^p$ is similar. Intuitively, this semantics distinguishes between three cases:

1. If program P_k is ahead of the other program in the input sequence, or at the same point, then a new successful input read operation produces a fresh input value, and adds it on top of the queue, discarding the value at the bottom at the queue.
2. If program P_k is behind the other program in the input sequence, and the delay is less than the size of the input queue, then a new successful input

$$\underline{\hat{\mathbb{S}}_1^p[\![s]\!] \in \mathcal{P}(\hat{\mathcal{E}}_p \times \hat{\mathcal{E}}_p)}$$

$$\begin{aligned}
&\hat{\mathbb{S}}_1^p[\![V \leftarrow \textbf{input}(a,b)]\!] \triangleq \\
&\quad \{ ((\rho_1,\delta,q\cdot v),(\rho_1[V_1 \mapsto \nu],\delta-1,\nu\cdot q)) \mid (\rho_1,\delta,q) \in \mathcal{E}_{p-1} \wedge \delta \leq 0 \wedge a \leq \nu \leq b \wedge v \in \mathbb{R} \} \\
&\cup \left\{ ((\rho_1,\delta,q\cdot v\cdot r),(\rho_1[V_1 \mapsto v],\delta-1,q\cdot 0\cdot r)) \;\middle|\; \begin{array}{l} (\rho_1,\delta,q) \in \mathcal{E}_{|\delta|-1} \wedge 0 < \delta \leq p \wedge a \leq v \leq b \\ r \in \mathbb{R}^{p-2} \wedge \forall\, 0 \leq n < p-2 : r_n = 0 \end{array} \right\} \\
&\cup \{ ((\rho_1,\delta,q),(\rho_1[V_1 \mapsto \nu],\delta-1,q)) \mid (\rho_1,\delta,q) \in \mathcal{E}_p \wedge \delta > p \wedge a \leq \nu \leq b \}
\end{aligned}$$

Fig. 12. Abstract semantics of simple program P_1 with queues of length $p \geq 1$. The case of P_2 is similar.

read operation retrieves the value in the queue indexed by this delay, and resets this value to zero.

3. If program P_k is behind the other program in the input sequence, and the delay is more than the size of the input queue, then a new successful input read operation produces a fresh input value, and leaves the queue unchanged.

In any case, an input read operation is only successful if the value read matches the bounds specified for the **input** statement. We do not display the semantics for other commands, as the semantics for assignments and tests are standard for memory environments, and leave input index differences and queues unchanged. For instance, $\hat{\mathbb{S}}_k^p[\![V \leftarrow e]\!] \triangleq \{((\rho,\delta,q),(\rho[V \mapsto v],\delta,q)) \mid (\rho,\delta,q) \in \mathcal{E}_p \wedge v \in \mathbb{E}[\![e]\!]\rho\}$.

Double Programs. We then lift the semantics $\hat{\mathbb{S}}_1^p[\![s]\!]$ and $\hat{\mathbb{S}}_2^p[\![s]\!]$ to double programs. The definition of $\hat{\mathbb{D}}^p[\![s]\!] \in \mathcal{P}(\hat{\mathcal{D}}_p \times \hat{\mathcal{D}}_p)$ is very similar to that of $\hat{\mathbb{D}}[\![s]\!]$. The main change is that $\hat{\mathbb{D}}_k^p[\![s]\!]$ is defined with $\hat{\mathbb{S}}_k^p[\![s]\!]$, where $\hat{\mathbb{D}}_k[\![s]\!]$ is defined with $\hat{\mathbb{S}}_k[\![s]\!]$. We thus only show the definitions of some relations on Fig. 13. These definitions are very similar to those of $\hat{\mathbb{D}}[\![s]\!]$ on Fig. 10. The semantics for double statements and conditions compose the semantics of their left and right projections. The order of the composition is arbitrary, but significant for statements, as $\hat{\mathbb{D}}_1^p[\![s]\!] \fatsemi \hat{\mathbb{D}}_2^p[\![t]\!] \neq \hat{\mathbb{D}}_2^p[\![t]\!] \fatsemi \hat{\mathbb{D}}_1^p[\![s]\!]$. Both composition orders, however, are sound. A way to make the analyse precise and independent on the order would be to compute the intersection of the compositions with the two orders. The order is in constrast not significant for conditions, as $\hat{\mathbb{F}}_1^p[\![c]\!] \fatsemi \hat{\mathbb{F}}_2^p[\![d]\!] = \hat{\mathbb{F}}_2^p[\![d]\!] \fatsemi \hat{\mathbb{F}}_1^p[\![c]\!]$.

Finally, we formalize the relation between the abstract semantics $\hat{\mathbb{D}}^p$ and the previous abstraction $\hat{\mathbb{D}}$ of the concrete collecting semantics.

Proposition 4. *For all $p \geq 1$, $\hat{\mathbb{D}}^p$ is a sound and optimal abstraction of $\hat{\mathbb{D}}$: $\hat{\mathbb{D}}^p = \alpha_p(\hat{\mathbb{D}})$.*

3.3 Numerical Abstraction

We now rely on numeric abstractions to abstract further $\hat{\mathbb{D}}^p[\![s]\!]$ into a computable abstract semantics $\hat{\mathbb{D}}^{\sharp p}[\![s]\!]$, resulting in an effective static analysis.

$$\underline{\hat{\mathbb{D}}^p\llbracket s \rrbracket \in \mathcal{P}(\hat{\mathcal{D}}_p \times \hat{\mathcal{D}}_p)}$$

$$\begin{array}{ll}
\hat{\mathbb{D}}^p\llbracket s_1 \parallel s_2 \rrbracket \triangleq \hat{\mathbb{D}}_1^p\llbracket s_1 \rrbracket \mathbin{;} \hat{\mathbb{D}}_2^p\llbracket s_2 \rrbracket & \\
\hat{\mathbb{D}}_1^p\llbracket s \rrbracket & \triangleq \{ ((\rho_1, \rho_2, \delta, q), (\rho_1', \rho_2, \delta', q')) \mid ((\rho_1, \delta, q), (\rho_1', \delta', q')) \in \hat{\mathbb{S}}_1^p\llbracket s \rrbracket \wedge \rho_2 \in \mathcal{E} \} \\
\hat{\mathbb{D}}_2^p\llbracket s \rrbracket & \triangleq \{ ((\rho_1, \rho_2, \delta, q), (\rho_1, \rho_2', \delta', q')) \mid ((\rho_2, \delta, q), (\rho_2', \delta', q')) \in \hat{\mathbb{S}}_2^p\llbracket s \rrbracket \wedge \rho_1 \in \mathcal{E} \} \\
\hat{\mathbb{F}}^p\llbracket c_1 \parallel c_2 \rrbracket \triangleq \hat{\mathbb{F}}_1^p\llbracket c_1 \rrbracket \mathbin{;} \hat{\mathbb{F}}_2^p\llbracket c_2 \rrbracket & \\
\hat{\mathbb{F}}_k^p\llbracket c \rrbracket & \triangleq \{ ((\rho_1, \rho_2, \delta, q), (\rho_1, \rho_2, \delta, q)) \mid (\rho_1, \rho_2, \delta, q) \in \hat{\mathcal{D}}_p \wedge \text{true} \in \mathbb{C}\llbracket c \rrbracket \rho_k \} \;;\; k \in \{1; 2\}
\end{array}$$

Fig. 13. Abstract semantics of double programs with queues of length $p \geq 1$

Connecting to Numeric Domains. As $\hat{\mathcal{D}}_p \approx \mathbb{R}^{2|\mathcal{V}|+p+1}$, any numeric abstract domain with $2|\mathcal{V}|+p+1$ dimensions may be used, such as polyhedra [5]. Let $\mathcal{N}$ be such an abstract domain, with values in $\mathcal{D}^\sharp$, order $\sqsubseteq^\sharp$, concretization $\gamma_\mathcal{N} \in \mathcal{D}^\sharp \rightarrow \mathcal{P}(\mathbb{R}^{2|\mathcal{V}|+p+1})$, and operators $\hat{\mathbb{S}}^{\sharp p}\llbracket s \rrbracket, \hat{\mathbb{C}}^{\sharp p}\llbracket c \rrbracket \in \mathcal{D}^\sharp \rightarrow \mathcal{D}^\sharp$ for assignments and tests of simple programs over variables in $\mathcal{V}_1 \cup \mathcal{V}_2 \cup \mathcal{Q}$, where $\mathcal{V}_k \triangleq \{ x_k \mid x \in \mathcal{V} \}$, and $\mathcal{Q} \triangleq \{\delta, (q_n)_{0 \leq n < p}\}$. Let $\cup^\sharp$ and $\cap^\sharp$ be the abstractions of set union and intersection of domain $\mathcal{N}$, and $\triangledown$ be its widening operator.

We abstract $\hat{\mathbb{D}}^p\llbracket s \rrbracket \in \mathcal{P}(\hat{\mathcal{D}}_p \times \hat{\mathcal{D}}_p)$ by $\hat{\mathbb{D}}^{\sharp p}\llbracket s \rrbracket \in \mathcal{D}^\sharp \rightarrow \mathcal{D}^\sharp$, with the soundness condition $\forall X^\sharp \in \mathcal{D}^\sharp : \hat{\mathbb{D}}^p\llbracket s \rrbracket(\gamma_\mathcal{N}(X^\sharp)) \subseteq \gamma_\mathcal{N}(\hat{\mathbb{D}}^{\sharp p}\llbracket s \rrbracket(X^\sharp))$. As $\hat{\mathbb{D}}^p\llbracket s \rrbracket$ is defined by induction on the syntax, the definition for $\hat{\mathbb{D}}^{\sharp p}\llbracket s \rrbracket$ is straightforward: the abstract semantics needs only be defined for the composition of syntactically different statements $s_1 \parallel s_2$ and conditions $c_1 \parallel c_2$. Figure 14 shows definitions for associate transfer functions, as well as the transfer functions for some of the other syntactic constructs. We use the syntactic renaming operator τ_1 (resp. τ_2), defined by induction on the syntax, to distinguish the variables of the left (resp. right) projection of a double program, with suffix 1 (resp. 2). For instance, $\hat{\mathbb{D}}^{\sharp p}\llbracket c \leftarrow 1 \parallel 0 \rrbracket = \hat{\mathbb{S}}^{\sharp p}\llbracket c_2 \leftarrow 0 \rrbracket \circ \hat{\mathbb{S}}^{\sharp p}\llbracket c_1 \leftarrow 1 \rrbracket$.

Leveraging Standard Numeric Domains. Coming back to the example Unchloop from Fig. 3, recall that the relation between c and i is non linear: $c_1 = i_1 \times b_1 + 1$ and $c_2 = i_2 \times b_2$ from line 4 to line 9. Thus, a separate analysis of programs P_1 and P_2 would require a non linear abstract domain to compare r_1 and r_2. In contrast, our joint analysis of P_1 and P_2 will be sufficiently precise, even when using linear numeric domains, because the difference between the values of the variables in P_1 and in P_2 remains linear. For instance, the polyhedra domain [5] is able to infer that the invariant $-c_1 + c_2 + 1 = 0$ holds from line 3 to 9, hence $r_1 = r_2$ at line 9, although it is not able to discover any interval for r_1 or r_2. The octagon domain [18] is also able to express these invariants, but its transfer function for assignment is not precise enough to infer them. Indeed, $x \leftarrow a - b$ cannot be exactly abstracted by the domain, and currently proposed transfer functions fall back to plain interval arithmetics in that case, so that the domain cannot exploit the bound it infers on $a - b$ to bound x, for efficiency reasons. The interval domain is not able to express the invariants, hence it cannot be used directly for a conclusive analysis.

$$\hat{\mathbb{D}}^{\sharp p}[\![s]\!] \in \mathcal{D}^\sharp \to \mathcal{D}^\sharp$$

$$\hat{\mathbb{D}}^{\sharp p}[\![s_1 \parallel s_2]\!] \triangleq \hat{\mathbb{D}}_2^{\sharp p}[\![s_2]\!] \circ \hat{\mathbb{D}}_1^{\sharp p}[\![s_1]\!]$$
$$\hat{\mathbb{D}}_k^{\sharp p}[\![s]\!] \triangleq \hat{\mathbb{S}}^{\sharp p}[\![\tau_k(s)]\!] \; ; \; k \in \{1;2\}$$

$$\hat{\mathbb{F}}^{\sharp p}[\![c_1 \parallel c_2]\!] \triangleq \hat{\mathbb{F}}_2^{\sharp p}[\![c_2]\!] \circ \hat{\mathbb{F}}_1^{\sharp p}[\![c_1]\!]$$
$$\hat{\mathbb{F}}_k^{\sharp p}[\![c]\!] \triangleq \hat{\mathbb{C}}^{\sharp p}[\![\tau_k(c)]\!] \; ; \; k \in \{1;2\}$$

$$\hat{\mathbb{D}}^{\sharp p}[\![V \leftarrow e_1 \parallel e_2]\!] \triangleq \hat{\mathbb{S}}^{\sharp p}[\![V_2 \leftarrow \tau_2(e_2)]\!] \circ \hat{\mathbb{S}}^{\sharp p}[\![V_1 \leftarrow \tau_1(e_1)]\!]$$

$$\begin{aligned}\hat{\mathbb{D}}_1^{\sharp p}[\![V \leftarrow \mathbf{input}(a,b)]\!] \triangleq \hat{\mathbb{S}}^{\sharp p}[\![\delta \leftarrow \delta - 1]\!] \circ \\ \begin{pmatrix} \hat{\mathbb{S}}^{\sharp p}[\![V_1 \leftarrow q_0]\!] \circ \hat{\mathbb{S}}^{\sharp p}[\![q_0 \leftarrow \mathbf{rand}(a,b)]\!] \circ \hat{\mathbb{S}}^{\sharp p}[\![q_1 \leftarrow q_0]\!] \circ \cdots \circ \hat{\mathbb{S}}^{\sharp p}[\![q_{p-1} \leftarrow q_{p-2}]\!] \circ \hat{\mathbb{C}}^{\sharp p}[\![\delta \leq 0]\!] \quad \cup^\sharp \\ \hat{\mathbb{S}}^{\sharp p}[\![q_{\delta-1} \leftarrow 0]\!] \circ \hat{\mathbb{S}}^{\sharp p}[\![V_1 \leftarrow q_{\delta-1}]\!] \circ \hat{\mathbb{C}}^{\sharp p}[\![q_{\delta-1} \leq b]\!] \circ \hat{\mathbb{C}}^{\sharp p}[\![q_{\delta-1} \geq a]\!] \circ \hat{\mathbb{C}}^{\sharp p}[\![\delta \leq p]\!] \circ \hat{\mathbb{C}}^{\sharp p}[\![\delta > 0]\!] \cup^\sharp \\ \hat{\mathbb{S}}^{\sharp p}[\![V_1 \leftarrow \mathbf{rand}(a,b)]\!] \circ \hat{\mathbb{C}}^{\sharp p}[\![\delta > p]\!] \end{pmatrix}\end{aligned}$$

$$\begin{aligned}\hat{\mathbb{D}}_2^{\sharp p}[\![V \leftarrow \mathbf{input}(a,b)]\!] \triangleq \hat{\mathbb{S}}^{\sharp p}[\![\delta \leftarrow \delta + 1]\!] \circ \\ \begin{pmatrix} \hat{\mathbb{S}}^{\sharp p}[\![V_2 \leftarrow q_0]\!] \circ \hat{\mathbb{S}}^{\sharp p}[\![q_0 \leftarrow \mathbf{rand}(a,b)]\!] \circ \hat{\mathbb{S}}^{\sharp p}[\![q_1 \leftarrow q_0]\!] \circ \cdots \circ \hat{\mathbb{S}}^{\sharp p}[\![q_{p-1} \leftarrow q_{p-2}]\!] \circ \hat{\mathbb{C}}^{\sharp p}[\![\delta \geq 0]\!] \quad \cup^\sharp \\ \hat{\mathbb{S}}^{\sharp p}[\![q_{-\delta-1} \leftarrow 0]\!] \circ \hat{\mathbb{S}}^{\sharp p}[\![V_2 \leftarrow q_{-\delta-1}]\!] \circ \hat{\mathbb{C}}^{\sharp p}[\![q_{-\delta-1} \leq b]\!] \circ \hat{\mathbb{C}}^{\sharp p}[\![q_{-\delta-1} \geq a]\!] \circ \hat{\mathbb{C}}^{\sharp p}[\![\delta \geq -p]\!] \circ \hat{\mathbb{C}}^{\sharp p}[\![\delta < 0]\!] \cup^\sharp \\ \hat{\mathbb{S}}^{\sharp p}[\![V_2 \leftarrow \mathbf{rand}(a,b)]\!] \circ \hat{\mathbb{C}}^{\sharp p}[\![\delta < -p]\!] \end{pmatrix}\end{aligned}$$

$$\text{where} \quad \tau_k(x) \triangleq \begin{cases} x_k & \mathbf{if}\ x \in \mathcal{V} \\ x & \mathbf{if}\ x \in \mathcal{Q} \end{cases}$$

Fig. 14. Abstract semantics of double programs with a standard numeric domain

$$(\mathcal{P}(\hat{\mathcal{D}}_p \times \hat{\mathcal{D}}_p), \subseteq) \xrightleftharpoons[\alpha_-]{\gamma_-} (\mathcal{P}(\hat{\mathcal{D}}_p \times \hat{\mathcal{D}}_p), \subseteq)$$

$$\alpha_-(R) \triangleq \{ ((\rho_1, \rho_2 - \rho_1, \delta^\star, q), (\rho_1', \rho_2' - \rho_1', \delta^{\star\prime}, q')) \mid ((\rho_1, \rho_2, \delta^\star, q), (\rho_1', \rho_2', \delta^{\star\prime}, q')) \in R \}$$

$$\gamma_-(\Delta) \triangleq \{ ((\rho_1, \rho_1 + \delta_\rho, \delta^\star, q), (\rho_1', \rho_1' + \delta_\rho', \delta^{\star\prime}, q')) \mid ((\rho_1, \delta_\rho, \delta^\star, q), (\rho_1', \delta_\rho', \delta^{\star\prime}, q')) \in \Delta \}$$

Fig. 15. Abstraction of double environments with environment differences

3.4 Introducing a Dedicated Numeric Domain

However, we remark that it is sufficient to bound the difference $x_2 - x_1$ for any variable x to express the necessary invariants, where x_1 (resp. x_2) represents the value of x for the left (resp. right) projection P_1 (resp. P_2) of a double program P. Thus, we now design an abstract domain that is specialized to infer these bounds. We abstract the values x_1 and x_2 by the pair $(x_1, \delta x)$, where $\delta x \triangleq x_2 - x_1$. This abstraction amounts to changing the representation of states of double program P. It does not lose information. A formalization of this abstraction is shown on Fig. 15. Note that we extend operators $+$ and $-$ to functions (pointwise lifting).

Proposition 5. *The pair (α_-, γ_-) defined in Fig. 15 is a Galois isomorphism.*

Let $\mathbb{\Delta}^p \triangleq \alpha_-(\hat{\mathbb{D}}^p)$. $\mathbb{\Delta}^p$ is able to represent two-variable equalities $x_1 = x_2 \Leftrightarrow \delta x = 0$, even after numeric abstraction using non relational domains, such as intervals. Transfer functions rely on symbolic simplifications to let such equalities propagate through linear expressions. The semantics $\mathbb{\Delta}^p$ of statements 6 and 9 of the UnchLoop example are shown for instance on Fig. 16, before and after simple symbolic simplifications of affine expressions.

Like for $\hat{\mathbb{D}}^p$, any numeric domain over variables in $\mathcal{V}_1 \cup \mathcal{V}_\delta \cup \mathcal{Q}$, where $\mathcal{V}_\delta \triangleq \{ \delta x \mid x \in \mathcal{V} \}$, can be used to abstract $\mathbb{\Delta}^p$. Therefore the definition for $\mathbb{\Delta}^{\sharp p}$ is

$$
\begin{aligned}
&\mathbb{\Delta}^p[\![c \leftarrow c + b]\!] \\
&\quad = \{\, (s_1, (((a_1, b_1, c_1 + b_1, i_1, r_1), ((a_1 + \delta a) - a_1, (b_1 + \delta b) - b_1, \\
&\qquad\qquad ((c_1 + \delta c) + (b_1 + \delta b)) - (c_1 + b_1), (i_1 + \delta i) - i_1, (r_1 + \delta r) - r_1), \delta, q)) \mid H_1 \,\} \\
&\quad = \{\, (s_1, ((a_1, b_1, c_1 + b_1, i_1, r_1), (\delta a, \delta b, \delta c + \delta b, \delta i, \delta r), \delta, q)) \mid H_1 \,\} \\
&\mathbb{\Delta}^p[\![r \leftarrow c \parallel c + 1]\!] \\
&\quad = \{\, (s_1, ((a_1, b_1, c_1, i_1, c_1), ((a_1 + \delta a) - a_1, (b_1 + \delta b) - b_1, ((c_1 + \delta c) - c_1, \\
&\qquad\qquad (i_1 + \delta i) - i_1, (c_1 + \delta c + 1) - c_1)), \delta, q) \mid H_1 \,\} \\
&\quad = \{\, (s_1, ((a_1, b_1, c_1, i_1, c_1), (\delta a, \delta b, \delta c, \delta i, \delta c + 1), \delta, q)) \mid H_1 \,\} \\
&\text{where } s_1 \triangleq ((a_1, b_1, c_1, i_1, r_1), (\delta a, \delta b, \delta c, \delta i, \delta r), \delta, q) \\
&\text{and} \quad H_1 \triangleq s_1 \in \mathbb{R}^{10} \times \mathbb{N} \times \mathbb{R}^p
\end{aligned}
$$

Fig. 16. Examples of $\mathbb{\Delta}^p$ semantics

$$
\begin{aligned}
&\mathbb{\Delta}^{\sharp p}[\![V \leftarrow \mathbf{input}(a, b)]\!] \triangleq \\
&\left(\begin{array}{r} \hat{\mathbb{S}}^{\sharp p}[\![\delta V \leftarrow 0]\!] \circ \hat{\mathbb{S}}^{\sharp p}[\![V_1 \leftarrow q_0]\!] \circ \hat{\mathbb{S}}^{\sharp p}[\![q_0 \leftarrow \mathbf{rand}(a, b)]\!] \circ_{i=0}^{p-2} \hat{\mathbb{S}}^{\sharp p}[\![q_{i+1} \leftarrow q_i]\!] \circ \hat{\mathbb{C}}^{\sharp p}[\![\delta^\star = 0]\!] \cup^\sharp \\
\mathbb{\Delta}_2^{\sharp p}[\![V \leftarrow \mathbf{input}(a, b)]\!] \circ \mathbb{\Delta}_1^{\sharp p}[\![V \leftarrow \mathbf{input}(a, b)]\!] \circ \hat{\mathbb{C}}^{\sharp p}[\![\delta^\star \neq 0]\!] \end{array} \right)
\end{aligned}
$$

$$
\mathbb{\Delta}^{\sharp p}[\![V \leftarrow e]\!] \triangleq \mathbb{\Delta}_2^{\sharp p}[\![V \leftarrow e]\!] \circ \hat{\mathbb{S}}^{\sharp p}[\![V_1 \leftarrow (\tau_1 \circ \pi_1)(e)]\!]
$$

where

$$
\mathbb{\Delta}_2^{\sharp p}[\![V \leftarrow e]\!] \triangleq \begin{cases} \hat{\mathbb{S}}^{\sharp p}[\![\delta V \leftarrow 0]\!] & \textbf{if } \text{is\_deterministic}(e) \wedge \forall x \in \text{Vars}(e) : \delta x = 0 \\ \hat{\mathbb{S}}^{\sharp p}[\![\delta V \leftarrow \sum_{x \in \mathcal{V}} \lambda_x \delta x]\!] & \textbf{if } \exists (\mu, (\lambda_x)_{x \in \mathcal{V}}) \in \mathbb{R}^{|\mathcal{V}|+1} : e = \mu + \sum_{x \in \mathcal{V}} \lambda_x x \\ \hat{\mathbb{S}}^{\sharp p}[\![\delta V \leftarrow (\tau_2' \circ \pi_2)(e) - (\tau_1 \circ \pi_1)(e)]\!] & \textbf{otherwise} \end{cases}
$$

$$
\tau_2'(x) \triangleq \begin{cases} x_1 + \delta x & \textbf{if } x \in \mathcal{V} \\ x & \textbf{if } x \in \mathcal{Q} \end{cases}
$$

Fig. 17. Symbolic simplifications in $\mathbb{\Delta}^{\sharp p}$

straightforward, by induction on the syntax of double programs. We also define the semantics for the $s_1 \parallel s_2$ construct as $\mathbb{\Delta}^{\sharp p}[\![s_1 \parallel s_2]\!] \triangleq \mathbb{\Delta}_2^{\sharp p}[\![s_2]\!] \circ \mathbb{\Delta}_1^{\sharp p}[\![s_1]\!]$, where $\mathbb{\Delta}_1^p[\![s]\!] \triangleq \mathbb{\Delta}^p[\![s \parallel \mathbf{skip}]\!]$, and $\mathbb{\Delta}_2^p[\![s]\!] \triangleq \mathbb{\Delta}^p[\![\mathbf{skip} \parallel s]\!]$, for simple statement s. Nonetheless, we add some particular cases, to gain both efficiency and precision on δV, for all variables V, through simple symbolic simplifications. These particular cases are displayed on Fig. 17. Note that we use the syntactic renaming operator τ_2', defined by induction on the syntax, to replace variables V_2 of the right projection of a double program by their abstraction $V_1 + \delta V$.

The first particular case is that of input statements $V \leftarrow \mathbf{input}(a, b)$ for both programs, in environments such that both programs have read the same number of input values, *i.e.* $\delta^\star = 0$, where $\delta^\star$ represents the difference between input indexes. In this case, we may assign $\delta V \leftarrow 0$ directly, and leave $\delta^\star$ unchanged. For instance, after statement $a \leftarrow \mathbf{input}(-1000, 1000)$ at line 1 of the Unchloop example on Fig. 3, we have $a \in [-1000, 1000]$, and $\delta a = 0$. The second particular case is that of affine assignments $V \leftarrow e$, where $e = \mu + \sum_{x \in \mathcal{V}} \lambda_x \times x$. We call such expressions "differentiable", as it is easy to compute δV directly as a function of all the δx variables. A third particular case is that of arbitrary (non necessarily affine) assignments $V \leftarrow e$, when e is deterministic, and all the occurring variables x satisfy $\delta x = 0$. Then $\delta V = 0$, as we know that both expressions always evaluate to equal values in P_1 and P_2.

To further enhance precision on some examples, we slightly generalize these particular cases to double assignments $V \leftarrow e_1 \parallel e_2$, when expressions e_1 and e_2 are found syntactically equal, modulo some semantics preserving transformations, such as associativity, commutativity, and distributivity. We also generalize symbolic simplifications based on expression differentiation to some double assignments $V \leftarrow e \parallel e + e'$, in particular when e' is a constant. For instance, for line 9 of the Unchloop example on Fig. 3, we have $\mathbb{\Delta}_2^{\sharp p}[\![r \leftarrow c \parallel c+1]\!] = \hat{\mathbb{S}}^{\sharp p}[\![\delta r \leftarrow \delta c + 1]\!]$.

As a consequence, the interval domain is able to infer the invariant $\delta r = 0$ for semantics $\mathbb{\Delta}^{\sharp p}$ at line 10 of this example, resulting a conclusive analysis with linear cost, which is much more efficient than using polyhedra with $\hat{\mathbb{D}}^{\sharp p}$.

4 Evaluation

We implemented a prototype abstract interpreter for the semantics $\hat{\mathbb{D}}^{\sharp p}$ and $\mathbb{\Delta}^{\sharp p}$ of the toy language introduced in this paper. It is about 2,500 lines of OCaml source code. It uses the APRON [12] library to experiment with the polyhedra and octagon abstract domains, and the BDDAPRON [13] library to implement state partitioning.

4.1 Benchmarking

We compare results on small examples selected from other authors' benchmarks [21,22,24]. Note that some of these benchmarks originate from real patches in GNU core utilities. We added a larger benchmark (also from a Coreutils patch), to evaluate scalability. For most benchmarks, patches preserve most of the loop and branching structure, except for the seq benchmark from [21,22], which features deep modifications of the control structure. The related works do not address streams. As a consequence, these benchmarks do not feature unbounded reads into input streams, except for the remove benchmark, which we presented in the introduction: see Fig. 1 and Fig. 2. Note that we simplified this benchmark to fstatat caching for a single file, in order to compare with [21].

[21,22,24] deal with C programs directly, while we encode their benchmarks in our toy language. In addition, these references not only prove equivalences, but also characterize differences, while we focus on equivalence for now. We therefore selected benchmarks relevant to equivalence only, except for the so-called the [24, Fig. 2] example, which we modified slightly to restore equivalence of terminating executions: see Fig. 4. On the other hand, [24] gives several versions of their benchmarks, depending on the maximum numbers of loop iterations of the examples. Indeed, the symbolic execution technique they use is very sensitive to this parameter. We do not have this constraint, as we use widening instead of fully unrolling loops, so that we handle directly unbounded loops in a sound way.

Figure 18 summarises the results of our analysis. It shows the analysis timings and results of our prototype, as well as timings of the analyses the related work, when they are available (their analyses are all successful). All experiments were conducted on a Intel® Core-i7™ processor. Our results are comparable with those of the original authors, with speedups of one order of magnitude or more. Some timing differences, of the order of milliseconds, cannot be considered significant, especially as the experiments are not performed on the same machines. A significant point, however, is that benchmark LoopMult takes 49 seconds in [24], which is 2 orders of magnitude slower than benchmark Const, while, with our method, both Const and LoopMult are analyzed at roughly the same speed. This difference in behaviors can be explained as a benefit of widening over unrolling loops. Hence, our timing comparison proves that our method can achieve at worst a similar speed, and it is also much more scalable for problems difficult in previous work. Note that [24] compared their method to well-established tools, such as Symdiff [14] and RVT [8], and observed speedups of one order of magnitude and more with respect to them. Therefore, it is not useful to compare our prototype with these tools on these benchmarks.

Most benchmarks are analyzed successfully with the polyhedra domain, without partitioning. The seq benchmark, for instance, is analyzed precisely despite significant changes in the control structure, as the matching of statements is established as part of the syntax of double programs. Only the remove benchmark requires partitioning for a successful analysis with the polyhedra domain. Four other benchmarks are analyzed very efficiently with the non relational interval domain, thanks to the $\mathbb{\Delta}^{\sharp p}$ semantics. Partitioning improves the precision on three other, but reduces efficiency. Nonetheless, some benchmarks, such as LoopSub, cannot be analysed conclusively using a non relational numeric domain with semantics $\hat{\mathbb{D}}^{\sharp p}$ or $\mathbb{\Delta}^{p}$ Indeed, related patches exchange the roles of two variables a and b, so that the challenge is not to infer $a_1 = a_2 \wedge b_1 = b_2$, but $a_1 = b_2 \wedge b_1 = a_2$. We therefore developed a dedicated abstract domain, to refine $\hat{\mathbb{D}}^{\sharp p}$ with automatically inferred variable equalities. This domain is based on union-find data structure that maintains a partitioning of the set $\mathcal{V}_1 \cup \mathcal{V}_2 \cup \mathcal{Q}$ of program variables. Two variables are part of the same equivalence class if they are guaranteed to be equal. The associate abstract lattice is the dual of the standard geometric lattice of partitions of a finite set: $a \sqsubseteq b$ means that partition b refines partition a, *i.e.* every equivalence class of a is a union of classes of b; $\top$ is the set of singleton variables; and the smallest non $\bot$ element is the whole set of variables. This abstract lattice has finite height, so we use union in place of widening. The LoopSub benchmark is analysed successfully using a reduced product between intervals and this domain.

4.2 Handling Streams

All benchmarks of Fig. 18 were analyzed using fixed-length queues of length 1, as the related works do not handle input streams. Note that abstracting infinite input streams with fixed-length queues of length 1 is also enough to analyze some patches of infinite-state programs with unbounded loops reading from a

Related origin	Benchmark	LOC	Related time	$\mathbb{D}^{\sharp 1}$(polyhedra) Partitioning No	Yes	$\mathbb{D}^{\sharp 1}$(octagon) Partitioning No	Yes	$\Delta^{\sharp 1}$(interval) Partitioning No	Yes
[24]	Comp	13	539 ms	14 ms ✓		18 ms ✗		2 ms ✗	
	Const	9	541 ms	7 ms ✓		17 ms ✓		1 ms ✓	
	Fig. 2	14	–	4 ms ✓		5 ms ✓		1 ms ✓	
	LoopMult	14	49[2] s	20 ms ✓		56 ms ✗		1 ms ✗	
	LoopSub	15	1.2 s	19 ms ✓		53 ms ✗		2 ms ✗	
	UnchLoop	13	2.8[3] s	15 ms ✓		36 ms ✗		2 ms ✓	
[21]	sign	12	–	6 ms ✓		8 ms ✗	420 ms ✓	2 ms ✗	400 ms ✓
	sum	14	4 s	14 ms ✓		30 ms ✓		6 ms ✗	3.2 s ✓[4]
	copy[1]	37	7 s	102 ms ✓		60 ms ✓		2 ms ✗	430 ms ✓
	remove[1]	19	1 s	31.6 s ✗	481 ms ✓	42 ms ✗	322 ms ✓	7 ms ✗	
[21,22]	seq[1]	41	11 s	75 ms ✓		500 ms ✗		2 ms ✗	
	test[1]	158	–	96 ms ✓		521 ms ✓		4 ms ✓	

Fig. 18. Benchmarks

```
s = input(−5,5);
b = input(0,1);
{ x = input(0,10); } || {/* skip */}
while ( b == 1 ) {
  {/* skip */} || { x = input(0,10); }
  s = s + x;
  b = input(0,1);
  { x = input(0,10); } || {/* skip */}
}
assert_sync(s);
```

Fig. 19. Reordering reads from an input stream

stream (e.g. a file), even when patches reorder input statements across the body of unbounded loops.

Figure 19 shows an example. This patch reorders input statements in the loop, and changes the number of input statements in terminating executions. The loop is unbounded, and the program is infinite-state. Terminating executions of the left and right projections compute equal values for s, though possibly not for x. This double program is analyzed successfully with $\mathbb{D}^{\sharp 1}$, using any relational numerical domain: 33 ms for polyhedra, 43 ms for octagon, and 18 ms for the reduced product between the domains of intervals and variable equalities. To the best of our knowledge, no previous work has sound and precise automatic analyses for patches of this type.

In the bounded abstraction of streams, the unbounded FIFO queue represents the subsequence of input values read by the program ahead in the sequence, and not yet read by the program behind. Though we are bounding this queue in the abstract, we retain precise information on executions reading arbitrary long input sequences. The bounded queue allows retaining relational information between all input values read with delays less or equal to the bound, while non relational

```
{ a = input(0,5); a = input(−5,0); } || {/* skip */}
x = input(0,5);
x = input(−5,0);
s = a || x;
assert(−5 <= s && s <= 0); // inferred with with a queue of length p ≥ 1
assert_sync(s); // inferred with a queue of length p ≥ 2
```

Fig. 20. Relational and non relational information versus lengths of queues

(interval) information is retained for values read with larger delays. Figure 20 shows a simple example. Using a queue of length 1 is enough to infer the range of variable s in both projections of the double program. On the contrary, a queue of length at least 2 is necessary to prove that both programs compute equal values for s.

5 Conclusion

We presented a static analysis for software patches. Our method is based on abstract interpretation, and parametric in the choice of an abstract domain. We presented a novel concrete collecting semantics, expressing the behaviors of two syntactically close versions of a program at the same time. This semantics deals with programs reading from unbounded input streams. We also introduced a novel numeric domain to bound differences between the values of the variables in the two programs, which has linear cost. We implemented a prototype and experimented on a few small examples from the literature.

In future work, we will consider extensions to larger, and non purely numeric programs, towards the analysis of realistic patches. We will also extend our method to characterize the semantic differences between two non equivalent versions of program. We will also investigate to what extend our approach could generalize to portability analysis, a dual problem where we wish to compare the semantics of the same program in two different environments. We plan to experiment with other abstract domains for our analysis, such as zonotopes. Finally, we will investigate the connections between our semantics and information flow problems. Indeed, as a side-effect of our method, our analysis is able to prove that two sets of executions of the same program compute equal values for some outputs. This is useful for proving some information flow properties, such as secrecy. For instance, Fig. 21 shows two programs with public variable pub and secret variable sec. These programs read pub as an input value, and choose sec non-deterministically, For all pairs of executions reading equal values in pub, but possibly different values in sec, Program 21(a) computes equal values for pub. hence ensuring secrecy. On the contrary, Program 21(b) leaks the sign of sec. Our analysis is able to distinguish these two programs. Indeed, it compares the semantics of two versions of each program. In this case, both versions have exactly the same code, which is a form of self-composition [3,20].

```
pub = input(−10,10);
sec = rand(−5,5);
if (sec < 0) pub = 1;
pub = 0;
assert_sync(pub); // OK
```

(a) secure program

```
pub = input(−10,10);
sec = rand(−5,5);
if (sec < 0) pub = 1;
pub = pub + 1;
assert_sync(pub); // failed
```

(b) insecure program

Fig. 21. Proving information flow properties

Data Availability Statements. The datasets/code generated during and/or analysed during the current study are available in the Figshare repository: https://doi.org/10.6084/m9.figshare.9860972.v1

References

1. The Be Book. https://www.haiku-os.org/legacy-docs/bebook/index.html
2. The Haiku Operating System. https://www.haiku-os.org/
3. Barthe, G., D'argenio, P.R., Rezk, T.: Secure information flow by self-composition. Math. Struct. Comput. Sci. **21**(6), 1207–1252 (2011)
4. Cousot, P., Cousot, R.: Abstract interpretation: a unified lattice model for static analysis of programs by construction or approximation of fixpoints. In: POPL 1977, pp. 238–252. ACM, January 1977
5. Cousot, P., Halbwachs, N.: Automatic discovery of linear restraints among variables of a program. In: POPL 1978. pp. 84–97. ACM (1978)
6. Delmas, D., Miné, A.: Analysis of program differences with numerical abstract interpretation. In: PERR 2019, Prague, Czech Republic, April 2019
7. Floyd, R.W.: Assigning meanings to programs. Proc. Symp. Appl. Math. **19**, 19–32 (1967)
8. Godlin, B., Strichman, O.: Regression verification. In: Proceedings of DAC 2009, pp. 466–471. ACM, New York (2009)
9. Goubault, E., Putot, S.: Static analysis of finite precision computations. In: Jhala, R., Schmidt, D. (eds.) VMCAI 2011. LNCS, vol. 6538, pp. 232–247. Springer, Heidelberg (2011). https://doi.org/10.1007/978-3-642-18275-4_17
10. Goubault, E., Putot, S.: Robustness analysis of finite precision implementations. In: Programming Languages and Systems, pp. 50–57 (2013)
11. Jackson, D., Ladd, D.A.: Semantic diff: a tool for summarizing the effects of modifications. In: Proceedings of ICSM 1994, pp. 243–252 (1994)
12. Jeannet, B., Miné, A.: Apron: a library of numerical abstract domains for static analysis. In: Bouajjani, A., Maler, O. (eds.) CAV 2009. LNCS, vol. 5643, pp. 661–667. Springer, Heidelberg (2009). https://doi.org/10.1007/978-3-642-02658-4_52
13. Jeannet, B.: Bddapron: A logico-numerical abstract domain library (2009). http://pop-art.inrialpes.fr/˜bjeannet/bjeannet-forge/bddapron/
14. Lahiri, S.K., Hawblitzel, C., Kawaguchi, M., Rebêlo, H.: SYMDIFF: a language-agnostic semantic diff tool for imperative programs. In: Madhusudan, P., Seshia, S.A. (eds.) CAV 2012. LNCS, vol. 7358, pp. 712–717. Springer, Heidelberg (2012). https://doi.org/10.1007/978-3-642-31424-7_54
15. Lahiri, S.K., McMillan, K.L., Sharma, R., Hawblitzel, C.: Differential assertion checking. Proc. ESEC/FSE **2013**, 345–355 (2013)

16. Marinescu, P.D., Cadar, C.: KATCH: high-coverage testing of software patches. Proc. ESEC/FSE **2013**, 235–245 (2013)
17. Martel, M.: Propagation of roundoff errors in finite precision computations: a semantics approach. In: Le Métayer, D. (ed.) ESOP 2002. LNCS, vol. 2305, pp. 194–208. Springer, Heidelberg (2002). https://doi.org/10.1007/3-540-45927-8_14
18. Miné, A.: The octagon abstract domain. High. Order Symb. Comput. **19**(1), 31–100 (2006)
19. Mora, F., Li, Y., Rubin, J., Chechik, M.: Client-specific equivalence checking. Proc. ASE **2018**, 441–451 (2018)
20. Müller, C., Kovács, M., Seidl, H.: An analysis of universal information flow based on self-composition. In: CSF 2015, pp. 380–393 (2015)
21. Partush, N., Yahav, E.: Abstract semantic differencing for numerical programs. In: Logozzo, F., Fähndrich, M. (eds.) SAS 2013. LNCS, vol. 7935, pp. 238–258. Springer, Heidelberg (2013). https://doi.org/10.1007/978-3-642-38856-9_14
22. Partush, N., Yahav, E.: Abstract semantic differencing via speculative correlation. In: Proceedings of OOPSLA 2014, pp. 811–828 (2014)
23. Person, S., Dwyer, M.B., Elbaum, S., Păsăreanu, C.S.: Differential symbolic execution. In: Proceedings of the 16th ACM SIGSOFT 2008/FSE-16, pp. 226–237 (2008)
24. Trostanetski, A., Grumberg, O., Kroening, D.: Modular Demand-Driven Analysis of Semantic Difference for Program Versions. In: Ranzato, F. (ed.) SAS 2017. LNCS, vol. 10422, pp. 405–427. Springer, Cham (2017). https://doi.org/10.1007/978-3-319-66706-5_20

Verifying Numerical Programs via Iterative Abstract Testing

Banghu Yin[1,2(✉)], Liqian Chen[1], Jiangchao Liu[1], Ji Wang[1,2(✉)], and Patrick Cousot[3]

[1] College of Computer, National University of Defense Technology, Changsha, China
{bhyin,wj}@nudt.edu.cn

[2] State Key Laboratory of High Performance Computing, Changsha, China

[3] New York University, New York, USA

Abstract. When applying abstract interpretation to verification, it may suffer from the problem of getting too conservative over-approximations to verify a given target property, and being hardly able to generate counter-examples when the property does not hold. In this paper, we propose iterative abstract testing, to create a property-oriented verification approach based on abstract interpretation. Abstract testing employs forward abstract executions (i.e., forward analysis) together with property checking to mimic (regular) testing, and utilizes backward abstract executions (i.e., backward analysis) to derive necessary preconditions that may falsify the target property, and be useful for reducing the input space that needs further exploration. To verify a property, we conduct abstract testing in an iterative manner by utilizing dynamic partitioning to split the input space into sub-spaces such that each sub-space involves fewer program behaviors and may be easier to verify. Moreover, we leverage bounded exhaustive testing to verify bounded small sub-spaces, as a means to complement abstract testing based verification. The experimental results show that our approach has comparable strength with several state-of-the-art verification tools.

Keywords: Program verification · Abstract interpretation · Abstract testing · Input space partitioning

1 Introduction

Abstract interpretation [18] has been successfully applied to static analysis, due to its soundness guarantee and scalability. It can automatically handle loops generally in a terminate and sound way, compared to other approaches such as bounded model checking and symbolic execution. And it allows the use of infinite abstract domains of program properties. In this paper, we focus on applying abstract interpretation to verify properties in numerical programs.

However, in the context of verification, there still exist several limitations over current abstract interpretation based approaches [25]. One limitation is

B.-Y. E. Chang (Ed.): SAS 2019, LNCS 11822, pp. 247–267, 2019.
https://doi.org/10.1007/978-3-030-32304-2_13

that the generated invariants may be not precise enough to prove the target property, due to the too conservative over-approximation of the concrete semantics of the program. More clearly, the major sources of imprecision of abstract interpretation come from the following aspects: (1) Most widely used abstract domains (such as intervals [18], octagons [41] and polyhedra [22]) have limitations in expressing disjunctive or non-linear properties, which are common in programs, for instance, at the joins of control-flows; (2) The widening operator in abstract interpretation which ensures the convergence of fixpoint iteration may bring severe precision loss, because widening often aggressively weakens unstable predicates in each iteration. Moreover, when one pass of the analysis does not provide precise enough invariants to prove the target property, it lacks a systematic approach (like counterexample-guided refinement) to refine the abstractions. Another limitation of most current abstract interpretation based approaches is that it can hardly generate counter-examples when a property does not hold.

In this paper, we propose an iterative approach to verify properties of numerical programs by exploiting iterative abstract testing based on abstract interpretation. We leverage the notion of "abstract testing" [19] to denote the process of abstract execution (i.e., forward analysis) of a program with an given abstract input (which represents a set of concrete inputs) and the checking of whether the abstract output satisfies the target property. The key idea of our approach is to perform abstract testing iteratively in a top-down manner, by refining the abstract input via partitioning, wherein the refinement process also makes use of the computed necessary precondition of violating the target assertion via the "inverse" abstract execution (i.e., backward analysis [21]). When the property has been checked to hold for all abstract sub-inputs in the partition, the iterative process stops and gives a proof. Another benefit of partitioning is that it enables to conduct verification via bounded exhaustive testing [11,38] over an abstract sub-input of small size. The use of bounded exhaustive testing allows our approach to generate counter-examples when the target property does not hold. Overall, our approach not only can give a proof when the property holds, but also can supply a concrete counter-example when the property does not hold.

This paper makes the following contributions.

- We propose an iterative abstract testing based program verification algorithm with dynamic input partitioning. The partitioning enables our analysis to focus on smaller input spaces in each of which the program may involve fewer disjunctive or non-linear behaviors and thus may be easier to verify.
- We propose to use bounded exhaustive testing to complement abstract testing based verification. When the considered input space after partitioning is of small enough size, we could utilize bounded exhaustive testing to replace abstract testing. Bounded exhaustive testing can completely verify the target program even when it involves very complicated behaviors (which may be out of the verification capability of abstract interpretation), and can supply a concrete counterexample when the property does not hold.

- We have implemented the proposed approach in a tool called VATer and conducted experimental comparison between VATer and other available state-of-the-art verification tools. Our experiments on a set of verification benchmarks show that our approach is promising.

The rest of this paper is organized as follow: Sect. 2 gives an overview of our approach. Section 3 presents the main approach based on iterative abstract testing. Section 4 presents how to utilize bounded exhaustive testing. Section 5 provides the experimental results on the benchmarks. Section 6 discusses related work. Finally, the conclusions as well as future work are given in Sect. 7.

2 Overview

2.1 The Framework

First, we give an overview of our verification framework, namely Verification based on Abstract Testing (VAT), as shown in Fig. 1. Overall, given a numerical program P (in which each variable is of machine-bounded numerical type) and a property represented as an assertion ψ, VAT gives a proof when the assertion holds or generates concrete counter-examples when the assertion does not hold. In detail, VAT involves the iteration of the following phases.

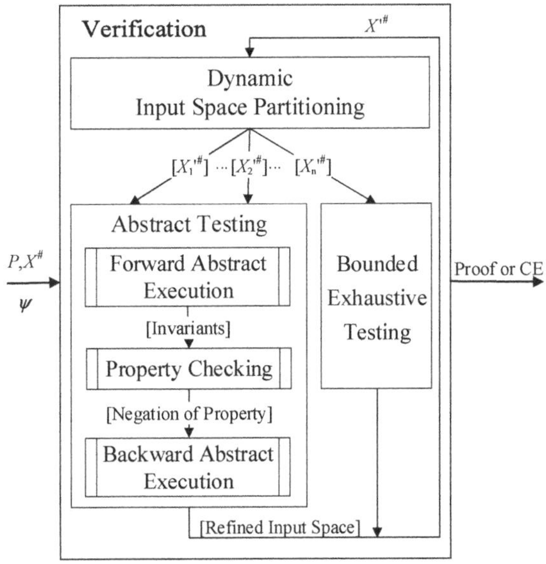

Fig. 1. The main framework of our approach.

Forward Abstract Execution. It acts as the abstract execution engine of abstract testing, which takes (one pass) forward abstract interpretation to generate program invariants under the given abstract input $X^\sharp$. Forward abstract execution "executes" a program in the sense of an abstract semantics instead of a concrete one, thus has the ability to consider several (possibly unbounded) concrete executions at a time.

Property Checking. It mimics the oracle of abstract testing. It checks the logic relation between the invariants generated by forward abstract execution and the assertion ψ. In concrete testing, the verifying result can be only "True" or "False" for each test case. However, in abstract testing, three possible verifying results may be returned: "True", "False" or "Unknown". If the result is "Unknown", we need further exploration on $X^\sharp$.

Backward Abstract Execution. It performs a backward analysis based on abstract interpretation for $X^\sharp$ that needs further exploration, starting from the assertion location and assuming that the negation of the target assertion holds. It essentially computes the necessary precondition for the failure of the target assertion, which results in a refined abstract input $X'^\sharp \subseteq X^\sharp$ at the program entry. If $X'^\sharp$ is the empty set, it means that the assertion holds true for the abstract input $X^\sharp$. Otherwise, we need continue to explore $X'^\sharp$.

Input Space Partitioning. To further explore the abstract input case $X'^\sharp$, VAT partitions $X'^\sharp$ into a set of sub-inputs $\{X_1'^\sharp, X_2'^\sharp, ..., X_n'^\sharp\}$. Then VAT checks further for each sub-input $X_i'^\sharp$ separately. For a sub-input $X_i'^\sharp$, if its size is small enough, VAT uses bounded exhaustive testing, otherwise it uses abstract testing (on top of forward and backward abstract execution and property checking). This phase mimics the abstract test case generation of abstract testing.

Bounded Exhaustive Testing. When the number of concrete inputs in the considered abstract input $X_i'^\sharp$ is small, VAT uses bounded exhaustive testing to check the assertion for all possible concrete inputs. The rationale behind bounded exhaustive testing is that the failure of assertions can be mainly revealed within small bounds, and exhaustively testing within the bounds ensures that no "corner case" is missed [33].

When this whole verification process terminates, VAT will find a concrete counter-example, or provide a complete proof, or a resource limit is reached.

2.2 An Illustrating Example

Now we illustrate our approach by verifying the assertion ψ (i.e., *y != 1225*) in the example P shown in Fig. 2(a). P implements the mathematical function shown in Fig. 2(b). From the mathematical function, one could know that when the input is $n = 49$ and *flag* $= 1$, the program will result in $y = 1225$ at Line 10 (while all other inputs will satisfy the assertion ψ). Thus the assertion ψ actually does not hold in program P.

Verifying ψ (whether it holds or not) in P automatically and completely is challenging for the following reasons. First, there is no restriction given on the input variables n and *flag*. Thus, without considering any mathematical background behind the program, $2^{32} * 2^{32}$ cases of possible values of the input variables need to be considered if they are 32-bit integers. Directly using exhaustive

```
1  void fun(int n, int flag){
2    int x = 0,y = 0;
3    while(x < n){
4      x = x + 1;
5      if(flag == 1)
6        y = y + x;
7      else
8        y = y - x * x;
9    }
10   assert(y != 1225);
11 }
```

(a)

$$y = \begin{cases} 0 & n \leq 0 \\ \frac{1}{2}n(n+1) & 1 \leq n, flag = 1 \\ -\frac{1}{6}n(n+1)(2n+1) & 1 \leq n, flag \neq 1 \end{cases}$$

(b)

Fig. 2. An illustrating example.

testing to verify ψ in P would cause too much overhead. Second, the loop condition at Line 3 (i.e., $x < n$) depends on the symbolic input variable n. Symbolically executing all feasible program paths (through unrolling) is not possible, owing to the potentially infinite number of paths. Thus symbolic execution or bounded model checking can hardly verify ψ in P automatically and completely. Third, P involves disjunctive and non-linear behaviors, which is out of the expressiveness of most widely used numerical abstract domains [40]. And the non-linear behaviors also make most SMT solvers hard or even unable to verify the assertion. Hence, it is also difficult to verify the assertion by using abstraction and SMT based techniques, such as CEGAR based software model checking [17].

We now illustrate step by step how VAT verifies the assertion ψ in P. First, since there is no constraint over the input variables n and $flag$, VAT starts from the initial abstract input $X^\sharp = \top$. Suppose we use here the octagon abstract domain [41] to perform abstract interpretation. Abstract execution with abstract input $X^\sharp = \top$ will result in the following invariant (namely $Inv^{X^\sharp}$) at the assertion location (at Line 10): $n - x \leq 0 \wedge x \geq 0$. Then our analysis performs property checking and finds that this invariant is not strong enough to prove ψ or $\neg\psi$. Thus we perform a backward analysis starting from the assertion location assuming that $y == 1225$ (that is the negation of the original assertion). However, this round of backward analysis results in $\top$ at program entry and does not help in refining the necessary precondition to falsify the assertion. Then we partition the current abstract input $\top$ into several sub-inputs. Here, we use a predicate based partitioning strategy (which will be described in Sect. 3.3) to partition $\top$ into the following 6 abstract sub-inputs: $\{X_1^\sharp : n \leq 0 \wedge flag \leq 0; X_2^\sharp : n \leq 0 \wedge flag == 1; X_3^\sharp : n \leq 0 \wedge flag \geq 2; X_4^\sharp : n \geq 1 \wedge flag \leq 0; X_5^\sharp : n \geq 1 \wedge flag == 1; X_6^\sharp : n \geq 1 \wedge flag \geq 2\}$. Then verifying ψ on abstract input $X^\sharp$ boils down to verifying ψ on each abstract sub-input.

For $X_1^\sharp$, we perform forward abstract execution and get the invariant $\{Inv^{X_1^\sharp} : y == 0 \wedge \ldots\}$ at the assertion location. After performing property checking, we find that $Inv^{X_1^\sharp} \Rightarrow \psi$, which imply that ψ holds for the abstract input $X_1^\sharp$. Similarly, for the other abstract inputs $X_2^\sharp$, $X_3^\sharp$, $X_4^\sharp$ and $X_6^\sharp$, the invariants generated by abstract execution at the assertion location are respectively $\{Inv^{X_2^\sharp} : y == 0 \wedge \ldots; Inv^{X_3^\sharp} : y == 0 \wedge \ldots; Inv^{X_4^\sharp} : y \leq -1 \wedge \ldots; Inv^{X_6^\sharp} : y \leq -1 \wedge \ldots\}$, which implies that ψ holds for all these abstract sub-inputs.

Now we consider the more complicated case, i.e., the abstract sub-input $X_5^\sharp$. We perform abstract execution on $X_5^\sharp$ and get invariant $Inv^{X_5^\sharp} : \{n - 1 \geq 0 \wedge -n + y \geq 0 \wedge x - 1 \geq 0 \wedge -x + y \geq 0\}$. Unfortunately, $Inv^{X_5^\sharp}$ is not precise enough to prove ψ or $\neg\psi$. Then we perform backward analysis assuming that $y == 1225$ at the assertion location and get a refined abstract input $X_{51}^\sharp : \{n \geq 1 \wedge n \leq 1225 \wedge flag == 1\}$. In other words, inside $X_5^\sharp$, only those inputs in $X_{51}^\sharp$ may cause the assertion ψ to fail, thus we only need to check $X_{51}^\sharp$ for the case $X_5^\sharp$. Since now the abstract sub-input $X_{51}^\sharp$ contains only 1225 concrete inputs, we employ the bounded exhaustive testing to check the case $X_{51}^\sharp$. Then we will find the concrete counter-example input $n = 49, flag = 1$ in $X_{51}^\sharp$ that falsifies the assertion ψ.

To summarize, for the illustrating example shown in Fig. 2(a), we totally partition the whole input space $X^\sharp$ into 6 abstract sub-inputs such that $X^\sharp = X_1^\sharp \cup \ldots \cup X_6^\sharp$, where $X_1^\sharp, X_2^\sharp, X_3^\sharp, X_4^\sharp, X_6^\sharp$ are verified by abstract testing and we use bounded exhaustive testing to find a concrete counter-example in $X_{51}^\sharp$ which is a refinement substitution of $X_5^\sharp$.

3 Property-Oriented Iterative Abstract Testing

In this section, we formalize the main idea of iterative abstract testing. Section 3.1 gives the background of abstract testing. Section 3.2 introduces our framework of iterative abstract testing. Section 3.3 presents the algorithm of partitioning on abstract input.

3.1 Abstract Testing

With the abstract semantics, sound program invariants can be computed automatically in finite steps by forward abstract interpretation [18] (denoted as Forward_AI) and backward abstract interpretation [21] (denoted as Backward_AI) respectively. The computation with abstract interpretation is parameterized by abstract domains specifying the considered approximated properties. Note that backward abstract execution also makes use of the invariants generated by the aforementioned forward abstract execution. In this paper, we combine forward and backward abstract execution to generate for each program location those constraints that describe states which are reachable from the abstract input and may cause the target assertion fail.

The process of *Abstract testing* (denoted as AbstractTesting()) is built on top of Forward_AI and Backward_AI, as defined in Algorithm 1. Abstract testing takes a program P, a target property ψ to verify, a chosen abstract domain D and an abstract input $X^\sharp$. Abstract testing first calls Forward_AI (at Line 1), which computes the invariants (denoted as $Inv^{X^\sharp}$) on program P with initial state $X^\sharp$.

Algorithm 1. Abstract Testing Algorithm

Input: program P, property ψ, abstract input $X^\sharp$, abstract domain D
Output: result res, refined abstract input $X'^\sharp$, program invariant $Inv_b^{X^\sharp}$
1: $Inv^{X^\sharp} \leftarrow$ Forward_AI($P, X^\sharp, D$)
2: $Inv_b^{X^\sharp} \leftarrow Inv^{X^\sharp}$
3: **if** $Inv^{X^\sharp}(l_\psi) \Rightarrow \psi$ **then**
4:     res $\leftarrow$ True
5:     $X'^\sharp \leftarrow \perp$
6: **else**
7:     **if** $Inv^{X^\sharp}(l_\psi) \Rightarrow \neg\psi$ **then**
8:         $res \leftarrow$ False
9:         $X'^\sharp \leftarrow \perp$
10:     **else**
11:         $Inv_b^{X^\sharp} \leftarrow$ Backward_AI($P, Inv^{X^\sharp}(l_\psi) \sqcap \neg\psi, D$)
12:         **if** $X^\sharp \sqcap Inv_b^{X^\sharp}(l_{ent}) == \perp$ **then**
13:             $res \leftarrow$ True
14:             $X'^\sharp \leftarrow \perp$
15:         **else**
16:             $res \leftarrow$ Unknown
17:             $X'^\sharp \leftarrow X^\sharp \sqcap Inv_b^{X^\sharp}(l_{ent})$
18:         **end if**
19:     **end if**
20: **end if**
21: **return** $res, X'^\sharp, Inv_b^{X^\sharp}$

To check whether the property ψ holds, abstract testing extracts $Inv^{X^\sharp}(l_\psi)$ of $Inv^{X^\sharp}$ at the location (i.e., l_ψ) before the assertion $assert(\psi)$. Three cases may arise after the checking: (a) the property ψ is surely true (Line 3 in Algorithm 1); (b) the property ψ is surely false (Line 7); (c) whether the property ψ holds or not can not be determinated yet by $Inv^{X^\sharp}(l_\psi)$ (Line 10). In the third case, a backward abstract execution Backward_AI is launched to refine the abstract input $X^\sharp$. Backward_AI takes the program and the error state $Inv^{X^\sharp}(l_\psi) \sqcap \neg\psi$ as input and computes backward the necessary pre-condition $Inv_b^{X^\sharp}$ that may cause the property to fail. If $X^\sharp \sqcap Inv_b^{X^\sharp}(l_{ent})$ (where l_{ent} is the entry location of P) is $\perp$ (which means there is no concrete input in $X^\sharp$ that violates ψ), ψ must be true (Lines 12). Otherwise, whether ψ holds is still unknown (Line 15) within $X^\sharp$, and in this case a refined input $X'^\sharp$ is generated as a refinement substitution of $X^\sharp$ (Line 17).

3.2 Algorithm of Iterative Abstract Testing

One iteration of abstract testing may fail to verify the given property due to the over-approximation. In this paper, we propose to partition the input space to refine the computed invariants on demand.

Definition 1 (*Partition of abstract input*). *A partition of an abstract input $X^\sharp$ is a set of sub-inputs $\{X_1^\sharp, X_2^\sharp, \ldots, X_n^\sharp\}$ such that*

$$\begin{cases} \forall i \in \{1, 2, ..., n\}, X_i^\sharp \neq \perp \\ \forall i, j \in \{1, 2, ..., n\}, i \neq j \Rightarrow X_i^\sharp \sqcap X_j^\sharp = \perp \\ \sqcup_{i \in \{1,2,...,n\}} X_i^\sharp = X^\sharp. \end{cases}$$

Let $P(X^\sharp)$ denote the program P, whose initial state of input variables are constrained by $X^\sharp$. Then we have the following proposition.

Proposition 1 (*Soundness of verification by partitioning*). *Let $\{X_1^\sharp, X_2^\sharp, \ldots, X_n^\sharp\}$ be a partition of abstract input $X^\sharp$. If for any $i \in \{1, 2, ..., n\}$, assertion ψ is proved to be true in program $P(X_i^\sharp)$, then ψ must be true in $P(X^\sharp)$.*

Proof. We assume ψ is false in $P(X^\sharp)$, then there must exists a concrete input x that satisfies the constraint of $X^\sharp$, but makes ψ false. From Definition 1, we know $\sqcup_{i \in \{1,2,...,n\}} X_i^\sharp = X^\sharp$, thus there exists $k \in \{1, 2, ..., n\}$ such that $x \in X_k^\sharp$, which means ψ is false in $P(X_k^\sharp)$. This conflicts with the assumption. Thus ψ is true in $\mathrm{P}(X^\sharp)$. □

Algorithm 2. Iterative Abstract Testing Algorithm

Input: program P, property ψ, abstract domain D
Output: True or False or Timeout
1: worklist $L \leftarrow \{\top\}$
2: **while** $L \neq \varnothing$ **do**
3:　　$X^\sharp \leftarrow$ Remove(L)　 //get and remove an element from L
4:　　$(res, X'^\sharp, Inv_b^{X^\sharp}) \leftarrow$ AbstractTesting($P, \psi, X^\sharp, D$)
5:　　**if** $res ==$ False **then**
6:　　　　Terminate with counter-example in $X^\sharp$
7:　　**else**
8:　　　　**if** $res ==$ True **then**
9:　　　　　*skip*
10:　　　　**else**
11:　　　　　$X\_list \leftarrow$ Partition($X'^\sharp, Inv_b^{X^\sharp}$)
12:　　　　　$L \leftarrow$ Insert(L, X_list)
13:　　　　**end if**
14:　　**end if**
15:　　**if** Timeout **then**
16:　　　　Terminate with Timeout
17:　　**end if**
18: **end while**
19: Terminate with ψ proved

Intuitively, our framework partitions an abstract input $X^\sharp$ when one iteration of abstract testing cannot prove whether the property holds or not, and then applies abstract testing further on the partitioned sub-inputs separately. The overall iterative algorithm is shown in Algorithm 2, which fits into a conventional worklist algorithm. In the beginning, the only element in the worklist

L is the initial input space I. For the sake of simplicity, in this paper we assume $I = \top$ (which means there is no restriction over the input). Then the algorithm copes with the abstract inputs in the worklist L one by one (in Lines 2–18). For each abstract input $X^\sharp$ in the worklist L (Line 3), the algorithm calls AbstractTesting(), which is detailed in Algorithm 1, trying to prove the property ψ with respect to the abstract input $X^\sharp$. If it fails, AbstractTesting() will return a refined abstract input $X'^\sharp$. Then Algorithm 2 partitions $X'^\sharp$ at Line 11 (where the Partition() procedure will be detailed in Algorithm 3), and puts all the newly split abstract sub-inputs into the worklist and repeats the process again (starting from Line 2). Until a counter-example is found or the property is proved true over all abstract inputs in the worklist, or a time limit is reached, the algorithm terminates.

Algorithm 3. Partitioning Algorithm

Input: abstract input $X^\sharp$, program invariant $Inv_b^{X^\sharp}$
Output: abstract input list X_list
1: $PS_0 \leftarrow \varnothing; X\_list = \{X^\sharp\}$
2: **for each** $l \in Lc(P)$ **do**
3: $\quad PS_0 \leftarrow PS_0 \bigcup \text{Project}(Inv_b^{X^\sharp}, l)$
4: **end for**
5: **for each** $p_0 \in PS_0$ **do**
6: $\quad p \leftarrow \text{Rename}(p_0)$
7: $\quad$ **for each** $X \in X\_list$ **do**
8: $\quad\quad X\_list \leftarrow (X\_list \setminus X) \cup \{X \wedge p, X \wedge \neg p\}$
9: $\quad$ **end for**
10: **end for**
11: **if** $X\_list = \{X^\sharp\}$ **then**
12: $\quad Itvs \leftarrow \text{Interval\_Hull}(X^\sharp)$
13: $\quad v \leftarrow \text{Var\_of\_Largest\_Range}(Itvs)$
14: $\quad X\_list \leftarrow \{X^\sharp \wedge v_{inf} \le v \le \frac{v_{inf}+v_{sup}}{2}, X^\sharp \wedge \frac{v_{inf}+v_{sup}}{2} < v \le v_{sup}\}$
15: **end if**
16: **return** X_list

3.3 Partitioning

Input partitioning plays an important role in the iterative abstract testing. Depending on the target programs, we employ two strategies for dynamic input partitioning as shown in Algorithm 3: predicate based strategy (from Lines 2 to 10) and dichotomy strategy (from Lines 11 to 15).

Predicate-Based Strategy. The main idea of this strategy is to first derive a set of predicates over the symbolic initial values of the input variables and then to partition the input space $X^\sharp$ into a set of sub-inputs based on these predicates. To this end, first, as a preprocessing step, for every input parameter (e.g., x) in the program P, we introduce a symbolic input variable (e.g., x_0) and insert an assignment statement (e.g., $x_0 = x$;) to symbolically record its initial value.

AbstractTesting() (at Line 4 of Algorithm 2) analyzes the instrumented program and returns the program invariant $Inv_b^{X^\sharp}$, which records all the constraints between the original variables of P and the introduced symbolic input variables.

In Algorithm 3, to derive interesting predicates, we only consider predicates at those program locations after conditional tests (which are represented as *Lc(P)* at Line 2). Moreover, we are only interested in predicates over symbolic input variables, the set of which is denoted as PS_0. Then for each program location l in *Lc(P)*, we project out all other variables (except symbolic input variables) from the computed invariants $Inv_{\bar{b}}^{X^\sharp}$ by function Project() at Line 3. Project() returns a set of predicates over symbolic input variables, which are all collected into PS_0. Note that the projection operator is a default operator in each abstract domain and implemented efficiently using algorithms tailored to the specific constraint representation of the abstract domain. Then for each predicate p_0 in PS_0, we rename all the symbolic input variables (e.g., x_0) as the original input variables (e.g., x) by function Rename() at Line 6. It returns a splitting predicate p on input variables, which is used to split all the abstract inputs in X_list (from Lines 7 to 9). For each X in X_list, our algorithm first deletes X from X_list, then splits X into two abstract inputs (i.e., $X \wedge p$, $X \wedge \neg p$), and adds them into X_list at Line 8. Note that, in the worst case, 2^n abstract inputs can be generated based on n predicates. To prevent partition explosion, we need to bound the number of predicates used for partitioning. Our immediate idea chooses a limited number of those predicates that emerge early in the forward AI analysis.

Take our illustrating program in Fig. 2(a) for example. First, as shown in Fig. 3, at Line 2, our preprocess defines two symbolic input variables for the input parameters n and $flag$, and assigns them with the initial values of n and $flag$. Then abstract testing generates invariants as well as necessary precondition of property violation for the program using the Octagon abstract domain. After projecting out other variables, the invariants on n_0 and $flag_0$ are derived, which is shown as annotations in Fig. 3 at Lines 4, 6 and 11. After renaming, our analysis collects two meaningful atomic predicates $\{n \geq 1, flag = 1\}$. Based on them, the following 6 abstract sub-inputs are generated: $\{X_1^\sharp : n \leq 0 \wedge flag \leq 0; X_2^\sharp : n \leq 0 \wedge flag = 1; X_3^\sharp : n \leq 0 \wedge flag \geq 2; X_4^\sharp : n \geq 1 \wedge flag \leq 0; X_5^\sharp : n \geq 1 \wedge flag = 1; X_6^\sharp : n \geq 1 \wedge flag \geq 2\}$.

```
1   void fun(int n, int flag){
2     int n0=n, flag0=flag;
3     int x = 0,y = 0;
4     while(x < n){  // n0 ≥ 1 ∧
5       x = x + 1;
6       if(flag == 1)   // n0 ≥ 1 ∧ flag0=1
7         y = y + x;
8       else
9         y = y - x * x;
10    }
11    assert(y != 1225);   // top }
```

Fig. 3. The illustrating example with predicates annotated.

Given an abstract input $X^\sharp$, if no useful predicate on the symbolic input variables can be found, predicate based partitioning would fail (i.e., the condition at Line 11 in Algorithm 3 holds). In this case, our framework employs the dichotomy strategy (from Lines 12 to 14).

Dichotomy Strategy. This strategy projects every input variable in the abstract input $X^\sharp$ into an interval (e.g., we treat $\top$ as [-max_int,max_int-1] for Integer type) by function Interval_Hull() at Line 12, which returns interval hulls of all input variables. Then it chooses the variable of the largest range as the variable (i.e., v) to be split, which is done by function Var_of_Largest_Range() at Line 13. After that, it conducts splitting evenly on the interval range of v, and $X^\sharp$ is split into two abstract sub-inputs at Line 14, where v_{inf} and v_{sup} represent the lower bound and upper bound of v respectively.

3.4 Sorting of Abstract Inputs

This subsection elaborates the sorting of the elements in the worklist L in Algorithm 2 in the framework of iterative abstract testing. This operation is necessary in the sense that, if an abstract input that violates the property ψ can be put in the front of the worklist, then the verification process can terminate earlier.

To perform sorting, we define a fitness function for each abstract input $X^\sharp$ as $fit(X^\sharp) = \frac{|\gamma(Inv_{l_\psi}^{X^\sharp} \sqcap \neg\psi)|}{|\gamma(Inv_{l_\psi}^{X^\sharp} \sqcap \psi)|}$, where $Inv_{l_\psi}^{X^\sharp}$ is the invariant at the assertion location computed by Forward_AI, and γ is a concrete function mapping abstract states to concrete states soundly. Here we assume that if the value returned by $fit(X^\sharp)$ is larger, then it is more likely to find a property violation within $X^\sharp$. Since $|\gamma(Inv_{l_\psi}^{X^\sharp} \sqcap \neg\psi)|$ and $|\gamma(Inv_{l_\psi}^{X^\sharp} \sqcap \psi)|$ are usually too costly to compute, in practice, we use $fit'(X^\sharp) = \frac{|\gamma(\text{Interval\_Hull}(Inv_{l_\psi}^{X^\sharp} \sqcap \neg\psi))|}{|\gamma(\text{Interval\_Hull}(Inv_{l_\psi}^{X^\sharp} \sqcap \psi))|}$, where $|\gamma(\text{Interval\_Hull}(Y^\sharp))|$ represents the number of points in the interval hull of $Y^\sharp$. The value of $|\gamma(\text{Interval\_Hull}(Y^\sharp))|$ is computed by projecting each input variable y into its interval bound $[a_y, b_y]$, and multiplying the widths of all these intervals. In other words, the value of $|\gamma(\text{Interval\_Hull}(Y^\sharp))|$ is computed as the volume of the interval hull of $Y^\sharp$.

In iterative abstract testing, our algorithm computes $fit'(X^\sharp)$ for each generated abstract input $X^\sharp$, and adds them into the worklist satisfying the decreasing order according to their fitness values (in Line 12 of Algorithm 2).

4 Combination with Bounded Exhaustive Testing

When the considered abstract input $X^\sharp$ is bounded and of small size (which means that the number of concrete inputs inside $X^\sharp$ is small), a good alterative of verifying the program on such an abstract input $X^\sharp$ is to use bounded exhaustive testing (BET) [11,38], which is complete, sound, and able to find counter-examples if they exist. In this section, we extend our framework by combining with bounded exhaustive testing.

4.1 Synergic Verification Framework

Our synergic verification framework (denoted by SynergicVerification()) is based on Algorithm 2, while the only change is replacing function AbstractTesting() (at Line 4 in Algorithm 2) with SynergicTesting() described in Algorithm 4. Compared with Algorithm 2 that uses solely abstract testing, the key difference in Algorithm 4 is that we add a decision module SizeChecking() to decide whether to take abstract testing or bounded exhaustive testing (at Line 1) and a module BETesting() to conduct bounded exhaustive testing (at Line 2).

Algorithm 4. Synergic Testing Algorithm

Input: program P, property ψ, abstract input $X^\sharp$, abstract domain D
Output: result res, refined abstract input $X'^\sharp$, program invariant $Inv_b^{X^\sharp}$
1: **if** SizeChecking($X^\sharp$) **then**
2: $\quad res = \text{BETesting}(P, X^\#)$
3: $\quad X'^\# \leftarrow \bot$
4: $\quad Inv_b^{X^\sharp} \leftarrow \bot$
5: **else**
6: $\quad \langle res, X'^\#, Inv_b^{X^\sharp} \rangle = \text{AbstractTesting}(P, \psi, X^\#, D)$
7: **end if**
8: **return** $res, X'^\#, Inv_b^{X^\sharp}$

Decision Module. Function SizeChecking() is implemented by just checking the size of the abstract input (i.e., $|\gamma(X^\sharp)|$): If the size is under a threshold, we adopt bounded exhaustive testing, otherwise we use abstract testing. In practice, $|\gamma(X^\sharp)|$ could be hard to be precisely computed, and hence we utilize $|\gamma(\text{Interval\_Hull}(X^\sharp))|$ as a compromise.

Bounded Exhaustive Testing Module. Bounded exhaustive testing aims to achieve exhaustive coverage of all the concrete inputs in the given abstract input $X^\sharp$. We exhaustively generate concrete input cases not directly from $X^\sharp$, but from its interval hull, and then filter out those that are not in $\gamma(X^\sharp)$ by checking whether they satisfy the constraints representing $X^\sharp$. During bounded exhaustive testing, once a concrete input is found as a counter-example that violates the target property, we will terminate the whole verification process.

4.2 Soundness Discussion

Theorem 1 *(Soundness of the synergic verification). Suppose that we use the synergic verification algorithm (i.e., Algorithm 2 wherein Line 4 is replaced with SynergicTesting()) to verify whether an assertion ψ holds in program P. If the algorithm terminates with ψ proved (or terminates with a counter-example found), then ψ must be true (or false) in program P with any (or some) inputs.*

Proof. First, we consider the case that Algorithm 2 combined with bounded exhaustive testing terminates with a counter-example found in abstract input $X^\sharp$. Since the counter-example must belong to the initial input space (i.e., $\top$), thus it is also a counter-example input to make P violate ψ.

The more complicated case is when Algorithm 2 terminates with ψ proved. To prove ψ must be true in P, we first briefly explain the soundness of abstract testing and bounded exhaustive testing. (1) The soundness of abstract testing (Algorithm 1) is guaranteed by the soundness of abstract interpretation [18], since it applies forward and backward abstract interpretation, which essentially compute over-approximations of the concrete reachable states. (2) The soundness of bounded exhaustive testing is obvious since BET has tested all the possible input cases (within the given bounded abstract input space) under the most precise (i.e., concrete) semantics. In Algorithm 2, the initial input space is partitioned into a set of sub-inputs, and each sub-input is proved by abstract testing or BET, or further partitioned into smaller sub-inputs, which are further coped with by Algorithm 2. According to Proposition 1 and the soundness of abstract testing and BET, we can conclude that ψ is true in P. □

Note that in this paper, as normal abstract interpretation-based verification [28,32], we assume the absence of undefined behaviors and runtime errors in statements before the assertion location. The unsoundness of verification due to undefined behaviors and runtime errors has been handled in [16], which is orthogonal to our work. Moreover, in this paper, a non-deterministic variable is treated as an interval of its whole valid input range (e.g., $[-\infty, +\infty]$) in abstract testing and a fresh random value in concrete testing. For non-deterministic programs, bounded exhaustive testing is used to verify false assertions only when it finds a counter-examples (but not used to provide proof for true assertions).

5 Experiments and Evaluation

We have implemented a prototype tool, namely VATer, based on our verification approach utilizing both iterative abstract testing (IAT) and bounded exhaustive testing (BET). We will evaluate VATer along the following three experimental questions (EQs). VATer can verify programs through refining abstract interpretation by dynamic input partitioning. We want to know whether VATer can prove more true assertions than abstract interpretation based tools (which may use other refinement techniques) (EQ1). We also hope to know the performance of VATer comparing with other widely used verification techniques in practice (EQ2). VATer utilizes bounded exhaustive testing to help abstract interpretation to prove "corner cases" or generate counter-examples. We should know whether the use of bounded exhaustive testing can help verify more assertions in practice (EQ3).

5.1 Experimental Setup

VATer is constructed based on the APRON numerical abstract domain library [36] (which includes the abstract domains of intervals [18], octagons [41], polyhedra [22], and linear congruence abstract domain [27]), and the Fixpoint Solver Library [1]. Moreover, VATer syntactically supports both C programs (by using the front-end CIL [42]) and the SPL language (by using the static analyzer Interproc [35] as the front-end). The upper bound of the number of splitting predicates chosen each time is 10, and the threshold for BET is set as 2500, which are both set according to our timeout bound empirically.

To address these experimental questions, we run our tool VATer, abstract interpretation involved tools (e.g., Interproc [35], SeaHorn [32]) and three tools participating in SV-COMP'18 [2] (i.e., VeriAbs [14], ULTIMATE Taipan [28] (which obtained the highest scores in the *ReachSafety-Loops* category), CPAchecker [9] (which won the gold medal overall in SV-COMP'18)). We use three numerical loop benchmark sets: (1) all the 46 programs from HOLA [24]; (2) all the 35 programs from C4B [13]. (3) all the 152 programs from the verification tasks of six folders in ReachSafety-Loops category of SV-COMP'18 [2]. Note that we used the version of HOLA and C4B from [23].

Different sets of benchmarks and tools are chosen to answer different experimental questions (EQ). To answer EQ1, benchmarks (C4B and Hola) with only true assertions and tools involving abstract interpretation technique (i.e., Interproc, SeaHorn, ULTIMATE Taipan) are used. To answer EQ2 and EQ3, benchmarks from SV-COMP'18 (which contain both true and false assertions) are more suitable, and we chose to compare with three state-of-the-art tools (i.e., ULTIMATE Taipan, VeriAbs, CPAchecker) for EQ2.

All the experiments are carried out with a timeout limit of 900 s for each benchmark program on a machine with Ubuntu 16.04 which has 16GB RAM and a 3.6 GHz octa-core Intel® Core^{TM} i7-7700U host CPU.

5.2 EQ1: Does VATer Strengthen the Ability of Proving True Assertions over Abstract Interpretation Based Techniques?

Table 1 shows the verification results on the HOLA and C4B benchmarks. It lists the number of verified programs (sub-column "#V") together with the total time for verified programs in seconds (column "#T(s)") for each tool. For VATer, it also lists the number of times using abstract testing (sub-column "#AT") and bounded exhaustive testing (sub-column "#BET") for the verified programs. We compare VATer with three available abstract interpretation based verification tools, i.e., Interproc (based on pure abstract interpretation), SeaHorn (combining Horn-clause solving and abstract interpretation) and ULTIMATE Taipan (combining CEGAR based software model checking and abstract interpretation).

All the specified assertions hold in the programs from HOLA and C4B. Table 1 shows that VATer can correctly verify 76 programs out of 81 with total 16.4 s consumed (0.22 s per program on average). Comparing with Interproc (one pass forward analysis), which can verify 19 programs with average 0.16 s, VATer achieves significant improvements on proving true assertions without too much extra time overhead. It indicates that our technique strengthens the ability of proving true assertions over standard abstract interpretation. And considering

Table 1. Comparison results with abstract interpretation involved tools.

Benchmark	Interproc		SeaHorn		UTaipan		VATer			
	#V	T(s)	#V	T(s)	#V	T(s)	#V	T(s)	#AT	#BET
HOLA(46)	17	2.9	34	298.5	38	805.2	**44**	14.1	64	1
C4B(35)	2	0.1	24	274.9	17	1277.4	**32**	2.3	85	0
Total(81)	19	3.0	58	573.4	51	2082.6	**76**	16.4	149	1

the iterations of abstract testing and BET, we find that this strengthening mainly comes from the iterative abstract testing through dynamic input partitioning.

VATer can verify 18 (31%) and 25 (49%) more programs than SeaHorn and ULTIMATE Taipan, respectively. Concerning timing, for those verified programs, VATer (on average 0.22 s) has an average 46X, 190X speedups over SeaHorn (on average 9.9 s) and ULTIMATE Taipan (on average 40.8 s) respectively. This improvement is achieved since most of the programs in HOLA and C4B have complex input-data dependent loops with disjunctive or non-linear properties. They are difficult to verify as a whole. While VATer utilizes partitioning techniques to simplify the program behaviors for each abstract input. This result reflects that VATer performs more effectively and efficiently than abstract interpretation based tools that use forward analysis only (e.g., SeaHorn and ULTIMATE Taipan) on these benchmarks.

Table 2. Comparison results with state-of-the-art verification tools.

Folder	P	IAT		VATer(IAT+BET)				VeriAbs		UTaipan		CPAChecker	
		#V	T(s)	#V	T(s)	#AT	#BET	#V	T(s)	#V	T(s)	#V	T(s)
Loops(67)	T(35)	21	4.2	23	5.0	23	2	26	749.9	25	400.3	**27**	1281.6
	F(32)	7	2.4	18	55.0	145	11	24	416.4	25	1080.7	**29**	550.3
Loop-new(8)	T(8)	4	4.7	**7**	5.8	7	3	2	21.9	4	187.1	2	710
	F(0)	0	0	0	0	0	0	0	0	0	0	0	0
Loop-lit(16)	T(15)	9	2.3	13	2.7	15	4	12	304.9	**14**	388.5	6	27.1
	F(1)	0	0	**1**	0.2	1	1	**1**	13.4	**1**	4.5	**1**	3.9
Loop-inv(19)	T(18)	**15**	32.6	**15**	32.6	16	0	8	144.7	10	253.4	5	440.6
	F(1)	0	0	**1**	11.9	86	1	**1**	17.1	**1**	7.7	**1**	5.4
Loop-craft(7)	T(6)	2	0.2	**4**	0.6	4	2	3	33.7	2	9.2	3	520.5
	F(1)	0	0	0	0	0	0	1	555.8	1	4.5	1	4.2
Loop-acc(35)	T(19)	9	0.9	**16**	96.2	78	38	12	132.9	13	510.7	10	663.9
	F(16)	1	0.1	**16**	9.0	43	15	13	290.1	6	84.2	8	946.8
Total(152)	T(101)	60	44.9	**78**	142.9	143	49	63	1388	68	1749.2	53	3643.7
	F(51)	8	2.5	36	76.1	275	28	**40**	1292.8	34	1181.6	**40**	1510.6

5.3 EQ2 – How Does VATer Work Comparing with Other Verification Techniques

We compare VATer with three state-of-the-art verification tools participating in SV-COMP'18: VeriAbs, ULTIMATE Taipan, CPAchecker. Table 2 shows the comparison result. The column "Folder" shows the names of all the folders and the number of programs included in each folder. The column "Property" distinguishes the programs with true assertions and false assertions in each folder.

For the programs with true assertions (totally 101 programs), VATer can verify 15 (24%), 10 (15%) and 25 (47%) more programs than VeriAbs, ULTIMATE Taipan and CPAchecker respectively. This improvement is achieved mainly due to the fact that most of these programs have input-data dependent loops and loop-result dependent branches. These program characteristics may result in infinite number of program states and make the precise (enough) loop invariants difficult to find by software model checking based tools. However, for these programs, VATer can always utilize input partitioning to get refined abstract inputs to help forward and backward abstract interpretation to generate sound invariants and necessary preconditions, which may be precise enough to prove the assertions finally. For the programs with false assertions (totally 51 programs), VATer finds counter-examples for 36 programs, which is less than VeriAbs (40 programs), CPAchecker (40 programs) but more than ULTIMATE Taipan (33 programs). We have further investigated those false-assertion programs for which other tools succeed but VATer fails. We found that for false-assertion programs we rely on bounded exhaustive testing to ensure the soundness of VATer, but if iterative abstract testing cannot reduce the search space into a small-size region then bounded exhaustive testing may take too much overhead to do dynamic testing exhaustively. For all the programs with true or false assertions (totally 152 programs), compared with these alternatives, VATer achieves 11%, 13%, 22% improvement respectively. Concerning timing, for those verified programs, VATer (on average 1.9 s) at least has an average 13.6X, 15.2X, and 29.2X speedups over VeriAbs (on average 26.0 s), ULTIMATE Taipan (on average 28.8 s), CPAChecker (on average 55.4 s) respectively. The results indicate that VATer also significantly outperforms other three tools on efficiency for these benchmarks.

5.4 EQ3: Does BET Help VATer Generate Counter-Examples over Abstract Testing?

In Table 2, the column "IAT" gives results where only iterative abstract testing is used. Comparing IAT and VATer, we can see that: (1) Considering the 101 programs with true assertions, IAT can verify 60, while VATer can successfully verify 78 programs, achieving a 30% improvement. We have inspected those programs with true assertions that only VATer successfully verified, and found that all of them have "corner cases" that cannot be verified by abstract testing solely, while testing can handle them quickly. (2) Considering 51 programs with false assertions, IAT finds counter-examples for 8 programs, while VATer generates counter-examples for 36 programs. The result indicates that bounded exhaustive testing makes significant contribution to generate counter-examples for programs with false assertions. (3) Overall, VATer can verify 114 programs with the average time of 1.9 s, while IAT can verify 68 programs with average time of 0.7 s. Hence, VATer achieves 68% improvement on IAT without much extra time overhead. This achievement mainly owes to the fact that VATer combines the advantages of both iterative abstract testing and bounded exhaustive testing. Considering the "#AT" and "#BET" column, VATer can verify 46 programs more than IAT with 77 (average 1.7) times of BET used. It indicates that, for these programs, iterative abstract testing has restricted the unverified input spaces into small sizes, thus only a few numbers of BET are conducted to prove the true assertions or generate counter-examples for false assertions.

6 Related Work

Abstract interpretation based verification. Many efforts [6,30,31,37] have been devoted to combine the strengths of over and under approximation. They mainly used model checking based techniques as over approximation engines. While this paper has used abstract interpretation, which can handles loops automatically in a terminate and sound way. Abstract interpretation is one of the fundamental techniques for automatic program verification [20,25]. Many recent approaches and tools for program verification use abstract interpretation. SeaHorn [32] combines Horn-clause solving techniques with abstract interpretation based analyzer IKOS [12], where IKOS is mainly used to supply program invariants to other techniques. ULTIMATE Taipan [28] is a CEGAR-based software model checker for verifying C programs, where abstract interpretation is used to derive loop invariants for the path program corresponding to a given spurious counterexample. A series of works have used interpolation technique to recover the imprecision due to widening and improved the verification ability of abstract interpretation based techniques, such as DAGGER [29], VINTA [4], UFO [5]. Unlike the above works, we use input space partitioning to refine abstract interpretation on-demand iteratively, and use bounded exhaustive testing to complement abstract interpretation.

Recently, combining abstract interpretation with dynamic analysis has received increasing attention. Most of these works combine abstract interpretation with symbolic execution [3,15,16,26], which mainly combine them in a two-stage manner and use (non-iterative) abstract interpretation as a black-box. While our work aims at program verification by performing abstract interpretation in an iterative way and makes use of the results of dynamic testing to complement abstract interpretation. Quite interestingly, Toman et al. [43] have recently presented the Concerto system for analyzing framework-based applications by combining concrete and abstract interpretation, which analyzes framework implementations using concrete interpretation and analyzes application code using abstract interpretation. Compared with their work, our work uses dynamic testing and abstract interpretation to verify the same code, rather than different parts of the target program. The closest work to ours is [19], in which Cousot and Cousot propose first the notion of "abstract testing", and compare abstract testing with classical program debugging and model checking. Our work is inspired by this work [19], but we further propose to conduct abstract testing iteratively with respect to the target property with the help of dynamic input partitioning. Moreover, we also propose to combine abstract testing with bounded exhaustive testing.

Partitioning Techniques. There exist several partitioning techniques in the context of abstract interpretation. Bourdoncle [10] presents a partitioning method in the context of analyzing recursive functions, to allow the dynamic determination of interesting abstract domains using data structures built over simpler domains. Jeannet [34] proposes a method to dynamically select a suitable partitioning according to the property to be proved, which relies on the use of a new abstract lattice combining Boolean and numerical properties. These partitioning techniques belong to state partitioning, while this paper only partitions input and then conducts abstract interpretation separately for each partition. Mauborgne and Rival [39] propose a systematic framework to utilize trace partitioning for managing disjunctions. Their trace partitioning techniques rely on heuristics or annotations to specify partition creation and merge points, while our approach only chooses program entries as the partitioning points, which makes our partitioning strategy fully automatic and easier to deploy. Another benefit of input space partitioning lies in that it can help to recover the precision loss as early as possible during generating invariants. Thus it can generate more precise invariants than partitioning intermediate states. Conditional model checking [7,8] combines the verification abilities of several different model checkers. Each model checker generates a condition to describe the successfully verified state space. Thus, utilizing this condition, the later verifiers only focus on verifying the yet unverified state space. These conditions generated by model checkers can be considered as a partition of state space. Compared with their work, we perform partitioning dynamically and iteratively according to the need of the current verification task and we only consider partitioning the inputs at the entry point of a program.

7 Conclusion

We have presented a property-oriented verification approach based on iterative abstract testing, to verify properties of numerical programs. Our approach iterates forward abstract execution (to compute invariants) and backward abstract execution (to compute necessary pre-condition for property violation) to verify the target property. The key point behind our iterative mechanism is the utilization of dynamic input space partitioning to split an abstract input that needs further exploration into sub-inputs such that each sub-input involves less program behaviors and may be easier to verify. The partitioning is conducted dynamically (on demand) according to the needs of the sub-goal of the verification. Moreover, the partitioning enables the verification to be achieved via bounded exhaustive testing over an abstract sub-input of small size, which complements the abstract testing and is able to generate counter-examples when the property does not hold. Finally, we have shown promising experimental results comparing against several state-of-the-art program verification tools.

For future work, we plan to investigate other dynamic analysis techniques to complement our abstract testing, especially for the cases that the property to be checked does not hold. Also, our approach is highly parallelizable by nature thanks to the partitioning, and thus we plan to develop a parallel version for speedup.

Acknowledgment. This work is supported by the National Key R&D Program of China (No. 2017YFB1001802), the NSFC Program (Nos. 61872445, 61532007), and the NSF under Grants CNS-1446511 and CCF-1617717. This work is also supported by the Hunan Key Laboratory of Software Engineering for Complex Systems, China.

Data Availability Statements. The datasets/code generated during and/or analysed during the current study are available in the Figshare repository: https://doi.org/10.6084/m9.figshare.9861095.v1

References

1. http://pop-art.inrialpes.fr/people/bjeannet/bjeannet-forge/fixpoint/index.html
2. SV-COMP 2018. 7th international competition on software verification. https://sv-comp.sosy-lab.org/2018/
3. Alatawi, E., Søndergaard, H., Miller, T.: Leveraging abstract interpretation for efficient dynamic symbolic execution. In: Proceedings of the 32nd IEEE/ACM International Conference on Automated Software Engineering, pp. 619–624. IEEE Press (2017)
4. Albarghouthi, A., Gurfinkel, A., Chechik, M.: Craig interpretation. In: Miné, A., Schmidt, D. (eds.) SAS 2012. LNCS, vol. 7460, pp. 300–316. Springer, Heidelberg (2012). https://doi.org/10.1007/978-3-642-33125-1_21
5. Albarghouthi, A., Li, Y., Gurfinkel, A., Chechik, M.: Ufo: a framework for abstraction- and interpolation-based software verification. In: Madhusudan, P., Seshia, S.A. (eds.) CAV 2012. LNCS, vol. 7358, pp. 672–678. Springer, Heidelberg (2012). https://doi.org/10.1007/978-3-642-31424-7_48
6. Beckman, N.E., Nori, A.V., Rajamani, S.K., Simmons, R.J., Tetali, S.D., Thakur, A.V.: Proofs from tests. IEEE Trans. Softw. Eng. **36**(4), 495–508 (2010)
7. Beyer, D., Henzinger, T.A., Keremoglu, M.E., Wendler, P.: Conditional model checking: a technique to pass information between verifiers. In: Proceedings of the ACM SIGSOFT 20th International Symposium on the Foundations of Software Engineering, p. 57. ACM (2012)
8. Beyer, D., Jakobs, M.C., Lemberger, T., Wehrheim, H.: Reducer-based construction of conditional verifiers. In: Proceedings of the 40th International Conference on Software Engineering, pp. 1182–1193. ACM (2018)
9. Beyer, D., Keremoglu, M.E.: CPAchecker: a tool for configurable software verification. In: Gopalakrishnan, G., Qadeer, S. (eds.) CAV 2011. LNCS, vol. 6806, pp. 184–190. Springer, Heidelberg (2011). https://doi.org/10.1007/978-3-642-22110-1_16

10. Bourdoncle, F.: Abstract interpretation by dynamic partitioning. J. Funct. Program. **2**(4), 407–435 (1992)
11. Boyapati, C., Khurshid, S., Marinov, D.: Korat: automated testing based on Java predicates. In: ACM SIGSOFT Software Engineering Notes, vol. 27, pp. 123–133. ACM (2002)
12. Brat, G., Navas, J.A., Shi, N., Venet, A.: IKOS: a framework for static analysis based on abstract interpretation. In: Giannakopoulou, D., Salaün, G. (eds.) SEFM 2014. LNCS, vol. 8702, pp. 271–277. Springer, Cham (2014). https://doi.org/10.1007/978-3-319-10431-7_20
13. Carbonneaux, Q., Hoffmann, J., Shao, Z.: Compositional certified resource bounds. ACM SIGPLAN Not. **50**(6), 467–478 (2015)
14. Chimdyalwar, B., Darke, P., Chauhan, A., Shah, P., Kumar, S., Venkatesh, R.: VeriAbs: verification by abstraction (competition contribution). In: Legay, A., Margaria, T. (eds.) TACAS 2017. LNCS, vol. 10206, pp. 404–408. Springer, Heidelberg (2017). https://doi.org/10.1007/978-3-662-54580-5_32
15. Christakis, M.: On narrowing the gap between verification and systematic testing. IT Inf. Technol. **59**(4), 197–202 (2017)
16. Christakis, M., Müller, P., Wüstholz, V.: Guiding dynamic symbolic execution toward unverified program executions. In: Proceedings of the 38th International Conference on Software Engineering, pp. 144–155. ACM (2016)
17. Clarke, E., Grumberg, O., Jha, S., Lu, Y., Veith, H.: Counterexample-guided abstraction refinement for symbolic model checking. J. ACM (JACM) **50**(5), 752–794 (2003)
18. Cousot, P., Cousot, R.: Abstract interpretation: a unified lattice model for static analysis of programs by construction or approximation of fixpoints. In: POPL 1977, pp. 238–252. ACM (1977)
19. Cousot, P., Cousot, R.: Abstract interpretation based program testing. In: Proceedings of the SSGRR 2000 Computer & eBusiness International Conference. Scuola Superiore G. Reiss Romoli L'Aquila, Italy (2000)
20. Cousot, P., Cousot, R.: On abstraction in software verification. In: Brinksma, E., Larsen, K.G. (eds.) CAV 2002. LNCS, vol. 2404, pp. 37–56. Springer, Heidelberg (2002). https://doi.org/10.1007/3-540-45657-0_3
21. Cousot, P., Cousot, R., Fähndrich, M., Logozzo, F.: Automatic inference of necessary preconditions. In: Giacobazzi, R., Berdine, J., Mastroeni, I. (eds.) VMCAI 2013. LNCS, vol. 7737, pp. 128–148. Springer, Heidelberg (2013). https://doi.org/10.1007/978-3-642-35873-9_10
22. Cousot, P., Halbwachs, N.: Automatic discovery of linear restraints among variables of a program. In: Proceedings of the 5th ACM SIGACT-SIGPLAN Symposium on Principles of Programming Languages, pp. 84–96. ACM (1978)
23. Cyphert, J., Breck, J., Kincaid, Z., Reps, T.: Refinement of path expressions for static analysis. Proc. ACM Program. Lang. **3**(POPL), 45 (2019)
24. Dillig, I., Dillig, T., Li, B., McMillan, K.: Inductive invariant generation via abductive inference. ACM SIGPLAN Not. **48**, 443–456 (2013)
25. D'silva, V., Kroening, D., Weissenbacher, G.: A survey of automated techniques for formal software verification. IEEE Trans. Comput. Aided Des. Integr. Circuits Syst. **27**(7), 1165–1178 (2008)
26. Ge, X., Taneja, K., Xie, T., Tillmann, N.: DyTa: dynamic symbolic execution guided with static verification results. In: Proceedings of the 33rd International Conference on Software Engineering, pp. 992–994. ACM (2011)
27. Granger, P.: Static analysis of arithmetical congruences. Int. J. Comput. Math. **30**(3–4), 165–190 (1989)

28. Greitschus, M., et al.: Ultimate Taipan: trace abstraction and abstract interpretation. In: Legay, A., Margaria, T. (eds.) TACAS 2017. LNCS, vol. 10206, pp. 399–403. Springer, Heidelberg (2017). https://doi.org/10.1007/978-3-662-54580-5_31
29. Gulavani, B.S., Chakraborty, S., Nori, A.V., Rajamani, S.K.: Automatically refining abstract interpretations. In: Ramakrishnan, C.R., Rehof, J. (eds.) TACAS 2008. LNCS, vol. 4963, pp. 443–458. Springer, Heidelberg (2008). https://doi.org/10.1007/978-3-540-78800-3_33
30. Gulavani, B.S., Henzinger, T.A., Kannan, Y., Nori, A.V., Rajamani, S.K.: Synergy: a new algorithm for property checking. In: Proceedings of the 14th ACM SIGSOFT International Symposium on Foundations of Software Engineering, pp. 117–127. ACM (2006)
31. Gunter, E., Peled, D.: Model checking, testing and verification working together. Form. Asp. Comput. **17**(2), 201–221 (2005)
32. Gurfinkel, A., Kahsai, T., Komuravelli, A., Navas, J.A.: The SeaHorn verification framework. In: Kroening, D., Păsăreanu, C.S. (eds.) CAV 2015. LNCS, vol. 9206, pp. 343–361. Springer, Cham (2015). https://doi.org/10.1007/978-3-319-21690-4_20
33. Jagannath, V., Lee, Y.Y., Daniel, B., Marinov, D.: Reducing the costs of bounded-exhaustive testing. In: Chechik, M., Wirsing, M. (eds.) FASE 2009. LNCS, vol. 5503, pp. 171–185. Springer, Heidelberg (2009). https://doi.org/10.1007/978-3-642-00593-0_12
34. Jeannet, B.: Dynamic partitioning in linear relation analysis: application to the verification of reactive systems. Form. Methods Syst. Des. **23**(1), 5–37 (2003)
35. Jeannet, B.: Interproc analyzer for recursive programs with numerical variables. INRIA, software and documentation are available at the following, pp. 06-11 (2010). http://pop-art.inrialpes.fr/interproc/interprocweb.cgi
36. Jeannet, B., Miné, A.: APRON: a library of numerical abstract domains for static analysis. In: Bouajjani, A., Maler, O. (eds.) CAV 2009. LNCS, vol. 5643, pp. 661–667. Springer, Heidelberg (2009). https://doi.org/10.1007/978-3-642-02658-4_52
37. Kroening, D., Groce, A., Clarke, E.: Counterexample guided abstraction refinement via program execution. In: Davies, J., Schulte, W., Barnett, M. (eds.) ICFEM 2004. LNCS, vol. 3308, pp. 224–238. Springer, Heidelberg (2004). https://doi.org/10.1007/978-3-540-30482-1_23
38. Marinov, D., Khurshid, S.: TestEra: a novel framework for automated testing of Java programs. In: Proceedings of the 16th Annual International Conference on Automated Software Engineering (ASE 2001), pp. 22–31. IEEE (2001)
39. Mauborgne, L., Rival, X.: Trace partitioning in abstract interpretation based static analyzers. In: Sagiv, M. (ed.) ESOP 2005. LNCS, vol. 3444, pp. 5–20. Springer, Heidelberg (2005). https://doi.org/10.1007/978-3-540-31987-0_2
40. Miné, A.: Tutorial on static inference of numeric invariants by abstract interpretation. Found. Trends Program. Lang. (FnTPL) **4**(3–4), 120–372 (2017)
41. Miné, A.: The octagon abstract domain. High.-Order Symb. Comput. **19**(1), 31–100 (2006)
42. Necula, G.C., McPeak, S., Rahul, S.P., Weimer, W.: CIL: intermediate language and tools for analysis and transformation of C programs. In: Horspool, R.N. (ed.) CC 2002. LNCS, vol. 2304, pp. 213–228. Springer, Heidelberg (2002). https://doi.org/10.1007/3-540-45937-5_16
43. Toman, J., Grossman, D.: Concerto: a framework for combined concrete and abstract interpretation. Proc. ACM Program. Lang. **3**(POPL), 43 (2019)

Trends: Assuring Machine Learning

Robustness Verification of Support Vector Machines

Francesco Ranzato(✉) and Marco Zanella

Dipartimento di Matematica, University of Padova, Padova, Italy
ranzato@math.unipd.it

Abstract. We study the problem of formally verifying the robustness to adversarial examples of support vector machines (SVMs), a major machine learning model for classification and regression tasks. Following a recent stream of works on formal robustness verification of (deep) neural networks, our approach relies on a sound abstract version of a given SVM classifier to be used for checking its robustness. This methodology is parametric on a given numerical abstraction of real values and, analogously to the case of neural networks, needs neither abstract least upper bounds nor widening operators on this abstraction. The standard interval domain provides a simple instantiation of our abstraction technique, which is enhanced with the domain of reduced affine forms, an efficient abstraction of the zonotope abstract domain. This robustness verification technique has been fully implemented and experimentally evaluated on SVMs based on linear and nonlinear (polynomial and radial basis function) kernels, which have been trained on the popular MNIST dataset of images and on the recent and more challenging Fashion-MNIST dataset. The experimental results of our prototype SVM robustness verifier appear to be encouraging: this automated verification is fast, scalable and shows significantly high percentages of provable robustness on the test set of MNIST, in particular compared to the analogous provable robustness of neural networks.

1 Introduction

Adversarial machine learning [10,17,38] is an emerging hot topic studying vulnerabilities of machine learning (ML) techniques in adversarial scenarios and whose main objective is to design methodologies for making learning tools robust to adversarial attacks. Adversarial examples have been found in diverse application fields of ML such as image classification, speech recognition and malware detection [10]. Current defense techniques include adversarial model training, input validation, testing and automatic verification of learning algorithms (see the recent survey [10]). In particular, formal verification of ML classifiers started to be an active field of investigation [1,8,9,12,15,16,19,23,26,27,31,32,39,40] within the verification and static analysis community. Robustness to adversarial inputs is an important safety property of ML classifiers whose formal verification has been investigated for (deep) neural networks [1,9,26,31,32,40]. A classifier

B.-Y. E. Chang (Ed.): SAS 2019, LNCS 11822, pp. 271–295, 2019.
https://doi.org/10.1007/978-3-030-32304-2_14

is robust to some (typically small) perturbation of its input objects representing an adversarial attack when it assigns the same class to all the objects within that perturbation. Thus, slight malicious alterations of input objects should not deceive a robust classifier. Pulina and Tacchella [26] first put forward the idea of a formal robustness verification of neural network classifiers by leveraging interval-based abstract interpretation for designing a sound abstract classifier. This abstraction-based verification approach has been pushed forward by Vechev et al. [9,31,32], who designed a scalable robustness verification technique which relies on abstract interpretation of deep neural networks based on a specifically tailored abstract domain [32].

While all the aforementioned verification techniques consider (deep) neural networks as ML model, in this work we focus on support vector machines (SVMs), which is a major learning model extensively and successfully used for both classification and regression tasks [7]. SVMs are widely applied in different fields where adversarial attacks must be taken into account, notably image classification, malware detection, intrusion detection and spam filtering [2]. Adversarial attacks and robustness issues of SVMs have been defined and studied by some authors [2,3,24,37,41,43,46], in particular investigating robust training and experimental robustness evaluation of SVMs. To the best of our knowledge, no formal and automatic robustness certification technique for SVMs has been studied.

Contributions. A simple and standard model of adversarial region for a ML classifier $C : X \to L$, where $X \subseteq \mathbb{R}^n$ is the input space and L is the set of classes (or labels), is based on a set of perturbations $P(\mathbf{x}) \subseteq X$ of an input $\mathbf{x} \in X$ for C, which typically exploits some metric on $\mathbb{R}^n$ to quantify a similarity to $\mathbf{x}$. A classifier C is robust on an input $\mathbf{x}$ for a perturbation P when for all $\mathbf{x}' \in P(\mathbf{x})$, $C(\mathbf{x}') = C(\mathbf{x})$ holds, meaning that the adversary cannot attack the classification of $\mathbf{x}$ made by C by selecting input objects from $P(\mathbf{x})$ [4]. We consider the most effective SVM classifiers based on common linear and nonlinear kernels, in particular polynomial and Gaussian radial basis function (RBFs) [7]. Our technique for formally verifying the robustness of C is quite standard: by leveraging a numerical abstraction A of sets of real vectors in $\wp(\mathbb{R}^n)$, we define a sound abstract classifier $C^\sharp : A \to \wp(L)$ and a sound abstract perturbation $P^\sharp : X \to A$, in such a way that if $C^\sharp(P^\sharp(\mathbf{x})) = \{C(\mathbf{x})\}$ holds then C is proved to be robust on the input $\mathbf{x}$ for the adversarial region P. As usual in static analysis, scalability and precision are the main issues in SVM verification. A robustness verifier has to scale with the number of support vectors of the SVM classifier C, which in turn depends on the size of the training dataset for C, which may be huge (easily tens/hundreds of thousands of samples). Moreover, the precision of a verifier may crucially depend on the relational information between the components, called features in ML, of input vectors in $\mathbb{R}^n$, whose number may be quite large (easily hundreds/thousands of features). For our robustness verifier, we used an abstraction which is a product of the standard nonrelational interval domain [6] and of the so-called reduced affine form (RAF) abstraction, a relational domain representing the dependencies from the components of input vectors. A RAF for vectors in $\mathbb{R}^n$ is given by $a_0 + \sum_{i=1}^{n} a_i \epsilon_i + a_r \epsilon_r$, where ϵ_i's are symbolic variables ranging in $[-1, 1]$ and representing a dependence from the i-th component of the vector, while ϵ_r is a further symbolic variable in $[-1, 1]$ which accumulates all the approximations introduced by nonlinear operations such as multiplication and exponential. RAFs can be viewed as a restriction to a given length (here the dimension n of $\mathbb{R}^n$) of the zonotope domain used in static program analysis [13], which features an optimal abstract multiplication [33], the crucial operation of abstract nonlinear SVMs. We implemented our robustness verification method for SVMs in a tool called *SAVer* (*S*vm *A*bstract *Ver*ifier), written in C. Our experimental evaluation of SAVer employed the popular MNIST [18] image dataset and the recent and more challenging alternative Fashion-MNIST dataset [42]. Our benchmarks provide the percentage of samples of the full test sets for which a SVM is proved to be robust (and, dually, vulnerable) for a given perturbation, the average verification times per sample, and the scalability of the robustness verifier w.r.t. the number of support vectors. We also compared SAVer to DeepPoly [32], a robustness verification tool for deep neural networks based on abstract interpretation. Our experimental results indicate that SAVer is fast and scalable and that the percentage of robustness provable by SAVer for SVMs is higher than the robustness provable by DeepPoly for deep neural networks.

Illustrative Example. The figure below shows a toy binary SVM classifier for input vectors in $\mathbb{R}^2$, with four support vectors $\mathbf{sv_1} = (8, 7)$, $\mathbf{sv_2} = (10, -4)$, $\mathbf{sv_3} = (8, 1)$, $\mathbf{sv_4} = (9, -5)$ for a polynomial kernel of degree 2. The corresponding binary classifier $C : \mathbb{R}^2 \to \{-1, +1\}$ is the following function:

$$\begin{aligned} C(\mathbf{x}) &= \text{sign}(\textstyle\sum_{i=1}^{4} \alpha_i y_i (\mathbf{sv_i} \cdot \mathbf{x})^2 + b) \\ &= \text{sign}(\alpha_1(8x_1{+}7x_2)^2{-}\alpha_2(10x_1-4x_2)^2{-}\alpha_3(8x_1{+}x_2)^2{+}\alpha_4(9x_1-5x_2)^2 + b) \end{aligned}$$

where y_i and α_i are, resp., the classes (± 1) and weights of the support vectors $\mathbf{sv_i}$, with: $\alpha_1 \approx 5.36 \times 10^{-4}$, $\alpha_2 \approx -3.78 \times 10^{-3}$, $\alpha_3 \approx -9.23 \times 10^{-4}$, $\alpha_4 \approx 4.17 \times 10^{-3}$, $b \approx 3.33$. The set of vectors $\mathbf{x} \in \mathbb{R}^2$ such that $C(\mathbf{x}) = 0$ defines the decision curve between labels -1 and $+1$. We consider a point $\mathbf{p} = (5, 1)$ and an adversarial region $P_1(\mathbf{p}) = \{\mathbf{x} \in \mathbb{R}^2 \mid \max(|x_1 - p_1|, |x_2 - p_2|) \leq 1\}$, which is the L_∞ ball of radius 1 centered in $\mathbf{p}$ and can be exactly represented by the interval in $\mathbb{R}^2$ (i.e., box) $P_1(\mathbf{p}) = (x_1 \in [4, 6], x_2 \in [0, 2])$. As shown by the figure, this classifier C is robust on $\mathbf{p}$ for this perturbation because for all $\mathbf{x} \in P_1(\mathbf{p})$, $C(\mathbf{x}) = C(\mathbf{p}) = +1$. However, it turns out that the interval abstraction $C^\sharp_{\text{Int}}$ of this classifier cannot prove the robustness of C:

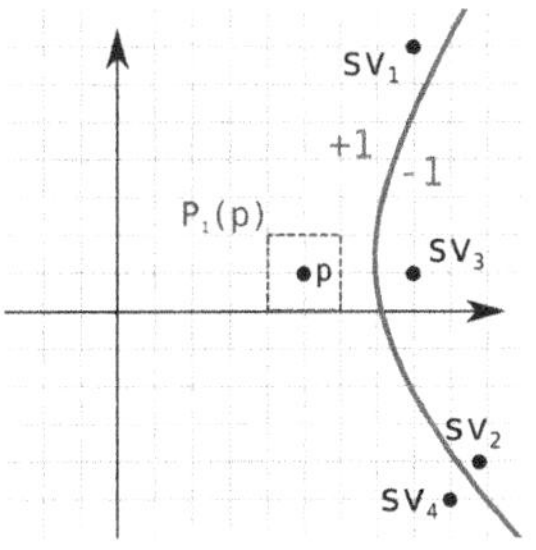

$$\begin{aligned} C^\sharp_{\text{Int}}(P_1(\mathbf{p})) &= \text{sign}(\textstyle\sum_{i=1}^{4} \alpha_i y_i ((\mathbf{sv_i})_1[4, 6] + (\mathbf{sv_i})_2[0, 2])^2 + b) \\ &= \text{sign}(\alpha_1 y_1[1024, 3844] + \alpha_2 y_2[1024, 3600] + \alpha_3 y_3[1024, 2500] + \alpha_4 y_4[676, 2916] + b) \\ &= \text{sign}([-9.231596, 12.735958]) = \top \end{aligned}$$

Instead, the reduced affine form abstraction $C^{\sharp}_{\text{RAF}_2}$ allows us to prove the robustness of C on $\mathbf{p}$. Here, the perturbation $P_1(\mathbf{p})$ is exactly represented by the RAF ($\tilde{x}_1 = 5 + \epsilon_1, \tilde{x}_2 = 1 + \epsilon_2$), where $\epsilon_1, \epsilon_2, \epsilon_r \in [-1, 1]$, and the abstract computation is as follows:

$$
\begin{aligned}
C^{\sharp}_{\text{RAF}_2}(P_1(\mathbf{p})) &= \text{sign}(\textstyle\sum_{i=1}^{4} \alpha_i y_i [(\mathbf{sv_i})_1(5+\epsilon_1) + (\mathbf{sv_i})_2(1+\epsilon_2)]^2 + b) \\
&= \text{sign}(\alpha_1 y_1 (47 + 8\epsilon_1 + 7\epsilon_2)^2 + \alpha_2 y_2 (46 + 10\epsilon_1 - 4\epsilon_2)^2 \\
&\qquad + \alpha_3 y_3 (41 + 8\epsilon_1 + \epsilon_2)^2 + \alpha_4 y_4 (40 + 9\epsilon_1 - 5\epsilon_2)^2 + b) \\
&= \text{sign}(\alpha_1 y_1 (2322 + 752\epsilon_1 + 658\epsilon_2 + 112\epsilon_r) + \alpha_2 y_2 (2232 + 920\epsilon_1 - 368\epsilon_2 + 80\epsilon_r) \\
&\qquad + \alpha_3 y_3 (1746 + 656\epsilon_1 + 82\epsilon_2 + 16\epsilon_r) + \alpha_4 y_4 (1706 + 720\epsilon_1 - 400\epsilon_2 + 90\epsilon_r) + b) \\
&= \text{sign}(1.635264 - 0.680779\epsilon_1 + 0.001047\epsilon_2 + 0.753025\epsilon_r) = +1
\end{aligned}
$$

Hence, the RAF analysis is able to prove that C is robust on $\mathbf{p}$ for P_1, since the final RAF has an interval range $[0.200413, 3.070115]$ consisting of positive numbers.

2 Background

Notation. If $\mathbf{x}, \mathbf{y} \in \mathbb{R}^n$, $z \in \mathbb{R}$ and $i \in [1, n]$ then $\mathbf{x}_i = \pi_i(\mathbf{x}) \in \mathbb{R}$, $\mathbf{x} \cdot \mathbf{y} \triangleq \sum_i \mathbf{x}_i \mathbf{y}_i \in \mathbb{R}$, $\mathbf{x} + \mathbf{y} \in \mathbb{R}^n$, $z\mathbf{x} \in \mathbb{R}^n$, $\|\mathbf{x}\|_2 \triangleq \sqrt{\mathbf{x} \cdot \mathbf{x}} \in \mathbb{R}$, $\|\mathbf{x}\|_\infty \triangleq \max\{|\mathbf{x}_i| \mid i \in [1, n]\} \in \mathbb{R}$, denote, resp., i-th component, dot product, vector addition, scalar multiplication, L_2 (i.e., Euclidean) and L_∞ (i.e., maximum) norms in $\mathbb{R}^n$. If $h : X \to Y$ is any function then $h^c : \wp(X) \to \wp(Y)$ defined by $h^c(S) \triangleq \{h(x) \mid x \in S\}$ denotes the standard collecting lifting of h, and, when clear from the context, we slightly abuse notation by using $h(S)$ instead of $h^c(S)$.

Classifiers and Robustness. Consider a training dataset $T = \{(\mathbf{x}_1, y_1), ..., (\mathbf{x}_N, y_N)\} \subseteq X \times L$, where $X \subseteq \mathbb{R}^n$ is the input space, $\mathbf{x}_i \in X$ is called feature (or attribute) vector and y_i is its label (or class) ranging into the output space L. A supervised learning algorithm $\mathcal{SL} : \wp(X \times L) \to (X \to L)$ (also called trainer) computes a classifier function $\mathcal{SL}(T) : X \to L$ ranging in some function subspace (also called hypothesis space). The learned classifier $\mathcal{SL}(T)$ is a function that best fits the training dataset T according to a principle of empirical risk minimization. The machine learning algorithm $\mathcal{SL}$ computes a classifier $\mathcal{SL}(T)$ by solving a complex optimization problem. The output space is assumed to be represented by real numbers, i.e., $L \subseteq \mathbb{R}$, and for binary classifiers with $|L| = 2$, the standard assumption is that $L = \{-1, +1\}$.

The standard threat model [4,10] of untargeted adversarial examples for a generic classifier $C : X \to L$ is as follows. Given a valid input object $\mathbf{x} \in X$ whose correct label is $C(\mathbf{x})$, an adversarial example for $\mathbf{x}$ is a legal input $\mathbf{x}' \in X$ such that $\mathbf{x}'$ is a small perturbation of (i.e., is similar to) $\mathbf{x}$ and $C(\mathbf{x}') \neq C(\mathbf{x})$. An adversarial region is the set of perturbations $P(\mathbf{x}) \subseteq X$ that the adversary is allowed to make to $\mathbf{x}$, meaning that a function $P : X \to \wp(X)$ models an adversarial region. A perturbation $P(\mathbf{x})$ is typically modeled by some distance metric to quantify a similarity to $\mathbf{x}$, usually a p-norm, and the most general model of perturbation simply requires that for all $\mathbf{x} \in X$, $\mathbf{x} \in P(\mathbf{x})$. A classifier C is defined to be robust on an input vector $\mathbf{x}$ for an adversarial region P when for all $\mathbf{x}' \in P(\mathbf{x})$, $C(\mathbf{x}') = C(\mathbf{x})$ holds, denoted by $\text{Rob}(C, \mathbf{x}, P) \stackrel{\triangle}{\Leftrightarrow} \{C(\mathbf{x}') \mid \mathbf{x}' \in P(\mathbf{x})\} = \{C(\mathbf{x})\}$. This means that the adversary cannot attack the classification of $\mathbf{x}$ made by C by selecting input objects from the region $P(\mathbf{x})$.

Support Vector Machines. Several strategies and optimization techniques are available to train a SVM, but they are not relevant for our purposes ([7] is a popular standard reference for SVMs). A SVM classifier partitions the input space X into regions, each representing a class of the output space L. In its simplest formulation, the learning algorithm produces a linear SVM binary classifier with $L = \{-1, +1\}$ which relies on a hyperplane of $\mathbb{R}^n$ that separates training vectors labeled by -1 from vectors labeled $+1$. The training phase consists in finding (i.e., learning) this hyperplane. While many separating hyperplanes may exist, the SVM separating hyperplane has the maximum distance (called margin) with the closest vectors in the training dataset, because a maximum-margin learning algorithm statistically reduces the generalization error. This SVM hyperplane is univocally represented by its normal vector $\mathbf{w} \in \mathbb{R}^n$ and by a displacement scalar $b \in \mathbb{R}$, so that the hyperplane equation is $\mathbf{w} \cdot \mathbf{x} = b$. The classification of an input vector $\mathbf{x} \in X$ therefore boils down to determining the half-space containing $\mathbf{x}$, namely, the linear binary classifier is the decision function $C(\mathbf{x}) = \text{sign}(\mathbf{w} \cdot \mathbf{x} - b)$, where the case $\text{sign}(0) = 0$ is negligible (e.g. $\text{sign}(0)$ may assign the class $+1$). This linear classifier $\text{sign}(\mathbf{w} \cdot \mathbf{x} - b)$ is in so-called primal form, while nonlinear classifiers are instead in dual form and based on a so-called kernel function.

When the training set T cannot be linearly separated in a satisfactory way, T is projected into a much higher dimensional space through a projection map $\varphi : \mathbb{R}^n \to \mathbb{R}^k$, with $k > n$, where $\varphi(T)$ may become linearly separable. Training a SVM classifier boils down to a high-dimensional quadratic programming problem which can be solved either in its primal or dual form. When solving the dual problem, the projection function φ is only involved in dot products $\varphi(\mathbf{x}) \cdot \varphi(\mathbf{y})$ in $\mathbb{R}^k$, so that this projection is not actually needed if these dot products in $\mathbb{R}^k$ can be equivalently formulated through a function $k : \mathbb{R}^n \times \mathbb{R}^n \to \mathbb{R}$, called kernel function, such that $k(\mathbf{x}, \mathbf{y}) = \varphi(\mathbf{x}) \cdot \varphi(\mathbf{y})$. Given a dataset $T = \{(\mathbf{x_1}, y_1), ..., (\mathbf{x}_N, y_N)\}$, with $y_i \in \{-1, +1\}$, solving the dual problem for training the SVM classifier means finding a set $\{\alpha_i\}_{i=1}^N \subseteq \mathbb{R}$, called set of weights, which maximizes the following function $f : \mathbb{R}^N \to \mathbb{R}$:

$$\max f(\alpha_1, ..., \alpha_N) \triangleq \textstyle\sum_{i=1}^N \alpha_i - \frac{1}{2} \sum_{i,j=1}^N \alpha_i \alpha_j y_i y_j k(\mathbf{x_i}, \mathbf{x_j})$$

subject to: for all i, $0 \leq \alpha_i \leq c$, where $c \in \mathbb{R}_{>0}$ is a tuning parameter, and $\sum_{i=1}^N \alpha_i y_i = 0$. This set of weights defines the following SVM binary classifier C: for all input $\mathbf{x} \in X \subseteq \mathbb{R}^n$,

$$C(\mathbf{x}) \triangleq \text{sign}([\textstyle\sum_{i=1}^N \alpha_i y_i k(\mathbf{x_i}, \mathbf{x})] - b) \tag{1}$$

for some offset parameter $b \in \mathbb{R}$. By defining $D_k(\mathbf{x}) \triangleq \sum_{i=1}^N \alpha_i y_i k(\mathbf{x_i}, \mathbf{x})$, this classifier will be also denoted by $C(\mathbf{x}) = \text{sign}(D_k(\mathbf{x}) - b)$. In practice most weights α_i are 0, hence only a subset of the training vectors $\mathbf{x_i}$ is actually used by the SVM classifier C, and these are called support vectors. By a slight abuse of notation, we will assume that $\alpha_i \neq 0$ for all $i \in [1, N]$, namely $\{\mathbf{x_i}\}_{i=1}^{N} \subseteq \mathbb{R}^n$ denotes the set of support vectors extracted from the training set by the SVM learning algorithm for some kernel function. We will consider the most common and effective kernel functions used in SVM training: (i) linear kernel: $k(\mathbf{x}, \mathbf{y}) = \mathbf{x} \cdot \mathbf{y}$; (ii) d-polynomial kernel: $k(\mathbf{x}, \mathbf{y}) = (\mathbf{x} \cdot \mathbf{y} + c)^d$ (common powers are $d = 2, 3, 9$); (iii) Gaussian radial basis function (RBF): $k(\mathbf{x}, \mathbf{y}) = e^{-\gamma\|\mathbf{x}-\mathbf{y}\|_2^2}$, for some $\gamma > 0$.

SVM Multiclass Classification. Multiclass datasets have a finite set of labels $L = \{y_1, ..., y_m\}$ with $m > 2$. The standard approach to multiclass classification problems consists in a reduction into multiple binary classification problems using one of the following two simple strategies [14]. In the "one-versus-rest" (ovr) strategy, m binary classifiers are trained, where each binary classifier $C_{i,\bar{i}}$ determines whether an input vector $\mathbf{x}$ belongs to the class $y_i \in L$ or not by assigning a real confidence score for its decision rather than just a label, so that the class y_j with the highest-output confidence score is the class assigned to $\mathbf{x}$. Multiclass SVMs using this ovr approach might not work satisfactorily because the ovr approach often leads to unbalanced datasets already for a few classes due to unbalanced partitions into y_i and $L \smallsetminus \{y_i\}$.

The most common solution [14] is to follow a "one-versus-one" (ovo) approach, where $m(m-1)/2$ binary classifiers $C_{\{i,j\}}$ are trained on the restriction of the original training set to vectors with labels in $\{y_i, y_j\}$, with $i \neq j$, so that each $C_{\{i,j\}}$ determines whether an input vector belongs (more) to the class y_i or (more to) y_j. Given an input vector $\mathbf{x} \in X$ each of these $m(m-1)/2$ binary classifiers $C_{\{i,j\}}(\mathbf{x})$ assigns a "vote" to one class in $\{y_i, y_j\}$, and at the end the class with the most votes wins, i.e., the argmax of the function $\text{votes}(\mathbf{x}, y_i) \triangleq |\{j \in \{1, ..., m\} \mid j \neq i,\ C_{\{i,j\}}(\mathbf{x}) = y_i\}|$ is the winning class of $\mathbf{x}$. Draw is a downside of the ovo strategy because it may well be the case that for some (regions of) input vectors multiple classes collect the same number of votes and therefore no classification can be done. In case of draw, a common strategy [14] is to output any of the winning classes (e.g., the one with the smaller index). However, since our primary focus is on soundness of abstract classifiers, we need to model an ovo multiclass classifier by a function $M_{\text{ovo}} : X \to \wp(L)$ defined by $M_{\text{ovo}}(\mathbf{x}) \triangleq \{y_k \in L \mid k \in \text{argmax}_{i\in\{1,...,m\}}\text{votes}(\mathbf{x}, y_i)\}$, so that $|M_{\text{ovo}}(\mathbf{x})| > 1$ models a draw in the ovo voting.

Numerical Abstractions. According to the most general definition, a numerical abstract domain is a tuple $\langle A, \leq_A, \gamma\rangle$ where $\langle A, \leq_A\rangle$ is at least a preordered set and the concretization function $\gamma : A \to \wp(\mathbb{R}^n)$, with $n \geq 1$, preserves the relation $\leq_A$, namely, $a \leq_A a'$ implies $\gamma(a) \subseteq \gamma(a')$ (i.e., γ is monotone). Thus, A plays the usual role of set of symbolic representations for sets of vectors of $\mathbb{R}^n$. Well-known examples of numerical abstract domains include intervals, zonotopes, octagons, convex polyhedra (we refer to the tutorial [22]). Some numerical domains just form preorders (e.g., standard representations of octagons by DBMs allow multiple representations) while other domains give rise to posets (e.g., intervals). While a monotone concretization γ is enough for reasoning about soundness of static analyses on numerical domains, the notion of best correct approximation of concrete sets relies on the existence of an abstraction function $\alpha : \wp(\mathbb{R}^n) \to A$ which requires that $\langle A, \leq_A \rangle$ is (at least) a poset and that the pair (α, γ) forms a Galois connection/insertion. Consider a concrete k-ary real operation $f : \wp(\mathbb{R}^n)^k \to \wp(\mathbb{R}^n)$, for some $k \in \mathbb{N}_{>0}$, and a corresponding abstract map $f^\sharp : A^k \to A$. Then, $f^\sharp$ is a correct (or sound) approximation of f when $f \circ \langle \gamma, ..., \gamma \rangle \subseteq \gamma \circ f^\sharp$ holds, while $f^\sharp$ is exact (or γ-complete) when $f \circ \langle \gamma, ..., \gamma \rangle = \gamma \circ f^\sharp$ holds. When a Galois connection (α, γ) for A exists, if $f^\sharp$ is exact then it coincides with the best correct approximation (bca) of f on A, which is the abstract function $\alpha \circ f \circ \langle \gamma, ..., \gamma \rangle : A^k \to A$ [28]. The abstract domain Int of numerical intervals on the poset of real numbers $\langle \mathbb{R} \cup \{-\infty, +\infty\}, \leq \rangle$ is defined as usual [6]:

$$\text{Int} \triangleq \{\bot, [-\infty, +\infty]\} \cup \{[l, u] \mid l, u \in \mathbb{R}, l \leq u\} \cup \{[-\infty, u] \mid u \in \mathbb{R}\} \cup \{[l, +\infty] \mid l \in \mathbb{R}\}.$$

The concretization map $\gamma : \text{Int} \to \wp(\mathbb{R})$ is standard. Intervals admit an abstraction map $\alpha : \wp(\mathbb{R}) \to \text{Int}$ such that $\alpha(X)$ is the least interval containing X, so that (α, γ) defines a Galois insertion between $\langle \text{Int}, \sqsubseteq \rangle$ and $\langle \wp(\mathbb{R}), \subseteq \rangle$.

3 Abstract Robustness Verification Framework

Let us describe a sound abstract robustness verification framework for binary and multiclass SVM classifiers. We consider a general classifier $C : X \to L$, where L is a set of labels, and an adversarial region $P : X \to \wp(X)$ for C. Consider a numerical abstract domain $\langle A, \leq_A \rangle$ whose abstract values represent sets of input vectors for a binary classifier C, namely $\gamma : A \to \wp(X)$, where X is the input space of C. We use A_n to emphasize that A is used as an abstraction of properties of n-dimensional vectors in $\mathbb{R}^n$, so that A_1 denotes that A is used as an abstraction of sets of scalars in $\wp(\mathbb{R})$.

Definition 3.1 (Sound Abstract Classifier). A *sound abstract classifier* on A is an algorithm $C^\sharp : A \to \wp(L)$ such that, for all $a \in A$, $\{C(\mathbf{x}) \in L \mid \mathbf{x} \in \gamma(a)\} \subseteq C^\sharp(a)$ holds. □

Thus, $C^\sharp$ is a sound abstraction of a classifier C when, given an abstract value $a \in A$ representing a set of concrete inputs, $C^\sharp(a)$ computes a superset of the labels computed by C on inputs ranging in $\gamma(a)$. In particular, the output $C^\sharp(a) = L$ plays the role of a "don't know" answer, while if $|C^\sharp(a)| = 1$ then every sample in $\gamma(a)$ must necessarily be classified by C with a same label $C^\sharp(a)$.

Definition 3.2 (Sound Abstract Perturbation). A *sound abstract perturbation* is a function $P^\sharp : X \to A$ which is sound for P, i.e., for all $\mathbf{x} \in X, P(\mathbf{x}) \subseteq \gamma(P^\sharp(\mathbf{x}))$. □

A sound abstract classifier and a sound abstract perturbation $\langle C^\sharp, P^\sharp \rangle$ allows us to define a robustness verifier as follows.

Theorem 3.3 (Robustness Verifier). *If $C^\sharp$ and $P^\sharp$ are sound then $\langle C^\sharp, P^\sharp\rangle$ is a sound robustness verifier, namely, for all $\mathbf{x} \in X$, $|C^\sharp(P^\sharp(\mathbf{x}))| = 1 \Rightarrow Rob(C, \mathbf{x}, P)$.*

As multiclass SVMs combine the outputs of a number of binary classifiers, let us focus on binary classifiers $C : X \to \{-1, +1\}$, where $C(\mathbf{x}) = \text{sign}(D(\mathbf{x}) - b)$ and $D : X \to \mathbb{R}$ has been trained for some kernel function k. For the sake of clarity we will use a slightly different notation for $C^\sharp : X \to \{-1, +1, \top\}$, where $\top$ is an abstract "don't know" value representing $\{-1, +1\}$. Of course, the key step for defining an abstract robustness verifier is to design a sound abstract version of the trained function $D : X \to \mathbb{R}$ on some abstraction A, namely an algorithm $D^\sharp : A_n \to A_1$ such that, for all $a \in A_n$, $D^c(\gamma(a)) \subseteq \gamma(D^\sharp(a))$. We also need that the abstraction A is endowed with a sound approximation of the Boolean test $\text{sign}_b(\cdot) : \mathbb{R} \to \{-1, +1\}$ for any bias $b \in \mathbb{R}$, where $\text{sign}_b(x) \triangleq$ **if** $x \geq b$ **then** $+1$ **else** -1. Hence, we require a computable abstract function $\text{sign}_b^\sharp : A_1 \to \{-1, +1, \top\}$ which is sound for sign_b, that is, for all $a \in A_1$, $\text{sign}_b^\sharp(a) \neq \top \Rightarrow \forall x \in \gamma(a).\text{sign}_b(x) = \text{sign}_b^\sharp(a)$. These hypotheses therefore provide a straightforward sound abstract classifier $C^\sharp : A \to \{-1, +1, \top\}$ defined as follows: $C^\sharp(a) \triangleq \text{sign}_b^\sharp(D^\sharp(a))$. It turns out that these hypotheses entail the soundness of the robustness verifier.

Lemma 3.4. *If $P^\sharp$ is a sound abstract perturbation then $\langle C^\sharp, P^\sharp\rangle$ is a sound robustness verifier.*

If T is a test set for the classifier C then we may correctly assert that C is provably $q\%$-robust on T for the perturbation P when a sound abstract robustness verifier is able to check that C is robust on $q\%$ of the test samples in T. Of course, by soundness, this means that C is certainly robust on *at least* $q\%$ of the inputs in T, while on the remaining $(100 - q)\%$ of T we do not know: these could be spurious or real unrobust input vectors.

In order to design a sound abstract version of $D(\mathbf{x}) = \sum_{i=1}^N \alpha_i y_i k(\mathbf{x_i}, \mathbf{x})$ we surely need sound approximations on A_1 of scalar multiplication and addition. We thus require a sound abstract scalar multiplication $\lambda a.za : A_1 \to A_1$, for any $z \in \mathbb{R}$, such that for all $a \in A_1$, $z\gamma(a) \subseteq \gamma(za)$, and a sound addition $+^\sharp : A_1 \times A_1 \to A_1$ such that for all $a, a' \in A_1$, $\gamma(a) + \gamma(a') \subseteq \gamma(a +^\sharp a')$, and we use $\sum_{i \in I}^\sharp a_i$ to denote an indexed abstract summation.

Linear Classifiers. Sound approximations of scalar multiplication and addition are enough for designing a sound robustness verifier for a linear classifier. As a preprocessing step, for a binary classifier $C(\mathbf{x}) = \text{sign}([\sum_{i=1}^N \alpha_i y_i (\mathbf{x_i} \cdot \mathbf{x})] - b)$ which has been trained for the linear kernel, we preliminarly compute the hyperplane normal vector $\mathbf{w} \in \mathbb{R}^n$: for all $j \in [1, n]$, $\mathbf{w}_j \triangleq \sum_{i=1}^N \alpha_i y_i \mathbf{x_i}_j$, so that for all $\mathbf{x} \in \mathbb{R}^n$, $\mathbf{w} \cdot \mathbf{x} = \sum_{j=1}^n \mathbf{w}_j \mathbf{x}_j = \sum_{i=1}^N \alpha_i y_i (\mathbf{x_i} \cdot \mathbf{x})$. Thus, $C(\mathbf{x}) = \text{sign}([\sum_{j=1}^n \mathbf{w}_j \mathbf{x}_j] - b)$ is the linear classifier in primal form, whose robustness can be abstractly verified by resorting to just sound abstract scalar multiplication and addition on A_1. The noteworthy advantage of abstracting a classifier in primal form is that each component of the input vector $\mathbf{x}$ occurs just once in $\text{sign}([\sum_{j=1}^{n} \mathbf{w}_j \mathbf{x}_j] - b)$, while in the dual form $\text{sign}([\sum_{i=1}^{N} \alpha_i y_i (\mathbf{x_i} \cdot \mathbf{x})] - b)$ each component $\mathbf{x}_j$ occurs exactly N times (one for each support vector), so that a precise abstraction of this latter dual form should be able to represent the correlation between (the many) multiple occurrences of each $\mathbf{x}_j$.

Nonlinear Classifiers. Let us consider a nonlinear kernel binary classifier $C(\mathbf{x}) = \text{sign}(D(\mathbf{x}) - b)$, where $D(\mathbf{x}) = \sum_{i=1}^{N} \alpha_i y_i k(\mathbf{x_i}, \mathbf{x})$ and $\{\mathbf{x_i}\}_{i=1}^{N} \subseteq \mathbb{R}^n$ is the set of support vectors for the kernel function k. Thus, what we additionally need here is a sound abstract kernel function $k^\sharp : \mathbb{R}^n \times A_n \to A_1$ such that for any support vector $\mathbf{x_i}$ and $a \in A_n$, $\{k(\mathbf{x_i}, \mathbf{x}) \mid \mathbf{x} \in \gamma(a)\} \subseteq \gamma(k^\sharp(\mathbf{x_i}, a))$. Let us consider the polynomial and RBF kernels.

For a d-polynomial kernel $k(\mathbf{x}, \mathbf{y}) = (\mathbf{x} \cdot \mathbf{y} + c)^d$, we need sound approximations of the unary dot product $\lambda \mathbf{y}. \mathbf{x} \cdot \mathbf{y} : \mathbb{R}^n \to \mathbb{R}$, for any given $\mathbf{x} \in \mathbb{R}^n$, and of the d-power function $(\cdot)^d : \mathbb{R} \to \mathbb{R}$. Of course, a sound nonrelational approximation of $\lambda \mathbf{y}. \mathbf{x} \cdot \mathbf{y} = \sum_{j=1}^{n} \mathbf{x}_j \mathbf{y}_j$ can be obtained simply by using sound abstract scalar multiplication and addition on A_1. Moreover, a sound abstract binary multiplication provides a straightforward definition of a sound abstract d-power function $(\cdot)^{d^\sharp} : A_1 \to A_1$. If $*^\sharp : A_1 \times A_1 \to A_1$ is a sound abstract multiplication such that for all $a, a' \in A_1$, $\gamma(a) * \gamma(a') \subseteq \gamma(a *^\sharp a')$, then a sound abstract d-power procedure can be defined simply by iterating the abstract multiplication $*^\sharp$.

For the RBF kernel $k(\mathbf{x}, \mathbf{y}) = e^{-\gamma \|\mathbf{x} - \mathbf{y}\|_2^2} = e^{-\gamma (\mathbf{x} - \mathbf{y}) \cdot (\mathbf{x} - \mathbf{y})}$, for some $\gamma > 0$, we need sound approximations of the self-dot product $\lambda \mathbf{x}. \mathbf{x} \cdot \mathbf{x} : \mathbb{R}^n \to \mathbb{R}$, which is the squared Euclidean distance, and of the exponential $e^x : \mathbb{R} \to \mathbb{R}$. Let us observe that sound abstract addition and multiplication induce a sound nonrelational approximation of the self-dot product: for all $\langle a_1, ..., a_n \rangle \in A_n$, $\langle a_1, ..., a_n \rangle \cdot^\sharp \langle a_1, ..., a_n \rangle \triangleq \sum_{j=1}^{\sharp n} a_j *^\sharp a_j$. Finally, we require a sound abstract exponential $e^{\sharp(\cdot)} : A_1 \to A_1$ such that for all $a \in A_1$, $\{e^x \mid x \in \gamma(a)\} \subseteq \gamma(e^{\sharp a})$.

Abstract Multi-classification. Let us consider multiclass classification for a set of labels $L = \{y_1, ..., y_m\}$, with $m > 2$. It turns out that the multi-classification approaches based on a reduction to multiple binary classifications such as ovr and ovo introduce a further approximation in the abstraction process, because these reduction strategies need to be soundly approximated.

Let us first consider the ovr strategy and, for all $j \in [1, m]$, let $C_{j,\bar{j}} : X \to \mathbb{R}$ denote the binary scoring classifier of y_j-versus-rest where $C_{j,\bar{j}}(\mathbf{x}) \triangleq D_j(\mathbf{x}) - b_j$. In order to have a sound approximation of ovr multi-classification, besides having m sound abstract classifiers $C^\sharp_{j,\bar{j}} : A_n \to A_1$ such that for all $a \in A_n$, $\{C_{j,\bar{j}}(\mathbf{x}) \in \mathbb{R} \mid \mathbf{x} \in \gamma(a)\} \subseteq \gamma(C^\sharp_{j,\bar{j}}(a))$, we need an abstract maximum function $\max^\sharp : (A_1)^m \to \{1, ..., m, \top\}$ which is sound, namely, if $(a_1, ..., a_m) \in (A_1)^m$ and $(z_1, ..., z_m) \in \gamma(a_1) \times ... \times \gamma(a_m)$ then $\max^\sharp(a_1, ..., a_m) \neq \top \Rightarrow \max(z_1, ..., z_m) \in \gamma(a_{\max^\sharp(a_1, ..., a_m)})$ holds. Clearly, as soon as the abstract function $\max^\sharp$ outputs $\top$, this abstract multi-classification scheme is inconclusive.

Example 3.5. Let $m = 3$ and assume that an ovr multi-classifier M_{ovr} is robust on $\mathbf{x}$ for some adversarial region P as a consequence of the following ranges of scores: for all $\mathbf{x}' \in P(\mathbf{x})$, $-0.5 \leq C_{1,\bar{1}}(\mathbf{x}') \leq -0.2$, $3.5 \leq C_{2,\bar{2}}(\mathbf{x}') \leq 4$ and

$2 \leq C_{3,\bar{3}}(\mathbf{x}') \leq 3.2$. In fact, since the least score of $C_{2,\bar{2}}$ on the region $P(\mathbf{x})$ is greater than the greatest scores of $C_{1,\bar{1}}$ and $C_{3,\bar{3}}$ on $P(\mathbf{x})$, these ranges imply that for all $\mathbf{x}' \in P(\mathbf{x})$, $M_{\text{ovr}}(\mathbf{x}') = y_2$. However, even in this advantageous scenario, on the abstract side we could not be able to infer that $C_{2,\bar{2}}$ always prevails over $C_{1,\bar{1}}$ and $C_{3,\bar{3}}$. For example, for the interval abstraction, some interval binary classifiers for a sound perturbation $P^\sharp(\mathbf{x})$ could output the following sound intervals: $C^\sharp_{1,\bar{1}}(P^\sharp(\mathbf{x})) = [-1, -0.1]$, $C^\sharp_{2,\bar{2}}(P^\sharp(\mathbf{x})) = [3.4, 4.2]$ and $C^\sharp_{3,\bar{3}}(P^\sharp(\mathbf{x})) = [1.5, 3.5]$. In this case, despite that each abstract binary classifier $C^\sharp_{i,\bar{i}}$ is able to prove that $C_{i,\bar{i}}$ is robust on $\mathbf{x}$ for P (because the output intervals do not include 0), the ovr strategy here does not allow to conclude that the multi-classifier M_{ovr} is robust on $\mathbf{x}$, because the lower bound 3.4 of the interval approximation provided by $C^\sharp_{2,\bar{2}}$ is not above the interval upper bound 3.5 of $C^\sharp_{3,\bar{3}}$. In such a case, a sound abstract multi-classifier based on ovr cannot prove the robustness of M_{ovr} for $P(\mathbf{x})$. □

Let us turn to the ovo approach which relies on $m(m-1)/2$ binary classifiers $C_{\{i,j\}} : X \to \{i, j\}$. Let us assume that for all the pairs $i \neq j$, a sound abstract binary classifier $C^\sharp_{\{i,j\}} : A \to \{y_i, y_j, \top\}$ is defined. Then, an abstract ovo multi-classifier $M^\sharp_{\text{ovo}} : A \to \wp(L)$ can be defined as follows. For all $i \in \{1, ..., m\}$ and $a \in A$, let $\text{votes}^\sharp(a, y_i) \in \text{Int}_{\mathbb{N}}$ be an interval of nonnegative integers used by the following abstract voting procedure AV, where $+^{\text{Int}}$ denotes standard interval addition:

$$
\begin{array}{l}
\textbf{forall } i \in [1, m] \textbf{ do } \text{votes}^\sharp(a, y_i) := [0, 0];\\
\textbf{forall } i, j \in [1, m] \textbf{ s.t. } i \neq j \textbf{ do}\\
\quad \textbf{if } C^\sharp_{\{i,j\}}(a) = y_i \textbf{ then } \text{votes}^\sharp(a, y_i) := \text{votes}^\sharp(a, y_i) +^{\text{Int}} [1, 1];\\
\quad \textbf{elseif } C^\sharp_{\{i,j\}}(a) = y_j \textbf{ then } \text{votes}^\sharp(a, y_j) := \text{votes}^\sharp(a, y_j) +^{\text{Int}} [1, 1];\\
\quad \textbf{else } \text{votes}^\sharp(a, y_i) := \text{votes}^\sharp(a, y_i) +^{\text{Int}} [0, 1]; \text{votes}^\sharp(a, y_j) := \text{votes}^\sharp(a, y_j) +^{\text{Int}} [0, 1];
\end{array}
\tag{2}
$$

Let us notice that the last else branch is taken when $C^\sharp_{\{i,j\}}(a) = \top$, meaning that the abstract classifier $C^\sharp_{\{i,j\}}(a)$ is not able to decide between y_i and y_j, so that in order to preserve the soundness of the abstract voting procedure, we need to increment just the upper bounds of the interval ranges of votes for both classes y_i and y_j while their lower bounds are left unchanged. Let us denote $\text{votes}^\sharp(a, y_i) = [v_i^{\min}, v_i^{\max}]$. Hence, at the end of the AV procedure, $[v_i^{\min}, v_i^{\max}]$ provides an interval approximation of concrete votes as follows:

$$
\begin{aligned}
|\{j \neq i \mid \forall \mathbf{x} \in \gamma(a).\, C_{\{i,j\}}(\mathbf{x}) = i\}| &\geq v_i^{\min},\\
|\{j \neq i \mid \exists \mathbf{x} \in \gamma(a).\, C_{\{i,j\}}(\mathbf{x}) = i\}| &\leq v_i^{\max}.
\end{aligned}
$$

The corresponding abstract multi-classifier is then defined as follows:

$$
M^\sharp_{\text{ovo}}(a) \triangleq \{y_i \in L \mid \forall j \neq i.\, v_j^{\min} \leq v_i^{\max}\}.
$$

Hence, one may have an intuition for this definition by considering that a class y_i is not in $M^\sharp_{\text{ovo}}(a)$ when there exists a different class y_k whose lower bound of votes is certainly strictly greater than the upper bound of votes for y_i. For example, for $m = 4$, if $\text{votes}^\sharp(a, y_1) = [4, 4]$, $\text{votes}^\sharp(a, y_2) = [0, 2]$, $\text{votes}^\sharp(a, y_3) = [4, 5]$, $\text{votes}^\sharp(a, y_4) = [1, 3]$ then $M^\sharp_{\text{ovo}}(a) = \{y_1, y_3\}$.

Example 3.6. Assume that $m = 3$ and for all $\mathbf{x}' \in P(\mathbf{x})$, $M_{\text{ovo}}(\mathbf{x}') = \{y_3\}$ because we have that $\text{argmax}_{i=1,2,3}\text{votes}(\mathbf{x}', y_i) = \{3\}$. This means that a draw never happens for M_{ovo}, so that for all $\mathbf{x}' \in P(\mathbf{x})$, $C_{\{1,3\}}(\mathbf{x}') = y_3$ and $C_{\{2,3\}}(\mathbf{x}') = y_3$ certainly hold (because $m = 3$). Let us also assume that $\{C_{\{1,2\}}(\mathbf{x}') \mid \mathbf{x}' \in P(\mathbf{x})\} = \{y_1, y_2\}$. Then, for a sound abstract perturbation $P^\sharp(\mathbf{x})$, we necessarily have that $C^\sharp_{\{1,2\}}(P^\sharp(\mathbf{x})) = \top$. If we assume that $C^\sharp_{\{1,3\}}(P^\sharp(\mathbf{x})) = y_3$ and $C^\sharp_{\{2,3\}}(P^\sharp(\mathbf{x})) = \top$ then we have that $M^\sharp_{\text{ovo}}(P^\sharp(\mathbf{x})) = \{y_1, y_2, y_3\}$ because $\text{votes}(P^\sharp(\mathbf{x}), y_1) = [0, 1]$, $\text{votes}(P^\sharp(\mathbf{x}), y_2) = [0, 2]$ and $\text{votes}(P^\sharp(\mathbf{x}), y_3) = [1, 2]$. Therefore, in this case, $M^\sharp_{\text{ovo}}$ is not able to prove the robustness of M_{ovo} on $\mathbf{x}$. Let us notice that the source of imprecision in this multi-classification is confined to the binary classifier $C^\sharp_{\{2,3\}}$ rather than the abstract voting AV strategy. In fact, if we have that $C^\sharp_{\{1,3\}}(P^\sharp(\mathbf{x})) = \{y_3\}$ and $C^\sharp_{\{2,3\}}(P^\sharp(\mathbf{x})) = \{y_3\}$ then $M^\sharp_{\text{ovo}}(P^\sharp(\mathbf{x})) = \{y_3\}$, thus proving the robustness of M. □

Lemma 3.7. *Let M_{ovo} be an ovo multi-classifier based on binary classifiers $C_{\{i,j\}}$. If the abstract ovo multi-classifier $M^\sharp_{ovo}$ is based on sound abstract binary classifiers $C^\sharp_{\{i,j\}}$ then $M^\sharp_{ovo}$ is sound for M_{ovo}.*

In our experimental evaluation we will follow the ovo approach for concrete multi-classification, which is standard for SVMs [14], and consequently we will use this abstract ovo multi-classifier for robustness verification.

On Completeness. Let $C : X \to \{-1, +1\}$ be a binary classifier, $P : X \to \wp(X)$ a perturbation and $C^\sharp : A \to \{-1, +1, \top\}$, $P^\sharp : X \to A$ be a corresponding sound abstract binary classifier and perturbation on some abstraction A.

Definition 3.8 (Complete Abstract Classifiers and Robustness Verifiers). $C^\sharp$ is *complete* for C when for all $a \in A$, $C^\sharp(a) = \top \Rightarrow \exists \mathbf{x}, \mathbf{x}' \in \gamma(a). C(\mathbf{x}) \neq C(\mathbf{x}')$.
$\langle C^\sharp, P^\sharp \rangle$ is a (sound and) *complete robustness verifier* for C w.r.t. P when for all $\mathbf{x} \in X$, $C^\sharp(P^\sharp(\mathbf{x})) = C(\mathbf{x})$ iff $\text{Rob}(C, \mathbf{x}, P)$. □

Complete abstract classifiers can be obtained for linear binary classifiers once these linear classifiers are in primal form and the abstract operations are exact. We therefore consider a linear binary classifier in primal form $C_{\text{pr}}(\mathbf{x}) \triangleq \text{sign}_b(\sum_{j=1}^{n} \mathbf{w}_j \pi_j(\mathbf{x}))$ and an abstraction A of $\wp(X)$ with concretization $\gamma : A \to \wp(X)$. Let us consider the following exactness conditions for the abstract functions on A needed for abstracting C_{pr} and the perturbation P:

(E_1) Exact projection $\pi^\sharp_j$: For all $j \in [1, n]$ and $a \in A_n$, $\gamma(\pi^\sharp_j(a)) = \pi_j(\gamma(a))$;
(E_2) Exact scalar multiplication: For all $z \in \mathbb{R}$ and $a \in A_1$, $\gamma(za) = z\gamma(a)$;
(E_3) Exact scalar addition $+^\sharp$: For all $a, a' \in A_1$, $\gamma(a +^\sharp a') = \gamma(a) + \gamma(a')$;
(E_4) Exact $\text{sign}^\sharp_b$: For all $b \in \mathbb{R}$, $a \in A_1$, $(\forall x \in \gamma(a). \text{sign}_b(x) = s) \Rightarrow \text{sign}^\sharp_b(a) = s$;
(E_5) Exact perturbation $P^\sharp$: For all $\mathbf{x} \in X$, $\gamma(P^\sharp(\mathbf{x})) = P(\mathbf{x})$.

Then, it turns out that the abstract classifier $C^\sharp_{\text{pr}}(a) \triangleq \text{sign}^\sharp_b(\sum^{\sharp n}_{j=1} \mathbf{w}_j \pi^\sharp_j(a))$ is complete and induces a complete robustness verifier.

Lemma 3.9. *Under hypotheses* (E_1)–(E_5), $C^\sharp_{\text{pr}}$ *is (sound and) complete for* C_{pr} *and* $\langle C^\sharp_{\text{pr}}, P^\sharp\rangle$ *is a complete robustness verifier for* C_{pr} *w.r.t.* P.

Let us now focus on multi-classification. It turns out that completeness does not scale from binary to multi-classification, that is, even if all the abstract binary classifiers are assumed to be complete, the corresponding abstract multi-classification could lose the completeness. This loss is not due to the abstraction of the binary classifiers, but it is an intrinsic issue of a multi-classification approach based on binary classification. Let us show how this loss for ovr and ovo can happen through some examples.

Example 3.10 Consider $L = \{y_1, y_2, y_3\}$ and assume that for two different inputs $\mathbf{x}, \mathbf{x}' \in X$, the scoring ovr binary classifiers $C_{i,\bar{i}}$ are as follows: $C_{1,\bar{1}}(\mathbf{x}) = 3$, $C_{2,\bar{2}}(\mathbf{x}) = -1$, $C_{3,\bar{3}}(\mathbf{x}) = 2$, $C_{1,\bar{1}}(\mathbf{x}') = 1$, $C_{2,\bar{2}}(\mathbf{x}') = -1$, $C_{3,\bar{3}}(\mathbf{x}) = 0.5$. Hence, $M_{\text{ovr}}(\mathbf{x}) = M_{\text{ovr}}(\mathbf{x}') = \{y_1\}$, meaning that M_{ovr} is robust on $\mathbf{x}$ for a perturbation $P(\mathbf{x}) = \{\mathbf{x}, \mathbf{x}'\}$. However, it turns out that the mere collecting abstraction of binary classifiers $C_{i,\bar{i}}$, although being trivially complete according to Definition 3.8, may well lead to a (sound but) incomplete multi-classification. In fact, even if we consider no abstraction of sets of vectors/scalars and an abstract binary classifier is simply defined by a collecting abstraction $C^\sharp_{i,\bar{i}}(Y) \triangleq \{C_{i,\bar{i}}(\mathbf{x}) \in \mathbb{R} \mid \mathbf{x} \in Y\}$, then we have that while each $C^\sharp_{i,\bar{i}}$ is complete the corresponding abstract ovr multi-classifier turns out to be sound but not complete. In our example, we have that: $C^\sharp_{1,\bar{1}}(P(\mathbf{x})) = \{1, 3\}$, $C^\sharp_{2,\bar{2}}(P(\mathbf{x})) = \{-1\}$, $C^\sharp_{3,\bar{3}}(P(\mathbf{x})) = \{0.5, 2\}$. Hence, the ovr strategy can only derive that both y_1 and y_2 are feasible classes for $P(\mathbf{x})$, namely, $M^\sharp_{\text{ovr}}(\{\mathbf{x}, \mathbf{x}'\}) = \{y_1, y_2\}$, meaning that $M^\sharp_{\text{ovr}}$ cannot prove the robustness of M. □

The above example shows that the loss of relational information between input vectors and corresponding scores is an unavoidable source of incompleteness when abstracting ovr multi-classification. An analogous incompleteness happens in ovo multi-classification.

Example 3.11 Consider $L = \{y_1, y_2, y_3, y_4, y_5\}$ and assume that for some $\mathbf{x}, \mathbf{x}' \in X$, the ovo binary classifiers $C_{\{i,j\}}$ give the following outputs:

	$C_{\{1,2\}}$	$C_{\{1,3\}}$	$C_{\{1,4\}}$	$C_{\{1,5\}}$	$C_{\{2,3\}}$	$C_{\{2,4\}}$	$C_{\{2,5\}}$	$C_{\{3,4\}}$	$C_{\{3,5\}}$	$C_{\{4,5\}}$
$\mathbf{x}$	y_1	y_1	y_1	y_5	y_2	y_2	y_5	y_3	y_3	y_4
$\mathbf{x}'$	y_1	y_1	y_4	y_1	y_2	y_4	y_2	y_3	y_5	y_5

so that $M_{\text{ovo}}(\mathbf{x}) = M_{\text{ovo}}(\mathbf{x}') = \{y_1\}$, meaning that M_{ovo} is robust on $\mathbf{x}$ for the perturbation $P(\mathbf{x}) = \{\mathbf{x}, \mathbf{x}'\}$. Similarly to Example 3.10, the collecting abstractions of binary classifiers $C_{\{i,j\}}$ are trivially complete but define a (sound but) incomplete multi-classification. In fact, even with no numerical abstraction, if we consider the abstract collecting binary classifiers $C^\sharp_{\{i,j\}}(Y) \triangleq \{C_{\{i,j\}}(\mathbf{x}) \mid \mathbf{x} \in Y\}$ then we have that:

	$C_{\{1,2\}}$	$C_{\{1,3\}}$	$C_{\{1,4\}}$	$C_{\{1,5\}}$	$C_{\{2,3\}}$	$C_{\{2,4\}}$	$C_{\{2,5\}}$	$C_{\{3,4\}}$	$C_{\{3,5\}}$	$C_{\{4,5\}}$
$P(\mathbf{x})$	$\{y_1\}$	$\{y_1\}$	$\{y_1, y_4\}$	$\{y_1, y_5\}$	$\{y_2\}$	$\{y_2, y_4\}$	$\{y_2, y_5\}$	$\{y_3\}$	$\{y_3, y_5\}$	$\{y_4, y_5\}$

Thus, the ovo voting for $P(\mathbf{x})$ in order to be sound necessarily has to assign 4 votes to both classes y_1 and y_5, meaning that $M^\sharp_{\text{ovo}}(P(\mathbf{x})) = \{y_1, y_5\}$. As a consequence, $M^\sharp_{\text{ovr}}$ cannot prove the robustness of M_{ovo}. Here again, this is a consequence of the collecting abstraction which looses the relational information between input vectors and corresponding classes, and therefore is an ineluctable source of incompleteness when abstracting ovo multi-classification. □

Let us observe that when all the abstract binary classifiers $C^\sharp_{\{i,j\}}$ are complete, then in the abstract voting procedure AV defined by (2), for all $\text{votes}^\sharp(a, y_i) = [v_i^{\min}, v_i^{\max}]$, we have that $|\{j \neq i \mid \exists \mathbf{x} \in \gamma(a).\ C_{\{i,j\}}(\mathbf{x}) = i\}| = v_i^{\max}$ holds, meaning that the hypothesis of completeness of abstract binary classifiers strengthens the upper bound $v_i^{\max}$ to a precise equality, although this is not enough for preserving the completeness.

4 Numerical Abstractions for Classifiers

Interval Abstraction. The n-dimensional interval abstraction domain Int_n is simply defined as a nonrelational product of Int, i.e., $\text{Int}_n \triangleq \text{Int}^n$ (with $\text{Int}_1 = \text{Int}$), where $\gamma_{\text{Int}_n} : \text{Int}_n \to \wp(\mathbb{R}^n)$ is defined by $\gamma_{\text{Int}_n}(I_1, ..., I_n) \triangleq \times_{i=1}^n \gamma_{\text{Int}}(I_i)$, and, by a slight abuse of notation, this concretization map will be denoted simply by γ. In order to abstract linear and nonlinear classifiers, we will use the following standard interval operations based on real arithmetic operations.

- Projection $\pi_j : \text{Int}_n \to \text{Int}$ defined by $\pi_j(I_1, ..., I_n) \triangleq I_j$, which is trivially exact because Int_n is nonrelational.
- Scalar multiplication $\lambda\mathbf{I}.z\mathbf{I} : \text{Int}_n \to \text{Int}_n$, with $z \in \mathbb{R}$, is defined as componentwise extension of scalar multiplication $\lambda I.zI : \text{Int}_1 \to \text{Int}_1$ given by: $z\bot = \bot$ and $z[l, u] \triangleq [zl, zu]$, where $z(\pm\infty) = \pm\infty$ for $z \neq 0$ and $0(\pm\infty) = 0$. This is an exact abstract scalar multiplication, i.e., $\{z\mathbf{x} \mid \mathbf{x} \in \gamma(\mathbf{I})\} = \gamma(z\mathbf{I})$ holds.
- Addition $+^\sharp : \text{Int}_n \times \text{Int}_n \to \text{Int}_n$ is defined as componentwise extension of standard interval addition, that is, $\bot +^\sharp I = \bot = I +^\sharp \bot$, $[l_1, u_1] +^\sharp [l_2, u_2] = [l_1 + l_2, u_1 + u_2]$. This abstract interval addition is exact, i.e., $\{\mathbf{x}_1 + \mathbf{x}_2 \mid \mathbf{x}_i \in \gamma(\mathbf{I}_i)\} = \gamma(\mathbf{I}_1 +^\sharp \mathbf{I}_2)$ holds.
- One-dimensional multiplication $*^\sharp : \text{Int}_1 \times \text{Int}_1 \to \text{Int}_1$ is enough for our purposes, whose definition is standard: $\bot *^\sharp I = \bot = I *^\sharp \bot$, $[l_1, u_1] *^\sharp [l_2, u_2] = [\min(l_1l_2, l_1u_2, u_1l_2, u_1u_2),\ \max(l_1l_2, l_1u_2, u_1l_2, u_1u_2)]$. As a consequence of the completeness of real numbers, this abstract interval multiplication is exact, i.e., $\{x_1x_2 \mid x_i \in \gamma(I_i)\} = \gamma(I_1 *^\sharp I_2)$.

It is worth remarking that since all these abstract functions on real intervals are exact and real intervals have the abstraction map, it turns out that all these abstract functions are the best correct approximations on intervals of the corresponding concrete functions.

For the exponential function $e^x : \mathbb{R} \to \mathbb{R}$ used by RBF kernels, let us consider a generic real function $f : \mathbb{R} \to \mathbb{R}$ which is assumed to be continuous and monotonically either increasing ($x \leq y \Rightarrow f(x) \leq f(y)$) or decreasing ($x \leq y \Rightarrow f(x) \geq f(y)$). Its collecting lifting $f^c : \wp(\mathbb{R}) \rightarrow \wp(\mathbb{R})$ is approximated on the interval abstraction by the abstract function $f^\sharp : \mathrm{Int}_1 \rightarrow \mathrm{Int}_1$ defined as follows: for all possibly unbounded intervals $[l, u]$ with $l, u \in \mathbb{R} \cup \{-\infty, +\infty\}$,

$$f_i([l,u]) \triangleq \inf\{f(x) \in \mathbb{R} \mid x \in \gamma([l,u])\} \in \mathbb{R} \cup \{-\infty\}$$
$$f_s([l,u]) \triangleq \sup\{f(x) \in \mathbb{R} \mid x \in \gamma([l,u])\} \in \mathbb{R} \cup \{+\infty\}$$
$$f^\sharp([l,u]) \triangleq [\min(f_i([l,u]), f_s([l,u])), \max(f_i([l,u]), f_s([l,u]))] \qquad f^\sharp(\bot) \triangleq \bot$$

Therefore, for bounded intervals $[l, u]$ with $l, u \in \mathbb{R}$, $f^\sharp([l,u]) = [\min(f(l), f(u)), \max(f(l), f(u))]$. As a consequence of the hypotheses of continuity and monotonicity of f, it turns out that this abstract function $f^\sharp$ is exact, i.e., $\{f(x) \in \mathbb{R} \mid x \in \gamma([l,u])\} = \gamma(f^\sharp([l,u]))$ holds, and it is the best correct approximation on intervals of f^c.

Reduced Affine Arithmetic Abstraction. Even if all the abstract functions of the interval abstraction are exact, it is well known that the compositional abstract evaluation of an inductively defined expression *exp* on Int can be imprecise due to the so-called dependency problem, meaning that if the syntactic expression *exp* includes multiple occurrences of a variable x and the abstract evaluation of *exp* is performed by structural induction on *exp*, then each occurrence of x in *exp* is taken independently from the others and this can lead to a significant loss of precision in the output interval. This loss of precision may happen both for addition and multiplication of intervals. For example, the abstract compositional evaluations of the simple expressions $x - x$ and $x * x$ on an input interval $[-c, c]$, with $c \in \mathbb{R}_{>0}$, yield, resp., $[-2c, 2c]$ and $[-c^2, c^2]$, rather than the exact results $[0, 0]$ and $[0, c^2]$. This dependency problem can be a significant source of imprecision for the interval abstraction of a polynomial SVM classifier $C(\mathbf{x}) = \mathrm{sign}([\sum_{i=1}^{N} \alpha_i y_i (\sum_{j=1}^{n} (\mathbf{y_i})_j \mathbf{x}_j + c)^d] - b)$, where each attribute $\mathbf{x}_j$ of an input vector $\mathbf{x}$ occurs for each support vector $\mathbf{y_i}$. The classifiers based on RBF kernels suffer from an analogous issue.

Affine Forms. Affine arithmetic [35,36] mitigates this dependency problem of the nonrelational interval abstraction. An interval $[l, u] \in \mathrm{Int}$ which approximates the range of some variable x is represented by an *affine form* (AF) $\hat{x} = a_0 + a_1 \epsilon_x$, where $a_0 = (l + u)/2$, $a_1 = (u - l)/2$ and ϵ_x is a symbolic (or "noise") real variable ranging in $[-1, 1] \in \mathrm{Int}$ which explicitly represents a dependence from the parameter x. This solves the dependency problem for a linear expression such as $x - x$ because the interval $[-c, c]$ for x is represented by $0 + c\epsilon_x$ so that the compositional evaluation of $x - x$ for $0 + c\epsilon_x$ becomes $(0 + c\epsilon_x) - (0 + c\epsilon_x) = 0$, while for nonlinear expressions such as $x * x$, an approximation is still needed.

In general, the domain AF_k of affine forms with $k \geq 1$ noise variables consists of affine forms $\hat{a} = a_0 + \sum_{i=1}^{k} a_i \epsilon_i$, where $a_i \in \mathbb{R}$ and each ϵ_i represents either an external dependence from some input variable or an internal approximation dependence due to a nonlinear operation. An affine form $\hat{a} \in \mathrm{AF}_k$ can be abstracted to a real interval in Int, as given by a map $\alpha_{\mathrm{Int}} : \mathrm{AF}_k \rightarrow \mathrm{Int}$ defined as follows: for all $\hat{a} = a_0 + \sum_{i=1}^{k} a_i \epsilon_i \in \mathrm{AF}_k$, $\alpha_{\mathrm{Int}}(\hat{a}) \triangleq [c_{\hat{a}} - \mathrm{rad}(\hat{a}), c_{\hat{a}} + \mathrm{rad}(\hat{a})]$, where $c_{\hat{a}} \triangleq a_0$ and $\mathrm{rad}(\hat{e}) \triangleq \sum_{i=1}^{k} |a_i|$ are called, resp., center and radius of the affine form $\hat{a}$. This, in turn, defines the interval concretization $\gamma_{\mathrm{AF}_k} : \mathrm{AF}_k \to \mathbb{R}$ given by $\gamma_{\mathrm{AF}_k}(\hat{a}) \triangleq \gamma_{\mathrm{Int}\to\mathbb{R}}(\alpha_{\mathrm{Int}}(\hat{a}))$. Vectors of affine forms may be used to represent zonotopes, which are center-symmetric convex polytopes and have been used to design an abstract domain for static program analysis [13] endowed with abstract functions, joins and widening.

Reduced Affine Forms. It turns out that affine forms are exact for linear operations, namely additions and scalar multiplications. If $\hat{a}, \hat{b} \in \mathrm{AF}_k$ and $c \in \mathbb{R}$ then abstract additions and scalar multiplications are defined as follows: $\hat{a} +^\sharp \hat{b} \triangleq (a_0 + b_0) + \sum_{j=1}^{k} (a_j + b_j)\epsilon_j$ and $c\hat{a} \triangleq ca_0 + \sum_{j=1}^{k} ca_j \epsilon_j$. They are exact, namely, $\{x + y \in \mathbb{R} \mid x \in \gamma_{\mathrm{AF}_k}(\hat{a}), y \in \gamma_{\mathrm{AF}_k}(\hat{b})\} = \gamma_{\mathrm{AF}_k}(\hat{a} +^\sharp \hat{b})$ and $c\gamma_{\mathrm{AF}_k}(\hat{a}) = \gamma_{\mathrm{AF}_k}(c\hat{a})$.

For nonlinear operations, in particular multiplication, in general the result cannot be represented exactly by an affine form. Then, the standard strategy for defining the multiplication of affine forms is to approximate the precise result by adding a fresh noise symbol whose coefficient is typically computed by a Taylor or Chebyshev approximation of the nonlinear part of the multiplication (cf. [13, Section 2.1.5]). Similarly, for the exponential function used in RBF kernels, an algorithm for computing an affine approximation of the exponential e^x evaluated on an affine form $\hat{x}$ for the exponent x is given in [35, Section 3.11] and is based on an optimal Chebyshev approximation (that is, w.r.t. L_∞ distance) of the exponential which introduces a fresh noise symbol. However, the need of injecting a fresh noise symbol for each nonlinear operation raises a critical space and time complexity issue for abstracting polynomial and RBF classifiers, because this would imply that a new but useless noise symbol should be added for each support vector. For example, for a 2-polynomial classifier, we need to approximate a square operation $x * x$ for each of the N support vectors, and a blind usage of abstract multiplication for affine forms would add N different and useless noise symbols. This drawback would be even worse for d-polynomial classifers with $d > 2$, while an analogous critical issue would happen for RBF classifiers. This motivates the use of so-called *reduced affine forms* (RAFs), which have been introduced in [20] as a remedy for the increase of noise symbols due to nonlinear operations and still allow us to keep track of correlations between the components of the input vectors of classifiers.

A reduced affine form $\tilde{a} \in \mathrm{RAF}_k$ of length $k \geq 1$ is defined as a sum of a standard affine form in AF_k with a specific rounding noise ϵ_a which accumulates all the errors introduced by nonlinear operations. Thus, $\mathrm{RAF}_k \triangleq \{a_0 + \sum_{j=1}^{k} a_j \epsilon_j + a_r \epsilon_a \mid a_0, a_1, ..., a_k \in \mathbb{R}, a_r \in \mathbb{R}_{\geq 0}\}$. The key point is that the length of $\tilde{a} \in \mathrm{RAF}_k$ remains unchanged during the whole abstract computation and $a_r \in \mathbb{R}_{\geq 0}$ is the radius of the accumulative error of approximating all nonlinear operations during abstract computations. Of course, each $\tilde{a} \in \mathrm{RAF}_k$ can be viewed as a standard affine form in AF_{k+1} and this allows us to define the interval concretization $\gamma_{\mathrm{RAF}_k}(\tilde{a})$ and the linear abstract operations of addition and scalar multiplication of RAFs simply by considering them as standard affine forms. In particular, linear abstract operations in RAF_k are exact w.r.t. interval concretization γ_{RAF_k}.

Nonlinear abstract operations, such as multiplication, must necessarily be approximated for RAFs. Several algorithms of abstract multiplication of RAFs are available, which differ in precision, approximation principle and time complexity, ranging from linear to quadratic complexities [33, Section 3]. Given $\tilde{a}, \tilde{b} \in \text{RAF}_k$, we need to define an abstract multiplication $\tilde{a} *^\sharp \tilde{b} \in \text{RAF}_k$ which is sound, namely, $\{xy \in \mathbb{R} \mid x \in \gamma_{\text{RAF}_k}(\tilde{a}),\ y \in \gamma_{\text{RAF}_k}(\tilde{b})\} \subseteq \gamma_{\text{RAF}_k}(\tilde{a} *^\sharp \tilde{b})$, where it is worth pointing out that this soundness condition is given w.r.t. interval concretization γ_{RAF_k} and scalar multiplication. Time complexity is a crucial issue for using $*^\sharp$ in abstract polynomial and RBF kernels, because in these abstract classifiers at least an abstract multiplication must be used for each support vector, so that quadratic time algorithms in $O(k^2)$ cannot scale when the number of support vectors grows, as expected for realistic training datasets. We therefore selected a recent linear time algorithm by Skalna and Hladík [33] which is optimal in the following sense. Given $\tilde{a}, \tilde{b} \in \text{RAF}_k$, we have that their concrete symbolic multiplication is as follows:

$$\begin{aligned}\tilde{a} * \tilde{b} &= (a_0 + \textstyle\sum_{j=1}^k a_j \epsilon_j + a_r \epsilon_a) * (b_0 + \textstyle\sum_{j=1}^k b_j \epsilon_j + b_r \epsilon_b)\\ &= a_0 b_0 + \textstyle\sum_{j=1}^k (a_0 b_j + b_0 a_j)\epsilon_j + (a_0 b_r \epsilon_b + b_0 a_r \epsilon_a) \ + f_{\tilde{a},\tilde{b}}(\epsilon_1, ..., \epsilon_k, \epsilon_a, \epsilon_b)\end{aligned}$$

where $f_{\tilde{a},\tilde{b}}(\epsilon_1, ..., \epsilon_k, \epsilon_a, \epsilon_b) \triangleq (\sum_{j=1}^k a_j \epsilon_j + a_r \epsilon_a)(\sum_{j=1}^k b_j \epsilon_j + b_r \epsilon_b)$. An abstract multiplication $*_e^\sharp$ on RAF_k can be defined as follows: if $R_{\max}, R_{\min} \in \mathbb{R}$ are, resp., the minimum and maximum of $\{f_{\tilde{a},\tilde{b}}(\mathbf{e}) \in \mathbb{R} \mid \mathbf{e} \in [-1,1]^{k+2}\}$ then

$$\begin{aligned}\tilde{a} *_e^\sharp \tilde{b} \triangleq a_0 b_0 + 0.5(R_{\max} + R_{\min}) + \textstyle\sum_{j=1}^k (a_0 b_j + b_0 a_j)\epsilon_j +\\ (|a_0| b_r + |b_0| a_r + 0.5(R_{\max} - R_{\min}))\epsilon_{a*b}\end{aligned}$$

where $0.5(R_{\max}+R_{\min})$ and $0.5(R_{\max}-R_{\min})$ are, resp., the center and the radius of the interval range of $f_{\tilde{a},\tilde{b}}(\epsilon_1, ..., \epsilon_k, \epsilon_a, \epsilon_b)$. As argued in [33, Proposition 3], this defines an optimal abstract multiplication of RAFs. Skalna and Hladík [33] put forward two algorithms for computing $R_{\max}$ and $R_{\min}$, one with $O(k)$ time bound and one in $O(k \log k)$: the $O(k)$ bound is obtained by relying on a linear time algorithm to find a median of a sequence of real numbers, while the $O(k \log k)$ algorithm is based on (quick)sorting that sequence of numbers. The details of these algorithms are here omitted and can be found in [33, Section 4]. In abstract interpretation terms, it turns out that this abstract multiplication algorithm $*_e^\sharp$ of RAFs provides the best approximation among the RAFs which correctly approximate the multiplication with the same coefficients for ϵ_1,...,ϵ_k of $\tilde{a} *_e^\sharp \tilde{b}$.

Finally, let us consider the exponential function e^x used in RBF kernels. The algorithm in [35, Section 3.11] for computing the affine form approximation of e^x and based on Chebyshev approximation of e^x can be also applied when the exponent is represented by a RAF $\tilde{x} = x_0 + \sum_{j=1}^k x_j \epsilon_j + x_r \epsilon_x \in \text{RAF}_k$, provided that the radius of the fresh noise symbol produced by computing $e^{\tilde{x}}$ is added to the coefficient of the rounding noise ϵ_x of $\tilde{x}$.

Floating Point Soundness. The interval and RAF abstractions and the corresponding abstract functions described above rely on precise real arithmetic on

$\mathbb{R}$, in particular soundness and exactness of abstract functions depend on real arithmetic. These abstract functions may yield unsound results for floating point arithmetic such as the standard IEEE 754 [34]. These domains therefore need some suitable adjustments to make them "floating-point" sound [21], which are described in the full version of this paper [29].

5 Verifying SVM Classifiers

Perturbations. We consider robustness of SVM classifiers against a standard adversarial region defined by the L_∞ norm, as considered in Carlini and Wagner's robustness model [4] and used by Vechev et al. [9,31,32] in their verification framework. Given a generic classifier $C : X \to L$ and a constant $\delta \in \mathbb{R}_{>0}$, a L_∞ δ-perturbation of an input vector $\mathbf{x} \in \mathbb{R}^n$ is defined by $P_\delta^\infty(\mathbf{x}) \triangleq \{\mathbf{x}' \in X \mid \|\mathbf{x}' - \mathbf{x}\|_\infty \leq \delta\}$. Thus, if the space X consists of n-dimensional real vectors normalized in $[0,1]$ (our datasets follow this standard) and $\delta \in (0,1]$ then $P_\delta^\infty(\mathbf{x}) = \{\mathbf{x}' \in \mathbb{R}^n \mid \forall i.\ \mathbf{x}'_i \in [\mathbf{x}_i - \epsilon, \mathbf{x}_i + \epsilon] \cap [0,1]\}$. Let us observe that, for all $\mathbf{x}$, $P_\delta^\infty(\mathbf{x})$ is an exact perturbation for intervals and therefore for RAFs as well (cf. (E_5)). The datasets of our experiments consist of $h{\times}w$ grayscale images (with 8 bits per pixel, i.e., the pixel depth allows 256 different gray intensities) where each image is represented as a normalized real vector in $[0,1]^{hw}$ whose components encode the light values of pixels. Increasing (decreasing) the value of a vector component means brightening (darkening) that pixel, so that a brightening of $+0.01$ means $+2.55$ pixel depth. Hence, a perturbation $P_\delta^\infty(\mathbf{x})$ of an image $\mathbf{x}$ represents all the images where every possible subset of pixels is brightened or darkened up to δ.

We also consider robustness of image classifiers for the so-called *adversarial framing* on the border of images, which has been recently shown to represent an effective attack for deep convolutional networks [44]. Consider an image represented as a $h \times w$ matrix $M \in \mathbb{R}_{h,w}$ with normalized real values in $[0,1]$. Given an integer framing thickness $t \in [1, \min(h,w)/2]$, the "occlude" t-framing perturbation of M is defined by

$$\begin{aligned} P_t^{\mathrm{frm}}(M) \triangleq \{M' \in \mathbb{R}_{h,w} \mid\ & \forall i \in [t+1, h-t], j \in [w+1, w-t].\ M'_{i,j} = M_{i,j}, \\ & \forall i \notin [t+1, h-t], j \notin [w+1, w-t].\ M'_{i,j} \in [0,1]\}. \end{aligned}$$

This framing perturbation models the uniformly distributed random noise attack in [44]. Also in this case $P_t^{\mathrm{frm}}(M)$ is a perturbation which can be exactly represented by intervals and consequently by RAFs.

Linear Classifiers. As observed in Sect. 4, for the interval abstraction it turns out that all the abstract functions which are used in abstract linear binary classifiers in primal form are exact, so that, by Lemma 3.9, these abstract linear binary classifiers are complete. This completeness implies that there is no need to resort to the RAF abstraction for linear binary classifiers. However, as argued in Sect. 3, this completeness for binary classifiers does not scale to multi-classification. Nevertheless, it is worth pointing out that for each binary classifier $C_{\{i,j\}}$ used in ovo multi-classification, since L_∞ and frame perturbations are exact for intervals, we have a complete robustness verifier for each $C_{\{i,j\}}$. As a consequence, this makes feasible to find adversarial examples of linear binary classifiers as follows. Let us consider a linear binary classifier in primal form $C(\mathbf{x}) = \text{sign}([\sum_{j=1}^{n} \mathbf{w}_j \mathbf{x}_j] - b)$ and a perturbation P which is exact on intervals, i.e., for all $\mathbf{x}$, $P(\mathbf{x}) = \gamma_{\text{Int}_n}(P^\sharp(\mathbf{x}))$, where $P^\sharp(\mathbf{x}) = \langle [l_1, u_1], ..., [l_n, u_n] \rangle \in \text{Int}_n$. Completeness of robustness linear verification means that if the interval abstraction $\sum_{j=1}^{\sharp n} \mathbf{w}_j [l_j, u_j]$ outputs an interval $[l, u] \in \text{Int}_1$ such that $0 \in [l, u]$, then C is surely not robust on $\mathbf{x}$ for P. It is then easy to find two input vectors $\mathbf{y}, \mathbf{z} \in P(\mathbf{x})$ which provide a concrete counterexample to the robustness, namely such that $C(\mathbf{y}) \neq C(\mathbf{z})$. For all $i \in [1, n]$, if $\mathbf{y}_i \triangleq$ **if** $\text{sign}(\mathbf{w}_i) \geq 0$ **then** u_i **else** l_i and $\mathbf{z}_i \triangleq$ **if** $\text{sign}(\mathbf{w}_i) \geq 0$ **then** l_i **else** u_i then we have defined $\mathbf{y}, \mathbf{z} \in P(\mathbf{x})$ such that $\sum_{j=1}^{n} \mathbf{w}_j \mathbf{y}_j = u$ and $\sum_{j=1}^{n} \mathbf{w}_j \mathbf{z}_j = l$, so that $C(\mathbf{y}) = +1$ and $C(\mathbf{z}) = -1$. This pair of inputs $(\mathbf{y}, \mathbf{z})$ therefore represents the strongest adversarial example to the robustness of C on $\mathbf{x}$.

Nonlinear Classifiers. Let us first point out through an example that interval and RAF abstractions are incomparable for nonlinear operations.

Example 5.1 Consider the 2-polynomial in two variables $f(x_1, x_2) \triangleq (1+2x_1-x_2)^2 - \frac{1}{4}(2+x_1+x_2)^2$, which could be thought of as a 2-polynomial classifier in $\mathbb{R}^2$. Assume that x_1 and x_2 range in the interval $[-1, 1]$. The abstract evaluation of f on the intervals $I_{x_1} = [-1, 1] = I_{x_2}$ is as follows:

$$\begin{aligned} f^\sharp_{\text{Int}}(I_{x_1}, I_{x_2}) &= (1 + 2[-1,1] - [-1,1])^2 - \tfrac{1}{4}(2 + [-1,1] + [-1,1])^2 \\ &= [-2,4]^2 - \tfrac{1}{4}[0,4]^2 = [0,16] + [-4,0] = [-4,16] \end{aligned}$$

On the other hand, for the RAF_2 abstraction we have that $\tilde{x}_1 = \epsilon_1$, $\tilde{x}_2 = \epsilon_2$ and the abstract evaluation of f is as follows:

$$\begin{aligned} f^\sharp_{\text{RAF}_2}(\tilde{x}_1, \tilde{x}_2) &= (1 + 2\epsilon_1 - \epsilon_2)^2 - \tfrac{1}{4}(2 + \epsilon_1 + \epsilon_2)^2 \\ &= [1 + 0.5(R_{1\,\max} + R_{1\,\min}) + 4\epsilon_1 - 2\epsilon_2 + 0.5(R_{1\,\max} - R_{1\,\min})\epsilon_r] \\ &\quad - \tfrac{1}{4}[4 + 0.5(R_{2\,\max} + R_{2\,\min}) + 4\epsilon_1 + 4\epsilon_2 + 0.5(R_{2\,\max} - R_{2\,\min})\epsilon_r] \\ \text{where} \quad & R_{1\,\max} = \max((2\epsilon_1 - \epsilon_2)^2) = 9,\ R_{1\,\min} = \min((2\epsilon_1 - \epsilon_2)^2) = 0, \\ & R_{2\,\max} = \max((\epsilon_1 + \epsilon_2)^2) = 4,\ R_{2\,\min} = \min((\epsilon_1 + \epsilon_2)^2) = 0 \\ &= [5.5 + 4\epsilon_1 - 2\epsilon_2 + 4.5\epsilon_r] - \tfrac{1}{4}[6 + 4\epsilon_1 + 4\epsilon_2 + 2\epsilon_r] \\ &= [5.5 + 4\epsilon_1 - 2\epsilon_2 + 4.5\epsilon_r] + [-1.5 - \epsilon_1 - \epsilon_2 - 0.5\epsilon_r] \\ &= 4 + 3\epsilon_1 - 3\epsilon_2 + 4\epsilon_r \end{aligned}$$

Thus, it turns out that $\gamma_{\text{RAF}_2}(f^\sharp_{\text{RAF}_2}(\tilde{x}_1, \tilde{x}_2)) = [4-10, 4+10] = [-6, 14]$, which is incomparable with $\gamma_{\text{Int}}(f^\sharp_{\text{Int}}(I_{x_1}, I_{x_2})) = [-4, 16]$. □

In view of Example 5.1, for a nonlinear binary classifier $C(\mathbf{x}) = \text{sign}(D(\mathbf{x}) - b)$, with $D(\mathbf{x}) = \sum_{i=1}^{N} \alpha_i y_i k(\mathbf{x}_i, \mathbf{x})$, we will use both the interval and RAF abstractions of C in order to combine their final abstract results. More precisely, if $D^\sharp_{\text{Int}_n}$ and $D^\sharp_{\text{RAF}_n}$ are, resp., the interval and RAF abstractions of D, assume that $P : X \to \wp(X)$ is a perturbation for C which is soundly approximated by $P^\sharp_{\text{Int}} : X \to \text{Int}_n$ on intervals and by $P^\sharp_{\text{RAF}} : X \to \text{RAF}_n$ on RAFs, so that

$P^\sharp : X \to \text{Int}_n \times \text{RAF}_n$ is defined by $P^\sharp(\mathbf{x}) \triangleq \langle P^\sharp_{\text{Int}}(\mathbf{x}), P^\sharp_{\text{RAF}}(\mathbf{x})\rangle$. Then, for each input vector $\mathbf{x} \in X$, our combined verifier first will run both $D^\sharp_{\text{Int}_n}(P^\sharp_{\text{Int}}(\mathbf{x}))$ and $D^\sharp_{\text{RAF}_n}(P^\sharp_{\text{RAF}}(\mathbf{x}))$. Next, the output $D^\sharp_{\text{RAF}_n}(P^\sharp_{\text{RAF}}(\mathbf{x})) = \hat{a} \in \text{RAF}_n$ is abstracted to the interval $[c_{\hat{a}} - \text{rad}(\hat{a}), c_{\hat{a}} + \text{rad}(\hat{a})]$ which is then intersected with the interval $D^\sharp_{\text{Int}_n}(P^\sharp_{\text{Int}}(\mathbf{x})) = [l, u]$. Summing up, our combined abstract binary classifier $C^\sharp : \text{Int}_n \times \text{RAF}_n \to \{-1, +1, \top\}$ is defined as follows:

$$C^\sharp(P^\sharp(\mathbf{x})) \triangleq \begin{cases} +1 \text{ if } \max(l, c_{\hat{a}} - \text{rad}(\hat{a})) \geq 0 \\ -1 \text{ if } \min(u, c_{\hat{a}} + \text{rad}(\hat{a})) < 0 \\ \top \;\; \text{otherwise} \end{cases}$$

As shown in Sect. 4, it turns out that all the linear and nonlinear abstract operations for polynomial and RBF kernels are sound, so that by Lemma 3.4, this combined abstract classifier $C^\sharp$ induces a sound robustness verifer for C. Finally, for multi-classification, in both linear and nonlinear cases, we will use the sound abstract ovo multi-classifier defined in Lemma 3.7.

6 Experimental Results

We implemented our robustness verification method for SVM classifiers in a tool called *SAVer* (*S*vm *A*bstract *Ver*ifier), which has been written in C (approximately 2.5k LOC) and whose source code together with all the datasets, trained SVMs and results is available on GitHub [30]. We assessed the percentage of samples of the full test sets for which a SVM classifier is proved to be robust (and, dually, vulnerable) for a given perturbation, as well as the average verification time per sample. We also evaluated the impact of using subsets of the training set on the robustness of the corresponding classifiers and on verification times. We compared SAVer to DeepPoly [32], a robustness verification tool for convolutional deep neural networks based on abstract interpretation. Our experimental results indicate that SAVer is fast and scalable and that the percentage of robustness provable by SAVer for SVMs on MNIST is higher than the robustness provable by DeepPoly for deep neural networks. Our experiments were run on a AMD Ryzen 7 1700X 3.0 GHz CPU.

Datasets and Classifiers. For our experimental evaluation of SAVer we used the standard and widespread MNIST [18] image dataset together with the recent alternative Fashion-MNIST (F-MNIST) image dataset [42]. They both contain grayscale images of $28 \times 28 = 784$ pixels (of depth 256) which are represented as normalized vectors of floating-point numbers in $[0, 1]^{784}$ (0 is black, 1 is white). MNIST contains images of handwritten digits, while F-MNIST comprises professional images of fashion dress products from 10 categories taken from the popular Zalando's e-commerce website. F-MNIST has been recently put forward as a more challenging alternative for the original MNIST dataset for benchmarking machine learning algorithms, since the extensive experimental results reported in [42] showed that the test accuracy of most machine learning classifiers significantly decreases (a rough average is about 10%) from MNIST to F-MNIST.

In particular, [42] reports that the average test accuracy (on the whole test set) of linear, polynomial and RBF SVMs on MNIST is 95.4% while for F-MNIST drops to 87.4%, where RBF SVMs are reportedly the most precise classifiers on F-MNIST with an accuracy of 89.7%. Both datasets include a training set of 60000 images and a test set of 10000 images, with no overlap. Our tests are run on the whole test set, where, following [32], these 10000 images of MNIST and F-MNIST have been filtered out of those misclassified by the SVMs (ranging from 3% of RBF and polynomial kernels to 7% for linear kernel), while the experiments comparing SAVer with DeepPoly are conducted on the same small test subset of MNIST used in [32]. We trained a number of SVM classifiers using different subsets of the training sets and different kernel functions. We trained our SVMs with linear, RBF and (2, 3 and 9°) polynomial kernels, and in order to benchmark the scalability of the verifiers we used the first 1k, 2k, 4k, 8k, 16k, 30k, 60k samples of the training set (training times never exceeded 3). For training we used Scikit-learn [25], a popular machine learning library for Python, which relies on the standard Libsvm C library [5].

Results. The results of our experimental evaluation are summarized by the following tables and charts.

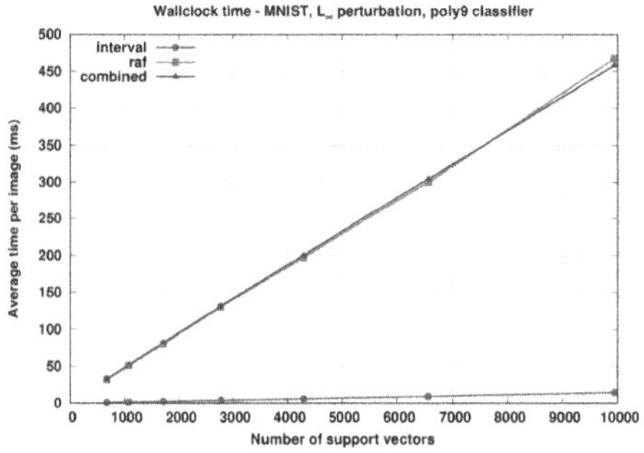

(g)

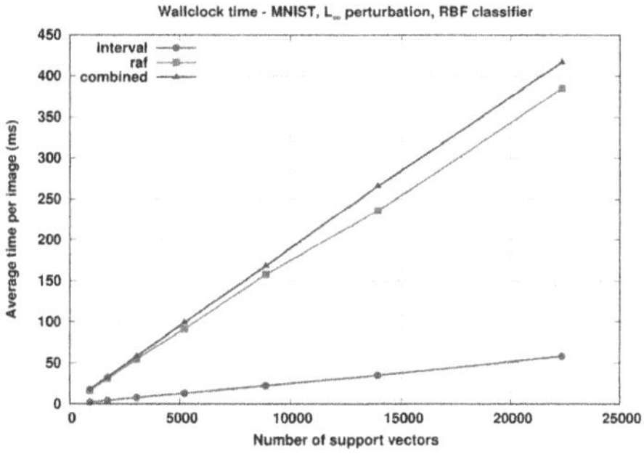

(h)

Table (a) compares the provable robustness to a P_δ^∞ adversarial region of SVMs which have been trained with different kernels. It turns out that the RBF classifier is the most provably robust: even with $\delta = 0.03$, meaning a perturbation of pixel depth of ± 7, SAVer can prove that more than 99% of the full test set of MNIST is robust. The RBF classifier is therefore taken as reference classifier for the successive experiments. Table (b) compares the relative precisions of robustness verification which can be obtained by changing the abstraction of the RBF classifier. As expected, the relational information of the RAF abstraction makes it significantly more precise than interval abstraction, although in a few cases (which do not affect the reported percentages) intervals can help in refining RAF analysis, and this justifies their combined use. Table (c) shows how the provable robustness depends on the size of the training subset. We may observe here that using more samples for training a SVM classifier tends to overfit the model, making it more sensitive to perturbations, i.e. less robust. Table (d) shows what we call *provable vulnerability* of a classifier C: we first consider all the samples

P_δ^∞	Provable Robustness %				
	Linear	Poly2	Poly3	Poly9	RBF
0.01	82.23	98.64	99.07	98.51	99.83
0.02	38.95	94.82	96.96	96.34	99.57
0.03	12.77	82.14	91.80	92.85	99.19
0.04	3.22	57.44	78.95	87.33	97.27
0.05	0.71	30.52	57.31	77.69	93.58
0.06	0.13	14.89	34.80	61.12	82.21
0.07	0.00	7.89	18.36	39.75	67.76
0.08	0.00	4.08	10.64	23.70	48.02
0.09	0	1.61	6.28	12.86	28.10
0.10	0	0.58	3.33	7.18	16.38

(a): Comparison of kernel functions

P_δ^∞	Provable Robustness %		
	Interval	RAF	Combined
0.01	47.73	99.83	99.83
0.02	14.95	99.57	99.57
0.03	6.26	99.19	99.19
0.04	2.42	97.27	97.27
0.05	0.82	93.58	93.58
0.06	0.17	82.21	82.21
0.07	0.04	67.76	67.76
0.08	0	48.02	48.02
0.09	0	28.10	28.10
0.10	0	16.38	16.38

(b): Comparison of abstractions for RBF kernel

P_δ^∞	Provable Robustness %						
	1k	2k	4k	8k	16k	30k	60k
0.01	99.50	99.72	99.69	99.74	99.73	99.77	99.83
0.02	99.01	99.20	99.36	99.35	99.49	99.42	99.57
0.03	98.28	98.58	98.81	98.80	98.95	98.94	99.19
0.04	97.01	97.73	97.91	97.99	98.02	97.71	97.27
0.05	95.28	96.42	96.71	96.50	96.32	95.73	93.58
0.06	93.15	94.69	95.13	94.33	93.90	91.72	82.21
0.07	90.30	92.15	91.16	91.07	88.51	84.43	67.76
0.08	86.69	87.92	87.89	84.86	78.40	66.84	48.02
0.09	81.79	82.47	81.01	74.29	62.38	49.45	28.10
0.10	75.45	74.66	70.83	58.80	45.87	30.86	16.38

(c): Comparison of training set sizes (thousands of samples)

P_δ^∞	Provable Robustness %		Provable Vulnerability %	
	MNIST	F-MNIST	MNIST	F-MNIST
0.01	99.83	88.59	94.48	39.20
0.02	99.57	60.63	73.62	11.80
0.03	99.19	42.13	48.47	5.50
0.04	97.27	27.24	32.51	3.00
0.05	93.58	18.36	20.25	1.50
0.06	82.21	12.18	9.86	0.90
0.07	67.76	8.22	3.68	0.60
0.08	48.02	5.23	0.61	0.40
0.09	28.10	1.96	0	0.10
0.10	16.38	0.48	0	0

(d): MNIST vs F-MNIST

P_t^{frm}	Provable Robustness	
	MNIST	F-MNIST
1	100.00%	49.56%
2	99.64%	4.71%
3	87.34%	0.00%
4	40.35%	0.00%

(e): MNIST vs F-MNIST

P_δ^∞	SAVer		DeepPoly	
	poly9	RBF	Sigmoid	Small
0.005	100%	100%	100%	100%
0.010	98.9%	100%	98%	95%
0.015	98.9%	100%	97%	75%
0.020	97.8%	100%	95%	50%
0.025	97.8%	100%	92%	25%
0.030	96.7%	100%	80%	10%

(f): SAVer vs DeepPoly

$(\mathbf{x}, y)$ in the test set which are misclassified by C, i.e., $C(\mathbf{x}) = y' \neq y$ holds, then our robustness verifier is run on the perturbations $P_\delta^\infty(\mathbf{x})$ of these samples for checking whether the region $P_\delta^\infty(\mathbf{x})$ can be proved to be consistently misclassified by C to y'. Provable vulnerability is significantly lower than provable robustness, meaning that when the classifier is wrong on an input vector, it is more likely to assign different labels to similar inputs, rather than assigning the same (wrong) class. Charts (g) and (h) show the average verification time per image, in milliseconds, with respect to the size of the classifier, given by the number of support vectors, and compared for different abstractions. Let N and n denote, resp., the number of support vectors and the size of input vectors. The interval-based abstract d-polynomial classifier is in $O(dN)$ time, while the RBF classifier is in $O(N)$, because the interval multiplication is constant-time. Hence, interval analysis is very fast, just a few milliseconds per image. On the other hand, the RAF-based abstract d-polynomial and RBF classifiers are, resp., in $O(dNn \log n)$ and $O(Nn \log n)$, since RAF multiplication is in $O(n \log n)$, so that RAF-based verification is slower although it never takes more than 0.5 s.

The same experiments have been replicated on the F-MNIST dataset and Table (d) shows a comparison of the results between MNIST and F-MNIST. As expected, robustness is harder to prove (and very likely to achieve) on F-MNIST than on MNIST, while SAVer proved that F-MNIST is less vulnerable than MNIST. Moreover, Table (e) shows the percentage of provable robustness for MNIST and F-MNIST for the frame adversarial region defined in Sect. 5, for some widths of the frame. F-MNIST is significantly harder to prove robust under this attack than MNIST: this is due to the fact that the borders of MNIST images do not contain as much information as their centers so that classifiers can tolerate some perturbation in the border. By contrast, F-MNIST images often carry information on their borders, making them less robust to adversarial framing. Finally, Table (f) compares SAVer with DeepPoly, a robustness verifier for feedforward neural networks [32]. This comparison used the same test set of DeepPoly, consisting of the first 100 images of the MNIST test set, and the same perturbations P_{δ}^{∞}. Although a strict comparison is not possible, as SAVer and DeepPoly operates on different ML models, we argue that percentages of provable robustness achieved by SAVer are competitive with respect to other state-of-the-art tools. Moreover, we point out the fact that a verification of a single image by DeepPoly can take as long as 10s [32], while the maximum verification time per image on SAVer is 0.5s. Among the benchmarks reported in [32, Section 6], we selected the FFNNSmall and FFNNSigmoid deep neural networks, denoted, resp., by DeepPoly Small and Sigmoid. FFNNSmall has been trained using a standard technique and achieved the best accuracies in [32], while FFNNSigmoid was trained using PGD-based adversarial training, a technique explicitly developed to make a classifier more robust. It turns out that the percentages of robustness provable by SAVer are higher than those provable by DeepPoly (precise percentages are not provided in [32], we extrapolated them from the charts). In particular, both 9-polynomial and RBF SVMs can be proved more robust that FFNNSigmoid networks, despite the fact that these classifiers are defended by a specific adversarial training.

7 Future Work

We believe that this work represents a first step in applying formal analysis and verification techniques to machine learning based on support vector machines. We envisage a number of challenging research topics as subject for future work. Generating adversarial examples to machine learning methods is important for designing more robust classifiers [11,41,45] and we think that the completeness of robustness verification of linear binary classifiers (cf. Sect. 3) could be exploited for automatically detecting adversarial examples in linear multiclass SVM classifiers. The main challenge here is to design more precise, ideally complete, techniques for abstracting multi-classification based on binary classification. Adversarial SVM training is a further stimulating research challenge. Mirman et al. [23] put forward an abstraction-based technique for adversarial training of robust neural networks. A similar approach could also work for SVMs, namely applying abstract interpretation to SVM training models rather than to SVM classifiers.

Acknowledgements. We are grateful to the anonymous referees for their helpful remarks. The doctoral fellowship of Marco Zanella is funded by Fondazione Bruno Kessler (FBK), Trento, Italy. This work has been partially funded by the University of Padova, under the SID2018 project "Analysis of STatic Analyses (ASTA)" and by the Italian Ministry of Research MIUR, under the PRIN2017 project no. 201784YSZ5 "AnalysiS of PRogram Analyses (ASPRA)".

Data Availability Statements. The datasets/code generated during and/or analysed during the current study are available in the Figshare repository: https://doi.org/10.6084/m9.figshare.9861029.v1

References

1. Anderson, G., Pailoor, S., Dillig, I., Chaudhuri, S.: Optimization and abstraction: a synergistic approach for analyzing neural network robustness. In: Proceedings of the 40th ACM SIGPLAN Conference on Programming Language Design and Implementation (PLDI2019), pp. 731–744. ACM (2019)
2. Biggio, B.: Security evaluation of support vector machines in adversarial environments. In: Ma, Y., Guo, G. (eds.) Support Vector Machines Applications, pp. 105–153. Springer, Cham (2014). https://doi.org/10.1007/978-3-319-02300-7_4
3. Biggio, B., Nelson, B., Laskov, P.: Support vector machines under adversarial label noise. In: Proceedings of the 3rd Asian Conference on Machine Learning (ACML2011), pp. 97–112 (2011)
4. Carlini, N., Wagner, D.A.: Towards evaluating the robustness of neural networks. In: Proceedings of the 2017 IEEE Symposium on Security and Privacy (SP2017), pp. 39–57 (2017)
5. Chang, C.-C., Lin, C.-J.: LIBSVM: a library for support vector machines. ACM Trans. Intell. Syst. Technol. **2**(3):27:1–27:27 (2011)
6. Cousot, P., Cousot, R.: Abstract interpretation: a unified lattice model for static analysis of programs by construction or approximation of fixpoints. In: Proceedings of the 4th ACM SIGACT-SIGPLAN Symposium on Principles of Programming Languages (POPL1977), pp. 238–252. ACM (1977)
7. Cristianini, N., Shawe-Taylor, J.: An Introduction to Support Vector Machines and OtherKernel-based Learning Methods. Cambridge University Press, Cambridge (2000)
8. Ehlers, R.: Formal verification of piece-wise linear feed-forward neural networks. In: Proceedings of the 15th International Symposium on Automated Technology for Verification and Analysis (ATVA2017), pp. 269–286 (2017)
9. Gehr, T., Mirman, M., Drachsler-Cohen, D., Tsankov, P., Chaudhuri, S., Vechev, M.T.: AI2: safety and robustness certification of neural networks with abstract interpretation. In: Proceedings of the 2018 IEEE Symposium on Security and Privacy (SP2018), pp. 3–18 (2018)
10. Goodfellow, I., McDaniel, P., Papernot, N.: Making machine learning robust against adversarial inputs. Commun. ACM **61**(7), 56–66 (2018)
11. Goodfellow, I.J., Shlens, J., Szegedy, C.: Explaining and harnessing adversarial examples. In: Proceedings of the International Conference on Learning Representations (ICLR2015) (2015)

12. Gopinath, D., Katz, G., Păsăreanu, C.S., Barrett, C.: DeepSafe: a data-driven approach for assessing robustness of neural networks. In: Lahiri, S.K., Wang, C. (eds.) ATVA 2018. LNCS, vol. 11138, pp. 3–19. Springer, Cham (2018). https://doi.org/10.1007/978-3-030-01090-4_1
13. Goubault, E., Putot, S.: A zonotopic framework for functional abstractions. Form. Methods Syst. Des. **47**(3), 302–360 (2015)
14. Hsu, C.-W., Lin, C.-J.: A comparison of methods for multiclass support vector machines. IEEE Trans. Neur. Netw. **13**(2), 415–425 (2002)
15. Huang, X., Kwiatkowska, M., Wang, S., Wu, M.: Safety verification of deep neural networks. In: Majumdar, R., Kunčak, V. (eds.) CAV 2017. LNCS, vol. 10426, pp. 3–29. Springer, Cham (2017). https://doi.org/10.1007/978-3-319-63387-9_1
16. Katz, G., Barrett, C., Dill, D.L., Julian, K., Kochenderfer, M.J.: Reluplex: an efficient SMT solver for verifying deep neural networks. In: Majumdar, R., Kunčak, V. (eds.) CAV 2017. LNCS, vol. 10426, pp. 97–117. Springer, Cham (2017). https://doi.org/10.1007/978-3-319-63387-9_5
17. Kurakin, A., Goodfellow, I.J., Bengio, S.: Adversarial machine learning at scale. In: Proceedings of the 5th International Conference on Learning Representations (ICLR2017) (2017)
18. LeCun, Y., Bottou, L., Bengio, Y., Haffner, P.: Gradient-based learning applied to document recognition. Proc. IEEE **86**(11), 2278–2324 (1998)
19. Leofante, F., Tacchella, A.: Learning in physical domains: mating safety requirements and costly sampling. In: Adorni, G., Cagnoni, S., Gori, M., Maratea, M. (eds.) AI*IA 2016. LNCS (LNAI), vol. 10037, pp. 539–552. Springer, Cham (2016). https://doi.org/10.1007/978-3-319-49130-1_39
20. Messine, F.: Extentions of affine arithmetic: application to unconstrained global optimization. J. Univers. Comput. Sci. **8**(11), 992–1015 (2002)
21. Miné, A.: Relational abstract domains for the detection of floating-point run-time errors. In: Schmidt, D. (ed.) ESOP 2004. LNCS, vol. 2986, pp. 3–17. Springer, Heidelberg (2004). https://doi.org/10.1007/978-3-540-24725-8_2
22. Miné, A.: Tutorial on static inference of numeric invariants by abstract interpretation. Found. Trends Program. Lang. **4**(3–4), 120–372 (2017)
23. Mirman, M., Gehr, T., Vechev, M.: Differentiable abstract interpretation for provably robust neural networks. In: Proceedings of the International Conference on Machine Learning (ICML2018), pp. 3575–3583 (2018)
24. Nam, G.P., Kang, B.J., Park, K.R.: Robustness of face recognition to variations of illumination on mobile devices based on SVM. KSII Trans. Internet Inf. Syst. **4**(1), 25–44 (2010)
25. Pedregosa, F.: Scikit-learn: machine learning in Python. J. Mach. Learn. Res. **12**, 2825–2830 (2011)
26. Pulina, L., Tacchella, A.: An abstraction-refinement approach to verification of artificial neural networks. In: Touili, T., Cook, B., Jackson, P. (eds.) CAV 2010. LNCS, vol. 6174, pp. 243–257. Springer, Heidelberg (2010). https://doi.org/10.1007/978-3-642-14295-6_24
27. Pulina, L., Tacchella, A.: Challenging SMT solvers to verify neural networks. AI Commun. **25**(2), 117–135 (2012)
28. Ranzato, F.: Complete abstractions everywhere (invited paper). In: Giacobazzi, R., Berdine, J., Mastroeni, I. (eds.) VMCAI 2013. LNCS, vol. 7737, pp. 15–26. Springer, Heidelberg (2013). https://doi.org/10.1007/978-3-642-35873-9_3
29. Ranzato, F., Zanella, M.: Robustness verification of support vector machines. http://arxiv.org/abs/1904.11803, CoRR arXiv, April 2019

30. Ranzato, F., Zanella, M.: SAVer GitHub Repository (2019). https://github.com/svm-abstract-verifier
31. Singh, G., Gehr, T., Mirman, M., Püschel, M., Vechev, M.T.: Fast and effective robustness certification. In: Advances in Neural Information Processing Systems 31: Proceedings of the Annual Conference on Neural Information Processing Systems 2018, (NeurIPS2018), pp. 10825–10836 (2018)
32. Singh, G., Gehr, T., Püschel, M., Vechev, M.: An abstract domain for certifying neural networks. Proc. ACM Program. Lang. **3**(POPL2019), 41:1–41:30 (2019)
33. Skalna, I., Hladík, M.: A new algorithm for Chebyshev minimum-error multiplication of reduced affine forms. Numer. Algorithms **76**(4), 1131–1152 (2017)
34. IEEE Computer Society: IEEE standard for binary floating-point arithmetic. Institute of Electrical and Electronics Engineers, New York (1985). Note: Standard 754–1985
35. Stolfi, J., de Figueiredo, L.H.: Self-Validated Numerical Methods and Applications. Brazilian Mathematics Colloquium Monograph, IMPA, Rio de Janeiro, Brazil (1997)
36. Stolfi, J., de Figueiredo, L.H.: Affine arithmetic: concepts and applications. Numer. Algorithms **37**(1), 147–158 (2004)
37. Trafalis, T.B., Gilbert, R.C.: Robust support vector machines for classification and computational issues. Optim. Methods Softw. **22**(1), 187–198 (2007)
38. Vorobeychik, Y., Kantarcioglu, M.: Adversarial machine learning. In: Synthesis Lectures on Artificial Intelligence and Machine Learning, vol. 12, no. 3, pp. 1–169. Morgan & Claypool Publishers, August 2018
39. Wang, S., Pei, K., Whitehouse, J., Yang, J., Jana, S.: Formal security analysis of neural networks using symbolic intervals. In: Proceedings of the 27th USENIX Conference on Security Symposium, (SEC2018), pp. 1599–1614. USENIX Association (2018)
40. Weng, T., et al.: Towards fast computation of certified robustness for ReLU networks. In: Proceedings of the 35th International Conference on Machine Learning, (ICML2018), pp. 5273–5282 (2018)
41. Xiao, H., Biggio, B., Nelson, B., Xiao, H., Eckert, C., Roli, F.: Support vector machines under adversarial label contamination. Neurocomputing **160**, 53–62 (2015)
42. Xiao, H., Rasul, K., Vollgraf, R.: Fashion-MNIST: A novel image dataset for benchmarking machine learning algorithms. CoRR arXiv, abs/1708.07747 (2017)
43. Xu, H., Caramanis, C., Mannor, S.: Robustness and regularization of support vector machines. J. Mach. Learn. Res. **10**, 1485–1510 (2009)
44. Zajac, M., Zolna, K., Rostamzadeh, N., Pinheiro, P.O.: Adversarial framing for image and video classification. In: Proceedings of the 33rd AAAI Conference on Artificial Intelligence (AAAI2019) (2019)
45. Zhao, Z., Dua, D., Singh, S.: Generating natural adversarial examples. In: Proceedings of the 6th International Conference on Learning Representations (ICLR2018) (2018)
46. Zhou, Y., Kantarcioglu, M., Thuraisingham, B., Xi, B.: Adversarial support vector machine learning. In: Proceedings of the 18th ACM SIGKDD International Conference on Knowledge Discovery and Data Mining (KDD2012), pp. 1059–1067. ACM (2012)

Analyzing Deep Neural Networks with Symbolic Propagation: Towards Higher Precision and Faster Verification

Jianlin Li[1,2], Jiangchao Liu[3], Pengfei Yang[1,2], Liqian Chen[3(✉)], Xiaowei Huang[4,5], and Lijun Zhang[1,2,5]

[1] State Key Laboratory of Computer Science, Institute of Software, Chinese Academy of Sciences, Beijing, China
[2] University of Chinese Academy of Sciences, Beijing, China
[3] National University of Defense Technology, Changsha, China
lqchen@nudt.edu.cn
[4] University of Liverpool, Liverpool, UK
[5] Institute of Intelligent Software, Guangzhou, China

Abstract. Deep neural networks (DNNs) have been shown lack of robustness, as they are vulnerable to small perturbations on the inputs, which has led to safety concerns on applying DNNs to safety-critical domains. Several verification approaches have been developed to automatically prove or disprove safety properties for DNNs. However, these approaches suffer from either the scalability problem, i.e., only small DNNs can be handled, or the precision problem, i.e., the obtained bounds are loose. This paper improves on a recent proposal of analyzing DNNs through the classic abstract interpretation technique, by a novel symbolic propagation technique. More specifically, the activation values of neurons are represented *symbolically* and propagated forwardly from the input layer to the output layer, on top of abstract domains. We show that our approach can achieve significantly higher precision and thus can prove more properties than using only abstract domains. Moreover, we show that the bounds derived from our approach on the hidden neurons, when applied to a state-of-the-art SMT based verification tool, can improve its performance. We implement our approach into a software tool and validate it over a few DNNs trained on benchmark datasets such as MNIST, etc.

1 Introduction

During the last few years, deep neural networks (DNNs) have been broadly applied in various domains including nature language processing [1], image classification [15], game playing [26], etc. The performance of these DNNs, when measured with the prediction precision over a test dataset, is comparable to, or even better than, that of manually crafted software. However, for safety-critical applications, it is required that the DNNs are certified against properties related to its safety. Unfortunately, DNNs have been found lack of robustness.

B.-Y. E. Chang (Ed.): SAS 2019, LNCS 11822, pp. 296–319, 2019.
https://doi.org/10.1007/978-3-030-32304-2_15

Specifically, [29] discovers that it is possible to add a small, or even imperceptible, perturbation to a correctly classified input and make it misclassified. Such adversarial examples have raised serious concerns on the safety of DNNs. Consider a self-driving system controlled by a DNN. A failure on the recognization of a traffic light may lead to a serious consequence because human lives are at stake.

Algorithms used to find adversarial examples are based on either gradient descent, see e.g., [2,29], or saliency maps, see e.g., [22], or evolutionary algorithm, see e.g., [21], etc. Roughly speaking, these are heuristic search algorithms without the guarantees to find the optimal values, i.e., the bound on the gap between an obtained value and its ground truth is unknown. However, the certification of a DNN needs provable guarantees. Thus, techniques based on formal verification have been developed. Up to now, DNN verification includes constraint-solving [5,7,14,17,19,23,33], layer-by-layer exhaustive search [11,31,32], global optimization [24], abstract interpretation [9,27,28], etc. Abstract interpretation is a theory in static analysis which verifies a program by using sound approximation of its semantics [3]. Its basic idea is to use an abstract domain to over-approximate the computation on inputs. In [9], this idea has first been developed for verifying DNNs. However, abstract interpretation can be imprecise, due to the non-linearity in DNNs. [27] implements a faster Zonotope domain for DNN verification. [28] puts forward a new abstract domain specially for DNN verification and it is more efficient and precise than Zonotope.

The first contribution of this paper is to propose a novel symbolic propagation technique to enhance the precision of abstract interpretation based DNN verification. For every neuron, we *symbolically* represent, with an expression, how its activation value can be determined by the activation values of neurons in previous layers. By both illustrative examples and experimental results, we show that, comparing with using only abstract domains, our new approach can find significantly tighter constraints over the neurons' activation values. Because abstract interpretation is a sound approximation, with tighter constraints, we may prove properties that cannot be proven by using only abstract domains. For example, we may prove a greater lower bound on the robustness of the DNNs.

Another contribution of this paper is to apply the value bounds derived from our approach on hidden neurons to improve the performance of a state-of-the-art SMT based DNN verifier Reluplex [14].

Finally, we implement our approach into a software tool and validate it with a few DNNs trained on benchmark datasets such as MNIST, etc.

2 Preliminaries

We recall some basic notions on deep neural networks and abstract interpretation. For a vector $\bar{x} \in \mathbb{R}^n$, we use x_i to denote its i-th entry. For a matrix $W \in \mathbb{R}^{m \times n}$, $W_{i,j}$ denotes the entry in its i-th row and j-th column.

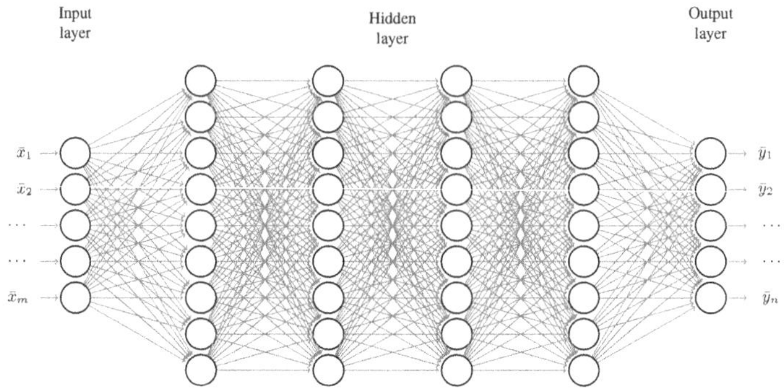

Fig. 1. A fully connected network: Each layer performs the composition of an affine transformation $\text{Affine}(\bar{x}; W, b)$ and the activated function, where on edges between neurons the coefficients of the matrix W are recorded accordingly.

2.1 Deep Neural Networks

We work with deep feedforward neural networks, or DNNs, which can be represented as a function $f : \mathbb{R}^m \to \mathbb{R}^n$, mapping an input $\bar{x} \in \mathbb{R}^m$ to its corresponding output $\bar{y} = f(\bar{x}) \in \mathbb{R}^n$. A DNN has in its structure a sequence of layers, including an input layer at the beginning, followed by several hidden layers, and an output layer in the end. Basically the output of a layer is the input of the next layer. To unify the representation, we denote the activation values at each layer as a vector. Thus the transformation between layers can also be seen as a function in $\mathbb{R}^{m'} \to \mathbb{R}^{n'}$. The DNN f is the composition of the transformations between layers, which is typically composed of an affine transformation followed by a non-linear activation function. In this paper we only consider one of the most commonly used activation function – the rectified linear unit (ReLU) activation function, defined as

$$\text{ReLU}(x) = \max(x, 0)$$

for $x \in \mathbb{R}$ and $\text{ReLU}(\bar{x}) = (\text{ReLU}(x_1), \ldots, \text{ReLU}(x_n))$ for $\bar{x} \in \mathbb{R}^n$.

Typically an affine transformation is of the form $\text{Affine}(\bar{x}; W, b) = W\bar{x} + b : \mathbb{R}^m \to \mathbb{R}^n$, where $W \in \mathbb{R}^{n \times m}$ and $b \in \mathbb{R}^n$. Mostly in DNNs we use a **fully connected layer** to describe the composition of an affine transformation $\text{Affine}(\bar{x}; W, b)$ and the activation function, if the coefficient matrix W is not sparse and does not have shared parameters. We call a DNN with only fully connected layers a fully connected neural network (FNN). Figure 1 gives an intuitive description of fully connected layers and fully connected networks. Apart from fully connected layers, we also have affine transformations whose coefficient matrix is sparse and has many shared parameters, like **convolutional layers**. Readers can refer to e.g. [9] for its formal definition. In our paper, we do not special deal with convolutional layers, because they can be regarded as common affine transformations. In the architecture of DNNs, a convolutional layer is often followed by a non-linear **max pooling layer**, which takes as an input a three dimensional vector $\bar{x} \in \mathbb{R}^{m \times n \times r}$ with two parameters p and q which divides m and n respectively, defined as

$$\mathrm{MaxPool}_{\mathrm{p,q}}(\bar{x})_{i,j,k} = \max\{x_{i',j',k} \mid i' \in (p \cdot (i-1), p \cdot i] \ \wedge \ j' \in (q \cdot (i-1), q \cdot i]\}.$$

We call a DNN with only fully connected, convolutional, and max pooling layers a convolutional neural network (CNN).

In the following of the paper, we let the DNN f have N layers, each of which has m_k neurons, for $0 \le k < N$. Therefore, $m_0 = m$ and $m_{N-1} = n$.

2.2 Abstract Interpretation

Abstract interpretation is a theory in static analysis which verifies a program by using sound approximation of its semantics [3]. Its basic idea is to use an abstract domain to over-approximate the computation on inputs and propagate it through the program. In the following, we describe its adaptation to work with DNNs.

Generally, on the input layer, we have a concrete domain $\mathcal{C}$, which includes a set of inputs X as one of its elements. To enable an efficient computation, we choose an abstract domain $\mathcal{A}$ to infer the relation of variables in $\mathcal{C}$. We assume that there is a partial order $\le$ on $\mathcal{C}$ as well as $\mathcal{A}$, which in our settings is the subset relation $\subseteq$.

Definition 2.1. *A pair of functions $\alpha : \mathcal{C} \to \mathcal{A}$ and $\gamma : \mathcal{A} \to \mathcal{C}$ is a Galois connection, if for any $a \in \mathcal{A}$ and $c \in \mathcal{C}$, we have $\alpha(c) \le a \Leftrightarrow c \le \gamma(a)$.*

Intuitively, a Galois connection (α, γ) expresses abstraction and concretization relations between domains, respectively. Note that, $a \in \mathcal{A}$ is a sound abstraction of $c \in \mathcal{C}$ if and only if $c \le \gamma(a)$.

In abstract interpretation, it is important to choose a suitable abstract domain because it determines the efficiency and precision of the abstract interpretation. In practice, we use a certain type of constraints to represent the abstract elements. Geometrically, a certain type of constraints correspond to a special shape. E.g., the conjunction of a set of arbitrary linear constraints correspond to a polyhedron. Abstract domains that fit for verifying DNN include Intervals, Zonotopes, and Polyhedra, etc.

- **Box.** A box B contains bound constraints in the form of $a \le x_i \le b$. The conjunction of bound constraints express a box in the Euclid space. The form of the constraint for each dimension is an interval, and thus it is also named the Interval abstract domain.
- **Zonotope.** A zonotope Z consists of constraints in the form of $z_i = a_i + \sum_{j=1}^{m} b_{ij}\epsilon_j$, where a_i, b_{ij} are real constants and ϵ_j is bounded by a constant interval $[l_j, u_j]$. The conjunction of these constraints express a center-symmetric polyhedra in the Euclid space.
- **Polyhedra.** A Polyhedron P has constraints in the form of linear inequalities, i.e. $\sum_{i=1}^{n} a_i x_i + b \le 0$ and it gives a closed convex polyhedron in the Euclid space.

The following example shows intuitively how these three abstract domains work:

Example 2.2. Let $\bar{x} \in \mathbb{R}^2$, and the range of $\bar{x}$ be $X = \{(1,0),(0,2),(1,2),(2,1)\}$. With Box, we can abstract the inputs X as $[0,2] \times [0,2]$, and with Zonotope, X can be abstracted as $\left\{x_1 = 1 - \frac{1}{2}\epsilon_1 - \frac{1}{2}\epsilon_3,\ \ x_2 = 1 + \frac{1}{2}\epsilon_1 + \frac{1}{2}\epsilon_2\right\}$. where $\epsilon_1, \epsilon_2, \epsilon_3 \in [-1,1]$. With Polyhedra, X can be abstracted as $\{x_2 \leq 2,\ x_2 \leq -x_1+3,\ x_2 \geq x_1 - 1,\ x_2 \geq -2x_1+2\}$. Figure 2 (left) gives an intuitive description for the three abstractions.

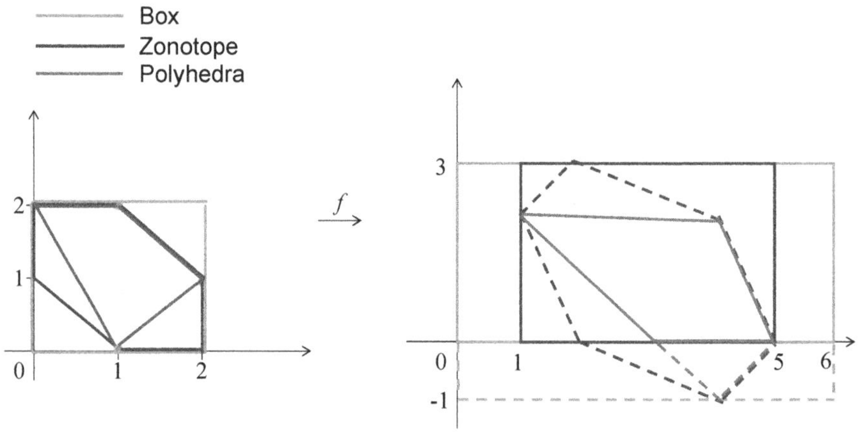

Fig. 2. An illustration of Examples 2.2 and 3.4, where on the right the dashed lines gives the abstraction region before the ReLU operation and the full lines gives the final abstraction $f^\sharp(X^\sharp)$.

3 Symbolic Propagation for Abstract Interpretation Based DNN Verification

In this section, we first describe how to use abstract interpretation to verify DNNs. Then we present a symbolic propagation method to enhance its precision.

3.1 Abstract Interpretation Based DNN Verification

The DNN Verification Problem. The problem of verifying DNNs over a property can be stated formally as follows.

Definition 3.1. *Given a function $f : \mathbb{R}^m \to \mathbb{R}^n$ which expresses a DNN, a set of the inputs $X_0 \subseteq \mathbb{R}^m$, and a property $C \subseteq \mathbb{R}^n$, verifying the property is to determine whether $f(X_0) \subseteq C$ holds, where $f(X_0) = \{f(\bar{x}) \mid \bar{x} \in X_0\}$.*

Local robustness property can be obtained by letting X_0 be a robustness region and C be $C_l := \{\bar{y} \in \mathbb{R}^n \mid \arg\max_{1 \le i \le n} y_i = l\}$. where y denotes an output vector and l denotes a label.

A common way of defining robustness region is with norm distance. We use $\|\bar{x} - \bar{x}_0\|_p$ with $p \in [1, \infty]$ to denote the L_p norm distance between two vectors $\bar{x}$ and $\bar{x}_0$. In this paper, we use L_∞ norm defined as follows.

$$\|\bar{x}\|_\infty = \max_{1 \le i \le n} |x_i|.$$

Given an input $\bar{x}_0 \in \mathbb{R}^m$ and a perturbation tolerance $\delta > 0$, a local robustness region X_0 can be defined as $B(\bar{x}_0, \delta) := \{\bar{x} \mid \|\bar{x} - \bar{x}_0\|_p \le \delta\}$.

Verifying DNNs via Abstract Interpretation. Under the framework of abstract interpretation, to conduct verification of DNNs, we first need to choose an abstract domain $\mathcal{A}$. Then we represent the set of inputs of a DNN as an abstract element (value) $X_0^\sharp$ in $\mathcal{A}$. After that, we pass it through the DNN layers by applying abstract transformers of the abstract domain. Recall that N is the number of layers in a DNN and m_k is the number of nodes in the k-th layer. Let f_k (where $1 \le k < N$) be the layer function mapping from $\mathbb{R}^{m_{k-1}}$ to $\mathbb{R}^{m_k}$. We can lift f_k to $T_{f_k} : \mathcal{P}(\mathbb{R}^{m_{k-1}}) \to \mathcal{P}(\mathbb{R}^{m_k})$ such that $T_{f_k}(X) = \{f_k(\bar{x}) \mid \bar{x} \in X\}$.

Definition 3.2. *An abstract transformer $T_{f_k}^\sharp$ is a function mapping an abstract element $X_{k-1}^\sharp$ in the abstract domain $\mathcal{A}$ to another abstract element ${X^\sharp}_k$. Moreover, $T_{f_k}^\sharp$ is sound if $T_{f_k} \circ \gamma \subseteq \gamma \circ T_{f_k}^\sharp$.*

Intuitively, a sound abstract transformer $T_{f_k}^\sharp$ maintains a sound relation between the abstract post-state and the abstract pre-state of a transformer in DNN (such as linear transformation, ReLU operation, etc.).

Let $X_k = f_k(...(f_1(X_0)))$ be the exact set of resulting vectors in $\mathbb{R}^{m_k}$ (i.e., the k-th layer) computed over the concrete inputs X_0, and ${X^\sharp}_k = {T_{f_k}}^\sharp(...({T_{f_1}}^\sharp({X^\sharp}_0)))$ be the corresponding abstract value of the k-th layer when using an abstract domain $\mathcal{A}$. Note that $X_0 \subseteq \gamma({X^\sharp}_0)$. We have the following conclusion.

Proposition 1. *If $X_{k-1} \subseteq \gamma({X^\sharp}_{k-1})$, then we have $X_k \subseteq \gamma({X^\sharp}_k) = \gamma \circ T_{f_k}^\sharp({X^\sharp}_{k-1})$.*

Therefore, when performing abstract interpretation over the transformations in a DNN, the abstract pre-state ${X^\sharp}_{k-1}$ is transformed into abstract post-state ${X^\sharp}_k$ by applying the abstract transformer $T_{f_k}^\sharp$ which is built on top of an abstract domain. This procedure starts from $k = 1$ and continues until reaching the output layer (and getting ${X^\sharp}_{N-1}$). Finally, we use ${X^\sharp}_{N-1}$ to check the property C as follows:

$$\gamma({X^\sharp}_{N-1}) \subseteq C. \tag{1}$$

The following theorem states that this verification procedure based on abstract interpretation is sound for the DNN verification problem.

Theorem 3.3. *If Eq. (1) holds, then* $f(X_0) \subseteq C$.

It's not hard to see that the other direction does not necessarily hold due to the potential incompleteness caused by the over-approximation made in both the abstract elements and the abstract transformers $T^\sharp_{f_k}$ in an abstract domain.

Example 3.4. Suppose that $\bar{x}$ takes the value in X given in Example 2.2, and we consider the transformation $f(\bar{x}) = \text{ReLU}\left(\begin{pmatrix}1 & 2\\ 1 & -1\end{pmatrix}\bar{x} + \begin{pmatrix}0\\1\end{pmatrix}\right)$. Now we use the three abstract domains to calculate the resulting abstraction $f^\sharp(X^\sharp)$

- Box. The abstraction after the affine transformation is $[0,6]\times[-1,3]$, and thus the final result is $[0,6]\times[0,3]$.
- Zonotope. After the affine transformation, the zonotope abstraction can be obtained straightforward:

  $$\left\{y_1 = 3 + \frac{1}{2}\epsilon_1 + \epsilon_2 - \frac{1}{2}\epsilon_3,\ y_2 = 1 - \epsilon_1 - \frac{1}{2}\epsilon_2 - \frac{1}{2}\epsilon_3 \mid \epsilon_1,\epsilon_2,\epsilon_3 \in [-1,1]\right\}.$$

  The first dimension y_1 is definitely positive, so it remains the same after the ReLU operation. The second dimension y_2 can be either negative or non-negative, so its abstraction after ReLU will become a box which only preserves the range in the non-negative part, i.e. $[0,3]$, so the final abstraction is

  $$\left\{y_1 = 3 + \frac{1}{2}\epsilon_1 + \epsilon_2 - \frac{1}{2}\epsilon_3,\ y_2 = \frac{3}{2} + \frac{3}{2}\eta_1 \mid \epsilon_1,\epsilon_2,\epsilon_3,\eta_1 \in [-1,1]\right\},$$

  whose concretization is $[1,5]\times[0,3]$.
- Polyhedra. It is easy to obtain the polyhedron before $P_1 = \text{ReLU}\ \{y_2 \leq 2, y_2 \geq -y_1+3, y_2 \geq y_1 - 5, y_2 \leq -2y_1+10\}$. Similarly, the first dimension is definitely positive, and the second dimension can be either negative or non-negative, so the resulting abstraction is $(P_1 \wedge (y_2 \geq 0)) \vee (P_1 \wedge (y_2 = 0))$, i.e. $\{y_2 \leq 2, y_2 \geq -y_1+3, y_2 \geq 0, y_2 \leq -2y_1+10\}$.

Figure 2 (the right part) gives an illustration for the abstract interpretation with the three abstract domains in this example.

The abstract value computed via abstract interpretation can be directly used to verify properties. Take the local robustness property, which expresses an invariance on the classification of f over a region $B(\bar{x}_0,\delta)$, as an example. Let $l_i(\bar{x})$ be the confidence of $\bar{x}$ being labeled as i, and $l(\bar{x}) = \text{argmax}_i l_i(\bar{x})$ be the label. It has been shown in [24,29] that DNNs are Lipschitz continuous. Therefore, when δ is small, we have that $|l_i(\bar{x}) - l_i(\bar{x}_0)|$ is also small for all labels i. That is, if $l_i(\bar{x}_0)$ is significantly greater than $l_j(\bar{x}_0)$ for $j \neq i$, it is highly likely that $l_i(\bar{x})$ is also significantly greater than $l_j(\bar{x})$. It is not hard to see that the more precise the relations among $l_i(\bar{x}_0), l_i(\bar{x}), l_j(\bar{x}_0), l_j(\bar{x})$ computed via abstract interpretation, the more likely we can prove the robustness. Based on this reason, this paper aims to derive techniques to enhance the precision of abstract interpretation such that it can prove some more properties that cannot be proven by the original abstract interpretation.

3.2 Symbolic Propagation for DNN Verification

Symbolic propagation can ensure soundness while providing more precise results. In [30], a technique called symbolic interval propagation is present and we extend it to our abstraction interpretation framework so that it works on all abstract domains. First, we use the following example to show that using only abstract transformations in an abstract domain may lead to precision loss, while using symbolic propagation could enhance the precision.

Example 3.5. Assume that we have a two-dimensional input $(x_1, x_2) \in [0,1] \times [0,1]$ and a few transformations $y_1 := x_1 + x_2$, $y_2 := x_1 - x_2$, and $z := y_1 + y_2$. Suppose we use the Box abstract domain to analyze the transformations.

- When using only the Box abstract domain, we have $y_1 \in [0,2]$, $y_2 \in [-1,1]$, and thus $z \in [-1,3]$ (i.e., $[0,2] + [-1,1]$).
- By symbolic propagation, we record $y_1 = x_1 + x_2$ and $y_2 = x_1 - x_2$ on the neurons y_1 and y_2 respectively, and then get $z = 2x_1 \in [0,2]$. This result is more precise than that given by using only the Box abstract domain.

Non-relational (e.g., intervals) and weakly-relational abstract domains (e.g., zones, octagons, zonotopes, etc.) [18] may lose precision on the application of the transformations from DNNs. The transformations include affine transformations, ReLU, and max pooling operations. Moreover, it is often the case for weakly-relational abstract domains that the composition of the optimal abstract transformers of individual statements in a sequence does not result in the optimal abstract transformer for the whole sequence, which has been shown in Example 3 when using only the Box abstract domain. A choice to precisely handle general linear transformations is to use the Polyhedra abstract domain which uses a conjunction of linear constraints as domain representation. However, the Polyhedra domain has the worst-case exponential space and time complexity when handling the ReLU operation (via the join operation in the abstract domain). As a consequence, DNN verification with the Polyhedra domain is impractical for large scale DNNs, which has been also confirmed in [9].

In this paper, we leverage symbolic propagation technique to enhance the precision for abstract interpretation based DNN verification. The insight behind is that affine transformations account for a large portion of the transformations in a DNN. Furthermore, when we verify properties such as robustness, the activation of a neuron can often be deterministic for inputs around an input with small perturbation. Hence, there should be a large number of linear equality relations that can be derived from the composition of a sequence of linear transformations via symbolic propagation. And we can use such linear equality relations to improve the precision of the results given by abstract domains. In Sect. 6, our experimental results confirm that, when the perturbation tolerance δ is small, there is a significant proportion of neurons whose ReLU activations are consistent.

First, given X_0, a ReLU neuron $y := \text{ReLU}(\sum_{i=1}^{n} w_i x_i + b)$ can be classified into one of the following 3 categories (according to its range information):

(1) definitely-activated, if the range of $\sum_{i=1}^{n} w_i x_i + b$ is a subset of $[0, \infty)$, (2) definitely-deactivated, if the range of $\sum_{i=1}^{n} w_i x_i + b$ is a subset of $(-\infty, 0]$, and (3) uncertain, otherwise.

Now we detail our symbolic propagation technique. We first introduce a symbolic variable s_i for each node i in the input layer, to denote the initial value of that node. For a ReLU neuron $d := \mathrm{ReLU}(\sum_{i=1}^{n} w_i c_i + b)$ where c_i is a symbolic variable, we make use of the resulting abstract value of abstract domain at this node to determine whether the value of this node is definitely greater than 0 or definitely less than 0. If it is a definitely-activated neuron, we record for this neuron the linear combination $\sum_{i=1}^{n} w_i c_i + b$ as its symbolic representation (i.e., the value of symbolic propagation). If it is a definitely-deactivated neuron, we record for this neuron the value 0 as its symbolic representation. Otherwise, we cannot have a linear combination as the symbolic representation and thus a fresh symbolic variable s_d is introduced to denote the output of this ReLU neuron. We also record the bounds for s_d, such that the lower bound for s_d is set to 0 (since the output of a ReLU neuron is always non-negative) and the upper bound keeps the one obtained by abstract interpretation.

To formalize the algorithm for ReLU node, we first define the abstract states in the analysis and three transfer functions for linear assignments, condition tests and joins respectively. An abstract state in our analysis is composed of an abstract element for a numeric domain (e.g., Box) $\mathbf{n}^{\#} \in \mathbf{N}^{\#}$, a set of free symbolic variables $\mathbf{C}$ (those not equal to any linear expressions), a set of constrained symbolic variables $\mathbf{S}$ (those equal to a certain linear expression), and a map from constrained symbolic variables to linear expressions $\xi ::= \mathbf{S} \Rightarrow \{\sum_{i=1}^{n} a_i x_i + b \mid x_i \in \mathbf{C}\}$. Note that we only allow free variables in the linear expressions in ξ. In the beginning, all input variables are taken as free symbolic variables. In Algorithm 1, we show the transfer functions for linear assignments $[\![y := \sum_{i=1}^{n} w_i x_i + b]\!]^{\sharp}$ which over-approximates the behaviors of $y := \sum_{i=1}^{n} w_i x_i + b$. If $n > 0$ (i.e., the right value expression is not a constant), variable y is added to the constrained variable set $\mathbf{S}$. All constrained variables in $\mathbf{expr} = \sum_{i=1}^{n} w_i x_i + b$ are replaced by their corresponding expressions in ξ, and the map from y to the new $\mathbf{expr}$ is recorded in ξ. Abstract numeric element $\mathbf{n}^{\#}$ is updated by the transfer function for assignments in the numeric domain $[\![y := \mathbf{expr}]\!]^{\sharp}_{\mathbf{N}^{\#}}$. If $n \leq 0$, the right-value expression is a constant, then y is added to $\mathbf{C}$, and is removed from $\mathbf{S}$ and ξ.

The abstract transfer function for condition test is defined as

$$[\![\mathbf{expr} \leq 0]\!]^{\sharp}(\mathbf{n}^{\#}, \mathbf{C}, \mathbf{S}, \xi) ::= ([\![\mathbf{expr} \leq 0]\!]^{\sharp}_{\mathbf{N}^{\#}}(\mathbf{n}^{\#}), \mathbf{C}, \mathbf{S}, \xi),$$

which only updates the abstract element $\mathbf{n}^{\#}$ by the transfer function in the numeric domain $\mathbf{N}^{\#}$.

The join algorithm in our analysis is defined in Algorithm 2. Only the constrained variables arising in both input $\mathbf{S}_0$ and $\mathbf{S}_1$ are with the same corresponding linear expressions are taken as constrained variables. The abstract element in the result is obtained by applying the join operator in the numeric domain $\sqcup_{\mathbf{N}^{\#}}$.

Algorithm 1. Transfer function for linear assignments $[\![y := \sum_{i=1}^{n} w_i x_i + b]\!]^\sharp$

Input: abstract numeric element $\mathbf{n}^\# \in \mathbf{N}^\#$, free variables $\mathbf{C}$, constrained variables $\mathbf{S}$, symbolic map ξ

expr $\leftarrow \sum_{i=1}^{n} w_i x_i + b$
When the right value expression is not a constant
if $n > 0$ **then**
  for $i \in [1, n]$ **do**
    if $x_i \in \mathbf{S}$ **then**
      $\mathbf{expr} = \mathbf{expr}_{|x_i \leftarrow \xi(x_i)}$
    end
  end
  $\xi = \xi \cup \{y \mapsto \mathbf{expr}\}$ $\quad \mathbf{S} = \mathbf{S} \cup \{y\}$ $\quad \mathbf{C} = \mathbf{C}/\{y\}$ $\quad \mathbf{n}^\# = [\![y := \mathbf{expr}]\!]^\sharp_{\mathbf{N}^\#}$
else
  $\xi = \xi/(y \mapsto *)$ $\quad \mathbf{C} = \mathbf{C} \cup \{y\}$ $\quad \mathbf{S} = \mathbf{S}/\{y\}$ $\quad \mathbf{n}^\# = [\![y := \mathbf{expr}]\!]^\sharp_{\mathbf{N}^\#}$
end
return $(\mathbf{n}^\#, \mathbf{C}, \mathbf{S}, \xi)$

The transfer function for a ReLU node is defined as

$$[\![y := \mathrm{ReLU}(\sum_{i=1}^{n} w_i x_i + b)]\!]^\sharp(\mathbf{n}^\#, \mathbf{C}, \mathbf{S}, \xi) ::= \mathbf{join}([\![y > 0]\!]^\sharp(\psi), [\![y := 0]\!]^\sharp([\![y < 0]\!]^\sharp)(\psi)),$$

where $\psi = [\![y := \sum_{i=1}^{n} w_i x_i + b]\!]^\sharp(\mathbf{n}^\#, \mathbf{C}, \mathbf{S}, \xi)$.

Algorithm 2. Join algorithm **join**

Input: $(\mathbf{n}_0^\#, \mathbf{C}_0, \mathbf{S}_0, \xi_0)$ and $(\mathbf{n}_1^\#, \mathbf{C}_1, \mathbf{S}_1, \xi_1)$

$\mathbf{n}^\# = \mathbf{n}_0^\# \sqcup_{\mathbf{N}^\#} \mathbf{n}_1^\#$
$\xi = \xi_0 \cap \xi_1$
$\mathbf{S} = \{x \mid \exists \mathbf{expr}, x \rightarrow \mathbf{expr} \in \xi\}$
$\mathbf{C} = \mathbf{C}_0 \cup (\mathbf{S}_0/\mathbf{S})$
return $(\mathbf{n}^\#, \mathbf{C}, \mathbf{S}, \xi)$

For a max pooling node $d := \max_{1 \le i \le k} c_i$, if there exists some c_j whose lower bound is larger than the upper bound of c_i for all $i \neq j$, we set c_j as the symbolic representation for d. Otherwise, we introduce a fresh symbolic variable s_d for d and record its bounds wherein its lower (upper) bound is the maximum of the lower (upper) bounds of c_i's. Note that the lower (upper) bound of each c_i can be derived from the abstract value for this neuron given by abstract domain.

The algorithm for max-pooling layer can be defined with the three aforementioned transfer functions as follows:

$$\mathbf{join}(\phi_1, \mathbf{join}(\phi_2, \ldots, \mathbf{join}(\phi_{k-1}, \phi_k))),$$
$$\text{where} \quad \phi_i = [\![d := c_i]\!]^\sharp [\![c_i \ge c_1]\!]^\sharp \ldots [\![c_i \ge c_k]\!]^\sharp(\mathbf{n}^\#, \mathbf{C}, \mathbf{S}, \xi)$$

Example 3.6. For the DNN shown in Fig. 3(a), there are two input nodes denoted by symbolic variables x and y, two hidden nodes, and one output node. The initial ranges of the input symbolic variables x and y are given, i.e., $[4, 6]$ and $[3, 4]$ respectively. The weights are labeled on the edges. It is not hard to see that, when using the Interval abstract domain, (the inputs of) the two hidden nodes have bounds $[17, 24]$ and $[0, 3]$ respectively. For the hidden node with $[17, 24]$, we know that this ReLU node is definitely activated, and thus we use symbolic propagation to get a symbolic expression $2x + 3y$ to symbolically represent the output value of this node. Similarly, for the hidden node with $[0, 3]$, we get a symbolic expression $x - y$. Then for the output node, symbolic propagation results in $x + 4y$, which implies that the output range of the whole DNN is $[16, 22]$. If we use only the Interval abstract domain without symbolic propagation, we will get the output range $[14, 24]$, which is less precise than $[16, 22]$.

For the DNN shown in Fig. 3(b), we change the initial range of the input variable y to be $[4.5, 5]$. For the hidden ReLU node with $[-1, 1.5]$, it is neither definitely activated nor definitely deactivated, and thus we introduce a fresh symbolic variable s to denote the output of this node, and set its bound to $[0, 1.5]$. For the output node, symbolic propagation results in $2x + 3y - s$, which implies that the output range of the whole DNN is $[20, 27]$.

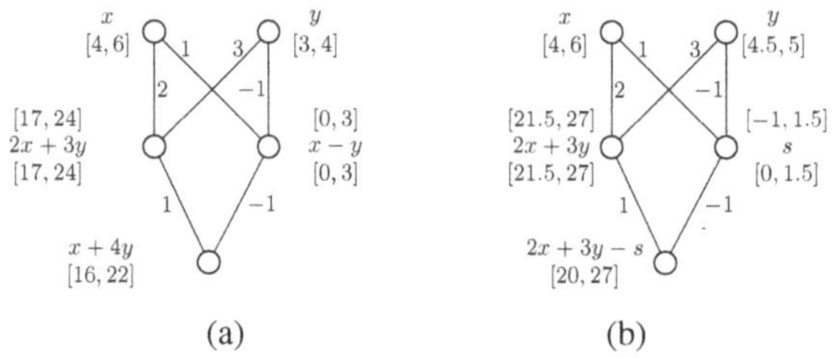

Fig. 3. An illustrative example of symbolic propagation

For a definitely-activated neuron, we utilize its symbolic representation to enhance the precision of abstract domains. We add the linear constraint $d == \sum_{i=1}^{n} w_i c_i + b$ into the abstract value at (the input of) this node, via the meet operation (which is used to deal with conditional test in a program) in the abstract domain [3]. If the precision of the abstract value for the current neuron is improved, we may find more definitely-activated neurons in the subsequent layers. In other words, the analysis based on abstract domain and our symbolic propagation mutually improves the precision of each other on-the-fly.

After obtaining symbolic representation for all the neurons in a layer k, the computation proceeds to layer $k+1$. The computation terminates after completing the computation for the output layer. All symbolic representations in the output layer are evaluated to obtain value bounds.

The following theorem shows some results on precision of our symbolic propagation technique.

Theorem 3.7. *(1) For an FNN $f : \mathbb{R}^m \to \mathbb{R}^n$ and a box region $X \subseteq \mathbb{R}^m$, the Box abstract domain with symbolic propagation can give a more precise abstraction for $f(X)$ than the Zonotope abstract domain without symbolic propagation.*
(2) For an FNN $f : \mathbb{R}^m \to \mathbb{R}^n$ and a box region $X \subseteq \mathbb{R}^m$, the Box abstract domain with symbolic propagation and the Zonotope abstract domain with symbolic propagation gives the same abstraction for $f(X)$.
(3) There exists a CNN $g : \mathbb{R}^m \to \mathbb{R}^n$ and a box region $X \subseteq \mathbb{R}^m$ s.t. the Zonotope abstract domain with symbolic propagation give a more precise abstraction for $g(X)$ than the Box abstract domain with symbolic propagation.

Proof. (1) Since an FNN only contains fully connected layers, we just need to prove that, Box with symbolic propagation (i.e., BoxSymb) is always more precise than Zonotope in the transformations on each RELU neuron $y := \mathrm{ReLU}(\sum_{i=1}^n w_i x_i + b)$. Assume that before the transformation, BoxSymb is more precise or as precise as Zonotope. Since the input is a Box region, the assumption is valid in the beginning. Then we consider three cases: (a) in BoxSymb, the sign of $\sum_{i=1}^n w_i x_i + b$ is uncertain, then it must also be uncertain in Zonotope. In both domains, a constant interval with upper bound computed by $\sum_{i=1}^n w_i x_i + b$ and lower bound as 0 is assigned to y (this can be inferred from our aforementioned algorithms and [10]). With our assumption, the upper bound computed by BoxSymb is more precise than that in Zonotope; (b) in BoxSymb, the sign of $\sum_{i=1}^n w_i x_i + b$ is always positive, then it must be always positive or uncertain in Zonotope. In the former condition, BoxSymb is more precise because it loses no precision, while Zonotope can lose precision because of its limited expressiveness. In the later condition, BoxSymb is more precise obviously; (c) in BoxSymb, the sign of $\sum_{i=1}^n w_i x_i + b$ is always negative, then it must be always negative or uncertain in Zonotope. Similar to case (b), BoxSymb is also more precise in this case.
(2) Assume that before each transformation on a ReLU neuron $y := \mathrm{ReLU}(\sum_{i=1}^n w_i x_i + b)$, BoxSymb and ZonoSymb (Zonotope with symbolic propagation) are with same precision. This assumption is also valid when the input is a Box region. Then the evaluation of $\sum_{i=1}^n w_i x_i + b$ is same in BoxSymb and ZonoSymb, thus in the three cases:(a) the sign of $\sum_{i=1}^n w_i x_i + b$ is uncertain, they both compute a same constant interval for y; (b) and (c) $\sum_{i=1}^n w_i x_i + b$ is always positive or negative, they both lose no precision.
(3) It is easy to know that, ZonoSymb is more precise or as precise as BoxSymb in all transformations. In CNN, with Max-Pooling layer, we just need to give an example that ZonoSymb can be more precise. Let the Zonotope $X' = \{x_1 = 2 + \epsilon_1 + \epsilon_2,\ x_2 = 2 + \epsilon_1 - \epsilon_2 \mid \epsilon_1, \epsilon_2 \in [-1, 1]\}$ and the max pooling node $y = \max\{x_1, x_2\}$. Obviously X' can be obtained through a linear transformation on some box region X. With Box with symbolic propagation, the abstraction of y is $[0, 4]$, while Zonotope with symbolic propagation gives the abstraction is $[1, 4]$.

Theorem 3.7 gives us some insights: Symbolic propagation technique has a very strong power (even stronger than Zonotope) in dealing with ReLU nodes, while Zonotope gives a more precise abstraction on max pooling nodes. It also provides a useful instruction: When we work with FNNs with the input range being a box, we should use Box with symbolic propagation rather than Zonotope with symbolic propagation since it does not improve the precision but takes more time. Results in Theorem 3.7 will also be illustrated in our experiments.

4 Abstract Interpretation as an Accelerator for SMT-Based DNN Verification

In this section we briefly recall DNN verification based on SMT solvers, and then describe how to utilize the results by abstract interpretation with our symbolic propagation to improve its performance.

4.1 SMT Based DNN Verification

In [7,14], two SMT solvers Reluplex and Planet were presented to verify DNNs. Typically an SMT solver is the combination of a SAT solver with the specialized decision procedures for other theories. The verification of DNNs uses linear arithmetic over real numbers, in which an atom may have the form of $\sum_{i=1}^{n} w_i x_i \leq b$, where w_i and b are real numbers. Both Reluplex and Planet use the DPLL algorithm to split cases and rule out conflict clauses. They are different in dealing with the intersection. For Reluplex, it inherits rules from the Simplex algorithm and adds a few rules dedicated to ReLU operation. Through the classical pivot operation, it searches for a solution to the linear constraints, and then apply the rules for ReLU to ensure the ReLU relation for every node. Differently, Planet uses linear approximation to over-approximate the DNN, and manage the conditions of ReLU and max pooling nodes with logic formulas.

4.2 Abstract Interpretation with Symbolic Propagation as an Accelerator

SMT-based DNN verification approaches are often not efficient, e.g., relying on case splitting for ReLU operation. In the worst case, case splitting is needed for each ReLU operation in a DNN, which leads to an exponential blow-up. In particular, when analyzing large-scale DNNs, SMT-based DNN verification approaches may suffer from the scalability problem and account time out, which is also confirmed experimentally in [9].

In this paper, we utilize the results of abstract interpretation (with symbolic propagation) to accelerate SMT-based DNN verification approaches. More specifically, we use the bound information of each ReLU node (obtained by abstract interpretation) to reduce the number of case-splitting, and thus accelerate SMT-based DNN verification. For example, on a neuron $d := \text{ReLU}(\sum_{i=1}^{n} w_i c_i + b)$, if we know that this node is a definitely-activated node according to the bounds given by abstract interpretation, we only consider the case $d := \sum_{i=1}^{n} w_i c_i + b$ and thus no split is applied. We remark that, this does not compromise the precision of SMT-based DNN verification while improving their efficiency.

5 Discussion

In this section, we discuss the soundness guarantee of our approach. Soundness is an essential property of formal verification.

Abstract interpretation is known for its soundness guarantee for analysis and verification [18], since it conducts over-approximation to enclose all the possible behaviors of the original system. Computing over-approximations for a DNN is thus our soundness guarantee in this paper. As shown in Theorem 3.3, if the results of abstract interpretation show that the property C holds (i.e., $\gamma(X^{\sharp}{}_N) \subseteq C$ in Eq. 1), then the property also holds for the set of actual executions of the DNN (i.e., $f(X_0) \subseteq C$). If the results of abstract interpretation can not prove that the property C holds, however, the verification is inconclusive. In this case, the results of the chosen abstract domain are not precise enough to prove the property, and thus more powerful abstract domains are needed. Moreover, our symbolic propagation also preserves soundness, since it uses symbolic substitution to compute the composition of linear transformations.

On the other hand, many existing DNN verification tools do not guarantee soundness. For example, Reluplex [14] (using GLPK), Planet [7] (using GLPK), and Sherlock [4] (using Gurobi) all rely on the floating point implementation of linear programming solvers, which is unsound. Actually, most state-of-the-art linear programming solvers use floating-point arithmetic and only give approximate solutions which may not be the actual optimum solution or may even lie outside the feasible space [20]. It may happen that a linear programming solver implemented via floating point arithmetic wrongly claims that a feasible linear system is infeasible or the other way round. In fact, [4] reports several false positive results in Reluplex, and mentions that this comes from unsound floating point implementation.

6 Experimental Evaluation

We present the design and results of our experiments.

6.1 Experimental Setup

Implementation. AI^2 [9] is the first to utilize abstract interpretation to verify DNNs, and has implemented all the transformers mentioned in Sect. 3.1. Since the implementation of AI^2 is not available, we have re-implemented these transformers and refer to them as AI^2-r. We then implemented our symbolic propagation technique based on AI^2-r and use AI^2-r as the baseline comparison in the experiments. Both implementations use general frameworks and thus can run on various abstract domains. In this paper, we chose Box (from Apron[1]), T-Zonotope (Zonotope from Apron (see Footnote 6)) and E-Zonotope (Elina Zonotope with the join operator[2]) as the underlying domains.

[1] https://github.com/ljlin/Apron_Elina_fork.

[2] https://github.com/eth-sri/ELINA/commit/152910bf35ff037671c99ab019c1915e93dde57f.

Datasets and DNNs. We use MNIST [16] and ACAS Xu [8,12] as the datasets in our experiments. MNIST contains 60,000 28×28 grayscale handwritten digits. We can train DNNs to classify the pictures by the written digits on them. The ACAS Xu system is aimed to avoid airborne collisions and it uses an observation table to make decisions for the aircraft. In [13], the observation table can be realized by training a DNN instead of storing it.

On MNIST, we train seven FNNs and two CNNs. The seven FNNs are of the size 3×20, 6×20, 3×50, 3×100, 6×100, and 9×200, where $m \times n$ refers to m hidden layers with n neurons in each hidden layer. The CNN1 consists of 2 convolutional, 1 max-pooling, 2 convolutional, 1 max-pooling, and 3 fully connected layers in sequence, for a total of 12,412 neurons. The CNN2 has 4 convolutional and 3 fully connected layers (89572 neurons). On ACAS Xu, we use the same networks as those in [14].

Properties. We consider the local robustness property with respect to the input region defined as follows:

$$X_{\bar{x},\delta} = \{\bar{x}' \in \mathbb{R}^m \mid \forall i.1 - \delta \leq x_i \leq x_i' \leq 1 \vee x_i = x_i'\}.$$

In the experiments, the optional robustness bounds are $0.1, 0.2, 0.3, 0.4, 0.5, 0.6$. All the experiments are conducted on an openSUSE Leap 15.0 machine with Intel i7 CPU@3.60 GHz and 16 GB memory.

6.2 Experimental Results

We compare seven approaches: AI^2-r with Box, T-Zonotope and E-zonotope as underlying domains and Symb (i.e., our enhanced abstract interpretation with symbolic propagation) with Box, T-Zonotope and E-zonotope as underlying domains, and Planet [7], which serves as the benchmark verification approach (for its ability to compute bounds).

Improvement on Bounds. To see the improvement on bounds, we compare the output ranges of the above seven approaches on different inputs $\bar{x}$ and different tolerances δ. Table 1(a) reports the results on three inputs $\bar{x}$ (No.767, No.1955 and No.2090 in the MNIST training dataset) and six tolerances $\delta \in \{0.1, 0.2, 0.3, 0.4, 0.5, 0.6\}$. In all our experiments, we set TIMEOUT as one hour for each FNN and eight hours for each CNN for a single run with an input, and a tolerance δ. In the table, TZono and EZono are shorts for T-Zonotope and E-Zonotope.

For each running we get a gap with an upper and lower bound for each neuron. Here we define the *the bound proportion* to statistically describe how precise the range an approach gives. Basically given an approach (like Symb with Box domain), the bound proportion of this approach is the average of the ratio of the gap length of the neurons on the output layer and that obtained using AI^2-r with Box. Naturally AI^2-r with Box always has the bound proportion 1, and the smaller the bound proportion is, the more precise the ranges the approach gives are.

Table 1. Experimental results of abstract interpretation for MNIST DNNs with different approaches

	AI^2-r		Symb			Planet
	TZono	EZono	Box	TZono	EZono	
FNN1	28.23348%	28.02098%	9.69327%	9.69327%	9.69327%	7.05553%
FNN2	24.16382%	22.13319%	1.76704%	1.76704%	1.76704%	0.89089%
FNN3	26.66453%	26.30852%	6.88656%	6.88656%	6.88656%	4.51223%
FNN4	28.47243%	28.33535%	5.13645%	5.13645%	5.13645%	2.71537%
FNN5	35.61163%	35.27187%	3.34578%	3.34578%	3.34578%	0.14836%
FNN6	38.71020%	38.57376%	7.12480%	7.12480%	7.12480%	1.94230%
FNN7	41.76517%	41.59382%	5.52267%	5.52267%	5.52267%	1h TIMEOUT
CNN1	24.19607%	24.13725%	21.78279%	7.58917%	7.56223%	8h TIMEOUT
CNN2	OOM	OOM	1.09146%	OOM	OOM	8h TIMEOUT

(a) Bound proportions (smaller is better) of different abstract interpretation approaches with the robustness bound $\delta \in \{0.1, 0.2, 0.3, 0.4, 0.5, 0.6\}$, and the fixed input pictures 767, 1955, and 2090;

	AI^2-r						Symb						Planet	
	Box		TZono		EZono		Box		TZono		EZono			
FNN1	11.168	0.2	13.482	0.5	44.05	0.5	12.935	0.6	17.144	0.6	45.88	0.6	20.179	0.6
FNN2	12.559	0	16.636	0.2	50.59	0.2	15.075	0.5	22.333	0.5	49.92	0.5	35.84	0.6
FNN3	12.699	0.2	18.748	0.3	49.812	0.3	19.042	0.6	28.128	0.6	54.77	0.6	76.106	0.6
FNN4	15.583	0.1	29.495	0.3	58.892	0.3	37.716	0.6	56.47	0.6	76.00	0.6	351.139	0.6
FNN5	28.963	0	81.49	0.2	149.791	0.2	90.268	0.4	154.222	0.4	173.263	0.4	1297.485	0.6
FNN6	62.766	0	398.565	0.1	538.076	0.1	323.328	0.3	650.629	0.3	745.454	0.3	15823.208	0.3
FNN7	111.955	0	1674.465	0	1627.72	0	642.978	0.3	1524.975	0.3	1489.604	0.3	1h TIMEOUT	
CNN1	2340.828	0	6717.57	0.2	94504.195	0.2	5124.681	0.2	8584.555	0.3	45452.102	0.3	8h TIMEOUT	
CNN2	41292.291	0	OOM	0	OOM	0	105850.271	0.3	OOM	0	OOM	0	8h TIMEOUT	

(b) The time (in second) and the maximum robustness bound δ which can be verified through the abstract interpretation technique and the planet bound, with optional $\delta \in \{0.1, 0.2, 0.3, 0.4, 0.5, 0.6\}$ and the fixed input picture 2090;

	AI^2-r			Symb			Planet
	Box	TZono	EZono	Box	TZono	EZono	
FNN1(60)	57 44 34	59 52 38	59 52 38	59 53 44	59 53 44	59 53 44	59 56 55
FNN2(120)	103 59 38	118 109 66	118 111 66	118 113 107	118 113 107	118 113 107	119 114 110
FNN3(150)	136 93 66	141 127 85	141 127 85	143 133 110	143 133 110	143 133 110	146 142 135
FNN4(300)	250 144 105	294 209 130	294 209 130	295 254 182	295 254 182	295 254 182	296 276 254
FNN5(600)	289 160 106	513 200 125	513 200 125	589 510 236	589 510 236	589 510 236	593 558 493
FNN6(1200)	472 247 181	782 339 195	782 339 195	1176 790 250	1176 790 250	1176 790 250	1189 1089 772
FNN7(1800)	469 271 177	770 350 200	775 350 200	1773 741 263	1773 741 263	1773 741 263	1h TIMEOUT
CNN1(12412)	12226 11788 11280	12371 12119 11786	12371 12122 11786	12373 12094 11659	12376 12193 11877	12376 12196 11877	8h TIMEOUT
CNN2(89572)	85793 77241 70212	OOM	OOM	89190 86910 81442	OOM	OOM	8h TIMEOUT

(c) The number of hidden ReLU neurons whose behavior can be decided with the bounds our abstract interpretation technique and Planet provide, with optional robustness bound $\delta \in \{0.1, 0.4, 0.6\}$ and the fixed input picture 767.

In Table 1(a), every entry is the average bound proportion over three different inputs and six different tolerances. OOM stands for out-of-memory, 1h TIMEOUT for the one-hour timeout, and 8h TIMEOUT for the eight-hour timeout. We can see that, in general, Symb with Box, T-Zonotope and E-zonotope can achieve much better bounds than AI^2-r with Box, T-Zonotope and E-zonotope do. These bounds are closer to what Planet gives, except for FNN5 and FNN6. E-zonotope is slightly more precise than T-Zonotope. On the other hand, while Symb can return in a reasonable time in most cases, Planet cannot terminate in an hour (resp. eight hours) for FNN7 (resp. CNN1 and CNN2), which have $1,800$, $12,412$ and $89,572$ hidden neurons, respectively. Also we can see that results in Theorem 3.7 are illustrated here. More specifically, (1) Symb with Box domain is more precise than AI^2-r with T-Zonotope and E-Zonotope on FNNs; (2) Symb with Box, T-Zonotope and E-Zonotope are with the same precision on FNNs; (3) Symb with T-Zonotope and E-Zonotope are more precise than Symb with Box on CNNs.

According to memory footprint, both AI^2-r and Symb with T-Zonotope or E-Zonotope need more memory than them with Box do, and will crash on large networks, such as CNN2, because of running out of memory. Figure 4 shows how CPU and resident memory usage change over time. The horizontal axis in the figure is the time, in seconds, the vertical axis corresponding to the red line is the CPU usage percentage, and the vertical axis corresponding to the blue line is the memory usage, in MB.

Greater Verifiable Robustness Bounds. Table 1(b) shows the results of using the obtained bounds to help verify the robustness property. We consider a few thresholds for robustness tolerance, i.e., $\{0.1, 0.2, 0.3, 0.4, 0.5, 0.6\}$, and find that Symb can verify many more cases than AI^2-r do with comparable time consumption (less than 2x in most cases, and sometimes even faster).

Proportion of Activated/Deactivated ReLU Nodes. Table 1(c) reports the number of hidden neurons whose ReLU behaviour (i.e., activated or deactivated) has been consistent within the tolerance δ. Compared to AI^2-r, our Symb can decide the ReLU behaviour with a much higher percentage.

We remark that, although the experimental results presented above are based on 3 fixed inputs, more extensive experiments have already been conducted to confirm that the conclusions are general. We randomly sample 1000 pictures (100 pictures per label) from the MNIST dataset, and compute the bound proportion for each of the pair (m, δ) where m refers to the seven approaches in Table 1 and $\delta \in \{0.1, 0.2, 0.3, 0.4, 0.5, 0.6\}$ on FNN1. Each entry corresponding to (m, δ) in Table 2 is the average of bound proportions of approach m over 1000 pictures and fixed tolerance δ. Then we get the average of the bound proportion of AI^2-r with TZono/EZono, Symb with Box/TZono/EZono, and Planet over six different tolerances are 27.98623%, 27.44977%, 11.02104%, 11.02104%, 11.02104%, 7.08377%, respectively, which are very close to the first row of Table 1(a).

Comparison with the Bounded Powerset Domain. In AI^2 [9], the bounded powerset domains are used to improve the precision. In AI^2-r, we also implemented such bounded powerset domains instantiated by Box, T-Zonotope and E-Zonotope domains, with 32 as the bound of the number of the abstract elements in a disjunction. The comparison of the performance on the powerset domains with our

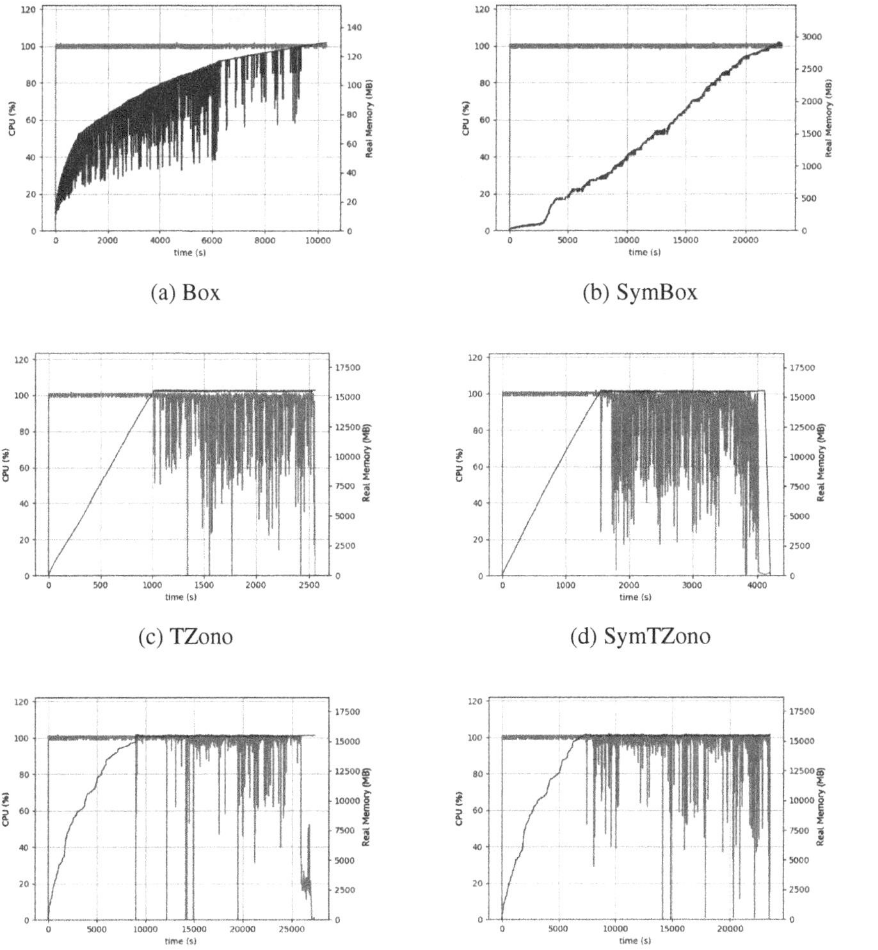

(a) Box (b) SymBox

(c) TZono (d) SymTZono

(e) EZono (f) SymEZono

Fig. 4. CPU and memory usage

symbolic propagation technique (with underlying domains rather than powerset domains) is shown in Table 3. We can see that our technique is much more precise than the powerset domains. The time and memory consumptions of the powerset domains are both around 32 times as much as the underlying domains, which are more than those of our technique.

Faster Verification. In this part we use the networks of ACAS Xu. To evaluate the benefits of tighter bounds for SMT-based tools, we give the bounds obtained by abstract interpretation (on Box domain with symbolic propagation) to Reluplex [14] and observe the performance difference. The results are shown in Table 4. Each cell shows the satisfiability (i.e., SAT if an adversarial

Table 2. Bound proportions (smaller is better) for 1000 randomly sampled pictures from MNIST testing set on FNN1 with $\delta \in \{0.1, 0.2, 0.3, 0.4, 0.5, 0.6\}$.

δ	AI^2-r		Symb			Planet
	TZono	EZono	Box	TZono	EZono	
0.1	7.13046%	7.08137%	6.15622%	6.15622%	6.15622%	5.84974%
0.2	11.09230%	10.88775%	6.92011%	6.92011%	6.92011%	6.11095%
0.3	18.75853%	18.32059%	8.21241%	8.21241%	8.21241%	6.50692%
0.4	30.11872%	29.27580%	10.31225%	10.31225%	10.31225%	7.04413%
0.5	45.13963%	44.25026%	14.49276%	14.49276%	14.49276%	7.96402%
0.6	55.67772%	54.88288%	20.03251%	20.03251%	20.03251%	9.02688%

Table 3. Bound proportions (smaller is better) of different abstract interpretation approaches with the robustness bound $\delta \in \{0.1, 0.2, 0.3, 0.4, 0.5, 0.6\}$, and the fixed input pictures 767, 1955, and 2090. Note that each entry gives the average bound proportion over six different tolerance and three pictures.

	AI^2-r			Symb			Planet
	Box32	TZono32	EZono32	Box	TZono	EZono	
FNN1	89.65790%	20.68675%	15.87726%	9.69327%	9.69327%	9.69327%	7.05553%
FNN2	89.42070%	16.27651%	8.18317%	1.76704%	1.76704%	1.76704%	0.89089%
FNN3	89.43396%	21.98109%	12.42840%	6.88656%	6.88656%	6.88656%	4.51223%
FNN4	89.44806%	25.97855%	13.05969%	5.13645%	5.13645%	5.13645%	2.71537%
FNN5	89.16034%	29.61022%	17.88676%	3.34578%	3.34578%	3.34578%	0.14836%
FNN6	89.30790%	OOM	22.60030%	7.12480%	7.12480%	7.12480%	1.94230%
FNN7	88.62267%	OOM	1 h TIMEOUT	5.52267%	5.52267%	5.52267%	1 h TIMEOUT

example is found) and the running time without or with given bounds. The experiments are conducted on different δ values (as in [14]) and a fixed network (nnet1_1 [14]) and 5 fixed points (Point 1 to 5 in [14]). The running time our technique spends on deriving the bounds are all less than 1 second. Table 4 shows that tighter initial bounds bring significant benefits to Reluplex with an overall $(\frac{1}{5076} - \frac{1}{32992})/\frac{1}{32992} = 549.43\%$ speedup (9.16 h compared to 1.41 h). However, it should be noted that, on one specific case (i.e., $\delta = 0.1$ at Point 1 and $\delta = 0.075$ at point 4), the tighter initial bounds slow Reluplex, which means that the speedup is not guaranteed on all cases. For the case $\delta = 0.05$ at point 4, Reluplex gives SAT and Reluplex+ABS gives UNSAT. This may result from a floating point arithmetic error.

Table 4. The satisfiability on given δ, and the time (in second) with and without bounds generated by abstract interpretation with symbolic propagation on the Box domain.

		$\delta = 0.1$		$\delta = 0.075$		$\delta = 0.05$		$\delta = 0.025$		$\delta = 0.01$		Total Time
		Result	Time	Result	Time	Result	Time	Result	Time	Result	Time	
Point 1	Reluplex	SAT	39	SAT	123	SAT	14	UNSAT	638	UNSAT	64	879
	Reluplex + ABS	SAT	45	SAT	36	SAT	14	UNSAT	237	UNSAT	36	368
Point 2	Reluplex	UNSAT	6513	UNSAT	1559	UNSAT	319	UNSAT	49	UNSAT	11	8451
	Reluplex + ABS	UNSAT	141	UNSAT	156	UNSAT	75	UNSAT	40	UNSAT	0	412
Point 3	Reluplex	UNSAT	1013	UNSAT	422	UNSAT	95	UNSAT	79	UNSAT	6	1615
	Reluplex + ABS	UNSAT	44	UNSAT	71	UNSAT	0	UNSAT	0	UNSAT	0	115
Point 4	Reluplex	SAT	3	SAT	5	SAT	1236	UNSAT	579	UNSAT	8	1831
	Reluplex + ABS	SAT	3	SAT	7	UNSAT	442	UNSAT	31	UNSAT	0	483
Point 5	Reluplex	UNSAT	14301	UNSAT	4248	UNSAT	1392	UNSAT	269	UNSAT	6	20216
	Reluplex + ABS	UNSAT	2002	UNSAT	1402	UNSAT	231	UNSAT	63	UNSAT	0	3698

7 Related Work

Verification of neural networks can be traced back to [23], where the network is encoded after approximating every sigmoid activation function with a set of piecewise linear constraints and then solved with an SMT solver. It works with a network of 6 hidden nodes. More recently, by considering DNNs with ReLU activation functions, the verification approaches include constraint-solving [7,14,17,19], layer-by-layer exhaustive search [11], global optimisation [4,24,25], abstract interpretation [9,27,28], functional approximation [35], and reduction to two-player game [32,34], etc. More specifically, [14] presents an SMT solver Reluplex to verify properties on DNNs with fully-connected layers. [7] presents another SMT solver Planet which combines linear approximation and interval arithmetic to work with fully connected and max pooling layers. Methods based on SMT solvers do not scale well, e.g., Reluplex can only work with DNNs with a few hidden neurons.

The above works are mainly for the verification of local robustness. Research has been conducted to compute other properties, e.g., the output reachability. An exact computation of output reachability can be utilised to verify local robustness. In [4], Sherlock, an algorithm based on local and global search and mixed integer linear programming (MILP), is put forward to calculate the output range of a given label when the inputs are restricted to a small subspace. [24] presents another algorithm for output range analysis, and their algorithm is workable for all Lipschitz continuous DNNs, including all layers and activation functions mentioned above. In [30], the authors use symbolic interval propagation to calculate output range. Compared with [30], our approach fits for general abstract domains, while their symbolic interval propagation is designed specifically for symbolic intervals.

[9] is the first to use abstract interpretation to verify DNNs. They define a class of functions called conditional affine transformations (CAT) to characterize DNNs containing fully connected, convolutional and max pooling layers with

the ReLU activation function. They use Interval and Zonotope as the abstract domains and the powerset technique on Zonotope. Compared with AI^2, we use symbolic propagation rather than powerset extension techniques to enhance the precision of abstract interpretation based DNN verification. Symbolic propagation is more lightweight than powerset extension. Moreover, we also use the bounds information given by abstract interpretation to accelerate SMT based DNN verification. DeepZ [27] and DeepPoly [28] propose two specific abstract domains tailored to DNN verification, in order to improve the precision of abstract interpretation on the verification on DNNs. In contrast, our work is a general approach that can be applied on various domains.

8 Conclusion

In this paper, we have explored more potential of abstract interpretation on the verification over DNNs. We have proposed to use symbolic propagation on abstract interpretation to take advantage of the linearity in most part of the DNNs, which achieved significant improvements in terms of the precision and memory usage. This is based on a key observation that, for local robustness verification of DNNs where a small region of the input space is concerned, a considerable percentage of hidden neurons remain active or inactive for all possible inputs in the region. For these neurons, their ReLU activation function can be replaced by a linear function. Our symbolic propagation iteratively computes for each neuron this information and utilize the computed information to improve the performance.

This paper has presented with formal proofs three somewhat surprising theoretical results, which are then affirmed by our experiments. These results have enhanced our theoretical and practical understanding about the abstract interpretation based DNN verification and symbolic propagation.

This paper has also applied the tighter bounds of variables on hidden neurons from our approach to improve the performance of the state-of-the-art SMT based DNN verification tools, like Reluplex. The speed-up rate is up to 549% in our experiments. We believe this result sheds some light on the potential in improving the scalability of SMT-based DNN verification: In addition to improving the performance through enhancing the SMT solver for DNNs, an arguably easier way is to take an abstract interpretation technique (or other techniques that can refine the constraints) as a pre-processing.

Acknowledgements. This work is supported by the Guangdong Science and Technology Department (No. 2018B010107004) and the NSFC Program (No. 61872445). We also thank anonymous reviewers for detailed comments.

Data Availability Statements. The datasets/code generated during and/or analysed during the current study are available in the Figshare repository: https://doi.org/10.6084/m9.figshare.9861059.v1

References

1. Deep neural networks for acoustic modeling in speech recognition: the shared views of four research groups. IEEE Signal Process. Mag. **29**(6), 82–97 (2012). https://doi.org/10.1109/MSP.2012.2205597
2. Carlini, N., Wagner, D.: Towards evaluating the robustness of neural networks. In: 2017 IEEE Symposium on Security and Privacy (SP), pp. 39–57. IEEE (2017)
3. Cousot, P., Cousot, R.: Abstract interpretation: a unified lattice model for static analysis of programs by construction or approximation of fixpoints. In: Fourth ACM Symposium on Principles of Programming Languages (POPL), pp. 238–252 (1977)
4. Dutta, S., Jha, S., Sankaranarayanan, S., Tiwari, A.: Output range analysis for deep feedforward neural networks. In: Dutle, A., Muñoz, C., Narkawicz, A. (eds.) NFM 2018. LNCS, vol. 10811, pp. 121–138. Springer, Cham (2018). https://doi.org/10.1007/978-3-319-77935-5_9
5. Dvijotham, K., Stanforth, R., Gowal, S., Mann, T.A., Kohli, P.: A dual approach to scalable verification of deep networks. CoRR abs/1803.06567 (2018). http://arxiv.org/abs/1803.06567
6. Dy, J.G., Krause, A. (eds.): Proceedings of the 35th International Conference on Machine Learning, ICML 2018, Stockholmsmässan, Stockholm, Sweden, 10–15 July 2018, JMLR Workshop and Conference Proceedings, vol. 80. JMLR.org (2018). http://proceedings.mlr.press/v80/
7. Ehlers, R.: Formal verification of piece-wise linear feed-forward neural networks. In: D'Souza, D., Narayan Kumar, K. (eds.) ATVA 2017. LNCS, vol. 10482, pp. 269–286. Springer, Cham (2017). https://doi.org/10.1007/978-3-319-68167-2_19
8. von Essen, C., Giannakopoulou, D.: Analyzing the next generation airborne collision avoidance system. In: Ábrahám, E., Havelund, K. (eds.) TACAS 2014. LNCS, vol. 8413, pp. 620–635. Springer, Heidelberg (2014). https://doi.org/10.1007/978-3-642-54862-8_54
9. Gehr, T., Mirman, M., Drachsler-Cohen, D., Tsankov, P., Chaudhuri, S., Vechev, M.: AI^2: safety and robustness certification of neural networks with abstract interpretation. In: 2018 IEEE Symposium on Security and Privacy (S&P 2018), pp. 948–963 (2018)
10. Ghorbal, K., Goubault, E., Putot, S.: The zonotope abstract domain taylor1+. In: Bouajjani, A., Maler, O. (eds.) CAV 2009. LNCS, vol. 5643, pp. 627–633. Springer, Heidelberg (2009). https://doi.org/10.1007/978-3-642-02658-4_47
11. Huang, X., Kwiatkowska, M., Wang, S., Wu, M.: Safety verification of deep neural networks. In: Majumdar, R., Kunčak, V. (eds.) CAV 2017. LNCS, vol. 10426, pp. 3–29. Springer, Cham (2017). https://doi.org/10.1007/978-3-319-63387-9_1
12. Jeannin, J., et al.: Formal verification of ACAS x, an industrial airborne collision avoidance system. In: Girault, A., Guan, N. (eds.) 2015 International Conference on Embedded Software, EMSOFT 2015, Amsterdam, Netherlands, 4–9 October 2015, pp. 127–136. IEEE (2015). https://doi.org/10.1109/EMSOFT.2015.7318268
13. Julian, K.D., Kochenderfer, M.J., Owen, M.P.: Deep neural network compression for aircraft collision avoidance systems. CoRR abs/1810.04240 (2018). http://arxiv.org/abs/1810.04240
14. Katz, G., Barrett, C., Dill, D.L., Julian, K., Kochenderfer, M.J.: Reluplex: an efficient SMT solver for verifying deep neural networks. In: Majumdar, R., Kunčak, V. (eds.) CAV 2017. LNCS, vol. 10426, pp. 97–117. Springer, Cham (2017). https://doi.org/10.1007/978-3-319-63387-9_5

15. Krizhevsky, A., Sutskever, I., Hinton, G.E.: Imagenet classification with deep convolutional neural networks. In: Bartlett, P.L., Pereira, F.C.N., Burges, C.J.C., Bottou, L., Weinberger, K.Q. (eds.) Advances in Neural Information Processing Systems 25: 26th Annual Conference on Neural Information Processing Systems 2012. Proceedings of a meeting held, Lake Tahoe, Nevada, United States, 3–6 December 2012, pp. 1106–1114 (2012). http://papers.nips.cc/paper/4824-imagenet-classification-with-deep-convolutional-neural-networks
16. Lécun, Y., Bottou, L., Bengio, Y., Haffner, P.: Gradient-based learning applied to document recognition. Proc. IEEE **86**(11), 2278–2324 (1998)
17. Lomuscio, A., Maganti, L.: An approach to reachability analysis for feed-forward ReLU neural networks. In: KR2018 (2018)
18. Miné, A.: Tutorial on static inference of numeric invariants by abstract interpretation. Found. Trends Program. Lang. **4**(3–4), 120–372 (2017)
19. Narodytska, N., Kasiviswanathan, S.P., Ryzhyk, L., Sagiv, M., Walsh, T.: Verifying properties of binarized deep neural networks. arXiv preprint arXiv:1709.06662 (2017)
20. Neumaier, A., Shcherbina, O.: Safe bounds in linear and mixed-integer linear programming. Math. Program. **99**(2), 283–296 (2004). https://doi.org/10.1007/s10107-003-0433-3
21. Nguyen, A., Yosinski, J., Clune, J.: Deep neural networks are easily fooled: high confidence predictions for unrecognizable images. In: Proceedings of the IEEE Conference on Computer Vision and Pattern Recognition, pp. 427–436 (2015)
22. Papernot, N., McDaniel, P.D., Jha, S., Fredrikson, M., Celik, Z.B., Swami, A.: The limitations of deep learning in adversarial settings. CoRR abs/1511.07528 (2015). http://arxiv.org/abs/1511.07528
23. Pulina, L., Tacchella, A.: An abstraction-refinement approach to verification of artificial neural networks. In: Touili, T., Cook, B., Jackson, P. (eds.) CAV 2010. LNCS, vol. 6174, pp. 243–257. Springer, Heidelberg (2010). https://doi.org/10.1007/978-3-642-14295-6_24
24. Ruan, W., Huang, X., Kwiatkowska, M.: Reachability analysis of deep neural networks with provable guarantees. In: Lang, J. (ed.) Proceedings of the Twenty-Seventh International Joint Conference on Artificial Intelligence, IJCAI 2018, Stockholm, Sweden, 13–19 July 2018, pp. 2651–2659. ijcai.org (2018). https://doi.org/10.24963/ijcai.2018/368
25. Ruan, W., Wu, M., Sun, Y., Huang, X., Kroening, D., Kwiatkowska, M.: Global robustness evaluation of deep neural networks with provable guarantees for the hamming distance. In: IJCAI2019 (2019)
26. Silver, D., et al.: Mastering the game of go with deep neural networks and tree search. Nature **529**(7587), 484–489 (2016). https://doi.org/10.1038/nature16961
27. Singh, G., Gehr, T., Mirman, M., Püschel, M., Vechev, M.T.: Fast and effective robustness certification. In: Bengio, S., Wallach, H.M., Larochelle, H., Grauman, K., Cesa-Bianchi, N., Garnett, R. (eds.) Advances in Neural Information Processing Systems 31: Annual Conference on Neural Information Processing Systems 2018, NeurIPS 2018, Montréal, Canada, 3–8 December 2018, pp. 10825–10836 (2018). http://papers.nips.cc/paper/8278-fast-and-effective-robustness-certification
28. Singh, G., Gehr, T., Püschel, M., Vechev, M.T.: An abstract domain for certifying neural networks. PACMPL **3**(POPL), 41:1–41:30 (2019). https://dl.acm.org/citation.cfm?id=3290354
29. Szegedy, C., et al.: Intriguing properties of neural networks. In: International Conference on Learning Representations (ICLR2014) (2014)

30. Wang, S., Pei, K., Whitehouse, J., Yang, J., Jana, S.: Formal security analysis of neural networks using symbolic intervals. CoRR abs/1804.10829 (2018). http://arxiv.org/abs/1804.10829
31. Weng, T., Zhang, H., Chen, H., Song, Z., Hsieh, C., Daniel, L., Boning, D.S., Dhillon, I.S.: Towards fast computation of certified robustness for relu networks. In: Dy and Krause [7], pp. 5273–5282. http://proceedings.mlr.press/v80/weng18a.html
32. Wicker, M., Huang, X., Kwiatkowska, M.: Feature-guided black-box safety testing of deep neural networks. In: Beyer, D., Huisman, M. (eds.) TACAS 2018. LNCS, vol. 10805, pp. 408–426. Springer, Cham (2018). https://doi.org/10.1007/978-3-319-89960-2_22
33. Wong, E., Kolter, J.Z.: Provable defenses against adversarial examples via the convex outer adversarial polytope. In: Dy and Krause [7], pp. 5283–5292. http://proceedings.mlr.press/v80/wong18a.html
34. Wu, M., matthew Wicker, Ruan, W., Huang, X., Kwiatkowska, M.: A game-based approximate verification of deep neural networks with provable guarantees. Theor. Comput. Sci. (2019)
35. Xiang, W., Tran, H., Johnson, T.T.: Output reachable set estimation and verification for multilayer neural networks. IEEE Trans. Neural Netw. Learn. Syst. **29**(11), 5777–5783 (2018). https://doi.org/10.1109/TNNLS.2018.2808470

Synthesis and Security

SORCAR: Property-Driven Algorithms for Learning Conjunctive Invariants

Daniel Neider[1(✉)], Shambwaditya Saha[2], Pranav Garg[3], and P. Madhusudan[2]

[1] Max Planck Institute for Software Systems, Kaiserslautern, Germany
neider@mpi-sws.org
[2] University of Illinois at Urbana-Champaing, Champaign, USA
[3] Amazon Web Services, Seattle, USA

Abstract. We present a new learning algorithm SORCAR to synthesize conjunctive inductive invariants for proving that a program satisfies its assertions. The salient property of this algorithm is that it is *property-driven*, and for a fixed finite set of n predicates, guarantees convergence in $2n$ rounds, taking only polynomial time in each round. We implement and evaluate the algorithm and show that its performance is favorable to the existing HOUDINI algorithm (which is not property-driven) for a class of benchmarks that prove data race freedom of GPU programs and another class that synthesizes invariants for proving separation logic properties for heap manipulating programs.

Keywords: Invariant synthesis · Machine learning · Horn-ICE learning · Conjunctive formulas

1 Introduction

The deductive verification approach for proving imperative programs correct is one of the most well-established and effective methods, and automating program verification using this method has been studied extensively. This approach can be seen as consisting of two parts: (a) writing inductive invariants in terms of loop invariants, class invariants, and method contracts, and (b) proving that these annotations are indeed correct using theorem proving. Automation of the latter has seen tremendous progress in the last two decades through the identification of decidable logical theories, theory combinations, heuristics for automatically reasoning with quantified theories, and their realization using efficient SMT solvers [5,34]. There has also been significant progress on automating the former problem of discovering inductive invariants [3,7,8,12–20,23,24,27,32,40–43,48], with varying degrees of success.

In this paper, we are interested in a class of or *learning-based* techniques for invariant generation [8,16,20,48]. In this context, the invariant synthesis engine is split into two components, a learner and a teacher, who work in rounds. In each round, the teacher examines the invariant produced by the learner and produces counterexamples that consist of concrete program configurations that

B.-Y. E. Chang (Ed.): SAS 2019, LNCS 11822, pp. 323–346, 2019.
https://doi.org/10.1007/978-3-030-32304-2_16

show why the proposed formulas are not inductive invariants. The learner then uses these concrete program configurations to synthesize new proposals for the invariant, *without* looking at the program. The teacher, on the other hand, does look at the program and produces counterexamples based on failed verification attempts.

The choice to separate the learner and teacher—and not give the learner access to the program—may seem strange at first. However, a rationale for this choice has emerged over the years, and the above choice is in fact the de facto approach for synthesis in various other domains, including program synthesis, where it is usually called counter-example guided inductive synthesis [1,44,45].

Horn-ICE Learning. In a paper at CAV 2014, Garg et al. [20] studied the above learning model and identified the precise form of counterexamples needed for synthesizing invariants. Contrary to usual classification learning where one is given positive and negative examples only, the authors argued that implication counterexamples (ICE) are needed, and coined the term *ICE learning* for such a learning model. More recently, it has been recognized that program verification problems can be cast as solving *Horn implication constraints* [22]. Consequently, the implication counterexamples returned by the teacher are naturally Horn implications (*Horn-ICE*), involving concrete program configurations. New algorithms for learning from such Horn counterexamples have recently been studied [8,16].

Learning Conjunctions Over a Fixed Set of Predicates. While one can potentially learn/synthesize invariants in complex logics, one technique that has been particularly effective and scalable is to fix a finite set of predicates $\mathcal{P}$ over the program configurations and only learn inductive invariants that can be expressed as a conjunction of predicates over $\mathcal{P}$. For particular domains of programs and types of specifications, it is possible to identify classes of candidate predicates that are typically involved in invariants (e.g., based on the code of the programs and/or the specification), and learning invariants over such a class of predicates has proven very effective. A prominent example is device drivers, and Microsoft's Static Driver Verifier [28,33] (specifically the underlying tool CORRAL [29]) is an industry-strength tool that leverages exactly this approach.

In this paper, we are mainly motivated by two other domains where learning conjunctive invariants is very effective. The first is the class of programs handled by GPUVerify [6,9], which considers GPU programs, reduces the problem to a sequential verification problem (by simulating two threads at each parallel fork), and proceeds to find conjunctive invariants over a fixed set $\mathcal{P}$ of predicates to prove the resulting sequential program correct. The second class is the class of programs considered by Neider et al. [35], where the authors synthesize invariants in order to prove the correctness of programs that dynamically update heaps against specifications in separation logic. The verification engine in the former is an SMT solver that returns concrete Horn-ICE counterexamples. In the latter, predicates involve *inductively defined relations* (such as a list-segment, the

Table 1. Comparison of HOUDINI [18] and SORCAR

Learning algorithm	**Property driven?**	**Complexity per round**	**Maximum # rounds**	**Final conjunct**
HOUDINI	No	Polynomial	$\|\mathcal{P}\|$	Largest set
SORCAR	Yes	Polynomial	$2 \cdot \|\mathcal{P}\|$	Bias towards weaker invariants (smaller sets of conjunctions) involving only relevant predicates

heaplet associated with it, or the set of keys stored in it), and validating verification conditions is undecidable in general. Hence, the verification engine is a sound but incomplete verification engine (based on "natural proofs") that returns abstract counterexamples that can be interpreted to be Horn-ICE counterexamples. In both domains, the set $\mathcal{P}$ consists of hundreds of candidate predicates, which makes invariant synthesis challenging (as there are $2^{|\mathcal{P}|}$ possible conjunctive invariants).

HOUDINI and SORCAR. The classical algorithm for learning conjunctive invariants over a finite class of predicates is the HOUDINI algorithm [18], which mimics the *elimination algorithm* for learning conjuncts in classical machine learning [26]. HOUDINI starts with a conjectured invariant that contains *all* predicates in $\mathcal{P}$ and, in each round, uses information from a failed verification attempt to remove predicates. The most salient aspect of the algorithm is that it is guaranteed to converge to a conjunctive invariant, if one exists, in $n = |\mathcal{P}|$ rounds (which is logarithmic in the number of invariants, as there are 2^n of them). However, the HOUDINI algorithm has disadvantages as well. Most notably, it is not property-driven as it does not consider the assertions that occur in the program (which is a consequence of the fact that it was originally designed to infer invariants of unannotated programs). In fact, one can view the HOUDINI algorithm as a way of computing the least fixed point in the abstract interpretation framework, where the abstract domain consists of conjunctions over the candidate predicates.

In this paper, we develop a new class of learning algorithms for conjunctions, named SORCAR[1], *that is property-driven.*

The primary motivation to build a property-driven learning algorithm is to explore invariant generation techniques that can be potentially more efficient in proving programs correct. The SORCAR algorithm presented in this paper has the following design features (also see Table 1). First, it is property-driven—in other words, the algorithm tries to find conjunctive inductive invariants that are sufficient to prove the assertions in the program. By contrast, HOUDINI computes the *tightest* inductive invariant. Since SORCAR is property-driven, it can find weaker inductive invariants (i.e., invariants with fewer conjuncts). Our intuition is that by synthesizing weaker, property-driven invariants, we can verify programs more efficiently.

[1] Houdini and Sorcar were both magicians!

Second, SORCAR guarantees that the number of rounds of interaction with the teacher is still linear ($2n$ rounds compared to HOUDINI's promise of n rounds). Third, SORCAR promises to do only polynomial amount of work in each round (i.e., polynomial in n and in the number of current counterexamples), similar to HOUDINI.

The SORCAR algorithm works, intuitively, by finding conjunctive invariants over a set of *relevant predicates* $R \subseteq \mathcal{P}$. This set is grown slowly (but monotonically, as monotonic growth is crucial to ensure that the number of rounds of learning is linear) by adding predicates only when they were found to be relevant to prove assertions. More specifically, predicates are considered relevant based on information gained from counterexamples of failed verification conditions that involve assertions in the program. The precise mechanism of growing the set of relevant predicates can vary, and we define four variants of SORCAR (e.g., choosing all predicates that show promise of relevance or greedily choosing a minimal number of relevant predicates). The SORCAR suite of algorithms is hence a new class of property-driven learning algorithms for conjunctive invariants with different design principles.

Experimental Evaluation. We have implemented SORCAR as a Horn-ICE learning algorithm on top of the BOOGIE program verifier [4] and have applied it to verify both GPU programs for data races [6,9] and heap manipulating programs against separation logic specifications [35]. To assess the performance of SORCAR, we have compared it to the current state-of-the-art tools for these programs, which use the HOUDINI algorithm. Though SORCAR did not work more efficiently on every program, our empirical evaluation shows that it is overall more competitive than HOUDINI. In summary, we found that (a) SORCAR worked more efficiently overall in verifying these programs, and (b) SORCAR verified a larger number of programs than HOUDINI did (for a suitably large timeout).

Related Work

Invariant synthesis lies at the heart of automated program verification. Over the years, various techniques have been proposed, including abstract interpretation [13], interpolation [32], IC3 [7], predicate abstraction [3], abductive inference [14], as well as synthesis algorithms that rely on constraint solving [12,17,23,24]. Complementing these techniques are data-driven approaches that are based on machine learning. Examples include DAIKON [15] and HOUDINI [18], the ICE learning framework [20] and its successor Horn-ICE learning [8,16], as well as numerous other techniques that employ machine learning to synthesize inductive invariants [19,27,40–43,48].

One potentially interesting question is whether ICE/Horn-ICE algorithms (and in particular, HOUDINI and SORCAR) are qualitatively related to algorithms such as IC3 for synthesizing invariants. For programs with Boolean domains, Vizel et al. [47] study this question and find that the algorithms are quite different. In fact, the authors propose a new framework that generalizes both. In the setting of this paper, however, there are too many differences to reconcile with: (a) IC3 finds invariants by bounded symbolic exploration, forward from initial configurations and backward from bad configurations (hence inherently unfolding loops), while ICE/Horn-ICE algorithms do not do that, (b) ICE/Horn-ICE algorithms instead use implication/Horn counterexamples, which can relate configurations arbitrarily far away from initial or bad configurations, and there seems to be no analog to this in IC3, (c) it is not clear how to restrict IC3 to finding invariants in a particular hypothesis class, such as conjunctions over a particular set of predicates, (d) IC3 works very closely with a SAT solver, whereas ICE/Horn-ICE algorithms are essentially independent, communicating with the SAT/SMT engine only indirectly, and (e) we are not aware of any guarantees that IC3 can give in terms of the number of rounds/conjectures, whereas the ICE/Horn-ICE algorithms HOUDINI and SORCAR give guarantees that are linear in the number of predicates. We believe that the algorithms are in fact very different, though more general algorithms that unify them would be interesting to study.

Learning of conjunctive formulas has a long history. An early example is the so-called elimination algorithm [26], which operates in the Probably Approximately Correct Learning model (PAC). DAIKON [15] was the first technique to apply the elimination algorithm in a software setting, learning likely invariants from dynamic traces. Later, the popular HOUDINI [18] algorithm built on top of the elimination algorithm to compute inductive invariants in a fully automated manner. In fact, as Garg et al. [21] and later Ezudheen et al. [16] argued, HOUDINI can be seen as a learning algorithm for conjunctive formulas in both the ICE and the Horn-ICE learning framework.

Using HOUDINI to compute conjunctive invariants over a finite set of candidate predicates is extremely scalable and has been used with great success in several practical settings. For example, CORRAL [29], which uses HOUDINI internally, has replaced SLAM [2] and YOGI [36], and is currently shipped as part of Microsoft's industrial-strength Static Driver Verifier (SDV) [28,33]. GPUVerify [6,9] is another example that uses HOUDINI with great success to prove race freedom of GPU programs.

2 Background

In this section, we provide the background on learning-based invariant synthesis. In particular, we briefly recapitulate the Horn-ICE learning framework (in Sect. 2.1) and discuss the HOUDINI algorithm (in Sect. 2.2), specifically in the context of the Horn-ICE framework.

To make the Horn-ICE framework mathematically precise, let P be the program (with assertions) under consideration and $\mathcal{C}$ the set of all program configurations of P. Furthermore, let us fix a finite set $\mathcal{P}$ of *predicates* $p\colon \mathcal{C} \to \mathbb{B}$ over the program configurations, where $\mathbb{B} = \{\mathit{true}, \mathit{false}\}$ is the set of Boolean values. These predicates capture interesting properties of the program and serve as the basic building blocks for constructing invariants. We assume that the values of these predicates can either be obtained directly from the program configurations or that the program is instrumented with ghost variables that track the values of the predicates at important places in the program (e.g., at the loop header and immediately after the loop). As notational convention, we write $c \models p$ if $p(c) = \mathit{true}$ and $c \not\models p$ if $p(c) = \mathit{false}$. Moreover, we lift this notation to formulas φ over $\mathcal{P}$ (i.e., arbitrary Boolean combinations of predicates from $\mathcal{P}$) and use $c \models \varphi$ ($c \not\models \varphi$) to denote that c satisfies φ (c does not satisfy φ).

To simplify the presentation in the remainder of this paper, we use conjunctions $p_1 \wedge \cdots \wedge p_n$ of predicates over $\mathcal{P}$ and the corresponding sets $\{p_1, \ldots, p_n\} \subseteq \mathcal{P}$ interchangeably. In particular, for a (sub-)set $X = \{p_1, \ldots, p_n\} \subseteq \mathcal{P}$ of predicates and a program configuration $c \in \mathcal{C}$, we write $c \models X$ if and only if $c \models p_1 \wedge \cdots \wedge p_n$.

2.1 The Horn-ICE Learning Framework

The Horn-ICE learning framework [8,16] is a general framework for learning inductive invariants in a black-box setting. We here assume without loss of generality that the task is to synthesize a single invariant. In the case of learning multiple invariants, say at different program locations, one can easily expand the given predicates to predicates of the form $(pc = l) \rightarrow p$ where pc refers to the program counter, l is the location of an invariant in the program, and $p \in \mathcal{P}$. Learning a conjunctive invariant over this extended set of predicates then corresponds to learning multiple conjunctive invariants at the various locations.

As sketched in Fig. 1, the Horn-ICE framework consists of two distinct entities—the *learner* and the *teacher*—and proceeds in rounds. In each round, the teacher receives a candidate invariant φ from the learner and checks whether φ proves the program correct. Should φ not be adequate to prove the program correct, the learner replies with a counterexample, which serves as a means to correct inadequate invariants and guide the learner towards a correct one. More precisely, a counterexample takes one of three forms:[2]

- If the pre-condition α of the program does not imply φ, then the teacher returns a *positive counterexample* $c \in \mathcal{C}$ such that $c \models \alpha$ but $c \not\models \varphi$.
- If φ does not imply the post-condition β of the program, then the teacher returns a *negative counterexample* $c \in \mathcal{C}$ such that $c \models \varphi$ but $c \not\models \beta$.
- If φ is not inductive, then the teacher returns a *Horn counterexample* $(\{c_1, \ldots, c_n\}, c) \in 2^{\mathcal{C}} \times \mathcal{C}$ such that $c_i \models \varphi$ for each $i \in \{1, \ldots, n\}$ but $c \not\models \varphi$. (We encourage the reader to think of Horn counterexamples as constraints of the form $(c_1 \wedge \cdots \wedge c_n) \rightarrow c$.)

A teacher who returns counterexamples as described above always enables the learner to make *progress* in the sense that every counterexample it returns is inconsistent with the current conjecture (i.e., it violates the current conjecture). Moreover, the Horn-ICE framework requires the teacher to be *honest*, meaning that each counterexample needs to be consistent with *all* inductive

[2] By abuse of notation, we write $c \models \alpha$ ($c \not\models \alpha$) to denote that c satisfies (violates) the formula α even if α contains predicates that do not belong to $\mathcal{P}$.

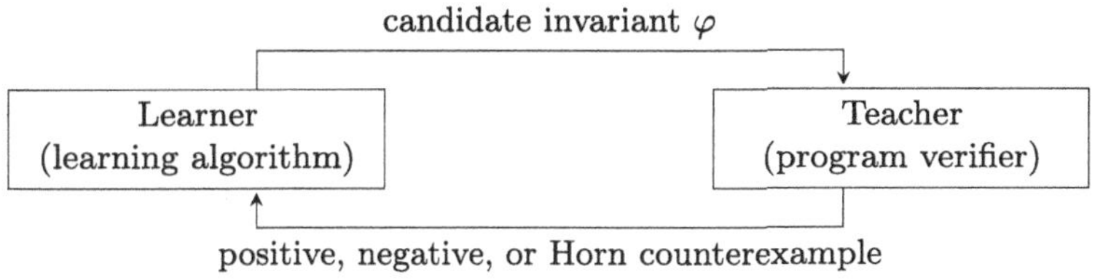

Fig. 1. The Horn-ICE learning framework [8,16]

invariants that prove the program correct (i.e., the teacher does not rule out possible solutions). Finally, note that such a teacher can indeed be built since program verification can be stated by means of *constrained Horn clauses* [22]. When the candidate invariant does not make such clauses true, some Horn clause failed, and the teacher can find a Horn counterexample using a logic solver (positive counterexamples arise when the left-hand-side of the Horn counterexample is empty, while negative counterexamples arise when the left-hand-side has one element and the-right-hand side is *false*).

The objective of the learner, on the other hand, is to construct a formula φ over $\mathcal{P}$ from the counterexamples received thus far. For the sake of simplicity, we assume that the learner collects all counterexamples in a data structure $\mathcal{S} = (S_+, S_-, S_H)$, called *Horn-ICE sample*, where

1. $S_+ \subseteq \mathcal{C}$ is a finite set of positive counterexamples;
2. $S_- \subseteq \mathcal{C}$ is a finite set of negative counterexamples; and
3. $S_H \subseteq 2^{\mathcal{C}} \times \mathcal{C}$ is a finite set of Horn counterexamples.

To measure the complexity of a sample, we define its *size*, denoted by $|\mathcal{S}|$, to be $|S_+| + |S_-| + \sum_{(L,c) \in S_H} (|L| + 1)$.

Given a Horn-ICE sample $\mathcal{S} = (S_+, S_-, S_H)$, the learner's task is then to construct a formula φ over $\mathcal{P}$ that is *consistent* with $\mathcal{S}$ in that

1. $c \models \varphi$ for each $c \in S_+$;
2. $c \not\models \varphi$ for each $c \in S_-$; and
3. for each $(\{c_1, \ldots, c_n\}, c) \in S_H$, if $c_i \models \varphi$ for all $i \in \{1, \ldots, n\}$, then $c \models \varphi$.

This task is called *passive Horn-ICE learning*, while the overall learning setup can be though of as *iterative (or online) Horn-ICE learning*. In the special case that the learner produces conjunctive formulas, we say that a set $X \subseteq \mathcal{P}$ is consistent with $\mathcal{S}$ if and only if the corresponding conjunction $\bigwedge_{p \in X} p$ is consistent with $\mathcal{S}$.

In general, the Horn-ICE learning framework permits arbitrary formulas over the predicates as candidate invariants. In this paper, however, we exclusively focus on conjunctive formulas (i.e., conjunctions of predicates from $\mathcal{P}$). In fact, conjunctive invariants form an important subclass in practice as they are sufficient to prove many programs correct [18,35] (also see our experimental evaluation in Sect. 4). Moreover, one can design efficient learning algorithms for conjunctive Boolean formulas, as we show next.

2.2 HOUDINI as a Horn-ICE Learning Algorithm

HOUDINI [18] is a popular algorithm to synthesize conjunctive invariants in interaction with a theorem prover. For our purposes, however, it is helpful to think of HOUDINI as an adaptation of the classical elimination algorithm [26] to the Horn-ICE learning framework that is modified to account for Horn counterexamples. To avoid confusion, we refer to algorithmic component that the HOUDINI learning algorithm as the *"elimination algorithm"* and the implementation of the elimination algorithm as a learner in the context of the Horn-ICE framework as HOUDINI-ICE.

Let us now describe the elimination algorithm as it is used in the design of SORCAR as well. Given a Horn-ICE sample $\mathcal{S} = (S_+, S_-, S_H)$, the elimination algorithm computes the largest conjunctive formula $X \subseteq \mathcal{P}$ in terms of the number of predicates in X (i.e., the semantically smallest set of program configurations expressible by a conjunctive formula) that is consistent with $\mathcal{S}$. Starting with the set $X = \mathcal{P}$ of all predicates, the elimination algorithm proceeds as follows:

1. The elimination algorithm removes all predicates $p \in X$ from X that violate a positive counterexample (i.e., there exists a positive counterexample $c \in S_+$ such that $c \not\models p$). The result is the unique largest set X of predicates—alternatively the largest conjunctive formula—that is consistent with S_+ (i.e., $c \models X$ for all $c \in S_+$).
2. The elimination algorithm checks whether all Horn counterexamples are satisfied. If a Horn counterexample $(\{c_1, \ldots, c_n\}, c) \in S_H$ is not satisfied, it means that each program configuration c_i of the left-hand-side satisfies X, but the configuration c on the right-hand-side does not. However, X corresponds to the semantically smallest set of program configurations expressible by a conjunctive formula that is consistent with S_+. Moreover, all program configurations c_i on the left-hand-side of the Horn counterexample also satisfy X. Thus, the right-hand-side c necessarily has to satisfy X as well (otherwise X would not satisfy the Horn counterexample). To account for this, the elimination algorithm adds c as a new positive counterexample to S_+.
3. The elimination algorithm repeats Steps 1 and 2 until a fixed point is reached. Once this happens, X is the unique largest set of predicates that is consistent with S_+ and S_H.

Finally, the elimination algorithm checks whether each negative counterexample violates X (i.e., $c \not\models X$ for each $c \in S_-$). If this is the case, X is the largest set of predicates that is consistent with $\mathcal{S}$; otherwise, no consistent conjunctive formula exists. Note that the elimination algorithm does not learn from negative counterexamples.

It is not hard to verify that the time the elimination algorithm spends in each round is *polynomial* in the number of predicates and the size of the Horn-ICE sample (provided predicates can be evaluated in constant time). If the elimination algorithm is employed in the iterative Horn-ICE setting (as HOUDINI-ICE), it is guaranteed to converge in at most $|\mathcal{P}|$ rounds, or it reports that no conjunctive invariant over $\mathcal{P}$ exists.

The property that HOUDINI-ICE converges in at most $|\mathcal{P}|$ rounds is of great importance in practice. One can, for instance, in every round learn the *smallest* set of conjuncts satisfying the sample, say using a SAT solver. Doing so would not significantly increase the time taken for learning in each round (thanks to highly-optimized SAT solvers), but the worst-case number of iterations to converge to an invariant becomes exponential. An exponential number of rounds, however, makes learning invariants often intractable in practice (we implemented such a SAT-based learner, but it performed poorly on our set of benchmarks). Hence, it is important to keep the number of iterations small when learning invariants. Note that HOUDINI-ICE does not use *negative examples* to learn formulas and, hence, is *not property-driven* (negative examples come from configurations that lead to violating assertions). The SORCAR algorithm, which we describe in the next section, has this feature and aims for potentially weaker invariants that are sufficient to prove the assertions in the program. Note, however, that HOUDINI-ICE is complete in the sense that it is guaranteed to find an inductive invariant that proves the program correct against its assertions, if one exists that can be expressed as a conjunction over the given predicates.

3 The SORCAR Horn-ICE Learning Algorithm

One disadvantage of HOUDINI-ICE is that it learns in each round the largest set of conjuncts, *independent* of negative counterexamples, and, hence, independent of the assertions and specifications in the program—in fact, it learns the semantically smallest inductive invariant expressible as a set of conjuncts over $\mathcal{P}$. As a consequence, HOUDINI-ICE may spend a lot of time finding the tightest invariant (involving many predicates) although a simpler and weaker invariant suffices to prove the program correct. This motivates the development of our novel SORCAR Horn-ICE learning algorithm for conjuncts, which is property-driven (i.e., it also considers the assertions in the program) and has a bias towards learning conjunctions with a smaller number of predicates.

The salient feature of SORCAR is that it always learns invariants involving what we call *relevant* predicates, which are predicates that have shown some evidence to affect the assertions in the program. More precisely, we say that a predicate is *relevant* if it evaluates to *false* on some negative counterexample or on a program configuration appearing on the left-hand-side of a Horn counterexample. This indicates that *not* assuming this predicate leads to an assertion violation or the invariant not being inductive, and is hence deemed important as a candidate predicate in the synthesized invariant. However, naively choosing relevant predicates does, in general, lead to an exponential number of rounds. Thus, SORCAR is designed to select relevant predicates carefully and requires at most $2|\mathcal{P}|$ rounds to converge to an invariant (which is twice the number that HOUDINI-ICE guarantees). Moreover, the set of predicates learned by SORCAR is always a subset of those learned by HOUDINI-ICE.

Algorithm 1. The SORCAR Horn-ICE learning algorithm

1 **Function** `Relevant-Predicates` *(N, H, X, R)*:
2   **return** *a set of* $R' \subseteq \mathcal{P}$ *of relevant predicates such that* $R' \setminus R \neq \emptyset$;
3 **end**

4 **Procedure** `Sorcar-Passive` $\mathcal{S} = (S_+, S_-, S_H)$, R:
5   Run the elimination algorithm to compute the set $X = \{p_1, \ldots, p_n\}$, corresponding to the largest conjunctive formula $\bigwedge_{i=1}^{n} p_i$ over $\mathcal{P}$ that is consistent with $\mathcal{S}$ (**abort** if no such formula exists);
6   **while** $X \cap R$ *is not consistent with* $\mathcal{S}$ **do**
7         $N \leftarrow \emptyset$;   // Stores inconsistent negative counterexamples
8         $H \leftarrow \emptyset$;   // Stores inconsistent Horn counterexamples
9   **foreach** *negative counterexample* $c \in S_-$ *not consistent with* $X \cap R$ **do**
10             $N \leftarrow N \cup \{c\}$;
11   **end**
12   **foreach** *Horn counterexample* $(L, c) \in S_H$ *not consistent with* $X \cap R$ **do**
13             $H \leftarrow H \cup \{(L, c)\}$;
14   **end**
15         $R \leftarrow R \cup$ `Relevant-Predicates` (N, H, X, R);
16   **end**
17   **return** $(X \cap R, R)$;
18 **end**

19 **static** $R \leftarrow \emptyset$;   // Stores relevant predicates across rounds
20 **Procedure** `Sorcar-Iterative`$\mathcal{S}$:
21     $(Y, R) \leftarrow$ `Sorcar-Passive`$\mathcal{S}, R$;
22   **return** Y;
23 **end**

Algorithm 1 presents the SORCAR Horn-ICE learner in pseudo code. In contrast to HOUDINI-ICE, it is not a purely passive learning algorithm but is divided into a passive part (`Sorcar-Passive`) and an iterative part (`Sorcar-Iterative`), the latter being invoked in every round of the Horn-ICE framework. More precisely, `Sorcar-Iterative` maintains a state in form of a set $R \subseteq \mathcal{P}$ in the course of the iterative learning, which is empty in the beginning and used to accumulate *relevant predicates* (Line 19). The exact choice of relevant predicates, however, is delegated to an external function `Relevant-Predicates`. We treat this function as a parameter for the SORCAR algorithm and discuss four possible implementations at the end of this section. Let us now present SORCAR in detail.

3.1 The Passive SORCAR Algorithm

Given a Horn-ICE sample $\mathcal{S}$ and a set $R \subseteq \mathcal{P}$, `Sorcar-Passive` first constructs the largest conjunction $X \subseteq \mathcal{P}$ that is consistent with $\mathcal{S}$ (Line 5). This construction follows the elimination algorithm described in Sect. 2.2 and ensures that X is consistent with all counterexamples in $\mathcal{S}$. Since X is the largest set of predicates consistent with $\mathcal{S}$, it represents the smallest consistent set of program configurations expressible as a conjunction over $\mathcal{P}$. As a consequence, it follows that $X \cap R$—in fact, any subset of X—is consistent with S_+. However, $X \cap R$ might not be consistent with S_- or S_H. To fix this problem, `Sorcar-Passive` collects all inconsistent negative counterexamples in a set N and all inconsistent Horn counterexamples in a set H (Lines 7 to 14). Based on these two sets, `Sorcar-Passive` then computes a set of relevant predicates, which it adds to R (Line 15). As mentioned above, the exact computation of relevant predicates is delegated to a function `Relevant-Predicates`, which we treat as a parameter. The result of this function is a set $R' \subseteq \mathcal{P}$ of predicates that needs to contain at least one new predicate that is not yet present in R. Once such a set has been computed and added to R, the process repeats (R grows monotonically larger) until a consistent conjunctive formula is found. Then, `Sorcar-Passive` returns both the conjunction $X \cap R$ as well as the new set R of relevant predicates. Note that the resulting conjunction is always a subset of the relevant predicates.

The condition of the loop in Line 6 immediately shows that the set $X \cap R$ is consistent with the Horn-ICE sample $\mathcal{S}$ once `Sorcar-Passive` terminates. The termination argument, however, is less obvious. To argue termination, we first observe that X is consistent with each positive counterexample in S_+ and, hence, $X \cap R$ remains consistent with all positive counterexamples during the run of `Sorcar-Passive`. Next, we observe that the termination argument is independent of the exact choice of predicates added to R—in fact, the predicates need not even be relevant in order to prove termination of `Sorcar-Passive`. More precisely, since the function `Relevant-Predicates` is required to return a set $R' \subseteq \mathcal{P}$ that contains at least one new (relevant) predicate not currently present in R, we know that R grows strictly monotonically. In the worst case, the loop in Lines 6 to 16 repeats $|\mathcal{P}|$ times until $R = \mathcal{P}$; then, $X \cap R = X$, which is guaranteed to be consistent with $\mathcal{S}$ by construction of X (see Line 5). Depending on the implementation of `Relevant-Predicates`, however, `Sorcar-Passive` can terminate earlier with a much smaller consistent set $X \cap R \subsetneq X$. Since the time spent in each iteration of the loop in Lines 6 to 16 is proportional to $|\mathcal{P}| \cdot |\mathcal{S}| + f(|\mathcal{S}|)$, where f is a function capturing the complexity of `Relevant-Predicates`, the overall runtime of `Sorcar-Passive` is in $\mathcal{O}\big(|\mathcal{P}|^2 \cdot |\mathcal{S}| + |\mathcal{P}| \cdot f(|\mathcal{S}|)\big)$. This is summarized in the following theorem.

Theorem 1 (Passive SORCAR algorithm). *Given a Horn-ICE sample $\mathcal{S}$ and a set $R \subseteq \mathcal{P}$ of relevant predicates, the passive* SORCAR *algorithm learns a consistent set of predicates (i.e., a consistent conjunction over $\mathcal{P}$) in time $\mathcal{O}\big(|\mathcal{P}|^2 \cdot |\mathcal{S}| + |\mathcal{P}| \cdot f(|\mathcal{S}|)\big)$ where f is a function capturing the complexity of the function* `Relevant-Predicates`.

Before we continue, let us briefly mention that the set of predicates returned by SORCAR is always a subset of those returned by HOUDINI-ICE.

3.2 The Iterative SORCAR Algorithm

`Sorcar-Iterative` maintains a state in form of a set $R \subseteq \mathcal{P}$ of relevant predicates in the course of the learning process (Line 19). In each round of the Horn-ICE learning framework, the learner invokes `Sorcar-Iterative` with the current Horn-ICE sample $\mathcal{S}$ as input, which contains all counterexamples that the learner has received thus far. Internally, `Sorcar-Iterative` calls `Sorcar-Passive`, updates the set R, and returns a new conjunctive formula, which the learner then proposes as new candidate invariant to the teacher. If `Sorcar-Passive` aborts (because no conjunctive formula over $\mathcal{P}$ that is consistent with $\mathcal{S}$ exists), so does `Sorcar-Iterative`.

To ease the presentation in the remainder of this section, let us assume that the program under consideration can be proven correct using an inductive invariant expressible as a conjunction over $\mathcal{P}$. Under this assumption, the iterative SORCAR algorithm identifies such an inductive invariant in at most $2|\mathcal{P}|$ rounds, as stated in the following theorem.

Theorem 2 (Iterative SORCAR algorithm). *Let P be a program and $\mathcal{P}$ a finite set of predicates over the configurations of P. When paired with an honest teacher that enables progress, the iterative* SORCAR *algorithm learns an inductive invariant (in the form of a conjunctive formula over $\mathcal{P}$) that proves the program correct in at most $2|\mathcal{P}|$ rounds, provided that such an invariant exists.*

Proof (of Theorem 2). We first observe that the computation of the set X in Line 5 of `Sorcar-Passive` always succeeds. This is a direct consequence of the honesty of the teacher (see Sect. 2.1) and the assumption that at least one inductive invariant exists that is expressible as a conjunction over $\mathcal{P}$. This observation is essential as it shows that `Sorcar-Iterative` does not abort.

Next, recall that the teacher enables progress in the sense that every counterexample is inconsistent with the current conjecture (see Sect. 2.1). We use this property to argue that the number of iterations of `Sorcar-Iterative` has an upper bound of at most $2|\mathcal{P}|$, which can be verified by carefully examining the updates of X and R as counterexamples are added to the Horn-ICE sample $\mathcal{S}$:

- If a positive counterexample c is added to $\mathcal{S}$, then it is added because $c \not\models X \cap R$ (as the teacher enforces progress). This implies $c \not\models X$, which in turn means that there exists a predicate $p \in X$ with $c \not\models p$. In the subsequent round of the passive SORCAR algorithm, p is no longer present in X (see Line 5) and $|X|$ decreases by at least one as a result.
- If a negative counterexample c is added to $\mathcal{S}$, then it is added because $c \models X \cap R$ (as the teacher enforces progress). This means that the set X remains unchanged in the next iteration but at least one relevant predicate is added to R in order to account for the new negative counterexample (Line 15). This increases $|R|$ by at least one.
- If a Horn counterexample $(\{c_1, \dots, c_n\}, c)$ is added to $\mathcal{S}$, then it is added because $c_i \models X \cap R$ for each $i \in \{1, \dots, n\}$ but $c \not\models X \cap R$ (as the teacher enforces progress). In this situation, two distinct cases can arise:

1. If $(\{c_1, \dots, c_n\}, c)$ is not consistent with X (i.e., $c_i \models X$ for each $i \in \{1, \dots, n\}$ but $c \not\models X$), the computation in Line 5 identifies and removes a predicate $p \in X$ with $c \not\models X$ in order to make X consistent with $\mathcal{S}$. This means that $|X|$ decreases by at least one.
2. If $(\{c_1, \dots, c_n\}, c)$ is consistent with X but not with $X \cap R$, then X remains unchanged. However, at least one new relevant predicate is added to R in order to account for the new Horn counterexample (Line 15). This means that $|R|$ increases by at least one.

Thus, either $|X|$ decreases or $|R|$ increases by at least one.

In the worst case, `Sorcar-Iterative` arrives at a state with $X = \emptyset$ and $R = \mathcal{P}$ (if it does not find an inductive invariant earlier). Since the algorithm starts with $X = \mathcal{P}$ and $R = \emptyset$, this worst-case situation occurs after at most $2|\mathcal{P}|$ iterations.

Let us now assume that `Sorcar-Iterative` indeed arrives at a state with $X = \emptyset$ and $R = \mathcal{P}$. Then, we claim that the result of `Sorcar-Iterative`, namely $X \cap R = \emptyset$, is an inductive invariant. To prove this claim, first recall that Theorem 1 shows that `Sorcar-Passive` always learns a set of predicates that is consistent with the given Horn-ICE sample $\mathcal{S}$. In particular, Line 5 of `Sorcar-Passive` computes the (unique) largest set $X \subseteq \mathcal{P}$ that is consistent with $\mathcal{S}$. Second, we know that every inductive invariant $X^\star$ is consistent with $\mathcal{S}$ because the teacher is honest. Thus, we obtain $X^\star \subseteq X = \emptyset$ and, hence, $X^\star = X$ because both X and $X^\star$ are consistent with $\mathcal{S}$ and X is the largest consistent set. This means that X is an inductive invariant because $X^\star$ is one.

Note, however, that `Sorcar-Iterative` might terminate earlier, in which case the current conjecture is an inductive invariant by definition of the Horn-ICE framework. In summary, we have shown that `Sorcar-Iterative` terminates in at most $2|\mathcal{P}|$ iterations with an inductive invariant (if one is expressible as an conjunctive formula over $\mathcal{P}$). □

Finally, let us note that `Sorcar-Iterative` can also detect if no inductive invariant exists that is expressible as a conjunction over $\mathcal{P}$. In this case, the computation of X in Line 5 of `Sorcar-Passive` fails and the algorithm aborts.

3.3 Computing Relevant Predicates

In the following, we develop *four* different implementations of the function `Relevant-Predicates`. All of these functions share the property that the search for relevant predicates is limited to the set $X \setminus R$ because only predicates in this set can help making $X \cap R$ consistent with negative and Horn counterexamples (cf. Line 6 of Algorithm 1). Moreover, recall that we define a predicate to be relevant if it evaluates to *false* on some negative counterexample or on a program configuration appearing on the left-hand-side of a Horn counterexample. Intuitively, these are predicates in $\mathcal{P}$ that have shown some relevancy in the sense that they can be used to establish consistency with the Horn-ICE sample.

`Relevant-Predicates-Max`. The function `Relevant-Predicates-Max`, shown as Algorithm 2, computes the maximal set of relevant predicates from $X \setminus R$

Algorithm 2. Computing the maximal set of relevant predicates

Function `Relevant-Predicates-Max` *(N, H, X, R)*:
  $R' \leftarrow \emptyset$;
  foreach *negative counterexample* $c \in N$ **do**
    $R' \leftarrow R' \cup \{p \in X \setminus R \mid c \not\models p\}$;
  end
  foreach *Horn counterexample* $(\{c_1, \ldots, c_n\}, c) \in H$ **do**
    $R' \leftarrow R' \cup \bigcup_{i=1}^{n} \{p \in X \setminus R \mid c_i \not\models p\}$;
  end
  return R';
end

with respect to the negative counterexamples in N and the Horn counterexamples in H. To this end, it accumulates all predicates that evaluate to *false* on a negative counterexample in N or on a program configuration appearing on the left-hand-side of a Horn counterexample in H. The resulting set R' can be large, but $X \cap R'$ is guaranteed to be consistent with N and H (because each negative counterexample and each program configuration on the left-hand-side of a Horn counterexample violates at least one predicates in R', the latter causing each Horn counterexample to be violated). Since $X \cap R$ was neither consistent with N nor with H, and since $R' \subseteq X \setminus R$, it follows that R' must contain at least one relevant predicate not in R, thus satisfying the requirement of `Relevant-Predicates`. Finally, the runtime of `Relevant-Predicates-Max` is in $\mathcal{O}(|\mathcal{P}| \cdot |\mathcal{S}|)$ since $X \setminus R \subseteq \mathcal{P}$, $N \subseteq S_-$, and $H \subseteq S_H$.

`Relevant-Predicates-First`. The function `Relevant-Predicates-First` is shown as Algorithm 3. Its goal is to select a smaller set of relevant predicates than `Relevant-Predicates-Max`, while giving the user some control over which predicates to choose. More precisely, `Relevant-Predicates-First` selects for each negative counterexample and each Horn counterexample only one relevant predicate $p \in X \setminus R$. The exact choice is determined by a total ordering $<_{\mathcal{P}}$ over the predicates, which reflects a preference among predicates and which we assume to be a priori given by the user. Using the same arguments as for the function `Relevant-Predicates-Max`, it is not hard to verify that the resulting set R' contains at least one additional relevant predicate not in R and that $X \cap R'$ is consistent with N and H. Moreover, R' clearly contains only a subset of the predicates returned by `Relevant-Predicates-Max`. Again, the runtime is in $\mathcal{O}(|\mathcal{P}| \cdot |\mathcal{S}|)$.

`Relevant-Predicates-Min`. The function `Relevant-Predicates-Min`, shown as Algorithm 4, takes the idea of `Relevant-Predicates-First` one step further and computes a (not necessarily unique) *minimum* set of relevant predicates with respect to N and H. It does so by means of a reduction to a well-known optimization problem called *minimum hitting set* [25].[3] For a collection

[3] Note that the corresponding decision problem is NP-complete.

Algorithm 3. Computing relevant predicates based on a preference ordering

Function `Relevant-Predicates-First` *(N, H, X, R)*:
  Define a total order $<_\mathcal{P}$ over $\mathcal{P}$;
  $R' \leftarrow \emptyset$;
  foreach *negative counterexample* $c \in N$ **do**
    $R' \leftarrow R' \cup \{p\}$ where p is the $<_\mathcal{P}$-smallest predicate with $p \in X \setminus R$ and $c \not\models p$;
  end
  foreach *Horn counterexample* $(\{c_1, \ldots, c_n\}, c) \in H$ **do**
    $R' \leftarrow R' \cup \{p\}$ where p is the $<_\mathcal{P}$-smallest predicate from the set $\bigcup_{i=1}^{n} \{p \in X \setminus R \mid c_i \not\models p\}$;
  end
  return R';
end

Algorithm 4. Computing a minimal set of relevant predicates

Function `Relevant-Predicates-Min` *(N, H, X, R)*:
  For each $c \in N$, construct $A_c := \{p \in X \setminus R \mid c \not\models p\}$;
  For each $(L, c) \in H$, construct $A_{(L,c)} := \{p \in X \setminus R \mid \exists c' \in L \colon c' \not\models p\}$;
  Compute a minimal hitting set R' for the instance $Q := \{A_c \mid c \in N\} \cup \{A_{(L,c)} \mid (L, c) \in H\}$ (e.g., using a SAT solver);
  return R';
end

$\{A_1, \ldots, A_\ell\}$ of finite sets, a set B is a *hitting set* if $B \cap A_i \neq \emptyset$ for all $i \in \{1, \ldots, \ell\}$, and the minimum hitting set problem asks to compute a hitting set of minimum cardinality. In the first step of the reduction, the function `Relevant-Predicates-Min` constructs for each negative counterexample $c \in N$ the set A_c of all predicates $p \in X \setminus R$ violating c and for each Horn counterexample $(L, c) \in H$ the set $A_{(L,c)}$ of all predicates $p \in X \setminus R$ violating some program configuration $c' \in L$. In a second step, it uses an exact algorithm (e.g., a SAT solver) to find a minimum hitting set R' for the problem instance $Q := \{A_c \mid c \in N\} \cup \{A_{(L,c)} \mid (L, c) \in H\}$. By construction of the sets A_c and $A_{(L,c)}$, the resulting minimum hitting set R' then is a minimum set of relevant predicates guaranteeing that $X \cap R'$ is consistent with N and H. Moreover, R' contains at least one relevant predicate not in R. However, the downside of approach is that it is not a polynomial time algorithm as the underlying decision problem is NP-complete.

`Relevant-Predicates-Greedy`. The key idea underlying the function `Relevant-Predicates-Greedy`, which is shown as Algorithm 5, is to replace the exact computation of a minimum hitting set with a polynomial-time approximation algorithm. More precisely, `Relevant-Predicates-Greedy` implements a

Algorithm 5. Greedily computing a "small" set of relevant predicates

Function `Relevant-Predicates-Greedy` (N, H, X, R):
 For each $c \in N$, construct $A_c := \{p \in X \setminus R \mid c \not\models p\}$;
 For each $(L, c) \in H$, construct $A_{(L,c)} := \{p \in X \setminus R \mid \exists c' \in L \colon c' \not\models p\}$;
 $R' \leftarrow \emptyset$;
 $Q \leftarrow \{A_c \mid c \in N\} \cup \{A_{(L,c)} \mid (L, c) \in H\}$;
 while $Q \neq \emptyset$ **do**
  Pick $p \in X \setminus (R \cup R')$ such that $|\{A \in Q \mid p \in A\}|$ is maximal;
  $R' \leftarrow R' \cup \{p\}$;
  $Q \leftarrow Q \setminus \{A \in Q \mid p \in A\}$;
 end
 return R';
end

straightforward greedy heuristic that successively chooses predicates $p \in X \setminus R$ that have the largest number of a non-empty intersections with sets in Q. This heuristic is essentially the dual of the well-known greedy algorithm for the minimum set cover problem [10] and guarantees to find a solution that is at most logarithmically larger than the optimal one. Apart from being an approximation of the minimal set, choosing relevant predicates greedily based on the *number* of sets it hits also has a statistical bias (choosing predicates more commonly occurring in the sets). Otherwise, except for a runtime in $\mathcal{O}(|\mathcal{P}| \cdot |\mathcal{S}|^2)$ and an approximation factor of $\log |\mathcal{S}|$, `Relevant-Predicates-Greedy` shares the same properties as the function `Relevant-Predicates-Min`.

4 Experimental Evaluation

To evaluate the performance of SORCAR, we implement a prototype, featuring all four variants of SORCAR (as well as more heuristics, which we do not discuss here).[4] This prototype is built on top of the program verifier BOOGIE [4], which natively supports HOUDINI and provides a so-called "Abstract-Houdini framework" [46] on top of which we have implemented ICE/Horn-ICE algorithms, including SORCAR. Consequently, SORCAR can easily be integrated into existing, BOOGIE-based verification tool chains.

We compared SORCAR with two HOUDINI-based tools: GPUVerify [6,9], a tool for checking data race freedom in GPU kernels, and a tool by Neider et al. [35] for verifying programs that dynamically manipulate heaps against specifications in separation logic. Since separation logic is undecidable in general, the latter tool is designed to work in tandem with a sound-but-incomplete verification engine rather than a complete decision procedure. To the best of our knowledge, both tools are the best ones available for their respective domains.

[4] The sources of SORCAR are publicly available at https://github.com/horn-ice/sorcar.

We have evaluated our implementation on two benchmarks suites: the first suite is shipped with GPUVerify, while the second is included in Neider et al.'s tool. As both of these tools use HOUDINI, all benchmarks were already equipped with a large number of predicates (often several hundred). We describe each benchmark suite in more detail shortly.

The goal of our experimental evaluation was twofold: (a) to determine whether SORCAR can prove programs correct that the HOUDINI-based tools cannot (and vice versa) as well as (b) to assess the performance of SORCAR in comparison to these two tools. Since one of the key design principles of SORCAR is to improve verification by constructing weaker invariant (smaller sets of conjuncts), we also report on the size of the invariants (number of conjuncts) inferred by SORCAR and compare to the other tools.

Benchmarks and Compared Tools. The first benchmark suite originates from GPUVerify [6,9] and was obtained from GPU kernels written in OpenCL and CUDA. GPUVerify processes such programs automatically by means of a complex process, involving sequentialization and compilation to the BOOGIE programming language. After removing all programs that did not have loops or recursion, this benchmark suite contained 287 programs.

GPUVerify proceeds in three stages. The first stage compiles an OpenCL or CUDA program into a BOOGIE program. The second stage uses HOUDINI in a custom version of BOOGIE to infer an inductive invariant; in this phase, the assertions are in fact removed as HOUDINI is anyway agnostic to the property being verified. Finally, the third phase substitutes the synthesized invariants, inserts the assertions back into the BOOGIE program, and verifies it.

The second benchmark suite is taken from Neider et al. [35]. It consists of 62 heap manipulating programs, written in C and are equipped with specifications in DRYAD, a dialect of separation logic that allows expressing second order properties using recursive functions and predicates.

Neider et al.'s tool uses the following verification tool chain. First, an extension of VCC [11], called VCDRYAD [37], compiles the C code into a BOOGIE program by unfolding recursive definitions, modeling heaplets as sets, and applying frame reasoning using a technique called natural proofs [31,37,38]. The tool then poses the verification problem as an invariant synthesis problem over a class of predicates that express complex properties of the heap (such as whether the heaplets of two data structures are disjoint, whether a list is sorted, and so on). Finally, Neider et al.'s tool uses HOUDINI to infer a loop invariant.

Note that the final phase of both tools is to synthesize a conjunctive invariant over a fixed set of predicates using HOUDINI. In our experiments, we have replaced HOUDINI with SORCAR.

Evaluation. All experiments were conducted on an Intel Xeon E7-8857 v2 CPU at 3,6 GHz, running Debian GNU/Linux 9.5. The timeout limit was 1200 s. So as to not clutter the following presentation too much, we only report on the version of SORCAR that performed best: SORCAR-MAX (using

`Relevant-Predicates-Max`). Additionally, we briefly compare SORCAR-MAX to SORCAR-GREEDY, the latter using `Relevant-Predicates-Greedy`.

Figures 2a and 2b compare SORCAR-MAX and GPUVerify on the first benchmark suite consisting of GPU kernels. Figure 2a compares the time taken to verify a program, while Fig. 2b compares the number of predicates in the final invariant (there is only one loop invariant in these programs). As can be seen from the figures, SORCAR-MAX compares highly favorably in efficiency. Specifically, SORCAR-MAX was able to verify 15 programs that GPUVerify could not verify, whereas GPUVerify verified only 2 programs that SORCAR-MAX could not verify. SORCAR-MAX was also able to show 9 programs to not have a conjunctive invariant that GPUVerify could not (GPUVerify was not able to show this for any program that SORCAR-MAX could not). On programs that both tools were able to verify (216 programs in total), SORCAR-MAX took on average 34 s per program (and synthesized invariants with an average number of 12 predicates). GPUVerify, on the other hand, took on average 89 s per program (and synthesized invariants with an average number of 23 predicates).

Additionally (not depicted in the scatter plots), we increased the time limit for programs that only one tool could verify from 1200 s to 3600 s. GPUVerify was able to verify 8 additional programs within this time limit. SORCAR, on the other hand, verified both programs that it had timed out on previously. Thus, with this larger timeout, SORCAR was able to verify a proper superset of programs that GPUVerify verified.

Figures 2c and 2d compare SORCAR-MAX to the tool of Neider et al. [35] on the second benchmark suite of programs with DRYAD specifications. Again, SORCAR-MAX outperformed the HOUDINI-based tool. Specifically, SORCAR-MAX was able to verify 3 programs that Neider et al.'s tool could not verify, whereas Neider et al.'s tool verified 2 programs that SORCAR-MAX could not verify. On programs that both tools were able to verify (57 programs in total), SORCAR-MAX took on average 20 s per program (and synthesized invariants with an average number of 19 predicates). On the other hand, Neider et al.'s tool took on average 45 s per program (and synthesized invariants with an average number of 37 predicates).

Figures 2e and 2f compare SORCAR-MAX and SORCAR-GREEDY on both benchmark suits. The latter was slightly slower overall, but synthesized invariants with fewer predicates.

Comparison of SORCAR and HOUDINI-ICE. Close to the time of writing the final version of this paper, we performed further experiments with HOUDINI-ICE (i.e., an implementation of HOUDINI as a Horn-ICE learning algorithm based on the elimination algorithm), as suggested by the reviewers. This allowed us to force the number of counterexamples returned by BOOGIE in each round to be the same for SORCAR and HOUDINI-ICE (a parameter over which we do not have control in BOOGIE's implementation of HOUDINI).

On the GPUVerify benchmark suite, SORCAR-MAX verified 5 programs that HOUDINI-ICE could not, whereas HOUDINI-ICE was able to verify 1 program that SORCAR-MAX could not. HOUDINI-ICE was also able to show 2 programs to

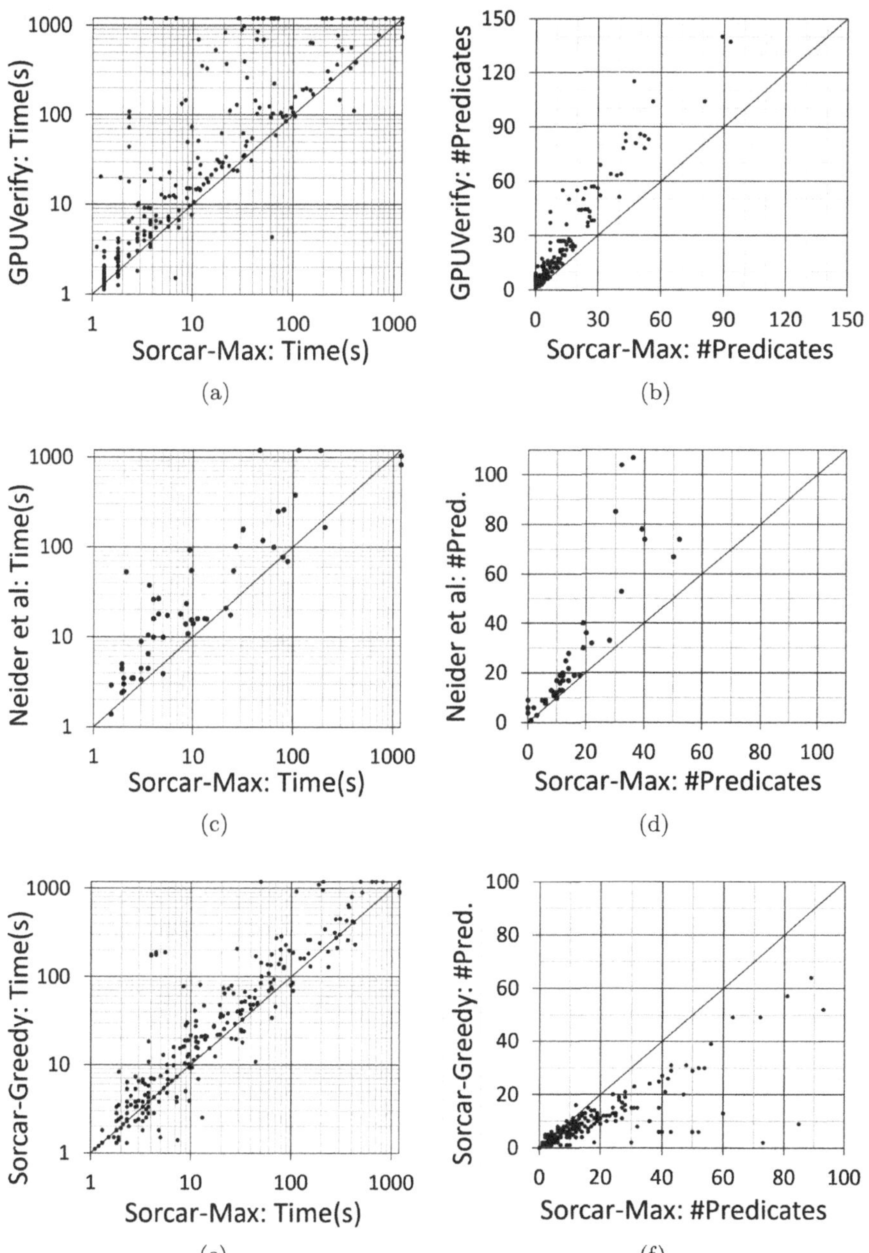

Fig. 2. Comparison of the time taken to verify a benchmark and the number of predicates in the final invariant. Subfigures (a) and (b) compare SORCAR-MAX and GPUVerify on the first benchmark suite. Subfigures (c) and (d) compare SORCAR-MAX and Neider et al.'s tool on the second benchmark suite. Subfigures (e) and (f) compare SORCAR-MAX and SORCAR-GREEDY on both benchmark suites.

not have a conjunctive invariant, which SORCAR-MAX could not. On programs that both were able to verify (233 programs in total), both algorithms performed with similar times.

On the DRYAD benchmark suite, SORCAR-MAX was able to solve 1 more program than HOUDINI-ICE (and verified all programs that HOUDINI-ICE verified). On the 59 programs that both could verify, SORCAR-MAX was roughly twice as fast (averaging 24 s per program for SORCAR-MAX vs. 51 s per program for HOUDINI-ICE).

While SORCAR-MAX still emerges better overall than HOUDINI-ICE, we are not entirely sure why implementing HOUDINI as an external Horn-ICE learning algorithm makes it perform much better than the internal implementation of HOUDINI in BOOGIE (the internal HOUDINI algorithm within BOOGIE is embedded deep and is very hard to configure or control). For the GPUVerify benchmarks, the tool GPUVerify does invariant synthesis without assertions and then inserts assertions to verify the program, and this could be one difference. We leave answering this question for future work.

5 Conclusion

In this paper, we have developed a new class of learning algorithms for conjunctions, named SORCAR, which are biased towards the simplest conjunctive invariant that can prove the assertions correct. SORCAR is parameterized by functions to identify relevant predicates and guarantees to learn an invariant in a linear number of rounds (if one exists). We have shown that SORCAR proves programs correct significantly faster than state-of-the-art HOUDINI-based tools.

There are several future directions to pursue. First, we believe that further algorithms for learning conjunctions need to be explored. For instance, the Winnow algorithm [30] learns from positive and negative samples in time $\mathcal{O}(r \log n)$, where r is the size of the final formula and n is the number of predicates. Finding Horn-ICE learning algorithms that have such sublinear round guarantees can be very interesting as r is often much smaller than n in verification examples. Second, we would like to use the new SORCAR algorithms in specification mining settings where smaller invariants are valuable as they are read by humans. Third, there are several types of inference algorithms similar to HOUDINI (see [39]), and it would be interesting to explore how well SORCAR performs in such settings.

Acknowledgements. We thank the reviewers for their many valuable suggestions that helped improve this paper. This material is based upon work supported by the National Science Foundation under Grant No. 1527395.

References

1. Alur, R., et al.: Syntax-guided synthesis. In: Dependable Software Systems Engineering, NATO Science for Peace and Security Series, D: Information and Communication Security, vol. 40, pp. 1–25. IOS Press (2015)

2. Ball, T., Levin, V., Rajamani, S.K.: A decade of software model checking with SLAM. Commun. ACM **54**(7), 68–76 (2011)
3. Ball, T., Majumdar, R., Millstein, T.D., Rajamani, S.K.: Automatic predicate abstraction of C programs. In: Proceedings of the 2001 ACM SIGPLAN Conference on Programming Language Design and Implementation (PLDI), Snowbird, Utah, USA, 20–22 June 2001, pp. 203–213. ACM (2001)
4. Barnett, M., Chang, B.-Y.E., DeLine, R., Jacobs, B., Leino, K.R.M.: Boogie: a modular reusable verifier for object-oriented programs. In: de Boer, F.S., Bonsangue, M.M., Graf, S., de Roever, W.-P. (eds.) FMCO 2005. LNCS, vol. 4111, pp. 364–387. Springer, Heidelberg (2006). https://doi.org/10.1007/11804192_17
5. Barrett, C., et al.: CVC4. In: Gopalakrishnan, G., Qadeer, S. (eds.) CAV 2011. LNCS, vol. 6806, pp. 171–177. Springer, Heidelberg (2011). https://doi.org/10.1007/978-3-642-22110-1_14
6. Betts, A., Chong, N., Donaldson, A.F., Qadeer, S., Thomson, P.: GPUVerify: a verifier for GPU kernels. In: Proceedings of the 27th Annual ACM SIGPLAN Conference on Object-Oriented Programming, Systems, Languages, and Applications, OOPSLA 2012, part of SPLASH 2012, Tucson, AZ, USA, 21–25 October 2012, pp. 113–132. ACM (2012)
7. Bradley, A.R.: SAT-based model checking without unrolling. In: Jhala, R., Schmidt, D. (eds.) VMCAI 2011. LNCS, vol. 6538, pp. 70–87. Springer, Heidelberg (2011). https://doi.org/10.1007/978-3-642-18275-4_7
8. Champion, A., Chiba, T., Kobayashi, N., Sato, R.: ICE-based refinement type discovery for higher-order functional programs. In: Beyer, D., Huisman, M. (eds.) TACAS 2018. LNCS, vol. 10805, pp. 365–384. Springer, Cham (2018). https://doi.org/10.1007/978-3-319-89960-2_20
9. Chong, N., Donaldson, A.F., Kelly, P.H.J., Ketema, J., Qadeer, S.: Barrier invariants: a shared state abstraction for the analysis of data-dependent GPU kernels. In: Proceedings of the 2013 ACM SIGPLAN International Conference on Object Oriented Programming Systems Languages & Applications, OOPSLA 2013, part of SPLASH 2013, Indianapolis, IN, USA, 26–31 October 2013, pp. 605–622. ACM (2013)
10. Chvátal, V.: A greedy heuristic for the set-covering problem. Math. Oper. Res. **4**(3), 233–235 (1979)
11. Cohen, E., et al.: VCC: a practical system for verifying concurrent C. In: Berghofer, S., Nipkow, T., Urban, C., Wenzel, M. (eds.) TPHOLs 2009. LNCS, vol. 5674, pp. 23–42. Springer, Heidelberg (2009). https://doi.org/10.1007/978-3-642-03359-9_2
12. Colón, M.A., Sankaranarayanan, S., Sipma, H.B.: Linear invariant generation using non-linear constraint solving. In: Hunt, W.A., Somenzi, F. (eds.) CAV 2003. LNCS, vol. 2725, pp. 420–432. Springer, Heidelberg (2003). https://doi.org/10.1007/978-3-540-45069-6_39
13. Cousot, P., Cousot, R.: Abstract interpretation: a unified lattice model for static analysis of programs by construction or approximation of fixpoints. In: Conference Record of the Fourth ACM Symposium on Principles of Programming Languages, Los Angeles, California, USA, January 1977, pp. 238–252. ACM (1977)
14. Dillig, I., Dillig, T., Li, B., McMillan, K.L.: Inductive invariant generation via abductive inference. In: Proceedings of the 2013 ACM SIGPLAN International Conference on Object Oriented Programming Systems Languages & Applications, OOPSLA 2013, part of SPLASH 2013, Indianapolis, IN, USA, 26–31 October 2013, pp. 443–456. ACM (2013)

15. Ernst, M.D., Czeisler, A., Griswold, W.G., Notkin, D.: Quickly detecting relevant program invariants. In: Proceedings of the 22nd International Conference on on Software Engineering, ICSE 2000, Limerick Ireland, 4–11 June 2000, pp. 449–458. ACM (2000)
16. Ezudheen, P., Neider, D., D'Souza, D., Garg, P., Madhusudan, P.: Horn-ICE learning for synthesizing invariants and contracts. PACMPL **2**(OOPSLA), 131:1–131:25 (2018)
17. Fedyukovich, G., Kaufman, S.J., Bodík, R.: Sampling invariants from frequency distributions. In: 2017 Formal Methods in Computer Aided Design, FMCAD 2017, Vienna, Austria, 2–6 October 2017, pp. 100–107. IEEE (2017)
18. Flanagan, C., Leino, K.R.M.: Houdini, an annotation assistant for ESC/Java. In: Oliveira, J.N., Zave, P. (eds.) FME 2001. LNCS, vol. 2021, pp. 500–517. Springer, Heidelberg (2001). https://doi.org/10.1007/3-540-45251-6_29
19. Garg, P., Löding, C., Madhusudan, P., Neider, D.: Learning universally quantified invariants of linear data structures. In: Sharygina, N., Veith, H. (eds.) CAV 2013. LNCS, vol. 8044, pp. 813–829. Springer, Heidelberg (2013). https://doi.org/10.1007/978-3-642-39799-8_57
20. Garg, P., Löding, C., Madhusudan, P., Neider, D.: ICE: a robust framework for learning invariants. In: Biere, A., Bloem, R. (eds.) CAV 2014. LNCS, vol. 8559, pp. 69–87. Springer, Cham (2014). https://doi.org/10.1007/978-3-319-08867-9_5
21. Garg, P., Neider, D., Madhusudan, P., Roth, D.: Learning invariants using decision trees and implication counterexamples. In: Proceedings of the 43rd Annual ACM SIGPLAN-SIGACT Symposium on Principles of Programming Languages, POPL 2016, pp. 499–512 (2016)
22. Grebenshchikov, S., Lopes, N.P., Popeea, C., Rybalchenko, A.: Synthesizing software verifiers from proof rules. In: ACM SIGPLAN Conference on Programming Language Design and Implementation, PLDI 2012, Beijing, China, 11–16 June 2012, pp. 405–416. ACM (2012)
23. Gulwani, S., Srivastava, S., Venkatesan, R.: Program analysis as constraint solving. In: Proceedings of the ACM SIGPLAN 2008 Conference on Programming Language Design and Implementation, Tucson, AZ, USA, 7–13 June 2008, pp. 281–292. ACM (2008)
24. Gupta, A., Rybalchenko, A.: InvGen: an efficient invariant generator. In: Bouajjani, A., Maler, O. (eds.) CAV 2009. LNCS, vol. 5643, pp. 634–640. Springer, Heidelberg (2009). https://doi.org/10.1007/978-3-642-02658-4_48
25. Karp, R.M.: Reducibility among combinatorial problems. In: Proceedings of a symposium on the Complexity of Computer Computations, held March 20–22, 1972, at the IBM Thomas J. Watson Research Center, Yorktown Heights, New York, USA, pp. 85–103. The IBM Research Symposia Series, Plenum Press, New York (1972)
26. Kearns, M.J., Vazirani, U.V.: An Introduction to Computational Learning Theory. MIT Press, Cambridge (1994)
27. Krishna, S., Puhrsch, C., Wies, T.: Learning invariants using decision trees. CoRR abs/1501.04725 (2015). http://arxiv.org/abs/1501.04725
28. Lal, A., Qadeer, S.: Powering the static driver verifier using corral. In: Proceedings of the 22nd ACM SIGSOFT International Symposium on Foundations of Software Engineering, (FSE-22), Hong Kong, China, 16–22 November 2014, pp. 202–212. ACM (2014)
29. Lal, A., Qadeer, S., Lahiri, S.K.: A solver for reachability modulo theories. In: Madhusudan, P., Seshia, S.A. (eds.) CAV 2012. LNCS, vol. 7358, pp. 427–443. Springer, Heidelberg (2012). https://doi.org/10.1007/978-3-642-31424-7_32

30. Littlestone, N.: Learning quickly when irrelevant attributes abound: a new linear-threshold algorithm. Mach. Learn. **2**(4), 285–318 (1987)
31. Löding, C., Madhusudan, P., Peña, L.: Foundations for natural proofs and quantifier instantiation. Proc. ACM Program. Lang. **2**(POPL), 10 (2017)
32. McMillan, K.L.: Interpolation and SAT-based model checking. In: Hunt, W.A., Somenzi, F. (eds.) CAV 2003. LNCS, vol. 2725, pp. 1–13. Springer, Heidelberg (2003). https://doi.org/10.1007/978-3-540-45069-6_1
33. Microsoft: Static driver verifier. https://docs.microsoft.com/en-us/windows-hardware/drivers/devtest/static-driver-verifier. Accessed 26 Apr 2019
34. de Moura, L., Bjørner, N.: Z3: an efficient SMT solver. In: Ramakrishnan, C.R., Rehof, J. (eds.) TACAS 2008. LNCS, vol. 4963, pp. 337–340. Springer, Heidelberg (2008). https://doi.org/10.1007/978-3-540-78800-3_24
35. Neider, D., Garg, P., Madhusudan, P., Saha, S., Park, D.: Invariant synthesis for incomplete verification engines. In: Beyer, D., Huisman, M. (eds.) TACAS 2018. LNCS, vol. 10805, pp. 232–250. Springer, Cham (2018). https://doi.org/10.1007/978-3-319-89960-2_13
36. Nori, A.V., Rajamani, S.K., Tetali, S.D., Thakur, A.V.: The YOGI project: software property checking via static analysis and testing. In: Kowalewski, S., Philippou, A. (eds.) TACAS 2009. LNCS, vol. 5505, pp. 178–181. Springer, Heidelberg (2009). https://doi.org/10.1007/978-3-642-00768-2_17
37. Pek, E., Qiu, X., Madhusudan, P.: Natural proofs for data structure manipulation in C using separation logic. In: Proceedings of the 35th ACM SIGPLAN Conference on Programming Language Design and Implementation, PLDI 2014, pp. 440–451. ACM (2014)
38. Qiu, X., Garg, P., Ştefănescu, A., Madhusudan, P.: Natural proofs for structure, data, and separation. In: Proceedings of the 34th ACM SIGPLAN Conference on Programming Language Design and Implementation, PLDI 2013, pp. 231–242. ACM, New York (2013). https://doi.org/10.1145/2491956.2462169
39. Rondon, P.M., Kawaguchi, M., Jhala, R.: Liquid types. In: Proceedings of the ACM SIGPLAN 2008 Conference on Programming Language Design and Implementation, Tucson, AZ, USA, 7–13 June 2008, pp. 159–169. ACM (2008)
40. Sharma, R., Aiken, A.: From invariant checking to invariant inference using randomized search. In: Biere, A., Bloem, R. (eds.) CAV 2014. LNCS, vol. 8559, pp. 88–105. Springer, Cham (2014). https://doi.org/10.1007/978-3-319-08867-9_6
41. Sharma, R., Gupta, S., Hariharan, B., Aiken, A., Liang, P., Nori, A.V.: A data driven approach for algebraic loop invariants. In: Felleisen, M., Gardner, P. (eds.) ESOP 2013. LNCS, vol. 7792, pp. 574–592. Springer, Heidelberg (2013). https://doi.org/10.1007/978-3-642-37036-6_31
42. Sharma, R., Gupta, S., Hariharan, B., Aiken, A., Nori, A.V.: Verification as learning geometric concepts. In: Logozzo, F., Fähndrich, M. (eds.) SAS 2013. LNCS, vol. 7935, pp. 388–411. Springer, Heidelberg (2013). https://doi.org/10.1007/978-3-642-38856-9_21
43. Sharma, R., Nori, A.V., Aiken, A.: Interpolants as classifiers. In: Madhusudan, P., Seshia, S.A. (eds.) CAV 2012. LNCS, vol. 7358, pp. 71–87. Springer, Heidelberg (2012). https://doi.org/10.1007/978-3-642-31424-7_11
44. Solar-Lezama, A.: Program Synthesis by Sketching. Ph.D. thesis, University of California at Berkeley (2008)

45. Solar-Lezama, A., Tancau, L., Bodík, R., Seshia, S.A., Saraswat, V.A.: Combinatorial sketching for finite programs. In: Proceedings of the 12th International Conference on Architectural Support for Programming Languages and Operating Systems, ASPLOS 2006, San Jose, CA, USA, 21–25 October 2006, pp. 404–415. ACM (2006)
46. Thakur, A., Lal, A., Lim, J., Reps, T.: Posthat and all that: automating abstract interpretation. Electron. Notes Theor. Comput. Sci. **311**, 15–32 (2015)
47. Vizel, Y., Gurfinkel, A., Shoham, S., Malik, S.: IC3 - flipping the E in ICE. In: Bouajjani, A., Monniaux, D. (eds.) VMCAI 2017. LNCS, vol. 10145, pp. 521–538. Springer, Cham (2017). https://doi.org/10.1007/978-3-319-52234-0_28
48. Zhu, H., Magill, S., Jagannathan, S.: A data-driven CHC solver. In: Proceedings of the 39th ACM SIGPLAN Conference on Programming Language Design and Implementation, PLDI 2018, Philadelphia, PA, USA, 18–22 June 2018, pp. 707–721. ACM (2018)

Direct Manipulation for Imperative Programs

Qinheping Hu[1], Roopsha Samanta[2], Rishabh Singh[3], and Loris D'Antoni[1](✉)

[1] University of Wisconsin-Madison, Madison, USA
loris@cs.wisc.edu
[2] Purdue University, West Lafayette, USA
[3] Google, Hanover, USA

Abstract. Direct manipulation is a programming paradigm in which the programmer conveys the intended program behavior by modifying program values at runtime. The programming environment then finds a modification of the original program that yields the manipulated values. In this paper, we propose the first framework for direct manipulation of imperative programs. First, we introduce *direct state manipulation*, which allows programmers to visualize the trace of a buggy program on an input, and modify variable values at a location. Second, we propose a synthesis technique based on program sketching and quantitative objectives to efficiently find the "closest" program to the original one that is consistent with the manipulated values. We formalize the problem and build a tool JDiAL based on the SKETCH synthesizer. We investigate the effectiveness of direct manipulation by using JDiAL to fix benchmarks from introductory programming assignments. In our evaluation, we observe that direct state manipulations are an effective specification mechanism: even when provided with a single state manipulation, JDiAL can produce desired program modifications for 66% of our benchmarks while techniques based only on test cases *always* fail.

1 Introduction

Direct manipulation [1–4] is a programming paradigm in which the programmer conveys the intended program behavior by modifying program values at runtime. The programming environment then finds a modification of the original program that yields the manipulated values. This paradigm has been successfully applied to drawing editors [5,6] to provide programming capabilities that allow users to interact directly with the displayed graphics.

In this paper, we propose the first framework for direct manipulation of imperative programs. We start by introducing *direct state manipulation*, a specification mechanism in which users can describe the intended program behavior by directly manipulating intermediate variable values in buggy program traces. We propose a workflow in which the user traverses the step-by-step visualization of the execution of the buggy program on a certain input to identify a location where the values of the program variables do not correspond to the ones

B.-Y. E. Chang (Ed.): SAS 2019, LNCS 11822, pp. 347–367, 2019.
https://doi.org/10.1007/978-3-030-32304-2_17

she expects. At this point, we allow the user to *manipulate* the variable values at the identified location and modify them. We then treat this manipulation as a specification and use it to synthesize a program that, on the same input, can reach the location identified by the user with the new variable values she provided.

We formalize our synthesis problem and present a constraint-based synthesis technique for computing programs consistent with direct state manipulations. Solving this problem requires addressing two key challenges. First, the execution step manipulated by the user in the buggy trace might appear at a different point in the trace of the synthesized program—e.g., when the modified program uses more/fewer loop iterations than the original one. Second, since a single program execution under-specifies the overall program behavior, there can be many possible programs that agree with the manipulated trace. To address the first challenge, given a manipulated location ℓ, we design an encoding that "guesses" in what occurrence of the location ℓ in the trace of the synthesized program the desired variable values are produced. To address the second challenge, we augment our synthesis problem with quantitative objectives [7] to prefer programs that produce execution traces similar to those of the original program—i.e., the goal is to compute a modified program that on the input provided by the user produces an execution trace similar to the one in the original program.

We implemented our synthesis technique in a tool called JDIAL, which is built on top of the SKETCH [8] synthesizer. JDIAL supports several program transformation models—i.e., descriptions of how the program can be modified—and program distances, and can handle Java programs containing loops, arrays, and recursion. To handle programs containing library functions such as `Math.pow`, JDIAL introduces a synthesis algorithm that uses concrete program executions to "discover" partial interpretations of external functions and uses such interpretations to synthesize modifications to the whole program. For the common case in which producing a new program only requires modification of a single statement, JDIAL uses a data flow analysis based on program slicing to summarize and reduce parts of the program for which the corresponding traces will not be affected by the code modification.

We evaluate JDIAL on a set of representative program repair benchmarks. We observe that direct state manipulations are an effective specification mechanism: even when provided with a single manipulation, JDIAL can produce desired program modifications for 66% of our benchmarks while techniques based only on test cases *always* fail and produce undesirable programs.

Contributions. We make the following key contributions.

- We introduce the specification mechanism of *direct state manipulation* and a corresponding synthesis problem in which the goal is to find a program that produces the variable values specified by the user at a certain point in the program execution trace and that has minimal distance from the original program according to some metric (Sect. 3).
- We propose a framework based on program sketching for synthesizing programs using direct state manipulations (Sect. 4).

- We instantiate our framework in JDIAL, a tool that supports direct state manipulations for simple Java programs (Sect. 5).
- We evaluate JDIAL on 17 representative benchmarks and show JDIAL computes good program modifications in cases where specifications based on test cases produce undesirable ones (Sect. 6).

```
1 int largestGap(int[] x){
2  int N = x.length;
3  int max = x[N-1];
4  int min = x[N-1];
5  for(int i=1; i<N-1; i++){
6   if(max < x[i])
7     max = x[i];
8   if(min > x[i])
9     min = x[i];
10 }
11 int res = max - min;
12 return res; }
```

	max	min	i
value	5	4	1
change to	**9**	?	?

Test case: `largestsGap([9,5,4]) = 5`

a) Direct state manipulation on failing test

JDIAL ⟶

```
int largestGapFix(int[] x){
  int N = x.length;
  int max = x[N-1];
  int min = x[N-1];
- for(int i=1; i<N-1; i++){
+ for(int i=0; i<N-1; i++){
    if(max < x[i])
      max = x[i];
    if(min > x[i])
      min = x[i];
  }
  int res = max - min;
  return res; }
```

b) Program computed by JDIAL

Fig. 1. Examples of synthesis using direct manipulation in JDIAL.

2 Illustrative Example

In this section, we illustrate our direct manipulation framework using an example student attempt to an introductory programming exercise. In this domain, automatic program repair—i.e., finding program transformations that fix the program—has been used to provide personalized feedback to students [9–11]. We show how direct state manipulations can be used an alternative to test-cases for program repair in this domain.

Consider the example in Fig. 1(a) where a student is trying to write a program `largestGap` for finding the *largest gap* in a non-empty array of integers—i.e., the difference between the maximum and minimum values in the array. In the following, we assume that the student has discovered that the program behavior on test `[9,5,4]` is incorrect and is trying to get a suggestion from the tool on how she could fix the program.

Specification via Test Cases. Several tools support test cases as a way to express the correct behaviour of the program. In this case, the student can specify that on the input `[9,5,4]`, the correct output should be 5. However, even the tool QLOSE [7], which can often find correct program modifications using a small number of test cases, will return the following wrong modification to line 11:

```
int res = max - min;  ⟶  int res = max - min + 4;
```

For this example, QLOSE requires two additional carefully selected test cases to find the correct program transformation.

Specification via Direct State Manipulation. Direct state manipulations allow programmers to convey *more information about the behavior of a test case*, rather than only its final output. Our proposal to use direct state manipulations in this domain is inspired by Guo's observation [12] that students find it beneficial to visualize concrete program executions and observe discrepancies between the variable values they observe and those they expect. For example, while debugging the `largestGap` program, the student notices that in the first iteration of the loop, right before executing line 8, variable `max` has value 5 instead of the expected value 9. While visualizing the trace, the student can directly modify the value of `max` as shown in the figure and JDIAL will synthesize the program `largestGapFix` consistent with the manipulation (Fig. 1(b))—i.e., when running `largestGapFix` with input `[9,5,4]`, there is a point in the execution where the variable `max` contains value 9 right before executing line 8. Why does this new specification mechanism lead to the desired program? First, by modifying the program's trace and its value at line 8, the student implicitly states that certain lines do not need modification—e.g., lines 11 and 12. Second, the modification provides information about an intermediate state of the program that a tool cannot access through just an input/output example. Besides the variable `max`, the student can modify the value of `i` from 1 to 0 or the values of both `i` and `max` at the same position and JDIAL will produce the same program.

Remarkably, direct state manipulation can also help debug partial implementations. Consider, for example, an incomplete version of the program `largestGap` in which lines 8–9 are missing because the student has not implemented the logic for min yet. The test case in Fig. 1(a) is essentially useless. On the other hand, the same direct manipulation shown in Fig. 1(a) will yield a good program.

3 Problem Definition

In this section, we define the class of programs we consider, the notion of direct state manipulation, and our synthesis problem.

3.1 Programs and Traces

We consider a simple imperative language in which a program P consists of a function definition $f(i_1, \dots, i_q) : o$ with input variables $I = \{i_1, \dots, i_q\}$ and output variable o (`NULL` for void functions), a set of program variables V such that $V \cap I = \emptyset$, and a sequence of labeled statements $\sigma = s_1 \dots s_n$. A statement is one of the following: `return`, assignment, conditional or loop statement. Each statement in σ is labeled with a unique location identifier from the set $L = \{\ell_0, \ell_1, \dots, \ell_p, exit\}$. We assume a universe $\mathcal{U}$ of values. We also assume variables are associated with types and assignments are consistent with these types.

Without loss of generality, we assume that executing a `return` statement assigns a value to the output variable and transfers control to a designated location *exit*. A program configuration η is a pair (ℓ, ν) where $\ell \in L$ is a location and $\nu : I \cup \{o\} \cup V \mapsto \mathcal{U} \cup \{\bot\}$ is a valuation function that assigns values to all variables. The element $\bot$ indicates that a variable has not been assigned a value yet or is out of scope. We write $(\ell, \nu) \rightarrow (\ell', \nu')$ if executing the statement at location ℓ under variable valuation ν transfers control to location ℓ' with variable valuation ν'. The execution trace $\pi_P(\nu_0)$ of the program P on an initial valuation ν_0 is a sequence of configurations $\eta_0, \eta_1, \ldots,$ where $\eta_0 = (\ell_0, \nu_0)$ and for each h, we have $\eta_h \rightarrow \eta_{h+1}$. An execution terminates once the location *exit* is reached and we only consider programs that terminate on all inputs. We use $\pi_P(\nu_0)_l = \eta_l$ to denote the configuration at index l and $\pi_P(\nu_0)_{[l,h]}$ to denote the subsequence of configurations between index l and h—e.g., $\pi_P(\nu_0)_{[3,5]} = \eta_3\eta_4\eta_5$.

Consider the program `largestGap` in Fig. 1. The input variable set I is $\{$x$\}$ and the output variable is `res`. The set of program variables is $\{$`i`,`max`,`min`$\}$. Let ν_0 be the initial valuation such that $\nu_0(x) = [9, 5, 4]$ and $\nu_0(w) = \bot$ for every other variable w. The execution of `largestGap` on ν_0 is shown in Fig. 2.

	η_0	η_1	η_2	η_3	η_4	η_5	η_6	η_7	η_8	η_9	η_{10}
loc	2	3	4	5	6	7	8	5	10	11	*exit*
`N`	$\bot$	3	3	3	3	3	3	3	3	3	3
`i`	$\bot$	$\bot$	$\bot$	$\bot$	1	1	1	1	$\bot$	$\bot$	$\bot$
`max`	$\bot$	$\bot$	4	4	4	4	5	5	5	5	5
`min`	$\bot$	$\bot$	$\bot$	4	4	4	4	4	4	4	4
`res`	$\bot$	$\bot$	$\bot$	$\bot$	$\bot$	$\bot$	$\bot$	$\bot$	$\bot$	$\bot$	1

Fig. 2. Execution of `largestGap` on ν_0. We omit valuations of the input variable x as $\nu_h(x) = \nu_0(x)$ for all h.

3.2 Synthesis for Direct State Manipulation

We define the notion of direct state manipulation, which allows users to express their intent by modifying variable values in intermediate configurations. We assume a fixed program P. A *direct state manipulation* $\mathcal{M}$ is a tuple (ν_0, k, ν') where ν_0 is an initial valuation, k is an index s.t. $k \leq |\pi_P(\nu_0)|$, and $\nu' : V \cup \{o\} \mapsto \mathcal{U} \cup \{?\}$ is a new partial variable valuation. Intuitively, the manipulation replaces the configuration $\pi_P(\nu_0)_k = (\ell, \nu)$ at location ℓ with the new partial configuration (ℓ, ν'). Notice that a partial configuration cannot change the values of the variables in I and it can assign a special value ? to certain variables. This value is used to denote that the manipulation "does not care" about the specific values of certain variables. We say that a valuation ν *satisfies* a partial valuation ν', denoted $\nu \vdash \nu'$, iff for every variable $x \in V \cup \{o\}$, if $\nu(x) \neq ?$ then $\nu(x) = \nu'(x)$.

Example 1. The direct state manipulation in Fig. 1(a) is formally defined as the pair $(\nu_0, 6, \nu')$ where ν_0 is the same as at the end of Sect. 3.1, $\nu'(max) = 9$ and $\nu'(i) = \nu'(min) = \nu'(o) = ?$. This manipulation, which modifies η_6, only sets the value of `max` to 9 at location 8 and leaves all other variables unconstrained.

Given a program P, a direct state manipulation $\mathcal{M} = (\nu_0, k, \nu')$ such that $\pi_P(\nu_0)_k = (\ell, \nu)$, we say that a program P' *satisfies the manipulation* $\mathcal{M}$, if there exists an index j such that $\pi_{P'}(\nu_0)_j = (\ell, \nu_j)$ and $\nu_j \vdash \nu'$—i.e., a program P' satisfies a direct state manipulation if there exists some configuration in the execution trace of P' satisfying the manipulated valuation ν' at location ℓ.

The synthesis problem is to find a program that satisfies a given manipulation. In what follows, we fix a *transformation model*, which is a function $\mathcal{RM}$ that assigns to a program a corresponding *synthesis space* $\mathcal{P}$. The synthesis space represents a set of programs from which we can draw candidate programs.

Definition 1 (Synthesis for Direct State Manipulation). *Given a program P and a direct state manipulation $\mathcal{M} = (\nu_0, k, \nu')$, the* synthesis for direct state manipulation *problem is to find a program $P' \in \mathcal{RM}(P)$ that satisfies the manipulation $\mathcal{M}$.*

Informally, a direct state manipulation (ν_0, k, ν') at location ℓ is a *reachability specification* requiring that a configuration (ℓ, ν') is *eventually* reached along an execution from the initial valuation ν_0. This specification mechanism is orthogonal to *assertions*, which require a property φ at location ℓ to be an *invariant*—i.e., each time an execution reaches location ℓ, the property φ holds. For instance, in Fig. 1(a), placing the assertion `max = 9` at location 8 would specify that the value of `max` should be 9 at location 8 across all loop iterations in an execution. The astute reader may suggest that for some suitably chosen predicate *condition* over the loop counter, an assertion of the form *condition* $\Rightarrow$ `(max = 9)` at location 8 could encode the direct state manipulation in Fig. 1. However, a direct state manipulation does not explicitly indicate what such a predicate *condition* should be. In particular, a direct state manipulation does not specify what the manipulation-satisfying index j should be.

Handling Test Cases. Definition 1 can be generalized to the problem of synthesising a program P given a direct state manipulation and a set of tests. A test t is a pair (ν^I, ν^O) where ν^I and ν^O are valuations over the input variables I and the output variable o, respectively. Let ν_0^I denote an initial valuation such that $\nu_0^I(w) = \nu^I(w)$ if $w \in I$ and $\bot$ otherwise. Program P satisfies a test t if the value of the output variable o at the end of an execution $\pi_P(\nu_0^I)$ of P on valuation ν_0^I is ν^O—i.e., if $j = |\pi_P(\nu_0^I)| - 1$, $\eta_j = (\ell, \nu)$ and $\nu(o) = \nu^O$. Program P satisfies a set of tests T if it satisfies all the tests $t \in T$. The synthesis problem is then to find a program that satisfies both the direct state manipulation and the tests.

Cost-aware Synthesis. Among the many programs that satisfy a given state manipulation we would like to pick the "best" one. To define what it means for a program to be better than another one, we use the notions of program distances proposed in [7]. We define two types of distances: syntactic and semantic distances. Given a program P, a syntactic distance is a function $f_{syn}^P : \mathcal{P} \to \mathbb{N}$ that maps each program in the synthesis space to a quantity capturing its syntactic similarity to the original program P. We define semantic distances using distance functions over execution traces. Let $dist(\pi, \pi')$ denote a distance function mapping a pair of traces to a non-negative integer. Intuitively, $dist$ captures the similarity between execution traces of P and P' on the same initial valuation ν_0. Given a program P and a direct state manipulation $\mathcal{M} = (\nu_0, k, \nu')$, a semantic distance function $f_{sem}^{P,\mathcal{M}} : \mathcal{P} \to \mathbb{N}$ maps a synthesized program P' to $dist(\pi_P(\nu_0)_{[0,k]}, \pi_{P'}(\nu_0)_{[0,j]})$ capturing the similarity between the manipulated trace $\pi_P(\nu_0)_{[0,k]}$ of P and the corresponding *manipulation-satisfying trace* $\pi_{P'}(\nu_0)_{[0,j]}$ of P' with manipulation-satisfying index j. An aggregation function $\text{AGGR} : \mathbb{N} \times \mathbb{N} \to \mathbb{N}$ is used to combine the two distance functions.

Example 2. An example of syntactic distance between two programs P and P' is the number of node edits needed to transform the abstract syntax tree P into the one P'. According to this distance, the change from `i=1` to `i=0` showed in Fig. 1 has syntactic distance 1. An example semantic distance is the sum of the differences in variable valuations in program configurations of the execution traces $\pi_P(\nu_0)_{[0,k]}$ and $\pi_{P'}(\nu_0)_{[0,j]}$ (with j as defined above).

For a program P and direct state manipulation $\mathcal{M}$, we can define the *cost* of a synthesized program P' as $cost(P') = \text{AGGR}(f_{syn}^{P}(P'), f_{sem}^{P,\mathcal{M}}(P'))$. The following definition can be generalized to incorporate a set of tests.

Definition 2 (Cost-aware Synthesis for Direct State Manipulation). *Given a program P and a direct state manipulation $\mathcal{M}$, the* Cost-aware synthesis for direct state manipulation *problem is to find a program $P' \in \mathcal{RM}(P)$ that satisfies the manipulation $\mathcal{M}$ and such that, for every $P'' \in \mathcal{RM}(P)$ that satisfies the manipulation $\mathcal{M}$, we have $cost(P') \leq cost(P'')$.*

4 JDIAL's Architecture

In this section, we describe the architecture of JDIAL and the sketching-based approach JDIAL employs to synthesize programs (Fig. 3).

JDIAL takes as input a buggy program, a direct state manipulation on an input trace, and (optionally) a set of test cases (left of Fig. 3). As described in Sect. 3, the synthesis problem is defined using four components: a transformation model, a syntactic distance function, a semantic distance function, and a cost-aggregation function. In JDIAL, these components are modular and defined independently from the underlying synthesis engine (grey boxes at the top of Fig. 3). The transformation model is given as a program GetSynthesisSpace that, given a program, returns a sketched version of it—i.e., a program with unknown holes of the form `??`. In Fig. 3, this program simply replaces each constant with a hole. By instantiating the holes in the sketched program with concrete values we obtain a program in the synthesis space. The syntactic distance is given as a program that computes a non-negative integer based on the values of the holes in the sketched program—e.g., how many constants were changed or by how much they were changed. The semantic distance is given as a program that computes a non-negative integer based on the value of two traces—e.g., the Hamming distance.

4.1 Synthesis via Sketching

To solve the synthesis problem, JDIAL computes a sketched program together with a set of assertions (blue box in Fig. 3). The solution to this sketched program—i.e., values for the holes that satisfy the assertions and minimize the given objective function—is the solution to our synthesis problem.

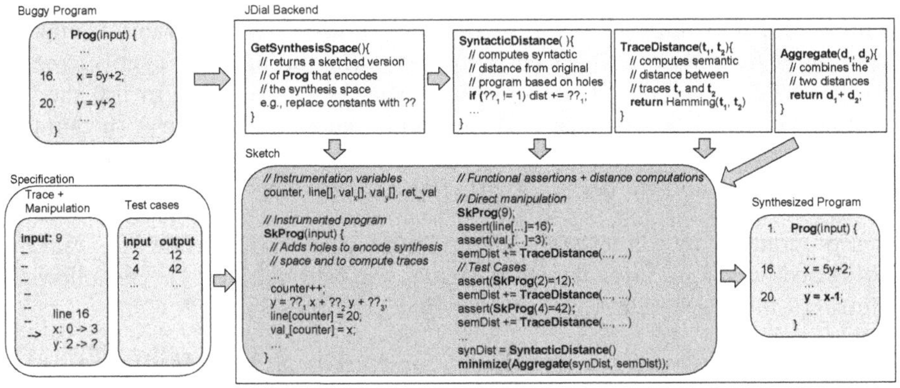

Fig. 3. Architecture of JDIAL. Grey components can be modified without having to modify the synthesis algorithm. (Color figure online)

Background on Sketching. Program sketching is a technique for specifying a parametric set of programs. This is done by allowing programs to contain holes (denoted by ??). When one provides a specification—e.g., test cases, assertions, minimization objectives—the sketching problem is to find (typically integer) values of the holes that satisfy the given specification. State-of-the-art sketching tools support complex program constructs, such as arrays, strings, and recursive functions, as well as complex specification mechanisms, such as Boolean assertions and quantitative optimization constraints over the values of the holes [8].

Computing Distances and Guessing Trace Lengths. The GetSynthesisSpace component, given the buggy program, adds holes to generate a sketched program encoding the synthesis space—e.g., `y = ??_1 * x + ??_2 * y + ??_3` in Fig. 3 (blue-box). JDIAL then generates a function that uses the values placed in the holes to compute the syntactic distance (Fig. 3(top)).

To compute the semantic distance JDIAL symbolically extracts traces by instrumenting the sketched program with a counter to measure the length of the trace, an array to record the values of each variable in the original program, and an array for the line numbers.[1] After each instruction, the arrays are updated to

[1] We assume that the length of the trace in the synthesized program is at most twice the length of the original trace and we use this assumption to initialize the length of the arrays. This constant is parametric and can be modified.

reflect the current variable values (Fig. 3(blue-box)). JDIAL then computes the semantic distance using the traces extracted from such arrays.

The key difficulty in encoding our synthesis problem is that there can be many ways to "align" the location manipulated by the user with a location in the sketched program—e.g., the execution of one synthesized program might reach the desired manipulated value the second time the manipulated location is visited, while another candidate program might reach the desired value the tenth time the manipulated location is visited. JDIAL must be able to consider all these possibilities.

Example 3. Consider the manipulation described in Fig. 1(a). The execution of the synthesized program `largestGapFix` presented in Fig. 1(b) on input [9, 5, 4] hits the manipulated location with `max=9` the first time line 8 is traversed. However, another correct program which changes the loop in line 5 to `i=N-2; i>=0; i--`, hits the manipulated location with `max=9` the second time line 8 is traversed.

Our key idea is to introduce an existential variable—i.e., a hole—in our sketched program to guess at what visit time the manipulated line is reached with the variable values provided by the user. Concretely, we define a global variable `int visit_time=??` to guess the number of visits of the manipulated line and modify the sketched program right before the sketched version of the manipulated line to interrupt the trace at the correct time (see Fig. 4). Thus, every time the manipulated line is reached, `visit_time` is decremented and, when the counter hits zero, the execution has reached the guessed number of visit times.

```
...
if(visit_time==0){
   // record state
   return; }
else
   visit_time--;
//Sketch of
//manipulated line
...
```

Fig. 4. Instrumentation to guess visiting times.

Finally, JDIAL adds assertions to guarantee the sketch solution satisfies the manipulation and a minimization objective to ensure the returned solution is optimal with respect to the given distances (see right of blue box in Fig. 3).

4.2 Correctness of the Synthesis Procedure

We now state the correctness of our encoding. Given a program P and a direct state manipulation $\mathcal{M}$, we call $\textsc{sket}(P, \mathcal{M})$ the sketched program computed by JDIAL. Recall the definition of cost-aware synthesis for direct state manipulation in Definition 2. Theorem 1 states that JDIAL correctly encodes the problem of cost-aware synthesis for direct state manipulation. We say an algorithm for this problem is *sound* if it only produces solutions in $\mathcal{RM}(P)$ that have minimal cost and satisfy $\mathcal{M}$, and *complete* if it produces a solution whenever one exists. Moreover, a program sketching solver is sound and complete if it can correctly solve all program sketches.

Theorem 1. JDIAL *is sound and complete for the problem of cost-aware synthesis for direct state manipulation iff the program sketching solver it uses is sound and complete.*

5 Implementation and Optimizations

JDIAL is composed of a frontend, which allows to visualize program traces and manipulate intermediate states, and a backend, which synthesizes the transformed programs. JDIAL can handle Java programs over integers, characters, Booleans, and arrays over these basic types. In its default mode, JDIAL only tries to modify statements in the function in which the manipulated line appears. In this section, we describe the concrete transformation model and distance functions JDIAL uses as well as several optimizations employed by JDIAL.

$$\mathtt{R}(\mathtt{e}_1 \ \mathtt{bop}\ \mathtt{e}_2) \ \rightarrow\ \mathtt{R}(\mathtt{e}_1)\ \mathtt{bop}\ \mathtt{R}(\mathtt{e}_2) + (\textstyle\sum_{\mathtt{v}\in V} ??_b\mathtt{v}+??)$$

$$\begin{array}{rcl@{\qquad}rcl}
\mathtt{R(x = e)} & \rightarrow & \mathtt{x} = \mathtt{R(e)} + (\sum_{\mathtt{v}\in V} ??_b\mathtt{v}+??) & \mathtt{R(c)} & \rightarrow & \mathtt{c} \\
\mathtt{R(return\ e)} & \rightarrow & \mathtt{R(e)} + (\sum_{\mathtt{v}\in V} ??_b\mathtt{v}+??) & \mathtt{R(x)} & \rightarrow & ??_b\mathtt{x} \\
\mathtt{R(c*e)} & \rightarrow & \mathtt{c} * (\mathtt{R(e)} + (\sum_{\mathtt{v}\in V} ??_b\mathtt{v}+??)) & \mathtt{R}(\mathtt{e}_1\mathtt{+e}_2) & \rightarrow & \mathtt{R}(\mathtt{e}_1) + \mathtt{R}(\mathtt{e}_2) \\
\mathtt{R(x[e])} & \rightarrow & ??_b\mathtt{x}[??_b\mathtt{*e}+??] & \mathtt{R(f(e))} & \rightarrow & ??_b\mathtt{f(e)}
\end{array}$$

Fig. 5. JDIAL's transformation model.

5.1 Transformation Model and Syntactic Distance

JDIAL supports complex transformation models—e.g., it can allow statements to be added to the program. However, overly expressive transformation models will often lead to undesired programs that overfit to the given manipulation. In fact, existing tools for automatically fixing introductory programming assignments typically employ several transformation models, each tailored to a particular programming assignment [9,13].

Transformation Model. Since in our application domain we do not know a priori what program the programmer is trying to write, JDIAL's default transformation model only allows to rewrite constants in linear arithmetic expressions. Figure 5 illustrates JDIAL's default transformation model and Fig. 6 illustrates an example of how the transformation model generates a Sketch from a program.

First, any variable in any expression is multiplied by a hole $??_b$ that only takes values from the set $\{-1, 0, 1\}$. These holes can be used to remove variables and negate their coefficients. Second, the term $\sum_{\mathtt{v}\in V} ??_b\mathtt{v}+??$, where V is the set of variables, is added to each expression appearing in an assignment or in a Boolean comparison. These terms can be used to add new variables, further increase/decrease the coefficients of variables appearing in the expression, or add new constants—e.g., turn `x<0` into `x>y`. This transformation model permits modifications of multiple expressions and it subsumes the default error model of the AUTOGRADER tool, which, despite its simplicity, was shown to be able to automatically fix 30%–60% of edX student submissions depending on the problem type [9].

Syntactic Distance. JDIAL's syntactic distance computes the difference between the synthesized hole values and the original ones. For example, in the expression

$??_b$x < 0 + $\sum_{v \in V}$$??_b$v+?? (corresponding to original expression x<0), the original value of the first hole $??_b$ is 1, while the original value of all the other holes is 0. The syntactic distance is the sum of the absolute difference between each hole's synthesized value and the original one. Intuitively, this distance penalizes modifications that introduce new variables and modify constants by large amounts.

5.2 Semantic Distance over Traces

When computing the distance from the original program traces, JDIAL ignores the variables that have been manipulated because they are likely to contain "incorrect" values that are not necessary to preserve. JDIAL first computes the restricted traces where the values of the manipulated variables are omitted and then uses a modified version of the Hamming distance to compute their distance. In the following definitions, we assume Boolean tests return 1 when true and 0 when false. Given two configurations $\eta = (l, \nu)$ and $\eta' = (l', \nu')$ over a set of variables V, the distance between the two configurations is defined as $H(\eta, \eta') = (l \neq l') + \sum_{w \in V} \nu(w) \neq \nu'(w)$. Finally, JDIAL computes the distance between two traces $\pi = \eta_1 \cdots \eta_s$ and $\pi' = \eta'_1 \cdots \eta'_t$, where $m = min(s, t)$ and $M = max(s, t)$ as the quantity $H(\eta_1, \eta'_1) + \cdots + H(\eta_m, \eta'_m) + M - m$.

```
int triple(int x){            int SkTriple(int x){
  int y = 3 * x;               int y=3*(??_bx+(??_bx+??))+(??_b*x+??);
  if(x == 10)         R        if(??_bx == 10 + (??_bx+??_by+??))
    y = 30;          -->        y = 30 + (??_bx+??_by+??);
  return y; }                  return ??_by + (??_bx+??_by+??); }
```

Fig. 6. A sketched program obtained from applying the transformation model to a program. Holes of the form ?? can be instantiated with arbitrary integers. Holes of the form $\sum_{v \in V}$$??_b$v+?? can only be instantiated with values in $\{-1, 0, 1\}$.

Example 4. Consider again the example described in Fig. 1. The restricted trace of the synthesized program up to the manipulation-satisfying index has distance 3 from the original trace since it only changes the value of the variable i in the last three steps and it has the same length as the original program trace.

JDIAL contains other implementations of trace distances—e.g., longest common subsequences. Since the distance presented above yields good results and performance in practice, we use it as default and in our experiments. JDIAL aggregates the syntactic and semantic distances by taking their sum.

5.3 Handling External Functions

JDIAL employs a new Counterexample-Guided Inductive Synthesis (CEGIS) scheme to handle programs that contain external functions for which semantics might be unknown or expensive to encode directly in SKETCH. Given the input program with an external function ext and the manipulated trace, JDIAL creates a sketched program that assigns a partial interpretation to the external function using the set of concrete values obtained from the input trace execution—i.e., for every call of the function observed in the input trace. JDIAL then computes a solution for the sketched program using this partial definition of ext. If synthesizing the program requires knowing the interpretation of ext on inputs that have not been observed yet, JDIAL lets SKETCH "guess" an interpretation for the function ext on such inputs. JDIAL can then execute the function ext and check whether the guesses were correct. If they are not correct, JDIAL modifies the new sketched program to incorporate the partial interpretation to the external function ext on the newly discovered inputs. The process continues until JDIAL finds a program that respects the semantics of ext.

```
// Test case
// sumPow(3)=15
int sumPow(int x){
  int sum = 1;
  for(int i=1;i<x;i++){
    sum+=Math.pow(2,i);
  }
  return sum;
}
```

(a)

```
// Partial interpretation
// of Mathpow
int Mathpow(a, b){
  if(a==2 && b==1)
    return 2;
  if(a==2 && b==2)
    return 4;
  if(a==?? && b==??)
    return ??; }
```

(b)

1. JDIAL guesses `Mathpow(2,3)=14`
2. Is `Math.pow(2,3)=14`?
3. No, modify `Mathpow`

(c)

```
// Refined interpretation
// of Mathpow
int Mathpow(a, b){
  if(a==2 && b==1)
    return 2;
  if(a==2 && b==2)
    return 4;
  if(a==2 && b==3)
    return 8;
  if(a==?? && b==??)
    return ??; }
```

(d)

Fig. 7. Given an example with an incorrect for-condition and an input test (a), JDIAL uses the execution of sumPow on the test to learn an initial partial interpretation of the function Math.pow (b). JDIAL then produces a proposed program and guesses the interpretation of Math.pow to be such that Math.pow(2,3)=14 (c). After executes Math.pow in Java, JDIAL discovers that Math.pow(2,3)=8, and refines the interpretation of Math.pow for the next round of synthesis (d).

Example 5. Consider the program sumPow in Fig. 7(a), which should compute the sum of powers of 2 up to x, but instead it only computes the sum up to x-1. By running the program on the given input 3, JDIAL can obtain the output of the

`Math.pow` function on input values 1 and 2, and constructs a SKETCH function that describes a partial interpretation of `Math.pow` as shown in Fig. 7(b). To synthesize the program, JDIAL needs to change the condition of the for loop, but this transformation requires knowing the output of the function `Math.pow` on arguments (2,3) and our partial interpretation of `Math.pow` does not contain this information. JDIAL synthesizes a transformation for the function `sumPow` and, while doing so, it assigns an interpretation to the inputs for which the behaviour of the function `Math.pow` is unknown (Fig. 7(c)). JDIAL then uses the concrete execution of the function `Math.pow` to check whether the synthesized interpretation is incorrect, and in this case it modifies the partial interpretation of `Math.pow` in the sketched program.

```
1 // input: [3,2,7]
2 int[] subLargestGap(int[] a){
3   int N=a.length;
4   int min=max=a[0];
5   for(int i=0; i<N; i++){
6     if(max<a[i]) max=a[i];
7     if(min>a[i]) min=a[i];}
8   int largestgap = max-min;
9  R:for(int i=1; i<N; i++){
10    a[i]=a[i]-largestgap;
11 M:}
12  return a; }
```

```
1 void sliced(int[] a){
2   int N=3;
3   int largestgap=5;
4   for(int i=1; i<N; i++)
5     a[i]=a[i]-largestgap;
6   return a; }
```

Fig. 8. Program `subLargestGap` and its `sliced` version when the manipulation happens at line 11 and only line 9 can be modified.

5.4 Additional Features and Optimizations

Specified Transformation Range. Since the programmer might want to prevent JDIAL from modifying certain program statements, JDIAL's frontend allows the programmer to specify what statements the tool is allowed to modify.

Single Statement Transformations. Since most synthesized programs only require transforming a single statement, JDIAL supports this restricted transformation model and it uses an optimized solver that, for each line of code, builds a separate sketched program that is only allowed to modify that line. The separate sketched programs are solved in parallel and JDIAL outputs the program of least cost. For each sketch that can only modify a certain line of code, JDIAL uses program slicing [14] to summarize parts of the program that will not be affected by the line modification. Concretely, let $\ell_{\mathcal{M}}$ be the location at which the manipulation is performed and ℓ_R be the location JDIAL is allowed to modify. By computing a *backward* slice of the manipulated location $\ell_{\mathcal{M}}$, we obtain the statements that can affect the values of the manipulated variables. Similarly, only statements that are reachable from location ℓ_R in the control-flow graph of the program are affected by modifications to line ℓ_R. Finally, the intersection of the two sets gives us the statements where variable values may vary as a result of a transformation. All other statements are irrelevant and can be removed or summarized.

Example 6. Consider the program `subLargestGap` in Fig. 8 that returns a new array obtained by subtracting the largest gap of the input array from all its elements. This program contains a mistake in the second for loop. Assume a student is trying to fix it by manipulating the variable `a[0]` at location 11 on input `[3,2,7]` and that the transformation model only allows modification to location 9. The backward slice of location 11 contains all the statements in the program except the return statement and the lines 9 to 12 are the only lines reachable from location 9. Using this information, JDIAL summarizes all other statements' values. For example, the whole computation of the variable `largestGap` is replaced by the constant assignment `largestGap=5`.

Table 1. Effectiveness and performance of JDIAL. ✗ denotes out of memory.

	Problem	**LOC**	**Vars**	**|Trace|**	**Time** [sec]	**Time single line** [sec]	
						JDIAL$_1$	JDIAL$_1^{o}$
QLOSE [7]	`largestGap-1.1`	7	4	11	3.8	1.6	1.0
	`largestGap-1.2`	7	4	10	2.2	0.8	0.6
	`largestGap-2`	7	4	15	4.2	1.1	0.5
	`largestGap-3.1`	7	4	10	1.8	1.1	0.5
	`largestGap-3.2`	7	4	10	2.8	1.0	0.6
	`tcas`	10	4	7	0.8	0.4	0.4
	`max3`	5	3	3	0.5	0.3	0.3
	`iterPower-1`	5	3	14	0.4	0.6	0.4
	`iterPower-2`	5	3	14	0.7	0.4	0.3
	`ePoly-1`	6	4	12	4.6	3.7	1.3
	`ePoly-2`	6	4	12	2.5	1.7	0.9
	`multIA`	4	4	9	1.3	0.8	1.1
New	`ePoly-3`	7	4	13	2.9	2.8	2.5
	`max4`	7	4	4	0.3	0.2	0.3
	`bubbleSort`	7	5	12	3.1	1.3	0.6
	`subLargestGap`	13	6	35	✗	✗	0.7
	`maxMin`	13	6	37	✗	✗	0.9

6 Evaluation

We evaluate the effectiveness of JDIAL through the following questions.

Q1 Can JDIAL yield desirable programs more often than test-based techniques?
Q2 Is the optimized version of JDIAL presented in Sect. 5.4 effective?
Q3 How sensitive is JDIAL w.r.t. the location of the manipulation?
Q4 Can JDIAL handle programs that contain external functions?

We perform our evaluation on 17 Java programs: 12 from QLOSE [7] and 5 new programs. All benchmarks and the corresponding Sketch files are available at this url: https://tinyurl.com/yd6bp3dx. The five variants of the `largestGap` problem presented in Sect. 2 are taken from the CodeHunt platform [15], The `tcas-semfix` program is a toy traffic collision avoidance system from [16]. The `max`, `iterPower`, `ePoly`, and `multIA` problems are taken from the Introduction to Python Programming course taught on edX [17]. Two of the new programs we consider are variations of QLOSE benchmarks. The other three `bubbleSort`, `subLargestGap`, and `maxMin` are larger programs that contain multiple loops, which are more complex than the benchmarks considered in [7].

Table 1 shows detailed metrics for each benchmark and the average runtime of JDIAL when performing synthesis on five randomly generated failing inputs. All experiments were performed on an Intel Core i7 4.00 GHz CPU with 32GB/RAM.

6.1 Comparison to Test-Based Tools

We compare JDIAL against the tool QLOSE to see if synthesis via direct manipulation can find meaningful programs more often than synthesis via test cases. We compare against QLOSE because it is the only test-based tool that uses semantic distances and it produces "good" programs when using a small number of test cases more often than tools that only use syntactic distances [7].

For each benchmark, we randomly generate 5 input tests that result in incorrect outputs. For each failing test, we run QLOSE using the test as a specification

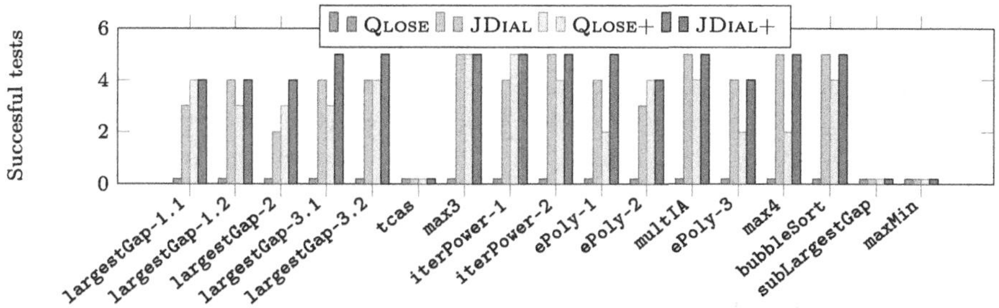

Fig. 9. Correct transformations out of 5 randomly generated tests for JDIAL vs QLOSE. Additional test provided in JDIAL+ and QLOSE+.

and run JDIAL by manually constructing a manipulation: we identify the first location in the execution trace where a variable has the wrong value and modify it to the correct one. Figure 9 illustrates the results of this comparison (JDIAL and QLOSE bars). JDIAL generates the desired transformations in 66% (56/85) of the cases while QLOSE never produces a correct program. When given only one test case, QLOSE always modifies the return statement of the program.

We perform another study where, for each previous experiment, we provide JDIAL and QLOSE with an additional (failing or passing) test—i.e., we provide QLOSE with two tests and JDIAL with one test and one manipulation. Figure 9 illustrates the results of this comparison (cf. JDIAL+ and QLOSE+ bars). JDIAL generates the intended transformations for 75% (64/85) of the cases while QLOSE produces the intended transformations on 58% (49/85) of the cases. While QLOSE performs better than when given a single test, for every input on which QLOSE produces the correct transformation, JDIAL also does so. Remarkably, when given a single manipulation and nothing more, JDIAL produces correct transformations more often than QLOSE, even when the latter is provided with 2 tests. To answer **Q1**, **JDial produces meaningful programs more often than techniques that only use tests**.

Before concluding, we explain why both tools performed poorly on some benchmarks. For the `tcas` program, the desired fix modifies an expression by adding a large constant that can only be synthesized from a very specific test case. Additionally, `subLargestGap` and `maxMin` benchmarks are too large. For the instances for which JDIAL produces the incorrect program, we evaluate whether JDIAL produces correct transformations if it is allowed further "attempts". Whenever an undesired transformation is generated at a location ℓ, we disallow JDIAL to transform location ℓ again or reject the proposed transformation and ask for a different one. This approach correctly synthesizes an additional 6 failing benchmarks with an average of 2.2 user interactions.

6.2 Optimizations for Single-Line Transformations

We repeat the previous experiment using the single-line transformation model described in Sect. 5.4. We refer to the version of JDIAL with this restricted transformation model as JDIAL_1 and its optimized version as JDIAL_1°. All our benchmarks can be fixed using a single-line transformation so both JDIAL_1 and JDIAL_1° find the same transformation. The last two columns of Table 1 show the running times. JDIAL_1 is generally faster than the version of JDIAL that uses the more complex transformation model. However, the optimized version JDIAL_1° is on average 1.37x faster than JDIAL_1. Moreover, for `subLargestGap` and `maxMin`, JDIAL_1° finds transformations in $<$ 1 second while JDIAL_1 times out. The improvement is due to the slicing-based data-flow analysis, which, can reduce the number of lines in the sketched program from 25 to 8.

To answer **Q2**, **the optimization from** Sect. 5.4 **is beneficial** for single-line transformations. This transformation model is very practical and our results hint that our slicing technique can make JDIAL scale to larger programs.

6.3 Sensitivity of Manipulated Location

One of the key aspects of JDIAL is that the user has to find a "good" location to perform the desired transformation. In this experiment, we evaluate how sensitive JDIAL is with respect to the location choice. We consider the experiment we performed against test-based tools and for each test case on which JDIAL and JDIAL+ successfully found a correct transformation, we then perform the following analysis: if the manipulation was performed at step i in the program trace, we measure after how many steps the generated transformation is "lost"—i.e., we compute the smallest k for which performing the manipulation at position $i + k$ would yield a wrong transformation.

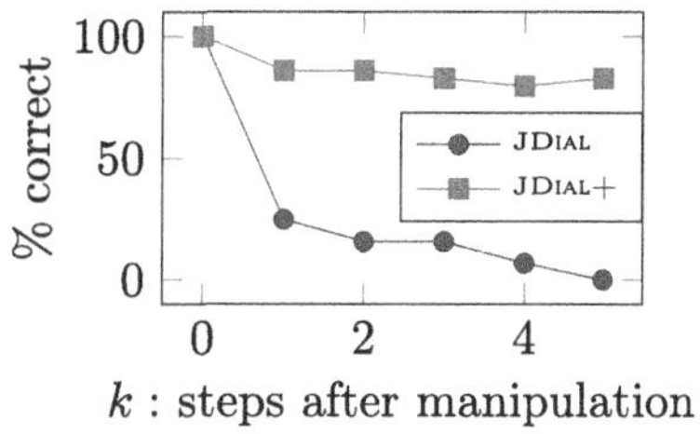

Fig. 10. Correct transformation if manipulating k steps after first point of error.

Figure 10 shows the results. In 80% of the cases, if JDIAL is provided only with a manipulation and the manipulation is performed one step later, JDIAL returns an incorrect transformation. However, when provided with one additional test case JDIAL returns the correct transformation in 80% of the cases, even when the manipulation is performed 5 steps after the ideal location. Even in these extreme conditions, JDIAL returns correct transformations more often than QLOSE does when provided with two test cases. To answer **Q3**, **JDIAL is sensitive with respect to the manipulation location only if no additional tests are provided**, but it is still more precise than QLOSE.

6.4 Ability to Handle External Functions

We evaluate if JDIAL can handle programs with external functions. `ePoly-1` and `ePoly-2`, contain the function `Math.pow` and JDIAL is able to produce a transformation for them using between 2 and 5 iterations (average 4.2), of the CEGIS algorithm presented in Sect. 5.3.

To better evaluate the algorithm, we design two more families of benchmarks. The first family of programs tries to compute $\sum_{i=0}^{n} \texttt{Math.pow}(2, i)$ for values of n between 2 and 8. The bug in this benchmark is the one shown in Fig. 7. For inputs 2 and 3, JDIAL can find the correct transformation that is compliant with the external function after 2 CEGIS iterations, while for inputs 4 through 8, JDIAL requires 3 iterations. The second family of programs computes the maximum value in an array using the `Math.max` function for different incorrect initializations of the variable `max`. In this case, the size of the initial constant affects the number of required CEGIS iterations. While incorrectly initializing `max` to 2 only requires a couple of iterations to produce the correct transformation, if we incorrectly initialize `max` to 100, computing the transformation requires guessing many new interpretations of the function `Math.max` that did not appear in the original trace, resulting in more than 90 iterations.

To answer **Q4, JDIAL can handle programs that contain external functions**, but in certain pathological cases it requires many CEGIS iterations.

7 Related Work

Direct Manipulation. Direct manipulation has been used in drawing editors [1–4]. The most relevant work in this space is SKETCH-N-SKETCH [5,6], which uses program synthesis to apply direct manipulation to scalable vector graphics (SVG)—i.e., constants in the program can be modified conforming to the direct manipulations. SKETCH-N-SKETCH and JDIAL tackle different domains. Unlike JDIAL, SKETCH-N-SKETCH can only rename constants defined at the top of the program and cannot handle complex updates involving changes in the program structure—e.g., replacing $x = y$ with $x = y - z$. Finally, SKETCH-N-SKETCH uses heuristics to select the "right" fix, while JDIAL does so using program distances.

In Wolverine [18], the user can modify a graphical abstract representation of a data structure such as a linked list and the tool will attempt to find a program modification consistent with the modification. Similar to SKETCH-N-SKETCH, Wolverine's technique is specific to certain families of data structure transformations and relies on the graphical abstraction used for the manipulation.

CODEHINT [19] synthesizes simple Java expressions—e.g., library calls—at user-set breakpoints using partial specifications—e.g., variable types. It uses information from the execution to construct expressions of a user-provided type. CODEHINT is different from JDIAL in two main aspects: (*i*) CODEHINT helps programmers auto-complete function calls given some expected type at a given location, whereas JDIAL transforms the original program using a global analysis. (*ii*) CODEHINT performs brute-force search while JDIAL uses constraint-based search with optimization objectives.

Personalized Education. There are many tools for teaching programming that help with grading (see [20] for a survey), personalized feedback [7,9,13,21,22], and visualization [12]. Several works have dealt with transforming synthesis tools into feedback generators [11]. Here, we discuss tools relevant to our work.

AUTOGRADER [9] and QLOSE [7] repair incorrect student solutions to introductory programming assignments. These systems require a reference implementation or a comprehensive set of test cases while JDIAL also allows students to discover potential transformations using direct manipulations. JDIAL extends QLOSE's technique to compute minimal program transformations. In particular, JDIAL encodes the problem of finding good stop points for aligning partial program traces, which is a new problem arising from our specification mechanism.

Program Repair. Program repair is the problem of automatically fixing bugs in large pieces of code. This topic has been studied extensively and researchers have proposed techniques based on constraint-solving [16,23], abstractions [24], and genetic algorithms [25]. These tools are mostly interested in fixing particular types of bugs—e.g., null-pointer exceptions. JDIAL uses constraint solving, but it would be interesting to investigate if other techniques work in our domain.

There are program repair approaches that find repaired programs that are syntactically close [23,26] or semantically close [27] to the original program. It was demonstrated in [7] that transformations generated using a combination of syntactic and semantic program distances are, in general, more *desirable* although more expensive to compute. Hence, JDIAL chooses this last approach and only compares against Qlose [7] since other tools rely on high-quality test suites.

Existing tools use test cases [7,16,28], logic specifications [29], or reference programs [9]. Direct manipulation "augments" a test case by allowing the user to specify intermediate information about the run of the program on a certain input. Moreover, direct manipulations can be used to debug incomplete implementations. Finally, it is important to note that direct manipulation is not directly expressible using assertions or test cases: while an assertion at a certain location is valid if *every* time the location is traversed the predicate in the assertion is true, a direct manipulation at a certain location only requires that *at some point* in the trace the variables evaluate to the manipulated values at that location.

Several tools use fault localization to find likely locations to modify [30–32]. The work on angelic debugging [33] is particularly relevant, where possible faulty expressions in a program are inferred by replacing them with an alternate concrete value (oracle) that makes all the tests pass. However, the burden on repairing the program with the correct expression still lies with the programmer.

The CEGIS refinement of external functions in Sect. 5.3 is related to the notion of SKETCH models [34], which allow one to specify certain properties (such as associativity, idempotence, etc.) to provide richer interpretations to uninterpreted functions. In contrast, JDIAL iteratively builds a model of the auxiliary function directly in the synthesis process.

Acknowledgment. This work was supported by NSF under grants CNS-1763871, CCF-1704117 and CCF-1846327; and by the UW-Madison OVRGE with funding from WARF.

References

1. Victor, B.: Drawing dynamic visualizations (2013). http://worrydream.com/
2. Schachman, T.: Apparatus (2015). http://aprt.us/
3. Hottelier, T., Bodik, R., Ryokai, K.: Programming by manipulation for layout. In: UIST, pp. 231–241 (2014)
4. Shneiderman, B.: Direct manipulation: a step beyond programming languages. ACM SIGSOC Bullstin, vol. 13, no. 2–3, p. 143 (1982)
5. Chugh, R., Hempel, B., Spradlin, M., Albers, J.: Programmatic and direct manipulation, together at last. In: Proceedings of the 37th ACM SIGPLAN Conference on Programming Language Design and Implementation, pp. 341–354. ACM (2016)
6. Hempel, B., Chugh, R.: Semi-automated SVG programming via direct manipulation. In: Proceedings of the 29th Annual Symposium on User Interface Software and Technology, pp. 379–390. ACM (2016)

7. D'Antoni, L., Samanta, R., Singh, R.: QLOSE: program repair with quantitative objectives. In: Chaudhuri, S., Farzan, A. (eds.) CAV 2016. LNCS, vol. 9780, pp. 383–401. Springer, Cham (2016). https://doi.org/10.1007/978-3-319-41540-6_21
8. Solar-Lezama, A.: Program sketching. Int. J. Softw. Tools Technol. Transfer **15**(5–6), 475–495 (2013)
9. Singh, R., Gulwani, S., Solar-Lezama, A.: Automated feedback generation for introductory programming assignments. In: ACM SIGPLAN Notices, vol. 48, no. 6, pp. 15–26 (2013)
10. Yi, J., Ahmed, U.Z., Karkare, A., Tan, S.H., Roychoudhury, A.: A feasibility study of using automated program repair for introductory programming assignments. In: Proceedings of the 2017 11th Joint Meeting on Foundations of Software Engineering, ser. ESEC/FSE 2017, pp. 740–751. ACM (2017)
11. Suzuki, R., et al.: Tracediff: debugging unexpected codebehavior using synthesized code corrections. In: VL/HCC 2017 (2017)
12. Guo, P.J.: Online python tutor: embeddable web-based program visualization for CS education. In: Proceeding of the 44th ACM Technical Symposium on Computer Science Education, pp. 579–584. ACM (2013)
13. Rolim, R., et al.: Learning syntactic program transformations from examples. In: Proceedings of the 39th International Conference on Software Engineering, ser. ICSE 2017, pp. 404–415. IEEE Press, Piscataway (2017)
14. Weiser, M.: Program slicing. In: Proceedings of the 5th International Conference on Software Engineering, pp. 439–449. IEEE Press 1981
15. Tillmann, N., De Halleux, J., Xie, T., Bishop, J.: Code hunt: gamifying teaching and learning of computer science at scale. In: Proceedings of the First ACM Conference on Learning@ Scale Conference, pp. 221–222. ACM (2014)
16. Nguyen, H.D.T., Qi, D., Roychoudhury, A., Chandra, S.: Semfix: program repair via semantic analysis. In: Proceedings of the 2013 International Conference on Software Engineering, pp. 772–781. IEEE Press (2013)
17. edX: Introduction to computer science and programming using python (2017). https://www.edx.org/course/introduction-computer-science-mitx-6-00-1x-10
18. Verma, S., Roy, S.: Synergistic debug-repair of heap manipulations. In: Proceedings of the 2017 11th Joint Meeting on Foundations of Software Engineering, ser. ESEC/FSE 2017, pp. 163–173. ACM (2017)
19. Galenson, J., Reames, P., Bodik, R., Hartmann, B., Sen, K.: Codehint: dynamic and interactive synthesis of code snippets. In: Proceedings of the 36th International Conference on Software Engineering, pp. 653–663. ACM (2014)
20. Striewe, M., Goedicke, M.: A review of static analysis approaches for programming exercises. In: Kalz, M., Ras, E. (eds.) CAA 2014. CCIS, vol. 439, pp. 100–113. Springer, Cham (2014). https://doi.org/10.1007/978-3-319-08657-6_10
21. Gulwani, S., Radiček, I., Zuleger, F.: Automated clustering and program repair for introductory programming assignments. arXiv preprint arXiv:1603.03165 (2016)
22. Kim, D., et al.: Apex: automatic programming assignment error explanation. In: ACM SIGPLAN International Conference on Object-Oriented Programming, Systems, Languages, and Applications, ser. OOPSLA 2016, pp. 311–327. ACM (2016)
23. Mechtaev, S., Yi, J., Roychoudhury, A.: Directfix: Looking for simple program repairs. In: Proceedings of the 37th International Conference on Software Engineering-Volume 1, pp. 448–458. IEEE Press (2015)
24. Logozzo, F., Ball, T.: Modular and verified automatic program repair. In: ACM SIGPLAN Notices, vol. 47, no. 10, pp. 133–146. ACM (2012)

25. Le Goues, C., Dewey-Vogt, M., Forrest, S., Weimer, W.: A systematic study of automated program repair: fixing 55 out of 105 bugs for $8 each. In: International Conference on Software Engineering (ICSE), pp. 3–13. IEEE Press (2012)
26. Samanta, R., Olivo, O., Emerson, E.A.: Cost-aware automatic program repair. In: Müller-Olm, M., Seidl, H. (eds.) SAS 2014. LNCS, vol. 8723, pp. 268–284. Springer, Cham (2014). https://doi.org/10.1007/978-3-319-10936-7_17
27. Von Essen, C., Jobstmann, B.: Program repair without regret. Formal Meth. Syst. Des. **47**(1), 26–50 (2015)
28. Le, X.-B.D., Chu, D.-H., Lo, D., Le Goues, C., Visser, W.: S3: syntax- and semantic-guided repair synthesis via programming by examples. In: Proceedings of the 2017 11th Joint Meeting on Foundations of Software Engineering, ser. ESEC/FSE 2017, pp. 593–604. ACM (2017)
29. Koukoutos, M., Kneuss, E., Kuncak, V.: An update on deductive synthesis and repair in the leon tool. arXiv preprint arXiv:1611.07625 (2016)
30. Ball, T., Naik, M., Rajamani, S.K.: From symptom to cause: localizing errors in counterexample traces. In: ACM SIGPLAN Notices, vol. 38, no. 1, pp. 97–105. ACM (2003)
31. Jose, M., Majumdar, R.: Cause clue clauses: error localization using maximum satisfiability. In: ACM SIGPLAN Notices vol. 46. no. (6), pp. 437–446 (2011)
32. Könighofer, R., Bloem, R.: Automated error localization and correction for imperative programs. In: Formal Methods in Computer-Aided Design (FMCAD), pp. 91–100. IEEE (2011)
33. Chandra, S., Torlak, E., Barman, S., Bodik, R.: Angelic debugging. In: 2011 33rd International Conference on Software Engineering (ICSE), pp. 121–130. IEEE (2011)
34. Singh, R., Singh, R., Xu, Z., Krosnick, R., Solar-Lezama, A.: Modular synthesis of sketches using models. In: McMillan, K.L., Rival, X. (eds.) VMCAI 2014. LNCS, vol. 8318, pp. 395–414. Springer, Heidelberg (2014). https://doi.org/10.1007/978-3-642-54013-4_22

Responsibility Analysis by Abstract Interpretation

Chaoqiang Deng and Patrick Cousot(✉)

Computer Science Department, New York University, New York, USA
{deng,pcousot}@cs.nyu.edu

Abstract. Given a behavior of interest in the program, statically determining the corresponding responsible entity is a task of critical importance, especially in program security. Classical static analysis techniques (e.g. dependency analysis, taint analysis, slicing, etc.) assist programmers in narrowing down the scope of responsibility, but none of them can explicitly identify the responsible entity. Meanwhile, the causality analysis is generally not pertinent for analyzing programs, and the structural equations model (SEM) of actual causality misses some information inherent in programs, making its analysis on programs imprecise. In this paper, a novel definition of responsibility based on the abstraction of event trace semantics is proposed, which can be applied in program security and other scientific fields. Briefly speaking, an entity E_{R} is responsible for behavior $\mathcal{B}$, if and only if E_{R} is free to choose its input value, and such a choice is the first one that ensures the occurrence of $\mathcal{B}$ in the forthcoming execution. Compared to current analysis methods, the responsibility analysis is more precise. In addition, our definition of responsibility takes into account the cognizance of the observer, which, to the best of our knowledge, is a new innovative idea in program analysis.

Keywords: Responsibility · Abstract interpretation · Static analysis · Dependency · Causality · Program security

1 Introduction

For any behavior of interest, especially potentially insecure behaviors in the program, it is essential to determine the corresponding responsible entity, or say, the root cause. Contrary to accountability mechanisms [15,23,40] that track down perpetrators after the fact, the goal of this paper is to detect the responsible entity and configure its permission before deploying the program, which is important for safety and security critical systems. Due to the massive scale of modern software, it is virtually impossible to identify the responsible entity manually. The only solution is to design a static analysis of responsibility, which can examine all possible executions of a program without executing them.

The cornerstone of designing such an analysis is to define responsibility in programming languages. It is surprising to notice that, although the concepts

B.-Y. E. Chang (Ed.): SAS 2019, LNCS 11822, pp. 368–388, 2019.
https://doi.org/10.1007/978-3-030-32304-2_18

of causality and responsibility have been long studied in various contexts (law sciences [36], artificial intelligence [30], statistical and quantum mechanics, biology, social sciences, etc. [4]), none of these definitions is fully pertinent for programming languages. Take the actual cause [19,20] as an example, its structural equations model (SEM) [10] is not suitable for representing programs: the value of each endogenous variable in the model is fixed once it is set by the equations or some external action, while the value of program variables can be assigned for unbounded number of times during the execution. In addition, the SEM cannot make use of the temporal information or whether an entity is free to make choices, which plays an indispensable role in determining responsibility.

There do exist techniques analyzing the influence relationships in programs, such as dependency analysis [1,7,37], taint analysis [31] and program slicing [39], which help in narrowing down the scope of possible locations of responsible entity. However, no matter whether adopting semantic or syntactic methods, these techniques are not precise enough to explicitly identify responsibility.

To solve the above problems, we propose a novel definition of responsibility based on the event trace semantics, which is expressive and generic to handle computer programs and other scientific fields. Roughly speaking, an entity E_{R} is responsible for a given behavior $\mathcal{B}$ in a certain trace, if and only if E_{R} can choose various values at its discretion (e.g. inputs from external subjects), and such a choice is the first one that guarantees the occurrence of $\mathcal{B}$ in that trace. Such a definition of responsibility is an abstract interpretation [11,12] of event trace semantics, taking into account both the temporal ordering of events and the information regarding whether an entity is free to choose its value. Moreover, an innovative idea of cognizance is adopted in this definition, which allows analyzing responsibility from the perspective of various observers. Compared to current techniques, our definition of responsibility is more generic and precise.

The applications of responsibility analysis are pervasive. Although an implementation of responsibility analyzer is not provided here, we have demonstrated its effectiveness by examples including access control, "negative balance" and information leakage. In addition, due to the page limit, a sound framework of abstract responsibility analysis is sketched in the extended version of this paper [13], which is the basis of implementing a responsibility analyzer. It is guaranteed that the entities that are found definitely responsible in the abstract analysis are definitely responsible in the concrete, while those not found potentially responsible in the abstract analysis are definitely not responsible in the concrete.

To summarize, the main contributions of this work are: (1) a completely new definition of responsibility, which is based on the abstract interpretation of event trace semantics, (2) the adoption of observers' cognizance in program analysis for the first time, (3) various examples of responsibility analysis, and (4) a sound framework for the abstract static analysis of responsibility.

In the following, Sect. 2 discusses the distinctions between responsibility and current techniques via an example, and sketches the framework of responsibility analysis. Section 3 formally defines responsibility as an abstraction of event trace semantics. Section 4 exemplifies the applications of responsibility analysis. Section 5 summarizes the related work.

2 A Glance at Responsibility

Given a behavior of interest (e.g. security policy violation), the objective of responsibility analysis is to automatically determine which entity in the system has the primary control over that behavior. Then security admins could decide either to keep or to deny the responsible entity's permission to perform the behavior of interest. Take the information leakage in a social network as an example: if the information's owner is responsible for the leakage (e.g. a user shares his picture with friends), then it is safe to keep its permission to perform such a behavior; otherwise, if anyone else is responsible for the leakage, it could be a malicious attacker and its permission to do so shall be removed. Such human decisions can only be done manually and are beyond the scope of this paper. In addition, it is worthwhile to note that responsibility analysis is not the same as program debugging, since the analyzed program code is presumed to be unmodifiable and the only possible change is on the permissions granted to entities in the system.

In order to give an informal introduction to responsibility, as well as its main distinctions with dependency, causality and other techniques in detecting causes, this section starts with a simple example, which is used throughout the paper.

2.1 Discussion of an Access Control Program Example

Example 1 (Access Control). Consider the program in Fig. 1, which essentially can be interpreted as an access control program for an object o (e.g. a secret file), such that o can be read if and only if both two admins approve the access and the permission type of o from system settings is greater than or equal to "read": the first two inputs correspond to the decisions of two independent admins, where 1 represents approving the access to o, and 0 represents rejecting the access; the third input stored in typ represents the permission type of o specified in the system settings, where 1 represents "read", 2 represents "read and write" (this is similar to the file permissions system in Linux, but is simplified for the sake of clarity); by checking the value of acs at line 10, the assertion can guarantee both admins approve the access and the permission type of o is at least 1. □

```
1:  apv = 1; //1: Approval, 0: Rejection
2:  i1 = input_1(); //Input 0 or 1 from 1st admin
3:  if (i1 == 0) {
4:    apv = 0; }
5:  i2 = input_2(); //Input 0 or 1 from 2nd admin
6:  if (apv != 0 && i2 == 0) {
7:    apv = 0; }
8:  typ = input_3(); //Input 1 or 2 from system settings
9:  acs = apv * typ;
10: assert(acs >= 1); //Check if the read access is granted
11: /* Read an object o here */
```

Fig. 1. Access control program example

Here the question we are interested is: when the assertion fails (referred as "Read Failure" in the following, i.e. the read access to o fails to be granted), which entity (entities) in the program shall be responsible? The literature has several possible answers. By the definition of dependency ([1,7,37]), the value of `acs` depends on the value of `apv` and `typ`, which further depend on all three inputs. That is to say, the read failure depends on all variables in the program, thus program slicing techniques (both syntactic slicing [39] and semantic slicing [35]) would take the whole program as the slice related with read failure. Such a slice is useful in debugging in the sense that it rules out parts of the program that are completely irrelevant with the failure, and modifying any code left in the slice may prevent the failure, e.g. replacing "`acs=apv*typ`" with "`acs=2`" trivially fixes the read failure problem. However, this paper presumes the program code to be unmodifiable, hence a statement like "`acs=apv*typ`", which is fully controlled by others and acts merely as the intermediary between causes and effects, shall not be treated as responsible. In addition, the third input (i.e. the system setting of o's permission type) is also included in the slice. Although it does affect `acs`'s value, it is not decisive in this case (i.e. no matter it is 1 or 2, it could not either enforce or prevent the failure). Therefore, the dependency analysis and slicing are not precise enough for determining responsibility.

Causation by counterfactual dependency [28] examines the cause in every single execution and excludes non-decisive factors (e.g. the third input in this example), but it is too strong in some circumstances. For example, in an execution where both the first two inputs are 0, neither of them would be determined as the cause of read failure, because if one input is changed to value 1, the failure would still occur due to the other input 0.

Actual cause introduced in [19,20] is based on the structural equations model (SEM) [10], and extends the basic notion of counterfactual dependency to allow "contingent dependency". For this example here, it is straightforward to create a SEM to represent the access control program (although it is not always the case): three inputs are represented by exogenous variables, and five program variables are represented by endogenous variables, in which the value of `apv` is `i1*i2`. Consider an execution where both the first two inputs are 0, no matter what value the third input takes, the actual causes of read failure (i.e. `acs<1`) would be determined as "`i1=0`", "`i2=0`", "`apv=0`" and "`acs=0`", since the failure counterfactually depends on each of them under certain contingencies. Thus, both two admins are equally determined as causes of failure, as well as two intermediary variables. This structural-model method has allowed for a great progress in causality analysis, and solved many problems of previous approaches. However, as an abstraction of concrete semantics, the SEM unnecessarily misses too much information, including the following three important points.

(P1) *Time (i.e. the temporal ordering of events) should be taken into account.* For example, the SEM does not keep the temporal ordering of first two inputs (i.e. the information that "`i1=0`" occurs before "`i2=0`" is missed), hence it determines both of them equally as the cause of assigning `0` to `apv`, further as the cause of read failure. However, in the actual execution where first two inputs are 0, the first input already decides the value of `apv` before the second input is entered and the assignment at line 7 is not even executed, thus it is unnecessary to take the second input as a cause of assigning `0` to `apv` or the read failure. To deal with this difficulty, Pearl's solution is to modify the model and introduce new variables [6] to distinguish whether `apv` is assigned by `i1` or `i2`. However, a much simpler method is to keep the temporal ordering of events, such that only the first event that ensures the behavior of interest is counted as the cause. Therefore, in an execution where both the first two inputs are 0, the first input ensures the read failure before the second input is entered, hence only the first input is responsible for failure; meanwhile, in another execution where the first input is 1 and the second one is 0, the second input is the first and only one that ensures the failure hence shall take the responsibility.

(P2) *The cause must be free to make choices.* For example, `acs=0` is determined as an actual cause of read failure, based on the reasoning that if the endogenous variable `acs` in SEM is assigned a different value, say 2, then the read failure would not have occurred. But such a reasoning ignores a simple fact that `acs` is not free to choose its value and acts merely as an intermediary between causes and effects. Thus, only entities that are free to make choices can possibly be causes, and they include but are not limited to user inputs, system settings, files read, parameters of procedures or modules, returned values of external functions, variable initialization, random number generations and the parallelism. To be more accurate, it is the external subject (who does the input, configures the system settings, etc.) that is free to make choices, but we say that entities like user inputs are free to make choices, as an abuse of language.

(P3) *It is necessary to specify "to whose cognizance/knowledge" when identifying the cause.* All the above reasoning on causality is implicitly based on an omniscient observer's cognizance (i.e. everything that occurred is known), yet it is non-trivial to consider the causality to the cognizance of a non-omniscient observer. Reconsider the access control program example, and suppose we adopt the cognizance of the second admin who is in charge of the second input. If she/he is aware that the first input is already 0, she/he would not be responsible for the failure; otherwise she/he does not know whether the first input is 0 or 1, then she/he is responsible for ensuring the occurrence of failure. In most cases, the cognizance of an omniscient observer will be adopted, but not always.

2.2 An Informal Definition of Responsibility

To take the above three points into account and build a more expressive framework, this paper proposes *responsibility*, whose informal definition is as follows.

Definition 1 (Responsibility, informally). *To the cognizance of an observer, the entity E_{R} is responsible for a behavior $\mathcal{B}$ of interest in a certain execution, if and only if, according to the observer's observation, E_{R} is free to choose its value, and such a choice is the first one that guarantees the occurrence of $\mathcal{B}$ in that execution.*

It is worth mentioning that, for the whole system whose semantics is a set of executions, there may exist more than one entities that are responsible for $\mathcal{B}$. Nevertheless, in every single execution where $\mathcal{B}$ occurs, there is only one entity that is responsible for $\mathcal{B}$. To decide which entity in an execution is responsible, the execution alone is not sufficient, and it is necessary to reason on the whole semantics to exhibit the entity's "free choice" and guarantee of $\mathcal{B}$. Thus, responsibility is not a trace property (neither safety nor liveness property).

To put such a definition into effect, our framework of responsibility analysis is designed as Fig. 2, which essentially consists of three components: (1) *System semantics*, i.e. the set of all possible executions, each of which can be analyzed individually. (2) *A lattice of system behaviors of interest*, which is ordered such that the stronger a behavior is, the lower is its position in the lattice. (3) *An observation function for each observer*, which maps every (probably unfinished) execution to a behavior in the lattice that is guaranteed to occur, even though such a behavior may have not occurred yet. These three components are formally defined in Sect. 3, and their abstractions are sketched in [13].

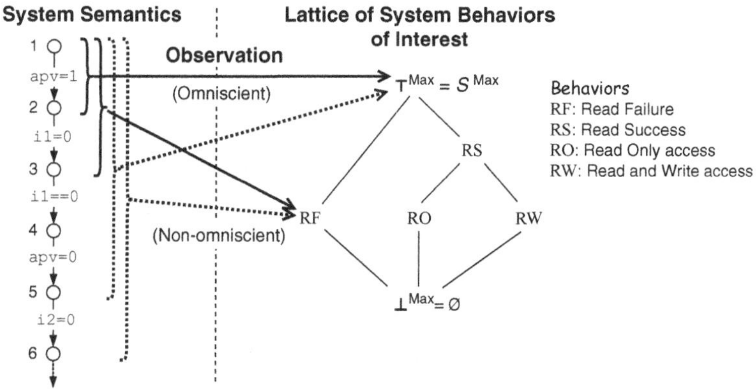

Fig. 2. Framework of responsibility analysis for Example 1

In this framework, if an observer's observation finds that the guaranteed behavior grows stronger after extending an execution, then the extension part of execution must be responsible for ensuring the occurrence of the stronger behavior. Consider the example in Fig. 2 which sketches the analysis for a certain execution of the access control program. Suppose $\top^{\mathsf{Max}}$ in the lattice represents "not sure if the read access fails or not" and `RF` represents the behavior of read failure, whose formal definitions are given in Sect. 3.2. The solid arrow from executions to the lattice stands for the observation of an omniscient observer, while the dashed arrow stands for the observation of the second admin who is unaware of the first input. As illustrated in the figure, the omniscient observer finds that the execution from point 1 to point 2 can guarantee only $\top^{\mathsf{Max}}$, while the stronger behavior `RF` is guaranteed if the execution reaches point 3.

Thus, to the cognizance of the omniscient observer, "`i1=0`" between point 2 and 3 is responsible for the read failure. Meanwhile, the second admin observes that all the executions upto point 5 guarantee $\top^{\mathsf{Max}}$, and **RF** is guaranteed only after point 6 is reached. Hence, to the cognizance of the second admin, "`i2=0`" between point 5 and point 6 is responsible for the read failure. For the sake of completeness, the entire desired analysis result for Example 1 is included in the following.

Example 2 (Access Control, Continued). To the cognizance of an omniscient observer: for any execution, if the first input is 0, no matter what the other two inputs are, only the first admin is responsible for the read failure; if the first input is 1 and the second one is 0, the second admin is responsible.

To the cognizance of the second admin, two cases need to be considered separately. If she/he is aware of the input of first admin, the analysis result is exactly the same as the omniscient observer. Otherwise, she/he does not know the first input: in every execution where the second input is 0, the second admin is responsible, no matter what the first and third input are; in every execution where the second input is 1, nobody shall be responsible for the failure, since whether the failure occurs or not is uncertain from the second admin's perspective. □

After finishing responsibility analysis, it is time for the security admin to configure permissions granted to each responsible entity at her/his discretion. If the behavior of interest is desired or the responsible entity is authorized, the permissions granted to the responsible entity can be kept. On the contrary, if that behavior is undesired or it is against the policy for the responsible entity to control it, the permissions granted to the responsible entity shall be confined. For instance, in the access control program, if the first two inputs are from admins who are authorized to control the access, their permissions to input 0 and 1 can be kept; if those two inputs come from ordinary users who have no authorization to deny other users' access, their permissions to input 0 shall be removed.

3 Formal Definition of Responsibility

In order to formalize the framework of responsibility analysis, this section introduces event traces to represent the system semantics, builds a lattice of system behaviors by trace properties, proposes an observation function that derives from the observer's cognizance and an inquiry function on system behaviors. Furthermore, this section formally defines responsibility as an abstraction of system semantics, using the observation function. To strengthen the intuition of responsibility analysis, the analysis of Example 1 will be illustrated step by step.

3.1 System Semantics

Generally speaking, no matter what system we are concerned with and no matter which programming language is used to implement that system, the system's semantics can be represented by event traces.

Event Trace. In general, an *event* could be used to represent any action in the system, such as "input an integer", "assign a value to a variable", or even "launch the program". Take the classic While programming language as an example, there are only three types of events: skip, assignment, and Boolean test. In order to make the definition of responsibility as generic as possible, here we do not adopt a specific programming language or restrict the range of possible events.

A *trace* σ is a sequence of events that represents an execution of the system, and its length $|\sigma|$ is the number of events in σ. If σ is infinite, then its length $|\sigma|$ is denoted as ∞. A special trace is the empty trace ε, whose length is 0. A trace σ is $\preceq$ - less than or equal to another trace σ', if and only if, σ is a prefix of σ'. The *concatenation* of a finite trace σ and an event e is simply defined by juxtaposition $\sigma\, e$, and the *concatenation* of a finite traces σ and another (finite or infinite) trace σ' is denoted as $\sigma\sigma'$.

$$
\begin{array}{llr}
e \in \mathrm{E} & & \text{event} \\
\sigma \in \mathrm{E}^{+\infty} & \triangleq \bigcup_{n \geqslant 1} \{[0, n-1] \mapsto \mathrm{E}\} \cup \{\mathbb{N} \mapsto \mathrm{E}\} & \text{nonempty trace} \\
\sigma \in \mathrm{E}^{*\infty} & \triangleq \{\varepsilon\} \cup \mathrm{E}^{+\infty} & \text{empty or nonempty trace} \\
\sigma \preceq \sigma' & \triangleq |\sigma| \leqslant |\sigma'| \wedge \forall 0 \leqslant i \leqslant |\sigma| - 1 : \sigma_i = \sigma'_i & \text{prefix ordering of traces}
\end{array}
$$

The function $\mathsf{Pref}(P)$ returns the prefixes of every trace in the set P of traces.

$$
\begin{array}{llr}
\mathsf{Pref} \in \wp(\mathrm{E}^{*\infty}) \mapsto \wp(\mathrm{E}^{*\infty}) & & \text{prefixes of traces} \\
\mathsf{Pref}(P) \triangleq \{\sigma' \in \mathrm{E}^{*\infty} \mid \exists \sigma \in P.\ \sigma' \preceq \sigma\} & &
\end{array}
$$

Trace Semantics. For any system that we are concerned with, its *maximal trace semantics*, denoted as $\mathcal{S}^{\mathsf{Max}} \in \wp(\mathrm{E}^{*\infty})$, is the set of all possible maximal traces of that system. Especially, the maximal trace semantics of an empty program is $\{\varepsilon\}$. Correspondingly, the *prefix trace semantics* $\mathcal{S}^{\mathsf{Pref}} \in \wp(\mathrm{E}^{*\infty})$ is the set of all possible prefix traces, which is an abstraction of maximal trace semantics via Pref, i.e. $\mathcal{S}^{\mathsf{Pref}} = \mathsf{Pref}(\mathcal{S}^{\mathsf{Max}})$. Besides, a trace σ is said to be *valid* in the system, if and only if $\sigma \in \mathcal{S}^{\mathsf{Pref}}$. Obviously, both maximal and prefix trace semantics do preserve the temporal ordering of events, which is missed by the SEM.

Example 3 (Access Control, Continued). For the program in Fig. 1, only two types of events are used: assignment (e.g. `apv=1`) and Boolean test (e.g. `i1==0` and `¬(acs>=1)`, where ¬ denotes the failure of a Boolean test). To clarify the boundary among events, the triangle ▷ is used in the following to separate events in the trace. The access control program has three inputs, each of which has two possible values, thus its maximal trace semantics $\mathcal{S}^{\mathsf{Max}}$ consists of 8 traces (`T1`-`T8`), each of which is represented as a path in Fig. 3 starting at the entry point of program and finishing at the exit point. E.g. `T1` = `apv=1` ▷ `i1=0` ▷ `i1==0` ▷`apv=0` ▷ `i2=0` ▷ `¬(apv!=0&&i2==0)`▷ `typ=1` ▷ `acs=0` ▷ `¬(acs>=1)` denotes the maximal where the first two inputs are 0 and the third input is 1. Meanwhile, the prefix trace semantics $\mathcal{S}^{\mathsf{Pref}} = \mathsf{Pref}(\mathcal{S}^{\mathsf{Max}})$ are represented by the paths that start at the entry point and stop at any point (including the entry point for the empty trace ε). $\square$

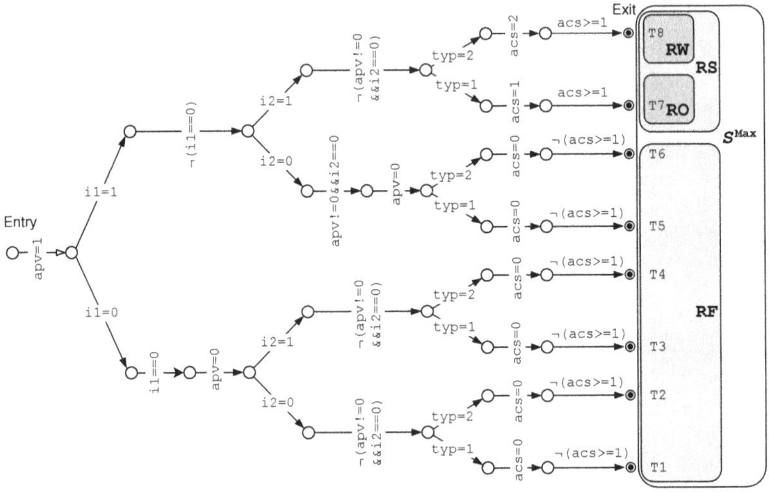

Fig. 3. Trace semantics and properties of Example 1

3.2 Lattice of System Behaviors of Interest

Trace Property. A *trace property* is a set of traces in which a given property holds. Most behaviors of a given system, if not all, can be represented as a maximal trace property $\mathcal{P} \in \wp(\mathcal{S}^{\mathsf{Max}})$.

Example 4 (Access Control, Continued). As illustrated in Fig. 3, the behavior "Read Failure" RF is represented as a set of maximal traces such that the last event is $\neg$(acs>=1), i.e. $\texttt{RF} = \{\sigma \in \mathcal{S}^{\mathsf{Max}} \mid \sigma_{|\sigma|-1} = \neg\texttt{(acs>=1)}\} = \{\texttt{T1}, \texttt{T2}, \texttt{T3}, \texttt{T4}, \texttt{T5}, \texttt{T6}\}$; the behavior "Read Success" RS (i.e. the read access succeeds to be granted) is the complement of RF, i.e. $\texttt{RS} = \mathcal{S}^{\mathsf{Max}} \setminus \texttt{RF} = \{\texttt{T7}, \texttt{T8}\}$, whose subset $\texttt{RO} = \{\texttt{T7}\}$ and $\texttt{RW} = \{\texttt{T8}\}$ represent stronger properties "Read Only access is granted" and "Read and Write access is granted", respectively. $\square$

Complete Lattice of Maximal Trace Properties of Interest. We build a complete lattice of maximal trace properties, each of which represents a behavior of interest. Typically, such a lattice is of form $\langle \mathcal{L}^{\mathsf{Max}}, \subseteq, \top^{\mathsf{Max}}, \bot^{\mathsf{Max}}, \Cup, \Cap \rangle$, where

- $\mathcal{L}^{\mathsf{Max}} \in \wp(\wp(\mathrm{E}^{*\infty}))$ is a set of behaviors of interest, each of which is represented by a maximal trace property;
- $\top^{\mathsf{Max}} = \mathcal{S}^{\mathsf{Max}}$, i.e. the top is the weakest maximal trace property which holds in every valid maximal trace;

- $\bot^{\mathsf{Max}} = \emptyset$, i.e. the bottom is the strongest property such that no valid trace has this property, hence it is used to represent the property of invalidity;
- $\subseteq$ is the standard set inclusion operation;
- $\Cup$ and $\Cap$ are join and meet operations, which might not be the standard $\cup$ and $\cap$, since $\mathcal{L}^{\mathsf{Max}}$ is a subset of $\wp(\mathcal{S}^{\mathsf{Max}})$ but not necessarily a sublattice.

For any given system, there is possibly more than one way to build the complete lattice of maximal trace properties, depending on which behaviors are of interest. A special case of lattice is the power set of maximal trace semantics, i.e. $\mathcal{L}^{\mathsf{Max}} = \wp(\mathcal{S}^{\mathsf{Max}})$, which can be used to examine the responsibility for every possible behavior in the system. However, in most cases, a single behavior is of interest, and it is sufficient to adopt a lattice with only four elements: $\mathcal{B}$ representing the behavior of interest, $\mathcal{S}^{\mathsf{Max}} \backslash \mathcal{B}$ representing the complement of the behavior of interest, as well as the top $\mathcal{S}^{\mathsf{Max}}$ and bottom $\emptyset$. Particularly, if $\mathcal{B}$ is equal to $\mathcal{S}^{\mathsf{Max}}$, i.e. every valid maximal trace in the system has this behavior of interest, then a trivial lattice with only the top and bottom is built, from which no responsibility can be found, making the corresponding analysis futile.

Example 5 (Access Control, Continued). We assume that "Read Failure" is of interest, as well as the behavior of granting write access. As illustrated by the lattice in Fig. 2, regarding whether the read access fails or not, the top $\top^{\mathsf{Max}}$ is split into two properties "Read Failure" `RF` and "Read Success" `RS`, which are defined in Example 4 such that $\mathtt{RF} \Cup \mathtt{RS} = \mathcal{S}^{\mathsf{Max}}$ and $\mathtt{RF} \Cap \mathtt{RS} = \emptyset$. Furthermore, regarding whether the write access is granted or not, `RS` is split into "Read Only access is granted" `RO` and "Read and Write access is granted" `RW`. Now every property of interest corresponds to an element in the lattice, and the bottom $\bot^{\mathsf{Max}} = \emptyset$ is the meet $\Cap$ of `RF`, `RO` and `RW`. In addition, if "Read Failure" is the only behavior of interest, `RO` and `RW` can be removed from the lattice. □

Prediction Abstraction. Although the maximal trace property is well-suited to represent system behaviors, it does not reveal the point along the maximal trace from which a property is guaranteed to hold later in the execution. Thus, we propose to abstract every maximal trace property $\mathcal{P} \in \mathcal{L}^{\mathsf{Max}}$ isomorphically into a set $\mathcal{Q}$ of prefixes of maximal traces in $\mathcal{P}$, excluding those whose maximal prolongation may not satisfy the property $\mathcal{P}$. This abstraction is called *prediction abstraction*, and $\mathcal{Q}$ is a *prediction trace property* corresponding to $\mathcal{P}$. It is easy to see that $\mathcal{Q}$ is a superset of $\mathcal{P}$, and is not necessarily prefix-closed.

$$\alpha_{\mathsf{Pred}}[\![\mathcal{S}^{\mathsf{Max}}]\!] \in \wp(\mathrm{E}^{*\infty}) \mapsto \wp(\mathrm{E}^{*\infty}) \qquad \text{prediction abstraction}$$
$$\alpha_{\mathsf{Pred}}[\![\mathcal{S}^{\mathsf{Max}}]\!](\mathcal{P}) \triangleq \{\sigma \in \mathsf{Pref}(\mathcal{P}) \mid \forall \sigma' \in \mathcal{S}^{\mathsf{Max}}.\ \sigma \preceq \sigma' \Rightarrow \sigma' \in \mathcal{P}\}$$
$$\gamma_{\mathsf{Pred}}[\![\mathcal{S}^{\mathsf{Max}}]\!] \in \wp(\mathrm{E}^{*\infty}) \mapsto \wp(\mathrm{E}^{*\infty}) \qquad \text{prediction concretization}$$
$$\gamma_{\mathsf{Pred}}[\![\mathcal{S}^{\mathsf{Max}}]\!](\mathcal{Q}) \triangleq \{\sigma \in \mathcal{Q} \mid \sigma \in \mathcal{S}^{\mathsf{Max}}\} = \mathcal{Q} \cap \mathcal{S}^{\mathsf{Max}}$$

We have a Galois isomorphism between maximal trace properties and prediction trace properties:

$$\langle \wp(\mathcal{S}^{\mathsf{Max}}),\ \subseteq\rangle \xleftrightarrow[\alpha_{\mathsf{Pred}}[\![\mathcal{S}^{\mathsf{Max}}]\!]]{\gamma_{\mathsf{Pred}}[\![\mathcal{S}^{\mathsf{Max}}]\!]} \langle \bar{\alpha}_{\mathsf{Pred}}[\![\mathcal{S}^{\mathsf{Max}}]\!](\wp(\mathcal{S}^{\mathsf{Max}})),\ \subseteq\rangle \tag{1}$$

where the abstract domain is obtained by a function $\bar{\alpha}_{\mathsf{Pred}}[\![\mathcal{S}^{\mathsf{Max}}]\!] \in \wp(\wp(\mathrm{E}^{*\infty})) \mapsto \wp(\wp(\mathrm{E}^{*\infty}))$, which is defined as $\bar{\alpha}_{\mathsf{Pred}}[\![\mathcal{S}^{\mathsf{Max}}]\!](\mathfrak{X}) \triangleq \{\alpha_{\mathsf{Pred}}[\![\mathcal{S}^{\mathsf{Max}}]\!](\mathcal{P}) \mid \mathcal{P} \in \mathfrak{X}\}$. The following lemma immediately follows from the definition of $\alpha_{\mathsf{Pred}}[\![\mathcal{S}^{\mathsf{Max}}]\!]$.

Lemma 1. *Given a prediction trace property $\mathcal{Q}$ that corresponds to a maximal trace property $\mathcal{P}$, if a prefix trace σ belongs to $\mathcal{Q}$, then σ guarantees the satisfaction of property $\mathcal{P}$ (i.e. every valid maximal trace that is greater than or equal to σ is guaranteed to have property $\mathcal{P}$).*

Example 6 (Access Control, Continued). By α_{Pred}, each behavior in the lattice $\mathcal{L}^{\mathsf{Max}}$ of Example 5 can be abstracted into a prediction trace property:

- $\alpha_{\mathsf{Pred}}[\![\mathcal{S}^{\mathsf{Max}}]\!](\top^{\mathsf{Max}}) = \mathcal{S}^{\mathsf{Pref}}$, i.e. every valid trace in $\mathcal{S}^{\mathsf{Pref}}$ guarantees $\top^{\mathsf{Max}}$.
- $\alpha_{\mathsf{Pred}}[\![\mathcal{S}^{\mathsf{Max}}]\!](\texttt{RF}) = \{\sigma \in \mathcal{S}^{\mathsf{Pref}} \mid \texttt{apv=1} \rhd \texttt{i1=0} \preceq \sigma \vee \texttt{apv=1} \rhd \texttt{i1=1} \rhd \neg\texttt{(i1==0)} \rhd \texttt{i2=0} \preceq \sigma\ \}$, i.e. for any valid trace, if at least one of first two inputs is 0, then it guarantees "Read Failure" RF.
- $\alpha_{\mathsf{Pred}}[\![\mathcal{S}^{\mathsf{Max}}]\!](\texttt{RS}) = \{\sigma \in \mathcal{S}^{\mathsf{Pref}} \mid \texttt{apv=1} \rhd \texttt{i1=1} \rhd \neg\texttt{(i1==0)} \rhd \texttt{i2=1} \preceq \sigma\}$, i.e. for any valid trace, if first two inputs are 1, it guarantees "Read Success" RS.
- $\alpha_{\mathsf{Pred}}[\![\mathcal{S}^{\mathsf{Max}}]\!](\texttt{RO}) = \{\sigma \in \mathcal{S}^{\mathsf{Pref}} \mid \texttt{apv=1} \rhd \texttt{i1=1} \rhd \neg\texttt{(i1==0)} \rhd \texttt{i2=1} \rhd \neg\texttt{(apv!=0\&\&i2==0)} \rhd \texttt{typ=1} \preceq \sigma\}$, i.e. for any valid trace, if first two inputs are 1 and the third input is 1, then it guarantees "Read Only access is granted" RO.
- $\alpha_{\mathsf{Pred}}[\![\mathcal{S}^{\mathsf{Max}}]\!](\texttt{RW}) = \{\sigma \in \mathcal{S}^{\mathsf{Pref}} \mid \texttt{apv=1} \rhd \texttt{i1=1} \rhd \neg\texttt{(i1==0)} \rhd \texttt{i2=1} \rhd \neg\texttt{(apv!=0\&\&i2==0)} \rhd \texttt{typ=2} \preceq \sigma\}$, i.e. for any valid trace, if first two inputs are 1 and the third is 2, then it guarantees "Read and Write access is granted" RW.
- $\alpha_{\mathsf{Pred}}[\![\mathcal{S}^{\mathsf{Max}}]\!](\bot^{\mathsf{Max}}) = \emptyset$, i.e. no valid trace can guarantee $\bot^{\mathsf{Max}}$. □

3.3 Observation of System Behaviors

Let $\mathcal{S}^{\mathsf{Max}}$ be the maximal trace semantics and $\mathcal{L}^{\mathsf{Max}}$ be the lattice of system behaviors designed as in Sect. 3.2. Given any prefix trace $\sigma \in \mathrm{E}^{*\infty}$, an observer can learn some information from it, more precisely, a maximal trace property $\mathcal{P} \in \mathcal{L}^{\mathsf{Max}}$ that is guaranteed by σ from the observer's perspective. In this section, an *observation* function $\mathbb{O}$ is proposed to represent such a "property learning process" of the observer, which is formally defined in the following three steps.

Inquiry Function. First, an *inquiry function* $\mathbb{I}$ is defined to map every trace $\sigma \in \mathrm{E}^{*\infty}$ to the strongest maximal trace property in $\mathcal{L}^{\mathsf{Max}}$ that σ can guarantee.

$$\mathbb{I} \in \wp(\mathrm{E}^{*\infty}) \mapsto \wp(\wp(\mathrm{E}^{*\infty})) \mapsto \mathrm{E}^{*\infty} \mapsto \wp(\mathrm{E}^{*\infty}) \qquad \text{inquiry (2)}$$
$$\mathbb{I}(\mathcal{S}^{\mathsf{Max}}, \mathcal{L}^{\mathsf{Max}}, \sigma) \triangleq$$
$$\quad \mathit{let}\ \alpha_{\mathsf{Pred}}[\![\mathcal{S}]\!](\mathcal{P}) = \{\sigma \in \mathsf{Pref}(\mathcal{P}) \mid \forall \sigma' \in \mathcal{S}.\ \sigma \preceq \sigma' \Rightarrow \sigma' \in \mathcal{P}\}\ \mathit{in}$$
$$\qquad \Cap\{\mathcal{P} \in \mathcal{L}^{\mathsf{Max}} \mid \sigma \in \alpha_{\mathsf{Pred}}[\![\mathcal{S}^{\mathsf{Max}}]\!](\mathcal{P})\}$$

Specially, for an invalid trace $\sigma \notin \mathcal{S}^{\mathsf{Pref}}$, there does not exist any $\mathcal{P} \in \mathcal{L}^{\mathsf{Max}}$ such that $\sigma \in \alpha_{\mathsf{Pred}}[\![\mathcal{S}^{\mathsf{Max}}]\!](\mathcal{P})$, therefore $\mathbb{I}(\mathcal{S}^{\mathsf{Max}}, \mathcal{L}^{\mathsf{Max}}, \sigma) = \emptyset = \bot^{\mathsf{Max}}$.

Corollary 1. *Given the semantics $\mathcal{S}^{\mathsf{Max}}$ and lattice $\mathcal{L}^{\mathsf{Max}}$ of system behaviors, if the inquiry function $\mathbb{I}$ maps a trace σ to a maximal trace property $\mathcal{P} \in \mathcal{L}^{\mathsf{Max}}$, then σ guarantees the satisfaction of $\mathcal{P}$ (i.e. every valid maximal trace that is greater than or equal to σ is guaranteed to have property $\mathcal{P}$).*

Lemma 2. *The inquiry function $\mathbb{I}(\mathcal{S}^{\mathsf{Max}}, \mathcal{L}^{\mathsf{Max}})$ is decreasing on the inquired trace σ: the greater (longer) σ is, the stronger property it can guarantee.*

Example 7 (Access Control, Continued). Using $\mathcal{S}^{\mathsf{Max}}$ defined in Example 3 and $\mathcal{L}^{\mathsf{Max}}$ defined in Example 5, the inquiry function $\mathbb{I}$ of definition (2) is such that:

- $\mathbb{I}(\mathcal{S}^{\mathsf{Max}}, \mathcal{L}^{\mathsf{Max}}, \texttt{apv=1}) = \top^{\mathsf{Max}}$, i.e. `apv=1` can guarantee only $\top^{\mathsf{Max}}$.
- $\mathbb{I}(\mathcal{S}^{\mathsf{Max}}, \mathcal{L}^{\mathsf{Max}}, \texttt{apv=1} \rhd \texttt{i1=0}) = \texttt{RF}$, i.e. after setting the first input as 0, "Read Failure" `RF` is guaranteed.
- $\mathbb{I}(\mathcal{S}^{\mathsf{Max}}, \mathcal{L}^{\mathsf{Max}}, \texttt{apv=1} \rhd \texttt{i1=1}) = \mathbb{I}(\mathcal{S}^{\mathsf{Max}}, \mathcal{L}^{\mathsf{Max}}, \texttt{apv=1} \rhd \texttt{i1=1} \rhd \neg\texttt{(i1==0)}) = \top^{\mathsf{Max}}$, i.e. if the first input is 1, only $\top^{\mathsf{Max}}$ is guaranteed before entering the second input.
- $\mathbb{I}(\mathcal{S}^{\mathsf{Max}}, \mathcal{L}^{\mathsf{Max}}, \texttt{apv=1} \rhd \texttt{i1=1} \rhd \neg\texttt{(i1==0)} \rhd \texttt{i2=0}) = \texttt{RF}$, i.e. if the second input is 0, "Read Failure" `RF` is guaranteed.
- $\mathbb{I}(\mathcal{S}^{\mathsf{Max}}, \mathcal{L}^{\mathsf{Max}}, \texttt{apv=1} \rhd \texttt{i1=1} \rhd \neg\texttt{(i1==0)} \rhd \texttt{i2=1}) = \texttt{RS}$, i.e. if first two inputs are 1, "Read Success" `RS` is guaranteed.
- $\mathbb{I}(\mathcal{S}^{\mathsf{Max}}, \mathcal{L}^{\mathsf{Max}}, \texttt{apv=1} \rhd \texttt{i1=1} \rhd \neg\texttt{(i1==0)} \rhd \texttt{i2=1} \rhd \neg\texttt{(i2==0)} \rhd \texttt{typ=2}) = \texttt{RW}$, i.e. if first two inputs are 1, after the third input is set to be 2, a stronger property "Read and Write access is granted" `RW` is guaranteed. □

Cognizance Function. As discussed in (P3) of Sect. 2.1, it is necessary to take the observer's cognizance into account. Specifically, in program security, the observer's cognizance can be used to represent attackers' capabilities (e.g. what they can learn from the program execution). Given a trace σ (not necessarily valid), if the observer cannot distinguish σ from some other traces, then he does not have an omniscient cognizance of σ, and the *cognizance* function $\mathbb{C}(\sigma)$ is defined to include all traces indistinguishable from σ.

$$\mathbb{C} \in \mathrm{E}^{*\infty} \mapsto \wp(\mathrm{E}^{*\infty}) \qquad \text{cognizance (3)}$$
$$\mathbb{C}(\sigma) \triangleq \{\sigma' \in \mathrm{E}^{*\infty} \mid \text{observer cannot distinguish } \sigma' \text{ from } \sigma\}$$

Such a cognizance function is extensive, i.e. $\forall\sigma \in \mathrm{E}^{*\infty}.\ \sigma \in \mathbb{C}(\sigma)$. In particular, there is an *omniscient observer* and its corresponding cognizance function is denoted as $\mathbb{C}_o$ such that $\forall\sigma \in \mathrm{E}^{*\infty}.\ \mathbb{C}_o(\sigma) = \{\sigma\}$, which means that every trace is unambiguous to the omniscient observer.

To facilitate the proof of some desired properties for the observation function defined later, two assumptions are made here without loss of generality:

(A1) The cognizance of a trace $\sigma\sigma'$ is the concatenation of cognizances of σ and σ'. I.e. $\forall\sigma,\sigma' \in \mathrm{E}^{*\infty}.\ \mathbb{C}(\sigma\sigma') = \{\tau\tau' \mid \tau \in \mathbb{C}(\sigma) \wedge \tau' \in \mathbb{C}(\sigma')\}$.
(A2) Given an invalid trace, the cognizance function would not return a valid trace. I.e. $\forall\sigma \in \mathrm{E}^{*\infty}.\ \sigma \notin \mathcal{S}^{\mathsf{Pref}} \Rightarrow \mathbb{C}(\sigma) \cap \mathcal{S}^{\mathsf{Pref}} = \emptyset$.

To make the assumption (A1) sound, we must have $\mathbb{C}(\varepsilon) = \{\varepsilon\}$, because otherwise, for any non-empty trace σ, $\mathbb{C}(\sigma) = \mathbb{C}(\sigma\varepsilon) = \{\tau\tau' \mid \tau \in \mathbb{C}(\sigma) \wedge \tau' \in \mathbb{C}(\varepsilon)\}$ does not have a fixpoint. In practice, $\{\langle\sigma,\sigma'\rangle \mid \sigma' \in \mathbb{C}(\sigma)\}$ is an equivalence relation, but the symmetry and transitivity property are not used in the proofs.

Example 8 (Access Control, Continued). Consider two separate observers.

(i) For an omniscient observer: $\forall\sigma \in \mathrm{E}^{*\infty}.\ \mathbb{C}_o(\sigma) = \{\sigma\}$.
(ii) For an observer representing the second admin who is unaware of the first input: $\mathbb{C}(\texttt{i1=0} \triangleright \texttt{i1==0} \triangleright \texttt{apv=0}) = \mathbb{C}(\texttt{i1=1} \triangleright \neg\texttt{(i1==0)}) = \{\texttt{i1=0} \triangleright \texttt{i1==0} \triangleright \texttt{apv=0},\ \texttt{i1=1} \triangleright \neg\texttt{(i1==0)}\}$, i.e. this observer cannot distinguish whether the first input is 0 or 1. Thus, for a prefix trace in which the first two inputs are 0, $\mathbb{C}(\texttt{apv=1} \triangleright \texttt{i1=0} \triangleright \texttt{i1==0} \triangleright \texttt{apv=0} \triangleright \texttt{i2=0}) = \{\texttt{apv=1} \triangleright \texttt{i1=0} \triangleright \texttt{i1==0} \triangleright \texttt{apv=0} \triangleright \texttt{i2=0},\ \texttt{apv=1} \triangleright \texttt{i1=1} \triangleright \neg\texttt{(i1==0)} \triangleright \texttt{i2=0}\}$, where `apv=1` and `i2=0` are known by this observer. In the same way, its cognizance on other traces can be generated. □

Observation Function. For an observer with cognizance function $\mathbb{C}$, given a single trace σ, the observer cannot distinguish σ with traces in $\mathbb{C}(\sigma)$. In order to formalize the information that the observer can learn from σ, we apply the inquiry function $\mathbb{I}$ on each trace in $\mathbb{C}(\sigma)$, and get a set of maximal trace properties. By joining them together, we get the strongest property in $\mathcal{L}^{\mathsf{Max}}$ that σ can guarantee from the observer's perspective. Such a process is defined as the *observation* function $\mathbb{O}(\mathcal{S}^{\mathsf{Max}}, \mathcal{L}^{\mathsf{Max}}, \mathbb{C}, \sigma)$.

$$\mathbb{O} \in \wp(\mathrm{E}^{*\infty}) \mapsto \wp(\wp(\mathrm{E}^{*\infty})) \mapsto (\mathrm{E}^{*\infty} \mapsto \wp(\mathrm{E}^{*\infty})) \mapsto \mathrm{E}^{*\infty} \mapsto \wp(\mathrm{E}^{*\infty})$$

$$\mathbb{O}(\mathcal{S}^{\mathsf{Max}}, \mathcal{L}^{\mathsf{Max}}, \mathbb{C}, \sigma) \triangleq \qquad \text{observation (4)}$$
$$\mathit{let}\ \alpha_{\mathsf{Pred}}[\![\mathcal{S}]\!](\mathcal{P}) = \{\sigma \in \mathsf{Pref}(\mathcal{P}) \mid \forall\sigma' \in \mathcal{S}.\ \sigma \preceq \sigma' \Rightarrow \sigma' \in \mathcal{P}\}\ \mathit{in}$$
$$\mathit{let}\ \mathbb{I}(\mathcal{S}, \mathcal{L}, \sigma) = \Cap\{\mathcal{P} \in \mathcal{L} \mid \sigma \in \alpha_{\mathsf{Pred}}[\![\mathcal{S}]\!](\mathcal{P})\}\ \mathit{in}$$
$$\Cup\{\mathbb{I}(\mathcal{S}^{\mathsf{Max}}, \mathcal{L}^{\mathsf{Max}}, \sigma') \mid \sigma' \in \mathbb{C}(\sigma)\}.$$

From the above definition, it is easy to see that, for every invalid trace σ, $\mathbb{O}(\mathcal{S}^{\mathsf{Max}}, \mathcal{L}^{\mathsf{Max}}, \mathbb{C}, \sigma) = \bot^{\mathsf{Max}}$, since every trace σ' in $\mathbb{C}(\sigma)$ is invalid by (A2) and $\mathbb{I}(\mathcal{S}^{\mathsf{Max}}, \mathcal{L}^{\mathsf{Max}}, \sigma') = \bot^{\mathsf{Max}}$. In addition, for an omniscient observer with cognizance function $\mathbb{C}_o$, its observation $\mathbb{O}(\mathcal{S}^{\mathsf{Max}}, \mathcal{L}^{\mathsf{Max}}, \mathbb{C}_o, \sigma) = \mathbb{I}(\mathcal{S}^{\mathsf{Max}}, \mathcal{L}^{\mathsf{Max}}, \sigma)$.

Corollary 2. *For any observer with cognizance $\mathbb{C}$, if the corresponding observation function maps a trace σ to a maximal trace property $\mathcal{P} \in \mathcal{L}^{\mathsf{Max}}$, then σ guarantees the satisfaction of property $\mathcal{P}$ (i.e. every valid maximal trace that is greater than or equal to σ is guaranteed to have property $\mathcal{P}$).*

Lemma 3. *The observation function $\mathbb{O}(\mathcal{S}^{\mathsf{Max}}, \mathcal{L}^{\mathsf{Max}}, \mathbb{C})$ is decreasing on the observed trace σ: the greater (longer) σ is, the stronger property it can observe.*

Example 9 (Access Control, Continued). For an omniscient observer, the observation function is identical to the inquire function in Example 7. If the cognizance of the second admin defined in Example 8 is adopted, we get an observation function that works exactly the same as the dashed arrows in Fig. 2:

- $\mathbb{O}(\mathcal{S}^{\mathsf{Max}}, \mathcal{L}^{\mathsf{Max}}, \mathbb{C}, \texttt{apv=1} \triangleright \texttt{i1=0}) = \mathbb{I}(\mathcal{S}^{\mathsf{Max}}, \mathcal{L}^{\mathsf{Max}}, \texttt{apv=1}\triangleright\texttt{i1=0}) \uplus \mathbb{I}(\mathcal{S}^{\mathsf{Max}}, \mathcal{L}^{\mathsf{Max}}, \texttt{apv=1} \triangleright \texttt{i1=1}) = \texttt{RF} \uplus \top^{\mathsf{Max}} = \top^{\mathsf{Max}}$, i.e. even if the first input is already 0 in the trace, no property except $\top^{\mathsf{Max}}$ can be guaranteed for the second admin.
- $\mathbb{O}(\mathcal{S}^{\mathsf{Max}}, \mathcal{L}^{\mathsf{Max}}, \mathbb{C}, \texttt{apv=1} \triangleright \texttt{i1=0} \triangleright \texttt{i1==0} \triangleright \texttt{apv=0} \triangleright \texttt{i2=1}) = \mathbb{I}(\mathcal{S}^{\mathsf{Max}}, \mathcal{L}^{\mathsf{Max}}, \texttt{apv=1} \triangleright \texttt{i1=0} \triangleright \texttt{i1==0} \triangleright \texttt{apv=0} \triangleright \texttt{i2=1}) \uplus \mathbb{I}(\mathcal{S}^{\mathsf{Max}}, \mathcal{L}^{\mathsf{Max}}, \texttt{apv=1} \triangleright \texttt{i1=1} \triangleright \neg\texttt{(i1==0)} \triangleright \texttt{i2=1}) = \texttt{RF} \uplus \top^{\mathsf{Max}} = \top^{\mathsf{Max}}$, i.e. if the second input is 1, only $\top^{\mathsf{Max}}$ can be guaranteed.
- $\mathbb{O}(\mathcal{S}^{\mathsf{Max}}, \mathcal{L}^{\mathsf{Max}}, \mathbb{C}, \texttt{apv=1} \triangleright \texttt{i1=0} \triangleright \texttt{i1==0} \triangleright \texttt{apv=0} \triangleright \texttt{i2=0}) = \mathbb{I}(\mathcal{S}^{\mathsf{Max}}, \mathcal{L}^{\mathsf{Max}}, \texttt{apv=1} \triangleright \texttt{i1=0} \triangleright \texttt{i1==0} \triangleright \texttt{apv=0} \triangleright \texttt{i2=0}) \uplus \mathbb{I}(\mathcal{S}^{\mathsf{Max}}, \mathcal{L}^{\mathsf{Max}}, \texttt{apv=1} \triangleright \texttt{i1=1} \triangleright \neg\texttt{(i1==0)} \triangleright \texttt{i2=0}) = \texttt{RF} \uplus \texttt{RF} = \texttt{RF}$, i.e. RF is guaranteed only after the second input is entered 0. □

3.4 Formal Definition of Responsibility

Using the three components of responsibility analysis introduced above, responsibility is formally defined as the *responsibility abstraction* α_R in (5). Specifically, the first parameter is the maximal trace semantics $\mathcal{S}^{\mathsf{Max}}$, the second parameter is the lattice $\mathcal{L}^{\mathsf{Max}}$ of system behaviors, the third parameter is the cognizance function of a given observer, the fourth parameter is the behavior $\mathcal{B}$ whose responsibility is of interest, and the last parameter is the analyzed traces $\mathcal{T}$.

Consider every trace $\sigma_{\mathrm{H}}\sigma_{\mathrm{R}}\sigma_{\mathrm{F}} \in \mathcal{T}$ where H, R and F respectively stand for *History*, *Responsible part* and *Future*. If $\emptyset \subsetneq \mathbb{O}(\mathcal{S}^{\mathsf{Max}}, \mathcal{L}^{\mathsf{Max}}, \mathbb{C}, \sigma_{\mathrm{H}}\sigma_{\mathrm{R}}) \subseteq \mathcal{B} \subsetneq \mathbb{O}(\mathcal{S}^{\mathsf{Max}}, \mathcal{L}^{\mathsf{Max}}, \mathbb{C}, \sigma_{\mathrm{H}})$ holds, then σ_{H} does not guarantee the behavior $\mathcal{B}$, while $\sigma_{\mathrm{H}}\sigma_{\mathrm{R}}$ guarantees a behavior which is at least as strong as $\mathcal{B}$ and is not the invalidity property represented by $\bot^{\mathsf{Max}} = \emptyset$. Therefore, σ_{R} is said to be *responsible* for ensuring behavior $\mathcal{B}$ in the trace $\sigma_{\mathrm{H}}\sigma_{\mathrm{R}}\sigma_{\mathrm{F}}$.

In particular, the length of σ_{R} is restricted to be 1 (i.e. $|\sigma_{\mathrm{R}}| = 1$), such that the responsible entity σ_{R} must be a single event and the responsibility analysis could be as refined as possible. Otherwise, if we do not have such a restriction, then for every analyzed trace $\sigma \in \mathcal{T}$ where the behavior $\mathcal{B}$ holds, the responsibility analysis may split the trace σ into three parts $\sigma = \sigma_{\mathrm{H}}\sigma_{\mathrm{R}}\sigma_{\mathrm{F}}$ such that $\sigma_{\mathrm{H}} = \varepsilon$, $\sigma_{\mathrm{R}} = \sigma$ and $\sigma_{\mathrm{F}} = \varepsilon$. In such a case, $\emptyset \subsetneq \mathbb{O}(\mathcal{S}^{\mathsf{Max}}, \mathcal{L}^{\mathsf{Max}}, \mathbb{C}, \sigma_{\mathrm{H}}\sigma_{\mathrm{R}}) \subseteq \mathcal{B} \subsetneq \mathbb{O}(\mathcal{S}^{\mathsf{Max}}, \mathcal{L}^{\mathsf{Max}}, \mathbb{C}, \sigma_{\mathrm{H}})$ holds, and the whole trace σ would be found responsible for $\mathcal{B}$. This result is trivially correct, but too coarse to be useful in practice.

Responsibility Abstraction α_R

$$\alpha_R \in \wp(\mathrm{E}^{*\infty}) \mapsto \wp(\wp(\mathrm{E}^{*\infty})) \mapsto (\mathrm{E}^{*\infty} \mapsto \wp(\mathrm{E}^{*\infty})) \mapsto \wp(\mathrm{E}^{*\infty}) \mapsto \wp(\mathrm{E}^{*\infty}) \mapsto \wp(\mathrm{E}^{*\infty} \times \mathrm{E} \times \mathrm{E}^{*\infty}) \tag{5}$$

$$\begin{aligned}
&\alpha_R(\mathcal{S}^{\mathsf{Max}}, \mathcal{L}^{\mathsf{Max}}, \mathbb{C}, \mathcal{B}, \mathcal{T}) \triangleq \\
&\quad \mathit{let}\ \alpha_{\mathsf{Pred}}[\![\mathcal{S}]\!](\mathcal{P}) = \{\sigma \in \mathsf{Pref}(\mathcal{P}) \mid \forall \sigma' \in \mathcal{S}.\, \sigma \preceq \sigma' \Rightarrow \sigma' \in \mathcal{P}\}\ \mathit{in} \\
&\quad\quad \mathit{let}\ \mathbb{I}(\mathcal{S}, \mathcal{L}, \sigma) = \Cap\{\mathcal{P} \in \mathcal{L} \mid \sigma \in \alpha_{\mathsf{Pred}}[\![\mathcal{S}]\!](\mathcal{P})\}\ \mathit{in} \\
&\quad\quad\quad \mathit{let}\ \mathbb{O}(\mathcal{S}, \mathcal{L}, \mathbb{C}, \sigma) = \Cup\{\mathbb{I}(\mathcal{S}, \mathcal{L}, \sigma') \mid \sigma' \in \mathbb{C}(\sigma)\}\ \mathit{in} \\
&\quad\quad\quad\quad \{\langle \sigma_{\mathrm{H}}, \sigma_{\mathrm{R}}, \sigma_{\mathrm{F}} \rangle \mid \sigma_{\mathrm{H}}\sigma_{\mathrm{R}}\sigma_{\mathrm{F}} \in \mathcal{T} \wedge |\sigma_{\mathrm{R}}| = 1 \wedge \\
&\quad\quad\quad\quad\quad \emptyset \subsetneq \mathbb{O}(\mathcal{S}^{\mathsf{Max}}, \mathcal{L}^{\mathsf{Max}}, \mathbb{C}, \sigma_{\mathrm{H}}\sigma_{\mathrm{R}}) \subseteq \mathcal{B} \subsetneq \mathbb{O}(\mathcal{S}^{\mathsf{Max}}, \mathcal{L}^{\mathsf{Max}}, \mathbb{C}, \sigma_{\mathrm{H}})\}
\end{aligned}$$

Since $\alpha_R(\mathcal{S}^{\mathsf{Max}}, \mathcal{L}^{\mathsf{Max}}, \mathbb{C}, \mathcal{B})$ preserves joins on analyzed traces $\mathcal{T}$, we have a Galois connection: $\langle \wp(\mathrm{E}^{*\infty}), \subseteq \rangle \xleftarrow[\alpha_R(\mathcal{S}^{\mathsf{Max}}, \mathcal{L}^{\mathsf{Max}}, \mathbb{C}, \mathcal{B})]{\gamma_R(\mathcal{S}^{\mathsf{Max}}, \mathcal{L}^{\mathsf{Max}}, \mathbb{C}, \mathcal{B})} \langle \wp(\mathrm{E}^{*\infty} \times \mathrm{E} \times \mathrm{E}^{*\infty}), \subseteq \rangle$.

Lemma 4. *If σ_R is said to be responsible for a behavior $\mathcal{B}$ in a valid trace $\sigma_H\sigma_R\sigma_F$, then $\sigma_H\sigma_R$ guarantees the occurrence of behavior $\mathcal{B}$, and there must exist another valid prefix trace $\sigma_H\sigma'_R$ such that the behavior $\mathcal{B}$ is not guaranteed.*

Recall the three desired points (time, free choices and cognizance) for defining responsibility in Sect. 2.1. It is obvious that α_R has taken both the temporal ordering of events and the observer's cognizance into account. As for the free choices, it is easy to find from Lemma 4 that, if σ_{R} is determined by its history trace σ_{H} and is not free to make choices (i.e. $\forall \sigma_{\mathrm{H}}\sigma_{\mathrm{R}}, \sigma_{\mathrm{H}}\sigma'_{\mathrm{R}} \in \mathcal{S}^{\mathsf{Pref}}.\ \sigma_{\mathrm{R}} = \sigma'_{\mathrm{R}}$), then σ_{R} cannot be responsible for any behavior in the trace $\sigma_{\mathrm{H}}\sigma_{\mathrm{R}}\sigma_{\mathrm{F}}$.

3.5 Responsibility Analysis

To sum up, the responsibility analysis typically consists of four steps: **(I)** collect the system's trace semantics $\mathcal{S}^{\mathsf{Max}}$ (in Sect. 3.1); **(II)** build the complete lattice of maximal trace properties of interest $\mathcal{L}^{\mathsf{Max}}$ (in Sect. 3.2); **(III)** derive an inquiry function $\mathbb{I}$ from $\mathcal{L}^{\mathsf{Max}}$, define a cognizance function $\mathbb{C}$ for each observer, and create the corresponding observation function $\mathbb{O}$ (in Sect. 3.3); **(IV)** specify the behavior $\mathcal{B}$ of interest and the analyzed traces $\mathcal{T}$, and apply the responsibility abstraction $\alpha_R(\mathcal{S}^{\mathsf{Max}}, \mathcal{L}^{\mathsf{Max}}, \mathbb{C}, \mathcal{B}, \mathcal{T})$ to get the analysis result (in Sect. 3.4). Hence, the responsibility analysis is essentially an abstract interpretation of the event trace semantics.

In the above definition of responsibility, the semantics and lattice of system behaviors are concrete, and they are explicitly displayed in the access control example for the sake of clarity. However, they may be uncomputable in practice, and we do not require programmers to provide them in the implementation of responsibility analysis. Instead, they are provided in the abstract, using an abstract interpretation-based static analysis that is sketched in [13].

Example 10 (Access Control, Continued). Using the observation functions created in Example 9, the abstraction α_R can analyze the responsibility of a certain behavior $\mathcal{B}$ in the set $\mathcal{T}$ of traces. Suppose we want to analyze "Read Failure" in every possible execution, then $\mathcal{B}$ is RF, and $\mathcal{T}$ includes all valid maximal traces, i.e. $\mathcal{T} = \mathcal{S}^{\text{Max}}$. Thus, $\alpha_R(\mathcal{S}^{\text{Max}}, \mathcal{L}^{\text{Max}}, \mathbb{C}, \text{RF}, \mathcal{S}^{\text{Max}})$ computes the responsibility analysis result, which is essential the same as desired in Example 2.

Furthermore, the responsibility of "granting write access" can be analyzed by setting the behavior $\mathcal{B}$ as RW instead, and we get the following result. To the cognizance of an omniscient observer, in every execution that both the first two inputs are 1, the third input (i.e. system setting of permission type) is responsible for RW. Meanwhile, to the cognizance of the second admin who is unaware of the first input, no one is found responsible for RW, because whether the write access fails or not is always uncertain, from the second admin's perspective.   □

4   Examples of Responsibility Analysis

Responsibility is a broad concept, and our definition of responsibility based on the abstraction of event trace semantics is universally applicable in various scientific fields. We have examined every example supplied in actual cause [19, 20] and found that our definition of responsibility can handle them well, in which actions like "drop a lit match in the forest" or "throw a rock at the bottle" are treated as events in the trace. In the following, we will illustrate the responsibility analysis by two more examples: the "negative balance" problem of a withdrawal transaction, and the information leakage problem.

4.1   Responsibility Analysis of "Negative Balance" Problem

Example 11 (Negative Balance). Consider the withdrawal transaction program in Fig. 4 in which the query_database() function gets the balance of a certain bank account before the transaction, and input() specifies the withdrawal amount that is positive. When the withdrawal transaction completes, if the balance is negative, which entity in the program shall be responsible for it?   □

It is not hard to see that, the "negative balance" problem can be transformed into an equivalent buffer overflow problem, where the memory of size balance is allocated and the index at n-1 is visited. Although this problem has been well studied, it suffices to demonstrate the advantages of responsibility analysis over dependency/causality analysis.

$$\top^{\text{Max}} = \mathcal{S}^{\text{Max}}$$
$$\diagup \qquad \diagdown$$
$$\text{NB} \qquad \neg\text{NB}$$
$$\diagdown \qquad \diagup$$
$$\bot^{\text{Max}} = \emptyset$$

```
1:  balance = query_database();
2:  n = input();  //Positive
3:  balance -= n;
```

Fig. 4. Withdrawal transaction program   **Fig. 5.** Lattice of behaviors

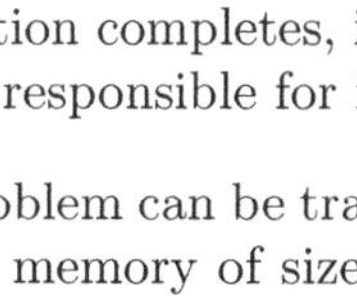

As discussed in Sect. 3.5, the responsibility analysis consists of four steps. For the sake of simplicity, we consider only the omniscient observer here.

(1) Taking each assignment as an event, each maximal trace in this program is of length 3, and the program's maximal trace semantics consists of infinite number of such traces. E.g. `balance=0` $\triangleright$ `n=5` $\triangleright$ `balance=-5` denotes a maximal execution, in which the balance before the transaction is 0 and the withdrawal amount is 5 such that "negative balance" occurs.
(2) Since "negative balance" is the only behavior that we are interested here, a lattice $\mathcal{L}^{\mathsf{Max}}$ of maximal trace properties in Fig. 5 with four elements can be built, where `NB` (Negative Balance) is the set of maximal traces where the value of `balance` is negative at the end, and $\neg$`NB` is its complement.
(3) Using the omniscient observer's cognizance $\mathbb{C}_o$, the observation function $\mathbb{O}$ can be easily derived from the lattice $\mathcal{L}^{\mathsf{Max}}$, such that:
   - $\mathbb{O}(\mathcal{S}^{\mathsf{Max}}, \mathcal{L}^{\mathsf{Max}}, \mathbb{C}_o, \varepsilon) = \top^{\mathsf{Max}}$;
   - $\mathbb{O}(\mathcal{S}^{\mathsf{Max}}, \mathcal{L}^{\mathsf{Max}}, \mathbb{C}_o, \texttt{balance=i}) = \texttt{NB}$ where $\texttt{i} \leq 0$, i.e. if the balance before the transaction is negative or 0, the occurrence of "negative balance" is guaranteed before the withdrawal amount `n` is entered;
   - $\mathbb{O}(\mathcal{S}^{\mathsf{Max}}, \mathcal{L}^{\mathsf{Max}}, \mathbb{C}_o, \texttt{balance=i}) = \top^{\mathsf{Max}}$ where $\texttt{i} > 0$, i.e. if the balance before the transaction is strictly greater than 0, whether "negative balance" occurs or not has not been decided;
   - $\mathbb{O}(\mathcal{S}^{\mathsf{Max}}, \mathcal{L}^{\mathsf{Max}}, \mathbb{C}_o, \texttt{balance=i} \triangleright \texttt{n=j}) = \texttt{NB}$ where $\texttt{i} > 0$ and $\texttt{j} > \texttt{i}$, i.e. "negative balance" is guaranteed to occur immediately after `input()` returns a value strictly greater than `balance`;
   - $\mathbb{O}(\mathcal{S}^{\mathsf{Max}}, \mathcal{L}^{\mathsf{Max}}, \mathbb{C}_o, \texttt{balance=i} \triangleright \texttt{n=j}) = \neg\texttt{NB}$ where $\texttt{i} > 0$ and $\texttt{j} \leq \texttt{i}$, i.e. "negative balance" is guaranteed not to occur immediately after `input()` returns a value less than or equal to `balance`.
(4) Suppose the behavior $\mathcal{B} = \texttt{NB}$ and the analyzed traces $\mathcal{T} = \mathcal{S}^{\mathsf{Max}}$, the abstraction $\alpha_R(\mathcal{S}^{\mathsf{Max}}, \mathcal{L}^{\mathsf{Max}}, \mathbb{C}_o, \mathcal{B}, \mathcal{T})$ gets the following result. If `query_database()` returns 0 or a negative value, no matter what value `input()` returns, the function `query_database()` (i.e. event `balance=i`) is responsible for "negative balance", and further responsibility analysis shall be applied on the previous transactions of the database. Otherwise, if `query_database()` returns a value strictly greater than 0, the function `input()` (i.e. event `n=j`) takes the responsibility for "negative balance", thus "negative balance" can be prevented by configuring the permission granted to `input()` such that its permitted return value must be less than or equal to the returned value of `query_database()`.

4.2 Responsibility Analysis of Information Leakage

Essentially, responsibility analysis of information leakage is the same as read failure or "negative balance" problem, and the only significant distinction is on defining the behaviors of interest. Here we adopt the notion of non-interference [16] to represent the behavior of information leakage.

In the program, the inputs and outputs are classified as either *Low* (public, low sensitivity) or *High* (private, high sensitivity). For a given trace σ, if there is another trace σ' such that they have the same low inputs but different low outputs, then the trace σ is said to leak private information. If no trace in the program leaks private information (i.e. every two traces with the same low inputs have the same low outputs, regardless of the high inputs), the program is secure and has the non-interference property. Thus, for any program with maximal trace semantics $\mathcal{S}^{\mathsf{Max}}$, the behavior of "Information Leakage" IL is represented as the set of leaky traces, i.e. $\mathtt{IL} = \{\sigma \in \mathcal{S}^{\mathsf{Max}} \mid \exists \sigma' \in \mathcal{S}^{\mathsf{Max}}. low\_inputs(\sigma) = low\_inputs(\sigma') \wedge low\_outputs(\sigma) \neq low\_outputs(\sigma')\}$, where functions *low_inputs* and *low_outputs* collects low inputs and outputs along the trace, respectively. The behavior of "No information Leakage" NL is the complement of IL, i.e. $\mathtt{NL} = \{\sigma \in \mathcal{S}^{\mathsf{Max}} \mid \forall \sigma' \in \mathcal{S}^{\mathsf{Max}}. low\_inputs(\sigma) = low\_inputs(\sigma') \Rightarrow low\_outputs(\sigma) = low\_outputs(\sigma')\}$. Thus, the lattice $\mathcal{L}^{\mathsf{Max}}$ of maximal trace properties regarding information leakage can be built as in Fig. 6. Further, the corresponding observation function $\mathbb{O}$ can be created, and the analysis result can be obtained by applying the responsibility abstraction.

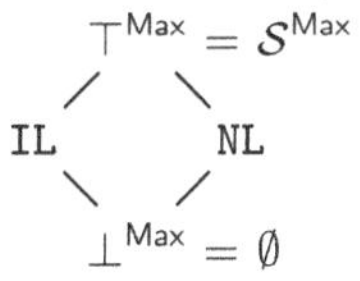

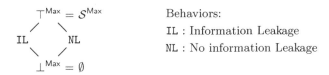

Behaviors:
IL : Information Leakage
NL : No information Leakage

Fig. 6. Lattice of behaviors regarding information leakage

Notice that we are interested in analyzing only the insecure programs in which some traces leak private information while others do not, i.e. $\mathtt{IL} \subsetneq \top^{\mathsf{Max}}$. For the erroneous programs where every trace leaks private information, i.e. $\mathtt{IL} = \top^{\mathsf{Max}}$, we need to admit that our responsibility analysis cannot identify any entity responsible for the leakage, unless "launching the program" is treated as an event and it would be found responsible for leaking private information.

5 Related Work

Definition of Causality and Responsibility. Hume [22] is the first one to specify causation by counterfactual dependence [29]. The best known counterfactual theory of causation is proposed by Lewis [28], which defines causation as a transitive closure of counterfactual dependencies. Halpern and Pearl [19,20,30] defines actual causality based on SEM and extends counterfactual dependency to allow "contingent dependency". Chockler and Halpern [8] defines responsibility to have a quantitative measure of the relevance between causes and effects, and defines blame to consider the epistemic state of an agent. Their application of actual causality, responsibility and blame is mainly on artificial intelligence.

Our definition of responsibility also adopts the idea of counterfactual dependence in the sense that, suppose an event σ_{R} is said to be responsible for behavior $\mathcal{B}$ in the trace $\sigma_{\mathrm{H}}\sigma_{\mathrm{R}}$, there must exist another event σ'_{R} such that, if σ_{R} is replaced by σ'_{R}, then $\mathcal{B}$ is not guaranteed (by Lemma 4).

Error Cause Localization. Classic program analysis techniques, e.g. dependency analysis [1,7,37] and program slicing [2,27,38,39], are useful in detecting the code that may be relevant to errors, but fail to localize the cause of error.

In recent years, there are many papers [3,17,18,24,25,32–34] on fault localization for counterexample traces, and most of them compare multiple traces produced by a model checker and build a heuristic metric to localize the point from which error traces separate from correct traces. Other related papers include error diagnosis by abductive/backward inference [14], tracking down bugs by dynamic invariant detection [21]. Actual causality is applied to explain counterexamples from model checker [5] and estimate the coverage of specification [9]. Besides, there are researches on analyzing causes of specific security issues. E.g. King et al. [26] employ a blame dependency graph to explain the source of information flow violation and generate a program slice as the error report.

Compared to the above techniques, this paper succeeds to formally define the cause or responsibility, and the proposed responsibility analysis, which does not require a counterexample from the model checker, is sound, scalable and generic to cope with various problems.

6 Conclusion and Future Work

This paper formally defines responsibility as an abstraction of event trace semantics. Typically, the responsibility analysis consists of four steps: collect the trace semantics, build a lattice of behaviors of interest, create an observation function for each observer, and apply the responsibility abstraction on analyzed traces. Its effectiveness has been demonstrated by several examples.

In the future, we intent to: (1) formalize the abstract responsibility analysis that is sketched in [13], (2) build a lattice of responsibility abstractions to cope with possible alternative weaker or stronger definitions of responsibility, (3) generalize the definition of cognizance function as an abstraction of system semantics, and (4) study the responsibility analysis of probabilistic programs.

Acknowledgment. This work was supported in part by NSF Grant CNS-1446511. Any opinions, findings, and conclusions or recommendations expressed in this material are those of the authors and do not necessarily reflect the views of the National Science Foundation. P. Cousot thanks Marco Pistoia for initial discussions on responsibility while visiting the Thomas J. Watson Research Center at Hawthorne in 2005.

References

1. Abadi, M., Banerjee, A., Heintze, N., Riecke, J.G.: A core calculus of dependency. In: POPL, pp. 147–160. ACM (1999)

2. Agrawal, H., Horgan, J.R.: Dynamic program slicing. In: PLDI, pp. 246–256. ACM (1990)
3. Ball, T., Naik, M., Rajamani, S.K.: From symptom to cause: localizing errors in counterexample traces. In: POPL, pp. 97–105. ACM (2003)
4. Beebee, H., Hitchcock, C., Menzie, P.: The Oxford Handbook of Causation. Oxford University Press, Oxford (2009)
5. Beer, I., Ben-David, S., Chockler, H., Orni, A., Trefler, R.J.: Explaining counterexamples using causality. Form. Methods Syst. Des. **40**(1), 20–40 (2012)
6. Chen, B., Pearl, J., Bareinboim, E.: Incorporating knowledge into structural equation models using auxiliary variables. In: IJCAI, pp. 3577–3583. IJCAI/AAAI Press (2016)
7. Cheney, J., Ahmed, A., Acar, U.A.: Provenance as dependency analysis. Math. Struct. Comput. Sci. **21**(6), 1301–1337 (2011)
8. Chockler, H., Halpern, J.Y.: Responsibility and blame: a structural-model approach. J. Artif. Intell. Res. **22**, 93–115 (2004)
9. Chockler, H., Halpern, J.Y., Kupferman, O.: What causes a system to satisfy a specification? ACM Trans. Comput. Log. **9**(3), 20:1–20:26 (2008)
10. Christopher, W.J.: Structural Equation Models, From Paths to Networks. Studies in Systems, Decision and Control, vol. 22. Springer, Cham (2015). https://doi.org/10.1007/978-3-319-16507-3
11. Cousot, P., Cousot, R.: Abstract interpretation: a unified lattice model for static analysis of programs by construction or approximation of fixpoints. In: POPL, pp. 238–252. ACM (1977)
12. Cousot, P., Cousot, R.: Systematic design of program analysis frameworks. In: POPL, pp. 269–282. ACM Press (1979)
13. Deng, C., Cousot, P.: Responsibility analysis by abstract interpretation. arXiv:1907.08251 [cs.PL] (2019)
14. Dillig, I., Dillig, T., Aiken, A.: Automated error diagnosis using abductive inference. In: PLDI, pp. 181–192. ACM (2012)
15. Frankle, J., Park, S., Shaar, D., Goldwasser, S., Weitzner, D.J.: Practical accountability of secret processes. In: USENIX Security Symposium, pp. 657–674. USENIX Association (2018)
16. Goguen, J.A., Meseguer, J.: Security policies and security models. In: IEEE Symposium on Security and Privacy, pp. 11–20. IEEE Computer Society (1982)
17. Griesmayer, A., Staber, S., Bloem, R.: Automated fault localization for C programs. Electr. Notes Theor. Comput. Sci. **174**(4), 95–111 (2007)
18. Groce, A., Chaki, S., Kroening, D., Strichman, O.: Error explanation with distance metrics. STTT **8**(3), 229–247 (2006)
19. Halpern, J.Y., Pearl, J.: Causes and explanations: a structural-model approach: Part 1: Causes. In: UAI, pp. 194–202. Morgan Kaufmann (2001)
20. Halpern, J.Y., Pearl, J.: Causes and explanations: a structural-model approach. Part I: causes. The Br. J. Philos. Sci. **56**(4), 843–887 (2005)
21. Hangal, S., Lam, M.S.: Tracking down software bugs using automatic anomaly detection. In: ICSE, pp. 291–301. ACM (2002)
22. Hume, D.: An Enquiry Concerning Human Understanding. A. Millar, London (1748). http://www.davidhume.org/texts/ehu.html
23. Jagadeesan, R., Jeffrey, A., Pitcher, C., Riely, J.: Towards a theory of accountability and audit. In: Backes, M., Ning, P. (eds.) ESORICS 2009. LNCS, vol. 5789, pp. 152–167. Springer, Heidelberg (2009). https://doi.org/10.1007/978-3-642-04444-1_10

24. Jin, H.S., Ravi, K., Somenzi, F.: Fate and FreeWill in error traces. In: Katoen, J.-P., Stevens, P. (eds.) TACAS 2002. LNCS, vol. 2280, pp. 445–459. Springer, Heidelberg (2002). https://doi.org/10.1007/3-540-46002-0_31
25. Jose, M., Majumdar, R.: Cause clue clauses: error localization using maximum satisfiability. In: PLDI, pp. 437–446. ACM (2011)
26. King, D., Jaeger, T., Jha, S., Seshia, S.A.: Effective blame for information-flow violations. In: SIGSOFT FSE, pp. 250–260. ACM (2008)
27. Korel, B., Rilling, J.: Dynamic program slicing methods. Inf. Softw. Technol. **40**(11–12), 647–659 (1998)
28. Lewis, D.: Causation. J. Philos. **70**(17), 556–567 (1973)
29. Menzies, P.: Counterfactual theories of causation. In: Zalta, E.N. (ed.) The Stanford Encyclopedia of Philosophy. Metaphysics Research Lab, Stanford University, Winter 2017 edn. (2017)
30. Pearl, J.: Causality: Models, Reasoning and Inference, 2nd edn. Cambridge University Press, Cambridge (2013)
31. Pistoia, M., Flynn, R.J., Koved, L., Sreedhar, V.C.: Interprocedural analysis for privileged code placement and tainted variable detection. In: Black, A.P. (ed.) ECOOP 2005. LNCS, vol. 3586, pp. 362–386. Springer, Heidelberg (2005). https://doi.org/10.1007/11531142_16
32. Qi, D., Roychoudhury, A., Liang, Z., Vaswani, K.: Darwin: an approach for debugging evolving programs. In: ESEC/SIGSOFT FSE, pp. 33–42. ACM (2009)
33. Ravi, K., Somenzi, F.: Minimal assignments for bounded model checking. In: Jensen, K., Podelski, A. (eds.) TACAS 2004. LNCS, vol. 2988, pp. 31–45. Springer, Heidelberg (2004). https://doi.org/10.1007/978-3-540-24730-2_3
34. Renieris, M., Reiss, S.P.: Fault localization with nearest neighbor queries. In: ASE, pp. 30–39. IEEE Computer Society (2003)
35. Rival, X.: Understanding the Origin of Alarms in Astrée. In: Hankin, C., Siveroni, I. (eds.) SAS 2005. LNCS, vol. 3672, pp. 303–319. Springer, Heidelberg (2005). https://doi.org/10.1007/11547662_21
36. van Sliedregt, E.: Individual Criminal Responsibility in International Law. Oxford Monographs in International Law. Oxford University Press, Oxford (2012)
37. Urban, C., Müller, P.: An abstract interpretation framework for input data usage. In: Ahmed, A. (ed.) ESOP 2018. LNCS, vol. 10801, pp. 683–710. Springer, Cham (2018). https://doi.org/10.1007/978-3-319-89884-1_24
38. Weiser, M.: Program slicing. In: ICSE, pp. 439–449. IEEE Computer Society (1981)
39. Weiser, M.: Program slicing. IEEE Trans. Softw. Eng. **10**(4), 352–357 (1984)
40. Weitzner, D.J., Abelson, H., Berners-Lee, T., Feigenbaum, J., Hendler, J.A., Sussman, G.J.: Information accountability. Commun. ACM **51**(6), 82–87 (2008)

Abstract Semantic Dependency

Patrick Cousot
Courant Institute of Mathematical Sciences, New York University, New York, USA
pcousot@cs.nyu.edu

Abstract. Dependency is a prevalent notion in computer science. There have been numerous informal or formal attempts to define viable syntactic and semantic concepts of dependency in programming languages with subtle variations and limitations. We develop a new value dependency analysis defined by abstract interpretation of a trace semantics. A sound approximate dependency algorithm is formally derived by calculational design. Further abstractions provide information flow, slicing, non-interference, dye, and taint analyses.

1 Introduction

Motivation: Dependency is a prevalent notion in computer science. For example it is useful in program development [14], it is an important part of any parallelizing compiler [54]. It appears in dataflow analysis [51,64], (abstract) program slicing [68,56,49,5], program refactoring [7], hardware design [2] and debugging [46]. It is prevailing in security, [30,12] including privacy analysis [59,47], and in data bases [27].

Context: There have been numerous attempts to define a viable semantic concept of dependency in programming languages. For example they are purely syntactic, not taking data into account [68]. Or they are postulated on programs [26,6,1] or on one execution trace [69] rather than derived from a definition of dependency and a definition of the program semantics. Or they are limited to one [17] or a few [48] of the many possible definitions of dependency based on a specific instrumentation of the semantics of a given language. Or they make assumptions of when dependencies are observed *e.g.* on program termination only [30,8,11] maybe including nontermination [5,64]. These are typical limitations that we would like to overcome.

Objective: Our aim is to introduce, justify, and illustrate a methodology to define flexible concepts of dependency and corresponding static analyzes that can be adapted to various contexts of use, each context requiring different notions of dependency, sometimes with subtle variations.

The general idea of dependency is that modifying something in an execution will later modify some other thing in the execution. This involves comparing at least two executions, the original and the modified one. Therefore dependency is not a property of a trace (such as invariance and termination) but a property of a set of traces (such as program equivalence), sometimes called hyperproperty [18].

Previous definitions of dependency (and related notions such as interference) have called for changing the description of program executions by considering multisemantics [16] or multilogics [31] handling more than one execution at a time. Other abstract interpretation-based definitions of dependency consider

B.-Y. E. Chang (Ed.): SAS 2019, LNCS 11822, pp. 389–410, 2019.
https://doi.org/10.1007/978-3-030-32304-2_19

only one execution trace (by postulating dependency on that execution trace [69] or by annotating the semantics [17,28]). When considering several execution traces, dependency can be defined by abstracting to functional dependency [56]. Otherwise, one can provide an hypercollecting semantics [8,64] which then abstracted.

As usual in abstract interpretation [23], we represent properties of entities in a universe $\mathbb{U}$ by a subset of this universe. So a property of elements of $\mathbb{U}$ belongs to $\wp(\mathbb{U})$. For example "to be a natural" is the property $\mathbb{N} \triangleq \{n \in \mathbb{Z} \mid n \geqslant 0\}$ of the integers $\mathbb{Z}$. The property "n is a natural" is "$n \in \mathbb{N}$".

Given a program component S which semantics $\mathcal{S}[\![\mathsf{S}]\!]$ is an element of the semantic domain $\mathcal{D}[\![\mathsf{S}]\!]$, we understand a program component property P as a property of its semantics $\mathcal{S}[\![\mathsf{S}]\!] \in \mathcal{D}[\![\mathsf{S}]\!]$ so $P \in \wp(\mathcal{D}[\![\mathsf{S}]\!])$ and $\mathcal{S}[\![\mathsf{S}]\!] \in P$ means that $\mathcal{S}[\![\mathsf{S}]\!]$ has property P. The *collecting semantics* is the strongest program property, that is the singleton $\{\mathcal{S}[\![\mathsf{S}]\!]\}$.

For example, the semantics we consider is a relation between a finite execution trace representing a past computation into its continuation into the future which may not terminate so $\mathcal{D}[\![\mathsf{S}]\!] = \wp(\mathbb{T}^+ \times \mathbb{T}^{+\infty})$ where $\mathbb{T}^+$ is the set of all finite execution traces and $\mathbb{T}^{+\infty}$ the set of all finite or infinite execution traces. So program properties belong to $\wp(\wp(\mathbb{T}^+ \times \mathbb{T}^{+\infty}))$. They are often called "hyper properties", after [18]. This terminology is supposed to rectify a previous misunderstanding of program properties in [3], where property stands for a trace property. More precisely, a program semantics is a set of execution traces in $\wp(\mathbb{T}^{+\infty})$ and a program property is also a set of execution traces in $\wp(\mathbb{T}^{+\infty})$. So a semantics and its properties belong to the same semantic domain, which is apparently incoherent.

Considering a property as a set of entities (with this property) has several advantages. It applies to languages which semantics are not naturally defined as traces *e.g.* [51] for logic programs. It avoids the definition of program properties through program transformation (like [10] duplicating programs which can compare one execution to another one but not one too many other ones). It eliminates the expressivity problems of logics (which can always be taken into account by a further abstraction). It eliminates the need to define different notions of properties for different notions of entities. In particular, the abstraction of a property is a property such as $\langle \wp(\wp(\mathbb{T}^{+\infty})), \subseteq\rangle \xrightleftharpoons[\alpha_\cup]{\gamma_\cup} \langle \wp(\mathbb{T}^{+\infty}), \subseteq\rangle$ with $\alpha_\cup(X) \triangleq \cup X$, thus solving the apparent incoherence of [3]. Finally, and more importantly, it aims at avoiding to create different theories for concepts that are the same.

One difficulty encountered *e.g.* by [8,64] to define dependency is to lift the structural trace semantics of a program component in $\wp(\mathbb{T}^+ \times \mathbb{T}^{+\infty})$ into a structural collecting semantics in $\wp(\wp(\mathbb{T}^+ \times \mathbb{T}^{+\infty}))$. For example, [8] has $\mathcal{D}[\![\mathsf{S}]\!] = \mathbf{Trc}_\perp \to \mathbf{Trc}_\perp$ (where $\mathbf{Trc}$ is a set of pairs of initial-final states augmented by $\perp$ for non-termination) while the (hyper-)collecting semantics is in $\wp(\wp(\mathbf{Trc})) \to \wp(\wp(\mathbf{Trc}))$ not in $\wp(\mathbf{Trc}_\perp \to \mathbf{Trc}_\perp)$. This is a strict approximation (as shown by [8, Theorem 1] which is an inclusion not an equality). Similarly, [64] uses an "outcome semantics" which approximates the (hyper-)collecting semantics.

These collecting semantics are specialized for dependency and lack generality since traces are approximated by a relation or function, but the advantage is that dependency boils down to functional dependency, which is easy to define [56]. We show that, for dependency, we can dispense with the formal structural definition of the (hyper-)collecting semantics $\{\mathcal{S}[\![\mathsf{S}]\!]\}$ (since it is trivially isomorphic to $\mathcal{S}[\![\mathsf{S}]\!]$ by the singleton map $\bullet \rightarrow \{\bullet\}$).

Content: We consider the syntax and trace semantics of iterative programs as defined in [20, Section **2**] in this volume. Traces are necessary to allow us to observe sequences of values of variables, in particular infinite ones. More abstract input/output semantics (such as denotational, natural, or axiomatic semantics) would not be adequate since intermediate or infinite computations are abstracted away. Informal requirements on the semantic definition of dependency are illustrated in Section **3**. The formal definition of value dependency is in Section **4**. We prove that this definition is valid both for prefix and maximal trace semantics hence excludes timing channels including empty observations. The calculational design of the structural static potential value dependency analysis is in Section **5**. It is not postulated without justification but designed by abstract interpretation of the semantics, handling uniformly the control and data dependency notions of [26]. Dye and tracking analysis are further abstractions described in Section **7**. We discuss related work and conclude in Section **2**.

2 Syntax and Trace Semantics

We consider a subset of `C` with simple variables, arithmetic and boolean expressions, assignment, skip (`;`), conditionals, **`while`** iterations, break, compound statement, statement lists. The syntax, program labelling, prefix trace semantics, and maximal trace semantics of this subset of `C` is defined in [20, Section **2**] in this volume. The main idea is that $\langle \pi_0, \pi_1 \rangle \in \mathcal{S}[\![\mathsf{S}]\!]$ if and only if the trace π_0 representing a past computation arriving at `S` is continued within `S` by π_1 resulting in a computation $\pi_0 \mathbin{\hat{}} \pi_1$. The continuation trace π_1 is finite prefix of the whole computation when $\mathcal{S}[\![\mathsf{S}]\!] = \mathcal{S}^*[\![\mathsf{S}]\!]$. π_1 is finite maximal or infinite when $\mathcal{S}[\![\mathsf{S}]\!] = \mathcal{S}^{+\infty}[\![\mathsf{S}]\!]$. $\varrho(\pi)\mathsf{x}$ denotes the value of a variable `x` at the end of the trace π.

3 Informal Requirements for a Semantic Definition of Dependency

According to [26], "Information *flows* from object `x` to object `y`, denoted $\mathsf{x} \rightsquigarrow \mathsf{y}$, whenever information stored in `x` is transferred to, or used to derive information transferred to, object `y`". When $\mathsf{x} \rightsquigarrow \mathsf{y}$ we say that `x` *flows* to `y` or, when considering the inverse relation, that `y` *depends* on `x`. To make this information flow clear, most definitions of in/dependency [17,65,64]) are of the form "changing (part of) the input (say `x`) may/should not change (part of) the output (say `y`)", sometimes including nontermination [64]. For example, a pure function depends on a parameter if and only if changing only this parameter changes the result of the function. In non-interference [30,48] changing private/untrusted input data should not change public/trusted output data. This shows that two different executions reflecting the change should be involved in the definition of dependency (or secrecy in [65]).

Dependency is usually *static* (valid for any execution of the program). The dependency relation $\rightsquigarrow$ can be *global* (valid anywhere in the program as in [26]) or *local* (that is relative to a correspondence between initial values of variables and their values when reaching a program point, if ever, including for nonterminating executions). We consider a *static* and *local* definition of dependency. The following examples illustrate this intuition and show how it may be made more precise.

Example 1 (explicit dependency). Consider ℓ_1 `y = x ;` ℓ_2. Changing the initial value y_0 of `y` will change the value of `y` at the entry point ℓ_1. Changing the initial value x_0 of `x` will not change the value of `y` at ℓ_1. So at the entry point ℓ_1, `y` depends on y_0 but not on x_0.

The value of `y` at exit point ℓ_2 is x_0 so changing the initial value y_0 of `y` will not change the value of `y` at ℓ_2. Changing the initial value x_0 of `x` will change the value of `y` at ℓ_2. So at ℓ_2, `y` depends on x_0 but not on y_0. Such a dependency at ℓ_2 is called explicit in [26] since it does not depend on the program control.

Dependency is local since `x` $\not\rightsquigarrow$ `y` at ℓ_1 but `x` $\rightsquigarrow$ `y` at ℓ_2. We write `x` $\not\rightsquigarrow^{\ell_2}$ `y` and `x` $\rightsquigarrow^{\ell_2}$ `y` to show the program point where dependency is specified □

Example 2 (implicit dependency). Consider $\mathtt{P_a} \triangleq \ell_1$ `y = 1 ;if` ℓ_2 `(x == 0) { ;`ℓ_4 `}`ℓ_5. Changing the initial value x_0 of `x` will change whether program control ℓ_4 is reached or not. If ℓ_4 is reached then the value of `y` at ℓ_4 will always be 1 so `y` does not depend on x_0 at ℓ_4 (and neither at ℓ_5).

Consider now $\mathtt{P_b} \triangleq \ell_1$ `y = 1 ;if` ℓ_2 `(x == 0) {` ℓ_3 `y = x ;`ℓ_4 `}`ℓ_5. Changing the initial value x_0 of `x` will change whether program control points ℓ_3 and ℓ_4 are reached or not. If ℓ_4 is reached then the value of `y` at ℓ_4 will always be 0 so `y` does not depend on x_0 at ℓ_4. However, depending on the initial value x_0 of `x`, the value of `y` at ℓ_5 will be either 1 (when $x_0 \neq 0$) or 0 (when $x_0 = 0$) so `y` depends on x_0 at ℓ_5. Such a dependency at ℓ_5 is called implicit in [26] since it depends on the program control. □

Our formalization of dependency does not need to distinguish implicit dependency (Ex. 2) from explicit dependency (Ex. 1) since the definition is the same in both cases.

Example 3 (timely dependency). Consider the program **`while`** `(0 == 0)` ℓ `y = x ;`. The sequence of values taken by `x` at ℓ is $x_0, x_0, x_0, \ldots$while it is $y_0, x_0, x_0, \ldots$for `y`. So `x` depends on x_0 while `y` depends on x_0 and y_0 at ℓ. For `y` considering only one possible value during the iterations would be insufficient to determine the dependency upon initial values and, in general, we have to consider the full sequence of successive values of `y` at a given program point ℓ. □

Example 4 (value dependency). Consider the program `while (0 == 0) { ℓ x = x - 1 ;if (x == 0) y = y + 1 ; }`. If $x_0 \leqslant 0$, the sequence of values of `y` at ℓ is the infinite sequence $y_0, y_0, y_0, ...$ If $x_0 > 0$, it is $\overbrace{y_0, \ldots, y_0}^{x_0 \texttt{times}}, y_0 + 1, y_0 + 1, ...$ So we can find two executions of the program with different initial values x_0 of `x` such that the sequences of values of `y` at ℓ have a common prefix but differ at least by one value after that prefix. So `y` depends on x_0 at ℓ. □

Example 5 (timing channel). Consider the program `int x, y; while (x > 0) ℓ x = x - 1 ;` (where we have added a declaration to show that the program involves variable `y`). If the initial value of `x` is $x_0 \leqslant 0$ then the sequence of values taken by `y` at ℓ is empty. Otherwise, if $x_0 > 0$, it is $y_0 \cdot y_0 \cdot \ldots \cdot y_0$ repeated x_0 times. So changing x_0 changes this sequence of values. Depending on x_0 we can find sequences of values of at ℓ that differ in length, but along these sequences we cannot find a point where they differ in value.

In security, this is a covert channel [44] (more precisely a timing channel [58]) which may or may not be considered as observable, the choice being application-dependent.

Traditionally, in dependency analysis, timing channels are not considered to be at the origin of dependencies [26], in particular when dependency is used in the context of compilation. □

Example 6 (empty observation). Consider the program `if (x==0) { ℓ₁ y = x ;ℓ₂ }ℓ₃`. What are the values of `y` observed at ℓ_2? If `x == 0` this is 0 while if `x != 0` there is no possible observation `y` at ℓ_2. So we may consider that an empty observation is a valid observation in which case `y` depends on `x` at ℓ_2. This is certainly a frequent point of view in security. On the contrary, we may exclude empty observations, in which case `y` does not depend on `x` at ℓ_2. This is more common in compilation (since `y` is constant at ℓ_2). Notice that in both cases `y` depends on `x` at ℓ_3 since we can observe different values of `y` depending on the test on `x`. □

Our definition of dependency relies on the timely observation of values but excludes timing channels and empty observations. This is an arbitrary choice that follows the implicit tradition in compilation.

4 Formal semantic definition of value dependency

Informally, we say that the initial value x_0 of variable `x` flows to variable `y` at program point ℓ (or `y` depends on the initial value of `x`), written $\mathtt{x} \overset{\ell}{\rightsquigarrow} \mathtt{y}$, if and only if changing the initial value x_0 of `x` will change the sequence of values taken by `y` whenever execution reaches program point ℓ.

Sequence of values of a variable at a program point Given an initialization trace $\pi_0 \in \mathbb{T}^+$ followed by a nonempty trace $\pi \in \mathbb{T}^{+\infty}$, let us define the sequence $\mathsf{seqval}[\![\mathtt{y}]\!]\ell(\pi_0, \pi)$ of values of the variable `y` at program point ℓ along the trace π continuing π_0 as follows.

$$\begin{aligned}
\mathsf{seqval}[\![\mathsf{y}]\!]\ell(\pi_0, \ell) &\triangleq \varrho(\pi_0)\mathsf{y} && (1)\\
\mathsf{seqval}[\![\mathsf{y}]\!]\ell(\pi_0, \ell') &\triangleq \ni && \text{when } \ell' \neq \ell\\
\mathsf{seqval}[\![\mathsf{y}]\!]\ell(\pi_0, \ell \xrightarrow{a} \ell''\pi) &\triangleq \varrho(\pi_0)\mathsf{y} \cdot \mathsf{seqval}[\![\mathsf{y}]\!]\ell(\pi_0 \mathbin{\bar{\,}} \ell \xrightarrow{a} \ell'', \ell''\pi)\\
\mathsf{seqval}[\![\mathsf{y}]\!]\ell(\pi_0, \ell' \xrightarrow{a} \ell''\pi) &\triangleq \mathsf{seqval}[\![\mathsf{y}]\!]\ell(\pi_0 \mathbin{\bar{\,}} \ell' \xrightarrow{a} \ell'', \ell''\pi) && \text{when } \ell' \neq \ell
\end{aligned}$$

$\mathsf{seqval}[\![\mathsf{y}]\!]\ell(\pi_0, \pi)$ is the empty sequence $\ni$ when ℓ does not appear in π. We rely on intuition that this definition applies to finite and infinite traces (by passing to the limit as in [20, Section **2.5**]).

The sequence of values of variable y at a program point ℓ abstracts away the position in traces where the values are observed. So execution time (represented as the number of steps that have been executed to reach a given position in the trace) is abstracted away.

Differences between sequences of values of a variable at a program point The definition of dependency of y on the initial value of x involves the comparison of sequences ω and ω' of the successive values of variable y taken at some program point for two different executions that differ on the initial value of x. By "differ", we mean that the sequences may have a common prefix but must eventually have a different value at some position in the sequences.

$$\mathsf{diff}(\omega, \omega') \triangleq \exists \omega_0, \omega_1, \omega'_1, \nu, \nu' \;.\; \omega = \omega_0 \cdot \nu \cdot \omega_1 \wedge \omega' = \omega_0 \cdot \nu' \cdot \omega'_1 \wedge \nu \neq \nu' \qquad (2)$$

Observe that $\neg\mathsf{diff}(\omega, \omega')$ implies either that $\omega = \omega'$ (the futures are the same so there is no dependency) or one is a strict prefix of the other (this is a timing channel abstracted away in this definition (2) of dependency). Because ω and ω' in (2) must contain at least one value, they cannot be empty (thus excluding Ex. 6).

Definition of value dependency Let us define $\mathcal{D}\ell\langle \mathsf{x}, \mathsf{y}\rangle$ to mean that "the sequence of values of variable y at ℓ depends upon the initial value of x", also written $\mathsf{x} \rightsquigarrow^{\ell} \mathsf{y}$ to mean that the initial value of x flows to y. So there are two execution traces whose initial values are the same but for x for which the sequences of values of y at program point ℓ on these two execution traces do differ.

Definition 1 (Dependency $\mathcal{D}$).

$$\begin{aligned}
\mathcal{D}\ell\langle \mathsf{x}, \mathsf{y}\rangle \triangleq \{\Pi \in \wp(\mathbb{T}^+ \times \mathbb{T}^{+\infty}) \mid{}& \exists \langle \pi_0, \pi_1\rangle, \langle \pi'_0, \pi'_1\rangle \in \Pi \,. && (3)\\
& (\forall \mathsf{z} \in \mathcal{V} \setminus \{\mathsf{x}\} \,.\, \varrho(\pi_0)\mathsf{z} = \varrho(\pi'_0)\mathsf{z}) \wedge\\
& \quad \mathsf{diff}(\mathsf{seqval}[\![\mathsf{y}]\!]\ell(\pi_0, \pi_1), \mathsf{seqval}[\![\mathsf{y}]\!]\ell(\pi'_0, \pi'_1))\} && \square
\end{aligned}$$

We do not need to require $\varrho(\pi_0)\mathsf{x} \neq \varrho(\pi'_0)\mathsf{x}$ in (3), since, the language being deterministic, the computations would be the same for the same initial values of variables.

Dependency in (3) defines (a) an abstraction of the past (the initial value of variables), (b) an abstraction of the future (seqval⟦y⟧), (c) the difference between past abstractions (the initial values of variables only differ for x), (d) the difference between futures (diff). It states that the abstraction of the future depends on the abstraction of the past if and only if there exist two executions with different past abstractions and different future abstractions.

Definition 2 (Value dependency flow). *At program point* ℓ *of program* P, *variable* y *depends on the initial value of variable* x *(or* $\mathsf{x} \overset{\ell}{\rightsquigarrow}_{\mathsf{P}} \mathsf{y}$ *i.e. the initial value of variable* x *flows to variable* y *at program point* ℓ*) if and only if*

$$\mathsf{x} \overset{\ell}{\rightsquigarrow}_{\mathsf{P}} \mathsf{y} \triangleq (\mathcal{S}^{+\infty}[\![\mathsf{P}]\!] \in \mathcal{D}\ell\langle\mathsf{x},\ \mathsf{y}\rangle). \tag{4}$$ □

The definition of seqval in (1) accounts for timely dependency (Ex. 3) while that of diff in (2) accounts for value dependency (Ex. 4) but excludes timing channels (Ex. 5) and empty observations (Ex. 6). Contrary to [26] there is no need for an artificial distinction between explicit (Ex. 1) and implicit flows (Ex. 2). In (3) and (4) both explicit and implicit flows are comprehended in exactly the same definition.

Notice that definition (4) of dependency is semantic-based and explicitly depends upon the program semantics. The notation $\mathsf{x} \overset{\ell}{\rightsquigarrow}_{\mathcal{S}^{+\infty}[\![\mathsf{P}]\!]} \mathsf{y}$ would be more precise.

Prefix versus maximal trace semantics based dependency The use of the prefix trace semantics $\mathcal{S}^{*}[\![\mathsf{P}]\!]$ is equivalent to that of the maximal trace semantics $\mathcal{S}^{+\infty}[\![\mathsf{P}]\!]$ in the definition (4) of dependency. This is formally stated by the following

Lemma 1 (Value dependency for finite prefix traces).

$$\mathsf{x} \overset{\ell}{\rightsquigarrow}_{\mathsf{P}} \mathsf{y} = (\mathcal{S}^{*}[\![\mathsf{P}]\!] \in \mathcal{D}\ell\langle\mathsf{x},\ \mathsf{y}\rangle).$$ □

Value dependency abstraction The value dependency abstraction of a semantic property $\mathcal{S} \in \wp(\wp(\mathbb{T}^{+} \times \mathbb{T}^{+\infty}))$ is

$$\alpha^{\mathrm{d}}(\mathcal{S})\ell \triangleq \{\langle\mathsf{x},\ \mathsf{y}\rangle \mid \mathcal{S} \subseteq \mathcal{D}\ell\langle\mathsf{x},\ \mathsf{y}\rangle\} \tag{5}$$

Lemma 2. *There is a Galois connection* $\langle\wp(\wp(\mathbb{T}^{+}\times\mathbb{T}^{+\infty})), \subseteq\rangle \underset{\alpha^{\mathrm{d}}}{\overset{\gamma^{\mathrm{d}}}{\leftrightarrows}} \langle\mathbb{P}^{\mathrm{d}}, \dot{\supseteq}\rangle$ *where* $\mathbb{P}^{\mathrm{d}} \triangleq \mathbb{L} \to \wp(\mathbb{V} \times \mathbb{V})$ *is ordered pointwise and the concretization of a dependency property* $\mathbf{D}$ *is*

$$\gamma^{\mathrm{d}}(\mathbf{D}) \triangleq \bigcap_{\ell\in\mathbb{L}} \bigcap_{\langle\mathsf{x},\ \mathsf{y}\rangle\in\mathbf{D}(\ell)} \mathcal{D}\ell\langle\mathsf{x},\ \mathsf{y}\rangle$$ □

The intuition is that the more semantics $\mathcal{S}$ have semantic property $\mathcal{S}$, the less dependencies can be found *i.e.* $\mathcal{S} \subseteq \mathcal{S}' \Rightarrow \alpha^{\mathrm{d}}(\mathcal{S})\ell \supseteq \alpha^{\mathrm{d}}(\mathcal{S}')\ell$. This is because the dependencies must exist for all semantics $\mathcal{S}$ having semantic property $\mathcal{S}$. Otherwise stated, the less dependencies you consider, the more semantics will exactly have these dependencies.

This is different from the observation than larger semantics have more dependencies $\mathcal{S} \subseteq \mathcal{S}' \Rightarrow \alpha^{\mathrm{d}}(\{\mathcal{S}\})\ell \subseteq \alpha^{\mathrm{d}}(\{\mathcal{S}'\})\ell$ since $\mathcal{S} \in \mathcal{D}\ell\langle \mathtt{x}, \mathtt{y}\rangle \Rightarrow \mathcal{S}' \in \mathcal{D}\ell\langle \mathtt{x}, \mathtt{y}\rangle$.

Value dependency semantics is an abstraction of the collecting trace semantics.

Corollary 1 (Value dependency for finite prefix traces).

$$\lambda \ell \bullet \{\langle \mathtt{x}, \mathtt{y}\rangle \mid \mathtt{x} \rightsquigarrow^{\ell}_{\mathtt{P}} \mathtt{y}\} = \alpha^{\mathrm{d}}(\{\mathcal{S}^{+\infty}[\![\mathtt{P}]\!]\}) = \alpha^{\mathrm{d}}(\{\mathcal{S}^{*}[\![\mathtt{P}]\!]\}) \qquad \square$$

Exact, definite, and potential value dependency semantics The exact value dependency semantics $\overline{\mathcal{S}}^{\,\mathrm{diff}}$ abstracts the maximal trace semantics, or equivalently, by Lem. 1, the prefix trace semantics by the dependency abstraction. By Rice theorem [55], $\{\mathcal{S}^{*}[\![\mathtt{S}]\!]\}$ is not computable so $\overline{\mathcal{S}}^{\,\mathrm{diff}}$ is not computable in this way. Therefore, static analysis must content itself with approximations (or unsoundness that we disapprove of). There are two possibilities. Definite value dependency is an under-approximation of value dependency (so $\emptyset$ is a correct under-approximation). Potential value dependency is an over-approximation of value dependency (so $\mathbb{V} \times \mathbb{V}$ is a correct over-approximation). Formally,

$$\begin{aligned}
\overline{\mathcal{S}}^{\,\mathrm{diff}}[\![\mathtt{S}]\!] &\triangleq \alpha^{\mathrm{d}}(\{\mathcal{S}^{+\infty}[\![\mathtt{S}]\!]\}) = \alpha^{\mathrm{d}}(\{\mathcal{S}^{*}[\![\mathtt{S}]\!]\}) && \text{exact dependency}\\
\overline{\mathcal{S}}^{\,\mathrm{diff}}_{\forall}[\![\mathtt{S}]\!] &\mathrel{\dot{\subseteq}} \alpha^{\mathrm{d}}(\{\mathcal{S}^{+\infty}[\![\mathtt{S}]\!]\}) && \text{definite dependency}\\
\alpha^{\mathrm{d}}(\{\mathcal{S}^{+\infty}[\![\mathtt{S}]\!]\}) &\mathrel{\dot{\subseteq}} \overline{\mathcal{S}}^{\,\mathrm{diff}}_{\exists}[\![\mathtt{S}]\!] && \text{potential dependency} \qquad (6)
\end{aligned}$$

We choose potential value dependency, which is an over-approximation of value dependency needed *e.g.* in compilation or security, looking for more dependencies than there are actually.

5 Calculational Design of the Structural Static Potential Value Dependency Analysis

Value dependency abstract domain An abstract property $\mathbf{D} \in \mathbb{P}^{\mathrm{d}}$ of the value dependency abstract domain $\mathbb{P}^{\mathrm{d}}$ tracks at each program point in $\ell \in \mathbb{L}$ the flows $\langle \mathtt{x}, \mathtt{y}\rangle \in \mathbf{D}\ell$ the initial value of $\mathtt{x}$ to the value of $\mathtt{y}$ at ℓ, that is $\mathtt{x} \rightsquigarrow^{\ell} \mathtt{y}$.

$$\mathbf{D} \in \mathbb{P}^{\mathrm{d}} \triangleq \mathbb{L} \to \wp(\mathbb{V} \times \mathbb{V}) \qquad (7)$$

$\langle \mathbb{P}^{\mathrm{d}}, \dot{\subseteq}, \dot{\bot}, \dot{\top}, \dot{\cap}, \dot{\cup}\rangle$ is a finite complete lattice partially ordered by pointwise subset inclusion $\dot{\subseteq}$. As in [26], values of variables are not taken into account in this abstraction. The Ex. 7 below shows that this introduces imprecision. This imprecision can be recovered by a reduced product [23,24] with a relational value analysis, which is an orthogonal problem.

Example 7 (structural compositionality). In the following statement, x and y at ℓ_1 depend on x at ℓ_0.

```
                                   /* x = x0, y = y0 */
ℓ0 y = x ;
ℓ1                                 /* x = x0, y = x0 */
```

In the following statement, x and y at ℓ_2 depend on x at ℓ_1.

```
                                   /* x = x0, y = y0 */
ℓ1 y = y-x ;
ℓ2                                 /* x = x0, y = y0 - x0 */
```

In the sequential composition of the two statements

```
                                   /* x = x0, y = y0 */
ℓ0 y = x ;                         /* x = x0, y = x0 */
ℓ1 y = y-x ;                       /* x = x0, y = 0 */
ℓ2
```

y at ℓ_2 depends on x at ℓ_1 which depends on x at ℓ_0 so, by composition, y at ℓ_2 depends on x at ℓ_0. However, y = 0 at ℓ_2 so y at ℓ_2 does not depend on x at ℓ_0.

For a more precise analysis, the reduced product of the dependency analysis and the linear equality analysis [40] will find $\exists x'_0, y'_0 \,.\, x'_0 = x_0 \wedge y'_0 = x_0 \wedge x = x'_0, y = y'_0 - x'_0$, that is, by projection, $x = x_0, y = 0$ so y at ℓ_2 does not depend on x at ℓ_0. □

Value dependency abstract semantics Whenever some term is not computable because it uses values, the calculational design of the potential value dependency semantics $\overline{\mathcal{S}}_{\exists}^{\text{diff}}[\![\mathsf{S}]\!]$ will over-approximated it (as required by (6)). Therefore $\overline{\mathcal{S}}_{\exists}^{\text{diff}}[\![\mathsf{S}]\!]$ is sound by construction. Besides the reduction with abstractions of values, this calculational design of $\overline{\mathcal{S}}_{\exists}^{\text{diff}}[\![\mathsf{S}]\!]$ shows that it is possible to improve the precision of the analysis by taking the symbolic constancy of expressions into account.

Theorem 1. *For all program components* S*, the abstract value dependency semantics* $\overline{\mathcal{S}}_{\exists}^{\text{diff}}[\![\mathsf{S}]\!]$ *defined by* (8) *to* (17) *is sound as specified by* (6) *of potential dependency.*

We obtain an abstract semantics operating by structural induction and computing fixpoints in a finite domain. It is therefore computable and directly yields an effective algorithm. We show the calculational design for the assignment, the other cases are similar.

- The **abstract potential dependency semantics at a statement S which is not an iteration**, variables have their initial value so only depend on themselves. (For loops (17) more dependencies may originate from the iterations.)

$$\overline{\mathcal{S}}_{\exists}^{\text{diff}}[\![\mathsf{S}]\!]\ \mathsf{at}[\![\mathsf{S}]\!] \triangleq \mathbb{1}_{\mathbb{V}} \tag{8}$$

where $\mathbb{1}_S \triangleq \{\langle \mathsf{x}, \mathsf{x}\rangle \mid \mathsf{x} \in S\}$ is the identity relation on set S and $\mathbb{V}$ is the set of program variables.

- The **abstract potential dependency semantics outside a statement**, there is no possible potential dependency since executions never reach that point.

$$\ell \notin \mathsf{labs}[\![\mathsf{S}]\!] \Rightarrow \overline{\mathcal{S}}^{\mathsf{diff}}_{\exists}[\![\mathsf{S}]\!]\, \ell \triangleq \varnothing \tag{9}$$

- The **abstract potential dependency semantics after an assignment** $\mathsf{S} ::= \mathsf{x} = \mathsf{A}\ ;$, the unmodified variables $\mathsf{y} \neq \mathsf{x}$ depend upon their initial value at $\mathsf{at}[\![\mathsf{S}]\!]$. The assigned-to variable x depends on $\overline{\mathcal{S}}^{\mathsf{diff}}_{\exists}[\![\mathsf{A}]\!]$ defined as the variables on which the assigned expression A does depend.

$$\begin{aligned}\overline{\mathcal{S}}^{\mathsf{diff}}_{\exists}[\![\mathsf{S}]\!]\, \ell \;&\triangleq\; (\!\!|\, \ell = \mathsf{at}[\![\mathsf{S}]\!] \;?\; \mathbb{1}_{\mathcal{V}} \\ &\quad\;\; \|\; \ell = \mathsf{aft}[\![\mathsf{S}]\!] \;?\; \{\langle \mathsf{y}, \mathsf{x}\rangle \mid \mathsf{y} \in \overline{\mathcal{S}}^{\mathsf{diff}}_{\exists}[\![\mathsf{A}]\!]\} \cup \{\langle \mathsf{y}, \mathsf{y}\rangle \mid \mathsf{y} \neq \mathsf{x}\} \\ &\quad\;\; \text{:}\; \varnothing \,|\!\!) \\ \overline{\mathcal{S}}^{\mathsf{diff}}_{\exists}[\![\mathsf{A}]\!] \;&\triangleq\; \{\mathsf{y} \mid \exists \rho \in \mathbb{E}\mathrm{v} \,.\, \exists \nu \in \mathbb{V} \,.\, \mathcal{A}[\![\mathsf{A}]\!]\rho \neq \mathcal{A}[\![\mathsf{A}]\!]\rho[\mathsf{y} \leftarrow \nu]\} \subseteq \mathbb{vars}[\![\mathsf{A}]\!]\end{aligned} \tag{10}$$

The functional dependency $\overline{\mathcal{S}}^{\mathsf{diff}}_{\exists}[\![\mathsf{A}]\!]$ of expression A is traditionally over-approximated syntactically by the set of variables $\mathbb{vars}[\![\mathsf{A}]\!]$ of this expression A [68,26]. This is very coarse since *e.g.* if A is constant (such as $\mathsf{y = x - x}\ ;$), $\overline{\mathcal{S}}^{\mathsf{diff}}_{\exists}[\![\mathsf{A}]\!]$ is empty. For a trivial improvement, we can define

$$\overline{\mathcal{S}}^{\mathsf{diff}}_{\exists}[\![1]\!] \triangleq \varnothing \qquad \overline{\mathcal{S}}^{\mathsf{diff}}_{\exists}[\![\mathsf{x}]\!] \triangleq \{\mathsf{x}\} \qquad \overline{\mathcal{S}}^{\mathsf{diff}}_{\exists}[\![\mathsf{A}_1 - \mathsf{A}_2]\!] \triangleq \{\mathsf{y} \in \mathbb{vars}[\![\mathsf{A}_1]\!] \cup \mathbb{vars}[\![\mathsf{A}_2]\!] \mid \mathsf{A}_1 \neq \mathsf{A}_2\}.$$

The analysis looks quite imprecise. Further precision can be obtained by a reduced product with a value analysis, as examplified in Ex. 7 and later discussed in Section **6**.

The interest of the proof of (10) is to show that the value dependency algorithm follows by calculus from the trace semantics of [20, Section **2**] and the abstraction (5). By varying the semantics this can be applied to other languages. By varying the abstraction, one can consider the different variants of dependency. In another context of safety analysis, such proofs have been shown to be machine checkable [39] and hopefully, in the future, automatisable.

Proof (of (10)). The cases $\ell = \mathsf{at}[\![\mathsf{S}]\!]$ was handled in (8) and $\ell \notin \mathsf{labs}[\![\mathsf{S}]\!]$ in (9). It remains the case $\ell = \mathsf{aft}[\![\mathsf{S}]\!]$.

$$\begin{aligned}&\alpha^{\mathrm{d}}(\{\mathcal{S}^{+\infty}[\![\mathsf{S}]\!]\})\,\mathsf{aft}[\![\mathsf{S}]\!] \\ =\;& \alpha^{\mathrm{d}}(\{\mathcal{S}^{*}[\![\mathsf{S}]\!]\})\,\mathsf{aft}[\![\mathsf{S}]\!] && \text{(Lem. 1)} \\ =\;& \{\langle \mathsf{x}', \mathsf{y}\rangle \mid \mathcal{S}^{*}[\![\mathsf{S}]\!] \in \mathcal{D}(\mathsf{aft}[\![\mathsf{S}]\!])\langle \mathsf{x}', \mathsf{y}\rangle\} && \text{(def. (5) of } \alpha^{\mathrm{d}} \text{ and def. } \subseteq\text{)} \\ =\;& \{\langle \mathsf{x}', \mathsf{y}\rangle \mid \exists \langle \pi_0, \pi_1\rangle, \langle \pi_0', \pi_1'\rangle \in \mathcal{S}^{*}[\![\mathsf{S}]\!] \,.\, \forall \mathsf{z} \in \mathcal{V} \setminus \{\mathsf{x}'\} \,.\, \varrho(\pi_0)\mathsf{z} = \varrho(\pi_0')\mathsf{z} \,\wedge \\ & \mathsf{diff}(\mathsf{seqval}[\![\mathsf{y}]\!](\mathsf{aft}[\![\mathsf{S}]\!])(\pi_0, \pi_1), \mathsf{seqval}[\![\mathsf{y}]\!](\mathsf{aft}[\![\mathsf{S}]\!])(\pi_0', \pi_1'))\} \\ & && \text{(def. } \in \text{ and (3) of } \mathcal{D}\ell\langle \mathsf{x}', \mathsf{y}\rangle\text{)} \\ =\;& \{\langle \mathsf{x}', \mathsf{y}\rangle \mid \exists \langle \pi_0, \pi_1\rangle, \langle \pi_0', \pi_1'\rangle \in \{\langle \pi\mathsf{at}[\![\mathsf{S}]\!], \mathsf{at}[\![\mathsf{S}]\!] \xrightarrow{\mathsf{x} = \mathcal{A}[\![\mathsf{A}]\!]\varrho(\pi\mathsf{at}[\![\mathsf{S}]\!])} \\ & \mathsf{aft}[\![\mathsf{S}]\!]\rangle \mid \pi\mathsf{at}[\![\mathsf{S}]\!] \in \mathbb{T}^{+}\} \,.\, \forall \mathsf{z} \in \mathcal{V} \setminus \{\mathsf{x}'\} \,.\, \varrho(\pi_0)\mathsf{z} = \varrho(\pi_0')\mathsf{z} \,\wedge \\ & \mathsf{diff}(\mathsf{seqval}[\![\mathsf{y}]\!](\mathsf{aft}[\![\mathsf{S}]\!])(\pi_0, \pi_1), \mathsf{seqval}[\![\mathsf{y}]\!](\mathsf{aft}[\![\mathsf{S}]\!])(\pi_0', \pi_1'))\}\end{aligned}$$

⟨def. ([20].3) of the assignment prefix finite trace semantics⟩

$= \{\langle \mathsf{x}', \mathsf{y}\rangle \mid \exists \langle \pi_0 \mathsf{at}[\![\mathsf{S}]\!], \mathsf{at}[\![\mathsf{S}]\!] \xrightarrow{\mathsf{x}=\mathcal{A}[\![\mathsf{A}]\!]\varrho(\pi_0\mathsf{at}[\![\mathsf{S}]\!])} \mathsf{aft}[\![\mathsf{S}]\!]\rangle, \langle \pi_0' \mathsf{at}[\![\mathsf{S}]\!], \mathsf{at}[\![\mathsf{S}]\!] \xrightarrow{\mathsf{x}=\mathcal{A}[\![\mathsf{A}]\!]\varrho(\pi_0'\mathsf{at}[\![\mathsf{S}]\!])} \mathsf{aft}[\![\mathsf{S}]\!]\rangle \,.\, \forall \mathsf{z} \in \mathbb{V} \setminus \{\mathsf{x}'\} \,.\, \varrho(\pi_0 \mathsf{at}[\![\mathsf{S}]\!])\mathsf{z} = \varrho(\pi_0' \mathsf{at}[\![\mathsf{S}]\!])\mathsf{z} \wedge \mathsf{diff}(\mathsf{seqval}[\![\mathsf{y}]\!](\mathsf{aft}[\![\mathsf{S}]\!])(\pi_0 \mathsf{at}[\![\mathsf{S}]\!], \mathsf{at}[\![\mathsf{S}]\!] \xrightarrow{\mathsf{x}=\mathcal{A}[\![\mathsf{A}]\!]\varrho(\pi_0\mathsf{at}[\![\mathsf{S}]\!])} \mathsf{aft}[\![\mathsf{S}]\!]), \mathsf{seqval}[\![\mathsf{y}]\!](\mathsf{aft}[\![\mathsf{S}]\!])(\pi_0' \mathsf{at}[\![\mathsf{S}]\!], \mathsf{at}[\![\mathsf{S}]\!] \xrightarrow{\mathsf{x}=\mathcal{A}[\![\mathsf{A}]\!]\varrho(\pi_0'\mathsf{at}[\![\mathsf{S}]\!])} \mathsf{aft}[\![\mathsf{S}]\!]))\}$ ⟨def. $\in$⟩

$= \{\langle \mathsf{x}', \mathsf{y}\rangle \mid \exists \langle \pi_0 \mathsf{at}[\![\mathsf{S}]\!], \mathsf{at}[\![\mathsf{S}]\!] \xrightarrow{\mathsf{x}=\mathcal{A}[\![\mathsf{A}]\!]\varrho(\pi_0\mathsf{at}[\![\mathsf{S}]\!])} \mathsf{aft}[\![\mathsf{S}]\!]\rangle, \langle \pi_0' \mathsf{at}[\![\mathsf{S}]\!], \mathsf{at}[\![\mathsf{S}]\!] \xrightarrow{\mathsf{x}=\mathcal{A}[\![\mathsf{A}]\!]\varrho(\pi_0'\mathsf{at}[\![\mathsf{S}]\!])} \mathsf{aft}[\![\mathsf{S}]\!]\rangle \,.\, (\forall \mathsf{z} \in \mathbb{V} \setminus \{\mathsf{x}'\} \,.\, \varrho(\pi_0 \mathsf{at}[\![\mathsf{S}]\!])\mathsf{z} = \varrho(\pi_0' \mathsf{at}[\![\mathsf{S}]\!])\mathsf{z}) \wedge \mathsf{diff}(\varrho(\pi_0 \mathsf{at}[\![\mathsf{S}]\!] \xrightarrow{\mathsf{x}=\mathcal{A}[\![\mathsf{A}]\!]\varrho(\pi_0\mathsf{at}[\![\mathsf{S}]\!])} \mathsf{aft}[\![\mathsf{S}]\!])\mathsf{y}, \varrho(\pi_0' \mathsf{at}[\![\mathsf{S}]\!] \xrightarrow{\mathsf{x}=\mathcal{A}[\![\mathsf{A}]\!]\varrho(\pi_0'\mathsf{at}[\![\mathsf{S}]\!])} \mathsf{aft}[\![\mathsf{S}]\!])\mathsf{y})\}$

⟨def. (1) of the future $\mathsf{seqval}[\![\mathsf{y}]\!]$⟩

$= \{\langle \mathsf{x}', \mathsf{y}\rangle \mid \exists \langle \pi_0 \mathsf{at}[\![\mathsf{S}]\!], \mathsf{at}[\![\mathsf{S}]\!] \xrightarrow{\mathsf{x}=\mathcal{A}[\![\mathsf{A}]\!]\varrho(\pi_0\mathsf{at}[\![\mathsf{S}]\!])} \mathsf{aft}[\![\mathsf{S}]\!]\rangle, \langle \pi_0' \mathsf{at}[\![\mathsf{S}]\!], \mathsf{at}[\![\mathsf{S}]\!] \xrightarrow{\mathsf{x}=\mathcal{A}[\![\mathsf{A}]\!]\varrho(\pi_0'\mathsf{at}[\![\mathsf{S}]\!])} \mathsf{aft}[\![\mathsf{S}]\!]\rangle \,.\, (\forall \mathsf{z} \in \mathbb{V} \setminus \{\mathsf{x}'\} \,.\, \varrho(\pi_0 \mathsf{at}[\![\mathsf{S}]\!])\mathsf{z} = \varrho(\pi_0' \mathsf{at}[\![\mathsf{S}]\!])\mathsf{z}) \wedge ((\varrho(\pi_0 \mathsf{at}[\![\mathsf{S}]\!])\mathsf{y} \neq \varrho(\pi_0' \mathsf{at}[\![\mathsf{S}]\!])\mathsf{y}) \vee (\varrho(\pi_0 \mathsf{at}[\![\mathsf{S}]\!])\mathsf{y} = \varrho(\pi_0' \mathsf{at}[\![\mathsf{S}]\!])\mathsf{y} \wedge \varrho(\pi_0 \mathsf{at}[\![\mathsf{S}]\!] \xrightarrow{\mathsf{x}=\mathcal{A}[\![\mathsf{A}]\!]\varrho(\pi_0\mathsf{at}[\![\mathsf{S}]\!])} \mathsf{aft}[\![\mathsf{S}]\!])\mathsf{y} \neq \varrho(\pi_0' \mathsf{at}[\![\mathsf{S}]\!] \xrightarrow{\mathsf{x}=\mathcal{A}[\![\mathsf{A}]\!]\varrho(\pi_0'\mathsf{at}[\![\mathsf{S}]\!])} \mathsf{aft}[\![\mathsf{S}]\!])\mathsf{y})\}$

⟨(2) so that $\mathsf{diff}(a \cdot b, c \cdot d)$ if and only if (1) $a \neq c$ or (2) $a = c \wedge b \neq d$.⟩

$= \{\langle \mathsf{x}', \mathsf{y}\rangle \mid \exists \langle \pi_0 \mathsf{at}[\![\mathsf{S}]\!], \mathsf{at}[\![\mathsf{S}]\!] \xrightarrow{\mathsf{x}=\mathcal{A}[\![\mathsf{A}]\!]\varrho(\pi_0\mathsf{at}[\![\mathsf{S}]\!])} \mathsf{aft}[\![\mathsf{S}]\!]\rangle, \langle \pi_0' \mathsf{at}[\![\mathsf{S}]\!], \mathsf{at}[\![\mathsf{S}]\!] \xrightarrow{\mathsf{x}=\mathcal{A}[\![\mathsf{A}]\!]\varrho(\pi_0'\mathsf{at}[\![\mathsf{S}]\!])} \mathsf{aft}[\![\mathsf{S}]\!]\rangle \,.\, (\forall \mathsf{z} \in \mathbb{V} \setminus \{\mathsf{x}'\} \,.\, \varrho(\pi_0 \mathsf{at}[\![\mathsf{S}]\!])\mathsf{z} = \varrho(\pi_0' \mathsf{at}[\![\mathsf{S}]\!])\mathsf{z}) \wedge ((\mathsf{y} = \mathsf{x}') \vee (\mathsf{y} = \mathsf{x} \wedge \mathcal{A}[\![\mathsf{A}]\!]\varrho(\pi_0 \mathsf{at}[\![\mathsf{S}]\!]) \neq \mathcal{A}[\![\mathsf{A}]\!]\varrho(\pi_0' \mathsf{at}[\![\mathsf{S}]\!])))\}$ ⟨def. (2) of ϱ⟩

$\subseteq \{\langle \mathsf{x}', \mathsf{y}\rangle \mid ((\mathsf{y} = \mathsf{x}') \vee (\mathsf{y} = \mathsf{x} \wedge \exists \rho, \nu \,.\, \mathcal{A}[\![\mathsf{A}]\!]\rho \neq \mathcal{A}[\![\mathsf{A}]\!]\rho[\mathsf{x}' \leftarrow \nu]))\}$ (11)

⟨letting $\rho = \varrho(\pi_0 \mathsf{at}[\![\mathsf{S}]\!])$ and $\nu = \varrho(\pi_0' \mathsf{at}[\![\mathsf{S}]\!])(\mathsf{x}')$ so that $\forall \mathsf{z} \in \mathbb{V} \setminus \{\mathsf{x}'\} \,.\, \varrho(\pi_0 \mathsf{at}[\![\mathsf{S}]\!])\mathsf{z} = \varrho(\pi_0' \mathsf{at}[\![\mathsf{S}]\!])\mathsf{z}$ implies that $\varrho(\pi_0' \mathsf{at}[\![\mathsf{S}]\!]) = \rho[\mathsf{x}' \leftarrow \nu]$.⟩

$= \{\langle \mathsf{x}', \mathsf{x}'\rangle \mid \mathsf{x}' \neq \mathsf{x}\} \cup \{\langle \mathsf{x}', \mathsf{x}\rangle \mid \exists \rho, \nu \,.\, \mathcal{A}[\![\mathsf{A}]\!]\rho \neq \mathcal{A}[\![\mathsf{A}]\!]\rho[\mathsf{x}' \leftarrow \nu]\}$ ⟨case analysis⟩

$= \{\langle \mathsf{x}', \mathsf{x}'\rangle \mid \mathsf{x}' \neq \mathsf{x}\} \cup \{\langle \mathsf{x}', \mathsf{x}\rangle \mid \mathsf{x}' \in \overline{\mathcal{S}}^{\mathsf{diff}}_{\exists}[\![\mathsf{A}]\!]\}$

⟨by defining the functional dependency of an expression A as $\overline{\mathcal{S}}^{\mathsf{diff}}_{\exists}[\![\mathsf{A}]\!] \triangleq \{\mathsf{x}' \mid \exists \rho, \nu \,.\, \mathcal{A}[\![\mathsf{A}]\!]\rho \neq \mathcal{A}[\![\mathsf{A}]\!]\rho[\mathsf{x}' \leftarrow \nu]\}$ in (10)⟩ □

Equality holds in (11) if every environment is computable *i.e.* $\forall \rho \in \mathbb{E}\mathbf{v} \,.\, \exists \pi \in \mathbb{T}^+ \,.\, \varrho(\pi) = \rho$. Then imprecision comes only from $\overline{\mathcal{S}}^{\mathsf{diff}}_{\exists}[\![\mathsf{A}]\!]$ *i.e.* when it is impossible to evaluate A in all possible environments. Notice that a reduced product with a reachability analysis providing an invariant $\mathsf{at}[\![\mathsf{S}]\!]$ will limit the possible values of the environments ρ and $\rho[\mathsf{x}' \leftarrow \nu]$ in $\overline{\mathcal{S}}^{\mathsf{diff}}_{\exists}[\![\mathsf{A}]\!]$ and therefore make the dependency analysis more precise.

- The **abstract potential value dependency semantics of a conditional statement** `S ::= if (B) S`$_t$ is specified in (12) below. It was discovered by calculational design. (The left restriction $r \rceil S$ of a relation $r \in \wp(S_1 \times S_2)$ to a set S is $\{\langle x, y\rangle \in r \mid x \in S\}$.)

$$\begin{aligned}
\overline{\mathcal{S}}_{\exists}^{\mathrm{diff}}[\![\mathsf{S}]\!]\,\ell \triangleq \{\!\!\{\ &\ell = \mathsf{at}[\![\mathsf{S}]\!] \ ?\ \mathbb{1}_{\mathcal{V}} && \text{(a)} \quad (12)\\
\|\ &\ell \in \mathsf{in}[\![\mathsf{S}_t]\!] \ ?\ \overline{\mathcal{S}}_{\exists}^{\mathrm{diff}}[\![\mathsf{S}_t]\!]\,\ell \rceil \mathsf{nondet}(\mathsf{B},\mathsf{B}) && \text{(b)}\\
\|\ &\ell = \mathsf{aft}[\![\mathsf{S}]\!] \ ?\ \overline{\mathcal{S}}_{\exists}^{\mathrm{diff}}[\![\mathsf{S}_t]\!]\,\mathsf{aft}[\![\mathsf{S}_t]\!] \rceil \mathsf{nondet}(\mathsf{B},\mathsf{B}) && \text{(c.1)}\\
&\qquad \cup \mathbb{1}_{\mathcal{V}} \rceil \mathsf{nondet}(\neg\mathsf{B},\neg\mathsf{B}) && \text{(c.2)}\\
&\qquad\quad \cup \mathsf{nondet}(\neg\mathsf{B},\neg\mathsf{B}) \times \mathsf{mod}[\![\mathsf{S}_t]\!] && \text{(c.3)}\\
:\ &\varnothing\ \}\!\!\} && \text{(d)}
\end{aligned}$$

On entry (12.a), which is an instance of (8), variables in $\mathcal{V}$ only depend upon themselves as specified by the identity relation $\mathbb{1}_{\mathcal{V}}$.

The reasoning in (12.b) is that if a variable y depends at ℓ on the initial value of a variable x at $\mathsf{at}[\![\mathsf{S}_t]\!]$, it depends in the same way on that initial value of the variable x at $\mathsf{at}[\![\mathsf{S}]\!]$ since the test B has no side effect. However, (12.b) also takes into account that if S_t can only be reached for a unique value of the variable x and the branch is not taken for all other values of x then the variable y does not depend on x in S_t since empty observations are disallowed by the abstraction (5) using the definition (2) of diff.

[Non-]determinacy $\mathsf{det}(\mathsf{B}_1,\mathsf{B}_2)$ [$\mathsf{nondet}(\mathsf{B}_1,\mathsf{B}_2)$] is defined *s.t.*

$$\begin{aligned}
&\mathsf{det}(\mathsf{B}_1,\mathsf{B}_2) \subseteq \{\mathsf{x} \mid \forall \rho,\rho' \,.\, (\mathcal{B}[\![\mathsf{B}_1]\!]\rho \wedge \mathcal{B}[\![\mathsf{B}_2]\!]\rho') \Rightarrow (\rho(\mathsf{x}) = \rho'(\mathsf{x}))\} && (13)\\
&\mathsf{nondet}(\mathsf{B}_1,\mathsf{B}_2) \supseteq \mathcal{V} \setminus \mathsf{det}(\mathsf{B}_1,\mathsf{B}_2)
\end{aligned}$$

So if $\mathsf{x} \in \mathsf{det}(\mathsf{B}_1,\mathsf{B}_2)$ in (13) then B_1 and B_2 can both be true for at most one value of x (*e.g.* det(x==1,x==1) = {x} and det(x==1,x!=1) = ∅). It is under-approximated by ∅. Its complement $\mathsf{nondet}(\mathsf{B}_1,\mathsf{B}_2)$ in (13) is the set of variables for which B_1 and B_2 may both be true for different values of variable x. It is over-approximated by all variables $\mathcal{V}$. A better solution is to use a reduced product with a value or symbolic constant propagation analysis as in Section **6**.

If $\mathsf{x} \notin \mathsf{nondet}(\mathsf{B},\mathsf{B})$ in (12.b) then $\mathsf{x} \in \mathsf{det}(\mathsf{B},\mathsf{B})$ so the value of x is constant in S_t so no variable y in S_t can depend on x. For example dependency at ℓ in `if (x == 1) { y = x ; ℓ }` is the same as `x = 1 ;y = x ; ℓ`, which is the same as `y = 1 ; ℓ` so y does not depends on x at ℓ.

(12.c) determines dependencies after S so compare two possible executions of that statement. In case (12.c.1) both executions go through the true branch. In case (12.c.2) both executions go through the false branch, while in case (12.c.3) the executions take different branches.

In case (12.c.1) when the test is true tt for both executions, the executions of the true branch S_t terminate and control after S_t reaches the program point after S (recall that $\mathsf{aft}[\![\mathsf{S}_t]\!] = \mathsf{aft}[\![\mathsf{S}]\!]$). The dependencies after S_t propagate after S but only in case of non-determinism, *e.g.* for variables that are not constant.

The second case in (12.c.2) is for those executions for which the test B is false ff. Variables depend on themselves $\mathsf{at}[\![\mathsf{S}]\!]$ and control moves to $\mathsf{aft}[\![\mathsf{S}]\!]$ so that dependencies are the same there, but only for variables that can reach $\mathsf{aft}[\![\mathsf{S}]\!]$ with different values on different executions as indicated by the restriction to $\mathsf{nondet}(\neg\mathsf{B},\neg\mathsf{B})$.

The third case in (12.c.3) is for pairs of executions, one through the true branch and the other through the false branch. In that case y depends on x only if x does not force execution to always take the same branch, meaning that $x \in \text{nondet}(\neg B, \neg B)$. If y is not modified by the execution through S_t then its value after S is always the same as its value at⟦S⟧ (since y is not modified on the false branch either). In that case changing y at⟦S⟧ would not change y after S so that, in that situation, y does not depend on x. Therefore (12.c.3) requires that $y \in \text{mod}[\![S_t]\!]$.

The variables mod⟦S⟧ modified by a statement S are

$$\text{mod}[\![S]\!] \supseteq \{x \mid \exists \pi_0, \pi_1 \,.\, \langle \pi_0 \text{at}[\![S]\!], \text{at}[\![S]\!]\pi_1 \text{aft}[\![S]\!]\rangle \in \mathcal{S}^{+\infty}[\![S]\!] \\ \wedge\, \varrho(\pi_0 \text{at}[\![S]\!]\pi_1 \text{aft}[\![S]\!])x \neq \varrho(\pi_0 \text{at}[\![S]\!])x\} \qquad (14)$$

In the style of [26], a purely syntactic and very rough over-approximation would be

$$\begin{array}{ll} \text{mod}[\![x = E\ ;]\!] \triangleq \{x\} & \text{mod}[\![\texttt{if (B) } S_t \texttt{ else } S_f]\!] \triangleq \text{mod}[\![S_t]\!] \cup \text{mod}[\![S_f]\!] \\ \text{mod}[\![\{\ Sl\ \}]\!] \triangleq \text{mod}[\![Sl]\!] & \text{mod}[\![\texttt{while (B) } S]\!] \triangleq \text{mod}[\![\texttt{if (B) } S]\!] \triangleq \text{mod}[\![S]\!] \\ \text{mod}[\![Sl\ S]\!] \triangleq \text{mod}[\![Sl]\!] \cup \text{mod}[\![S]\!] & \text{mod}[\![;]\!] \triangleq \text{mod}[\![\epsilon]\!] \triangleq \text{mod}[\![\texttt{break ;}]\!] \triangleq \emptyset \end{array} \qquad (15)$$

Again Section **6** applies. A reduced product with a reachability analysis would be more precise *e.g.* because the variable is constant on exit of S or a relational analysis such that linear equalities [40] shows that it is equal to its initial value.

Finally in case (12.d) the program point ℓ is not reachable in S so, as stated in (9) there is not dependency at ℓ originating from S.

Example 8. Consider $S ::= \ell\ L = H\ ;\ell'$. We have $\overline{\mathcal{S}}^{\text{diff}}_{\exists}[\![S]\!]\,\ell = \{\langle x, x\rangle \mid x \in \mathbb{V}\}$ and $\overline{\mathcal{S}}^{\text{diff}}_{\exists}[\![S]\!]\,\ell' = \{\langle H, L\rangle\} \cup \{\langle x, x\rangle \mid x \in \mathbb{V} \setminus \{L\}\}$.

We have $\text{nondet}(H, H) = \text{nondet}(H, \neg H) = \text{nondet}(\neg H, \neg H) = \{H\}$ so that for the statement $S' ::= \{\ \texttt{if}\ \ell_1\ (H)\ \ell_2\ L = H\ ;\ell_3\ \texttt{else}\ \ell_4\ L = H\ ;\ell_5\ \}\ell_6$, we have

$$\begin{aligned} \overline{\mathcal{S}}^{\text{diff}}_{\exists}[\![S']\!]\,\ell_1 &= \{\langle x, x\rangle \mid x \in \mathbb{V}\} \\ \overline{\mathcal{S}}^{\text{diff}}_{\exists}[\![S']\!]\,\ell_2 = \overline{\mathcal{S}}^{\text{diff}}_{\exists}[\![S']\!]\,\ell_4 &= \{\langle x, x\rangle \mid x \in \mathbb{V} \setminus \{H\}\} \\ \overline{\mathcal{S}}^{\text{diff}}_{\exists}[\![S']\!]\,\ell_3 = \overline{\mathcal{S}}^{\text{diff}}_{\exists}[\![S']\!]\,\ell_5 &= \{\langle x, x\rangle \mid x \in \mathbb{V} \setminus \{L\}\} \\ \overline{\mathcal{S}}^{\text{diff}}_{\exists}[\![S']\!]\,\ell_6 &= \{\langle H, L\rangle\} \cup \{\langle x, x\rangle \mid x \in \mathbb{V} \setminus \{L\}\} \end{aligned}$$

This is different and more precise than *e.g.* [5,26] since L does not depend on H at ℓ_3 and ℓ_5 since, by def. nondet, L is constant at ℓ_3 and ℓ_5. So this is equivalent to ℓ_2 `L = true ;`ℓ_3 and ℓ_4 `L = false ;`ℓ_5 which obviously would create no dependency. In contrast [5,26] maintain an imprecise control dependence context, denoting (a superset of) the variables that at least one test surrounding S depends on. Section **6** provides other examples of increased precision when taking values of variables into account. □

r • The **abstract potential dependency semantics of a statement list** $Sl ::= Sl'\ S$ is

$$\overline{\mathcal{S}}_{\exists}^{\text{diff}}[\![\mathtt{Sl}]\!]\, \ell \triangleq (\![\ell \in \mathsf{labs}[\![\mathtt{Sl'}]\!] \mathrel{?} \overline{\mathcal{S}}_{\exists}^{\text{diff}}[\![\mathtt{Sl'}]\!]\, \ell \tag{16.a}$$

$$[\![\ell \in \mathsf{labs}[\![\mathtt{S}]\!] \setminus \{\mathsf{at}[\![\mathtt{S}]\!]\} \mathrel{?} \overline{\mathcal{S}}_{\exists}^{\text{diff}}[\![\mathtt{Sl'}]\!]\, \mathsf{at}[\![\mathtt{S}]\!] \mathbin{;} \overline{\mathcal{S}}_{\exists}^{\text{diff}}[\![\mathtt{S}]\!]\, \ell \tag{16.b}$$

$$\mathrel{:} \varnothing)\!)$$

where the composition $;$ of relations is $r_1 \mathbin{;} r_2 \triangleq \{\langle x, y\rangle \mid \exists z \,.\, \langle x, z\rangle \in r_1 \wedge \langle z, y\rangle \in r_2\}$.

The first case (16.a) looks for dependencies at a program point ℓ inside $\mathtt{Sl'}$ so, by structural induction, this is $\overline{\mathcal{S}}_{\exists}^{\text{diff}}[\![\mathtt{Sl'}]\!]\, \ell$.

The second case (16.b) looks for dependencies at a program point ℓ inside $\mathtt{S}$. We exclude the case $\ell = \mathsf{at}[\![\mathtt{S}]\!]$ since $\mathsf{at}[\![\mathtt{S}]\!] = \mathsf{aft}[\![\mathtt{Sl'}]\!] \in \mathsf{labs}[\![\mathtt{Sl'}]\!]$ so this case has already been handled in the previous case (16.a).

Otherwise in (16.b), a variable $\mathtt{y}$ at ℓ in $\mathtt{S}$ depends on the initial value of a variable $\mathtt{x}$ on entry $\mathsf{at}[\![\mathtt{Sl} ::= \mathtt{Sl'}\ \mathtt{S}]\!] = \mathsf{at}[\![\mathtt{Sl'}]\!] \in \mathsf{labs}[\![\mathtt{Sl'}]\!]$ if and only if $\mathtt{y}$ at ℓ in $\mathtt{S}$ depends on the initial value of some variable $\mathtt{z}$ on entry $\mathsf{at}[\![\mathtt{S}]\!] = \mathsf{aft}[\![\mathtt{Sl'}]\!]$ of statement $\mathtt{S}$ and the value of $\mathtt{z}$ at that point depends on the initial value of a variable $\mathtt{x}$ on entry $\mathsf{at}[\![\mathtt{Sl}]\!]$ of the statement list $\mathtt{Sl}$. So there exists $\mathtt{z}$ such that $\langle \mathtt{y}, \mathtt{z}\rangle \in \overline{\mathcal{S}}_{\exists}^{\text{diff}}[\![\mathtt{Sl'}]\!]\, \mathsf{aft}[\![\mathtt{Sl'}]\!] = \overline{\mathcal{S}}_{\exists}^{\text{diff}}[\![\mathtt{Sl'}]\!]\, \mathsf{at}[\![\mathtt{S}]\!]$ and $\langle \mathtt{z}, \mathtt{y}\rangle \in \overline{\mathcal{S}}_{\exists}^{\text{diff}}[\![\mathtt{S}]\!]\, \ell$, meaning that $\langle \mathtt{x}, \mathtt{y}\rangle \in \overline{\mathcal{S}}_{\exists}^{\text{diff}}[\![\mathtt{Sl'}]\!]\, \mathsf{at}[\![\mathtt{S}]\!] \mathbin{;} \overline{\mathcal{S}}_{\exists}^{\text{diff}}[\![\mathtt{S}]\!]\, \ell$ is in their composition. As shown by Ex. 7, the precision can be improved by a reduced product with a value analysis.

- The **abstract potential dependency semantics of an iteration statement** $\mathtt{S} ::= \mathtt{while}\ \ell\ \mathtt{(B)}\ \mathtt{S}_b$ is the following

$$\overline{\mathcal{S}}_{\exists}^{\text{diff}}[\![\mathtt{S}]\!]\, \ell' = (\mathsf{lfp}^{\dot{\subseteq}}\, \mathcal{F}_{\exists}^{\text{diff}}[\![\mathtt{while}\ \ell\ \mathtt{(B)}\ \mathtt{S}_b]\!])\, \ell' \tag{17}$$

$$\mathcal{F}_{\exists}^{\text{diff}}[\![\mathtt{while}\ \ell\ \mathtt{(B)}\ \mathtt{S}_b]\!]\, X\, \ell' =$$

$$(\![\ell' = \ell \mathrel{?} \mathbb{1}_{\mathbb{V}} \cup (X(\ell) \mathbin{;} (\overline{\mathcal{S}}_{\exists}^{\text{diff}}[\![\mathtt{S}_b]\!]\, \ell \rceil \mathsf{nondet}(\mathtt{B}, \mathtt{B}))) \tag{a}$$

$$[\![\ell' \in \mathsf{in}[\![\mathtt{S}_b]\!] \mathrel{?} X(\ell) \mathbin{;} (\overline{\mathcal{S}}_{\exists}^{\text{diff}}[\![\mathtt{S}_b]\!]\, \ell' \rceil \mathsf{nondet}(\mathtt{B}, \mathtt{B})) \tag{b}$$

$$[\![\ell' = \mathsf{aft}[\![\mathtt{S}]\!] \mathrel{?} X(\ell) \cup (X(\ell) \mathbin{;} (\mathbb{V} \times \mathsf{mod}[\![\mathtt{S}_b]\!])) \cup \tag{c}$$

$$X(\ell) \mathbin{;} \Big(\Big(\bigcup_{\ell'' \in \mathsf{brks\text{-}of}[\![\mathtt{S}_b]\!]} \overline{\mathcal{S}}_{\exists}^{\text{diff}}[\![\mathtt{S}_b]\!]\, \ell''\Big) \rceil \mathsf{nondet}(\mathtt{B}, \mathtt{B})\Big)$$

$$\mathrel{:} \varnothing)\!) \tag{d}$$

Since $\mathcal{F}_{\exists}^{\text{diff}}[\![\mathtt{S}]\!] \in \mathbb{P}^{\mathrm{d}} \longrightarrow \mathbb{P}^{\mathrm{d}}$ is $\dot{\subseteq}$-monotone and the abstract domain $\langle \mathbb{P}^{\mathrm{d}}, \dot{\subseteq}, \lambda \ell \bullet \varnothing, \lambda \ell \bullet \mathbb{V} \times \mathbb{V}, \dot{\cup}, \dot{\cap}\rangle$ in (7) is a complete lattice, the least fixpoint $\mathsf{lfp}^{\dot{\subseteq}}\, \mathcal{F}^{*}[\![\mathtt{S}]\!]$ of $\mathcal{F}^{*}[\![\mathtt{S}]\!]$ exists by Tarski's fixpoint theorem [62]. Moreover, since $\mathbb{P}^{\mathrm{d}}$ is finite (at least when considering only the program labels $\mathbb{L}$ and variables $\mathbb{V}$ occurring in a program), the abstract properties of $\mathbb{P}^{\mathrm{d}}$ have a finite computer memory representation and the limit of iterates [22] can be computed in finitely many iterations, which yields an effective static analysis algorithm.

$\mathsf{lfp}^{\dot{\subseteq}}\, \mathcal{F}_{\exists}^{\text{diff}}[\![\mathtt{while}\ \ell\ \mathtt{(B)}\ \mathtt{S}_b]\!]$ is the least solution to the system of equations

$$\begin{cases} X(\ell') = \mathcal{F}_{\exists}^{\text{diff}}[\![\mathtt{while}\ \ell\ \mathtt{(B)}\ \mathtt{S}_b]\!]\, X\, \ell' \\ \ell' \in \mathbb{L} \end{cases}$$

which can be understood as follows.

(a) On loop entry the variables depend on themselves. After several iterations the dependency is the composition of the dependencies of the previous iterations $X(\ell)$ composed with those $\overline{\mathcal{S}}_{\exists}^{\mathrm{diff}}[\![\mathsf{S}_b]\!]\,\ell$ created by one more iteration. The composition $\fatsemi$ is that used for a list of statements in (16). The restriction $\rceil\mathsf{nondet}(\mathsf{B},\mathsf{B})$ eliminates dependencies on variables with a single possible value on loop [re-]entry;

(b) The initial value of a variable x on loop entry flows to a variable z at $\ell' \in \mathsf{in}[\![\mathsf{S}_b]\!]$ in the loop body if and only if the initial value of a variable x on loop entry flows to some variable y at loop entry ℓ after 0 or more iterations (so $\langle\mathsf{x},\ \mathsf{y}\rangle \in X(\ell)$) and the value of variable y at the loop body flows to z at ℓ' (so $\langle\mathsf{y},\ \mathsf{z}\rangle \in \overline{\mathcal{S}}_{\exists}^{\mathrm{diff}}[\![\mathsf{S}_b]\!]\,\ell'$). Moreover the restriction $\mathsf{nondet}(\mathsf{B},\mathsf{B})$ eliminates the case when x is constant after the loop test B. (The case when y is constant after the loop test B has been recursively eliminated by $\overline{\mathcal{S}}_{\exists}^{\mathrm{diff}}[\![\mathsf{S}_b]\!]\,\ell'$));

(c) This case determines the dependencies on loop exit $\ell' = \mathsf{aft}[\![\mathsf{S}]\!]$, not knowing the values of variables, so the number of iterations and how the loop is exited is unknown. Therefore all cases must be considered.
   - The term $X(\ell)$ (where $\ell \triangleq \mathsf{at}[\![\mathsf{S}]\!] = \mathsf{aft}[\![\mathsf{S}_b]\!]$) corresponds to the case when the loop is entered and iterated 0 or more times before exiting so either the loop is never entered so each variable depends on itself by (17.a) or the dependencies on exit of the loop are those after the last iteration of the body;
   - The term $(X(\ell) \fatsemi (\mathbb{V} \times \mathsf{mod}[\![\mathsf{S}_b]\!]))$ covers dependencies originating from two executions decided by the initial values of a variable x such that in one case the loop is entered and exited and for another value it is immediately exited. The variables y modified in the loop body depend on x, as was the case in (12.c.3) for the conditional;
   - The term $\bigcup_{\ell'' \in \mathsf{brks\text{-}of}[\![\mathsf{S}]\!]}(X(\ell) \fatsemi \overline{\mathcal{S}}_{\exists}^{\mathrm{diff}}[\![\mathsf{S}_b]\!]\,\ell'')$ propagates the dependencies at the **break ;** statements within the loop body to the break point $\mathsf{aft}[\![\mathsf{S}]\!]$ after the loop;
   - The term (17.c) can be refined to take the test determinism into account more precisely, by eliminating those cases for which it is sure that no two distinct executions can be found in the definition of dependency;

(d) The iteration statement **while** ℓ **(B)** S_b introduces no dependency outside its reachable points.

- The remaining cases of the conditional with alternative, empty statement list, skip, break, and compound statements are similar.

6 Reduced product with a relational value analysis

$\overline{\mathcal{S}}_{\exists}^{\mathrm{diff}}[\![\mathsf{A}]\!]$ in (10) handles the case $\overline{\mathcal{S}}_{\exists}^{\mathrm{diff}}[\![\mathsf{x} - \mathsf{x}]\!] = \emptyset$ while $\mathbb{vars}[\![\mathsf{x} - \mathsf{x}]\!] = \{\mathsf{x}\}$. As shown in Ex. 7, even more precision can be achieved by considering reachable environments only. The abstraction $\alpha_r(\mathcal{S}[\![\mathsf{S}]\!])\ell$ of the trace semantics $\mathcal{S}[\![\mathsf{S}]\!]$ of a program component S by the classical relation abstraction

$$\alpha_r(\mathcal{S}) \triangleq \lambda\,\ell \in \mathbb{L} \bullet \{\langle\varrho(\pi_0),\ \varrho(\pi_0 \mathbin{\widehat{\ }} \pi_1\ell)\rangle \mid \langle\pi_0,\ \pi_1\ell\rangle \in \mathcal{S}\}$$

provides a relation between the initial value of variables and their value at a program point ℓ of S (the relation is empty if ℓ is not in S).

Then the dependency analysis can be refined using this relational value information.

- For the assignment (10), the imprecision is only due to the term $\overline{\mathcal{S}}^{\text{diff}}_{\exists}[\![\mathsf{A}]\!]$ because it is impossible to evaluate the arithmetic expression A in all reachable environments on entry of the assignment (see step (11) of the calculation design). However, a relational value static analysis can provide relevant information.
  For example, using a constant propagation either cartesian [41,67] or relational in [40,42,52], or a zone/octagon analysis [50], $\mathsf{y} \in \overline{\mathcal{S}}^{\text{diff}}_{\exists}[\![\mathsf{A}_1 - \mathsf{A}_2]\!]$ only if this analysis cannot prove that $\mathsf{A}_1 - \mathsf{A}_2$ is constant.
- For the conditional (12) and the iteration (17), the relational value static analysis can provide relevant information on non-determinacy nondet in (13).
- For sequential composition, conditionals, and iteration, it is also possible to refine the calculational design to improve compositionality. For example, in `if (H) L=X; else L=X;`, the above relational value analyzes yield $\mathsf{L}=\mathsf{X}_0$ on exit of the conditional so L does not depend on H.

This is better implemented by a reduced product [23,69,19] and side conditions in the dependency analysis (such as $\overline{\mathcal{S}}^{\text{diff}}_{\exists}[\![\mathsf{A}]\!]$ and nondet) refining dependencies using relational value information provided by the other domains in the product. This separation of concerns greatly simplifies the design of the analysis [25].

7 Examples of derived dependency semantics and analyzes

Independence Definite independence is the complement of potential dependency. [53,4,5] introduced a Hoare-like logic to statically check independences. It also takes nontermination into account so relies on a different definition of $\neg\mathcal{D}\ell\langle \mathsf{x}, \mathsf{y}\rangle$. It is recognized that definite independence is an abstract interpretation but this is not used to design the logic which remains empirical.

Abstract non-interference/dependency The abstraction $\alpha^{\mathrm{d}}(\mathcal{S})$ of the semantic property $\mathcal{S}$ in (5) is meaningful for any semantic property $\mathcal{S}$, including abstract ones, as considered in abstract non-interference/dependency [29]. Given a structural semantic definition of this abstract property, the principle of design by calculational design of the abstract dependency remains the same.

Forward and backward dependency Dependency information is useful for program slicing [68]. The semantics ([20].3)—([20].9) considered in Section **2** is forward, defining the continuation in a program component of an initialization computation ending on entry of that program component. This forward dependency is adequate for forward slicing [5]. The dependency abstraction may be applied to a backward semantics defining the reachability in a program component of an finalization computation starting at that end of a program component or on a break. This backward dependency would certainly be more useful as a basis for slicing [68], or abstract slicing [37,57,49].

Dye instrumented semantics By analogy with dye-tracer tests in hydrology to determine the possible origins of spring discharges or resurgences by water source coloring and flow tracing [43], it has been suggested to decorate the initial values of variables with labels such as color annotations and to track their diffusion and mixtures to determine dependencies [17]. This postulated definition of dependency can be proved sound by observing that the initial color of variables can be designated by the name of these variables and that the color mix at point ℓ for variable y is $\{\mathsf{x} \mid \mathcal{S}^{+\infty}[\![\mathsf{P}]\!] \in \mathcal{D}\ell\langle \mathsf{x},\ \mathsf{y}\rangle\}$. Note that in the postulated instrumented semantics, the choice of diff remains implicit as defined by the arbitrarily selected color mixing rules. Otherwise the instrumented semantics [38] need to be semantically justified with respect to the non-instrumented semantics, in which case the non-instrumented semantics can be used as well to justify dependency, as we do.

Tracking analysis Assume the initial values of variables (more generally inputs) are partitioned into tracked $\mathbb{T}$ and untracked $\mathbb{U}$ variables, $\mathbb{V} = \mathbb{T} \cup \mathbb{U}$ and $\mathbb{T} \cap \mathbb{U} = \emptyset$. The tracking abstraction $\alpha^{\tau}(\mathbf{D})$ of a dependency property $\mathbf{D} \in \mathbb{L} \to \wp(\mathbb{V} \times \mathbb{V})$ (7) attaches to each program point ℓ the set of variables y which, at that program point ℓ, depend upon the initial value of at least one tracked variable $\mathsf{x} \in \mathbb{T}$.

$$\alpha^{\tau}(\mathbf{D})\ell \triangleq \{\mathsf{y} \mid \exists \mathsf{x} \in \mathbb{T}\ .\ \langle \mathsf{x},\ \mathsf{y}\rangle \in \mathbf{D}(\ell)\}$$

A tracking analysis is an over-approximation of the abstract tracking semantics

$$\mathcal{S}^{\tau}[\![\mathsf{S}]\!] \supseteq \alpha^{\tau}(\alpha^{\mathrm{d}}(\{\mathcal{S}^{+\infty}[\![\mathsf{S}]\!]\}))$$

assigning the each program point ℓ, a set $\mathcal{S}^{\tau}[\![\mathsf{S}]\!]\ell \in \wp(\mathbb{V})$ of variables potentially depending on tracked variables. Examples are taint analysis in privacy/security checks [28,61] (tracked is tainted, untracked is untainted); binding time analysis in offline partial evaluation [33] (tracked is dynamic, untracked is static) and absence of interference [30,66,15,36,45] (tracked is high (private/untrusted), untracked is low (public/trusted)).

8 Conclusion

Related work Definitions of dependency follow one of the approaches below[1].

[1] Some approaches are a mix of these cases. For example [69,19] postulates dependency on one trace as in 1. and then abstracts for a set of traces as in 3. and so uses the "Merge over all paths" approach of dataflow analysis [23], with no semantics justification of soundness.

1. Dependency is postulated for a given programming language by specifying an algorithm [68,26] or a calculus [1] which is claimed, a priori, to define dependency. Since the definition is not semantic, it hides (and does not allow to discuss) important details and so is hardly transferable to other languages.
2. Dependency is incorporated in a semantics of the language instrumented with a policy [65] or flows [17]. The problem is that changing slightly the instrumentation definitely changes the variety of dependency which is defined. In particular, it does not guarantee that the notion of dependency is defined uniformly all over the language (*e.g.* conditionals and iterations might be handled using different notions of dependency).
3. Dependency is defined as an abstract interpretation of properties of a formal semantics [65,8,64], although the abstraction originally remained completely implicit [30,66].

Our approach is in the category 3. Besides a generalization beyond input-output dependency, we have shown that, although dependency is an "hyperproperty" (*i.e.* a property of the semantics which is a set of traces), we don't need a different abstract interpretation theory for that case (as in [8,64] introducing specific collecting semantics abstracting general semantic properties). The classical approach [21,23] directly applies whichever kind of property is considered.

Achievements We have designed by calculus a new potential value dependency analysis between the initial value of variables and their value when reaching a program point during execution. It follows and formalizes the intuition provided by [26], "Information flows from object x to object y, denoted $\mathsf{x} \rightsquigarrow \mathsf{y}$, whenever information stored in x is transferred to, or used to derive information transferred to, object y. A program statement specifies a flow $\mathsf{x} \rightsquigarrow \mathsf{y}$ if execution of the statement could result in a flow $\mathsf{x} \rightsquigarrow \mathsf{y}$." "Information flow" is formalized as "changing initial values will change the non-empty sequence of values observed at a program point".

An alternative [32,13,35] is to monitor an abstraction of the program semantics at runtime (Lem. 1 on prefix observation is not valid for all definitions of dependency so dynamic checking might be unsound [60,9]).

The analysis is not postulated but derived formally by abstract interpretation of the trace semantics. So our definition is concise and coherent. We found no need for extra notions like (hyper)^{n}properties [8], non-standard abstract interpretation [64], postulated instrumented semantics [70, Sect. 4], multisemantics [16], monadic reification [31], *etc.*

As shown by [13,34] and Ex. 7, taking values into account will definitely improve the precision of the dependency analysis. As noticed in Section **6**, one possible implementation is by a reduced product of a dependency analysis with a reachability analysis [69,19].

The data-dependence analysis used to detect parallelism in sequential code [54] is also an abstract interpretation, see [63].

Future work The Def. 1 of $\mathcal{D}$ is certainly not unique. For example replacing diff in (3) by equality would take into consideration timing dependencies (Ex. 5) and empty observations (Ex. 6). The methodology that we proposed in this paper can, in our opinion, be applied to a wide variety of definitions of dependency, as follows.

The semantics is a set of executions by pairs $\langle \pi^{\ell}, {}^{\ell}\pi' \rangle$ where π^{ℓ} is the past before reaching ℓ and ${}^{\ell}\pi'$ is the continuation. We define an abstraction of the past π^{ℓ} (*e.g.* the initial value of variables in our case). We define an abstraction of the continuation (*e.g.* seqval (1) in our case). We define the difference between past abstractions (the initial values of variables only differ for one variable in our case). We define the difference between futures (diff in our case). Then the abstraction of the future depends on the abstraction of the past if and only if there exist two executions with different past abstractions and different future abstractions. We conjecture that by varying the past/future abstractions and their difference, we can express the dependency abstractions introduced in the literature. Good examples are [29] for (abstract) non-interference and [12] for mitigation against side-channel attacks.

Acknowledgement. I thank the reviewers for their comments. This work was supported in part by NSF Grant CCF-1617717. Any opinions, findings, and conclusions or recommendations expressed in this material are those of the author and do not necessarily reflect the views of the National Science Foundation.

References

1. Abadi, M., Banerjee, A., Heintze, N., Riecke, J.G.: A core calculus of dependency. In: POPL, pp. 147–160. ACM (1999)
2. Alglave, J., Maranget, L., Sarkar, S., Sewell, P.: Fences in weak memory models (extended version). Formal Methods Syst. Des. **40**(2), 170–205 (2012)
3. Alpern, B., Schneider, F.B.: Recognizing safety and liveness. Distrib. Comput. **2**(3), 117–126 (1987)
4. Amtoft, T., Bandhakavi, S., Banerjee, A.: A logic for information flow in object-oriented programs. In: POPL, pp. 91–102. ACM (2006)
5. Amtoft, T., Banerjee, A.: A logic for information flow analysis with an application to forward slicing of simple imperative programs. Sci. Comput. Program. **64**(1), 3–28 (2007)
6. Andrews, G.R., Reitman, R.P.: An axiomatic approach to information flow in programs. ACM Trans. Program. Lang. Syst. **2**(1), 56–76 (1980)
7. Apel, S., Kästner, C., Batory, D.S.: Program refactoring using functional aspects. In: GPCE, pp. 161–170. ACM (2008)
8. Assaf, M., Naumann, D.A., Signoles, J., Totel, É., Tronel, F.: Hypercollecting semantics and its application to static analysis of information flow. In: POPL, pp. 874–887. ACM (2017)
9. Balliu, M., Schoepe, D., Sabelfeld, A.: We are family: relating information-flow trackers. In: Foley, S.N., Gollmann, D., Snekkenes, E. (eds.) ESORICS 2017. LNCS, vol. 10492, pp. 124–145. Springer, Cham (2017). https://doi.org/10.1007/978-3-319-66402-6_9

10. Barthe, G., Crespo, J.M., Kunz, C.: Relational verification using product programs. In: Butler, M., Schulte, W. (eds.) FM 2011. LNCS, vol. 6664, pp. 200–214. Springer, Heidelberg (2011). https://doi.org/10.1007/978-3-642-21437-0_17
11. Barthe, G., D'Argenio, P.R., Rezk, T.: Secure information flow by self-composition. Math. Struct. Comput. Sci. **21**(6), 1207–1252 (2011)
12. Barthe, G., Grégoire, B., Laporte, V.: Provably secure compilation of side-channel countermeasures. IACR Cryptology ePrint Archive 2017, 1233 (2017)
13. Bock, P.B., Schürmann, C.: A contextual logical framework. In: Davis, M., Fehnker, A., McIver, A., Voronkov, A. (eds.) LPAR 2015. LNCS, vol. 9450, pp. 402–417. Springer, Heidelberg (2015). https://doi.org/10.1007/978-3-662-48899-7_28
14. Bergeretti, J., Carré, B.: Information-flow and data-flow analysis of while-programs. ACM Trans. Program. Lang. Syst. **7**(1), 37–61 (1985)
15. Bowman, W.J., Ahmed, A.: Noninterference for free. In: ICFP, pp. 101–113. ACM (2015)
16. Cabon, G., Schmitt, A.: Annotated multisemantics to prove non-interference analyses. In: PLAS@CCS, pp. 49–62. ACM (2017)
17. Cheney, J., Ahmed, A., Acar, U.A.: Provenance as dependency analysis. Math. Struct. Comput. Sci. **21**(6), 1301–1337 (2011)
18. Clarkson, M.R., Schneider, F.B.: Hyperproperties. J. Comput. Secur. **18**(6), 1157–1210 (2010)
19. Cortesi, A., Ferrara, P., Halder, R., Zanioli, M.: Combining symbolic and numerical domains for information leakage analysis. In: Gavrilova, M.L., Tan, C.J.K., Chaki, N., Saeed, K. (eds.) Transactions on Computational Science XXXI. LNCS, vol. 10730, pp. 98–135. Springer, Heidelberg (2018). https://doi.org/10.1007/978-3-662-56499-8_6
20. Cousot, P.: Syntactic and semantic soundness of structural dataflow analysis. In: B.-Y. E. Chang (ed.) SAS 2019. LNCS, vol. 11822, pp. 96–117. Springer, Cham (2019)
21. Cousot, P., Cousot, R.: Abstract interpretation: a unified lattice model for static analysis of programs by construction or approximation of fixpoints. In: POPL, pp. 238–252. ACM (1977)
22. Cousot, P., Cousot, R.: Constructive versions of Tarski's fixed point theorems. Pac. J. Math. **81**(1), 43–57 (1979)
23. Cousot, P., Cousot, R.: Systematic design of program analysis frameworks. In: POPL, pp. 269–282. ACM (1979)
24. Cousot, P., Cousot, R., Mauborgne, L.: Theories, solvers and static analysis by abstract interpretation. J. ACM **59**(6), 31:1–31:56 (2012)
25. Cousot, P., Cousot, R., Feret, J., Mauborgne, L.: Minée scale up? Formal Methods Syst. Des. **35**(3), 229–264 (2009)
26. Denning, D.E., Denning, P.J.: Certification of programs for secure information flow. Commun. ACM **20**(7), 504–513 (1977)
27. Fagin, R., Vardi, M.Y.: The theory of data dependencies - a survey. In: Mathematics of Information Processing. Proceedings of Symposia in Applied Mathematics, vol. 34, pp. 19–71. AMS (1986)
28. Ferrara, P., Olivieri, L., Spoto, F.: Tailoring taint analysis to GDPR. In: Medina, M., Mitrakas, A., Rannenberg, K., Schweighofer, E., Tsouroulas, N. (eds.) APF 2018. LNCS, vol. 11079, pp. 63–76. Springer, Cham (2018). https://doi.org/10.1007/978-3-030-02547-2_4
29. Giacobazzi, R., Mastroeni, I.: Abstract non-interference: a unifying framework for weakening information-flow. ACM Trans. Priv. Secur. **21**(2), 9:1–9:31 (2018)

30. Goguen, J.A., Meseguer, J.: Unwinding and inference control. In: IEEE Symposium on Security and Privacy, pp. 75–87. IEEE Computer Society (1984)
31. Grimm, N., et al.: A monadic framework for relational verification: applied to information security, program equivalence, and optimizations. In: CPP, pp. 130–145. ACM (2018)
32. Guernic, G.L.: Confidentiality enforcement using dynamic information flow analyses. Ph.D. thesis, Kansas State University, United States of America (2007)
33. Hatcliff, J.: An introduction to online and offline partial evaluation using a simple flowchart language. In: Hatcliff, J., Mogensen, T.Æ., Thiemann, P. (eds.) DIKU 1998. LNCS, vol. 1706, pp. 20–82. Springer, Heidelberg (1999). https://doi.org/10.1007/3-540-47018-2_2
34. Hedin, D., Bello, L., Sabelfeld, A.: Value-sensitive hybrid information flow control for a Javascript-like language. In: CSF, pp. 351–365. IEEE Computer Society (2015)
35. Hedin, D., Bello, L., Sabelfeld, A.: Information-flow security for Javascript and its APIs. J. Comput. Secur. **24**(2), 181–234 (2016)
36. Heinze, T.S., Turker, J.: Certified information flow analysis of service implementations. In: SOCA, pp. 177–184. IEEE Computer Society (2018)
37. Hong, H.S., Lee, I., Sokolsky, O.: Abstract slicing: a new approach to program slicing based on abstract interpretation and model checking. In: SCAM, pp. 25–34. IEEE Computer Society (2005)
38. Jones, N.D., Nielson, F.: Abstract interpretation: a semantics-based tool for program analysis. In: Abramsky, S., Gabbay, D.M. (eds.) Handbook of Logic in Computer Science, Volume 4, Semantic Modelling, pp. 527–636. Oxford University Press, Oxford (1995)
39. Jourdan, J., Laporte, V., Blazy, S., Leroy, X., Pichardie, D.: A formally-verified C static analyzer. In: POPL, pp. 247–259. ACM (2015)
40. Karr, M.: Affine relationships among variables of a program. Acta Informatica **6**, 133–151 (1976)
41. Kildall, G.A.: A unified approach to global program optimization. In: POPL, pp. 194–206. ACM (1973)
42. Knoop, J., Rüthing, O.: Constant propagation on the value graph: simple constants and beyond. In: Watt, D.A. (ed.) CC 2000. LNCS, vol. 1781, pp. 94–110. Springer, Heidelberg (2000). https://doi.org/10.1007/3-540-46423-9_7
43. Kranjc, A.: Tracer Hydrology 97. CRC Press, Boca Raton (1997)
44. Lampson, B.W.: A note on the confinement problem. Commun. ACM **16**(10), 613–615 (1973)
45. Lourenço, L., Caires, L.: Dependent information flow types. In: POPL, pp. 317–328. ACM (2015)
46. Malburg, J., Finder, A., Fey, G.: Debugging hardware designs using dynamic dependency graphs. Microprocess. Microsyst. Embed. Hardw. Des. **47**, 347–359 (2016)
47. Mandal, A.K., Cortesi, A., Ferrara, P., Panarotto, F., Spoto, F.: Vulnerability analysis of Android auto infotainment apps. In: CF, pp. 183–190. ACM (2018)
48. Mantel, H.: A uniform framework for the formal specification and verification of information flow security. Dr.-ing. thesis, Fakultät I der Universität des Saarlandes, Saarbrücken, Germany, July 2003
49. Mastroeni, I., Zanardini, D.: Abstract program slicing: an abstract interpretation-based approach to program slicing. ACM Trans. Comput. Log. **18**(1), 7:1–7:58 (2017)

50. Miné, A.: The octagon abstract domain. High.-Order Symb. Comput. **19**(1), 31–100 (2006)
51. Muthukumar, K., Hermenegildo, M.V.: Compile-time derivation of variable dependency using abstract interpretation. J. Log. Program. **13**(2&3), 315–347 (1992)
52. Müller-Olm, M., Rüthing, O.: On the complexity of constant propagation. In: Sands, D. (ed.) ESOP 2001. LNCS, vol. 2028, pp. 190–205. Springer, Heidelberg (2001). https://doi.org/10.1007/3-540-45309-1_13
53. Ngo, M., Naumann, D.A., Rezk, T.: Typed-based relaxed noninterference for free. CoRR abs/1905.00922 (2019)
54. Padua, D.A., Wolfe, M.: Advanced compiler optimizations for supercomputers. Commun. ACM **29**(12), 1184–1201 (1986)
55. Rice, H.G.: Classes of recursively enumerable sets and their decision problems. Trans. Am. Math. Soc. **74**(1), 358–366 (1953)
56. Rival, X.: Abstract dependences for alarm diagnosis. In: Yi, K. (ed.) APLAS 2005. LNCS, vol. 3780, pp. 347–363. Springer, Heidelberg (2005). https://doi.org/10.1007/11575467_23
57. Rival, X.: Understanding the origin of alarms in ASTRÉE. In: Hankin, C., Siveroni, I. (eds.) SAS 2005. LNCS, vol. 3672, pp. 303–319. Springer, Heidelberg (2005). https://doi.org/10.1007/11547662_21
58. Sabelfeld, A., Myers, A.C.: Language-based information-flow security. IEEE J. Sel. Areas Commun. **21**(1), 5–19 (2003)
59. Sadeghi, A., Bagheri, H., Garcia, J., Malek, S.: A taxonomy and qualitative comparison of program analysis techniques for security assessment of Android software. IEEE Trans. Software Eng. **43**(6), 492–530 (2017)
60. Schoepe, D., Balliu, M., Pierce, B.C., Sabelfeld, A.: Explicit secrecy: a policy for taint tracking. In: EuroS&P, pp. 15–30. IEEE (2016)
61. Spoto, F., et al.: Static identification of injection attacks in Java. ACM Trans. Program. Lang. Syst. **41**(3), 18:1–18:58 (2019)
62. Tarski, A.: A lattice theoretical fixpoint theorem and its applications. Pac. J. Math. **5**, 285–310 (1955)
63. Tzolovski, S.: Data dependences as abstract interpretations. In: Van Hentenryck, P. (ed.) SAS 1997. LNCS, vol. 1302, pp. 366–366. Springer, Heidelberg (1997). https://doi.org/10.1007/BFb0032756
64. Urban, C., Müller, P.: An abstract interpretation framework for input data usage. In: Ahmed, A. (ed.) ESOP 2018. LNCS, vol. 10801, pp. 683–710. Springer, Cham (2018). https://doi.org/10.1007/978-3-319-89884-1_24
65. Volpano, D.: Safety versus secrecy. In: Cortesi, A., Filé, G. (eds.) SAS 1999. LNCS, vol. 1694, pp. 303–311. Springer, Heidelberg (1999). https://doi.org/10.1007/3-540-48294-6_20
66. Volpano, D.M., Irvine, C.E., Smith, G.: A sound type system for secure flow analysis. J. Comput. Secur. **4**(2/3), 167–188 (1996)
67. Wegman, M.N., Zadeck, F.K.: Constant propagation with conditional branches. ACM Trans. Program. Lang. Syst. **13**(2), 181–210 (1991)
68. Weiser, M.: Program slicing. IEEE Trans. Software Eng. **10**(4), 352–357 (1984)
69. Zanioli, M., Cortesi, A.: Information leakage analysis by abstract interpretation. In: Černá, I., et al. (eds.) SOFSEM 2011. LNCS, vol. 6543, pp. 545–557. Springer, Heidelberg (2011). https://doi.org/10.1007/978-3-642-18381-2_45
70. Ørbæk, P.: Can you trust your data. In: Mosses, P.D., Nielsen, M., Schwartzbach, M.I. (eds.) CAAP 1995. LNCS, vol. 915, pp. 575–589. Springer, Heidelberg (1995). https://doi.org/10.1007/3-540-59293-8_221

Temporal Properties and Termination

Temporal Verification of Programs via First-Order Fixpoint Logic

Naoki Kobayashi[1(✉)], Takeshi Nishikawa[2], Atsushi Igarashi[2], and Hiroshi Unno[3,4]

[1] The University of Tokyo, Tokyo, Japan
koba@is.s.u-tokyo.ac.jp
[2] Kyoto University, Kyoto, Japan
{igarashi,nishikawa}@fos.kuis.kyoto-u.ac.jp
[3] University of Tsukuba, Tsukuba, Japan
uhiro@cs.tsukuba.ac.jp
[4] RIKEN AIP, Tokyo, Japan

Abstract. This paper presents a novel program verification method based on Mu-Arithmetic, a first-order logic with integer arithmetic and predicate-level least/greatest fixpoints. We first show that linear-time temporal property verification of first-order recursive programs can be reduced to the validity checking of a Mu-Arithmetic formula. We also propose a method for checking the validity of Mu-Arithmetic formulas. The method generalizes a reduction from termination verification to safety property verification and reduces validity of a Mu-Arithmetic formula to satisfiability of CHC, which can then be solved by using off-the-shelf CHC solvers. We have implemented an automated prover for Mu-Arithmetic based on the proposed method. By combining the automated prover with a known reduction and the reduction from first-order recursive programs above, we obtain: (i) for while-programs, an automated verification method for arbitrary properties expressible in the modal μ-calculus, and (ii) for first-order recursive programs, an automated verification method for arbitrary linear-time properties expressible using Büchi automata. We have applied our Mu-Arithmetic prover to formulas obtained from various verification problems and obtained promising experimental results.

1 Introduction

Several researchers have recently advocated the use of fixpoint logics in program verification. The idea at least goes back to the early work of Blass [10], who showed that the weakest preconditions of while-loops can be expressed by using a fixpoint logic. Bjorner et al. [5,8,9,22] advocated a reduction from program verification problems to the satisfiability of Constrained Horn Clauses (CHC), which is essentially the validity checking for a restricted fragment of first-order fixpoint logic. Burn et al. [12] have recently extended the approach to a higher-order extension of Constrained Horn Clauses. Kobayashi et al. [26,41] have shown

B.-Y. E. Chang (Ed.): SAS 2019, LNCS 11822, pp. 413–436, 2019.
https://doi.org/10.1007/978-3-030-32304-2_20

that temporal verification problems for higher-order functional programs can be reduced to validity checking problems in a higher-order fixpoint logic. Nanjo et al. [32] also proposed an approach to temporal verification based on a fixpoint logic. One of the main advantages common to those approaches is that a fixpoint logic prover can be used as a common, language-independent backend tool for a variety of verification problems (not only safety properties but also arbitrary regular temporal properties, including liveness). Fixpoint logic provers have not, however, been available yet with the full generality.

Based on the observation above, in the present paper, we propose a method for automatically checking the validity of first-order fixpoint logic formulas. The first-order fixpoint logic (with integer arithmetic) we consider has been studied before albeit in different contexts and with different syntax [11,30]. Following Bradfield [11], we call the logic Mu-Arithmetic. For while-programs (with unbounded integers), the formulas generated by the aforementioned translations of Kobayashi et al. [26,41] are actually Mu-Arithmetic formulas. The core logic used by Nanjo et al. [32] is also Mu-Arithmetic. Thus, by combining those previous studies with our procedures for proving Mu-Arithmetic formulas, we can obtain an automated tool for temporal program verification.

Our method, called Mu2CHC, reduces the validity of a Mu-Arithmetic formula to the satisfiability of CHC (in a sound but incomplete manner). The reduction has been inspired by reductions from termination verification to safety property verification [21,35]. More precisely, we generalize the termination verification method of Fedyukovich et al. [21] to underapproximate a least fixpoint formula by a greatest fixpoint formula. Given a formula φ consisting of both least and greatest fixpoints, we convert it to a stronger formula φ' (in the sense $\varphi' \Rightarrow \varphi$) that consists of only greatest fixpoint formulas. We then transform it to a set $\mathcal{C}$ of CHCs, so that $\mathcal{C}$ is satisfiable if and only if φ' is valid. This provides a sound method for proving the validity of the original Mu-Arithmetic formula. The main advantages of this approach are: (i) the reduction is fairly simple and easy to implement, and (ii) we can use off-the-shelf CHC solvers [13,27,38], avoiding replicated work for, e.g., invariant inference.

We have implemented the proposed approach, and confirmed its effectiveness. The benchmark problems used for experiments contain those beyond the capabilities of the existing related tools (such as CHC solvers and program verification tools).

Another main contribution of the present paper is a sound and complete reduction from linear-time properties (expressible using Büchi automata) of first-order recursive programs to the validity of Mu-Arithmetic formulas. This can be considered a generalization of reductions from safety properties of first-order recursive programs to CHC satisfiability (see [6], Sect. 3.2). Kobayashi et al. [26] have shown a reduction from linear-time properties of higher-order programs to the validity of *higher-order* fixpoint logic formulas, but for first-order recursive programs, their translation yields a formula of a second-order fixpoint logic, not a first-order one. We also show a reduction from the modal μ-calculus model checking of while-programs to the validity of Mu-Arithmetic formulas. Such a reduction can in principle be obtained from the general reduction of Watanabe et al. [41], but our reduction is more direct.

The rest of the paper is organized as follows. Section 2 defines Mu-Arithmetic, the first-order fixpoint logic with integer arithmetic. Section 3 discusses applications of the fixpoint logic to program verification; in particular, we show that linear-time properties of first-order recursive programs can be reduced to the validity of Mu-Arithmetic formulas. We propose our method Mu2CHC in Sect. 4. Section 5 reports on the implementation and experimental evaluation of our methods. We discuss related work in Sect. 6 and conclude the paper in Sect. 7.

2 First-Order Fixpoint Logic with Integer Arithmetic

This section introduces the first-order fixpoint logic with integer arithmetic. Following Bradfield [11], we call the logic Mu-Arithmetic (though the syntax is different). We define the syntax and semantics of fixpoint logic in the form of *hierarchical equation systems*, following [37].

2.1 Syntax

The set of *formulas*, ranged over by φ is given by:

$$\begin{aligned}\varphi &::= a_1 \geq a_2 \mid P(a_1, \ldots, a_k) \mid \varphi_1 \vee \varphi_2 \mid \varphi_1 \wedge \varphi_2 \mid \exists x.\varphi \mid \forall x.\varphi \\ a &::= x \mid n \mid a_1 \,\mathbf{op}\, a_2\end{aligned}$$

Here, P ranges over a set of predicate names. We have only $\geq$ as a primitive predicate; in examples, we shall use other integer predicates like $=$ (which can be expressed in terms of $\geq$ and other logical operators).

A *hierarchical equation system* (HES) Φ is a pair $(\mathcal{E}, \mathcal{H})$. Here, $\mathcal{E}$ is a set of equations of the form $\{P_1(\widetilde{x}_1) = \varphi_1, \cdots, P_m(\widetilde{x}_m) = \varphi_n\}$, where $\widetilde{x}$ stands for a sequence of variables, and $\mathcal{H}$ is a sequence $(\mathcal{P}_k, \alpha_k); \cdots; (\mathcal{P}_1, \alpha_1)$, where $\mathcal{P}_k, \ldots, \mathcal{P}_1$ are mutually disjoint sets of predicate names such that $\mathcal{P}_k \cup \cdots \cup \mathcal{P}_1 = \{P_1, \ldots, P_m\}$, and $\alpha_i \in \{\mu, \nu\}$. We write $\mathcal{P}_\Phi$, $\mathcal{P}_{\leq i}$, and $\mathcal{P}_{\geq i}$ for $\bigcup_j \mathcal{P}_j$, $\bigcup_{j \leq i} \mathcal{P}_j$, and $\bigcup_{j \geq i} \mathcal{P}_j$, respectively. We often write $\mathcal{P}$ for $\mathcal{P}_\Phi$ if Φ is clear from the context. We also write $\mathcal{E}_{\mathcal{P}_i}$, or just $\mathcal{E}_i$ to denote the subset of equations $\{P(\widetilde{x}) = \varphi \in \mathcal{E} \mid P \in \mathcal{P}_i\}$. We sometimes write

$$\begin{aligned}&\{P_{k,1}(\widetilde{x}_{k,1}) =_{\alpha_k} \varphi_{k,1}, \ldots, P_{k,\ell_k}(\widetilde{x}_{k,\ell_k}) =_{\alpha_k} \varphi_{k,\ell_k}\}; \cdots; \\ &\{P_{1,1}(\widetilde{x}_{1,1}) =_{\alpha_1} \varphi_{1,1}, \ldots, P_{1,\ell_1}(\widetilde{x}_{1,\ell_1}) =_{\alpha_1} \varphi_{1,\ell_1}\}\end{aligned}$$

for $(\mathcal{E}, \mathcal{H})$ where $\mathcal{E} = \{P_{i,j}(\widetilde{x}_{i,j}) =_{\alpha_i} \varphi_{i,j} \mid i \in \{1, \ldots, k\}, j \in \{1, \ldots, \ell_i\}\}$ and $\mathcal{H} = (\{P_{k,1}, \ldots, P_{k,\ell_k}\}, \alpha_k); \cdots; (\{P_{1,1}, \ldots, P_{1,\ell_1}\}, \alpha_1)$. When $P(\widetilde{x}) = \varphi \in \mathcal{E}$, we write $\mathtt{ar}_\mathcal{E}(P)$ for the length $|\widetilde{x}|$ of the sequence $\widetilde{x}$; we often omit the subscript when $\mathcal{E}$ is clear from context.

Bound (integer) variables in a formula are defined as usual. Integer variables $\{\widetilde{x}\}$ are bound in an equation $P(\widetilde{x}) = \varphi$. We assume that a given HES is closed: free predicate variables in each formula are defined in the HES.

Intuitively, $(\{P_{i,1},\ldots,P_{i,\ell_i}\},\alpha_i)$ where $\alpha_i = \mu$ ($\alpha_i = \nu$, resp.) means that $P_{i,1},\ldots,P_{i,\ell_i}$ are the *least* (*greatest*, resp.) predicates that satisfy the corresponding equations. In $\mathcal{H} = (\{P_{k,1},\ldots,P_{k,\ell_k}\},\alpha_k);\cdots;(\{P_{1,1},\ldots,P_{1,\ell_1}\},\alpha_1)$, the predicates in $\{P_{k,1},\ldots,P_{k,\ell_k}\}$ ($\{P_{1,1},\ldots,P_{1,\ell_1}\}$, resp.) are bound in the outermost (innermost, resp.) position.

Example 1. Consider the HES[1] $\Phi = (\mathcal{E},\mathcal{H})$ with $\mathcal{H} = (\{P_2\},\nu);(\{P_1\},\mu)$ and

$$\mathcal{E} = \{P_2(x) = P_2(x+1) \wedge P_1(x,0), P_1(x,y) = (y = x \vee P_1(x,y+1))\}.$$

Since $P_1(x,y)$ can be expanded to:

$$P_1(x,y) \equiv y = x \vee P_1(x,y+1) \equiv y = x \vee y+1 = x \vee P_1(x,y+2) \equiv \cdots,$$

$P_1(x,y)$ is equivalent to $x \geq y$. Thus, $P_2(x)$ is equivalent to:

$$P_2(x+1) \wedge x \geq 0 \equiv P_2(x+2) \wedge x+1 \geq 0 \wedge x \geq 0 \equiv \cdots.$$

Therefore, $P_2(x)$ is equivalent to $x \geq 0$. □

Remark 1. We do not have the negation operator as a primitive, but it can be expressed by using de Morgan duality [29]. The quantifiers $\forall, \exists$ could also be removed: A formula $\exists x.\varphi$ with the free variables $\widetilde{y}$ can be expressed by $P(0,\widetilde{y})$ where P is defined by $P(x,\widetilde{y}) =_\mu \varphi \vee P(x+1,\widetilde{y}) \vee P(x-1,\widetilde{y})$; similarly for $\forall x.\varphi$.

2.2 Semantics

We now define the formal semantics of HES. Let $\mathbf{Z}$ and $\mathbf{B} = \{\mathtt{tt},\mathtt{ff}\}$ be the sets of integers and Booleans, respectively. We consider the partial order $\mathtt{ff} \sqsubseteq \mathtt{tt}$ on $\mathbf{B}$, and write $\sqcup$ ($\sqcap$, resp.) for the least upper (greatest lower, resp.) bound with respect to $\sqsubseteq$. Given Φ and $\mathcal{P} \subseteq \mathcal{P}_\Phi$, we write $\Gamma_\mathcal{P}$ for the set of maps ρ such that $dom(\rho) = \mathcal{P}$ and $\rho(P) \in \mathbf{Z}^{\mathrm{ar}(P)} \to \mathbf{B}$ for $P \in dom(\rho)$. $(\Gamma_\mathcal{P}, \sqsubseteq_{\Gamma_\mathcal{P}})$ forms a complete lattice, where $\Gamma_\mathcal{P}$ is the pointwise ordering on the elements of $\Gamma_\mathcal{P}$.

Given a map ρ such that $dom(\rho) = \mathcal{P} \cup \mathcal{X}$, where $\mathcal{X}$ is a finite subset of integer variables, and $\rho(P) \in \mathbf{Z}^{\mathrm{ar}(P)} \to \mathbf{B}$ for $P \in \mathcal{P}$ and $\rho(x) \in \mathbf{Z}$ for $x \in \mathcal{X}$, the semantics $[\![\varphi]\!]_\rho \in \mathbf{B}$ of a formula φ is defined by:

$$[\![a_1 \geq a_2]\!]_\rho = \begin{cases} \mathtt{tt} \text{ if } [\![a_1]\!]_\rho \geq [\![a_2]\!]_\rho \\ \mathtt{ff} \text{ otherwise} \end{cases} \qquad [\![P(a_1,\ldots,a_m)]\!]_\rho = \rho(P)([\![a_1]\!]_\rho,\ldots,[\![a_m]\!]_\rho)$$

$$[\![\varphi_1 \vee \varphi_2]\!]_\rho = [\![\varphi_1]\!]_\rho \sqcup [\![\varphi_1]\!]_\rho \qquad [\![\varphi_1 \wedge \varphi_2]\!]_\rho = [\![\varphi_1]\!]_\rho \sqcap [\![\varphi_1]\!]_\rho$$

$$[\![\exists x.\varphi]\!]_\rho = \bigsqcup_{z \in \mathbf{Z}} [\![\varphi]\!]_{\rho\{x \mapsto z\}} \qquad [\![\forall x.\varphi]\!]_\rho = \bigsqcap_{z \in \mathbf{Z}} [\![\varphi]\!]_{\rho\{x \mapsto z\}}$$

$$[\![x]\!]_\rho = \rho(x) \qquad [\![n]\!]_\rho = n \qquad [\![a_1 \,\mathbf{op}\, a_2]\!]_\rho = [\![a_1]\!]_\rho [\![\mathbf{op}]\!] [\![a_2]\!]_\rho.$$

Here, $[\![\mathbf{op}]\!]$ denotes the binary function on integers represented by $\mathbf{op}$.

[1] We remark that, for those who are familiar with fixpoint logics, $P_2(x)$ can be written as $\nu P_2.\lambda x.P_2(x+1) \wedge (\mu P_1.\lambda y.y = x \vee P_1(y+1))\,0$ in the ordinary syntax of Mu-Arithmetic [11] or HFL [40].

Given an HES Φ, $\mathcal{P}_i$ and $\rho \in \Gamma_{\mathcal{P}_\Phi}$, the semantics $[\![\mathcal{E}_i]\!]_\rho \in \Gamma_{\mathcal{P}_i}$ is defined by:

$$[\![\mathcal{E}_i]\!]_\rho = \{P \mapsto \lambda\widetilde{z} \in \mathbf{Z}^{\mathrm{ar}(P)}.[\![\varphi_P]\!]_{\rho\{\widetilde{x}\mapsto\widetilde{z}\}} \mid P(\widetilde{x}) = \varphi_P \in \mathcal{E}_i\}.$$

We are now ready to define the semantics of HES. By abuse of notation, we write Γ_i, $\Gamma_{\geq i}$, and $\Gamma_{\leq i}$ for $\Gamma_{\mathcal{P}_i}$, $\Gamma_{\mathcal{P}_{\geq i}}$, and $\Gamma_{\mathcal{P}_{\leq i}}$ respectively. The semantics $[\![\Phi]\!]_i \in \Gamma_{\geq i+1} \to \Gamma_i$ and $[\![\Phi]\!]_{\leq i} \in \Gamma_{\geq i+1} \to \Gamma_{\leq i}$ are defined by induction on i, as follows.

$$\begin{array}{ll} [\![\Phi]\!]_0 = [\![\Phi]\!]_{\leq 0} = \lambda\rho \in \Gamma_{\geq 1}.\emptyset & \\ [\![\Phi]\!]_i = \lambda\rho \in \Gamma_{\geq i+1}.\mathbf{FP}^{\Gamma_i}_{\alpha_i}(\lambda\rho' \in \Gamma_i.[\![\mathcal{E}_i]\!]_{\rho\cup\rho'\cup[\![\Phi]\!]_{\leq i-1}(\rho\cup\rho')}) & (\text{for } i > 0) \\ [\![\Phi]\!]_{\leq i} = \lambda\rho \in \Gamma_{\geq i+1}.[\![\Phi]\!]_i(\rho) \cup [\![\Phi]\!]_{\leq i-1}(\rho \cup [\![\Phi]\!]_i(\rho)) & (\text{for } i > 0) \end{array}$$

Here, $\mathbf{FP}^{\Gamma}_{\mu}, \mathbf{FP}^{\Gamma}_{\nu} \in (\Gamma \to \Gamma) \to \Gamma$ (the superscript Γ is often omitted) are the least and greatest fixpoint operators defined by:

$$\mathbf{FP}^{\Gamma}_{\mu}(F) = \textstyle\bigsqcap_{\Gamma}\{f \in \Gamma \mid f \sqsupseteq_{\Gamma} F(f)\} \qquad \mathbf{FP}^{\Gamma}_{\nu}(F) = \textstyle\bigsqcup_{\Gamma}\{f \in \Gamma \mid f \sqsubseteq_{\Gamma} F(f)\}.$$

Note that the semantics $[\![\Phi]\!]_i$ of the predicates in $\mathcal{P}_i$ is parameterized by the semantics of predicates of higher levels (as indicated by $\lambda\rho \in \Gamma_{\geq i+1}.\cdots$). To evaluate $[\![\mathcal{E}_i]\!]$ in the definition of $[\![\Phi]\!]_i$, we need an environment on all the predicate variables; ρ, ρ', and $[\![\Phi]\!]_{\leq i-1}(\rho \cup \rho')$ respectively provide the environment on the predicates of higher levels, the current level i, and lower levels. We write $[\![\Phi]\!]$ for $[\![\Phi]\!]_{\leq k}(\emptyset)$ (where k is the highest level) and write $\Phi \models \varphi$ if $[\![\varphi]\!]_{[\![\Phi]\!]} = \mathtt{tt}$.

Example 2. Recall Example 1, with $\mathcal{P}_1 = \{P_1\}$ and $\mathcal{P}_2 = \{P_2\}$.

$$\begin{aligned} [\![\Phi]\!]_1 &= \lambda\rho \in \Gamma_{\geq 2}.\mathbf{FP}_\mu(\lambda\rho' \in \Gamma_1.\{P_1 \mapsto \lambda(x,y).y = x \vee \rho'(P_1)(x, y+1)\}) \\ &= \lambda\rho \in \Gamma_{\geq 2}.\{P_1 \mapsto \lambda(x,y).x \geq y\}. \\ [\![\Phi]\!]_{\leq 1} &= \lambda\rho \in \Gamma_{\geq 2}.[\![\Phi]\!]_1(\rho) \cup [\![\Phi]\!]_{\leq 0}(\rho \cup [\![\Phi]\!]_1(\rho)) = [\![\Phi]\!]_1. \\ [\![\Phi]\!]_2 &= \lambda\rho \in \Gamma_{\geq 3}.\mathbf{FP}_\nu(\lambda\rho' \in \Gamma_2.\{P_2 \mapsto \lambda x.\rho'(P_2)(x+1) \wedge x \geq 0\}) \\ &= \lambda\rho \in \{\emptyset\}.\{P_2 \mapsto \lambda x.x \geq 0\}. \\ [\![\Phi]\!]_{\leq 2} &= \lambda\rho \in \{\emptyset\}.\{P_2 \mapsto \lambda x.x \geq 0, P_1 \mapsto \lambda(x,y).x \geq y\}. \end{aligned}$$

Thus, we have $[\![\Phi]\!] = \{P_2 \mapsto \lambda x.x \geq 0, P_1 \mapsto \lambda(x,y).x \geq y\}$, hence $\Phi \models P_2(0)$. □

Example 3. To understand the importance of the order of equations, let us consider $\Phi_1 = (\mathcal{E}, \mathcal{H}_1)$ and $\Phi_2 = (\mathcal{E}, \mathcal{H}_2)$, where:

$$\begin{array}{ll} \mathcal{E} = \{X = X \wedge Y, Y = X \vee Y\} & \\ \mathcal{H}_1 = (\{X\}, \nu); (\{Y\}, \mu) & \mathcal{H}_2 = (\{Y\}, \mu); (\{X\}, \nu). \end{array}$$

Note that Φ_2 is obtained from Φ_1 by just swapping the order of X and Y. Yet, their semantics are completely different: $[\![\Phi_1]\!] = \{X \mapsto \mathtt{tt}, Y \mapsto \mathtt{tt}\}$ but $[\![\Phi_2]\!] = \{X \mapsto \mathtt{ff}, Y \mapsto \mathtt{ff}\}$. To see this, for Φ_1, we have:

$$\begin{aligned} [\![\Phi_1]\!]_1 &= \lambda\rho \in \Gamma_{\geq 2}.\mathbf{FP}_\mu(\lambda\rho' \in \Gamma_1.[\![Y = X \vee Y]\!]_{\rho\cup\rho'}) = \lambda\rho \in \Gamma_{\geq 2}.\{Y \mapsto \rho(X)\} \\ [\![\Phi_1]\!]_2 &= \lambda\rho \in \{\emptyset\}.\mathbf{FP}_\nu(\lambda\rho' \in \Gamma_2.[\![X = X \wedge Y]\!]_{\rho'\cup\{Y\mapsto\rho(X)\}}) \\ &= \lambda\rho \in \{\emptyset\}.\{X \mapsto \mathtt{tt}\}. \end{aligned}$$

In contrast, for Φ_2, we have:

$$\begin{aligned}
[\![\Phi_2]\!]_1 &= \lambda\rho \in \Gamma_{\geq 2}.\mathbf{FP}_\nu(\lambda\rho' \in \Gamma_1.[\![X = X \wedge Y]\!]_{\rho\cup\rho'}) = \lambda\rho \in \Gamma_{\geq 2}.\{X \mapsto \rho(Y)\}\\
[\![\Phi_2]\!]_2 &= \lambda\rho \in \{\emptyset\}.\mathbf{FP}_\mu(\lambda\rho' \in \Gamma_2.[\![Y = X \vee Y]\!]_{\rho'\cup\{X\mapsto\rho(Y)\}})\\
&= \lambda\rho \in \{\emptyset\}.\{Y \mapsto \mathtt{ff}\}.
\end{aligned}$$

□

2.3 Relationship with Other Logics

We comment on the relationship between our logic and other logics used in the context of program verification. As indicated already, our fixpoint logic in the form of HES is essentially equi-expressive as Bradfield's original Mu-Arithmetic [11]. Any formula of HES can be translated to a formula of the original Mu-Arithmetic in the same way as the translation from HES for higher-order fixpoint logic to HFL formulas [25].

Our Mu-Arithmetic can be considered a restriction of $\mathrm{HFL}_\mathbf{Z}$ [26] (which is an extension of HFL [40] with integers), obtained by (i) restricting predicates to those on integers, and (ii) removing modal operators.

HES can also be considered an extension of Constrained Horn Clauses (CHC) [6], obtained by allowing fixpoint alternations. In fact, the satisfiability problem of CHC (i.e., whether there is a substitution for the predicate variables $P_1, \ldots, P_n$ that makes all the clauses valid):

$$P_1(\widetilde{x}_1) \Leftarrow \varphi_1 \qquad \cdots \qquad P_n(\widetilde{x}_n) \Leftarrow \varphi_n \qquad \mathtt{ff} \Leftarrow P_1(\widetilde{x}_1)$$

(where we allow disjunctions in $\varphi_1, \ldots, \varphi_n$, and assume that $P_1, \ldots, P_n$ are mutually distinct) is equivalent to the validity of $\forall\widetilde{x}_1.\overline{P}_1(\widetilde{x}_1)$, where $\overline{P}_i$ is defined by HES: $(\{\overline{P}_1(\widetilde{x}_1) = \overline{\varphi}_1, \ldots, \overline{P}_n(\widetilde{x}_n) = \overline{\varphi}_n\}, (\{\overline{P}_1, \ldots, \overline{P}_n\}, \nu))$. Here, $\overline{\varphi}_i$ is the de Morgan dual of φ_i, and $\overline{P}_i$ intuitively represents the negation of P_i.

Conversely, the validity checking problem for any HES without μ or $\exists$ can be transformed to the satisfiability problem for CHC, by just reversing the above transformation. In fact, let Φ be an HES of the form

$$(\{P_1(\widetilde{x}_1) = \forall\widetilde{y}_1.\varphi_1, \ldots, P_n(\widetilde{x}_n) = \forall\widetilde{y}_n.\varphi_n\}, (\{P_1, \ldots, P_n\}, \nu)),$$

where $\varphi_1, \ldots, \varphi_n$ are quantifier-free formulas. Then, $\Phi \models \forall\widetilde{x}.P_i(\widetilde{x})$ if and only if the followings are satisfiable:

$$\overline{P}_1(\widetilde{x}_1) \Leftarrow \exists\widetilde{y}_1.\overline{\varphi}_1 \qquad \cdots \qquad \overline{P}_n(\widetilde{x}_n) \Leftarrow \exists\widetilde{y}_n.\overline{\varphi}_n \qquad \mathtt{ff} \Leftarrow \exists\widetilde{x}.\overline{P}_i(\widetilde{x}).$$

Since $\overline{P}_i(\widetilde{x}_i) \Leftarrow \exists\widetilde{y}_i.\overline{\varphi}_i$ is equivalent to $\forall\widetilde{y}_i.(\overline{P}_i(\widetilde{x}_i) \Leftarrow \overline{\varphi}_i)$ (assuming that $\widetilde{x}_i \cap \widetilde{y}_i = \emptyset$), one can transform the conditions above to CHC.

3 From Temporal Property Verification to First-Order Fixpoint Logic

This section discusses applications of the fixpoint logic to temporal verification of programs. As we mentioned in Sect. 1, Watanabe et al. [41] have shown that temporal verification of higher-order recursive programs can be reduced in a sound and complete manner to validity checking of *higher-order* fixpoint logic formulas. For while-programs (i.e., imperative programs without recursion), their translations actually produce formulas within our fixpoint logic. Thus, by combining their translations with the procedures for our fixpoint logic given in Sect. 4, we obtain an automated temporal verification method for while-programs, which can deal with arbitrary temporal properties that can be expressed in modal μ-calculus. The reduction of Watanabe et al. [41] is, however, indirect: one has to first transform a while-program to a tree-generating grammar $\text{HORS}_{\mathbf{Z}}$ that generates a computation tree of the program, and a temporal property to a tree automaton. We thus present a direct reduction from modal μ-calculus model checking of imperative programs to validity checking of Mu-Arithmetic formulas in Sect. 3.1 below.

For linear-time temporal properties, we can also deal with first-order programs with arbitrary recursion (not just while-loops). More precisely, given a first-order (possibly non-deterministic) recursive program D (that contains special primitives called *events*) and a Büchi automaton $\mathcal{A}$, one can construct an HES $\Phi_{D,\mathcal{A}}$, such that $\Phi_{D,\mathcal{A}} \models \mathbf{main}_{q_I,\texttt{tt}}()$ (where q_I is the initial state of $\mathcal{A}$) holds, if and only if some (infinite) event sequence generated by D is accepted by $\mathcal{A}$. We formalize the reduction in Sect. 3.2, which is one of the main contributions of the present paper.

3.1 Modal μ-Calculus Model Checking of Imperative Programs

We model an imperative program as a tuple $\mathbf{P} = (\mathbf{PC}, \mathbf{Vars}, \mathbf{Code})$, where $\mathbf{PC}$ is a finite set consisting of non-negative integers (which intuitively represent program counters), $\mathbf{Vars}$ is a finite set of variables, and $\mathbf{Code}$ is a map from $\mathbf{PC}$ to the set $\mathcal{I}_{\mathbf{Vars}}$ of instructions, consisting of:

- $x := a;$ **goto** i: update the value of $x \in \mathbf{Vars}$ to that of a, and then go to $i \in \mathbf{PC}$.
- $x := *;$ **goto** i: update the value of $x \in \mathbf{Vars}$ to an arbitrary integer in a non-deterministic manner, and then go to $i \in \mathbf{PC}$.
- **if** $a_1 \geq a_2$ **then goto** i **else goto** j: go to $i \in \mathbf{PC}$ if $a_1 \geq a_2$ and $j \in \mathbf{PC}$ otherwise.
- **if** $*$ **then goto** i **else goto** j: non-deterministically go to i or j.

Here, a ranges over the set of arithmetic expressions, like the meta-variable a in Sect. 2.

A program $\mathbf{P} = (\mathbf{PC}, \mathbf{Vars}, \mathbf{Code})$, with $\mathbf{Vars} = \{x_1, \ldots, x_n\}$ can be viewed as a Kripke structure $K_{\mathbf{P}} = (\mathbf{AP}, S, s_0, \longrightarrow, L)$, where: (i) $\mathbf{AP}$ is a set of constraints on $\mathbf{Vars}$ (such as $x_1 \geq 0$), (ii) the set S of states is $\mathbf{PC} \times (\mathbf{Vars} \to \mathbf{Z})$, (iii) the initial state $s_0 \in S$ is $(0, \{x_1 \mapsto 0, \ldots, x_n \mapsto 0\})$, (iv) the labeling function $L \in S \to \mathbf{AP}$ is given by: $L(i, \sigma) = \{p \in \mathbf{AP} \mid\models \sigma(p)\}$. Here, $\sigma(p)$ is the closed formula obtained by replacing each variable x_i in p with $\sigma(x_i)$, and $\models \sigma(p)$ means that the resulting formula evaluates to true, and (v) $\longrightarrow \subseteq S \times S$ is the transition relation (see [33] for the definition). We represent modal μ-calculus formulas in the form of hierarchical equation systems, following [37]. We call them *hierarchical modal equation systems (HMES)*, to distinguish them from the HES for Mu-Arithmetic introduced in Sect. 2.

The set of (fixpoint-free) modal formulas, ranged over by ψ, is defined by:

$$\psi ::= p \mid X \mid \psi_1 \vee \psi_2 \mid \psi_1 \wedge \psi_2 \mid \diamond\psi \mid \Box\psi$$
$$a ::= n \mid x \mid a_1 \,\mathbf{op}\, a_2.$$

A *hierarchical modal equation system* (HMES) Ξ is a pair $(\mathbf{E}, \mathbf{H})$, where $\mathbf{E}$ is a set of equations for the form $\{X_1 = \psi_1, \cdots, X_m = \psi_n\}$, where $\mathbf{H}$ is a sequence $(\mathcal{P}_k, \alpha_k); \cdots ; (\mathcal{P}_1, \alpha_1)$, where $\mathcal{P}_k, \ldots, \mathcal{P}_1$ are mutually disjoint sets of variables such that $\mathcal{P}_k \cup \cdots \cup \mathcal{P}_1 = \{X_1, \ldots, X_m\}$, and $\alpha_i \in \{\mu, \nu\}$. We write $\mathcal{P}_{\geq i}$ and $\mathcal{P}_{\leq i}$ for $\bigcup_{j \geq i} \mathcal{P}_j$ and $\bigcup_{j \leq i} \mathcal{P}_j$ respectively.

The semantics of HMES Ξ is defined in a way analogous to that of HES in Sect. 2, as a function that maps each propositional defined in Ξ to the set of states that satisfy the proposition; see [33] for details.

Given a program $\mathbf{P}$ with variables $\{x_1, \ldots, x_n\}$ and an HMES Ξ with $X \in \mathcal{P}_\Xi$, we say that a program $\mathbf{P}$ satisfies (Ξ, X), written $\mathbf{P} \models (\Xi, X)$, if the initial state $(0, \{x_1 \mapsto 0, \ldots, x_n \mapsto 0\})$ belongs to $[\![\Xi]\!](X)$. The goal of verification is to check whether $\mathbf{P} \models (\Xi, X)$ holds.

We now reduce the problem of checking whether $\mathbf{P} \models (\Xi, X)$ to the validity checking problem for Mu-Arithmetic. For the convenience of presenting the reduction, we assume without loss of generality that the righthand side of each equation in HMES is restricted to the following syntax.

$$\psi ::= a_1 \geq a_2 \mid X \mid X_1 \vee X_2 \mid X_1 \wedge X_2 \mid \diamond X \mid \Box X.$$

Let $\mathbf{Vars} = \{x_1, \ldots, x_n\}$ and $\widetilde{x}$ be the sequence $x_1, \ldots, x_n$. For each equation $X = \psi$ and $i \in \mathbf{PC}$, we define the equation $[\![X = \psi]\!]_i$ of Mu-Arithmetic by:

$$[\![X = (a_1 \geq a_2)]\!]_i = (X^{(i)}(\widetilde{x}) = a_1 \geq a_2) \qquad [\![X = X_1]\!]_i = (X^{(i)}(\widetilde{x}) = X_1^{(i)})$$
$$[\![X = X_1 \vee X_2]\!]_i = (X^{(i)}(\widetilde{x}) = X_1^{(i)}(\widetilde{x}) \vee X_2^{(i)}(\widetilde{x}))$$
$$[\![X = X_1 \wedge X_2]\!]_i = (X^{(i)}(\widetilde{x}) = X_1^{(i)}(\widetilde{x}) \wedge X_2^{(i)}(\widetilde{x}))$$
$$[\![X = \diamond X_1]\!]_i = \begin{cases} X^{(i)}(\widetilde{x}) = X_1^{(k)}(x_1, \ldots, x_{j-1}, a, x_{j+1}, \ldots, x_n) \\ \qquad\qquad \text{if } \mathbf{Code}(i) = x_j := a; \mathbf{goto}\ k \\ X^{(i)}(\widetilde{x}) = \exists m. X_1^{(k)}(x_1, \ldots, x_{j-1}, m, x_{j+1}, \ldots, x_n) \\ \qquad\qquad \text{if } \mathbf{Code}(i) = x_j := *; \mathbf{goto}\ k \\ X^{(i)}(\widetilde{x}) = (a_1 \geq a_2 \wedge X_1^{(j)}(\widetilde{x})) \vee (a_2 \geq a_1 + 1 \wedge X_1^{(k)}(\widetilde{x})) \\ \qquad\qquad \text{if } \mathbf{Code}(i) = \mathbf{if}\ a_1 \geq a_2\ \mathbf{then\ goto}\ j\ \mathbf{else\ goto}\ k \\ X^{(i)}(\widetilde{x}) = X_1^{(j)}(\widetilde{x}) \vee X_1^{(k)}(\widetilde{x}) \\ \qquad\qquad \text{if } \mathbf{Code}(i) = \mathbf{if}\ *\ \mathbf{then\ goto}\ j\ \mathbf{else\ goto}\ k \end{cases}$$

$$[\![X = \Box X_1]\!]_i = \begin{cases} X^{(i)}(\widetilde{x}) = X_1^{(k)}(x_1, \ldots, x_{j-1}, a, x_{j+1}, \ldots, x_n) \\ \qquad\qquad \text{if } \mathbf{Code}(i) = x_j := a; \mathbf{goto}\ k \\ X^{(i)}(\widetilde{x}) = \forall m. X_1^{(k)}(x_1, \ldots, x_{j-1}, m, x_{j+1}, \ldots, x_n) \\ \qquad\qquad \text{if } \mathbf{Code}(i) = x_j := *; \mathbf{goto}\ k \\ X^{(i)}(\widetilde{x}) = (a_1 \geq a_2 \wedge X_1^{(j)}(\widetilde{x})) \vee (a_2 \geq a_1 + 1 \wedge X_1^{(k)}(\widetilde{x})) \\ \qquad\qquad \text{if } \mathbf{Code}(i) = \mathbf{if}\ a_1 \geq a_2\ \mathbf{then\ goto}\ j\ \mathbf{else\ goto}\ k \\ X^{(i)}(\widetilde{x}) = X_1^{(j)}(\widetilde{x}) \wedge X_1^{(k)}(\widetilde{x}) \\ \qquad\qquad \text{if } \mathbf{Code}(i) = \mathbf{if}\ *\ \mathbf{then\ goto}\ j\ \mathbf{else\ goto}\ k. \end{cases}$$

Given $\Xi = (\mathbf{E}, \mathbf{H})$ with $\mathbf{H} = (\mathcal{P}_1, \alpha_1); \cdots; (\mathcal{P}_\ell, \alpha_\ell)$, and $\mathbf{P} = (\mathbf{PC}, \mathbf{Vars}, \mathbf{Code})$, we define HES $\Phi_{\Xi,\mathbf{P}}$ as $(\mathcal{E}_{\Xi,\mathbf{P}}, \mathcal{H}_{\Xi,\mathbf{P}})$, where:

$$\mathcal{E}_{\Xi,\mathbf{P}} = \{[\![X = \psi]\!]_i \mid (X = \psi) \in \mathbf{E}, i \in \mathbf{PC}\},$$

and $\mathcal{H}_{\Xi,\mathbf{P}} = (\{X^{(i)} \mid X \in \mathcal{P}_1, i \in \mathbf{PC}\}, \alpha_1); \cdots; (\{X^{(i)} \mid X \in \mathcal{P}_\ell, i \in \mathbf{PC}\}, \alpha_\ell)$.

By the translation, it is not difficult to observe that $(j, \{x_1 \mapsto m_1, \ldots, x_n \mapsto m_n\}) \in [\![\Xi]\!](X_i)$ if and only if $[\![\Phi_{\Xi,\mathbf{P}}]\!](X_i^{(j)})(m_1, \ldots, m_n) = \mathtt{tt}$. Thus, $\mathbf{P} \models (\Xi, X_1)$ if and only if $\mathcal{H}_{\Xi,\mathbf{P}} \models X_1^{(0)}(0, \ldots, 0)$.

Example 4. Consider the program $\mathbf{P}_0 = (\{0,1\}, \{x,y\}, \mathbf{Code}_0)$, where:

$$\mathbf{Code}_0 = \{0 \mapsto (x := x-1; \mathbf{goto}\ 1),\ 1 \mapsto (y := y+1; \mathbf{goto}\ 1)\}.$$

The modal μ-calculus formula $\nu X.(x + y \geq 0 \wedge \diamond\diamond X)$ expresses the property "there exists an execution sequence in which $x + y \geq 0$ holds after any even number of steps." This is a property that cannot be expressed in CTL*. The corresponding HMES Ξ_0 is $(\mathbf{E}_0, \mathbf{H}_0)$ where

$$\mathbf{E}_0 = \{X = x + y \geq 0 \wedge \diamond Y, Y = \diamond X\} \qquad \mathbf{H}_0 = (\{X, Y\}, \nu).$$

By the translation above, we obtain $\Phi_{\Xi_0,\mathbf{P}_0} = (\mathcal{E}_0, \mathcal{H}_0)$ where $\mathcal{H}_0 = (\{X^{(0)}, X^{(1)}, Y^{(0)}, Y^{(1)}\}, \nu)$ and $\mathcal{E}_0$ consists of:

$$X^{(0)}(x,y) = x + y \geq 0 \wedge Y^{(1)}(x-1, y) \quad X^{(1)}(x,y) = x + y \geq 0 \wedge Y^{(0)}(x, y+1)$$
$$Y^{(0)}(x,y) = X^{(1)}(x-1, y) \qquad Y^{(1)}(x,y) = X^{(0)}(x, y+1)$$

3.2 Linear-Time Property Verification of Recursive Programs

Target Language and Verification Problem. We first define a language of first-order recursive programs with non-determinism. The syntax of programs is given by:

$$\begin{aligned} &D(\text{programs}) ::= \{f_1(x_1, \ldots, x_{k_1}) = e_1, \ldots, f_\ell(x_1, \ldots, x_{k_\ell}) = e_\ell\} \\ &e(\text{expressions}) ::= a \mid * \mid A; e \mid f(v_1, \ldots, v_k) \mid \mathbf{let}\ x = e_1\ \mathbf{in}\ e_2 \\ &\qquad\qquad \mid \mathbf{if}\ v \geq 0\ \mathbf{then}\ e_1\ \mathbf{else}\ e_2 \\ &a ::= v \mid a_1\, \mathbf{op}\, a_2 \qquad v ::= n \mid x \end{aligned}$$

The expression $*$ evaluates to an integer in a non-deterministic manner. The expression $A; e$ raises an *event* A and evaluates e. Here, we assume a finite set of events; they are referred to by temporal property specifications (expressed by Büchi automata below). The other expressions are standard and should be self-explanatory. In a function definition $f_i(x_1, \ldots, x_{k_i}) = e_i$, variables $x_1, \ldots x_{k_i}$ and functions $f_1, \ldots, f_\ell$ are bound in e_i and we assume a given program is closed.

In a program $D = \{f_1(x_1, \ldots, x_{k_1}) = e_1, \ldots, f_\ell(x_1, \ldots, x_{k_\ell}) = e_\ell\}$, we assume that $\{f_1, \ldots, f_\ell\}$ contains the special function name **main** of the "main" function with arity 0, that **main**() never terminates, and every infinite reduction sequence generates an infinite sequence of events.[2]

$$\frac{n \in Z}{E[*] \xrightarrow{\epsilon}_D E[n]} \qquad \frac{(f(x_1, \ldots, x_k) = e) \in D}{E[f(n_1, \ldots, n_k)] \xrightarrow{\epsilon}_D E[[n_1/x_1, \ldots, n_k/x_k]e]}$$

$$\frac{a \notin Z \quad \mathbf{val}(a) = n}{E[a] \xrightarrow{\epsilon}_D E[n]} \qquad \frac{}{E[\mathbf{let}\ x = n\ \mathbf{in}\ e] \xrightarrow{\epsilon}_D E[[n/x]e]}$$

$$\frac{}{E[A; e] \xrightarrow{A}_D E[e]} \qquad \frac{n \geq 0}{E[\mathbf{if}\ n \geq 0\ \mathbf{then}\ e_1\ \mathbf{else}\ e_2] \xrightarrow{\epsilon}_D E[e_1]}$$

$$\frac{n < 0}{E[\mathbf{if}\ n \geq 0\ \mathbf{then}\ e_1\ \mathbf{else}\ e_2] \xrightarrow{\epsilon}_D E[e_2]}$$

Fig. 1. Operational Semantics. E ranges over the set of evaluation contexts, defined by $E ::= [\,] \mid \mathbf{let}\ x = E\ \mathbf{in}\ e$.

Operational Semantics. The transition relation $e \xrightarrow{\xi}_D e'$ (where ξ is either A or ϵ) is defined in Fig. 1. Here, $\mathbf{val}(a)$ denotes the value of an integer arithmetic expression a. We write $e \xRightarrow{w}_D e'$ if $w = \xi_1 \cdots \xi_\ell$ and $e_{i-1} \xrightarrow{\xi_i}_D e_i$ for each $i \in \{1, \ldots, \ell\}$, with $e = e_0$ and $e' = e_i$. Here, we treat ϵ as the empty word.

We write $\mathcal{L}(D)$ for the set of infinite sequences $A_1 A_2 A_3 \cdots$ such that

$$\mathbf{main}() \xRightarrow{A_1}_D e_1 \xRightarrow{A_2}_D e_2 \xRightarrow{A_3}_D \cdots.$$

Example 5. Consider the program D_0 consisting of the following function definitions.

$$\mathbf{main}() = \mathbf{let}\ x = *\ \mathbf{in}\ \mathtt{f}(x)$$
$$\mathtt{f}(x) = \mathbf{let}\ r = \mathtt{g}\ x\ \mathbf{in}\ (\mathtt{A}; \mathtt{f}(r)) \qquad \mathtt{g}(x) = \mathtt{B}; \mathbf{if}\ x \geq 0\ \mathbf{then}\ \mathtt{g}\ (x-1)\ \mathbf{else}\ 5$$

It has, for example, the following reduction sequence:

$$\mathbf{main}() \xRightarrow{\epsilon} \mathtt{f}(0) \xrightarrow{\epsilon} \mathbf{let}\ r = \mathtt{g}(0)\ \mathbf{in}\ (\mathtt{A}; \mathtt{f}(r)) \xrightarrow{\mathtt{B}} \mathbf{let}\ r = \mathtt{g}(-1)\ \mathbf{in}\ (\mathtt{A}; \mathtt{f}(r))$$
$$\xRightarrow{\epsilon} \mathtt{A}; \mathtt{f}(5) \xrightarrow{\mathtt{A}} \mathtt{f}(5) \xrightarrow{\epsilon} \cdots$$

The set $\mathcal{L}(D_0)$ of infinite event sequences generated by D_0 is $\{\mathtt{B}^n(\mathtt{AB}^6)^\omega \mid n \geq 1\}$.

[2] The assumption on non-termination is guaranteed by renaming **main** to **main**′, and adding the function definitions $\mathbf{main}() = \mathbf{let}\ x = \mathbf{main}'()\ \mathbf{in}\ loop()$ and $loop() = A_{call}; loop$; the last assumption is guaranteed by restricting the righthand side of each function definition to an expression of the form $A_{call}; e$.

Verification Problem. We are interested in the verification of linear-time properties, expressible by using Büchi automata. Let us recall the definition of Büchi automata.

Definition 1 (Büchi automata). *A (non-deterministic)* Büchi automaton $\mathcal{A}$ *is a quintuple* $(\Sigma, Q, \Delta, q_0, F)$, *where (i)* Σ *is a set of input symbols, (ii)* Q *is a set of states, (iii)* $\Delta \in Q \times \Sigma \to 2^Q$ *is the transition function, (iv)* $q_0 \in Q$ *is the initial state, and (v)* $F \subseteq Q$ *is the set of final states. An* ω*-word* $w = A_1 A_2 \cdots \in \Sigma^\omega$ *is* accepted *by* $\mathcal{A}$ *if there exists an infinite sequence of states* $q'_0 q'_1 q'_2 \cdots \in Q^\omega$, *such that (i)* $q'_0 = q_0$, *(ii)* $q'_j \in \Delta(q'_{j-1}, A_j)$ *for each* $j \geq 1$, *and (iii)* $\forall j \in J. q'_j \in F$ *holds for an infinite subset* J *of natural numbers (in other words, final states are visited infinitely often). We write* $\mathcal{L}(\mathcal{A})$ *for the set of* ω*-words accepted by* $\mathcal{A}$.

Example 6. Let $\mathcal{A}_0 = (\{\mathtt{A}, \mathtt{B}\}, \{q_A, q_B\}, \Delta, q_A, \{q_A\})$ where $\Delta(q_A, \mathtt{A}) = \Delta(q_B, \mathtt{A}) = \{q_A\}$ and $\Delta(q_A, \mathtt{B}) = \Delta(q_B, \mathtt{B}) = \{q_B\}$. The automaton is depicted as follows.

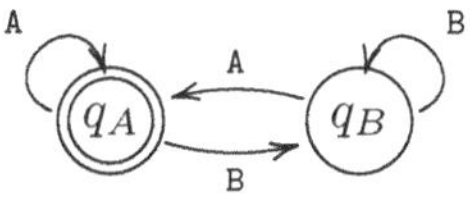

$\mathcal{A}_0$ accepts an infinite word $w \in \{\mathtt{A}, \mathtt{B}\}^\omega$ just if w contains infinitely many A's.

We are interested in the following verification problem: Given a program D and a Büchi automaton $\mathcal{A}$, does $\mathcal{L}(D) \cap \mathcal{L}(\mathcal{A}) \neq \emptyset$ hold? In a typical verification context, $\mathcal{L}(\mathcal{A})$ denotes the set of *invalid* infinite sequences of events, and the question $\mathcal{L}(D) \cap \mathcal{L}(\mathcal{A}) \overset{?}{\neq} \emptyset$ asks whether D may generate an invalid infinite sequence. The goal of the rest of this section is to characterize the condition $\mathcal{L}(D) \cap \mathcal{L}(\mathcal{A}) \neq \emptyset$ by a fixpoint formula $\varphi_{D,\mathcal{A}}$.

Overview of the Reduction Through an Example. Consider the program D_0 and automaton $\mathcal{A}_0$ in Examples 5 and 6. Suppose we wish to verify that $\mathcal{L}(D_0) \cap \mathcal{L}(\mathcal{A}_0) \neq \emptyset$.

For each function $f \in \{\mathbf{main}, \mathtt{f}, \mathtt{g}\}$, we construct the following predicates:

- $f_{q,b,q'}(x, r)$ for each $q, q' \in \{q_A, q_B\}, b \in \mathbf{B}$. Intuitively, $f_{q,b,q'}(x, r)$ means that $f(x)$ may generate an event sequence that changes the state of the automaton from q to q', and returns r. The Boolean value b represents whether a final state is visited by the automaton during the state changes from q to q' (excluding the state q). For example, since $\mathtt{g}(-1) \xrightarrow{\mathtt{B}}_{D_0} 5$, $\mathtt{g}_{q,\mathtt{ff},q_B}(-1, 5)$ should hold for $q \in \{q_A, q_B\}$.
- $f_{q,b}(x)$ for each $q \in \{q_A, q_B\}, b \in \mathbf{B}$. Intuitively, $f_{q,b}(x)$ means that $f(x)$ may generate an event sequence that can be accepted by the automaton from the state q. The Boolean value b is determined by the calling context of f; it represents whether a final state has been visited since the parent recursive call of f. For example, $f_{q,b}(n)$ should hold for any integer n, $q \in \{q_A, q_B\}$,

and $b \in \mathbf{B}$, as $f(n)$ generates an event sequence that contains infinitely many A's, which is accepted by $\mathcal{A}_0$. On the other hand, $\mathtt{g}_{q,b}(n)$ does not hold, as $\mathtt{g}(n)$ cannot generate an infinite sequence.

The predicates above can be systematically constructed from function definitions. For our running example, let us first construct $\mathtt{g}_{q,b,q'}$. Since $\mathtt{g}(x)$ generates only events B and returns r if either (i) $x \geq 0$ and $g(x-1)$ returns r, or (ii) $x < 0$ and $r = 5$. Thus, $\mathtt{g}_{q,b,q'}$ should satisfy:

$$\begin{aligned}
\mathtt{g}_{q_A,\mathtt{ff},q_B}(x,r) &= (x \geq 0 \wedge \mathtt{g}_{q_B,\mathtt{ff},q_B}(x-1,r)) \vee (x < 0 \wedge r = 5)\\
\mathtt{g}_{q_B,\mathtt{ff},q_B}(x,r) &= (x \geq 0 \wedge \mathtt{g}_{q_B,\mathtt{ff},q_B}(x-1,r)) \vee (x < 0 \wedge r = 5)\\
\mathtt{g}_{q,b,q'}(x,r) &= \mathtt{ff} \quad (\text{if } q' = q_A \text{ or } b = \mathtt{tt}).
\end{aligned}$$

Notice that the above equations are recursive. Since we are concerned about termination, $\mathtt{g}_{q,b,q'}$ is defined as the *least* solution of the equations above.

Using $\mathtt{g}_{q,b,q'}$ above, the equation for $\mathtt{f}_{q_A,\mathtt{tt}}$ is given as follows.

$$\mathtt{f}_{q_A,\mathtt{tt}}(x) = \exists r.(\mathtt{g}_{q_A,\mathtt{ff},q_B}(x,r) \wedge \mathtt{f}_{q_A,\mathtt{tt}}(r)).$$

This is because $\mathtt{f}(x)$ generates an infinite event sequence accepted from q_A by $\mathcal{A}_0$ if $\mathtt{g}(x)$ terminates and returns some r, and then $\mathtt{f}(r)$ generates an event sequence accepted from q_A. This time, $\mathtt{f}_{q_A,\mathtt{tt}}$ should be defined as the *greatest* solution for the above equation, since the automaton visits a final state (as indicated by the subscript tt for the predicate $\mathtt{f}_{q_A,\_}$) each time f is expanded. In general, $f_{q,b}$ is defined as the *greatest* solution if $b = \mathtt{tt}$, and as the *least* solution if $b = \mathtt{ff}$.

Based on the discussion above, $\Phi_{D_0,\mathcal{A}_0}$ is given as:

$$\begin{aligned}
&\{\mathbf{main}_{q_A,\mathtt{tt}}() =_\nu \exists x.\mathtt{f}_{q_A,\mathtt{ff}}(x),\\
&\quad \mathtt{f}_{q_A,\mathtt{tt}}(x) =_\nu \exists r.(\mathtt{g}_{q_A,\mathtt{ff},q_B}(x,r) \wedge \mathtt{f}_{q_A,\mathtt{tt}}(r))\};\\
&\{\mathtt{f}_{q_A,\mathtt{ff}}(x) =_\mu \exists r.(\mathtt{g}_{q_A,\mathtt{ff},q_B}(x,r) \wedge \mathtt{f}_{q_A,\mathtt{tt}}(r)),\\
&\quad \mathtt{g}_{q_A,\mathtt{ff},q_B}(x,r) =_\mu (x \geq 0 \wedge \mathtt{g}_{q_B,\mathtt{ff},q_B}(x-1,r)) \vee (x < 0 \wedge r = 5),\\
&\quad \mathtt{g}_{q_B,\mathtt{ff},q_B}(x,r) =_\mu (x \geq 0 \wedge \mathtt{g}_{q_B,\mathtt{ff},q_B}(x-1,r)) \vee (x < 0 \wedge r = 5)\}.
\end{aligned}$$

General Construction of $\Phi_{D,\mathcal{A}}$. We now formalize the general construction of the HES $\Phi_{D,\mathcal{A}}$. Below we fix a Büchi automaton $\mathcal{A} = (\Sigma, Q, \Delta, q_0, F)$.

As explained in the overview, for each function definition $f(\widetilde{x}) = e_f$, we construct predicates $f_{q,b,q'}(\widetilde{x}, r)$ and $f_{q,b}(\widetilde{x})$. To obtain equations for those predicates, we convert each subexpression e of e_f to formulas $[e]_{q,b,q',r}$ and $[e]_{q,b}$, where $q, q' \in Q$, $b \in \mathbf{B}$ and r is an integer variable. Intuitively, the formula $[e]_{q,b,q',r}$ means that there is a terminating execution sequence of e which generates a finite sequence of events that changes the state of $\mathcal{A}$ from q to q', and returns the integer r. The Boolean parameter b expresses whether an accepting state is visited during the automaton's transitions from q to q' (excluding the start state q). $[e]_{q,b}$ means that there is an infinite execution sequence of e that generates an infinite sequence of events accepted from q. The Boolean parameter b records information on whether an accepting state has been visited since the parent recursive call; the Boolean parameter is used to choose the Boolean parameter b' of $f_{q,b'}$.

The formula $[e]_{q,b,q',r}$ is defined by induction on the structure of e, as follows.

$$[a]_{q,b,q',r} = \begin{cases} a = r \text{ if } q = q' \text{ and } b = \texttt{ff} \\ \texttt{ff} \quad \text{otherwise} \end{cases} \qquad [*]_{q,b,q',r} = \begin{cases} \texttt{tt} \text{ if } q = q' \text{ and } b = \texttt{ff} \\ \texttt{ff} \text{ otherwise} \end{cases}$$

$$[A; e]_{q,b,q',r} = \bigvee\{[e]_{q'',b',q',r} \mid q'' \in \Delta(q, A), b' \in \mathbf{B}, b' \vee (q'' \in F) = b\}$$

$$[f(a_1, \ldots, a_k)]_{q,b,q',r} = f_{q,b,q'}(a_1, \ldots, a_k, r)$$

$$[\mathbf{let}\ x = e_1\ \mathbf{in}\ e_2]_{q,b,q',r} = \bigvee\{\exists x.([e_1]_{q,b_1,q'',x} \wedge [e_2]_{q'',b_2,q',r}) \mid q'' \in Q, b_1, b_2 \in \mathbf{B}, b = b_1 \vee b_2\}$$

$$[\mathbf{if}\ a \geq 0\ \mathbf{then}\ e_1\ \mathbf{else}\ e_2]_{q,b,q',r} = (a \geq 0 \wedge [e_1]_{q,b,q',r}) \vee (a < 0 \wedge [e_2]_{q,b,q',r})$$

We explain a few cases. Since a immediately evaluates to an integer, $[a]_{q,b,q',r}$ is true just if $a = r$, $q = q'$, and $b = \texttt{ff}$. In the translation of $A; e$, q'' is the state of $\mathcal{A}$ after the event A has occurred. The case for a function call $f(a_1, \ldots, a_k)$ is based on the intuition on the predicate $f_{q,b,q'}$ explained in Sect. 3.2. The translation for $e \equiv \mathbf{let}\ x = e_1\ \mathbf{in}\ e_2$ is based on the intuition that e evaluates to r just if e_1 evaluates to some integer x, and then e_2 evaluates to r; q'' is the intermediate state of $\mathcal{A}$ when e_1 has been evaluated.

The formula $[e]_{q,b}$ is also inductively defined as follows.

$$[a]_{q,b} = \texttt{ff} \qquad [*]_{q,b} = \texttt{ff} \qquad [A; e]_{q,b} = \bigvee\{[e]_{q',b \vee (q' \in F)} \mid q' \in \Delta(q, A)\}$$

$$[f(a_1, \ldots, a_k)]_{q,b} = f_{q,b}(a_1, \ldots, a_k)$$

$$[\mathbf{let}\ x = e_1\ \mathbf{in}\ e_2]_{q,b} = [e_1]_{q,b} \vee (\bigvee\{\exists x.[e_1]_{q,b',q',x} \wedge [e_2]_{q',b \vee b'} \mid q' \in Q, b' \in \mathbf{B}\})$$

$$[\mathbf{if}\ a \geq 0\ \mathbf{then}\ e_1\ \mathbf{else}\ e_2]_{q,b} = (a \geq 0 \wedge [e_1]_{q,b}) \vee (a < 0 \wedge [e_2]_{q,b})$$

When $e = a$ or $*$, $[e]_{q,b} = \texttt{ff}$ since e does not generate an infinite event sequence. In the translation of $A; e$, we update the state and accumulate (by $b \vee (q' \in F)$) information on whether an accepting state has been visited. For a function call $f(a_1, \ldots, a_k)$, the Boolean parameter b is used to annotate f, so that $f_{q,b}$ is defined as the greatest fixpoint if $b = \texttt{tt}$ (which means that an accepting state has been visited since the last recursive call), and otherwise defined as the least fixpoint. The translation for $e \equiv \mathbf{let}\ x = e_1\ \mathbf{in}\ e_2$ is based on the intuition that e diverges either if e_1 diverges, or if e_1 evaluates to an integer x and e_2 diverges.

Using $[e]_{q,b,q',r}$ and $[e]_{q,b}$, we define $\mathcal{E}_{D,b}, \mathcal{P}_{D,\texttt{fin}}, \mathcal{E}_{D,\texttt{fin}}$ and $\mathcal{P}_{D,b}$ ($b \in \mathbf{B}$) by:

$$\begin{aligned} \mathcal{E}_{D,b} &= \{f_{q,b}(\widetilde{x}) = [e]_{q,\texttt{ff}} \mid (f(\widetilde{x}) = e) \in D, q \in Q\} \\ \mathcal{P}_{D,b} &= \{f_{q,b} \mid (f(\widetilde{x}) = e) \in D, q \in Q\} \\ \mathcal{E}_{D,\texttt{fin}} &= \{f_{q,b,q'}(\widetilde{x}, r) = [e]_{q,b,q',r} \mid (f(\widetilde{x}) = e) \in D, q, q' \in Q, b \in \mathbf{B}\} \\ \mathcal{P}_{D,\texttt{fin}} &= \{f_{q,b,q'} \mid (f(\widetilde{x}) = e) \in D, q, q' \in Q, b \in \mathbf{B}\}. \end{aligned}$$

Finally, we define $\Phi_{D,\mathcal{A}} = (\mathcal{E}_D, \mathcal{H}_D)$ by:

$$\mathcal{E}_D = \mathcal{E}_{D,\texttt{tt}} \cup \mathcal{E}_{D,\texttt{ff}} \cup \mathcal{E}_{D,\texttt{fin}} \qquad \mathcal{H}_D = (\mathcal{P}_{D,\texttt{tt}}, \nu); (\mathcal{P}_{D,\texttt{ff}} \cup \mathcal{P}_{D,\texttt{fin}}, \mu).$$

As indicated above, the alternation depth (between ν and μ) of $\Phi_{D,\mathcal{A}}$ is 2.

The following theorem states the correctness of the construction of $\Phi_{D,\mathcal{A}}$. A proof is given in [33].

Theorem 1. *Let D be a program and $\mathcal{A}$ be a Büchi automaton. Then $\mathcal{L}(D) \cap \mathcal{L}(\mathcal{A}) \neq \emptyset$ if and only if $\Phi_D \models \mathbf{main}_{q_0,\mathtt{tt}}()$.*

Example 7. We have already given an example of the construction of $\Phi_{D,\mathcal{A}}$ in Sect. 3.2. We give another simple example here, which may help the reader understand the role of the Boolean parameter b in $f_{q,b}$. Recall the automaton $\mathcal{A}_0$ in Example 6, and consider the program D_1 that consists of the single function definition $\mathbf{main}() = \mathtt{A}; \mathbf{main}()$. Then, $\Phi_{D_1,\mathcal{A}_0}$ is:

$$\{\mathbf{main}_{q_A,\mathtt{tt}}() =_\nu \mathbf{main}_{q_A,\mathtt{tt}}()\}; \{\mathbf{main}_{q_A,\mathtt{ff}}() =_\mu \mathbf{main}_{q_A,\mathtt{tt}}()\}.$$

(We omit the equations for $\mathbf{main}_{q_B,b}$.) Thus, $\Phi_{D_1,\mathcal{A}_0} \models \mathbf{main}_{q_A,\mathtt{tt}}()$. Indeed, D_1 generates $\mathtt{A}^\omega$, which is accepted by $\mathcal{A}_0$. The reason why $\mathbf{main}_{q_A,-}$ in the bodies of the equations is annotated with $\mathtt{tt}$ is that an event $\mathtt{A}$ occurs (so, the automaton visits the accepting state q_A) before **main** is called in the body of the function definition.

In contrast, the program D_2 consisting of $\mathbf{main}() = \mathtt{B}; \mathbf{main}()$ is translated to: $\{\mathbf{main}_{q_A,\mathtt{tt}}() =_\nu \mathbf{main}_{q_B,\mathtt{ff}}()\}; \{\mathbf{main}_{q_B,\mathtt{ff}}() =_\mu \mathbf{main}_{q_B,\mathtt{ff}}()\}$. Thus, $\Phi_{D_2,\mathcal{A}_0} \not\models \mathbf{main}_{q_A,\mathtt{tt}}()$. Indeed, D_2 only generates $\mathtt{B}^\omega$, which is not accepted by $\mathcal{A}_0$. Note that $\mathbf{main}_{q_B,-}$ in the bodies of the equations is annotated with $\mathtt{ff}$ because each call of $\mathbf{main}()$ is only preceded by an event $\mathtt{B}$; so, the automaton does not visit q_A. □

4 Proving Fixpoint Formulas by Reduction to CHC Solving

In this section, we describe our Mu2CHC approach to validity checking of fixpoint formulas. The method is based on a reduction to CHC solving [5]. As mentioned in Sect. 1, a main advantage of the approach is that we can reuse off-the-shelf CHC solvers such as Spacer [27] and HoIce [13].

Suppose that we wish to prove $\Phi \models \mathbf{main}()$. Without loss of generality, we can assume that the predicate **main** is bound by ν in Φ (otherwise, just introduce a fresh predicate $\mathbf{main}'$, and prove $\{\mathbf{main}'() =_\nu \mathbf{main}()\}; \Phi \models \mathbf{main}()$). We can also assume that Φ contains no existential quantifiers, as existential quantifiers can be encoded by using μ; recall Remark 1. Below we present a method to transform Φ to another HES Φ' so that $\Phi' \models \mathbf{main}()$ implies $\Phi \models \mathbf{main}()$, and Φ' contains neither μ nor existential quantifiers. By the observation in Sect. 2.3, $\Phi' \models \mathbf{main}()$ can be reduced to CHC solving. Using a CHC solver as a backend, we obtain a sound procedure for proving $\Phi \models \mathbf{main}()$. To disprove $\Phi \models \mathbf{main}()$, it suffices to prove the dual problem $\overline{\Phi} \models \overline{\mathbf{main}}()$ (where $\overline{\mathbf{main}}$ is the predicate symbol that denotes the negation of **main** in $\overline{\Phi}$); thus, by running the sound procedure for proving $\Phi \models \mathbf{main}()$ and $\overline{\Phi} \models \overline{\mathbf{main}}()$ in parallel, we obtain a sound (but incomplete) decision procedure.

Inspired by methods for proving termination by reduction to safety properties [35], we approximate μ-formulas (which can be considered generalization of the termination property) by ν-formulas (which can be considered generalization of safety properties). In particular, we pick the recent termination verification method of Fedyukovich et al. [21] and generalize it for our context.

Let us first consider a special case, where an HES consists of a single equation: $P(\widetilde{x}) =_\mu \varphi$. Recall that the semantics of P is the least fixpoint of $F = \lambda f \in \mathbf{Z}^k \to \mathbf{B}.\lambda\widetilde{v} \in \mathbf{Z}^k.[\![\varphi]\!]_{\{P\mapsto f,\widetilde{x}\to\widetilde{v}\}}$, where $k = \mathtt{ar}(P)$. Thus, the semantics of P can be under-approximated by $F^y(\lambda\widetilde{v}.\mathtt{ff})$ for any $y \geq 0$, and a greater value of y gives a better approximation. With this in mind, we prepare a new predicate P' and construct a new equation:

$$P'(y, \widetilde{x}) =_\nu y > 0 \wedge \varphi',$$

where φ' is the formula obtained from φ by replacing each formula of the form $P(\widetilde{t})$ with $P'(y-1, \widetilde{t})$. The predicate $\lambda\widetilde{x}.P'(y,\widetilde{x})$ corresponds to $F^y(\lambda\widetilde{v}.\mathtt{ff})$ above (in fact, one can prove that the semantics of $\lambda\widetilde{x}.P'(y,\widetilde{x})$ is equivalent to $F^y(\lambda\widetilde{v}.\mathtt{ff})$ by induction on y), and thus $P'(y,\widetilde{x}) \Rightarrow P(\widetilde{x})$ for any $y \in \mathbf{Z}$. To prove a formula of the form $C[P(\widetilde{a})]$ (here, C is a formula with a hole, and we write $C[\varphi]$ for the formula obtained by filling the hole with φ), it suffices to prove $C[\forall y.(y \geq a'_1 \wedge \cdots \wedge y \geq a'_k \Rightarrow P'(y,\widetilde{a}))]$, where $a'_1, \ldots, a'_k$ are arbitrary arithmetic expressions constructed by using variables available in the hole of C. Note that $\forall y.(y \geq a'_1 \wedge \cdots \wedge y \geq a'_k \Rightarrow P'(y,\widetilde{a}))$, which is equivalent to $P'(\max(a'_1, \ldots, a'_k), \widetilde{a})$, implies $P(x)$, and that (the semantics of) C is monotonic with respect to the hole position, since there is no connective for negation. Thus, we have reduced the validity checking problem for a least fixpoint formula with that of a greatest fixpoint formula in a sound (but incomplete) manner.

Remark 2. In $\forall y.(y \geq a'_1 \wedge \cdots \wedge y \geq a'_k \Rightarrow P'(y,\widetilde{a}))$, the bounds $a'_1, \ldots, a'_k$ can be chosen heuristically. A nice point about using multiple bounds is that we can monotonically increase the precision of approximation, by adding new elements to the set $\{a'_1, \ldots, a'_k\}$. This advantage is analogous to that of disjunctive well-founded relations over well-founded relations in the context of termination verification [35].

Example 8. Consider:

$$P(x) =_\mu x = 0 \vee P(x-1)$$

and suppose that we wish to prove $\forall z.z < 0 \vee P(z)$. We define a new predicate P' by:

$$P'(y,x) =_\nu y > 0 \wedge (x = 0 \vee P'(y-1, x-1)),$$

and change the goal to $\forall z.z < 0 \vee (\forall y.y \geq z+1 \Rightarrow P'(y,z))$. One can reduce its validity to the satisfiability of the following CHC:

$$\begin{array}{l} \overline{P'}(y,x) \Leftarrow y \leq 0 \vee (x \neq 0 \wedge \overline{P'}(y-1, x-1)) \\ \mathtt{ff} \Leftarrow z \geq 0 \wedge y \geq z+1 \wedge \overline{P'}(y,z). \end{array}$$

It is satisfiable with $\overline{P'}(y,x) \equiv y \leq 0 \vee x < 0 \vee y < x+1$; hence we know the original formula $\forall z.z < 0 \vee P(z)$ is valid. □

In the general case, we replace each layer of μ-equations with ν-equations one by one. Assume that a given HES Φ is

$$\begin{array}{l}\Phi_1; \{P_1(\widetilde{x}_1) =_\mu \varphi_1, \dots, P_k(\widetilde{x}_k) =_\mu \varphi_k\};\\ \qquad \{P_{k+1}(\widetilde{x}_{k+1}) =_\nu \varphi_{k+1}, \dots, P_{k+\ell}(\widetilde{x}_{k+\ell}) =_\nu \varphi_{k+\ell}\}.\end{array}$$

As in the special case, we approximate the least fixpoint $\mathbf{FP}_\mu(F)$ for the values of $P_1, \dots, P_k$ with a finite approximation $F^y(\bot)$. To this end, we replace Φ with the following HES Φ':

$$\begin{array}{l}\Phi'_1; \{P'_1(y, \widetilde{x}_1) =_\mu y > 0 \wedge \varphi'_1, \dots, P'_k(y, \widetilde{x}_k) =_\mu y > 0 \wedge \varphi'_k\};\\ \qquad \{P'_{k+1}(y, \widetilde{x}_{k+1}) =_\nu \varphi'_{k+1}, \dots, P'_{k+\ell}(y, \widetilde{x}_{k+\ell}) =_\nu \varphi'_{k+\ell}\}.\end{array}$$

Here,

- φ'_i $(1 \le i \le k+\ell)$ is the formula obtained from φ_i by replacing each subformula of the form $P_j(\widetilde{a})$ with $P'_j(y-1, \widetilde{a})$ if $1 \le j \le k$, and with $P'_j(y, \widetilde{a})$ if $k+1 \le j \le k+\ell$). Intuitively, $P'_i(y, \_)$ $1 \le i \le k$ is the y-th approximation $F^y(\bot)$ of the least fixpoint of F; hence y is decremented each time P_i is recursively called. For $P'_i(y, \widetilde{x}_i)$ for $k+1 \le i \le k+\ell$ approximates $P_i(\widetilde{x}_i)$ by approximating $P_j(\widetilde{x}_j)$ with $P'_j(y, \widetilde{x}_j)$ for $1 \le j \le k$ (recall that the semantics of $P_{k+1}, \dots, P_{k+\ell}$ are parameterized by those of $P_1, \dots, P_k$).
- Φ'_1 is the HES obtained from Φ_1 by replacing each formula of the form $P_i(\widetilde{a})$ $(1 \le i \le k+\ell)$ with $\forall y.y \ge a'_1 \wedge \dots \wedge y \ge a'_m \Rightarrow P'_i(y, \widetilde{a})$, where $a'_1, \dots, a'_m$ are expressions consisting of the variables available at the position of $P_i(\widetilde{a})$.

By the construction above, $P'_i(y, \widetilde{x}_i) \Rightarrow P_i(\widetilde{x}_i)$ holds for every $y, \widetilde{x}_1 \in \mathbf{Z}$; hence Φ' is an under-approximation of Φ. By repeatedly applying the transformation above to Φ, we get an HES Φ' such that Φ' contains neither μ nor $\exists$, and $[\![\Phi']\!] \sqsubseteq [\![\Phi]\!]$.

Example 9. Recall the HES Φ_1 in Sect. 3.2 (with some simplification):

$$\begin{array}{l}\{\mathbf{main}_{q_A,\mathtt{tt}}() =_\nu \exists x.\mathtt{f}_{q_A,\mathtt{tt}}(x), \quad \mathtt{f}_{q_A,\mathtt{tt}}(x) =_\nu \exists r.(\mathtt{g}_{q_A,\mathtt{ff},q_B}(x,r) \wedge \mathtt{f}_{q_A,\mathtt{tt}}(r))\};\\ \{\mathtt{g}_{q_A,\mathtt{ff},q_B}(x,r) =_\mu (x \ge 0 \wedge \mathtt{g}_{q_B,\mathtt{ff},q_B}(x-1,r)) \vee (x < 0 \wedge r = 5),\\ \ \mathtt{g}_{q_B,\mathtt{ff},q_B}(x,r) =_\mu (x \ge 0 \wedge \mathtt{g}_{q_B,\mathtt{ff},q_B}(x-1,r)) \vee (x < 0 \wedge r = 5)\}.\end{array}$$

By encoding $\exists$ with μ, we obtain:

$$\begin{array}{l}\{\mathbf{main}_{q_A,\mathtt{tt}}() =_\nu P(0), \quad \mathtt{f}_{q_A,\mathtt{tt}}(x) =_\nu Q(0,x)\};\\ \{P(x) =_\mu \mathtt{f}_{q_A,\mathtt{tt}}(x) \vee P(x+1) \vee P(x-1),\\ \ Q(r,x) =_\mu (\mathtt{g}_{q_A,\mathtt{ff},q_B}(x,r) \wedge \mathtt{f}_{q_A,\mathtt{tt}}(r)) \vee Q(r+1,x) \vee Q(r-1,x),\\ \ \mathtt{g}_{q_A,\mathtt{ff},q_B}(x,r) =_\mu (x \ge 0 \wedge \mathtt{g}_{q_B,\mathtt{ff},q_B}(x-1,r)) \vee (x < 0 \wedge r = 5),\\ \ \mathtt{g}_{q_B,\mathtt{ff},q_B}(x,r) =_\mu (x \ge 0 \wedge \mathtt{g}_{q_B,\mathtt{ff},q_B}(x-1,r)) \vee (x < 0 \wedge r = 5)\}.\end{array}$$

By the transformation above, we obtain Φ_1':

$$
\begin{aligned}
\{&\mathbf{main}_{q_A,\mathtt{tt}}() =_\nu \forall y.(y \geq 1 \Rightarrow P'(y,0)),\\
&\mathtt{f}_{q_A,\mathtt{tt}}(x) =_\nu \forall y.(y \geq x+6 \Rightarrow Q'(y,0,x)),\\
&P'(y,x) =_\nu y > 0 \land (\mathtt{f}_{q_A,\mathtt{tt}}(x) \lor P'(y-1,x+1) \lor P'(y-1,x-1)),\\
&Q'(y,r,x) =_\nu y > 0 \land ((\mathtt{g}_{q_A,\mathtt{ff},q_B}(y-1,x,r) \land \mathtt{f}_{q_A,\mathtt{tt}}(y-1,r))\\
&\qquad\qquad \lor Q'(y-1,r+1,x) \lor Q'(y-1,r-1,x)),\\
&\mathtt{g}'_{q_A,\mathtt{ff},q_B}(y,x,r) =_\nu y > 0\\
&\qquad\qquad \land((x \geq 0 \land \mathtt{g}'_{q_B,\mathtt{ff},q_B}(y-1,x-1,r)) \lor (x < 0 \land r = 5)),\\
&\mathtt{g}'_{q_B,\mathtt{ff},q_B}(y,x,r) =_\nu y > 0\\
&\qquad\qquad \land((x \geq 0 \land \mathtt{g}'_{q_B,\mathtt{ff},q_B}(y-1,x-1,r)) \lor (x < 0 \land r = 5))\}.
\end{aligned}
$$

Since $\Phi_1' \models \mathbf{main}_{q_A,\mathtt{tt}}()$, we know $\Phi_1 \models \mathbf{main}_{q_A,\mathtt{tt}}()$. □

Remark 3. As explained above, the idea of our translation is to approximate the least fixpoint $\mathbf{FP}_\mu(F)$ with $F^k(\bot)$. This is too conservative, when (i) the least fixpoint is not reached in the ω-step (i.e., when $\mathbf{FP}_\mu(F) \neq F^\omega(\bot)$), or (ii) the bound k is too large to express it and for the underlying CHC solver to reason about (e.g. when k is expressed by the Ackermann function). One way to overcome this problem is to represent a bound as a tuple of integers. For example, $P(\widetilde{x}) =_\mu \varphi$ can be approximated by $P'(y_1, y_2, \widetilde{x})$, which is defined by:

$$P'(y_1, y_2, \widetilde{x}) =_\nu y_1 > 0 \land y_2 > 0 \land \varphi',$$

where φ' is the formula obtained from φ' by replacing each subformula of the form $P(\widetilde{a})$ with

$$P'(y_1, y_2 - 1, \widetilde{a}) \lor \forall y_2'.(y_2' \geq \max(a_1', \ldots, a_k') \Rightarrow P'(y_1 - 1, y_2', \widetilde{a})).$$

Note that when the value of y_1 is decreased, the value of y_2 can be reset. This corresponds to the use of a lexicographic ranking function in termination verification. □

```
CheckValidity(Φ, main){ /* Φ: HES, main: Entry formula */
  if Φ is a ν-only HES then return CHCsolver(toCHC(MakeDual(Φ,main)))
  else if Φ is a μ-only HES then return not(CHCsolver(toCHC(Φ,main)))
  else return (CheckSub(Φ, main) || not(CheckSub(MakeDual(Φ,main))));
}
CheckSub(Φ, main){
  (Φ',main') := ElimMu(Φ,main)
  while(true) {
    if CHCsolver(toCHC(Φ',main')) then return true
    else (Φ',main') := IncreaseBounds(Φ',main'); }
}
```

Fig. 2. Mu2CHC procedure

Figure 2 shows pseudo code of our overall procedure. The procedure `CheckValidity` takes as input an HES Φ and an entry predicate **main** and returns whether $\Phi \models \mathbf{main}()$ holds. If Φ is ν-only (i.e., it contains neither $\exists$ nor μ), then the procedure converts the problem to the corresponding CHC satisfiability problem, and calls a backend CHC solver. Similarly, if Φ is μ-only (i.e., it contains neither $\forall$ nor ν), then the procedure makes the de Morgan dual of the problem by `MakeDual`, converts it to CHC, and calls a CHC solver; in this case, the final result is the negation of the output of the CHC solver. The remaining is the case where Φ has alternations between μ and ν. In this case, the procedure runs the subprocedure `CheckSub` for proving the original problem and its dual in parallel. As described above, `CheckSub` approximates a given HES Φ to a ν-only HES Φ' and then converts Φ' to CHC. Due to the under-approximation, the result is valid only if the CHC solver returns true (which means the formula is valid); if the CHC solver returns false or time-outs, the procedure increases bounds ($a'_1, \ldots, a'_k$ used for eliminating μ) and repeats the loop.

5 Implementation and Evaluation

We have implemented a validity checking tool MU2CHC for the fixpoint logic in OCaml, based on the method in Sect. 4. We use Spacer [27] and HoIce [13] as the backend CHC solvers of MU2CHC. In addition, we have also implemented a translator from CTL verification problems for C programs to Mu-Arithmetic formulas, which supports only a very small subset of C, just large enough to cover the benchmark programs of [17]. We have not yet implemented the translations described in Sects. 3.1 and 3.2 (implementing them for a full-scale language is not difficult but tedious); thus, the outputs of those translations used in the experiments below have been obtained by hand.

As the set of bounds $\{a'_1, \ldots, a'_k\}$ used for approximating μ-formulas by ν-formulas (recall Remark 2), MU2CHC uses $\{c_1x_1+...+c_nx_n+B \mid c_i \in \{-A, A\}\}$ where A, B are positive integers, and $x_1, \ldots, x_n$ are the variables in scope. Those bounds are equivalent to the single bound $A(|x_1| + ... + |x_n|) + B$. MU2CHC first sets $A = 1, B = 10$, and doubles them each time the `IncreaseBounds` procedure in Fig. 2 is called. In the implementation, an existentially-quantified formula $\exists x.\varphi$ is directly approximated by the formula $\forall x.x \geq a'_1 \wedge \cdots \wedge x \geq a'_k \Rightarrow P(x)$, where $P(x) =_\nu x \geq 0 \wedge (\varphi \vee [-x/x]\varphi \vee P(x-1))$ (rather than encoding it using μ as in Remark 1 and then approximating μ by ν). Note that $\forall x.x \geq a'_1 \wedge \cdots \wedge x \geq a'_k \Rightarrow P(x)$ is equivalent to $\exists x.x \leq \max(a'_1, \ldots, a'_k) \wedge \varphi$.

We have tested MU2CHC against our own benchmark set, and the standard benchmark set for CTL verification [17]. The tool was run on an Intel Core i5 2.7 GHz dual-core processor with main memory of 8 GB.

The first table in Table 1 shows the results on our own benchmark set. The columns Exp. and Act. show expected and actual results, respectively, where ✓, ✗, and ? denote "valid", "invalid", and "unknown", respectively. All the problems except ex4 contain nested ν and μ. The problems 1–6 encode some properties of integer arithmetic in the fixpoint logic. The problems 7–22 encode linear-time properties of recursive programs, based on the translation in Sect. 3 (with some hand-optimizations). In particular, 7 and 8 are $\Phi_{D_0,\mathcal{A}_0}$ in Sect. 3.2 and a variation of it. The problems 9–14 are from [23,28,31]. For those problems, the formulas encode the property "there is an (infinite) error trace that violates an expected linear-time property." Those formulas are *invalid*, since the original programs have actually no error trace. The rest of the problems (23–28) encode temporal property of while-programs, based on the translation in Sect. 3.1. Among them, the problems 23 and 24 verify the properties $\nu X.(x + y \geq 0 \wedge \diamond \diamond X)$ and $\nu X.\mu Y.\Box Y \vee (0 \geq x \wedge (\mu Z. \diamond Z \vee (x \geq 1 \wedge X)))$ respectively, which we believe cannot be expressed in CTL*. The problem ex5 has been taken from a test case[3] of T2 [15], and verifies the CTL* property $\mathtt{AG}(\mathtt{AFG}(x = 0) \vee \mathtt{AFG}(x = 1))$. See [33] for more details on the benchmark set. Our tool could successfully check the validity of Mu-Arithmetic formulas, except the problem 22. It requires a reasoning about the divisibility predicate, which is not well handled by the underlying CHC solvers.

The table below in Table 1 shows the result for the "industrial" benchmark set from [17]; the result for the "small" benchmark set is provided in [33]. For comparison, we take the results from [17] verbatim (note that the execution time is measured by using a different processor).[4] As the table shows, our tool could successfully solve all the problems and outperforms [17] in most cases (note however the difference in the experimental environments). This may be a bit surprising, as our tool is not customized for CTL verification.

6 Related Work

As already mentioned, our work has been motivated by recent proposals of reductions from program verification to validity/satisfiability checking in fixpoint logics [3,5,7–9,22,26,32,41]. The idea of using CHC in program analysis or verification can actually be further traced back to earlier studies on constraint logic programming [19,24,34].

The combination of our method for proving Mu-Arithmetic formulas with the translation given in Sect. 3.1 yields an automated verification method for the full modal μ-calculus model checking of while-programs with infinite data. In contrast, the previous temporal verification methods have been restricted to less expressive temporal logics such as CTL [3,17,18,39], CTL* [14], and linear-time logics such as LTL [16,20,31]. As already mentioned, the translation given

[3] https://github.com/hkhlaaf/T2/blob/master/test/ctlstar_test.t2.

[4] There are some discrepancies on the verification results among [17], [3] and ours. We are not sure about this, but it is most likely because the benchmark set has accidentally been modified when it was passed around. We have taken the industrial set from that of E-HSF [3] provided by Andrey Rybalchenko. Note, however, that we found some discrepancies between the C programs and their encodings in the E-HSF; that explains the difference between the outputs of our tool and those of E-HSF [3]. The "small" set was provided by Eric Koskinen. For 26–28, the results are "invalid" for both φ and $\neg\varphi$ (as in [3]); this is not a contradiction, as the checked properties are of the form "*for all the initial states*, φ (or $\neg\varphi$) holds.".

Table 1. Experimental Results. The upper table shows the results for our own benchmark set, and the lower table shows the results for the Industrial Set from [17].

Benchmark Name	Exp.	Act.	Time[s]	Benchmark Name	Exp.	Act.	Time[s]
1. simple-nest	✓	✓	0.21	15. infinite1	✓	✓	1.58
2. simple-nest-inv	✓	✓	0.19	16. infinite1b	✓	✓	2.97
3. lines1	✓	✓	1.72	17. infinite1c-invalid	✗	✗	1.64
4. lines2-invalid	✗	✗	0.27	18. infinite2	✓	✓	0.36
5. lines3	✓	✓	1.95	19. infinite3	✓	✓	0.13
6. lines4	✓	✓	1.66	20. intfun1-invalid	✗	✗	0.06
7. ex3	✓	✓	9.36	21. intfun2-invalid	✗	✗	0.06
8. ex3-forall	✓	✓	22.87	22. intfun3-invalid	✗	?	-
9. hofmann1	✗	✗	0.17	23. ex4	✓	✓	0.09
10. hofmann2	✗	✗	0.48	24. ex4	✓	✓	0.13
11. koskinen1_fo	✗	✗	0.27	25. ex5	✗	✗	1.58
12. koskinen2	✗	✗	1.50	26. ctl1	✓	✓	0.79
13. koskinen3	✗	✗	0.46	27. ctl2	✓	✓	5.50
14. intro	✗	✗	1.96	28. ctl2b-invalid	✗	✗	1.72

Problem ID and Property φ	$\models \varphi$					$\models \neg\varphi$				
	Exp.	[17]		MU2CHC		Exp.	[17]		MU2CHC	
		Act.	Time[s]	Act.	Time[s]		Act.	Time[s]	Act.	Time[s]
1. $\mathtt{AG}(p \Rightarrow \mathtt{AF}q)$	✓	✓	4.6	✓	0.40	✗	✗	12.5	✗	0.41
2. $\mathtt{AG}(p \Rightarrow \mathtt{AF}q)$	✗	✗	9.1	✗	0.10	✓	✓	3.5	✓	0.32
3. $\mathtt{AG}(p \Rightarrow \mathtt{EF}q)$	✓	✓	9.5	✓	0.23	✗	✗	18.1	✗	1.57
4. $\mathtt{AG}(p \Rightarrow \mathtt{EF}q)$	✗	✗	1.5	✗	0.65	✓	✓	105.7	✓	0.82
5. $\mathtt{AG}(p \Rightarrow \mathtt{AF}q)$	✓	✓	2.1	✓	0.49	✗	✗	6.5	✗	3.91
6. $\mathtt{AG}(p \Rightarrow \mathtt{AF}q)$	✗	✗	1.8	✗	0.15	✓	✓	1.2	✓	2.91
7. $\mathtt{AG}(p \Rightarrow \mathtt{EF}q)$	✓	✓	3.7	✓	4.91	✗	✗	8.7	✗	6.33
8. $\mathtt{AG}(p \Rightarrow \mathtt{EF}q)$	✗	✗	1.5	✗	5.55	✓	✓	5.6	✓	4.25
9. $\mathtt{AG}(p \Rightarrow \mathtt{AF}q)$	✓	✓	38.9	✓	0.65	✗	✗	1930.9	✗	3.27
10. $\mathtt{AG}(p \Rightarrow \mathtt{AF}q)$	✗	✗	148.0	✗	28.20	✓	✓	1680.7	✓	29.53
11. $\mathtt{AG}(p \Rightarrow \mathtt{EF}q)$	✓	✓	90.0	✓	0.42	✗	?	-	✗	2.69
12. $\mathtt{AG}(p \Rightarrow \mathtt{EF}q)$	✓	✗	107.8	✓	0.52	✗	?	-	✗	2.92
13. $\mathtt{AF}q \vee \mathtt{AF}p$	✗	✓	34.3	✗	0.16	✓	✗	62.3	✗	14.62
14. $\mathtt{AF}q \vee \mathtt{AF}p$	✗	✗	18.8	✗	0.20	✓	✓	7.6	✓	1.91
15. $\mathtt{EF}q \wedge \mathtt{EF}p$	✓	✓	1261.0	✓	21.87	✗	✗	0.9	✗	0.14
16. $\mathtt{EF}q \wedge \mathtt{EF}p$	✗	?	-	✗	1.80	✓	✓	0.6	✓	0.16
17. $\mathtt{AGAF}p$	✓	✓	596.7	✓	0.58	✗	✗	1471.7	✗	2.39
18. $\mathtt{AGAF}p$	✗	✗	65.1	✗	0.07	✓	✓	351.1	✓	0.23
19. $\mathtt{AGEF}p$	✗	?	-	✗	0.46	✓	✗	85.5	✓	0.38
20. $\mathtt{AGEF}p$	✗	?	-	✗	0.89	✓	✓	255.8	✓	0.52
21. $\mathtt{AGAF}p$	✗	?	-	✗	1.22	✓	✗	45.3	✓	0.29
22. $\mathtt{AGAF}p$	✗	✗	38.1	✗	0.13	✓	✓	35.2	✓	0.32
23. $\mathtt{AGEF}p$	✗	?	-	✗	0.11	✓	?	-	✓	0.11
24. $\mathtt{AGEF}p$	✗	✗	42.7	✗	0.11	✓	✓	30.2	✓	1.62
25. $p \Rightarrow \mathtt{AF}q$	✓	✓	70.2	✓	17.17	✗	✗	0.4	✗	0.13
26. $p \Rightarrow \mathtt{AF}q$	✗	✗	32.4	✗	0.84	✗	✓	4.5	✗	0.09
27. $p \Rightarrow \mathtt{EF}q$	✗	✓	18.5	✗	0.94	✗	✗	0.5	✗	0.09
28. $p \Rightarrow \mathtt{EF}q$	✗	✗	1.3	✗	0.07	✗	✓	0.3	✗	0.11

in Sect. 3.1 can be considered a special case of the translation of Watanabe et al. [41] for higher-order programs. For imperative programs, however, our translation in Sect. 3.1 is more direct. Our translation for infinite-data programs may also be viewed as a generalization of Andersen's translation from modal μ-calculus model checking of finite-state systems to Boolean graphs [2].

The reduction from linear-time properties of first-order recursive programs to the validity checking problem in a first-order fixpoint logic is new, to our knowledge. Kobayashi et al. [26] proposed a translation from linear-time properties of higher-order programs to the validity checking in a *higher-order* fixpoint logic (called HFL), but their translation yields second-order fixpoint logic formulas for first-order recursive programs. Combined with our Mu-Arithmetic prover, the translation yields a new automated method for proving linear-time properties of first-order recursive programs. Our translation may be considered a generalization of the technique for LTL model checking of recursive state machines [1], to deal with infinite-data programs.

Our approach of Mu2CHC described in Sect. 4 has been inspired by termination verification methods [21,35] and generalizes the method of Fedyukovich et al. [21]. A related technique has been proposed by Biere et al. [4] for finite-state model checking. The Mu2CHC approach also much relies on the recent advance of CHC solving techniques [5,13,27,38]. An alternative approach to approximate μ-formulas by ν-formulas would be to generalize the termination verification method based on transition invariants [36], as sketched in [41].

As discussed in Sect. 2.3, the validity checking problem for Mu-Arithmetic may be seen as a generalization of the satisfiability problem for CHC [8,9]. A few extensions of CHC have been previously studied [3,7]. To encode CTL verification problems, Beyene et al. [3] extended CHC with a special predicate dwf such that $dwf(r)$ if and only if r is disjunctively well-founded. This fragment is close to Mu-Arithmetic, in that, as an alternative to the method in Sect. 4, we can replace a μ-equation $P(\widetilde{x}) =_{\mu} \varphi$ with $P(\widetilde{x}) =_{\nu} \varphi'$, where φ' is the formula obtained from φ by replacing each subformula of the form $P(\widetilde{a})$ with $r(\widetilde{a}, \widetilde{x}) \wedge P(\widetilde{a})$ for a well-founded relation r. Allowing universal quantifiers in bodies of CHC [7] corresponds to allowing existential quantifiers in our HES (recall that we took de Morgan dual in the conversions between a fragment of Mu-Arithmetic and CHC in Sect. 2.3). In contrast, there is no counterpart of the extension with existential quantifiers (in head positions of CHC) [3] in our fixpoint logic, which indicates that such an extension is unnecessary for the μ-calculus model checking of while programs.

7 Conclusion

We have proposed a method for proving validity of first-order fixpoint logic with integer arithmetic. Combined with the reduction in Sect. 3.1, the proposed methods yield an automated, unifying verification method for temporal properties of while-programs, supporting all the properties expressive in the modal μ-calculus. We have also presented a reduction from linear-time properties of first-order recursive programs to validity of fixpoint formulas, which also yields an automated method for temporal properties of first-order recursive programs, supporting all the properties expressive by Büchi automata. Future work includes further refinement of our verification method (e.g., on the point discussed in Remark 3), and an extension of our tool lo support data types other than integers. Extending our methods in Sects. 3 and 4 to support algebraic data types is not difficult, but the CHC solving phase may become a bottleneck, as the current CHC solvers are not very good at dealing with algebraic data types.

Acknowledgments. We would like to thank anonymous referees for useful comments. This work was supported by JSPS KAKENHI Grant Number JP15H05706 and JP16H05856.

References

1. Alur, R., Benedikt, M., Etessami, K., Godefroid, P., Reps, T.W., Yannakakis, M.: Analysis of recursive state machines. ACM Trans. Program. Lang. Syst. **27**(4), 786–818 (2005)
2. Andersen, H.R.: Model checking and boolean graphs. Theor. Comput. Sci. **126**(1), 3–30 (1994)
3. Beyene, T.A., Popeea, C., Rybalchenko, A.: Solving existentially quantified horn clauses. In: Sharygina, N., Veith, H. (eds.) CAV 2013. LNCS, vol. 8044, pp. 869–882. Springer, Heidelberg (2013). https://doi.org/10.1007/978-3-642-39799-8_61
4. Biere, A., Artho, C., Schuppan, V.: Liveness checking as safety checking. Electr. Notes Theor. Comput. Sci. **66**(2), 160–177 (2002)
5. Bjørner, N., Gurfinkel, A.: Property directed polyhedral abstraction. In: D'Souza, D., Lal, A., Larsen, K.G. (eds.) VMCAI 2015. LNCS, vol. 8931, pp. 263–281. Springer, Heidelberg (2015). https://doi.org/10.1007/978-3-662-46081-8_15
6. Bjørner, N., Gurfinkel, A., McMillan, K., Rybalchenko, A.: Horn clause solvers for program verification. In: Beklemishev, L.D., Blass, A., Dershowitz, N., Finkbeiner, B., Schulte, W. (eds.) Fields of Logic and Computation II. LNCS, vol. 9300, pp. 24–51. Springer, Cham (2015). https://doi.org/10.1007/978-3-319-23534-9_2
7. Bjørner, N., McMillan, K., Rybalchenko, A.: On solving universally quantified horn clauses. In: Logozzo, F., Fähndrich, M. (eds.) SAS 2013. LNCS, vol. 7935, pp. 105–125. Springer, Heidelberg (2013). https://doi.org/10.1007/978-3-642-38856-9_8
8. Bjørner, N., McMillan, K.L., Rybalchenko, A.: Program verification as satisfiability modulo theories. In: 10th International Workshop on Satisfiability Modulo Theories, SMT 2012, pp. 3–11. EasyChair (2012)
9. Bjørner, N., McMillan, K.L., Rybalchenko, A.: Higher-order program verification as satisfiability modulo theories with algebraic data-types. CoRR abs/1306.5264 (2013)
10. Blass, A., Gurevich, Y.: Existential fixed-point logic. In: Börger, E. (ed.) Computation Theory and Logic. LNCS, vol. 270, pp. 20–36. Springer, Heidelberg (1987). https://doi.org/10.1007/3-540-18170-9_151
11. Bradfield, J.C.: Fixpoint alternation and the game quantifier. In: Flum, J., Rodriguez-Artalejo, M. (eds.) CSL 1999. LNCS, vol. 1683, pp. 350–361. Springer, Heidelberg (1999). https://doi.org/10.1007/3-540-48168-0_25
12. Burn, T.C., Ong, C.L., Ramsay, S.J.: Higher-order constrained horn clauses for verification. PACMPL **2**(POPL), 11:1–11:28 (2018)

13. Champion, A., Chiba, T., Kobayashi, N., Sato, R.: ICE-based refinement type discovery for higher-order functional programs. In: Beyer, D., Huisman, M. (eds.) TACAS 2018. LNCS, vol. 10805, pp. 365–384. Springer, Cham (2018). https://doi.org/10.1007/978-3-319-89960-2_20
14. Cook, B., Khlaaf, H., Piterman, N.: Fairness for infinite-state systems. In: Baier, C., Tinelli, C. (eds.) TACAS 2015. LNCS, vol. 9035, pp. 384–398. Springer, Heidelberg (2015). https://doi.org/10.1007/978-3-662-46681-0_30
15. Cook, B., Khlaaf, H., Piterman, N.: Verifying increasingly expressive temporal logics for infinite-state systems. J. ACM **64**(2), 15:1–15:39 (2017)
16. Cook, B., Koskinen, E.: Making prophecies with decision predicates. In: POPL 2011, pp. 399–410. ACM (2011)
17. Cook, B., Koskinen, E.: Reasoning about nondeterminism in programs. In: PLDI 2013, pp. 219–230. ACM (2013)
18. Cook, B., Koskinen, E., Vardi, M.: Temporal property verification as a program analysis task. In: Gopalakrishnan, G., Qadeer, S. (eds.) CAV 2011. LNCS, vol. 6806, pp. 333–348. Springer, Heidelberg (2011). https://doi.org/10.1007/978-3-642-22110-1_26
19. Delzanno, G., Podelski, A.: Constraint-based deductive model checking. STTT **3**(3), 250–270 (2001)
20. Dietsch, D., Heizmann, M., Langenfeld, V., Podelski, A.: Fairness modulo theory: a new approach to LTL software model checking. In: Kroening, D., Păsăreanu, C.S. (eds.) CAV 2015. LNCS, vol. 9206, pp. 49–66. Springer, Cham (2015). https://doi.org/10.1007/978-3-319-21690-4_4
21. Fedyukovich, G., Zhang, Y., Gupta, A.: Syntax-guided termination analysis. In: Chockler, H., Weissenbacher, G. (eds.) CAV 2018. LNCS, vol. 10981, pp. 124–143. Springer, Cham (2018). https://doi.org/10.1007/978-3-319-96145-3_7
22. Grebenshchikov, S., Lopes, N.P., Popeea, C., Rybalchenko, A.: Synthesizing software verifiers from proof rules. In: Proceedings of PLDI 2012, pp. 405–416 (2012)
23. Hofmann, M., Chen, W.: Abstract interpretation from Büchi automata. In: CSL-LICS 2014, pp. 51:1–51:10. ACM (2014)
24. Jaffar, J., Santosa, A.E., Voicu, R.: A CLP method for compositional and intermittent predicate abstraction. In: Emerson, E.A., Namjoshi, K.S. (eds.) VMCAI 2006. LNCS, vol. 3855, pp. 17–32. Springer, Heidelberg (2005). https://doi.org/10.1007/11609773_2
25. Kobayashi, N., Lozes, É., Bruse, F.: On the relationship between higher-order recursion schemes and higher-order fixpoint logic. In: Proceedings of the 44th ACM SIGPLAN Symposium on Principles of Programming Languages, POPL 2017, Paris, France, January 18–20, 2017, pp. 246–259. ACM (2017)
26. Kobayashi, N., Tsukada, T., Watanabe, K.: Higher-order program verification via HFL model checking. In: Ahmed, A. (ed.) ESOP 2018. LNCS, vol. 10801, pp. 711–738. Springer, Cham (2018). https://doi.org/10.1007/978-3-319-89884-1_25
27. Komuravelli, A., Gurfinkel, A., Chaki, S.: SMT-based model checking for recursive programs. In: Biere, A., Bloem, R. (eds.) CAV 2014. LNCS, vol. 8559, pp. 17–34. Springer, Cham (2014). https://doi.org/10.1007/978-3-319-08867-9_2
28. Koskinen, E., Terauchi, T.: Local temporal reasoning. In: CSL-LICS 2014. pp. 59:1–59:10. ACM (2014)
29. Lozes, É.: A type-directed negation elimination. In: Matthes, R., Mio, M. (eds.) Proceedings Tenth International Workshop on Fixed Points in Computer Science, FICS 2015, Berlin, Germany, September 11–12, 2015. EPTCS, vol. 191, pp. 132–142 (2015)

30. Lubarsky, R.S.: μ-definable sets of integers. J. Symbolic Logic **58**(1), 291–313 (1993)
31. Murase, A., Terauchi, T., Kobayashi, N., Sato, R., Unno, H.: Temporal verification of higher-order functional programs. In: Proceedings of POPL 2016 (2016, to appear)
32. Nanjo, Y., Unno, H., Koskinen, E., Terauchi, T.: A fixpoint logic and dependent effects for temporal property verification. In: LICS 2018, pp. 759–768. ACM, July 2018
33. Kobayashi, N., Nishikawa, T., A.I., Unno, H.: Temporal verification of programs via first-order fixpoint logic. A longer version, available from the first author's web page (2019)
34. Peralta, J.C., Gallagher, J.P., Sağlam, H.: Analysis of imperative programs through analysis of constraint logic programs. In: Levi, G. (ed.) SAS 1998. LNCS, vol. 1503, pp. 246–261. Springer, Heidelberg (1998). https://doi.org/10.1007/3-540-49727-7_15
35. Podelski, A., Rybalchenko, A.: Transition invariants. In: LICS 2004, pp. 32–41. IEEE (2004)
36. Podelski, A., Rybalchenko, A.: Transition invariants. In: 19th IEEE Symposium on Logic in Computer Science (LICS 2004), 14–17 July 2004, Turku, Finland, Proceedings, pp. 32–41 (2004)
37. Seidl, H., Neumann, A.: On guarding nested fixpoints. In: Flum, J., Rodriguez-Artalejo, M. (eds.) CSL 1999. LNCS, vol. 1683, pp. 484–498. Springer, Heidelberg (1999). https://doi.org/10.1007/3-540-48168-0_34
38. Unno, H., Torii, S., Sakamoto, H.: Automating induction for solving horn clauses. In: Majumdar, R., Kunčak, V. (eds.) CAV 2017. LNCS, vol. 10427, pp. 571–591. Springer, Cham (2017). https://doi.org/10.1007/978-3-319-63390-9_30
39. Urban, C., Ueltschi, S., Müller, P.: Abstract interpretation of CTL properties. In: Podelski, A. (ed.) SAS 2018. LNCS, vol. 11002, pp. 402–422. Springer, Cham (2018). https://doi.org/10.1007/978-3-319-99725-4_24
40. Viswanathan, M., Viswanathan, R.: A higher order modal fixed point logic. In: Gardner, P., Yoshida, N. (eds.) CONCUR 2004. LNCS, vol. 3170, pp. 512–528. Springer, Heidelberg (2004). https://doi.org/10.1007/978-3-540-28644-8_33
41. Watanabe, K., Tsukada, T., Oshikawa, H., Kobayashi, N.: Reduction from branching-time property verification of higher-order programs to HFL validity checking. In: PEPM 2019. ACM (2019)

A Temporal Logic for Higher-Order Functional Programs

Yuya Okuyama, Takeshi Tsukada(✉), and Naoki Kobayashi

The University of Tokyo, Tokyo, Japan
{okuyama,tsukada,koba}@kb.is.s.u-tokyo.ac.jp

Abstract. We propose an extension of linear temporal logic that we call Linear Temporal Logic of Calls (LTLC) for describing temporal properties of higher-order functions, such as "the function calls its first argument before any call of the second argument." A distinguishing feature of LTLC is a new modal operator, the call modality, that checks if the function specified by the operator is called in the current step and, if so, describes how the arguments are used in the subsequent computation. We demonstrate expressiveness of the logic, by giving examples of LTLC formulas describing interesting properties. Despite its high expressiveness, the model checking problem is decidable for deterministic programs with finite base types.

1 Introduction

Specifications of programs (or other systems) are often described by temporal or modal logics such as linear temporal logic (LTL), computational tree logic (CTL) and modal μ-calculus [2,8,12,16,19,22]. Formulas of these logics are built from atomic propositions representing basic properties of run-time states, e.g. whether the control is at a certain program point and whether the value of a certain global variable is positive. The set of atomic propositions in these logics is *static* in the sense that it remains unchanged during evaluation of programs.

We are interested in verification of higher-order functional programs, and logics suitable for describing temporal properties of such programs. For example, consider a function $g : (\texttt{unit} \to \texttt{string}) \to (\texttt{int} \to \texttt{int})$, which takes (the reader function of) a read-only file and creates a function on integers. The following is a possible specification for g:

- g is allowed to access the reader function only until it returns.

The implementation

$$\mathbf{let}\, g\, r \;=\; (\mathbf{let}\, w \;=\; \mathit{int\_of\_string}\,(r\,())\,\mathbf{in}\,\lambda x.x + w)$$

meets the specification, whereas

$$\mathbf{let}\, g\, r \;=\; \lambda x.x + (\mathit{int\_of\_string}\,(r\,()))$$

B.-Y. E. Chang (Ed.): SAS 2019, LNCS 11822, pp. 437–458, 2019.
https://doi.org/10.1007/978-3-030-32304-2_21

violates it.

Properly describing this specification is difficult because the property refers to *dynamic* notions such as "the argument of the first call of g." The program

$$\begin{array}{l}\textbf{let}\, g\, r \;=\; \big(\textbf{let}\, w \;=\; \mathit{int\_of\_string}\,(r\,())\, \textbf{in}\, \lambda x.x + w\big)\ \textbf{in}\\ \textbf{let}\, \mathit{fp} = \mathit{open\ filename}\ \textbf{in}\\ \textbf{let}\, r = \lambda\_.\mathit{read\_line}\ \mathit{fp}\ \textbf{in}\\ \textbf{let}\, v_1 = g\, r\ \textbf{in}\\ \textbf{let}\, v_2 = g\, r\ \textbf{in}\\ \quad \textbf{print}\,(v_1\, 1 + v_2\, 2)\end{array}$$

is an example that calls g twice. The sequence of call and return events of g and r in the evaluation is written as

$$\textbf{call}\, g_1 \rightarrow \textbf{call}\, r_1 \rightarrow \textbf{ret}\, r_1 \rightarrow \textbf{ret}\, g_1 \rightarrow \textbf{call}\, g_2 \rightarrow \textbf{call}\, r_2 \rightarrow \textbf{ret}\, r_2 \rightarrow \textbf{ret}\, g_2,$$

where g_1 means the first call of g and r_1 is its argument and similarly for g_2 and r_2. The above program satisfies the property since there is no $\textbf{call}\, r_i$ after $\textbf{ret}\, g_i$ for $i = 1, 2$. However, by ignoring the subscripts, i.e. confusing the first call of g with the second call, the program may seem to violate the specification since there is $\textbf{call}\, r_2$ after $\textbf{ret}\, g_1$. This means that references to dynamic notions like the subscripts in the above sequence are inevitable for precise description of the specification. For this reason, the specification does not seem to be expressible in the standard logics listed above.

This paper proposes a new temporal logic, named *Linear Temporal Logic of Calls* (*LTLC* for short), by which one can describe the above property. The logic is an extension of Linear Temporal Logic (LTL) with a new operator $\mathit{call}\, f(x_1, \ldots, x_n).\varphi$, the *call operator*, where the occurrences of $x_1, \ldots, x_n$ are binding occurrences. Intuitively this formula is true just if the function f is called in the current step (i.e. the current expression is of the form $E[f\, e_1\, \ldots\, e_n]$) and $\varphi[e_1/x_1, \ldots, e_n/x_n]$ holds at the next step.[1] We shall see in Example 2 an LTLC formula describing the above property.

LTLC is expressive. One can describe properties written by dependent refinement types in the form of [21], relational properties [1,5] (e.g. monotonicity of a given function) and some examples in resource usage analysis [10].

Furthermore LTLC is tractable. The LTLC model-checking problem is not more difficult than the standard temporal verification problem, because the LTLC model-checking problem is effectively reducible to the standard temporal verification of programs. In particular, for programs over finite types,[2] the LTLC model-checking is reducible to higher-order model checking [12,17] and thus decidable.

[1] Here is a subtlety. We should distinguish different occurrences of the same expression, and here e_i means the occurrence of e_i as the i-th argument of this function call. See Sects. 3.2 and 3.3.

[2] This finiteness condition is obviously necessary, because most verification problems are undecidable for programs with infinite types, such as integers.

Organisation of this Paper. After defining the target language in Sect. 2, we present the syntax and semantics of LTLC in Sect. 3. Section 4 shows examples of properties expressible by LTLC. Section 5 proves the reducibility result. Section 6 gives a brief discussion on other topics. After discussing related work in Sect. 7, Sect. 8 concludes the paper.

2 Target Language

This section describes the target language of this paper, which is a simply-typed call-by-name higher-order functional programming language with recursion.

We assume a set of *base types*, ranged over by b, as well as a set V_b of values for each base type b. We require that $V_b \cap V_{b'} = \emptyset$ whenever $b \neq b'$. Examples of base types are boolean type and (bounded or unbounded) integer type. We assume the set of base types contains the boolean type $\mathtt{Bool}$ and $V_{\mathtt{Bool}} = \{ tt, ff \}$.

We also assume a set of binary operators Op. Each binary operator $op \in Op$ is associated with their *sort* $b_1, b_2 \to b_3$, meaning that it takes two arguments of types b_1 and b_2 and yields a value of type b_3. Examples of binary operations are $+, -, \times$ (of sort $\mathtt{Int}, \mathtt{Int} \to \mathtt{Int}$) and $=_{\mathtt{Int}}$ (of sort $\mathtt{Int}, \mathtt{Int} \to \mathtt{Bool}$).

Most results of this paper are independent of the choice of basic types and operators. The only exception is the decidability of model checking (Theorem 4) for which we assume base types are finite (i.e. V_b is finite for each base type b).

The set of *types* is given by:

$$\tau := \star \mid \sigma \to \tau \qquad\qquad \sigma := b \mid \tau.$$

A type is the unit type $\star$, a base type b or a function type $\sigma \to \tau$. For a technical convenience, the above syntax requires that the return type of a function is not a base type. Therefore a type τ must be of the form $\sigma_1 \to \cdots \to \sigma_n \to \star$ for some $n \geq 0$ and σ_i, $1 \leq i \leq n$. This does not lose generality because this requirement can be fulfilled by applying the CPS translation.

Assume disjoint sets V of variables and F of function names. The set of *expressions* is defined by the following grammar:

$$e \quad := \quad () \mid c \mid x \mid f \mid e_1\, e_2 \mid \mathbf{op} \mid \mathbf{if}$$

where x and f are meta-variables ranging respectively over variables and function names. The expression $()$ is the unit value and $c \in \bigcup_b V_b$ is a constant of a base type. Each binary operation $op \in Op$ has the associated constructor **op**, which is in CPS (see the type system below) for a technical convenience. We also have a constructor **if** of conditional branching.

A *function definition* $\mathcal{P}$ is a finite set of equations of the form $f\, x_1\, \ldots\, x_n = e$, where f is the name of the function, $x_1, \ldots, x_n$ $(n \geq 0)$ are formal parameters and e is the body of the function. We assume that a function definition $\mathcal{P}$ contains at most one equation for each function name f. A *program* is a pair $(\mathcal{P}, e)$ of a function definition and an expression.

We shall consider only well-typed programs. A *type environment* is a finite set of type bindings of the form $x \colon \sigma$ or $f \colon \tau$. We shall use Δ for type environments of function names, and Γ for variables. A *type judgement* is a tuple $\Delta \mid \Gamma \vdash e : \sigma$. The typing rules for expressions are straightforward, e.g.,

$$\frac{f : \tau \in \Delta}{\Delta \mid \Gamma \vdash f : \tau} \qquad \frac{}{\Delta \mid \Gamma \vdash \mathbf{if} : \mathtt{Bool} \to \star \to \star \to \star}$$

$$\frac{op \in Op \text{ has sort } b_1, b_2 \to b_3}{\Delta \mid \Gamma \vdash \mathbf{op} : b_1 \to b_2 \to (b_3 \to \star) \to \star}.$$

Some notable points are (1) the then- and else-branches of an if-expression have to be of unit type, and (2) the binary operation $\mathbf{op}\, e_1\, e_2\, e_3$ in CPS takes two arguments $e_1 : b_1$ and $e_2 : b_2$ of base types and a continuation $e_3 : b_3 \to \star$. We say that a function definition $f\, x_1 \ldots x_n = e$ defines a function of type τ under the type environment Δ, written $\Delta \vdash f\, x_1 \ldots x_n = e : \tau$, if $\tau = \sigma_1 \to \cdots \to \sigma_n \to \star$ and $\Delta \mid x_1 : \sigma_1, \ldots, x_n : \sigma_n \vdash e : \star$. Note that the function body e is required to have type $\star$ (this restriction can be fulfilled by η-expanding the definition, which does not change the meaning of a function in the call-by-name setting). A function definition $\mathcal{P} = \{ f_i\, \widetilde{x}_i = e_i \}_{1 \le i \le m}$ is *well-typed* under $\Delta = \{ f_1 : \tau_1, \ldots, f_m : \tau_m \}$, written $\Delta \vdash \mathcal{P}$, if $\Delta \vdash f_i\, \widetilde{x}_i = e_i : \tau_i$ for every i. A program $(\mathcal{P}, e)$ is *well-typed* if there exists Δ such that $\Delta \vdash \mathcal{P}$ and $\Delta \mid \emptyset \vdash e : \star$.

The operational semantics of the language is fairly straightforward. We define the *small-step reduction relation* $\longrightarrow$ by the following rules:

$$\frac{c_1\ op\ c_2 = c}{\mathbf{op}\, c_1\, c_2\, e \longrightarrow e\, c} \qquad \frac{}{\mathbf{if}\ tt\, e_1\, e_2 \longrightarrow e_1} \qquad \frac{}{\mathbf{if}\ f\!f\, e_1\, e_2 \longrightarrow e_2}$$

$$\frac{(f\, x_1 \ldots x_n = e) \in \mathcal{P}}{f\, e_1 \ldots e_n \longrightarrow [e_1/x_1, \ldots, e_n/x_n]e} \qquad \frac{}{() \longrightarrow ()}$$

The last rule is an artificial rule, which ensures that every well-typed expression has an infinite reduction sequence, somewhat simplifying some definitions in the next section. We write $\longrightarrow^*$ for the reflexive, transitive closure of $\longrightarrow$.

If V_b is finite and the equality $=_b$ on b is in Op, the case analysis of values of type b is definable in the language. We write

$$\mathbf{case}\, e\, \mathbf{of}\, c_1 \to e_1 \mid \cdots \mid c_n \to e_n,$$

where $e, c_1, \ldots, c_n : b$ and $e_1, \ldots, e_n : \star$, for the expression

$$\mathbf{if}\,(=_b\ e\, c_1)\, e_1 (\mathbf{if}\,(=_b\ e\, c_2)\, e_2\, (\ldots (\mathbf{if} (=_b\ e\, c_n)\, e_n\, ())\ldots)).$$

Example 1. Recall the example in Introduction, which was written in direct style. By abstracting unimportant details and transforming it into CPS, we obtain the following program:

$$\begin{aligned}
&\mathbf{let}\, g\, r\, k \ = \ r\, (\lambda w.k\, (\lambda x h.h\, (x + w)))\ \mathbf{in}\\
&\mathbf{let}\, r\, k \ = \ k\, 0\ \mathbf{in}\\
&\mathbf{let}\, p\, x \ = \ ()\ \mathbf{in}\\
&\quad g\, r\, (\lambda v_1.g\, r\, (\lambda v_2.v_1\, 1\, (\lambda u_1.v_2\, 2\, (\lambda u_2.p\, (u_1 + u_2)))))
\end{aligned}$$

Here r is a function reading the value from a file (consisting of only 0 s) and passing it to the continuation k; p is the function that prints the argument (but formally does nothing). This program can be seen as a program in our language,[3] of which functions definitions are given by sequences of **let** and the initial expression e is that in the last line. The type environment for functions is given by

$$r\colon (\mathtt{Int} \to \star) \to \star, \qquad p\colon \mathtt{Int} \to \star,$$
$$g\colon ((\mathtt{Int} \to \star) \to \star) \to ((\mathtt{Int} \to (\mathtt{Int} \to \star) \to \star) \to \star) \to \star$$

The evaluation of the program is

$$\begin{array}{lllllll} g\, r\, k_1 & \longrightarrow & r\,(\lambda w.k_1\,(\lambda xh.h(x+w))) & \longrightarrow^* & k_1\,(\lambda xh.h(x+0)) & \longrightarrow \\ g\, r\, k_2 & \longrightarrow & r\,(\lambda w.k_2\,(\lambda xh.h(x+w))) & \longrightarrow^* & k_2\,(\lambda xh.h(x+0)) & \longrightarrow \cdots \end{array}$$

where

$$\begin{aligned} k_1 &= (\lambda v_1.g\, r\,(\lambda v_2.v_1\, 1\,(\lambda u_1.v_2\, 2\,(\lambda u_2.p\,(u_1+u_2))))) \\ k_2 &= [(\lambda xh.h(x+0))/v_1]\,(\lambda v_2.v_1\, 1\,(\lambda u_1.v_2\, 2\,(\lambda u_2.p\,(u_1+u_2)))). \end{aligned}$$

Note that r is called twice: The first (resp. the second) call of r is between the first (resp. the second) call of g and the call of the corresponding continuation k_1 (resp. k_2).

3 Linear Temporal Logic of Calls

This section defines a novel temporal logic that we call *Linear Temporal Logic of Calls* (*LTLC* for short). It is an extension of the standard linear temporal logic (LTL) by a modal operator, called the *call operator*, which describes a property on function calls. Let $\mathcal{P}$ be a function definitions and Δ be the type environment for functions, fixed in the sequel.

3.1 Syntax

Assume a set L of *variables* that is disjoint from the sets of function names and of variables in expressions. We use α, β and γ for variables in L. The set of *LTLC formulas* is defined by the following grammar:

$$\varphi := \mathit{true} \mid \mathit{false} \mid \neg\varphi \mid \varphi \vee \varphi \mid \varphi \wedge \varphi \mid \bigcirc\varphi \mid \varphi\,\mathbf{U}\,\varphi \mid \varphi\,\mathbf{R}\,\varphi \mid \mathit{call}\,\xi(\widetilde{\beta}).\varphi \mid p(\widetilde{\beta})$$

where ξ is either a function name f or a variable $\alpha \in L$. It is the standard LTL with next $\bigcirc$, (strong) until $\mathbf{U}$ and release $\mathbf{R}$ extended by the *call operator* $\mathit{call}\,\xi(\widetilde{\beta}).\varphi$ and predicates $p(\widetilde{\beta})$ on values of base types (such as the order $<$

[3] Strictly speaking, we need to do lambda-lifting as the lambda abstraction is not in the syntax.

and equivalence $=$ of integers). The occurrences of variables $\widetilde{\beta}$ in $call\,\xi(\widetilde{\beta}).\varphi$ are binding occurrences, and ξ is free.

The meaning of formulas should be clear except for $call\,\xi(\widetilde{\beta}).\varphi$. Intuitively $call\,f(\widetilde{\beta}).\varphi$ is true just if the current expression is of the form $f\,\widetilde{e}$ and $\varphi\{\widetilde{e}/\widetilde{\beta}\}$ holds in the next step $e_f\{\widetilde{e}/\widetilde{x}\}$ (where $f\,\widetilde{x} = e_f \in \mathcal{P}$), although here is a subtle point that we shall discuss in the next subsection.

Each variable β in a formula naturally has its type, and a formula should respect the types to make sense. For example, $call\,f(\beta).\varphi$ would be nonsense if the function f has two arguments. We use a type system to filter out such meaningless formulas. We write Θ for a type environment for variables in L. A type judgement is of the form $\Delta \mid \Theta \vdash \varphi$, meaning that φ is well-formed under Δ and Θ. Here Δ and Θ declares the types for function names and variables in L, respectively. Examples of typing rules are as follows:

$$\frac{}{\Delta \mid \Theta \vdash \mathit{false}} \qquad \frac{\Delta \mid \Theta \vdash \varphi}{\Delta \mid \Theta \vdash \bigcirc\varphi} \qquad \frac{\Delta \mid \Theta \vdash \varphi_1 \qquad \Delta \mid \Theta \vdash \varphi_2}{\Delta \mid \Theta \vdash \varphi_1 \,\mathbf{U}\, \varphi_2}$$

$$\frac{f : \sigma_1 \to \cdots \to \sigma_n \to \star \in \Delta \qquad \Delta \mid \Theta \cup \{\beta_i : \sigma_i\}_{1 \le i \le n} \vdash \varphi}{\Delta \mid \Theta \vdash call\,f(\beta_1, \ldots, \beta_n).\varphi}.$$

We shall use the following abbreviations. As usual, the temporal operators "future" **F** and "always" **G** are introduced as derived operators, defined by

$$\mathbf{F}\varphi := \mathit{true}\,\mathbf{U}\,\varphi \qquad \text{and} \qquad \mathbf{G}\varphi := \mathit{false}\,\mathbf{R}\,\varphi.$$

We also use a derived operator *ifcall* given by

$$\mathit{ifcall}\,\xi(\widetilde{\beta}).\varphi \quad := \quad \neg\mathbf{F}\,call\,\xi(\widetilde{\beta}).(\neg\varphi)$$

meaning that $call\,\xi(\widetilde{\beta}).\varphi$ holds for every call of ξ in the future. This operator can alternatively be defined by

$$\mathit{ifcall}\,\xi(\widetilde{\beta}).\varphi \quad = \quad \mathbf{G}(call\,\xi(\widetilde{\beta}).\varphi \vee \neg call\,\xi(\widetilde{\beta}).\mathit{true}).$$

We write $\bigcirc^n\varphi$ for $\underbrace{\bigcirc\cdots\bigcirc}_{n}\varphi$, meaning that φ holds after n steps.

Example 2. Recall the program in Example 1. The formula meaning "g does not call its first argument after returning the value" can be written as follows:

$$\mathit{ifcall}\,g(\alpha,\beta)\;.\;\mathit{ifcall}\,\beta(\gamma)\;.\;(\neg\mathbf{F}\,call\,\alpha(\delta)\;.\;\mathit{true}).$$

Since the programs are now written in CPS, "returning the value" means "calling the continuation β." The above formula says that, for every call of g, if it returns the value (via the continuation β), then it will never call the first argument α.

3.2 Naïve Semantics and a Problem

Every closed expression $\Delta \mid \emptyset \vdash e : \star$, possibly using functions in $\mathcal{P}$, induces the unique infinite reduction sequence

$$e = e_0 \longrightarrow e_1 \longrightarrow e_2 \longrightarrow \ldots \longrightarrow e_n \longrightarrow \cdots.$$

An LTLC formula φ describes a property on such infinite reduction sequences. Thus the *satisfaction relation* $e \models \varphi$ is defined as a relation between an expression $\Delta \vdash e : \star$ and an LTLC formula $\Delta \vdash \varphi$.

The definition of the relation for logical connectives from the standard LTS is straightforward. For example, $\bigcirc\varphi$ means that φ holds in the next step, and thus $e \models \bigcirc\varphi$ if and only if $e' \models \varphi$ for the unique e' such that $e \longrightarrow e'$.

The main issue is how to define the semantics of $\mathit{call}\, f(\widetilde{\beta}).\varphi$. Intuitively $e \models \mathit{call}\, f(\beta_1, \ldots, \beta_n).\varphi$ holds if and only if $e = f\, e_1 \ldots e_n$ and $e_f[e_1/x_1, \ldots, e_n/x_n] \models \varphi[e_1/\beta_1, \ldots, e_n/\beta_n]$, where e_f is the body of the definition of f. However this naïve definition has a problem.

Let us explain the problem by using an example. Consider the function *doTask* defined by

$$\mathit{doTask}\, f\, g \quad = \quad f\,(g\,()).$$

It would be natural to expect that "*doTask* does not call the second argument unless it does not call the first argument" should be true independent of the context in which *doTask* is used. Formally we expect $C[\mathit{doTask}] \models \varphi$ for every context C, where φ is the formula given by

$$\varphi \quad = \quad \mathit{call}\ \mathit{doTask}(\alpha, \beta)\ .\ \big((\neg\, \mathit{call}\, \beta(\gamma).\mathit{true})\ \mathbf{U}\ (\mathit{call}\, \alpha(\delta).\mathit{true})\big).$$

However it is not true. Consider, for example, $C = [\,]\, h\, h$ where h is an arbitrary function. Then

$$\mathit{doTask}\, h\, h \models \varphi \quad \Leftrightarrow \quad h\,(h\,()) \models (\neg\, \mathit{call}\, h(\gamma).\mathit{true})\ \mathbf{U}\ (\mathit{call}\, h(\delta).\mathit{true})$$

but the right-hand-side is false because $h\,(h\,()) \models \mathit{call}\, h(\gamma).\mathit{true}$ and thus $h\,(h\,()) \not\models \neg\, \mathit{call}\, h(\gamma).\mathit{true}$.

The problem is caused by confusion between h as the first argument and h as the second argument. In the formula φ, the first and second arguments of *doTask* are distinguished by their names, α and β. However they become indistinct by the substitution $[h/\alpha, h/\beta]$.

3.3 Formal Semantics

We use labels to correctly keep track of expressions. A *label* is just a variable $\alpha \in L$ in a formula. *Labelled expressions* are those obtained by extending expressions with the *labelling* construct, as follows:

$$e ::= \cdots \mid e^{\alpha}, \qquad \alpha \in L.$$

$$
\begin{array}{lll}
e, \rho \models \mathit{true} & & \text{always holds} \\
e, \rho \models \mathit{false} & & \text{never holds} \\
e, \rho \models \neg\varphi & \iff & e, \rho \not\models \varphi \\
e, \rho \models \varphi_1 \vee \varphi_2 & \iff & e, \rho \models \varphi_1 \text{ or } e, \rho \models \varphi_2 \\
e, \rho \models \varphi_1 \wedge \varphi_2 & \iff & e, \rho \models \varphi \text{ and } e, \rho \models \varphi_2 \\
e, \rho \models \bigcirc\varphi & \iff & (\exists e')[e \longrightarrow e' \text{ and } e', \rho \models \varphi] \\
e, \rho \models \varphi_1 \,\mathbf{U}\, \varphi_2 & \iff & (\exists j)[e, \rho \models \bigcirc^j \varphi_2 \text{ and } (\forall i < j)[e, \rho \models \bigcirc^i \varphi_1]] \\
e, \rho \models \varphi_1 \,\mathbf{R}\, \varphi_2 & \iff & (\forall j)[e, \rho \models \bigcirc^j \varphi_2 \text{ or } (\exists i < j)[e, \rho \models \bigcirc^i \varphi_1]] \\
e, \rho \models p(\alpha_1, \ldots, \alpha_k)a & \iff & p(\natural\rho(\alpha_1), \ldots, \natural\rho(\alpha_k)) \text{ is true} \\
e, \rho \models \mathit{call}\, \alpha(\beta_1, \ldots, \beta_k).\varphi & \iff & e = (\ldots(e_0^{S_0}\, e_1)^{S_1} \ldots e_k)^{S_k} \text{ and } \alpha \in S_0 \text{ and} \\
 & & e_0\, e_1^{\beta_1} \ldots e_k^{\beta_k} \longrightarrow e' \text{ and } e', \rho \cup \{\beta_i \mapsto e_i\}_{1 \le i \le k} \models \varphi \\
e, \rho \models \mathit{call}\, f(\beta_1, \ldots, \beta_k).\varphi & \iff & e = (\ldots(f^{S_0}\, e_1)^{S_1} \ldots e_k)^{S_k} \text{ and} \\
 & & e_0\, e_1^{\beta_1} \ldots e_k^{\beta_k} \longrightarrow e' \text{ and } e', \rho \cup \{\beta_i \mapsto e_i\}_{1 \le i \le k} \models \varphi
\end{array}
$$

Fig. 1. Semantics of formulas. The operation $\natural$ removes labels from a given expression.

For a possibly empty sequence $S = \alpha_1 \ldots \alpha_n$, we write e^S for $((e^{\alpha_1})\ldots)^{\alpha_n}$. Given a labelled expression e, we write $\natural e$ for the (ordinary) expression obtained by removing labels in e.

The labels do not affect reduction. For example,

$$(((f^{S_0}\, e_1)^{S_1}\, e_2)^{S_2} \ldots e_n)^{S_n} \quad \longrightarrow \quad e_f[e_1/x_1, \ldots, e_n/x_n]$$

provided that $f\, x_1\, \ldots\, x_n = e_f \in \mathcal{P}$. Therefore, if $e \longrightarrow e'$ as labelled expressions, then $\natural e \longrightarrow \natural e'$.

Now we formally define the satisfaction relation $\models$. It is a ternary relation $e, \rho \models \varphi$ on a labelled expression $e : \star$, a valuation map ρ from free variables in φ to labelled expressions, and an LTLC formula φ. It is defined by induction on the complexity[4] of formulas by the rules in Fig. 1.

Remark 1. Given a judgement $e, \rho \models \varphi$, one can remove the following data without changing the meaning of the judgement:

- mapping $\alpha \mapsto e$ from ρ if α is not of a base type, and
- label β in $(d)^\beta$ from e if d is an expression of a base type.

This is because the information on a base-type variable β is recorded in ρ, and the information on a non-base-type variable α is tracked by labels in the expression. We put both information to both ρ and e just to simplify the definition (by avoiding the case split by types).

The main difference from the naïve semantics is the meaning of the call operator. Instead of substituting β_i in the formula to the actual argument e_i in the expression, we annotate the actual argument e_i by β_i.

[4] We define the *complexity* of a formula φ as the pair of numbers (n, m) ordered by the lexicographic ordering, where n is the sum of the numbers of occurrences of **U** and **R** in φ and m is the size of φ.

We see how the labelling works by using the example in the previous subsection. By the labelling semantics, we have

$$(doTask\,h\,h), \emptyset \models \varphi \quad \Leftrightarrow \quad h^{\alpha}\,(h^{\beta}\,()), \rho \models (\neg\, call\,\beta(\gamma).true)\ \mathbf{U}\ (call\,\alpha(\delta).true)$$

for some ρ (whose contents are not important here). Notice that h as the first argument of *doTask* can be distinguished from h as the second argument of *doTask*: the former has the label α whereas the latter is annotated by β. Now $h^{\alpha}\,(h^{\beta}\,()), \rho \not\models call\,\beta(\gamma).true$ and $h^{\alpha}\,(h^{\beta}\,()), \rho \models \neg call\,\beta(\gamma).true$ as expected. It is not difficult to see that $doTask\,h\,h, \emptyset \models \varphi$ indeed holds, whatever h is.

3.4 Negation Normal Form

The negation $\neg$ in a formula can be pushed inwards in many cases, without changing the meaning of the formula. For example,

$$\neg true = false \qquad \neg(\varphi_1\,\mathbf{U}\,\varphi_2) = (\neg\varphi_1)\,\mathbf{R}\,(\neg\varphi_2) \quad \text{and} \quad \neg\bigcirc\varphi = \bigcirc\neg\varphi.$$

Unfortunately the negation of the call operator $\neg call\,\xi(\widetilde{\beta}).\varphi$ cannot be pushed inwards in general, but we can restrict the shape of the formula to which the negation is applied. The formula $call\,\xi(\widetilde{\beta}).\varphi$ does *not* hold if either (a) ξ is now called but the following computation violates φ or (b) ξ is not called in the current step. This observation can be expressed by the equation

$$\neg call\,\xi(\widetilde{\beta}).\varphi \quad = \quad call\,\xi(\widetilde{\beta}).(\neg\varphi)\ \vee\ \neg call\,\xi(\widetilde{\beta}).true.$$

We shall abbreviate $\neg call\,\xi(\widetilde{\beta}).true$ as $\neg call\,\xi$.

The above argument gives an effective rewriting process, yielding a formula in the following syntax that we call the *negation normal form*:

$$\begin{aligned}\varphi := {} & true \mid false \mid \varphi \vee \varphi \mid \varphi \wedge \varphi \mid \bigcirc\varphi \mid \varphi\,\mathbf{U}\,\varphi \mid \varphi\,\mathbf{R}\,\varphi \\ \mid {} & call\,\xi(\widetilde{\beta}).\varphi \mid \neg call\,\xi \mid p(\widetilde{\beta}) \mid \neg p(\widetilde{\beta}).\end{aligned}$$

We shall use this normal form in the following section.

4 Expressiveness

This section briefly explains the expressiveness of LTLC.

4.1 Dependent Refinement Types

Properties described by dependent refinement types in the form of [21] are expressible by LTLC formulas.

Example 3. Consider the type

$$T_0 \quad := \quad (x\colon \{\texttt{Int} \mid \nu \geq 0\}) \to \{\texttt{Int} \mid \nu > x\}$$

for call-by-value programs. This is the type for functions f on integers such that $f(x) > x$ for every positive x. As the target language of this paper is call-by-name, we need to apply the CPS translation to call-by-value programs of interest and the corresponding translation to dependent types. The resulting type is

$$T \quad := \quad (x\colon \{\texttt{Int} \mid \nu \geq 0\}) \to \big(\{\texttt{Int} \mid \nu \geq x\} \to \star\big) \to \star.$$

The LTLC formula φ_T corresponding to the judgement $\vdash f : T$ is

$$\varphi_T \quad := \quad \mathit{ifcall} f(\alpha, \beta)\ .\ \big(\alpha \geq 0 \Rightarrow \mathit{ifcall}\ \beta(\gamma)\ .\ \alpha < \gamma\big).$$

We explain the general rule of the translation, focusing on the image of function types by the call-by-value CPS translation. The syntax of dependent refinement types is given by

$$T, S \ ::= \ (\alpha : U) \to \big(V \to \star\big) \to \star \qquad\qquad U, V \ ::= \ \{\texttt{Int} \mid \vartheta(\nu)\} \ \mid \ T$$

where ν is a distinguished variable and $\vartheta(\nu)$ is a formula of the underlying logic. The occurrence of α is a binding occurrence and ϑ may contain variables other than ν. The LTLC formula Φ_U is defined by the following rules:

$$\Phi_{\{\texttt{Int}\mid\vartheta(\nu)\}}(\alpha) := \vartheta(\alpha)$$
$$\Phi_{(\beta:U)\to(V\to\star)\to\star}(\alpha) := \mathit{ifcall}\ \alpha(\beta,\kappa).\ \big(\Phi_U(\beta) \Rightarrow \mathit{ifcall}\ \kappa(\gamma)\,.\,\Phi_V(\gamma)\big).$$

A judgement $\vdash f : T$ corresponds to the LTLC formula $\Phi_T(f)$.

4.2 Relational Property

Some *relational properties* [1,5], such as the relationship between two functions and that between two calls of a function, can be described by LTLC. An example of relational property is monotonicity; if a given function f is not monotone, one can find two inputs $x \leq y$ such that $f(x) \not\leq f(y)$. Monotonicity can be naturally expressed by LTLC.

Example 4 (Monotonicity). Assume a function $f\colon \texttt{Int} \to (\texttt{Int} \to \star) \to \star$. This function is *monotone* if $n \leq n'$, $f\,n\,k$ calls the continuation k with the value m and $f\,n'\,k'$ calls k' with m', then $m \leq m'$. (Recall that f is in CPS and thus "calling k with m" can be understood as "returning m".) If f is assumed to be non-recurrent, this property can be written as

$$\mathit{ifcall}\ f(\alpha, \beta)\ .\ \mathit{ifcall}\ \beta(\gamma)\ .\ \mathit{ifcall}\ f(\alpha', \beta')\ .\ \mathit{ifcall}\ \beta'(\gamma')\ .\ \psi(\alpha, \gamma, \alpha', \gamma')$$

where $\psi(\alpha, \gamma, \alpha', \gamma') = (\alpha \leq \alpha' \Rightarrow \gamma \leq \gamma') \wedge (\alpha \geq \alpha' \Rightarrow \gamma \geq \gamma')$. The meaning of this formula can be expressed by a natural language as follows:

Let α be the argument to the first call of f, and γ be the "return value" of the first call. Similarly let α' be the argument to the second call of f, and γ' be the "return value" of the second call. We require that $\alpha \leq \alpha'$ implies $\gamma \leq \gamma'$, and that $\alpha \geq \alpha'$ implies $\gamma \geq \gamma'$.

A formula applicable to the case of f being recurrent is a bit complicated, since the order of two calls and returns is not determined. The formula applicable to the general case is

$$\begin{aligned} & \mathit{ifcall}\, f(\alpha,\beta)\,.\,\mathit{ifcall}\, f(\alpha',\beta')\,.\,\mathit{ifcall}\,\beta(\gamma)\,.\,\mathit{ifcall}\,\beta'(\gamma')\,.\,\psi(\alpha,\gamma,\alpha',\gamma') \\ \wedge\, & \mathit{ifcall}\, f(\alpha,\beta)\,.\,\mathit{ifcall}\, f(\alpha',\beta')\,.\,\mathit{ifcall}\,\beta'(\gamma')\,.\,\mathit{ifcall}\,\beta(\gamma)\,.\,\psi(\alpha,\gamma,\alpha',\gamma') \\ \wedge\, & \mathit{ifcall}\, f(\alpha,\beta)\,.\,\mathit{ifcall}\,\beta(\gamma)\,.\,\mathit{ifcall}\, f(\alpha',\beta')\,.\,\mathit{ifcall}\,\beta'(\gamma')\,.\,\psi(\alpha,\gamma,\alpha',\gamma') \end{aligned}$$

The conjunction enumerates all possible orders of two calls and returns of f.

4.3 Resource Usage Verification

The final example is verification/analysis of programs using resources, known as *resource usage analysis* [10]. An example of resource is read-only files. For simplicity, we focus on the verification of usage of read-only files.

Let us first consider the simplest case in which a program generates a unique resource only at the beginning. In this case, a target is a program with distinguished functions $r, c : \star \to \star$ for reading and closing the file. The specification requires (1) the program does not read the file after closing it, and (2) the file must be closed before the termination of the program. The specification can be described by an LTLC formula:

$$\varphi(r,c) \quad := \quad \mathbf{G}(\mathit{call}\, c \Rightarrow \neg\mathbf{F}\,\mathit{call}\, r) \wedge (\neg\texttt{end}\;\mathbf{U}\;\mathit{call}\, c),$$

where `end` is the event meaning the termination. Indeed this is an LTL formula when one regards $\mathit{call}\, c$ and $\mathit{call}\, r$ as atomic propositions.

In the general case, a program can dynamically create read-only file resources. The target program has a distinguished type `File` for file resources and a distinguished function $\mathit{gen} : (\texttt{File} \to \star) \to \star$. Since the possible operations for `File` is read and close, we identify the type `File` as $(\star \to \star) \times (\star \to \star)$, the pair of reading and closing functions. The specification requires that, for each call of gen, the created resource should be used in the manner following φ; this specification can be written by an LTLC formula as

$$\mathit{ifcall}\;\mathit{gen}(\alpha)\,.\,\mathit{ifcall}\;\alpha(r,c)\,.\,\varphi(r,c).$$

Note that $\mathit{ifcall}\,\alpha(r,c)$ intuitively means that "if the function gen returns the value (r,c)" since gen is in CPS and α is the continuation.

5 LTLC Model Checking

This section focuses on the LTLC model-checking problem, i.e. the problem to decide, given a program $\mathcal{P}$, an expression e and an LTLC formula φ, whether

$e, \emptyset \models \varphi$ (where $\emptyset$ is the empty valuation). The main result of this section is that the LTLC model-checking problem is effectively reducible to the standard temporal verification problem, which could be solved by model checkers for higher-order programs. In particular, for programs and expressions over finite types, this reduction yields an instance of higher-order model checking [12,17], for which several model-checkers are available [6,20].

5.1 Preliminaries: Higher-Order Model Checking

Higher-order model checking is a problem to decide, given a higher-order tree grammar and an ω-regular tree property, whether the (possibly infinite) tree generated by the grammar satisfies the property. Higher-order model checking has been proved to be decidable by Ong [17][5] and applied to many verification problems of higher-order programs (see, e.g., [12]). We prove that LTLC model checking is decidable by reducing it to higher-order model checking.

This subsection briefly reviews higher-order model checking, tailored to our purpose. See [12,17] for formal definitions and general results.

Let Σ be a ranked alphabet defined by

$$\Sigma := \{\top, \bot \mapsto 0, \;\; \sqcup, \sqcap \mapsto 2, \;\; \mathtt{U}, \mathtt{R} \mapsto 3\}.$$

This means that $\top$ is a leaf and $\sqcup$ (resp. $\mathtt{U}$) is a binary (resp. ternary) branching tree constructor, and so on. A *Σ-labelled tree* is a possibly infinite tree of which each node is labelled by a symbol in Σ. We shall consider only *well-ranked trees*: we require that the number of children of a node labelled by $\sqcap$ is 2, for example. We shall often use the infix notation for $\sqcup$ and $\sqcap$, e.g. $T_1 \sqcup T_2$ is the tree whose root is $\sqcup$ and its children are T_1 and T_2.

A *nondeterministic Büchi automaton* is a tuple (Q, q_0, δ, F), where Q is a finite set of *states*, $q_0 \in Q$ is an *initial state*, $\delta \colon \prod_{a \in \mathrm{dom}(\Sigma)}(Q \to \mathcal{P}(Q^{\Sigma(a)}))$ is a *transition function* and $F \subseteq Q$ is the set of *accepting states*. A *run-tree* of $\mathcal{A}$ over a tree T is an association of states $q \in Q$ to nodes in T that respects the transition function in a certain sense. A run-tree is *accepting* if each infinite branch contains infinitely many occurrences of an accepting state. A tree T is *accepted* by $\mathcal{A}$ if there is an accepting run-tree over T.

A *tree-generating program* is a variant of programs introduced in Sect. 2, but has different set of operators on type $\star$. The syntax of expressions is

$$e \quad := \quad \top \mid \bot \mid \sqcup \mid \sqcap \mid \mathtt{U} \mid \mathtt{R} \mid c \mid x \mid f \mid e_1\, e_2 \mid \mathbf{op}\, e_1\, e_2\, e_3 \mid \mathbf{if}\, e_1\, e_2\, e_3,$$

obtained by replacing () with the tree constructors in Σ. Their types are

$$\top, \bot \colon \star \qquad\qquad \sqcup, \sqcap \colon \star \to \star \to \star \qquad \text{and} \qquad \mathtt{U}, \mathtt{R} \colon \star \to \star \to \star \to \star.$$

[5] The original definition (as in [17]) considers only programs without data types, but the decidability result can be easily extended to programs with finite data types. We shall consider a generalised version, in which programs may contain infinite data types. Of cause, the decidability result fails for the generalised version.

So $\star$ should be now regarded as the type for *trees*. The notion of function definition remains unchanged, except that the body of a function is now an expression with tree constructors.

The operational semantics is basically the same as before. The only difference is that reduction may occur under tree constructors, i.e. the following rules

$$\frac{e_1 \longrightarrow e_1'}{(e_1 \sqcup e_2) \longrightarrow (e_1' \sqcup e_2)} \quad \text{and} \quad \frac{e_2 \longrightarrow e_2'}{(e_1 \sqcup e_2) \longrightarrow (e_1 \sqcup e_2')}$$

are added, as well as similar rules for other constructors. A program $(\mathcal{P}, e)$ generates a possibly infinite tree as a result of possibly infinite steps of reduction.

Higher-order model checking asks to decide, given a program $(\mathcal{P}, e)$ and a nondeterministic Büchi automaton $\mathcal{A}$, whether the tree generated by $(\mathcal{P}, e)$ is accepted by $\mathcal{A}$.

Theorem 1 (Ong [17]). *Given a tree-generating program $(\mathcal{P}, e)$, of which all basic data types are finite, and a nondeterministic Büchi automaton $\mathcal{A}$, one can effectively decide whether the tree generated by $(\mathcal{P}, e)$ is accepted by $\mathcal{A}$.*

5.2 Satisfaction Tree

Let $\mathcal{P}$ be a function definition, fixed in this subsection. Given an expression $e\colon \star$, a valuation ρ and an LTLC formula φ in negation normal form, we define a tree $\mathcal{T}(\varphi, \rho, e)$, called the *satisfaction tree*, which represents the process evaluating $e, \rho \models \varphi$. This subsection shows that the satisfaction tree correctly captures the satisfaction relation, in the sense that $e, \rho \models \varphi$ if and only if $\mathcal{T}(\varphi, \rho, e)$ belongs to a certain ω-regular tree language.

A satisfaction tree is a Σ-labelled tree. The meaning of $\top, \bot, \sqcup$ and $\sqcap$ should be obvious. The trees $\top$ and $\bot$ represent immediate truth and falsity. The tree $T_1 \sqcap T_2$ means that the evaluation process invokes two subprocess, represented by T_1 and T_2, and the result is true just if the results of both subprocesses are true. The meaning of $\sqcup$ is similar.

The constructors $\mathtt{U}$ and $\mathtt{R}$, corresponding respectively to $\mathbf{U}$ and $\mathbf{R}$, require some expositions. The meaning of $\mathtt{U}$ is based on a classical but important observation: whether $e, \rho \models \varphi_1 \mathbf{U} \varphi_2$ or not is completely determined by three judgements, namely $e, \rho \models \varphi_1$, $e, \rho \models \varphi_2$ and $e, \rho \models \bigcirc(\varphi_1 \mathbf{U} \varphi_2)$. That means, $e, \rho \models \varphi_1 \mathbf{U} \varphi_2$ if and only if either (a) $e, \rho \models \varphi_1$ and $e, \rho \models \varphi_2$, or (b) $e, \rho \models \varphi_1$ and $e, \rho \models \bigcirc(\varphi_1 \mathbf{U} \varphi_2)$. So the process of checking $e, \rho \models \varphi_1 \mathbf{U} \varphi_2$ invokes three subprocesses; the three subtrees of $\mathtt{U}$ correspond to these judgements. A similar observation applies to $\mathbf{R}$.

The definition of satisfaction trees is co-inductively defined by the rules in Figs. 2, 3, 4 and 5. The meaning of the rules in Fig. 2 should now be clear. For example, the rule for $\varphi_1 \mathbf{U} \varphi_2$ says that $e, \rho \models \varphi_1 \mathbf{U} \varphi_2$ depends on satisfaction of $e, \rho \models \bigcirc(\varphi_1 \mathbf{U} \varphi_2)$, $e, \rho \models \varphi_1$ and $e, \rho \models \varphi_2$.

Figure 3 defines the rules for the call modality $\mathit{call}\,\alpha(\widetilde{\beta}).\varphi$. The first two rules check if e is calling an expression labelled by α. If one finds the label α, then

$$
\begin{aligned}
\mathcal{T}[e,\rho \models \mathit{true}] &:= \top\\
\mathcal{T}[e,\rho \models \mathit{false}] &:= \bot\\
\mathcal{T}[e,\rho \models \varphi_1 \vee \varphi_2] &:= \mathcal{T}[e,\rho \models \varphi_1] \sqcup \mathcal{T}[e,\rho \models \varphi_2]\\
\mathcal{T}[e,\rho \models \varphi_1 \wedge \varphi_2] &:= \mathcal{T}[e,\rho \models \varphi_1] \sqcap \mathcal{T}[e,\rho \models \varphi_2]\\
\mathcal{T}[e,\rho \models \varphi_1 \mathbf{U}\, \varphi_2] &:= \mathbf{U}(\mathcal{T}[e,\rho \models \bigcirc(\varphi_1 \mathbf{U}\, \varphi_2)],\ \mathcal{T}[e,\rho \models \varphi_1],\ \mathcal{T}[e,\rho \models \varphi_2])\\
\mathcal{T}[e,\rho \models \varphi_1 \mathbf{R}\, \varphi_2] &:= \mathbf{R}(\mathcal{T}[e,\rho \models \bigcirc(\varphi_1 \mathbf{R}\, \varphi_2)],\ \mathcal{T}[e,\rho \models \varphi_1],\ \mathcal{T}[e,\rho \models \varphi_2])\\
\mathcal{T}[e,\rho \models p(\alpha_1,\ldots,\alpha_n)] &:= \begin{cases} \top & (\text{if } p(\natural\rho(\alpha_1),\ldots,\natural\rho(\alpha_n)) \text{ is true})\\ \bot & (\text{if } p(\natural\rho(\alpha_1),\ldots,\natural\rho(\alpha_n)) \text{ is false})\end{cases}\\
\mathcal{T}[e,\rho \models \neg p(\alpha_1,\ldots,\alpha_n)] &:= \begin{cases} \top & (\text{if } p(\natural\rho(\alpha_1),\ldots,\natural\rho(\alpha_n)) \text{ is false})\\ \bot & (\text{if } p(\natural\rho(\alpha_1),\ldots,\natural\rho(\alpha_n)) \text{ is true})\end{cases}
\end{aligned}
$$

Fig. 2. Satisfaction tree: (1) Boolean connectives, until and release.

the arguments are recorded to ρ and labelled by $\widetilde{\beta}$ as required. In this case, we also change the target formula to $\bigcirc\varphi$. In the second rule, a label other than α should be simply ignored. The last three rules deal with the case of α not being annotated; then $e, \rho \models \mathit{call}\,\alpha(\widetilde{\beta}).\varphi$ is immediately false.

$$
\begin{aligned}
\mathcal{T}[e^{\alpha}\, e_1\, \ldots\, e_n,\ \rho \models \mathit{call}\,\alpha(\widetilde{\beta}).\varphi] &:= \mathcal{T}[e\, e_1^{\beta_1}\, \ldots\, e_n^{\beta_n},\ \rho \cup \{\beta_i \mapsto e_i\}_{1\leq i\leq n} \models \bigcirc\varphi]\\
\mathcal{T}[e^{\gamma}\, e_1\, \ldots\, e_n,\ \rho \models \mathit{call}\,\alpha(\widetilde{\beta}).\varphi] &:= \mathcal{T}[e\, e_1\, \ldots\, e_n,\ \rho \models \mathit{call}\,\ell(\widetilde{x}).\varphi]\\
\mathcal{T}[f\, e_1\, \ldots\, e_n,\ \rho \models \mathit{call}\,\alpha(\widetilde{\beta}).\varphi] &:= \bot\\
\mathcal{T}[\mathbf{if}\, e_1\, e_2\, e_3,\ \rho \models \mathit{call}\,\alpha(\widetilde{\beta}).\varphi] &:= \bot\\
\mathcal{T}[\mathbf{op}\, e_1\, e_2\, e_3,\ \rho \models \mathit{call}\,\alpha(\widetilde{\beta}).\varphi] &:= \bot\\
\mathcal{T}[(),\rho \models \mathit{call}\,\alpha(\widetilde{\beta}).\varphi] &:= \bot
\end{aligned}
$$

Fig. 3. Satisfaction tree: (2) Call modality. We assume $\gamma \neq \alpha$. The satisfaction tree for $\mathit{call}\, f(\widetilde{\beta}).\varphi$ is similar; we omit the rules here.

Figure 4 defines the rules for the negation of call. If e is calling an expression labelled by α, then $e, \rho \models \neg\mathit{call}\,\alpha(\_)$ is obviously false. The last three rules describe the case of α not being found, in which case $\neg\mathit{call}\,\alpha(\_)$ holds.

Figure 5 defines the rules for the next modality. It simply ignores labels and reduces the expression in one step.

We omit the rules for $\mathit{call}\, f(\widetilde{\beta}).\varphi$ and $\neg\mathit{call}\, f(\_)$, which are basically the same as those for $\mathit{call}\,\alpha(\widetilde{\beta}).\varphi$ and $\neg\mathit{call}\,\alpha(\_)$.

We formalise the meaning of a satisfaction tree by giving a nondeterministic Büchi automaton. The definition of the automaton is basically straightforward, but there is a subtlety in the meaning of $\mathtt{U}$. Recall that $\varphi_1\, \mathbf{U}\, \varphi_2$ holds if either

$$\mathcal{T}[e^{\alpha}\, e_1\, \dots\, e_n,\ \rho \models \neg\, call\, \alpha(\_)] := \bot$$
$$\mathcal{T}[e^{\gamma}\, e_1\, \dots\, e_n,\ \rho \models \neg\, call\, \alpha(\_)] := \mathcal{T}[e\, e_1\, \dots\, e_n,\ \rho \models \neg call\, \ell(\_)]$$
$$\mathcal{T}[f\, e_1\, \dots\, e_n,\ \rho \models \neg call\, \alpha(\_),\ \rho,] := \top$$
$$\mathcal{T}[\mathbf{if}\, e_1\, e_2\, e_3,\ \rho \models \neg call\, \alpha(\_)] := \top$$
$$\mathcal{T}[\mathbf{op}\, e_1\, e_2\, e_3,\ \rho \models \neg call\, \alpha(\_)] := \top$$
$$\mathcal{T}[(), \rho \models \neg call\, \alpha(\_)] := \top$$

Fig. 4. Satisfaction tree: (3) Negation of call modality. We assume $\gamma \neq \alpha$. The satisfaction tree for $\neg call\, f(\_)$ is similar; we omit the rules here.

$$\mathcal{T}[e^{\alpha}\, e_1\, \dots\, e_n,\ \rho \models \bigcirc\varphi] := \mathcal{T}[e\, e_1\, \dots\, e_n,\ \rho \models \bigcirc\varphi]$$
$$\mathcal{T}[f\, e_1\, \dots\, e_n,\ \rho \models \bigcirc\varphi] := \mathcal{T}[e_f[e_1/x_1, \dots, e_n/e_n],\ \rho \models \varphi]$$
$$\mathcal{T}[\mathbf{if}\ tt\, e\, e,\ \rho \models \bigcirc\varphi] := \mathcal{T}[e, \rho \models \varphi]$$
$$\mathcal{T}[\mathbf{if}\ ff\, e\, e',\ \rho \models \bigcirc\varphi] := \mathcal{T}[e', \rho \models \varphi]$$
$$\mathcal{T}[\mathbf{op}\, e_1\, e_2\, e_3,\ \rho \models \bigcirc\varphi] := \mathcal{T}[e_3\, c',\ \rho \models \varphi] \qquad \text{where } c' = (\natural e_1)\ op\ (\natural e_2)$$
$$\mathcal{T}[(), \rho \models \bigcirc\varphi] := \mathcal{T}[(), \rho \models \varphi]$$

Fig. 5. Satisfaction tree: (4) Next modality. It ignores labels and reduces the expression in one step. We assume that $(f\, x_1\, \dots\, x_n = e_f) \in \mathcal{P}$.

1. both φ_1 and φ_2 hold, or
2. both φ_1 and $\bigcirc(\varphi_1\, \mathbf{U}\, \varphi_2)$ hold.

Similarly $\varphi_1\, \mathbf{R}\, \varphi_2$ holds if and only if

1. both φ_1 and φ_2 hold, or
2. both φ_2 and $\bigcirc(\varphi_1\, \mathbf{U}\, \varphi_2)$ hold.

The condition for $\mathbf{U}$ quite resembles that for $\mathbf{R}$, but there is a crucial difference which cannot be captured by the above descriptions. That is, $\varphi_1\, \mathbf{U}\, \varphi_2$ requires that φ_2 eventually holds, but $\varphi_1\, \mathbf{R}\, \varphi_2$ is true even if φ_1 never becomes true. This difference should be captured by the acceptance condition of the Büchi automaton.

The Büchi automaton $\mathcal{A}$ has three states, q_0, q_1 and $*$. The states q_0 and q_1 have the same behaviour except that q_0 is accepting and q_1 is not accepting. The state $*$ accepts every tree; this state is used to describe a rule which ignores some of children. The set of accepting states is $\{q_0, *\}$ and the initial state is q_0. The transition rules are given by:

$$\delta_{\top}(q) := \{()\} \qquad \delta_{\bot}(q) := \{()\}$$
$$\delta_{\sqcap}(q) := \{(q_0, q_0)\} \qquad \delta_{\sqcup}(q) := \{(q_0, *), (*, q_0)\}$$
$$\delta_{\mathtt{U}}(q) := \{(q_1, q_0, *), (*, q_0, q_0)\} \qquad \delta_{\mathtt{R}}(q) := \{(q_0, *, q_0), (*, q_0, q_0)\},$$

where $q = q_0$ or q_1. We omit the rules for the state $*$, which accepts every tree. The tree $\mathtt{U}(T_1, T_2, T_3)$ is accepted from q_0 if T_1 is accepted from q_1 and T_3 is accepted from q_0; note that we assign q_1 to T_1, instead of q_0, because the until formula $\varphi_1 \mathbf{U} \varphi_2$ expects φ_2 eventually holds.

The following theorem is the first half of the reduction.

Theorem 2. *$e, \rho \models \varphi$ if and only if $\mathcal{T}[e, \rho \models \varphi]$ is accepted by $\mathcal{A}$.*

5.3 A Tree-Generating Program Generating the Satisfaction Tree

The previous subsection introduced satisfaction trees, which concern only about LTL features of LTLC, i.e. the tree does not have any information on the call nor next modality, which are related to reduction of programs.

This subsection discusses a way to deal with these features missing in satisfaction trees. Technically, given a program $(\mathcal{P}, e)$ and a formula φ, we construct a tree-generating program $(\mathcal{P}^\#, e')$ that generates the satisfaction tree $\mathcal{T}[e, \emptyset \models \varphi]$. The construction of $(\mathcal{P}^\#, e')$ is effective, and if the original program and the formula use only finite base types, then so does $(\mathcal{P}^\#, e')$. Therefore this construction, together with the result of the previous subsection, shows that the LTLC model checking is decidable for programs and formulas over finite data types.

We first give the formal statement of the theorem, which shall be proved in the rest of this subsection.

Theorem 3. *Given a program $(\mathcal{P}, e_0)$ and an LTLC formula φ, one can effectively construct a tree-generating program $(\mathcal{P}^\#, e_0')$ that generates the satisfaction tree $\mathcal{T}[e, \emptyset \models \varphi]$. Furthermore, if both the program $(\mathcal{P}, e)$ and the formula φ contain only finite base types, then so does $(\mathcal{P}^\#, e_0')$.*

Let φ_0 be a formula of interest, fixed in the sequel. By renaming bound variables if necessary, we can assume without loss of generality that different variables in φ_0 have different names. Let $L_0 \subseteq L$ be the finite set of bound variables in φ_0. Note that each $\alpha \in L_0$ is associated to its type in φ_0.

The idea of the translation, written #, is as follows. Recall that the satisfaction tree $\mathcal{T}[e, \rho \models \varphi]$ is determined by the three data, namely an expression $e : \star$, a valuation ρ and a formula φ. Hence the translation $e^\#$ of the expression e should take two extra arguments ρ and φ to compute $\mathcal{T}[e, \rho \models \varphi]$.

Let us first consider the translation of types. Because the translation of an expression e of unit type $\star$ takes two additional arguments, namely a formula and a valuation, the translation of the unit type should be given by

$$\star \quad \stackrel{\#}{\longmapsto} \quad (\mathit{valuation} \to \mathit{formula} \to \star),$$

where *valuation* and *formula* are the "types" for valuations and formulas, which shall be described below. The translation can be naturally extended to base types and function types by

$$b^\# := b \quad \text{and} \quad (\sigma \to \tau)^\# := \sigma^\# \to \tau^\#.$$

The "type" *formula* can be defined as an additional finite base type. An important observation is that only finitely various formulas are reachable by unfolding the definition of $\mathcal{T}[e, \emptyset \models \varphi_0]$. It is easy to see that the following set

$$\{\,\psi, \bigcirc\psi \mid \psi \text{ is a subformula of } \varphi_0\,\}$$

is an overapproximation. So we define the values in $V_{formula}$ as this set. We shall write $\lfloor\psi\rfloor$ for the formula ψ seen as a value in $V_{formula}$. We assume an operation $=_{formula}$ to compare formulas. Since *formula* is now a finite base type, one can define a function by using pattern matching of formulas.

The "type" *valuation* can be implemented as a tuple. Note that valuations ρ reachable from $\mathcal{T}[e, \emptyset \models \varphi_0]$ have subsets of L_0 as their domains. So a reachable valuation ρ can be represented as a tuple of length $|L_0|$, where $|L_0|$ is the number of elements in L_0. If $\rho(\alpha)$ is undefined for some $\alpha \in L_0$, one can fill the corresponding place in a tuple by an arbitrary expression.

Summarising the above argument, the translation of the unit type is

$$\star \quad \overset{\#}{\longmapsto} \quad (\sigma_1 \to \sigma_2 \to \cdots \to \sigma_n \to \mathit{formula} \to \star)$$

if the set of variables L_0 in φ_0 is $\{\,\alpha_1, \dots, \alpha_n\,\}$ and σ_i is the type for α_i, $1 \le i \le n$. We shall fix the enumeration $\alpha_1, \dots, \alpha_n$ of L_0 in the sequel.

We give the translation of expressions. The function definition $\mathcal{P}^{\#}$ after translation defines the following functions:

- $f^{\#} : \tau^{\#}$ for each function f defined in $\mathcal{P}$,
- $\alpha^{\#} : \tau^{\#} \to \tau^{\#}$ for each variable $\alpha \in L_0$ of type τ,
- $\mathbf{op}^{\#} : b_1 \to b_2 \to (b_3 \to \star^{\#}) \to \star^{\#}$ for each operation $op \in Op$,
- $\mathbf{if}^{\#} : \mathtt{Bool} \to \star^{\#} \to \star^{\#} \to \star^{\#}$, the translation of **if**, and
- $()^{\#} : \star^{\#}$, the translation of the unit value.

Note that $\alpha \in L_0$ does not have the translation if α has a base type; the label $(-)^{\alpha}$ is simply ignored by the translation (see Remark 1). Using these functions, the translation of expressions is given as follows:

$$c^{\#} := c \qquad x^{\#} := x \qquad (e_1\, e_2)^{\#} := e_1^{\#}\, e_2^{\#} \qquad (e^{\alpha})^{\#} := \alpha^{\#}\, e^{\#} \quad \text{and} \quad (e^{\beta})^{\#} := e^{\#}$$

where α (resp. β) is a variable in L_0 of a non-base type (resp. a base type). Other cases have already given by $\mathcal{P}^{\#}$: for example, $() \overset{\#}{\mapsto} ()^{\#}$ and $f \overset{\#}{\mapsto} f^{\#}$. A notable point is that the label annotation e^{α} is translated to application to $\alpha^{\#}$.

The translation of valuations should now be clear. A valuation is translated to a sequence of expressions, defined by

$$\rho \quad \overset{\#}{\longmapsto} \quad \rho(\alpha_1)^{\#} \,\dots\, \rho(\alpha_n)^{\#}.$$

If $\rho(\alpha_i)$ is undefined, then $\rho(\alpha_i)^{\#}$ can be arbitrary (but fixed a priori) expression of the required type. We use ϱ for sequences of this kind. We write $\varrho[\alpha_i \mapsto e]$ for the sequence obtained by replacing the ith element in ϱ with e.

What remains is to give definitions of functions $\mathcal{P}^{\#}$ so that the value tree of $e^{\#}\, \rho^{\#}\, \lfloor\varphi\rfloor$ will coincide with the satisfaction tree $\mathcal{T}[e, \rho \models \varphi]$. Each function definition is of the form $h\, \widetilde{x}\, \varrho\, \lfloor\varphi\rfloor = e$, where $\widetilde{x}$ is a sequence of arguments in the original definition, ϱ is a sequence representation of a tuple of type *valuation*, and $\lfloor\varphi\rfloor \in V_{formula}$ is the value of type *formula*. All functions in $\mathcal{P}^{\#}$ are defined by pattern matching on the final argument $\lfloor\varphi\rfloor$. For example, consider the case of the final argument being $\lfloor\psi_1 \wedge \psi_2\rfloor$. Because

$$\mathcal{T}[h\, \widetilde{e}, \rho \models \psi_1 \wedge \psi_2] \quad = \quad \mathcal{T}[h\, \widetilde{e}, \rho \models \psi_1] \sqcap \mathcal{T}[h\, \widetilde{e}, \rho \models \psi_2],$$

the definition[6] of h for this case has to be

$$h\, \widetilde{x}\, \varrho\, \lfloor\psi_1 \wedge \psi_2\rfloor \quad = \quad (h\, \widetilde{x}\, \varrho\, \lfloor\psi_1\rfloor) \sqcap (h\, \widetilde{x}\, \varrho\, \lfloor\psi_2\rfloor).$$

As an example of more complicated case, let us consider the rule

$$\mathcal{T}[e^{\alpha}\, e_1\, \dots\, e_n,\ \rho \models \mathit{call}\, \alpha(\beta_1, \dots, \beta_n).\varphi] \quad = \quad \mathcal{T}[e\, e_1^{\beta_1}\, \dots\, e_n^{\beta_n},\ \rho' \models \bigcirc\varphi]$$

where $\rho' = \rho \cup \{\beta_i \mapsto e_i\}_{1 \leq i \leq n}$. Because

$$(e^{\alpha}\, e_1\, \dots\, e_n)^{\#} \quad = \quad \alpha^{\#}\, e^{\#}\, e_1^{\#}\, \dots\, e_n^{\#},$$

the above rule can be seen as (a part of) the definition of $\alpha^{\#}$:

$$\alpha^{\#}\, g\, \widetilde{x}\, \varrho\, \lfloor\mathit{call}\, \alpha(\beta_1, \dots, \beta_n).\varphi\rfloor \quad = \quad g\, (\beta_1^{\#}\, x_1)\, \dots\, (\beta_n^{\#}\, x_n)\, \varrho'\, \lfloor\bigcirc\varphi\rfloor$$

where $\varrho' = \varrho[\beta_1 \mapsto x_1] \dots [\beta_n \mapsto x_n]$. It is easy to check that

$$(e^{\alpha}\, e_1\, \dots\, e_n)^{\#}\, \rho^{\#}\, \lfloor\mathit{call}\, \alpha(\beta_1, \dots, \beta_n).\varphi\rfloor \quad \longrightarrow^{*} \quad (e\, e_1^{\beta_1}\, \dots\, e_n^{\beta_n})^{\#}\, \rho'^{\#}\, \lfloor\bigcirc\varphi\rfloor$$

as expected. All other cases are given in the same way.

Now the definition of the translation has been given in sufficient detail, we believe. It is not difficult to establish the following lemma.

Lemma 1. *The value tree of $e^{\#}\, \rho^{\#}\, \lfloor\varphi\rfloor$ is equivalent to $\mathcal{T}[e, \rho \models \varphi]$, provided that ρ and φ are reachable from the definition of $\mathcal{T}[e_1, \emptyset \models \varphi_0]$ for some expression e_1 of type $\star$.*

Theorem 3 is a consequence of this lemma: e_0' can be defined as $e_0^{\#}\, \emptyset^{\#}\, \lfloor\varphi_0\rfloor$.

The decidablity result is a corollary of Theorems 2 and 3.

Theorem 4. *Let $(\mathcal{P}, e)$ is a program and φ is an LTLC formula. If $(\mathcal{P}, e)$ and φ contain only finite base types, then one can effectively decide whether $e, \emptyset \models \varphi$.*

---

[6] Strictly speaking, the "function definition" here does not precisely follow the syntax of function definition in our language, as we do not allow pattern matching on the left-hand-side of a definition, but we expect that the reader can fill the gap.

Remark 2. Let us briefly discuss the time complexity of the algorithm. The cost of the translation is negligible; we estimate the running time of the higher-order model checking. If we fix the property automaton to $\mathcal{A}$ in Theorem 2, the higher-order model checking be solved in time $O(P^2\,\mathbf{exp}_N(poly(A\,D)))$ for some polynomial *poly* ([13, Section 5] adopted to our setting), where P, N, A and D are parameters determined by the program after translation; P is the size, N is the order, A is the maximum arity of types and D is the maximum number of values in base types. Easy calculation shows that

$$P = O(|(\mathcal{P}, e)| \times |\varphi|) \qquad N \leq order(\mathcal{P}, e) + 2 \qquad N = O(|\varphi|) \qquad A = O(|\varphi|)$$

where $|(\mathcal{P}, e)|$ and $|\varphi|$ are the sizes of the program and of the formula.

6 Discussions

Compositional Reasoning. LTLC model checking is a kind of whole-program verification. Actually $C[f], \rho \models \Phi_T(f)$, where Φ_T is the LTLC formula corresponding to a dependent type T (see Sect. 4.1), only means that the behaviour of f *in the context* C does not violate the specification T; it does not ensure that f meets T in other contexts as well.

This is in contrast to a compositional approach such as a type-based one, in which $\vdash t : T$ means that t satisfies the specification T in whatever the context t is used. In this sense $\Phi_T(f)$ is not like a type judgement but like dynamic monitoring of a contract [9].

A way to fill the gap is to consider all possible contexts. That means, we define $\models f : T$ to mean that $C[f], \emptyset \models \Phi_T(f)$ for every context C. In a sufficiently expressive programming language, $\forall C.(\,C[f], \emptyset \models \Phi_T(f)\,)$ is equivalent to $C_0[f], \emptyset \models \Phi_T(f)$ for a certain "worst" context C_0; this observation gives us a way to reduce compositional reasoning to whole-program analysis. This strategy is actually used in [23], for example.

A typical way to construct the "worst" context C_0 is to use nondeterminism [23]; intuitively C_0 is a "maximally" nondeterministic context, which may do anything allowed. Unfortunately this construction is not directly applicable to our case, since our reducibility result (in particular, Theorem 2) essentially relies on the determinism of programs.

Non-deterministic Programs. Determinism of programs is essential to our reducibility result. In fact, even the definition of the satisfaction relation becomes "incorrect" in the presence of non-determinism.

To see the reason, consider an LTLC formula

$$\varphi \quad := \quad \mathit{ifcall}\, f \vee \neg \mathit{ifcall}\, f,$$

which is obviously true for every program. By definition, we have

$$e, \rho \models \mathit{ifcall}\, f \vee \neg \mathit{ifcall}\, f \qquad \text{iff} \qquad e, \rho \models \mathit{ifcall}\, f \quad \text{or} \quad e, \rho \models \neg \mathit{ifcall}\, f,$$

for every expression e. This rule is problematic in the presence of nondeterminism. For example, consider $e = (f\,()) \oplus ()$ where $\oplus$ is the nondeterministic branching. This expression decides nondeterministically whether it calls f or not. Then $e, \rho \models \mathit{ifcall}\,f \vee \neg\mathit{ifcall}\,f$ but neither $e, \rho \models \mathit{ifcall}\,f$ nor $e, \rho \models \neg\mathit{ifcall}\,f$.

This problem can be easily fixed by changing the definition of the satisfaction relation. It should be a relation $\pi, \rho \models \varphi$ on an infinite reduction sequence π (instead of an expression e), a valuation and a formula in the presence of nondeterminism.

However Theorem 2 cannot be modified accordingly to the new definition. The definition of $\mathcal{T}[e, \rho \models \varphi]$ is so deeply related to the current definition of the satisfaction that we cannot obtain a variant of Theorem 2 applicable to nondeterministic setting.

Actually we conjecture that LTLC model-checking for nondeterministic programs is undecidable even for programs with only finite data types. The proof of the conjecture is left for future work.

7 Related Work

LTLC model checking is a kind of temporal verification of higher-order programs, which has been extensively studied [11,12,14,15,22]. The temporal properties of higher-order programs have also been studied in the context of contracts, named *temporal higher-order contracts* [7].

Alur et al. proposed a linear temporal logic called CARET [2], which is designed for specifying properties for first-order programs modeled by Recursive State Machines [3] and Pushdown Sytems [16]. Neither CARET nor LTLC subsumes the other. On the one hand, CARET cannot describe properties of higher-order functions, such as "a function argument of some function is eventually called." On the other hand, CARET can describe *caller* properties such as "a caller function of the function currently invoded is never returned," which cannot be expressed in LTLC. An extension of LTLC for specifying caller properties is left for future work. Alur and Madhusudan proposed Visibly Pushdown Languages (VPL) [4], which can specify properties of function calls and returns, and subsumes CARET. Like CARET, VPL is for first-order programs, not for higher-order programs.

Recently Satake and Unno proposed a dynamic logic for higher-order programs, named HOT-PDL [22]. Their logic is not directly comparable to ours, as their logic is for call-by-value programs. The gap can be partially filled by applying the CPS translation, and the formulas in their logic can be translated to LTLC formulas in many cases, although we need to extend LTLC by *anonymous call operator* $\mathit{call}\ \_(\vec{\beta}).\varphi$ to fully capture their logic. Many LTLC formulas such as those in Example 2 and Sect. 4.3 cannot be expressed in HOT-PDL.

Applications of HORS model checking to program verification has been studied [11,12,14,15,17,18,22]. Decidability of resource usage verification has been proved in [12] by using a program translation tailor-made for the resource usage verification problem. The argument in Sect. 4.3 together with Theorem 4 gives another, more principled proof of the decidability result, although the current argument proves only a partial result of [12].

8 Conclusion

We have proposed a temporal logic called LTLC, which is an extension of LTL and can specify properties for call-by-name higher-order programs. Thanks to the call operator, LTLC can describe properties of arguments of function currently called. For example, LTLC can specify the order of function calls such as "the first argument passed to the function f is called before the call of the second argument passed to f." We have shown that LTLC model checking is decidable for a finite-data deterministic programs via a reduction to HORS model checking.

The most important future work is to prove the undecidability (possibly, the decidability) of LTLC model checking for non-deterministic programs. To further widen the scope of our method, it is worth extending LTLC for specifying branching properties by embedding the call operator into CTL* or modal μ-calculus.

References

1. Aguirre, A., Barthe, G., Gaboardi, M., Garg, D., Strub, P.: A relational logic for higher-order programs. PACMPL **1**(ICFP), 21:1–21:29 (2017)
2. Alur, R., Etessami, K., Madhusudan, P.: A temporal logic of nested calls and returns. In: Jensen, K., Podelski, A. (eds.) TACAS 2004. LNCS, vol. 2988, pp. 467–481. Springer, Heidelberg (2004). https://doi.org/10.1007/978-3-540-24730-2_35
3. Alur, R., Etessami, K., Yannakakis, M.: Analysis of recursive state machines. In: Berry, G., Comon, H., Finkel, A. (eds.) CAV 2001. LNCS, vol. 2102, pp. 207–220. Springer, Heidelberg (2001). https://doi.org/10.1007/3-540-44585-4_18
4. Alur, R., Madhusudan, P.: Visibly pushdown languages. In: Babai, L. (ed.) Proceedings of the 36th Annual ACM Symposium on Theory of Computing, Chicago, IL, USA, June 13–16, 2004. pp. 202–211. ACM (2004)
5. Asada, K., Sato, R., Kobayashi, N.: Verifying relational properties of functional programs by first-order refinement. Sci. Comput. Program. **137**, 2–62 (2017)
6. Broadbent, C.H., Kobayashi, N.: Saturation-based model checking of higher-order recursion schemes. In: Rocca, S.R.D. (ed.) Computer Science Logic 2013 (CSL 2013), CSL 2013, September 2–5, 2013, Torino, Italy. LIPIcs, vol. 23, pp. 129–148. Schloss Dagstuhl - Leibniz-Zentrum fuer Informatik (2013)
7. Disney, T., Flanagan, C., McCarthy, J.: Temporal higher-order contracts. In: Chakravarty, M.M.T., Hu, Z., Danvy, O. (eds.) Proceeding of the 16th ACM SIGPLAN International Conference on Functional Programming, ICFP 2011, Tokyo, Japan, September 19–21, 2011, pp. 176–188. ACM (2011)
8. Emerson, E.A., Halpern, J.Y.: "Sometimes" and "not never" revisited: on branching versus linear time temporal logic. J. ACM (JACM) **33**(1), 151–178 (1986)
9. Findler, R.B., Felleisen, M.: Contracts for higher-order functions. In: Wand, M., Peyton Jones, S.L. (eds.) Proceedings of the Seventh ACM SIGPLAN International Conference on Functional Programming (ICFP 2002), Pittsburgh, Pennsylvania, USA, October 4–6, 2002, pp. 48–59. ACM (2002)

10. Igarashi, A., Kobayashi, N.: Resource usage analysis. ACM Trans. Program. Lang. Syst. **27**(2), 264–313 (2005)
11. Kobayashi, N.: Types and higher-order recursion schemes for verification of higher-order programs. In: Shao, Z., Pierce, B.C. (eds.) Proceedings of the 36th ACM SIGPLAN-SIGACT Symposium on Principles of Programming Languages, POPL 2009, Savannah, GA, USA, January 21–23, 2009. pp. 416–428. ACM (2009)
12. Kobayashi, N.: Model checking higher-order programs. J. ACM **60**(3), 20:1–20:62 (2013)
13. Kobayashi, N., Ong, C.L.: A type system equivalent to the modal mu-calculus model checking of higher-order recursion schemes. In: Proceedings of the 24th Annual IEEE Symposium on Logic in Computer Science, LICS 2009, 11–14 August 2009, Los Angeles, CA, USA. pp. 179–188. IEEE Computer Society (2009)
14. Lester, M.M., Neatherway, R.P., Ong, C.L., Ramsay, S.: Model checking liveness properties of higher-order functional programs. In: Proceedings of ML Workshop, vol. 2011 (2011)
15. Murase, A., Terauchi, T., Kobayashi, N., Sato, R., Unno, H.: Temporal verification of higher-order functional programs. In: Bodík, R., Majumdar, R. (eds.) Proceedings of the 43rd Annual ACM SIGPLAN-SIGACT Symposium on Principles of Programming Languages, POPL 2016, St. Petersburg, FL, USA, January 20–22, 2016, pp. 57–68. ACM (2016)
16. Nguyen, H., Touili, T.: CARET model checking for pushdown systems. In: Seffah, A., Penzenstadler, B., Alves, C., Peng, X. (eds.) Proceedings of the Symposium on Applied Computing, SAC 2017, Marrakech, Morocco, April 3–7, 2017, pp. 1393–1400. ACM (2017)
17. Ong, C.L.: On model-checking trees generated by higher-order recursion schemes. In: 21th IEEE Symposium on Logic in Computer Science (LICS 2006), 12–15 August 2006, Seattle, WA, USA, Proceedings, pp. 81–90. IEEE Computer Society (2006)
18. Ong, C.L., Ramsay, S.J.: Verifying higher-order functional programs with pattern-matching algebraic data types. In: Ball, T., Sagiv, M. (eds.) Proceedings of the 38th ACM SIGPLAN-SIGACT Symposium on Principles of Programming Languages, POPL 2011, Austin, TX, USA, January 26–28, 2011, pp. 587–598. ACM (2011)
19. Pnueli, A.: The temporal logic of programs. In: In: 18th Annual Symposium on Foundations of Computer Science, pp. 46–57. IEEE (1977)
20. Ramsay, S.J., Neatherway, R.P., Ong, C.L.: A type-directed abstraction refinement approach to higher-order model checking. In: Jagannathan, S., Sewell, P. (eds.) The 41st Annual ACM SIGPLAN-SIGACT Symposium on Principles of Programming Languages, POPL 2014, San Diego, CA, USA, January 20–21, 2014, pp. 61–72. ACM (2014)
21. Rondon, P.M., Kawaguchi, M., Jhala, R.: Liquid types. In: Gupta, R., Amarasinghe, S.P. (eds.) Proceedings of the ACM SIGPLAN 2008 Conference on Programming Language Design and Implementation, Tucson, AZ, USA, June 7–13, 2008, pp. 159–169. ACM (2008)
22. Satake, Y., Unno, H.: Propositional dynamic logic for higher-order functional programs. In: Chockler, H., Weissenbacher, G. (eds.) CAV 2018. LNCS, vol. 10981, pp. 105–123. Springer, Cham (2018). https://doi.org/10.1007/978-3-319-96145-3_6
23. Sato, R., Asada, K., Kobayashi, N.: Refinement type checking via assertion checking. JIP **23**(6), 827–834 (2015)

Multiphase-Linear Ranking Functions and Their Relation to Recurrent Sets

Amir M. Ben-Amram[1], Jesús J. Doménech[2], and Samir Genaim[2(✉)]

[1] School of Computer Science, The Tel-Aviv Academic College, Tel Aviv, Israel
[2] DSIC, Complutense University of Madrid (UCM), Madrid, Spain
genaim@gmail.com

Abstract. Multiphase ranking functions (MΦRFs) are used to prove termination of loops in which the computation progresses through a number of phases. They consist of linear functions $\langle f_1, \ldots, f_d \rangle$ where f_i decreases during the ith phase. This work provides new insights regarding MΦRFs for loops described by a conjunction of linear constraints (*SLC* loops). In particular, we consider the existence problem (does a given *SLC* loop admit a MΦRF). The decidability and complexity of the problem, in the case that d is restricted by an input parameter, have been settled in recent work, while in this paper we make progress regarding the existence problem without a given depth bound. Our new approach, while falling short of a decision procedure for the general case, reveals some important insights into the structure of these functions. Interestingly, it relates the problem of seeking MΦRFs to that of seeking recurrent sets (used to prove nontermination). It also helps in identifying classes of loops for which MΦRFs are sufficient, and thus have linear runtime bounds. For the depth-bounded existence problem, we obtain a new polynomial-time procedure that can provide *witnesses* for negative answers as well. To obtain this procedure we introduce a new representation for *SLC* loops, the *difference polyhedron* replacing the customary *transition polyhedron*. We find that this representation yields new insights on MΦRFs and *SLC* loops in general, and some results on termination and nontermination of bounded *SLC* loops become straightforward.

1 Introduction

Proving that a program will not go into an infinite loop is one of the most fundamental tasks of program verification, and has been the subject of voluminous research. Perhaps the best known, and often used, technique for proving termination is that of *ranking functions*. This consists of finding a function that maps program states into the elements of a well-founded ordered set, such that its value decreases when applied to consecutive states. This implies termination since infinite descent is impossible in a well-founded order.

This work was funded partially by the Spanish MICINN/FEDER, UE project RTI2018-094403-B-C31, the MINECO project TIN2015-69175-C4-2-R, the CM project S2018/TCS-4314 and by the pre-doctoral UCM grant CT27/16-CT28/16.

B.-Y. E. Chang (Ed.): SAS 2019, LNCS 11822, pp. 459–480, 2019.
https://doi.org/10.1007/978-3-030-32304-2_22

Unlike termination of programs in general, which is undecidable, the algorithmic problems of detection (deciding the existence) or generation (synthesis) of a ranking function can well be solvable, given certain choices of the program representation, and the class of ranking function. There is a considerable amount of research in this direction, in which different kinds of ranking functions for different kinds of program representations were considered. In some cases the algorithmic problems have been completely settled, and efficient algorithms provided, while other cases remain open.

The program representation we study is *single-path linear-constraint loops* (*SLC* loops), where a state is described by the values of numerical variables, and the effect of a transition (one iteration) is described by a conjunction of *linear constraints*. We consider the settings of integer-valued variables and rational-valued (or real-valued) variables. Here is an example of this loop representation; primed variables $x_1', x_2', \ldots$ refer to the state following the transition.

$$\texttt{while } (x_1 \geq -x_3) \texttt{ do } x_1' = x_1 + x_2,\ x_2' = x_2 + x_3,\ x_3' = x_3 - 1 \quad (1)$$

Note that $x_1' = x_1 + x_2$ is an equation, not an assignment. The description of a loop may involve linear inequalities rather than equations, and consequently be nondeterministic. It is a standard procedure to compile sequential code (or approximate it) into such representation using various techniques. We assume the "constraint loop" to be given, and do not concern ourselves with the orthogonal topic of extracting such loops from general programs. The loop is called *simple* since branching in the loop body is not represented. Despite this restriction, *SLC* loops are important, e.g., in approaches that reduce a question about a whole program to questions about simple loops [14–16,21,27]; see [29] for references that show the importance of such loops in other fields.

Several types of ranking functions have been suggested for *SLC* loops; linear ranking functions (*LRFs*) are probably the most known. In this case, we seek a function $\rho(x_1, \ldots, x_n) = a_1x_1 + \cdots + a_nx_n + a_0$ such that (i) $\rho(\mathbf{x}) \geq 0$ for any valuation $\mathbf{x} = \langle x_1, \ldots, x_n\rangle$ that satisfies the loop constraints (i.e., an enabled state); and (ii) $\rho(\mathbf{x}) - \rho(\mathbf{x}') \geq 1$ for any transition leading from $\mathbf{x}$ to $\mathbf{x}' = \langle x_1', \ldots, x_n'\rangle$. The algorithmic problems of existence and synthesis of *LRFs* have been completely settled [5,12,18,31,33], for both integer-valued and rational-valued variables, not only for *SLC* loops but rather for control-flow graphs.

LRFs do not suffice for all terminating *SLC* loops, e.g., Loop (1) does not have a *LRF*, and in such case, one may resort to an argument that combines several linear functions to capture a more complex behavior. A common such argument is one that uses *lexicographic ranking functions*, where a tuple of linear functions is required to decrease lexicographically when moving from one state to another. In this paper we are interested in a special case of the lexicographic order argument that is called *Multiphase ranking functions* (MΦRF for short). Intuitively, a MΦRF is a tuple $\langle f_1, \ldots, f_d\rangle$ of linear functions that define phases of the loop that are linearly ranked, as follows: f_1 decreases on all transitions, and when it becomes negative f_2 decreases, and when f_2 becomes negative, f_3 will decrease, etc. Loop (1) has the MΦRF $\langle x_3+1, x_2+1, x_1\rangle$. The parameter d is called the *depth* of the MΦRF, intuitively the number of phases.

The decision problem *Existence of a MΦRF* asks to determine whether a *SLC* loop has a MΦRF. The *bounded* decision problem restricts the search to MΦRFs of depth d, where d is part of the input. The complexity and algorithmic aspects of the bounded version of the MΦRF problem were completely settled in [6]. The decision problem is PTIME for *SLC* loops with rational-valued variables, and coNP-complete for *SLC* loops with integer-valued variables; synthesizing MΦRFs, when they exist, can be performed in polynomial and exponential time, respectively. In addition, [6] shows that for *SLC* loops MΦRFs have the same power as general lexicographic-linear ranking functions, and that, surprisingly, MΦRFs induce linear iteration bounds. The problem of deciding if a given *SLC* admits a MΦRF, without a given bound on the depth, is still open.

In practice, termination analysis tools search for MΦRFs starting by depth 1 and incrementally increase the depth until they find one, or reach a predefined limit, after which the returned answer is *don't know*. Clearly, finding a theoretical upper-bound on the depth of a MΦRF, given the loop, would also settle this problem. As shown in [6], such bound must depend not only on the number of constraints or variables, but also on the coefficients used in the constraints.

In this paper we make progress towards solving the problem of *existence of a MΦRF*, i.e., seeking a MΦRF without a given bound on the depth. In particular, we present an algorithm for seeking MΦRFs that reveals new insights on the structure of these ranking functions. In a nutshell, the algorithm starts from the set of transitions of the given *SLC* loop, which is a polyhedron, and iteratively removes transitions $(\mathbf{x}, \mathbf{x}')$ such that $\rho(\mathbf{x})-\rho(\mathbf{x}') > 0$ for some function $\rho(\mathbf{x}) = \vec{a} \cdot \mathbf{x} + b$ that is *nonnegative on all enabled states*. The process continues iteratively, since after removing some transitions, more functions ρ may satisfy the nonnegativity condition, and they may eliminate additional transitions in the next iteration. When all transitions are eliminated in a finite number of iterations, we can construct a MΦRF using the ρ functions; and when reaching a situation in which no transition can be eliminated, we prove that we have actually reached a recurrent set that witnesses nontermination.

The algorithm always finds a MΦRF if one exists, and in many cases it finds a recurrent set (see experiments in Sect. 5) when the loop is nonterminating, however, it is not a decision procedure as it diverges in some cases. Nonetheless, our algorithm provides important insights on the structure of MΦRFs. Apart from revealing a relation between seeking MΦRFs and seeking recurrent sets, these insights are useful for finding classes of *SLC* loops for which, when terminating, there is always a MΦRF and thus have linear runtime bound.

Our research has, in addition, led to a new representation for *SLC* loops, that we refer to as the *displacement* representation, that provides us with new tools for studying termination of *SLC* loops in general, and existence of a MΦRF in particular. In this representation a transition $(\mathbf{x}, \mathbf{x}')$ is represented as $(\mathbf{x}, \mathbf{y})$ where $\mathbf{y} = \mathbf{x}' - \mathbf{x}$. Using this representation our algorithm can be formalized in a simple way that avoids computing the ρ functions mentioned above (which might be expensive), and reduces the existence of a MΦRF of depth d to unsatisfiability of a certain linear constraint system. Moreover, any satisfying assignment is a witness that explains why the loop has no MΦRF of depth d. As an evidence on the usefulness of this representation in general, we also show that some nontrivial observations on termination of bounded *SLC* loops are made straightforward in this representation, while they are not easy to see in the normal representation.

The article is organized as follows. Section 2 gives precise definitions and necessary background. Section 3 describes our algorithm and its possible outcomes. Section 4 discusses the displacement representation for *SLC* loops. Section 5 discusses some experiments. Finally, in Sect. 6 we conclude and discuss related work.

2 Preliminaries

Polyhedra. A *rational convex polyhedron* $\mathcal{P} \subseteq \mathbb{Q}^n$ (*polyhedron* for short) is the set of solutions of a set of inequalities $A\mathbf{x} \leq \mathbf{b}$, namely $\mathcal{P} = \{\mathbf{x} \in \mathbb{Q}^n \mid A\mathbf{x} \leq \mathbf{b}\}$, where $A \in \mathbb{Q}^{m \times n}$ is a rational matrix of n columns and m rows, $\mathbf{x} \in \mathbb{Q}^n$ and $\mathbf{b} \in \mathbb{Q}^m$ are column vectors of n and m rational values respectively. We say that $\mathcal{P}$ is specified by $A\mathbf{x} \leq \mathbf{b}$. If $\mathbf{b} = \mathbf{0}$, then $\mathcal{P}$ is a *cone*. The set of *recession directions* of a polyhedron $\mathcal{P}$ specified by $A\mathbf{x} \leq \mathbf{b}$, also known as its *recession cone*, is the set $\texttt{rec.cone}(\mathcal{P}) = \{\mathbf{y} \in \mathbb{Q}^n \mid A\mathbf{y} \leq \mathbf{0}\}$. Polyhedra also have a *generator representation* in terms of vertices and rays, written as $\mathcal{P} = \text{conv.hull}\{\mathbf{x}_1, \ldots, \mathbf{x}_m\} + \text{cone}\{\mathbf{y}_1, \ldots, \mathbf{y}_t\}$. This means that $\mathbf{x} \in \mathcal{P}$ iff $\mathbf{x} = \sum_{i=1}^m a_i \cdot \mathbf{x}_i + \sum_{j=1}^t b_j \cdot \mathbf{y}_j$ for some rationals $a_i, b_j \geq 0$, where $\sum_{i=1}^m a_i = 1$. Note that $\mathbf{y}_1, \ldots, \mathbf{y}_t$ are the recession directions of $\mathcal{P}$, i.e., $\mathbf{y} \in \texttt{rec.cone}(\mathcal{P})$ iff $\mathbf{y} = \sum_{j=1}^t b_j \cdot \mathbf{y}_j$ for some rationals $b_j \geq 0$. For a given polyhedron $\mathcal{P} \subseteq \mathbb{Q}^n$ we let $I(\mathcal{P})$ be $\mathcal{P} \cap \mathbb{Z}^n$, i.e., the set of integer points of $\mathcal{P}$. The *integer hull* of $\mathcal{P}$, commonly denoted by $\mathcal{P}_I$, is defined as the convex hull of $I(\mathcal{P})$.

Let $\mathcal{P} \subseteq \mathbb{Q}^{n+m}$ be a polyhedron, and let $\binom{\mathbf{x}}{\mathbf{y}} \in \mathcal{P}$ be such that $\mathbf{x} \in \mathbb{Q}^n$ and $\mathbf{y} \in \mathbb{Q}^m$. The *projection* of $\mathcal{P}$ onto the $\mathbf{x}$-space is defined as $\texttt{proj}_{\mathbf{x}}(\mathcal{P}) = \{\mathbf{x} \in \mathbb{Q}^n \mid \exists \mathbf{y} \in \mathbb{Q}^m \text{ such that } \binom{\mathbf{x}}{\mathbf{y}} \in \mathcal{P}\}$. We will need the following lemmas later.

Lemma 1. $\texttt{proj}_{\mathbf{x}}(\texttt{rec.cone}(\mathcal{P})) = \texttt{rec.cone}(\texttt{proj}_{\mathbf{x}}(\mathcal{P}))$.

Proof. A polyhedron $\mathcal{P}$ whose variables are split into two sets, $\mathbf{x}$ and $\mathbf{y}$, can be represented in the form $A\mathbf{x} + G\mathbf{y} \leq \mathbf{b}$ for matrices A, G and a vector $\mathbf{b}$ of matching dimensions. Then [13, Theorem 11.11] states that $\texttt{proj}_{\mathbf{x}}(\mathcal{P})$ is specified by the constraints $V(\mathbf{b} - A\mathbf{x}) \geq \mathbf{0}$ for a certain matrix V determined by G only. From this it follows that $\texttt{rec.cone}(\texttt{proj}_{\mathbf{x}}(\mathcal{P})) = \{\mathbf{x} \;:\; VA\mathbf{x} \leq \mathbf{0}\}$. But we can also apply the theorem to $\texttt{rec.cone}(\mathcal{P})$, which is specified by $A\mathbf{x} + G\mathbf{y} \leq \mathbf{0}$, and we get the same result $\texttt{proj}_{\mathbf{x}}(\texttt{rec.cone}(\mathcal{P})) = \{\mathbf{x} \;:\; VA\mathbf{x} \leq \mathbf{0}\}$. □

Lemma 2 (Lemma 1 in [6]). *Given a polyhedron* $\mathcal{P} \neq \emptyset$, *and linear functions* $\rho_1, \ldots, \rho_k$ *such that*

(i) $\mathbf{x} \in \mathcal{P} \rightarrow \rho_1(\mathbf{x}) > 0 \vee \cdots \vee \rho_{k-1}(\mathbf{x}) > 0 \vee \rho_k(\mathbf{x}) \geq 0$
(ii) $\mathbf{x} \in \mathcal{P} \not\rightarrow \rho_1(\mathbf{x}) > 0 \vee \cdots \vee \rho_{k-1}(\mathbf{x}) > 0$

There exist nonnegative constants $\mu_1, \ldots, \mu_{k-1}$ *such that* $\mathbf{x} \in \mathcal{P} \rightarrow \mu_1\rho_1(\mathbf{x}) + \cdots + \mu_{k-1}\rho_{k-1}(\mathbf{x}) + \rho_k(\mathbf{x}) \geq 0$.

Single-Path Linear-Constraint Loops. A *single-path* linear-constraint loop (*SLC* loop) over n variables $x_1, \ldots, x_n$ has the form

$$\textit{while } (B\mathbf{x} \leq \mathbf{b}) \textit{ do } A\mathbf{x} + A'\mathbf{x}' \leq \mathbf{c} \tag{2}$$

where $\mathbf{x} = (x_1, \ldots, x_n)^{\mathrm{T}}$ and $\mathbf{x}' = (x'_1, \ldots, x'_n)^{\mathrm{T}}$ are column vectors, and for some $p, q > 0$, $B \in \mathbb{Q}^{p \times n}$, $A, A' \in \mathbb{Q}^{q \times n}$, $\mathbf{b} \in \mathbb{Q}^p$, $\mathbf{c} \in \mathbb{Q}^q$. The constraint $B\mathbf{x} \leq \mathbf{b}$ is called *the loop guard* and the other constraint is called *the update*. The update is *deterministic* if, for any given $\mathbf{x}$ (satisfying the guard) there is at most one $\mathbf{x}'$ satisfying the update, and is *affine linear* if it can be rewritten as $\mathbf{x}' = U\mathbf{x}+\mathbf{c}$. We say that there is a transition from a state $\mathbf{x} \in \mathbb{Q}^n$ to a state $\mathbf{x}' \in \mathbb{Q}^n$, if $\mathbf{x}$ satisfies the loop condition and $\mathbf{x}$ and $\mathbf{x}'$ satisfy the update constraint. A transition can be seen as a point $\binom{\mathbf{x}}{\mathbf{x}'} \in \mathbb{Q}^{2n}$, where its first n components correspond to $\mathbf{x}$ and its last n components to $\mathbf{x}'$. For ease of notation, we denote $\binom{\mathbf{x}}{\mathbf{x}'}$ by $\mathbf{x}''$. The set of all transitions $\mathbf{x}'' \in \mathbb{Q}^{2n}$, of a given *SLC* loop, will be denoted by $\mathcal{Q}$ and is specified by the set of inequalities $A''\mathbf{x}'' \leq \mathbf{c}''$ where

$$A'' = \begin{pmatrix} B & 0 \\ A & A' \end{pmatrix} \qquad\qquad \mathbf{c}'' = \begin{pmatrix} \mathbf{b} \\ \mathbf{c} \end{pmatrix}$$

and B, A, A', $\mathbf{c}$ and $\mathbf{b}$ are those of (2). We call $\mathcal{Q}$ *the transition polyhedron*. An *integer loop* is a *SLC* loop restricted to integer values, i.e., the set of transitions is $I(\mathcal{Q})$.

Multi-Phase Ranking Functions. An affine linear function $\rho : \mathbb{Q}^n \rightarrow \mathbb{Q}$ is a function of the form $\rho(\mathbf{x}) = \vec{a} \cdot \mathbf{x} + b$ where $\vec{a} \in \mathbb{Q}^n$ is a row vector and $b \in \mathbb{Q}$. For a given function ρ, we define the function $\Delta\rho : \mathbb{Q}^{2n} \mapsto \mathbb{Q}$ as $\Delta\rho(\mathbf{x}'') = \rho(\mathbf{x}) - \rho(\mathbf{x}')$.

Definition 1. *Given a set of transitions* $T \subseteq \mathbb{Q}^{2n}$, *we say that* $\tau = \langle\rho_1, \ldots, \rho_d\rangle$ *is a MΦRF (of depth d) for T if for every* $\mathbf{x}'' \in T$ *there is index i such that:*

$$\forall j \leq i.\ \Delta\rho_j(\mathbf{x}'') \geq 1, \tag{3}$$

$$\rho_i(\mathbf{x}) \geq 0, \tag{4}$$

$$\forall j < i. \quad \rho_j(\mathbf{x}) \leq 0. \tag{5}$$

We say that $\mathbf{x}''$ *is* ranked by ρ_i *(for the minimal such i).*

It is not hard to see that a MΦRF $\langle\rho_1\rangle$ of depth $d = 1$ is a linear ranking function (*LRF*). If the MΦRF is of depth $d > 1$, it implies that if $\rho_1(\mathbf{x}) \geq 0$, transition $\mathbf{x}''$ is ranked by ρ_1, while if $\rho_1(\mathbf{x}) < 0$, $\langle\rho_2, \ldots, \rho_d\rangle$ becomes a MΦRF. This agrees with the intuitive notion of "phases." We say that τ is *irredundant* if removing any component invalidates the MΦRF. Finally, it is convenient to allow an empty tuple as a MΦRF, of depth 0, for the empty set.

The decision problem *Existence of a MΦRF* asks to determine whether a given *SLC* loop admits a MΦRF. The *bounded* decision problem restricts the search to MΦRFs of depth at most d, where d is part of the input.

Recurrent Sets. A recurrent set is a set of states that witnesses nontermination of a given *SLC* loop $\mathcal{Q}$. It is commonly defined as a set of states $S \subseteq \texttt{proj}_{\mathbf{x}}(\mathcal{Q})$ where for any $\mathbf{x} \in S$ there is $\mathbf{x}' \in S$ such that $(\mathbf{x}, \mathbf{x}') \in \mathcal{Q}$. This clearly proves the existence of an infinite run. In this article we use a slightly different notion.

Definition 2. *Give a SLC loop $\mathcal{Q}$, we say that $S \subseteq \mathcal{Q}$ is a* recurrent set of transitions *if* $\texttt{proj}_{\mathbf{x}'}(S) \subseteq \texttt{proj}_{\mathbf{x}}(S)$.

Clearly, both notions are equivalent: if S is a recurrent set of transitions then $\texttt{proj}_{\mathbf{x}}(S)$ is a recurrent set of states, and if S is a recurrent set of states then $\mathcal{Q} \cap (S \times S)$ is a recurrent set of transitions. Note that both notions correspond to what is known as *existential recurrent sets*, i.e., they guarantee the existence of nonterminating runs starting in some initial states, however, due to nondeterminism, these initial states might have terminating runs as well.

3 An Algorithm for Inferring MΦRFs

In this section we describe our algorithm for deciding the existence of (and constructing) MΦRFs, which is also able to find recurrent sets for certain nonterminating *SLC* loops. In what follows we assume a given *SLC* loop $\mathcal{Q}$ where variables range over the rationals (or reals), the case of integer variables is discussed after considering the rational case.

Let us start with an intuitive description of the algorithm and its possible outcomes. Our work started with the following crucial observation: given linear functions $\rho_1, \dots, \rho_l$ such that

- $\rho_1, \dots, \rho_l$ are nonnegative over $\texttt{proj}_{\mathbf{x}}(\mathcal{Q})$, i.e., over all enabled states;
- for some ρ_i, we have $\Delta\rho_i(\mathbf{x}'') > 0$ for at least one transition $\mathbf{x}'' \in \mathcal{Q}$; and
- $\mathcal{Q}' = \mathcal{Q} \wedge \Delta\rho_1(\mathbf{x}'') \leq 0 \wedge \cdots \wedge \Delta\rho_l(\mathbf{x}'') \leq 0$ has a MΦRF of depth d

then $\mathcal{Q}$ has a MΦRF of depth at most $d+1$. The proof of this observation is constructive, i.e., given a MΦRF τ' for $\mathcal{Q}'$, we can construct a MΦRF τ for $\mathcal{Q}$ using conic combinations of the components of τ' and $\rho_1, \dots, \rho_l$.

Let us assume that we have a procedure $F(\mathcal{Q})$ that picks some candidate functions $\rho_1, \dots, \rho_l$, i.e., nonnegative over $\texttt{proj}_{\mathbf{x}}(\mathcal{Q})$, and computes $F(\mathcal{Q}) = \mathcal{Q} \wedge \Delta\rho_1(\mathbf{x}'') \leq 0 \wedge \cdots \wedge \Delta\rho_l(\mathbf{x}'') \leq 0$. Clearly, if $F^d(\mathcal{Q}) = \emptyset$, for some $d > 0$, then using the above observation we can conclude that $\mathcal{Q}$ has a MΦRF of depth at most d. Obviously, the difficult part in defining F is how to pick functions $\rho_1, \dots, \rho_l$, and, moreover, how to ensure that if $\mathcal{Q}$ has a MΦRF of optimal depth d then $F^d(\mathcal{Q}) = \emptyset$, i.e., to find the optimal depth. For this, we observe that the set of all nonnegative functions over $\texttt{proj}_{\mathbf{x}}(\mathcal{Q})$ is a polyhedral cone, and thus it has generators $\rho_1, \dots, \rho_l$ that can be effectively computed. These $\rho_1, \dots, \rho_l$ turn out to be the right candidates to use. In addition, when using these candidates, we prove that if we cannot make progress, i.e., we get $F^{i-1}(\mathcal{Q}) = F^i(\mathcal{Q})$, then we have actually reached a recurrent set that witnesses nontermination.

In Sect. 3.1 we present the algorithm and discuss how it is used to decide existence of MΦRFs; in Sect. 3.2 we discuss how the algorithm can infer recurrent sets; and in Sect. 3.3 we discuss cases where the algorithm does not terminate and raise some questions on what happens in the limit.

3.1 Deciding Existence of MΦRFs

Definition 3. *The set of all nonnegative functions over a polyhedron $\mathcal{S} \subseteq \mathbb{Q}^n$, is defined as $\mathcal{S}^{\#} = \{(\vec{a}, b) \in \mathbb{Q}^{n+1} \mid \forall \mathbf{x} \in \mathcal{S}.\ \vec{a} \cdot \mathbf{x} + b \geq 0\}$.*

It is known that $\mathcal{S}^{\#}$ is a polyhedral cone [32, p. 112]. Equivalently, it is generated by a finite set of rays $(\vec{a}_1, b_1), \ldots, (\vec{a}_l, b_l)$. The cone generated by $\vec{a}_1, \ldots, \vec{a}_l$ is known as the dual of the cone $\texttt{rec.cone}(\mathcal{S})$ – we make use of this in Sect. 4. These rays are actually the ones that are important for the algorithm, as can be seen in the definition below, however, in the definition of $\mathcal{S}^{\#}$ we included the b_i's as they makes some statements smoother. Since $\mathcal{S}$ is a closed convex set, it is known that it is equal to the intersection of all half-spaces defined by the elements of $\mathcal{S}^{\#}$, i.e., $\mathcal{S} = \wedge\{\vec{a} \cdot \mathbf{x} + b \geq 0 \mid (\vec{a}, b) \in \mathcal{S}^{\#}\}$.

Definition 4. *Let $\mathcal{Q}$ be a SLC loop, and define*

$$F(\mathcal{Q}) = \mathcal{Q} \ \wedge \ \vec{a}_1 \cdot \mathbf{x} - \vec{a}_1 \cdot \mathbf{x}' \leq 0 \ \wedge \ \cdots \ \wedge \ \vec{a}_l \cdot \mathbf{x} - \vec{a}_l \cdot \mathbf{x}' \leq 0$$

where $(\vec{a}_1, b_1), \ldots, (\vec{a}_l, b_l)$ are the generators of $\texttt{proj}_{\mathbf{x}}(\mathcal{Q})^{\#}$.

It is easy to see that each $\vec{a}_i \cdot \mathbf{x} - \vec{a}_i \cdot \mathbf{x}' \leq 0$ above is actually $\Delta\rho_i(\mathbf{x}'') \leq 0$ where $\rho_i = \vec{a}_i \cdot \mathbf{x} + b_i \leq 0$. Intuitively, $F(\mathcal{Q})$ removes from $\mathcal{Q}$ all transitions $\mathbf{x}''$ for which there is $(\vec{a}, b) \in \texttt{proj}_{\mathbf{x}}(\mathcal{Q})^{\#}$ such that $\vec{a} \cdot \mathbf{x} - \vec{a} \cdot \mathbf{x}' > 0$. This is because any $(\vec{a}, b) \in \texttt{proj}_{\mathbf{x}}(\mathcal{Q})^{\#}$ is a conic combination of $(\vec{a}_1, b_1), \ldots, (\vec{a}_l, b_l)$, and thus for some i we must have $\vec{a}_i \cdot \mathbf{x} - \vec{a}_i \cdot \mathbf{x}' > 0$, otherwise we would have $\vec{a} \cdot \mathbf{x} - \vec{a} \cdot \mathbf{x}' = 0$.

Example 1. Consider Loop (1), whose transition polyhedron is defined by $\mathcal{Q} = \{x_1 \geq -x_3, x_1' = x_1 + x_2,\ x_2' = x_2 + x_3,\ x_3' = x_3 - 1\}$. The generators of $\texttt{proj}_{\mathbf{x}}(\mathcal{Q})^{\#}$ are $\{(1, 0, 1, 0), (0, 0, 0, 1)\}$—the last component of each generator is the free constant b, and the rest is $\vec{a}$. The corresponding nonnegative functions are $\rho_1(x_1, x_2, x_3) = x_1 + x_3$ and $\rho_2(x_1, x_2, x_3) = 1$. Computing $F(\mathcal{Q})$ results in:

$$\mathcal{Q}' = \mathcal{Q} \wedge \Delta\rho_1(\mathbf{x}'') \leq 0 \wedge \Delta\rho_2(\mathbf{x}'') \leq 0 = \mathcal{Q} \wedge (x_1 + x_3) - (x_1' + x_3') \leq 0 \quad (6)$$

This eliminates any transition for which the quantity $x_1 + x_3$ decreases. □

In what follows we aim at showing that $\mathcal{Q}$ has a MΦRF of optimal depth d iff $F^d(\mathcal{Q}) = \emptyset$. We first state some auxiliary lemmas.

Lemma 3. *If $\mathcal{Q}' = F(\mathcal{Q})$ has a MΦRF of depth at most d, then $\mathcal{Q}$ has a MΦRF of depth at most $d + 1$.*

Proof. Consider the generators $(\vec{a}_1, b_1), \ldots, (\vec{a}_l, b_l)$ used in Definition 4, and let $\rho_i(\mathbf{x}) = \vec{a}_i \cdot \mathbf{x} + b_i$. We have $\mathcal{Q}' = \mathcal{Q} \wedge \Delta\rho_1(\mathbf{x}'') \leq 0 \wedge \cdots \wedge \Delta\rho_l(\mathbf{x}'') \leq 0$. Let $\tau = \langle g_1, \ldots, g_d \rangle$ be a MΦRF for $\mathcal{Q}'$, and w.l.o.g. assume that it is of optimal depth. Next, we show how to construct a MΦRF $\langle g_1' + 1, \ldots, g_d' + 1, g_{d+1} \rangle$ for $\mathcal{Q}$. Note that simply appending $\rho_1, \ldots, \rho_l$ to τ does not always produce a MΦRF for $\mathcal{Q}$, since the components of τ are not guaranteed to decrease over $\mathcal{Q} \setminus \mathcal{Q}'$.

If g_1 is decreasing over $\mathcal{Q}$, we define $g_1'(\mathbf{x}) = g_1(\mathbf{x})$, otherwise we have

$$\mathbf{x}'' \in \mathcal{Q} \rightarrow \Delta\rho_1(\mathbf{x}'') > 0 \vee \cdots \vee \Delta\rho_l(\mathbf{x}'') > 0 \vee \Delta g_1(\mathbf{x}'') - 1 \geq 0 \tag{7}$$
$$\mathbf{x}'' \in \mathcal{Q} \not\rightarrow \Delta\rho_1(\mathbf{x}'') > 0 \vee \cdots \vee \Delta\rho_l(\mathbf{x}'') > 0 \tag{8}$$

and by Lemma 2 there are nonnegative constants $\mu_1, \ldots, \mu_l$ such that

$$\mathbf{x}'' \in \mathcal{Q} \rightarrow \Delta g_1(\mathbf{x}'') - 1 + \sum_{i=1}^{l} \mu_i \Delta\rho_i(\mathbf{x}'') \geq 0. \tag{9}$$

Define $g_1'(\mathbf{x}) = g_1(\mathbf{x}) + \sum_{i=1}^{l} \mu_i \rho_i(\mathbf{x})$. Clearly, $\mathbf{x}'' \in \mathcal{Q} \rightarrow \Delta g_1'(\mathbf{x}'') \geq 1$. Moreover, since $\rho_1, \ldots, \rho_l$ are nonnegative on all enabled states, g_1' is nonnegative on the states on which g_1 is nonnegative. If $d > 1$, we proceed with

$$\mathcal{Q}^{(1)} = \mathcal{Q} \cap \{\mathbf{x}'' \mid g_1'(\mathbf{x}) \leq (-1)\}. \tag{10}$$

If g_2 is decreasing over $\mathcal{Q}^{(1)}$, let $g_2' = g_2$, otherwise, since transitions in $\mathcal{Q}' \cap \mathcal{Q}^{(1)}$ are ranked by $\langle g_2, \ldots, g_d \rangle$ we have

$$\mathbf{x}'' \in \mathcal{Q}^{(1)} \rightarrow \Delta\rho_1(\mathbf{x}'') > 0 \vee \cdots \vee \Delta\rho_l(\mathbf{x}'') > 0 \vee \Delta g_2(\mathbf{x}'') - 1 \geq 0 \tag{11}$$
$$\mathbf{x}'' \in \mathcal{Q}^{(1)} \not\rightarrow \Delta\rho_1(\mathbf{x}'') > 0 \vee \cdots \vee \Delta\rho_l(\mathbf{x}'') > 0 \tag{12}$$

and again by Lemma 2 we can construct the desired g_2' as we did for g_1'. In general, for any $j \leq d$ we construct g_{j+1}' such that $\Delta g_{j+1}'(\mathbf{x}'') \geq 1$ over

$$\mathcal{Q}^{(j)} = \mathcal{Q} \cap \{\mathbf{x}'' \in \mathbb{Q}^{2n} \mid g_1'(\mathbf{x}) \leq (-1) \wedge \cdots \wedge g_j'(\mathbf{x}) \leq (-1)\} \tag{13}$$

and $\mathbf{x}'' \in \mathcal{Q} \wedge g_j(\mathbf{x}) \geq 0 \rightarrow g_j'(\mathbf{x}) \geq 0$. Finally we define

$$\mathcal{Q}^{(d)} = \mathcal{Q} \cap \{\mathbf{x}'' \in \mathbb{Q}^{2n} \mid g_1'(\mathbf{x}) \leq (-1) \wedge \cdots \wedge g_d'(\mathbf{x}) \leq (-1)\} \tag{14}$$

and note that

$$\mathbf{x}'' \in \mathcal{Q}^{(d)} \rightarrow \Delta\rho_1(\mathbf{x}'') > 0 \vee \cdots \vee \Delta\rho_l(\mathbf{x}'') > 0 \tag{15}$$

We assume that no ρ_i is redundant in (15), otherwise we take an irredundant subset. Now from (15) we get

$$\mathbf{x}'' \in (\mathcal{Q}^{(d)} \wedge \Delta\rho_1(\mathbf{x}'') \leq 0 \wedge \cdots \wedge \Delta\rho_{l-1}(\mathbf{x}'') \leq 0) \rightarrow \Delta\rho_l(\mathbf{x}'') > 0 \tag{16}$$

and since the left-hand side is a polyhedron, there is a constant $c > 0$ such that

$$\mathbf{x}'' \in (\mathcal{Q}^{(d)} \wedge \Delta\rho_1(\mathbf{x}'') \leq 0 \wedge \cdots \wedge \Delta\rho_{l-1}(\mathbf{x}'') \leq 0) \rightarrow \Delta\rho_l(\mathbf{x}'') \geq c. \tag{17}$$

W.l.o.g. we may assume that $c \geq 1$, otherwise we divide ρ_l by c. Then we have

$$\mathbf{x}'' \in \mathcal{Q}^{(d)} \rightarrow \Delta\rho_1(\mathbf{x}'') > 0 \vee \cdots \vee \Delta\rho_{l-1}(\mathbf{x}'') > 0 \vee \Delta\rho_l(\mathbf{x}'') - 1 \geq 0 \tag{18}$$
$$\mathbf{x}'' \in \mathcal{Q}^{(d)} \not\rightarrow \Delta\rho_1(\mathbf{x}'') > 0 \vee \cdots \vee \Delta\rho_{l-1}(\mathbf{x}'') > 0 \tag{19}$$

By Lemma 2 we can construct $g_{d+1} = \rho_l + \sum_{i=1}^{l-1} \mu_i \rho_i$ such that $\mathbf{x}'' \in \mathcal{Q}^{(d)} \rightarrow \Delta g_{d+1}(\mathbf{x}'') \geq 1$. Moreover, g_{d+1} is nonnegative over $\mathcal{Q}^{(d)}$ and thus it ranks all $\mathcal{Q}^{(d)}$. Now, by construction, $\tau' = \langle g_1' + 1, \ldots, g_d' + 1, g_{d+1} \rangle$ is a MΦRF for $\mathcal{Q}$. □

Algorithm 1. Deciding existence of MΦRFs and inferring recurrent sets

`FindMLRF`($\mathcal{Q}$)
begin
1 **if** ($\mathcal{Q}$ is empty) **then return** $\emptyset$
2 **else**
3 Compute the generators $(\vec{a}_1, b_1), \ldots, (\vec{a}_l, b_l)$ of $\mathtt{proj}_{\mathbf{x}}(\mathcal{Q})^{\#}$
4 Let $\mathcal{Q}' = \mathcal{Q} \wedge \vec{a}_1 \cdot \mathbf{x} - \vec{a}_1 \cdot \mathbf{x}' \leq 0 \wedge \cdots \wedge \vec{a}_l \cdot \mathbf{x} - \vec{a}_l \cdot \mathbf{x}' \leq 0$
5 **if** ($\mathcal{Q}' == \mathcal{Q}$) **then return** $\mathcal{Q}$
6 **else return** `FindMLRF` ($\mathcal{Q}'$)

Lemma 4. *If $\mathcal{Q}$ has a MΦRF of depth d then $\mathcal{Q}' = F(\mathcal{Q})$ has a MΦRF of depth at most $d-1$.*

Proof. Let $\tau = \langle \rho_1, \ldots, \rho_k \rangle$ be an MΦRF for $\mathcal{Q}$, of optimal depth $k \leq d$. As shown in [6], there is no loss of generality in assuming a special form of MΦRF (nested MΦRF [25]) in which the last component is nonnegative; so we assume $\rho_k(\mathbf{x}) \geq 0$ over $\mathtt{proj}_{\mathbf{x}}(\mathcal{Q})$. Clearly $\tau' = \langle \rho_1, \ldots, \rho_{k-1} \rangle$ is a MΦRF for $\mathcal{Q} \wedge \Delta\rho_k(\mathbf{x}'') \leq 0$. Now since ρ_k is a conic combination of the generators of $\mathtt{proj}_{\mathbf{x}}(\mathcal{Q})^{\#}$ we have $\mathcal{Q}' = F(\mathcal{Q}) \subseteq \mathcal{Q} \wedge \Delta\rho_k(\mathbf{x}'') \leq 0$ and thus τ' is a MΦRF for $\mathcal{Q}'$ as well. □

Lemma 5. *$\mathcal{Q}$ has a MΦRF of depth d iff $F^d(\mathcal{Q}) = \emptyset$.*

Proof. For the first direction, suppose that $\mathcal{Q}$ has a MΦRF of depth at most d, then applying Lemma 4 iteratively we must reach $F^k(\mathcal{Q}) = \emptyset$ for some $k \leq d$, thus $F^d(\mathcal{Q}) = \emptyset$. For the other direction, suppose $F^d(\mathcal{Q}) = \emptyset$, then using Lemma 3 we can construct a MΦRF of depth d. □

Procedure `FindMLRF`($\mathcal{Q}$) of Algorithm 1 implements the above idea, it basically applies F (lines 3–4) iteratively until it either reaches an empty set (Line 1) or stabilizes (Line 5). If it returns $\emptyset$ then $\mathcal{Q}$ has a MΦRF and we can construct one simply by invoking the polynomial-time procedure for synthesizing nested MΦRFs as described in [6], or construct one as in the proof of Lemma 3. Note that, by Lemma 5, if we bound the recursion depth by a parameter d, then the algorithm is actually a decision procedure for the existence of MΦRFs of depth at most d. The case in which it returns a nonempty set is discussed in Sect. 3.2.

The complexity of Algorithm 1 is exponential since computing the generators at Line 3 might take exponential time. In Sect. 4 we provide a polynomial-time implementation that avoids computing the generators.

Example 2. Let us apply Algorithm 1 to Loop (1). We start by calling `FindMLRF` with $\mathcal{Q} = \{x_1 \geq -x_3, x_1' = x_1 + x_2, x_2' = x_2 + x_3, x_3' = x_3 - 1\}$ and proceed as follows ($\mathcal{Q}_i$ represents the polyhedron passed in the i-th call to `FindMLRF`):

$\mathcal{Q}_i$	Generators of $\mathtt{proj}_{\mathbf{x}}(\mathcal{Q}_i)^{\#}$
$\mathcal{Q}_0 = \mathcal{Q}$	$\{(\mathbf{1},\mathbf{0},\mathbf{1},\mathbf{0}),(\mathbf{0},\mathbf{0},\mathbf{0},\mathbf{1})\}$
$\mathcal{Q}_1 = \mathcal{Q}_0 \wedge (x_1+x_3)-(x_1'+x_3') \leq 0$	$\{(\mathbf{0},\mathbf{1},\mathbf{0},-\mathbf{1}),(1,0,1,0),(0,0,0,1)\}$
$\mathcal{Q}_2 = \mathcal{Q}_1 \wedge x_2 - x_2' \leq 0$	$\{(\mathbf{0},\mathbf{0},\mathbf{1},\mathbf{0}),(0,1,0,-1),(1,0,1,0),(0,0,0,1)\}$
$\mathcal{Q}_3 = \mathcal{Q}_2 \wedge x_3 - x_3' \leq 0 = \emptyset$	

Explanation:

- $\mathcal{Q}_0$ is not empty. We compute the generators of $\mathtt{proj}_{\mathbf{x}}(\mathcal{Q}_0)^{\#}$, which define the nonnegative functions $\rho_1(x_1,x_2,x_3)=x_1+x_3$ and $\rho_2(x_1,x_2,x_3)=1$, and then compute $\mathcal{Q}_1 = \mathcal{Q}_0 \wedge \Delta\rho_1(\mathbf{x}'') \leq 0 \wedge \Delta\rho_2(\mathbf{x}'') \leq 0$; and since it differs from $\mathcal{Q}_0$ we recursively call $\mathtt{FindMLRF}(\mathcal{Q}_1)$.
- $\mathcal{Q}_1$ is not empty. We compute the generators of $\mathtt{proj}_{\mathbf{x}}(\mathcal{Q}_1)^{\#}$, which define the nonnegative function $\rho_3(x_1,x_2,x_3)=x_2-1$, and then compute $\mathcal{Q}_2 = \mathcal{Q}_1 \wedge \Delta\rho_3(\mathbf{x}'') \leq 0$; and since it differs from $\mathcal{Q}_1$ we recursively call $\mathtt{FindMLRF}(\mathcal{Q}_2)$. Note that the only new generator wrt. the previous iteration is the one in bold font, the others are ignored as they have been used for computing $\mathcal{Q}_1$.
- $\mathcal{Q}_2$ is not empty. We compute the generators of $\mathtt{proj}_{\mathbf{x}}(\mathcal{Q}_2)^{\#}$, which define the nonnegative function $\rho_4(x_1,x_2,x_3)=x_3$, and then compute $\mathcal{Q}_3 = \mathcal{Q}_2 \wedge \Delta\rho_4(\mathbf{x}'') \leq 0$; and since it differs from $\mathcal{Q}_2$ we recursively call $\mathtt{FindMLRF}(\mathcal{Q}_3)$.
- $\mathcal{Q}_3$ is empty, so we return $\emptyset$.

Since we have reached an empty set in 3 iterations, we conclude that Loop (1) has a MΦRF of optimal depth 3, e.g., $\langle x_3+1, x_2+1, x_1+x_3+1\rangle$. □

For the case of integer-valued variables, i.e., when considering $I(\mathcal{Q})$, it is know that $I(\mathcal{Q})$ has a MΦRF iff the integer hull $\mathcal{Q}_I$ of $\mathcal{Q}$ has a MΦRF (over the rationals) [6, Sect. 5]. Thus, $I(\mathcal{Q})$ has a MΦRF of depth d iff $F^d(\mathcal{Q}_I)=\emptyset$.

3.2 Inference of Recurrent Sets

Next we discuss the case in which $\mathtt{FindMLRF}(\mathcal{Q})$ returns a nonempty set of transition $\mathcal{S} \subseteq \mathcal{Q}$ (Line 5), and show that $\mathcal{S}$ is always a recurrent set, implying that $\mathcal{Q}$ is nonterminating. In Sect. 5 we discuss an experimental evaluation regarding the use of Algorithm 1 for proving nontermination of control-flow graphs.

Lemma 6. *Let $\mathcal{S} \subseteq \mathbb{Q}^{2n}$ be a polyhedron, if $\mathcal{S}=F(\mathcal{S})$ then $\mathcal{S}$ is a recurrent set.*

Proof. According Definition 2, we need to show that $\mathtt{proj}_{\mathbf{x}'}(\mathcal{S}) \subseteq \mathtt{proj}_{\mathbf{x}}(\mathcal{S})$. Since $\mathtt{proj}_{\mathbf{x}}(\mathcal{S})$ and $\mathtt{proj}_{\mathbf{x}'}(\mathcal{S})$ are closed convex sets, each is an intersection of half-spaces that are defined by the corresponding sets $\mathtt{proj}_{\mathbf{x}}(\mathcal{S})^{\#}$ and $\mathtt{proj}_{\mathbf{x}'}(\mathcal{S})^{\#}$, e.g., $\mathtt{proj}_{\mathbf{x}}(\mathcal{S}) = \wedge\{\vec{a}\cdot\mathbf{x}+b \geq 0 \mid (\vec{a},b) \in \mathtt{proj}_{\mathbf{x}}(\mathcal{S})^{\#}\}$. Thus, it is enough to show that $\mathtt{proj}_{\mathbf{x}}(\mathcal{S})^{\#} \subseteq \mathtt{proj}_{\mathbf{x}'}(\mathcal{S})^{\#}$.

Let $(\vec{a},b) \in \mathtt{proj}_{\mathbf{x}}(\mathcal{S})^{\#}$, we show that $(\vec{a},b) \in \mathtt{proj}_{\mathbf{x}'}(\mathcal{S})^{\#}$ as well. Define $\rho(\mathbf{x}) = \vec{a}\cdot\mathbf{x}+b$. Since $\mathcal{S}=F(\mathcal{S})$, by definition of F we have

$$\mathbf{x}'' = (\mathbf{x},\mathbf{x}') \in \mathcal{S} \models \rho(\mathbf{x}) - \rho(\mathbf{x}') \leq 0 \tag{20}$$

which together with the fact that ρ is nonnegative over $\mathtt{proj}_{\mathbf{x}}(\mathcal{S})$ implies that $\rho(\mathbf{x}') \geq 0$ holds for any $\mathbf{x}' \in \mathtt{proj}_{\mathbf{x}'}(\mathcal{S})$, and thus $(\vec{a}, b) \in \mathtt{proj}_{\mathbf{x}'}(\mathcal{S})$. □

Corollary 1. *If* `FindMLRF`$(\mathcal{Q})$ *returns* $\mathcal{S} \neq \emptyset$ *then* $\mathcal{S}$ *is a recurrent set, and thus* $\mathcal{Q}$ *is nonterminating.*

Proof. This follows from Lemma 6, since the algorithm returns a nonempty set $\mathcal{S} \subseteq \mathcal{Q}$ iff it finds one such that $\mathcal{S} = F(\mathcal{S})$ (Line 5 of `FindMLRF`). □

Example 3. Let us apply Algorithm 1 to the following loop, from [34]:

$$\mathtt{while}\ (x_1 - x_2 \geq 1)\ \mathtt{do}\ x_1' = -x_1 + x_2,\ x_2' = x_2 \tag{21}$$

This loop does not terminate, e.g., for $x_1 = -1, x_2 = -2$. We call `FindMLRF` with $\mathcal{Q} = \{x_1 - x_2 \geq 1, x_1' = -x_1 + x_2, x_2' = x_2\}$, and proceed as in Example 2:

$\mathcal{Q}_i$	Generators of $\mathtt{proj}_{\mathbf{x}}(\mathcal{Q}_i)^{\#}$
$\mathcal{Q}_0 = \mathcal{Q}$	$\{(\mathbf{1}, \mathbf{-1}, \mathbf{-1}), (\mathbf{0}, \mathbf{0}, \mathbf{1})\}$
$\mathcal{Q}_1 = \mathcal{Q}_0 \wedge (x_1 - x_2) - (x_1' - x_2') \leq 0$	$\{(\mathbf{-2}, \mathbf{1}, \mathbf{0}), (1, -1, -1), (0, 0, 1)\}$
$\mathcal{Q}_2 = \mathcal{Q}_1 \wedge (-2x_1 + x_2) - (-2x_1' + x_2') \leq 0$	$\{(\mathbf{2}, \mathbf{-1}, \mathbf{0}), (\mathbf{-1}, \mathbf{0}, \mathbf{-1}), (-2, 1, 0), (0, 0, 1)\}$
$\mathcal{Q}_3 = \mathcal{Q}_2 \wedge (2x_1 - x_2) - (2x_1' - x_2') \leq 0 \wedge (-x_1) - (-x_1') \leq 0$	

Explanation:

- $\mathcal{Q}_0$ is not empty. We compute the generators of $\mathtt{proj}_{\mathbf{x}}(\mathcal{Q}_0)^{\#}$, which define the nonnegative functions $\rho_1(x_1, x_2, x_3) = x_1 - x_2 - 1$ and $\rho_2(x_1, x_2, x_3) = 1$, and then compute $\mathcal{Q}_1 = \mathcal{Q}_0 \wedge \Delta\rho_1(\mathbf{x}'') \leq 0 \wedge \Delta\rho_2(\mathbf{x}'') \leq 0$; and since it differs from $\mathcal{Q}_0$ we recursively call `FindMLRF`$(\mathcal{Q}_1)$.
- $\mathcal{Q}_1$ is not empty. We compute the generators of $\mathtt{proj}_{\mathbf{x}}(\mathcal{Q}_1)^{\#}$, which define the nonnegative function $\rho_3(x_1, x_2, x_3) = -2x_1 + x_2$, and then compute $\mathcal{Q}_2 = \mathcal{Q}_1 \wedge \Delta\rho_3(\mathbf{x}'') \leq 0$; and since it differs from $\mathcal{Q}_1$ we invoke `FindMLRF`$(\mathcal{Q}_2)$.
- $\mathcal{Q}_2$ is not empty. We compute the generators of $\mathtt{proj}_{\mathbf{x}}(\mathcal{Q}_2)^{\#}$, which define the nonnegative functions $\rho_4(x_1, x_2, x_3) = 2x_1 - x_2$ and $\rho_5(x_1, x_2, x_3) = -x_1 - 1$, and then compute $\mathcal{Q}_3 = \mathcal{Q}_2 \wedge \Delta\rho_4(\mathbf{x}'') \leq 0 \wedge \Delta\rho_5(\mathbf{x}'') \leq 0$; and since it is equal to $\mathcal{Q}_2$ ($\Delta\rho_4(\mathbf{x}'') \leq 0$ and $\Delta\rho_5(\mathbf{x}'') \leq 0$ are implied by $\mathcal{Q}_2$) we return $\mathcal{Q}_2$.

Thus, $\mathcal{Q}_2$ is a recurrent set of transitions and we conclude that Loop (21) is nonterminating. Projecting $\mathcal{Q}_2$ on x_1 and x_2 we get $\{x_1 \leq -1, 2x_1 - x_2 = 0\}$, which is the corresponding recurrent set of states.

We remark that Loop (21) has a fixed point $(-1, -2)$, i.e., from state $x_1 = -1, x_2 = -2$ we have a transition to $x_1 = -1, x_2 = -2$. The algorithm also detects nontermination of loops that do not have fixed points. For example, if we change $x_2' = x_2$ in Loop (21) by $x_2' = x_2 - 1$, we obtain a recurrent set of transitions $\mathcal{S}$ such that $\mathtt{proj}_{\mathbf{x}}(\mathcal{S}) = \{-2x_2 \geq 3, 4x_1 - 2x_2 = 1\}$. □

Now that we have seen the possible outcomes of the algorithm (in case it terminates), we see that this approach reveals an interesting relation between seeking MΦRFs and seeking recurrent sets. A possible view is that the algorithm seeks a recurrent set (of a particular form) and when it concludes that no such set exists, i.e., reaching $\emptyset$, we can construct a MΦRF.

The recurrent sets inferred by Algorithm 1 belong to a narrower class than that of Definition 2. In fact, the condition in Definition 2 is equivalent to requiring that if $\rho(\mathbf{x}) \geq 0$ over $\mathtt{proj}_{\mathbf{x}}(\mathcal{S})$ then $\rho(\mathbf{x}) \geq 0$ over $\mathtt{proj}_{\mathbf{x}'}(\mathcal{S})$. In our recurrent sets, we further have $\rho(\mathbf{x}') \geq \rho(\mathbf{x})$ for any $(\mathbf{x}, \mathbf{x}') \in \mathcal{S}$. We call a recurrent set satisfying this stronger condition *monotonic*.

Example 4. Consider the following *SLC* loop:

$$\mathtt{while}\ (x \geq 0)\ \mathtt{do}\ x' = 1 - x \tag{22}$$

The largest recurrent set of transitions for this loop is $\{x \geq 0, x \leq 1, x' = 1-x\}$, and it is not monotonic. Algorithm 1 infers the largest *monotonic* recurrent set $\{x = \frac{1}{2}, x' = \frac{1}{2}\}$, where it first eliminates all transitions for which $x - x' > 0$, i.e., $x \in (\frac{1}{2}, \infty)$, and then those for which $(-x) - (-x') > 0$, i.e., $x \in [0, \frac{1}{2})$. □

At this point, it is natural to explore the difference between the two kinds recurrent sets. The most intriguing question is if nonterminating *SLC* loops always have monotonic recurrent sets. This is true for loops that have a fixed point, i.e., there is $\mathbf{x}$ such that $(\mathbf{x}, \mathbf{x}) \in \mathcal{Q}$, however, this question is left open for the general case. We note that the *geometric nontermination argument* introduced in [26] is also related to monotonic recurrent sets. Specifically, it is easy to show that in some cases (when the nonnegative coefficients μ_i and λ_i, in Def. 5 of [26], are either 0 or at least 1), we can construct a monotonic recurrent set.

Let us discuss now the case of integer loops. First, the difference between the two kinds of recurrent sets is clear in the integer case: Loop (22) of Example 4 has a recurrent set of integers $\{(0,1), (1,0)\}$, but does not have a monotonic recurrent set of integers. Apart from this difference, a natural question is whether the recurrent set $\mathcal{S}$ returned by $\mathtt{FindMLRF}(\mathcal{Q}_I)$, or more precisely $I(\mathcal{S})$, witnesses nontermination of $I(\mathcal{Q})$. This is not true in general (see Example 5 below), however, there are practical cases for which it is true.

Lemma 7. *Let $\mathcal{Q}$ be a SLC loop with affine update $\mathbf{x}' = U\mathbf{x} + \mathbf{c}$, and assume the coefficients of U and $\mathbf{c}$ are integer. If $\mathcal{S}$ is a recurrent set for $\mathcal{Q}$, and $I(\mathcal{S})$ is not empty, then $I(\mathcal{S})$ is recurrent for $I(\mathcal{Q})$.*

Proof. Since the update is affine with integer coefficients, it follows that any state in $\mathtt{proj}_{\mathbf{x}}(I(\mathcal{S}))$ has a successor in $\mathtt{proj}_{\mathbf{x}'}(I(\mathcal{S})) \subseteq \mathtt{proj}_{\mathbf{x}}(I(\mathcal{S}))$, which is the definition of a recurrent set. □

In the context of the above lemma, assuming that $\mathcal{S} = \mathtt{FindMLRF}(\mathcal{Q}_I)$, if $\mathcal{S} \neq \emptyset$ and $I(\mathcal{S}) = \emptyset$ all we can conclude (when the algorithm is applied to $\mathcal{Q}_I$) is that $I(\mathcal{Q})$ does not have a MΦRF, we cannot conclude anything about nontermination as in the rational case. For example, for the loop $\mathcal{Q}_I = \mathcal{Q} = \{x \geq 0, x' = 10 - 2x\}$ we have $\mathcal{S} = \{(3\frac{1}{3}, 3\frac{1}{3})\}$ and $I(\mathcal{S}) = \emptyset$ and the loop is terminating over the integers, and for the loop $\mathcal{Q}_I = \mathcal{Q} = \{x \geq 0, x' = 1 - x\}$

we have $\mathcal{S} = \{(\frac{1}{2}, \frac{1}{2})\}$ and $I(\mathcal{S}) = \emptyset$ and the loop is nonterminating over the integers.

The next example demonstrates that the above lemma does not extend to *SLC* loops in general, even when the algorithm is applied to the integer hull $\mathcal{Q}_I$. This is because it is not guaranteed that any integer state $\mathbf{x} \in I(\mathtt{proj}_{\mathbf{x}}(\mathcal{S}))$ has an integer successor $\mathbf{x}' \in I(\mathtt{proj}_{\mathbf{x}'}(\mathcal{S}))$.

Example 5. Consider the following loop

$$\mathtt{while}\ (x \geq 2)\ \mathtt{do}\ x' = \frac{3}{2}x \tag{23}$$

which is nonterminating over the rationals, for any $x \geq 2$, and is terminating over the integers. For the integer case, the loop stops (or blocks) if for some integer x, there is no integer x' such that that equality $x' = \frac{3}{2}x$ holds. The algorithm returns $\mathcal{Q}$ as a recurrent set, but $I(\mathcal{Q})$, which is not empty, is not a recurrent set as the loop is terminating over the integers. Note that the transition polyhedron is integral, i.e., $\mathcal{Q} = \mathcal{Q}_I$. □

3.3 Cases in Which Algorithm 1 Does Not Terminate

When Algorithm 1 terminates, it either finds a MΦRF or proves nontermination of the given loop. This means that if applied to a terminating loop that has no MΦRF, Algorithm 1 will not terminate, e.g., for the loop $\mathcal{Q}_t = \{x_1 \geq x_2, x_2 \geq 1, x_1' = 2x_1, x_2' = 3x_2\}$, which is terminating [25]. Algorithm 1 might also fail to terminate when applied to some nonterminating loops, e.g., the nonterminating loop [26] $\mathcal{Q}_{nt} = \{x_1 + x_2 \geq 3, x_1' = 3x_1 - 2,\ x_2' = 2x_2\}$.

When the algorithm does not terminate, the iterates $F^i(\mathcal{Q})$ converge to $\mathcal{Q}_\omega = \cap_{i \geq 0} F^i(\mathcal{Q})$. For example, for the terminating loop $\mathcal{Q}_t$ above, we have $\mathcal{Q}_\omega = \emptyset$, and for the nonterminating loop $\mathcal{Q}_{nt}$ above, we have $\mathcal{Q}_\omega = \{x_1 \geq 1, x_2' = 2x_2,\ x_1' = 3x_1 - 2\}$ which is a monotonic recurrent set. Given these examples, we ask: (i) is it true that $\mathcal{Q}_\omega = \emptyset$ iff $\mathcal{Q}$ is terminating? (ii) is it true that if $\mathcal{Q}_\omega \neq \emptyset$ then it is a (monotonic) recurrent set? For *deterministic* loops, it is easy to show that termination implies $\mathcal{Q}_\omega = \emptyset$, and that if $\mathcal{Q}_\omega \neq \emptyset$ then $\mathcal{Q}_\omega$ is a monotonic recurrent set. The general questions are left open.

4 MΦRFs and the Displacement Polyhedron

In this section we introduce an alternative representation for *SLC* loops, that we refer to as the *displacement polyhedron*, and show that Algorithm 1, or more precisely the check $F^k(\mathcal{Q}) = \emptyset$, has a simple encoding in this representation that can be preformed in polynomial time, specifically, we show that it is equivalent to checking for unsatisfiability of a particular linear constraint system. Note that we already know that deciding the existence of a MΦRF of depth d can be done in polynomial time [6], so in this sense we do not provide new knowledge. However, apart from the efficient encoding of the check $F^k(\mathcal{Q}) = \emptyset$, the new formulation has some importance advantages:

- Unlike existing algorithms for inferring MΦRFs [6, 26], it allows synthesizing witnesses for the *nonexistence* of a MΦRF of a given depth, see Sect. 4.1.
- It provides a new tool for addressing the general MΦRF problem, i.e., without a depth bound, that is still open, see Sect. 4.2.
- Some nontrivial observations about termination and nontermination *SLC* loops are made straightforward through this representation, see Sect. 4.3.

Next, we define the notion of the *displacement polyhedron*, show how the check $F^d(\mathcal{Q}) = \emptyset$ can be encoded in this representation, and then discuss each of the above points.

Definition 5. *Given a SLC loop* $\mathcal{Q} \subseteq \mathbb{Q}^{2n}$*, we define its* displacement polyhedron *as* $\mathcal{R} = \mathtt{proj}_{\mathbf{x},\mathbf{y}}(\mathcal{Q} \wedge \mathbf{x}' = \mathbf{x} + \mathbf{y}) \subseteq \mathbb{Q}^{2n}$.

Note that the projection drops $\mathbf{x}'$. Intuitively, an execution step using $\mathcal{Q}$ starts from a state $\mathbf{x}$, and chooses a state $\mathbf{x}'$ such that $\binom{\mathbf{x}}{\mathbf{x}'} \in \mathcal{Q}$. To perform the step using $\mathcal{R}$, select $\mathbf{y}$ such that $\binom{\mathbf{x}}{\mathbf{y}} \in \mathcal{R}$ and let the new state be $\mathbf{x} + \mathbf{y}$. By definition, we obtain the same transitions. The constraint representation of $\mathcal{R}$ can be derived from that of $\mathcal{Q}$ as follows. Let $\mathcal{Q} \equiv [A''\binom{\mathbf{x}}{\mathbf{x}'} \leq \mathbf{c}'']$ where A'' is the matrix below on the left (see Sect. 2), then $\mathcal{R} \equiv [R\binom{\mathbf{x}}{\mathbf{y}} \leq \mathbf{c}'']$ where R is the matrix below on the right:

$$A'' = \begin{pmatrix} B & 0 \\ A & A' \end{pmatrix} \qquad R = \begin{pmatrix} B & 0 \\ A + A' & A' \end{pmatrix} \tag{24}$$

Example 6. Consider Loop (1) which is defined by $\mathcal{Q} = \{x_1 \geq -x_3, x_1' = x_1 + x_2, x_2' = x_2 + x_3, x_3' = x_3 - 1\}$. The corresponding displacement polyhedron is $\mathcal{R} = \{x_1 \geq -x_3, y_1 = x_2, y_2 = x_3, y_3 = -1\}$. □

We will show that the displacement polyhedron $\mathcal{R}_k$ of $\mathcal{Q}_k = F^k(\mathcal{Q})$ is equivalent to the following polyhedron projected onto $\mathbf{x}$ and $\mathbf{y}_0$

$$\widehat{\mathcal{R}}_k \equiv\ R\tbinom{\mathbf{x}}{\mathbf{y}_0} \leq \mathbf{c}'' \ \wedge\ R\tbinom{\mathbf{y}_0}{\mathbf{y}_1} \leq \mathbf{0} \wedge\ R\tbinom{\mathbf{y}_1}{\mathbf{y}_2} \leq \mathbf{0}\ \wedge\ \dots\ \wedge\ R\tbinom{\mathbf{y}_{k-1}}{\mathbf{y}_k} \leq \mathbf{0} \tag{25}$$

Now since, by Definition 5, $\mathcal{Q}_k$ is empty iff $\mathcal{R}_k$ is empty, the check $F^k(\mathcal{Q}) = \emptyset$ is reduced to checking that (25) is empty, which can be done in polynomial time in the bit-size of the constraint representation of $\mathcal{Q}$ and the parameter k. It is important to observe that the first conjunct $R\binom{\mathbf{x}}{\mathbf{y}_0} \leq \mathbf{c}''$ of (25) is actually $\mathcal{R}$, and that each $R\binom{\mathbf{y}_i}{\mathbf{y}_{i+1}} \leq \mathbf{0}$ is actually $\mathtt{rec.cone}(\mathcal{R})$. Observe also how the conjuncts of (25) are connected, i.e., that the lower part of the variables vector of each conjunct is equal to the upper part of the next one.

We first show how $\mathcal{R}_{k+1}$ can be obtained from $\mathcal{R}_k$ similarly to $\mathcal{Q}_{k+1} = F(\mathcal{Q}_k)$.

Lemma 8. *Let* $(\vec{a}_1, b_1), \dots, (\vec{a}_l, b_l)$ *generate the cone* $\mathtt{proj}_{\mathbf{x}}(\mathcal{R})^{\#}$. *Then* $\mathcal{R}_{k+1} = \mathcal{R}_k \wedge -\vec{a}_1 \cdot \mathbf{y} \leq 0 \wedge \cdots \wedge -\vec{a}_l \cdot \mathbf{y} \leq 0$.

Proof. Follows from the fact that $\mathtt{proj}_{\mathbf{x}}(\mathcal{Q}_k) = \mathtt{proj}_{\mathbf{x}}(\mathcal{R}_k)$, and thus $\mathtt{proj}_{\mathbf{x}}(\mathcal{Q}_k)^{\#}$ and $\mathtt{proj}_{\mathbf{x}}(\mathcal{R}_k)^{\#}$ are the same, and that for $\rho(\mathbf{x}) = \vec{a} \cdot \mathbf{x} + b$ we have $\Delta\rho(\mathbf{x}'') = \rho(\mathbf{x}) - \rho(\mathbf{x}') = -\vec{a} \cdot \mathbf{y}$, by definition of the displacement polyhedron. □

Lemma 9. *Let $(\vec{a}_1, b_1), \ldots, (\vec{a}_l, b_l)$ generate the cone $\texttt{proj}_{\mathbf{x}}(\mathcal{R})^{\#}$. Then the condition $-\vec{a}_1 \cdot \mathbf{y} \leq 0 \wedge \cdots \wedge -\vec{a}_l \cdot \mathbf{y} \leq 0$ of Lemma 8 is equivalent to $M\mathbf{y} \leq 0$, where M is such that $\texttt{proj}_{\mathbf{x}}(\mathcal{R}) \equiv [M\mathbf{x} \leq \mathbf{b}]$.*

Proof. Consider $(\vec{a}, b) \in \texttt{proj}_{\mathbf{x}}(\mathcal{Q})^{\#} = \texttt{proj}_{\mathbf{x}}(\mathcal{R})^{\#}$. By Farkas' lemma, a function $f(\mathbf{x}) = \vec{a} \cdot \mathbf{x} + b$ is nonnegative over $\texttt{proj}_{\mathbf{x}}(\mathcal{R})$ iff there are nonnegative $\vec{\lambda} = (\lambda_1, \ldots, \lambda_m)$ such that $\vec{\lambda} \cdot M = -\vec{a} \wedge \vec{\lambda} \cdot \mathbf{b} \leq b$. Note that any (nonnegative) values for $\vec{\lambda}$ define corresponding values for $\vec{a}$ and b. Thus the valid values for $\vec{a}$ are all conic combinations of the rows of $-M$, i.e., this cone is generated by the rows of $-M$. Hence $-\vec{a}_1 \cdot \mathbf{y} \leq 0 \wedge \cdots \wedge -\vec{a}_l \cdot \mathbf{y} \leq 0$ is equivalent to $M\mathbf{y} \leq \mathbf{0}$. □

We use the above lemma to show that $\mathcal{R}_k$ can be represented as in (25), without the need to compute M explicitly. We first note that using Lemmas 8 and 9, we have $\mathcal{R}_{k+1} = \mathcal{R}_k \cap \mathcal{D}_k$, where

$$\begin{aligned} \mathcal{D}_k &= \{ \left(\begin{smallmatrix}\mathbf{x}\\ \mathbf{y}\end{smallmatrix}\right) \in \mathbb{Q}^{2n} \mid M\mathbf{y} \leq \mathbf{0} \} && \text{(M as in Lemma 9)} \\ &= \{ \left(\begin{smallmatrix}\mathbf{x}\\ \mathbf{y}\end{smallmatrix}\right) \in \mathbb{Q}^{2n} \mid \mathbf{y} \in \texttt{rec.cone}(\texttt{proj}_{\mathbf{x}}(\mathcal{R}_k)) \}. \end{aligned}$$

Lemma 10. $\mathcal{R}_k = \texttt{proj}_{\mathbf{x},\mathbf{y}_0}(\widehat{\mathcal{R}}_k)$ *where* $\widehat{\mathcal{R}}_k$ *is defined by* (25).

Proof. We use induction on k. For $k = 0$ the lemma states that $\mathcal{R}_0$ is specified by $R\left(\begin{smallmatrix}\mathbf{x}\\ \mathbf{y}_0\end{smallmatrix}\right) \leq \mathbf{c}''$, which is correct since by definition $\mathcal{R}_0 = \mathcal{R}$. Assume the lemma holds for $\mathcal{R}_k$, we prove it for $\mathcal{R}_{k+1} = \mathcal{R}_k \cap \mathcal{D}_k$. By the induction hypothesis,

$$\mathcal{R}_k = \{ \left(\begin{smallmatrix}\mathbf{x}\\ \mathbf{y}_0\end{smallmatrix}\right) \in \mathbb{Q}^{2n} \mid R\left(\begin{smallmatrix}\mathbf{x}\\ \mathbf{y}_0\end{smallmatrix}\right) \leq \mathbf{c}'' \wedge R\left(\begin{smallmatrix}\mathbf{y}_0\\ \mathbf{y}_1\end{smallmatrix}\right) \leq \mathbf{0} \wedge \ldots \wedge R\left(\begin{smallmatrix}\mathbf{y}_{k-1}\\ \mathbf{y}_k\end{smallmatrix}\right) \leq \mathbf{0} \} \quad (26)$$

and

$$\begin{aligned} \mathcal{D}_k &= \{ \left(\begin{smallmatrix}\mathbf{x}\\ \mathbf{y}_0\end{smallmatrix}\right) \in \mathbb{Q}^{2n} \mid \mathbf{y}_0 \in \texttt{rec.cone}(\texttt{proj}_{\mathbf{x}}(\mathcal{R}_k)) \} && \text{by definition} \\ &= \{ \left(\begin{smallmatrix}\mathbf{x}\\ \mathbf{y}_0\end{smallmatrix}\right) \in \mathbb{Q}^{2n} \mid \mathbf{y}_0 \in \texttt{rec.cone}(\texttt{proj}_{\mathbf{x}}(\texttt{proj}_{\mathbf{x},\mathbf{y}_0}(\widehat{\mathcal{R}}_k))) \} && \text{by IH} \\ &= \{ \left(\begin{smallmatrix}\mathbf{x}\\ \mathbf{y}_0\end{smallmatrix}\right) \in \mathbb{Q}^{2n} \mid \mathbf{y}_0 \in \texttt{rec.cone}(\texttt{proj}_{\mathbf{x}}(\widehat{\mathcal{R}}_k)) \} \\ &= \{ \left(\begin{smallmatrix}\mathbf{x}\\ \mathbf{y}_0\end{smallmatrix}\right) \in \mathbb{Q}^{2n} \mid \mathbf{y}_0 \in \texttt{proj}_{\mathbf{x}}(\texttt{rec.cone}(\widehat{\mathcal{R}}_k)) \} && \text{by Lemma 1} \\ &= \{ \left(\begin{smallmatrix}\mathbf{x}\\ \mathbf{y}_0\end{smallmatrix}\right) \in \mathbb{Q}^{2n} \mid R\left(\begin{smallmatrix}\mathbf{y}_0\\ \mathbf{y}_1\end{smallmatrix}\right) \leq \mathbf{0} \wedge R\left(\begin{smallmatrix}\mathbf{y}_1\\ \mathbf{y}_2\end{smallmatrix}\right) \leq \mathbf{0} \wedge \cdots \wedge R\left(\begin{smallmatrix}\mathbf{y}_k\\ \mathbf{y}_{k+1}\end{smallmatrix}\right) \leq \mathbf{0} \} \end{aligned}$$

Note that in the last step, we incorporated the recession cone of $\widehat{\mathcal{R}}_k$ as in (25), after renaming $\mathbf{y}_i$ to $\mathbf{y}_{i+1}$, and $\mathbf{x}$ to $\mathbf{y}_0$ just to make it easier to read in the next step. Now, let us compute $\mathcal{R}_{k+1} = \mathcal{R}_k \cap \mathcal{D}_k$. Note that any $\left(\begin{smallmatrix}\mathbf{x}\\ \mathbf{y}_0\end{smallmatrix}\right) \in \mathcal{R}_{k+1}$ must satisfy the constraint $R\left(\begin{smallmatrix}\mathbf{x}\\ \mathbf{y}_0\end{smallmatrix}\right) \leq \mathbf{c}''$ that comes form $\mathcal{R}_k$. Adding this constraint to $\mathcal{D}_k$ above we clearly obtain a subset of $\mathcal{R}_k$, and thus

$$\mathcal{R}_{k+1} = \{ \left(\begin{smallmatrix}\mathbf{x}\\ \mathbf{y}_0\end{smallmatrix}\right) \mid R\left(\begin{smallmatrix}\mathbf{x}\\ \mathbf{y}_0\end{smallmatrix}\right) \leq \mathbf{c}'' \wedge R\left(\begin{smallmatrix}\mathbf{y}_0\\ \mathbf{y}_1\end{smallmatrix}\right) \leq \mathbf{0} \wedge \cdots \wedge R\left(\begin{smallmatrix}\mathbf{y}_k\\ \mathbf{y}_{k+1}\end{smallmatrix}\right) \leq \mathbf{0} \}$$

which is exactly $\texttt{proj}_{\mathbf{x},\mathbf{y}_0}(\widehat{\mathcal{R}}_{k+1})$, justifying the lemma's statement for $k+1$. □

Lemma 11. *$\mathcal{Q}$ has a MΦRF of depth d iff $\widehat{\mathcal{R}}_d$ is empty.*

Proof. By Lemma 5, $\mathcal{Q}$ has a MΦRF of depth d iff $\mathcal{Q}_d = F^d(\mathcal{Q})$ is empty, and by Definition 5, $\mathcal{Q}_d$ is empty iff $\mathcal{R}_d$ is empty. Since $\mathcal{R}_d$ is empty iff $\widehat{\mathcal{R}}_d$ is empty the lemma follows. □

Example 7. Consider Loop (1) and the corresponding displacement polyhedron as in Example 6. As notation, let $\mathbf{x}_0 = (x_1, x_2, x_3)$, $\mathbf{y}_0 = (y_1, y_2, y_3)$, $\mathbf{y}_1 = (w_1, w_2, w_3)$, $\mathbf{y}_2 = (z_1, z_2, z_3)$, and $\mathbf{y}_3 = (v_1, v_2, v_3)$. Then $\widehat{\mathcal{R}}_2 = \{x_1 \geq -x_3, y_1 = x_2, y_2 = x_3, y_3 = -1\} \wedge \{y_1 \geq -y_3, w_1 = y_2, w_2 = y_3, w_3 = 0\} \wedge \{w_1 \geq -w_3, z_1 = w_2, z_2 = w_3, z_3 = 0\}$ is satisfiable, e.g., for $\mathbf{x}_0 = (0,1,0)$, $\mathbf{y}_0 = (1,0,-1)$, $\mathbf{y}_1 = (0,-1,0)$ and $\mathbf{y}_2 = (-1,0,0)$, and thus, as expected, the loop does not have a MΦRF of depth 2. On the other hand, $\widehat{\mathcal{R}}_3 = \widehat{\mathcal{R}}_2 \wedge \{z_1 \geq -z_3, v_1 = z_2, v_2 = z_3, v_3 = 0\}$ is not satisfiable, and thus the loop has a MΦRF of depth 3. □

4.1 Witnesses for the Nonexistence of MΦRFs of a Given Depth

Existing algorithm for deciding whether a given loop has a MΦRF of depth d [6,26] synthesize a MΦRF in the case of success, but in the case of failure they do not provide any further knowledge on why the loop does not have such a MΦRF. In this section we show that any satisfying assignment for $\widehat{\mathcal{R}}_k$ (as defined in (25)) witnesses the nonexistence of MΦRF of depth k, i.e., it can be used to explains the reason why the loop does not have such MΦRF.

To gain intuition into the next idea let us start with the case $k = 1$, i.e., the case of *LRFs*. If $\mathbf{x}_0, \mathbf{y}_0, \mathbf{y}_1$ is a satisfying assignment for $\widehat{\mathcal{R}}_1$, then by construction

$$\binom{\mathbf{x}_0}{\mathbf{y}_0} \in \mathcal{R} \qquad \binom{\mathbf{y}_0}{\mathbf{y}_1} \in \texttt{rec.cone}(\mathcal{R}) \tag{27}$$

Observe that for $b \geq 0$, $\binom{\mathbf{x}_0}{\mathbf{y}_0} + b \cdot \binom{\mathbf{y}_0}{\mathbf{y}_1} \in \mathcal{R}$. If $\mathcal{R}$ has a *LRF* ρ, then ρ ranks $\binom{\mathbf{x}_0}{\mathbf{y}_0}$ and $\binom{\mathbf{x}_0}{\mathbf{y}_0} + b \cdot \binom{\mathbf{y}_0}{\mathbf{y}_1} \in \mathcal{R}$ for any $b > 0$. This requires $\rho(\mathbf{y}_0) \leq -1$ and $\rho(\mathbf{x}_0) + b \cdot \rho(\mathbf{y}_0) \geq 0$, which contradict for b large enough. Thus the point $\binom{\mathbf{x}_0}{\mathbf{y}_0}$ and ray $\binom{\mathbf{y}_0}{\mathbf{y}_1}$ form a witness that explains why the loop does not have a *LRF*. More precisely, the loop generated by the point and ray of (27), i.e., conv.hull$\{\binom{\mathbf{x}_0}{\mathbf{y}_0}\}+$ cone$\{\binom{\mathbf{y}_0}{\mathbf{y}_1}\} \subseteq \mathcal{R}$, cannot have a *LRF*.

Let us generalize the above intuition for MΦRFs. Assume the loop has a MΦRF $\langle \rho_1, \ldots, \rho_k \rangle$, and let $\mathbf{x}_0, \mathbf{y}_0, \ldots, \mathbf{y}_k$ be an assignment satisfying $\widehat{\mathcal{R}}_k$, then

$$\binom{\mathbf{x}_0}{\mathbf{y}_0} \in \mathcal{R} \quad \binom{\mathbf{y}_0}{\mathbf{y}_1} \in \texttt{rec.cone}(\mathcal{R}) \quad \cdots \quad \binom{\mathbf{y}_{k-1}}{\mathbf{y}_k} \in \texttt{rec.cone}(\mathcal{R}) \tag{28}$$

We may assume that $\binom{\mathbf{x}_0}{\mathbf{y}_0}$ is ranked by ρ_1.

Let $\mathcal{R}' = \mathcal{R} \wedge \rho_1(\mathbf{x}) \leq -1$. Note that none of the transitions of $\mathcal{R}'$ are ranked by ρ_1. Since ρ_1 is decreasing on all transitions of $\mathcal{R}$, we must have $\rho_1(\mathbf{y}_0) \leq -1$ and $\rho_1(\mathbf{y}_i) \leq 0$ for $1 \leq i \leq k$. This means that the rays $\binom{\mathbf{y}_0}{\mathbf{y}_1} \cdots \binom{\mathbf{y}_{k-1}}{\mathbf{y}_k}$ are in $\texttt{rec.cone}(\mathcal{R}')$ too. Moreover, for some $b > 0$ large enough, the point $\binom{\mathbf{x}_0 + b \cdot \mathbf{y}_0}{\mathbf{y}_0 + b \cdot \mathbf{y}_1}$ is in $\mathcal{R}'$ since ρ_1 can be made arbitrarily negative by increasing b. Now we have

$$\binom{\mathbf{x}_0 + b \cdot \mathbf{y}_0}{\mathbf{y}_0 + b \cdot \mathbf{y}_1} \in \mathcal{R}' \; \binom{\mathbf{y}_0 + b \cdot \mathbf{y}_1}{\mathbf{y}_1 + b \cdot \mathbf{y}_2} \in \texttt{rec.cone}(\mathcal{R}') \; \cdots \; \binom{\mathbf{y}_{k-2} + b \cdot \mathbf{y}_{k-1}}{\mathbf{y}_{k-1} + b \cdot \mathbf{y}_k} \in \texttt{rec.cone}(\mathcal{R}')$$

It has the same form as in (28), i.e., the lower part of each point/ray is equal to the upper part of the next one, but the number of rays is reduced by 1, and since $\langle \rho_2, \dots, \rho_k \rangle$ is a MΦRF for $\mathcal{R}'$ we can apply the same reasoning again and reduce the number of rays to $k-2$. Repeating this, we arrive to a point and ray as in (27) that are supposed to be ranked by ρ_k, but we know that they cannot have a *LRF* so we need at least one more component in the MΦRF. Thus, we conclude that the solution of (28) is a witness that suffices to prohibit a MΦRF of depth k. In fact, the loop generated by this witness, i.e., conv.hull$\{\binom{\mathbf{x}_0}{\mathbf{y}_0}\}$ + cone$\{\binom{\mathbf{y}_0}{\mathbf{y}_1}, \dots, \binom{\mathbf{y}_{k-1}}{\mathbf{y}_k}\} \subseteq \mathcal{R}$, cannot have a M$\Phi$RF of depth k.

Example 8. The satisfying assignment for $\widehat{\mathcal{R}}_2$ in Example 7 is a witness for the nonexistence of *MΦRF* of depth 2 for Loop (1). The transition polyhedron corresponding to this witness is $\{\underline{x_1 = -x_3, x_2 \leq 1, x_3 \leq 0}, x_1' = x_1 + x_2, x_2' = x_2 + x_3, x_3' = x_3 - 1\}$. Note how the guard is strengthened wrt. $x_1 \geq -x_3$ of Loop (1). □

Finally, observe that any polyhedral subset of $\mathcal{R}$ that is disjoint from $\mathcal{R}_k$ has a MΦRF of depth at most k.

Example 9. Consider Loop (1), for which $\widehat{\mathcal{R}}_2$ is satisfiable as we have seen in Example 7. Computing $\mathcal{R}_2 = \mathtt{proj}_{\mathbf{x}_0,\mathbf{y}_0}(\widehat{\mathcal{R}}_2)$ results in $\{x_3 \geq 0, x_2 \geq 1, x_1 + y_2 \geq 0, y_1 = x_2, y_2 = x_3, y_3 = -1\}$. For $\epsilon > 0$, any subset of $\mathcal{R}$ that includes $x_3 \leq -\epsilon$ or $x_2 \leq 1 - \epsilon$ is disjoint from $\mathcal{R}_2$. Adding either constraint to Loop (1) results in loops that have MΦRFs of optimal depth 1 and 2 respectively. □

4.2 New Directions for Addressing the General MΦRF Problem

We believe that the displacement polyhedra representation, in particular the check induced by Lemma 10, provides us with new tools that can be used for addressing the problem of deciding whether a given *SLC* loop has a *MΦRF* of any depth, which is still an open problem. Next we discuss some directions.

One direction is to come up with conditions on the matrices A'' (or equivalently R) and $\mathbf{c}''$, that define the loop, under which it is guaranteed that if $\widehat{\mathcal{R}}_k$ is empty then k must be smaller than some d, i.e., bounding the depth of MΦRFs for classes of loops that satisfy these conditions.

Let $\mathcal{C} \equiv [R\binom{\mathbf{y}}{\mathbf{y}'} \leq \mathbf{0}]$ and $\mathcal{C}^i$ be the i-fold composition of $\mathcal{C}$. Consider the problem of seeking N, such that $\mathcal{C}^N = \mathcal{C}^{N+1}$. This is a sufficient condition for Algorithm 1 to terminate in at most N iterations (either with a recurrent set or with a MΦRF), since then $\mathcal{R}_N = \mathcal{R}_{N+1}$. This is particularly interesting if the loop has an affine update $\mathbf{x}' = U\mathbf{x} + \mathbf{c}$. In such case $\mathcal{C} \equiv [B\mathbf{y} \leq 0 \wedge \mathbf{y}' = (U - I)\mathbf{y}]$, where $I \in \mathbb{Q}^{n \times n}$ is the identity matrix, and thus if the matrix $(U - I)$ is nilpotent, for example, then there is N such that $\mathcal{C}^N = \mathcal{C}^{N+1}$. This also holds when matrix $(U - I)$ satisfies the finite-monoid property [8].

Another tantalizing observation reduces the existence of d such that $\widehat{\mathcal{R}}_d$ is empty to the question whether a related *SLC* loop terminates, for a given polyhedron of initial states, in a bounded number of steps. Specifically, the loop:

$$\mathtt{while}\ (B\mathbf{y} \leq \mathbf{0})\ \mathtt{do}\ (A + A')\mathbf{y} + A'\mathbf{y}' \leq \mathbf{0}.$$

where B, A and A' are those used in the definition of R in (24), and the question whether it terminates in at most d steps for all $\mathbf{y} \in \{\mathbf{y} \in \mathbb{Q}^n \mid R\binom{\mathbf{x}}{\mathbf{y}} \leq \mathbf{c}''\}$. This is because $\widehat{\mathcal{R}}_d$ as in (25) is equivalent to unrolling the above loop d times. If the update is affine, i.e., $\mathbf{x}' = U\mathbf{x} + \mathbf{c}$, then the above loop is equivalent to the following loop: `while` $(B\mathbf{y} \leq \mathbf{0})$ `do` $\mathbf{y}' = (U - I)\mathbf{y}$.

4.3 Termination and Nontermination of Bounded *SLC* Loops

To further demonstrate the usefulness of the displacement polyhedra, in this section we provide some observations, regarding *SLC* loops whose set of enabled states are defined by bounded polyhedra, that are easy to see using the displacement polyhedron and are much less obvious using the transition polyhedron. A polyhedron is bounded if its recession cone consists of a single point $\mathbf{0}$.

Lemma 12. *Let $\mathcal{Q}$ be a SLC loop such that the set of enabled states* $\mathtt{proj}_{\mathbf{x}}(\mathcal{Q})$ *is a bounded polyhedron, then $\mathcal{Q}$ is nonterminating iff it has a fixpoint* $\binom{\mathbf{x}}{\mathbf{x}} \in \mathcal{Q}$*, and it is terminating iff it has a LRF.*

Proof. Let $\mathcal{R}$ be the displacement polyhedron of $\mathcal{Q}$. Since $\mathtt{proj}_{\mathbf{x}}(\mathcal{Q})$ is bounded, $\mathtt{proj}_{\mathbf{x}}(\mathcal{R})$ is bounded. This means that its recession cone $R\binom{\mathbf{x}}{\mathbf{y}} \leq \mathbf{0}$ consists of points of the form $\binom{\mathbf{0}}{\mathbf{y}}$. From the form of $\widehat{\mathcal{R}}_k$, which is a conjunction of instances of $R\binom{\mathbf{y}_i}{\mathbf{y}_{i+1}} \leq \mathbf{0}$, it is easy to see that $\mathcal{R}_2 = \mathcal{R}_1$. This means that the algorithm will terminate in at most two iterations with one of the following outcomes: (i) $\mathcal{R}_0 = \mathcal{R}_1$; (ii) $\mathcal{R}_2 = \mathcal{R}_1$; or (iii) $\mathcal{R}_1$ is empty. In the first two cases all transitions of $\mathcal{R}_1$ or $\mathcal{R}_2$ are of the form $\binom{\mathbf{x}}{\mathbf{0}}$, and thus $\binom{\mathbf{x}}{\mathbf{x}} \in \mathcal{Q}$; in the third case we have found a MΦRF of depth 1, i.e., *LRF*. Note that the part that relates nontermination to the existence of a fixpoint follows also from [26]. □

5 Implementation and Experimental Evaluation

For experimentally evaluating Algorithm 1 for *nontermination*, we have integrated it in a version of iRankFinder which is available at http://irankfinder.loopkiller.com. It takes as input a control-flow graph, and proves nontermination as follows: when it fails to prove termination, it enumerates closed walks (which are basically *SLC* loops) using only transitions whose termination was not proven, and then applies Algorithm 1 to seek recurrent sets. For now it does not check that the recurrent set is reachable, which is an orthogonal problem.

We have analyzed 436 benchmarks that we have taken from TPDB [35] and for which iRankFinder fails to prove termination, and for 412 it finds recurrent sets. These recurrent sets are valid over the rationals, however, at least for 223 benchmarks that satisfy the condition of Lemma 7, they are also valid over the integers. The raw data of the experiments is available at http://irankfinder.loopkiller.com/papers/extra/sas19. Since we do not check reachability, we cannot compare numbers to the other tools, however, in the link above we also provide the results for some other tools when applied to these examples.

We also provide an implementation of Algorithm 1 in a light version of iRankFinder that accepts *SLC* loops as input, which is adequate for experimenting with the algorithm both for finding MΦRFs and recurrent sets – it is available at http://www.loopkiller.com/irankfinder by selecting options $M\Phi RF(\mathbb{Q})$ or $M\Phi RF(\mathbb{Z})$.

6 Conclusion

The purpose of this work has been to improve our understanding of MΦRFs, in particular of the problem of deciding whether a given *SLC* loop has a MΦRF without a given bound on the depth. The outcomes are important insights that shed light on the structure of these ranking functions.

At the heart of our work is an algorithm that seeks MΦRFs, which is based on iteratively eliminating transitions, until eliminating them all or stabilizing on a set of transitions that cannot be reduced anymore. In the first case, a MΦRF can be constructed, and, surprisingly, in the second case the stable set of transitions turns to be a recurrent set that witnesses nontermination. This reveals an equivalence between the problems of seeking MΦRFs and seeking recurrent sets of a particular form.

Apart from the relation to seeking recurrent sets, the insights of our work are helpful for characterizing classes of loops for which there is always a MΦRF, when terminating. In addition, our insights led to a new representation for *SLC* loops in which our algorithm has a very simple formalization that, unlike previous algorithms, yields witnesses for the nonexistence of MΦRFs of a given depth. Moreover, this new representation makes some nontrivial observations regarding (bounded) *SLC* loop straightforward. We believe that this representation can be useful for other related problems. Our research leaves a number of *new open questions*, which we hope will trigger the interest of the community.

The problem of seeking MΦRFs with a given bound on the depth has been considered in several works. The complexity of the problem for *SLC* loops was settled in [6]. MΦRFs for general loops are considered in [25,28], both using non-linear constraint solving. In [2] the notion of "eventual linear ranking functions," which are MΦRFs of depth 2, was studied. The method in [7] can infer MΦRFs for general loops incrementally, by solving safety problems using Max-SMT. Lexicographic ranking function are closely related. Their algorithmic aspects are considered in [1,5,9,19,23]. There are other works [17,36,37] that address the problem of prove termination by ranking functions, in particular [37] that combines piecewise-linear functions with lexicographic orders. None considers recurrent sets together with ranking-function termination proofs. The combination of piecewise-linear functions with lexicographic orders as in [37] subsumes multiphase ranking functions, however, being more general, and using an approach which is more generic, [37] does not offer any particular insights about multiphase ranking functions and makes no claims of completeness.

Nontermination provers are described in several works. Some techniques are based on finding recurrent sets in one form or another [3,4,8,10,20,22,26,30];

while others are based on reducing the problem to proving non-reachability of terminating states [11, 24, 38]. The idea of shrinking a set of states until finding a recurrent set can be found in several of these works, the main difference is that they typically remove states that ensure termination while our procedure might remove nonterminating states (so that, when it finds a recurrent set, it is not necessarily the largest one).

References

1. Alias, C., Darte, A., Feautrier, P., Gonnord, L.: Multi-dimensional rankings, program termination, and complexity bounds of flowchart programs. In: Cousot, R., Martel, M. (eds.) SAS 2010. LNCS, vol. 6337, pp. 117–133. Springer, Heidelberg (2010). https://doi.org/10.1007/978-3-642-15769-1_8
2. Bagnara, R., Mesnard, F.: Eventual linear ranking functions. In: Proceedings of the 15th International Symposium on Principles and Practice of Declarative Programming, PPDP 2013, pp. 229–238. ACM Press (2013)
3. Bakhirkin, A., Berdine, J., Piterman, N.: A forward analysis for recurrent sets. In: Blazy, S., Jensen, T. (eds.) SAS 2015. LNCS, vol. 9291, pp. 293–311. Springer, Heidelberg (2015). https://doi.org/10.1007/978-3-662-48288-9_17
4. Bakhirkin, A., Piterman, N.: Finding recurrent sets with backward analysis and trace partitioning. In: Chechik, M., Raskin, J.-F. (eds.) TACAS 2016. LNCS, vol. 9636, pp. 17–35. Springer, Heidelberg (2016). https://doi.org/10.1007/978-3-662-49674-9_2
5. Ben-Amram, A.M., Genaim, S.: Ranking functions for linear-constraint loops. J. ACM **61**(4), 26:1–26:55 (2014)
6. Ben-Amram, A.M., Genaim, S.: On multiphase-linear ranking functions. In: Majumdar, R., Kunčak, V. (eds.) CAV 2017. LNCS, vol. 10427, pp. 601–620. Springer, Cham (2017). https://doi.org/10.1007/978-3-319-63390-9_32
7. Borralleras, C., Brockschmidt, M., Larraz, D., Oliveras, A., Rodríguez-Carbonell, E., Rubio, A.: Proving termination through conditional termination. In: Legay, A., Margaria, T. (eds.) TACAS 2017. LNCS, vol. 10205, pp. 99–117. Springer, Heidelberg (2017). https://doi.org/10.1007/978-3-662-54577-5_6
8. Bozga, M., Iosif, R., Konečný, F.: Deciding conditional termination. In: Flanagan, C., König, B. (eds.) TACAS 2012. LNCS, vol. 7214, pp. 252–266. Springer, Heidelberg (2012). https://doi.org/10.1007/978-3-642-28756-5_18
9. Bradley, A.R., Manna, Z., Sipma, H.B.: Linear ranking with reachability. In: Etessami, K., Rajamani, S.K. (eds.) CAV 2005. LNCS, vol. 3576, pp. 491–504. Springer, Heidelberg (2005). https://doi.org/10.1007/11513988_48
10. Brockschmidt, M., Ströder, T., Otto, C., Giesl, J.: Automated detection of non-termination and NullPointerExceptions for Java bytecode. In: Beckert, B., Damiani, F., Gurov, D. (eds.) FoVeOOS 2011. LNCS, vol. 7421, pp. 123–141. Springer, Heidelberg (2012). https://doi.org/10.1007/978-3-642-31762-0_9
11. Chen, H.-Y., Cook, B., Fuhs, C., Nimkar, K., O'Hearn, P.: Proving nontermination via safety. In: Ábrahám, E., Havelund, K. (eds.) TACAS 2014. LNCS, vol. 8413, pp. 156–171. Springer, Heidelberg (2014). https://doi.org/10.1007/978-3-642-54862-8_11
12. Colón, M.A., Sipma, H.B.: Synthesis of linear ranking functions. In: Margaria, T., Yi, W. (eds.) TACAS 2001. LNCS, vol. 2031, pp. 67–81. Springer, Heidelberg (2001). https://doi.org/10.1007/3-540-45319-9_6

13. Conforti, M., Cornuéjols, G., Zambelli, G.: Polyhedral approaches to mixed integer linear programming. In: Jünger, M., et al. (eds.) 50 Years of Integer Programming 1958–2008, pp. 343–386. Springer, Heidelberg (2010). https://doi.org/10.1007/978-3-540-68279-0_11
14. Cook, B., Gotsman, A., Podelski, A., Rybalchenko, A., Vardi, M.Y.: Proving that programs eventually do something good. In: Proceedings of the 34th ACM SIGPLAN-SIGACT Symposium on Principles of Programming Languages, POPL 2007, Nice, France, 17–19 January 2007, pp. 265–276 (2007)
15. Cook, B., Gulwani, S., Lev-Ami, T., Rybalchenko, A., Sagiv, M.: Proving conditional termination. In: Gupta, A., Malik, S. (eds.) CAV 2008. LNCS, vol. 5123, pp. 328–340. Springer, Heidelberg (2008). https://doi.org/10.1007/978-3-540-70545-1_32
16. Cook, B., Podelski, A., Rybalchenko, A.: Termination proofs for systems code. In: Schwartzbach, M.I., Ball, T. (eds.) Programming Language Design and Implementation, PLDI 2006, pp. 415–426. ACM (2006)
17. Cousot, P., Cousot, R.: An abstract interpretation framework for termination. In: Field, J., Hicks, M. (eds.) Symposium on Principles of Programming Languages, POPL 2012, pp. 245–258. ACM (2012)
18. Feautrier, P.: Some efficient solutions to the affine scheduling problem. I. One-dimensional time. Int. J. Parallel Program. **21**(5), 313–347 (1992)
19. Gonnord, L., Monniaux, D., Radanne, G.: Synthesis of ranking functions using extremal counterexamples. In: Grove, D., Blackburn, S. (eds.) Programming Language Design and Implementation, PLDI 2015, pp. 608–618. ACM (2015)
20. Gupta, A., Henzinger, T.A., Majumdar, R., Rybalchenko, A., Xu, R.-G.: Proving non-termination. In: Necula, G.C., Wadler, P. (eds.) Symposium on Principles of Programming Languages, POPL 2008, pp. 147–158 (2008)
21. Harrison, M.: Lectures on Sequential Machines. Academic Press, New York (1969)
22. Larraz, D., Nimkar, K., Oliveras, A., Rodríguez-Carbonell, E., Rubio, A.: Proving non-termination using Max-SMT. In: Biere, A., Bloem, R. (eds.) CAV 2014. LNCS, vol. 8559, pp. 779–796. Springer, Cham (2014). https://doi.org/10.1007/978-3-319-08867-9_52
23. Larraz, D., Oliveras, A., Rodríguez-Carbonell, E., Rubio, A.: Proving termination of imperative programs using Max-SMT. In: Formal Methods in Computer-Aided Design, FMCAD 2013, pp. 218–225. IEEE (2013)
24. Le, T.C., Qin, S., Chin, W.-N.: Termination and non-termination specification inference. In: Grove, D., Blackburn, S. (eds.) Programming Language Design and Implementation, PLDI 2015, pp. 489–498. ACM (2015)
25. Leike, J., Heizmann, M.: Ranking templates for linear loops. Log. Methods Comput. Sci. **11**(1), 1–27 (2015)
26. Leike, J., Heizmann, M.: Geometric nontermination arguments. In: Beyer, D., Huisman, M. (eds.) TACAS 2018. LNCS, vol. 10806, pp. 266–283. Springer, Cham (2018). https://doi.org/10.1007/978-3-319-89963-3_16
27. Leroux, J., Sutre, G.: Flat counter automata almost everywhere!. In: Peled, D.A., Tsay, Y.-K. (eds.) ATVA 2005. LNCS, vol. 3707, pp. 489–503. Springer, Heidelberg (2005). https://doi.org/10.1007/11562948_36
28. Li, Y., Zhu, G., Feng, Y.: The L-depth eventual linear ranking functions for single-path linear constraint loops. In: 10th International Symposium on Theoretical Aspects of Software Engineering (TASE 2016), pp. 30–37. IEEE (2016)
29. Ouaknine, J., Worrell, J.: On linear recurrence sequences and loop termination. ACM SIGLOG News **2**(2), 4–13 (2015)

30. Payet, É., Mesnard, F., Spoto, F.: Non-termination analysis of Java bytecode. CoRR, abs/1401.5292 (2014)
31. Podelski, A., Rybalchenko, A.: A complete method for the synthesis of linear ranking functions. In: Steffen, B., Levi, G. (eds.) VMCAI 2004. LNCS, vol. 2937, pp. 239–251. Springer, Heidelberg (2004). https://doi.org/10.1007/978-3-540-24622-0_20
32. Schrijver, A.: Theory of Linear and Integer Programming. Wiley, New York (1986)
33. Sohn, K., Van Gelder, A.: Termination detection in logic programs using argument sizes. In: Rosenkrantz, D.J. (ed.) Symposium on Principles of Database Systems, pp. 216–226. ACM Press (1991)
34. Tiwari, A.: Termination of linear programs. In: Alur, R., Peled, D.A. (eds.) CAV 2004. LNCS, vol. 3114, pp. 70–82. Springer, Heidelberg (2004). https://doi.org/10.1007/978-3-540-27813-9_6
35. The Termination Problems Data Base. http://termination-portal.org/wiki/TPDB
36. Urban, C.: The abstract domain of segmented ranking functions. In: Logozzo, F., Fähndrich, M. (eds.) SAS 2013. LNCS, vol. 7935, pp. 43–62. Springer, Heidelberg (2013). https://doi.org/10.1007/978-3-642-38856-9_5
37. Urban, C., Miné, A.: An abstract domain to infer ordinal-valued ranking functions. In: Shao, Z. (ed.) ESOP 2014. LNCS, vol. 8410, pp. 412–431. Springer, Heidelberg (2014). https://doi.org/10.1007/978-3-642-54833-8_22
38. Velroyen, H., Rümmer, P.: Non-termination checking for imperative programs. In: Beckert, B., Hähnle, R. (eds.) TAP 2008. LNCS, vol. 4966, pp. 154–170. Springer, Heidelberg (2008). https://doi.org/10.1007/978-3-540-79124-9_11

Author Index

Printed in the United States
By Bookmasters